THE PAPERS OF

James Madison

SPONSORED BY
THE UNIVERSITY OF VIRGINIA

THE PAPERS OF

James Madison

SECRETARY OF STATE SERIES

VOLUME 10

1 JULY 1805–31 DECEMBER 1805

EDITED BY

MARY A. HACKETT

J. C. A. STAGG   MARY PARKE JOHNSON

ANNE MANDEVILLE COLONY   KATHARINE E. HARBURY

UNIVERSITY OF VIRGINIA PRESS

CHARLOTTESVILLE AND LONDON

This volume of *The Papers of James Madison* has been edited with financial aid from the National Endowment for the Humanities, an independent federal agency, the National Historical Publications and Records Commission, and the University of Virginia. Financial support has also been provided by Founding Fathers Papers, Inc. and the Packard Humanities Institute. The publication of this volume has been supported by a grant from the National Historical Publications and Records Commission.

UNIVERSITY OF VIRGINIA PRESS

First published in 2014

The paper used in this publication meets the minimum requirements
of ANSI/NISO Z39.48–1992(R 1997) (Permanence of Paper).

1 3 5 7 9 8 6 4 2

Library of Congress Cataloging-in-Publication Data
Madison, James, 1751–1836.
  The papers of James Madison: secretary of state series.
  Vol. 10 edited by Mary A. Hackett and others.
  Includes bibliographical references and index.
  Contents: v. 1. 4 March–31 July 1801—[etc.]—v. 10.
1 July 1805–31 December 1805.
    1. United States—Foreign relations—1801–1809—Sources.
  2. United States—Politics and government—1801–1809—Sources.
  3. United States—History—1801–1809—Sources. 4. Madison, James,
  1751–1836—Correspondence. I. Stagg, J. C. A. II. Hackett, Mary A.
E302.M19 1986 973.46 85-29516
ISBN 0-8139-1093-5 (v. 1)
ISBN 0-8139-3571-3 (v. 10)

Contents

1805

CONTENTS

CONTENTS

CONTENTS

CONTENTS

CONTENTS

CONTENTS

CONTENTS

Preface

The documents in this volume cover the period from 1 July 1805 to 31 December 1805. The Madisons were unable to make their usual summer visit to Montpelier because they spent several months in Philadelphia where James took his wife to have her ulcerated knee treated by the highly regarded physician, Philip Syng Physick. The Madisons left Washington on 25 July, and Madison returned there on 26 October, leaving Dolley Madison in Philadelphia for another month to complete her recovery. The letters exchanged by the couple during their month-long separation reflect largely the warm and loving nature of their relationship. After his return from Philadelphia and while he was living alone in Washington, Madison arranged for his stepson, John Payne Todd, to enter St. Mary's College in Baltimore (*PJM-SS*, 8:xxv; Wagner to JM, 5 Aug., 26 Sept., 9, 14, and 17 Oct. 1805; JM to Jefferson, 16 Oct. 1805).

Madison spent much of his time in Philadelphia researching and beginning to write his pamphlet, *An Examination of the British Doctrine, Which Subjects to Capture a Neutral Trade, Not Open in Time of Peace*, which he completed after his return to Washington. Letters from Peter S. Du Ponceau in July, and Madison's own notes, filed in September and November, show the depth of his research. State Department Chief Clerk Jacob Wagner, who during Madison's absence in Philadelphia continued to exercise considerable autonomy in writing letters, dealing with visitors, offering suggestions on correspondence and appointments, also provided research assistance from Washington. Although the pamphlet was printed anonymously and laid on the desks of Congress on 16 January 1806, the author's identity was no secret. Madison mentioned to both Thomas Jefferson and James Monroe his intention to argue against the increasing severity of Great Britain's policy of limiting neutral trade with belligerent colonies in wartime (Du Ponceau to JM, 8, 15, and 23 July 1805; "Extracts from Longs Hist. Jamaica," ca. 14 Sept. 1805; Notes on Neutral Trade, ca. 14 Sept. 1805; Madison's Notes on Neutral Trade With Belligerents, ca. 11 Nov. 1805; Wagner to JM, 14 and 17 Oct. 1805; Brown, *William Plumer's Memorandum of Proceedings in the U.S. Senate*, 388; Diary 27, 16 Jan. 1806, *The Diaries of John Quincy Adams: A Digital Collection*. [Boston: Massachusetts Historical Society, 2005] 201 http://www .masshist.org/jqadiaries).

James Monroe had returned to London, having passed through Paris where he learned that Charles-Maurice Talleyrand maintained the position he had conveyed in his reply to the note Monroe wrote him on Monroe's way to Spain in December 1804: France would not support the

American position on the eastern boundary of Louisiana. Learning of a suggestion made by former American minister Robert R. Livingston that the United States should lend Spain money to pay U.S. claims for illegal seizures of American ships—money which France could then siphon into its own treasury—Monroe blamed French lack of cooperation and the failure of the Spanish negotiation on Livingston. Monroe believed Livingston had tried to deny him credit for the Louisiana Purchase and also, by his interference with the French, had denied Monroe credit for an agreement with Spain. In London, Monroe was faced with British intransigence on the "Rule of 1756" which decreed that a trade forbidden in peace was also forbidden in war, therefore, neutral trade between a mother country and its colonies not allowed in peace could not be allowed in war. Monroe's repeated attempts to discuss this issue with British foreign secretary Lord Mulgrave were evaded, as were Monroe's attempts to negotiate on the impressment of American seamen and the boundaries between British North America and the United States. The British defeat of the combined French and Spanish fleets at Trafalgar on 21 October 1805 left Great Britain as the only outstanding European sea power and intensified British imposition of its regulations on neutral vessels. It appeared that Monroe's efforts to reach agreement with Great Britain were to be as unsuccessful as his efforts to reach an agreement with Spain (Thomas Auldjo to JM, 22 Sept. 1805; Monroe to JM, 6 July, 6 Aug. and n. 9, 16 Aug. and n. 2, 25 Sept. and n. 2, 18 Oct. and n. 3, 6 Nov. 1805; George W. Erving to JM, 28 Oct. 1805, and n. 12).

In France, American minister John Armstrong continued drawing bills against the U.S. Treasury for the settlement of claims under the Louisiana Purchase Claims Convention while also receiving new complaints about French seizures of American ships. In nearly every letter to Madison, Armstrong provided news of the battles taking place between the armies of France and those of its enemies as Napoleon consolidated his power on the continent. Armstrong also transmitted his correspondence with Talleyrand on the trade between American merchants and the black rebels of Haiti, which France still regarded as its colony of Saint-Domingue. Talleyrand continued, much to Armstrong's annoyance, to meddle in American relations with Spain, his goal being to persuade the United States to pay Spain millions of dollars, which could be transferred to France (Armstrong to JM, 3 July, 10 Aug., 10 Sept., 14 Sept. and n. 1, and 3 Oct. 1805).

Minister to Spain James Bowdoin, who had fallen ill immediately after landing in Spain and who departed for England for treatment, recovered sufficiently to embark for Paris where he intended to stay awaiting instructions from Madison and Jefferson. His decision not to return to Spain was reinforced by his agreement with Monroe that sending a minister to

Madrid so soon after the failure of negotiations would indicate that the United States was too eager for a settlement. It was decided instead that the newly appointed legation secretary, George W. Erving, should go to Madrid as chargé des affaires. In Paris, Bowdoin meddled, as he had agreed not to do, in the situation created by French efforts to influence Spanish policy toward the United States, which eventually led to a serious rift between him and Armstrong.

Former minister to Spain Charles Pinckney, after waiting for the arrival of either Bowdoin or Erving, finally departed for America via Lisbon in late October, just as Erving arrived. Pinckney had, on the advice of Monroe, and contrary to instructions the latter had received from Madison and Jefferson, remained in Madrid to participate in the Spanish negotiations. Pinckney's limitations as a diplomat were remarked upon years later by John Quincy Adams when he recorded in his 14 November 1822 diary entry: "after the rest of the company went away, Pinckney remained, and entertained us with music. He sings in French, German, Italian, Russian and English with equal facility, and with self-accompaniment on the Piano. He has turned his time and opportunities to excellent account at least for the acquisition of ornamental accomplishments" (Bowdoin to JM, 8 and 31 July, 3 Sept., 7 Dec. 1805; Monroe to JM, 6 Nov. 1805, and nn. 4–5; Erving to JM, 25 Oct. 1805; Jefferson to JM, 16 Sept. 1805; *PJM-SS*, 8:xxvii; Diary 32, 14 Nov. 1822, *The Diaries of John Quincy Adams: A Digital Collection*, 416, http://www.masshist.org/jqadiaries).

U.S. affairs in the Mediterranean were improved by the treaty Tobias Lear had signed with Yusuf Qaramanli, pasha of Tripoli, in June 1805. When sending Madison a copy of the treaty, Lear mentioned that the pasha had insisted that "time should be allowed for the delivery of the wife and family" of his exiled brother Ahmad, who had marched against Derna, Tripoli, with William Eaton in the spring of 1805. What Lear neglected to tell Madison, and what the Americans did not learn until George Davis arrived in Tripoli as consul in 1807, was that Lear had signed a secret agreement with the pasha giving him four years to return Ahmad's family. Hammuda Bey of Tunis reiterated his demands for the return of Tunisian ships seized while trying to enter the blockaded port of Tripoli, and decided to send an ambassador to the United States to discuss the matter. The ambassador, Soliman Melimeni, arrived at Hampton Roads in the *Congress* on 4 November 1805 and, after being delayed by contrary winds, arrived in Washington where he had an audience with Madison on 30 November.

On 14 January 1806, Melimeni gave Madison copies of a list of the names and duties of the members of his suite in both English and Arabic. On the English list, which is in the hand of former consul general at Algiers Richard O'Brien, is the name of "Georgia, a Greek taken into Service at

Washington." Rumors that the Tunisian ambassador desired to be supplied with a harem and reports of State Department financial support for Melimeni and his suite were printed in newspapers across the nation. The realities of the situation were less lurid. Madison's 27 September 1806 letter to Jefferson, written shortly before Melimeni's departure for Tunis, stated that "it is not amiss to avoid narrowing too much the scope of the *appropriations to foreign intercourse*, which are terms of great latitude, and may be drawn on by very urgent & unforeseen occurrences." Irving Brant, a later biographer of Madison, conflated the rumors, Madison's letter, and O'Brien's list into the assertion that Madison had hired a female companion for the ambassador. Madison's 27 September 1806 letter, however, dealt with a 13 September request from Louis-Marie Turreau for a loan of over $120,000 needed for repairs to three French warships damaged in a hurricane the previous month and, while agreeing with Jefferson that the loan should be refused because Congress had not appropriated funds for such a purpose, Madison added the comment about avoiding narrowing the scope of "foreign intercourse." Furthermore, a translation of the Arabic version of the household list reveals that the person in question was a man named George, a drogerman or translator. Thus, not only did Madison not hire female company for the ambassador, the person listed was not a woman, and the letter regarding the scope of "the *appropriations to foreign intercourse*," was written months after the ambassador had left Washington. The entire tale, titillating though it may be, is based on a faulty contemporary translation of the Arabic list and a misinterpretation of Madison's later letter to Jefferson about the French loan request (Lear to JM, 5 July 1805; *ASP, Foreign Relations*, 2:724–25; Davis to JM, 31 Aug. and 5 Nov. 1805; Philadelphia *United States' Gazette*, 7 Jan. 1806; *Portland Gazette, and Maine Advertizer*, 17 Mar. 1806; Brown, *William Plumer's Memorandum of Proceedings in the U.S. Senate*, 336, 359; JM to Jefferson, 22 and 27 Sept. 1806 [DLC: Jefferson Papers]; Louis-Marie Turreau to JM, 13 Sept. 1806 [DNA: RG 59, NFL, France, vol. 2–3]; Melimeni to JM, 14 Jan. 1806 [DNA: RG 59, CD, Tunis, vol. 3]; Norwich *Connecticut Centinel*, 18 Mar. 1806; Brant, *Madison*, 4:306; Ketcham, *James Madison*, 447).

During this period Madison was, as always, regularly apprised of affairs in Orleans Territory by Gov. William C. C. Claiborne, who continued his habit of writing frequently in spite of seldom receiving a reply. Claiborne's main concerns were Spanish troop movements in Texas and West Florida—territories claimed by the United States as part of Louisiana—and the removal of Spanish officers who had remained there well beyond the time allotted in the purchase treaty for them to leave. Although Madison, Jefferson, and Claiborne fretted over Spanish activities in the region, they dismissed as of little or no consequence Spanish complaints about Americans invading Spanish territory in West Florida. In Louisiana Territory, James Wilkinson, serving in his capacity as both civil governor and military leader, introduced the French settlers to American governance. He was also confronted with incursions by British soldiers and traders seeking to continue their commerce with the Indians as well as by opposition from other Americans within his jurisdiction. Michigan Territory governor William Hull and secretary Stanley Griswold informed Madison of the pitiful state of Detroit following a disastrous fire there in June 1805 and of transgressions committed by British soldiers from Canada (William C. C. Claiborne to JM, 29 July 1805, 16 Aug. 1805, and n. 1; JM to Claiborne, 18 and 25 Nov. 1805; JM to Jefferson, 16 Oct. 1805; *U.S. Statutes at Large*, 2:283, 287; William Hull to JM, 3 Aug. 1805, n. 3; Wilkinson to JM, 28 July and 6 Nov. 1805; John B. C. Lucas to JM, 12 Nov. 1805).

Other matters demanding Madison's attention during these months were Lafayette's requests that Madison attend to the grants of land given him by Congress, Aaron Burr's visit to New Orleans, the intransigence of Spanish minister Carlos Fernando Martínez de Yrujo, who refused to leave the United States in spite of his recall having been requested, and the behavior of belligerents' ships in American waters. The usual applications for employment, appointments, orders for wine, and sales of tobacco engaged Madison during the second half of 1805 as well (Lafayette to Madison, 3 Aug. and 16 Oct. 1805; William C. C. Claiborne to JM, 6 Aug. 1805; JM to Jefferson, 16 Oct. 1805; Anthony Merry to JM, 9 July [second letter] and 25 July 1805).

Acknowledgments

The editors extend their thanks for the assistance of Timothy D. W. Connelly and the staff of the National Historical Publications and Records Commission; David Langbart, Richard Peusor, and the staff at the Reading Room at the National Archives in College Park, Maryland; William Davis, Jessica Kratz, and Richard McCulley at the National Archives in Washington, D.C.; Julie Miller at the Library of Congress; and Peter Drummey at the Massachusetts Historical Society. We would also like to thank the following people for their advice and assistance: Tricia T. Pyne, Director of the Associated Archives at St. Mary's Seminary & University, Baltimore, Maryland; Dr. Mohammed Sawaie, Department of Middle Eastern and South Asian Languages and Cultures, and the staffs of Alderman Library and the Albert and Shirley Small Special Collections Library at the University of Virginia, especially Jared Loewenstein for help with Portuguese translation; our colleagues at the Papers of Thomas Jefferson, the Papers of Thomas Jefferson: Retirement Series, the Papers of

George Washington, and Daniel Preston of the Papers of James Monroe; John Hackett for photography of the George Davis Letterbooks at the New-York Historical Society; and our transcriber, Sarah Marshall, whose language skills in Greek, Latin, French, and Spanish, have added immeasurably to the volume.

Editorial Method

The guidelines used in editing *The Papers of James Madison* were explained in volumes 1 and 8 of the congressional series (1:xxxiii–xxxix and 8:xxiii), in the first volume of the secretary of state series (1:xxv–xxvii), and in volume 6 of the presidential series (6:xxxii–xxxiii). Considerable effort has been made to render the printed texts as literal, faithful copies of the original manuscripts, but some exceptions must be noted. Characters and words that are missing owing to damage to the manuscript are indicated by [. . .]; those that are obscured by binding, tape, or blots are restored by conjecture within angle brackets. Words consistently spelled incorrectly, as well as variant or antiquated spellings, are left as written; however, words that may appear to be printer's errors are corrected through additions in square brackets or followed by the device [*sic*]. The brackets used by Madison and other correspondents have been rendered as parentheses. Slips of the pen and minor errors in encoding and decoding letters have been silently corrected, but substantial errors, discrepancies, or omissions have been noted.

The amount of material in the period covered by the secretary of state years has led the editors to adopt a policy of increased selectivity. The primary consideration in choosing whether to print, abstract, or omit a document is its degree of relevance to Madison's thoughts or actions in his official and personal life as recipient or sender. Other considerations, though not paramount, are whether the document is of a routine nature, or adds a new dimension to our understanding of the man, or in the case of a lengthy document, whether it has been previously published in an easily accessible source such as *American State Papers* or the *Territorial Papers of the United States*. A large number of bureaucratic documents were generated as a result of the broad responsibilities of Madison's office; those that produce little useful information, such as ship's papers and patents, are silently omitted.

In preparing abstracts the editors have in most cases quoted the entire body of the document, or substantial portions thereof, ignoring salutations and complimentary closes. Editorial additions to the abstracts appear in brackets or in notes. Datelines have been standardized and placed at the heads of the abstracts; variant spellings of personal and place-names have been standardized as well.

Because of the nature of the office, this series includes more letters in foreign languages than our other series; when printed in full, such letters are followed by a condensed translation. Where documents appear in languages with which Madison was relatively unfamiliar, the clerical translation he used is included when available. Otherwise, translations are by the editors.

Pertinent information related to the documents is set forth in the provenance notes. Routine endorsements are not noted except in the case of State Department clerks Jacob Wagner and Daniel Brent. Most of the information on the covers of documents (such as addresses) is ignored unless of particular interest; postmarks are noted only when three or more days have elapsed before posting or when used to support conjectural dating of undated letters. When the enclosures mentioned are newspapers or other ephemeral publications that would have been immediately separated from the document, the absence of such items has not been noted in the provenance.

Where identifications of persons are made without source citations, the relevant material has been taken from the *Biographical Directory of the American Congress*, the *Dictionary of American Biography*, or the *Dictionary of National Biography*. Wherever possible, names and dates have been verified from the *Library of Congress Authorities* (authorities.loc.gov).

The order of documents continues unchanged from previous series.

Depository Symbols

In the provenance section following each document the first entry indicates the source of the text. If the document was in private hands when copied for this edition, the owner and date of ownership are indicated. If the document was in a private or public depository in the United States, the symbol listed in the Library of Congress's *MARC Code List for Organizations* (2000 ed.) is used. (For recent updates, see http://www.loc.gov/marc/organizations/). When standing alone, the symbol DLC is used to cite the Madison Papers in the Library of Congress. The location symbols for depositories used in this volume are:

AAE	Archives du Ministère des Affaires Étrangères, Paris
AGI	Archivo General de Indias, Seville
CCamarSJ	St. John's Seminary, Camarillo, California
CLjC	Copley Newspapers Inc., James S. Copley Library, La Jolla, California
CLO	Occidental College, Los Angeles, California
CSmH	Huntington Library, San Marino, California
CtHi	Connecticut Historical Society, Hartford
DLC	Library of Congress, Washington, D.C.
DNA	National Archives, Washington, D.C.
	CD Consular Despatches
	DD Diplomatic Despatches

	DL	Domestic Letters
	IC	Instructions to Consuls
	IM	Instructions to Ministers
	LAR	Letters of Application and Recommendation
	LOAG	Letters from and Opinions of Attorneys General
	LRD	Letters of Resignation and Declination
	LRRS	Letters Received by the Secretary of War, Registered Series
	LRUS	Letters Received by the Secretary of War, Unregistered Series
	ML	Miscellaneous Letters
	NFC	Notes from Foreign Consuls
	NFL	Notes from Foreign Legations
	PPR	Presidential Pardons and Remissions
	TP	Territorial Papers
ICHi		Chicago Historical Society, Illinois
LNT		Tulane University, New Orleans, Louisiana
MdAA		Maryland, Hall of Records Commission, Annapolis
MdBS		Saint Mary's Seminary and University, Baltimore, Maryland
MeB		Bowdoin College, Brunswick, Maine
MHi		Massachusetts Historical Society, Boston
Ms-Ar		Mississippi Department of Archives and History, Jackson
NhCSp		Saint Paul's School, Concord, New Hampshire
NHi		New-York Historical Society, New York City
NjP		Princeton University, Princeton, New Jersey
NN		New York Public Library, New York City
NNC		Columbia University, New York City
OClWHi		Western Reserve Historical Society, Cleveland, Ohio
PHi		Historical Society of Pennsylvania, Philadelphia
PPAmP		American Philosophical Society, Philadelphia
PPGi		Girard College, Philadelphia
PU-Sp		University of Pennsylvania, Van Pelt Library, Special Collections, Philadelphia
PWbW		Wilkes College, Wilkes-Barre, Pennsylvania
TU		University of Tennessee, Knoxville Libraries
UkLPR		Public Record Office, London
Vi		Library of Virginia, Richmond
ViFreJM		James Monroe Museum and Memorial Library, Fredericksburg, Virginia
ViHi		Virginia Historical Society, Richmond

ViU   University of Virginia, Charlottesville
ViW   College of William and Mary, Williamsburg, Virginia

Abbreviations

FC File copy. A copy of a letter or other document retained by the sender for his own files and differing little if at all from the final version. A draft, on the other hand, is a preliminary version of a document, typically either incomplete, varying in content or expression from the final version, or bearing marks of emendation. Unless otherwise noted, both are in the sender's hand. A letter-book copy is a retained duplicate, often bound in a chronological file, and usually in a clerk's hand.

JM James Madison.

Ms Manuscript. A catchall term describing numerous reports and other papers written by JM, as well as items sent to him which were not letters.

RC Recipient's copy. The copy of a letter intended to be read by the addressee. If the handwriting is not that of the sender, this fact is noted in the provenance.

Tr Transcript. A copy of a manuscript, or a copy of a copy, customarily handwritten and ordinarily not by its author or by the person to whom the original was addressed.

Abstracts and Missing Letters. In most cases a document is presented only in abstract form because of its trivial nature, its great length, or a combination of both. Abstracted letters are noted by the symbol §.

The symbol ¶ indicates a "letter not found" entry, giving the name of the writer or intended recipient, the date, and such other information as can be surmised from the surviving evidence. If nothing other than the date of the missing item is known, however, it is mentioned only in the notes to a related document.

Short Titles for Books and Other Frequently Cited Materials

In addition to these short titles, bibliographical entries are abbreviated if a work has been cited in a previous volume of the series.

Annals of Congress.   *Debates and Proceedings in the Congress of the United States . . .* (42 vols.; Washington, 1834–56).

Annual Register. The Annual Register, or a View of the History, Politics, and Literature, for the Year . . . (80 vols.; London, 1758–1837).

ASP. American State Papers: Documents, Legislative and Executive, of the Congress of the United States . . . (38 vols.; Washington, 1832–61).

Boyd, *Papers of Thomas Jefferson.* Julian P. Boyd et al., eds., *The Papers of Thomas Jefferson* (39 vols. to date; Princeton, N.J., 1950–).

Brant, *Madison.* Irving Brant, *James Madison* (6 vols.; Indianapolis, 1941–61).

Brigham, *American Newspapers.* Clarence S. Brigham, *History and Bibliography of American Newspapers, 1690–1820* (2 vols.; Worcester, Mass., 1947).

Carter, *Territorial Papers.* Clarence Carter et al., eds., *The Territorial Papers of the United States* (28 vols.; Washington, 1934–75).

Cranch. William Cranch, *Reports of Cases Argued and Decided in the Supreme Court of the United States* (9 vols.; Washington, 1804–17).

DLC: Jefferson Papers, Epistolary Record. DLC: Jefferson Papers, Epistolary Record or Summary Journal of Letters, 1783–1826.

DMDE. The Dolley Madison Digital Edition, ed. Holly C. Shulman (Charlottesville: University of Virginia Press, Rotunda, 2004), http://rotunda.upress.virginia.edu/dmde/default.xqy.

Evans. Charles Evans, ed., *American Bibliography . . . from . . . 1639 . . . to . . . 1820* (12 vols.; Chicago, 1903–34).

Ford, *Writings of Thomas Jefferson.* Paul Leicester Ford, ed., *The Writings of Thomas Jefferson* (10 vols.; New York, 1892–99).

Hamilton, *Writings of James Monroe.* Stanislaus Murray Hamilton, ed., *The Writings of James Monroe . . .* (7 vols.; 1898–1903; reprint, New York, 1969).

Kline, *Papers of Aaron Burr.* Mary-Jo Kline, ed., *Political Correspondence and Public Papers of Aaron Burr* (2 vols.; Princeton, N.J., 1983).

Knox, *Naval Documents, Barbary Wars.* Dudley W. Knox, ed., *Naval Documents Related to the United States Wars with the Barbary Powers* (6 vols.; Washington, 1939–44).

Knox, *Naval Documents, Quasi-War.* Dudley W. Knox, ed., *Naval Documents Related to the Quasi-War between the United States and France* (7 vols.; Washington, 1935–38).

Looney et al., *Papers of Thomas Jefferson: Retirement Series.* J. Jefferson Looney et al., eds., *The Papers of Thomas Jefferson: Retirement Series* (6 vols. to date; Princeton, N.J., 2004–).

Madison, *Letters* (Cong. ed.). [William C. Rives and Philip R. Fendall, eds.], *Letters and Other Writings of James Madison* (published by order of Congress; 4 vols.; Philadelphia, 1865).

Miller, *Treaties.* Hunter Miller, ed., *Treaties and Other International Acts of the United States of America* (8 vols.; Washington, 1930–48).

OED Online.   *Oxford English Dictionary,* www.oed.com.

PJM.   William T. Hutchinson et al., eds., *The Papers of James Madison* (1st ser., vols. 1–10, Chicago, 1962–77; vols. 11–17, Charlottesville, Va., 1977–91).

PJM-PS.   Robert A. Rutland et al., eds., *The Papers of James Madison: Presidential Series* (7 vols. to date; Charlottesville, Va., 1984–).

PJM-RS.   David B. Mattern et al., eds., *The Papers of James Madison: Retirement Series* (2 vols. to date; Charlottesville, Va., 2009–).

PJM-SS.   Robert J. Brugger et al., eds., *The Papers of James Madison: Secretary of State Series* (10 vols. to date; Charlottesville, Va., 1986–).

PMHB.   *Pennsylvania Magazine of History and Biography.*

Preston, *Catalogue of the Correspondence and Papers of James Monroe.* Daniel Preston, *A Comprehensive Catalogue of the Correspondence and Papers of James Monroe* (2 vols.; Westport, Conn., 2001).

Rand.   Peyton Randolph, comp., *Reports of Cases Argued and Determined in the Court of Appeals of Virginia* (6 vols.; Richmond, Va., 1823–29).

Rowland, *Claiborne Letter Books.*   Dunbar Rowland, ed., *Official Letter Books of W. C. C. Claiborne, 1801–1816* (6 vols.; Jackson, Miss., 1917).

Senate Exec. Proceedings.   *Journal of the Executive Proceedings of the Senate of the United States of America* (3 vols.; Washington, 1828).

Shaw and Shoemaker.   R. R. Shaw and R. H. Shoemaker, comps., *American Bibliography: A Preliminary Checklist for 1801–1819* (22 vols.; New York, 1958–66).

U.S. Statutes at Large.   *The Public Statutes at Large of the United States of America . . .* (17 vols.; Boston, 1848–73).

VMHB.   *Virginia Magazine of History and Biography.*

WMQ.   *William and Mary Quarterly.*

Madison Chronology

1805

24 July	James Monroe arrives in London
25 July	James and Dolley Madison leave for Philadelphia
23 October	Madison leaves Philadelphia for Washington
26 October	Madison arrives in Washington
25 November	Dolley Madison leaves Philadelphia for Washington
30 November	Madison meets with Sidi Soliman Melimeni

THE PAPERS OF

James Madison

Circular Letter to American Consuls and Commercial Agents

SIR,   DEPARTMENT OF STATE, July 1st, 1805.

I have directed to be transmitted herewith a copy of the laws passed at the last session of Congress.

In the act passed the 27th March 1804,[1] it is provided, that no vessel shall be entitled to a register, or if already registered, to the benefits thereof, if owned wholly or in part by any naturalized person who shall have resided for one year in his native country, or two years in any other foreign country, unless such person be a public agent of the United States. As at the custom-houses of the United States not only registers but sea letters are refused to vessels thus owned, it has been judged expedient to instruct you equally to withhold from them certificates of ownership and of other facts, implying that the vessel is American property.

Doubts having been suggested whether in case of a discharge of the seamen in consequence of a vessel being stranded or condemned as unfit for service, three months' extra pay is to be received by the consuls and commercial agents, in pursuance of the 3d section of the act of the 28th February 1803,[2] supplementary to the consular act; you are informed that the construction of the late attorney general restricts the provision to voluntary sales of vessels and discharges of their crews in the ordinary course of trade. But it is conceived, that where, on account of a sale of the vessel or an alteration of the original voyage, the persons having charge of her are willing to procure for the men return passages on as good terms as they shipped for, you are nevertheless bound to demand three months' extra wages.

When registered vessels are lost, condemned as not sea-worthy, or are sold to foreigners, you will, with the consent of the captain, or other person representing the former owner, cancel the register and return it to the Treasury department; but if such consent is withheld, you will in lieu of the register transmit information of the circumstance, that recourse may be had to the bond. When the sale is made to a citizen of the United States, you are not to oppose the register's being returned in the vessel to which it belongs, as otherwise the purchaser may be exposed to weighty inconveniences, whilst the bond will operate as a safeguard against fraud.

To remove a misconception which seems to have partially taken place, you are advised that no judicial authority belongs to your office, except what may be expressly given by a law of the United States, and may be tolerated by the government in whose jurisdiction you reside. On the contrary, all incidents of a nature to call for judicial redress, must be submitted to the local authorities, if they cannot be composed by your recommendatory intervention.

The official bonds given by the Consuls and Commercial agents require, considering the personal character of the security, periodical renewals; therefore every such bond now of a date older than one year, is to be replaced by a new one, in which the sureties, who join the Consul or Commercial agent in its execution, must be citizens of sufficient solidity, or if not citizens, they must have property or a commercial establishment in the United States.

In order to[3] the protection of our country from disease, and that the means practised in other countries for its cure may be added to the existing stock of knowledge, you are requested to procure and transmit to this Department, from time to time, such newspapers, pamphlets and collections of facts as may make their appearance on the subject of epidemical disorders and quarantine regulations, during your actual residence at your respective stations. It has been thought necessary to limit the expence you may incur in carrying this request into effect to five[4] dollars annually, but in instances where it may seem expedient to increase the sum, you will be pleased first to state the matter specially to this Department; and in order that the same communication may not be made by several, you will each confine yourself to publications in the limits of your district.

To treat with deference the authorities constituted over the place of your residence, and to abstain from all irritating and disrespectful expressions or demeanor towards them is prescribed in your standing instructions. The necessity and importance of observing this duty induce me to recall it to your view, and to request, that whenever your official applications are followed by inattention or unsatisfactory results of a nature to excite your sensibility, you will content yourselves with reporting the circumstances, in order that if a different manner of application should be necessary, it may be sanctioned by your government. *I have the honor to be,* Sir, *Very respectfully, Your most obedient servant,*

JAMES MADISON

RC, four copies (NjP: Jasper E. Crane Collection of James and Dolley Madison; owned by Marshall B. Coyne, Washington, D.C., 1992; offered for sale by Richard D. Wolffers Auctions, Inc., San Francisco, Calif., 17 Mar. 1993, item 1003; offered for sale by James D. Julia, Inc., Fairfield, Maine, 4–5 Feb. 2010, lot 2043); FC (DNA: RG 59, Circulars of the Department of State, vol. 1); letterbook copy (DNA: RG 59, IC, vol. 1). RCs and FC are printed copies, signed by JM.

1. For the 27 Mar. 1804 "Act to amend the act intituled 'An act concerning the registering and recording of ships and vessels,'" see *U.S. Statutes at Large*, 2:296–97.

2. For section 3 of the 28 Feb. 1803 "Act supplementary to the 'act concerning Consuls and Vice-Consuls, and for the further protection of American Seamen,'" see ibid., 203–4.

3. A word was apparently omitted here.

4. Left blank in printed copy. The first three RCs have "five" inserted here in a clerk's hand. The letterbook copy has an asterisk here with the added note: "5 dollars except those at London & Paris which are 10." inserted below.

To John Langdon

DEAR SIR: WASHINGTON, July 1, 1805.

According to your request the letter to you from Mr. Griswold is now returned.[1] It was duly communicated with your letter to me, to the President. I had previously received your favor on the subject of a successor to Mr. Erving.[2] But the appointment had before it came to hand, been conferred on Mr. Wm. Lyman; so that the door was not open for taking into consideration the merits of the gentlemen recommended by you. With sentiments of great esteem and regard I remain Dear Sir very sincerely Yr. mo. obed. servt.

JAMES MADISON

Printed copy (Alfred Langdon Elwyn, ed., *Letters by Washington, Adams, Jefferson, and Others, Written during and after the Revolution, to John Langdon, New Hampshire* [Philadelphia, 1880], 51).

1. See Langdon to JM, 20 Dec. 1805, *PJM-SS*, 8:411.
2. Letter not found.

§ To John Gill. *1 July 1805, Department of State.* "I have received your letter of the 28th. ult, and its enclosures, which ought to have been sent to the Treasury Department; I have therefore referred them thither, with a request that the compensation found due to Capt. Driggs[1] may be remitted to you.

"A list of the Consuls, Commercial Agents and Agents for Seamen will be published in the Newspapers in the course of a few days."[2]

Letterbook copy (DNA: RG 59, DL, vol. 15). 1 p.

1. Gill's 28 June letter has not been found, but it may have referred to compensation due to Captain Driggs of the *Mary*, which arrived at Baltimore carrying the mate of the schooner *Potomac*, Captain Dye. The mate had been placed on board Driggs's ship by the captain of the French privateer that had captured the *Potomac* in the Windward Passage between Cuba and Haiti (*New-York Commercial Advertiser*, 24 June 1805).
2. The list of consuls and commercial agents was published in the 12 July 1805 *National Intelligencer.*

§ From Josiah Blakeley. *1 July 1805, Santiago de Cuba.* "My last to you was dated 7th. June last,[1] which I hope has reached you. Since my last to you, I have received a letter from Mr. Henry Hill at Havana, informing me of his arrival there with the Commission of Consul. But, that the Capt General refused to receive him.[2] He requested me to Continue Charge of the Consulate office here. Also, to name Some one to act for our Nation at Baracoa. But, I know of no one here I could recommend. The scenes of robery, destruction, evasion, perjury, Cruelty & insult to which the americans Captured by French Privateers, & brought into this, & the adjacent ports, have been subjected, perhaps, has not been equalled in a Cent[u]ry past. The american Consulate here is forbidden by the Spanish Govt., insulted by the French, Complained of for want of liberality by the americans, & possibly will be censured by Govt. for want of promptitude. Mr. Hill wrote me it was then a little uncertain if he Should act or not in the Consulate office. That he Should write & advise me on the Subject, to which I Shall attend.

"You will have been informed of what has taken place with Mr. Gray.[3] They have placed him in the *Crucible* through which they compelled me to pass, at the expense & loss of more than $20,000. Their real motive for these arrests they neve(r) declare.

"With this I forward you my third acct. against the U. S., amounting to $3317.7 Continued unto the last June [not found]. Whilst this port Continues open 'tis not probable it will be necessary to again put govt. to a like expense. A number of American vessels were here during part of the time I was feeding those distressed Seamen. But, the masters refused feeding them onboard their vessels, Saying they had no work for them to do & had only provisions sufficient for their voyage. Many of the Seamen were Sick, with Veneral Complaints & fevers Some had lock-jaw many had been wounded. More than Sixty were landed here & arrived from other parts of the Island, within a few days when they moved together as they Sometimes would they appeared quite firmidable. Many of the masters Complained that I would advance them no more. The Seamen that I would give them no more clothes, All were fed, none naked, Such people will co(m)plain.

"The French Cruisers here are using every possible excitement to prevail on american seamen here, to enter on board their privateers. Some have gone with them. Had not those captured & brought into this been well fed & attended to many more would have gone. Sickness here is very expensive. I have used all the economy I could the govr. of the hospital is my friend & I employed a Surgeon physician by the month or the Charges for the wounded & Sick would have been much more very few have died I have given them but few clothes, but sufficient to accomodate them to the U. S. The list of Captured vessels Contains all I can officially name.[4] Tho I am pretty Certain others have been brought into bye ports & unloaded. The govr. here & Dn. Duhart the high judge are good men & would restrain these french privateers had they power. They are our friends but want authority to act.

"Capt Hathaway's vessel the Snow Cornelia was not released.[5] I intended Sending you a Copy of his protest, but on his leaving this he told me he should wait on you in person with it & other papers I have not been informed if my last acct. dated 3d. April 1805 have ever reached you.[6] My Confidence in administration excludes fear for its fate."

RC and enclosure (DNA: RG 59, CD, Santiago de Cuba, vol. 1); extract and copy of enclosure (DNA: RG 233, President's Messages, 9A–D1); extract and copy of enclosure (DNA: RG 46, President's Messages, 9B–B1). RC 3 pp.; marked "Duplicate"; in a clerk's hand, signed by Blakeley; docketed by Wagner as received 7 Oct. 1805. Extract printed in *ASP, Foreign Relations*, 2:670. For surviving enclosure, see n. 4.

1. *PJM-SS*, 9:441.

2. For the marqués de Someruelos's refusal to recognize Hill as consul, see Hill to JM, 12 June 1805, ibid., 460–61, and 463 nn. 2–3.

3. For Vincent Gray's detention and the seizure of his papers, see John Morton to JM, 26 Apr. 1805, and Gray to JM, 4 May 1805, ibid., 289, 290 n. 1, 320–21.

4. The enclosure (1 p.; docketed by Wagner; printed in *ASP, Foreign Relations*, 2:671) is a list of captured U.S. ships, showing the name of each ship, its captain, home port, port of departure, destination, date of capture, cargo, and the name of the capturing privateer and its captain; the list was published in the 16 Dec. 1805 *National Intelligencer*.

5. Shadrach Hathaway in the *Cornelia* was on route from Kronstadt, Russia, to Providence, Rhode Island, when he encountered a series of storms that damaged the ship severely and delayed its progress for so long that his supplies of food and water were depleted. After spending several months fighting the weather, Captain Hathaway headed south along the American coast only to be captured on 8 Mar. 1805 by the French privateer *General Ernouf*, Capt. L. Boyer, and taken to Santiago de Cuba. In his protest Hathaway stated that he was also robbed of his clothing, possessions, and papers. He added that Boyer repeatedly offered him money to sign a paper in French saying that the *Cornelia* was bound for New Providence and carrying British goods, but Hathaway refused. After an extra-legal hearing before French agent J. Audebut, Hathaway was persuaded to sign statements releasing his captor from liability after which his papers, cargo, and vessel, which he heard had been sent to Baracoa, would be returned. When they were not, Hathaway appealed to Governor Someruelos, who said he had instructions "not to interfere in any differences between the French and Americans." Hathaway remained in Santiago de Cuba negotiating the return of his ship and papers but at last departed for Rhode Island without them on 2 June. In late March 1805, the "*General Ernouf*, of Guadeloupe" was captured by the British and taken to Barbados (New York *Morning Chronicle*, 9 May 1805; *Providence Gazette*, 30 Mar., and 3 and 10 Aug. 1805).

6. *PJM-SS*, 9:207–8.

§ From James Maury. *1 July 1805, Liverpool.* "My last letter to you was of the 7th instant.[1]

"I have the honor to inclose an abstract of sundry late quarantine regulations under which all vessels from any Port of the United States arriving in this country, on, or after the 1st day of next October, with any of the articles enumerated in the appendix will be subjected to that restraint, unless they produce a declaration upon oath made by the Owner, Proprietor, shipper or consignor, stating either that such articles are not the growth, produce or manufacture of Turkey or of any other place in Africa within the streights of Gibraltar or in the West Barbary on the Atlantic Ocean.[2]

"Mr Murray, our late Consul at Glasgow, being dead,[3] & that part of the country become within my district, I have appointed a deputy at Greenock, where so many of our vessels now resort that I beg leave, with all due deference, to submit to you the propriety of suggesting to the President a direct appointment.

"Inclosed is a price current for the exports of the United States [not found]."

RC (DNA: RG 59, CD, Liverpool, vol. 2). RC 2 pp.; in a clerk's hand, signed by Maury; docketed by Wagner, with his note: "Consul wanting at Glasgow."

1. No 7 July 1805 letter from Maury has been found; see Maury to JM, 7 June 1805, *PJM-SS*, 9:442.

2. The enclosure has not been found, but the 10 Sept. 1805 *New-York Commercial Advertiser* contained an extract of a 5 July 1805 letter from Thomas Auldjo to Benjamin Lincoln enclosing a form of the required declaration to be attested to by the British consul or vice-

consul at the port of departure or, if none such existed, by "two known British merchants." The regulation covered "cotton, hoofs, horns and tips, hides, (and a number of other articles not usually exported from the United-States)."

3. For the death of John J. Murray, see Murray to JM, 13 Mar. 1805, *PJM-SS*, 9:133 n. 1.

§ From William Riggin. *1 July 1805, Trieste.* "I had this Honor on the 1st January,[1] and have now that of enclosing to you the Report of Vessels arrived in this district up to the 30h, June this year.

"A considerable number of Troops have latterly marched from the interior of Germany into the Austrian Venetian territory, an army of reserve is about forming in the neighbourhood of Laibach and military movements in general indicate a war between this country and the Emperor of the French, common opinion concurs with this Idea, but what are the real sentiments of the austrian Cabinet I am not prepared to say, my opinion is they will preserve their neutrality, if they can do so without degradation.

"We enjoy perfect Salubrity here, the quarantine on Vessels direct from the United States, with clean Bills of Health, without having touched at any intermediate Port, or been boarded by any Vessel on the Passage has been reduced to Seven days.

"In my last I had the honor to enclose my account against the United States Amounting to ƒ357:47 and praying that the Ambassador in London might be desired, to Liquidate my account.

"Inclosed is a Price Current."

RC (DNA: RG 59, CD, Trieste, vol. 1). 3 pp. Enclosures not found.

1. *PJM-SS*, 8:442–43.

§ From Jonathan Trumbull. *1 July 1805, Lebanon, Connecticut.* "I have received your Letter of the 29th May[1] wth. The several inclosures. I shall pay attention to the Request of the President, communicated by you, whenever any occurrence takes place within my Jurisdiction, which shall require it."

FC (CtHi). 1 p.

1. See JM's 29 May 1805 Circular Letter to the Governors, *PJM-SS*, 9:413–14.

§ To Robert Patterson.[1] *2 July 1805, Department of State.* "The President of the United States being desirous of availing the public of your services as Director of the Mint of the United States, I have the pleasure to inclose your Commission."

RC (PPAmP). 1 p.; in a clerk's hand, signed by JM.

1. Scotch-Irish Revolutionary War veteran Robert Patterson (1743–1824) was named professor of mathematics at the University of Pennsylvania in 1779, a position he held until 1814 while also serving as director of the Mint. He was a member of and, after 1819, president of the American Philosophical Society. He remained director of the Mint until shortly before his death. His son, Robert M. Patterson, who had previously filled the university

position left vacant by his father's resignation, was also director of the Mint from 1835 to 1851 (George Greenlief Evans, ed., *Illustrated History of the United States Mint with Short Historical Sketches and Illustrations of the Branch Mints and Assay Offices, and a Complete Description of American Coinage . . .* [Philadelphia, 1898], 84–85).

From John Armstrong

SIR,   PARIS 3 July 1805.

Before the receit of your letter of the 5th. of March,[1] I had drawn a few Bills which were made payable at sight. This mode was adopted under a beleif of it's greater conformity to the provisions of the Convention, than that of paying at different dates and long intervals; and from my not having the smallest suspicion, that any embarrasment would have followed to the Treasury or the Banks. I have since under some degree of obstruction, as well from the claimants as the Government, accomodated the drafts as nearly as possible to your first suggestion; dividing the credits, in most cases, into four parts, and drawing one fourth at sight, 1 Do, at 30, 1 Do, at 60 and the remaining fourth at 90 days. The exceptions to this rule are few and made up of small demands for which I have taken the mean of 45 days. This arrangement will I hope be satisfactory. It was all I could effect without a controversy, doubtful in its issue and unpleasant in it's temper, and which, on many other accounts, I wished to avoid. The amount already drawn and which (from Mr. Marbois absence) cannot be encreased for a month to come, is about ten millions of francs. I send herewith a list of the bills;[2] reserving the vouchers untill some safe and direct conveyance to the United States shall present itself.

Of the case mentioned in your letter of the 26th. of March and transmitted to Mr. Livingston in October 1803,[3] I have neither seen nor heard anything. No papers of the late Minister have been left with me, and Mr. Skipwith's memory does not supply the defect. Everingham's Memorial[4] has been handed to the Agent of claims—but, being entirely unsupported by proofs, no step can be taken with regard to it, except meerly to have it placed on the rolls of the Tribunal. Mr. Skipwith has written to Mr. Everingham instructing him in the kind and degree of evidence necessary to the farther prosecution of the cause.

I have lost no opportunity of presenting as favourably as I could and as the policy itself deserved, the "Act for the Clearance of Merchant Armed vessels."[5] Of this Law, the estimate formed here is tolerably correct. They admit the restriction to have been carried as far as was consistent with our interests or our rights, and as such, receive it as sufficient evedence of the friendly dispositions of the Government—but at the same Time they anticipate outrages of it which, they say, we cannot prevent, and Which will go far to destroy its effect. On this head I make no promises, believing it to be the safest course to permit both parts of Their creed to remain undiminished. On the return of Mr. Talleyrand I shall resume the subject generally, but With little hope of getting Any other answer than—"Have your Government received the propositions suggested last winter? Do they approve the idea on which they were founded?"

Mr. Monroe's return to this place and the facility with which he Will now be able to communicate our common views & knowlege, Makes it unnecessary for me to say much on the turn his late negociation has taken. In it's relation to this Country, there is no Shade of difference in our opinions; and so little in the Course to be persued with regard to Spain, that it is scarcely worth noting. The whole may be reduced to this, that, instead of assailing the Spanish posts in West Florida or even indicating an intention to do so, I would, (from motives growing more peculiarly out of the Character of the Emperor) restrict the operation to such as may have been established in Louisiana. This, with some degree of demonstration that we meditate an embargo on our commercial intercourse with Spain and her colonies, would compel this Government to interpose promptly and efficiently and with dispositions to prevent the quarrel from going farther.

You will have heard through the public papers that Genoa has become a part of France[6]—Parma Placentia &c. are also to be added to the masse—Switzerland will have the same fate and Batavia, it is said, is only to preserve her name, as a province of the Empire.

Of the Allied fleet, we know nothing certainly. The most probable Conjecture now is, that Trinidad or Jamaica is their destination. Nothing can exceed the activity (unless it be the expence) employed in the Ports of the Channel, & the return of the fleet will probably be the Signal for a descent upon England.

The English Alliances on the Continent go on slowly— Russia and Austria, like old Frederick of Prussia on another occasion, wish to see her (England) throw sixes before they take their stand at the table.[7] With the highest respect, I have the honor to be, Sir, Your Most Obedient & very humble servant

JOHN ARMSTRONG.

RC and enclosures (DNA: RG 59, DD, France, vol. 10). For enclosures, see n. 2.

1. *PJM-SS*, 9:104–7.

2. Armstrong enclosed a list (7 pp.; docketed by Wagner; printed in the 18 Sept. 1805 *National Intelligencer*) of persons to whom bills had been issued, the amounts paid, and the dates of issue. He also enclosed copies of (1) his 9 May 1805 letter to François Barbé-Marbois (2 pp.) listing exceptions to the general rule that payments should be made to

claimants and not to their agents and asking Barbé-Marbois's opinion on whether payments should be made directly to claimants or to legal creditors of claimants; (2) Barbé-Marbois to Armstrong, 10 May 1805 (3 pp.), agreeing that payments should generally go to the claimants and not to their agents, stating that proven creditors of the claimants should receive the payments in their own names not the name of the claimant, listing acceptable forms of proof under French law, and stating that cases in which the claimants and their creditors disagreed about the validity of the debt would be judged by himself and Armstrong; (3) Armstrong to Barbé-Marbois, 11 May 1805 (7 pp.; marked "Duplicate"), disagreeing with the latter's implied statement that French law was the deciding factor for proof of the legitimacy of claims covered by the terms of an international treaty, giving an anecdotal example from his own experience of how this could lead to fraud, citing articles 3 and 6 of the Claims Convention of 1803 in support of his position, and presenting several other arguments showing why Barbé-Marbois's position was untenable; (4) Barbé-Marbois to Armstrong, 26 Floreal an XIII [16 May 1805] (4 pp.), rejecting Armstrong's interpretation of his words, stating that the treaty presumed that the claims would be paid exactly as they would have had France done so directly except that the funds were now coming from the U.S. Treasury, denying that Armstrong would be held accountable for the disbursements of the funds, rejecting Armstrong's concerns about possible frauds and asking him to refrain from listing more hypothetical examples, repeating that claimants would be paid in full except in the minority of cases where they had creditors in France, in which case those debts would be deducted from the sums due them, and agreeing to send Armstrong, as requested, all the details of such cases; (5) Armstrong to Barbé-Marbois, 20 May 1805 (3 pp.; marked "*Duplicate.*"), disagreeing again with Barbé-Marbois's interpretation of article 3 of the convention, insisting that the United States and not France was the ultimate payer of the claims, denying any intention of giving offense, and stating that his respect for Barbé-Marbois and Napoleon could not deter him from performing his public duty. On the verso of the letter's last page is Armstrong's note: "I did not think it prudent, in this letter, to touch Mr. Marbois's second Argument Viz: the Emperor's Sovereignty over the claims; but in an interview which took place between us on the 22d. of May, I stated to him fully & freely my opinion on that point, which differed widely from his and which restricted that sovereignty to the twenty four cases on which the Agent had reported to the Commissioners & the Commissioners to me &c.&c.

"In this interview it was agreed, that payment of the Clear and unembarrassed Cases should go on & With regard to oppositions, that none should be maintained but upon *Titres pares.*" Also on the verso is Wagner's note: "Correspondence between Genl. Armstrong and Mr. Marbois respecting attachments on and deductions from claims liquidated under the Louisiana Convention. 1805."

Armstrong also enclosed copies (8 pp.; docketed by Wagner) of: (1) M. Forestier, agent of Rubot & Lorando, to Armstrong, 13 Mar. 1805, stating that the schooner *Wilmington Packet*, owner Jeremiah Condy, Capt. Moses Andrews, left Bordeaux in 1793 for Saint-Domingue carrying cargo belonging to Rubot & Lorando and Andrews and was seized by a Dutch privateer; that Williams Vans Murray reported the case to the Batavian government, which decreed it an illegal seizure and granted an indemnity of 20,000 florins that was deposited with bankers Willinks, Van Staphorsts, and Hubbard for distribution to the interested parties, that the bankers had refused to release the funds without authorization from the U.S. government, and asking Armstrong to order them to do so; (2) Willinks and Van Staphorsts to Armstrong, 2 May 1805, stating that when Murray deposited the money with them in February 1800, they had credited it to the State Department account and that those concerned in the *Wilmington Packet*, instead of applying to them, should apply to JM, who "disposed of those monies" after Murray had deposited them (for the case of the

9

Wilmington Packet, see *PJM-SS*, 2:103 and n. 1, 161, 3:104 and n. 2, 459, 521 and n. 1, 4:27, 8:545–46); (3) Thomas Appleton to Armstrong, 24 May 1805, informing him that the Danes and Swedes had once had a plan to replace Yusuf Qaramanli with his deposed brother, Ahmad, but had given it up as impracticable, that it had been renewed by James Leander Cathcart and put into action by William Eaton supported by Samuel Barron and the squadron, that he had heard Yusuf was aware of the American plans and was making extensive preparation for defense, and that the king of Naples had refused to lend gunboats to the U.S. Navy as he had done the previous year.

3. For the details of William Lewis's claim on France, see Lewis to JM, 15 Oct. 1804, *PJM-SS*, 8:176–77. For JM to Robert R. Livingston, 27 Oct. 1803, and to Armstrong, 26 Mar. 1805, see ibid., 5:579–80 and 9:178.

4. The memorial has not been identified but presumably was one of those enclosed in JM to Livingston, 27 Oct. 1803 (see n. 3 above).

5. See JM to Armstrong, 5 Mar. 1805, *PJM-SS*, 9:104–7 and n. 4.

6. For France's annexation of Genoa, see Peter Kuhn Jr. to JM, 29 May 1805, ibid., 417–18 and n. 1.

7. For a discussion of Frederick the Great's relationship with England during the Seven Years' War, see J. Holland Rose, "Frederick the Great and England, 1756–1763," *English Historical Review* 29 [1914]: 79–93, 257–75.

§ To Jacob Crowninshield. *3 July 1805, Department of State.* "I have the honor to inform you, in answer to your letter of the 25 ult. [not found] that no information respecting the service of the monition in the case of the Hector, Smith, or any subsequent proceeding respecting it, exists in this Department.[1] Mr. Wm. Lyman, as the Agent for such claims in London, will have it in his power to furnish the statement you desire."

RC (DLC: Stone Autograph Collection); letterbook copy (DNA: RG 59, DL, vol. 15). RC 1 p.; in Wagner's hand, signed by JM. Minor differences between the copies have not been noted.

1. According to a "List of Cases not coming within the Treaty" that were pending on 1 Oct. 1801, enclosed in George W. Erving to William Lyman, 28 May 1805, the schooner *Hector*, Captain Smith, was the property of Robert Stone, John Ropes, and Ebenezer Putnam of Salem, Massachusetts, and was carrying a cargo of coffee, cotton, and sugar when it was seized by the British sloop of war *Bulldog*, Capt. John Dick, on 26 Feb. 1796, while en route from Gonaïves to St. Thomas. The ship and the cargo, which belonged to the owners of the vessel and to Thomas G. Waite of Lyme, Connecticut, were condemned at Tortola on 29 Mar. 1796. Erving noted that a monition had been issued but never returned (DNA: RG 76, Preliminary Inventory 177, entry 179, Great Britain, Treaty of 1794 [Art. VII], British Spoliations, ca. 1790–1820, Unbound Records, box 4).

§ From Robert Smith. *3 July 1805, Navy Department.* "Will you be pleased to send me an order on the director of the mint, to permit George Harrison esquire navy agent at Philadelphia, or an artist under his direction to use the machine for striking coins in the case of the medal for commre. Preble—& to furnish the necessary aid in preparing the steel to sink the die on."[1]

RC (DNA: RG 59, ML); letterbook copy (DNA: RG 45, Letters to Secretary of State). RC 1 p.; in a clerk's hand, signed by Smith.

1. On 3 Mar. 1805 Congress passed a resolution that the president be asked to present Commodore Edward Preble with a gold medal in recognition of his actions in the U.S. attack on Tripoli. Smith sent the medal to Preble on 17 May 1806 (*Annals of Congress*, 8th Cong., 2d sess., 1703; *PJM-PS*, 5:519 and n. 1, 520 n. 2).

§ From Thomas Auldjo.[1] *4 July 1805, Cowes.* "I have the honor of your circular of 31st of January last from the department of Treasury[2] with the forms of accounts to be rendered of the monies that may be received & disbursed for American Seamen which shall be duly attended to—But as no discharges of Seamen have ever yet taken place here to entitle me to demand of the Captains the monies prescribed by Law, I have nothing hitherto to account for on that Score.

"Very Strict laws having passed lately in this Country in regard to quarantine, which will probably very much inconvenience Ships from America, till the Shippers & Captains are informed of the documents necessary to keep them clear of the restrictions, I have as Soon as possible had a number of the inclosed papers printed off[3] which if properly attended to, will be a prevention to their meeting any trouble in these ports—If it meets with your concurrence, may I request you will give this paper the necessary publicity.

"Our prices of Wheat are here 11/ a 11/6 ℔ bushel weighing 60 pounds—Fine flour 30/ a 33/ ℔ 112 lbs.

"The navigation of the U.S. goes on uninterrupted in these parts—Only one Ship the Augusta Capt Harradin from Cadiz for Boston has been sent into any port in my district within the present year—this vessel has been released & is gone on her voyage."[4]

RC, two copies, and enclosures (DNA: RG 59, CD, Southampton, vol. 1). First RC 2 pp. Second RC 2 pp.; marked "(Du)plicate"; in a clerk's hand, except for Auldjo's complimentary close and signature. Minor differences between the copies have not been noted. For enclosures, see n. 3.

1. Thomas Auldjo (ca. 1757–1823), "the first merchant at Cowes," was named consul at Poole in 1791 after the British government objected to a foreign consul being appointed to Cowes (*Times* [London], 22 Nov. 1823; Boyd, *Papers of Thomas Jefferson*, 19:314, 316, 319; 29:583, 584 n.).

2. Albert Gallatin's 31 Jan. 1805 circular instructed consuls and vice-consuls to report in three forms to the Treasury Department on funds collected from the masters of vessels who discharged sailors according to the third section of the 28 Feb. 1803 act for the further protection of seamen. The first was to be an account of funds received from masters of vessels belonging to U.S. citizens; the second, an account of funds paid to seamen who were U.S. citizens; and the third, the officials' accounts current with the United States, to be updated semiannually and sent to the Treasury for settlement together with the previous two accounts (DNA: RG 84, Records of the Foreign Service Posts, France, Consular Letters Received, vol. 1795–1809). For the "Act supplementary to the 'act concerning Consuls and Vice-Consuls, and for the further protection of American Seamen,'" see *U.S. Statutes at Large*, 2:203–4.

3. Auldjo enclosed copies, docketed by Wagner, of: (1) a printed certificate (1 p.), to be signed by the local British consul, certifying that none of the cargo was from Turkey, the Barbary regencies, or Egypt or, alternatively, that the cargo was the produce of America or of the country from which the ship sailed, with a handwritten added note: "All Ships

provided with a Certificate agreeable to above Form may have communication at *Cowes* without being subject to any Quarantine Restriction or detention, whether they come in to *Import* Goods, to *receive Orders*, by *distress*, or *contrary Winds*"; (2) Auldjo's printed notice of the restrictions in the quarantine act, with an appended list of articles that would subject all ships carrying them to detention unless the captain could produce the above form (2 pp.; signed and dated 1 July 1805 by Auldjo). For the 12 Mar. 1805 Quarantine Act, see 45 Geo. 3, c. 10, printed in Tomlins et al., *Statutes of the United Kingdom*, 2:261–71. For earlier notice of the act, see James Maury to JM, 1 July 1805, and n. 2.

4. On 5 July, Auldjo wrote again (DNA: RG 59, CD, Southampton, vol. 1; 1 p., two copies; the second copy is written as a postscript to the duplicate of Auldjo's 4 July dispatch), saying: "I have already troubled you with a printed paper relative to the quarantine regulations soon to be enforced in this Country. I now beg leave to inclose a form of the declaration required [not found], which please to affix to the paper already furnished."

§ From Return Jonathan Meigs Jr. *4 July 1805, Saint Charles.* "I had the honour of receiving yours of the 27th. of March [not found] enclosing a Commission to me as one of the Judges of the Territory of Louisiana.[1] Having accepted the Commission— and taken the necessary Oaths before the Governour I shall endeavour to discharge the Duties of the Office."

RC (DNA: RG 59, TP, Louisiana, vol. 1). 1 p.; docketed by Wagner as received 31 Aug.

1. Meigs's commission is printed in Carter, *Territorial Papers, Louisiana-Missouri*, 13:100.

To Robert R. Livingston

DEAR SIR   July 5. 1805.

Your favor of the 29 Ulto.[1] was duly handed to me by Mr. Townsend. I congratulate Mrs. Livingston & yourself on your safe arrival, and the shortness of the passage. Your trip up the river was but a reasonable preliminary to your Visit to Washington, and was advised also by the approaching departure of the President, which will take place in 8 (or) 10 days. Mine will be a few days before or after his. Our return will be the last of Sepr. or the first of October, where we shall see you with the greater pleasure, as being more convenient to yourself.

The communications from Genl. Armstrong are not later than May 4.[2] Those from Madrid are nearly about the same date. They concur in shewing that Spain struggles much against our demands, & that France has her views in embarrassing, if not in defeating the negociation. What the end will be remains to be seen. Altho' appearances are not flattering, is there not some room to calculate, that when France finds that she cannot get her hand into our pocket, & that our disputes with Spain may involve herself, and throw the U.S. into the British scale, she will, unless events shall place her above all such considerations promote an adjustment of our affairs with her ally? Whether Madrid or Paris, be the Theatre, the issue, in[3] would seem, equally depends on her influence, or rather authority over the Spanish Cabinet.[4] With sentiments of great esteem & consideration, I remain Dear Sir Your most Obedt. sert

JAMES MADISON

RC (NHi: Livingston Papers); draft (DLC). RC docketed by Livingston. Minor differences between the copies have not been noted.

1. *PJM-SS*, 9:501–2.
2. See John Armstrong to JM, 6 May 1805, ibid., 326.
3. Draft has "it" here.
4. JM added here in the draft but crossed out and omitted from the RC: "And that nothing is now essential but those provisional arrangments which may prevent collisions, particularly in W. Florida and on the Mobille. Should Spain refuse to concur in these, serious questions will arise, such as Congress alone can p⟨rov⟩ide for."

From William Jarvis

SIR   LISBON 5 July 1805.

I should have done myself the pleasure to have answered your private favour of the 12th. May[1] by the Aurora (by which Vessel my Official letter of the 28th. Ulto. went)[2] had want of time not prevented. But there being only three Vessels in port bound to America, I without delay set about fulfilling your Commission; and by the Ship Robert, Captn Alcorn, for Baltimore, have shipped a pipe of old Bucellos & an other of Termo Wine,[3] which I hope will prove to your satisfaction. As I expected the Vessel would sail the 2nd., time would not allow of cases being made, but this will be of less consequence as the Captain appears to be a very honest Man & has promised to be very careful of them. I have sent a small bottle out of each Cask, sealed with the initials of my name, in a small box also sealed, to your address. Inclosed goes a Bill of Lading.[4] The cost of the Bucellos is one hundred & the Termo ninety Milreis, which I shall draw for the first occasion that offers, agreeable to your wishes. There not being any good Port here, except at a high price, (for the feudal custom of paying duties from one province to the other still prevails in this Kingdom) I have written to Mr Clamouse Brown of Porto[5] to send by the first conveyance a quarter Cask of the best.

Do me the favour Sir to make my respects to Mrs Madison, and assure her that I feel myself much indebted to her politeness for accepting the trifles I took the liberty to send the last fall.[6] Assuring you of my very great Respect & Esteem I am sir Your Mo: Ob: Servt.

WILLIAM JARVIS

RC and enclosure (DLC: Rives Collection, Madison Papers). RC cover marked "(Private)"; docketed by Wagner as received 30 Aug. For enclosure, see n. 4.

    1. On 12 May 1805 JM wrote Jarvis about the importation of dry Portuguese wines, as well as best red port (Parke-Bernet Catalogue No. 939 [1–2 Mar. 1948], item 289).

    2. The letter has not been found, but the *Aurora*, Webb, arrived at Salem, Massachusetts, on 18 Aug. 1805, in forty-five days from Lisbon (New York *Mercantile Advertiser*, 23 Aug. 1805).

    3. Bucellas is a white wine produced from the Arinto grape in a region north of Lisbon. In JM's time it was frequently fortified with brandy. Termo is a dry white wine also produced in the vicinity of Lisbon. The *Robert*, Alcorn, arrived in Baltimore about 28 Aug. 1805, forty-eight days after leaving Lisbon (John Hailman, *Thomas Jefferson on Wine* [Jackson, Miss., 2006], 276, 279; New York *Morning Chronicle*, 2 Sept. 1805).

    4. The enclosure (1 p.) is a 6 July 1805 bill of lading from Jarvis for "One Pipe Bucellos Wine, & one Ditto Lisbon" and "1 small Box with 2 Sample bottles" shipped on the *Robert* to JM's account at Baltimore. The shipping charge was $14. plus five per cent primage.

    5. Jarvis probably referred to Peter de Clamouse Brown, the U.S. vice-consul at Oporto, or his father, a British merchant (Rogers, *Evolution of a Federalist*, 322).

    6. See Jarvis to JM, 6 Oct. 1804 (first letter), *PJM-SS*, 8:128.

From Tobias Lear

No. 10.   On board the U States Frigate Constitution
Sir   Syracuse Harbour July 5th. 1805

    Since I had the honor of addressing You under date of the 3d. of November,[1] I have thought it my duty to remain in the Vicinity of Tripoli, that I might be at hand for entering into a negociation with the Bashaw; whenever he Shd. give evidence of his disposition to do so on proper terms; and I accordingly took up my residence in Malta; being well assured that nothing would occur to make my presence necessary: at Algiers during the Winter, and knowing that the Dey was perfectly satisfied as to the cause of my extended absence from his dominions.

    On the 28th. of Decr. I received a letter from Don Gerardo Joseph De Souza, the Spanish Consul at Tripoli, stating, that on the 17th. of Decr. he had a private audience with the Bashaw of Tripoli on the business of his Nation, which being over, the Bashaw introduced the Subject of this War with the U. States, and expressed his willingness to conclude it, if the Americans were disposed to come forward on proper grounds. The Sp. Consul answered that he presumed they would have no objections to finish the war upon honorable terms. There, he says, the Subject was droped; and he took the liberty of making this communication to me, having heard that I was in Malta; adding, as his own opinion, that if I would come over to Tripoli, in a Flag of Truce, he had no doubt but a peace might soon be concluded on honorable & satisfactory terms. As I had reason to believe that this communication was made to me with the knowledge; if not the express desire of the Bashaw, I felt in no haste to reply to it, as I was persuaded that, if he then discovered a desire to terminate the business, he would be more anxious to do so when the Season for active operations Shd. approach. On the 28th of March Commodore Barron sent a Small Vessel to Tripoli with Cloathing &c. for our Captive Countrymen, and by that occasion, I acknowledged the receipt of the Sp: Consul's letter; and observed to him that as we had last year made several overtures to the Bashaw for peace, which had been rejected, he might be assured that we Should never make the first advance again on that Subject. But that, notwithstanding our Force in this Sea was very considerable, and would, at the proper Season, act with decided vigour; Yet we Shd. be ready to receive and consider any propositions which might come from the Bashaw before that Season arrived; provided such propositions were compatable with the dignity and rising character of our Nation, and tending to an honorable and permanent peace.

On the 21st. of Apl. I received by the return of the same Vessel from Tripoli, another letter from the Sp: Consul, saying that he had communicated to the Bashaw the contents of my letter of the 28th. of March, who had directed him to inform me, that to shew his disposition to end the War he would make a proposition Viz. That the U. S should pay him 200,000 for peace & ransom and deliver up to him, gratis, all his subjects in their power, and make full restitution of the property taken from them. The Sp: Consul added, that he considered the propositions of the Bashaw rather intended to form the basis for opening a negociation, than made with an expectation of being granted—At the Same time he mentioned the mode of communication which might be pursued, if I shd. think proper to come off Tripoli with a view to open a negociation. These propositions were so completely inadmissable that after communicating them to Commodore Barron, I thought no more of them, fully expecting further advances either through the same, or some other channel; as it evidently appeared to be the wish of the Bashaw to open a negociation.

Between the time last mentioned, and the 18th. of May, there were intimations made, in various ways, of the disposition of the Bashaw to treat; but none in a direct or official manner. On that day Commodore Barron wrote me the letter No. 1. to which on the 19th. I returned the answer No. 2.[2] And on the 22d, he informed me he had relinquished the command of the Squadron to Captn. Rodgers.[3] On the 24 I embarked on bd. the U.S. Frigate Essex, Captn. James Barron to proceed to Tripoli. On the 26th. in the morng. we saw the Town of Tripoli distant about 10 miles, & at the same time the U.S. Frigates Constitution & President. At 10 A M. Captn. Barron & myself went onboard the former when Captain Rodgers received the letter of Commodore Barron relinquishing to him the command of

the Squadron &c. He returned with us to the Essex, when we stood in for
the Town, and within a short distance from the Battery hoisted the white
flag, which was immediately answered by the same from the Bashaw's Castle. In half an hour a boat came off with the Spanish Consul and an Officer of the Bashaw. I informed the Sp: Consul that I had, agreeably to the
desire of the Bashaw to treat, come for that purpose; but that the propositions which had been made through him (the Sp: Consul) were totally out
of the question, and must be relinquished before I wd. consent to move
one step in the business; and that if I had not the most unequivocal evidence that they would be put a side in toto, I would not go on Shore, and
told him he had better return with my determination, and come off again
the next day, if the Bashaw was desireous of having peace on terms which
we could admit. He left the Ship, and the Wind during the night blew so
heavily on shore that the Ships were obliged to Stand off; and were not
able to come in near the Town again untill the 29th. when at 9 AM the Sp:
Consul came on board bringing the Tiscara or Commission of the Bashaw
to treat on his part, on the principal points of accommodations. We now
removed from the Essex to the Constitution. The Bashaw relinquished all
pretentions to a paymt. for peace or any future demand of any nature
whatever; but demanded the Sum of 130,000 dollars for the ransom of our
Countrymen, and the delivery of his subjects gratis. To this I objected as
Strongly as to the first propositions; and after some time spent in discussing the subject I told the Sp: Consul, that to prevent unnecessary delay &
altercation I would give him in writing my *ultimatum* which must be at
once decided upon. Viz—That there Should be an exchange of Prisoners,
man for man so far as they would go—that the Bashaw Should Send all the
Americans now in his power on board the Squadron now off Tripoli—that
his Subjects should be brought over from Syracuse, and delivered to him
with all convenient speed and as he had 300 Americans more or less—and
We 100 Tripolines more or less, I would engage to give him for the balance in his favour 60,000 Dollars. That a treaty of peace should be made
upon honorable and mutually beneficial terms. With this he went on shore
in the Evening; but apparently without any expectation of its being
accepted.

On the 30th. At 11 A.M the Sp: Consul came again on bd. the Constitution, and urged me very strongly to go on Shore, where everything, he
said, Should be Satisfactorily arranged; but as I had determined not to deviate from the ground I had taken, I declined, Stating to him that it now
depended on the Bashaw to terminate the business by a single word and
that very little time more would be given for that purpose. He requested
permission to send a letter on shore, to which he would await an answer.
This was granted; and on receiving an answer to his letter he again urged
my going on Shore in the Strongest terms. This I Steadily refused to do.

The Wind increasing obliged the Ship to Stand off, and prevented the Sp: Consul from going on shore this night.

At 8 AM. on the 31 of May, the Sp. Consul went on shore, promising to come off again in a few hours with the Bashaw's answer. At noon he came off again, and said that the Bashaw had at length agreed to the sum of 60,000 dollars for the balance of the prisoners; but that he could not think of delivering up the Americans until his Subjects were ready to be delivered to him, and again urging me to go on shore. I told him, in one word, that the business had already been protracted beyond what I conceived a reasonable time; but as the weather yesterday would not admit of our Countrymen being sent on board, I would allow the Bashaw 24 hours, from this time, to agree to my propositions in toto, or reject them. He begged for further time; but without effect; and left the Ship at 5 P.M.

At 11 A.M. June 1st. our unfortunate Countryman, Capt. Bainbridge came on board, who had been permitted to come off, under the guarantee of the Danish Consul and Sidi Mahomet Dghies, the Minister of foreign affairs. He assured me that the Americans would not be delivered up until a treaty of peace should be made with the Bashaw, as peace was more his object than the sum he might get for the Captives; and as it was our intention to conclude a treaty, it would be cruel to let our Countrymen languish in Captivity merely on the punctillio of negociating the treaty before or after their delivery; as whatever related to them was already understood. I informed him of all which had passed between the Sp. Consul and myself; and told him that as the Sp. Consul had come on board as the Commissioner of the Bashaw, with his credentials, which he had delivered to me, I considered the business as now brought nearly to a close, and that a very short time remained for the Bashaw to make up his mind. However, as I shd. make no difference in the terms of the treaty, whether it shd. be drawn up before or after the delivery of the Prisoners, I would enter into an immediate negociation for that purpose, with any proper Character whom the Bashaw might send on board duly authorized; but I would have nothing more to do with the Sp. Consul. But the Americans Should be sent on board without waiting the arrival of the Tripolines from Syracuse. Captain B. left us in the evening and went onshore.

In the forenoon of the 2d. of June, M. Nissen, His Danish Majesty's Consul at Tripoli, came off to the Constitution, bringing a Commission from the Bashaw to negociate with me on the articles of the Treaty. As I had a sketch prepared I communicated it to Mr. Nissen, who observed that there were some articles more favourable to us than were to be found in any treaty which the Bashaw had with any other nation; yet he would take them on shore and submit them to the Bashaw. He did so, and returned on board again about 4 PM. saying that the Bashaw had consented to the Articles;[5] but was very desireous of having an article expressive of our determination to withdraw our forces &c. from Derne, and that we should endeavour to persuade his brother to leave his dominions.[4] To the first I could have no objection, as it would be a natural consequence of peace; but I insisted that if his brother should leave his territory, he should have his wife and children restored to him. Mr. Nissen thought this latter clause would meet objection. However, he took it on shore.

On the morning of the 3d of June Mr. Nissen came off again, and declared that the Bashaw would not agree to deliver the Wife and Children of his brother. I Adhered to that part of the Article, and after some little time he return'd on shore. When Mr Nissen had left the Ship, I told Commodore Rodgers, and Captn. Smith of the Vixen, who was on board, that if the Bashaw should persist in his opposition to that article, I would not suffer the business to be broken off and leave our Countrymen in Slavery; but would, at all hazards, take a boat and go on shore, if the white flag should be haul'd down, which Mr. N. said would be the signal, if the Bashaw persisted in his determination. At 4 P. M. Mr. Nissen came off again with the seal of the Bashaw to the preliminary Articles;[5] but with a condition that time should be allowed for the delivery of the wife and family of his Brother. I consented to it, and we went on board the Vixen to stand in near the harbour. When we were close to the Town, we fired a gun and hauled down the white flag. A salute of 21 Guns was fired from the Batteries, and answered by the Constitution. I went into the harbour in the Constitution's barge with the flag of the United States display'd, and was received at the landing place by the American officers who had been in captivity, with a sensibility more easily to be conceived than described. An immense concourse of people crowded the shore and filled the streets, all signifying their pleasure on the conclusion of the peace.

This, I beleive, is the first instance where a peace has been concluded by any of the Barbary States on board a ship of war. I must here pay a tribute of Justice to Commodore Rodgers, whose conduct, during the negociation on board, was mixed with that manly firmness and evident wish to continue the war, if it could be done with propriety, while he display'd the magnanimity of an American in declaring that we fought not for conquest, but to maintain our just rights and national dignity, as fully convinced the negociators that we did not ask, but grant peace. You will pardon me if I here introduce a circumstance evincive of the spirits of our Countrymen. At Breakfast this morning, Commodore Rodgers observed, that if the Bashaw would consent to deliver up our Countrymen, without making peace, he would engage to give him 200,000 dolls. instead of 60,000, and raise the difference between the two sums from the officers of the Navy, who, he was perfectly assured, would contribute to it with the highest satisfaction.

In the evening I visited Sidi Mahomet Dghies, whom I found a sensible, liberal and well informed man. He is a great friend of our's, and has always been opposed to the War with us.

On the 4h of June, at 11 AM. the Flag staff was raised on the American House, and the Flag of the United States display'd, which was immediately saluted with 21 Guns from the Castle and Forts, and was returned by the Constitution; and all our unfortunate Countrymen sent off on board their Ships.[6] At noon I had an Audience of the Bashaw, by Appointment, and was received with every mark of respect and attention. He paid me many compliments, and expressed himself on the peace with much manliness. He is a man of a very good presence, manly & dignified, and has not in his appearance so much of the *Tyrant* as he has been represented to be. His Court was much more superb than that of Algiers. We spoke but little on the subject of the Treaty &c. He observed that he had given stronger evidences of his confidence in us than he had ever before given to any nation. He had delivered our people before he had received his own; and as to the money he was to receive it was merely nominal—the sum was nothing; but it was impossible to deliver them without something. The other articles of the Treaty I might form as I pleased; being convinced I would not insert anything which was not just. I returned his Compliments, and assured him he would find our nation as just as he had found them brave and persevering.

On the 6h of June the Constitution sailed for Malta and Syracuse, to return to Tripoli with the money and the Tripoline prisoners. The Constellation sailed also for Derne, to bring off the few of our Countrymen who might be there. I remained in Tripoli 'till the return of the Constitution to establish an Agent and make a final settlement of our business there. Dr. John Ridgely of Maryland, late Surgeon of the Philadelphia was strongly recommended as a proper person to reside at Tripoli till the pleasure of the President was Known, and I accordingly appointed him, as will be seen by the inclosed power and letter of instructions.[7]

On the 10th. I sent to the Bashaw two Copies of the Treaty, with translations in the Arabic language, to be signed by him and his Divan. He requested me to attend the Divan & see the form of business there; and as this was a favour never before granted to a Christian he gave it as an evidence of his respect &c. I accordingly attended, and was seated on the same seat with the Bashaw, on his right hand. Great order and solemnity were observed. I presented the Treaty to the Bashaw, who delivered it to his first Secretary to read, article by article. Some observations and short debates took place on several of the Articles; but the Bashaw appeared to explain them satisfactorily. After the whole was read, the form of its presentation and acceptance was written by the Secretary, and the Seals of the Bashaw and Members of the Divan affixed to the two Copies, one of which the Bashaw delivered to me in a solemn manner, and with many expressions of friendship;[8] (He speaks good Italian).

On the 17th. the Constitution arrived; but the wind was too high to admit of her landing the Tripolines or money. On the 18th. both were sent on shore; but instead of 100 Tripolines there were only 48, and 41 Blacks. Seven had been carried to the U.S. by Commodore Preble, and I could never obtain an accurate account of the whole number. I had the Bashaws Tiscara respecting those who had been taken by Commo. Dale, which had been left in hands of Mr. Nissan, which I found expressed 21 Tripolines & Turks, for whom, and their goods, 7 Americans were to have been delivered. I was therefore obliged to make it appear that the Blacks were his Subjects, and were to be included in the exchange. I found no difficulty in the case, tho' I am sure he was not *convinced* of the propriety of it. Those in the U. S. I assured him would be returned by the first opportunity. The 60,000 Dollars were paid, and a receipt therefor given on the treaty left with Dr. Ridgely, and a duplicate therefor which is enclosed.[9] No Consular Present is mentioned in the Treaty; but that it is understood will be given as is usual with *all* Nations when a Consul shall be sent, it does not exceed 6,000 Dollars, and the particulars I shall send in my next, as I shall also my accounts, which can not yet be adjusted, as our quarantine at Malta did not admit of my having that communication with Mr Higgins which was necessary for settling, as I had given him Bills on the House of Sir Francis Baring & Co. in London for the money sent to Tripoli &c.

On the 20th Commodore Rodgers came on shore, and had an audience of the Bashaw, where the assurances of friendship &c were repeated by the Bashaw.

On the 21st. in the Evening we sailed for Malta and Syracuse; arrived on the former on the morning of the 24th., where we remained two days, and sailed for this place.

I shall, in a future letter, give a more particular account of Tripoli &c. At present I confine myself to the subject of the negociation & Treaty. As I have always been opposed to the Egyptian & Derne expedition, I shall say nothing on that subject, especially as I presume there will be full communications respecting it from other quarters.

On the 5th. of March last we were indebted to Algiers for one years annuity, deducting the Cargo of Timber &c. which had been sent. I had learned that they were in great want of wheat at that place, and it struck me that if a Cargo of that Article was sent to them on account of our Annuity, it would be received with gratitude, and be a great saving to the U. S. I therefor(e) purchased a Cargo of about 12.000 bushels at Malta, which cost, with charges about 32,000. Dollars, and sent it to Algiers with a proper letter on the occasion; And I am happy to inform you that it arrived in good time, and in fine order, and was more valuable, as it relates to the U. S., than a cargo of money would have been at that time. It was received, as intended, as a proof of friendship, and an evidence of good faith; and will settle our accounts for one year at least.

As our force in this Sea is now so respectable, Commodore Rodgers has determined to go to Tunis, not to defy the Bey to War, but to have all differences with that regency settled on a basis that will ensu[r]e us future tranquility from that power, and place our national honor on a permanent ground, The Bey has lately been threatning us very hard; but I presume he will now be as submissive as he has been presumptuous. I shall go with him to that place on my way to Algiers, and notwithstanding what Mr. Davis says of the Bey's resolution not to discuss the affairs of the U.S. with any other person but himself,[10] I am persuaded I shall find no difficulty in convincing him that the President of the U. S. will chuse whomsoever he may think proper to settle our national Affairs, provided there be no well grounded personal objections to the man. With sentiments of the highest respect and consideration I have the honor, to be, Sir, Your most faithful &. Obed. Sert[11]

TOBIAS LEAR

RC and enclosures (DNA: RG 46, President's Messages, 9B–B5); RC and enclosures (DNA: RG 59, CD, Algiers, vol. 7, pt. 1); FC (CLjC); letterbook copy (owned by Stephen Decatur, Garden City, N.Y., 1961); extract (DNA: RG 46, President's Messages, 10B–B2). First RC partially in Lear's hand and partially in a clerk's hand, with Lear's emendations, complimentary close, and signature; docketed by Wagner as received 17 Sept. Second RC marked "(*Duplicate*)." FC in a clerk's hand, emended and signed by Lear. Differences between the copies have not been noted. For surviving enclosures, see nn. 2, 5, 7, and 11.

  1. *PJM-SS*, 8:255–58.
  2. Enclosure "no. 1" is a copy of Samuel Barron's 18 May 1805 letter (4 pp.; docketed by Wagner; printed in Knox, *Naval Documents, Barbary Wars*, 6:22–23) saying that the "declining state" of his health would force him to relinquish command of the squadron to John Rodgers; that, based on letters from William Eaton and information Barron had received about Ahmad Qaramanli's character, he no longer considered Ahmad "a fit subject for our support and Cooperation"; that he believed Eaton's expedition and the capture of Derna had "a powerful effect upon the reigning Bashaw"; and that it was his "earnest wish" that Lear "meet the overture" made by Yusuf Qaramanli through the Spanish consul. Enclosure "no. 2" is a copy of Lear to Barron, 19 May 1805 (2 pp.; printed ibid., 24), agreeing to go to Tripoli to begin negotiations with the bashaw.
  3. For Barron's 22 May 1805 letter informing Lear that he had resigned his command to John Rodgers, see *ASP, Foreign Relations*, 2:712.
  4. For William Eaton's march across North Africa with Ahmad Qaramanli to attack Derna, see Eaton to JM, 18 Sept. 1804, *PJM-SS*, 8:66–67 and n. 2. For his agreement to place Ahmad on the throne, see Eaton to JM, 4 Mar. 1805, ibid., 9:101 and n. 1.
  5. Filed with the first RC is a copy (2 pp.) of "Preliminary articles of a Treaty of Peace," dated 2 June 1805, that contains the first three articles of the final treaty.
  6. On 4 June 1805 Lear wrote John Rodgers that "the people will not be ready to go off till Afternoon, as the intoxication of Liberty & Liquor has deranged the faculties as well as

dresses of many of the Sailors, and Captn. B. wishes them all on board quite clean and in Order" (Knox, *Naval Documents, Barbary Wars*, 6:82).

7. With the first RC, Lear enclosed a copy of his 6 June 1805 letter to John Ridgely (3 pp.; marked "No. 3"; extract printed in *ASP, Foreign Relations*, 2:713–14), naming him agent at Tripoli, giving him instructions on his duties, and recommending Nicolai C. Nissen to him as a source of advice on consular proceedings there; and a copy (2 pp.; printed ibid., 714) of Lear's 6 June 1805 public announcement of Ridgely's appointment.

8. For the treaty, see Miller, *Treaties*, 2:529–54. Although article 3 of the treaty required the return of Ahmad Qaramanli's wife and children, Lear signed another agreement, which he kept secret from the U.S. government, allowing the bashaw to hold them for four more years (ibid., 554–56).

9. Enclosure not found.

10. For George Davis's reports that the bey rejected Lear as negotiator, see Davis to JM, 8 Apr. 1804, and 26 Sept. 1804, *PJM-SS*, 7:20–21, 8:93.

11. Filed with the second RC are copies (82 pp.) of George Davis to Lear, 17 Oct. 1804, 9 Nov. 1804, 19 and 25 Nov. 1804 (printed in Knox, *Naval Documents, Barbary Wars*, 5:150, 160–61), 9 Dec. 1804 (printed ibid., 179–80), 16 Dec. 1804, 11 Jan. 1805, 30 Jan. 1805 (printed ibid., 321), 31 Jan. 1805, 17 Feb. 1805, 8 Mar. 1805 (two letters), 19 and 30 Mar. 1805, 13 and 21 Apr. 1805, 14 May 1805, and 23 May 1805 (printed ibid., 6:44); Lear to Davis, 20 Nov. 1804 (printed ibid., 5:153–54), 24 Dec. 1804, 31 Jan. 1805, 15 May 1805 (printed ibid., 6:16–17), 19 May 1805 (two letters, the first printed ibid., 26), and 30 June 1805; William Bainbridge to Lear, 11 Nov. 1804 (printed ibid., 5:135–37), 19 Dec. 1804 (two letters, printed ibid., 201–2), 27 Jan. 1805 (printed ibid., 311–12), 11 Apr. 1805 (two letters, printed ibid., 500–502); Samuel Barron to Lear, 13 Nov. 1804 (printed ibid., 139) and 18 May 1805, and Lear to Barron, 19 May 1805 (see n. 2 above); a translated extract from Spanish consul Gerardo José de Souza to Lear, 18 Dec. 1804; Nicolai C. Nissen to Samuel Barron, 18 Mar. 1805 (printed in Knox, *Naval Documents, Barbary Wars*, 5:421–23); Lear to John Ridgely, 6 June 1805; Lear's 6 June 1805 proclamation of Ridgely's appointment (see n. 7 above); and John Ridgely to Lear, 6 June 1805, thanking Lear for his appointment as consul.

§ From Thomas Appleton.[1] *5 July 1805, Leghorn.* "My last respects were in date of the 11th. of June,[2] in which I inclos'd a translation into our language of the considerations which the government of Genova publish'd as reasons for annexing their territory to the empire of France. His majesty is now at Genova, but he has not as yet publickly made known the limits of his new Kingdom—very lately he invested Eugenio Beauharnais with the vice-royalty,[3] and it is confidently Asserted that the King of Spain has approv'd the propos'd marriage with his daughter the Queen of Etruria.

"On the evening previous to the corronation of the King of Italy at Milan, Mr. Saml. Purviance of Baltimore and Mr. Nathaniel amory of Boston were arrested in that city, and kept under close confinement during fifteen days[4]—the original cause of Suspicion was nothing more I am inclin'd to believe, than an excess of vigilance of the police, over all those who Speak the english language(;) in addition to this circumstance, that from their spies they had learnt the uncommon price they had paid for tickets of admittance to the Cathedral, in order to be present at the Ceremony of incorronation.

"On examination of their papers Mr. Purviance was liberated, with injunctions to leave the City in 24 hours, but among those of Mr. Amory was found a letter from Mr. Gibbs a merchant of Palermo, in which he had in the most unqualified manner spoken of the Emperor Napoleone—giving way to a licence of expression at all times unbecoming, but peculiarly improper in the present conjuncture—this unhappy circumstance has been the cause that Mr. Amory has been convey'd under an escort to Paris.[5] I have been since inform'd that the Emperor has order'd his minister at Naples to demand of the government to deliver up the person of Mr. Gibbs.

"This is the second instance where our Citizens have been imprison'd in Lombardy; and As there is no Agent of the U:states from hence to Paris, to recognize the passports of distant ministers and Consuls, I have well-grounded reason to believe, we may frequently have occasion to lament the want of it—on the 9th of June the Ship Eagle Nathl. Shaler master, was brought to on her passage from Algesiras to this port, by his Britanick majesty's Ship the Phoebe, The Hble. Thos. Cassel commander; and forcibly impress'd, John Kelly a native of Connecticut, and Alexander Fisk, native of Rhode-island; both of whom were provided with protections from the collector of Middletown in the State of Connecticut.

"In consequence of letters I have receiv'd from my brother-in-law Samuel Emery of Philadelphia, I now inclose you, sir, duplicates of my Accounts for disbursements to seamen &c. in 1800. and 1803.[6]—the original Accounts at the close of those years were regularly transmitted with the necessary documents; and As the orders which I drew for their amounts in favor of Saml. Emery were forwarded by the Same conveyances, I Could not doubt of the punctual delivery of my accounts to the department of State—those for 1800. went by the Brig Maria Louisa, Nathl. Bouche master for Norfolk, and sail'd on the 10th. of January 1801.—those for 1803 went by the Hannah, Capt. Yeardsley for Phila. on the 20th of January 1804.[7]—as no letters have reach'd my hands from the department of State since the year 1799, it was difficult to foresee the unpardonable negligence of those Captains. I have been able to procure from the father of the hospital duplicates for the most Considerable charges; but the English Consular-fees for the interrment of divers seamen Are now impossible to obtain, as at present there is no british Consul residing here.

"The medical attendance of Doctor Blay which comprises a number of the items, are still more impracticable to procure, as he died in the course of the last year.

"The great number of other Small Sums which Are in my Accounts, and paid to distress'd seamen, who arrived from the extremes of Italy, and Istria, you are at once, sensible, that it is now totally out of my power to furnish duplicate vouchers.

"After this undisguis'd statement of facts, I am persuaded sir that I need only address myself to those sentiments of equity which so eminently distinguish you, in order that the amount of the inclos'd duplicate accounts for 1800. and 1803 may be pass'd to my credit. Inclos'd is the list of American Vessels arriv'd in this port from the 1st. of January to the 30th. of June of the present year, their numbers and amount of Value is much greater than during any Similar period, since seven years I have held this Consulate! I have made Known to both the ministers, and to the principal Consuls from the U:states in Europe the peace which was concluded by Coll' Lear at Tripoli on the 3d. of June last."

Adds in a postscript: "1. The amount of imports from the U: States in six months being for the immense sum of One million, Nine hundred and forty seven thousand, five hundred Dollars."

RC (DNA: RG 59, CD, Leghorn, vol. 1). 7 pp.; docketed by Wagner as received 24 Sept. Enclosures not found.

1. Thomas Appleton (1763–1840) was a member of the poorer branch of a prominent Boston family. In 1786 he went to France where he met Thomas Jefferson, who recommended him as consul at Leghorn in 1797. American trade at Leghorn was scanty and declined over time, and Appleton received most of his income from commissions on orders from wealthy Americans for Italian alabaster art pieces and marble busts and mantelpieces (Philipp Fehl, "The Account Book of Thomas Appleton of Livorno: A Document in the History of American Art, 1802–1825," *Winterthur Portfolio* 9 [1974]: 123–35).

2. *PJM-SS*, 9:454–55.

3. For the appointment of Eugène de Beauharnais as viceroy in Italy, see Peter Kuhn Jr. to JM, 8 June 1805 (first letter), ibid., 444, 445 n. 3.

4. Boston merchant Nathaniel Amory (b. 1777) had been traveling through Mediterranean Europe. Previous to his arrival at Milan he had been with Abraham Gibbs, U.S. consul at Palermo (Washington Irving, *Journals and Notebooks*, ed. Nathalia Wright, vol. 1, 1803–1806 [Madison, Wisc., 1969], 216 and n. 149).

5. Amory was released at Paris and by August 1805 was in the Netherlands planning to sail to England. Samuel Purviance's 8 June 1805 letter to a friend said that he was to be sent to Paris also but "through the interest of a friend this measure, as it respected me, was relinquished. . . ." Purviance apparently remained in Leghorn until at least 1806 (Boston *New-England Palladium*, 29 Oct. 1805; New York *Morning Chronicle*, 27 Aug. 1805; Janet A. Headley, "The Monument without a Public: The Case of the Tripoli Monument," *Winterthur Portfolio* 29 [1994]: 250 n. 10, 251 n. 12).

6. For earlier correspondence regarding Appleton's accounts, see *PJM-SS*, 5:152–53, 6:426–27, 430.

7. Ibid., 6:369.

§ From Robert Bowie. *5 July 1805, "Council Chamber Annapolis."* "Your (Circular) letter of the 19th Ultimo[1] was duly received, and in reply I have the pleasure of assuring you, that the request of the President shall be promptly attended to, should any occurrence render the aid of the Militia of this State, necessary to the support of the authority and laws of the United States."

Letterbook copy (MdAA: Executive Letter Book, fol. 158). 1 p.

1. Bowie presumably referred to JM's 29 May 1805 Circular Letter to the Governors, *PJM-SS*, 9:413–14.

§ From William C. C. Claiborne. *5 July 1805, New Orleans.* "In a former Letter, I advised you of the departure of Captain Carmick for Pensacola with a communication from me to Governor Folch upon the Subject of the Post Road through West Florida.[1] Captain Carmick was detained much longer than was expected, and has returned without Governor Folch's Answer. A Copy of Captain Carmicks Letter to me on the occasion is herewith enclosed;[2] He was detained at Pensacola by the Spanish Authorities, and I am inclined to think that to their Jealousy and

Suspicion, may be attributed the loss of the Dispatches with which the Captain was charged. I learn however, that Governor Folch had no objection to the Post Route, and that his protection would be afforded the Post Riders.

"I fear it will be some time before this new Route will become Safe and expeditious; The Rider a Mr. Abrahams has been twice here, and he represents the road from thence to Fort Stoddart, as being difficult and often interrupted by High Waters."

RC and enclosure (DNA: RG 59, TP, Orleans, vol. 7); letterbook copy and letterbook copy of enclosure (Ms-Ar: Claiborne Executive Journal, vol. 15). RC 1 p.; in a clerk's hand, emended and signed by Claiborne; docketed by Wagner as received 13 Aug. For enclosure, see n. 2.

1. See Claiborne to JM, 29 Apr. 1805, *PJM-SS*, 9:300.

2. The enclosure (3 pp.; printed in Rowland, *Claiborne Letter Books*, 3:113–14) is a copy of Daniel Carmick to Claiborne, 4 July 1805, saying that he had delivered Claiborne's letter to Juan Vicente Folch at Pensacola on 2 June and had requested a prompt response so he could return on a ship leaving on 6 June; that after receiving Folch's letters, he was denied a passport until a privateer Folch was outfitting was ready for sea; that he at last left overland without a passport for Mobile, where he arrived on 30 June and, after embarking for New Orleans, discovered that his pocketbook with Folch's letters was missing and had probably been stolen at Mobile. He said he continued on to Pass Christian, where he sent a message to Folch explaining the situation and asking for duplicates of the missing dispatches.

§ From John Delafield. *5 July 1805, New York.* "In behalf of the United Insurance Company in the City of Newyork, I have the honor to transmit to you an account of Captures illegally made by certain french Privateers, of property insured by the said Company.[1] We have no reason to believe that the property was ever condemned by any competent tribunal, on the contrary we apprehend the same was converted to the private use of the Captors, without the form of a judicial proceeding.

"Captures of a similar nature having frequently occurred, the United Insurance Company have felt it their duty to transmit to the Government of the United States a correct Statement of the circumstances, accompanying the violation of our Neutral Commerce, and a full detail of the Facts will be found in the enclosed Documents. They confide in the wisdom & justice of Government to adopt all necessary measures for their indemnity for past injuries, and for their security against future ones of a similar nature."[2]

RC (DLC: Causten-Pickett Papers, box 7); Tr and enclosures (DNA: RG 46, President's Messages, 9A–E3). RC 2 pp. Undated; date assigned based on the date of the Tr; docketed by Wagner as received 9 July 1805, with his note: "French & Spanish Union Insurance Company of New York's losses." Tr dated 5 July 1805; printed in *ASP, Foreign Relations*, 2:768–69.

1. The enclosures have not been found, but they probably included the list of captures by French privateers filed with the Tr (4 pp.; printed in *ASP, Foreign Relations*, 2:767–68) that described the amounts paid out by the company for the *Almy*, Crowe, the *Andromache*, Heckle, the *Eagle*, Barber, the *Hector*, Harding, the *Polly*, Bigley, and the *Twins*, Crowe. Details of the cases are in Williams, *French Assault on American Shipping*, 51, 58, 123, 176, 286, 346.

2. On 11 July 1805 JM replied: "I have duly received your letter enclosing documents respecting several captures, made by French privateers, of property insured by the company of which you are President. As far as they may support the measures deemed necessary to be taken in order to procure a general arrangement for restitution and the means of security against a repetition of similar aggressions, these documents are properly deposited in the Department of State; but it is necessary that you should bear in mind that the judicial pursuit of the captors and their sureties, as far as practicable, may prove a precaution not to be safely neglected" (DNA: RG 59, DL, vol. 15; 1 p.).

§ From William Kirkpatrick. *5 July 1805, Málaga.* "Nothing particular having occurred here, since the date of my last 31st. January,[1] I have not considered it necessary to address you. I now inclose the semi annual Return of arrivals in this Port, from the begining of the Year 'till the 30: ulto, in conformity to your orders.

"On the 29: ulto. the Brig Washington, Captain Atkins Adams was brought into this Port, by a Spanish Gun Boat, on her voyage from Leghorn to Boston; her Papers which I have had the inspection of, are in the most perfect order, and I consequently expected she would be immediately set at Liberty, but I find myself disappointed; for the Marine Tribunal has taken cognizance of the Case, and has begun taking declarations from the Captors, who insist on the Brig being brought to trial; I have however no doubt but that she will be set at Liberty, tho' some days will elapse before the many requisite formalities can be got through.[2]

"I am extremely sorry to observe many of our Vessels are carried into Algeceras, and frequently experience a condemnation of their Cargos, contrary to the spirit of the Treaty.

"We continue to enjoy here the most compleat state of health—No symptoms whatever of the cruel Epidemy have made their appearance, and our Physicians are generally of opinion there will be none this Season."

Adds in a postscript: "I inclose a copy of my accot of disbursement for account of Governmt. transmitted to Mr Pinckney, dated 31 March last, & amounting to $75.43."[3]

RC and enclosure (DNA: RG 59, CD, Málaga, vol. 1). 2 pp. For enclosure, see n. 3.

1. *PJM-SS*, 8:520. For a later private letter, see Kirkpatrick to JM, 22 Mar. 1805, ibid., 9:165–66.
2. The *Washington* was held for three weeks at Málaga, where Adams was "treated with great impoliteness. . . . The keys of his trunk were detained from him," and he had to pay over twelve hundred dollars before being released (Charleston *City Gazette*, 23 Aug. and 19 Sept. 1805).
3. The enclosure (1 p.) is a 1 Apr. 1804 to 30 Mar. 1805 account, dated 31 Mar. 1805, of Kirkpatrick's "Disbursements for Account of the Government of the United States," amounting to $75.43, that includes charges for food for the crew of the foundered American ship *Fortune*, who were put on board a Swedish ship, a coil of rope for the naval brig *Scourge*, and stationery and postage.

§ From James Simpson. *5 July 1805, Tangier.* No. 96. "Seeing very little chance of a direct conveyance offering for forwarding to you the sundry Accounts stated so long ago for that purpose and the Channels of Gibraltar and Cadiz having become very hazardous, without hopes of their being other for some time, I have determined on sending them by the way of Lisbon, availing of the occasion of a Portuguese Vessel about to sail from hence for Faro, as the most probable safe Route in these times.

"The Accounts are as follows—

"No 1— disbursements in Morocco Consulate   17th August 1797
    2   Receipt and distribution ⎫ do.   to
        of Articles for Presents   ⎭   30th June 1798
    3   disbursements   ⎫ do   1st July to 31st Decemr 1798
    4   Receipt and distribution ⎭
    5   disbursements   ⎫ do   1st Jany to 31st Decemr 1799
    6   Receipt and distribution ⎭
    7   disbursements   ⎫ do   1st Jany to 31st Decemr 1800
    8   Receipt and distribution ⎭
    9   disbursements   ⎫ do   1st Jany to 31st Decemr 1801
   10   Receipt and distribution ⎭
   11   distribution of Articles remained 7th Septemr 1795 dated
                                   31st Decemr 1801
   12   Extra disbursements in Morocco Consulate 23d June to
                                   29t Decemr 1802
   13   disbursements   ⎫ do   1st Jany to 31st Decemr 1802
   14   Receipt and distribution ⎭
"No 15—Extra disbursements in Morocco Consulate 1st Sepr to
                                   31st Octor 1803.
   16   disbursements   ⎫ do   1st Jany to 31st Decemr 1803.
   17   Receipt and distribution ⎭
   18   disbursements for Crews of Ship Oswego
   19   and Schooner Betsey in Morocco Consulate   29th February 1804.
   20   disbursements   ⎫ do   1st Jany to 31st Decr. 1804.
   21   Receipt and distribution ⎭
   22   General Statement of Receipts and payments in Morocco Consulate from
                    17h August 1797 to 31st December 1804.

"The Sheet of elucidations and the Vouchers, I retain to be sent by the first Vessel of War of The United States may return to America. I am very sensible that untill these be received the proper Officers cannot proceed to determine on the propriety of the Accounts I now transmit, but I could not for that reason Keep them any longer from being laid before you, for your information. I have the conscious satisfaction of Knowing that the Public money with which I have been entrusted has been expended with the strictest attention to the Interest of the Nation so far as my judgement has been able to guide me and that my sole pursuit has been to benefit the Service under my charge, to the utmost of my power."

RC (DNA: RG 59, CD, Tangier, vol. 2). 2 pp.; marked "duplicate."

From James Monroe

DEAR SIR   PARIS July 6th. 1805

Since my letter of the 30th. ulto.[1] some facts have come to my knowledge which it may be of advantage to you to know. I have been told *that
mister T—D[2] has replied when pres[s]ed to aid the negotiation at Madrid that it
could not be expected of him as a project of a very different character countenanced by our agent meaning mister L—N[3] was before our government—this
fact is* unquestionable, as I have it from authority too *direct and deserving of
confidence* in every view *to be doubted.* Thus it appears by the clearest demonstration, *that the failure of the negotiation is* entirely *owing to[4] facts go to
prove that the many acts of his misconduct while here are not attributable to folly
alone.* I have heretofore thought *him entitled to that apology but I am far from*
thinking so *at present;* indeed there *is much reason to suspect him of the grossest iniquity I give you this hint to put you on your guard be assured that he will
poison what he* touches. *His object is to obtain some appointment of the president
to England if possible.* Counting *on it he has proposed a change to* Genl. Armstrong *here to get back to this place to* pursue *the same game that he has heretofore done.* I should *not be surprised if this[5] government on seeing the stand made
here and at Madrid against the project submitted by him to our government
apprehending its failure in that extent had charged him with some other more
reasonable in the hope of better success. If he is admitted in the least degree into
confidence or if cause is given him to infer that sacrefices would be made for peace
or that our councils balance and are not decided he will communicate the same
here.* In *short he is the man of all others whom you should avoid* as deserving *the
execrations of his Country.* These ideas *were never expressed before because
some of the facts which inspire them were not known even when I wrote you last.*
I write you in haste to take advantage of a private conveyance to Bordeaux.
Genel. Armstrong and myself have united in a letter to Mr. Pinckney for
Mr. Bowdoin, to advise *that he decline treating with the government of Spain,*
should his powers authorise it (which however we presume cannot be the
case) till he hears from you, after the receipt of the result of the negotiation at Madrid. I shall leave this on Wednesday next, by the way of Antwerp for London. The above is of course *confidential,* being intended solely
for the purpose of putting you on *your guard.* Very sincerely yours.

                                                              JAS. MONROE

RC (DLC: Rives Collection, Madison Papers); draft (NN). RC in a clerk's hand, with
Monroe's complimentary close and signature. RC in code; decoded interlinearly by JM,
and decoded here by the editors. For the code, see *PJM-SS*, 4:352 n. 1). Draft docketed by
Monroe, with his note: "respecting Mr Livingston confidential, to be kept within the most
c[*illegible*]d limit."

1. *PJM-SS*, 9:503–7.
2. Talleyrand.
3. Robert R. Livingston.
4. Draft has "the misconduct of that individual. Many" inserted here, which was omitted in the RC.
5. Draft has "this"; encoded "thirteen"; decoded "this."

§ From Sylvanus Bourne. *6 July 1805, Amsterdam.* "I have this day been honored by your favr of the 28h May[1] & I hasten to reply thereto that although I have not copies of my letters which Mr Damon refers to in his publication I believe them generally correct. Indeed the Confidence I placed in Mr D at that time & before was more fully evidenced by having left my consular Powers on both my visits to the UStates namely in 1797 & 1802—and it was not till sometime after my return here that I became acquainted my confidence had been misplaced—the first thing that alarmed my suspicions arose from having heard that he had reappointed Mr Hooglant as Consular Agent at the Helder during my absence to answer his private purposes nothwithstanding [*sic*] he knew that I had dismissed him from said place for improper conduct—this naturally led me to make inquiry not only into his Official Conduct but as to the general tenor of his conduct in transacting the Affairs of his brokerag⟨e⟩ house as a thing of essential importance to the interest of all americans trading here—& the result of my inquiries on this head was of the following kind that there existed between him & some Houses here & the Officers of the Customs a secret & improper connection relative to the entry of mercha. the payt of duties thereon &c—such pr example as debiting ƒ100 to the Consignor w[h]ere only ƒ50 was paid while the Balce remained with the Contracting parties. And that in the more detail part of their concerns—it has been understood that in connect⟨ion⟩ with the Sellers not a pound of Sugar or Candles up to a Cab⟨le⟩ & anchor & a Suit of Sails—fictitious or Simulated Accounts are made to the purchasers expressing more than is paid while the Ballen⟨ce⟩ ⟨or⟩ Surplus is held by D & O. You will readily conceive that such like connect⟨ions⟩ are so made as to preclude the chance of procuring legal proof. Although the mind may be quite convinced indeed I have substantial grounds of th⟨e⟩ belief thereof deduced from various sources—permit me to quote two or three to you in corroboration of my assertions—Capt Smith from Phila (addressed to D & O) called at my office one ⟨day⟩ with an Account in his hand of about ƒ1500 made out ⟨by⟩ an Inn Keeper for the support at his House of a number of Germans who were bound to the UStates which he inform⟨ed⟩ me he had been correctly informed was paid by D & O with 900—while the Balce remained he had no doubt in th⟨e⟩ hands of D & O their Agents as the Passengers were debit⟨ed⟩ ⟨for⟩ the Whole amot—he also at the same time related to me a transaction of his own with said House—viz tha⟨t⟩ he had been to examine two parc[e]lls of Beef one of which was ƒ38 Pr Bbl & the other ƒ44—& that D & O advised him by all means to take that of ƒ44 because said they it is better beef & better packed for the long voyage which he w⟨as⟩ bound—some circumstances how ever led him to suspe⟨ct⟩ that all was not right & he went to the Store w[h]ere the Beef was to be had at ƒ38 & desired leave to exam⟩ine⟩ it & said during

the examination he with his pen k⟨nife⟩ made a secret mark on the Blls—after
which he went to the other Store where the Beef was at *f*44 & agreed to take a
number of Blls thereof to be dld in 2 or 3 days & that when they were dld he found
the Blls that he had marked at the other Store which had been bought up at *f*38 &
thus imposed on him—but as he was in time to correct the *mistake*—Mess D & O
did not at that time get their part of the difference between *f*38 & *f*44. 3dly I have
a letter from Mr. James Biass of Baltimore[2] since my return here last covering his
power to me to close his accots with said House wherein he says 'They have
Swindled & cheated me out of a little fortune since my connection with them.'
These items I believe my respected Sir will be sufficient to convince of the correctness of the Character I give them in my letter of 13 March[3] & also that it was
high time that means should be used to correct so great an evil & that this cou⟨ld⟩
not be more effectually accomplished than by the establishment of an other House
in that line under my guarantee for the correct & faithfull managment of all concerns entrusted to them: such is indeed the House of Haines & Co. but let me here
explain that I have no funds in said House & that they have no connection whatever with the powers functions & emoluments of my Office which I found on reflection would be incorrect. My only connection therewith is the allowance of a
Commission for my guarantee on a Mercantile principle in like Cases & this
guarantee was *absolutely necessary* to the very existence of the house & to give it
the chance of any profit whatever—as two houses of the kind had before set ⟨in⟩
that since some years & were sucessively crushed by the Col⟨o⟩ssal Weight of the
antient monopoly—I have only through infinite *trouble & Chagrin* suceeded to
effe⟨ct⟩ a counter establishment which has already had & must continue to have the
most beneficial & permanent advantages to the Amn. trade here this is the uniform opinion of all amn Masters & Supercargoes (who w[h]ere they are left to act
for themselves uniformly give their business to Haines & Co[)] & ough⟨t⟩ I to be
condemned for the exertions I have made to effect so valuable an object. I regret
only having exposed myself by my Zeal herein to the Obse[r]vation⟨s⟩ of Mess
D&O but I shall soon prepare & send out such a statement of the matter as will
correct any unfavorable impressions produced by their advertist[4]—which must
operate towards my [*illegible*] with you & the preservation of a place on which I
alon⟨e⟩ rely to support my distressed family & which I have filled (I am led to hope)
with honor & integrity & to public advantage. Whatever propositio⟨ns⟩ I may have
made to Mr D. at a time when I thought him to merit my confidence & which my
embarrassed situation suggested the idea of, if not incorrect in themselves will not
meet your disapprobation. Let me then examine in to the principles or causes
which led me to make the propositions. I had by the long & distressing sickness of
my late dear friend[5] been exposed to expences & sacrifices of a heavy kind, my
commercial house here was in the decay & many of our important fri[e]nds in the
U States in a like situation I was therefore neceessitated [*sic*] to seek a substitute to
revive my drooping prospects & looked to Mr D for several reasons such as that he
was the person who first introduced me to my acquaintean[c]e & connection with
Mr Lange my then partner in buisness & I presumed he might be disposed to
agree to some plan favorable to the interest of L & B. & as Nineteen twentieths of
the documents legalized at my Office are made out [by] the Brokers [*sic*] who is the
merchants Agent in such Cases I thought a general convenience to all parties con-

cerned might arise from having the Offices under the same roof & my intention of conferring joint Consular Powers on Mr D was merely that of giving him the title or Character of Chancellor to the Consulate as is practised in many of our Consular Offices in France & as a base of that pecuniary reciprocity which might induce him to consent to my views I was led to offer him a share of my revenues *which was all I had to offer* but nothing in the whole thing was intended by me that could in any manner divert the Consular Powers from their regular & proper Channels or in any way increase its emoluments or operate as an aditional weight on my Countrymen—should you doubt this fact I will appeal for proof to a convincing truth which Cannot avoid having a full & most favorable effect in my Case—viz that I have never in the case of outward or export documents charged more than *half* what the Law would ju(s)tify me in doing in the case of inward ones 15s less than Others Charge in the Cr: Offices. No sir had interest eve(r) been capable of causing me to swerve from my duties I should now have been a rich man instead of the contrary. I call with confidence on every man who has had to deal with me in my private or public capacity since I have had the honor of serving th(e) UStates for proof to say if I have not ever conducted on My affairs on the Strictest & *most scrupulous* principl(es) of honor & integrity—Merchant, Citizen & Sailor I feel & know will come forward as my advoc(ates) While in the opinion of the Govt here I am bold to say I stand on firm & solid grounds as I have not only its respect but warm Affection & regard. My sy[s]tem of nerves full of sensibility by nature— have been Strung & extended by a series of bitter misfortunes & I feel most deeply even the *appearance* of any thing which might sully my reputation as it is all I possess in the world. I have been the victim of those whom I have had to deal with & although my means of gain have been circumscribed what little I had honestly earned I have lost by the perfidy of others[6] & I now alone depend on my little Official income for the maintenance of my distressed family & motherless infants but if I have forfeited your confidence by the violation of either private faith or public duty, it becomes your duty to treat me accordingly whatever may be the event.

"That my zeal may have led me into some indiscretions in the case in question may be true but the Object was important & I have ensured it I have suceeded to fix an establishment which will operate *the most essential benefits to the trade of my Country here*—& I shall if doomed to retire have the Consolation of an approving mind & if permitted to remain I shall strive to render myself worthy of your Confidence & that of the Govt of the U States by my honest [*illegible*]able & able exertion to fullfill my duties with honor."

Adds in a postscript: "Among other proofs of the intrigues of Mr D may I mention the following lately discovered viz that he to serve his own view sent an agent into Germany with a printed advertist purporting that the Govt of the UStates had resolved to people the Country of Louisiana with sober industrio(us) Inhabitants & conveying the belief that he was commissioned to send them on to America free of Charge—what an infamou(s) what a daring prostitution of the Character of a Nation & Govt for private purposes! but the artfull fellow takes care not to compromise himself by putting his name to the advertist which task he imposes on his agent who has been in that sort of employ for him some years.

"Mr. D conscious that a new Brokerage house would tend to break up his System left no means untried to prevent its establishment even to buying off a person who had priorly to Mr H. shewn Intentions of undertaking the thing & he has said he would spend ƒ[*illegible*]0,000 to ruin me—but in case I meet the dissaprobation of Govt his Object would be effected at a cheaper rate & his triumph would be Complete."

Adds in a second postscript, dated 9 July: "[*illegible*] Cargoes had been nearly Completed by the means within alluded to of the Advertist but both the french & Batavian Authorities were so piquéd at the thing & the general complexion of the buisness that they sent soldiers on board the Ships discharged the passengers & broke the voyages up While they have since permitted Mess Haines & Co to put the greater part of them on board of another vessel & send them on to the UStates they sailed in the Venus Capt King for Phila by whom I wrote my first reply."[7]

RC, three copies (DNA: RG 59, CD, Amsterdam, vol. 1). First RC 9 pp.; marked "Copy/ *with additions*"; cover marked "*private*"; docketed by Wagner as received 4 Oct. 1805. First RC appears to be the third copy Bourne sent. Second RC docketed by Wagner. With the exception of that noted in n. 6 below, differences between the copies, in which Bourne defends his conduct and blames Damen and Van Oliver, have not been noted.

1. See JM to Bourne, 23 May 1805, *PJM-SS*, 9:379–80.
2. Fells Point merchant and shipowner James Biays (d. 1822) served on the local health committee from 1795 to 1796. He was also named port warden in 1796, served as a militia captain, and later was a director of the Deptford Fire Company (*Federal Gazette & Baltimore Daily Advertiser*, 16 Apr. and 14 Oct. 1796, *Maryland Herald, and Elizabeth-Town Advertiser*, 18 July 1799, *Baltimore Patriot & Mercantile Advertiser*, 10 Feb. 1819, 30 Sept. 1822).
3. *PJM-SS*, 9:131–32.
4. Bourne's 1 Aug. 1805 letter replying to Damen and Van Oliver was printed in the 18 Oct. 1805 *National Intelligencer*.
5. Bourne's wife, Rebecca Haslett Bourne, died in March 1805 (*PJM-SS*, 4:59 n. 1; *Newburyport Herald*, 17 May 1805).
6. In the second RC, Bourne listed his losses as 13,000 florins in property condemned by the British Admiralty, 27,000 florins through the failure of James Greenleaf, and 25,000 florins by his "late Partner" J. W. Lange, for a total loss of 65,000 florins.
7. The *Venus*, King, arrived at the Philadelphia lazaretto on 2 Sept. 1805, but there is no indication that the letter it carried from Bourne arrived at the State Department before the first RC. The "GERMAN REDEMPTIONERS, of different ages and professions," were "to be disposed of on board the ship VENUS from Amsterdam" after 5 Sept. (*New-York Commercial Advertiser*, 3 Sept. 1805; Philadelphia *Aurora General Advertiser*, 17 Sept. 1805).

§ From William C. C. Claiborne. *6 July 1805, New Orleans.* "On the third Instant the Legislative Council was pror[o]gued Sine die, and I have the Honor to enclose for your perusal a Copy of a Short address which I made on the occasion.[1] Perhaps you will perceive on my part a greater share of feeling than ought to have been manifested; but the late *State* of party here was Such, that I could not well have omitted noticing *it*, and I am persuaded that the allusions made to the efforts of, *calumniators* may have a good effect; not on *Them*, for they are callous to every virtuous impulse, but with the people; whom I trust will not for the future be as easily imposed upon by pretended Patriots. Finding that reports still existed relative to the retrocession of Louisiana to Spain, and that Such reports tended to lessen the confidence and Affections of the Citizens for the American Government, I thought it proper to express the Sentiments contained in the latter part of the address, and I flatter myself you will not Suppose that I said too much on the Subject.

"I have received no recent dispatches from the Seat of Government."

RC and enclosure (DNA: RG 59, TP, Orleans, vol. 7); letterbook copy (Ms-Ar: Claiborne Executive Journal, vol. 15). RC 1 p.; docketed by Wagner as received 13 Aug. For enclosure, see n. 1.

1. The enclosure is a broadside of Claiborne's 3 July 1805 address to the legislative council (1 p.; printed in Rowland, *Claiborne Letter Books*, 3:108–13), in which he defends himself against his critics, criticizes those who are trying to stir up political problems in the territory, praises the council for the acts passed at their session, and assures the members that, in spite of rumors to the contrary, neither Louisiana nor any part of it will be returned by the United States to any foreign power.

§ From Harry Toulmin. *6 July 1805, Fort St. Stephen's, Mississippi Territory.* "Some time since, previously to my leaving the state of Kentucky, I observed a statement in the National Intelligencer, of my having been appointed to the office of receiver of public monies on the east side of Pearl river.[1] Not receiving any personal information of the kind, I regarded it only as a mistake in the printer of the paper: but finding on my arrival here that no other person had been appointed to that office, that the duties of it must shortly commence, and that it was the general idea here, that they were to be discharged by myself; I have thought it not improper to state the difficulty to you, under the idea that it is possible that a commission may have been forwarded, but, in consequence of the great irregularity of the mail through the last winter, never reached me.

"Indeed the circumstance of receiving such an addition to a salary very inadequate to the support of a family in this southern country, would have been highly agreable to me, and my residence at this place where the register likewise lives, would place it in my power to execute the duties of the office with promptness and convenience.

"Whilst at New Orleans I took the liberty of drawing on you for 100$ in favour of Mr. John Clay, in addition to 400$ at Natchez of which I duly advised you, being part of my compensation as a Judge of the Missi. Territory (from which I dated it) from the middle of August last to the 1st. of April.

"I am informed by my friend Judge Bruin, that you do not consider any letter of advice as necessary, & shall therefore, unless otherwise instructed, in future draw on you as my salary becomes due, without that formality."

RC (DNA: RG 59, LAR, 1801–9, filed under "Toulmin"). 2 pp.; docketed by Jefferson.

1. For Toulmin's initial appointment as receiver of public monies at Fort Stoddert, the announcement of which was printed in the 12 Oct. 1804 *National Intelligencer*, see Jefferson to JM, 4 Oct. 1804, *PJM-SS*, 8:120–21. It appears the appointment was never submitted to the Senate, and the commission expired (Carter, *Territorial Papers, Mississippi*, 5:418–19).

§ From Harry Toulmin. *6 July 1805.* "You are informed, no doubt, that all the Vessels to and from the Country, even though bound to Fort Stoddart and clearing out from Fort Stoddart, are obliged to come to at Mobille, and to pay twelve per centum ad valorem, on their Cargoes, according to the estimate of the Spanish Officers.

"Such an exaction as this you may well conceive must be ruinous to this Country, and is moreover the Source of perpetual heart-burnings and contention between our Citizens and the Subjects of his Catholic Majesty.

"There are two Vessels which have lately undertaken, as I am told, to pass without calling at Mobille, from this Country, laden with Cotton. I cannot but anticipate unpleasant consequences, but will inform you of the result when acquainted with it."

Extract (DNA: RG 233, President's Messages, 9A–D1); letterpress copy of extract (DNA: RG 46, President's Messages, 9B–B1). Extract 1 p.

From James Bowdoin

Sir,   ST. ANDER July 8th. 1805.

I had the honour to inform you the 18th. Ulto.[1] of my arrival at this place, & of my determination to pursue my Journey to Madrid with all expedition: Since which, I have been taken down with a fever, which for a number of days threatened my Life; & has so reduced me, as to put it out of my power to pursue my Journey to Madrid. In consequence of which, I have written to Madrid for a Passport to go out of Spain for a few months for the recovery of my health; and it is my intention when I receive it, to embark for England to procure medical advice: Shd. the voyage & the medical advice prove salutary, so as to enable me to return to Spain, without danger of a Relapse, in the course of two or three months, I shall in that case return, or otherwise I shall think myself obliged to resign my Commission. Mr. Erving is not at Madrid, & I apprehend, that he has not yet left England: Mr. Munroe, instead of being at Madrid, as I was informed when I last wrote to you, is at Paris, waiting the return of the Emperor from Italy: Mr. Pinkney is at madrid, & will continue there as he writes to me, "*as yet for some time.*" Under these circumstances & the peculiar situation in which the negociations of the U.S. with the Government of Spain actually are, I can see no advantage from being at Madrid at this moment: on the contrary, I conceive my situation would be an awkward & an embarrassing one, and attended with but little public advantage. But be the advantage what it might, it would not be in my power to go there, in the weak state in which I find myself. Lest from the state of my health, I shd. find myself constrained to relinquish my Commission, I have not touched any part of my Salary or outfitt, nor shall I, untill the state of my health shall ultimately determine me to execute or relinquish my appointment: in the latter case, I shall expect a reasonable part of my Expences to be allowed by Government.

I shall take care to keep you duely informed of my situation & circumstances, that as few inconveniences may arise, as the State of my health will permit.

Before I conclude, I would inform you, that the Governmt. of Spain has withdrawn from the province of Biscay its peculiar priveleges;[2] & to make sure of the object, sent thither 12,000 regular Troops, who met no manner of Resistance: some of the principal inhabitants of Bilboa have been taken up, imprisoned & condemned to exile in the Phillipine islands. A military Governmt. is now established at Bilboa, where the Kings Custom house will be soon put upon the same footing, as in the other ports of Spain. In this situation of things, in case the United States shall not be embroiled with Spain, I think it my duty to remind you, that a Consul of the U.S. will be immediately required at the Port of Bilboa. We recd. accts. last Evening of an american Ship being carried in there by a spanish privateer, it is said she was bound to Liverpool from some port of the U.S. & is carried in, on acco. of english property, wch. is said to be on board. Neither the name of the Ship nor of the Captain have I been yet able to obtain.[3] It wd. be fortunate for the owners of the Ship, if there was a Consul of the U.S. at the port of Bilboa! Mr. John Erving some time since a mercht. in Boston, where he now has a number of Children, is very solicitous for the Office of Consul at the port of Bilboa: he was unfortunate when in business in Boston, but has been carrying on Trade between Bordeaux & some of the Atlantic ports of Spain: he speaks french well, & has some knowledge of the Spanish language: if the President shd. have no better Person suggested to him, Mr. Erving will very gratefully accept the appointment, & I believe him capable to perform the necessary duties of the office. Mr. Erving is a Cousin of mine, & also to the Secretary of Legation.[4]

Permit me to suggest that any Letters or instructions you may see fit to send to me had best for the present to be transmitted undercover to Mr. Munroe, at London. I have the honour to subscribe myself most respectfully, Sir, Yr most obedt Servt.

JAMES BOWDOIN

RC (DNA: RG 59, DD, Spain, vol. 9). Docketed by Wagner as received 9 Oct.

1. *PJM-SS*, 9:478.
2. In May 1805, following a minor revolt the previous year, the Spanish central government under Manuel Godoy began to dismantle the fuero system that had allowed the Basque province of Vizcaya a great degree of autonomy (Renato Barahona, *Vizcaya on the Eve of Carlism: Politics and Society, 1800–1833* [Reno, Nev., 1989], 18–22).
3. The ship was the *Mary*, Captain Brown, owned by Minturn and Champlin of New York. The vessel was still being held in mid-September, but an order had been received from

Madrid to try the ship at Bilbao, and Captain Brown was confident that the *Mary* "should be cleared, in 15 or 20 days." In spite of the captain's optimism, the ship and cargo were reported to have been condemned (*New-York Commercial Advertiser*, 9 Aug. and 30 Oct. 1805; *New-York Gazette & General Advertiser*, 24 Oct. 1805).

4. Bowdoin presumably referred to the John Erving who was a son of George W. Erving's uncle John Erving. Like George W. Erving's father, John Erving Sr. was a Loyalist who moved to England during the Revolution, and died there in 1816 (*PJM-SS*, 8:37 n. 2; *Proceedings of the Massachusetts Historical Society*, 2d ser., 5 [1890]: 10–11).

From Peter S. Du Ponceau

SIR   PHILADELPHIA, 8th. July 1805.

Agreeably to your desire communicated to me by Mr. Wagner,[1] I have Sat down to collect & put together in the form of Notes, the facts which had struck me in the course of my reading as throwing light on the history & motives of the British prohibition of the Trade of neutrals with the Colonies of her Enemies. The Subject being very interesting has grown upon me, & this interest, added to an indisposition of Some days has been the cause of its taking up more time than I expected. Having divided my enquiry under three periods, I take the liberty, lest you Should Suspect that I have neglected your intimation, to enclose the first which is completed,[2] & the others will Shortly follow. My object has Simply been to refresh your memory as to a variety of facts, to which, not having at hand the books in which they are recorded, you cannot easily recur. I shall be happy if I can Succeed in convincing you of my Zeal in any thing that may be agreeable to you & of my profound respect. I have the honor to be Sir Your most obedient humble Servant

PETER S. DUPONCEAU

[Enclosure]

Notes on the restrictions imposed by Great Britain,
on the commerce of neutrals with the Colonies
of their Enemies, in time of War.

———

It is expected that the result of these notes will Shew

1st That the restrictions alluded to were not thought of by Great Britain, nor by any other power until the War which began in 1756.

2. That the alledged principle on which those restrictions are founded, was first broached by the British jurists at the period of that War, and has not been advanced or acted upon, either before or Since by any other power.

3dly. That the reasons alledged by Great Britain in Support of those restrictions are merely colourable, while the true reason, which is carefully kept concealed, is a desire to monopolize in time of war, the trade of the French & Spanish American colonies, and therefore that those restrictions are not a measure of war against their Enemies, but a direct hostility upon neutral States.

They are not a measure of war against their Enemies to prevent their colonies from being Strengthened by Supplies from abroad, Since she Supplies them herself with the same articles which She prevents neutrals from furnishing.

They are an act of direct hostility upon neutrals, Since they intercept and destroy their Commerce in order to make room for their own.

These points will be attempted to be elucidated by a recurrence to historical facts.

We shall consider this Subject under three distinct periods.

1. From the reign of Queen Elizabeth to the peace of Utrecht in 1713.

2. From the peace of Utrecht to that of Aix La Chapelle in 1748.

3. From the peace of Aix La Chapelle to the present time.

———

First Period
From the reign of Queen Elizabeth to the peace of Utrecht

It is in vain to look into the Works of the writers of that period for principles particularly applicable to the commerce of neutrals with the Colonies of Belligerents in time of War, and the reason of it Seems to be that the nations who possessed Colonies in America, & particularly Spain & Portugal, were much more jealous of their Commercial monopoly than they are at present, it does not appear that any contraband Trade was carried on with them by neutrals in time of War, & therefore the state of things was not Such as to give rise to discussions Similar to the present.

We find, indeed, that at that time, Belligerent nations were equally jealous of the commerce & prosperity of neutrals in time of war, as they are now, and that they endeavoured to prevent their deriving profit from trading with their enemies, but among the various prohibitions of neutral trade which took place in that interval of time, there is none to be found directed particularly against the Trade to or with enemy's colonies.

The Law of nations as to the Trade of neutrals with Belligerents, appears to have been at that period very much undefined, & indeed, the Subject of Neutrality in general, had not yet sufficiently drawn the attention of the publicists, for we find it barely touched upon, even by Grotius, who collected the Scattered principles of the Law of nations, & reduced it into a regular System.

How vague & how unsettled those principles were during the period that we are Speaking of, & what was the general Spirit of the prohibitions of Belligerent powers at that time, will best appear by a recapitulation in chronological order of the most prominent actes of the European Governments, in respect to the Commerce of Neutrals in time of war.

In 1551. The Hanse Towns required of Denmark that they Should not trade with the Dutch, with whom they were at war. 1. Hubner 78.[3]

In 1572. John, King of Sweden being at war with Russia, issued an Edict, prohibiting all nations from Trading with Livonia and the port of Nerva— Thuan. B: 96.[4]

Poland issued a Similar prohibition, & many Vessels were captured in consequence of it—Marquard. de jure mercat: p. 149[5]—La Liberté de la navigation & du commerce & ca. p: 155.[6]

In 1584. The States of Holland, & in 1586 The Earl of Leicester, who governed that country, prohibited all nations from Trading with Spanish Flanders—(The pretence was—a blockade of the whole coast) Bynk: Quæst: Jur. pub. B. 1. Cap: 11.[7]

In 1597. Queen Elizabeth prohibited neutrals from trading with the Dominions of Spain. Thuan: B. 119. Camden annal, Sub anno 1597.[8] Some writers have pretended that she only prohibited the carrying of provisions, naval Stores & contraband articles, but Thuanus gives us at length her answer to the complaint of the Ambassadors of the King of Poland, on this Subject, in which she is made to say "Navigationem Mercatorium Osterlingorum, quod impediat, frumento *præsertim* & apparatu bellico hostes adjuventium, multas justasque causas habere"[9] nor Says She, do the particular privileges granted to the Easterlings, interfere with this prohibition, for this Special clause has been very properly inserted in them "Ne ad regni hostes commercii Specie *commeare* liceat."[10] And she quotes the Example of Sweden & Poland in 1572. Thuan: Ibidem.

In 1599. The States genl. issued an Edict, prohibiting all nations from trading with Spain. Grot: Hist: Book 8. P: 371. La Liberté &ca. p. 157.[11]

In 1610. Charles IX of Sweden, being at war with Poland, interdicted all Commerce with Riga, which then belonged to that Republic, & with the Dutchy of Courland. La Liberté &ca. page 154. marquard p: 148.

In 1625 Charles I of England made a Treaty with the Dutch by which they agreed to unite their endeavours to prevent neutrals from trading with Spain or her Dominions, by fair means, if possible, that is to say, by obtaining from the Sovereigns of Europe a prohibition of that Trade to their Subjects, otherwise by arresting Searching &ca. the Vessels when suspected of being bound to Spain or the ports of her Dominions. Such is the Spirit of the articles 20. 23. of that Treaty, which is to be found in Dumont, Corps Diplom: Tom 5. Part 2. p. 478.[12] Its execution and the measures of retaliation which France pursued in consequence of it, were, says the author of *La Liberté* &a. p. 160. The cause or rather the pretext of the war between France & England in 1627.

In 1652. The Dutch being at war with the commonwealth of England, prohibited all nations from Trading with the British Dominions. Bynk: Quæst: Jur: Pub: B. 1. C 10.

In 1663. The Spaniards issued a Similar prohibition against trading with Portugal. Bynk: Ibid: C 4.

In 1689. The English made a Treaty with the Dutch, by which it was Stipulated that all vessels found trading with France or her Dominions Should be condemned as prize. The Dutch Plenipotentiaries did not much relish the Article, & remonstrated against it "il faut que cela Soit ainsi," answered King William, "C'est le droit Comun."[13] La liberté &a. p: 163.

The above instances will be Sufficient to shew what was the Spirit of the prohibitions of Belligerent nations against neutral Trade, during the period that we are treating of—There is not to be found in the whole history of those times (at least as far as we have been able to investigate) a Single instance of a prohibition particularly directed against trading with the colonies of Enemies. Of course as the Subject never came under discussion, the writer who treated on the Law of nations did not make it the object of their enquiries. Those that we have at hand have been particularly examined with that view, &, as was expected, nothing has been found in them bearing directly upon the present question.

And, indeed, there was nothing in the State of Colonial commerce at that time, that could give rise to a discussion of this kind. The colonies of the nations of Europe in America, except those of Spain, were yet in their infancy. Spain of course, excited the jealousy of all the other Nations, & particularly by her extravagant pretention of the exclusive Sovereignty of the American Seas. It was well known that she denied to other nations the right of navigating those Seas without her permission. When Oliver Cromwell remonstrated against that claim to Don Alonzo De Cardenas, the Spanish Ambassador, when he complained that the English were treated as Enemies wherever they were met with in the American Seas, and that the English Subjects were liable to be molested by the Inquisition the ambassador answered: "That to ask a liberty from the inquisition and free Sailing in the West Indies, was to ask his master two eyes; and that nothing could be done on these points, but according to the practice of former times." Long's Hist: of Jamaica, Vol: 1. p: 291.[14]

Spain, therefore in war, as well as in peace, watched her Colonies with the most jealous eye, and did not Suffer this Sanctum Sanctorum to be approached by adventurers from other Countries.

The other nations on their parts had but two objects in view.

1st. To colonize Such parts of the American Continent & Islands, as they could take possession of—2dly. To annoy by all the means in their power, & destroy, if possible the Colonies of Spain.

Hence it happened that France and England, tho' at peace with Spain in Europe, were perpetually at war with her in America—Anderson on Trade, Vol: 2 p. 139.[15]

It is now well known the Buccaneers who in the 17th. century, did so much mischief to the trade and Colonies of Spain in America, were protected & encouraged by the Governments of France & England. Sir Henry Morgan,[16] the great English leader of those daring men acted by virtue of a regular commission 1. Long. 301. 2. Anders: 140. and the King Charles 2. himself Shared in the Booty. 1 Long, 626.

The total destruction, therefore, of the Spanish Establishmts. in America, & not a participation in their advantages by means of a contraband Trade, were at that time the object both of France & of Great Britain, while, on the other hand the avenues to those countries, were so well watched by Spain, that contraband was if not altogether impossible, at least very difficult to be carried on, nor does it appear to have been thought of at that time, as an object for mercantile enterprize.

Such was the State of things during the greatest part of the period which we have before us. It continued so until the year 1670 when another Scene began gradually to unfold itself, and to prepare the events which happened in the Subsequent period. Spain and England, tired of mutual hostility, concluded on the 18th. of July of that year, a Treaty to restore peace and good understanding between them in America. By the 9th. Article of that treaty, it was Stipulated, that the Subjects of both parties should abstain from Sailing & trafficking to the ports of each other in the West Indies, & by the 15th. That it was nevertheless to be understood that the freedom of navigation Should not be interrupted, when nothing was attempted contrary to the 9th. article. 2d. Chalmers 34.[17] 1 Long 305.

The French continued longer to disturb the trade of the Spaniards in the American Seas, but the British Government began from that time to turn their thoughts from the project of destroying that trade, to that of participating in it, that project however was not fully matured until the next period.

The Spaniards compelled by actual necessity, had now begun for the first time to shew to foreigners the way to their American ports. On this Subject we shall here Copy a note from Long Vol: 1. page 598. "In 1669. Spain for want of Ships & Sailors of her own, began openly to hire Dutch Shipping to Sail to the Indies, tho' formerly so careful to exclude all foreigners from thence, and so great was the Supply of Dutch manufactures to Spain &ca. that all the merchandize brought from the Spanish West Indies, was not sufficient to make returns for them, So that the Dutch carried home the ballance in money." The English then began to see that it was better to endeavour to profit by the Spanish Colonies, than to attempt to destroy them.

The new System of Measures which afterwards developed itself on the part of Great Britain appears to have been pointed out to the ministry by an intelligent Gentleman, of the name of Nevil, who resided at Jamaica. In a letter which he wrote to the Earl of Carlisle,[18] about the year 1677. which is recorded in Long's History, Vol: 1. page 596. he recommends the following plan:

1. To encourage the Settlement and Cultivation of the Island of Jamaica

2 To endeavour to obtain a *Trade with the Spaniards*, but Says he, so many obstructions will arise from their jealousies & interests in the beginning, as will require a more than ordinary Care in conducting it, & some assistance here & at home to make it practicable.

3 To make some Contract for Supplying their American Settlements with negroes. This he recommends as a means to gain a Trade with those Settlements.

4 To maintain bonâ fide the peace made with the Spaniards & not to Suffer the French to molest or disturb their Trade in the West Indies.

5 To drive the French, if possible, entirely from the Island of St. Domingo, where they had begun to make Settlements, which promised to rise into importance.

These hints appear to have Sunk deep into the minds of the ministry of Great Britain, & we find Mr. Nevil's plan begun to be carried into effect in the famous Asiento Treaty, concluded in 1713.[19]

RC (DLC); letterbook copy and letterbook copy of enclosure (PHi: Peter S. Du Ponceau Letterbook, 1777–1839). In the margin of the letterbook copy of enclosure is a note in Du Ponceau's hand: "2d Period Sent 15 July / 3d Period Sent 23 July."

1. Jacob Wagner had written Du Ponceau on 27 June, asking for the information (Du Ponceau to Wagner, 29 June 1805, PHi: Peter S. Du Ponceau Letterbook, 1777–1839).

2. JM presumably used Du Ponceau's notes while composing his own *Examination of the British Doctrine, Which Subjects to Capture a Neutral Trade, Not Open in Time of Peace* later in 1805 ([Washington, 1806]; Shaw and Shoemaker 10776).

3. Du Ponceau referred to Martin Hübner's 1759 *De la saisie des bâtimens neutres*, 1:78, in which Hübner actually says that the Hanseatic cities demanded that the *Dutch* stop trading with the *Danes*, but that the Dutch replied that such trade was their right and they would not refrain from exercising it. Hübner (1723–1795) was born in Hanover but raised and educated in Denmark, where he became a professor of history and philosophy at the University of Copenhagen from which he had graduated. He was a member of the Society of Arts and Letters in Paris and of the Royal Society in London (Ernest Nys, *Études de droit international et de droit politique*, 2d ser. [Brussels, 1901], 55 n. 2).

4. Du Ponceau referenced *Historiarum Sui Temporis* (5 vols.; Paris, 1604–20) by Jacques-Auguste de Thou (*PJM*, 10:309 n. 1; Sowerby, *Catalogue of Jefferson's Library*, 1:73 and n.). Jacques-Auguste de Thou (1553–1617) was educated in the law and was a member of the Parlement at Paris and the council of state. His history was placed on the Index Librorum Prohibitorum (List of Prohibited Books) in 1609 (Berard L. Marthaler et al., eds., *New Catholic Encyclopedia*, 2d ed., [Detroit, 2003], 14:61).

5. This was the *Tractatus Politico-Juridicus de Jure Mercatorum et Commerciorum Singulari . . . : Accesserunt in Fine Tractatus Ipsa Privilegiorum, Constitutionum, Statutorum,*

Pactorum, &c. Exemplaria . . . (2 vols. in 1; Frankfurt, 1662) by Johann Marquart. Johann Marquart (1610–68) studied law in Jena, Leipzig, and Padua. He was elected to the city council of Lübeck and became its mayor in 1663. As diplomatic representative for that city, he was renowned for his skill in negotiation and his knowledge of commercial law. He is considered to have written Europe's first comprehensive treatise on commercial law (Otto Stolberg-Wernigerode et al., eds., *Neue Deutsche Biographie* [24 vols. to date; Berlin, 1953—], 16:244–45).

6. Du Ponceau cited *La liberté de la navigation et du commerce des nations neutres, pendant la guerre, considerée selon le droit des gens universel, celui de l'Europe, et les traités . . .* (London, 1780) by Eobald Toze. However, what Toze says is that Sweden forbade all commerce with Polish territories in Latvia (ibid., 154). Toze (1715–1789) was a professor of public law and history at the University of Butzow, counselor to the duke of Mecklenburg-Schwerin, and a member of the Royal Academy of History in Göttingen (*Biographie universelle* [1843–65 ed.], 42:9).

7. Du Ponceau referenced *Quaestionum Juris Publici Libri Duo, Quorum Primus Est de Rebus Bellicis, Secundus de Rebus Varii Argumenti* (Leiden, 1737) by Cornelis van Bijnkershoek. Following the assassination of William of Orange in July 1584, which left the Dutch revolt against Spain leaderless, the States General offered the sovereignty of the region first to Henry III of France, then to Elizabeth I of England, both of whom refused, although the latter agreed to supply the states with military aid. Robert Dudley, Earl of Leicester, was placed in charge of the troops and named governor general, a position he held until late 1587. He imposed his embargo, which had a profound effect on Dutch trade and food prices, in April 1586. The Estates of Holland on 27 July 1584 had issued an earlier decree forbidding neutrals to trade with Spanish Flanders on pain of having their ships and cargoes confiscated. Dutch jurist Cornelis van Bijnkershoek (1673–1743) was first a member and later president of the supreme court of Holland and Zeeland, who wrote several seminal works on international law (Jonathan I. Israel, *The Dutch Republic: Its Rise, Greatness, and Fall, 1477–1806* [Oxford, 1995], 216, 219–20, 225–28, 230; Cornelius van Byjnkershoek, *Quaestionum Juris Publici Libri Duo,* Classics of International Law 14 [2 vols.; 1737; facsimile reprint, Oxford, 1930], 2:75; *Encyclopaedia Britannica* [11th ed.; 29 vols.; Cambridge, 1910–11], 4:896).

8. Du Ponceau here referenced William Camden's *Annales Rerum Anglicarum, et Hibernicarum, Regnante Elizabetha* (2 vols. in 1; Leiden, 1625). William Camden (1551–1623) was an English educator, historian, and herald who was educated at Oxford and taught for over twenty years at Westminster School. After he published a historical and geographical description of the British Isles in 1586, he was named senior herald in the College of Arms. His *Annales,* the first biography of Elizabeth I, was written in two parts; the first was published in 1615 and the second, posthumously, in 1625.

9. "Navigationem Mercatorium Osterlingorum, quod impediat, frumento *præsertim* & apparatu bellico hostes adjuventium, multas justasque causas habere." They had many just reasons to interfere with the merchant navigation of the Eastern people, who were helping the enemy, *especially* with grain & means of war (editor's translation).

10. "Ne ad regni hostes commercii Specie *commeare* liceat." Nor shall it be allowed to work together with the enemies of the kingdom under the appearance of trade (editor's translation).

11. Du Ponceau is citing Hugo Grotius's *Annales et historiae de rebus Belgicis* (1657). In the English translation by T. Manley (London, 1665) the referred matter is found in book 8, 639–40, which states that the States General sent copies of their decree to several countries "that none might pretend ignorance thereof." Hugo Grotius (1583–1645) was a Dutch diplomat and philosopher whose treatise on international law, *De Jure Belli ac Pacis,* is regarded as "an essential foundation" for the study of that subject (Paul Edwards et al., eds., *The Encyclopedia of Philosophy* [8 vols. in 4; 1967; reprint, New York, 1972], 3:393).

12. Du Ponceau cited *Corps universel diplomatique du droit des gens; contenant un recueil des traitez d'alliance, de paix, de treve, . . . faits en Europe, depuis le regne de l'empereur Charlemagne jusques à présent . . .* (8 vols. in 14; Amsterdam, 1726–31) by Jean Dumont. In articles 20–23 of the treaty, the signatories listed what was to be considered contraband, agreed to persuade all neutral rulers to forbid their subjects to trade with Spain, and further agreed that if those rulers would not do so, the signatories would seize any ships suspected of such trade and carry them into their own ports for inspection (Davenport and Paullin, *European Treaties,* 1:297–98). Jean Dumont (1667–1727) entered the army but left after having been tried and acquitted of espionage. He traveled through Italy, Malta, Turkey, and Germany, and wrote about his voyages. His book on the peace of Ryswick brought him to the attention of Count Zinzendorf, who recommended him to Emperor Joseph I, who charged Dumont to write a history of the battles of Prince Eugene of Savoy. Dumont was a counselor and historiographer to Charles VI, who named him baron de Carlscroon in 1725 (*Dictionnaire de biographie française,* 12:220–21).

13. "It is necessary for it to be that way" and "it is the common law." For the 1689 treaty between England and the United Provinces forbidding either signatory to trade with France, see Jenkinson, *Collection of All the Treaties between Great Britain and Other Powers* (1968 reprint), 1:292–95.

14. Du Ponceau cited Edward Long's *History of Jamaica. . . . with Reflections on Its Situation, Settlement, . . . Laws, and Government* (3 vols.; 1774; reprint, London, 1970), which said that Cromwell based his complaint on the 1630 treaty between England and Spain, which stated "that there should be a peace, amity, and friendship, between the two kings and their respective subjects, in all parts of the world." Cornish native Edward Long (1734–1813) belonged to a family that had for decades been connected with the Jamaican government. In 1757 he moved to Jamaica, where he was a judge of the vice-admiralty court and a member of the legislative assembly. He returned wealthy to England in 1769 and wrote a number of pamphlets on Jamaica before producing his epic work.

15. Du Ponceau referred to Adam Anderson's *Historical and Chronological Deduction of the Origin of Commerce from the Earliest Accounts Containing an History of the Great Commercial Interests of the British Empire* (4 vols.; 1801; reprint, New York, 1967), 2:493–94. Scottish-born Anderson (1692–1765) spent forty years in London's South Sea House, rising in the end to chief clerk. *An Historical and Chronological Deduction of the Origin of Commerce,* first published in two volumes in 1762, made his reputation as "one of the first serious historians of commerce." JM was familiar with Anderson's work and cited him often in the 1780s and 1790s (*PJM,* 13:208, 209, 211 n. 5, 366, 367 nn. 1, 3–9, 367–69 and nn.; 14:121, 122 n. 5; 15:170 n., 179, 189, 201 n. 8, 216, 224 n. 4; and 17:575).

16. Henry Morgan (ca. 1635–88) was a privateer who led plundering expeditions in the 1660s against Spanish territory in Portobelo in Panama and Maracaibo in Venezuela in the on-again, off-again Anglo-Spanish wars of the period. In 1671, with an army of over 2,000 volunteers, he captured and sacked Panama City. He was arrested in a campaign against privateering in 1672 and imprisoned in the Tower of London until 1674, after which he was named lieutenant governor of Jamaica and knighted. He returned to the island, where he also served as a council member and an admiralty court judge, and with the tacit approval of Charles II, encouraged privateering against Spain. He was acting governor from 1680 to 1682 but was suspended from office in 1683 when his political rivals gained power. He used his time in office to accumulate wealth and died one of the richest men in Jamaica.

17. Du Ponceau referred to George Chalmers's *Collection of Treaties between Great Britain and Other Powers* (2 vols.; London, 1790). It is the eighth article of the Anglo-Spanish treaty of 1670 that forbids subjects of each country from trading with the West Indian possessions of the other (ibid., 2:34, 37, 39). In his discussion of the treaty, Long also confuses the provisions of the eighth and ninth articles (*History of Jamaica* [1970 reprint], 1:305–7).

George Chalmers (1742–1825), was born and educated to the law in Scotland and emigrated to America in 1763, where he invested in land and practiced law in Baltimore. A Loyalist, he returned to England in 1775 and spent the next several years producing anti-American works. In 1786 he was named chief clerk of the Privy Council's Committee on Trade and Foreign Plantations, a position he held until his death, and in 1792 he was appointed London agent for the legislative assembly of the Bahamas. He was a prolific writer who researched and published several histories of Scotland while filling these two positions.

18. Charles Howard, 1st Earl of Carlisle (1628–1685), who held government and military offices under both Oliver Cromwell and Charles II, was governor of Jamaica from 1677 to 1681.

19. For the Asiento of 1713 between Spain and Great Britain allowing the British to import 4,800 slaves a year for thirty years into the Spanish colonies in the West Indies and South America, see Jenkinson, *Collection of All the Treaties between Great Britain and Other Powers* (1968 reprint), 1:375–99.

From Cato West

SIR   MISSISSIPPI TERRITORY July the 8th. 1805.
    I have lately receiv'd from the Secretary of the Treasury a letter, inform-ing me that he coud not pay towards the ordinary expences of my office as Secretary of this Territory, more than 72 dollars 22 Cents for the present year, owing (as I understand him) to the allowance for a Clerk to my office during the absense of the Govr having been paid out of the appropriation for the contingent expenses of the Executive department of this Government. I am of opinion Sir that the Secretary has not perfectly understood this affair, and I trust that you will be pleased to explain it to him, so that my bills drawn before the rect of his letter may be paid. Without your authority Sir,[1] I never shou'd have drawn on you for one dollar on that account, altho' the State of my health, and the situation of the Public business in which I was engag'd compelld me to employ a person to aid me in the discharge of the duties of my offices, as well as other important matters which I attended to for the U,S, in the course of my Administration of this Government.
    Various considerations have combind to induce me to retire from the office of Secretary of this Territory—you will therefore please to accept this as my resignation of that office. I am Sir very respectfully Your most obedient Servant

                                                                CATO WEST

RC (DNA: RG 59, TP, Mississippi, vol. 1). Docketed by Wagner as received 13 Aug., with his note: "Mem. that J Wagner permitted another of Mr. West's bills to be protested on account of the appropriation being exhausted."

1. On 21 May 1804, in response to a 19 Apr. 1804 letter from West (not found), State Department clerk Bernard Smith stated that he had been "directed to inform you that you

can draw on the Secretary of State, for the amount of the salary due the Clerk you were authorized to employ to aid you in the discharge of your duties during the absence of Governor Claiborne" (Carter, *Territorial Papers, Mississippi*, 5:326).

§ To Alexander J. Dallas. *8 July 1805, Department of State.* "The Commors. under the 7th. Art. of the British Treaty having awarded a considerable sum to Thomas & Philip Reily as owners of the Brig Sally & her Cargo,[1] which had been captured under circumstances requiring, by the provisions of the Treaty, that compensation should be made by the British Government, the two first instalments of it have been received by the public Agent, as doubtless the third will be in the course of this Month. On account of the complication of interests in the proceeds of the award, arising from insurances, failures & assignments, I judged it reasonable to require a bond of indemnity before the money was paid into the hands of the claimants, but one of them Mr. Clement Biddle, in lieu of it proposes the enclosed documents. I have therefore to request your opinion, whether they constitute such a title to the money as may admit of its being legally paid."

Letterbook copy (DNA: RG 59, DL, vol. 15). 1 p.

1. For the case of the *Sally*, Logan, see JM to Clement Biddle, *PJM-SS*, 8:353–54 and n. 2.

§ To Thomas FitzSimons. *8 July 1805, Department of State.* "In answer to your letter of the 4th. inst. [not found] I can only inform you, that it appears from a letter received from Genl. Armstrong, dated on the 6th. of May[1] that the drawing of the bills under the Louisiana Convention commenced on the 3d. of the same month. A letter from Mr. Livingston written to me since his arrival[2] is silent respecting the amount and description of the bills of which he was the bearer; it is therefore presumed that they were such only as were confnded [*sic*] to him by private persons."

Letterbook copy (DNA: RG 59, DL, vol. 15). 1 p.

1. *PJM-SS*, 9:326.
2. See Robert R. Livingston to JM, 29 June 1805, ibid., 501–2.

§ From Sylvanus Bourne. *8 July 1805, Amsterdam.* "I had the honor to address you on the 6th Inst on the interesting letter from you of the 23 May[1] & I have no doubt you will be convinced that I made no *misrepresentation* to you in the *Case in question.* Should you need a confirmation Mr. Biass of Baltimore will be ready I shou[l]d presume to give it as in a letter to me since my last arrival here in which he inclosed me powers to Settle his Accots with mess D& O he says 'they have infamously Swindled & cheated me out of a little fortune since my connection with them'—I shall ever regret that my peculiar situation at the time should have suggested to me the idea of making any proposition on the subject of buisness to them—but my mind was embarrassed by misfortune & objects did not present themselves in a clear & distinct light, you will perceive indeed by the tenor of my letters that I had no *fixed* plan in view as those letters refer to three distinct plans—& what regarded the Consular arrangment was merely on this ground that

as 19/20s of the papers which are legalized at the Consular Office are made out at the
Brokers—I thought it would be to the convenience of Citizens the Merchants
here & all parties to have the Offices under one roof & I intended to give him the
character of Chancellor agreably to the practice of some of our Consuls in France
but nothing was intended or implied in the thing which could in its tendency divert
the Consular Powers from their proper channell or incur a farthing aditional charge
on our trade—indeed in many instances since ⟨I⟩ have been in Offices my charges
have been less than what the Law allowed—Could interest have ever been able to
warp my judgm⟨en⟩t I shou[l]d have been a rich man now instead of the contrary.

"I have waded thro trouble & Chagrin to fix an establishment which has already
had & must continue to produce substantial & lasting Advantages—& cruel indeed
would it be should I become the victim thereto—as this would be my ruin while
it wou⟨ld⟩ add a new & splendid laurell to the brow of that monster of duplicity &
intrigue—I shall prepare & soon send on a Statement to be published which will
do away any unfavorable impressions from the public mind which his publication
may have caused which has indeed given me sufficient pain—but my zeal has
pr[*illegible*]red it to me.

"If you think me to have violated public duty or private faith—you certainly
would do wrong in suffer me to hold my place—but I am unconscious of any thing
of the Sort & shall [at] all Events have the Consolations de⟨riv⟩ed from an approving mind."

RC (DNA: RG 59, CD, Amsterdam, vol. 1). 2 pp.; docketed by Wagner "8 July 1805";
dated 8 July 1804 and filed there; date assigned here based on internal evidence and Wagner's docket.

1. *PJM-SS*, 9:379–80.

§ From Frances Smith Prevost.[1] *8 July 1805, New Orleans.* "On the 10. of last month
while in the discharge of his duties Mr. Prevost was attacked with a serious fever
which still confines him to his bed: And his Physicians are of opinion that he will
not regain his strength in this Country until the cold weather sets in, in Decembr.
It is therefore his wish, thro' you to obtain permission from the President to leave
the Colony on the arrival of Judge Duffield, and the moment that such leave is
obtained he will take the first vessel that offers whithersoever she may be bound.
The very great interest I take in this event induces me to solicit an early answer."

RC (DNA: RG 59, TP, Orleans, vol. 7). RC 1 p.; docketed by Wagner as received 13 Aug.,
with his note: "Quer. what controul has the President over the Judges?" The initials in the
signature are illegible. On 10 Mar. 1806 John B. Prevost wrote JM (DNA: RG 59, TP, Orleans, vol. 8) that his wife, Frances Ann Smith Prevost, had written JM the previous June
notifying him of Prevost's illness. On 7 May 1806 JM replied (DNA: RG 59, DL, vol. 15)
that the earlier letter had been received and answered. See JM to Prevost, 28 Aug. 1805.

§ From James Simpson. *8 July 1805, Tangier.* No. 97. "No. 96 by way of Faro and
Lisbon accompanied sundry Accounts up to the 31st December last year, sent to
the care of Consul Jarvis.[1] In attention to the very great difficulty there now is in

obtaining money from Gibraltar, with a prospect of encreasing, and the apprehension it may become not less so to pass Bills in Spain, I have this day taken the freedom of drawing a Bill on you for One thousand dollars on Account of Sallary, payable thirty days after presentation to the order of Richard W Meade Esqr of Cadiz. Altho' this Bill has been drawn with some anticipation of the usual period I have observed, for the reasons above assigned I beg you will be pleased to order its being paid, excusing the liberty I have taken."

RC (DNA: RG 59, CD, Tangier, vol. 2). 1 p.; docketed by Wagner.

1. See Simpson to JM, 5 July 1805.

From Anthony Merry

SIR,   WASHINGTON July 9th. 1805
    His Majesty's Consul at Norfolk in Virginia has transmitted to me a Copy of a printed Notice (a Transcript of which I have the Honor to enclose)[1] published by the Deputy Marshall of the United States for that District advertizing for Sale on the 12th. of this Month the Brigantine Transfer, which the Notice expresses to have been libelled and sold for a Breach of Blockade, informing me that he had good Reason to believe the Vessel in Question to be British, and that she is the same that, when taken, was called the Scourge, and arrived at Norfolk the Beginning of this Year under the name of the Transfer, which was said to have been captured several Months before in the Mediterranean by a Frigate of the United States, and to have been commissioned for their Service after some summary Form of Condemnation had been adopted by Means of a Board of Officers assembled for the Purpose from the American Squadron in that Sea.

    I have the Honor, Sir, to lay this Case before You, as it has been represented to me, because, if the Circumstances already stated, and those which I shall advert to presently, be correct, there would seem to be in it a great Want of that Formality which, according to Practice usually observed in similar Cases, and to the common Principles of Justice, is necessary to render the Condemnation legal.

    It would seem impossible that that which is said to have taken Place somewhere in the Mediterranean can be considered as such since it is not Known that the United States had at the Time a Court of Admiralty established there, and it would therefore appear to have been very unusual and irregular to alter the Name of the Vessel, and to commission her for the Service of the Government, before the necessary Formalities had been complied with. That a legal Condemnation had not in Fact taken place, and, consequently, that the Alteration in the Vessel's Name and her Employment in the Service was irregular, appears to be evident from the Circumstance of her having been libelled and condemned latterly in the District Court at Norfolk.

With Respect to the latter Proceeding, it is understood that the Vessel was libelled by the Name of the Transfer and not, as ought to have been the Case, by the name of the Scourge, and that Nobody on the Part of the Owners was present to defend their Cause. If these Circumstances should prove to be correct, I can safely trust, from the Known Sentiments of Justice of the Government of the United States, that the latter Proceeding will be considered by them as irregular as the former.

His Majesty's Consul has not been able to acquire any other or more positive Information on this Subject than that which I have had the Honor to state. I therefore take the Liberty, Sir, of submitting it to you, with the Observations which have naturally occurred to me on it, with a Request that you will be pleased to cause the necessary Inquiry to be made into the Matter. I have the Honor to be With high Consideration and Respect, Sir, Your most obedient humble Servant

ANT: MERRY

RC and enclosure (DNA: RG 59, NFL, Great Britain, vol. 3); Tr (UkLPR: Foreign Office, ser. 5, 45:242–243v.); letterbook copy (ibid., ser. 115, 14:113–115). RC in a clerk's hand, signed by Merry; docketed by Wagner: "Brige. Transfer." Tr enclosed in Merry to Mulgrave, 2 Aug. 1805 (ibid., ser. 5, 45:239–240v.). For enclosure, see n. 1.

1. The enclosure (1 p.; docketed by Wagner) is a transcript of a 28 June 1805 advertisement by Cary Selden for marshal Joseph Scott of the 12 July auction sale of "the Brig Transfer, her Tackle, Apparel, Furniture and Stores, as she came from Sea, libelled and sold for a Breach of Blockade." The *Transfer* had sailed to Tripoli from Malta carrying "powder & other stores belonging to the Tripoline Consul." After evading the blockade, delivering the powder to the pasha, and selling the other goods, the ship, now loaded with oil, sailed for Malta. On 17 Mar. 1804 it was seized by Lt. Charles Stewart of the *Syren*, who sent the *Transfer*'s papers to the United States for a condemnation he considered certain. Stewart sold the vessel to Edward Preble who renamed it *Scourge* and used it in the squadron. The ship arrived at Norfolk in February 1805, but its papers were not sent there for judgment from Washington until April 1805. On 12 July the *Transfer* was sold to Reeves Spalding for $596 and the guns to another buyer for $150 (Knox, *Naval Documents, Barbary Wars*, 3:495, 4:35–36, 5:344, 497–98, 506, 6:203).

From Anthony Merry

SIR,   WASHINGTON July 9th. 1805

I have the Honor to transmit to You enclosed the Copy of a Correspondence which has taken Place between His Majesty's Consul General at New York and the Mayor of that City[1] on the Subject of a Breach of Neutrality which the latter Officer has allowed to take Place on the Part of a

French Privateer by encreasing her Force in Guns, Ammunition and Men, in the Port of New York, where she entered with the Pretext of making some necessary Repairs.

It may be permitted to me to observe upon the Mayor's Reply to the Representation made to him by Mr. Barclay, that his Application for Information on the Subject of it to the Commissary of the French Government and to the Agent of the Privateer, and, above all, his being satisfied with the Assurances which he received from that interested Quarter, for he does not express to have made any other Inquiry, whilst the Circumstances stated by Mr. Barclay were so notorious as to have been remarked upon in the public Prints,[2] would seem to evince a very unfavorable Disposition on the Part of that Magistrate to observe that strict Neutrality to which I am persuaded that the Government of the United States would in every Instance wish to adhere.

This Persuasion, Sir, renders it unnecessary for me to make any Apology for troubling You on this Occasion; and I am equally convinced that it will be sufficient that you should be in Possession of the enclosed Correspondence for such an Animadversion to be made to the Mayor of New York upon his Conduct in this Instance as shall ensure a more strict Observance of Neutrality on his Part in Future. I have the Honor to be, with high Consideration and Respect, Sir, Your most obedient humble Servant[3]

ANT: MERRY

RC and enclosures (DNA: RG 59, NFL, Great Britain, vol. 3). RC in a clerk's hand, signed by Merry; docketed by Wagner: "Les Amies." For enclosures, see n. 1.

1. Merry enclosed copies of Thomas Barclay to DeWitt Clinton, 3 July 1805 (1 p.; docketed by Wagner), stating that since arriving at New York, the privateer *Les Amies* had augmented its guns and crew members and was said to have loaded gunpowder, and asking Clinton to take measures to prevent the ship's departure which was scheduled for the following morning; and Clinton to Barclay, 5 July 1805 (1 p.; docketed by Wagner), saying that he had "applied to the Commissary of the French Government, and the Agent of the French Privateer" and had "received their most explicit and satisfactory Assurance that the Information given to you is totally incorrect."

2. The 6 July 1805 *New-York Gazette & General Advertiser* reported: "The French privateer, which has been in this port for a month, having been repaired, and having taken in powder and guns, sailed on Wednesday last (through the Sound) on a cruize. We shall soon hear, no doubt, of her industry in the old trade of plundering defenceless vessels off Sandy Hook."

3. On 17 July 1805 JM wrote to collector David Gelston at New York: "Mr. Merry the British Minister, has transmitted to me a representation that the French privateer, Les Amies, has increased the number of her men & guns, in the Port of New York accompanied with a suggestion that she might have there also received some gun-powder on board. Though the Mayor appears to have been persuaded that these allegations were unfounded, as they in all probability will prove to be, yet as you are possessed of standing instructions to enquire into and prevent such breaches of neutrality, to ascertain which the Officers of the Customs have the best means, I request you to examine into the matter and report to me the result" (DNA: RG 59, DL, vol. 15; 1 p.).

§ To Albert Gallatin. *9 July 1805, Department of State.* "I have the honor to request that you will be pleased to issue your warrant, on the appropriations for Barbary Intercourse, for one thousand dollars, in favor of James Davidson, the holder of the enclosed bill of Exchange, drawn upon me on the 24th. Novr. last, for the same sum by James Simpson Esqr. Consul of the United States at Tangier in favor of Wm. Jarvis Esqr.:[1] said Simpson to be charged and held accountable for the same."

Letterbook copy (DNA: RG 59, DL, vol. 15). 1 p.

1. See Simpson to JM, 24 Nov. 1804, *PJM-SS*, 8:320.

§ From Jacob Crowninshield. *9 July 1805, Salem.* "You will oblige me very much by informing me whether the Island of Curacoa in the West Indies is in a state of actual blockade, or considered so by the Government. Several recent captures of vessels belonging to this quarter of the Union, under the charge of being bound to Curacoa, has caused much sensation among our Merchts and I have been repeatedly asked for information on the subject. We presume here that the Island is not blockaded as no official notice has been given it.

"Will you have the goodness to state if it is blockaded or not, & if blockaded please to give the time when it actually commenced."[1]

RC (DLC). 2 pp.; docketed by JM.

1. No reply to this request has been found. For the blockade of Curaçao, see JM to Snell, Stagg, & Co., 8 Oct. 1804, *PJM-SS*, 8:135–36.

§ From Frederick Jacob Wichelhausen. *9 July 1805, Bremen.* "I beg leave to confirm to you the contents of my last respects of the 20th March[1] when I had the honor to ⟨i⟩nclose you the usual semi-annual report, and to communicate to you at the same time the rigorous measures taken by the respective Governments of Germany and Denmark against Vessels coming from the different Sea-ports of the United States, in order to prevent the communication and extension of the yellow fever in those Countries.

"Till now the Quarantaine laws published by the Duke of Oldenburg continue to be in force: all vessels coming from the different Ports of the United States are obliged to perform a few days quarantaine, even being furnished with proper Certificates of health, and vessels coming from Charleston are not yet admitted at all⟨;⟩ on account of the proclamation of the Board of Health in Philadelphia, of last year⟨,⟩ wherein this place is proclaimed as an infected one.

"Three Bremen vessels and one vessel belonging to Oldenburg subjects which arrived lately from that Port were sent to Christiansand, where they are obliged to perform a Quarantaine agreeable to special circumstances from twenty to forty days.

"I entered into a very circumstancial Correspondence with Mr. Hentz: President of the Board of Quarantaine in Oldenburg, Wherein I endeavoured to shew the unjustness of the measures taken against Vessels coming from Charleston, as in England, France and Holland, all vessels arriving from this Port, were admitted without further examination or difficulty. I tried to convince him of the innocuousness of the malady which had prevailed last Summer in Charleston in so slight a degree, it being merely considered there as a seasonable fever, attributed to the hot climate, which immediately disappeared again when the cold weather commenced, that in general only foreigners not accustomed to the Climate were attacked by it, and that it wa⟨s⟩ not considered there as an infectious malady, as in the Country in the neighborhood of the City, never the Sickness had extended itself. All these different arguments could not prevail on the Government to alter its regulations in regard to Charleston; after alledging to me the different reasons for acting with such precaution, Mr. Hentz finally declared that the conduct adopted by France, England and Holland in regard to Quarantaine could be no rule to them, as all their regulations were made in concert with the northern powers, viz: Prussia, Denmark, Sweden and Russia, consequently they could make no alteration therein without it being previously done and officially communicated to them by one of those Powers, whose example they were obliged to follow. I have therefore wrote again to Mr Saabye, requesting his interference near the Government of Denmark, respecting Charleston, and I hope still that his renewed applications may be as successful as they have been in regard to New York, as by his exertions, occasioned by my informations and request, this City was scratched out again on the list of infectious places in the Royal Danish Quarantaine Ordinances.

"By the Prussian Royal Acad⟨emy⟩ of Sciences, a Premium of 200 Ducats is promised for the best comment on the nature and qualities of the yellow fever, if it be a contagious sickness, or if its poison can be transferred in lifeless substances, ⟨and⟩ for what space of time the substance may keep its destructive power &c &c, the answers are to be delive⟨re⟩d at the high medical college at Berlin, before the 1st. Jany 1807. You will please to perceive by this measure how desirous the King of Prussia is himself to have a clear and correct idea of the nature of this dreadful malady, in orde⟨r⟩ to take such constructive measures, which prevent the communication and exten⟨sion⟩ of it, without the interruption of Commerce and Navigation. Indeed th⟨e⟩ King of Prussia acts very proper in this respect, only the premium of 200 ducats is by no means adequate to the importance of the questions.

"In compliance with my Duty, I have the honor to transmit you again the semi annual report [not found], of American Vessels arrived at and sailed from the River Jahde in the first six months of the present year which is drawn out with the usual care and diligence. The number of American vessels is not large in this list, however a very considerable part of the Commerce between the United States and this City is still carried on in Bremen Vessels. The Jahde River being considered very dangerous in the winter season, keeps off foreigners from this Port as undoubtedly the Navigation of American Vessels to Bremen, would in the present war be much more considerable if the Weser was not blockaded, therefore this blockade is not only an inconvenience to this City, but also to foreign neutral Nations."

RC (DNA: RG 59, CD, Bremen, vol. 1). 3 pp.; docketed by Wagner.

1. *PJM-SS*, 9:160–63.

To Thomas Corbett

SIR, DEPARTMENT OF STATE July 10th. 1805.

I have received your letter of the 22d: ult.[1] enclosing the memorial of the Insurance Company of which you are President and of the Merchants and others interested in the commerce of Charleston.

Having been before made acquainted by the Collector of the Customs with the circumstances of the capture of the two Friends, I lost no time it[2] stating it to the French Minister, who has replied that the communication made to him respecting this affair by the Commissary of his Nation at Charleston, had enabled him to anticipate my desires,[3] by requesting the Captains of the French Colonies, to all of whom he had written respecting it, to obtain satisfaction for this violation of the Convention between France & the United States.

The observations contained in the memorial respecting the local situation and the protection necessary for the port of Charleston and the adjacent coast have been weighed by the President and in connection with other information will promote such measures as the nature of his functions, the existing laws, and the public good may be thought to admit and require. I am &c.

JAMES MADISON.

Letterbook copy (DNA: RG 59, DL, vol. 15).

1. See Thomas Corbett and others to JM, 12 June 1805, *PJM-SS*, 9:456–59 and n.
2. The clerk probably intended to write "in" here.
3. See Louis-Marie Turreau to JM, 24 June 1805, ibid., 493–94.

To Benjamin Lincoln

SIR. DEPARTMENT OF STATE. July 10th. 1805.

I request you to be pleased to cause to be purchased, as soon as possible, and delivered to the Assistant Military Agent at Fort Independence the following articles intended for Algiers and respecting which he will receive instructions.[1]

1 piece of fine muslin embroidered with small spots of Silver.

1 Do. embroidered in like manner with gold.

In case the latter cannot be procured you will substitute two pieces of very fine Indian Dimity, or a piece (10 yards) of very fine muslin.

About two hundred dollars worth of Sweetmeats prepared without any spirituous mixture.

50 lb of Coffee.

I shall be obliged by your taking care that they be chosen with particular attention & safely packed.

You may draw upon me for the expense, at sight, accompanying the draft will[2] a bill of parcells. I am &c.

JAMES MADISON.

Letterbook copy (DNA: RG 59, DL, vol. 15).

1. For the initial request for these items, see Timothy Mountford to JM, 3 Jan. 1805, *PJM-SS*, 8:446, 449 n. 4.

2. The clerk probably meant to write "with" here.

From Charles Pinckney

DEAR SIR,   MADRID 10th. July 1805.

In my last I informed you of the capture by the Spaniards of four American Vessels, and among them an American Gun-boat.[1] I have now to acquaint you that this week's posts brings us the disagreeable intelligence of *four more* being taken by the Spaniards likewise—to wit; the John, in the Mediterranean, not yet arrived—the Polly carried into Algeciras—the Washington carried into Malaga, & a large new ship bound from New York to Liverpool, (name unknown as we have no Consul at Bilbao,) and carried in there by the Adventure, Spanish Privateer of that Port. On these, as on the former cases, I have made the strongest Remonstrances, and urged their immediate release, & compensation for the detention—You are, however, to expect no satisfaction, but on the contrary, that the business of capturing our Vessels will go on rapidly, the same orders being issued as during the last war—In addition, I am informed, from two or three different sources, but all very respectable, that secret orders are issued to the Tribunals, in the Ports to be slow in deciding on these or any other cases that may arise, as this Government means to indemnify themselves by these means for the part they think you will find Yourselves obliged to act with respect to Spain, on the arrival of the Dispatches by Capt. Dulton[2]—of one thing, however, you may always be sure, that the moment an American Vessel & Cargo are captured & brought into a port of Spain, both are immediately & irrevocably lost. I expect Mr. Young or Mr. Erving here daily to relieve me & then I propose setting out immediately for you, to bring you my Accounts & my proceedings here, & to have the pleasure of seeing you, & then also I think you will confess you never had a Minister in Europe who has had more work or trouble than I have

53

had for the last four years. With my affectionate Respects to the President, I am always Dear Sir, Yours truly.

CHARLES PINCKNEY

RC (DNA: RG 59, DD, Spain, vol. 6A). In a clerk's hand, signed and addressed by Pinckney; docketed by Wagner as received 2 Sept.

1. See Pinckney to JM, 26 June 1805, *PJM-SS*, 9:494–95.
2. For Thomas Dulton's departure, see Pinckney to JM, 28 May 1805, ibid., 410–11. Dulton arrived at Plymouth, Massachusetts, shortly before 25 July (*New-York Commercial Advertiser*, 25 July 1805).

§ To Robert Patterson. *Ca. 10 July 1805, Department of State.* "I have the honor to request, that you will permit Mr. George Harrison, Agent of the Navy Department at Philadelphia, or an Artist under his direction, to make use of the machinery of the Mint for striking the medal voted to Commodore Preble, and that you will also be pleased to furnish from the Mint any aid which may be necessary in preparing the steel for the die."[1]

RC (PHi); letterbook copy (DNA: RG 59, DL, vol. 15). RC 1 p.; in Wagner's hand; addressed and franked by him; signature torn. Undated; conjectural date assigned based on docket: "0 July received 11 do 1805. requesting use of machinery in striking Medals." Letterbook copy dated "(supposed) 10 July 1805."

1. For the origin of this request, see Robert Smith to JM, 3 July 1805.

§ To Charles Simms. *10 July 1805, Department of State.* "I request you to be pleased to inform me whether there is at Alexandria any Vessel, bound to Boston; as I wish to Ship thither five pieces of brass cannon intended for Barbary."[1]

Letterbook copy (DNA: RG 59, DL, vol. 15). 1 p.

1. On 12 Aug. 1805 the War Department charged the State Department $8,664.99 for five brass eighteen-pound cannon including carriages and transport from Philadelphia to Boston (DNA: RG 59, ML). For the manufacture of the cannon, see JM to Tobias Lear, 20 Apr. 1805, *PJM-SS*, 9:261–62.

§ From Sylvanus Bourne. *10 July 1805, Amsterdam.* "This will serve to acquaint you that I have wrote you by Capt King on the 6h Inst & shall write you again *more amply* in a few days by Cap Allen to New york & via norfolk on the interesting Subject of your letter of May 23[1]—& by which I hope to explain fully & satisfactorily the apparent Solecism to which your Said Letter refers & convince you that the expressions on a certain head in my letter of 13 March[2] are intrinsically just & applicable to the Case—& also that the connection which I at the time proposed was from the purest motives & that nothing was intended thereby which could militate with my duty, divert the Consular Powers from their proper Channell, or involve one farthing additional Charge on our trade that God who knows & tries the hearts of men will be my judge as the perfect propriety & uprightness of my views—I have to regret the necessities which operated to induce the idea on my part of any connection with this intriguing fellow—as well as the effect which his jesuitical publication may have had on the minds of some, & I Shall send a statement for publication which will do away all unfavorable impressions—& restore me to the highest confidence which it has ever been my pride & anxious desire to conciliate & deserve from my fellow Citizens & my Govt.

"I am most deeply grieved that you should even for *a moment* have had re⟨ason⟩ Sir to doubt the propriety of my conduct—as a Man or public Officer—which not only Sentiment but my highest interest must operate in making me anxious to deserve seeing that on the preservation of your confidence depends the only source I have for the support of my moth⟨erless⟩ Infants an aged mother & my truly distressed family since the failure of my late commercial House. The person in question has said he would spend ƒ20,000 to ruin me but if I lost my place his object would be acquired at a cheap⟨er⟩ Rate & his triumph would be complete—I have waded through much trouble & chagrin to fix a buisness that has already had & will continue to offer the greatest benefits to our trade here—if my Zeal has led me into any indiscretion it ought to be viewed with indulgence & candor if the motives were correct as I feel them to be.

"The letters to which I refer will probably reach you about the time this does or a few days after please therefore wave any decisive judgment till you get them."

Adds in a postscript: "I shall most anxiously wait your reply."

RC (DNA: RG 59, CD, Amsterdam, vol. 1). 3 pp.; docketed by Wagner.

1. *PJM-SS*, 9:379–80.
2. Ibid., 131–32.

§ From George W. Erving.[1] *10 July 1805, London.* No. 62. "My letter No 59 (May 18th.) transmitted by original & duplicate,[2] acknowledged the receipt of yours dated March 19th. addressed to Mr. Purviance, and directing him to make a proposition to this government for paying in London, instead of at Washington, the third instalment becoming due to it from the United States, under the late Convention: With the same letter I inclosed a copy of Lord Mulgrave's Note acceding to the proposition. The payment will accordingly be made by Messrs. Baring on the 15th. of this month, to some person who will be properly authorized by the British government to receive it.

"I have now the honor to acknowledge the receipt of the following letters for the minister Vizt.

March 2d.   "   "
March 6. and its inclosures by original & duplicate[3]
March 11. by original, duplicate & triplicate[4]
March 15. by original and duplicate
March 25. by original, duplicate and triplicate
March 26. by original duplicate and triplicate
April 4.   "   "   "
April 12. duplicate and triplicate[5]

May 13. by original and duplicate[6]
and one from the Secretary of the Navy dated April 16th.[7]

"I have from time to time advised Mr. Monroe of the receipt of the most material of these dispatches, & that I shoud act on the directions which they contain as far as may be proper, during his absence. The important subject to which that of April 16th. relates, I presume it is not your wish that I shoud touch upon, but rather that Mr. Monroe shoud find it on his return in the same state which he left it in.

"I have duly communicated to this government, that the President has thought proper to revoke the commission of Mr. Harry Grant as Consul at Leith; & have written also to Mr. Grant to that effect, in such terms as you directed.[8]

"I have lost no time in taking measures to procure the documents referred to in the legislative resolve transmitted by your Letter of May 11;[9] the latter part of them are very difficult to be obtained, but yet I hope to be able to complete & send them in the course of a few weeks.

"Upon the subject of your letter of March 26h. I had an interview with Mr. DeRehausen the Swedish Minister on the 23d ultimo, in which I opened and urged the claims upon his government therein referred to: he expressed himself in terms of indignation and surprize at the proceeding of the Governor of St. Bartholomews—assured me that he woud transmit with great pleasure the note which I shoud address to him on the subject, and was persuaded that his government woud immediately attend to the representation: He found it the more difficult to conceive a *motive*[10] for the extraordinary conduct of the governor; since at that period, Sweden & France were not on an amicable footing; & he particularly desired, if I had any private information on the subject, and more especially in what related to the governor, that I woud communicate it, as it woud enable him to strengthen the representation which he shoud make: I replied that the conduct of the governor might certainly be considered as very mysterious, that we had no acquaintance however with his private motives, that I woud communicate in my note all the facts which had come to the knowledge of our government, by which he woud see that it was a pure case, unembarrassed with any questions or difficulties which coud impeach the justice of the claim. He again assured me that he woud do all in his power to promote the object, but observed that some considerable delay woud arise, from the necessity of sending out to St. Bartholomews to make formal investigations; to this I observed, that in consequence of Mr. Soderstrom's interference, all these preliminary steps had been taken, and therefore I did not doubt that the present application, thro' the channel of his representations, woud produce without much delay, the remuneration which the claimants had so long awaited. Mr. De Rehausen promised immediate attention to the subject, and on the 24. I addressed to him a note of which the inclosed is a copy.[11]

"Having received from Doctor Rush, answers to the enquiries made by the King of Prussia respecting the yellow fever, I took occasion in transmitting them to Baron Jacobi, to write to him further upon the subject, as I perceived by your letter of May 13. that the measures taken by his government had created a great deal of concern. Copy of that letter and his note in reply are herewith inclosed, as are also some Prize questions proposed by the medical college of Berlin, which he has since transmitted to me.[12] I made the alarms of Prussia upon this subject a topic of conversation with Mr. DeRehausen, and learnt from him, that not the least apprehension of a similar kind existed in Sweden; that so far from embarrassing our trade with restrictions of this sort, his countrymen regretted that we had so little intercourse with them, and were desirous, by affording us every possible facility & advantage, to invite us to their ports.

"I have scarcely heard any complaint here, as to the severity of the quarantine regulations, & see no reason to apprehend that this government has fallen into the views of Prussia, or is likely to enter into a concert with her to impose any similar restrictions on our trade, more strict than those which have hitherto been in use. On enquiry at Liverpool I learn from Mr. Maury that though fourteen days were added to the term of quarantine last year, yet that it was only applied to vessels arriving from Charleston, Georgia, & New Orleans, that they have not placed our vessels, arriving from all parts of the United States indiscriminately under quarantine, but those only coming from a state, in some part of which the disorder was known to exist; and that these restraints have been applied impartially to the[ir] own vessels: and with respect to this so far indiscriminate regulation, it has been intimated to me to have arisen from some discoveries of fraud in clearances, as tho' vessels actually from Philadelphia, had brought cl[e]arances from NewCastle.[13] Under these circumstances I have doubted whether it woud be your wish that any immediate representation should be made upon the subject, yet seeing that the general apprehension of importing the infection is greater than the real danger warrants, that this particular measure of the addition of fourteen days to the term of quarantine may be considered oppressive, and as you may also think that a more exact discrimination shoud be made of places deemed to be infected; I have concluded that you woud not disapprove of a communication adverting to those points, & covering the instructions of the Secretary of the Treasury to the Collectors of the customs which you have directed to be communicated to this government.[14] A Copy of my letter to Lord Mulgrave on this subject is herewith inclosed.[15]

"Mr. Lorentz Chargé d'Affaires of the Elector of Hesse, has requested me to obtain information respecting a Mr. George Gattere—this enquiry he is directed by his government to make: I have promised to transmit it to you, and that he woud be furnished with the information desired.[16]

"Count Staremburgh the Imperial Minister has also requested me to forward the two letters inclosed."

RC and enclosures (DNA: RG 59, CD, London, vol. 9). 4 pp.; in a clerk's hand, signed by Erving; docketed by Wagner as received 12 Sept. For surviving enclosures, see nn. 11–13 and 15–16.

1. Boston native George William Erving (1769–1850) was the son of Loyalist George Erving who moved to England during the American Revolution. The younger Erving was educated at Oriel College, Oxford, and at the age of twenty-one returned to the United States where he became a supporter of Thomas Jefferson. Erving served as agent for seamen and also chargé d'affaires in London. He was legation secretary and chargé d'affaires in Madrid from 1805 to 1809, and JM named him special minister to Denmark in 1810 and minister to Madrid in 1814. Erving resigned that post in 1819 and spent his remaining years traveling and translating a Spanish work of philology. He died in New York (*Senate Exec. Proceedings*, 2:156, 531).

2. *PJM-SS*, 9:368.

57

3. JM to James Monroe, ibid., 109–14.

4. See JM to John Henry Purviance, 11 Mar. 1805, ibid., 125–26.

5. Ibid., 135–36, 173, 179–80, 209, 234–39.

6. See JM to John Armstrong, James Bowdoin, and Monroe, 13 May 1805, ibid., 344–45.

7. Robert Smith's 16 Apr. 1805 letter to Monroe dealt with the apprehension of Mark Vigna who was suspected of a forgery committed in Edward Preble's name (Preston, *Catalogue of the Correspondence and Papers of James Monroe*, 1:167). For this case, see Monroe to JM, 18 June 1804, Erving to JM, 27 June 1804, and William Jarvis to JM, 19 Jan. 1805 (*PJM-SS*, 7:330 and n. 1, 380, 8:493–94).

8. See JM to Monroe, 25 Mar. 1805, ibid., 9:173.

9. Erving referred to JM's 11 Mar. 1805 letter to John Henry Purviance (see n. 4 above).

10. Wagner placed a cross here and another at the foot of the page with his note: "†The governor was the son-in-law of the Govr. of Guadeloupe, where the privateers were fitted out."

11. Erving enclosed a copy (3 pp.; docketed by Wagner) of his 24 June 1805 note to Baron Gotthard Mauritz von Rehausen, transmitting copies of protests made at St. Bartholomew on 27 June 1799 before U.S. consul Job Wall by Capt. Ira Canfield of the brig *Matilda* and Capt. Joseph Chandler of the schooner *Reliance*, both of which had been seized in St. Bartholomew waters by French privateers. Erving stated that although Wall had demanded restitution on the very day of the captures, the governor had ignored the request and allowed the sale of *Reliance* without condemnation; both vessels were later condemned at Guadeloupe. Erving added that the U.S. secretary of state had complained to the Swedish government through Swedish consul Richard Söderström, but since Söderström's notes had had no effect, JM had instructed Erving to apply through von Rehausen. For more information on the *Matilda* and the *Reliance*, see Söderström to JM, 10 Jan. 1805, *PJM-SS*, 8:465–66.

12. The enclosure is a copy of Erving's 24 June 1805 letter to baron Konstans Philipp Wilhelm von Jacobi-Kloest (2 pp.), enclosing a letter from Benjamin Rush with three of Rush's pamphlets and his answers to Jacobi-Kloest's questions. Erving added that the U.S. government had taken measures to monitor outbreaks of yellow fever in order to prevent frequent occurrences, to limit the spread of the disease, and to diminish its severity and mortality. For Jacobi-Kloest's original request for information, see Erving to JM, 24 Apr. 1805, ibid., 9:285–86 and nn. 3–4. For the yellow fever competition sponsored by the Prussian Royal Academy, see Frederick Jacob Wichelhausen to JM, 9 July 1805.

13. Erving enclosed copies of his 24 June 1805 letter to James Maury (2 pp.; docketed by Wagner), asking for information about quarantine and health regulations at Liverpool, how they differed from previous years, and if they applied to all vessels from the U.S. coast regardless of port of departure; and Maury's 27 June reply (2 pp.), stating that all ships arriving from New Orleans, Georgia, and Charleston had been required to undergo an extra fourteen days' quarantine, but that in January they had been allowed immediate discharge of their cargoes with permission, which was granted in all cases except those where there had been sickness or death on board. He added that Charleston had been so healthy the previous fall that many American and British captains had neglected to get clean bills of health, and their arrival without them had subjected them to a seven-shilling-per-ton duty surcharge, which he had heard would be returned. Maury said that all vessels from a state where yellow fever had been reported were subject to quarantine regardless of their port of departure, but those leaving from adjacent states were not. No distinction was made on this point between British and American ships.

14. See JM to Armstrong, Bowdoin, and Monroe, 13 May 1805, *PJM-SS*, 9:344–45 and n. 4.

15. Erving enclosed a copy of his 9 July 1805 letter to Lord Mulgrave (4 pp.; docketed by Wagner) that enclosed a copy of the Treasury circular to collectors (ibid., 2:1–4 and n. 1).

He told Mulgrave that the increased restrictions on ships from the United States were not lifted until late into the winter, and that steps taken by the U.S. government, including encouraging all government officials to report outbreaks promptly and to ensure that all bills of health were strictly accurate, had diminished the frequency and mortality of yellow fever. He observed that the length of the voyage between the United States and Great Britain made it unlikely that the disease could be unknowingly imported. He suggested that all these facts should lead to a shorter quarantine period, adding that since yellow fever in the United States never continued past the first frost in November, the same would apply to Great Britain, so there was no need to continue any quarantine after the start of cold weather. Erving stated that it was unnecessary to prohibit vessels from clean ports in states where yellow fever existed because it rarely spread beyond a narrow range, therefore it was highly unlikely the fever would be imported into Great Britain from these ports.

16. Erving enclosed a copy of Richard Lorentz's 22 June 1805 note (1 p.), inquiring about George Gatterer, a physician and apothecary from Göttingen whose sister was married to a privy councilor of Hesse-Cassel. Lorentz said Gatterer had been practicing in Savannah about two years previously, but was since said to have died, leaving an estate worth $20,000. Wagner noted on the verso: "wrote to the Coll. of Savannah 13 Septr 1805." George Gatterer, age thirty-six, "a native of Hanover," died at Savannah, Georgia, on 1 Sept. 1803 (New York *Daily Advertiser*, 24 Sept. 1803; New York *Morning Chronicle*, 24 Sept. 1803).

§ From Anne-Louis de Tousard. *10 July 1805, Philadelphia.* "I am Sorry it is not in my power to deliver my self to you the enclosed letter which Our friend the Marquis de Lafayette entrusted to my care.[1] From the contents of it you will percieve that he depends on a speedy answer, and that his private situation requires an immediate relief. Whether you will be able to promote his wishes, I do not Know, but from the confidence he placed in me and Knowledge of his private affairs, he depends much on your assistance.

"As Soon as I can go to Washington, where I propose going in a couple of weeks, I may give you on our friend's political and private affairs whatever information you may wish to receive; in the mean time you may command all my Services.

"With my best respects to Mrs. Madison I do remain with the greatest esteem & respect."

FC (PHi).

1. The enclosure presumably was Lafayette to JM, 22 Apr. 1805, *PJM-SS*, 9:276–79.

Circular Letter to American Consuls and Commercial Agents

SIR,   DEPARTMENT OF STATE, July 12th, 1805.

THE multiplied abuses of the certificates which the Consuls of the United States were, by the instructions of the 1st August, 1801,[1] authorized to give in the case of foreign vessels, purchased by a citizen of the United States, notwithstanding the precautions taken against them, have led to the conclusion, that a discontinuance of the certificates altogether, is the only effectual remedy. You will therefore forbear to grant any certificate whatever relative to such purchases, except to those who may satisfy you that the purchase was made without knowing this alteration in your instructions. Accordingly you will publicly advertise, that you are restrained from issuing certificates in such cases, with the sole exception just mentioned; and also from allowing the exception itself, after the expiration of two months from the date of the advertisement.

To the Commercial Agents in France new commissions, accommodated to the existing form of government therein, are enclosed herewith. *I have the honor to be, Very respectfully, Sir, Your most obedient servant,*

JAMES MADISON

RC, four copies (offered for sale in Paul C. Richards Autographs, Catalogue No. 265, item 119; R. M. Smythe Summer 1997 Autograph Auction, Public Sale No. 164, item 332; NHi: Gilder Lehrman Collection; LNT: George H. and Katherine M. Davis Collection); FC (DNA: RG 59, Circulars of the Department of State, vol. 1); letterbook copy (DNA: RG 59, IC, vol. 1). RCs and FC are printed copies, signed by JM. First RC is addressed to Robert C. Gardiner, U.S. consul at Gothenburg.

1. *PJM-SS*, 2:1–4.

§ To Francis Becker. *12 July 1805, Department of State.* "The Louisiana Convention not providing for admitting restitution in case of property being irreversibly condemned, the claim you refer to, in your letter of the 6th. inst. [not found], seems to be unprovided for."[1]

Letterbook copy (DNA: RG 59, DL, vol. 15). 1 p.

1. Becker had two claims against the French government. One was for the *Hannah*, Capt. William L. Fisher, for a loss he suffered at Bordeaux in 1797; the other was for the *Harmony*, Capt. Samuel Clapp, that was condemned at Saint-Domingue in 1797 for trading with the rebels (Williams, *French Assault on American Shipping*, 167, 170–71).

§ From Sylvanus Bourne. *12 July 1805, Amsterdam.* "You will not I hope that on accot of the many letters I have lately addressed you[1] in reply to yours of May 23 be disposed to apply to my Case the allusion conveyed by the french proverb which says *Celui qui s'excuse s'accuse.*

"I have indeed Suffered infinite pain & mortification that you Should *for a moment* have had an unfavorable impression in my regard in the transaction alluded to; and it is not to be wondered at that my nerves which have been wire drawn by a Series of almost unparrelled misfortunes & dissappointments for ten years past Should be affected on a Subject so unpleasant in its *prima facie* view & by which I might in the least degree have impaired that confidence in your mind & that of my fellow Citizens at large which it has ever been my desire to cultivate & my pride to have possessed & on which depend the only sure means I have (since the failure of my commercial house) for the support of a truly distressed family.[2]

"I therefore do trust that from the explanation given, you will be Completely satisfied that I have not done or contemplated doing any thing which could militate with my public duty or priva⟨te⟩ faith—& that I shall continue to possess *unimpair⟨e⟩d* the confidence of my Govt which I shall ever keep myself worthy of by a correct & faithfull discha⟨rge⟩ of every obligation imposed by my Official positi⟨on⟩."

Adds in a postscript: "My Antagonist has been heard to Say that he woud Spend ƒ20,000 to ruin me—Should I meet the disapprobation so far as to lose its confidence it would ruin me indeed & fullfill his views at a cheaper rate & afford him a *complete triumph.*

"Even allowing for a moment that my views *had been impure* a most substantial, pub⟨lic⟩ good has been effected—of which our trade must long feel the advantages— this is the uniform & unbiassed opinion of all americans coming here."

RC, two copies (DNA: RG 59, CD, Amsterdam, vol. 1). First RC 3 pp.; marked "Copy"; docketed by Wagner as received 20 Sept. Second RC marked "private"; docketed by Wagner. Minor differences between the copies have not been noted.

    1. See Bourne to JM, 6, 8, and 10 July 1805.
    2. From this point the RC marked "private" reads: "consisting of two motherless infants—my aged mother & a Sister & you may believe me when I say that was I recalled to morrow—I doubt of having a Surplus after settling my affairs here, sufficient to pay my passage to the U.States—unpleasant even as this position may be I am still of opinion that you ought not to continue me a day longer provided you believe me to have violated the principles of public duty or private faith—but I flatter myself you will on a view of the whole case regard it in its true & unaffe⟨cted⟩ light—viz—That as the person in question had my public Confidence at the time proved by my leaving the Consular Powers with him—it was not unnatural that I should hav⟨e⟩ proposed to him a connection in my private Affairs & that th⟨e⟩ idea was suggested & supported by the following Circumstance⟨s⟩ viz that as he was the person who first introduced me to the acquaintance of my late partner I had reason to suppos⟨e⟩ he might be inclined, to an arrangment which might end⟨eavor⟩ to revive the decaying prospects of L & B—which he would hav⟨e⟩ in his power to do by recommending commercial buisness which a Broker from his position has often opportunity to do as it is not customary for Brokers to transact such themselves—in short I thought to make Such an arrangment as might help my house out of its embarrassments—but you ca⟨n⟩ never believe that I should have proposed any connection a⟨t⟩ all with him had I hence been aware that matters were conducted by him as explained in my former letters—the *uniform* tenor of my conduct through life precludes such a belief or opinion altogether—& in respect to the junct⟨ure?⟩ of the Consular Powers I meant nothing more than for the convenience of the merchants & of the buisness generally to give him the character of Secy. or Chancellor as is practised by many of our Consuls in France but nothing thereby *was intended or could operate* to divert the Consular Powers from their true & proper Channell nor endanger my responsibility or the public interest or incur one farthing's aditional charge on our trade. Justice claims this intrepretation as the one due to the purity of my views & motives—such I doubt not you will be disposed to give—& that I shall remain in the full & unimpaired possession of your Confidence & you may rely that I shall continue to fullfill the duties of my Office as I have ever done with integrity & application to those duties in the most correct & rigid purity.
    "I solicit your excuse for the trouble I have given you herein."

§ From William C. C. Claiborne. *12 July 1805, New Orleans.* "I enclose for your perusal a Copy of a Letter, which I this day received from the Reverend Mr. Walsh, together with my answer thereto.[1] You will perceive that the Schism in the Church is not likely to be adjusted;[2] I consider it a *contest* of an extreme delicate nature, and *one* in which I shall very reluctantly take a part, but I suspect that the Marquis of Casa Calvo is the Foreign Agent alluded to by Mr. Walsh, and if I should be furnished with evidence of his Interference, I shall hasten to inform him that his conduct is viewed as indelicate, and improper. The Monk who heads the opposition to Mr. Walsh is a Spaniard, and devoted to the Spanish Government, & there can be little doubt, but the Monks from the Havanna will come hence with the like foreign attachments; but I cannot see how their residence among us can be prevented."

RC and enclosures (DNA: RG 59, TP, Orleans, vol. 7); letterbook copy (Ms-Ar: Claiborne Executive Journal, vol. 15). RC 1 p.; docketed by Wagner as received 20 Aug. For enclosures, see n. 1.

1. The enclosures are copies of Patrick Walsh to Claiborne, 11 July 1805 (3 pp.; docketed by Wagner; printed in Rowland, *Claiborne Letter Books*, 3:121–22), blaming the problems in the local church on "a refractory Monk," "the fanaticism of a Misguided Populace," and the interference of a private person, and stating that "two individuals (whom I can name) instigated by a certain foreign agent (whom I also can name) have gone to the Havannah with the express intent of procuring a reinforcement of Monks, to Support Father Antonio De Sedella in his rebellious conduct," that these monks were expected daily, and that in giving Claiborne this information he had acquitted himself of his duty; and Claiborne to Walsh, 12 July 1805 (2 pp.; docketed by Wagner; printed ibid., 122–23), deploring the upheaval in the church, reminding Walsh that under American law, government officials avoided interfering in religious disputes, and asking him to name the interfering private individual, the two who had gone to Havana, and the foreign agent.

2. For the dissension in the New Orleans Catholic community, see Claiborne to JM, 18, 24, 26 (second letter), 31 Mar., 1 Apr., and 16 June 1805, *PJM-SS*, 9:147–48 and n. 3, 169–70, 183, 195 and n. 1, 199, 200 n. 1, 473.

§ From John Gavino. *12 July 1805*. "I beg leave to congratulate you on the restoration of an honorable peace with Tripoli—adding thereto the agreeable account of capt. Bainbridge, with the other late captives, having got to Sicily."

Printed extract (*National Intelligencer*, 13 Sept. 1805). Printed with the extract are a copy of John Rodgers's 8 June 1805 circular letter (printed in Knox, *Naval Documents, Barbary Wars*, 6:99), which is described as having been transmitted to JM, announcing the peace and the arrival of the *Philadelphia* crew, and an 8 June 1805 letter from William Bainbridge saying he had requested a court of inquiry into his conduct, which he expected would be held in about a week.

§ From William Jarvis. *12 July 1805, Lisbon*. "I had this pleasure the 5 Instant by the ship Robert of Philadelphia Captn Alcorn bound for Baltimore & of executing your Commission for two pipes of Wine by the same Vessel. She sailed the sixth. Inclosed Sir is a Bill of Lading. I was sorry that time would not allow of casing them."

RC and enclosure (DLC: Rives Collection, Madison Papers). RC 1 p. The enclosed bill of lading (1 p.) is similar to that enclosed in Jarvis's 5 July 1805 letter to JM.

§ From Josef Yznardy. *12 July 1805, Madrid.* Came to this court on several matters both private and official when Monroe was here, continuing in his true desires of avoiding [causes of] dissatisfaction, and knowing himself with some power for persuasion in whatever way might be useful, he arrived when negotiations were broken off, with profound regret at having been unable to serve as he had done before now: since Pinckney's arrival, Yznardy had informed him of all military and naval occurrences in the ports of his district and considered JM informed of all that and himself free from all accusations of neglect; and now hastens to tell JM that the said Pinckney told Yznardy that he withdrew, leaving in charge Mr. Young who has not yet appeared there.

JM knows from Yznardy's different statements the wish he has to have named, or to be authorized to appoint, a vice-consul or agent at Algeciras in the proper form and that in the interim Miguel Colletly was there. Captain Stewart, influenced greatly by one Mr. Meade of Cádiz, who proclaims he will be the true consul, gave the appointment of which Yznardy encloses a copy.[1] Not knowing if he had the authority for it, Yznardy has left him until he might have the proper answer from JM to whom he sends two copies of a letter to the governor of Cádiz[2] about the events that [are happening] under the said Stewart. Having helped the said Mr. Pinckney on his way so that he might give JM Yznardy's proper complaint, as well as [news of] several seizures by French and Spanish privateers of American ships carried to the ports of his districts and principally about the brigantine of which the copy sent to the general of the marine speaks. Hopes all this will earn JM's approbation, knowing that in this he performed more immediate service of his position than he might in Cádiz. His vice-consul, to whom it appears that under the influence of Meade, representations have been made that seem to him dangerous, has given JM an official report of all that happened.

The news there is of the taking of Jamaica and [*illegible*] by a squadron of nineteen French and Spanish vessels; that Napoleon Bonaparte had joined Genoa to his territories [and will do?] the same with all the rest of Italy.

Forty Spanish gunboats have assembled in Algeciras where they have arrested our gunboat New York No. 3; the appropriate steps for obtaining its release have been taken.

There are nine Spanish warships ready at Cartagena, two- and three-deckers among them, under the command of Admiral Salcedo of the squadron. In Cádiz there are seven and in Ferrol are fifteen Spanish and French ships whose destination is unknown. The Spanish government seems to be sustaining the war with requisite firmness.

RC and enclosure (DNA: RG 59, CD, Cádiz, vol. 1). RC 3 pp.; in Spanish; in a clerk's hand, signed by Yznardy; docketed by Wagner as received 2 Sept. For enclosure, see n. 2.

1. For Charles Stewart's appointment of Pedro Porral as navy agent at Algeciras in May 1805, see Knox, *Naval Documents, Barbary Wars,* 6:13, 58, 65.

2. The enclosure (3 pp.; in Spanish) is a copy of Yznardy to general of the Cádiz marine Juan Joaquín Moreno, 28 June 1805.

§ To Henry Hill Jr. *13 July 1805, Department of State.* "I have lately received a letter from Mr Blakely late Consul at St Jago,[1] from which it appears that besides the ten-dollars allowed for the passage of seamen when put on board American vessels according to law, he has furnished them with provisions for their passage. You will therefore be pleased to take such steps as may prevent for the future, the furnishing of provisions since the law contemplates the compensation for them as included in the ten dollars passage money.[2]

"He also informs me that the masters of captured vessels have demanded from him from 50 to 100 dollars as a relief from Government. It would be a departure from the legal provisions to advance this. There is no distinction made in the laws between the masters and the men in the mode of administering to their distress."

Letterbook copy (DNA: RG 59, IC, vol. 1). 1 p.

1. JM probably referred to Josiah Blakeley's 7 June 1805 letter of which only an extract has been found (*PJM-SS*, 9:441 and nn.).
2. For section 4 of the 28 Feb. 1803 "Act supplementary to the 'act concerning Consuls and Vice-Consuls, and for the further protection of American Seamen,'" which states that the amount paid to captains for transporting destitute seamen to the United States could not exceed ten dollars, see *U.S. Statutes at Large*, 2:203–4.

§ From James Simpson. *13 July 1805, Tangier.* No. 98. "With this I beg leave to lay before you copy of No. 96 and triplicate of No. 97.[1] We have not had any intelligence of the Emperors Frigate Maimona since her departure from Sallé Roads;[2] there appears a probability she may have been sent to England as no advices have been received from His Majestys Agents there, since they left Lisbon.[3] A Gentleman in London writes me the 3d June that those Men had been looking out for some armed Vessels to purchase, that they had offered £4000 Stg for one, but that he did not know of their having at that time agreed for any. I am satisfied it was expected when they went from hence they would have done more than they have, with such a sum of money in their hands it is astonishing they have not. The difficulty appears to lay in finding Armed Vessels of a Construction and draft of Water suitable for the Bar Harbours of Larach and Sallé, where sharp built Vessels would be in constant danger at passing.

"At Tetuan the two Row Gallies are getting ready for Sea, but the Chief exertions there are applied to finishing a Xebeque to mount sixteen Guns, in order to its being sent to Sea the soonest possible: this Vessel has been hastily built and was lately put in the Water. A quantity of Sail cloth—Cordage and six Brass four pounders were sent from hence three days ago for her.

"You will no doubt have been advised from Spain the frequency with which the Privateers of that Nation have of late carried to their Ports Vessels of The United States, under the most frivolous pretexts. I have often the mortification of seeing them detained in the Straits and sent to Port by the Cruizers of Tariffa and Algeziras. It appears to me highly probable that had but one or two Vessels of War been left on this Station, these Privateers would have acted with more circumspection. I have not heard from Commodore Barron or his Squadron since the Siren went up with the Ann Storeship.[4] Mr Gavino in his Letter to me of the 5h Inst. observes that neither the Gun Vessel No. 7 or any of the Mortar Brigs had then reached Gibraltar, nor have I seen any Vessel of that description pass up since.[5]

"Alcayde Hashash is still here, I never am with him without his touching on subject of the Meshouda[6] and expressing His Majestys desire to send her home. In a late conversation he remarked the time was far past before which the Emperour was given to understand Peace would take place between The United States and Tripoly; he said the Ship would soon become totally useless and if so that it would be a means of fixing in Muley Solimans mind a lasting motive of disgust.

"That may probably be the case, since these people only allow themselves to view matters of such a Nature, on that side suits them. I know the Ship is suffering much because no care whatever has been taken of her since she was put in Larach River in October 1803. My Friend there lately assured me her Copper was geting loose and some of it in a state of dropping off. Whilst this ill fated Vessel remains in this Country we shall have constantly rancorous reflections respecting her. I wish to God the day was arrived when she might be sent from hence. In the course of the last ten days we have had a variety of Reports from Fez on subject of an incursion made by the Arabs of this Country into the Algerine Dominions near the East end of the Atlas; that such an occurrence has happened there is no doubt, but the particulars we have yet received are too vague to be given to you in detail.

"The affair does not appear to have been sanctioned by Muley Soliman, but the unauthorised act of his people to avenge Injuries Done to a Sheriff of this Country near Mascara when on a Journey towards Mecca some Months ago, and for satisfaction of which he had applied in Vain to the Governour of Oran. The Imperial Ambassador returned from Court on Friday last after having accomplished the busyness he went upon; himself and some of his Suite lay dangerously ill of Inflamatory Fevers, occasioned no doubt by the excessive heat of the Weather they experienced on their Journey.

"The Swedish Consul arrived here the 6h Inst from Stockholm, last from Lisbon in the Schooner Andromeda of Boston, bringing Forty thousand dollars for the last two years Subsidy from his Nation to Muley Soliman. Denmark is in arrear for the same time. The Andromeda has gone on to Mogadore in quest of a Cargo of Mules, or produce of this Country, being the first Vessel of the United States has attempted any Trade in this Empire since better than twenty Months back. I beg leave to mention that the Bill of Seven hundred and sixty dollars sixty nine Cents drawn by me the 4h November 1803[7] for ballance of the Amount of Extra disbursements stated the 2d that Month, has layen over untill now; in the first instance because Mr Humphry could not find an opportunity of passing it and latterly because of his death. That Bill will now pass into Mr Gavinos hands, who will recover the ballance due to me thereon. I therefor beg you will please direct its being paid."

RC (DNA: RG 59, CD, Tangier, vol. 2). 4 pp.; marked "Triplicate"; docketed by Wagner.

1. See Simpson to JM, 5 and 8 July 1805.
2. For the *Maimona*, see Simpson to JM, 22 June 1805, *PJM-SS*, 9:490.
3. For the Moroccan representatives, see Simpson to JM, 2 Apr. 1805, ibid., 206.

4. For the departure of these ships from Tangier, see Simpson to JM, 7 June 1805, ibid., 442.

5. For the gunboats sent to the Mediterranean, see JM to Tobias Lear, 20 Apr. 1805, ibid., 261–62.

6. For the *Meshouda*, see Simpson to JM, 26 Oct. and 24 Dec. 1804, ibid., 8:228–29, 421–22.

7. Ibid., 6:18.

From Charles Pinckney

(Private)

DEAR SIR   July 14: 1805 IN MADRID

I send you the contingencies of the six months from January to July which amount only to Two hundred & twenty five Dollars as all foreign Gazettes have been stopped for the last year & nearly all foreign Correspondence had ceased & no documents had arrived to me either from South America or the West Indies or any American Gazettes—the letters & dispatches to Mr Monroe & myself & to him solely on the special mission nearly all came under cover to Bankers & do not appear on the Post accounts.

I find in examining the sums paid by my Mayor Domo for letters—& other documents & packages in the three months from January to April 1804 there was a mistake in the account for that Quarter, of One hundred & sixteen Dollars which was paid on another account & by mistake included in the Postage—the sum to be charged for that Quarter therefore is One hundred & seventy two Dollars which I will thank you to have corrected.

There are considerable sums for Mule hire which I paid distinct from the above for which I have the Vouchers & charge them in the general account. In August last I drew for a sufficient sum to cover all the Debts of the Legation & contingencies up to the time the Bills I gave would become due as was then necessary & indispensable—of things which then took place You will be a better judge when You see me for I am not at liberty to put some of them on Paper even in cypher. Since this & for now nearly a Year I have not drawn for any thing for as I am hopeful to have money enough from the sale of my Effects to carry me home I would rather leave a Balance undrawn in my favour than place it in the power of any one to suppose I had drawn for a shilling I had not fully a right to draw for.

Mr Bowdoin is arrived at Santander but writes me he is sick & cannot come on during summer but that Mr Erving will to relieve me—if he does not I expect Mr Young up from Cadiz whom I mean to leave charged with the Papers until some of them arrive for nothing on Earth but a sacrifice to public duty & keeping the intercourse open (until the President decides what is to be done) could have detained me here until this time, or until some one arrives to relieve me. With my affectionate Respects to the President I remain dear sir with regard & Esteem Yours Truly

CHARLES PINCKNEY

RC (DNA: RG 59, DD, Spain, vol. 6A). Docketed by Wagner. Enclosure not found.

From John Pendleton

SIR   CITY OF RICHMOND July 15. 1805

Presuming on a slight acquaintance but more especially on your universal Civility I take the liberty of addressing you on a subject which gives me infinite concern: I Know sir it does not belong to your Department to attend to applications of this Nature but as the secretary of War is an entire Stranger to me I hope you will pardon me for the intrusion & that he will be so good as to excuse my addressing him through you. I have a son (an only son) who has long lead a very dissipated & irregular course of life, & not long since in the extravagancy of his imprudence & folly, without consulting me or advising with any of his friends enlisted into the Military Corps Stationed at Fort Nelson in the Vicinity of Norfolk in this State, & he has lately written to me to endeavour to procure for him a discharge from that Service; Conscious that he is totally unfit for the fatigue & duty of a soldiers life & hoping that the present moment (if he could be discharged from a situation which is mortifying & painful to him) might be so improved as to get him setled [sic] in business & effect a reformation I feel extremely anxious to obtain a discharge for him; I know sir that applications of this Kind must place the Secretary of War in a delicate situation but as I am confident that it was a precipitate act—that he is unfit from the delicacy of his consitution for the service—that he is very unhappy & that if he is confined to that situation it will soon cost him his life. I hope I shall be pardoned for entreating you sir to intercede with the Secretary at War for his discharge from the service; Your attention to this application will confer superior obligations on sir Your most obedt. & very h'ble Servant

JOHN PENDLETON[1]

RC (DLC).

1. John Pendleton (ca. 1749–1806) was Edmund Pendleton's nephew. He had been clerk of the Virginia Committee of Safety in 1775 and 1776, clerk of the state senate, auditor of public accounts, and was a member of the Council of State from 1796 to 1802. He died

intestate and deeply in debt (*New-York Gazette & General Advertiser*, 19 Aug. 1806; *PJM*, 1:190 n. 8; *PJM-SS*, 4:187 n. 2; Pickett et al. v. Stewart et al., 1 Rand. 478 [Peyton Randolph, comp., *Reports of Cases Argued and Determined in the Court of Appeals of Virginia* (6 vols.; Richmond, Va., 1823–29)]).

§ From William C. C. Claiborne. *15 July 1805, New Orleans.* "Your favor of the 2nd of June [not found] I have had the pleasure to receive. Your Letter to Mr. *Duplantier*[1] shall be delivered, and in his agency for *La Fayette, he* will receive all the aid in my power, for my friendship for that *unfortunate Patriot* is very Sincere, and I feel solicitous that the donation of Congress should prove a sure resource in providing for his own comfort and the establishment of his family. I am desirous to learn the final issue of the pending Negotiation at Madrid. I had Supposed that our Envoy would experience much difficulty and delay; The great *object* of Spain will be to make the Mississippi the Boundary. Her Agents here avow *it*, and hesitate not to Say, that on no other condition will Spain consent to an Amicable adjustment. But my impression is otherwise; If Spain should find that the United States will maintain their ground, and possess themselves by force of the Territory claimed, She will yield to our demands, unless indeed a contrary policy should be advised or prescribed by France, and I cannot conjecture any rational considerations which would lead the Emperor Napoleon to wish a War with the United States. I have not found on the part of Governor Folch, that Spirit of accommodation which I had anticipated; One American Vessel (with Public Stores) was permited to pass and repass the Fort of Mobile without interruption, but other's have been brought to, and duties exacted. The long and unnecesssary detention of Captain Carmick at Pensacola I consider as unfriendly, and the Robbing him of his Papers on his return (which I cannot but attribute to the Spanish Agents) evidences a Hostile Jealousy."[2]

RC (DNA: RG 59, TP, Orleans, vol. 7); letterbook copy (Ms-Ar: Claiborne Executive Journal, vol. 15). RC 2 pp.; marked "(Private)"; docketed by Wagner.

1. See JM to Armand Duplantier, 2 June 1805, *PJM-SS*, 9:424–26. JM's 2 June 1805 letter to Claiborne was presumably just a cover letter, ibid., 426 n.
2. For these incidents, see Claiborne to JM, 5 July 1805, and n. 2.

§ From Peter S. Du Ponceau. *15 July 1805, Philadelphia.* "I have the honor of enclosing to you the Continuation of my Notes &c. for the Second period.[1] I beg you will excuse me for Sending it thus by parcels, but living as I do at present partly in Town & partly in the Country, & not having before me at the same time all the Books that I have occasion to recur to, it necessarily requires more time than it would otherwise do, & correctness & accuracy being the only merit of these Notes, I would not wish to be deficient in this particular. The third & last period, I shall have the honor of Sending you with the least possible delay."

[Enclosure]

Second Period.
From the Peace of Utrecht to the peace of Aix La Chapelle

———

After the cessation of the hostilities between Spain & Great Britain in America, by the Treaty of 1670, commo[n]ly called the American Treaty,[2] a contraband commerce began to be carried on principally if not altogether by English Vessels, from the Island of Jamaica to the Colonies of Spain—This Commerce was already Very considerable at the time of the Treaty of Utrecht. Bryan Edwards tell[s] us that about the beginning of the last Century the Trade of the Spanish Colonies employed 4000 Tons of English Shipping & created a Vent for one million & a half of English merchandize (1. Edw: Hist: W.Ind: 284. Philad: Ed:).[3]

Of So much consequence was this Commerce already considered at that period by the British Government & so jealous were they of other Nations Sharing in it, that they insisted in their Treaty with the French at Utrecht & obtained an engagement on the part of the King of France "that he should not accept of any other usage of Navigation to Spain & the Spanish Indies, than what was practised there in the reign of Charles 2 of Spain, or than what Should likewise be fully given and granted at the same time to other Nations & people Concerned in Trade" See the Treaty art: 6. in 1st Chalm: 340.[4]

On the other hand Great Britain availed herself of the favorable Circumstances then existing to obtain from Spain all the Commercial advantages that she could in America. France in 1701 had made with Spain an Assiento Treaty for 10 years which were expired—Britain made one for thirty years on the same terms that France had had it before (See the Treaty Art: 12)[5] and obtained besides the Liberty of Sending annually to Porto Bello during that period, a Ship laden with her manufactures, which was called the annual Ship.

With these powerful means, it is well known in what manner Great Britain Contrived to encrease he[r] Contraband Trade with the Spanish Colonies, so that in the year 1739 the King of Spain thought himself authorized to assert in the manifesto which he published at that time, That that contraband Trade yielded annually. to the English by their own Confession Several millions—6 Lord's Debates 247.[6]

The English Writers themselves inform us to what a degree this Trade was then Carried. "The Assiento" Says Long, "became a great Source of improvement to Jamaica, Kingston became the *great Magazine* for Supplying British manufactures to the Spaniards; numberless merchants, factors & Traders were attracted by the gainful plan of business which then opened to view"—1 Long 297.

The English were now bent not only on forcing a direct Trade between their Colonies and those of Spain, but on being themselves the carriers of it. The Spaniards grew jealous, remonstrated, let loose their Guarda Costas, took all the English Vessels which they found in the American Seas and Suspected to be engaged in that Trade, the English complained; eleven years, from 1728 to 1739. were Spent in mutual complaint & negotiations (1. Long 293.) at last War broke out between the two nations, which was declared by Great Britain on the 19th. Octer. 1739. while this war continued France in 1744. became a party to it, & the two Wars, the Spanish War of 1739. & the French War of 1744. ended in 1748. by the Treaty of Aix-La Chapelle, which closes this period.[7]

During the Eleven years that these two Maritime Wars continued, we do not find that the British pretended to limit or restrain the Commerce of Neutrals with the Colonies of either Spain & France, on the contrary, we find that in the War of 1744. Ships taken on a voyage from the French Colonies were released before the Lords of appeal. 2 Robinson 122. Am: Ed:[8] And Sir William Scott, who traces the British prohibitions thro' all their different periods, does not speak of them previous to the war of 1756. The Immanuel 2. Rob: 156. Am: Ed.

Altho' it appears that Great Britain at that time had a Considerable interest (tho' not in the same degree as at present) to induce her to prevent the trade of other Nations with the Colonies of her enemies, & that she was fully as jealous of their interfering in it as she is at the present time, yet it Seems that Sufficient reasons may be assigned for the forbe[a]rance which She exercised during that War.

1. Great Britain was evidently making War upon Spain for the purpose of forcing a Trade with her Colonies. The Dutch & other Nations must have seen her efforts with pleasure, as long as She did not shew any disposition to monopolize it to herself. However she might have cloaked her prohibitions under Specious Arguments, the veil would have been seen thro', the Spirit of monopoly would have been perceived, & the objects which the War was intended to promote might have been frustrated by her displaying too Soon the whole of her ultimate views.

2 Great Britain was then feelingly alive to the fears of Popery & the Pretender. The Carrying Nations of the North of Europe were mostly Protestant States, & She had an evident interest in treating them with justice & with moderation.

Whatever may have been the cause of the moderation which Gt. Britain displayed in the Course of this War, it appears certain, that the idea of the trade of neutrals with the enemy's Colonies being a violation of the Laws of neutrality did not enter the minds of British Statesmen during this period, on the Contrary at the time of the breaking out of the war of 1739.

both the political parties which then divided Great Britain, appear to have entertained no other idea, but that it was a Legal Trade, altho' it militated against their commercial interests. In the Debates which took place in the British Parliament on the expediency of a war with Spain, a few days before the War was declared, this particular point came incidentally under consideration in the house of Lords, & we cannot give a better idea of the opinions which then prevailed, than by copying Extracts from the Speeches which were delivered on that occasion—they are taken from 6. Lord's Debates 136. 154.

Lord Hervey, against the War.

"Some People may perhaps imagine that great advantages might be made by our intercepting the Spanish Plate fleets, or the Ships that are employed in that trade with their Settlements in America, because none but Spanish Ships can be employed in that Trade; but even this could be precarious, & might in Several Shapes be entirely prevented; for, if they should open that Trade to the French and Dutch, it is what those two nations would be glad to accept of, *& we could not pretend to make prize of a French or Dutch Ship on account of her being bound to or from the Spanish Settlements in America, no more than we could make prize of her on account of her being bound to or from any port in Spain.*" ["]We could not so much as pretend to Seize any treasure or goods (Except Contraband) she had on board, unless we could prove that those goods or that Treasure actually belonged to the king or Subjects of Spain. Thus the Spanish treasure and effects might Safely be brought &ca."

Lord Bathurst, in answer.

"We may do the Spaniards much damage by privateering &a. If they bring their Treasure home in *flotas*, we intercept them by our Squadrons, if in Single Ships, our privateers take them.

They cannot bring it home either in French or Dutch Ships, because by the 6th. Article of the Treaty of Utrecht the King of France is expressly obliged not to accept of any other usage of navigation to Spain & the Spanish Indies—than What was practised there in the reign of Charles 2. of Spain or than what shall likewise be fully given & granted at the Same time to other Nations & people Concerned in Trade—*Therefore* the Spaniards could not Lay the Trade to their settlements in America open to the French, or at least the French could not accept of it, & if the Dutch should, *they would be opposed by the French as well as by us,* an opposition they would not, I believe chuse to struggle with."

The Subject is not taken up in the whole of this debate, on the ground of Belligerent right, or of neutral duty—The opposition of France, which was then Neutral, as well as that of Britain, to the Dutch interfering in that Trade, is Threatened Solely on the ground of *commercial jealousy,* the true and only real ground of the prohibitions which have taken place in Subsequent times.

Such appear to have been the prevailing ideas during the period before us—The trade of Neutrals with Enemies appears to have been considered by the publicists generally as Lawful, except in the two Cases of enemy's goods & contraband, no distinction is made between trading to the Colonies & trading to the mother Country. We have carefully looked into all the authors of this period that have come to our hands, & have not been able to find any traces of Such a distinction. We have not been able to find it even in the analogous case of the Coasting trade of Belligerents in Europe, not an idea is thrown out of its being prohibited to Neutrals in time of War. In the Debates which took place in the house of Lords respecting the Spanish Captures in america and the war which followed, Several of the Lords in their Speeches lay down in detail the particular Cases in which Belligerent Nations may Search, Capture & Confiscate neutral vessels in time of War; but altho' Colonial Trade was the immediate Subject of their discussions, the distinction alluded to, does not Seem to have been even Suspected to prevent, the Carrying of contraband of War is the only ground on which Spain is admitted to be allowed to Search & Capture Neutral Vessels in the American Seas in time of War—See the speech of Lord Carteret 5 Lord's Debates 402, 405. and the Speeches of Several other Lords on the Same question.

With regard to the practice of other Nations, we do not find either within this or the former period, that any nation confiscated neutral Vessels for the *Specific cause* of trading with Enemy's Colonies—But candor requires us to State that a still greater degree of Severity was then exercised by Some Nations upon Neutral Trade. Louis 14th. by his Marine Ordinance of 1681, had Established the monstrous principle "Que la robe d'ennemi confisque celle d'ami,"[9] See Ordinance *Title des Prises* art: 7 in 2 Valin 252.[10] by which principle if either Vessel or Cargo were enemy's property, the whole was liable to Confiscation. This was Copied by Spain in her ordinance concerning prizes of the year 1718. art: 9. (Chevalier d'Abreu on the Spanish Law of prizes, Vol 1. p. 144. French Translation)[11]—In the year 1705 France by another ordinance waived the above principle, but introduced another not less Severe, to wit; "That all Merchandize of the growth or manufactures of the Country of her Enemies found on board of Neutral Vessels was liable to Confiscation tho' the Vessel itself was to be released["]—(2 Valin 248)—By a Subsequent ordinance, at the breaking out of the war of 1744. She re-enacted the same Law, excepting only from its operation the Vessels of Denmark, Sweden, Holland & the Hanse Towns, in consequence of particular Treaties with those several powers (2 Valin 250.) The effect of these regulations might well prevent an intercourse between neutrals & the Colonies of the Enemies of France, but after all we have not been able to find any act either of that Country or any other, done with that direct substantive View, and the above ordinances were universally held to be contrary to the principles of the Law of nations.

We find indeed in the appendix to 4 Robinson, page 18. am: Ed: (note to document No. 3) that about the year 1705. The French tried the plan of Supplying their Colonies in America in time of War by means of Neutral Vessels, but the first Vessels which were fitted out *having been taken* they returned to the plan of Convoys—This may be true, but from the general Course of ideas and opinions which then prevailed in Europe respecting the Law of Nations & Neutral Trade, it seems morally impossible that they could have been taken on the fine Spun principle, of its not being Lawful for neutrals to carry on with Belligerents in time of war, a trade not permitted to them in time of peace, That these Captures originated in Commercial jealousy, there can be no doubt, & if the Vessels were condemned, pretences will not have been Wanting more suited to the opinions and to the spirit of the age.

The principle in question appears to be a modern refinemt. & Seems to have been very little known or understood even in the War of 1756. out of the British Cabinet. Long, an Englishman, who wrote after that war, & who residing at Jamaica, must have Witnessed the many Captures which were made by the British in those Seas, does not seem even to have been aware of it when he wrote the following anecdote with which we Shall conclude these notes for the present period.

"It was a shrewd remark of the Spanish Governor of St. Domingo, Don manuel Azlor, during the last War with france. At that time the Spanish Vessels were not allowed to trade with the French; but a Sloop having, Contrary to her Register, deviated to a French port, and there received a loading of French produce, was intercepted by one of our Cruizers, and carried into Jamaica for condemnation. The Spanish Governor immediately Sent to reclaim her; insisting that the Spanish Commerce in the West Indies being restrained by their Law to the Subjects of the King of Spain, all their Vessels, which had Registers to shew that they were dispatched from a Spanish port, ought to navigate freely and not be Stopped under pretence of Search; but their lading Should be suffered to pass untouched, even tho' belonging to the French—'If our Vessels, (added he) carried French effects to the British ports or to their Ships, I should not oppose their being Seized, & the effects Confiscated, if the Crews & Vessels were returned to us, as being Spanish, that we might Chastise our own Subjects for the transgression of our Laws, but the Ships of his Britannic Majesty are not Guarda Costas of the King of Spain, nor ought they to watch his Vessels, if they enter into an illicit trade; it belongs to me, and others, the respective Governors of the King my master, to prohibit it, to guard against, & to punish it, as we do upon all occasions. And the bad use which any Spaniard may make of his licences & passports cannot give a right, Nor legal authority to subjects of your Nation, to Seize & Carry them into your ports, and commence processes against them; by which they are ruined, even when the Cause is decided in their favour.[']" 1 Long. Hist: of Jam: 308.

RC (DLC); letterbook copy of enclosure (PHi: Peter S. Du Ponceau Letterbook, 1777–1839). RC 1 p.

1. For an earlier installment of the notes, see Du Ponceau to JM, 8 July 1805.

2. For the 1670 treaty of Madrid, see Jenkinson, *Collection of All the Treaties between Great Britain and Other Powers* (1968 reprint), 1:197–98.

3. In citing Bryan Edwards's *History, Civil and Commercial, of the British Colonies in the West Indies,* 4th ed. (4 vols.; Philadelphia, 1805–6; Shaw and Shoemaker 8375), Du Ponceau transposed the numbers; the correct page number is 248. Bryan Edwards (1743–1800) was born in England and in 1759 was sent to help manage an uncle's sugar plantations in Jamaica, where he continued his education. Given two estates by his uncle, he inherited several others in 1769 and eventually owned thousands of acres and 1,500 slaves. In 1765 he was elected to the Jamaica legislative assembly, where he supported the thirteen mainland colonies in their differences with Great Britain. In 1774 he was elected to the American Philosophical Society. From 1782 to 1787 he was in England, where he published a pamphlet calling for an expansion of trade between the British West Indian colonies and the newly independent United States. He published his highly acclaimed history in 1793 (Olwyn M. Blouet, "Bryan Edwards, F.R.S., 1743–1800," *Notes and Records of the Royal Society of London* 54 [2000]: 215–22). JM was familiar with Edwards's 1784 pamphlet on the trade between the United States and the West Indies (*PJM,* 8:91 n. 1, 102; and 13:208, 211 n. 7).

4. For article 6 of the Anglo-French Treaty of Peace and Friendship signed at Utrecht in 1713, see Chalmers, *Collection of Treaties between Great Britain and Other Powers,* 1:477–78.

5. The Franco-Spanish Asiento of 1701 granted the French a monopoly to import 4,800 slaves each year, from 1702 to 1712, from Corisco Island and Angola to the Spanish West Indian colonies (Hugh Thomas, *The Slave Trade: The Story of the Atlantic Slave Trade; 1440–1870* [New York, 1997], 227–28). For the Anglo-Spanish Asiento of 1713, see Du Ponceau to JM, 8 July 1805, n. 19.

6. Du Ponceau quoted from Ebenezer Timberland's *History and Proceedings of the House of Lords, from the Restoration in 1660, to the Present Time. . . .* (8 vols.; London, 1742–43).

7. The "Spanish War of 1739" was the War of Jenkins' Ear; after 1742 it merged with the War of the Austrian Succession, which involved most of Europe (Acton, *Cambridge Modern History* [1969 reprint], 6:64, 66, 68, 157, 228–29, 233, 236, 238, 239, 242, 248–49). For the 1748 Treaty of Aix-la-Chapelle that ended the wars, see de Clercq, *Recueil des traités de la France,* 1:65–79.

8. Du Ponceau cited the 1801 Philadelphia edition of Robinson's *Admiralty Reports* (Shaw and Shoemaker 584), 2:122.

9. *Que la robe d'ennemi confisque cette d'ami.* That the dress of an enemy condemns that of a friend (editor's translation).

10. Du Ponceau cited René-Josué Valin's *Nouveau commentaire sur l'ordonnance de la marine, du mois d'août 1681* (1766 reprint), 2:252.

11. Du Ponceau referred to Félix José de Abreu y Bertodano's *Tratado juridico-politico, sobre pressas de mar, y calidades, que deben concurrir para hacerse legitimamente el corso* (Cádiz, 1746). French translations were printed in Paris in 1753, 1758, and 1802 as *Traité juridico-politique sur les prises maritimes et sur les moyens qui doivent concourir pour rendre ces prises légi-*

times. Félix José de Abreu y Bertodano (ca. 1722–1766) was the Spanish envoy extraordinary to Britain from 1755 to 1760 and had held another diplomatic position in England before that (*The Biographical Dictionary of the Society for the Diffusion of Useful Knowledge* [4 vols. in 7; London, 1842–44], 1:178; Joseph Thomas, *Universal Pronouncing Dictionary of Biography and Mythology,* 3d ed. [2 vols.; Philadelphia, 1908], 1:39).

§ From William Lyman. *15 July 1805, London.* "On the 10th: Ultimo I had the Honor of addressing you[1] by the Ship *Otis* Captn. Phillips bound from this Port to New York a duplicate whereof I also transmitted a few days thereafter together with a Parcel of Newspapers by the Ship Planter Captn. Bush, also b(o)und from this Port to Norfolk Virginia, which Communication either has or doubtless will be received, so that no notice of the Purport thereof is now necessary.

"At this time I have also the Honor herewith to transmit a Report of the Vessels of the United States which have entered the Ports of this District for the Twelve Months preceeding, and closing the Thirtieth day of June last past [not found] I have included therein Twelve Months as my Predecessor States that the Six Months closing the Thirty-first day of December which he had transmitted has been lost in the Jupiter at Sea:[2] In the Form of the Report it will be observed that up to this time I have followed his Table in which there is neither a Column for the description of the Vessel or Number of her Men &c: which from the Consular Instructions appear to be required; in my next therefore I shall aim to embrace those points with such others as may seem proper.

"The Money either received or disbursed for the last Quarter after I came into the Office is so inconsiderable that I postpone transmitting any Account thereof or of services for settlement until the close of the present: I postpone also any return of the Impressed Seamen to the Same period, as a greater part of the former Quarter was included in the last return.

"As yet I have drawn on Sir Francis Baring & Co: for only one Hundred Pounds Sterling, of which I suppose you will also be advised by them: I wave at this time all remarks either Commercial or Political as my Predecessor who not only from the time of his residence but present station here, must be so much more competent thereto also writes by this opportunity."

RC (DNA: RG 59, CD, London, vol. 9). 2 pp.; in a clerk's hand, signed by Lyman.

1. *PJM-SS,* 9:449–50.
2. For the fate of the *Jupiter,* see George W. Erving to JM, 21 June 1805, ibid., 484, 487 n. 2.

To Anthony Merry

Sir, Department of State July 16th. 1805

I have had the Honor to receive your Letter of the 9th. Instant respecting the Brigantine Transfer.[1] By Information remaining in the Navy Department it appears, that though a Sale is ordered by an Interlocutory Decree, yet—Time has been given for a Claimant to appear until the next

Term, before which Time no Distribution can be made of the Proceeds. It also appears, that before she was temporarily taken into the Public Service by the American Commodore, her Value was ascertained by three impartial and respectable Persons; and that not a Doubt remained of the Truth of the Facts on which she was stopped, and that they would amount to such an unneutral Conduct as necessarily to produce a Condemnation. Of the su⟨mmary⟩ Condemnation in the Mediterranean noth⟨ing⟩ can be traced; and it is evident from ⟨the⟩ Vessel being sent to the United States fo⟨r⟩ Adjudication, that either such a Proced⟨ure⟩ did not take Place, or that however advisable in some Respects it might be ⟨deemed⟩ by the Commodore, it was not understo⟨od⟩ ⟨by⟩ him as in any Manner affecting the C⟨laims⟩ of the former Proprietors. It is moreove⟨r⟩ verbally reported to me, that an Offe⟨r⟩ ⟨was⟩ made to the Captain of the Transfer, of th⟨e⟩ Means of accompanying her to the Unit⟨ed⟩ States, which he declined. In Reference ⟨to⟩ the Facts of the Case, I shall only add, ⟨that⟩ the Transfer, the Name by which she h⟨as⟩ been proceeded against at Norfolk, ⟨is that⟩ which belonged to her at the Time of th⟨e⟩ Capture. In order however that every opp⟨ortunity⟩ may be afforded to the former Owner who resides at Malta, to make Claim even at this late stage of the Process, if he thinks it advisable, Instructions will be given to the Attorney of the United States for the District of Virginia, to apply to the Court to prolong the Term allowed for a Claimant to come in, for such an additional Space, as may be fully adequate for the Purpose.[2] Should this Application be allowed, as I make no Doubt it will, I flatter myself that your Views will be accomplished: and in the mean Time you may be assured of the sincere wish of the United States to promote on every proper Occasion such Measures as may secure to Foreigners Justice in its Forms as well as Substance, and more particularly to repair and rectify Irregularities in Cases of Marine Captures. I have the Honor to be &c.

(signed) JAMES MADISON

Tr (UkLPR: Foreign Office, ser. 5, 45:245–246; letterbook copy (ibid., ser. 115, 14:115–117). Tr marked "⟨Co⟩py," enclosed in Merry to Mulgrave, 2 Aug. 1805, ibid., ser. 5, 45: 239–240v. Words and parts of words in angle brackets have been supplied from the letterbook copy. Minor differences between the copies have not been noted.

1. See Merry to JM, 9 July 1805 (first letter).

2. On 17 July 1805 JM wrote to George Hay, U.S. district attorney for Virginia, stating: "In the course of the last year one of the Vessels under Commodore Preble in the Mediterranean captured the Brigantine Transfer bound to Tripoli, after having an estimate made of her value he took her temporalily [sic] into the public service, and she has since been proceeded against as prize at Norfolk, where an interlocutory decree for her sale has been made and time given till the 13th. day of the next term of the District Court for claimants to come in. Her late owner being a resident of Malta, and Mr. Merry, the British Envoy, supposing him to be a British subject, has addressed a letter to me on the subject of this capture, intimating a dissatisfaction that the prosecution should proceed without the presence of

any representative of the Owner. As it does not appear that the Master or any of the officers of the Transfer were brought to Norfolk with her, as she was converted to public use abroad when in strictness she should have been previously sent home for adjudication, it is thought to be not unreasonable in order to satisfy forms and repair any irregularity which might have taken place before the judicial proceedings commenced, that ample time should be given for the owner to make his claim if he should think proper. You will therefore be pleased to apply to the Court to prolong the time limited for the claim and to suspend the distribution of the proceeds of the sale for Six months or such other term as may be sufficient for notice to reach the Island of Malta" (DNA: RG 59, DL, vol. 15; 2 pp.).

§ From Thomas Auldjo. *16 July 1805, Cowes.* "I had the honor to address you on the 4th & 5th inst via Boston & having now an opportunity direct for Baltimore I take the liberty of sending you duplicates of the papers relative to the quarantine regulations & hoping that what I have done therein may be of some Service & meet your approbation."

RC (DNA: RG 59, CD, Southampton, vol. 1). 1 p.

§ From George W. Erving. *16 July 1805.* No. 33. "Since I wrote to you last the differences which have for a long time Existed between Mr Pitt & Lord Sidmouth, more especially in relation to the proceedings against Lord Melville, have produced a seperation.[1] Lord Sidmouth & his friends have resigned. Immediately after this Event the parliament was prorogued; which measure, as Mr Pitt has no prospect of filling the places of the seceders by any members from either branch of the opposition, was perhaps fortunately timed.

"His Majesty is gone to Weymouth; his Eyes are becoming Extremely bad; a cataract has certainly taken place in one of them, & the other is advancing to the same state; this disorder is attributed to too great Exertion & Exposure.[2] I have not heard a word of Mr Monroe since 26th May when he quitted Madrid. Mr Bowdoin had landed in Spain."

RC (MHi: Winthrop Family Papers). 1 p.; marked "*Private.*"

1. For the falling-out between William Pitt and Henry Addington, see Erving to JM, 21 June 1805, *PJM-SS,* 9:486, 487 n. 8.
2. George III had lost a great deal of the vision in his right eye in 1804, probably because of a cataract. The cataract forming at this time in the other eye caused him to stop writing by the end of 1805 and eventually led to his total blindness (Macalpine and Hunter, *George III and the Mad-Business,* 138–42).

§ From George W. Erving. *16 July 1805, London.* No. 63. "As Lord Mulgrave had not notified to me previous to the 11th Inst, the appointment of any person to receive the 200,000 £ becoming due from the United States to the British government,[1] & agreed by him to be received in London, I thought it proper to write to his Lordship on the subject; & having received his answer & communicated it to Sir Francis Baring & Co, the money was paid in pursuance of the desire therein Expressed, as appears by Messrs Barings letter to me of yesterday, copy of which together with copies of the notes referred to, I have the honor herewith to inclose.[2]

"I have also the Satisfaction to inform you that I received yesterday from the British government the third & last instalment on the awards made payable to me as Agent of the United States; the ballance of which amounting to 48979.3.4 I paid at the Same time to Messrs Barings: I shall during my stay here & up to the time limited for payments, Satisfy the claimants bills by dra[f]ts on this fund, & if I shoud leave this place before that period will deliver to Messrs Barings such documents as will Enable them to pay the remainder.

"I inclose herewith a proclamation just published[3] which is calculated to give facilities to the transporting & introducing upon the continent, the manufactured goods of this country &c &c. The loss of the Spanish trade added to the prohibitory measures taken by France & Holland, has certainly crowded this country with its own produce, as well as with its imports; for the manufacturer has not ceased to work, having always speculated upon these obstacles as temporary, or having calculated upon forcing a trade in defiance of them."

Adds in a postscript: "I inclose a very ingenious plan [not found] for reefing the sails of Ships which is submitted by Capt Cowan the pattentee."[4]

RC and enclosures (DNA: RG 59, CD, London, vol. 9). RC 2 pp.; docketed by Wagner as received 14 Sept., with his note: "Mem. the proclamation relaxing the navigation system of England *in time of war*." For surviving enclosures, see n. 2.

1. For the payment of the Jay Treaty claims, see Erving to JM, 18 May 1805 (second letter), *PJM-SS*, 9:368 and n. 2.

2. Erving enclosed copies of his 11 July 1805 letter to Lord Mulgrave (1 p.; docketed by Wagner), asking who had been appointed to receive the £200,000 due Great Britain under the terms of the Jay Treaty; Mulgrave's 13 July 1805 reply (1 p.), asking that the funds "be paid into the Bank of England on account of the 'Commissioners appointed by act of Parliament under the Convention with the United States of America[']"; Erving's 13 July 1805 letter to Francis Baring & Co. (1 p.), asking them to pay the money into the Bank of England on 15 July; and the Barings' 15 July reply (1 p.), informing Erving that they had done so.

3. The enclosure was a copy of the 29 June 1805 order in council, published in London on 10 July, stating that neutral ships "trading, directly or circuitously, between the Ports of our United Kingdom and the Enemy's Ports in Europe (such Ports not being blockaded), shall not be interrupted in their Voyages by our Ships of War, or Privateers. . . ." The order contained a list of articles that could be imported and exported to and from Holland, France, and Spain and stated that the neutral ships need not obtain licenses for such trade (*Naval Chronicle* 14 [1805]: 105–6; *National Intelligencer*, 6 Sept. 1805). A copy of the order in a clerk's hand, with Wagner's notes on additional laws governing imports during war, docketed by JM: "Additional examples of the Suppression of the British navigation laws in time of war," is filed in the Rives Collection, Madison Papers, at the Library of Congress.

4. Royal Navy commander Malcolm Cowan was granted a patent on 11 June 1805 "for improvements in the construction of sails for ships and vessels of all descriptions" (*Annual Register for 1805*, 851).

§ From John M. Forbes. *16 July 1805*. "My last Respects were under 4th. December last;[1] since which having no Political information of a decided nature to communicate, I have not thought it necessary to importune you with a Report of all the fleeting Conjectures and Rumors which have continued to perplex public opinion on the grand question of Peace or continental War. You will have been regularly informed no doubt through more direct Channels of the various measures of the french Governement. The long forbearance of the Russian Emperor and the naming of Monsieur de Novosilzoff to enter into Pacific explanations with the Emperor of the French, had given very ardent and well grounded hopes, not only of the Continuance of Peace on the Continent, but of its re-establishment between France and England. We have however, this day seen inserted in the official Gazette of this City, a Note from Mr. de Novosilzoff to Baron von Hardenberg one of the Prussian Ministers of State, which goes very far towards dissipating all the hopes hitherto conceived of the preservation of Peace on the Continent. I lose no time in transmitting to You by different Opportunities a Translation of this important docume⟨nt⟩² and as often as any Measures of a decided Characte⟨r⟩ come to my Knowledge, shall feel it my duty to communicate them."

RC and enclosure (DNA: RG 59, CD, Hamburg, vol. 1). RC 2 pp.; in a clerk's hand, with Forbes's complimentary close and signature. For enclosure, see n. 2.

1. *PJM-SS*, 8:350–51.
2. The undated enclosure (4 pp.; printed in the 20 Sept. 1805 *National Intelligencer*) is a translation of the 10 July 1805 note from Count Nikolai Novosiltsov, the Russian diplomat sent to negotiate between France and Russia, to Prussian foreign minister Baron Karl August von Hardenberg, stating that since the annexation of the Ligurian Republic showed that Napoleon did not truly desire peace, whatever his pronouncements may have indicated, Alexander I had ordered Novosiltsov to return the passport he had obtained from France through Prussian mediation, and end his mission.

§ From Peter Kuhn Jr. *16 July 1805, Genoa.* "I have the honor to confirm my respects of the 28th Ulto¹ and on the 30th in the morning arrived in this Town the French Emperor with the Empress and a Numerous suit; his residence here was only of Six days during which some magnificent entertainments and rejoicings were given; he seemed to grant particular attention to whatever might contribute to the future happiness and prosperity of this new acquired Territory, but instead of continuing his residence for some time in Italy, as was expected, he is, in consequence of some expresses receiv'd, return'd to France, and goes direct to the Army in the North. The Arch Treasurer LeBrun remains here, and is particularly charged with the organisation of these new Departments.

"By the most recent, and best grounded political reports several new changements seem to be imminent in the actual state of Europe such as the Union of Switzerland to France, and that of the Republic of Ragusa to the German Empire; other alterations are likewise talked of, but not with sufficient foundation to be mention'd as yet.

"A Vessel arrived at Leghorn in three days from Algiers brings the intelligence that the wild Arabs having made a sudden invasion from the mountains have renderd themselves masters of that City after having put to the sword all the Christian Slaves, and pillaged ⟨t⟩he houses of all the Jews established there; some hundreds of these unfortunate people have been able to escape, but the slaughter has been considerable.[2] The Bey is now in the hands of these Wretches, who have not yet murder'd him to find out first where he has concealed his treasures.

"In adherence to my instructions I have to acquaint you Sir that no American Vessels have been at this port within these eight months. The last was the Matilda Mathew Strong of Philadelphi⟨a⟩ in the Month of September, and as I do not find by the papers deliver'd me from Mr. Wollaston that he had ever made any report thereof, I think it my duty to inform you as per enclosed particulars.[3] I hope that before many months expire the American flag will make often it's appearance in this port, the blockade whereof never was but nominal, and by the new political changement can not even be considerd under that predicament. No Vessels of War whatsoever appear in this neighbourhood except the French, and they are constantly manouvering in and out of this port to exercise their Seamen."

RC, two copies, and enclosure (DNA: RG 59, CD, Genoa, vol. 1). First RC 2 pp.; docketed by Wagner. Second RC marked "*Duplicate.*" For enclosure, see n. 3.

1. *PJM-SS*, 9:500–501.
2. In late June 1805 Naphtali Busnach, a Jewish exporter who had great influence over Mustapha Dey, was murdered by a Turkish janissary, after which the janissaries invaded the Jewish quarter of Algiers, killing or driving into refuge in the consulates hundreds of the residents. The dey himself was killed several weeks later (Michael Berenbaum and Fred Skolnok, eds., *Encyclopaedia Judaica*, 2d ed. [22 vols.; Detroit, 2007], 4:316; Garrot, *Histoire générale de l'Algérie*, 614–16; Playfair, *Scourge of Christendom* [1972 reprint], 235–36).
3. The enclosure (1 p.) is an extract, dated 16 July 1805, of the 29 Sept. 1804 entry in the consular register recording the arrival at Genoa of the ship *Matilda*, "of & from Philadelphia," owned by Vanuxem and Clarke, consigned to Filippi and Company of Genoa, carrying a cargo of sugar, coffee, cocoa, fish, tobacco, and rum, and returning with a cargo of "Wine, oil, & Brandy for Messma [Messina] & America."

§ From William Lee. *16 July 1805, Bordeaux.* "I have the honor to enclose you a duplicate copy of my correspondence with General Armstrong concerning Consular Certificate Vessels[1] accompanied by a copy of my letter to the Secretary of the Treasury on the same subject."[2]

RC and enclosures (DNA: RG 59, CD, Bordeaux, vol. 2). RC 1 p.; docketed by Wagner as received 8 Oct. For enclosures, see nn.

1. The enclosures are copies of: (1) Lee to John Armstrong, 15 Apr. 1805 (4 pp.), enclosing a copy of his instructions from JM (not found, but see *PJM-SS*, 5:479 and n. 1) and a copy of the certificate (not found), stating that he had refused certificates for the *Susan* and *Olive Branch*, explaining the evasions of U.S. laws that often took place, and asking Armstrong's opinion as to whether or not he should refuse the certificate to ships that he was certain were not going directly to the United States as the law required; (2) a list (3 pp.) of eleven ships "fitting out at Bordeaux under the Consular Certificate April 16th. 1805," containing a paragraph on each vessel with the names of the owners and captains and the owners' cities of residence; and (3) Lee to Armstrong, 26 Apr. 1805 (3 pp.; docketed by Wagner), listing the names of five individuals who had applied for certificates for eight ships since Lee's 15 Apr. letter, adding that these made a total of fifty-one ships fitted out at Bordeaux "under american colours since the commenceme⟨nt⟩ of the present war, forty two of which appear to m⟨e⟩ to be on french Account." Lee also noted that such vessels often under-

cut legitimate American ships on pricing and enticed away crew members, and if the practice continued, American trade to Bordeaux would "sooner or later suffer greatly." He added that between 120 and 150 ships had sailed from Bordeaux and neighboring French ports "of which two thirds are owned by foreigners," and that if American consuls were allowed to charge for the certificates, it might check the practice.

2. Lee enclosed a copy (2 pp.) of his 10 July 1805 letter to Albert Gallatin, stating that on Armstrong's advice he now required the owner, captain, or consignee of any vessel to which he had issued a certificate, and which he suspected was not bound to the port for which it cleared, to post a bond of $2,000 that the ship would proceed directly to the United States. He enclosed two bonds, one for the *Mercury* and one for the *Olive Branch*, because he had heard that the former went to Portugal before sailing for New York and the latter was bound to Cádiz and then to Philadelphia. He asked Gallatin to transmit the bonds to the collectors at New York and Philadelphia with orders for them to prosecute the captains.

¶ To Anthony Merry. Letter not found. *16 July 1805.* Described in the index to Notes to Foreign Ministers and Consuls as "relative to the French privateer Les Amies" (DNA: RG 59, Notes to Foreign Ministers and Consuls, vol. 1). For *Les Amies*, see Merry to JM, *9 July 1805* (second letter), and nn.

§ To Silas Lee.[1] *17 July 1805, Department of State.* "I enclose a Certificate from the Consul at London of an oath taken before him, that the Brig Harry and Jane, said to belong to Portland, has been concerned in the Slave trade.[2] If on examining the circumstances of the case you are of opinion that it admits of a prosecution, and after enquiry you are led to believe, that you can be furnished with the evidence necessary to support it, I request you to lose no time in instituting one against every person and thing liable to it."

Letterbook copy (DNA: RG 59, DL, vol. 15). 1 p.

1. Harvard graduate Silas Lee (1760–1814) was admitted to the Massachusetts bar and served in the state legislature in 1793 and 1797–98. From 1799 to 1801 he was a Federalist in the U.S. House of Representatives. From 1802 until his death he was the federal district attorney for Maine, and from 1805 to 1814 he also served as probate judge.

2. For George W. Erving's report on the *Harry & Jane*, see Erving to JM, 20 Apr. 1805 (second letter), *PJM-SS*, 9:265. In April 1804 the *Harry & Jane*, Captain Turner, "arrived at Rio de Janeiro from the river Zaire (Congo) in Africa" (Chandler, "United States Merchant Ships in the Rio de La Plata," *Hispanic American Historical Review* 2 [1919]: 37, 39; Chandler, "List of United States Vessels in Brazil," ibid. 26 [1946]: 609).

§ From John Martin Baker.[1] *17 July 1805, Palma.* "I have the honor to refer you, and to confirm my last respects under date the Sixteenth of January last,[2] covering my Consular demi-annual report, closing on the thirty-first day of December 1804.

"Herewith have the honor to transmit You inclosed my Consular half yearly last report [not found], closing on the thirtieth day of June Ultimo.

"I have the satisfaction sir, to communicate for your information, that agreeable to every account received up to this day from the Continent of Spain, health continues to be enjoyed at the places, so much afflicted the last Year, with the contageous fever. On these Island(s) thank Providence good health (is) enjoyed."

RC, two copies (DNA: RG 59, CD, Port Mahon, vol. 1). First RC 2 pp.; marked "*duplicate.*" Second RC marked "*triplicate.*"

1. John Martin Baker (d. 1841) was named consul for the Balearic Islands in 1803 and in 1807 became consul for Tarragona, Spain. During 1808 and 1809 he served briefly as dispatch courier to France and also spent several months as a State Department clerk, after which he returned to Minorca. In 1813 he left Port Mahon with his family and spent the next few years in France, returning to Port Mahon in 1815 after peace was achieved between the United States and Great Britain. He returned to the United States again in 1817. In 1822 he received a clerkship in the State Department, where he remained until 1831 when he was named consul at Rio de Janeiro. In July 1840 he was named consul at Nuevitas, Cuba (*Daily National Intelligencer*, 21 July 1841; *PJM-SS*, 3:502 n. 2; John Martin Baker to Richard Rush, 18 Aug. 1817, DLC: Jefferson Papers; *Baltimore Patriot & Mercantile Advertiser*, 31 Oct. 1822; Elmer Plischke, *U.S. Department of State: A Reference History* [Westport, Conn., 1999], 121; *Senate Exec. Proceedings*, 4:178, 193, 5:298, 301).

2. *PJM-SS*, 8:481.

§ To Jeremiah Powell. *18 July 1805, Department of State.* "I have received your letter of the 10th. Ult. [not found] enclosing one to you from David G. Gillis,[1] who it appears, has been captured in a Vessel belonging to you and imprisoned at Guadaloupe. As relates to the property, it may be remarked, that if your Commercial House in St. Domingo is established in that part of the Island not possessed by the French, the ordinary laws of war would justify the capture in order to[2] the condemnation of such a portion of the property as might be found to belong to persons domiciled in the Country of an enemy to France: but the nature of the voyage, the place of capture, the conduct of the captured, the character of the Vessel & Cargo, the reasons if any which were assigned for the capture, being circumstances material to a just view of the transaction, and being omitted from your communication, no step can be at present taken on behalf of either the persons or property. Every document & elucidation however calculated more fully to develope the case, and serve as the foundation of the interposition it may call for, which you may think proper to transmit will receive due attention."

Letterbook copy (DNA: RG 59, DL, vol. 15). 2 pp. Addressed to Powell at New York.

1. Powell's 10 June 1805 letter probably dealt with the capture on 9 May 1805 of his schooner *Daphne*, Capt. David G. Gillers, by the French privateer *Grand Decide*. The *Daphne*, carrying coffee from Jacmel, Haiti, was captured with three other American ships bound from Port-au-Prince and carried into Point Petre, Guadaloupe, where the Americans, as the captain wrote Powell on 20 June 1805, were "put into the common prison, among mad men, witches, murderers, and people of every description" and not allowed contact with other Americans in the port. He added that they were "almost starved with hunger" and were all to be tried. In newspaper reports Gillers's surname is variously spelled *Gilles, Gillies, Gillus*, and *M'Giles* (*New-York Commercial Advertiser*, 10 July 1805; *New-York Gazette & General Advertiser*, 26 Apr. 1805).

2. The clerk apparently omitted a word here.

§ From DeWitt Clinton. *18 July 1805, New York.* "I enclose you certain depositions of the Mother & Wife of Nathaniel Moore an impressed American Citizen.[1]
In addition to other impressive considerations, permit me to assure you that your
favorable interposition will be an act of great benevolence to those very afflicted
relatives."

Letterbook copy (NNC: DeWitt Clinton Papers). 1 p.

1. According to the "Statement of applications in cases of impressment, made immediately to the Department of State, and not before reported to the House of Representatives,
or included in Mr. Erving's or Mr. Lyman's returns to this office," submitted to the House
in JM's letter of 5 Mar. 1806, Nathaniel Moore was impressed into the *Leander,* and it was
unknown if he had a protection (*ASP, Foreign Relations,* 2:776, 790, 794).

§ From George Davis. *18 July 1805, Tunis.* "I have the honor to inform you that
the United States Frigate Congress, Captain Decatur, eight days from Syracuse,
anchored in the Road of the Goletta on the 11th. instant. The same day I received
a letter from the Commodore, enclosing one for His Excellency the Bey of Tunis.
Copies of both I have the honor to transmit you [not found].[1]

"On the following morning was at Bardo, and informed the Sapatapa that I had
received a letter for his Master, which was written in English; and delivered it to
him. He spoke much of the detention of the captured Vessels[2] and of the disagreeable consequences which would necessarily arise therefrom. I informed him that
the Commodore with Consul General Lear, would shortly be here, and endeavour
to close all difficulties. He requested to know the object of their visit. I stated it
was probably for the final arrangement of our affairs, as well as for making some
changes in the Treaty. He answered that neither would be received until the captured Vessels were restored, and that Colo. Lear would never be Acknowledged as
one authorized to transact public business with him. That if he visited him as
Consul of Algiers, it was well—if he visited him as Interpreter of the Commodore,
wel⟨l;⟩ but never while there was another acknowledged Representative could a
Consul of Barbary come and talk with his Master on public affairs. The discussion
was continued for a long time without producing anything decisive.

"On the 13th was at Bardo. The Bey gave me a private audience. He said the
letter had been translated wh. I delivered his Minister, and that I should learn
hereafter what he thought of its contents; that he only wished to know why the
Vessels were not restored; if the act would be sanctioned by the Government, and
if he was to consider it as a declaration of war. I informed him that on all these
points satisfactory Answers should be given when the Commodore arrived. He
said the Commodore did not appear to be a man whose presence was necessary,
unless to produce an immediate declaration of War; that he must first repair the
injuries he had done, before he could expect that any negociation would be entered into—that on this point he shd. write His Excellency the President—that
with respect to the Consul of Algiers, he had already said in what capacity he
should consider him, and how he would be received; that he could not defend him
from visiting his Regency; but that he certainly should decline any conversation

with him relative to our affairs. With respect to a change in the Treaty that could not be done; he was satisfied with it as it was, and we had already expressed our approbation of it; if we wished to break any of the Articles of it, or make any new ones, the shortest way was to recall me, commence hostilities; and then make a new peace; when such Treaty should be concluded as we thought proper, *if we paid well for it*. In relation to a final arrangement on the score of his pretensions, this depended much on ourselves; that he would be treated as we treated the Dey of Algiers, to whom he never could feel himself inferior—that the insignificant offers made him, had and would be declined.

"On the morning of the 14th was again at Bardo—the conversation of the day before was talked over, when I assured the Sapatapa, that the Vessels could not be restored; that the Commodore would unquestionably visit this Bay with his Squadron; and with the expectation of seeing all difficulties arranged before he left it, and that unpleasant consequences might result from the Bey's refusal to receive Colo. Lear in the manner which the President expected—that for the arrangement of our Affairs no greater sacrifices could ever be made, and that it was the indispensable duty of the Commodore to Know the Bey's last expectations, always observing that nothing greater would be offered than those his Master had refused last year, and which indeed I was not authorized at the moment to repeat, or even accord, if the Bey would accept. He assured me that the final termination of the Affair must be war, unless our mode of negociation was wholly altered—that the first thing which ought to be done, was the restoration of the Vessels; a concession on our part indispensably necessary previous to his entering into any negociation with myself or the Commodore. After a lengthy conversation, the Bey again gave me a private audience. His Excellency observed, that he had supposed his observations of yesterday, as well as those of his Minister, would be sufficient; but as it seemed necessary for him to be more explicit, he should be so. That no remark ought to hurt[3] my feelings; for if I had asked of him, as an individual, a favour greater than the one my Gover(n)ment had to demand, it would have been accorded me; but he spoke as a Sovereign to the Representative of a *Government which* seemed ignorant of his Character, or rather *which* mixed him with the Common Herd of Barbary Princes. Your Commodore's letter ought not to be viewed in any other light than a declaration of War; and I certainly should have acted agreeably to such an impression, had not your Master assured me, that the hasty and rash acts of an Individual, which tend to produce such an event, would never be countenanced by him. Ask any of the Christian Consuls in this Regency, if Hamouda Bashaw has ever received such an insult from their Governments. The President of the United States must know that I am born a Prince—that my father and Grandfather have sat on the throne, and ruled a Kingdom. He shall learn from me that Hamouda is not yet dead; and every crowned head in Europe shall approve the eternal continuance of that war which you seem resolved to force me into; for I solemnly pledge myself, that if war is the result, never while I have a soldier to fire a gun will I accord a peace; you may form some idea of my Character from the difficulty you had to negociate a peace, because you weakly permitted the Dey of Algiers to interfere. You may also learn my conduct to the Venetians, who rashly forced me into a war, and if I am doomed to engage in another, it shall be continued to the last hour of my existence. I frankly tell you that the famine in my Country has prevented my declaring war against you, in order that I might convince my subjects that their miseries should not be increased, unless I was forced thereto; without such a motive you certainly never would have been asked the reason why you captured my Vessels; but the just motive to a protraction of our difficulties must be sacrificed to those considerations which I owe myself and all Europe.

"You are the first power which has ever captured a Tunesian Cruizer (in full peace) on any pretext whatever; you are the first that has ever offered unprovoked insults to Hamouda Bassa, who has ruled a Kingdom for twenty seven years, and been respected by all the world as a Souvreign; if I was tamely to submit to such acts of outrage, what should I expect from nations far more powerful than yourselves. You have seen what has been accorded me by Spain, Sweeden and Denmark, whose local situation and maritime force must render them more formidable Enemies than the United States. Abstracted from this, the measures you propose are such as do not permit me to enter into any negociation: Your Commodores have done me great & repeated injuries, for the last of which my political existance forces me to insist on a proper reparation.

"Nations who desire to arrange disputes which frequently arise, commence by offering *at least* a proper justification for the acts which produced the complaints; your Commodore commences by insults which even no crowned head would have offered me. You go further by informing me that your Commodore proposes coming here with his Squadron; this is not only blocking up every avenue to a reconcilement, but must certainly produce a declaration of War on my part; for it is saying to me, and shewing the world, that you hope to obtain by force of Arms what you could not by argument. You there attack that pride which is the support of my Throne, and consequently force me to repel your menaces with becoming vigour: for Europe shall never say that half a dozen frigates have overawed a prince who has Kept in subjection such superior Powers. From such considerations you will perceive the impossibility of arrangement on your present plan. I again repeat to you, it is my desire to retain the peace, particularly at this moment, because it is my interest to do so; but it is more my interest to run the chances of a war with you, even under such unpropitious circumstances, than by an acquiescence and tame submission to your insults excite the half of Europe to follow your Example.

"Your conduct has ever been marked with prudence and discretion, and whatever may be the result, you will always be considered by me as one, who has protracted, for a long time, this event. If you are finally obliged to leave my Regency, your person shall be respected in the highest manner. It now rests with you to make such representations, and take such measures as are deemed most expedient for the interest and honor of your Country. My position is known; my resolutions are taken, and from which I will never retract.

"It was impossible to conceive the painful embarrassment in which I was placed—the presence and advice of the Commodore and Consul General Lear, *the Authorized officers* of the Government were essentially necessary *to one* who had no instructions, powers, or authority to enter into any solid engagements with the Bey; or ward off, any longer, the painful event(,) which for eighteen months we ought to have expected. His Excellency had declared that neither would be received, and the arrival of the Commodore *with his Squadron*, might force him to a declaration of war, unless he came with assurances very different from those he had written. It is most certain that the Bey is not in a Situation to enter even into a defensive war, at this period—his Regency is still distressed with famine, and its consequent civil Commotion: his only hopes of succour, are from foreign powers, deprived of which half of his subjects must perish with want. His Cruizers, when unoccupied, flying[4] into the heart of his Country, a daring enemy, to wit, the whole body of Turks (hence every Barbary State is always at war with some Christian Power) all these serious and menacing evils must necessarily result from a War with us, and has heretofore induced me to beleive that the Bey's threats were wholly the result of fear; but these are considerations which I am not authorized to make for him *at such a moment*, I ought to be governed wholly by his declarations; and particularly so, from my knowledge of his Character: *He is avaricious & politic but proud and tenacious of his Royal Dignity*, and to which he will possibly sacrifice every other consideration. In order to avoid this last extremity, no resource presented itself, but that of visiting the Commodore and Colo. Lear, at Syracuse, where, after a full exposition of all circumstances, *they* could more readily decide on the measures which ought to be taken. I trust that the Honbe. the Secretary of State will see the just motives which induced me to take such a resolution; and that His Excellency the President will not disapprove of it.

"On the morning of the 16th was again at Bardo—and informed His Excellency the Bey, after mature reflection on his last conversation, I found but one means to avoid immediate hostilities; vizt. that of embarking on board the Frigate, in order to have a personal interview with the Commodore; to effect which, I beg'd his permission to leave his Regency forty days; and during which period he would accept my Secretary Mr. Ambo. Allegro, as Chargé d'Affaires; who should possess no power or authority beyond that of transacting the ordinary business of the Consulate.

"The Spanish and Dutch Consuls (who were at Bardo) were called for. His Excellency thus addressed them. 'In your presence, as the Representatives of different Governments I protest against the Commodore and Commander in Chief of the American forces in these seas, who has captured, and detains during full peace a Tunisian Corsair with two of her prizes; and who has augmented the injury by writing a letter unprecedented for its want of respect for me as a Souvreign, and declare to you, that unless full satisfaction be given Me by the President of the United States, for the insult, and reperation for the injuries committed by his Commodore, that I shall be compelled, in defence of my Regency and its dignity to wage war against him. I further declare that the American Chargè d'Affaires Mr. Davis, has permission to leave my Regency for forty days, in order to confer with his Commodore; and if the result shall be war, he may nevertheless visit my Kingdom at any time he thinks proper, without any risque for his personal safety; but shall ever be respected in the highest manner by myself and subjects.[']

"The following morning presented Mr. Allegro to the Bey and Sapatapa, and took my leave.

"In the evening received the enclosed letter for His Excellency the President."[5]

Tr (DNA: RG 59, CD, Tunis, vol. 2, pt. 2); Tr (DLC: John Rodgers Papers); letterbook copy (NHi: George Davis Letterbooks); enclosure (DNA: RG 59, CD, Tunis, vol. 3). First Tr 8 pp.; with a 9 Aug. 1805 note at the foot of the last page: "The foregoing is the true Copy of a letter sent to me by George davis Esq Charge d'Affaires of the U.States at Tunis. Jno

Rodgers." Letterbook copy marked "No. 30." Minor differences between the copies have not been noted. For surviving enclosure, see n. 5.

1. The enclosures were probably copies of Rodgers to Davis, 29 June 1805 (printed in Knox, *Naval Documents, Barbary Wars*, 6:143), refusing to return the Tunisian vessel captured by the United States (see n. 2 below), and adding that he would meet either warlike or peaceful overtures from the bey in the spirit in which they were offered; and Rodgers to Hammuda Bey, 1 July 1805 (printed in Knox, *Naval Documents, Barbary Wars*, 6:146–47), refusing to return the ship, and complaining that Tunisian vessels had been consistently violating his blockade of Tripoli.

2. For the Tunisian ship captured by the American navy, see Davis to JM, 20 June 1805, *PJM-SS*, 9:482–83 and n. 2.

3. In the first Tr, "wound" is interlined above "hurt."

4. Second Tr and letterbook copy have "fling."

5. The surviving enclosure is a copy of Hammuda Bey to Jefferson, 17 July 1805 (2 pp.; in Italian; translation printed in Knox, *Naval Documents, Barbary Wars*, 6:185), complaining of the American seizure of the Tunisian ship and its prizes and of Rodgers's letter, which the bey considered insulting enough to have led to war had he not earlier received from Jefferson assurance that the president would never approve the rash actions of one individual, and stating that Davis was going, with the bey's permission, to talk to Rodgers.

To Peter Muhlenberg

Sir.   Department of State. July 19th. 1805.

I have received information that some convict Negroes were last Month, forced on board the Schooner Juliana of Newbury Port, J. U. Horton, Master bound to Philadelphia, by the Government of Surinam.[1] It may be proper for you to make it known to the Government of the State, immediately on her arrival, and I request you also to report the circumstances to me, as well as the best evidence you can obtain that they were actually forced on board the Vessel at Surinam and by whom the measure was authorized and carried into effect. If she arrives without them, you will make a strict enquiry into the manner of their being disposed of. I am &c.

JAMES MADISON

Letterbook copy (DNA: RG 59, DL, vol. 15).

1. See Turell Tufts to JM, 13 June 1805, *PJM-SS*, 9:467–68 and n. 1. Capt. J. Haven Horton's deposition of his protest to Lt. Gov. William C. Hughes and Hughes's insistence that Horton carry to America a free black man and woman condemned to banishment was printed in the 2 Aug. 1805 Richmond *Enquirer*.

§ From George W. Erving. *19 July 1805*. No. 34. "In my[1] of the 16th I mentioned that Mr Monroe had quitted Madrid on the 26th May; this upon the authority of what he wrote to me on the 25th, Mr Pinkney on the 26th of the same & Mr Jarvis of Lisbon on the 28th of June. I have just now received a letter from Mr Sullivan the private Secretary of Mr Bowdoin, dated St Andero 20 June, where they arrived on the 12th, in which he says 'Mr Monroe is there (Madrid) nor have we heard of any intention of his to quit the kingdom.' Mr Bowdoin himself remains very unwell at St Andero, & for the present unable to proceed on his journey."

RC (MHi: Winthrop Family Papers). 1 p.; marked "*Private*" and "*Duplicate.*"

1. Erving evidently omitted a word here.

§ From John Mitchell. *19 July 1805, Havre.* "Since I had the honor to Write you,[1] this port has daily diminished in Consequence, from the effect of the Blockade, Commerce has totally desert(e)d it.

"The Armed Vessells fitted out here have all saild & arrived safe at their destination, (Boulogne) not a merchant Vessell has entered, Fecamp & Dieppe are Watched with equal strictness; that, I have no return to make from either place.

"Cherbourg remains open, I had directed returns to be forwarded from that to the end of the year. But I am Informed by Mr. Liaise My Substitute there that Mr. Barnet had appeard and taken from Him his register & Seal. And placed them with a Mr. Chanterenne from Him sir I presume you will receive the returns. Desirous to avoid all and evry difficulty I have passed over this Action of Mr. Barnet—and request you will favor Me with your opinion how far I have a right to Act. From the printed instructions I thought I had Authority to & that it was my Duty to name an Agent Where there was None & Where one was become Necessary from the Circomstance from Mr. Barnets Ideas—I may be called on tomorrow for My Register & Seals & My appointment be thus taken away; this I presume is not the intention of Goverment or, I should Not have received a Commission a Year after Mr. Barnet had His. Your Opinion will direct Me, it shall be strictly followed. If it is the intention in that way to remove me—it shall be Complyed with & When our Goverment will pleace to Confer on Me an other Appointment I will endeavor to deserve it by executing to the best of My Abilities."

RC (DNA: RG 59, CD, Havre, vol. 1). 3 pp.; docketed by Wagner, with his note: "To be answd."

1. See Mitchell to JM, 1 Feb. 1805, *PJM-SS*, 9:2–3.

§ From Francis J. Oliver.[1] *19 July 1805, Boston.* "The following extract from a protest signed at La Guayra by myself, Captain & crew of the Brig 'White Oak' of this town commanded by Joseph Mountfort, is forwarded to you in order that the Govt. of my country may be made acquainted with a wanton, & barbarous attack upon the lives & property of several of its citizens, & with the hope that some measures may be pursued to obtain redress for the injuries therein stated.

"'On the 13th March 1805 sailed from Demerary bound to a market; on the 20th: made Cape Codera bearg. S. W. distant 3 leagues, winds baffling; at 8 A.M. the wind springing up from the eastward, made all sail, & on the 21st. at 7 a. m. La Guayra bore S. W. by W. distant 3 leagues. On the 22d light winds from N. W. &

W. La Guayra distant 4. Leagues. On the 23d in the morning the wind, breezing from the eastward, set the American Ensign at the main-top-gallant-mast head, & made all sail, but owing to the strong weather current running to windward were not able to get within cannon shot of the fort at La Guayra untill about 15 minutes before sun-set when the wind left us becalmed, with a heavy swell heaving on shore. Half an hour before dark were hailed several times from the fort, in Spanish, to which the Captain replied in English, that we were Americans from Cayenne (having touched at that port previous to stopping at Demerary). At this period the Brig had drifted so near the fort that the voices of those on the walls were easily distinguished, & the boat was ordered ahead to tow her off. Several boats were seen coming towards us from the shore, the persons in which hailed & upon being answered suddenly retreated, after discharging a volley of musketry at the Brig; at the same moment also a ball was fired from the fort & immediately followed by several others, one of which passed through the foresail & cut away some of the rigging. Observing that the lights in the vessel served only as marks for the better directing of the guns, they were extinguished, & the Captain jumped into his boat with an intent to land but the balls flying in every direction, he was soon obliged to return.

"[']The firing from the fort, batteries, & several armed vessels in the harbor continued untill ten o'Colk P. M. previous to which hour the vessel having been hove to leeward by the sea, we came to anchor to avoid getting upon the lee shore, when an eighteen pound ball struck the Brig, carried away one of the top timbers, & passed through two water casks. At ten o'Clk the Captain effected a landing & was immediately taken before the Commandant who placed him in confinement for the night. The following morning the Brig's papers were ordered on shore & taken by the Commt. who directed that the vessel should be moored under the guns of one of the batteries untill orders were received from Caracas, observing that it was fortunate that the Captn. landed as he did, for that directions had been given to sink the vessel as soon as the moon rose.

"'Having waited three days & no orders received from Caracas I applied to the Intendant of the province for permission to land & sell the cargo & repair the vessel, which on the 4th April was refused & liberty granted only for the landing of such part of the property as should be sufficient to defray the charges, one of wch. was a demand by Govt. of four hundred & eight Dollars for powder and shot fired at us. The Brig being very leaky I made a second application stating her situation &c. and presented also a remonstrance to the Captain-General against his exaction of the $408. On the 22d Apl. a decree was received confirming that of the 4th. & peremptorily ordering payment for the powder & ball, with which I was obliged to comply.

"'The only reasons alledged by the Spanish Commt. in justification of his cruel and (the firing upon an unarmed vessel becalmed, may also with propriety be termed) cowardly conduct were, first, that it was well known to be contrary to the laws of Spain to permit foreigners to trade with her Colonies, & secondly, that we ought not to have attempted to enter their harbor after sun-set. To the former it may be replied that it was equally well known that during the last war the ports of La Guayra, Porto-Cavello, Barcelona & Cumana were opened to Neutrals, & that since the commencement of the present, a commercial intercourse is permitted with those in the islands of Porto Rico & Cuba. In addition to which Danish, Hamburg & American vessels were seen laying at La Guayra, at the time the Brig White-Oak was off the port. Under these circumstances it surely could not have been esteemed criminal to ask if permission was granted for neutral commerce. In reply to the second reason it is sufficient to say that, had the wind continued a few minutes longer we should have been within hail of their fort before sun-set, but it having become perfectly calm we were left entirely to the guidance of the waves.'

"Conceiving, Sir, that the abovementioned aggressions interest not myself only, but also the American Nation to whose flag no respect was paid, I deem myself justified in respectfully demanding of my Country that support & protection which every Government is bound to afford its citizens.

"The documents I can offer in evidence of the truth of my charges are, the pro-test, official copies of my correspondence with the Intendant & Captain-General of Caracas, & a Bill of the powder, shot, wadding, match rope &c. expended upon us, receipted by the Collector of the customs.

"I shall consider it a favor, Sir, to be informed whether this affair will be noticed by Government."[2]

RC (DNA: RG 76, Preliminary Inventory 177, entry 322, Spain, Treaty of 1819 [Art. XI] [Spoliation], Misc. Records, ca. 1801–24, box 5, folder "White Oak"). 5 pp.; docketed by Wagner as received on 27 July, with his note: "Brige. White Oak (Mountfort)."

1. Federalist Francis Johonnot Oliver (1777–1858) was born in Boston and educated at Boston Latin School. He graduated from Harvard College in 1795. He became a merchant in Boston in 1805 and from 1818 to 1835 served as president of the American Insurance Company, after which he was president of the City Bank of Boston from 1835 to 1840. From 1816 to 1818 he was grand master of Grand Lodge of Massachusetts Freemasons. He was a member of the Boston common council, 1823–25 and 1828, and a member of the state legis-lature, 1822–23. In 1840 he moved to Middletown, Connecticut, where he lived until his death (Middletown, Conn. *Constitution*, 8 Sept. 1858; William Sewall Gardner and Solon Thornton, *Proceedings of the Grand Lodge of the Most Ancient and Honorable Fraternity of Free and Accepted Masons of the Commonwealth of Massachusetts . . . From March 9 to December 27, 1870 . . .* [Boston, 1871], 490).

2. On 5 Aug. 1805 JM replied: "I have received your letter respecting the injury you sustained in the Brig Live Oak, at Laguira. Whatever documents you may think proper to transmit shall be placed among the files to which they bear an anology, in order that they may be ready for the benefit of some general arrangement with Spain, if any adapted to it should be effectuated; for the circumstances of this individual case are not thought to require a separate interposition" (DNA: RG 59, DL, vol. 15; 1 p.).

To James M. Henry

Sir,   Department of State July 20th. 1805

Mr Brent has communicatd your having declined the office of Agent for Seamen at Jamaica, but as it is possible that an explanation of its func-tions may remove your objections I have inclosed a copy of the letter which confers the appointment,[1] and which, tho' sent by Duplicates to Jamaica, absence may have prevented you from receiving. That no other Agent possessing commercial duties is to be appointed is an additional circumstance which may vary the view you have taken of the nature of the appointment. If you should accept it be pleased to inform me of the time of your return to the Island. I have the honor to be &c

JAMES MADISON

Letterbook copy (DNA: RG 59, IC, vol. 1).

1. For earlier mention of Henry's appointment, see Jefferson to JM, 11 Mar. 1805, and JM to Henry, 25 Mar. 1805, *PJM-SS*, 9:123, 125 n. 10, 171–72 and n.

To Walter Jones Jr.

SIR.   DEPARTMENT OF STATE, July 20th. 1805.

I enclose a certificate from the Consul at London[1] of an oath made before him, by Richard Christie, late mate of the Schooner Commerce of Alexandria, of which John Harper was Master, wherein it appears as from the Captain's confession that he maliciously represented at Cowes, that Wm. Gray, a Citizen of the U.States, and one of his Crew, was a British Subject in order to his impressment into the British service, and that in consequence he was actually so impressed. Though no criminal prosecution can perhaps be sustained upon the case for the principal act, yet he may be prosecuted under the 5th. & 6th. Sections of the Act of Congress of the 28th. May 1796 for not transmitting his protest, if he has returned; and if the Seamen in question was entered upon the list of his crew to be deliver'd to the Collector in virtue of the 1st. Section of the act of the 28th. Feby. 1803, his bond may also be sued for not bringing him back. Considering the enormity of Capt. Harper's conduct, I request you to confer with the Collector as to facts, and if these or any other penalties or prosecutions have been incurred in the case & its incidents to take the proper steps for making an example of the Offender.[2] I am &c.

JAMES MADISON

Letterbook copy (DNA: RG 59, DL, vol. 15).

1. See George W. Erving to JM, 20 Apr. 1805 (second letter), *PJM-SS*, 9:265.
2. Walter Jones Jr. (1776–1861), who was educated by a Scottish tutor and read law with Bushrod Washington, was admitted to the bar in the spring of 1796 when he was not yet twenty. He was named U.S. attorney for the District of Potomac in 1802 and for the District of Columbia in 1804. He resigned this federal position in 1821 and went on to have a long and distinguished career in private practice, arguing, among other cases, *McCulloch v. Maryland*. In his cases he joined with such famous contemporaries as Luther Martin, Edward

Livingston, Francis Scott Key, Daniel Webster, and Henry Clay. During the War of 1812, he fought in the Battle of Bladensburg; in 1821 Monroe appointed him brigadier general of militia; eventually he became major general of the District of Columbia. He was a founding member of both the American Colonization Society and the Washington National Monument Society and was strongly opposed to the secession movement that led to the Civil War.

To Peter Muhlenberg and David Gelston

SIR.　　　　　　　　　　DEPARTMENT OF STATE(,) July 20th. 1805.

I request that hereafter you will cause to be endorsed on the packets of Gazettes intended for the Ministers in Europe the words *"not to be put in a Post office*," taking care as often as practicable & necessary to arrange with those who take charge of them the means of otherwise conveying them to their destination after the arrival of the Vessel. Whenever the Vessel is bound to a port where we have a Consul (and such ports ought generally to be preferred) those means may be confided to them.[1] I am &c.

JAMES MADISON.

Letterbook copy (DNA: RG 59, DL, vol. 15). Addressed "To the Collectors of Philada. & N. York." RC (1 p.) sold at Swann Auction Galleries, 19 May 1949, lot 17 (*American Book-Prices Current* [1949] 55:ix, xxv, 483).

1. JM probably wrote this in response to a 30 Apr. 1805 letter from George W. Erving to Jacob Wagner (DNA: RG 59, CD, London, vol. 9; 2 pp.), reporting that dispatches he received from the State Department often had for cover only "one sheet of thin paper, which worn away at the Edges has sometimes left them so open, as that the inclosures might have been Easily taken out & restored without injury to the seal." Erving also complained that packages of newspapers sent to the consuls were sometimes directed *"to be put into the Post Office*," which on occasion led to postage charges as high as three, four, or even ten pounds, causing him to refuse delivery; he suggested that they be labeled as JM instructs here.

§ From Hodijah Baylies. *20 July 1805, Dighton, Massachusetts.* "On the 15th. instant, the schooner Joseph of Somerset in this District, John Trott Junr., master, from Martinique, via Antigua, was entered at this office. It appears by the declaration of Capt. Trott, that the Joseph was captured on her passage from Martinique, by His Britannic Majesty's schooner Netley, commanded by William Carr, & carried to the port of St. John's in Antigua; and that there, by order of the Court of Vice Admiralty, forty hogsheads of sugar, laden on board the Joseph at Martinique; viz. twenty hogsheads shipped by Samuel Newson & consigned to Miller, Son & Miller of N. York & twenty hogsheads shipped by Joseph Barret & consigned to Grant, Forbes & Co. of New York, were taken out of her on suspicion of its being French property. Captn. Trott was then permitted to proceed on his voyage homeward."

RC (DNA: RG 76, Preliminary Inventory 177, entry 180, Great Britain, Treaty of 1794 [Art. VII], British Spoliations, ca. 1794–1824, Unsorted Papers, box 3, folder J). 1 p.; docketed by Wagner as received 7 Aug., with his note: "British Sch'r Netley (Carr)."

§ From Sylvanus Bourne. *20 July 1805, Amsterdam.* "I had the honor to write you *fully* of late by Captains, King, Allen & Davis[1] on the Subject of the question made me in your favr of May 23 & I feel every confidence that those letters will serve to develope to you a Scene of intriguing & unfustiable[2] practices in a certain quarter that must tend to convince you that the appellation I gave in mine above referred to is in Strict conformity to the truth & that you will no longer doubt that in patronising the other establishment, I have been influenced by upright views & laudable Motives & (however an unpleasant appearance the first complexion of the matter may have Carried) that you will consider me acquitted me of any blame in this transaction & that I shall preserve *entire* that Confidence which it has been my boast to have deserved. Please turn over leaf."

Adds in a postscript: "The most displeasing part of the buisness to you must have doubtless appeared in the nature of the propositions I made Mr D as conveying the idea of exclusive buisness myself—but if you will be ⟨so⟩ kind to examine particularly the contents of the letters you will perceive that I had nothing of the sort in view to which I gave any importance or value or indeed any precise or fixed object whatever as the said let⟨ters⟩ refer to 2 or 3 distinct plans of buisness—the fact was that my mind was much embarrassed at the time & I was desirous to effect somethi⟨n⟩g which might prop up the decaying prospects of my commercial hous⟨e⟩ which shortly after failed & has left me nothing but my Consular income to rely on for the support of my family—you will in all events acquit me of any intentions of conducting my affairs in the manner which i⟨t⟩ appears the house in question has been accustomed to nor will you beleive that had I then the knowlege of those facts that I should never ever made any propositions of buisness to them whatever—I can say no more as before Observed I am free in my Conscience from any improper motives & must abide the result with Composure & fortitude— whatever decision may be made the interests of my Children & family will require that you let me have your reply as soon as possible & I doubt not your indulgence & candor will be exercised towards *a truly unfortunate man.*"

RC (DNA: RG 59, CD, Amsterdam, vol. 1). 2 pp.

1. See Bourne to JM, 6, 8, 10, and 12 July 1805.
2. Bourne probably meant to write "unjustifiable" here.

§ From Sylvanus Bourne. *20 July 1805, Amsterdam.* "In a letter I had the honor to write you not long since[1] I mentioned that there appeared to me to be a want of regularity in the Ships documents which come from New Orleans & I have this day met with a renewed example in the case of the Ship Sampson Capt Lovise Munroe, which has only a Sea Letter & Mediterranean pass & Roll of Seamen of April 26h. 1805 in due form but is without any *Certificate* of the *property* of the Vessel—so that I cannot ascertain to whom Said Vessel belongs—it has heretofore been uniformly the Custom—when vessels are not entitled to a *Register* though property of Citizens of the U States that they are furnished with a Certificate of Property from the Custom House, Shewing to whom the Vessel belongs. Whether any Change in that regard have been made by Law I know not—but I can hardly conceive that any regulation should have been made dispensing with the kind of Certificate alluded to. Indeed the difference of practice on many points in the Custom houses of the U States—makes it often difficult to ascertain wh⟨at⟩ are the precise rules of evidence presented by the Law & may lead to confusion & error. In the present instanc⟨e⟩ I am indeed at a loss to know how to act. Tho desirou⟨s⟩ to detect the fraud (if any exists) I shall be loth to take too great a responsibility on myself in any measures regarding the Vessell in question. If the Custom house Officers permit a Vessell to sail with improper papers What check have *I* on them towards Correcting the evil as they must be necessarily supposed to have the best information of the rules of the Law in like Cases—particularly in a quarter where many new rules have been lately established.

"I shall at any rate endeavor to procure from the parties the best possible proof (to be had here) of the Ownership or property of the Vessell & I hope it may be such as to convince me that there is no inca*[illegible]* in the transaction referred to."

Adds in a postscript: "If my instructions from the Secy of the Treasury had said—

"'You will not regard as regular any papers but such as are in the forms *which were by him presented* relative to vessells built in the U States & those that were only owned by Citizens of the U States' I should possess a more sure & perfect guide for the correction of any errors or fraudulent intentions."

RC (DNA: RG 59, CD, Amsterdam, vol. 1). 3 pp.; docketed by Wagner. Another docket in an unidentified hand reads: "Perused by the English Court of Admirlty."

   1. Bourne to JM, 12 May 1805, *PJM-SS*, 9:343.

§ From William Lee. *20 July 1805, Bordeaux.* "I have the honor herewith to transmit you a return of the Vessels, that have entered and cleared at this Consulate, from the 1st. of January to the 30th of June [not found]; together with a list, of those Vessels that have been expedited under the Consular Certificate,[1] accompanied by my account current with the United States [not found].

"You will perceive that my advances for distressed seamen, has been but trifling in comparison with former times. This arises from the efficacy of the new regulations concerning them, and the steady employment they can now easily procure which keeps them out of idleness, and preserves both their health, and morals. I am sorry however to be able to remark, that many of these thoughtless beings not content with the wages of thirty, and thirty five dollars per month, engage on board of privateers, and that I have continually from ten, to fifteen of them in prison, for this and other misdemeanors, some of which would more properly come under the cognizance of the criminal tribunal, but as the constituted authorities have given up the police of American Vessels to my direction, I have thought it most prudent in all cases of trifling theft, and embezzlement of the Cargo, to confine the sailors until the departure of the Vessels, leaving it with the Captains to take such measures on their return to the United S. as they may judge proper. I have been led to this arrangement from the extreme Severity of the Laws of this Country, which are by no means proportioned to the crime, and by the great demand, that has existed here since the war for American seamen.

"The existing difference between the United States & Spain, gives encouragement to privateersmen that ere long, their booty will be considerable from our unprotected commerce. Three privateers have been fitted out here lately under Spanish Colours, with these expectations, and I am told that eighteen, or twenty, of our Vessels have already been carried into the ports of Spain.

"One of these privateers, having shipped in this port eight Americans, I demanded them of the Commissary of marine, who agreed to deliver them up to me, but the Spanish Consul, interposed and prevented my visiting the privateer in order to arrest them: This brought on a discussion between us, and the Commissary doubtful of his competency, found it necessary to consult the minister of marine on the subject, in the mean time the Vessel put to sea and I lost my men. As this is an interesting point to our Commerce, I have thot. it my duty to mention the affair to Genl. Armstrong that if he thinks proper he may represent it to the minister of marine. Since the commencement of the war, I have arrested one hundred, and thirty seven Seamen who either were actually engaged on board of privateers or were secreted for that purpose. If such men found a door open, through which they could escape my vigilence, our vessels would be continually detained here for the want of seamen to the destruction of their voyages.

"I regret that my returns of our Commerce to this port is always imperfect, on account of the refusal of the Captains, to communicate the amount of their inward, and outward Cargoes, by which means a just computation of its advantages might be ascertained and I have no way of coming at this estimate, except thro' the Custom house, which is not a correct source nor is it agreeable to have recourse to that administration for information of this nature.

"I have taken the liberty to State to the Secretary of the Treasury, in some of my last letters the irregularity with which our Custom houses expedite the papers of foreign built ships, commonly called, Certificate, or sea letter Vessels. The Custom houses, of Boston, New York, (Baltimore in some instances) and norfolk, grant these Vessels a Sea Letter, and Mediterranean pass, accompanied with a Certificate, somewhat like a Register, describing the length, breadth, burthen, &c. of the Vessel. The Collectors of New Orleans, Savannah, Charleston and Philadelphia grant them only a Sea Letter, and Mediterranean pass, which not containing a particular description of the Vessel, and specifying only the Captains name and that she is owned by one or more citizens of the United States, may be applied to any Vessel, of nearly the same burthen: Thus it happens that so many of those papers are misapplied, and the legitimacy of all Vessels sailing under them rendered suspicious. The List of those papers, that I have found it necessary to take from the Captains, which you will find hereunto annexed[2] will explain on this head, and shew how necessary it is that the Consuls of the United States should be strict in their duties, particularly in time of war, when many of our shipping are detained, and if condemned are fitted out on Acct. of foreigners, with the same papers, or those papers are applied to more valuable Vessels.

"The Brig Hope of New York sailed from this on the 16th of April for New Orleans, and on the fourth of May put back in distress. On surveying this Vessel,

I found it necessary to condemn her as unfit for sea, and accordingly ordered her sold on account of the underwriters. The Captain and his friends purchased her in and demanded the papers of me, which I refused to grant them. They then presented a petition to Genl. Armstrong who confirmed my decision.

"The Brig Hamilton of New York was cast away at the mouth of this river some time since, and sold shortly after on Account of the Underwriters. The former owner Mr Waldron purchased her in, and on his departure for the United States left a power with the house of Gadiou & Co., of this City to fit her out on his account. These people now demand the papers of me and I have refused to comply with their request, under a firm belief, that the Vessel belongs to them, and because an attempt had been made to my knowledge by a Mr S B Wigginton of New York to apply these papers to the Brig Virginia, which on detecting I ordered Captain Thompson, the former commander of the Hamilton, and the then master of the Virginia, to deposit them in my Office where they now lay cancelled.

"The case of the Brig Ranger Capt Hooper I have made known to you by transmitting duplicate copies of my letters to the Collector of Boston on the subject.[3]

"I should not mention these trifling occurences but, that they form the ground work of many complaints and attacks against my Official conduct.

"During the last six months, several seizures of no moment have been made on American Vessels, by the marine, and Custom house, which have all been abandoned on proper representations being made, That on the Draper, which I had the honor to state to you on the 19th of May[4] was the most serious and so totally unjust, that I had thrown the Vessel on the hands of the Commissary of marine, when a letter was recd. by that Officer from the head of his department at Paris, ordering the ship released, and giving her permission to load.

"The Affair of the ship Easter which I mentioned in my respects of the 18th of May[5] has not terminated as I wished. I seized this Vessel on her arrival here and took possession of her papers, but in endeavouring to draw this case into the Tribunals, I found the same difficulties as attended my prosecuting last year that of the ship Mercury of Charleston.[6] The Easter proves to be the property of Gadiou & Co. a french house who it appears bought her papers of the Agent of Capt. Booth the former owner. As I could not with any hopes of success, according to the opinion of my Counsel, pursue a french merchant, before a french Tribunal, for a breach of the laws of the United States, I thought it most prudent to withdraw the action, and content myself with obtaining the papers.

"The move I took in this business has brought a transaction to light, which I think it not amiss to make known to you, as it will shew in a strong point of view the conduct of those Americans, who connect themselves with french houses for the purpose of doing business to great extent under the American flag.

"It appears that Gadiou & Co. were part owners both of the Easter, and of the Ship mercury, of New York, in which latter S B. Wigginton of New York had an interest. This Vessel on her arrival here from Baltimore, was laid up in a ship Yard to be repaired, but as freights were then brisk the papers of the mercury, were applied to the Easter and she was expedited as the mercury with a Cargo for Brest, and on entering the port met with some accident, which threw her into the Carpenters hands. While the Easter was on this Voyage with the mercurys papers, permission was given by this Government to export grain to Spain, which brought freights up to the enormous price of 160 fs. to 180 fs. per ton from this to Cadiz & probably gave Gadiou & Co. the idea of procuring of me the papers of the Easter, by Mr Wiggintons assistance through Mr Duballet the Agent of Booth. How they managed to accomplish their ends I have stated in my respects to you of the 20th of January last.[7]

"By a little address I have succeeded in getting possession of both sets of papers, and disconcerted their future plans of operation. These facts come to me through unquestionable sources but not accompanied with such substantial proof as would support an action against Wigginton and Duballet, under the act concerning the Registering and recording ships, or Vessels, passed the 2d. of March 1803.[8] I have some expectation of getting hold of this evidence, when I will Lay the affair before the Attorney General of the United States, that a proper example may be made of them for two more deceitful, and unprincipled men, I never met with.

"The very heavy charge of postage that I am subject to by receiving letters from Africa & all parts of France, the Mediterranean, & indeed Europe in General, to be forwarded to America has induced me, to carry out a sum in my A/C with the United States to meet this disbursement. I hope it will be found correct, and that you will order it to pass for adjustment.

"Permit me to close this letter by observing, that since the failure of my house of Perrot & Lee[9] there has been a continual system of intrigue, and calumny, carried on against me by a Set of unprincipled Office seekers, united with political opponents. Genl. Armstrong, Mr Monroe, & Mr Livingston, have successively heard their slanders and though solicited to favor their designs, have treated them as they merit. The friends of these men in London, Paris, New York, Philadelphia and particularly Baltimore, have been busy in their misrepresentations—I have been surrounded by spies in the garb of friends and every part of my official conduct has been scrutinized and censured and one of the most active of this party of calumniators, whose expences I am told are paid for the purpose, has been sent to America to lodge complaints with you. Such things are distressing to a man of an honest mind, who has a large family to provide for and no other means of support but his Office. I have however in the midst of this continual cabal felt secure, and gone on in the righteous discharge of my duty under the belief, that I shall not be censured without a hearing, and trusting in that justice which so eminently distinguishes the present administration of my Country."

RC and enclosures (DNA: RG 59, CD, Bordeaux, vol. 2). RC 11 pp.; docketed by Wagner. For surviving enclosures, see nn. 1–2.

1. The enclosure (1 p.; docketed by Wagner) is a "List of Vessels Cleared out at the Consulate of Borde(a)ux under the Consular Certificate from 1st. Jany. to 30. June 1805," naming sixteen ships, and showing the number and date of the consular certificate issued to the ship, the owner, the port to which it belonged, the tonnage, the destination port, the clearance date, the cargo, the captain, and what build, with remarks stating who fitted out the ship and for whom.

2. Lee enclosed two copies of a "List of Vessels Papers taken from the Captains by William Lee and sent to Genl. Armstrong at Paris May 20th. 1805" (2 pp. each; docketed by Wagner; minor differences between the copies have not been noted), naming seventeen ships, and showing the papers taken, the dates on and ports in which they were issued, the

port to which they belonged, the owners' names, and the captains' names, with remarks on each vessel explaining why Lee seized the papers.

3. For Lee's 15 June 1805 letter to Benjamin Lincoln discussing the *Ranger*, see Lee to JM, 18 June 1805, *PJM-SS*, 9:480 and n. 1.

4. Ibid., 372 and n. 1.

5. Ibid., 368–69.

6. For the *Mercury*, see Lee to JM, 11 Oct. 1804, ibid., 8:158, 159 n. 6.

7. Ibid., 497–98.

8. *U.S. Statutes at Large*, 2:209–10.

9. For the failure of Lee's mercantile house and his recovery from it, see *PJM-SS*, 7:92, 8:412.

§ From William Lee. *21 July 1805, Bordeaux*. No. 241. "I have the honor to transmit you enclosed a letter I have this moment recd. from the US. agents at Leghorn."[1]

RC and enclosure (DNA: RG 59, CD, Bordeaux, vol. 2). RC 1 p. For enclosure, see n. 1.

1. The enclosure (1 p.) is a copy of Degen, Purviance, & Co. to Lee, 1 July 1805, transmitting a copy of John Rodgers's 8 June 1805 letter to Frederick Degen (1 p.) announcing the peace arranged on 31 May between the United States and Tripoli by Tobias Lear, as well as the release of William Bainbridge and the *Philadelphia* crew members.

To Thomas Jefferson

Dear Sir   Washington July 22. 1805

By this Mail you will receive the letters last received from Mr. Erving. No others have come to hand from any quarter worth troubling you with.

Mr. Gallatin left Washington the day I believe you did. I am still detained here by the situation of Mrs. M's complaint.[1] The Doctr. does not claim less than seven or 8 days from this time, at least, in order to render the journey safe; and her recovery has been so much more slow than he calculated that I dare not be sanguine as to the time of my departure. I am not without apprehensions that the case may be of a very serious kind. Its appearance has changed for the better, during the state of absolute rest prescribed, but does not yet resemble that denoting the ordinary course of healing. With respectful attachment I remain always yours

James Madison

We had a fine shower yesterday, and a slight one a few days ago.

RC (DLC: Jefferson Papers). Docketed by Jefferson as received 25 July, with his note: "Erving's lre." The enclosures have not been identified.

1. Dolley Madison had been suffering for weeks from an ulcerated knee, and the Madisons had finally decided to go to Philadelphia where she could be treated by the celebrated doctor Philip Syng Physick. They left Washington on 25 July, and although JM returned to

the capital on 23 Oct., Dolley remained under Dr. Physick's care for another month (Mattern and Shulman, *Selected Letters of Dolley Payne Madison*, 61, 63, 64, 78; Wagner to Jefferson, 27 July 1805, DLC: Jefferson Papers).

§ To Albert Gallatin. *22 July 1805, Department of State.* "Be pleased to issue your warrant on the appropriation for the Contingent expences of the Department of State for Five Hundred Dollars in favor of C. S. Thom: he to be charged and held accountable for the same."[1]

    Letterbook copy (DNA: RG 59, DL, vol. 15). 1 p.

    1. On 12 Dec. 1805 JM again asked Gallatin to issue a warrant on the appropriation for the contingent expenses of the State Department for five hundred dollars to be also charged to Christopher S. Thom's account (DNA: RG 59, DL, vol. 15; 1 p.).

§ From Sylvanus Bourne. *22 July 1805, Amsterdam.* "Agreably to what I had the honor to write you sometime since[1] I have been to Rotterdam & made due inquiry into the affairs of the Consulate there & finding from the information given me both by the masters of Vessells & Merchants who have buisness at the Consular Office that the actual State of Mr Alexander's[2] enables to attend with propriety to the duties thereof & without injury to the public service—& there being no Other fit Character to my knowlege. I have concluded to let him hold the Agency *under my name & controul* till the pleasure of Govt Shall be known by a fixed appointment for said place—but I have at the same time given Mr Alexander to understand fully that he cannot ever expect said appointment & that he must employ the interim in Settling his Affairs so as to the [*sic*] leave the place with the least possible injury to himself—I hope this arrangment may meet your approbation."

    RC, two copies (DNA: RG 59, CD, Amsterdam, vol. 1). First RC 2 pp.; marked "*Copy.*" Second RC dated 23 July 1805. Minor differences between the copies have not been noted.

    1. Bourne to JM, 16 June 1805, *PJM-SS*, 9:472.
    2. Bourne presumably meant to write "Mr Alexander's health enables him" here.

§ From Sylvanus Bourne. *22 July 1805.* "Notwithstanding the Volumes I have lately addressed you on the subject of your favr of May 23[1]—I must beg leave to add a few more observations particularly as to the Contents of my letters to Mr D.

    "You will doubtless find it peculiar that I should have wished to Conciliate exclusive buisness (as you may construe those letters to express) while I condemn the like in others—but you will at the same time my respected Sir agree with me that the unfair or improper manner in which any buisness is conducted constitutes the obnoxious effects of it—& you will never consider me to have an idea of conducting any buisness on the principles which I have since found to have guided said house in their transactions—the whole tenor of my life forbids such an interpretation—I have already explained to you the embarrassed state of my mind at the time I made the propositions & when you come to examine them entirely For when I say that they really conveyed no precise correct or fixed meaning whatever for when I say that by combining the two Offices we should ensure *most* of the Shipping buisnes⟨s⟩ to ourselves I said nothing at all—for without any connection whatever between the two Offices Mr D had not only most but *every* Amn. Ship or Vessell coming here to his address as Broker & when I proposed allowing him half my Consular fees—I could only expect an equal sum from hi⟨s⟩ buisness in return & where was my gain⟨?⟩

"In fine I can but repeat that whatever ma⟨y⟩ have been my expressions, or however awkward the appearanc⟨e⟩ that I had no improper intentions that I meant nothing tha⟨t⟩ Could interfer[e] with my public obligations or have a tendency to injure the interest of another in the Slightest degree the genuine principles of honor & integrity have Stamped my conduct through life & I challenge any one to an⟨swer⟩ the contrary—& these principles have gained me the estee⟨m⟩ & respect of my own Countrymen in my public & priv⟨ate⟩ concerns and those of the Govt & individuals of this Country. When Since my establishment I have lost by failures & other like events about $30,000 have twice had my family broke up my [*sic*] sickness & misfortune—am now just a little settled again depending entirely on my Consular Income for my living & unconscious truly so of having forfeited my title thereto or even that your confidence or that of my Govt in me should be impaired—I therefore must confide on those just & candid interpretations of the whole matter which a liberal & enlightened mind is capable of forming & you shall ever find me scrupously continuing to perform every obligation—with integrity & Zeal—& my Children will bless the name of him who has preserved their father's honor & shewn himself their friend & protector."

RC, two copies (DNA: RG 59, CD, Amsterdam, vol. 1). First RC 3 pp.; marked *"Copy"*; docketed by Wagner. Second RC contains the same sentiments as Bourne's several other letters on the issue (see n. 1 below). Differences between the copies have not been noted.

1. See JM to Bourne, 23 May 1805, *PJM-SS*, 9:379–80, and Bourne to JM, 6, 8, 10, 12, and 20 July 1805 (first letter).

§ From William C. C. Claiborne. *22 July 1805, New Orleans.* "My last, upon the Subject of the Post Route thro' West Florida,[1] informed you, that Captain Carmick on his return from Pensacola, had unfortunately lost the answer of Governor Folch to my communication: But the enclosed Copy of a Letter from the Marquis of Casa Calvo to me,[2] will inform you that no objections will be made on the part of the Spanish Authorities to the proposed establishment."

RC and enclosure (DNA: RG 59, TP, Orleans, vol. 7); letterbook copy and letterbook copy of enclosure (Ms-Ar: Claiborne Executive Journal, vol. 15). RC 1 p.; in a clerk's hand, except for Claiborne's complimentary close and signature; docketed by Wagner as received 27 Aug., with his note: "Govr. Folch's consent to the mail passing through W. Florida." For enclosure, see n. 2.

1. Claiborne to JM, 5 July 1805.
2. The enclosure (1 p.; in Spanish; docketed by Wagner; translation printed in Rowland, *Claiborne Letter Books*, 8:130) is a copy of Casa Calvo's 16 July 1805 letter to Claiborne stating that he had heard from Governor Folch of West Florida who had received Clai-

borne's communication sent by Daniel Carmick and who had made no objection to the postal route through his territory that Claiborne desired.

§ From William C. C. Claiborne. *22 July 1805, New Orleans.* "I received by the last Mail My Commission as Governor of The Territory of Orleans, under the late act of Congress.[1] At any time, an evidence of the President's Confidence would Afford me Satisfaction; but I must confess, that the late renewal of my Commission, has excited in my breast, the liveliest emotions of gratitude and pleasure. An Approving Conscience, and *a hope*, that my Public Conduct would be acceptable to those, whose *approbation* I most desired, have hitherto enabled me to encounter many difficulties, and to pursue, amidst much opposition, the Policy which My judgment Sanctioned. The proof of that approbation has highly gratified me, and there now remains only one political object dear to my Heart, and that is to discharge *with fidelity*, the trust reposed, and thus to merit a continuance of the Esteem and Confidence of the present administration. I have received also by the last Mail, Commissions for Messrs. Prevost, Graham and Thruston;[2] the two first have been delivered, and the third will be presented on the arrival of the Gentleman for whom it is intended!"

RC (DNA: RG 59, TP, Orleans, vol. 7); letterbook copy (Ms-Ar: Claiborne Executive Journal, vol. 15). RC 2 pp.; in a clerk's hand, except for Claiborne's complimentary close and signature; docketed by Wagner as received 27 Aug. Minor differences between the copies have not been noted.

1. The passage of the "Act further providing for the government of the territory of Orleans" on 2 Mar. 1805 necessitated the reissuance of commissions for the territorial officials (*U.S. Statutes at Large*, 2:322–23).
2. For John B. Prevost's 10 June 1805 commission as judge, see Carter, *Territorial Papers, Orleans*, 9:350 n. 78, 455. For Buckner Thruston's, see JM to Thruston, 10 June 1805, *PJM-SS*, 9:447 and n. 1. A copy of John Graham's commission is filed with copies of Prevost's and Thruston's commissions in the National Archives, Record Group 59, Temporary Presidential Commissions.

§ From Henry Hill Jr. *22 July 1805, Havana.* "Some circumstances have occured since I last had the honor of addressing you, which concerns my official situation, and affects the interests of our Citizens, which it will become my duty to communicate; but as they are not yet brought to maturity, I defer it to a future opportunity.
   "Presuming that our Govt. will be disposed to aid me in the legal execution of my duty, is the object of this letter; in which I shall detail the cause which in my opinion renders such aid necessary.
   "My arrival here at a time when the public mind was still agitated by the recent arrest and imprisonment of Mr Gray, and the consequent seizure of the papers of this Consulate,[1] has militated much against me.
   "The evils that resulted therefrom to many of the merchants, had caused a considerable party among that class, in favor of the acknowledgment of a Consul from

the United States, to reside here so long as the port should continue open to our commerce; which they are sensible the Island is entirely dependent on for the supplies so necessary to its existence, and the present controul of public events. This but increased the fears and predjudices of the Govt against the acknowledgement of a consul, as the officers of one of the principal departments were deeply implicated in the measures against Mr Gray, which originated with them; and were desirous of throwing some responsability upon the Captn. Grnl. These circumstances awakened his fears, and caused him to publish officially that he had not, neither could he acknowledge any public agent from whatever nation, without special orders from his King; it being contrary to the laws of these dominions.

"On my being presented to His Excellency he repeated the same to me. This was the Situation of affairs on my arrival. Notwithstanding which, and although I considered my reception, the conduct pursued towards Mr Gray, and the existance of various flagrant abuses on our Commerce and citizens in this Island, insulting to my Country and humiliating to myself, I took upon me the duties of my office on the 10th. of June, from a conviction that Consular documents in many instances were indispensably necessary to those of my fellow citizens trading hither.

"It being generally understood from what had been made public, that I should receive no aid or protection from this Govt. in the execution of my duty, but be subject to the same arbitrary will which had thrown Mr Gray into prison, and at the mercy of any malicious informer, many citizens of the united States (masters of Vessels) were disposed from thier circumstances to dispute my authority, and commit acts in violation and contempt of the laws of their country.

"Among the most atrocious of these, was a Ralph Barber, master of the Schooner Alleghany of New York—proofs of whose conduct are contained in the inclosed Nos 1 & 2[2] As I doubt not but the said Barber is bad enough, to take pains on his arrival in the United States to represent this business very widely from the truth, and g⟨i⟩ve a coloring to it, which may make very unfavorable impressions upon the minds of those who are not intimately acquainted with me, I request in such case, that such part of this letter as will elucidat⟨e⟩ the transaction, with the document no 2 may receive equal publicity with his assertions. Also, that a suit may be instituted against the said Barber, for his just punishment, & recovery of the penalty the law affixes to him. For however this government may find it convenient to treat a commission from the President of the United States, I presume it will not be thought it should lessen the obligations of our own citizens.

"It was not my wish to prosecute said Barber in this Country for the personal abuse I recd from him, as he is too contemptible a character to excite my resentment; and it wou⟨l⟩d have materially injured his owners interests."

RC and enclosures (DNA: RG 59, CD, Havana, vol. 1). RC 4 pp.; docketed by Wagner. For enclosures, see n. 2.

1. For Vincent Gray's arrest, see John Morton to JM, 26 Apr. 1805, and Gray to JM, 4 May 1805, *PJM-SS*, 9:289, 290 n. 1, 320–21.

2. Enclosure no. 1 (1 p.) is Hill's 24 July 1805 certification that he enclosed a "true and correct transcript" from his consular diary and that his secretary John L. Ramage had sworn to the truth of the facts there transcribed. Enclosure no. 2 (3 pp.) is an 8 July 1805 statement, certified as true by Ramage, that Ralph Barber of the New York schooner *Alleghany* had

appeared at the consulate to register a protest, which Hill refused to accept unless Barber deposited his ship's papers. Barber insolently refused, saying his owners had forbidden him to do so, and Hill replied that he would fine Barber five hundred dollars and "not consider him an American." On 9 June, Barber returned with two witnesses and offered to show Hill the papers. Hill asked if he would deposit them and Barber replied he would if he received a receipt, which Hill refused to deliver. The situation deteriorated and Hill had his servants forcibly eject Barber from the house. On 11 June, Barber's representative appeared to deposit the papers, but Hill refused to receive them from anyone but Barber and further demanded an acknowledgment from Barber of "the insolence and abuse he had given" Hill, who added that his consular commission should receive the respect due to it.

§From John Pearson and James Kimball. *22 July 1805, Newburyport.* "We the Subscribers did in March last past Load and fix away the Brig Hannah, from this place, Isaac Bridges Master, with a Cargo of Boards, Staves, Oil & sundry other articles for the Island of Terciera, one of the Western Islands or Azores, the said Brig sailed from this port on the 13th. day of March, and nothing material occured untill the 30th. of the same Month, when a Sail was discovered a Stern which came alongside. She was the Cutter Providence of London, Commanded by Philip Le Roux, the said Captain Le Roux ordered Capt. Bridges to hoist out his Boat and come on board, Capt Bridges laid his Topsails aback, and told him that the Sea was so large and his Boat so small it was impossible to come on Board, he threatned him, if he did not come on board immediately he would Fire on him, Capt Bridges remonstrated against his Fireing, and told him he was at his Mercy, and would lay by all night untill the weather was more moderate, so that he could board him, and then hauled down his Colours, but the said Capt LeRoux still insisting he should get out his Boat, and began to Fire on him with Muskets & Great Guns, and after fireing sometime and still persisting in Capt Bridges getting out his Boat, and said Bridges remonstrating against such conduct and telling said L.Roux, that he was in a Lawful Trade, and no Treaty obliged him to risk his life in going on Board, & beging him not to Fire, but they continuing their Fire and threats, at length said Bridges was exasperated at such conduct, told him, as you will see in one of the Protests, to Fire, said L'Roux still firing at length Capt Bridges received two Shot one in his Groin and one in his thigh and was mortally wounded after the Captain was wounded the Mate found they persisted in Firing and he expected they should all be killed, and that he might as well be drowned as killed, lowered down the small Boat and fortunately got on Board the Cutter, at a Great hazard of his life, And the said Capt LeRoux told him he would have killed him likewise if he had not come on board, and said LeRoux-people told the Mate that said LeRoux ordered them to Fire at & kill said Capt Bridges: The Brig Hannah was however permitted to proceed. The Captain's being wounded & she being near Fayal, the next day the Mate went in there, and put the Captain on shore, where he lingered nineteen Days in great pain and distress and then Expired,[1] When the Captain got on Shore he knew the Voyage intended, could not be prosecuted, therefore sold the Cargo for the most that was offered there, to have it delivered at the Island of Graciosa, the Mate went there with the Brig and landed the Cargo and received the Wines on board which was received for it, and proceeded to Newburyport, where she arrived the 12th instant; in consequence of this Illegal, inhuman and barborous conduct of said LeRoux, a very worthy Man has lost his life and his fr(i)ends are deprived of his earnings, and in addition to this, We the said Owners have suffered a great Loss of property, say four or five thousand Dollars at least, the Brig We Chartered and in consequence of losing the Captain a considerable Loss of Charter was sustained and heavy expence, was incurred, and We can make it appear had our plan been executed in the manner We had directed, and which was every part of it lawful and proper, We should have received nearly double the amount of property we have, therefore, Sir, We feel very much injured and agreived and if satisfaction can be obtained, We expect to have it, it was the opinion of the British, French and American Consuls at Fayall, & the Merchants, that the said Capt LeRoux was liable for all damages sustained in Consequence of his unprece- dented and barbarous Conduct, although he cannot make amends for Capt. Bridge's Life, said Le Roux went into Fayall, and acknowledged that his conduct was wrong, and the Captains of several British Ships of War was of opinion that he would be Severely punished, and that all Loss & damages would be paid on representation being made to the British Goverment, we therefore Sir think this ought to be pur- sued by our Goverment as the Flag of the United States has been insulted, and a worthy Citizen deprived of his Life, as well as a great Loss of property to us, we would not Sir, dictate what measures sould be adopted, but ask your opinion and Assistance and wish to know wether our Goverment will pursue this Business and demand satis'faction through our Minister at London, or wether they will point out to us any other way of proceeding, we submit the whole Business to you hoping you will pursue this Business so degrading to the national Flag and to persons employed in a Lawful Commerce. We have a Protest made at Fayall, by said Capt Bridges, Mate & Crew, before the American Consul there, also a Protest made in Newbury- port by the Mate and some of the Crew, also two Certificates, one from a Gentle- man who was at Fayall, Merchant of Boston, & the Mates, Certifying the [. . .] have sustained in our Property in consequence of [. . .] not being pursued, these we have enclosed and [. . .] procure other documents if necessary."

RC (DNA: RG 76, Preliminary Inventory 177, entry 201, Great Britain, Misc. Claims, ca. 1797–1853, envelope 2, folder 21). 3 pp. Damaged by removal of seals; docketed by Wagner. Enclosures not found.

1. For more on this incident, see John Street to JM, 28 May 1805, *PJM-SS*, 9:413 and n. 1.

From Thomas Jefferson

MONTICELLO July 23. 05.

Th: Jefferson presents his affectionate salutations to mr. Madison and incloses him the extract of a letter from mr. Granger,[1] giving information of constant trespasses committing on a certain species of timber growing on the public lands on lake Erie, of great value, and which he presumes should be the subject of a charge from the Secretary of state to Governor Hull. He presumes the Governor should first warn all persons by proclamation from the commission of such trespass, and be afterwards watchful to have trespassers punished by[2] indictment according to law.

P.S. Th:J. sets out on the 26th. for Bedford & will be absent 10 days.

RC and enclosure (DNA: RG 59, ML); FC (DLC: Jefferson Papers). RC docketed by Wagner: "The President 23 July 1805. Recd 30 July"; marked "file," in a clerk's hand. For enclosure, see n. 1.

1. The enclosure (1 p.) is an extract of Gideon Granger to Jefferson, 19 July 1805, stating that "a very valuable pinery" belonging to the government and extending from "the North Side of Lake St Claer . . . up the river and Lake Huron, to a place call'd Whiterock" was being laid waste by both American and Canadian citizens; that its value appeared to him so great that he had asked the U.S. commissioner to extinguish Indian title to it; and that this tract and another, which he owned near Ashtabula, were the only stands of this valuable material that he was aware of in the area.
2. JM placed a cross here and wrote beneath Jefferson's postscript: "+Quer. whether it be indictable at Com Law, or a mere civil injury?"

§ From Sylvanus Bourne. *23 July 1805, Amsterdam.* "The inclosed Gazette contains a note of the Russian Minister[1] (who was as far [as] Berlin on his way to Paris to Converse on the subject of peace) of a nature to exclude for the present all hopes of accommodation—the probable result will be the vigorous renewal of the War on the Continent early in the ensuing Spring—but how far even their combined efforts may be effectual to check the imperious weight of Power now held by the Govt of France is indeed very problematical. It will all operate favorably to the interests of our Country & I hope may eventually produce the general good of Europe.

"I wrote you yesterday on the Subject of the Consulate at Rottm.[2] Stating the temporary arrangment I had made for Mr Alexanders holding the Agency—under my *Name* & *Controul* till the pleasure of Govt should be known by a fixed appointment there, giving him to understand that he must not look for it, or in any event expect it. It being necessary that some one Should act there & no person being found willing to take the place for a short time & Mr As actual state of health enabling him to fullfill the duties with propriety I have adopted this middle line & shall see that every thing there is conducted regularly & properly till the place is filled by Govt. Mr Clark our Consul at Emden heretofore suggested to me his hopes of said appointment and as his Claims thereto must be already known to you I decline all interference therein.

"My mind has been unpleasantly occupied by the subject of my late letters to you.[3] I however now have resumed the calmness & composure which conscious integrity inspires & shall wait your reply with confidence in the Justice & propriety of your decision."

Adds in a postscript: "I send you inclosed a Copy of my Letter to Mr Alexr."[4]

RC and enclosure (DNA: RG 59, CD, Amsterdam, vol. 1). RC 3 pp.; docketed by Wagner. For enclosure, see n. 4.

1. For Nikolai Novosiltsov's letter to Karl August von Hardenberg, see John M. Forbes to JM, 16 July 1805, and n. 2.

2. Bourne to JM, 22 July 1805 (first letter).

3. See Bourne to JM, 6, 8, 10, 12, 20 (first letter), and 22 July (second letter) 1805.

4. Bourne enclosed an undated copy (2 pp.) of his letter to Lawson Alexander listing the conditions under which the latter could continue to perform the consular duties at Rotterdam. Alexander was to have all official documents made out in Bourne's name as consul general and to sign himself as agent; to submit to Bourne's advice whenever it was required; and to be subject to Bourne's control, which would extend even to Alexander's recall should that become necessary. This arrangement was conditional on further instructions from the U.S. government. Bourne added "you ought by no means to flatter yourself with the hopes of a permanent appointment there but employ the interim in making such an arrangment of your affairs as will enable you to leave the place with the least possible inconvenience to yourself." Alexander remained in the post until 1807 (Alexander to JM, 1 July 1807, DNA: RG 59, LAR, 1801–9, filed under "Alexander"; JM to Alexander, 13 July 1807, DNA: RG 59, DL, vol. 15).

§ From George Duffield. *23 July 1805, "Territory of Orleans, near the City of Orleans."* "Although the period, since my arrival in this Territory, has been very short, the effect of the climate on my health, has been such, as to convince me, it will never be friendly to my constitution: I have therefore enclosed the Commission, with which, the President was pleased to honour me, and must respectfully request you, Sir, to inform him of my resignation of it.[1] With peculiar Satisfaction I am enabled to State, that no inconvenience will occur hereby, in the discharge of the public business of the Territory, as there is at present a Suspension of the judicial proceedings of the Court; which, it is presumed, will continue untill the month of November next, by reason of the sickly season, with the formality of opening & adjourning the Court in pursuance of the Act of Congress on the subject. I deemed it my duty to give the earliest intimation of my intention, that n⟨o⟩ possible inconvenience might result from it. Be pleased Sir, to honour me, with assuring the President of my most profound respect."

RC (DNA: RG 217, First Auditor's Accounts, no. 17,724). 1 p.; docketed by Wagner as received 27 Aug.; with Jefferson's docket and note: "I signed his commn. Mar. 11. it's date may vary a few days."

1. For Duffield's appointment as judge, see Jefferson to JM, 11 Mar. 1805, and Duffield to JM, 6 May 1805, *PJM-SS*, 9:123, 125 n. 10, 327.

§ From Peter S. Du Ponceau. *23 July 1805, Philadelphia.* "I have the honor of Sending you the conclusion of the Notes &c. with an Appendix of Documents & authorities.[1] I have endeavoured as much as has been in my power, to fulfill the object which you appeared to have in view; if I have not Succeeded, I rely upon your goodness to ascribe it solely to my want of abilities, not to a deficiency of Zeal. You will excuse me also if I have stated many facts which are already familiar to you, but it seemed to me necessary to connect together the whole of this little Sketch.

"The Gentleman to whom I alluded in the Course of the Notes, & from whom I have received the information respecting the proposals of Adml. Duckworth to Dessalines, is Capt. Lewis, of the Ship Hindostan, of New York, who is lately returned from St Domingo,[2] I had a full opportunity to obtain correct information there."

[Enclosure]

Third Period.
From the peace of Aix La Chapelle to the present time.

———

The War of 1739. which, as we have observed was undertaken by Great Britain in order to Secure an active Trade with the Spanish American Colonies, failed entirely of its principal and indeed its Sole object. The English at the Conclusion of this War found themselves quite fallen from the vantage ground which they Stood on at the conclusion of the Treaty of Utrecht, the right claimed by Spain to Search British vessels Navigating in the american Seas, was neither given up, explained or modified, the asiento, the term of which had expired about four years after the beginning of the war, was not renewed, the British were only allowed to continue it for the remainder of the term which the war had Suspended, & they even soon after commuted that right with Spain for a gross sum of money, so that the asiento, the annual Ship & the carrying trade to the Spanish Colonies were now at an end.

While Great Britain was thus endeavouring to obtain by force a Trade with the American Colonies of Spain, France had also aimed at the same object, but had pursued it by more pacific Means, She had Silently encouraged the Spanish Smugglers to come to the ports of her Colonies, where they brought in Small Vessels their valuable produce, and took away in return the manufactures of *France*. England had no resource left but to follow the same plan, & She wisely did it. The Court of Spain endeavoured to counteract it by relaxing in Some degree the Severity of her Laws concerning the Trade between her old and new possessions, & succeeded thereby so far as greatly to diminish the quantity of contraband Trade, nevertheless, Says Edwards, "the intercourse with Jamaica in—Spanish Vessels, was still very considerable, So late as the year 1764." 1. Edw: 249. Philada Ed.[3]

Besides this Trade Carried on between the British American Colonies in general, especially those of the West Indies, & the Spanish, there had for a long time Subsisted one equally extensive, between the British Colonies (especially those on the Continent of North America) and the French West Indies. This Trade was permitted to be carried on for a long time during the war (of 1756) between Great Britain & France, directly, by means of flags of Truce[(a)]; and in a round about way thro' the Dutch & Danish Islands, and at length thro' the Spanish port of Monte Christi, in the Island of Hispaniola; till a[t] last (Says the Annual Register) the vast

———

[(a)]French Flags of Truce Sent from time to time from St. Domingo to Jamaica, as the occasion of the War required, the merchants wh[o] owned the flags of Truce clandestinely put on board cotton & Indigo for the Jamaica market, not, perhaps, without the Connivance of the officers of the French Government.

advantages the French received from it, above what the English could expect, in Consequence of their having in a manner laid Siege to all the French West India Islands, determined the Government to put a Stop to it. Ann: Reg: 1765 p: 20–21.[4]

If the British Government really did put a Stop to that Trade, it must have been very late in the War, probably not until the year 1762. when it was declared against Spain & when the West India Islands became not only the Theatre of War, but the object of attack.

This Commerce while it continued was certainly of immense advantage to Great Britain. Long tells us that during the Six first years of the War (of 1756.) there were 640 thousand weight of French Indigo, imported from St. Domingo into the Island of Jamaica. 1. Long 499.[5] He tells us also (Same page) that in the years 1764–5. the Exports from Jamaica to England exceeded by more than one third the Sum which they amounted to in 1751.[6] So that the Colony must greatly have enriched itself during the War by the French & Spanish Colonial Trade. And when by the impolitic Conduct of the Government of Great Britain in the year 1765 which we Shall hereafter mention, a Stop was put to that lucrative Trade, the exports from Great Britain to Jamaica fell Short of what they were in 1763. by £168000 Sterlg. 1. Edw: 248.[7]

We can judge also of the immense importance of this Trade with the French West India Colonies by what took place in the British house of Commons in 1774. on the question of the renewal of the free port act, which was about to expire "It being,["] Says Edwards, "given in Evidence that thirty thousand people about Manchester, were employed in the Velvet manufactory, for which the St. Domingo Cotton was best adapted, & that Indigo had been imported from Jamaica at least Thirty per Cent cheaper than the same could have been procured at thro' France; the house, disregarding all Colonial opposition, came to a resolution 'that the continuance of free ports in Jamaica would be highly beneficial to the Trade and Manufactures of the Kingdom.' That act was thereupon renewed & has since been made perpetual." 1 Edw: 252.[8]

It is then an undoubted matter of fact, that at the breaking out of the War of 1756. the British were in possession of a very Lucrative Trade with the French & Spanish Colonies in America, that they continued it during the whole war (Except perhaps the last year, when they were laying actual Siege to the French and Spanish Islands[)], and that they derived a great profit from it during the War.

It is also a fact that the commerce while it was highly advantageous to Great Britain, was not less so to her enemies (See annual Register Loco citato) Hence when during the same war, she Seized & confiscated the Dutch & other Neutral Vessels, which were Seeking a participation in that beneficial Trade the cause of that prohibition must be looked for else-where, than in her fears, lest the strength & resources of her enemies should be thereby encreased; and the facts and circumstances which we have before us, point to commercial jealousy as the only motive that could actuate them.

The principles which governed the decisions of the British Courts dur-ing that War, as to this particular trade appear to have been fluctuating. We find in the case of Berens v. Rucker (in 1. Black: Rep: 313.)[9] which was the case of a Dutch Ship which had taken in Sugar at Sea off the Island of St Eustatius, which were brought along side of her by French boats from a French Island, and which was taken in 1758. on her return to Amsterdam with those Sugars on board, that Lord Mansfield in the year 1760. ex-presses himself as follows "This Capture was certainly unjust. The pre-tence was that part of this Cargo was put on board off St. Eustatius by French boats from a French Island. *This is now a Settled point by the Lords of appeals*, to be the same thing as if they had been landed on the Dutch Shore, & then put on board afterwards; in which case *there is no Colour for Seizure*. The Rule is, that if a neutral Ship Trades to a French Colony, with all the privileges of a French Ship, and is thus adopted and naturalized, it must be looked upon as a French Ship, & is liable to be taken—not so, if She has only French produce on board, *without taking it at a French port, for it may be purchased of Neutrals*."

It Seems that the French during that War gave licences to Neutrals to trade with their Colonies, & that Lord Mansfield, & (if he is Correct) the Lords of appeals considered the prohibition as applying only to those li-cenced Vessels, under the quaint Supposition of their being Naturalized as French bottoms, but that a trade carried on with the French Colonies in-directly thro the neutral Islands, or even, which makes the case much Stronger by waiting for the French boats in the open Sea, without touch-ing at the French port was perfectly lawful. Yet we find in Robinson that the French West India produce which was taken in Neutrals [*sic*] Vessels at Monte Christi, a Spanish Neutral port was uniformly condemned, it being considered as an evasion of the rule—The Providentia 2. Rob: 120. Am: Ed: Appendix to 4 Rob: A page 6. Am. Ed.[10]

We find also that the usage of Licences being discontinued by the French in the Course of that War, the Vessels which were taken in that trade, tho' without licences were nevertheless condemned. The Providentia 2. Rob: 120.

Yet if we are to credit the Annual Register, the English themselves car-ried on the same trade directly with the French Islands, by means of Flag of Truce, equivalent to Licences, and indirectly thro' the port of *Monte Christy* and other Neutral ports, while they confiscated the property of neutrals, for carrying on precisely the same trade & in the same Manner.

Sir William Scott has admitted that the English trading with Enemy's Colony, justifies neutrals for doing it *precisely* in the same degree. The Immanuel 2 Rob: 163. Am: Ed: This is sufficient to shew that the reason which they gave for condemning the Dutch and other Neutral Ships or Cargoes Carrying on the French West India trade from their own country, directly by means of Licences, or indirectly thro' the port of Monte Christi, was but mere Colour or pretence, & that the[y] were really making War upon Neutrals, while they pretended to be making it upon the French.

The English admit thus much, because they have Since the last war restricted their prohibition to the direct trade by Neutrals, between the Enemy's Colony & the mother country or other ports than those of the Nation to which the Vessel belongs. It is not within the Scope of these notes to point out the little essential difference in regard to the now assumed ground of Strenghtening [*sic*] the Enemy, that there is between that trade, and the trade which is carried on by the British themselves, perhaps that the considerable pains which appear to have been taken by Sir William Scott to avoid that delicate point, Speaks louder than any arguments that we may adduce on the Subject, & which we leave to those who are more adequate to the task. But see the Immanuel 2. Rob: 169. am: Ed.

If we have Succeeded thus far in proving that Commercial jealousy was the sole cause of the English prohibition in the War of 1756. Our object is fully attained. We shall now proceed with our historical narrative.

Soon after the peace of 1763. the British Ministry by a Series of impolitic measures lost what remained to them of the Commerce of the Spanish Colonies. "They gave directions" Says Edwards "to enforce their Laws of Navigation with the utmost rigour; and the Captains of British men of war had custom house Commissions given to them, with orders to Seize indiscriminately all foreign Vessels that should be found in the ports of our West India Islands, a measure which in reality Converted the British navy into *Guarda Costas* for the Spanish King. The Spaniards by these proceedings, were deterred from approaching near us; and in the year 1765 the exports from great Britain to Jamaica alone in the year 1765 fell short of the year 1763. £168000 Sterling.

"A wiser minister endeavoured to remedy the mischief by giving orders for the admission of Spanish Vessels as usual, but the Subject matter being canvassed in the British Parliament, the Nature and intent of those orders were so fully explained, that the Spanish Court, grown wise from experience, took the alarm, and immediately adopted a measure, equally prompt & prudent for counteracting them. This was laying open the trade to the Islands of Trinidad, Porto Rico, Hispaniola & Cuba 'to Every Province in Spain,['] & permitting goods of all kinds to be sent thither, on the payment of moderate Duties, Thus the temptation of an illicit commerce with foreign Nations being in a great measure removed, there was reason to believe that the effect would Cease with the Cause.

"Such, however, is the Superiority or comparative cheapness of British manufactures, that it is probable the Trade would have been revived to a Certain degree if the British Ministry of 1765 after giving orders for the admission of Spanish Vessels into our ports, had proceeded no further, but in the following year they obtained an Act from Parliament for opening the chief ports of Jamaica & Dominica, to all foreign Vessels of a certain description—The Jealousy of Spain was awakened, and the endeavours of the British Parliament on this occasion Served only to encrease the evil which was meant to be redressed—By an unfortunate over Sight the Collectors at the Several British free ports were instructed to keep regular accounts of the entry of all foreign Vessels, & of the bullion which they imported, together with the names of their Commanders. These accounts having been transmitted to England, copies of them were by Some means procured by the Court of Spain, and occasioned the absolute destruction of the poor people, who had been concerned in the business. Information of this being transmitted to the British ministry, the former Instructions were revoked, but the remedy came too late, for what else could be expected than that the Spaniards would naturally shun all intercourse with a people, whom neither the safety of their friends; nor their own evident interest, was sufficient to engage the Confidence and Secrecy?

"The little Trade therefore which now (about the year 1793.) Subsists with the Subjects of Spain in America, is chiefly carried on by small vessels from Jamaica, which contrive to elude the Vigilence of the *Guarda Costas*.["]
1. Edw: Hist: W. Ind: 249. Philada Ed.

Thus at the beginning of the war of 1778. The British by their own fault had lost their valuable Trade with the Spanish Colonies, their trade with the French possessions was chiefly carried on from the now United States, which being now separated from the mother Country, She no longer derived any benefit from it, the intercourse between Jamaica & the French part of St. Domingo still Subsisted by which they were enabled to procure cotton & Indigo for their manufactures at home, the war put an end to it, and they were obliged to obtain those Supplies in a less direct way.[a]

The Commerce of the French Colonies was opened to allies and Neutrals during that War. But we have not been able to ascertain by any authentic document the precise date when it began; it does not appear however, from the best information that we have been able to obtain, that there was much intercourse between them and Europe until about the year 1781. It is

[a] We are informed by a Gentleman, who himself carried on that trade, that flags of Truce were also made use of in this war to carry cotton and Indigo to Jamaica.

certain that in the year 1779. Coffee could be had at Cape François & Port au Prince at 4 to 5s French West India currency per pound (the Sol is $^1/_{165}$th. part of a Dollar) and the best brown Sugar at One Dollar ℔ Cwt., which shews that purchasers did not abound in the French Ports of St. Domingo.

While the Dutch remained Neutral, the Trade of the French Islands centered principally in the Dutch Island of St. Eustatius, which was made a free port, & was the great mart of West India produce to which all nations resorted, & the British as well as others. It is recollected that when the British forces under Adml. Rodney & Genl. Vaughan took that Island in 1781. the immense property which their Countrymen possessed there was involved in the general plunder.

After the Capture of that Island, the Emperor of Germany having made Ostend a free port, Several French houses, particularly from Dunkirk, established agents there, by whom a considerable trade was carried on with the French West Indies, under cover of the Imperial flag, the French Islands were then better Supplied, & their produce rose proportionally. The port of Ostend was opened on the 11th of June 1801. & peace was concluded between Great Britain and the allies on the 3d. of September 1803.

We have been informed by respectable Merchants who resided at St. Domingo at that time, that that trade between Ostend & that Island was very little interrupted by the British Cruizers, altho' the cloak of neutrality was so thin that it would hardly be called a disguise. That trade was chiefly carried on by French Vessels with French Owners, Masters, Crews & Cargoes, who had merely touched at Ostend to obtain an Imperial passport for the Vessel, & Letters of Burgership for the Captain.

In this state of things, we have it from British as well as from Neutral authority, that the application of the principle now contended for by Great Britain, & which is the object of these notes, was wholly intermitted. The Emanuel, 1. Robinson 252. Am: Ed:—Henning's Abhandlung über die neutralitæt, page 58.[11] The Courts of Admiralty released every neutral Vessel & Cargo which was brought in for having traded with the Enemy's Colonies. And it is remarkable that they did this in the face of an Act of Parliament passed during the same War, by which the Cargoes of Vessels thus taken, were declared to be liable to confiscation. This act, 20 Geo: 3. C. 29. was passed after the Capture of the Island of Grenada by the French, it made it lawful for Neutrals to trade to that Island, and the Grenadines, but at the same time declared that it was not to exempt from confiscation the Cargoes of Vessels found trading with the other enemy Islands. As this act was temporary, its Title only is to be found in Danby Pickering's Statutes at large,[12] but it is recorded at full length in 2. Henning's *Sammlung von Staatsschriften* (collection of State papers during the war of 1778.) page 114.[13] We Subjoin it to these notes, with other Documents, in an appendix No. 1.[14]

Sir William Scott, in the above cited case of the Emanuel, 1. Rob: 252. assigns as a reason for this toleration of the neutral Trade with Enemy's Colonies "That it was understood that France, in opening her Colonies during the war, had declared that this was not done with a temporary view, relative to the War, but on a general & permanent purpose of altering her Colonial System, & of admitting foreign Vessels universally & at all times to a participation of that Commerce."

We have not been able to find in the annals of the times any traces of Such a declaration made by France—indeed Sir William Scott himself does not State it as an absolute fact, for he Says *"Taking that to be the fact,* (however Suspicious its commencement might be during the existence of a war) there was no ground to say that neutrals were not engaged in an ordinary Commerce &c. & proceeds to say that on *that ground* the neutral Vessels were released."

It is impossible not to perceive that this Supposed declaration of France, So doubtful in its terms, according to the Statement of Sir William Scott, and so Suspicious on account of the time when it is said to have been made, cannot have been the real cause of the non condemnation of neutral Vessels trading with enemy Colonies during the War of 1778. It is at least, an object of curiosity to endeavour to find out what were the true motives which induced Great Britain to follow that line of conduct, during that War. We hope that we shall not be thought presumptuous if we collect here a few data, which may perhaps lead to a correct conjecture, we must for that purpose take a brief retrospect of the law & practice of nations for some time back with regard to neutral Commerce.

We have Seen in the former parts of these notes what were during the 17th Century the general prohibitions of Belligerent Nations in Europe, against trading with their Enemies. In the next Century we have seen what were the severe Laws of France & Spain on the same subject. During those periods England acted in the different Wars in which she was engaged, according as circumstances pointed out to her, Some times, as we have seen, issuing herself general prohibitions against neutrals, at other times retaliating upon them by her courts of Admiralty, the Severe Laws of her Enemies, of which we find Examples in Sir Leoline Jenkins,[15] some times also pursuing a milder line of Conduct. As she did not issue formal Edicts like other Nations, and as no records are Extant of the proceedings of her Courts of prize, during those times except the few Scattered cases which we find in the works of Jenkins, and a very few indeed in some other Books, we cannot trace her conduct with regard to neutrals, So precisely as we can that of other Nations. Holland also during those periods, issued some arbitrary Edicts, several of which are noticed and animadverted upon by Bynkershoek, in the first Book of his *Quæstiones Juris publici.*[16]

In the midst of all these irregularities, the principle of "free Ships make free goods" and the mitigated list of contraband articles, had begun, so early as the middle of the 17th Century, to introduce themselves among the nations of Europe. The *great Maritime powers* had successively adopted them in their Treaties *with each other,* and with those other nations which they wished particularly to favor, so that at last the *Weaker* Maritime powers were alone exposed to the effects of the arbitrary Edicts and proceedings of the Belligerent Nations.

Such was the State of things during the war of 1744. when Britain rigidly enforced what is called the *ancient Law of Nations,* upon the Subjects of those Sovereigns with whom She had no Treaty to the Contrary. Prussia had till then been considered as an insignificant State, particularly in a maritime point of view. But Frederick the Second by the force of his genius was rapidly raising her to the high rank which she has obtained among the powers of Europe. The British Government, however, did not immediately understand the line of Conduct that was to be followed with a country governed by such a man—His vessels were seized & brought into the English ports on various grounds, and particularly on that of being laden with enemy's property, & condemnations ensued. Frederick felt indignant at being assimilated to the lesser powers of the north of Europe, he Seized on the monies due to British Subjects which were mortgaged on the Dutchy of Silesia, & remonstrated afterwards. A legal discussion ensued, which was managed on the part of Prussia, by the celebrated Professor Cocceius, and on the part of England by Lord Mansfield, Sir Dudley Ryder[17] & the first civilians & common Lawyers of the day. The Memorial of professor Cocceius was written in the plain Style of a German jurist, while the answer of the British Government was adorned with all the elegancies of Style & language; Hence the latter is in every body's hands, while the former is read but by few. The issue, however, was not favorable to the English, altho' their political writers have taken great pains to insinuate that it was so[(a)] but the dispute ended in the payment by Great Britain to Prussia of £20,000. by way of indemnity for the unjust Captures made upon her Subjects. The Instrument by which the King of England agreed to this Settlement, has been kept out of view in the British publications, but it has found its way into the German Collections, and is published

[(a)]See Ward's Treatise on the right & duties of Belligerent & neutrals, London 1801. page 72.[19] To prove that all nations acquiesced in the claim of England to condemn enemy's property found on board of Neutral Ship, he Says, "The simple exception of Prussia in 1752 could never be counted in the Scale from the Circumstance of its being Single, *'but the conduct of that King, having as we have seen, been changed and totally relinquished, the claim itself mus[t] be considered as having been relinquished along with it.'*" This is hardly intelligible, but the author did not, perhaps wish to be understood.

at large in the Original French in 3d Wenck's Corpus juris Gentium[18] from
which we have Translated & inserted it in the appendix to these notes No. 2.

During the War of 1756. Prussia Was in alliance with Great Britain, &
of Course her Vessels were not molested by the British Cruizers; But they
were let loose upon other nations, & even upon some who were entitled
by Treaty to the benefit of the modern principles in a manner that excited
general indignation.[b] Several able writers took up their pens in vindication of neutral rights, and among others the celebrated Hubner—Others
wrote in favor of the British pretentions, & among those we are sorry to
find the Name of Vattel. Other measures than polemic writings, would
probably have been resorted to by the oppressed neutrals, but Britain was
victorious in every quarter of the glob[e]. France, in the course of that war
had followed, with respect to neutral nations a line of Conduct comparatively moderate. She had not expressly renewed her Severe Ordinance of
1744. & the decisions of her prize courts were dictated by the policy of the
Cabinet; Suited to times, cases & Circumstances. Thus the discontent of
neutrals was directed Solely against Great Britain, the State of the public
mind was Such, that it was easy to forsee that an explosion would take
place, whenever a favorable opportunity should offer. France understood
this very well, & by a stroke of Masterly policy, immediately on the breaking out of the War of 1778 proclaimed to all the world by a Solemn Edict,
the principles of the modern Law of nations. See her Edict of 23. July 1778.[20]

Here was neither a proper time nor proper Circumstances for Britain
to assert new or extravagant pretentions against neutral Trade—Her
Trade with foreign Colonies was almost entirely annihilated—She was
fighting for the recovery of her own Colonies, which had revolted from her
dominion. Her cause was not popular in Europe, her great maritime
power, & the tyranical use which she had made of it during the preceeding
War, had indisposed the other Nations against her, & she had no hopes of
being able to form continental alliances, but on the contrary She might
discover an enemy in every other Maritime power. France on the Contrary
had a powerful navy, a well managed Treasury, able Statesmen at the head
of her affairs, friends or at least well wishers in all the Sovereigns of Europe,
& the moderate conduct which she pursued with respect to neutral States
made it dangerous for Great Britain to adopt a different one.

When therefore we attend to the public acts of that Nation with regard
to neutral Nations during that War, we find them fraught with a Spirit of
Concession such as she had never exhibited in any former War, & Such as

[b]So early as 1758. the property captured from the Dutch only amounted to Several Millions, and at the end of the War, Say the Dutch merchants, it was beyond all computation.
Speech of the principal Merchants of Holland to the Stadtholder in 1778. 2. Hennings 359.

She has certainly not Shewn in any subsequent one. Let us be permitted to recapitulate here some of those public Acts.

1. Additional Instructions to privateers, dated 15th December 1778. Strictly charging them not to make illegal Captures. 2. Henning's Collection 59.

2. Explanatory Article of the Treaty with Denmark of the 11th. July 1670. By this Explanatory article, dated the 21 july 1780. the word *Contraband*, which in the Original Treaty was left unexplained, is construed according to the principles of the modern law of nations.[21] 2 Henning's. 16.

3. Additional Instructions to privateers, dated 20 Nover. 1800. charging them strictly to observe the 10th & 11th. Articles of the Treaty between Great Britain & Russia of the 20th of june 1766. founded on the principles of the modern Law of nations.[22] 2 Hennings 63.

4. Additional Instructions to privateers, dated 15 Feby 1801. warning all those who shall make illegal Captures, that they Shall "inevitably be compelled to the most Complete and ample restitution & amends."[23] 2. Hennings 106.

5. Additional Instructions to privateers, dated 20 April 1801. forbidding the making any Captures whatever in the Baltic Sea. 2 Hennings 105.

Among those public Acts of the Executive of Great Britain during the war of 1778. we find none relating to the trade with Enemy's Colonies, except an additional Instruction dated the 29 Decer. 1780. permitting the Dutch who were then Enemies, to trade freely with the Island of Grenada, the Grenadines, St. Vincent & Dominica, for the Space of four months, & to be while so engaged considered as neutral vessels going to neutral ports. 2 Hennings 117.

When we take into view this State of things, and the formidable combination of the Neutral powers which took place in the year 1780 under the name of the armed neutrality, we shall not perhaps be at a loss how to account for the conduct of the British Courts of Admiralty in not condemning Neutral Vessels trading with her enemy's Colonies. The General Conduct of England in this war with respect to Neutrals, tho' not free from blame, yet was in a degree moderate compared to what it was in the War of 1756. and to what it has been in subsequent wars. The recollection of past Sufferings, & the Spirit which they had excited contributed as much at least to produce the armed Neutrality as the actual irregularities of Great Britain during the war that gave it birth.

The Subject of the rights of Neutrals had taken possession of Men's mind, and Scarcely had the war of 1778 begun, when a multitude of writings appeared in various parts of Europe in which it was more or less ably discussed. Even the Writers of Italy came forward & took their parts in the important contest. Galiani at Naples, wrote a voluminous Treatise on the Laws of Neutrality in which he advocated the modern principles.[24]

Lampredi a celebrated Professor of the Law of Nations at the University of Pisa, in Tuscany, took up the other Side of the question.[25] Germany and the Northern States of Europe teemed with productions on the Same Subject—Among others Professor Busch of Hamburg, wrote a Spirited Treatise in which having collected a number of the decisions of the late judge of Admiralty of England, Sir James Marriott, he criticised them in such a severe manner as excited in the mind of that Judge, that strong antipathy to German Professors, which he has so ludicrously displayed in his decree on the Case of the Ship Columbus, which is recorded in the first Volume of *Collectanea Juridica*.[26]

We are now come down to the period of the War of 1793. the occurrences of which are still fresh in the recollection of every one. We shall therefore content ourselves with collecting and bringing together here within a narrow compass, a few of the most material facts in Support of our chief position. "That the restrictions imposed by the British on the Commerce of neutrals with the Colonies of their Enemies, *are founded on Commercial, & not in Belligerent interests*."

After the Conclusion of the peace of 1783. the British Governmt. thought Seriously of re-organising a Contraband Trade with the French & Spanish Colonies in America. In 1787 on an average of three years, Jamaica already imported £150,000: Sterlg. annually from foreign Colonies, under the free port Law &c. 1 Edw: 245. The French Revolution, & the Wars which it produced, soon furnished them with the means of exceeding in this respect even their most sanguine Expectations.

The objects recommended in 1677 by mr. nevil to the British Government,[27] had never been entirely lost Sight of. To drive the French, if possible, out of the Island of St. Domingo, & to obtain a Trade by all means with the Spanish Colonies.

The first of these objects appears to have been taken up by Great Britain early in the French Revolution & before the breaking out of war between the two Countries, for there are many who think, that the discussions provoked by mr. Pitt in the British Parliament respecting the abolition of the Slave trade, had for its object to encourage the enthusiastic spirit which had begun to appear in France on the Subject of the freedom of the blacks, and to lead that nation into those measures, which have proved So fatal in their consequences, & lost ultimately to them that beautiful & valuable Colony.[28]

If however the true motives which actuated mr. Pitt in this particular instance cannot be mathematically ascertained, & are involved in some degree of obscurity & doubt, their Conduct during the War, particularly in the time of General Toussaint point beyond all possibility of doubt to their true object. For what reason the American Nation was *then* permitted by Great Britain to participate in that trade, is a Subject which does not belong to us to touch upon.[29] It is enough for us to observe that the same indulgence was not shewn to other neutrals, their Vessels trading with St. Domingo were condemned on the identical pretence, on which our own have been lately adjudged as prize at Halifax and elsewhere, to wit; that that Island was still considered as a French Colony. The Immanuel, 2. Rob: 162 Am: Ed.

We have taken pains to procure sufficient data, from which not only to conjecture, but to ascertain, if possible the real Motives of the British lately capturing & condemning our Vessels & property met with in the St Domingo Trade, & we have obtained the following information on which we can entirely rely. The British have at present no direct Trade from Jamaica or elsewhere with the late French part of the Island of St. Domingo, they Supply themselves with Cotton & cocoa, indirectly thro' St. Thomas, from whence that trade is freely carried on. The reason why the British prohibit their Vessels from going to those ports is that they are afraid lest some of the Negroes shoul[d] conceal themselves on board of their Vessels, & Spread the Spirit of insurrection at Jamaica. At the same time, they are not insensible to the advantages of that trade, & are exerting themselves for obtaining it on a safe & advantageous footing. They have made the following proposals to Dessalines:[30] 1. To make a Treaty of Commerce with them whereby they shall be admitted to Supply them with their manufactures, & with every article that they may want, the Americans to be excluded from that Trade, except that they will be permitted to import articles of their own growth, but nothing else. 2d. To give possession to the British of two points on the Island, viz, Cape Nichola mole, & Cape Tiburon. Dessalines refused to accede to these terms, and the British in order to frighten him into compliance, threatened to cut off all Supplies from him by preventing the Trade between the United States & St. Domingo. This threat had no effect upon him, therefore the British to give it greater force, have carried it into execution by giving private instructions to the commanders of their Armed Vessels, to take & bring in for adjudication our vessels found in that trade.[(a)] What the result of this Measure will be, it is not yet known. The Gentleman, from whom, we have obtained this information, is an intelligent and well informed American on whom dependance Can be placed. He is just returned from St. Domingo, when he has had frequent & familiar access to the Emperor; he has told us that he translated a letter for him from Admiral Duckworth, by which that Admiral Offered to furnish him with every article that he might stand in need of, & particularly with arms, powder & other warlike Supplies.

[(a)]We have heard only as yet of the condemnation of Such Vessels as had contraband on board, it would be difficult to find a pretence for condemning others, but how many have been carried & detained, we do not know.

Thus we find still the same principle actuating the British prohibitions of neutral Trade, in the present War, as in the preceeding ones. We shall now proceed to consider them as they affect the trade with the Spanish Colonies.

At the beginning of the War of 1793. Britain had re-organized in some degree her contraband Trade with the Colonies of Spain. Her alliance with that power, gave it a greater extent & Spirit, & the Spanish possessions were inundated with English goods, when the peace took place between Spain & France. The two Nations lately in enmity soon became allies to each other, & Spain, Now desirous of diminishing the Contraband trade between the English possessions & her own, but yet being sensible that her Colonies could not do without the Supplies which they had been till then accustomed to receive from Great Britain, did by her decree of the 18th. of Nover. 1797. open her American ports to the Vessels of Neutral Nations, & prohibited the entry of English merchandize.[31]

This was a heavy stroke upon Great Britain, In order to counteract it, she issued in the year 1798. an order of Council, opening the ports of Jamaica & new Providence to the Spaniards, *then her enemies*, See the Pamphlet entitled "Observations on the Commerce of Spain with her Colonies, in time of War," which is attributed to the Marquis de Casa Yrujo, and was printed at Philadelphia in 1800. by James Carey, pages 37: 60.[32]

Not satisfied with this measure, Britain intrigued at the Court of Spain, & was so Successful in her machinations that the obnoxious Edict was repealed on the 23d of April 1799. The times were then exceedingly favorable to her purpose—The French had lost all their influence with the Courts of Europe, they were threatened with an Invasion from Italy, the Directory were hated & despised at home & abroad. So that but little resistance could be offered to the powerful arguments that she made use of. But after the overthrow of the directory, & the accession of Bonaparte to the Supreme power, the Spanish Colonies were again opened to neutrals, British merchandize was again prohibited & continued so to the end of the War.

It is remarkable that it was in the same year 1799. that Condemnations of neutrals began to take place in England for trading with Enemy's Colonies; See the case of the Immanuel, 2: Rob: 162. Am: Ed: where the counsel Say *arguendo* "With respect to authorities" (upon the main question of Neutral Trade with enemy Colonies) "It cannot be expected that there should be any. The question has not arisen in this War, or it would not be discussed So much at length in the present case."

It would Seem then, as if the Instructions of 1793. & 1794. were issued merely *in terrorem*, & to be only enforced when favorable circumstances should permit it, except perhaps in the West India Islands upon the Vessels of the United States against which the instructions of Nover. 1793. appear to have been more particularly, if not exclusively directed.

This Supposition is strengthened by what is also Stated by Counsel, in another Case, the Providentia, reported in 2. Rob: 122 Am: Ed: "But if it were granted that the interposition in the trade of a Belligerent, not before open to foreign Traders, made Some part of the principle of that war" (the War of 1756.) "it would not only apply to the cases of this War, for in the late practice of this Court during this War, there have been a Variety of cases from the French & Dutch Colonies, in which the Court has either ordered farther proof, or restored in the first instance, by no means considering them therefore as concluded by this circumstance." This case of the Providentia was adjudged on the 16th Augt. 1799.

To return to the British Trade with the Spanish Colonies, Since the year 1798. it has been regularly organized by the communication opened with the free ports established at Jamaica and other Islands, & lately with the Island of Trinidad. "These ports" Says the author of the Observations on the Commerce of Spain &c." are opened, altho' in time of War, to the Spanish Subjects, granting them protection, not only in the said Islands, but also in their voyages to and from the Spanish possessions, by means of Special passports Granted by the Governors of the said English Islands. The British Ships of War protect these Smuggling Vessels, & the privateers respect them." Observations &c. p. 37.

The nature of this Trade & its advantages to Great Britain are still more fully explained in a late work entitled "The claims of the British West India Colonists &c. in answer to Lord Sheffield's Strictures, by G. W. Jordan,[33] Colonial agent for Barbadoes." Some Extracts from this Work have been published in the London monthly Review for April 1805. a few paragraphs of which we shall here copy, from the Gazette of the United States, of Friday the 12th. of July instant.

"It is possible," Says mr. Jordan "to open a South American trade, as well as that of North America, which, without any respect to the nature of the Shipping employed, shall, by a due enumeration & restriction of the permitted articles of exchange or carriage, with perfect Safety & propriety encrease indefinitely the British import, export and carrying trade of the West India Islands.

"These Islands are so disposed along the coasts or Stretched across between the principal points of North & South America, that access to them from both the continents may at all times be had by the simplest & cheapest Species of Navigation. The approach [of] British vessels to the continent of South America is partially or totally forbidden by the Great European Powers who possess it—Under these circumstances British Vessels cannot be used in the intercourse with it. Great Britain, therefore of necessity indeed, but with her accustomed wisdom, has opened certain ports in the Colonies to Vessels of these foreign Countries, in order that they may bring in the enumerated Articles she desires to obtain, and that they cárry the enumerated Articles She wishes to dispose of, or such as are necessary to support the trade. The first enumeration contains articles of Territorial produce of that part of the continent, and bullion among the rest; the other consists of goods of British Manufactures, or import or articles of territorial produce of the Islands. Great Britain does not upon this occasion consider her navigation and colonial Systems, as not at any time, upon any occasion, or under any circumstances to be invaded. She looks to the objects and purposes of those Systems. She wants raw materials, She wants markets for her various articles of manufacture, commerce & produce; She wants encouragement & extensive employment for her Shipping. By neglecting all consideration of the use as militating against her navigation and colonial Systems, of those petty vessels which serve to associate her islands with the continent, She obtains all the objects of those Systems, materials, markets, and increased carriage. The ports of her Islands become ports of the continent, and those Vessels are only as the port Vessels and laden droghers of other countries. British Ships carry to and bring away from the Islands the commodities laden in and unladen from these Vessels, and neither their employment nor their Numbers is to be calculated upon by Great Britain, but as proofs of the extension of her own commerce and proper Navigation.

"Instead, therefore of a port in Grenada a port in Dominica Two in Jamaica, one in Tortola, one in the Bahamas, it might upon these principles well be recommended to Great Britain, to extend the provisions of the freeport Acts to all the Islands, or to the Custom house ports of all the Islands. It might further be proposed by enlarging and combining all the principles & practice which alike prevail in the West India intercourse with the Northern and Southern portions of America, to form a general, Simple & consolidated System, that should connect them all, which should embrace and comprehend the at present enumerated articles of import and export between the whole continent and the Islands, and permitt between them the employment jointly with British ships of one decked vessels of all the Countries growing the commodities imported into the Islands."

Thus far mr. Jordan—We hardly think it possible to prove more Completely that the prohibitions issued by Great Britain in the Wars of 1756, 1793. & in the present War against the Trade of neutrals with the Colonies of her enemies, have had no other object than to Secure that trade exclusively to themselves, Since they have carried it on in every one of these Wars, except in the War of 1778. during which their prohibitions were intermitted from a variety of powerful motives.

It therefore only remains for us now to Say Something respecting the practice of other Nations & the Opinions of publicists, on the Subject of the interference of Neutrals in the Commerce of the Enemy's Colonies.

I. As to the practice of other Nations.

We have before us all the Successive ordinances and Edicts of France respecting neutral Trade made during the whole of this period. We have also the Old and new *Code des Prises*,[34] in which are contained the principal decisions of their prize Courts before & Since the Revolution. We have the Works of their most approved authors upon prize Law, in which the Doctrines adopted by their Tribunals, are fully laid down & commented upon. With regard to Spain, we have also the successive Edicts & Ordinances on the Subject of neutral Trade during this period, & we have a late Edition of the Chevalier D'Abreu's Treatise upon prize Law.[35] We have also some Dutch Books on the subject, tho' the Dutch have ceased for a long time to give Laws to neutrals in time of war. Lastly we have a variety of German and French collections of Edicts, Ordinances & other State papers, issued by the different powers of Europe during the different Wars which took place within this period, & in none of these sources have we been able to find any thing like a direct or indirect prohibition to Neutrals from trading with enemy's Colonies, unless we are to consider in that light the Decree of the French Directory of the 29th Nivose, 6th. year, which revives the Edict of 1744. against goods of British growth or manufacture, with the additional Severity of the confiscation of the Ship. and innocent parts of the Cargo.[36] We say unless we Consider this Decree in that light, because Vessels trading with British Colonies, must necessarily on their return have been laden with British west India produce, & of course must have fallen with the general principle of the decree & been liable to Confiscation. But we have not found any Edict, Ordinance, State paper decision or even dictum of a Court of Judicature, directly applicable to the present point.

II. As to the Opinion of Writers.

We have taken the pains to collect, & have before us, the Writings of almost every publicist of note, who has written during the present period, either on the laws of nations in general or on the Law of neutrality in particular. It may be astonishing, but it is not less true, that after an accurate research, we have found only two of them who have touched at all on the subject in question. They are Hubner and Hennings, both Danes, the former of whom wrote during the war of 1756. & the latter between the war of 1778. & the wars of 1793.[37] We Subjoin their opinions in the appendix No. 3. 4. & 5.

It will be observed that Hubner gives but a kind of unsettled, hesitating opinion on the Subject, and it is not perhaps, to be wondered at. At the time when he wrote, the general principle of free Ships make free goods, & the List of Contrabands were the great points which agitated the Neutral world. Those two points alone are the subject of his Book, & the Trade of Neutrals to Enemy's Colonies is noticed only incidentally. The Carrying trade to Europe was then the great Subject of discussion, the carrying trade to America (which Trade was not then by far so considerable as it has become Since) was an object of inferior consequence, which had not yet attracted the general attention, & which the Neutral Nations of Europe would perhaps—at that moment have sacrificed for the sake of attaining the greater & more important object which then swallowed up all inferior considerations.

It is evident that Mr. Hubner did not pay much attention to this particular Subject, for the concessions which he makes in his 6th. Section, appendix No. 3. are in direct contradiction with the luminous principles which he lays down himself in his 5th. Section, which we have inserted in the appendix No. 4. that the two sections may be compared together.

With regard to mr. Hennings, as he wrote at a time when Great Britain was considered as having given up the point, it cannot be expected that he should have said much upon the Subject.

The latter Writers are altogether Silent upon it, & take no notice of it whatever.

There is a general principle, however, laid down in the works of almost every Neutral writer from Hubner down to the present time, which, if dextrously laid hold of, might afford an argument against the Trade of Neutrals with Enemy's Colonies. The principle is this: "That Neutrality is not a new State of things, but a continuation of that which existed before the War; hence, that Neutral Nations are entitled to carry on Commerce during the war precisely & on the same footing, as they did before the war, with the exception of Contraband, & trading to blockaded ports." This position being so often repeated by the neutral Writers, it may be said that the right of carrying on Trade during the War precisely as they did before the War, is all that they have ever contended for, that the prohibition of Trade with Enemy's Colonies, does not militate against this right, Since it is a different Trade from that which they carried on before the war, and *expressio unius, est exclusio alterius.*[38]

It Seems that this position of the Neutral Writers, is at once unguarded & inaccurate. It is *unguarded*, because, they had not in contemplation when they wrote every kind of neutral Trade which might take place during a war. It is *unaccurate* because Neutrality is not an *absolute*, but a *relative* State of things, & no definition of it can be correct, which loses Sight of its relative character. The neutral Writers, therefore Seem to have gone too far in representing it as the continuation of a fixed & permanent state of things, independent of the variations of external circumstances to which it is & will ever be Subordinate.

The application however of this principle as an argument against the Trade of Neutrals with Belligerent Colonies, would be a mere Sophism. For, before the War, it was lawful for Neutrals to trade with every nation which open their ports to them—They do no more in the present instance, and thus every argument founded upon this *dictum* of the neutral writers, would necessarily end in a dispute about words.

We ought to add, in conclusion, that after a minute research, we have not been able to find any authority or judicial decision out of England, by which it might appear that the coasting Trade of Belligerents, in time of war, So analogous to the Trade between the mother Country and the Colonies, is unlawful for neutrals, even tho' it be prohibited to foreigners in time of peace, & only permitted during the war; no distinction appears at all to be made between that & any other trade between Neutral & Belligerent Nations; & in England, we have not been able to find any thing on the Subject, prior to the decision of Sir William Scott, in the case of the Emanuel, Soderstrom in the year 1799. reported in 1. Rob: 249: Am: Ed: which appears on the face of it, to be a Case *of the first impression*, tho' it refers to a Decree of the Lords of Appeal in 1795. which from Sir W. Scott's embarrassed Statement, seems to have been given upon other grounds and to *more ancient judgments*, of which he neither Specifies the time nor the cases in which they were given.

Partial RC (DLC); letterbook copy of enclosure (PHi: Peter S. Du Ponceau Letterbook, 1777–1839). RC 1 p.; complimentary close and signature clipped; correspondent assigned based on the hand, and on the contents of Du Ponceau's 8 and 15 July 1805 letters to JM.

1. For earlier installments of the notes, see Du Ponceau to JM, 8 and 15 July 1805. The appendix has not been found.

2. The *Hindostan*, Captain Lewis, arrived at New York with "the Saint Domingo fleet" on 19 May 1805 (New York *Morning Chronicle*, 20 May 1805).

3. Edwards, *History, Civil and Commercial, of the British Colonies in the West Indies* (Shaw and Shoemaker 8375), 1:249.

4. *Annual Register for 1765*, 20–21.

5. Du Ponceau erred; the information is cited from note g on page 497 of the first volume of Long's *History of Jamaica* (1970 reprint).

6. Ibid., 499.

7. The correct page in volume one of Edwards, *History, Civil and Commercial, of the British Colonies in the West Indies*, for this information is 249.

8. For the matter quoted, see ibid., 252–53.

9. Du Ponceau referred to *Berens v. Rucker* in William Blackstone's *Reports of Cases Determined in the Several Courts of Westminster-Hall, from 1746 to 1779* (2 vols.; London, 1781), 1:313–15.

10. Robinson, *Admiralty Reports* (Shaw and Shoemaker 584), 2:120, and ibid. (Shaw and Shoemaker 6412), 4:appendix A, 6.

11. Du Ponceau cited August Adolph Friedrich von Hennings's *Abhandlung über die Neutralität und ihre Rechte, insonderheit bey einem Seekriege* (Altona, 1785).

12. Du Ponceau referred to Danby Pickering's *Statutes at Large, from the Magna Charta to the End of the Eleventh Parliament of Great Britain, Anno 1761* (46 vols. in 51; Cambridge, 1762–1807).

13. Du Ponceau referred to August Adolph Friedrich von Hennings's *Sammlung von Staatsschriften, die, während des Seekrieges von 1776 bis 1783, sowol von den kriegführenden, als*

auch von den neutralen Mächten, öffentlich bekannt gemacht worden sind; in so weit solche die Frei-
heit des Handels und der Schiffahrt betreffen (2 vols. in 1; Altona, 1784–85).

14. The appendix has not been found.

15. For the works of Sir Leoline Jenkins, see JM to John Henry Purviance, 24 Dec.
1804, *PJM-SS*, 8:416 and n. 1.

16. Bijnkershoek, *Quaestionum Juris Publici Libri Duo.*

17. Du Ponceau presumably referred to baron Samuel von Cocceji (1679–1755), a Prussian minister of state and chancellor under Frederick the Great. He compiled the Frederi-
cian Code in 1747. William Murray (1705–1793), first Earl Mansfield, was born in Scotland
and educated at Oxford and Lincoln's Inn. He practiced law successfully for several years
before becoming solicitor general and a member of Parliament in 1742. He succeeded Dudley
Ryder as attorney general in 1754 and as chief justice in 1756, when he was also created baron
Mansfield. He was a member of the House of Lords for thirty years and served on various
occasions as privy councilor, chancellor of the exchequer, and speaker of the House of Lords.
He was created Earl Mansfield in 1776. Sir Dudley Ryder (1691–1756) was a prosperous attorney who became a member of Parliament and solicitor general in 1733. He was appointed
attorney general in 1737, knighted in 1740, and named lord chief justice in 1754 (Hugh James
Rose, ed., *A New General Biographical Dictionary* [12 vols.; London, 1853], 6:384).

18. The appendix has not been found. For the 1756 agreement between Great Britain
and Prussia, see Friedrich August Wilhelm Wenck's *Codex Juris Gentium Recentissimi, è Tabu-
lariorum Exemplorumque Fide Dignorum Monumentis Compositus* (3 vols.; Leipzig, 1781–95),
3:84–87. Du Ponceau donated his copy to the American Philosophical Society's library in
1840, when he was president of the organization (*Proceedings of the American Philosophical
Society* 1 [1840]: 180).

19. Du Ponceau misquoted from Robert Ward's *Treatise of the Relative Rights and Duties
of Belligerent and Neutral Powers in Maritime Affairs. . . .* (London, 1801). The correct quotation from page 79 reads: "The single exception of Prussia, in 1752, to which we have adverted, could never be counted in the scale, from the very circumstance of its being single;
but the conduct of that King, which was founded upon the new claim, having, as we have
seen, been changed, and totally relinquished, the claim itself must be considered as having
been relinquished along with it."

20. The 26 July 1778 French edict concerning the trade of neutral vessels during a war
was printed in the *Pennsylvania Packet or the General Advertiser,* 14 Jan. 1779.

21. For the Explanatory Article of 4 July 1780 defining contraband, see Scott, *Armed
Neutralities of 1780 and 1800,* 295–96. For the 1670 Anglo-Danish treaty, see Dumont, *Corps
universel diplomatique du droit des gens,* 7, pt. 1:132–37.

22. For the tenth and eleventh articles of the 1766 Treaty of Commerce and Navigation
between Great Britain and Russia, see Jenkinson, *Collection of All the Treaties between Great
Britain and Other Powers* (1968 reprint), 3:224, 228–29.

23. These instructions appear to be a restatement of similar instructions issued on 15 Feb.
1781. For these, see Scott, *Armed Neutralities of 1780 and 1800,* 365.

24. Ferdinando Galiani (1728–1787) was a Neapolitan cleric, economist, diplomat, and
prolific writer who dealt with, among other topics, finance and the grain trade. He served
as secretary to the Neapolitan legation at Paris. Du Ponceau presumably referred to
Galiani's *De' doveri de' principi neutrali verso i principi guerreggianti, e di questi verso i neutrali*
([Naples], 1782) on the rights and duties of neutrals (*Grande Dizionario Enciclopedico,* 4th ed.
[23 vols.; Turin, 1984–2000], 9:25–26).

25. Giovanni Maria Lampredi (1732–1793) was a theologian and professor of canon law
at the University of Pisa. Du Ponceau had in mind Lampredi's *Del commercio dei popoli
neutrali in tempo di guerra* (2 vols.; Florence, 1788), "which was translated into various languages and occupies an important position in the literature of international law." Lampredi

argued that neutrals should be allowed to trade with all belligerents in a war provided they maintained impartiality (Edwin R. A. Seligman et al., eds., *Encyclopaedia of the Social Sciences* [15 vols.; New York, 1930–35], 9:28–29).

26. For the 18 Dec. 1789 decision in the case of the *Columbus*, Guerin master, see Francis Hargrave, ed., *Collectanea Juridica: Consisting of Tracts Relative to the Law and Constitution of England* (2 vols.; London, 1791–92), 1:88–128.

27. For Nevil's suggestion, see Du Ponceau to JM, 8 July 1805.

28. For William Pitt the Younger's efforts towards the abolition of the slave trade by Great Britain, see William Hague, *William Pitt the Younger* (New York, 2005), 247–58.

29. For the Maitland agreement allowing British and American trade with Saint-Domingue, see *PJM-SS*, 2:257 n. 2.

30. For British negotiations with Jean-Jacques Dessalines about a trade agreement, see ibid., 8:106 n. 1.

31. The 18 Nov. 1797 decree that allowed "a legal and heavily taxed trade" with the Spanish colonies was revoked on 20 Apr. 1799, but the revocation was widely ignored by both American shippers and citizens of the Spanish colonies (Leslie Bethell, ed., *The Independence of Latin America* (Cambridge, 1987), 20–21.

32. *Observations on the Commerce of Spain with Her Colonies, in Time of War* (Philadelphia, 1800; Evans 38142) is listed as written "By a Spaniard, in Philadelphia" and "Translated from the Original Manuscript, by another Spaniard."

33. *The Claims of the British West India Colonists to the Right of Obtaining Necessary Supplies from America*, by Gibbes W. Jordan, was printed in London in 1804.

34. Du Ponceau referred to Daniel Marc Antoine Chardon's *Code des prises ou Recueil des édits, déclarations, lettres patentes, arrêts, ordonnances, règlemens, et décisions sur la course et l'administration des prises, depuis 1400 jusqu' à présent* (2 vols., [Paris], 1784) and Sylvain Lebeau's *Nouveau code des prises: ou Recueil des édits, déclarations, lettres patentes, arrêts, ordonnances, réglemens et décisions sur la course et l'administration des prises, depuis 1400 jusqu'au mois de mai 1789 (v. st.); suivi de toutes les lois, arrêtés, messages, et autres actes qui ont paru depuis cette dernière époque jusqu'au 3 prairial an 8* (4 vols.; Paris, [1789–1801]).

35. Abreu y Bertodano, *Tratado juridico-politico*.

36. For the wording of the 18 Jan. 1798 decree, see *ASP, Foreign Relations*, 2:182. By 1 Aug. 1798 the Council of 500 was debating the repeal of the decree because of its deleterious effect on French trade with neutrals (*New-York Gazette and General Advertiser*, 18 Oct. 1798).

37. For Martin Hübner, see Du Ponceau to JM, 8 July 1805, n. 3. For Hennings, see nn. 11 and 13, above.

38. *Expressio unius, est exclusio alterius:* the expression of one thing is the exclusion of the other thing (editor's translation).

§ From Louis-Marie Turreau. *23 July 1805, Baltimore.* Encloses two of Napoleon's decrees naming François Louis Michel Chemin Deforgues commissary of commercial relations and Anne Louis de Tousard under-commissioner and chancellor of commercial relations at New Orleans.

Asks JM to present them to the president and obtain their exequatur in the usual form and to return them to him with the decrees of nomination.

RC (DNA: RG 59, NFL, France, vol. 2–3). 1 p.; in French; docketed by Wagner, with his note: "nomination of Messrs. Desforgues & Tousard for N. Orleans."

To Thomas Jefferson

DEAR SIR   WASHINGTON July 24. 1805

At the date of my last, I hoped by this time to be making ready for my journey on your track. A consultation of the Doctors We[e]ms & Elzey[1] on the situation of my wife's knee has ended in the joint opinion that an operation is indispensable which can best be performed at Philadelphia, and that it is prudent to avoid delay as much as possible. We shall accordingly set off tomorrow, in order to put her under the care of Docr. Physic.[2] No cause less urgent could have diverted me from my trip home, which had become very peculiarly desirable on several accounts. It is now altogether uncertain when I shall have that pleasure. If every thing goes well it is possible that the detention at Philada. may not exceed two or three weeks. I shall shorten it as much as can properly be done and then hasten to Virginia. In the mean time be pleased to address your public commands, which can not be fulfilled in the Office, to me at Philada. till otherwise advised, and freely add any private ones where I can be of service. With respectful attachment I remain always yrs.

JAMES MADISON

RC (DLC: Jefferson Papers). Docketed by Jefferson as received 2 Aug.

1. John Weems (d. 1808) of Maryland, who graduated with Philip Syng Physick from the University of Edinburgh in 1792, was living in Georgetown by 1801 and was elected an honorary member of the Philadelphia Medical Society in February 1805. Arnold Elzey (ca. 1758–1818) was a Maryland native who graduated from the College of New Jersey in 1775. He apparently studied medicine in Baltimore from 1779 to 1783. He served one term in the Maryland legislature in 1784, was one of the founders of the Medical and Chirurgical Faculty of Maryland in 1799, and was vice president of the Medical Society of the District of Columbia. In 1814 he was named garrison surgeon's mate at Greenleaf's Point in the District and in 1816 became post surgeon, a position he held until his death (Samuel Lewis, "List of the American Graduates in Medicine in the University of Edinburgh, from 1705 to 1866, with Their Theses," *New-England Historical and Genealogical Register* 42 [1888]: 159, 162; Alexandria *Times; and District of Columbia Daily Advertiser*, 29 Aug. 1801; Philadelphia *Aurora General Advertiser*, 15 Feb. 1805; *National Intelligencer*, 11 Nov. 1808; Harrison, *Princetonians, 1769–1775*, 478–80; Papenfuse et al., *Biographical Dictionary of the Maryland Legislature*, 1:304–5).

2. Philadelphia native Philip Syng Physick (1768–1837) graduated from the University of Pennsylvania in 1785 and was educated in medicine in London and Edinburgh. From 1794 until 1816 he served on the staff of the Pennsylvania Hospital, where his growing reputation led to the creation of a chair of surgery for him at the University of Pennsylvania in 1805. He was an innovative practitioner and introduced many improvements to surgery in America during his long career.

From Charles Pinckney

(Private)

DEAR SIR   July 24: 1805 IN MADRID

I wrote you ten days since acquainting you with what you doubtless heard before the Peace with Tripoli made by Colonel Lear on terms as it is said very honourable & advantageous[1]—I now send you duplicate of the last six months' contingencies for Postage &c which is exceedingly small on account of all foreign Gazettes & correspondence nearly having ceased for the last Year & the letters to Mr Monroe & self during the special mission having all come under cover to Bankers & do not appear in the Postage—in this there was a mistake I find in my Mayor Domos account to me of 116 Dollars in the beginning of 1804 in the Quarter between January & April which I wish you to correct.

It is now very near the month of August & I am still obliged to stay here contrary to my inclination & most ardent desire to return—nor do I know what to do—Mr Bowdoin is gone to England—Mr Erving is there also & Mr. Young is not arrived nor is there any one here to whom I can with the smallest propriety entrust the charge of our affairs—I really do not know what to do—to stay is the most distressing & inconvenient thing in the World to me & I have only to hope the speedy arrival of Mr Young with whom I propose leaving every thing until Mr Bowdoin or Mr Erving can arrive & you can determine what is to be done. I am so anxious to return that as I have often told you every day now I am obliged to remain looks like a month.

About a year agoë I drew for a sufficient sum to cover all the debts of the Legation & contingencies & my own salary & in short every thing then due as the then pressing & urgent state of affairs made necessary & of which you can only judge when You see me as things then passed which I am not at liberty to put on paper even in cypher—since this & for the whole of my last Year I have not drawn for a shilling on any account, either salary or contingencies, or special missions—extraordinary for as I am hopeful to have money enough from the sale of my Effects to carry me home, I would rather leave a Balance undrawn in my favour than to place it in the Power of any one to suppose I had drawn for a shilling I had not a right fully to draw. To our good President I always request you to remember me affectionately & respectfully & to believe me always dear sir With regard Yours Truly

CHARLES PINCKNEY

I have this moment recieved official information of the capture & carrying in to Algesires of three more American Ships, named the Recovery from Norfolk.[2] The ⟨B⟩erbish Packet from Charleston & a Ship name unknown bound from Faro to Malaga. I am making a proper representation on the subject to the secretary of state here & these make Eleven on which I have represented within a month.

I hear much of the Captures of our Vessels in the West Indies but of this You must know better than I as nothing official has Yet reached me on that subject.

RC (DNA: RG 59, DD, Spain, vol. 6A). Damaged by removal of seal; docketed by Wagner as received 17 Sept., with his note: "Mr. Bowdoin is gone to England." Enclosures not found.

1. Pinckney's 14 July 1805 letter, which enclosed his contingency accounts for the previous six months, does not mention the peace with Tripoli.

2. The *Recovery* of Norfolk, Capt. Nathaniel F. Adams, was carrying a cargo of flour, rice, rum, sugar, and coffee to Gibraltar when it was captured. The cargo was condemned by the Spanish court for lack of a Spanish consular certificate of neutrality, but the ship was restored (*Albany Gazette*, 16 Sept. 1805; *New-York Spectator*, 21 Sept. 1805).

§ Circular Letter to John Armstrong, James Bowdoin, and James Monroe. *24 July 1805, Department of State.* "I have the honor to inclose copies of the instructions transmitted by the Departments of State and the Treasury for carrying into effect the harbour-Act, passed at the last Session of Congress. They have been communicated to the Foreign Ministers in the United States.[1]

"I use the same occasion to transmit copies of the circular letters from this Department to the Consuls and Commercial Agents dated on the 1st and 12 inst."

FC (DNA: RG 59, Circulars of the Department of State, vol. 1); letterbook copy (DNA: RG 59, IM, vol. 6). FC 1 p.

1. The enclosures were the instruction and circular enclosed in JM's 11 June 1805 letter to the foreign ministers. See JM to Merry, 11 June 1805, *PJM-SS*, 9:451–52 and n. and n. 1, and Peder Pedersen's, Joseph Rademaker's, Louis-Marie Turreau's, and Carlos Martínez de Yrujo's 17 June 1805 letters to JM, ibid., 475–76.

§ From Sylvanus Bourne. *24 July 1805, Amsterdam.* "I hasten to forward you the inclosed important State document[1] & you will at once see into all the probable consequences thereof.

"I transmit also a Copy of my letter to mr Alexander on the subject of the Consulate at Rottm referred to in my late letters to you[2] & which I hope will meet your approbation.

"Mr Clark at Emden has expressed his hopes of this Appointment of his claims to which you must be duly acquainted—I therefore forbear any interference.

"My Mind has lately been much & very unpleasantly occupied on the Subject referred to in my many letters wrote you—but I now feel the Calmness & composure which a conscious integrity inspires & Shall wait with confidence for your decision not doubting it will be candid & just."[3]

RC and enclosures (DNA: RG 59, CD, Amsterdam, vol. 1). RC 1 p. For enclosures, see nn. 1–2.

1. The enclosure (13 pp., in French; marked *"Duplicate"*; docketed by Wagner) is a printed copy of the 10 Jan. 1805 *arrêté* of the Batavian Council of State containing the latest quarantine regulations.

2. Bourne enclosed a copy (1 p.) of his letter to Lawson Alexander. For an earlier copy, with slightly different wording, see Bourne to JM, 23 July 1805, and n. 4.

3. Bourne wrote JM again on 25 July 1805 (DNA: RG 59, CD, Amsterdam, vol. 1; 1 p.) to say: "A Correspondence Still Subsists between France & England but the precise object thereof remains unknown to the public—various Conjectures are daily formed on the subject but as none of them *can be relied on* I forbear to make any recital thereof."

§ From Philip Mazzei. *24 July 1805.* "In the above-mentioned copy[1] I included a sentence, in which I spoke of two of my works, consigned to Timpanari for you, and which I am not now able to send to you, because I am 50 miles from Pisa and on the point of leaving for Rome.

"I should like to know whether you received my long letter of December 28, 1803,[2] or even that of December 15, 1804.[3] I have reason to believe that you have received it and I attribute the fact of my not having received an answer to the confusion of your errands.

"Our esteemed President will tell you of the sad reason[4] which has caused me to send you copy of that of August 30, 1804. Attribute the inconsistencies of this letter to that reason, which drives me out of my mind, as my heart stops every time I think of it."

RC and enclosure (DLC). RC 1 p.; in Italian; written at the foot of Mazzei to JM, 30 Aug. 1804; docketed by JM.

1. See Mazzei to JM, 30 Aug. 1804, *PJM-SS*, 7:659–60.
2. Ibid., 6:240–43.
3. Ibid., 8:385.
4. In his 20 July 1805 letter to Jefferson, Mazzei expressed his fear that the *John Adams*, Captain Ramsdale, in which his friend Giuseppe Timpanari Viganò had sailed, carrying Mazzei's earlier letters, had been lost at sea. The ship left Gibraltar on 22 Sept. 1804 for Philadelphia (Marchione, *Philip Mazzei: Selected Writings*, 3:393; New York *Morning Chronicle*, 1 Dec. 1804).

§ From Audley Laurens Osborne. *24 July 1805, Salisbury, North Carolina.* "It is with considerable reluctance, that I again presume to intrude on the time of one to whom I am altogether a stranger. How anxious soever I might have expected an answer to my late letter,[1] I must acknowledge I was not disappointed. The various important avocations of men holding the higher offices of government, removes them so far beyond the reach of applications of this sort; and the course I took in my application was so much out of the ordinary track, I do not wonder it was not attended to. But the highest officer of government Should, I concieve, be accessible to a citizen of The United States; and on this Ground alone I expected an answer. I assure You Sir, it was with extreme diffidence, I undertook my own recomendation; but circumstances not to be explain'd within the compass of a letter, urged the measure. Apprehensive that my former letter did not reach You, I again state to you that it is my most ardent wish to become servicable to a government, to which I am attached by all the ties of birth & education, and to an administration for which I have allways expressd the most profound veneration. I have the will, and my utmost abilities shall be exerted to the performance of my duty, should I meet with your patronage. My desires are moderate. My only wish is to have it in my power to live decently in some post wherein the compensation shall equal the labour.

"I care not, whether I am established in the civil or military department. I will only suggest, that I feel myself better calculated to do the duties of the former.

"Could You procure for me, any imployment, reputable, under government, in Louisiana, The North Western Teritory or at the Seat of government, I shall hold myself bound to You by every tie of Gratitude. Should I meet Your approbation, I flatter myself I can produce testimonials which will justify Your interference in my behalf; and my conduct thereafter will not, I hope, discredit Your patronage. At any moment in which I am call'd on to act, I am ready to obey, as nothing detains me at Salisbury but an expectation of an answer."[2]

RC (DNA: RG 59, LAR, 1801–9, filed under "Osborne"). 3 pp.

1. See Osborne to JM, 3 May 1805, *PJM-SS*, 9:317.
2. This letter to JM was enclosed in Osborne's 24 July 1805 letter to Samuel Harrison Smith, editor of the *National Intelligencer* (DLC; 2 pp.).

From Thomas Jefferson

DEAR SIR   MONTICELLO July 25. 05.
Your letter of July 22. finds me in the hurry of my departure for Bedford. I return you Erving's letter, and inclose Rankin's petition for a pardon;[1] as also a correspondence sent me by Lee of Bordeaux,[2] which tho' a little long, is entitled to a reading, as it throws light on subjects we ought to understand. I sincerely regret that mrs. Madison's situation confines her & yourself so long at Washington. I think it very unsafe for both. The climate of our quarter is really like that of another country. I have not felt one moment of disagreeable warmth since I have been at home. The thermom. has generally been, at it's maximum from 86. down to 81. In hopes that on my return I shall learn that mrs. Madison is much better, & safely moored in Orange I tender you my affectionate salutations.

                                                    TH:JEFFERSON

P.S. I inclose you the list of the members appointed to the legislative council of Indiana, to be recorded.[3]

RC (DLC); FC (DLC: Jefferson Papers). Enclosures not found, but see nn.

1. On 30 July 1805 Jefferson pardoned Robert Rankin, who had been jailed at Alexandria, and remitted the fine and court costs associated with his sentence (DNA: RG 59, PPR).

2. This was probably William Lee's 17 May 1805 letter to Jefferson in which Lee enclosed copies of correspondence that he believed would vindicate his character and refute attacks made on him (DLC: Jefferson Papers).

3. This was probably the list of names contained in William Henry Harrison's 18 June 1805 letter that Jefferson received on 25 July (ibid.; printed in Carter, *Territorial Papers, Indiana*, 7:293–96).

From Anthony Merry

SIR,   WASHINGTON July 25th. 1805

I have the Honor to transmit to you enclosed the Copy of a Protest made by Francis Blair,[1] late Master of the British Ship Golden Grove, stating the particulars of the Capture of that Ship on the 9th. of May last by a Spanish Privateer Schooner called the Atrevido commanded by a Person of the Name of Hooper, said to be an American, that is declared to have sailed from Hampton Road, together with several other vessels, at the same Time that the British Ship put to Sea from thence, the English Captain not Knowing that the Schooner was an Enemy's armed Vessel from her Guns and Men having been concealed.

The Circumstance, Sir, of the Privateer having accompanied the British Ship out of the Port being an Infringement of the Rule of Twenty Four Hours,[2] renders the Capture of the latter illegal, and it is upon this Ground that I have the Honor to solicit of the American Government that the necessary Means may be employed to procure the Restitution of the Ship and Cargo, which the Protest states to have been carried into St Augustine.

In Addition to the Particulars recited in the enclosed Document, the Master of the Golden Grove declared verbally at his Arrival at Philadelphia to his Majesty's Consul General, who has reported the Case to me, that the Commander of the Privateer attended at the Custom House at Norfolk at the Time he was clearing out his Ship, by which Means he became acquainted with the Time of his intended departure; and it appears by a Report from His Majesty's Consul at Norfolk that the same Privateer also captured Two other British Vessels that sailed from thence for Bermuda at the same Time, which, although the Particulars of their Seizure have not as yet been ascertained, there is Reason to believe were taken under similar Circumstances, all the British Masters being ignorant, from the Schooner's Arms being so closely concealed, that an Enemy's Privateer was lying in Hampton Road.

The Schooner's Quality, as such, would seem in Fact to have been generally unknown at Norfolk. I therefore take the Liberty, Sir, of making you acquainted with the daring Imposition which has apparently been practised in this Instance, and of Submitting to you the Propriety of such

Means being adopted as in the Wisdom of the American Government may appear to be the most conducive for ascertaining the real Quality of the Vessels that enter the Ports of the United States. I have the Honor to be, with high Consideration and Respect, Sir, your most obedient humble Servant

ANT: MERRY.

RC and enclosure (DNA: RG 59, NFL, Great Britain, vol. 3). RC docketed by Wagner: "Capture of the Golden Grove." For enclosure, see n. 1.

1. The enclosure (4 pp.; docketed by Wagner; certified by notary Clement Biddle) is the 11 July 1805 protest of Francis Blair, stating that the *Golden Grove* left Hampton Roads for Liverpool on 8 May 1805 in company with several other ships, among them the *Atrevido*, under the command of an American named Hooper. A few miles out from port the *Atrevido* approached, unfurled Spanish colors, and uncovering cannon, fired a broadside into Blair's ship. Hooper sent the *Golden Grove* to St. Augustine, where the cargo was partly unloaded, the vessel and cargo condemned, and the *Golden Grove* sent into the St. Marys River. Blair reported that the privateer had lain in Hampton Roads for several days, keeping its guns and the crew of about forty men, many of whom were American, hidden while the officers visited many of the British ships in the harbor inquiring about passage to England. Blair also complained that the day after the capture, five of his own seamen had signed on with the prize master to sail the *Golden Grove* to St. Augustine. On 25 June he was allowed to leave St. Augustine for Philadelphia. The *Atrevido*, the *Golden Grove*, and a prize brig were retaken in the St. Marys River by a captured French ship fitted out by the British frigate *Cambrian* (Charleston *Carolina Gazette*, 19 July 1805; Maine *Kennebunk Gazette*, 31 July 1805; New York *Morning Chronicle*, 9 Aug. 1805).

2. For the rule of twenty-four hours, see JM to Merry, 25 June 1804, *PJM-SS*, 7:367–68.

From Philip Nicklin and Robert Eaglesfield Griffith

PHILADELPHIA July 25t. 1805.

The Memorial of Philip Nicklin and Robert Eaglesfield Griffith[1] of the City of Philadelphia Merchants
Respectfully sheweth

That your Memorialists are Natives of England, but that Philip Nicklin became a citizen of the United States on the eleventh day of October 1785, and that Robert Eaglesfield Griffith became a Citizen of the United States on the   [2] day of October 1785.

That Your Memorialists have carried on trade together in the City of Philadelphia for more than fourteen years, at first under the firm of Philip Nicklin & Co and since under the firm of Nicklin & Griffith; during which time they have been Owners of many Registered Vessels of the United States.

133

That in the year 1797 Your Memorialists were with the late Archibald McCall, the late George Plumsted, William Read and Mathew Pearce, (the two latter trading under the firm of William Read & Co) Owners of the Ship New Jersey, a duly Registered Vessel of the United States, and engaged in an adventure on board of that ship from Philadelphia to Canton and back again in company with the above named Archibald McCall, George Plumsted, and William Read & Co, all native citizens of the United States.

That the Cargo on the above mentioned Voyage was insured exclusively by the Insurance Companies of Philadelphia, New York and Baltimore, and sundry private Underwriters who were resident Citizens of the United States, but the insurance was not effected to the full value of the Property at risque.

That the Ship sailed on her voyage with all the customary documents to prove the American Ownership of Ship and Cargo, but in returning from Canton she was captured by a French privateer and carried into Porto Rico.[3]

That on receiving the account of this capture Your Memorialists and their Associates in the adventure abandoned their respective interests to the Insurers, but as a great part of the value of the Cargo was not insured, and the Ship totally uncovered, Your Memorialists and their associates sent an agent to St Domingo to negotiate as well on their behalf as on the behalf of the Underwriters, for a restitution of the property.

That with great trouble and expense the said Agent induced General Hidouville in the name of the French Government to accept of a deposit of Two hundred and three thousand and fifty dollars in lieu of the Ship and cargo, on th(e) express stipulation, that he would pay the money to whomsoever the Council of Prizes should eventually decree the payment to be made.

That matters remained in this situation until the convention and Treaty were successively made between the United States and France, in the Years   ,[4] by the first of which it was declared that all captured property not definitively condemned, should be reciprocally restored, and by the last a portion of the Louisiana purchase money was assigned for the payment (of) demands arising from the depredations committed by French privateers on the American Commerce.

That under the sanction of these Treaties your Memorialists, their Associates, and the greatest part of the Underwriters appointed Monsr. Du Pont De Nezmours to be their Attorney and representative, and the Insurances Companies of Pennsylvania and North America appointed Monsr. De la Grange, who proceeded to establish the illegality of the Capture of the Ship New Jersey, and obtained a definitive decree in favor of their constituents from the French Council of Prizes.

That the decree of restitution being thus pronounced it was submitted to the American Commission under the Louisiana Treaty, who did not hesitate to Admit and allow it as the foundation of a just and regular claim upon the Fund committed to their care.

That although it was deemed a matter almost of course to recognize the charges thus allowed by the American commission, unexpected and unmerited difficulties occurred upon the p[r]esent occasion in the French Council of Liquidation, upon the Suggestion that your Memorialists were Englishmen, that the Cargo of the New Jersey was English property, and that some of the underwriters were also Englishmen.

That while these suggestions proceeded from men obviously interested in fabricating and circulating them, the Attorneys of your Memorialists had little danger to apprehend; but it is Stated with equal surprize and affliction that having obtained the sanction of the Minister plenepotentiary of the United States at Paris, they threaten to involve your Memorialists their associates and the Underwriters in the absolute loss of the whole Sum already actually decreed, which Amounts to upwards of Two hundred thousand Dollars.

That under this impression your Memorialists on behalf of themselves, their associates, and the Underwriters, have deemed it a duty to submit the subject to the immediate consideration of the Government, from whose wisdom they may reasonably hope an effectual interposition to guide the conduct of their Minister, or from whose justice they shall confidently expect an ultimate indemnity against the ruinous consequences of his unauthorized acts.

That it appears from the documents which accompany this Memorial, (and to which the Secretary of State is respectfully refered for a detail of all the important circumstances of the case) that at the instance of one of the members of the French council of Liquidation an application was made to General Armstrong for information upon the difficulties that had occured.

That in answer to this application General Armstrong declared that Although he had no written document on the subject, and although his information was merely verbal, without the sanction of an oath, or the responsibility of a name, Yet, that, "he had much verbal information, which furnished strong presumptive evidence of two facts: First that the New Jersey was partially, or altogether, English property, and secondly that whether American or English she was insured and that no loss was sustained by the Ostensible Claimants."[5]

That Your Memorialists will not here condescend to refute the allegations on which the first of these positions is founded, nor will they discuss the extraordinary principle involved in the second, but it is material to remark that the effect produced by this diplomatic communication was such as even the recantation of the Minister himself could never eradicate.

That the Attornies of your Memorialists having obtained a knowledge of the opinions expressed by General Armstrong, hastened to convince him of their fallacy, and in a very short period he was induced to acknowledge explicitly that, "The Policies of insurance and other documents which they have Submitted to his inspection at different times, had entirely removed any doubt that he might have had with respect to the fact, that the ship New Jersey and her Cargo were American Property." It is to be lamented that General Armstro⟨n⟩g had not earlier called for those documents instead of listening to the invid⟨ious⟩ and sinister tales of Masked individuals, or that he had not extended his enquir⟨ies⟩ beyond the group of rival claimants to many other respectable American⟨s⟩ then in Paris, or that he had not even resorted to his own memory for a more accurate knowledge of men, neither of whom had lived in obscurity, and one of whom had been actually married for a period of eight years to a relation of his wife![6] But on this interesting occasion your Memorialists rather wish to pursue a remedy than to indulge in a reproach; to state facts, rather than to investigate motives.

That on the receipt of General Armstrong's communication the French Council of Liquidation at once condemned the claim of your Memorialists, their associates, and the Underwriters, but when Messrs Du Pont and Le Grange had discovered the cause of the condemnation, had obtained the recantation of General Armstrong on the question of property, and had in several successive Memorials developed the facts and principles of the case, the Council returned to its original favorable dispositions, and a decision (which required unanimity) was only suspended by a single voice.

That under these circumstances the French Council of Liquidati⟨on⟩ agreed to refer the subject conclusively to the ministers plenepotentiary of the two nations, and so auspicious was this reference deemed that the Attornies of your Memorialists felt no doubt of success, until it was discovered that General Armstrong retained the extraordinary idea that indemnity for Maritime spoliation, was not due to American Underwriters who had paid a loss to the original American owner; while the French Minister was unwilling in the case of a deficiency to apportion the Louisiana Fund among the claimants, and thought it better to reject an entire clas⟨s⟩ than to reduce the payment ratable on the claims that were admitted.

That this new source of danger and disappointment gave rise to the last Memorial E., which Messrs Du Pont and Le Grange have presented to the Ministers plenepotentiary under feelings of extreme Mortification and alarm, and which is submitted with deference to the consideration of the Secretary of State.

And Your Memorialists having concluded this recapitulation for themselves, their associates, and the Underwriters interested in the Ship New
Jersey and her Cargo, solicit the aid and authority of the Government to
rescue them from the impending misfortune.

1st. Because the justice of their claim is indisputable, has been declared
so by the Tribunals of France, and has been recognized by the American Commissioners.

2ndly. Because the suspicion cast upon their claim and the hazard to
which it is now exposed proceed from the unauthorized, mistaken,
and injurious, interposition of the Minister of the United States.

3rdly. Because the principles on which the American Minister continues to oppose the claim are as pernicious in point of public policy, as
they are oppressive in their operation upon private rights.

4thly. Because for the voluntary act of a public Minister which involves
his fellow Citizens in a heavy loss, his own fortune and the faith of
Government must furnish an ultimate indemnity.[7]

Tr (Rokeby Collection, Barrytown, Dutchess County, N.Y., courtesy of Richard Al-
drich and others, 1967). Enclosures not found.

1. Philip Nicklin (c. 1760–1806) was a Philadelphia merchant for over twenty years
whose "reputation for integrity, punctuality and intelligence, [had] never been impeached."
In 1794, 1796–97, 1802–4, and 1806, he was named a director for the Bank of Pennsylvania;
in 1797 and 1803 he was also elected a director of the Insurance Company of North America. In 1798 he was treasurer of the Society of the Sons of St. George, and in 1801 he was
elected vice president, a position he held until his death. He and Robert Eaglesfield Griffith
changed the name of their company to Nicklin & Griffith in early 1798, and Griffith continued the company alone after Nicklin died (*New-York Commercial Advertiser*, 5 Nov. 1806;
Philadelphia *Gazette of the United States*, 5 Feb. 1794, 24 Jan. 1798, 26 Mar. 1798, 15 Feb.
1804; *Philadelphia Gazette & Universal Daily Advertiser*, 25 Jan. 1796, 13 Jan. and 7 Feb. 1797;
New-York Gazette and General Advertiser, 28 Jan. 1801, 5 Feb. 1802; Philadelphia *Poulson's
American Daily Advertiser*, 8 Feb. 1803, 10 Nov. 1806; Philadelphia *Aurora General Advertiser*, 16 Feb. 1804; Philadelphia *United States' Gazette*, 5 Feb. and 19 Nov. 1806). Merchant
Robert Eaglesfield Griffith (1756–1833) was also a member of the Society of the Sons of
St. George, serving at various times as steward and as president. In 1803 he was named a di-
rector of the newly founded Phoenix Insurance Company of Philadelphia and was reelected
in 1805. During his lifetime he was also a manager of the Lehigh Navigation Company and a
member of the Philadelphia Chamber of Commerce (*Dorothy Wordsworth: The Grasmere
Journals*, ed. Pamela Woof [Oxford, 1991], 174; Philadelphia *Gazette of the United States*, 24
Jan. 1798, 19 Dec. 1803; *Philadelphia Gazette & Daily Advertiser*, 27 Jan. 1802; Philadelphia
Poulson's American Daily Advertiser, 26 Jan. 1807, 29 Mar. 1813; Philadelphia *United States'
Gazette*, 10 Jan. and 19 Feb. 1805).

2. Left blank in Tr.

3. For the capture of the *New Jersey*, see *PJM-SS*, 6:346 n. 1.

4. Left blank in Tr. The writers referred to article 4 of the Convention of 1800 between
the United States and France, and to the Louisiana Purchase Claims Convention of 1803
(see Miller, *Treaties*, 2:457, 459–62, 516–23).

5. Armstrong's 5 Dec. 1804 letter to François Barbé-Marbois containing this statement was printed in the 1 Jan. 1806 New York *Republican Watch-Tower*.

6. Griffith was married to Maria Thong Patterson whose mother, Catherine Livingston, was the second cousin of Armstrong's wife Alida Livingston (Charles Henry Hart, "Gilbert Stuart's Portraits of Women," *Century Illustrated Monthly Magazine*, 58 [1899]: 153; Dangerfield, *Chancellor Robert R. Livingston*, Genealogical Chart opposite p. 516).

7. Armstrong opposed the statement of Nicklin and Griffith, saying that the reasons their claim was rejected were quite different from what they had indicated (see Armstrong to JM, 26 Nov. 1805). In 1806 Nicklin and Griffith issued pamphlets expanding on and giving supporting documentation for their position on the *New Jersey* case (*Memorial of the Owners and Underwriters of the American Ship, the New Jersey* [Shaw and Shoemaker 10856]; *Examination of the Memorial of the Owners and Underwriters of the American Ship the New Jersey, and of the Documents Accompanying It as Presented to the Senate and House of Representatives of the United States of America at Their Late Session* [Philadelphia, 1806; Shaw and Shoemaker 10378]).

§ From George W. Erving. *25 July 1805, London*. No. 35. "Mr Monroe arrived here yesterday, & I have this day a letter from Mr Bowdoin dated Southampton at which place it appears he has just landed from St. Andero; Mr Bowdoin has not quitted Spain on account of any political circumstances, but as I learn by his letter, the ill State of his health has made it necessary for him to come hither for the benefit of medical advice."

RC (DNA: RG 59, CD, London, vol. 9); RC (MHi: Winthrop Family Papers). First RC 1 p.; marked "*Private*"; docketed by JM. Cover postmarked 10 Sept. and marked: "Liverpool 29th July 1805 In the packet Capt. Trott via Boston ⅌ H.M.O.S. for James Maury Thos: Bigland"; damaged by removal of seal. Second RC marked "*Private Duplicate: No 35*."

§ From William Lee. *25 July 1805, Bordeaux*. "Mr. John Erving of Boston, is desirous of being appointed Consul for the Port of Bilboa in Spain, and has shewn me a letter from his relation James Bowdoin, containing an extract from one which, that gentleman, has written to the President of the United States on the subject.[1]

"Presuming that testimonials respecting candidates for public office are acceptable to you, I have taken the liberty to mention, that I have known Mr Erving from my youth, to be a very honest, honourable man. His connections are very respectable, and having been educated at Cambridge University and regularly bred a merchant he is every way qualified to discharge the duties of such an office. Should there be other applicants for this place perhaps Mr Ervings having a family of Children in Boston to support will have some weight in his favor, and if he succeeds in his wishes I am persuaded he will conduct in such a manner as to merit the approbation of his Government."

RC (DNA: RG 59, LAR, 1801–9, filed under "John Erving"). 2 pp.; docketed by Jefferson as received 10 Oct.

1. No letter from Bowdoin to Jefferson recommending John Erving has been found. For Erving, see Bowdoin to JM, 8 July 1805, and n. 4.

§ From George Joy.[1] *26 July 1805, London.* "I have yet to thank you for your favor of the 10th Novr.[2] I had of course communicated to Mr. Monroe the information I possessed relative to the south American Claims, and I greatly regret that his Efforts in that business have been unavailing.

"Should any farther measures be adopted which can with propriety be communicated I should be greatly obliged by a line from you on the subject.

"Mr: Monroe from whom I have just parted has been kind enough to say what he could on the subject, and I have this day recd: a letter from my old friend Mr: Young at Cadiz by which, I am glad to find, he is returning to his post and the Government likely to have the benefit resulting from his long residence & approved fidelity. I presume the President will have taken some decided measures long before this can reach you, and having sought for redress in vain I cannot but apprehend the natural and usual result in such cases; but as Mr. Monroe observes that the Court of Spain brings no Charge against the U.S. and their Policy is Peace, I hope it will still be maintained: tho' I find it a very general opinion, and remember it to have been Mr Young's before he left Europe, that to effect anything with Spain a higher tone should be held than heretofore.

"I cover, lest Mr: Monroe should not be apprisd of this Conveyance, the Copy of a recent adjudication in the Court of Admiralty here, which is at this moment the subject of much Conversation;[3] & on which I have been conferring with Mr: Monroe this morning. I take the doctrine of the Law to be with the Judge; and should expect little advantage from combating the opinion as such; but for the expediency of a relaxation that will reach such cases there is much to be said; and much I think may be said with effect. A nation at war assumes and is generally allowed to possess a right to distress her enemy into reasonable terms of peace; and the politeness among nations (Comitas inter gentes) allows each to be judge of what is reasonable in his own cause, while they confine themselves to cutting each others throats. In the exercise of this right it cannot, I fear, be denied that the belligerent may distress and even destroy the Commerce of the Enemy; and the plea of the neutral that he is injured will hardly avail among Civilians when he can only alledge the prevention of a trade growing out of the War, denied him in time of peace, and allowed him for the express purpose of relieving the distressed party from that pressure for which the blood and treasure of the other are expended. Nor is it the relief of Individuals only that is effected by these new Channels of sale and supply; they carry the Duties and Imposts by a small detour into the public Coffers, without even the degree of diminution to which the property of the Citizen is subjected by extra freight and other Charges.

"On the other hand the Ideas that I formerly suggested to you, of the benefits derived to this Country from the increase of wealth in America, demand, in a political view, the adoption of other principles, and raise large considerations on the other side of the account.

"Without troubling you with a recapitulation of these motives, I will only say here that I had occasion to propound them in a late Correspondence with the Council thro' the Duke of Montrose, and, (whether from those motives or not I cannot say, for Ministers rarely assign their reasons,) the result of the discussion was that the privilege of neutrals in return Cargoes under licence from Enemy Colonies was extended from 50 to 200 ⅌Cent advance on their Exports from England.

"Now that this doctrine, of the benefit of one nation tending to that of another with whom she has intercourse, has obtained with the President, is evident from the first lines of the Message that you were so good to enclose me:[4] it must then be congenial with his views and may be fairly urged by him in the discussion of objects of reciprocal advantage.

"That Mr. Monroe entertains similar notions, in preference to the doctrine of rivalry and mutual annoyance, was apparent in the first half hour I ever spent with him, and on suggesting to him this morning the Ideas that I am now taking the liberty to trouble you with, I was glad to find him according with them, entertaining a high opinion of sir William Scott whom he knows personally, intending to treat the subject with moderation, and determined to do all in his power to remove the Evil. Besides the political Arguments for a Compact favorable to the navigation of the U.S. there are certain Claims of Justice resulting from a justifiabl(e) ignorance of the Law in this Case, which a common Arbiter, if such a thing could be between nations in the shape of a Lord Chancellor, would consider as mitigating the rigour of the Law—the doctrine of *Ignorantia Juris non excusat* may surely be combated in a case where the Judge has varied from himself, and where his former decisions may act as a snare[5] it is not however in the doctrine that sir Willm. differs from himself, or from the Lords, but in the Construction of Evidence; and since he is bound by the rule of Law where such rule exists, I confess I do not see how he could avoid the present decision.

"When Nat Fellowes of Boston[6] received Cargoes on one side of his wharf passed them thro' his Warehouses and into other ships on the other side; had I been a Judge of the Admiralty I should have pronounced it all Evasion; but had I once acquitted a ship under these Circumstances and my Judgement had been acted upon, if I were afterwards overruled and obliged to conform to a superior tribunal, I should feel it my duty to do all in my power to prevent the injury of those who were acting under the authority of my opinion; besides I am not a Judge of the Admiralty, but a Quaker, and disposed to favor the neutral at all points—when history shall furnish a fair average of examples in which Justice has been obtained by the sword—the Guilty punished and the Innocent relieved, I shall if I live, (after many transmigrations alas!) favor the Laws of war: but while one party is always and both are often in the wrong I shall be disposed to make the debatable objects of Life flourish on neutral ground. Nations are apt enough, God knows, to engage in wars without the stimuli of plunder; and rarely sheath the sword once drawn, till they are exhausted, without either having obtained its object—let the wise then flourish in abundance of peace as long as the moon endureth that the nations of the Earth may learn wisdom and War be Known no more. So much par parenthese; for these are sentiments that will hardly be allowed the place of a makeweight in political discussions, in which men must be considered as they are, not as they ought to be.

"Now as sir William Scott is esteemed on all sides an excellent man, and does not appear chargeable with any undue Bias, but on the contrary has shewn the most liberal dispositions towards neutral Claimants, I think it a circumstance favorable to negotiation on this subject that he is so highly respected in the Council and so much relied on in discussions on those points. I should think it probable, for instance, that he would admit the penalty of Confiscation in such cases to be too great, and consent to some defined evidence of the colonial property becoming part of the national stock of the U.S. that would prevent evasion on the one hand and litigation on the other; and as the changing of property is a matter of mere form attended with considerable expence and no benefit to any one I should hope it might be done away by agreement; but I should not in this case urge the direct voyage, lest it check the generation of seamen. The business requires management—the direct trade of the neutral to enemy Colonies and back to his own ports is a subject of relaxation from the principle, except so far as it was carried on in time of peace; and this including the smuggling of Coffee and sugar was trifling compared with the War trade. It requires promptitude also; for there is no Knowing what Russia may do and while she is neutral the possibility of an armed neutrality may have it's influence. The state of things in spain too, which it is a subject of serious regret were not followed up at the time of the Louisiana purchase, makes it desireable that there should be no cause of altercation here.

"Such are the opinions that I have taken the liberty to suggest to Mr: Monroe, Mr. Erving being present, and the inclination of my own opinion is that the difficulties will be removed, for I have no belief in any fresh orders from the Government here, tho' the Proctors at the Commons are no doubt sending Circulars to the Cruizers who will intercept any Ships they may meet under similar Circumstances."

RC and enclosure (DLC). RC 8 pp.; marked: "(Copy) 1st. ℔ Philadelphia." For enclosure, see n. 3.

1. George Joy (b. ca. 1760) was the son of a Massachusetts Loyalist who took his family to Great Britain at the outbreak of the American Revolution. Joy remained in London, where he wrote newspaper essays, pamphlets, and letters to American and British politicians in support of American neutral rights. In December 1807 he was named consul at Rotterdam. In extreme old age he spent a year and a half in debtor's prison. He wrote frequently and at length to JM, who seldom answered. He died sometime between February 1844 and February 1853 (*PJM-PS*, 1:30–31; *Senate Exec. Proceedings*, 2:60, 63; *Times* [London], 22 Nov. and 26 Dec. 1842, 22 Feb. 1844, 15 Feb. 1853).

2. Letter not found (calendared in *PJM-SS*, 8:280).

3. The enclosure (3 pp.) is a copy of the 23 July 1805 condemnation by Sir William Scott of part of the cargo of the *Enoch*, Doane, consisting of coffee, sugar, and barrel staves traded from Martinique to Antwerp, for carrying produce from an enemy colony to the United States and then reshipping it to the mother country, a trade that had been allowed under the *Polly* decision of 1800 but was forbidden by the *Essex* decision announced on 22 June 1805. Scott argued that unloading a cargo and paying duties did not alone prove that there was no intent to carry the cargo to the mother country, and other evidence must be considered. In the case of the *Enoch* the fact that a charter party existed to carry the cargo to Antwerp from Boston proved that the original intention was to make a continuous voyage (*Alexandria Daily Advertiser*, 20 Sept. 1805; Boston *Independent Chronicle*, 23 Sept. 1805). For a discussion of the *Polly* and *Essex* decisions, see Perkins, *First Rapprochement*, 88–89, 177–81.

4. For Jefferson's fourth annual message to Congress, see Ford, *Writings of Thomas Jefferson*, 8:323–32.

5. Joy placed an asterisk here and added at the bottom of the page: "*'An American has undoubtedly a right to import the produce of the spanish Colonies for his own use; and after it is imported *bona fide* into his own Country he should be at liberty to carry it on to the general Commerce of Europe.

'It is urged that it would not be sufficient that the duties should be paid and that the Cargo should be landed: if these Criteria are not to be resorted to I should be at a loss to Know what should be the Test; and I am strongly disposed to hold that it would be sufficient that the Goods should be landed and the Duties paid.' Polly-Laskey-feb: 5th 1800."

6. Nathaniel Fellowes (d. ca. 1806) was "a firm republican & one of the wealthiest merchants of Boston." In 1801, during Jefferson's reduction of the navy, he bought the sloops of war *Merrimack* and *Warren*. In 1804 he was one of the original incorporators of the Union Insurance Company (*PJM-SS*, 2:232; Boyd, *Papers of Thomas Jefferson*, 34:viii, 110–11, 398; New York *Mercantile Advertiser*, 25 June 1801; Boston *Columbian Centinel*, 9 May 1801; Boston *Independent Chronicle*, 4 Apr. 1804, 31 July 1806.

§ From Thomas Auldjo. *27 July 1805, Cowes.* "I had the honor to write you 16th inst & having had a little more time to consider of the form of a Certife for quarantine, I have drawn out the inclosed as being more Simple[1] & I think it will be usefull if sent to the Collrs of every port in the U.S.

"Several serious Admiralty Condemnations have taken place this Week in the Commons which establish that the Navigation of American Ships from Holland to the Dutch Colonies shall not be permitted longer[2] & also that the produce of the French & Spanish Colonies shall not come to Europe in the ship that first took it on board & that notwithstanding the produce shall have been landed in America, if reship into the same ship, it shall be considered a continuation of the Same voyage & be condemned.

"Our prices of Wheat are 10/ a 11/ ℔ bushel."

RC and enclosure (DNA: RG 59, CD, Southampton, vol. 1). RC 1 p.; docketed by Wagner. For enclosure, see n. 1.

1. The enclosure (1 p.) is a printed form on which captains or owners of ships could list the information required under the British quarantine act.
2. For one such decision, see George Joy to JM, 26 July 1805, and n. 3.

§ From Sylvanus Bourne. *27 July 1805, Amsterdam.* "I have now the pleasure to inclose you a Copy of an advertisement[1] to which I referred in some of my late letters[2] which has been circulated throughout all Germany in order to *entice* people to go to America or *elsewhere.* What a violation of truth? What a Vile prostitution of the Character & dignity of the Govt of the U States to *answer private purposes* Mrs D & O were Brokers for the Vessells which had the passengers on board—collected by *these measures* & mr Kurtz who signs one of the Advertists has for many years consecutive been in Germany as Agent for D&O to collect Emigrants & therefore (tho' they have had cunning enough not to have their names appear in the matter) must be supposed to have full & complete knowlege of the whole transaction & I doubt not they were *the planners of the Scheme* as it is truly conformable to their manner of doing business. All these things must tend my respected Sir to convince you that a remedy was required & I flatter myself it will be found in the conduct of the Other establishment whose success will depend however on my support & protection."

Adds in a postscript: "As before mentioned to you—the Govt here hint at the means which had been used to collect these passengers as well as suspicions of the objec⟨t⟩ & intent of the voyage—forcibly turned them ashore—while they permitted mess Haines & Co to ship the greater part of them in another vessell—Capt King—Ship Venus—to Phila."[3]

Adds in a second postscript: "I shall shortly send on my publication which will correctly explain all Circumstances & set every thing right in the minds of my fellow Citizens."

RC and enclosure (DNA: RG 59, CD, Amsterdam, vol. 1). RC 2 pp.; docketed by Wagner. For enclosure, see n. 1.

1. The enclosure (2 pp.; docketed by Wagner) is an English translation of a 20 Feb. 1804 advertisement by Casimir Kurz, announcing that the U.S. Congress had designated Wills & Co. of Amsterdam agents for encouraging emigration of "sober Industrious and honest Citizens" from Germany to Louisiana, Florida, and other regions of the United States. Five transports were to leave Frankfort between 12 Apr. and 30 June 1805. Emigrants were to be "furnished with abundant victuals, Eaten & Drink, good Loging and a free passage to America" as well as a complete outfit of clothing and free housing in the Netherlands while awaiting passage on the ship on which they would be provided with excellent food, "beer & Brandy and free purge Physians attendance in case of Sickness," and on which "no Arbitrary Punition or ill usages" would take place. On arrival in America they were to receive more free food, clothing, and lodging. They were to be bound workers for six years at good wages and would be free at the end of that time either to work for themselves or to engage again with the same employer. It was further stated that anyone who objected to these conditions on arrival in the United States could return to Europe after repaying his passage.

2. For an earlier mention of German emigrants, see the two postscripts to Bourne to JM, 6 July 1805.

3. The 28 Sept. 1805 Philadelphia *Aurora General Advertiser* announced the sale of "A NUMBER of German Redemptioners, to be disposed of on board ship Venus, from Amsterdam, consisting of farmers, tanners, curriers, morocco leather dressers, plaisterers, &c. &c. . . ."

§ From William C. C. Claiborne. *27 July 1805, New Orleans.* "In obedience to the Law providing for the further Government of the Territory of Orleans, I have laid out the Same into convenient Election Districts, and apportioned the representatives to the number of twenty five among the several Counties.[1] A Copy of my Proclamation upon this Subject and of my circular Letter to the Officers named to conduct the election, I now have the Honor to enclose you.[2]

"By an Ordinance of the City Council, certain repairs are directed to be made to the Side Walks of the Streets, and it was ordained that the owners of real property in the City Should difray the expense of Such improvements as were made in front of their respective Lots. By virtue of this regulation, improvements have been made in front of the Barracks, and the charge for the same amounts to Six Hundred Dollars;[3] The account was Exhibited to me, but I had no authority to pay it, nor had Colonel Freeman who was also apply'd to; The delay in the Settlement of this Account, it is fearrd may retard the completion of a Work, deemed necessary to the Health of the City; I therefore Sincerely wish, that the claim might be allowed and Speedily paid. I have however requested the Mayor of the City, to Suspend all further improvements to Lots claimed by the United States, until I hear from you on the Subject, and I therefore request an answer to this communication as early as may be convenient. The proposed improvements would probably cost the United States about three thousand Dollars *for their lots;* but would at the Same time add *to their* value. I cannot see any objection to the Expenditure, unless indeed it should be considered in the light of a Tax upon Public property, and unconstitutional. The Police of this City is becoming vigilant, and the Civil Authorities throughout the Territory are now organized. I can therefore no longer see a necessity of Stationing Regular Troops in the Interior of this Territory. In this City one Company might be usefully employed as a Guard for the Public Property, but a greater number appears to me unnecessary. The Strengthening of the Works at Plaquemine, or the Erecting of a New Fort at some strong position on the Mississippi below New Orleans, I consider an object worthy the attention of the Administration, and in this way I think a part of the Troops now here might be well employed, & that others might with propriety be sent to some Frontier Post. To guard however against any difficulties with Spain, it might be adviseable to have a regular Force so posted as to enable them, to Act with promptitude and effect, as well in attacking the Florida's, as in defending this City, and I know of no Position more eligible than Fort Adams!"

RC and enclosures (DNA: RG 59, TP, Orleans, vol. 7); letterbook copy (Ms-Ar: Claiborne Executive Journal, vol. 15). RC 3 pp.; in a clerk's hand, signed by Claiborne; docketed by Wagner as received 3 Sept., with his note: "Taxes laid upon Public property at New Orleans." Minor differences between the copies have not been noted. For enclosures, see nn. 2–3.

1. For section 2 of the act establishing a government for Orleans Territory, which deals with the creation of twenty-five districts for general assembly representatives, see *U.S. Statutes at Large,* 2:322.

2. Claiborne enclosed a copy (1 p.; printed in Carter, *Territorial Papers, Orleans,* 9:481) of his 26 July 1805 circular letter addressed to the mayor of New Orleans covering a copy (1 p.; printed ibid., 478–81) of his 26 July 1805 broadside proclamation describing the electoral districts, setting the election date for the third Monday in September, and requiring all the representatives thus elected to convene at New Orleans on the first Monday in November 1805. Enclosed with the proclamation is an extract (1 p.) from the 13 July 1787 Northwest Ordinance listing the requirements for eligibility for election to the general assembly, term limits, and duties.

3. The enclosures (2 pp.) are bills totaling $568.52 for the construction of sidewalks in front of the district court and government office buildings.

From Gideon Gooch

SIR   July 28th 1805

I Recd. yours To-day. I wrote you by the Satturdays mail[1] and in closed you forty dollars also in formd you that on Sunday I would Send you too hundred more for fear of a disapointment from mr: Richards but finding you will not come home as soon as I expected and gone To Pillidelpia I have declined for warding you any more money untill I hear from you for their may be Some Risk in the matter but if mr. Richards should. fail and you wish me to Send you money I can Send you too or 300 dollars But mr.

Richards will ceartainly not fail To comply with his promise. I went down
to see him last week and have wrote him to day on the subject he informd
me when I see him that he would get the money and you might look for it
by the first Or 2d mail I have been very closely ingagd for 7 or 8 weeks that
I could not give as full in for mation as I wishd and expectd. you home
Some Time past that I did not think my writeing would be of the same in
portace as I now find it will. I viewd. the several crops yester day and find
they Suffer very much for Rain at this Time if we could have penty of Rain
their will be good crops of corn Yates To bo is very large but if Seasonable
weather I think it w(ill) make a good crop Sawneys To bo is small and hi(s)
wheat will not make much over 300 Bus Ralphs about the Same we all
Secured but Sawneys he will get his secured this week I expect To be gin
to get out my wheat next week if the weather is favourable I be lieave the
mare put to clifden[2] is in foal I Send Sam To morrow for the others mares.
all is wel you will hear from me one a week and Sorry you will not be able
to get home Sooner Yours

JAMES MADISON[3]

I Shall soon expect to hear from you again.

RC (DLC). Docketed by JM.

1. Neither JM's nor Gooch's letter has been found.
2. For JM's continued use of Clifden's services, see *PJM-PS*, 2:112 and n. 1.
3. "James Madison" has been lined out and "Gideon Gooch" inserted in JM's hand.

From Jacob Wagner

DR. SIR   Sunday 28 July 1805.
   Capt. Dulton has arrived with the dispatches.[1] They confirm Young's
account in every respect:[2] the negotiation has failed altogether; but care
has been taken not to commit us to war by Mr. Pinckney's remaining for
the arrival of Mr. Bowdoin, by Mr. Monroe's leave from the King of Spain
&c. I send the copy of the enclosed to the President and retain the rest of
the dispatches for the purpose of making further copies for him, after
which they shall be sent to you to morrow. Dulton has it in confidence
from Mr. Pinckney that the Prince of Peace informed him, that the Deposit of N. Orleans was formerly taken away by a written demand from
the French government as a preparation for its possession of Louisiana.[3]
Dulton left Madrid 27th. May, the day after Mr. Monroe proceeded for
Paris. In great haste Your's affectionately

J. WAGNER[4]

RC (DLC).

1. See Monroe to JM, 26 May 1805 (two letters), and Pinckney to JM, 26 May 1805, *PJM-SS*, 9:404, 405–7, 408.

2. Letter not found (calendared ibid., 427).

3. For France's role in the closing of the U.S. deposit at New Orleans, see Charles Pinckney to JM, 28 Feb. 1805, ibid., 75. In the journal that he enclosed in his 26 May 1805 letter to JM, Monroe stated that Manuel de Godoy had told him the closing was done at France's instigation (ibid., 405, 407 n.).

4. Jacob Wagner (ca. 1772–1825) was admitted to the Philadelphia bar in 1793. He became a clerk at the State Department in 1794 and rose to chief clerk in 1798, a post he held until 1807, when he moved to Baltimore. From 1794 to 1798 he also served as deputy clerk to the Supreme Court. Between early 1807 and 1816 he published or edited pro-Federalist newspapers in Baltimore and in Georgetown in partnership with Alexander Contee Hanson. The office of his Baltimore paper was sacked and burned by a mob during the War of 1812 (Maeva Marcus et al., *The Documentary History of the Supreme Court of the United States, 1789–1800* [8 vols.; New York, 1985–2007], 1:162, 167 n. 28; Looney et al., *Papers of Thomas Jefferson: Retirement Series*, 3:262 n.; *Baltimore North American and Mercantile Daily Advertiser*, 11 Jan. 1808).

From James Wilkinson

SIR   ST: LOUIS July 28th: 1805.

I reached this place the 1st: Inst: And On the morning of the 4th: the Secretary of the Territory arrived just in season to attest the Enclosed Proclamation.[1]

My Predecessor having provided for the prevention of crimes, the maintenance of Order, the Organization of the Militia and the distribution of Justice, and having filled every appointment, it has been deemed adviseable to examine attentively, his systems and arrangements and to ascertain their effects, before we Should commence Legislation.

Deliberate enquiry into the State of Society and the merits of Individuals also, is rendered indispensable by the bitter animosities, and vindictive personal Factions which rend Several districts of this Territory, excited I have cause to beleive, by a few impatient, ambitious and perhaps Sordid Spirits, with whom I fear Several officers of the Government have been too deeply engaged; yet I flatter myself the force of admonition Supported by example, may soon produce a proper sense of Duty, correct the errors which have prevailed, and restore that general concord, to which the mass of the people, and particularly the Creoles, are certainly well disposed.

The transient intercourse which I had with the inhabitants pending my ascent of the River, discovered to me the divisions which agitated the community, and determined me to embrace the first occasion, to express my disapprobation thereof: I accordingly on the 3d: Inst: made the reply you will find under cover, to an address which I could not resist, without exciting false apprehensions and heavy disgust, and I hope my conduct in this instance may prove satisfactory.[2]

Attempts have been made to introduce here, the political distinctions of the union and to excite national prejudices, but without effect: the French are not able to distinguish between republicanism and federalism, and Our fugitive countrymen, who sought asylum here during the Spanish Government, wear their political Morality as loosely as they do their cloaths.

The interdiction of the British Commerce west of the Mississippi, becomes hourly more interesting, because it not only affects our Revenues, but discourages our own enterprize and industry, and supports the influence of a Foreign Power, within our own limits, which may hereafter be employed for distructive purposes.

Engageés are now daily arriving here, from Montreal "via" Michilimackanack and the Ouisconsin with merchandise not only for the Indians of the Missouri, but the Inhabitants of this Territory, and the Supplies for the former will I understand, be principally derived from that Source this Season; I beleive I should be justified were I to prohibit the introduction of this merchandise, into the rivers west of the Mississippi, but as such a measure would cut off the regular Supplies of the natives, it is at present forbidden by every consideration of Sound policy.

The President commanded me to carry my attention to this subject, and therefore I beg leave breifly to Submit to you my ideas, of the measures necessary to accomplish the desired prohibition, without giving just cause of complaint to any one.

The British Minister should be warned of the intentions of Government, to interdict this intercourse after a given period, and this warning Should be made Public, as well for the government of the British Merchants, as the encouragement of our own.

To guard the avenues from Canada, a Military post should be established near the mouth of the Ouisconsin, and an officer of the customs placed there, whose certificate shall be rendered necessary by Law, to the exemption from Seizure of all the goods and merchandise, which may pass that Post to the west Bank of the Mississippi, and a Similar arrangement should be made for Chicago—it must follow that none but goods of our own importation Shall receive this certificate, and all others carried across the river will of course be liable to Scizure: And to break up the contraband from the North west by the Ossiniboine River, a Garrison should be established at the mandan Towns or perhaps at the Falls of the Missouri, with an officer of the customs to seize whatever may be introduced by that Channel. But in aid of these measures, confidential agents should be established with the Scieoux, Saque and Renard indians on the waters of the Mississippi, and with the Scieoux and Mandanes of the Missouri. These arrangements being once accomplished, in a very few Years the trade of the Mississippi and Missouri, would take its ancient and natural course by New Orleans, to extend our foreign commerce, to augment our Revenues, to familiarize and facilitate the navigation of the Mississippi, and to co-operate with the Settlements of the Ohio, in rearing numerous bands of Hardy Boatmen, ever at hand for the protection and defence, of our weakest and most vulnerable points.

Colonel Meggs[3] one of the Judges of the Territory, is on a visit to his Family at Marietta, with intention to return before the Next Term of the Superior Court, he is a most valuable Officer, And is well calculated to conciliate and attach this mixt Community.

Colonel Hammand[4] arrived a few days Since, whose gentle manners, conciliatory deportment, correct Judgment and firm conduct, will contribute much to the preservation of Order and the restoration of Harmony. Doctor Browne the Secretary will also I flatter myself justify the Presidential Trust, he appears to be a man of Suavity, of intellectual force, polished education, and liberal views.

Judge Lucas has not arrived but I expect him with the Recorder[5] in Ten or Twelve days, after which we shall attempt a System of Jurisprudence, calculated to discourage litigation and discountenance pettifoggers who begin to swarm here like locusts, & may be considered the main Source of the discords which have obtained in this Territory. With much consideration & respect I am sir Your Mo. Obed Servt

JA: WILKINSON

RC and enclosures (DNA: RG 59, TP, Louisiana, vol. 1). In a clerk's hand, with Wilkinson's emendation, complimentary close, and signature. Docketed by Wagner as received 31 Aug., with his note: "British trade to the Territory." For enclosures, see nn. 1–2.

1. The enclosure (4 pp. on one folio sheet; in English and French; in a clerk's hand, signed by Wilkinson; countersigned by territorial secretary Joseph Browne; docketed by Wagner; printed in Carter, *Territorial Papers, Louisiana-Missouri*, 13:155–56) is a copy of Wilkinson's 4 July 1805 proclamation announcing that, in accordance with the law establishing a territorial government for Louisiana, he recognized and confirmed the appointments previously made in the district and authorized the appointed officers to continue their functions.

2. Wilkinson enclosed copies of the 3 July 1805 address to him of Charles Gratiot, Auguste Chouteau, Antoine Soulard, Robert Wescott, and Isaac Darneille (2 pp.; certified by territorial secretary Joseph Browne; printed ibid., 149–50), expressing on behalf of the citizens of St. Louis their delight at the arrival of "a Governor of known principles and worth" at the head of the new government, and Wilkinson's 3 July 1805 reply (4 pp.; in a clerk's hand, emended and signed by Wilkinson, and incorrectly dated 1804; docketed by Wagner; printed ibid., 150–51) promising to maintain an impartial, just, and firm course of action and calling "personal factions the bane of social harmony, and political Strife hostile to human felicity."

3. Return Jonathan Meigs Jr.

4. Samuel Hammond (1757–1842) was a Virginia native and Revolutionary War veteran who became a merchant in international trade in Savannah, Georgia, where he was sur-

veyor general and a member of the state legislature. He was elected to Congress in 1802 and served until Jefferson named him civil and military commander of Louisiana Territory in 1805, in which post he served until 1806. In 1811 he was named judge of the court of common pleas. After the establishment of the Missouri Territory, he was a member of the territorial council and of the 1820 constitutional convention. In 1824 he moved to South Carolina, where he served as surveyor general in 1827 and secretary of state in 1831.

5. Baltimore lawyer James Lowry Donaldson (d. 1814), who was born James Lowry but changed his name legally to inherit an estate, was named recorder of land titles in Louisiana Territory in the spring of 1805. He was criticized for his performance in office by both John B. Lucas and Jefferson, who replaced him with Frederick Bates in 1807. In 1805 he was named district attorney by James Wilkinson, but the appointment was nullified by the court (Benson J. Lossing, *The Pictorial Field-Book of the Revolution; or, Illustrations by Pen and Pencil . . . of the War for Independence* [2 vols.; New York, 1860], 2:183 n.; Carter, *Territorial Papers, Louisiana-Missouri*, 13:113, 115–16, 261–63, 545, 14:52–54, 58, 98).

§ From Sylvanus Bourne. *28 July 1805, Amsterdam.* "You will find on the other Side[1] which I send by way of triplicate the head of an advertisement which has been circulated in Germany to entice emigration to America by mess Wils & Co D&O—& Casimir Kurtz—Agent for the concern who has been for many years in the habits of travelling for Mess D&O in Germany to procure emigrants. What a vile prostitution of truth as well as of the Character of our Govt to answer their private purposes. I am now preparing advertists to be published in various parts of Germany to contradict that part of the said Advertist which relates to the Govt of our Country & which I think a regard to its reputation requires Should be done—you will see by this a new proof how matters have been conducted here & be convinced that what I have done towards counteracting (as far I may have the power) such proceedings is laudable & correct.

"I am now also employed in making such a Statement to be forwarded for publication in the UStates as will remove all unfavorable impressions which may have been inspired by Mr Ds jesuitical note & satisfactorily resolve the whole transaction."

RC (DNA: RG 59, CD, Amsterdam, vol. 1). 1 p.; docketed by Wagner.

1. Written on the verso of this letter is a translated extract from the advertisement enclosed in Bourne's 27 July 1805 dispatch.

From Jacob Wagner

DEAR SIR   DEPARTMENT OF STATE 29 July 1805.
    I have the honor to enclose the remainder of the dispatches from Madrid except such as had before come to hand.[1] Copies are likewise transmitted to the President. Genl. Dearborn has of course seen them. I have paid Dulton for his passage hither; and, as before, for his return, he having charged it on the principle that he ought to be restored to his concerns at Madrid,

from which according to the Statement in the close of the letter of the Ministers of May 23d. he was separated. I own I am not altogether satisfied with the latter charge but its allowance was in a measure unavoidable.

I have advanced Cathcart half the bills he wished to retain.

Dr. & Mrs. Thornton have arrived in good hea[l]th.

With my best wishes for the recovery of Mrs. Madison, I have the honor to remain, Dr Sir, faithfully, Your obed. servt.

JACOB WAGNER

RC (DLC).

1. See Wagner to JM, 28 July 1805.

§ From William C. C. Claiborne. *29 July 1805, New Orleans.* "I have the Honor to enclose you a Translation of a communication, I lately recieved from the Marquis of Casa Calvo,[1] together with a Copy of my answer thereto:[2] you shall be furnished also with Copies of Such other Letters as may pass upon the same Subject."

RC and enclosures (DNA: RG 59, TP, Orleans, vol. 7); letterbook copy and letterbook copy of enclosure (Ms-Ar: Claiborne Executive Journal, vol. 15). RC 1 p.; docketed by Wagner, with his note: "He was informed on the 7th. Jany. last that the Marquis' privileges did not continue." Minor differences between the copies have not been noted. For the 7 Jan. 1805 letter, see *PJM-SS*, 8:460–61. For JM's earlier objection to the delay in the Spanish officers' departure, see ibid., 7:643–44 and n. 1.

1. Claiborne enclosed a translation (1 p.; docketed by Wagner; printed in Rowland, *Claiborne Letter Books*, 3:138–39) of Casa Calvo's 27 July 1805 letter asking if his employees on the boundary commission and the officers and others vested with offices by Spain, who planned to depart soon or whenever they finished their business, were subject to the municipal tax on slaves or enjoyed an exemption like that granted by Spain to foreigners working or traveling in that country. If the latter, he would send Claiborne a list of all those entitled to such an exemption in order to avoid problems that might arise.

2. The enclosure is a copy (2 pp.; docketed by Wagner; printed ibid., 139–40) of Claiborne to Casa Calvo, 28 July 1805, stating that the Louisiana Purchase Treaty allowed a specific period of time for Spanish forces to depart from the territory. When that time had passed, Casa Calvo had been "urged to direct the departure of *certain officers*" who stayed on well beyond the deadline without any reason for remaining and who indeed appeared to be considering "permanent residence." Claiborne added that he could not see how such individuals could claim special exemptions and advised them to pay any tax they owed. He said he would submit to JM the question of whether Casa Calvo and the members of his family were exempt and asked Casa Calvo to send him the names of individuals employed on the commission as well as those of anyone "vested with *Public* offices" by Spain. For article 5 of the treaty, which stipulated that foreign troops should leave the territory within three months after ratification, see Miller, *Treaties*, 2:501–2.

§ To Anthony Merry. *30 July 1805, Department of State.* "I beg leave to trouble you with Duplicate Copies of a Document concerning Benjamin Moore,[1] who appears to have been impressed into the British frigate Leander, which is supposed to be still somewhere on the American Coast; and to ask the Interposition of your good Offices, to effect the release of this man, whose Citizenship is fully proved by the Document alluded to."

FC (DNA: RG 59, Notes to Foreign Ministers and Consuls, vol. 1). 1 p.; marked "(Office Copy)."

1. JM may have misremembered the name of Nathaniel Moore who was also impressed into the *Leander*. See DeWitt Clinton to JM, 18 July 1805, and n. 1.

§ From Stephen Cathalan Jr.[1] *30 July 1805, Marseilles.* "I embrace the opportunity of Mr. Julius Oliver[2] of Philadelphia who is ready to Sail on his Brig Jefferson for that port,[3] to Congratulate you on the Peace which has been Signed between the United States and the Bashaw of Tripoli on the 3d. June last,[4] which by the reports is an honorable and advantageous one, and produces the best effects for the energy the Government of the United States has Shewed in that Contest and the Valour of their officers and Seamen; I herein have the honor to inclose you the States of the American Vessels entered and Cleared from this port from the 1st. July 1804 to the 31, Decembr. with the States of those from the 1st. January to the 30th. June ulto. [not found]. You will observe that trade between united States in this Port has much encreased and it is hoped it will Continue more So as long as war will Continue between France & England.

"Mr. Julius Oliver who was my Chancellor will probably have to honor of presenting his Respects to you, Sir; I have been much Satisfy'd with his Services and take the Liberty of Recomending him to you, begging you to introduce him near the most Honble. President to whom he wishes much to present his best respects and mine also."

RC (DNA: RG 59, CD, Marseilles, vol. 2). 3 pp.; in a clerk's hand, signed by Cathalan.

1. Stephen Cathalan Jr. (1757–1819) was named vice-consul at Marseilles in 1790, a position he held until his death. In 1804 Washington Irving described him as: "a small man—a french man but talks English fluently. He has a great esteem and admiration of his own appearance and qualifications in which good opinion he is a little singular as I believe very few except himself intertain it" (André de Gasquet, *Étienne Cathalan, 1757–1819: Vice-consul des États-Unis à Marseille de 1789 à 1819* (Marseille, 1998); Looney et al., *Papers of Thomas Jefferson: Retirement Series*, 1:313 n.; Boston *Columbian Centinel*, 21 July 1819; Irving, *Journals and Notebooks*, ed. Wright, 1:81).

2. Julius Oliver, a protégé of Cathalan, was an orphan who had been sent to school in Philadelphia at Cathalan's expense. At this time he was also serving as chancellor of the Marseilles consulate (Boyd, *Papers of Thomas Jefferson*, 31:107–8; *PJM-SS*, 7:249).

3. On 14 Sept. 1805 the *Jefferson* was captured at the mouth of Delaware Bay and carried into Halifax for judgment (*New-York Gazette & General Advertiser*, 25 Oct. 1805).

4. For the peace treaty, see George Davis to JM, 20 June 1805, *PJM-SS*, 9:482–83 and n. 1.

§ From William C. C. Claiborne. *30 July 1805, New Orleans.* "I have this day drawn upon you in favor of Captain Daniel Carmick for 180 Dollars, payable at five days Sight; Captain Carmick was the Bearer of Dispatches from me to Governor Folch, upon the Subject *of the Post Route* through West Florida;[1] and I promised to defray his expences. I would willingly have paid this charge out of the Fund appropriated for the contingent expences of this Government; but that fund is so limitted that I fear, it will not meet the expenditures which must necessarily be made within the Territory. I had at one time Supposed that the receipt of Captain Carmick might be exhibited as a voucher in the Settlement of my accounts at the War Office. But upon reflection, it appeared to fall more properly under the Head of Foreign expenditures, and therefore chargeable to your department. Captain Carmick's receipt is herewith enclosed as my Voucher [not found]."

RC (DNA: RG 59, TP, Orleans, vol. 7); letterbook copy (Ms-Ar: Claiborne Executive Journal, vol. 15). RC 1 p.; docketed by Wagner. Minor differences between the copies have not been noted.

1. See Claiborne to JM, 5 July 1805.

From James Bowdoin

DEAR SIR,   No. 14 CONDUIT STRT. LONDO. July 31st. 1805.

I had the honour to write to you under date of the 12th of June last[1] & of the 8th. instant from St. Ander, to which please to be referred: since which I have taken passage & have happily arrived here with my family: I landed at So. hampton, & after a detention of a few days to procure my Passport from this Place, I came here, & have the satisfaction to inform you, that I am much better in health, & have a fair prospect in a short time of being perfectly restored: I have happily met both Colo. Munroe & Mr. Erving, who agree in the opinion, that independent of the situation of my health, they consider my coming here to be the best step I could have taken in the present posture of our affairs with Spain: that my being at Madrid at this moment could be attended with no public benefit; that my Situation wd. have been a perplexing & most embarrassing one, & would have had a tendency to impress the Spanish ministry, that our Governme. meant to remain easy & quiet under the ill success of its Negociations: I have had the fullest & most satisfactory conversation with Colo. Munroe respecting his and Mr. Pinkney's late negociations, & I expect to be furnished with the copies of the Details for my perusal in a day or two, when I shall put into the hands of Colo. Munroe for his consideration the records of my correspondence with you, of your instructions and of the several circumstances, which have occured, since my appointment as minister to the Court of his Catholic Majesty. In my next, I shall write to you fully & explicitly upon the subject of the late negociations. In the mean time, with the best wishes for your health, & happiness & for those of our worthy President. I have the honour to subscribe myself. Most respectfully, Dr. Sir, Your faithful and obedient Servant
JAMES BOWDOIN.

RC (DNA: RG 59, DD, Spain, vol. 9). Docketed by Wagner.

1. No letter of this date has been found. Bowdoin referred to his 18 June 1805 letter, *PJM-SS*, 9:478.

§ From Jacob Ridgway. *31 July 1805, Antwerp.* "I have the honor to acknowledge receipt of Your Letter of the 26th November 1804,[1] which Came to hand the 22d April last. I have taken due note of its dispositions to conform to the Same.

"Referring to my preceding respects of the 26th March[2] I now enclose Duplicate thereof and a report List of the American Vessels interred and Cleared at Antwerp from the 1st. January up to the 30th: June last [not found]."

RC (DNA: RG 59, CD, Antwerp, vol. 1). 1 p.

1. *PJM-SS*, 8:324.
2. Ibid., 9:183–84.

To William Hull

SIR.   DEPARTMENT OF STATE August 1st. 1805.
I enclose an extract of a letter from the Postmaster General to the President containing information that trespasses are committing on a certain species of timber, growing on the public lands near lake Erie.[1] It is the President's direction that you warn by proclamation all persons from committing such trespass, and that you be afterwards watchful to cause the trespassers to suffer proper legal animadversion. I am &c.

JAMES MADISON

Letterbook copy (DNA: RG 59, DL, vol. 15).

1. For the timber, see Thomas Jefferson to JM, 23 July 1805, and n. 1.

To an Unidentified Correspondent

DEAR SIR   PHILADA. Aug. 1 1805
Your favor with the note for 250 drs. on the Bank has been duly recd., for your attention to which be pleased to accept my thanks.

The weather was so favorable for travelling that we got thro' our journey in less time & with less difficulty than was expected. We are much encouraged by the opinion expressed on the complt.[1] of Mrs. M. by Docr Physic. He assures us that there is nothing very serious in it, and that altho' the knife would hasten the cure, it is not indispensable to it. Accept our joint respects & best wishes for yourself & those to whom they also belong. Yrs. respectfully

JAMES MADISON

RC (owned by Marshall B. Coyne, Washington, D.C., 1992).

1. Complaint.

From Charles J. Ingersoll

Sunday Evening [ca. 1 August–22 October 1805]
  In the 9th. vol. page 421 of Smollet's continuation of Hume[1] an account is given of the dispute with Spain in 1737. In the 5th. vol. page 313 of the Lords Debates the Motion of Lord Cholmendeley and Speech of Ld Carteret on this subject will be found. In page 333 Lord Carteret is thus reported "The Spanish Court says We have a right to search your ships But *no search* are the words that echo from shore to shore of this Island. Unless we obtain this concession from them of no search, *be the grounds & pretensions what they will*, we in effect give them such a right. But this takes away chicane, altercation and grounds of dispute about latitude, possessions and prohibited goods."[2]

SIR—The above references will lead to the speeches at large from which I have preserved only a short extract. With great respect and consideration your humble servant

C. J. INGERSOLL

RC (DLC). Undated; conjectural date assigned based on the probability that the letter was written during JM's stay in Philadelphia from 29 July to 23 Oct. 1805, when JM was researching and writing his pamphlet, *An Examination of the British Doctrine, Which Subjects to Capture a Neutral Trade, Not Open in Time of Peace.*

1. Ingersoll probably referred to Tobias Smollett's *A Complete History of England, from the Descent of Julius Caesar, to the Treaty of Aix la Chapelle, 1748: Containing the Transactions of One Thousand Eight Hundred and Three Years*, 2d. ed. (11 vols.; London, 1758–60). For the reference to the 1737 British dispute with Spain, see the 1800 edition (5 vols.; London), 3:7–8.
    2. Ingersoll has conflated and paraphrased the extracts from Lord Carteret's 2 May 1738 speech in a debate in Parliament on Spanish demands to search British ships suspected of trading with Spanish colonies. Carteret first made the statement about "no search" and several minutes later added "yet, my Lords, unless we obtain the concession from them of 'no search, be the grounds and pretensions what they will,' we, in effect, give them such a right," adding shortly after that: "Besides, my Lords, an absolute concession of this point from the Spaniards takes away chicane, it takes away all altercations, it takes away all grounds of dispute betwixt us and them, about latitude, possessions, prohibited goods, and all that" (*Parliamentary History of England*, 10:730, 745, 753).

From William Jarvis

SIR   LISBON 1st. August 1805

Before this reaches you I hope sir you will have received your two pipes of Wine ℔ the Ship Robert, Capen Alcorn that sailed for Baltimore the 8th. Ultimo.[1]

By the Brig Maria Capen Carew for Alexandria,[2] that arrived two days after the Robert sailed, I have taken the liberty to send a small box of Citron three boxes preserves & a basket of Almonds, address'd to Genl. Dearborn, for Mrs. Madison, which I hope she will do me the honor to accept. In quality of a Bachelor, from whom gallantry demands the first advances to a Lady, I was much disposed to address myself directly to her, but recollecting that one word from so powerful a solicitor would have more weight with her than a Volume from me, I prudently sacrificed my inclination in hopes to have the benefit of your good Offices to secure a favourable reception to these trifles. After such a strain of policy surely I may enjoy the pleasure of thinking that my humble present will be honored with a place amongst her desert, and may receive some praise with a view to compliment a Lady of so much merit. With perfect Respect I have the honor to be Sir Your Mo: Ob: servt.

WILLIAM JARVIS

RC (DLC: Rives Collection, Madison Papers).

1. See Jarvis to JM, 5 July 1805, and nn. 3–4.
2. The *Maria*, Captain Carew, arrived at Alexandria about 16 Sept. (*Alexandria Daily Advertiser*, 16 Sept. 1805).

To Albert Gallatin

DEAR SIR   PHILADA. Aug. 2. 1805

Before I left Washington I was called upon by Col. Tousard, who had been charged by Fayette with explanations &c. to his friends.[1] These confirm the need he is in of relief both permanent & present, with respect to his pecuniary affairs. The idea has been entertained by him and is strongly pressed by Toussard, that money can be got on loan from the Banks & that his friends here can greatly promote such an operation. Another idea, with Toussard at least, is that a club of voluntary loans may be brought about from his private friends. I have no doubt of the infinite distress of Fayette, and of the duty of his friends to do every thing possible for his relief, but I have not found myself authorized to give encouragement. Will it be possible to do any thing, or rather to get the Banks to do any thing? If it be you alone can give the requisite impetus? Toussard told me he should soon be with you in N. York, and wished me to prepare the way for his conversing with you on the subject. He will satisfy you, if any doubt remains, of the extreme urgency of Fayettes case, and as to term as well as to the amount of the succor.

I have just recd. from Washington the despatches by Dulton. The negociation was closed by a positive rejection of an offer from our Ministers, without a single proposition in place of it, on the other side, and in a stile not a little peremptory. The offer claimed at least a counter project, and would have produced one, if there had been no predetermination agst. it. The ratification of the Convention was also refused, but on the old conditions. The status quo, the navigation of the Mobille &c and the Spoliations subsequent to the Convention, have all passed as appears sub silentio.[2] The despatches are gone to the P. It is not impossible but he may ask the opinions of the Depts. If it be proper to make any new propositions, the points omitted in the negociation will facilitate the business. But if they be refused also, and even the provision for the claims embraced by the Convention, continue to be witheld, the question becomes pretty serious. In fact it is not a little so in its present form.

The obstinacy of Mrs. M's complaint, and the apprehension of its taking a worse form, brought us to this City, in pursuit of its medical skill. Docr. Physic signifies that a cure can certainly be effect[ed], in a short term with the use of the Knife, in a longer time without it. Mrs. M. joins in affectionate[3] to Mrs. Gallatin & to yourself.

JAMES MADISON

RC (NHi: Gallatin Papers).

1. For Anne-Louis de Tousard's involvement with Lafayette's affairs, see Lafayette to JM, 22 Apr. 1805, *PJM-SS*, 9:278–79 and n. 11.
2. *Sub silentio:* in silence.
3. JM omitted a word here.

To Thomas Jefferson

DEAR SIR   PHILADA. Aug. 2. 1805

Having passed Dulton on the road, I have received the despatches from M. & Pinkney under the delay of their coming hither from Washington. You will have recd. copies from Washington, according to instructions I left there. The business at Madrid has had an awkward termination, and if nothing, as may be expected, particularly in the absence of the Emperor, shd. alleviate it at Paris, involves some serious questions. After the parade of a Mission Extry. a refusal of all our overtures in a haughty tone, without any offer of other terms, and a perseverance in withdrawing a stipulated provision for claims admitted to be just, without ex post facto conditions manifestly unreasonable & inadmissible, form a strong appeal to the honor & sensibility of this Country. I find that, as was apprehended from the tenor of former communications, the military status quo in the Controverted districts, the navigation of the rivers running thro' W. Florida, and the spoliations subsequent to the Convention of 1802. have never had a place in the discussions. Bowdoin may perhaps be instructed, consistently with what has passed, to propose a suspension of the territorial questions, the deposit, and the French spoliations, on condition that those points be yielded, with an incorporation of the Convention of 1802 with a provision for the subsequent claims. This is the utmost within the Executive purview. If this experiment should fail, the question with the Legislature must be whether or not resort is to be had to force, to what extent, and in what mode. Perhaps the instructions to B. would be improved by including the idea of transfer[r]ing the sequel of the business hither. This would have the appearance of an advance on the part of Spain, the more so as it would be attended with a new Mission to this Country, and would be most convenient for us also, if not made by Spain a pretext for delay. It will be important to hear from Monroe, after his interviews at Paris. It is not impossible, if he should make an impression there, that without some remedy a rupture will be unavoidable, that an offer of medi[a]tion, or a promise of less formal interposition, may be given; And it will merit consideration, in what way, either should be met. Monroe talks as if he might take a trip from London home. If he comes, with a proper option to remain or return as may be thought proper, and so as not too much to commit the Govt. or himself, the trip may perhaps produce political speculations abroad, that may do no harm.

Inclosed are several letters from C. P: also a communication adding another instance to the provoking insults from British Commanders.[1] I am not able to say how far the insult was aggravated by a violation of our territorial rights.

We arrived here on monday last; and have fixt ourselves in a pleasant, and as is believed a very safe part of the City (between 7 & 8 Streets. and Walnut & Chesnut). Docr. Physic has no doubt of effecting the cure for which his assistance was required; and without the use of the knife. But this, if his patient could be reconciled to it, would greatly save time. Yrs. with respectful attachment

JAMES MADISON

RC (DLC: Jefferson Papers). Docketed by Jefferson as received 8 Aug., with his note: "Span. affairs." Enclosures not found.

1. The editors have been unable to identify which of Charles Pinckney's letters JM transmitted. For the incident with the British to which JM probably referred, see Jacob Wagner to JM, 5 Aug. 1805, n. 6.

§ From Robert W. Fox. *2 August 1805, Falmouth.* "Be pleased to receive enclosed a List of American Shipping arrived in this District for the last 6 Months ending the 25 June [not found]—many other ships have touched off this port, but having received orders to proceed to foreign ports, particular[l]y to Holland, France &c⟨e⟩. I had it not in my power to procure the particulars.

"The Seamen in this neighbourhood in general have been protected from the Impress, except in cases when they have not had Certificates, but Some of these have even been restored on the Regulating Captain for the Impress Service being assured that they were American Citizens, and Similar favours have been granted me by Captains of Ships of War.

"Our Harvest promises well, thoug⟨h⟩ Sound Wheat has got up to 12/ a 13/ ⅌ Bushel—Rice is also getting up.

"I expect this will be made a Naval po⟨rt⟩ as Moorings for Ships of the Line are laying down in our Road; and Government have also permitted Goods to be Bonded here without paying Duties."

Adds in a postscript: "Premiums of Insurance in Goods ⅌ American Vessels are advanced to 20 a 25 ⅌: in consequence of the Spaniards capturing Such Vessels loaden in England."

RC (DNA: RG 59, CD, Falmouth, vol. 2). 2 pp.; in a clerk's hand, signed by Fox.

§ From John Oakley. *2 August 1805.* "Finding the duties of a Justice of the peace for Washington County to interfere injuriously with my Office of Collector of the Customs for the District of George Town I beg leave through you to present my resignation of the Appointment of Justice of the peace to the President."[1]

RC (DNA: RG 59, LRD). 1 p.; docketed by Jefferson, with JM's note at foot of document: "Mr Wagner will inclose this to the President."

1. Oakley was named collector of customs at Georgetown, D.C., on 1 Oct. 1801 and justice of the peace for Washington County on 5 Apr. 1802 (Richard P. Jackson, *The Chronicles of Georgetown, D.C., from 1751 to 1878* [Washington, 1878], 101; *Senate Exec. Proceedings,* 1:417–18).

§ From Carlos Martínez de Yrujo. *2 August 1805, Philadelphia.* The governor of Pensacola, commander of West Florida, has informed him of the declaration made by Manuel Durante, captain of the Spanish schooner *Our Lady of Mount Carmel,* who has just arrived at Pensacola from New Orleans. It appears that toward the end of February, coming in distress from Dolphin Island[1] to Petitbois, and finding themselves in need of provisions, they headed for Francis Kreps's home. At their arrival Kreps told Durante that the American cutter, which had been off that coast for some days previously, had sent its whole crew ashore at the home of

Mr. Nicolle, armed with rifles, swords, and pistols; that they entered the house and took off the coffee and sugar deposited there,[2] which was the cargo of a vessel the name of which Yrujo has not heard. They forcibly took a boat from a neighbor to carry the coffee and sugar on board the cutter. They subsequently went to the farm of Jean Baptiste Bordereau, which is in the Pascagoula district, territory of Mobile, where they landed in the same way, firing as soon as they landed, and stealing the considerable quantity of fowl they lit upon, as well as whatever food-stuffs they found.

It likewise appears that the captain and crew of the cutter had landed at various points on the coast of the territory under the governor's command and tried to persuade the inhabitants that they were now not Spanish but Americans. They also held other talks of this nature with the inhabitants, the object of which cannot be ambiguous.

To the catalogue of these insults committed on the coasts of West Florida by this United States vessel, he adds the following report, which the governor of Pensacola sent him separately.

It seems that on returning from New Orleans to Pensacola, the Spanish schoo-ner *Magdalena* and sloop *Josefina*, commanded by the owners, Josef Galez and Benito García, met the American cutter in St. Louis Bay, territory of Mobile. The cutter fired one loaded and two blank volleys at them and as a result they headed alongside it. After they got there, the cutter fired three rounds of shot at them, one of which passed very close to García. The American cutter made them put astern and detained them for twenty-four hours, causing them to lose the favorable wind they had. The cutter did the same to seven more small craft, all Spanish. They put a passenger, who was traveling in one of them, on the sandbar and kept him there all night for no more reason than that, on another occasion, he had arrested three Americans who had stolen his boat.

This insulting and even hostile conduct on the part of a vessel in the service of the United States and in the waters and on the coasts of His Catholic Majesty cannot fail to fill with indignation the government of the United States, whose instructions for this vessel would have been peaceable and just. For this reason he refrains from making any comment, persuaded that the government of the United States will determine immediately on taking the necessary steps for investigating the truth and that, when the bad conduct of the commander of the American cut-ter is known, he will be duly punished.[3]

RC (DNA: RG 59, NFL, Spain, vol. 2). 4 pp.; in Spanish; in a clerk's hand, except for Yrujo's complimentary close and signature; docketed by Wagner, with his note: "Com-plaints against the Revenue Cutter on the N. Orleans Station."

1. A marginal note here in Wagner's hand reads: "near the mouth of Mobille."
2. For the seizure of the coffee and sugar, see William C. C. Claiborne to JM, 27 Feb. 1805, *PJM-SS*, 9:70–71.
3. JM's 6 Aug. 1805 reply to Yrujo has not been found but is calendared in the index to State Department notes to foreign legations (DNA: RG 59, Notes to Foreign Ministers and Consuls, vol. 1).

From William Hull

Sɪʀ   Dᴇᴛʀᴏɪᴛ 3d. Augt. 1805.

I arrived at this place on the evening of the 1st. of July, in company with Mr. Griswold, the Secretary of the Territory. Judge Woodward had arrived the day before, and Judge Bates was present. Having taken the Oaths before the Vice-President of the U.S., I administred the same to the two Judges and the Secretary in the presence of a number of Citizens who assembled on the occasion. The inclosed paper, marked No. 1.[1] is a copy of an address, which I delivered to a numerous assembly of the People. It has been translated into the french language, read in the churches, and communicated in various other ways. Nos. 2. 3. 4. & 5,[2] are mere complimentary addresses, with my answers, I inclose them for the purpose of shewing the disposition of the People towards the goverment.

The distruction of the Town of Detroit[3] has caused great distress to the people, and subjected the officers to great inconvenience. On my arrival every house was crouded, and it was more than a week before I could obtain the least accomodation.

I am now in a small farmers house, about a mile above the ruins, and must satisfy myself to remain in this situation, during the next winter at least. It has not been ascertained how the fire took place, but it is generally beleived, it was by design, and by persons interested in the lumber trade. Contracts had been previously made, for all the lumber at the mills, and which could be sawed this season, which was a novel arrangement in the Country. The People are daily recovering from their difficulties, they appear perfectly satisfied with the manner in which their goverment has commenced, and the most perfect harmony subsists among all the officers.

On my arrival, I found the Citizens of Detroit had laid out a new Town, nearly on a similar plan with the old one, and had included the common,[4] which they pretend to claim in consequence of a grant from the french goverment, and having used it as a common pasture, since the settlement of the Country. Their title to it, is at least doubtfull, and it will probably rest with Congress to determine what disposition shall be made of it. After a conversation with the Judges, it was determined to attempt to convince the proprietors of the impropriety of their proceedings. They observed it had arisen from the necessity of the case; that they were without houses, and their families must suffer, if they did not take measures, to prepare houses for the winter. We assured them, we would make it a primary object, and would make the best arrangements in our power for their accomodation. They very readily agreed to relinquish their plan, and wait for our arrangements. We immediately fixed on a plan, and employed the best Surveyor we could find in the Country to lay out the Streets, Squares and lots. If possible the plan shall be transmitted by this conveyance. I hope it will be approved by the goverment. The principal part of the grounds embraced by the plan belong to the U.S. without any question. Many of the lots in the old Town are cut up by the Streets, which has reduced us to the necessity of exchanging them for lots on the Domain or Common, we have likewise from the necessity of the case, concluded to sell as many lots on the Domain or Common, as will be necessary for the accomodation of those Citizens who wish to build this Season, and did not own lots in the Town. This rule, however we make, expressly subject to the ratification of Congress. We think, we have great reason to beleive, our conduct will be approved, because we obtain two important objects by it; first, a Town or City laid out on a regular plan; secondly the accommodation of those people, who have suffered by the late calamity. And I have no doubt, but a third will be obtained, viz, the value of the lands of the United States, will be greatly increased. I shall detail this subject more fully to the Secretary of the Treasury.

I have received no intimation whether a third Judge has been appointed. If not, I hope it will not be delayed. We have been in constant session in our legislative capacity, since the first of July. We find much embarrasment in the adoption of laws, only the laws of three or four states have arrived. They are not in all cases applicable to our situation. Can there be an objection to an alteration of the law, and giving us the powers of legislation, subject to the revision of Congress. On this subject, we shall make a representation to Congress.

In no part of the U.S. or Europe where I have resided, is the expence of living so great as at this place. It will be for Congress to judge whether it will not be expedient and indeed absolutely necessary to increase the Salaries of their Officers. The Secretary has been strongly inclined to resign immediately. I have persuaded him to remain untill the next Session of Congress. I owe it to Judge Woodward to say, that I receive great assistance from his talents, his zeal and Industry. Judge Bates is a young Man of good understanding, great purity of mind, and wants nothing but experience to render him eminently usefull. I am with very great respect your most obedt. Servt.

WM. HULL

P.S. We have adopted temporary Seals for the different departments of Goverment; we wait for permanent ones from your Office.

WH.

RC and enclosures (DNA: RG 59, TP, Michigan, vol. 1). RC docketed by Wagner as received 31 Aug., with his note: "Mem. The oaths are all informal, as the Vice President was incompetent to administer that to the Govr. The seals may be procured in Albany or elsewhere by the Govr. himself." For enclosures, see nn. 1–2.

1. Enclosure No. 1 (4 pp.; docketed by Wagner; undated; conjectural date assigned based on enclosure No. 4 [see n. 2 below]; printed in *Michigan Pioneer and Historical Collections* 31 [1902]: 531–35) is a copy of Hull's [8 July 1805] address to the people of the territory, listing the rights to which they were entitled under their new government, stressing the importance of "a well organized & disciplined Militia," discussing the ramifications of their being situated so close to Canada, and urging "reverence & gratitude . . . to God, and Justice to each other" as the guiding principles of the government.

2. Enclosure No. 2 (1 p.; docketed by Wagner; printed ibid., 526–27) is a copy of an undated letter of congratulations to Hull on his appointment signed by Francis Navarre, John Anderson, and Lewis Bond as representatives of the citizens of Sargent township. Enclosure No. 3 (1 p.; docketed by Wagner; printed ibid., 527–28) is Hull's 9 July 1805 reply. Enclosure No. 4 (2 pp.; docketed by Wagner; printed ibid., 529–30) is a 15 July 1805 reply to Hull's 8 July communication to the people (see n. 1 above), signed by James Henry, Elijah Brush, George McDougall, Chabert Joncaire, and George Meldrum on behalf of the inhabitants of Detroit, expressing satisfaction with the governor's goals, and a hope that the people of the United States would provide aid to sufferers from the fire (see n. 3 below). Enclosure No. 5 (1 p.; docketed by Wagner; printed ibid., 528–29) is Hull's 16 July 1805 response.

3. On 11 June 1805 a fire supposed to have begun in a livery stable destroyed every building in Detroit except the blockhouse (F. Clever Bald, *Detroit's First American Decade, 1796 to 1805* [Ann Arbor, Mich., 1948], 239–41).

4. The common was an open section of land outside the eastern part of the palisades surrounding the town. It extended from Detroit to the nearest farm (ibid., 23).

From Lafayette

MY DEAR FRIEND   MONT D'OR 15h Therm. 3d August 1805

Mr. David parish,[1] now a french Citizen, and Inhabitant of Antwerpt is Going to Visit America. The Character of His House, His family, and Himself will Sufficiently Introduce Him. But I am Happy in this Instance to Indulge a lively Sentiment of friendship, and a deep Sense of Obligations to Him and His Worthy parents. Mr. John parish His father, during our Captivity of olmütz, Was the American Consul at Hamburgh, and towards the End of it returned to His private Station of an Eminent Merchant at that place—in Both Capacities He Acquired an Everlasting Title to my Gratitude and that of Every friend Who is pleased to Have Some Concern for me. His local and personal Situation Gave Additional merit to those Acts of kindness fully and Affectionately Confered. They Have Been Continued as long as We Have Remained in a foreign land. My Wife; family, and Myself Have often Wished for Opportunities to Express the Grateful feelings of our Hearts. David parish His Son Has Been an Affectionate partaker in those Cares, of h[i]s. Let me Hope this Idea May With My American Friends, and particularly With You, My dear Madison, Contribute to the Good Reception to Which He is, in Every other Respect, fully Entitled.

I am Indebted to His father for a Sum of forty five thousand francs. He is Endeavouring to Make a Loan for me in Holland. Permit me to Refer Myself to the Letters of Which Mr. Livingston and Colonel touzard Have Been the Bearers.[2] My debt to Mr. John parish forms a part of the plan for a General Clearance Which the Munificence of Congress Has Enabled me to Submit to You. Perhaps While I am writing His Son david is Rendering me the Additional Service to increase their Claim Upon me By doing, Himself or through His friends, What Had Been Expected from Mess: Willink and Staphorst. That You Will Know When He Gets to Washington. But in all Events I must make Known to You My Original debt to the family.

I am Returned to the Hot Waters of Montd'or from Which My Broken Limb Has, Last Year, derived Great Benefit.[3] I shall from Here pay a Visit to My Aunt and Return to la Grange By the fi[r]st Vendemiair or Rather the 22d. September, for they Say our *New Calendar* will not Last Long. I am the More desirous to Be Nearer paris as My Son is in the Active Army of Holland. No Answer from the president and You Has Yet Come to Hand, Except A Very kind one to a short Letter from me dated 1st July Last Year.[4] I am Very Anxious to Hear of the Arrival of Mr. Livingston and Col Touzard.[5] May My Conduct, and My Motives, Have Met With Your Approbation. I Want it More than Words Can Express. As to pecuniary Interest I am Very Sure You are doing for the Best, and from an Affectionate Confidence in Your friendship I forbear Apologizing for the trouble I Give You.

Adieu, My dear friend, present My Affectionate Respects to our Worthy president to Whom I Have a few Weeks Ago Writen By Mr. parish. With Every Sentiment of tender and Grateful Regard I am Your old Constant friend

LAFAYETTE

RC (PHi: Dreer Collection; Lafayette Letters). Docketed by JM.

1. Antwerp merchant David Parish (d. 1826) arrived in New York in January 1806 to superintend the interests of a syndicate consisting of European financiers Gabriel-Julien Ouvrard, Hope & Co., and himself, with the aid of Baring Brothers & Co., in a plan to transfer Spanish gold and silver bullion in neutral vessels from Vera Cruz, Mexico, to Europe via the United States. The syndicate also received permission from the Spanish government to carry on trade with Mexico that had formerly been forbidden to foreigners. By November 1806 Parish, who had moved to Philadelphia, had received $1,250,000 in bullion that he transferred to Hope & Co. After the passage of the 1807 Embargo Act, Parish received permission from Treasury secretary Albert Gallatin for the syndicate's chartered American vessels to continue this exchange. By the fall of 1808 all the Spanish bullion had been transferred from Mexico, and operations ceased. Parish lived in the United States until 1816, buying and developing property along the St. Lawrence River in New York. He also played a principal role in raising funds to finance the War of 1812 (Walters and Walters,

"The American Career of David Parish," *Journal of Economic History* 4 [1944]: 149, 151–54, 156–61, 165).

2. For Lafayette's 22 Apr. 1805 letter carried by Anne-Louis de Tousard, a copy of which was probably also carried by Robert R. Livingston, see *PJM-SS*, 9:276–79.

3. In February 1803 Lafayette slipped on the ice in Paris and broke his thigh. He submitted to treatment by a new machine for bone-setting that a friend had invented, which caused him to be in extreme pain for forty days and left him with stiffness "and a permanent limp" (Olivier Bernier, *Lafayette: Hero of Two Worlds* [New York, 1983], 275).

4. No letter of 1 July 1804 from Lafayette to JM has been found, but Lafayette wrote to Jefferson on that date. Jefferson received the letter on 24 Oct.; he replied on 10 Mar. 1805 with information about locating Lafayette's lands near New Orleans (DLC: Jefferson Papers).

5. For Robert R. Livingston's arrival in the United States, see Livingston to JM, 29 June 1805, *PJM-SS*, 9:501–2. For Tousard's arrival, see Tousard to JM, 10 July 1805.

§ From William C. C. Claiborne. *3 August 1805, New Orleans*. "Having understood that Mr Moralis had been instructed by the King of Spain to despose of all, the vacant Lands in *East and West Florida*, and to open his office in this City, I immediatly addressed to the Marquis of Casa Calvo a Letter of which the enclosed is a Copy."[1]

RC and enclosure (DNA: RG 59, TP, Orleans, vol. 7); letterbook copy and letterbook copy of enclosure (Ms-Ar: Claiborne Executive Journal, vol. 15). RC 1 p.; in a clerk's hand, signed by Claiborne; docketed by Wagner as received 10 Sept. For enclosure, see n. 1.

1. The enclosure (1 p.; docketed by Wagner; printed in Rowland, *Claiborne Letter Books*, 3:146) is a copy of Claiborne to Casa Calvo, 3 Aug. 1805, stating that he understood that Juan Ventura Morales had received orders from the king "to dispose of all the vacant Lands in *West* and East Florida" and that Morales was opening an office for that purpose in New Orleans. He asked Casa Calvo if the information was correct and if Morales would "undertake to exercise his functions during his Continuance within this Territory."

§ From William C. C. Claiborne. *3 August 1805, New Orleans*. "On the 30th. ultimo, Mr. Gurley the Register of the Land Office, left this City, on a Visit to the several Counties of the Territory, with a view, of making such explanations of the late Act of Congress 'for ascertaining and adjusting the Titles, and Claims to Land within the Territory of Orleans,['] as may tend to check any disquietude which has arisen, and to insure the speedy execution of the Law. A letter from Mr. Gurley to me, announcing the Objects of his Journey, and a Copy of my answer are herewith enclosed for your perusal."[1]

RC and enclosures (DNA: RG 59, TP, Orleans, vol. 7); letterbook copy and letterbook copy of second enclosure (Ms-Ar: Claiborne Executive Journal, vol. 15). RC 1 p.; in a clerk's hand, signed and addressed by Claiborne; docketed by Wagner as received on 10 Sept. For enclosures, see n. 1.

1. The first enclosure is John Ward Gurley to Claiborne, 25 July 1805 (5 pp.; docketed by Wagner; printed in Carter, *Territorial Papers, Orleans*, 9:476–78), announcing his intention to tour "the western and northern part of this Territory" to explain the law regulating

land titles in Orleans Territory and to forestall efforts already being made to incite alarm among the populace. He added that he would not make the trip if Claiborne thought "any public inconvenience" would result from Gurley's absence from New Orleans. For the 2 Mar. 1805 "act for ascertaining and adjusting the titles and claims to land, within the territory of Orleans, and the district of Louisiana," see *U.S. Statutes at Large*, 2:324–29. The second enclosure (2 pp.; docketed by Wagner; printed in Rowland, *Claiborne Letter Books*, 3:140–41) is a copy of Claiborne's 28 July reply stating that he believed the proposed tour for the reasons given would be "highly useful" and adding that Gurley could "best determine" how far his duties as register would allow his absence from the city "for so short a time."

§ From William C. C. Claiborne. *3 August 1805, New Orleans.* "On the 6th of June last, I had the Honor to inclose you a Correspondence betwe[e]n Colonel Freeman and myself,[1] relative to a public building in his possession, which I desired the use of, for the accommadation of the Federal Court, but which the Colonel refused to evacuate, without orders from the Secretary of War.[2] I am daily in expectation, of hearing from you on that subject, and I flatter myself, that the Colonel will be directed to retire from a *building*, which for some weeks, he has retained in defiance to my Authority, and to the injury of the public Interest; but whither *it* should be appropriated to the sessions of the District Court, or to the purpose for which it was originally intended *a public School-Room*, the President will be pleased to decide.

"The Mayor of the City, solicits that the building in question, may not be deverted from the laudable object for which it was designed, and that until provision be made for a public School, he begs *it* may be used as a Library Hall, for the public Library about to be established in this City. A Copy of the Mayors *Letter* to me on this Occasion, and of my *answer*, are herewith enclosed,[3] which I pray you to lay before the President of the United States."

RC and enclosures (DNA: RG 59, TP, Orleans, vol. 7); letterbook copy and letterbook copy of second enclosure (Ms-Ar: Claiborne Executive Journal, vol. 15). RC 2 pp.; in a clerk's hand, signed and addressed by Claiborne; docketed by Wagner, with his note: "Schoolhouse occupied by Colo. Freeman." For enclosures, see n. 3.

1. *PJM-SS*, 9:437–38 and n. 1.
2. On 14 June 1805 Henry Dearborn wrote Lt. Col. Constant Freeman that if the building in question was "attached to the civil department, the governor had authority over it" (Carter, *Territorial Papers, Orleans*, 9:488 n. 36).
3. The first enclosure (3 pp.; docketed by Wagner; printed ibid., 487–88) is a copy of John Watkins to Claiborne, 2 Aug. 1805, stating that the building had been built as a free public school maintained at the Spanish king's expense, asking why the building "consacrated under the arbitrary goverment of Spain to the education of youth, be now under the peaceful goverm̃t. of the United States converted into the head quarters of a Military chief?," and suggesting that it be used to house a public library. The second enclosure (2 pp.; docketed by Wagner; printed in Rowland, *Claiborne Letter Books*, 3:147–48) is a copy of Claiborne to Watkins, 3 Aug. 1805, stating that he was aware the building had formerly been a schoolhouse, that Freeman had refused to move without orders from Dearborn, that the case had been referred to the president, and that Claiborne would refer Watkins's letter to him also.

§ From James Simpson. *3 August 1805, Tangier.* No. 99. "The United States Frigate President having only brought to off the Bay for a moment, prevents my addressing you so fully as I could have wished by so good an opportunity. I sincerely congratulate you on the re-establishment of Peace with Tripoly.[1] Mr Gavino advised me of it and it is now confirmed to me by Captain James Barron, which is the only intelligence (besides report) I have yet received of it.

"I did not however fail of acquainting His Imperial Majesty on the 24h. Ulto when I received Mr Gavinos Letter, as the Departure of the Meshouda (depending entirely on this happy event)[2] I knew was a matter he had much at heart, and it would not have been well to have allowed the news to reach him from any other person before myself.

"The Express I expect will return tomorrow or next day.

"A deputation from Tremcen and that Neighborhood have arrived at Mequinez to acquaint Muley Soliman the people of that Country had proclaimed him their Sovereign—he has sent his Brother Muley Mussa with a small Army to ascertain the fact.

"As the Frigate does not Anchor I can only repeat the assurance of my being Sir Your Most Obedt Servant."

RC (DNA: RG 59, CD, Tangier, vol. 2). 2 pp.; docketed by Wagner as received 17 Sept.

1. For the treaty of peace with Tripoli, see Tobias Lear to JM, 5 July 1805, and n. 8.

2. For the *Meshouda*, see Simpson to JM, 26 Oct. and 24 Dec. 1804, *PJM-SS*, 8:228–29, 421–22.

From Thomas Jefferson

DEAR SIR   MONTICELLO Aug. 4. 05

On my return from Bedford two days ago I recieved your favor of July 24 and learnt with sincere regret that mrs Madison's situation required her going to Philadelphia. I suppose the choice between Physic & Baynham[1] was well weighed. I hope the result will be speedy & salutary, and that we shall see you in this quarter before the season passes over.

A letter from Charles Pinckney of May 22.[2] informs me that Spain refuses to settle a limit, & perseveres in witholding the ratification of the convention. He says not a word of the status quo, from which I conclude it has not been proposed. I observe by the papers that Dulton is arrived with the public dispatches, from which we shall know the particulars. I think the status quo, if not already proposed, should be immediately offered through Bowdoin Should it even be refused, the refusal to settle a limit is not of itself a sufficient cause of war, nor is the witholding a ratification worthy of such a redress. Yet these acts shew a purpose both in Spain & France against which we ought to provide before the conclusion of a peace. I think therefore we should take into consideration whether we ought not immediately to propose to England an eventual treaty of alliance, to come into force when[e]ver (within   ³ years) a war shall take place with Spain or France. It may be proper for the ensuing Congress to make some preparations for such an event, and it should be in our power to shew we have done the same. This for your consideration.

Mr. Wagner writes me that two black convicts from Surinam are landed at Philadelphia.[4] Being on the spot you will have a better opportunity of judging what should be done with them. To me it seems best that we should send them to England with a proper representation against such a measure. If the transportation is not within any of the regular appropriations, it will come properly on the contingent fund. If the law does not stand in the way of such an act, & you think as I do, it may be immediately carried into execution. Accept for mrs Madison & yourself my affectionate salutations & assurances of constant esteem & respect.

TH: JEFFERSON

RC (DLC); FC (DLC: Jefferson Papers).

1. This was the "celebrated" Dr. William Baynham (1749–1814), an Essex, Virginia, physician who received his initial training in Virginia then went to England in 1769, where he studied and worked at St. Thomas's Hospital. Disappointed of a promised professorship in 1781, he became a fellow of the Royal College of Surgeons and practiced surgery in London before returning to the United States in 1785. He developed an extensive practice and was skilled at operations for "stone, cataract, and extra-uterine conception" (Wingfield, *History of Caroline County, Virginia*, 346).

2. Jefferson received Pinckney's 22 May 1805 letter on 2 Aug. 1805, DLC: Jefferson Papers.

3. Left blank in RC and FC.

4. For this incident, see Turell Tufts to JM, 13 June 1805, *PJM-SS*, 9:467–68, and JM to Peter Muhlenberg, 19 July 1805. Wagner reported the convicts' arrival in his 27 July letter to Jefferson, DLC: Jefferson Papers.

From Louis-Marie Turreau

A BALTIMORE le 16 Thermidor An 13,

MONSIEUR   2 de l'Empire [4 Aug. 1805]

Je viens de recevoir des plaintes de Mr. le Préfet colonial de la Martinique, Sur ce que le Capitaine Drummond, l'un des propriétaires et Commandant de Navire le *Fox* de Boston, abusant des facilités accordées aux Batiments de votre Nation d'aller prendre leur chargement dans tous les points accessibles de la Côte de Cette Isle, S'est évadé de la mode du *Robert* dans la nuit du 24 au 25 Avril sans payer les droits de Douane montant à 1241 Dollars.

En vous transmettant ci joint Monsieur copie de la lettre de ce Préfet à Mr. Le Commissaire des Relations Commerciales à Boston qui constate cette plainte,[1] J'ai moins l'intention de reclamer votre intervention dans la poursuite que ce Commissaire pourra prendre contre ce Captaine pour la restitution des droits, que de vous engager à prendre telles mesures que vous jugerez à propos pour empêcher la récidive d'un Semblable abus, qui certainement priverait votre Commerce des facilités qui lui ont été accordées jusqu'ici, ou qui l'entraverait de difficultés aussi désagréables qu'onéreuses. Je vous prie, Monsieur, d'agréer l'assurance de ma haute Considération

TURREAU

CONDENSED TRANSLATION

Has just received complaints from the colonial prefect of Martinique that Captain Drummond, one of the owners and master of the Ship *Fox* of Boston, abusing the privileges granted to American vessels of loading at all the accessible points on the island, escaped, like the *Robert*, on the night of 24 to 25 Apr., without paying customs duties amounting to $1,241.

In sending JM a copy of the prefect's letter to the commissary of commercial relations at Boston giving notice of this complaint, has the intention not so much of demanding JM's intervention in the action the commissary may undertake against Captain Drummond for payment of the duty but to call upon JM to take such measures as JM will judge proper to prevent the repetition of such abuses, which will certainly deprive U.S. commerce of the facilities which have been granted to it up to now, or involve it in difficulties equally disagreeable and burdensome.

RC and enclosure (DNA: RG 59, NFL, France, vol. 2–3). For enclosure, see n. 1.

1. The enclosure (2 pp.; in French; certified as correct by Laussat and Turreau) is a copy of a 27 May 1805 letter from Pierre Clément de Laussat to Marc Antoine Alexis Giraud asking him to inform the governor of Massachusetts and the judge of the court at Boston, and to publish the information in the newspapers.

§ From William C. C. Claiborne. *4 August 1805, New Orleans.* "I have the Honor to transmit You, a Copy of a Letter from the Mayor of this City, communicating to me, three Decrees of the City Council, (which in their execution required my co-operation) together with a Copy of my response.[1] Those papers sufficiently explain themselves, and it remains only for me to say, that the *evacuation* of the Forts alluded to in one of the Decrees, *is* considered by me as advisable. These Forts give no security to *the Town;* some eligible position for *its defence,* and *that* of *the Country generally on the Mississippi,* aught to be selected some where about the English turn,[2] and should be strongly fortified."

RC and enclosures (DNA: RG 59, TP, Orleans, vol. 7); letterbook copy and letterbook copy of fifth enclosure (Ms-Ar: Claiborne Executive Journal, vol. 15). RC 1 p.; in a clerk's hand, signed by Claiborne; docketed by Wagner as received 10 Sept., with his note: "Demolition of the fortifications, Custom house &c. requested by the Council." Minor differences between the copies have not been noted. For enclosures, see n. 1.

1. The enclosures (8 pp.; docketed by Wagner) are copies of (1) John Watkins to Claiborne, 26 July 1805, printed in Carter, *Territorial Papers, Orleans,* 9:481–82, stating that when he took possession of the mayor's office, he discovered three city council resolutions which he was enclosing to Claiborne for a decision, adding that the "riotous conduct of the Town guard" showed they should be "confined to close quarters" and placed under the control of their officers, and agreeing with the other two resolutions asking that the city receive possession of the property where the old customhouse and Spanish forts were located, which would enable the city to clear out the streets and fill in ditches of stagnant water; (2) a 20 July 1805 city council resolution, ibid., 482, asking that Claiborne order the old customhouse destroyed and the materials carried away; (3) a 20 July 1805 council resolution, ibid., 483, requesting the same to be done to the "forts and batteries Surrounding the City," thus allowing the city to expand and the water-filled ditches around the forts to be filled in; (4) a 20 July 1805 council resolution, ibid., 483, asking that the troops of the town guard be lodged in barracks as requested by their officers and that Claiborne order the removal of the regular army troops now occupying the guardhouse so the town guard could be housed there; and (5) Claiborne's 2 Aug. 1805 reply to Watkins, printed in Rowland, *Claiborne Letter Books,* 3:143–45, stating that the old customhouse had been delivered to him as national property, which he lacked the power to destroy, and suggesting that the council submit its request to the commissioners who would arrive soon to investigate the validity of land claims. He said that the same observation applied to the forts, but that since the stagnant water accumulating there did endanger public health, he would consent to the destruction of them all, except Fort Charles and Fort St. Louis, which were garrisoned by regular troops, and to the draining of the ditches around them. He added that he saw no need for a day guard at the city hall but that one might be needed at night to secure the property and the prisoners at the jail, to accommodate which he would consent to the removal of the regular troops; he further added that if it were determined that a guard was required both day and night, it might be more economical to use the services of the regular army for that purpose.

2. The English Turn, or English Bend, as it was better known, was a deep turn in the Mississippi about eighteen miles downriver from New Orleans (Carl J. Ekberg, "The English Bend: Forgotten Gateway to New Orleans," in *La Salle and His Legacy: Frenchmen and Indians in the Lower Mississippi Valley,* ed. Patricia K. Galloway [Jackson, Miss., 1982], 214).

§ From William Lee. *4 August 1805, Bordeaux.* "I take the liberty to enclose you a copy of my letters to Genl Lincoln the Collector of Boston concerning the Brig Ranger Capt Hooper."[1]

RC and enclosures (DNA: RG 59, CD, Bordeaux, vol. 2). RC 1 p. For enclosures, see n. 1.

1. For the *Ranger,* see William Lee to JM, 18 June 1805, *PJM-SS,* 9:480 and n. 1, and 20 July 1805. The enclosures (10 pp.) are copies of (1) Lee to Benjamin Lincoln, 25 July 1805, enclosing a copy of his 15 June letter to Lincoln, and stating that since Captain Hooper had produced the required bonds, Lee had allowed him to depart for a Spanish port and from there to Boston; that he was enclosing a copy of the bond; and that on Hooper's arrival Lincoln could decide on the case as he thought just; (2) Lee to Albert Gallatin, 17 June 1805,

enclosing a copy of Lee's 15 June letter to Lincoln, stating that he understood Hooper had written to the government on the matter, that others were urging Hooper to protest and to throw his ship on Lee's hands, and that Lee hoped that on reading the enclosure Gallatin would approve his conduct; (3) Lee to Lincoln, 15 June 1805 (see *PJM-SS*, 9:480 n. 1); (4) a 19 July 1805 bond for $4,000 signed by Benjamin Hooper, David Smith (who was then the captain of the *Ranger*), Joseph Nye Jr., and Penn Townsend, with an addendum by Lee, also signed by Hooper, Smith, Nye, and Townsend, ensuring that on arrival at Boston, Smith would deliver the *Ranger* and its papers to Lincoln, failing which, $2,000 of the stated funds would be paid to Lee for the use of the United States.

¶ From Seth Botts Wigginton. Letter not found. *4 August 1805*. Acknowledged in JM to Wigginton, 10 Aug. 1805, where it is described as requesting a copy of William Lee's dispatch to the State Department concerning the ship *Easter* and its papers.

To James Monroe

Sir,   Department of State August 5th. 1805
   There can be little doubt that the facts contained in the inclosed documents respecting the firing into the American Brig Hannah, whereby Isaac Bridges, the Master, came by his death, amount to murder in the Capt. of the British Cutter. You will therefore be pleased to lay them before the British Government as an additional example of the wanton barbarity with which our Citizens are treated at sea by its ships of war, and call upon it to bring the Offender to trial and punishment. Should this be declined, and you are advised by Counsel that the evidence you may be able to procure thro' the aid of Mr. Lyman, will justify a prosecution, you will cause it to be conducted at the expence of the United States. I have the honor to be &c

James Madison

Letterbook copy (DNA: RG 59, IM, vol. 6).

To John Pearson and James Kimball

Gentlemen.   Department of State August 5th 1805.
   I have received your letter of the 22d. ult, with its enclosures respecting the murder of Capt. Bridges of the Brig Hannah through the orders given by Capt. Le Roux of the British Cutter Providence of London to fire into the former vessel, and also representing that in consequence of this conduct of the British Captain, the Hannah's voyage being changed, a considerable loss accrued to you.

To the Minister of the U. States in London instructions will be given to make a statement of the affair to the British Government[1] in order that Capt. Le Roux may be brought to punishment, but for your pecuniary loss it is necessary that you should prosecute him in the ordinary course of the law. I am &c.

JAMES MADISON.

Letterbook copy (DNA: RG 59, DL, vol. 15).

1. See JM to James Monroe, 5 Aug. 1805.

From Anthony Merry

SIR,   WASHINGTON August 5th. 1805
I have received the Honor of your Letter of the 30th. of last Month requesting me to use my good offices to procure the Release of Benjamin Moore, an American Citizen, who is said to have been impressed, and to be on board His Majesty's Ship Liander.

I shall not fail, Sir, to transmit without Loss of Time the Document which your Letter inclosed, proving the Citizenship of the abovementioned Individual, to the Commander in Chief of His Majesty's Ships on the Halifax Station, and to accompany it with the Desire which you have expressed for his Discharge. I have the Honor to be, with high Respect and Consideration, Sir, your most obedient humble Servant

ANT: MERRY

RC (DNA: RG 59, NFL, Great Britain, vol. 3). 1 p.; in a clerk's hand, signed by Merry; docketed by Wagner, with his note: "impressment of Benj. Moore."

From Jacob Wagner

DEAR SIR   DEP. STATE 5 Augt. 1805.
I have been honored with your several favors of the 30th. ult. 1 & 2 currt.[1] When I conversed with Mr. Merry about the privateer Les Amies, he expressed no decided sentiment, on which account a communication for him is enclosed.[2] He proposed proceeding for Philada. to day or to morrow, whither, I am told, Mr. Foster is already gone. I have, as you directed, made the enquiry, respecting the Golden Grove, from the Collector of Norfolk.[3] An answer to Oliver is enclosed.[4] Lamson's account amounts to

about $1400 but it is altogether inadmissible, and the enclosed answer, which, if you approve it, I beg you to return, has been drafted on that idea.[5] Having in the office a survey of Passamaquoddy Bay taken by the Commors. who decided the Northern Boundary, I shall be able, on the return of the papers to ascertain, whether the place, where the Busy insulted the Revenue Boat and captured the Brig belonging to Newbury Port,[6] is within the jurisdiction of the U.States. The papers of Nicklin and Griffith being very voluminous, I had it not in my power to read more than the memorial.[7] It appears to me, that until Genl. Armstrong's report upon it is received, it would be unsafe to recommit it to him, more especially as it seems to have been definitively acted upon whether correctly or otherwise. How far they have fairly represented his impressions respecting the incapacity of insurers to step into the shoes of the insured in case of loss is to me very doubtful.

Mr. Lear has lately drawn £6000 Stg. on Baring & Co. on whom he had a credit to a considerable amount, but without a correspondent remittance having been made on account of their engaging to advance. Mr. Lear has not advised us of the purpose of his drafts nor indeed of their being made. As Mr. Gallatin will probably purchase the remittance at NewYork, the enclosed letter requesting it to be made is addressed to him there.[8] Mr. Sheldon's note will further explain the affair.[9]

Mr. Grainger has mentioned to me some circumstances with a view to guard against the appointment of a Mr. Seymour, who he understands is about to apply for a Consulate.[10] He observes that Mr. S. belongs to a very respectable family in Connecticut, but his own character is so much tainted as to render him unworthy of such a trust and as to justify the many criticisms which will doubtless be made upon him, if he should succeed in his expectations of an office.

The aid of Colo. Simms & Mr. Deblois has not been sufficient to enable me hitherto to obtain a passage for the five 18 pounders for Algiers, which are ready to be shipped to meet the other stores at Kennebec.[11] They shall be forwarded as soon as possible.

Capt. Murray's frigate is now proceeding down the River. When Dulton was here[12] he shewed me a letter from M. LaFayette to Genl. Moreau,[13] which he was to deliver; a proof that the latter may be expected.

It gives me the sincerest pleasure to hear the favourable opinion of Dr. Physic respecting the cause of your going to Philada. Be pleased to present my best respects to Mrs. Madison. Yesterday I saw Mrs. Payne and her grandson in good health. We had a severe gale of wind the day before yesterday, which blew down parts of several houses in the City between the office and Georgetown.

I enclose a letter from the Collector of Salem respecting the impressments from the fishing vessels.[14] The part which Mr. Allen[15] has taken in endeavouring to procure the release of the seamen affords a very favourable presage of his conduct, and it is the more valuable from his connection with the British office of Foreign Affairs. I have the honor to remain, with the highest respect, Dr. Sir, Yr. affecte. obed. servt.

Jacob Wagner

RC (DLC).

1. Letters not found.

2. The enclosure has not been found, but for the French privateer *Les Amies*, see Anthony Merry to JM, 9 July 1805 (second letter), and nn., and JM to Merry, 16 July 1805 (second letter).

3. For the capture of the *Golden Grove*, see Merry to JM, 25 July 1805, and n. 1. On 5 Aug. 1805 Wagner wrote to Wilson Cary Nicholas, enclosing a copy of Francis Blair's protest and asking Nicholas to report any information he had "respecting the abuse of the waters of the United States" by the privateer in question (DNA: RG 59, DL, vol. 15).

4. The enclosure was JM to Francis J. Oliver, 5 Aug. 1805 (see Oliver to JM, 19 July 1805, n. 2).

5. For John Lamson's account and JM's reply, see Lamson to JM, 31 May 1805, *PJM-SS*, 9:422, 423 n. 2.

6. Wagner may have referred to an incident in which the British armed brig *Busy* seized a Marblehead, Massachusetts, schooner that was drifting in Passamaquoddy Bay, and carried it into Saint John, New Brunswick, where the *Busy* had gone to impress men. The collector there refused to admit the schooner, and the *Busy*, whose press gang was driven back on board by the local citizens, carried it to Halifax, Nova Scotia (Boston *Columbian Centinel*, 31 July 1805).

7. See the 25 July 1805 memorial from Philip Nicklin and Robert Eaglesfield Griffith.

8. The enclosure was a letter from JM to Albert Gallatin, 5 Aug. 1805, stating: "Mr. Lear having lately drawn upon Sir Francis Baring & Co. for Six thousand pounds Sterling, it seems proper that the sum of about Sixteen thousand dollars should be remitted to those Bankers to answer it. It may be drawn from the appropriations for Barbary Intercourse" (DNA: RG 59, DL, vol. 15; 1 p.). For £5,000 of this money, see Francis Baring & Co. to JM, 7 June 1805, *PJM-SS*, 9:441. For its probable use, see Timothy Mountford to JM, 30 May 1805, ibid., 419.

9. This note has not been found.

10. This was Yale graduate Ledyard Seymour of Hartford, Connecticut (1771–1848). He established himself in business in New York but declared bankruptcy about 1797 after having several ships seized by the British in the West Indies. In 1800 he went to Havana, where he lived for three years. In June 1805 he had applied to Jefferson for appointment as a consul in any Spanish colony (Dexter, *Biographical Sketches of the Graduates of Yale*, 5:37–38; Seymour to Thomas Jefferson, 14 June 1805, DNA: RG 59, LAR, 1801–9, filed under "Seymour").

11. For the cannon for Algiers, see JM to Charles Simms, 10 July 1805, and n. 1.

12. See Wagner to JM, 28 and 29 July 1805.

13. Exiled French general Jean Victor Marie Moreau and his family arrived in Philadelphia on 25 Aug. 1805 (Philadelphia *United States' Gazette*, 26 Aug. 1805).

14. No letter from William R. Lee, collector at Salem, Massachusetts, has been found. In late July a dozen or more fishermen from Salem, Beverly, and Marblehead were impressed on the Grand Banks by Capt. Robert Laurie of the British frigate *Ville de Milan*. British consul Andrew Allen (see n. 15 below) advised Vice Adm. Andrew Mitchell at Halifax to return the men (*Salem Register*, 22 July 1805; *New-York Gazette & General Advertiser*, 29 July 1805).

15. Andrew Allen (d. 1850), British consul at Boston from 1805 to 1812, was the son of Pennsylvania Loyalist Andrew Allen (1740–1825). His sister Margaret was married to George Hammond, former British minister to the United States, and at this time undersecretary in the British Foreign Office (Emma Siggins White, comp., *Genealogical Gleanings of Siggins and Other Pennsylvania Families* . . . [Kansas City, Mo., 1918], 455; Charles P. Keith, "Andrew Allen," *PMHB* 10 [1887]: 361, 364–65).

§ From William C. C. Claiborne. *5 August 1805, New Orleans.* "On last Evening, I paid a visit to the Marquis of Casa Calvo. He acknowledged the receipt of my Letter of the 3rd Instant,[1] and told me 'that an answer should be returned, so soon as he had received from Morales a communication (which was momently expected) upon the Subject, to which I had alluded.' The Marquis added that 'he believed Morales had received instructions, to sell the Vacant Lands in West Florida,' but he (the Marquis) hoped 'no Sales would for the present be made; he thought that pending the Negociation, things should remain in their present state, and he persuaded himself, that the United States would on their part, make no disposition of the Lands West of the Mississippi.' I then observed, 'that Spain was in possession of a Vast Tract of Country, which was claimed by the United States, and until the dispute was adjusted, any Sale of Lands by the King of Spain, would be considered as highly indecorous, and opposed to that Spirit of Friendly accommodation, which it was the Interest of the two Nations to feel, and to manifest.' With respect to the Sales of Lands West of the Mississippi I remarked, that 'I did not believe that Lands without the acknowledged limits of the Ceded Territory, would for the present be disposed of by the United States, and therefore no possible exception could be taken.' The Marquis seemed unwilling to say any thing further upon this Point, but again expressed a Wish that no Lands in West Florida should be disposed of until the dispute was settled, and observed that Morales, whom he represented as an unprincipled Man, would alone be benefited by the proceeding. I must confess, that I feel much embarassment as to the conduct proper to be pursued on my part, in the event that Morales should, *recommence in this City, the Sales of Lands in West Florida; It* would be insulting to the Government, and might have injurious Consequences. That many Citizens would be found willing to purchase, I have no doubt, and others weak enough to draw from the proceeding—a conclusion, that Louisiana, or a portion of it, would soon change Masters. I have myself supposed, that Morales could not act in this Teritory, in his Official Character, without violating the general Law of Nations! I am also inclined to think, that the Selling of Lands to Citizens of the United States with a view to induce them to emigrate, is an offence at common Law, and which Law (as relates to Minor offences) was extended to this Teritory by an act of the Legislative Council.

"Thus impressed, I have contemplated having recourse to the Judiciary, in the event, that Morales should act the part conjectured. The absense from the City of the District Attorney (Mr. Brown) and the Attorney General for the Teritory (Mr. Gurley) leaves me on this occasion without the benefit of Counsel. But you may be assured that I will do nothing rashly, and that the Measures taken, will be the result of my best Judgment."

RC (DNA: RG 59, TP, Orleans, vol. 7); letterbook copy (Ms-Ar: Claiborne Executive Journal, vol. 15). RC 3 pp.; docketed by Wagner, with his note: "Morales sells lands in W. Florida." Minor differences between the copies have not been noted.

   1. See Claiborne to JM, 3 Aug. 1805 (first letter), and n. 1.

§ From Horatio Gates. *5 August 1805, Rose Hill.* "Saturdays News paper acquainted me with your Arrival at Philadelphia; if you intend farther Northward, I have the satisfaction to Offer you Rose Hill, during your stay near New York; there you will find ease, fine Air, fine Water, & every Accomodation you can desire; Mrs: Gates Joins me in presenting her kindest Compliments to Mrs. Maddison, and in our Assurances; to make R H as agreeable as you wish it."

   RC (PU-Sp: Hugenschmidt Autograph Collection). 1 p.

§ From Robert Montgomery. *5 August 1805, Alicante.* "I have the honor to hand you herewith Copy of a letter received this morning from Algiers;[1] I have Given every assistance and support to Capn John Allen of the Schooner Jane of Boston Captured by the Piratical Vessel mentioned in Mr Mountfords letter and sent him and his Mate to Malta where it is probable the Jane may have been sent to as I am well informed that the owners of the Cruiser live there and will be forced to make restitution.[2]

   "The Jane was on her Voyage from Boston to Marseille and on the Coast east of Valencia was hailed by a Vessel under Barbary Colours, the Master apprehending she was a Tripoline abandoned his Vessel and they Carried her off, when I learned this business I concluded the cruizer must be An Algerine as the Others had very little Chance of geting Clear of Our Blockade, in consequence I detained Capn Allen here and wrote Mr Mountford, who reply'd nearly as containd in his letter of which you have herewith Copy and I trust that Allen will find his Vessel altho much plundered."

   RC and enclosure (DNA: RG 59, CD, Alicante, vol. 1). RC 2 pp.; docketed by Wagner as received 15 Oct., with his note: "Transactions at Algiers." For enclosure, see n. 1.

   1. The enclosure (7 pp.; docketed by Wagner) is a copy of Timothy Mountford to Montgomery, 28 July 1805, in which Mountford acknowledged some previous correspondence between himself and Montgomery about the *Jane* and stated that the British consul at Algiers said the ship had been captured by the British polacre *Two Brothers*, Captain Cock, or Cook, of Malta, and had probably been sent to Sardinia. The captain and the crew were thought to be pirates and had been arrested and jailed by the British. It was believed there were several such ships in the Mediterranean, disguised as vessels from the Barbary regencies; an Imperial polacre had been reported taken by the same means. Mountford stated that the Jewish merchant [Naphtali] Busnach had been murdered by a Turkish soldier on 28 June, that the next day, soldiers had killed every Jew they met and plundered their houses, that they had been in rebellion since then, and that the whole country of the Moors, from Tlemcen to Constantine, had risen against the Turks. Tlemcen was taken by the Moorish army, and Oran was said to be unable to hold out much longer. Mountford added that every vessel that went to Oran was held by the dey in preparation for flight to Turkey when the

city at last fell. The city of Algiers had relieved Oran with grain but could do so no more, since it, too, was running short. After Oran had fallen the Moors would send all their troops to the city of Algiers, so all grain in the vicinity was being ordered to Algiers. On 25 July the Turkish soldiers marched out of town against the dey's orders, conferred for three hours, and returned; on 27 July they held another conference, the result of which was unknown. The dey and the divan feared for their own safety.

It was believed the soldiers intended to destroy the dey because he had ordered two soldiers strangled for the Jewish massacre, and to "create a new set of Rulers." The palace guard was doubled and all the street gates closed at sunset, which only happened in times of real danger. Mountford commented that Algiers was beset within and without by its own subjects, and "a scene of horror" would occur in a short time. He had been told Lear had concluded peace with Tripoli and so should be returning to Algiers where the scene about to unfold would require his presence to take steps in the American interest. Mountford asked that copies of his letter be sent to JM and to Lear, whose whereabouts were uncertain, adding that Montgomery was his only mode of conveyance, since the current state of affairs had caused the dey to "look sharp" that few letters got out of port. The sudden arrival and departure of a Spanish courier had left him unable to write to JM and Lear. In a postscript he suggested sending a copy to John Gavino also, so Gavino could give information to all Americans bound up the Mediterranean but without giving them any more than would put them on their guard against freebooters. He added that all the Algerian corsairs were in port except a xebec of 32 guns and 400 men which it was thought had been taken by the Portuguese or Neapolitans. He stated further that he was alone, with not another American in the entire regency.

2. On 26 Sept. 1805 Jacob Wagner wrote Benjamin Lincoln that Joseph Pulis, the American consul at Malta, had informed JM that the *Jane*, on its voyage from Boston to Marseilles, had been chased by a British privateer, and the *Jane*'s crew, supposing the pursuers to be Tripolitan, had abandoned ship, leaving only a Russian on board. Wagner said the *Jane* had been carried to Malta and asked Lincoln to notify the owners so they could make a claim (DNA: RG 59, DL, vol. 15). No letter to JM from Joseph Pulis about the *Jane* has been found.

From Albert Gallatin

DEAR SIR.   NEW YORK 6 August 1805

It cannot be expected that the Banks will make a loan to La Fayette:[1] they never lend on real property; of the value of the Louisiana lands no person can at present give them Sufficient assurance; and their answer will be that they are ready to make the requested advance on La Fayette notes *with two approved endorsers.* I will confer with Tousard on his arrival & give every assistance in my power: but every thing depends on some fortunate extraordinary location; for no lands, however fertile, will, merely as objects of common cultivation, realise his expectations.

The demands from Spain were too hard to have expected, even independent of French interference, any success from the negotiation. It could only be hoped that the tone assumed by our negociators might not be such as to render a relinquishment or suspension of some of our claims productive of some loss of reputation. If we are safe on that ground, it may be eligible to wait for a better opportunity before we again run the risk of lowering the national importance by pretensions which our strength may not at this moment permit us to support. If from the manner in which the negotiation has been conducted & has terminated, that effect has already been produced, how to save character without endangering peace, will be a serious & difficult question. Perhaps a law making efficient provision for building a dozen of ships of the line would be the most dignified & most forcible mode of re-opening the negotiation: but it will be a doubt with some whether the remedy be not worse than the disorder. At all events to go to war for the western boundary of Louisiana, or even for the country beween Mississippi & Perdido, after having omitted in our treaty of purchase to bind France to a certain construction of limits, never will do. The refusal to ratify the convention is, in my view of the subject, the most offensive part of the proceeding.

Mr. Randolph & Mr. Nicholson are both anxious to know with precision the time when Mr. Munroe may be expected in England; as they have both placed business of importance in his hands.[2] I will thank you to communicate your knowledge or conjectures on that point.

Mrs. Gallatin joins in affectionate compliments to you & to Mrs Madison, and sincerely hope that she will receive prompt & efficient relief in Philadelphia. If she is better, you should come & pay a visit to the American Tyre[3] which you would hardly recognize. Your's truly

ALBERT GALLATIN

I find that Lear has drawn £5000 Stg. on the Barings on the contingent credit of 100,000 dollars which had been given for the ransom in case of peace. Do you know for what reason? & was it not wrong to diminish that fund or rather to divert it from its intended object?[4]

RC (DLC).

1. For the suggestion of a bank loan for Lafayette, see JM to Gallatin, 2 Aug. 1805.

2. John Randolph's business with Monroe may have had to do with his deaf-mute nephew, St. George Randolph: Monroe had offered to oversee the boy's education in Europe, and St. George was sent from the United States to England probably early in 1806. On 22 May 1805 Joseph H. Nicholson had written to Monroe asking his help in investing the proceeds of the Maryland bank stock that had been returned to the state by Great Britain in 1804. On 7 Aug. 1805 Monroe replied that he had begun negotiations with Francis Baring & Co. (Randolph to Monroe, 20 July 1804, and 20 Mar. 1806, DLC: Monroe Papers; Radoff, *The Bank Stock Papers*, no. 5 of *Calendar of Maryland State Papers*, 45, 47). For the Maryland bank stock, see *PJM-SS*, 8:243–51 and nn.

3. New York, like the city of Tyre in Lebanon, was built on an island (John Barton and John Muddiman, eds., *The Oxford Bible Commentary* [Oxford, 2001], 552).

4. For Lear's bills on JM, see Jacob Wagner to JM, 5 Aug. 1805, and n. 8.

From James Monroe

London August 6th. 1805

I left Madrid on the 26 of May & arrived here on the 23d. ulto. by the route of Paris & Holland. I reached Paris on the 20th. June & left in [*sic*] on the 11th. of July. I shoud have remained there longer had I seen reasonable ⟨c⟩ause to presume that any advantage might have been derived from it in respect to our business with Spain. But none such occurred, & of course there was no motive ⟨fo⟩r delaying longer my journey here. The french governt ⟨h⟩ad been invited as I passed thro' Paris to aid our negotiation ⟨w⟩ith Spain according to its Engagement on a former ⟨o⟩ccasion; it was apprized in the progress of what occurred in it[,] knew the time of its conclusion & that I shoud return thro' Paris, so that had it been disposed even in that stage to interpose ⟨i⟩ts good offices to promote an adjustment of our differences ⟨wi⟩th that power, on such terms as we coud accept, ⟨i⟩t might have done it with Effect. I had flattered myself t⟨ha⟩t it woud have interposed at that period, & with a ⟨v⟩iew to draw its attention in an especial manner to the ⟨o⟩bject, had made such a communication to Genel Bournonville ⟨i⟩ts ambassador at madrid, as seemed most likely to Secure it. ⟨Of⟩ this & all other documents relative to the subject a copy ⟨w⟩as sent you from Madrid by Captn Dulton.[1] It is proper ⟨to⟩ add that when I delivered that communication to Genl Bournonville which I did in person, I intimated to him verbally that as I shoud take Paris on my return, the opportunity for such friendly interference on the part of his government woud again be presente⟨d⟩ to it: that I had a power to act singly & if a like one shoud be given to the Spanish Ambassador there, we might renew the business & conclude it. General Bournonville transmitted immediately this communication to his government then at Milan by a courier, so that it must have been received in a week after I left Madrid, & as I was more than three wee⟨ks⟩ on the rout from Madrid to Paris the French government had sufficient time to make an arrangement for the purpose even before my arrival at Paris. While there I was attentive to Every circumstance from which any inference could be drawn of the disposition of the French government on that head, & as I was frequantly in society with some of the members of the government who were left behind, especialy the archchancellor who is considered as its head in the absence of the Emperor, the opportunity to make a correct Estimate was a very favorable one. But nothing occurred to authorize an inference that it intended to make me any proposition on the subject. On the contrary I had sufficien⟨t⟩ reason to believe that the French government still indulged the Expectation that the proposition which Mr Livingston had submitted to you before I set out from this country to Spain woud finally be accepted.[2] As this fact had been avowed by the Minister of foreign affairs it coud not be questioned.

Having done every thing in my power to Expose the fallacy of this expectation in obedience to my instructions while at Paris in my way to Spain; & in Spain I was surprized that the idea shoud still be Entertained & the more so as Genl. Armstrong had Equally labord to remove it.

Under these circumstances it seemed highly improper for me to ⟨r⟩epeat again my application to the French government for its ⟨a⟩id in that business. It was sure to fail of success & therefore t⟨o⟩ be avoided.[3] But that was not the only objection to it. ⟨It⟩ seemed likely by weakening the force of the part which ⟨h⟩ad been taken at Madrid to diminish the good effect which ⟨w⟩e flattered ourselves might reasonably been expected from it. ⟨I⟩t was even probable in relation to what had passed, that it might ⟨b⟩e considered as betraying a want of just sensibility to what was due to the character of our government & country, & ⟨l⟩essen the effect of such measures as our government might t⟨h⟩ink proper to adopt on a view of the result & whole proceedings ⟨at⟩ Madrid. On full consideration therefore of all circumstances ⟨I⟩ deemed it most consistent with the publick honor & interest, ⟨a⟩fter waiting about three weeks at Paris & furnishing the ⟨o⟩pportunity & drawing the conclusions above stated of the indisposition of the French govt. to interfere in a suitable manner in our business with Spain, to proceed on my ⟨j⟩ourney here, without making any application for it, which I did accordingly.

I send you herewith a copy of Mr Livingstons letter t⟨o⟩ me of Novr. 12 & of my answer of 13th. which have reference ⟨to⟩ what occurred in that stage of this interesting concern ⟨a⟩t Paris. They were mentioned in mine to you of the 27th. ⟨b⟩ut by accident not then forwarded.[4]

Some days after my return here Mr Bowdoin arrived ⟨a⟩lso. He has I understand Explained to you fully the motives of this measure. In a political view I consider it a judicious one. Had he proceeded to Madrid from the port where he landed, he coud not in the present state of affairs have been able to render any service in the great object depending with Spain, while his arrival there at that moment being attributed to improper motives might have done harm in the view which has been already Explained. I shall avail myself of the opportunity it affords to give him all the light in my possession relative to our concerns with that power. I am persuaded that Mr Pinkney will hold the ground 'till his successor relieves him, tho⟨'⟩ he is desirous of withdrawing from it. It is not yet decided whether it will be most adviseable for Mr. Erving to proceed to Madrid or wait with Mr Bowdoin farther orders from you. Shoud he adopt the former course he wil⟨l⟩ probably proceed thro' Paris to confer with Genl Armstrong on the general subject & ascertain whether any change has taken place in the disposition of the French government respecting it. When I left Paris I intimated to Genl Armstrong who was then in the Country by letter, that I shoud be willing while here to return to Holland on a suitable inducement to conclude the business. I did so not in a presumption that there was any prospect of such an event, but as a measure of precaution to be taken advantage of in Case an opportunity offered.

While at Paris I recieved your letter of May 4th and since my return that of June 21st.[5] On the subject of the first I have to observe that under the discouraging ⟨c⟩ircumstances in which we commenced the negotiation with Spain we thought it best to adhere as closely as possible to the convention of Augt. 11. 1802 which had at one time been approved by her government. We ⟨f⟩lattered ourselves that if that government coud be induced to take a right course in the great points, it might be possible to prevail on it afterwards to accede to the modification suggested in the letter. We shoud have been ⟨a⟩ttentive to the subject had the occasion favor'd. Our reason for not entering more fully into some points, & among others that mentioned in the Extract of your letter to Genl Armstrong ⟨o⟩f June 6th[6] in our correspondence with Mr Cervallos was ⟨e⟩xplained in Mr Pinkneys & my joint letter from Madrid.[7] In addition to which it may be observed that much was said in conversation in reply to his subsequent notes ⟨w⟩hich the contents of the first had not permitted.

On the day of my return here one of our vessels the Enoch[8] under circumstances precisely similar to those in the ⟨c⟩ase of the Aurora[9] was condemned by the admiralty. Several ⟨o⟩thers have since been brought in on the same principle whose cases are now before the court. I have taken the ⟨s⟩ubject up in connection with the other topicks that were depending before I set out for Spain. I send you a copy of my letter to Lord Mulgrave & of his answer to it.[10] I beg to assure you that I shall push this business with promptitude and decision to some result, to place before the President a correct view of the policy of this governmen⟨t⟩ towards the United States. I am with great respect & esteem yr. most obt. humble servant

JAS. MONROE

RC, extract, and enclosures (DNA: RG 59, DD, Great Britain, vol. 12); letterbook copy (DLC: Monroe Papers); extract (MHi: Bowdoin and Temple Collection). RC in a clerk's hand, except for Monroe's complimentary close and signature. Minor differences between the copies have not been noted. For enclosures, see nn. 4 and 10.

1. For Thomas Dulton's arrival at Washington with dispatches, see Jacob Wagner to JM, 28 July 1805.

2. For Robert R. Livingston's plan for acquiring West Forida, see Livingston to JM, 10 Oct. 1804, and Monroe to JM, 16 Dec. 1804, *PJM-SS*, 8:150, 386–87, 397 n. 14.

3. The phrase "therefore to be avoided" is omitted from the letterbook copy.

4. The enclosures (6 pp.; docketed by Wagner), which Monroe had intended but failed to include in his 27 Nov. 1804 dispatch, are copies of Livingston to Monroe, 12 Nov. 1804, and Monroe to Livingston, 13 Nov. 1804. For Monroe's 27 Nov. dispatch, see *PJM-SS*, 8:329–33; for Livingston's letter and Monroe's reply, see Hamilton, *Writings of James Monroe*, 4:274–77, 306–7 and n. 1.

5. See *PJM-SS*, 9:319, 484.

6. See JM to Monroe, 21 June 1805, ibid., 484 and n. 1.

7. See Charles Pinckney and Monroe to JM, 23 May 1805, ibid., 385–92.

8. For the case, see George Joy to JM, 26 July 1805, and n. 3.

9. For the case of the *Aurora*, see JM to Monroe, 12 Apr. 1805, *PJM-SS*, 9:234–35, 237–38, 239 n. 1.

10. Monroe enclosed copies of: (1) Monroe to Lord Mulgrave, 31 July 1805 (2 pp.; docketed by Wagner; printed in *ASP, Foreign Relations*, 3:103), requesting an interview to renew the discussion on neutral rights, impressment, and American trade with colonies of Britain's enemies that had been postponed for Monroe's trip to Spain; (2) Mulgrave to Monroe, 5 Aug. 1805 (1 p.; printed ibid.), stating that he would designate a date after informing himself about the state of the pending business; (3) Monroe to Mulgrave, 8 Aug. 1805 (2 pp.; in a clerk's hand, except for Monroe's complimentary close and signature; docketed by Wagner; printed ibid., 104), stating that the recent British seizure of U.S. ships was so important and the causes of it so unknown to the U.S. representatives in Great Britain, that, although he would have preferred to wait for the pending interview to inquire about it, he could not justify a longer delay; and (4) Mulgrave to Monroe, 9 Aug. 1805 (1 p.; docketed by Wagner; printed ibid.), stating that because Monroe had not given either "the nature or the period of the transaction" to which he alluded, Mulgrave was unable to answer, and he was unaware of any recent events that were so pressing that a discussion of them could not wait until the following week. Filed with these documents is a transcript (1 p.) of the last paragraph of Monroe's 6 Aug. letter to JM.

§ From Sylvanus Bourne. *6 August 1805, Amsterdam.* "It appears that the British Govt flattered by the prospect of a new Coalition on the Continent against France begins to treat Neutrals with less delicacy than heretofore & several Amn. Vessells have lately been carried into the Ports of England tried & with their Cargoes condemned for reason of having been on voyages between the mother Countries & the Colonies of nations with which they are at war. And within a few days past several Vessells bound here direct from the UStates with West India produce on board have been taken in & it is said that orders are issued to send in all such for examination & adjudication.[1] On what grounds such orders can be predicated I am at a loss to conceive not believing that GB would presume to say that our vessells should under no circumstances be the carriers of WI produce to Europe as this would in effect be annihilating two thirds of our trade.

"GB has for many years been found to regulate her maritime judicial proceedings more by the circumstances attending her political position than by the rules or Laws of Nations—such a system however exposes neutral trade to constant risks & inconveniences & I doubt not that our Govt will assume that firm & decided aspect which its dignity & the interests of our commerce dictate."

Adds in a postscript: "I am on the whole led to suppose that the vessells referred to are carried in to obtain full proof whether the Cargo on board if taken in in a Dutch Colony was or not relanded in the UStates in order to render the voyage *legal* in their view of the Case & that if such fact can be proved that the vessells will be permitted to proceed hence with said Cargoes and it may be ⟨well⟩ that the public should be officially informed of the risk incurred by those who do not land their Cargoes in the UStates if brought from a Dutch Colony as in the cases of the Vessells & Cargoes that have been condemned—this rule it appears had not been complied with & the voyage was therefore regarded as one *continued voyage* from the Mother Country to the Colony."

RC (DNA: RG 59, CD, Amsterdam, vol. 1). 3 pp.; docketed by Wagner as received 10 Oct.

1. For the change in the British court decisions regarding neutral trade with the colonies of Britain's enemies, see George Joy to JM, 26 July 1805, and n. 3.

§ From William C. C. Claiborne. *6 August 1805, New Orleans.* "I am not yet favored with the Marquis's Answer to my Letter of the third instant.[1] It is (I believe) delayed, from Moralis's unwillingness to communicate the extent of his Orders, or the time and manner he proposes to execute them.

"Moralis has more information, *but less principle* than any Spanish Officer I ever met with; his Wealth enables him to make many *Friends*, and among *them* I am sorry to inform you, some of our own Countrymen are conspicuous.

"The day after the report was circulated, that Moralis's conduct was approved by his Court, and that he had Authority to continue his Sales in West Florida, he (Moralis) was (I learn) waited upon by many Persons, who congratulated him on the interesting Intelligence, and evidenced a Disposition to adventure in the Speculation. Many of the Emigrants thither, are, indeed mere Adventurers, the acquirement of Wealth is their object and as to the means, they seem to manifest much indifference.

"I must confess Sir, that the embarrassments which have attended our Negociation with Spain, have mortified me exceedingly—the People of West Florida, expected that the Country would certainly be delivered to the United States, and while the delay excites their regret and surprise, it tends to lessen the confidence of the Citizens of this Territory, in the American Government, and to encourage a belief that Louisiana will again fall under the Dominion of Spain!"

Adds in a postscript: "During Colo: Bur's continuance in this City, he was marked in his Attentions to Moralis, and was in habits of intimacy with Livingston, Clark & Jones."[2]

RC (DNA: RG 59, TP, Orleans, vol. 7). RC 3 pp.; marked "(Private)"; in a clerk's hand, except for Claiborne's complimentary close, signature, postscript, and address; docketed by Wagner.

1. See Claiborne to JM, 3 Aug. 1805 (first letter), and n. 1.
2. For Aaron Burr's arrival at New Orleans, see Claiborne to JM, 26 June 1805, *PJM-SS*, 9:495. Burr's visit to the city was part of his travels through the western territories, which later led to his arrest on charges of conspiracy. While in New Orleans, he also met with his stepson, John B. Prevost. Burr was gone by 14 July (Kline, *Papers of Aaron Burr*, 2:937–38 n., 943–44; Claiborne to Jefferson, 14 July 1805, Rowland, *Claiborne Letter Books*, 3:127). Daniel Clark, Evan Jones, and Edward Livingston were all opposed to Claiborne, with whom Clark fought a duel in 1807. For Clark and Livingston, see *PJM-SS*, 3:58 n. 3, 6:577 n. 4, 8:167, 490–91. New York native Evan Jones (1739–1813) had been a merchant trading with Spanish Louisiana and British Florida before moving to Louisiana sometime before 1780. In 1799 he was named U.S. consul at New Orleans. After the Orleans Territory was established, he was appointed to the legislative council but declined the post. From 1807 until his death he grew sugar profitably on his vast plantation, Evan Hall (Junius

P. Rodriguez, ed., *The Louisiana Purchase: A Historical and Geographical Encyclopedia* [Santa Barbara, Calif., 2002], 71, 163–64; *Senate Exec. Proceedings,* 1:326; Claiborne to JM, 13 and 29 Oct. 1804, *PJM-SS,* 8:139 n. 2, 167, 235).

§ From William C. C. Claiborne. *6 August 1805, New Orleans.* "I forgot to mention to you in my Letter of yeasterday, that in the course of my conversation with the Marquis of Casa Calvo, he mentioned to me, that 'his Conduct here, had been approved by the Minister of State, at Madrid, and his interference in the affair of the Negroes, who had escaped to Nacagdoches was particularly approbated by his Court.'[1] The Marquis also told me, that 'the Spanish Minister (D'Yrugo) had been instructed to have him (the Marquis) recognized by the President of the United States as Commissioner of Limits.'"

RC (DNA: RG 59, TP, Orleans, vol. 7); letterbook copy (Ms-Ar: Claiborne Executive Journal, vol. 15). RC 1 p.; in a clerk's hand, except for Claiborne's complimentary close, signature, and address; docketed by Wagner as received 17 Sept.

1. For the escaped slaves, see *PJM-SS,* 9:217.

From Thomas Jefferson

DEAR SIR   MONTICELLO Aug. 7. 05.

On a view of our affairs with Spain, presented me in a letter from C. Pinckney, I wrote you on the 23d. of July[1] that I thought we should offer them the status quo, but immediately propose a provisional alliance with England. I have not yet recieved the whole correspondence, but the portion of the papers now inclosed to you,[2] confirm me in the opinion of the expediency of a treaty with England, but make the offer of the status quo more doubtful. The correspondence will probably throw light on that question. From the papers already recieved I infer a confident reliance on the part of Spain on the ominipotence of Bonaparte, but a desire of procrastination till peace in Europe shall leave us without an ally. General Dearborne has seen all the papers. I will ask the favor of you to communicate them to Mr. Gallatin & Mr. Smith. From Mr. Gallatin I shall ask his first opinions, preparatory to the stating formal questions for our ultimate decision. I am in hopes you can make it convenient on your return to see & consult with Mr. Smith & Genl. Dearborne, unless the latter should be come on here, where I can do it myself. On the reciept of your own ideas Mr. Smith's and the other gentlemen I shall be able to form points for our final consideration & determination.

I inclose you some communications from the Mediterranean.[3] They shew Barron's understanding in a very favorable view. When you shall have perused them, be so good as to inclose them to the Secretary of the Navy. Accept my fervent wishes for the speedy recovery of Mrs. Madison, and your speedy visit to this quarter.

TH: JEFFERSON

RC (DLC: Rives Collection, Madison Papers); FC (DLC: Jefferson Papers); Tr (MHi).

1. Jefferson is referring to Charles Pinckney's 22 May 1805 letter, which Jefferson received on 2 Aug. 1805 and mentioned in his 4 Aug. letter to JM (DLC: Jefferson Papers). His 23 July 1805 letter to JM enclosed an extract of a letter from Gideon Granger.
2. For the dispatches from Spain that Jacob Wagner sent to JM and Jefferson, see Wagner to JM, 28 and 29 July 1805.
3. The enclosures have not been identified.

From Jacob Wagner

DEAR SIR   DEPARTMENT OF STATE 7 Augt. 1805.

I have had the honor to receive your favor of the 3rd. inst.[1] Mr. Gallatin has disapproved of the descent of the Revenue Cutter upon East Florida to seize the coffee and Sugar, mentioned in the letter of the Spanish Minister,[2] & ordered it to be returned; but as the complaint against the Captain is composed of many particulars beside that affair, it seems to me best to defer the answer until we obtain a report from the Collector of New Orleans under whose immediate orders the Cutter acts. I shall therefore translate the narrative part of the letter and request information upon it from the Collector to be transmitted to you.[3] Enclosed are letters to Genl. Turreau[4] (the enclosures in which require your signature) Marquis Yrujo,[5] Pierson & Kimball[6] & duplicates to Mr. Monroe.[7] I have retained copies of the three first & they may therefore be forwarded after obtaining your signature.

Mr. Merry does not approve of the interposition of Consul Allen in favor of the impressed fishermen,[8] as he thinks it ought to have come through himself, and not the Consul. He says he has obtained information from his government that a number of American fishermen have been detected in drying their fish on N. Foundland, which have consequently been seized, and that the Americans have enticed the British to serve them, which they have in several instances acceded to, carrying off at the same time the property of their former employers. These occurrences he supposes have occasioned the impressments; and thus we are likely to see all the oppressions founded on the pretext of reclaiming British *seamen* acted over again to obtain their *fishermen*. He confidentially read me a letter from Sir A. Mitchell respecting the complaint of the master of the Happy Couple of the impressment of his people and the very extraordinary language held to him,[9] in the presence of the Atty. Genl. by Captains Talbot and Bassford. Those captains were absent at the date of the Admiral's letter and he therefore reserves himself for a further answer, but at the same time so absolutely prejudges the matter, that I think we shall get no satisfaction.

The President was at Monticello when the last post left it, as he returned some papers with the Milton postmark.

The N. Orleans mail has not come in this week. With great respect & attachment Your ob. Servt.

J. WAGNER

RC (DLC). Docketed by JM.

1. Letter not found.
2. See Carlos Martínez de Yrujo to JM, 2 Aug. 1805, and n. 2.
3. On 5 Aug. 1805 Wagner wrote to William Brown, enclosing an extract from Yrujo's letter, and asking Brown "to make enquiry into the nature and truth of these imputations and report the result" (DNA: RG 59, DL, vol. 15).
4. The letter has not been found, but it was probably the 9 Aug. 1805 letter to Louis-Marie Turreau calendared in the index to the State Department notes to foreign legations as "enclosing two Exequaturs" (DNA: RG 59, Notes to Foreign Ministers and Consuls, vol. 1).
5. This was probably JM to Yrujo, 7 Aug. 1805, requesting a passport (not found). On 12 Aug., Yrujo replied, enclosing the passport (DNA: RG 59, NFL, Spain, vol. 2).
6. See JM to John Pearson and James Kimball, 5 Aug. 1805.
7. See JM to James Monroe, 5 Aug. 1805.
8. For this incident, see Wagner to JM, 5 Aug. 1805, and n. 14.
9. For the case of the *Happy Couple*, see Samuel Sterett to JM, 21 Apr. 1805, *PJM-SS*, 9:271, 272 n. 6.

§ From William C. C. Claiborne. *7 August 1805, New Orleans.* "In my communication of the 29 ultimo, was inclosed a *Letter to me*, from the Marquis of Casa Calvo, (soliciting that the Spanish Officers now in this Territory, may be exempted from the payment of the Municipal Tax) together with a Copy of my answer thereto.

"I now have the Honor to transmit you, a second Letter from the Marquis on the same subject, together with a list of the Officers alluded to;[1] and if it be not improper, I should be glad to hear your sentiment, as to the propriety of the exemtion solicited: my own opinion is, 'that the Officers generally who possess property within this Territory, are liable to Taxation; nor can exemtion be made in favor of the *Marquis* and the members of his Family, until *he* shall have been recognized by the President as an Agent of Spain.' You no doubt will be surprised to find so many Foreign Officers in this City; the fact is th⟨at⟩ they are wedded to Loisiana, and necessity alone will induce them to depart. I have repeatedly by Letter, and verbally, informed the Marquis, that the continuance in this Territory, of 'so many Spanish officers so long beyond the right occasion for it' was not seen with approbation, and urged their departure: The Marquis has as often assured me of his disposition to comply with my wishes, but you will percieve that the inconveniance is not yet remedied."

RC and enclosures (DNA: RG 59, TP, Orleans, vol. 7); letterbook copy (Ms-Ar: Claiborne Executive Journal, vol. 15); Tr and Tr of enclosures (DNA: RG 233, President's Messages, 9A–D1); Tr and Tr of enclosures (DNA: RG 46, President's Messages, 9B–B1). RC 2
pp.; in a clerk's hand, signed by Claiborne; docketed by Wagner as received 18 Oct.; printed
in Rowland, *Claiborne Letter Books*, 3:154. The second Tr and Tr of enclosures are letterpress copies of the first Tr and Tr of enclosures. Minor differences between the copies have
not been noted. For enclosures, see n. 1.

1. The enclosures (7 pp.; docketed by Wagner; printed in Carter, *Territorial Papers,
Orleans*, 9:484–87) are a translation, certified by interpreter Moreau Lislet, of Casa Calvo
to Claiborne, 2 Aug. 1805, enclosing translations certified by Lislet of 30 July 1805 lists
signed by Andrés López Armesto of (1) "individuals composing the expedition of the limits
of the province of Louisiana, as approved by his C. M.'s order of the 20th. august 1804";
(2) "Persons employed by his Catholic Majesty who are to depart as soon as their business
shall be terminated"; (3) "officers in his C. M.'s service, who are to Depart immediately
after having terminated their business"; and (4) "the retired officers and . . . other persons
employed in the service of his Catholic Majesty who are to remain in this Province, in order
to settle their business or on account of their old Age or usual infirmities," for a total of
fifty-eight persons, and nine widows who "are unable to Go to Pensacola." The first list
contains a note that a naval officer and his clerk were also there on a mission to purchase
timber for the navy, and the last list contains a note that a small number of retired sergeants
and privates were to go to Baton Rouge or Pensacola.

To Albert Gallatin

DEAR SIR   PHILADA. Aug. 8. 1805
    I am just favored with yours of the 6th: I have not seen Toussard since
my arrival here, and can not therefore say when you will have an oppy. of
conferring with him on the subject of Fayette. I wish most fervently that
something could be done for the latter, tho I can not pretend to say what
can. Notwithstanding the grant of Congs. I fear he must be ruined without some immediate relief in money, which can not be raised out of that
fund. Should a location as fortunate as that suggested last to his Agent at
N. O. take place, the unavoidable delay in turning it into cash would leave
him a prey to his actual difficulties.
    I send you the correspondence from Madrid. You will see that the status
quo, the Mobille, & the spoliations subsequent to the Convention of 1802,
have passed sub silentio. These topics may keep open the door for negociation if a return to it be invited by circumstances, and so far the omission of
them, may be turned to convenient account. It is certain that our posture
towards Spain is an awkward one. Your view of it appears to be just. I have
long been of opinion that it would be a wise & dignified course, to take
preparatory & provisional measures for a naval force, and the present crisis
gives a great[1] of urgency to such a policy. This depends on Congress. In the
mean time the instructions to Bowdoin involve delicate considerations.

Monroe left Madrid I understand on the 26 or 27th. of May. He meant to pass thro' Paris. As his family was there, and he would allow some time for discovering the final views of that Govt. but as not only the Empr. & Talleyrand, but as the papers say, Marbois also would be absent, it is probable that his stay would be shortened. I can no otherwise guess the time of his getting to London than by an estimate of these circumstances, which you can make as well as myself. I leave you to state them to Mr. R. & Mr. N. as I presume was reserved to yourself to do. The inclosed letter this moment recd. gives a probable clue to Lears Draught, concerning which no information has been recd from him.[2] The operation undertaken by him may perhaps have good effects but it is of a delicate sort for public functionaries.

Mrs. Madisons apprehensions have been much assuaged by Dr. Physic's encouraging language, and the commencement of her cure is I think perceptible under his process. I fear however it will be several weeks before he will be able to dismiss her. We should both be very happy to see our friends in N. York; but the trip hither being carved out of that to Virga. we must fly in that direction the moment the signal is given. Be so good as to return the letter from Algiers by the first mail. Accept for yourself & Mrs. Gallatin our affectionate respects. Yrs. truly

JAMES MADISON

RC (NHi: Gallatin Papers).

1. JM evidently omitted a word here.
2. The enclosed letter was probably Timothy Mountford to JM, 30 May 1805, *PJM-SS*, 9:419–20. For Lear's draft on JM, see Jacob Wagner to JM, 5 Aug. 1805, and n. 8.

To Horatio Gates

DEAR SIR   PHILADA. Aug 8. 1805

I have recd yours of the 5th. inst: containing the very kind invitation to Mrs. M. and myself to partake of your hospitality at Rose Hill. It would, as I hope you will not doubt, be particularly gratifying to both of us to avail ourselves of so favorable an opportunity of enjoying once more the society of those we so much esteem & regard. Unfortunately the circumstances in which we find ourselves form an insuperable bar to our inclinations. We were brought hither by the desire of obtaining the celebrated skill ⟨of⟩ Dr. Physic, for a complaint which Mrs. M. has had for some months near one of her knees, and which having baffled the ordinary treatment she was advised by her Physicians ⟨at⟩ Washington to place under his management: She has already felt a benefit from it, & has every prospect of a cure. But the time required is likely to be very inconvenient, and being carved out of that allotted for a trip to my farm so important to me in several respects, we shall be obliged to hasten to the Southward the moment the Docr. will grant her a clearance. She joins me in cordial & respectful acknowledgments for the friendly politeness of Mrs. Gates & yourself, and in tendering the best of wishes, with which I remain Dr. Sir Your friend & servt.

JAMES MADISON

RC (NN: Emmet Collection). Docketed by Gates.

From David Gelston

DEAR SIR,   NEW YORK August 8th. 1805

I have received your letter of the 31st ultimo,[1] it appears by the manifest of the Adventure from Halifax, that the wine &ca. was shipped by Gov: Wentworth. I was told that the Gov: finding sundry articles captured, were for the President of the United States & the Secretary of State, interfered and ordered them for N.York. I was also informed that the Adventure was in no case to enter or unlade here, but in the event of the french fleet being in the west Indies and no possibility of effecting reasonable insurance.

Mr Allen made an attempt to enter the Articles in question, and it appeared to me the object in view was to get the articles in his possession to indemnify for many charges. I judged it prudent to stop it, and gave an order to send all the articles to the public store.

I have obtained from Messrs. Robinson & Hartshorne a statement, copy enclosed, from the character of those Gentlemen I have no doubt the statement is correct. I am very respectfully, sir. your obedient servant

DAVID GELSTON

Amo. duties on all the articles	$45_5
deduct to receiv[e] of Mr Butler	8.14
	36.91

The expence of cartage & storage is not yet ascertained—the whole will be forwarded to you when the articles are sent on.

RC (DLC). Docketed by JM.

1. The letter has not been found, but for the seizure of goods sent by Stephen Cathalan Jr. to JM, Jefferson, and Pierce Butler, see Anthony Merry to JM, 30 June 1805, *PJM-SS*, 9:503 and n. 1.

From Jacob Wagner

Dear Sir   Department of State 8 Augt. 1805.

Mr. Deblois encourages me with the expectation of procuring a vessel in a day or two to carry the brass guns to Boston;[1] and as thereafter nothing will remain to prevent the vessel from sailing from Kennebec, I have enclosed letters requesting passports from the Foreign Ministers.[2] Mr. Merry proceeds on his journey for Philada. this afternoon: from Baltimore he crosses the Bay. He says Mrs. Turreau lodges at Evans' tavern in Baltimore and the General lives at a Country seat.

I have at length gone over all OBrien's accounts,[3] so as to enable him to return, and, as, I hope, to render his return unnecessary, having obtained all the light he can throw upon them. They will of course remain in their present state until you return.

A letter from the President for you goes in this mail. With respect & attachment Your obed. servt.

J. Wagner

P.S. Will you be pleased to cover the passports to Joshua Wingate Esqr. Hallowell, Maine.

RC (DLC).

1. For the cannon, see JM to Charles Simms, 10 July 1805, n. 1.
2. Letters not found.
3. For former consul Richard O'Brien's arrival in the United States, see *PJM-SS*, 9:263 n. 7. On 12 Aug. 1805 Wagner asked Albert Gallatin to issue a warrant for $1,500 in favor of O'Brien (DNA: RG 59, DL, vol. 15).

§ From Harry Toulmin. *8 August 1805.* "I mentioned to you in a letter some time since, that I understood that a Vessel then lying in the River was about to pass Mobille without calling.[1] Captain Schuyler (who is just now from Orleans) tells me that she passed Mobille in the Night—that the Spaniards were exceedingly irritated, and threatened to imprison the owner of the Cargo on his return from Orleans and to confiscate the Vessel, if she ever appeared there again. They also talked of building a Gun boat for the purpose of compelling Vessels to stop."

Extract (DNA: RG 233, President's Messages, 9A–D1); extract (DNA: RG 46, President's Messages, 9B–B1). 2 pp. The second extract is a letterpress copy of the first extract.

1. See Toulmin to JM, 6 July 1805 (second letter).

To Thomas Jefferson

Dear Sir   Philada. Aug. 9. 1805.

I select the enclosed papers relating the ship N. Jersey from a mass of which this is but a certain portion.[1] They will enable you to decide on the question to which alone the case is reduced. This is whether in the claims under the French Convention Insurers stand in the shoes of the insured. The printed memoire by Dupont (de Nemours) deserves to be read as a Chef d'oevre of the kind.[2] Whatever the merits of the question in the abstract may be, I should suppose that in relation to the present case it must have been decided by the decisions in many preceding ones, a great proportion of the claims, probably the greater part, having been in the hands of Insurers. It is surmised that Swann in connection with a Corrupt member of the Council of liquidation has created the difficulty in order to secure his own claims out of a fund that might not be equal to the aggregate of claims. It is more easy to suppose this than to account for the opinion of Armstrong as stated by Dupont, which if just ought to have been applied to all claims of the like sort, and whether just or not, can scarcely be proper in its application to one, as an exception to similar claims. I understand from the parties interested that in fact a considerable part of the indemnication [*sic*] in the case of the N. Jersey is due & claimed not by Insurers, but by the owners themselves in their own right. And they are very urgent that something should pass from the Executive which may possibly be in time to save them from the erroneous interposition of the agent of the U. States. I have explained to them the principles on which the Ex. has proceeded, and the little chance there is that the whole business will not have been closed before any communication can reach Genl. Armstrong. I have suggested also the repugnance to any communication previous to intelligence from himself on the subject. In reply they urge considerations which are as obvious as they are plausible. I shall do nothing in the case till I receive your sentiments. If these do not forbid, I shall transmit the case to Armstrong in a form which will merely glance at the point on which it is understood to turn, and will imply our confidence that he will do what is right on it.

I find by a postscript from Cadiz of June 28. that Bowdoin had arrived at Santander.[3] The time is not mentioned.

The wine &c. carried into Halifax[4] was sent by Govr. Wentworth with polite intentions, by a vessel going to N.Y. which had no occasion to enter on her own acct. The consequence has been that she was entered on ours, and the foreign tonnage advanced, amounting to $168. including Majr. Butlers share. The duties & other charges will add not less than $50 more. This being a debt of honor admits of no hesitation. I shall pay your part, and if necessary write to Barnes to replace it.[5] The articles are to go round to Washington.

Mrs. M. is in a course of recovery, according to appearances & the opinion of Docr. Physic. Unfortunately an essential part of the remedy, the Splinter & bandage, must it seems be continued till the cure is compleated. I fear therefore that our detention here will be protracted several weeks at least.

The drouth here is intense. The pastures have entirely failed, so as to drive the graziers to the Hay Stacks; and the evil is doubled by the failure of the 2d. Crops of Hay. Yrs. respectfully & faithfully

JAMES MADISON

RC (DLC: Jefferson Papers). Docketed by Jefferson as received on 15 Aug. Jefferson returned the enclosures in his letter to JM of 17 Aug. 1805.

1. For the *New Jersey*, see Philip Nicklin and Robert Eaglesfield Griffith's 25 July 1805 memorial to JM.

2. The editors have been unable to identify which of Samuel Du Pont de Nemours's five memorials concerning the *New Jersey* JM is referring to (Saricks, *Pierre Samuel Du Pont de Nemours*, 323–24, 422 n. 65).

3. The letter containing this postscript has not been found.

4. For the wine, see David Gelston to JM, 8 Aug. 1805.

5. John Barnes (ca. 1731–1826) had been a grocer in New York and Philadelphia before moving to Georgetown, D.C., in 1800 as a contractor for the Treasury Department. He was Jefferson's "banker and commission agent," and also "supplied him with groceries" until 1809 (Looney et al., *Papers of Thomas Jefferson: Retirement Series*, 1:32 n.; *National Intelligencer*, 30 Jan. 1804).

From Charles Pinckney

(Private)

DEAR SIR,   9 August 1805 IN MADRID.

I have written to you lately very often informing you of the Spaniards being now in the habit of capturing our Vessels as much as during the last war, & that this together with the non-arrival of either Messrs. Bowdoin or Erving, & the impossibility of my finding a proper person to leave our affairs with, had obliged me to remain so much longer than I wished. I am now preparing to leave this for Lisbon in a short time, & send you inclosed my Account Current for 4. Years & one Month.[1] As I am not well acquainted with the keeping of accounts, it is possible there may be some errors, for which reason I send it to you more as a pro forma account than any thing else, to keep until I arrive in Washington, when I shall be content to settle it on any terms the President & yourself shall consider as just &

liberal. I have sent it by Duplicate in case any accident should happen to me on the way home, & I have hitherto refrained from drawing a Shilling for the last year from those motives, I have already mentioned to you, the desire of never touching a farthing of Public Money, until I have proved my right to do so.

The following is the List transmitted to me of American Vessels taken by the Spaniards & sent into Algeciras for adjudication, since the date of my last to you.

Brigantine, Anne Isabel, of Virginia, Williams, Master.
Brigantine, Vervius Pesa.
Brigantine, Dido, Snail, Master, from Marblehead.[2]
Ship, Mary, Robert Stephenson.
Ship, Eagle, Nehemech Shaler, last from Liverpool.
Brigantine, Jefferson, Simon Richmond.
Brigantine, Polly & Nancy, of Baltimore, John Croan.
Schooner, Leffen, William Maret, of Virginia.
Schooner, Molengue, John Waterman of New York.
Brigante, Diana, Silvester Simmons, of New-Haven.[3]
Brigantine, Dru of Norfolk Hill Master.

On all these as in the antecedent ones I have made strong remonstrances to the Secretary of State here but it seems now to be a settled plan to disregard the article which makes the flag cover the property & You may be assured most of our Vessels will be brought in under pretence of having British Property on board. You see how they go on. I have been always & still am certain the more We submit to the more We shall have to submit to & that nothing but firmness & somber measures can obtain from this Court any thing like justice or even a decent observance of Treaty.

RC, two copies, and enclosure (DNA: RG 59, DD, Spain, vol. 6A); extract (DNA: RG 233, President's Messages, 9A–D1); extract (DNA: RG 46, President's Messages, 9B–B1). First RC unsigned; in a clerk's hand; docketed by Wagner as received 26 Oct. Second RC unsigned; in a clerk's hand; marked "(Triplicate)" by Pinckney and includes his postscript: "September 28. Since the above I find there is a small mistake in the account of Mule hire made by my Clerk in the case of the Charge in the name of Bengochea which ought not to have been charged to the United States—Bengochea did the service with Mules which is that charged & recieved the money, but it was on my own private account & the receipt he gave being mixed with the others has occasioned the mistake which I will rectify when I arrive." The enclosure (1 p.) in the second RC is a list of the ships carried into Algeciras, which was omitted from the body of the RC. The second extract is a letterpress copy of the first extract.

1. Not found.
2. The captain of the *Dido* was Samuel Stiness (Benjamin J. Lindsey, comp., *Old Marblehead Sea Captains and the Ships in Which They Sailed* [Marblehead, Mass., 1915], 121; Boston *Democrat*, 9 Nov. 1805).
3. Here the clerk's hand ends, and Pinckney's begins.

§ From William C. C. Claiborne. *9 August 1805, New Orleans.* "I have this day received a Duplicate of the communication to me from Governor Folch, which was lost by Captain Carmick on his passage from Pensacola to this City.[1] It bears date the 6th of June last, and Governor Folch thus expresses himself, 'Captain Carmick in the service of the United States delivered to me your Excellency's favor Dated the 26th. of April last, whereby your Excellency requests my protection for the persons employed in the Mail, which conformably to an order of the American Government is to be established from Washington City to New Orleans, and to go through his Majesty's Territory as far as seventy Miles. I do accede to the Solicitation of your Excellency, being Sensible of the advantage which may result from Such an establishment for the Public, and that it will tend to promote the good understanding which happily prevails between our respective Governments.' There are now Sir, no impediments to the running of the Mail from hence to Fort Stoddart, and I hope it may prove a Safe and expeditious conveyance for Letters."

RC (DNA: RG 59, TP, Orleans, vol. 7); letterbook copy (Ms-Ar: Claiborne Executive Journal, vol. 15). RC 1 p.; in a clerk's hand, signed by Claiborne; docketed by Wagner as received 17 Sept.

1. See Claiborne to JM, 5 July 1805, and n. 2.

§ From Robert Williams. *9 August 1805, Washington, Mississippi Territory.* "The Legislature of this Territory adjourned the 25 ulto after completing the objects for which it was convened.

"I have the honor to inclose you two laws relative to the publick officers of this Territory including that of the Secretary[1] the first originated in consequence of Mr Wests the Secretary's conduct in carrying that office from this place as you have been informed by my communication of the 17th of May[2] and also his never coming near the Legislature or Governor during their Session except the day it Met. The second imposing a penalty, was passed in consequence of his attempts to evade the first in a Manner which the inclosed documents marked No 1.2.3 [not found] will shew and in this event the Territory would have been deprived of its Laws passed during the late annual Session of the General Assembly to a period altogether uncertain and depending on the arrival of his successor as the printed copies had been deposited with him for distribution and which had not been done except in a few instances. The law you will observe is so worded as not to infringe any constitutional or Legal right. On a demand being made agreeable to the Documents here with inclosed marked No 4[3] the Colo delivered the whole of the Records and documents Colo West by his late conduct has lost all his popularity and compelled those who were disposed to adhere to him to relinquish and we are all becoming very quiet."

Adds in a postscript: "Mr [Thomas H.] Williams has received his commission as Secretary and has been prevailed on to accept conditionally I suppose he will write you on this subject."

Letterbook copy (Ms-Ar: Executive Journal, 1805–10).

1. The enclosures were doubtless copies of the 16 July 1805 act "Establishing the place at which the Officers therein named, shall keep their respective Offices, and for other purposes"

which required the treasurer, the auditor of public accounts, and "for the time being," the territorial secretary, to keep their offices and the public records belonging to the secretary's office at the place designated by law for holding general assembly sessions and allotted the first two officers fifty dollars a year for office rent; and the 25 July 1805 act "Concerning Public Officers" which stated that because the former act had not been complied with and because it appeared some officers had attempted to evade it, should the territorial secretary or the other two officers refuse or neglect to comply with the earlier act on or before 10 Aug. 1805, they should pay $3,000 to be recovered in court; and that if any person possessing any records or public documents belonging to the territorial government, to which they had no right, refused to deliver them on the governor's application, that person should pay $3,000 as above, and authorized the territorial attorney general to prosecute and recover the forfeited sums (*Acts Passed by the Third General Assembly of the Mississippi Territory during Their Extra Session Began and Held in the Town of Washington, on the First Monday in July* . . . [Natchez, 1805], in *Records of the States of the United States of America* [DLC microfilm ed.], Miss. B.2, reel 1, pp. 8–9, 31–32).

2. Williams's 17 May 1805 letter to JM presumably contained copies of his 14 May 1805 letter to Cato West asking when it would be convenient for the latter to deliver the public documents to him and regretting that business before the board of commissioners would prevent him from calling on West as they had discussed; Williams's 16 May 1805 letter to West stating that he had received West's reply through Parke Walton, that he believed the public documents existed and belonged at the seat of government, asking West to appear at Washington with the seal of office on 17 May, and stating that he would accommodate West as much as was commensurate with the public interest; and Walton's 16 May 1805 statement that he had delivered Williams's 14 May letter to West who said he would not write to Williams as that might lead to "serious embarrassments," that Williams might act as he thought proper and West would do the same. West asked if Walton would take the seal and when Walton refused West said he would send it next day "if he could or some time shortly" (Ms-Ar: Executive Journal, 1805–10).

3. Among the documents marked No. 4 Williams presumably enclosed his 30 July 1805 letter to West conveying a copy of the 25 July law and demanding the delivery of the public documents to Williams's secretary William B. Shields (ibid.).

To Seth Botts Wigginton

SIR.   DEPARTMENT OF STATE, August 10th. 1805.

I have received your letter of the 4th. inst. requesting a copy of the communication you were informed was made to the Department of State by Mr. Lee, the Commercial Agent at Bourdeaux, respecting the Ship Easter & her papers so far as it involves yourself.[1] In answer I must observe to you what you seem to have partly foreseen, that the rules of the Department, founded upon reasons of public expediency, forbid the granting of your request; but it may not be improper to acquaint you that the part which is attributed to you in the transaction is expressly stated by Mr. Lee to have come to his knowledge chiefly from the information of others. I have only to add that whatever well authenticated facts you may think proper to impute against the conduct of Mr. Lee will receive the attention they may merit, and which will be equally due to any counter proofs he may have to offer. I am &c.

JAMES MADISON.

Letterbook copy (DNA: RG 59, DL, vol. 15).

1. See William Lee to JM, 20 Jan. 1805, *PJM-SS*, 8:497–98, and Lee to JM, 20 July 1805. Wigginton was probably inquiring about the former letter.

From John Armstrong

SIR,   August 10th. 1805 PARIS.

I have had the honor of receiving your letters of the 23d. of May and 6th. of June[1] and shall loose no time in attending to the injunctions they convey. One of these, in relation to Gen. Ferrand's proclamation, has been anticipated, as you will perceive by my answer to Mr. Tallyrand's note of the 21st. of July.[2] The other, with respect to the claim upon the Batavian Government, must necessarily be suspended 'till Mr. Brantzan's arrival at Paris; the suspension of the Neapolitan business (were it in the power or disposition of His Sicilian M. to execute it on the principles we wish) would arise from a similar cause—the absence of Mr. de Gallo. Mr. Lewis's claim has been put into the hands of Mr. Skipwith who is charged with the prosecution of it in the Council of Prizes. The claimants ought to know, that whatever may be the Decision of this tribunal, the present state of the Treasury, with the multiplying demands of the war upon it, admits of no payments to foriegn creditors; and that unless we were in condition, and it had become our policy as well as duty to enforce the demands of our citizens, there is no use and some disadvantage, even to them, in pressing their claims. There is a degree of importunity that not only sours the temper but impairs the justice of a debtor, and it is not improbable that an error of this sort may be at the bottom of that indifference which has been shewn here to the reclamations of Denmark &c. for ten years past. In the last conversation I had with the Minister of the Treasury on the subject of Le Clerc's bills and other debts of similar character & standing, he assured me, there was no prospect of immediate payment, and recommended good humor & patience as the means best calculated for obtaining it eventually. What is true with respect to these, will be equally so with regard to debts arising from capture.

The first fruits of the late incorporation of the Ligurian Republic with France will in all probability be a war with Russia. The note, a copy of which is enclosed, though not acknowledged here, may be received as genuine, and will shew very clearly the temper & views of Russia.[3] It is

195

conjectured, that the language of this note would have been more guarded had not the Power employing it(,) pre-concerted with other powers, a system of hostility calculated on the continuance of what they call, French en-croachment;[4] a conjecture which takes additional probability from the encreased military activity & preparations of Austria, and from the new influences which the late Russian acquisition of Swedish Pomerania,[5] is so obviously calculated to produce upon Prussia. A few days will however put an end to conjecture & we shall then know whether this war with Russia, like that with England, is to consist only of angry words and impotent menaces, or whether, embracing the several Powers, it is destined to rivive all the calamities of Europe?

The Emperor is now at Bologne and looking towards England. If the explanations, which have been demanded, from Austria be satisfactory, it is probable that he will continue to look that way—but should they be hostile or even equivocal, he will instantly set his face towards Germany. In war, the first blow is sometimes decisive and of all men living he will perhaps be the last either to over:look an advantage, or to forbear to use it. The near-est column of the Russian Army (120,000) is in Polhenia—twenty six days march from Trieste; another heavy corps is forming on the borders of the Black Sea, whence they may be readily thrown into lower Italy or brought up to the head of the Adriatic; a third in Swedish Pomerania; a fourth of 45,000 already exists in Albania, and a fifth of 25,000, at Corfu. These are preparations worthy of an Alexander and when seen in connexion with those of Austria which has 300,000 men ready to take the field at a mo-ment's warning, would appal any man but Bonaparte and any nation but France. To this extraordinary man and more extraordinary people, they but appear as sources of new atchievements, new glories and a wider range of spoil and domination; nor are there wanting among them, men other-wise sober and enlightened, who consider the contest on which they are about to enter, as destined to verify all the dreams of Lewis the 14, and to render Bonaparte as absolute over every part of Europe, as he now is in the city of Paris. A fact highly propitious to this ambition, is, that every french-man identifies his chief and himself, and feels as proud under any new cir-cumstance of agrandizement to his Emperor, as if he himself were loaded with crowns & laurels. I am not sure however but that this vanity has in it-self the principle of a counter-action, which only waits a change of fortune to shew itself.

The English papers mention the capture of an American armed vessel off Giberaltar by the Spaniards.[6] This report has not reached us through any other channel—it is therefore to be doubted—but of their general disposition to injustice & insolence with regard to us, I have no doubt, and I now transmit the copy of a letter from Mr. Lee of Bourdeaux, which exhibits both under a new & very offensive shape.[7] I have not failed to remonstrate freely on the subject and am well enough assured, that the particular injury will be redressed—but whether this will be done in a way that will prevent a repitition of the offense, is very uncertain. For this purpose, our own endeavors would serve us best. Hints of this kind have so frequently escaped me, that you may perhaps begin to suspect, that I have caught a little of the influenza of Europe. This however is far from being the fact. It is here that a man of any tolerable degree of sense & soberness will soonest perceive how little is the good conferred, and how great & lasting are the mischiefs inflicted by war; but it is also here that he best discovers that in nine cases out of ten of national insult or injury, the motives to their perpetration have partaken more of the cowardice that believes it has nothing to fear, than of the intrepidity that fears nothing—& he will hence conclude that national, like personal spirit, is not only our best support under actual hostility, but our most substantial protection against it. With the highest possible respect, I am Sir, Your most Obedt. humb. Servant

JOHN ARMSTRONG

RC and enclosures (DNA: RG 59, DD, France, vol. 10). RC in a clerk's hand, signed by Armstrong; marked "(()Duplicate)." For enclosures, see nn. 2 and 7.

1. See *PJM-SS*, 9:378–79, 432–36.
2. The enclosures are (1) Talleyrand to Armstrong (3 pp.; undated; in French; printed in *ASP, Foreign Relations*, 2:726–27), protesting American trade with rebel-occupied ports of Haiti; stating that although these might be private ventures, the U.S. government was required to end them because the obligations of countries in a state of peace with each other meant that no such government could "second the spirit of revolt of the subjects of another power"; complaining that the U.S. government could no longer ignore this scandalously public trade in which merchant vessels were supported by armed ships, and the captains publicly feted on their return by dinners at which "the principles of the government of Haiti were celebrated" and "vows are made of its duration"; enclosing an extract from an American newspaper detailing such a dinner and listing the toasts; and stating that he gave this information to Armstrong so the latter could transmit it to his government, which Talleyrand had no doubt would take prompt and effectual measures to end the trade; and (2) Armstrong's undated reply (3 pp.) to Talleyrand's "of yesterday," stating that he was enclosing a second copy of the U.S. act of 3 Mar. 1805, which Talleyrand would find answered his demands and showed the U.S. government's respect and friendship for Napoleon; he noted that although national law only required leaving citizens engaged in illicit trade to the penalties attached to such trade, in this case the government had added new regulations prohibiting certain articles of trade. Armstrong asked Talleyrand to note that the commercial trip to which he referred had occurred before passage of the new law, and the public dinner, no matter how indecent and offensive to the U.S. and French governments, must be left to the mercies of public opinion, which, he further stated, could be seen in the new law. Armstrong decried General Ferrand's recent fiat ordering those who traded with Haiti to be treated like pirates as contrary to international law, and he was sure that Talleyrand would immediately overturn such an outrageous decree. For the 3 Mar. 1805 law forbidding the departure of armed merchant ships for the West Indies, see *U.S. Statutes at Large*, 2:342–43. For Ferrand's decree, see *PJM-SS*, 9:134 n. 2.

3. For the 10 July 1805 note from Count Nikolai Novosiltsov to Baron Karl August von Hardenberg, see John M. Forbes to JM, 16 July 1805, and n. 2.

4. For the coalition against France, see *PJM-SS*, 9:362 n. 1.

5. Prussian threats to invade Swedish Pomerania throughout the fall and early winter of 1804–5 culminated in a Russo-Swedish convention of 14 Jan. 1805 "to guarantee the independence of Germany" in which Russia agreed to send troops to Swedish Pomerania. During the summer of 1805 rumors spread through Europe concerning the sale of Swedish Pomerania, which the Swedish minister at Ratisbon denied, and Russian troops did not arrive in Pomerania until the fall of 1805 (John Holland Rose, ed., *Select Despatches from the British Foreign Office Archives Relating to the Formation of the Third Coalition against France, 1804–1805* [London, 1904], 52, 59, 86, 97 n. 2, 99, 103–4; *Times* [London], 9 Sept. and 22 Oct. 1805).

6. The 16 July 1805 edition of the London *Times* contains an extract of a 15 June letter from Gibraltar, describing the Spanish seizure of an American gunboat as a hostile act against the United States. For this incident, see *PJM-SS*, 9:495 n. 3.

7. The enclosure is a copy of William Lee to Armstrong, 3 Aug. 1805 (1 p.), describing a recent "very serious dispute" he had had with the commissary of marine and the Spanish consul about eight American seamen who had deserted their ships to sign on with a Spanish privateer. The commissary refused to order the men returned to their ships without permission from the Spanish consul, which the latter refused to give. Lee predicted similar difficulties in the future because there were several French privateers fitting out under the Spanish flag, "no doubt to capture American Vessels." Lee added that he could not remedy the evil and asked for Armstrong's advice. He said the commissary had promised to write to the minister of marine and added "doubtless he and the Span. Consul understand each other in the business."

§ From Sylvanus Bourne. *10 August 1805, Amsterdam.* "I embrace the opportunity by the return of Mr Rittenhouse to send for publication in the national Intelligencer at Washington & in the *Phila Gazette,* at Phila. a Statement relative to the subject of my late letters which I hope will prove Satisfactory to you & my fellow Citizens at large.[1] While I sincerely regret the unpleasant circumstances which call for this publication I must again aver that my embarrassments at the time could have alone suggested the idea of the proposed connection with Mr D—but as explained in my Statement—my motives & views were perfectly correct & nothing was intended by said arrangment that could possibly divert the Consular Powers from their true & proper Channell or involve one shilling aditional Charge on the commerce of the UStates—your conviction of this truth & the consequent purity of my motives in the matter must operate to restore me to your full confidence & such a conviction must arise from the uniform tenor of my conduct since I have had the honor of holding a Commission under Govt.

"I am not unacquainted that applications have heretofor been made to Govt: for the place I now occupy & that as I had given no cause of discontent to Govt it resolv⟨ed⟩ on permitting me to remain. I feel particularly gratefull for this decision & anxiously hope it will not be departed from as such an event would in⟨v⟩olve me *in great distress*—indeed my future welfare in life depends on the preservation of my place as it forms the material source for the support of my unfortunate family—the long time I have been absent from the U States would make me be as a Stranger in my own Country & I should be at a loss to know what plan of buisness to pursue— you may be persuaded my respected Sir that I Shall cautiously avoid in future even the *appearance* of impropriety or irregularity in my conduct & sedulo⟨usly⟩ Strive to perform every obligation imposed by my public situati(on) with becoming dignity & a true & constant regard to the interest of my Countrymen which indeed I have ever & scrupulou(sly) attended to—as they must be disposed to testify.

"My late letters will have acquainted you that as your desire for the removal of Mr. Alexander was predicated on his inability from ill health to perform properly the duties of his Office but which not being the case at this time I had concluded to continue him as my agent & under my controul till Govt. Should fill said place by a fixed appointment—& that I had informed Mr Alexr. that he ought not to expect said appointments by any means but prepare his affairs so as to quit the place with the least inconvenience to himself. I hope that the humane motives which have guided me in this temporary arrangment will be duly appreciated by you especially as the public service does not in the least Suffer therefrom.

"The present State of Affairs in Europe Seem Strongly to presage a long continued war & I have reason to beleive that the ensuing Spring will open with very active operations on all quarters. The British Govt. flattered by the prospect of important aid on the Continent begin to treat neutrals more roughly than they have done of late but I doubt not that our Govt will firmly assert the rights of our Commerce & not permit them to be trampled on with impunity.

"I shall anxiously wait your letters in reply to this & the others lately wrote you."

Adds in a postscript: "I have not in my publication noticed Mr Damens' conduct in conniving at the exercise of the Official functions by Mr Hooglant during my absence who had been dismissed by me for [*illegible*]ble reasons because the intriguing fellow has so arranged that matter as to put it out of my power to prove the fact in Law—though *no doubt exists thereof*—viz of his acting as agent & by Mr Damen('s) connivance Mr H being his particular friend & correspondent at the Helder & so late *as August 1804* I received a packett of letters sent up to my care from the Master of an American vessell on his arrival below among which letters was one addressed to Mr Hooglant as *Consular Agent of the UStates* tho he had been removed by me in *1801*. As Mr D has threatned to spend *f*20,000 to ruin me I thought best not to expose myself to him in any way—but you can rely my respected Sir on the fact of Mr H having acted agent in many cases during my absence & undoubtedly by Mr Damens advice as it gave him a conseque(nce) of importance to Mr Damen's interests in whose affairs he is Strongly connected & his right hand man in supporting the many impositions to which our commerce has been long subjected. The same principle has also prevented my taking notice of the intriguing business carried on for the procuring Passengers from Germany fully explained in my late letters to you."

RC (DNA: RG 59, CD, Amsterdam, vol. 1). 4 pp.; docketed by Wagner as received 15 Oct.

1. For the publication of Bourne's 1804 letters to Damen & Van Oliver suggesting they combine their businesses, see *PJM-SS*, 9:380 n. 2. In his 1 Aug. 1805 statement, Bourne argued that at that time he believed that Damen & Van Oliver were correct in their conduct, denied that the wording in his letters implied that he intended to share his consular powers with Herman Hendrik Damen, said that he no longer had confidence in Damen and that his sponsorship of another brokerage house was based not on resentment at Damen's refusal to the suggested combination but on that lack of confidence, asked where Damen had received the exclusive right to all American business in Amsterdam,

said that all the American captains, merchants, and seamen with whom he had transactions would support him, and expressed his hope that this statement would restore public confidence in him (*National Intelligencer*, 18 Oct. 1805).

§ From William C. C. Claiborne. *10 August 1805, New Orleans.* "I now transmit you a Copy of the Marquis's answer (marked No 1)[1] to my Letter of the 3rd. Inst. You will perceive Sir, that Morales has authority to continue his Sales in West Florida; that he contemplates residing in this City, and proposes to issue *Official orders from hence*, as *Intendant of East and West Florida*. I consider a conduct *of this kind*, not only disrespectful, but insulting to this Government, and I have accordingly addressed on this day a Letter to the Marquis, of which the enclosed (no 2)[2] is a copy. Since the possession of this Territory by the United States, the departure of Morales has several times been solicited; I considered him an unprincipled, intrigu'ing Man, and was persuaded that his views were Hostile to the Interest of the United States. His early departure was promised; He once assured me in person (in the month of May last) that his King had ordered him to Mexico, and that he would depart so soon as some necessary Business relating to the Kings revenue was adjusted. I requested him to expedite that Business, and in the mean time promised him protection, and this I presume is the 'assent' to which he alludes."

RC and enclosures (DNA: RG 59, TP, Orleans, vol. 7); letterbook copy and letterbook copy of enclosures (Ms-Ar: Claiborne Executive Journal, vol. 15). RC 2 pp.; in a clerk's hand, signed by Claiborne; docketed by Wagner as received 17 Sept. Minor differences between the copies have not been noted. For enclosures, see nn.

1. The enclosure (2 pp.; marked "*No. 1.*"; docketed by Wagner; printed in Rowland, *Claiborne Letter Books*, 3:159–60) is a copy of a translation, certified by interpreter Moreau Lislet, of Casa Calvo to Claiborne, 8 Aug. 1805, transmitting Juan Ventura Morales's statement that he had received a royal order that removed the obstacles to land transfers laid down by Vicente Folch, who had forbidden the governor of Baton Rouge to permit the survey or transfer of Spanish lands sold since 18 May 1803; that Morales had been instructed to bring to conclusion all pending land sale proceedings; that he would exercise his functions during his stay in the territory; that he had Claiborne's assent to this; and that he would fulfill his duties as intendant relative to the king's interests in Louisiana and West Florida.

2. Claiborne enclosed a 10 Aug. 1805 copy of his reply to Casa Calvo (2 pp.; marked "No. 2"; docketed by Wagner; printed ibid., 160–61, where it is dated 9 Aug.), repeating that the time prescribed by treaty for the withdrawal of Spanish authorities had long expired, stating that he could not see by what authority Morales presumed to exercise within U.S. territory his functions as intendant, asking Casa Calvo to close Morales's office and to direct him to repair to Spanish territory to transact his public business, adding that he considered Morales's remaining there and acting as intendant "not only as disrespectful, but a direct insult to this government." He requested that Casa Calvo, if he lacked the power to comply with Claiborne's wishes, inform him promptly so Claiborne might "have recourse to Such other measures as my duty shall enjoin."

§ From William Duane. *10 August 1805.* "Wm Duane's respects to Mr Maddison— Sends a paper in which there is an article, that it may be proper he should see— the same information is stated in other papers of N York, of not so hostile a character as the N York Gazette.[1]

"Wm D. would have waited on Mr Maddison before now, but was desirous not to intrude while there was likely to be any interruption of other company—and on the subject of Spanish affairs he refrained rather from saying any thing than endanger any erroneous or premature discussion."

RC (DLC). 1 p.

1. The enclosure has not been found, but Duane probably referred to an article in the 2 Aug. 1805 *New-York Gazette and General Advertiser* asking how the paragraph in Jefferson's 8 Nov. 1804 message to Congress which stated that Spanish objections to the validity of the American title to Louisiana had been withdrawn, but the question of the territory's exact limits remained to be settled, could be reconciled with the news that Monroe and Pinckney's negotiations had "failed in every point." The paper added: "An involved message, which may be read with equal chance of comprehension either backwards or forwards, will put every thing to rights."

§ From Peter Kuhn Jr. *10 August 1805, Genoa.* "My last respects were of the 16th Ulto as per Copy annexed, and have now the honor of confirming them in every particular. Since then nothing very material has occurred in this quarter worth your notice except the arrest of two French Engineers at Venice, which occasioned much alarm in the political sphere, especially as the German Agents here were insinuated to quit this place immediately, but as on the application of the French Court said Engineers have been since released, it is imagined that matters may yet for some time continue to hold in a state of Suspence.

"Notwithstanding the formal Union of this State to France the French System & Laws have not yet been enforced here, nor is the changement to take place as is reported till the 1st of Next Vendemmiaire or 22d Sepr."

RC (DNA: RG 59, CD, Genoa, vol. 1). 1 p.; docketed by Wagner "16 July & 10 Augt. 1805."

§ From John Sibley. *10 August 1805, Natchitoches.* "By the request of Governor Claiborne, I have the Honour of forwarding to you herewith, a coppy of a French Manuscript that by accident come into my possession.[1] It was found Amongst the papers of the late Governor Messier of the Province of Taxus;[2] he died at St. Antonio, & after his death his family return'd Again to Natchitoches where they had before lived, And this Manuscript was brought in amongst his private Books and papers, I procur'd it from his Son Athanaise de Messier esqr.[2] a very worthy Man now the Treasurer of this County. It is written in a clear handsome hand in a large folio Bound Volum, with wide margin. The Original is now in my possession. The expence of Coppying it is $85. (viz).

Pierre Graciole's acct. 25 days @$2.	$50
25 days boarding ditto	25
Paper Stationry &c	6
Mr. Vin P(ie)re. 2 days comparing the Coppy.	4
	$85."

RC and Tr (DLC: Jefferson Papers). RC 1 p.; docketed by Wagner. Tr docketed by Jefferson.

1. For the manuscript and Claiborne's request for a copy, see *PJM-SS*, 9:431 and nn. 1–2.

2. Parisian native Athanase de Mézières (d. 1779) was one of the French army officers retained by Spain after that country took control of Texas and Louisiana. A longtime resident of Natchitoches, he served as lieutenant governor of that district from 1769 to 1779 (*Athanase de Mézières and the Louisiana-Texas Frontier, 1768–1780*, trans. and ed. Herbert Eugene Bolton, 2 vols., Spain in the West [Cleveland, 1914], 1:79–80, 84 n. 104, 121).

§ From Elias Vander Horst. *10 August 1805, Bristol.* "The preceding is a Copy of my last of the 30h. of June ℔ the Louisa Capn. Wilson Via Philadelphia,[1] since which I have not been honored with any of your favors. The Affairs of Europe still continue to be involved in intrigue & mystery and whether Peace will be the result or the War become more general remains for time to determine. I am however not yet quite without hope ('though I confess I am now less sanguine than I was a short time since) that the ensuing Winter maybe productive of a general pacification, and the more so as the late stir that Russia has made seems better calculated to give weight to negociations at that period than to produce any other effect sooner.

"The Season hitherto has not been the most favorable for our growing Crops, which are at present uncommonly backward, but yet, if we should have a continuance of a month or Six weeks, of the warm weather that has but Just commenced, with less rain than before, the Harvest may still be tolerably productive, though, at any rate, I do not expect it will be abundant nor indeed by any means equal to the consumption of the Country, of this however it is impossible for anyone yet to be quite certain. I can therefore only further say that the Harvest will be late and I never yet knew a large [*sic*] Harvest a good one.

"Enclosed I beg leave to hand you a London Price Current [not found] & a few of our latest News-papers to which please be referred for what is now passing in this Quarter of a public nature."

RC (DNA: RG 59, CD, Bristol, vol. 2). 2 pp.; marked "(Duplicate)"; written above Vander Horst to JM, 28 Aug. 1805; docketed by Wagner "10. 28. 30. Aug 1805."

1. *PJM-SS*, 9:508. The *Louisa* arrived at Philadelphia on 3 Sept. (*New-York Price-Current*, 7 Sept. 1805).

§ From Thomas H. Williams.[1] *10 August 1805, Washington, Mississippi Territory.* "I had the honor to recieve a few days ago under cover from the Department of State, a Commission as Secretary of the Mississippi Territory.

"As my public engagements render any other than a temporary acceptance impracticable, I deem it proper to State to you candidly my Situation, in order that the necessity for the Speedy appointment of a Successor may be more apparent.

"I have been for some time past acting as Register and ex-officio Commissioner under the Act of Congress for the adjustment of land titles in this Territory. Various reasons have hitherto contributed to procrastinate the accomplishment of this business. It begins now to assume a progressive form; and I need not point out to you how essentially important it is both to the interest and honor of the united States that it Should be Speedily and with the least possible delay completed. The relations Subsisting between the General Government and the State of Georgia, render it not only extremely desirable but highly expedient, and the Solicitude of the people here, who are more directly interested, Still more so: for it is a Subject on which hang if not all their affections, at least all their anxieties.

"The labors of the Commissioners conjunctly and of the Register seperately, will be daily increasing: and I have every reason to calculate upon Such an accumulation of duty in the course of the ensuing autumn and winter, as will render it impossible for me to discharge with any degree of Credit to myself, or of utility to the Government the additional duties of Secretary of the Territory. I will therefore respectfully suggest the propriety, indeed the necessity, of Superceding me in that office by the first of November, or at any rate by the first of December next.

"In thus declining the acceptance of an office highly honorable in its nature, I am guided by an honest conviction that in doing so I shall be more useful to the Government. This consideration alone could have induced me to forego the pleasure of acting with my worthy friend at the head of the Government here, who by his inflexible integrity and patriotic devotion to the public weal, grows daily in the esteem of his friends, and of his fellow citizens in General.

"I beg leave to charge you with the office of making my acknowledgments to the President of the United States. In doing this you cannot use language too Strong to be expressive of my gratitude and esteem."

RC (DNA: RG 59, LRD). 3 pp.; docketed by Wagner as received 17 Sept., with Jefferson's added docket: "wishes a successor to be appointed." Printed in Carter, *Territorial Papers, Mississippi*, 5:417–18.

1. Attorney Thomas Hill Williams (1780–1840) was a North Carolina native who moved to Mississippi Territory in 1802. He continued to act as secretary until Cowles Mead of Georgia, who was named to replace him, arrived on 2 June 1806. Williams was again appointed secretary in 1807. He was named collector at New Orleans in 1810 but later returned to Mississippi, where he was elected senator from the new state in 1817. He moved to Tennessee in 1840 (Carter, *Territorial Papers, Mississippi*, 5:380 n. 71, 584–85; Claiborne, *Mississippi, as a Province, Territory and State* [1964 reprint], 1:258 n.; *PJM-SS*, 9:138 n. 2).

From Jacob Wagner

DR. SIR   DEP. STATE 11 Augt. 1805.

I have received your letter of the 6th. inst.[1] and enclose an answer for Mr. Wigginton.[2] Mr. Lee's statement accompanies it. If Mr. W. be innocent, it is necessary to suppose that his assurance to the latter was founded on a fraud of which he was made the dupe himself, and that his privity in the corrupt agreement, by drafting it, is falsly testified by Erving and the broker. Mr. Lee on a former occasion gave Erving a very bad character,[3] and the part taken by the broker includes the perfidy of disclosing the confidence of his employers, which may possibly discredit his allegations. I do not know Wigginton, otherwise than as the author of a letter or two, you received from him some time ago,[4] pointing out various deceptions practiced by foreigners with our neutral documents, a topic which may be considered as raising some little presumption in his favor on this occasion.

The guns for Algiers are shipped,[5] and I have desired Mr. Deblois to insure them to Boston, & the Navy Agent at the latter place to continue the insurance to Kennebec? I expect to send on Monday a letter for your signature, to accompany the shipment of the cargo. I have the honor to remain Yr. faithful obed. servt.

Jacob Wagner

RC (DLC). Postmarked 10 Aug.

1. Letter not found.
2. See JM to Seth Botts Wigginton, 10 Aug. 1805.
3. Wagner may have referred to William Lee's 20 Jan. 1805 letter, *PJM-SS*, 8:497–98.
4. See S. B. Wigginton to JM, 31 May and 9 June 1804, ibid., 7:269–70, 303.
5. See JM to Charles Simms, 10 July 1805, and n. 1, and Wagner to JM, 5 and 8 Aug. 1805.

From Albert Gallatin

Dear Sir   N. York Aug. 12th 1805

I return the Spanish correspondence & the Algiers letter.[1] Although there are some unpleasant circumstances in the manner in which the negotiation was carried and terminated, the situation of affairs is rather on a more decent footing than I had expected; but, as you observed, the instructions to Mr. Bowdoin & the conduct which he ought to pursue are very delicate & serious considerations.

It seems from Mountford's letter that Mr. Lear's draft was for the Algiers annuity. I immediately directed the purchase here of £5000 Stg. to be remitted to Baring & cover their advance. But the question occurs whether they should not be informed that they are still to keep the whole of the contingent credit of one hundred thousand dollars (22,500 Stg.) opened in Mr Lear's favor. Otherwise, that credit being reduced to less than 80,000 dollars by his wheat draft, some inconvenience may arise in the Tripolitan negotiation. Be pleased to communicate your opinion & I will write to the Barings accordingly.

We rejoice to hear of Mrs Madison's favorable symptoms & beg to be affectionately remembered. Your's truly

ALBERT GALLATIN

RC (DLC).

1. See JM to Gallatin, 8 Aug. 1805.

From Robert Purviance

SIR   BALTIMORE 12th Aug 1805

Agreeably to the enclosed Letter from Governor Claiborne,[1] I have just received from him by the Ship Comet, one Hogshead, three Boxes & two, cases directed "for the President of the United States";[2] which I have engaged with a Carter to take to Washington for 17 Drs. inclusive of Drayage from the Point.

I am sorry to inform you, that the surv[iv]ing magpie, according to the Captain's report, eat the other three on the passage. I find that he is remarkably voratious and can eat meat or any thing that is given him.

I suppose it probable that they must have been carried to New Orleans in seperate Cages.

I should have complied with Governor Claiborne's request, on Saturday last, by sending these things, but I could[3] succeed in getting the whole of them landed 'till this Afternoon.

I have directed Nath Peck, the Carter, to take with him a sufficient quantity of Corn for food for the Animals and to be careful in supplying them with water, while on his way to Washington. I have the honor to be Sir very respectfully Your ob Serv.

RT PURVIANCE
Collr

RC (DLC: Jefferson Papers). In a clerk's hand, signed by Purviance; docketed by Jefferson "Purviance to mr Madison."

1. For Claiborne's 23 July 1805 letter to Purviance, see Jackson, *Letters of the Lewis and Clark Expedition*, 1:253.
2. On 7 Apr. 1805 Meriwether Lewis wrote Jefferson, enclosing an invoice of the articles he was sending. Among them were the skins of antelope, mule deer, marten, Rocky Mountain squirrels, and coyote, Indian artifacts, a box of various earths and minerals, and "four liveing Magpies . . . a liveing burrowing squirel of the praries [prairie dog] [and] one liveing hen of the Prairie [sharp-tailed grouse]," ibid., 231, 234–36. The four magpies, the prairie dog, and the grouse were alive when they arrived at St. Louis forty-five days after leaving Fort Mandan in what is now North Dakota. It is unknown when the grouse died, but Claiborne told Purviance only that he was sending four magpies and the prairie dog

(Paul Russell Cutright, "The Odyssey of the Magpie and the Prairie Dog," *Missouri Historical Society Bulletin* 23 [1967]: 215–23).

3. Purviance presumably omitted the word "not" here.

§ From John F. Brown. *12 August 1805, New York.* "Since I had the Honor of addressing you last,[1] I find my health continues in a bad State, and the opinion of my physicians is, that a Warm Climate would operate against my Complaint, and advise my continuing in this Country, I am therefore under the Necessity of Requesting you, to Accept my Resignation of Consul at the Port of St. Thomas. Mr. Ewers will continue to Act for me in that Station, untill the last of December, at which time, the Returns will be made up, And the Accounts forwarded."

RC (DNA: RG 59, LRD). 1 p.

1. See Brown to JM, 28 Mar. 1805, *PJM-SS*, 9:189.

§ From James Leander Cathcart.[1] *12 August 1805, Washington.* "I have the honor to enclose Mr. Nissen⟨s⟩ receipt [not found] for security given for cloth taken from me by the Bashaw of Tripoli deposited in his hands by me in order that he might recover the amount upon account of the United States, & likewise his letter to me of the 14th. of January 1805 containing a list of the furniture left by me at Tripoli,[2] which with the paper⟨s⟩ & accounts already deposited in the office of the Department of State are incontestable proofs of the validity of the charge⟨s⟩ made by me for loss sustain'd on said Cloth furniture and difference of Exchange amounting in the aggregate to $ 1562 $^{80}/_{100}$ which was paid to me by way of advance until I procured the necessary vouchers to substantiate my claim, this being done, I request that I may be exonerated from the above charge as it still remains to my debit in the books of the Treasury. I likewise request you to have the goodness to advance me the remainder of the amount of the balance of my accounts which is stop'd in part payment of Robertsons bill, & to permit the whole amount of said bill $ 3383 $^{20}/_{100}$ to remain to my debit until I recover damages either from the Spanish government or the underwriters, in like manner as it h⟨as⟩ been permited to remain since the year 1797;[3] by granting my request you will render me a very particular favor & you may be persuaded Sir that I would not be so importunate if circumstances did not dictate the necessity; my acc⟨ts⟩ are all settled of every denomination the bill in question excepted, which is the only sum that will continue to my debit."

RC and enclosures (DNA: RG 59, CD, Tripoli, vol. 2). RC 1 p. For surviving enclosures, see n. 2.

1. James Leander Cathcart (1767–1843) was born in Ireland of Scots-Irish ancestry. He came to America with a relative and entered on the *Confederacy* as a midshipman in 1779. He was captured by the British and imprisoned at New York but escaped in 1782. In 1785, while serving on the merchant ship *Maria*, he was captured and enslaved by Algerians, rising through various positions until he became the dey's chief Christian clerk in 1792. In 1796, after a peace treaty was signed between Algiers and the United States, he returned to America. He was named consul at Tripoli the following year but stayed in Philadelphia to select tribute for Algiers. In 1798 he went to Tunis with William Eaton to renegotiate the

treaty of 1797 with that country, then went to Tripoli, where he remained until the pasha declared war on the United States in 1801. In 1802 he was named consul general at Algiers and in 1803 consul at Tunis, but the rulers of both countries rejected him. He was consul at Madeira from 1807 to 1815 and at Cádiz from 1815 to 1817. From 1818 to 1820 he was naval agent for timber in Florida. From 1823 to 1843 he worked in the second comptroller's office in the Treasury Department (Cathcart, *Captives*, iv).

2. The enclosures are (1) a copy of Nicolai C. Nissen to Cathcart, 14 Jan. 1805 (2 pp.), acknowledging receipt of Cathcart's 27 Aug. 1804 letter announcing his intention to return to the United States; protesting that Nissen's "few service[s]" merited neither the American government's "distinguhised [*sic*] acknowledgement" nor Cathcart's thanks; stating that the articles Cathcart had left in the American consular house were being used by the imprisoned American officers and could not be disposed of, that some were broken or destroyed by use but that he and William Bainbridge had agreed that the matter could be settled at a peace, or at the arrival of a new consul, and Cathcart paid their value, and that not knowing how long he would remain in Tripoli he was enclosing a copy of Cathcart's list of the items; and adding "out of Tripoly is the principal, that is like out of prison" and (2) a copy (1 p.) of a "Note of Articles left in the American house," which listed seven tables; thirty-six chairs and two small sofas; one iron bedstead with silk curtains; two sofas; one calico cover and four pillows, with Nissen's note "one Pillow was given to Capt. Morris"; one safe and two bottle racks; seven demijohns, with Nissen's note "must have been stolen as I could not find them;" twenty empty bottles; one roasting jack and trivet; twelve curtain rods and valance; one lustre in the parlor; several mats and "other trifling articles"; and two American flags, with Nissen's additional note "the Chairs will be broke in great part, being very Bad. The Remainder will remain in great part." On the verso of the list, Cathcart has written: "From Mr. Nissen Tripoli Jany. 14th recd at Washington July 26th. 1805. This contains an acct. of Furniture which I left at Tripoli, the most valuable are here inserted & cost much more than what I charged govt. for the whole, the reason it does not exactly correspond with my note is in consequence of the hurry Mrs. Cathcart was in when she took the Inventory of them on the eve of our departure but these alone are certainly worth more than $ 280."

3. In 1797 the *Independent*, a brig of which Cathcart was part-owner, and John Robertson master, was chartered by the U.S. government to carry presents to the dey of Algiers. It was seized by a Spanish privateer and brought into Cádiz, where it was released by the court. The French consul, claiming the rôle d'équipage was defective, refused to allow the ship to depart until Robertson drew a bill of exchange on Secretary of State Timothy Pickering charged to Cathcart. The money was then paid to ransom the *Independent*. The ship was seized again on 28 Apr. 1798 and condemned by the French consul at Málaga. Cathcart was eventually reimbursed $10,910.77 (Williams, *French Assault on American Shipping*, 189).

§ From Joshua Lewis. *12 August 1805, Lexington.* "I acknowledge the receipt of a commission appointing me Commr to the Eastern District of the New-Orlean territory from the President of the U. States. With gratitude I accept of it, and assure you that my best endeavours shall be used to discharge the same with fidelity."

RC (DNA: RG 59, TP, Orleans, vol. 7). 1 p.; docketed by Wagner as received 31 Aug. Printed in Carter, *Territorial Papers, Orleans*, 9:490.

§ From John Pendleton. *12 August 1805, Richmond.* "I had the honor of receiving your very polite favour of the 20th. ulto. [not found] & pray you to accept my best thanks for your kind attention to the subject of my former letter;[1] my absence from Town has occasioned a little delay. I have now written to the secretary at War."

RC (DLC). 1 p.

1. See Pendleton to JM, 15 July 1805.

§ From Henry Hill Jr. *13 August 1805, Havana.* "By the ship Voltaire[1] now on the eve of departure for Phila., I profit of a moment to inform you that I have this day closed the Consulate of the United States in this city, and suspended my official functions, in consequence of a note recd. from His Excy the Govr., of which I inclose you a copy.[2]

"The cause proceeds from a letter I wrote to His Excellency the 8th currt, informing him of the Capture of an am. Vessel and extreme bad treatment of the crew, by a spanish Privateer; proofs of which I inclosd him, made before a spanish notary.

"I shall tomorrow know the result of this business, and communicate without delay a detailed acct of my official conduct to your department.

"I hope my conduct hitherto, nor on this occasion, will be such as to disgrace or injure my Country, give cause to the ennimies of patriotism and Virtue to reflect on the power that appointed me, or dishonor to myself.

"I give you this early information, and have communicated a line to a friend, to prevent unfavorable impressions that reports going from here might cause, before the business is brought to a state of maturity sufficient to calculate on the consequences that may result."

RC and enclosure (DNA: RG 59, CD, Havana, vol. 1). RC 2 pp. For enclosure, see n. 2.

1. The *Voltaire* arrived at Philadelphia on 2 Sept. (Boston *Repertory,* 6 Sept. 1805).
2. The enclosure (1 p.; in Spanish; marked "copy"; docketed by Wagner as received in Hill's 13 Aug. 1805 dispatch) is the marqués de Someruelos to Hill, 13 Aug. 1805, stating that because Hill wrote about matters that he should not have and because of the terms Hill used in his 8 Aug. 1805 letter to Someruelos, he was being ordered to leave Cuba immediately.

§ From Louis-Marie Turreau. *13 August 1805, Baltimore.* Has the honor of enclosing the passport that JM requested in his 7 Aug. letter [not found] for the ship that will carry the naval and military stores and other articles to fulfill the conventions made between the United States and the Algerian regency from the Kennebec River to Algiers. To avoid all difficulties, thought it best the collector or customs officer at the port of departure should fill in the names of the ship and of the captain left blank.

RC (DNA: RG 59, NFL, France, vol. 2–3). 1 p.; in French; docketed by Wagner, with his note: "Passport for the vessel from Kennebec."

§ From James Leander Cathcart. *14 August 1805, Washington.* "It is some time since I had the honor to promise you document[s] to substantiate the justice of some personal remarks dispersed through the numerous communications which

I have had the honor to transmit to the Department of State,[1] The liquidation of my Accounts prevented me from presenting them prior to their final Settlement, neither was I very solicitous upon the subject, as my only wish at present is to prevent you from supposing me capable of misrepresentation.

"The enclosures A and B contain proof positive of the certainty of Mr. O Brien's connection with the Jews of Algiers and presumptive evidence of the many facts which I have reported relative to him in the course of my correspondence.[2]

"C; and D, are documents relative to Mr. Ingraham.[3] The former is a letter from him to Brien Mc.Donogh wherein the character of Leon Farfara is placed in a proper point of view and Mr. Ingraham eventually acknowledges having embezzel'd £1228.16. Sterling of the property of the United States, as it is well known that when Mr. Barlow, sent him to Tripoli, that he was not worth one dollar, that he did not continue there two years, and that he was only allowed at the rate of one hundred dollars per month, it is likewise known that he never entered into any trade, that he lived on a much larger establishment than there was occasion for, and that he set several bad precedents by lavishing money unnecessarily on unworthy objects; Mr. Ingraham covers the above expenditures by charging in his Accounts a sum for repairs more than sufficient to build the house he lived in, when three hundred dollars would more than indemnify him for all his expenses under that head. Farfara knowing how Ingraham came by the above sum has cheated him out of £728.16. Sterling and Brien Mc.Donogh having placed the Seal of the British Consulate upon Ingraham's Accounts, I conceive it highly probable that he has shared the plunder both with Ingraham and Farfara.

"The latter is a Certificate, the copy of which as well as the original are in the hand writing of Mr Eaton, which I obliged Mr. Ingraham to give me at Leghorn in consequence of the infamous proceedings of himself and Mc.Donogh, these are the characters with whom I have unfortunately & inevitably been connected with and on whom Mr. O Brien placed and advised me to place implicit confidence.

"Enclosure E, is Mr. Spence's Certificate relative to George Davis which with my despatch of September the 12th 1803 signed by Hugh G. Campbell Esqr. will substantiate whatever I have alledged against him.[4]

"F, contains W.Y Purviance's note requesting an Extract from Commodore Dale's letter to me, which he published in the Florence Gazette without my permission with an intention to enhance his own importance, which however had a contrary effect as I counteracted his views and made him appear extremely mean and ridiculous.[5]

"G. and H, are Copies of Degen & Purviance's Accounts which envolved me in a loss of dollars 1,551 $^{31}/_{100}$ which I was obliged to accede to in order to draw the balance of 37,000 dollars out of their hands which I could not effect for more than Seven months notwithstanding they had the greatest part of the above Sum in their hands for more than eighteen months free from interest merely to oblige them.[6]

"Exclusive of the observations which might be made on the charges, which are at more than double the just rate (of a private nature) I shall only observe that the 18. boxes of Tea when sold to me by them weighed 2.006lbs Net and that they only accounted to me for 1,046 lbs, saying the remainder was stolen out of their Store.

"Of a public nature it is necessary to observe that as Navy Agents they receive a Commission for purchasing provisions for our Squadron, and have no right to any other profit: now by these Accounts it appears that they had sold to me the following articles at the following prices and it is presumable from the tenor of their conduct that they had made a resonable profit on them Vizt.

97 Kegs of American split peas	֍ 116.10.5
50 Barrels of American Ship-bread	112.10.0
	֍ 229. 0.5

"It likewise appears that they sold the above mentioned articles after they were disembarked from the Ionic Ship Minerva to the American Squadron as follows.

97 Barrels of Peas sold to the American Squadron	֍ 185.11.3
50 Barrels of Biscuit sold to the Schooner Enterprize	259.14.2
	֍ 445. 5.5

"Thus making a profit including their Commission of more than one hundred ֍: Cent, and as vouchers are required for all expenditures at the Navy Department, if any has been forwarded they must be forged and the person or persons who may have sent them are entirely unworthy, either public or private confidence.

"It would be an endless task to describe to you the chicane deception and intrigue that is practised by the whole possé of itinerant adventurers who have settled at Naples, Leghorn and Mersailles. They are in general men of infamous characters who would do any thing for money within the pale of the law; they have long formed the plan of getting the American trade into their own hands, and all the public employments, to give them some degree of consideration and to enable them to commence a correspondence with the Merchants of the United States, they have admitted two young Americans into their firm, the one is in New York soliciting business for them, the other went to England apparently on the same business, but in reality a scheme had been formed by one of the partners to promote an union between him and his Sister, which succeeded to his no small satisfaction, but in reality adds but little to his respectability.

"The plan pursued to acquire recommendation is by inviting a number of American Citizens to their houses, and waiting an hour of hilarity to require it, but those who afterwards place business in their hands pay extremely dear for their entertainment.

"You would blush Sir, to see by what Men we are represented, and by what Agents we are served in the Mediterranean; and until government makes some provision for their Consuls which will put them on an equality with those of other Nations, and be an inducement to men of character to solicit for those posts, I can see no alternative."

RC and enclosures (DNA: RG 59, CD, Tripoli, vol. 2). RC 4 pp. For surviving enclosures, see nn. 3–4.

1. See Cathcart to JM, 27 Apr. 1805, *PJM-SS*, 9:291.

2. The enclosures have not been found, but for Cathcart's earlier criticism of Richard O'Brien, who had objected to Cathcart's appointment as consul general at Algiers, and of O'Brien's relations with the Jews there, see O'Brien to JM, 16 Sept. 1802, Cathcart to JM, 25 Jan. and 30 Mar. 1803, ibid., 3:585–86, 4:281–82, 463, 6:122 n. 12.

3. Joseph Ingraham had served as U.S. representative at Tripoli before and after Cathcart's arrival. Bryan McDonogh was the British consul there. Leon Farfara was a broker and a leader of the Tripoline Jewish community with whom Cathcart had business dealings (Knox, *Naval Documents, Barbary Wars*, 1:297–98, 314, 322, 331, 391–93, 566, 6:369). For Cathcart's earlier reference to Ingraham's embezzlement of funds, see *PJM-SS*, 6:174 n. 1. Enclosure "C" (2 pp.; with Cathcart's 14 Aug. 1805 note on the cover sheet: "Letter from Joseph Ingraham to Brien McDonogh wherein the former accuses Leon Farfara of having detain'd in his hands £728.16.0 Sterling being part of £1228.16.0 for which Ingraham gave bills upon Algiers to said Farfara or in other words Ingraham has cheated the United States out of £1228.16 & Farfara has kept as his share of the plunder £728.16 and as Brien McDonogh put the Consular Seal of the British Nation upon Ingrahams accounts it is presumeable that he came in for snacks"; filed at June 1802) is a copy of Ingraham's 29 June 1802 letter to McDonogh, complaining about several bills drawn payable at London by Farfara, who then gave such instructions to his London correspondent that prevented the bills from being paid to Ingraham. Enclosure "D" (2 pp.; in Eaton's hand, countersigned by Appleton and Eaton; with Cathcart's 14 Aug. 1805 statement that a confrontation took place between Cathcart and Ingraham in Leghorn in which it was revealed that Ingraham owed Cathcart $2,414.61, for which he gave Cathcart security on the underwriters, which was deposited at the American consulate in Leghorn, and in which Cathcart insisted on Ingraham's retracting the contents of a letter he had written Eaton about Cathcart's actions while consul; filed at 4 July 1802) is a copy of Joseph Ingraham's 22 Feb. 1802 testimony in the presence of Thomas Appleton and William Eaton that the copy of a 19 July 1801 letter to William Eaton signed by Ingraham had been composed by Bryan McDonogh, that the "defamatory insinuations" therein regarding Cathcart's agency at Tripoli were entirely fabricated by McDonogh and that he, Ingraham, was completely retracting them. An earlier copy of Ingraham's statement was enclosed in Cathcart's 5 Mar. 1802 letter, *ibid.*, 3:4–5 n.

4. Enclosure "E" (1 p.; with Cathcart's 14 Aug. 1805 note on the verso: "Mr. Spences certificate relative to George Davis—which with my dispatch of September the 12th. 1803 [Cathcart referred to his 9 Sept. 1803 dispatch, *PJM-SS*, 5:391–98 and n.] sign'd by Hugh G. Campbell Esqr. Captain in the United States Navy will place his character in a proper point of view & substantiate every charge which I have made against him"; filed at July 1804) is a copy of midshipman Robert T. Spence's 27 Apr. 1804 statement that "Mr. Ewer" of Degen & Co. at Naples declared in the presence of Cathcart and Spence that Davis, while in Naples, publicly stated that Aaron Burr was his uncle and called him Uncle Burr, that "Mr. Degen was undeceived" by a New Yorker about this and many other things Davis said, that Degen was "extremely mortified" at being so imposed on and said if Davis ever returned to Naples, he would get a far different reception than previously.

5. Enclosure not found. Filed at October 1804 is a copy of the 12 Sept. 1801 *Gazzetta universale* (8 pp.; in Italian), on the last page of which is a loosely translated extract from the beginning of Richard Dale's 25 Aug. 1801 letter to Cathcart, describing the capture of a Tripoline polacre by the U.S. schooner *Enterprize*. In the margin Cathcart wrote: "*This extract was from Commodore Dale to J L Cathcart was given ⟨to⟩ Mr. B[*illegible*]." Dale's letter is printed in Knox, *Naval Documents, Barbary Wars*, 1:560–61.

6. Enclosures not found.

§ From DeWitt Clinton. *14 August 1805, New York.* "I enclose certain documents to prove the impressment &. detention of an American Citizen.

"I also enclose a memorandum of the place &c. where he obtained his protection which may throw further light on the subject of his Citizenship."

Letterbook copy (NNC: DeWitt Clinton Papers). 1 p.

§ From Louis-Marie Turreau. *14 August 1805, Baltimore.* General Moreau, to whom His Imperial and Royal Majesty has granted the liberty to come to the United States, having left France under the disadvantage of a legal judgment entered against him, must not under any circumstances receive in foreign countries the honors to which the consideration of his services would formerly have entitled him, and it is fitting that his arrival and his stay in the United States should not be marked by any demonstrations which go beyond the limits of hospitality. But General Moreau is a Frenchman, and as one he must in all circumstances, receive the protection of the agents of the Imperial government, at any time he may address them, in order to claim it.[1]

These are, Sir, the instructions received from Moreau's government about him, and which Turreau hastens to communicate to JM, particularly because JM's presence in Philadelphia, where Moreau is about to arrive at any moment, might involve JM in some demonstrations, which according to what he has the honor to point out, JM will believe it his duty to keep within certain limits, in view of the situation in which he finds himself, and out of respect for a legal judgment.

RC (DNA: RG 59, NFL, France, vol. 2–3). 1 p.; in French; docketed by Wagner, with his note: "respecting the expected arrival of Genl. Moreau."

1. For Gen. Jean Victor Marie Moreau's arrest and trial for conspiring against Napoleon, see Robert R. Livingston to JM, 19 June 1804, *PJM-SS,* 7:341 and n. 9.

From John Armstrong

SIR,   PARIS 15th. August 1805.

Europe is on the eve of a war, which, from present appearances, will leave no power in it a mere Spectator of the Combat. On One side will be marshalled France, Spain, Portugal, Batavia Swisserland & the new Kingdom of Italy. On the Other, Austria, Russia, England, Prussia Sweden, Denmark, Naples and even Turkey. The Coalitions on both sides will have in them some very discordant materials and unwilling agents, & may perhaps equally suffer from this Cause. France will hersel(f) make prodigious efforts, and it is not either her policy or Usage to spare her Allies, nor is it likely that Austria England & Russia will be more indulgent to the wants wishes or interests of the smaller powers who they may influence. Thinking men, who abstract themselves from person(al) views, consider the crisis as extremely awful, and likely to bring afte(r) it changes of great interest & extent & even those most bent upon dissembling or concealing its' horrors, look forward to a struggle of longer duration & more sanguinary character, than has yet desolated Europe. These last, however, display nothing but confidence in its' issue. They believe, or affect to believe, that the Armies of France are irrisistab(le) & that they will achieve great things, cannot be doubted. Calamitous as this State of things may be for Europe—it effectually *does our business (I ha)ve not failed to employ and have hopes of making it* as *subservient in negotiations as it might be made to a cours(e) decisive* should that be preferred. These circumstances have authorized (me) to repeat an advice Already given by Mr. Monroe & myself, to *mister B———N not to commit you in any way with the government* of Spain in rela-*tion to the late negotiation at Madrid until he shall have received your instruc-tions on the final report made on that business.* Any steps in consequence of your letter of the 23d. of May to Mr. M.[1] *would defeat every hope from any degree of sensation excited here by the dang(er) to Spain of a rupture with us.* I need not tell you that we have *no hope from any other source.*

My last letter was dated on the 10th. With the highest possible respect, I am Sir, Your most Obedient & very humble Servant

JOHN ARMSTR(ONG)

RC (DNA: RG 59, DD, France, vol. 10). Docketed by Wagner as received 27 Oct. Italicized words are those encoded by Armstrong's clerk in a State Department code also used by John Quincy Adams at St. Petersburg and by Jacob Lewis at Saint-Domingue; key not found; copytext is Wagner's interlinear decoding.

1. See JM to Monroe, 23 May 1805, *PJM-SS*, 9:380–83.

§ From William C. C. Claiborne. *15 August 1805, New Orleans.* "A short time previous to the transfer of Louisiana to the United States, Governor Folch having doubted the Authority of Morales to sell lands in West Florida, without his (Folches) assent, would not permit the Surveyors to proceed. The consequence was, that Titles for vast Tracts of Land which had been enter'ed, remained incompleat: the Quantity of Land in this situation, and the names of the purchasers, you will find in the enclosed paper which I have obtained from a confidential source.[1] I have understood that Mr. Daniel Chark [*sic*] and other early Adventurers obtained complete Titles."

RC and enclosure (DNA: RG 59, TP, Orleans, vol. 7); letterbook copy (Ms-Ar: Claiborne Executive Journal, vol. 15). RC 1 p.; in a clerk's hand, signed by Claiborne; docketed by Wagner as received 24 Sept. Letterbook copy dated 16 Aug. For enclosure, see n. 1.

1. The enclosure (1 p.; in Spanish) is a list of land grants in Baton Rouge, Mobile, and along the Amite River totaling 1,249,272 arpents. Several Americans were among the grantees.

§ From Peder Pedersen. *15 August 1805, Philadelphia.* "A continuation of bad health having induced Mr. Blicher:Olsen to sollicit from His Majesty the King his recall from the appointment he hold near this Government as His Majesty's Minister Resident and Consul General, and the Same having most graciously been granted, I have herewith the honor to transmit to you His Majesty's letter on this occasion, (a copy of which is here enclosed:) for His Excellency the President of the United States which I shall beg leave to request may be forwarded to him as soon as convenient."

RC and enclosure (DNA: RG 59, NFL, Denmark, vol. 1). RC 1 p.; docketed by Wagner. The enclosure (2 pp.; in Latin; docketed by Wagner) is Peder Blicherolsen's 5 Apr. 1805 letter of recall.

To Tobias Lear

SIR,   DEPARTMENT OF STATE August 16th. 1805.

Since your last letter dated 3d. November from Malta,[1] I have received communications from Mr. Mountford of the 3 & 4 Jany. 1st. Feby. and 25 March.[2] You will receive the present by a store ship about to sail from Kennebec with a cargo of plank, timber, spars &c, an invoice of which will be transmitted to you by the Agent who collected it, and which it is hoped will be received upon the annuity, of which more than a year has now become due. To render them the more acceptable, they are accompanied with the five brass Eighteen pounders, with carriages and apparatus complete.[3] The remainder of the brass guns will be finished and forwarded without delay. Inclosed is a bill of the weight of the Guns which are correspondently marked, in order that if the practice be as is suggested to weigh but one as a criterion of the whole, such an one may be selected as may bear the nearest average proportion to the whole. This is the one numbered 4.

The reluctance manifested by the Regency to receive the Timber by the William and Mary,[4] is the more extraordinary as it was intended to replace that sent by the Sally, which went on shore at St. Lucar,[5] and as nothing existed to produce a doubt respecting the necessity of sending it. The present cargo of wood was collected last year and is composed of such an assortment as your communications have indicated as the next most desirable at Algiers. I have also directed to be shipped a piece of muslin embroidered with gold and another with silver, according to the Dey's request signified to Mr. Mountford;[6] but in case the latter piece cannot be obtained two pieces of fine India Dimity are to be sent in its stead. To these are added two hundred dollars worth of sweetmeats preserved without a spiritous mixture and fifty pounds of Coffee, which as well as the muslin and Dimity may be presented to the Dey. This and the former cargo of timber and the fifteen brass cannon when delivered, it is calculated will leave the Regency in our debt. If therefore the select quality and kinds of timber, plank &c composing this cargo and the circumstances of its having been procured before it was known that it would not be very acceptable and its being accompanied with the cannon and other articles so much desired, should not fully satisfy the Regency in accepting it, it may be observed that as nothing will probably be due on the annuities, we are justly entitled to more time to procure and forward the articles contained in the disadvantageous list, formerly dictated to you, if it be absolutely necessary to do so; but much reliance is placed in your exertions to have it retracted and to obtain a favorable substitute.

The articles you have on hand from the Consular present received from Mr. Cathcart and the Attagon by Commodore Barron,[7] if it can be disposed of according to its value, may constitute part of the biennial present due this year, and the remainder be obtained in Italy or from the Jews as may be deemed most advisable in referrence to the comparative cost of the articles and the necessity there may arise from circumstances of policy to deal with the Jews. I shall cause a remittance, to cover the expence of these supplemental articles in the present, to be made to Sir Francis Baring & Co. of London, on whom you will consequently draw for it. I have the honor to be &c

JAMES MADISON

Letterbook copy (DNA: RG 59, IC, vol. 1).

1. *PJM-SS*, 8:255–58.
2. For Timothy Mountford's letters of 3 and 4 Jan. 1805, see ibid., 445–48, 450–51. For the 1 Feb. 1805 letter, see John Gavino to JM, 12 Mar. 1805, ibid., 9:128 and n. 3. For Mountford's 25 Mar. 1805 letter, see ibid., 175–76.
3. See JM to Charles Simms, 10 July 1805, and n. 1, and Wagner to JM, 5 Aug. 1805.
4. See *PJM-SS*, 8:445.
5. See ibid., 6:154.
6. See ibid., 8:446.
7. For the consular presents that Lear received from James Leander Cathcart, see Lear to JM, 24 Dec. 1803, and Lear to JM, 7 May 1804, ibid., 6:205, 7:180, 181, 184 nn. 17, 19–20, 185 nn. 21 and 25. For the attagan, see JM to Lear, 6 June 1804, and Lear to JM, 3 Nov. 1804, ibid., 7:288, 291 n. 4, 8:257.

From James Monroe

No.[1]
Duplicate
Sir   London August 16. 1805.

I enclose you a copy of my letters to Lord Mulgrave relative to the late seizure of our vessels by his Majesty's cruizers, in the Channel and North Sea, and of his replies.[2] I had yesterday an interview with him on the subject, in which he gave me a report from each of the King's law-officers in the admiralty respecting the late decisions, and promised me another interview on that and the other topicks depending between our governments, as soon as I Should desire it after having perused the reports. By my note to him of this date you will find that I consider these documents unsatisfactory on the great question and have asked another interview. It appears however by them that no recent order has been issued by the government; hence it is probable that the late decisions on the point of Continuity of Voyage which have carried the restraints on that commerce to a greater extent than heretofore may have furnished to the parties interested a motive for these Seizures. It is equally probable that the decision of the Court of appeals in the case of the "Essex," as several of its members are also members of the Cabinet, may have been dictated by policy to promote the navigation of this country at the expence of that of the United States. In the late interview with Lord Mulgrave, much general conversation took place on the Subject, in which he assured me in the most explicit terms that nothing was more remote from the views of his government than to take an unfriendly attitude towards the U. States: he assured me also that no new orders had been issued, and that his government was disposed to do every thing in its power to arrange this and the other points to our Satisfaction, by which however I did not understand that the principle in this case would be abandoned; tho' I think it probable that in other respects much accommodation may be obtained in that commerce.

Affairs here seem to be approaching a crisis. It is Said that the combined fleets, having been previously joined by the Rochfort Squadron, have entered Ferrol, and that the force now there is 37 sail of the line. Sir Robert Calder has joined Adm. Cornwallis before Brest. The French fleet there consists of about 26. Sail of the line. This force so nearly united, is a very imposing one. The menace of invasion is Kept up and encreased; every thing Seems to indicate that an attempt will Soon be made. I have the honor to be with great respect & regard Sir, Your very obedient Servant.

Jas. Monroe

RC and enclosures (DNA: RG 46, President's Messages, 10B–B1); RC and Tr of enclosures (DNA: RG 233, President's Messages, 10A–D1); letterbook copy (DLC: Monroe Papers). First RC in a clerk's hand, signed by Monroe; docketed by Wagner. Minor differences between the copies have not been noted. For enclosures, see n. 2.

    1. Left blank in both RCs. Letterbook copy and Tr marked *"No. 32."*
    2. The enclosures (6 pp.; docketed by Wagner as received in Monroe's 6 Aug. dispatch); printed in *ASP, Foreign Relations*, 3:103–5) are copies of Monroe to Mulgrave, 31 July and 8 Aug. 1805, and Mulgrave to Monroe, 5 and 9 Aug. 1805 (see Monroe to JM, 6 Aug. 1805, n. 9), as well as copies of Monroe to Mulgrave, 12 Aug. 1805, stating that in recent weeks about twenty U.S. ships had been seized by the British in the Channel and the North Sea and carried into British ports, and that these acts seemed to be based on the *Essex* decision, which the United States considered to be a violation of neutral rights, since by it Great Britain asserted a right to control the sovereignty and the commerce of neutral nations; Mulgrave to Monroe, 12 Aug. 1805, appointing the following Thursday for their meeting; Monroe to Mulgrave, 12 Aug. 1805, accepting the time; and Monroe to Mulgrave, 16 Aug. 1805, returning documents he had received at the 15 Aug. 1805 meeting, expressing his disappointment that they gave no satisfactory explanation for U.S. complaints, and asking for another meeting.

§ From Sylvanus Bourne. *16 August 1805, Amsterdam.* "The advice I had the honor to communicate to you in a late letter relative to the conduct of the British towards our navigation Seems to be confirmed,[1] viz that their Cruisers have recd new orders to detain & convey into the Ports of G B for examination *All* our Vessells laden with Colonial produce of the french or Dutch Colonies—in order that it may-be ascertained whether their Cargoes were boná Shipped in the UStates or whether the papers only have been changed & that the voyages may be regarded as continued from any of said Colonies to the Mother Countries in Europe & of course liable *by their rules* to confiscation. It appears that the little rigor which has of late been used by the British Govt towards neutrals has led our Countrymen into a security in this regard which has been attended with unpleasant consequences as several of our Vessel(ls) have lately been condemned in England for not complying with the rule heretofore laid down by the British Govt for rendering such voyages legal that is to say by a discharge in the UStates of the Cargoes brought there from F or D Colonies—how far we ought to be bound in right by said Rules must of course be a ques(tion) between that Govt & ours—while it cannot escape now that the present proceedings of the British tend to expose our Commerce to Europe to great inconveniences & such as are peculiarly prejudicial to the interest of our Citizens & these inconvenienc(es) will dai(ly) become enhanced by the approach of the winter seas(on) when the detention of a vessell one day even may make the difference of the whole voyage to the owners. I have as yet no official advices from our Consul(s?) on the matt(er) here referred but wait for them with great impatience as the Capture of our vessells bound here causes a grea(t) sensation on the exchange.

"I hope my late letters w(ill) have reached you in safety as I flatter myself they tend to restore that perfect confidence in me which I shall not cease to cherish."

Adds in a postscript: "Capt Tripp of Ship Charles from Phila lately bound from this City to that Port has been carried into England & the Cargo taken out till further proofs can be obtained as to the neutrality of the property altho' said Cargo was accompanied by the usual Certificates to that effect—& it is said the vessell has been discharged without payt of Costs or the Allowance of any freight to the Ship. I do not indeed know what all this would say & I hope that our Govt will take a decided attitude."

RC (DNA: RG 59, CD, Amsterdam, vol. 1). 3 pp.; docketed by Wagner.

1. See Bourne to JM, 6 Aug. 1805.

§ From William C. C. Claiborne. *16 August 1805, New Orleans.* "The enclosure No, 1 is the last letter received from the Marquis on the subject of Mr. Moralis's continuance in this Territory, and No, 2 a Copy of my Answer.[1]

"I do not Know how far the part I have acted on this occasion will be approved of by the President; But I pray you to be assured that my conduct is directed by my best Judgment and a sincere disposition to protect the Interest of my Country."

RC and enclosures (DNA: RG 59, TP, Orleans, vol. 7); letterbook copy and letterbook copy of enclosures (Ms-Ar: Claiborne Executive Journal, vol. 15). RC 1 p.; in a clerk's hand, signed by Claiborne; docketed by Wagner as received 24 Sept. Filed with the enclosures is a note in Jefferson's hand: "the papers respecting Morales are retained Th: J. will be glad to see the Volume from Sibley." For that volume, see John Sibley to JM, 10 Aug. 1805. Minor differences between the copies have not been noted. For enclosures, see n. 1.

1. Enclosure No. 1 is a translation of Casa Calvo to Claiborne, 12 Aug. 1805 (3 pp.; printed in Rowland, *Claiborne Letter Books,* 3:170–72), stating that he had informed Morales of the demand in Claiborne's 9 Aug. 1805 letter (see Claiborne to JM, 10 Aug. 1805, n. 2), that Morales had replied that "great prejudice for the Spanish Government may be the consequence of Such a measure" and had asked Casa Calvo to ask Claiborne to stay his determination until Morales could execute the orders entrusted to him. Casa Calvo added that although Claiborne had been urging the departure of the Spanish officials since October 1804, and although he himself had repeatedly sent orders to the same effect, it had proven impossible to settle the business that was yet pending because of the "sudden change of Government, in a Country whither the Posts are placed at such a distance," giving as an example the evacuation of the troops from upper Louisiana which had only been completed in March 1805, adding that Morales's continued presence was not meant as a mark of disrespect but was necessitated by his duty to uphold the king's interests. Casa Calvo further added that he would do his best to remove any obstacles to the closing of the Spanish offices and the speedy termination of pending business in any way that would not prejudice the king's interest. Enclosure No. 2 is a copy of Claiborne's 14 Aug. 1805 reply (3 pp.; printed ibid., 167–68), stating that he had no desire to injure the king's interest except when it interfered with that of the United States; that in spite of the time for the departure of the Spanish officers having elapsed, he would allow them to remain a "reasonable time" to settle their business; that because of the pending negotiations between their countries, he could not "suffer a Foreign Officer to make any disposition of Lands" claimed by the United States; that Morales apparently fully intended to complete the sales he had made of Florida lands west of the Perdido River and to sell even more; and that the only basis on which he could allow Morales to remain was if Morales wrote him that "during his residence in this City no further disposition of Lands West of the Perdido" would be made by him. Claiborne expressed his appreciation for the frankness and sincerity of Casa Calvo's letters, which had disposed Claiborne to make allowance for the difficulties Casa Calvo had suggested.

From Thomas Jefferson

Dear Sir   Monticello Aug. 17. 05.

Yours of the 9th. has been duly recieved, & I now return the papers it covered, and particularly those respecting the ship New Jersey, on which I have bestowed due attention. I think the error of Genl. Armstrong a very palpable & unfortunate one;[1] but one not at all chargeable on our government. By the French Convention the council of Liquidation has certain functions assigned to them, of a judiciary nature. They are appointed by that government, and over their nomination or opinions we have no controul. Embarrassed to come to a conclusion in a particular case they transfer their functions to two other persons. These persons then stand in their place as the agents of the French government deriving their authorities from them, & responsible to them alone, not to us. It is true that to command our confidence they have appointed one of these, a person who holds our commission of Min. Pleny. but he does not act in this case under that commission. He is merely a French agent. Messrs. Nicklin & Griffith therefore may just as well suppose this government liable for all the errors of the council of liquidation, as for this; & that they are individually liable in their private fortunes of all their errors of judgment as General Armstrong for his. This renders it more delicate than usual to enter into explanations with Armstrong. Yet I think we may properly state to him our opinion. Honest men may justly be influenced by the opinion of those whose judgment they respect, especially where they are doubtful themselves. I hazard these things to you, not as decisions but for your own consideration & decision.

The conduct of Capt Drummond of the Fox in running away from Martinique without clearing or paying duties, is that of a rogue.[2] But every government must contrive means within itself to enforce it's own revenue laws; others cannot do it for them. I suppose Drummond might be sued here as other fugitive debtors, these actions being what the lawyers call transitory; and that it would be well for the French Consul at Boston or wherever he can be caught, to institute a suit.

I am anxious to recieve opinions respecting our procedure with Spain: as, should negociations with England be adviseable they should not be postponed a day unnecessarily, that we may lay their results before Congress before they rise next spring. Were the question only about the bounds of Louisiana, I should be for delay. Were it only for spoliations, just as this is as a cause of war, we might consider if no other expedient were more eligible for us. But I do not view peace as within our choice, I consider the cavalier conduct of Spain as evidence that France is to settle with us for her; and the language of France confirms it: and that if she can keep us insulated till peace, she means to enforce by arms her will, to which she foresees we will not trouble & therefore does not venture on the mandate now. We should not permit ourselves to be found off our guard and friendless.

I hear with great pleasure that mrs. Madison is on the recovery, but fear we shall not have the pleasure of having you in our neighborhood this season, as cases like hers are slow. We are extremely seasonable in this quarter. Better crops were never seen. I have bought my provision of corn @ 12/6. Accept for mrs. Madison & yourself affectionate salutations.

TH: JEFFERSON

RC (DLC: Rives Collection, Madison Papers); FC (DLC: Jefferson Papers).

1. For a discussion of John Armstrong's involvement in the *New Jersey* case, see Skeen, *John Armstrong*, 64–68.
2. See Louis-Marie Turreau to JM, 4 Aug. 1805.

§ To Albert Gallatin. *17 August 1805, Department of State.* "To enable Mr. Lear to make the biennial present which comes due to Algiers this fall, I request you to be pleased to provide him with a credit in the hands of Sir Francis Baring &Co. in London, to the amount of twelve thousand dollars."

Letterbook copy (DNA: RG 59, DL, vol. 15). 1 p.

§ To Robert Morris Jr.[1] *17 August 1805, Department of State.* "I have received your letter respecting Comfort Sand's, claim under the Louisiana convention,[2] but as the payments in such cases are made at the Treasury and the questions which may be raised in whom the real interest of the claim resides are consequently to be disposed of, I could not promote your wishes otherwise than by transmitting the letter to that Department."

Letterbook copy (DNA: RG 59, DL, vol. 15). 1 p.

1. Robert Morris Jr. (b. 1769) was the oldest son of Revolutionary financier Robert Morris. He and his younger brother Thomas were educated in Europe, where they were acquainted with Benjamin Franklin and John Jay. In 1823 Morris was sued by Comfort Sands for funds Sands believed were due to him and not to Morris, who was one of Sands's assignees in his bankruptcy (Ferguson et al., eds., *The Papers of Robert Morris, 1781–1784*, 3:58–59 n. 2; Thomas W. Waterman, *Reports of Cases Argued and Determined in the Circuit Court of the United States, for the Second Circuit, Comprising the Districts of New York, Connecticut and Vermont* [2 vols.; 1827–1856], 2:409–15).
2. Morris's letter has not been found, but it probably dealt with Sands's claim against the French government for his ship *Light Horse*, John Hoff master, which was captured in June 1797 while on a trading voyage from Bristol, England, to New York, and carried into Bordeaux, where the ship and cargo were condemned for lack of a proper rôle d'équipage (Williams, *French Assault on American Shipping*, 218). Comfort Sands (1748–1834) entered the mercantile line as a boy of twelve. At the age of twenty-one he opened his own store and quickly made a fortune in trade with the West Indies. He was a fervent patriot during the

Revolution and fled New York with his family when it was occupied by the British in 1776. He spent the next seven years moving about in the Philadelphia area and upstate New York. From 1776 to 1782 he served as auditor general of New York. In 1784 he was one of the founders of the Bank of New York, and from 1794 to 1798 he was president of the Chamber of Commerce. In spite of having bank deposits of over three million dollars earned from trade, he had so many ships seized by the British and French during their European war that he declared bankruptcy in June 1801. The final settlement left him with a surplus of $118,000, and he retired to a country estate in New Jersey.

§ From George Armroyd & Co. *17 August 1805, Philadelphia.* "We avail ourselves of your being at this moment in Philada. to address you upon a disastrous Occurrence to us as Merchants of this place trading to the Island of St Croix. It is such as induces us to solicit the interference of the Executive in our behalf, and we flatter ourselves that thro' your Kindness this interference may be accelerated and so prompt in the present Case as to counteract the Mischief with which we are threatned.

"We beg leave to inform you that we are One of the Houses of this place connected intimately with the above Island, and were yesterday expecting the Arrival from thence of a Vessel of ours, the Brig Neptune Captn. Ray, but of which the Paper enclosed now states the capture, by a french or Spanish Privateer. A Letter from Our friend & partner Captn. Joseph DaCosta, which we received yesterday and beg leave also to enclose for your perusal, states the particulars of our Vessel's Cargo.[1]

"We have long been in the habit of an uninterrupted Intercourse with the Danish Islands, particularly St Croix, and are at a loss to conjecture upon what ground we suffer in the present Instance, unless it is to be considered an act of Piracy.

"We know the Executive will in its Wisdom take such Measures as are proper to obtain redress when ever our innocent Trade is aggrieved. We beg leave in the Case at present, Knowing of no motive the Captors can be actuated by but a determination to plunder, and apprehensive of the worst from their irregular proceedings, to suggest that it might be extremely serviceable to us to be enabled to dispatch immediately Letters from the spanish Minister addressed to the Governor of Porto Rico directing the proper Enquiries and such Steps to be taken in the business as are necessary to justice."

RC and enclosure (DNA: RG 76, Preliminary Inventory 177, entry 322, Spain, Treaty of 1819 [Art. XI] [Spoliation], Misc. Records, ca. 1801–24, box 4). RC 2 pp. For enclosure, see n. 1.

1. The enclosure (1 p.) is an extract from a 28 July 1805 letter from Joseph Da Costa at St. Croix stating that the *Neptune* had sailed on the night of 26 July carrying 105 hogsheads of sugar and 14 puncheons of rum. Newspaper reports stated that the *Neptune* had been taken by a Spanish privateer "manned with people from all countries" and sent into the west end of Puerto Rico (*New-York Commercial Advertiser*, 15 Aug. 1805; New York *Morning Chronicle*, 19 Aug. 1805).

§ From William C. C. Claiborne. *17 August 1805, New Orleans.* "By the enclosed, you will perceive that the Correspondence between the Marquis of Casa Calvo and myself concerning Morales has not yet Closed.[1] If Morales should not abandon his project relative to the Sales of Florida Lands, I shall not cease to urge his immediate departure from the Territory.

"The Climate here is now excessively warm, and I fear the City will soon become Sickly; With a v[i]ew to my Health and to assist personally in Organizing the Militia I have contemplated a Journey to several of the interior Counties, but the pending correspondence with the Marquis, has hitherto delayed my departure."

RC and enclosures (DNA: RG 59, TP, Orleans, vol. 7); letterbook copy and letterbook copy of enclosures (Ms-Ar: Claiborne Executive Journal, vol. 15). RC 1 p.; in a clerk's hand, signed by Claiborne; docketed by Wagner as received 24 Sept. For enclosures, see n. 1.

1. Of the enclosures (8 pp.; in Spanish and English; printed in Rowland, *Claiborne Letter Books*, 3:172–75), the first is a copy of Casa Calvo to Claiborne, 17 Aug. 1805, stating that he had sent Claiborne's 14 Aug. resolution to Morales (see Claiborne to JM, 16 Aug. 1805, n. 1), and Morales had replied that if Claiborne did not allow him to collect the money for lands already surveyed and sold, he would be unable to adopt the measures Casa Calvo had suggested without causing the king's interest to suffer; he added that the business to be conducted at New Orleans required his presence and depended on events that he had not the power to accelerate, and even after those events occurred, he would require more time to conclude the business. Morales further added that Claiborne's conditions were injurious to his (Morales's) character and contrary to all rights, that he hoped Casa Calvo would insist that the king's interests not be harmed by hindering Morales in the performance of his duties, and that Morales's authority as respected those duties would not be shackled. Casa Calvo explained to Claiborne that he had suggested that Morales efficaciously conclude such matters as could not be done elsewhere and reserve everything else to be accomplished in Spanish territory, and that he (Casa Calvo) would explain to Claiborne that he could not disallow the collection of payments for such lands as had been already sold, since the funds were royal property; he added that he did not doubt Claiborne would allow this. As for the other functions which Morales proposed to exercise, Casa Calvo hoped Claiborne would adopt measures that would prevent both countries' interests from suffering and would maintain the existing harmony between them. The second enclosure is a copy of Claiborne to Casa Calvo, 17 Aug. 1805, stating that the conditions in his 14 Aug. letter were the only ones on which he would allow Morales's continued residence; that he cared nothing for Morales's opinion of them; that if they were not acceded to, he would demand Morales's immediate departure, adding that he did not know what faculties were conferred on Morales by the king, but he did know that the king could not authorize Morales to perform any official acts or open a land office within U.S. territory. He further added that if Morales desired his authority to remain unshackled, he could withdraw to Spanish territory. Claiborne expressed his unwillingness to injure the king's interests but stated that he could not allow a foreign officer to open a land office or issue titles, and if Morales persisted, Claiborne would require his immediate departure, would cheerfully prepare the customary passports, and afford Casa Calvo such assistance as he needed to bring about "the speedy and comfortable conveyance of [Morales] to some Post within the dominions of His Catholic Majesty."

§ From Henry Hill Jr. *17 August 1805, Havana.* "The above is duplicate of my respects of the 13th. currt which I confirm.

"Having replied to His Excellencys note above refered to, and recd. an answer wh⟨ich⟩ leaves the business open to a further corr⟨es⟩pondence, it is not yet brought to a conclusion. I therefore defer going into the detail of a business which must excite in you considerabl⟨e⟩ surprize and astonishment, and perhaps regret, before

I have it in my power to communicate the result; which must now be known in a day or two."

RC and enclosure (DNA: RG 59, CD, Havana, vol. 1). RC 2 pp.; written at the foot of a duplicate of Hill to JM, 13 Aug. 1805; docketed by Wagner as received 12 Sept. The enclosure (1 p.; docketed by Wagner) is a duplicate copy of the marqués de Someruelos to Hill, 13 Aug. 1805, which was also enclosed in Hill's 13 Aug. letter.

§ From Anthony Merry. *17 August 1805, Philadelphia.* "I received to-day the Honor of your Letter of the 7th. of this Month,[1] and have the Honor to transmit to you inclosed the Passport you have desired for an American Vessel bound from the River Kennebec to Algiers, with a Cargo of military and naval Stores, in Fulfilment of the Stipulations between the United States and the Regency of Algiers, having, agreeably to your Request, left Blanks for the Names of the Vessel and Master."

RC (DNA: RG 59, NFL, Great Britain, vol. 3). 1 p.; in a clerk's hand, signed by Merry; docketed by Wagner as received 22 Aug., with his note: "Passport for the Kennebec vessel."

1. See Wagner to JM, 8 Aug. 1805, and n. 2.

§ From Robert Williams. *17 August 1805, Washington, Mississippi Territory.* "Since I have been acting as Governor I have been under the necessity of employing a person in the Character of clerk or private Secretary to assist me in the discharge of the duties of that office can I be allowed for this. I find the Secretary Colo West was allowed, (whilst acting without the governor[)] in this respect I have been acting without a Secretary.

"I will farther observe that I am and shall be necessitated to continue to employ some person in that Character at all events as long as both Mr Williams the Secretary and Myself shall be engaged in the land busines as Commissioners—again having leave from the President to return to N. Carolina for my family which I shall do in a few months it will be almost impossible for the Secretary to perform those respective duties without some assistance—an allowance for a Clerk to the department of this Government will be so arranged between the Secretary and myself as to answer both of us. We hope this request will be thout reasonable and granted at least till the land Commission shall be over and until I can return from No Carolina. Colo West has had his political frolic over and all things are quiet."

Letterbook copy (Ms-Ar: Executive Journal, 1805–10). 2 pp.

To George Armroyd

SIR.   DEPARTMENT OF STATE August 18th. 1805.

In conformity to the request in yours of the   [1] instant I have made the capture of the Brig Neptune the subject of a representation to the Marquis de Casa Yrujo, as a ground for his interposition with the Govr. of Porto Rico: I enclose the letter with a request that you will convey it to him.[2] As no document proving the Citizenship of the Claimants or the ownership of the Vessel, accompanied your letter to me, and as these proofs may be necessary for the satisfaction of the Marquis, or to supply at Porto Rico, the loss or distruction of the Ships papers, I suggest the expediency of your annexing them to my letter. It may not be amiss to add proofs of the ownership of the Cargo: For altho' the Treaty of the United States with Spain, which makes the neutrality of the Flag a protection of the Cargo to whomsoever belonging, ought to supersede enquiries on that point, the precaution may not be without use in precluding vexatious pretexts. I am &c.

JAMES MADISON.

Letterbook copy (DNA: RG 59, DL, vol. 15).

1. Left blank in letterbook copy. See George Armroyd & Co. to JM, 17 Aug. 1805.
2. The letter has not been found, but its receipt was acknowledged in Carlos Martínez de Yrujo to JM, 25 Aug. 1805.

§ From Sylvanus Bourne. *18 August 1805, Amsterdam.* "We are at present quite in consternation here on account of the proceedings of the British Govt towards our flag as it appears they have ordered their Cruisers to take into their ports *all* Amn. vessells bound to the ports of France Spain or Holland laden with Colonial produce—& (as I was led to suppose) in order only to ascertain whether said Cargoes were bona fide taken on board in the UStates or whether the papers were only changed as in the latter cases they will be confiscated (as some have already been) on the principle of their being *continued* voyages from the Colonies to the Mother Countries. It appears however from a letter yesterday recd from Mr Patterson of Balto now in London to his Correspondent here that the late measures will not be long confined towards our Vessells destined for their enemies ports but after Novr. those even destined for the Ports of England with colonial produce will be subject to the same consequences do they indeed mean to declare war against the UStates? for they might as well do it at once as to pursue these measures which are calculated to destroy at once at least *one half* of the American Commerce—& indeed the most important part—much is said of the abuse of Power on the Continent by France but can less be said of the British at Sea & where indeed would any commerce exist bu⟨t⟩ in name except what belonged to England did not Fran⟨ce⟩ present a counterpart to the insolent Ambition & insatia⟨ble⟩ Cupidity of GB on that element—they are doubly jeal⟨ous⟩ of our progress & rivalship in Commerce & wish to check it but I hope we shall not be obliged to submit tamely to all the rules they may think proper to prescribe for the regulation of our trade. I have no doubt our Govt will take a firm & decided posture under these unpleasant ci⟨r⟩cumstances."

Adds in a postscript: "Just as I was closing this letter Mr Patterson's Correspondent referred to within—called on me & explains the matter thus—that the late proceedings of the British appear to have been instigated by the susp[i]cion of our Citizens having covered their enemies property & that to avoid the like as far as possible in future—property brought into the U.States from the Islands of their enemies must be there landed, Sold, & reshipped in a vessel different from the one that imported it—& after novr. Cargoes destined even for England must be under the same rules—this new doctrine will doubtless be more correctly communicated to you from England as it is of very great importance to be known officially by our merchants in the UStates to guide their future proceedings."[1]

RC (DNA: RG 59, CD, Amsterdam, vol. 1). 3 pp.; docketed by Wagner.

1. For the change in British Admiralty Court decisions regarding neutral trade with enemy colonies, see George Joy to JM, 26 July 1805, and n. 3.

From Jacob Wagner

DEAR SIR   DEPARTMENT OF STATE 19 Augt. 1805.

The enclosed requisition of money for the Algerine biennial present proceeds upon the supposition that the articles on hand will avail to the amount of at least 4 or 5000 dollars.[1] The shipment of wheat made by Mr Lear will of itself free us from all the arrears of the annuity, without computing the two cargoes of timber and the brass guns: we may, therefore, on the score of nothing being due as well as of the merit of saving the city from famine, fairly expect to get rid of the list furnished Mr. Lear in Decr. 1803.[2]

The President has returned the papers about the outrages in Passamaquoddy Bay;[3] but as the whole passed most decidedly within the British and not a common or American jurisdiction; as the men were returned; and as Genl. Dearborn says the fact is, what is very natural, that smuggling is much practised in that quarter, the complaint to be made to Mr. Merry ought not I think to be very animated. I shall therefore on to morrow send you a draft accommodated to this tone.

It is a curious circumstance, that Yrujo's questions to the lawyers and their answers[4] should be published at NewYork from a copy which must have come either directly or remotely from the Spanish officer. This latter circumstance I infer from the words "es *copia*" being annexed. The copies we have were as well as I remember in possession of the Senate, but I cannot suppose the members would have kept copies from them.

The city remains healthy, although we have had some very warm weather. Mrs. Paine was to set out for Virginia this morning. With much respect & esteem Your's

J. WAGNER

RC (DLC). Docketed by JM.

1. The enclosure was probably JM to Albert Gallatin, 17 Aug. 1805.
2. For the list, see Lear to JM, 24 Dec. 1803, *PJM-SS*, 6:205–6, 207 n. 2.
3. For this incident, see Wagner to JM, 5 Aug. 1805, and n. 6.
4. On 16 Aug. 1805 the New York *American Citizen* printed the November 1802 reply of Philadelphia lawyers Jared Ingersoll, William Rawle, Joseph Borden McKean, and Peter S. Du Ponceau to a hypothetical question regarding spoliation claims put to them probably by Carlos Martínez de Yrujo. For an earlier reference to the question, see *PJM-SS*, 5:266, 270 n. 9.

From John Willis

DR SIR,   ORANGE COURT HOUSE Aug. 19 [1805]

Application was made to me some time since by Captn. H. Lee through the medium of Mr Robt: Taylor for the renewal of a Deed for a Tract of Land situated in the County of Jefferson (State of Kentucky) stated to have been sold to Captn Lee by your Brother Mr. Ambrose Madison, and the Deed since lost. As you are equally interested with your Niece in all the Lands held in that State in name of your deceased Brother⟨,⟩ I deemd it improper to have any Deed executed until you had been consulted, and have hitherto defered writing under an expectation of seeing you at home; but since Mrs Madison's health has rendered a trip to Philadelphia necessary, and the time of your returning I presume uncertain⟨,⟩ I have considered it necessary to apply by Letter to be directed in what manner to proceed. If you think fit that a conveyance should be made, I will have it done immediately, or if on the contrary there are any reasons why it should not you will be so obliging as to communicate them. Being desirous of converting whatever interest My Wife may have in Kentucky into property in this State at a convenient distance from me where necessary attention may be paid to it, and having an offer to that effect I will esteem it a very particular favour in you to give me any information you may be possessed of respecting the quantity, situation, and value of each respective Tract, and at what price you think it would be advisable in me to exchange two or three thousand Acres gra[n]ting the privilege of selecting that quantity from her moiety. Be so good as to present our respects to Mrs Madison and accept our best wishes for the speedy restoration, of her health. I am Sir with great respect and esteem your obt. & very humb: Serv:

JOHN WILLIS[1]

RC (DLC: Papers of Dolley Madison). Year not indicated; Conjectural year assigned based on internal evidence. Docketed by JM.

1. John Willis (1774–1812) married Ambrose Madison's daughter and JM's niece and ward, Nelly Conway Madison, in 1804 (*PJM*, 15:378 n. 2; Ketcham, *James Madison*, 460). For Ambrose Madison's Kentucky lands, see *PJM*, 15:362–63 and nn. 1–2, 377–78 and nn. 1 and 4–5, 17:575–76; *PJM-SS*, 8:283–84 and n. 1; *PJM-RS*, 1:177 n. 1.

§ From George Armroyd & Co. *19 August 1805, Philadelphia.* "In additon to the Information we had the honor to transmit to you on Saturday respecting the Capture of our Brig the Neptune Capt. Ray, we beg leave now to enclose the Evidence of said Vessel being our property, in a Bill of Sale executed to us [not found]. As we at first were Charterers only of this Vessel, and became purchasers since the Voyage was begun, her Register & Papers are of course as yet in the name of Mr. Geisse her former Owner.

"Our friends in St Croix, the Shippers of her Cargo of Sugars &c from thence, will furnish every regular proof in the business there that may be requisite.

"We flatter ourselves that the prompt Measures, which thro' your kindness will be taken herein, may yet be in time to frustrate some of the Evil intended us by the Captors, and save or recover the property from their hands.

"We take the liberty further to suggest that it might be eligible, as a provision against the contingency of their carrying the Neptune to a french port in place of a Spanish, to have Letters from the French Minister addressed to the proper authorities in Sa Domingo &c on th⟨is⟩ Subject."

Adds in a postscript: "Since writing the above, we notice in the publick paper of this Morning under the Baltimore head, some further account of the Privateer in question, which is there called the french privateer Ressource, Capt. Janet. We enclose the Paper."[1]

RC (DNA: RG 76, Preliminary Inventory 177, entry 322, Spain, Treaty of 1819 [Art. XI] [Spoliation], Misc. Records, ca. 1801–24, box 4). 2 pp.; docketed by Wagner.

1. The enclosed paper probably contained the article with a Baltimore dateline, describing the plunder of the ship *Sally* by Captain Janet and the crew of the French privateer *Resource* (New York *Mercantile Advertiser*, 20 Aug. 1805).

§ From William Kirkpatrick. *19 August 1805, Málaga.* "My last Letter to you was under date 5th: July by duplicates, inclosing the Semi Annual Return of arrivals at this Port; I also mention'd that the Brig Washington, Captain Atkins Adams had been brought in for adjudication, on her Voyage from Leghorn to Boston; on the 12h: ulto. she was finally set at liberty, without Costs, but no damages were allowed.

"In consequence of the representation of our Minister in Madrid, a circular order has been pass'd to the Marine Tribunals in the different Ports of Spain, desiring that the American Vessels should not be detained without a just cause, and that the proceedings against them should be expeditiously dispatched, in conformity to the existing Treaty and Marine Ordinances, as you will observe by the enclos'd Copy[1] which I have succeeded in procuring.

"I enclose Copy of a Letter which the French under Commissary of Commercial Relations has address'd me, and of the Decree therein referr'd to.[2]

"You will before this reaches you, have had the pleasing information of Peace being happily restored with Tripoly, on the most honorable terms for the United States.

"Captain Bainbridge has advised me his arrival at Gibraltar on his way home in the Frigate President."

RC and enclosures (DNA: RG 59, CD, Málaga, vol. 1). RC 2 pp. For enclosures, see nn.

1. Kirkpatrick enclosed a copy (1 p.; in Spanish; docketed by Wagner) of a 25 July 1805 letter from Juan Joaquín Moreno to Pedro Guerrero conveying a message from Pedro Cevallos that because of Charles Pinckney's complaints about the seizure of American ships by Spanish privateers, most recently the cases of the *John*, the *Polly*, the *Washington*, and another ship at Bilbao, the king had ordered Spanish courts to proceed without delay to the investigation and decision in those cases in conformity with laws on the matter and with the treaty between the United States and Spain. Moreno added that he was sending this decree so Guerrero could communicate to owners and captains of privateers that the most effective method of complying with the order would be to give careful consideration to intercepting neutral vessels unless there were reasonable grounds for suspicion.

2. The enclosures (3 pp.) are copies of a 22 Thermidor an 13 (10 Aug. 1805) letter from French under-commissary Pierre Agaud to Kirkpatrick, enclosing Napoleon's 18 Prairial an 13 (7 June 1805) decree, which stated: "All privateers, the two thirds of whose crews are not natives of England or subjects of a power hostile to France, and who are Frenchmen, Genoese, or Neapolitans," would be considered pirates, the officers shot, and the crew condemned to the galleys. The minister of marine was charged with the execution of the decree, which was to be printed, publicly posted, translated into all European languages, and transmitted to all French commissaries of commercial relations. An English translation was printed in the 10 Oct. 1805 Philadelphia *Aurora General Advertiser.*

§ From Anthony Merry. *19 August 1805, Philadelphia.* "Mr Merry presents his best Respects to Mr Madison, and has the Honor to transmit to him annexed the Extract of a Letter which he has just received from Sir John Wentworth, Governor of His Majesty's Province of Nova Scotia, on the Subject of the Effects belonging to the President and Mr Madison, together with the Bill of Loading referred to in it. As only one of these Documents has been sent to Mr Merry, he is under the Necessity of taking the Liberty of referring Mr Butler for it to Mr Madison."[1]

RC and enclosures (DLC). RC 1 p. For enclosures, see n. 1.

1. The enclosures are an extract of a 23 June 1805 letter from Gov. John Wentworth to Merry (1 p.), enclosing a copy of Lawrence Hartshorne to Wentworth, 22 June 1805 (1 p.), which enclosed the bill of lading "of the Articles belonging to the President, Secy. &c, shipped onboard the Brig Adventure bound for NYork, and consignd to care of Mr. Allen Super Cargo & part owner of the New Orleans, in whose Charge they came from France— the Brig Adventure is expected to sail tomorrow Morning." For the goods listed in the bill of lading, see *PJM-SS*, 9:503 n. 1. For the wine shipped on board the *New Orleans* for JM, Jefferson, and Pierce Butler, see Stephen Cathalan Jr. to JM, 22 Sept., 21 Oct. and 8 Dec. 1804, ibid., 8:78, 197, 359–60.

To Thomas Jefferson

Dr. Sir   PHA. Aug. 20. 1805

Your two favors of the 4 & 7th. Instant have come duly to hand. Letters
from C. Pinkney to the 10th. Of June have been forwarded to You thro'
Washington.[1] They confirm the idea that Spain emboldened by France, is
speculating on the presumed aversion of this Country to war, and to the
military connection with G.B. They shew at the same time that Spain herself not only does not aim at war, but wishes to cover the unfriendly posture of things, with the appearances of an undiminished harmony. This
idea is confirmed by the behaviour of the Spanish functionaries here.
Yrujo particularly, has multiplied his attentions, and with an air of cordiality which I should have thought it not easy for him to assume. By associat-
ing me with the Govr. In an invitation to dinner, and by the manner of it,
a refusal was rendered unavoidable witht. Giving it a point & the occasion
an importance not due to it. I inclose the copy of a letter which I have since
been obliged to write to him, the tone of which he will probably regard as
too hard for that of our late intercourse.[2] He has not yet answered it; and I
have not seen him since he recd it; I inclose also a letter from Turreau.[3]
Shall it be answered or not, and if answered in what point of view.

I shall endeavor to see Mr. Smith on my return; and have sent him the
despatches from Madrid.[4] My present view of our affairs with Spain, suggests the expediency of such provisional measures as are within the Ex.
Authy., and when Congs. Meets, of such an extension of them as will prevent or meet an actual rupture. It deserves consideration also whether,
with a view to all the Belligerent powers⟨,⟩ the supply of their Colonies
from the U. States ought not to be made to depend on commercial justice.
Bowdoin I think should be instructed to let Spain understand the absolute
necessity of a Status quo, and the use of the Mobille, if not of an arbitra-
tion of acknowledged spoliations; but without any formal proposition or
negociation⟨,⟩ which if rejected would be the more mortifying to this
Country, & would not ⟨le⟩ave the ultimate question as free to Congress as
it ought to be. The conduct towards G. B. is delicate as it is important. No
engagement Can be expected from her if not reciprocal; and if reciprocal
would put us at once into the war. She would certainly not stipulate to
continue the war for a given period, without a stipulaton on our part that
within that period we would join in it. I think therefore that no formal
proposition ought to be made on the subject. If the war goes on, the time
will always be suitable for it. If peace is within her reach, & her deliberations, we can let the state of things between this Country & Spain have
their natural influence on her councils. For this purpose frank but informal
explanations of it, ought to be made; without commitments on our side,
but with every preparation for a hostile event short of them. This course

will have the further advantage of an appeal in a new form to the policy of Spain & France, from whom the growing communications with G.B. would not be concealed. An eventual alliance with G.B. if attainable from her without inadmissible conditions, would be for us the best of all possible measures; but I do not see the least chance of laying her under obligations to be called into force at our will, without correspondent obligations on our part.

I have kept so much from conversation on the politics of this State, that I can not give any very precise acct. of them.[5] It is much to be feared that the mutual repulsion between the two immediate parties, will drive them both into extremes of doctrine as well as animosity. Symptoms of them are shewing themselves in the reasonings & language they oppose to each other. The federal party are not as yet settled in their plan of operations. Some are ready to support McKean as a barrier agst. The tendency they apprehend in the views of his adversaries. Others are disposed to withold their votes from him, thro' personal & political dislike. And others taking a middle course are willing to join the Govrs. party, on condition of obtaining some share in the Legislature election. The event of the contest is uncertain. Both sides seem to be equally confident. Those most capable of a cool estimate seem to think that at this moment the Govrs. party is the stronger; but that the other is gaining ground. We have now been here three weeks, without being able to fix the time of departure. I have every reason to believe that Mrs. M. is in the sure road to perfect recovery; but it proceeds as yet slowly. The Aurora of this date gives the true state of the yellow fev⟨er.⟩[6] Yrs. As ever.

JAMES MADISON

RC (DLC: Jefferson Papers). Docketed by Jefferson as received on 26 Aug., with his note: "Span. affairs. Pensva. politics."

1. Pinckney's letters to JM of ca. 3–17 Mar., 22 May, and 26 May 1805 are docketed by Wagner as received on 27 and 29 July. Pinckney also wrote JM on 28 May, and 4 and 10 June. See *PJM-SS*, 9:91–97, 376–77, 408, 410–11, 428–29, and 446–47.

2. Letter not found.

3. JM enclosed Louis-Marie Turreau's 14 Aug. 1805 letter to him.

4. See Jefferson to JM, 7 Aug. 1805.

5. For the state of the Republicans in Pennsylvania, see *PJM-SS*, 9:421 n. 5.

6. The 20 Aug. 1805 Philadelphia *Aurora General Advertiser* stated that "several cases of yellow fever have appeared in the southern extremity of the suburbs" and two people had died.

From James Monroe

⟨No. 33⟩
⟨Du⟩plicate
S<small>IR</small>   L<small>ONDON</small> August 20. 1805

I had an interview with Lord Mulgrave yesterday on the late seizure of ⟨ou⟩r vessels,[1] which I am sorry to observe presented the prospect of a less favorable ⟨r⟩esult than I had anticipated from the preceeding one. He asserted the principle ⟨i⟩n the fullest extent, that a neutral power had no right to a commerce, with the colonies of an enemy in time of war, which it had not in time of peace; and that ⟨e⟩very extension of it in the former state, beyond the limit of the latter, was due to the concession of Great-Britain, not to the right of the neutral power. I denied ⟨t⟩he principle in equal extent and insisted that G. Britain had no more right ⟨in⟩ war to interfere with or controul the commerce of a neutral power with the ⟨co⟩lonies of an enemy, than she had in peace. As we could not agree on the ⟨p⟩rinciple, I asked on what footing his government was willing to place the trade? His reply shewed that it was not disposed to relax in the slightest degree from the ⟨d⟩octrine of the late decrees of the courts of admiralty and appeals; which go to ⟨cu⟩t up completely by the roots the whole Commerce of the U. States in the produce ⟨of⟩ the colonies of its enemies, other than for the home consumption of their citizens. ⟨I⟩ urged in as strong terms as I could the objections which occurred to me to this ⟨p⟩retention, but he shewed no disposition to accommodate, so that we parted ⟨a⟩s remote from an accord as possibly could be. I asked Lord Mulgrave ⟨wh⟩ether I should consider the sentiments which he expressed as those of his ⟨go⟩vernment? He said he had in the commencement expressed a desire that ⟨o⟩ur conversations Should be considered rather as informal, than official, ⟨a⟩s entered into more in the hope of producing an accord than in the expectation that we should ultimately disagree—that he was sorry to find that we could not agree; that however he should report the result to the cabinet, & ⟨gi⟩ve me such an answer to my letters, for my government, of the views of his own, ⟨a⟩s it might wish to be taken of its conduct and policy in this business. ⟨I⟩ do not state the arguments that were used in the conference on each side, because ⟨th⟩ose of Lord Mulgrave will probably be furnished by himself, and you will ⟨re⟩adily conceive those to which I resorted. What the ultimate decision of his government may be I cannot pretend to say. It is possible that he held the ⟨tone⟩ mentioned above, in the late conference, to see whether I could be prevailed ⟨on to⟩ accommodate with his views. It is difficult to believe that it will yeild ⟨no⟩ accommodation on its part to our just claims in the present State of pu⟨blick⟩ affairs.

In my former interview with Lord Mulgrave he informed me that I ⟨should⟩ find by the reports which he gave me, that most of the vessels had been dism⟨issed;⟩ and it appeared by the reports that some of them had been, one or two on the o⟨pinion⟩ of Docr Laurence counsel for the Captured, which had been taken in the a⟨bsence⟩ of the King's proctor. I returned to him the reports to obtain copies for yo⟨u.⟩ Genl Lyman had informed me that others have been since dismissed, and as ⟨he⟩ thought some that had been seized on the new doctrine of Continuity of Voy⟨age;⟩ tho' nothing to countenance such an expectation escaped from Lord Mu⟨lgrave⟩ in the last conference.

It is decided on consideration of all circumstances, that Mr Bowd⟨oin⟩ will repair to Paris where he will probably remain till he receives the ord⟨ers⟩ of the President, and that Mr Erving will proceed immediately to Mad⟨rid⟩ to relieve Mr. Pinckney. Mr Bowdoin by being on that ground will be ⟨more⟩ in the way of obeying such orders as he may receive than here; and bo⟨th he⟩ and Mr. Erving respectively may perhaps take their ground with greate⟨r⟩ propriety in this stage, while it is known that our government has not ⟨acted⟩ than afterwards. I am, Sir, with great respect and esteem, Your very obedt. ⟨Serv⟩

JAS. MONROE

RC (DNA: RG 59, DD, Great Britain, vol. 12); RC (DNA: RG 233, President's Messages, 10A–D1); RC (DNA: RG 46, President's Messages, 10B–B1); letterbook copy (DLC: Monroe Papers); extract (DLC: Monroe Papers). First RC in a clerk's hand, signed by Monroe. Words and parts of words in angle brackets in the first RC are supplied from the letterbook copy. Minor differences between the copies have not been noted.

1. For the seizure of U.S. ships, see Monroe to JM, 16 Aug. 1805, and n. 2.

§ From George Armroyd & Co. *20 August 1805, Philadelphia.* "We have not been able before this Morning to get the Vouchers respecting our Brig the Neptune compleated. We now transmit your Letter,[1] accompanied thereby, to the Marquis de Casa Yrujo: and beg leave to enclose a Second Set of the Papers for the inspection of the French Minister, to whom you will be kind enough to represent the Case also."[2]

RC (DNA: RG 76, Preliminary Inventory 177, entry 322, Spain, Treaty of 1819 [Art. XI] [Spoliation], Misc. Records, ca. 1801–24, box 4). 1 p. Enclosures not found.

1. See JM to George Armroyd & Co., 18 Aug. 1805.
2. JM's letter to Louis-Marie Turreau has not been found but was acknowledged in Turreau to JM, 26 Aug. 1805.

§ From William C. C. Claiborne. *20 August 1805, New Orleans.* "Mr. Moralis has at length acceeded to my wishes, And given an assurance in writing, that 'during his residence in this Territory no further Sales of Lands west of the Perdido shall be made by him'; nor will 'he complete the Titles for Land heretofore contracted for under the Spanish Government, and which lie within the Limits aforesaid.'

A Copy of the Instrument signed by Mr. Moralis and of the Marquis's last letter to me upon the subject, shall be transmited to you by the next Mail.

"The affairs of the Territory, being now in a situation to admit of my absence from this City for a short time, I propose seting out this afternoon, on a Journey to the several Counties. In making this excursion, I have two *objects* in view; the *one*, to benefit my Health, which is much impaired, and the *other*, to assist personally in organizing the Militia.

"During my absence, I shall receive regular communications from New Orleans, and if my presence in the City should be necessary, I shall hasten my return. I have also made arrangements for the immediate Conveyance to me of your despatches, and you may rely on my faithful attention to any Instructions which may be given me."

RC (DNA: RG 59, TP, Orleans, vol. 7); letterbook copy (Ms-Ar: Claiborne Executive Journal, vol. 15). RC 2 pp.; in a clerk's hand, signed by Claiborne; docketed by Wagner as received 1 Oct. 1805.

§ From Anthony Terry. *20 August 1805, Cádiz.* "I have the pleasure to inform you that this day arrived safe in our Bay the Combined fleet from Ferrol in Seven days composed of the following Vessels.

18 Ships	5. Frigates	3. Brigs	French
11 Dittos	1. Ditto	"	1. Corvette. Spanish

Under the Command of the French Admiral Monsr. de Villeneuve, it is reported that they will not remain long in Port, and that the Plan is to pass to Cartagena & join the Vessels that are ready there, which if takes place the whole will be.

44 Ships	10. Frigates	6. Brigs	2. Corvettes—vizt.
18 Ships	5. Frigates	3. Brigs	French
26 Ditto	5. Dittos	3. Dittos	2. Corvettes Spanish

"It is with grief I inclose you Copy of Mr. John Gavinos Letter to me,[1] by which you will be informed that sundry American Vessels that sailed from this Port homeward bound have been condemned for a breach of Blockade as they Say, but you will be perfectly informed ℔ the Copies remitted to you ℔ Duplicate of our representations to the Vice Admirl. that we had received no notification whatever, since that received from Vice Admiral Orde."

Adds in a postscript: "Governmt. Notes—42½—43%."

RC and enclosure (DNA: RG 59, CD, Cádiz, vol. 1). RC 2 pp.; in a clerk's hand, signed by Terry. For enclosure, see n. 1.

1. The enclosure (1 p.; docketed by Wagner) is a copy of John Gavino to Josef Yznardy, 16 Aug. 1805, acknowledging the latter's 29 July letter, and stating that all letters for the United States by the detained ships had been sent on by the *President.* Gavino added that the *Paulina,* Captain Choate, had gone to trial on 15 Aug., when the judge had shown a copy of Adm. Charles Collingwood's instructions stating that the foreign ministers at the British court had been notified on 18 Apr. 1805 of the blockade of Cádiz and Sanlúcar de Barrameda and that sufficient time had elapsed for the news to reach the various ports. The

Paulina and its cargo of salt were therefore condemned for breach of blockade. The *Betsy* and *Hermon* were to go to trial on 17 Aug. and were expected to share the same fate. Gavino added in a postscript that the ships and cargoes had been condemned except for 600 quarter-casks on board the *Betsy*, which would be subject to further discussion because it was stated that the owner at New York had given his orders about them before news of the blockade could have reached him. For the announcement of the blockade, see George Erving to JM, 27 Apr. 1805, *PJM-SS*, 9:292 and n. 1.

¶ To Anthony Merry. Letter not found. *20 August 1805*. Calendared in the index to the State Department notes to foreign legations as regarding the recapture of the schooner *John* (DNA: RG 59, Notes to Foreign Ministers and Consuls, vol. 1).

§ From William Sprigg.[1] *21 August 1805, Trumbull County, Ohio.* "On the 3d Inst. I received from the President of the United States the appointment of Judge in the Territory of Michigan. Having previously received Information of the Destruction of the Town of Detroit by fire I thought it best not to be precipitate but to take some time to consult and enquire. The Commission reached me just before the Commencement of our Circuit so that I cannot with propriety visit that Country without first resigning my Office here which I think under all Circumstances it would not be prudent in me to do at this time. I feel myself honoured and greatly obliged by the President of the United States for this Mark of his Confidence which had I accepted, it should have been my Study to endeavour to prove not wholly misplaced and undeserved. With Sincere thanks and assurances of profound respect for the President and yourself I beg leave to decline the honour of accepting this Commission."

RC (DNA: RG 59, LRD). 2 pp.; docketed by Wagner as received 14 Sept.; docketed by Jefferson.

1. Maryland native William Sprigg (b. ca. 1770) of Steubenville, Ohio, was appointed judge in Orleans Territory in 1806, from which position he resigned in 1807. At some point he returned to Ohio, where he again served on the supreme court until he and the other members of that court were removed by the legislature in 1809. In 1812 he was named judge in Louisiana Territory and resigned from that post in 1813. In that year he was named judge on the supreme court of Illinois Territory and served on that bench until 1818 (Sharon J. Doliante, *Maryland and Virginia Colonials: Genealogies of Some Colonial Families . . .* [Baltimore, 1991], 936; Carter, *Territorial Papers, Orleans,* 9:626, 753 and n. 13; Carter, *Territorial Papers, Louisiana-Missouri,* 14:547, 699–700; *Senate Exec. Proceedings,* 2:401, 418; James E. Babb, "The Supreme Court of Illinois," *Green Bag: A Useless but Entertaining Magazine for Lawyers* 3 [1891]: 221; James Harrison Kennedy and Wilson M. Day, *The Bench and Bar of Cleveland* [Cleveland, 1889], 167).

§ From Samuel Huntington,[1] William Sprigg, and Daniel Symmes.[2] *22 August 1805, Trumbull County, Ohio.* "The Subscribers beg leave to recommend to the President of the United States George Tod Esq.[3] of youngstown in the County of Trumbull & State of Ohio, to fill the vacancy in the General Court of the Michigan Territory. Mr. Tod has been regularly bred to the profession of Law, and has practised with reputation in this State—from our acquaintance with him we are led to believe he would discharge the duties of a Judge in that Territory with capacity and integrity, & that his unifo[r]m conduct would be such in that station as to justify the confidence placed in him by the Government."

RC (DNA: RG 59, LAR, 1801–9, filed under "Tod"). 1 p.; in a clerk's hand, signed by Huntington, Sprigg, and Symmes; docketed by Wagner as received 14 Sept.; docketed by Jefferson.

1. Connecticut native Samuel Huntington (1765–1817) attended Dartmouth College and graduated from Yale, after which he toured Europe. He was admitted to the Connecticut bar, and later moved to Ohio about 1800. He was prominent in the state constitutional convention in 1802 and was appointed to the state supreme court in 1803. Huntington, George Tod, and Return Jonathan Meigs Jr. were leaders in the conservative wing of the state Republicans. Huntington served as governor from 1808 to 1810, was a member of the state legislature from 1811 to 1812, and was district paymaster in the U.S. Army during the War of 1812.

2. Daniel Symmes (1772–1817), nephew of John Cleves Symmes, was born in New Jersey, educated at the College of New Jersey, and studied law in Ohio, where he was admitted to the bar. He was a member of the Ohio state senate, serving as speaker from December 1803 to February 1805, when he was appointed to the state supreme court on which he served until January 1808 (Fred J. Milligan, *Ohio's Founding Fathers* [New York, 2003], 121–23).

3. Connecticut-born George Tod (1773–1841) graduated from Yale in 1795 and moved to Youngstown, Ohio, in 1800. He was a state senator from 1804 to 1805 and in 1806 was named to the state supreme court. In 1809 he, Samuel Huntington, and William Sprigg were removed by the legislature for upholding the policy of judicial review. He was a lieutenant colonel in the regular army in the War of 1812. He was named presiding judge of the court of common pleas in 1815 and served there until 1834 (Alfred T. Goodman, "Judges of the Supreme Court of Ohio, under the First Constitution, 1803–1852," *Western Reserve and Northern Ohio Historical Society, Cleveland, Ohio* 2 [1870]: 3).

§ From James Maury. *22 August 1805, Liverpool.* "I had the honor of writing to you on the 1st. Ultimo.

"The person whom I have appointed my Deputy at Greenock for the ports of the Clyde is Mr James Likely. My reason for appointing a person at Greenock in preference to Glasgow was its appearing to me more convenient on account of our ships laying at Greenock.

"Ever since my being in Office, no American Vessel commanded by a person in the predicament of Captn. Williamson of the Leda, has been admitted to entry at this port, unless by a special act of grace; but, in this case, after the most deliberate investigation, it has been determined otherwise, from which I conclude it as established that an american vessel commanded by a natural born subject of this country, who has become a resident in the United States since the 3rd February 1783 & been admitted a citizen thereof in due form of Law, has the same rights of admission to entry as if the master had been a natural born citizen of the U. S. A. or in her allegiance previous to the aforesaid era. The inclosed papers contain the grounds on which the Privy council have made this decision,[1] &, with all due deference, I submit to you the propriety of making it public.

"Our ships at this port have been very numerou(s) during the summer & have in general been advantageously freighted for the United States with the products of this country. For the state of this market I beg leave to refer to the price current herewith [not found]."

RC and enclosure (DNA: RG 59, CD, Liverpool, vol. 2). RC 2 pp.; in a clerk's hand, signed by Maury. For surviving enclosure, see n. 1.

1. The enclosure is an undated copy (1 p.; docketed by Wagner; printed in the Philadelphia *United States' Gazette*, 4 Nov. 1805) of a letter from king's advocate John Nicholl, attorney general Spencer Perceval, and solicitor general Vicary Gibbs to the Lords of the Privy Council, stating that they had, as directed, considered the petition of Thomas and Isaac Littledale to allow the *Leda* to unload its cargo of flour and staves, which had been forbidden on the grounds that Captain Williamson, a native of Scotland, had not become a citizen of the United States at their independence as required by the act of 37 Geo. 3 c. 97. They suggested, on the basis of *Wilson v. Marryat* in 1798, and an Exchequer decision in 1799, that if Williamson had become a U.S. citizen and established a bona fide residence, he was entitled to be the master of a ship that could legally import goods into Great Britain. For the provisions of the act, see *PJM-SS*, 4:112 n. 3.

§ From William C. C. Claiborne. *23 August 1805, "County of Acadia Sixty Miles from New Orleans."* "In the course of my Journey I have found the Citizens much desturbed by a report of the retrocession to Spain of the Country west of the Mississippi. I have possitively asserted, that the *Report* was groundless; but *it* had acquired such general currency, that many good disposed Citizens cannot be made to think that their connexion with the United States is permanent.

"On my arrival at *Concordia* (opposit Natchez) *where* I shall remain for a few days, it is my Intention again to write You: In the mean time, I cannot deny myself the pleasure of informing you, that the most perfect good Order prevails thro'out my Government, and the various subordinate Civil Officers vie with each other, in a faithful discharge of their duties.

"I am fearful that my best efforts to render the Militia an efficient force, will for some time be unavailing. The various descriptions of Inhabitants; the difference in Language; and the aversion of the independent Farmers to serve in the Militia, unless in the higher grades are not my only difficulties.

"To meet the convenience of the Citizens, and to render them Justice, I am inclined to think, that some Amendments to the late law of Congress relative to the Titles of Lands in this Territory, will be found advisable, and upon this subject, I shall hereafter do myself the Honor to write you fully. I will at this time Only observe, that some Indulgence ought to be given to the Owners of land on the Mississippi, and particularly that they should be secured in *a right of preemption*, to *a certain Quantity of Acres lying in the rear of their present possessions.*

"Under the Government of Spain, it was customary to grant from Six to twenty Acres front and forty Deep. The Cypress Swamps which approach near the lands now in cultivation, were seldom included in the grant; but from time immorial [*sic*] the Timber has been at the disposition of the *Inhabitant* who owned the Land in front, and *he* was considered by the Spanish Government as possessing an equitable right to the Swamp.

"If Congress should not make some special provision on this point, much discontent will arise; for the large Cypress Swamps, which at present limit the valuable

Farms on the Mississippi will be monopolized by Speculators, and the present settlers greatly injured."

RC (DNA: RG 59, TP, Orleans, vol. 7); letterbook copy (Ms-Ar: Claiborne Executive Journal, vol. 15). RC 3 pp.; in a clerk's hand, signed by Claiborne; docketed by Wagner as received 1 Oct. Minor differences between the copies have not been noted.

§ From Hans Rudolph Saabye. *23 August 1805, Copenhagen.* "I hope my last respects of 12 April and 14 May,[1] are duly come to hand, since which I have received the letter of 2 May,[2] with which you have honoured me. You have already been apprized of my having taken all possible steps, to render the measures adopted against the spreading of the yellow fever as little detrimental to the trade of the U.S. as possible, and it is with the greatest pleasure I can say, that they hardly have been felt. Every Ship has been admitted in the danish ports without any difficulty, and likewise in the russian when they had bills of health from Elsinore or here.

"Charleston alone is excluded from this advantage, but Ships from there, which have no cotton onboard, are laid under a Quarantine of 14 days, in case of cotton being onboard on the contrary, they must submit to the strict Quarantine.

"At present it is impossible to obtain any alteration in this established rule, it being the time, the fever generally manifests itself, but I do not doubt, if this should not be the case in the course of the Summer, but I migh⟨t⟩ get an alteration made therein, to which I shall direc⟨t⟩ my whole attention.

"It is required that all Bills of health granted in the U.S. should hereafter be certified by the danish Consuls, where there are any, for which formality you will please give the nescessary orders.

"Inclosed I have the honour of sending you the same annual List of Ships passed the Sound from 1 January till 30 June [not found] and likewise of advising you that the Acts of Congress for last year, have not yet been communicated to me."

RC (DNA: RG 59, CD, Copenhagen, vol. 1). 2 pp.; in a clerk's hand, signed by Saabye.

1. *PJM-SS*, 9:246–47, 351.
2. Ibid., 308–9.

From James Wilkinson

No. 2

SIR,   ST. LOUIS Augt. 24th. 1805.

Since my last, bearing date the 28th. Ulto. the affairs of this Territory have progressed with tranquility. My neglect of the violent personal invectives, which were poured in upon me[1] by the adverse parties of the Country, appears to have abated the Zeal and ardor of the managers on either Side, and it would seem that a truce has succeeded at all points, excepting the district of St. Genevieve, where the contest has I fear derived support from an improper source, but even there we shall soon have concord. Judge Lucas arrived here on the 10th. or 11th. inst., and we have since adjusted general principles for the organization of our Courts, and the construction of the System of jurisprudence we propose to adopt, the leading features of which ⟨are⟩ ⟨brevity,⟩ ⟨sim⟩plicity, promptitude and economy; and thus far, I have much pleasure in assuring you, we have proceeded, not only in harmony, but with cordiality and a happy coincidence of Sentiment.

I am obliged to touch one of the three great objects to which the President directed my attention,[2] with extreme delicacy; that is the depopulation of the feeble scattered Settlements below, on the Mississippi and St. François Rivers, for the People of the Territory, however well satisfied with their present condition, look forward with much confidence to the period of their admission, to memberhood with the United States, and the sudden extinction of these views, would deeply affect the *Amour Propre*, and probably excite some seditious emotions; my course therefore in this respect must be rather indirect. Perceiving that the Judges were unapprised of the Presidential policy, and that one of them encouraged the popular expectations, I considered it proper to impart to them his injunctions to me, observing at the same time, that whatever might be our own feelings on the occasion, I considered it the solemn duty of every public functionary to maintain and promote the views of the executive with Zeal and assiduity. I was listened to with apparent Surprize, but experienced an accordance of Sentiment; yet Sir, I do believe a communication from you on the subject, would enable me to give additional force to my own observations. The result of the inquiries, which I have set on foot on the subject, favors the practibility of the proposition of the President, which I consider essentially connected, with the transfer of our Southern Indians to the West of the Mississippi. In fact the Settlements below Cape Girardeau are composed very generally, of a medley of our loose erratic countrymen, whose local attachments are as fluctuating, as their principles are unsteady.

The inclosed letter from a native of Baltimore County, Maryland, who has great influence over the most respectable settlements of the District in which he lives, will convey to you some idea of the dispositions, feelings and interests of the Inhabitants in that quarter.[3]

The projects of the British merchants on the Side of Canada, to monopolize at once the whole trade of the Missouri, menace such serious consequences, as to call forth my decisive interposition. This town is now almost filled, not only with merchandise imported from Montreal, but with merchants, Agents, Clerks, and engagés all British Subjects, who are here for the express purpose of carrying their enterprizes into a River, where they have no right and which they never before visited. At this moment our controul over the Indians of the Missouri is unrivalled, they repose with confidence on our protection, and invite us to establish factories, and military Posts, in the interior of their Country: Independent of commercial considerations, and the tranquility of this our feeble and exposed frontier, The proximity and relation of those Indians to Spanish America, their force, and the Safety with which their erratic habits, would enable them to make war upon us, point out the policy and expediency of our preserving their friendship, by every means in our power.

But if We admit the British trader to a free intercourse with them, we may reasonably expect, that from political rivalry or personal interest, he will oppose himself to our plans, and by a Single whisper he may destroy our present good understanding with the natives, defeat our future views and involve Calamitous consequences of permanent duration.

Jealousy is a prominent trait of In(dian) Character, and to excite it effectually among the Missourians, it is barely necessary to say to them, "Beware of the Americans. They mean to take your Country from you, as they have done that of your Red Bretheren East of the Mississippi; If you Suffer them to establish factories among you, it is to corrupt your Chiefs; and if you permit them to build forts in your Country, and Garrison them with their Warriors, they will make slaves of you"; Such artifices have heretofore been practised, and We have witnessed their pernicious effects.

The force of these reflections which are, I flatter myself sound, determined me to address a letter to the Congressional officers of the Territory now in this Place, of which you have a Copy under Cover,[4] I Shall wait for their answer to-morrow, and should they accord in the opinion, I will prohibit the entrance of British Merchandise into the Missouri; but let their Judgement be what it may, it is my intention the day after to-morrow to utter the Notification, of which you have also a Copy;[5] I know the measure will draw upon me a load of obloquy to which I must oppose the policy of the Step and the integrity of my motives, in the firm hope that my conduct may receive your approbation and that of the President. With perfect respect I am Sir, your Obdt. Servt.

JA: (WILKINSON)

NB. I herewith transmit you copies of the only official documents which I have uttered.[6]

RC and enclosures (DNA: RG 107, LRUS); RC (DNA: RG 59, TP, Louisiana, vol. 1); FC (ICHi); extract and copies of enclosures (DNA: RG 107, LRRS). First RC docketed by Wagner as received 3 Oct. Second RC marked "Duplicate"; in a clerk's hand, signed and addressed by Wilkinson; docketed by Wagner. Words and parts of words in angle brackets in the first RC are supplied from the second RC. FC in a clerk's hand, with Wilkinson's emendations. The extract consists of the last four paragraphs of the RCs. Minor differences between the copies have not been noted. For enclosures, see nn. 3–6.

1. In the second RC this sentence reads: "My utter neglect of the violent invectives which poured in upon me. . . ."

2. Jefferson had directed Wilkinson's attention to "the prevention of the Trade from Canada to the West of the Mississippi—the depopulation of our loose settlements below this on the Mississippi & its branches—and the transfer of the Southern Indians to this Territory" (Carter, *Territorial Papers, Louisiana-Missouri*, 13:266).

3. The enclosure is a copy (7 pp.; certified by Wilkinson; docketed by Wagner; printed ibid., 175–78) of Edward F. Bond to Wilkinson, 2 Aug. 1805, stating that he had settled at Cape Girardeau about five years previously, that he would be happy to move elsewhere if Jefferson and Congress "should think that Louisiana ought not to be settled," that "at least two thirds of the People would be Satisfied" to move into Spanish territory for various reasons, and that the population of the region was made up of "some old patriots, some old tories a few federalists and some with no Politics of their own."

4. The enclosure (3 pp.; docketed by Wagner; printed ibid., 188–89) is a copy of Wilkinson's 22 Aug. 1805 letter to the three judges, the secretary of the territory, and army colonels John B. Scott and Samuel Hammond, stating that before the Louisiana Purchase, the trade with the Indians up the Missouri river "was confined to a few licensed Spanish Subjects"; that it now appeared that "extensive arrangements" were underway in Canada for "a general trade with the Indians of the Missouri"; that "several Batteaux charged with merchandise, and navigated by the Subjects of a foreign power" had already come down the Mississippi; and asking his correspondents (1) if Canadian products should be allowed to enter the Missouri; (2) if firearms should be allowed to be carried up that river; and (3) if the subjects of any foreign power should be allowed to enter the river for the purpose of trade with the Indians. In their 24 Aug. 1805 reply (printed ibid., 200–201), the officials stated that only Canadian goods imported by U.S. citizens or residents of U.S. territories should be allowed to be traded up the Missouri, that firearms should not be allowed except in such quantities as Wilkinson might deem advisable, and that foreign subjects should not be allowed to enter the Missouri unless they were residents of the United States or its territories.

5. The enclosure (1 p.; docketed by Wagner) is a copy of Wilkinson's 24 Aug. 1805 proclamation stating that no foreign subjects would be permitted to enter the Missouri River "on any pretence whatever"; that licensed traders were forbidden to carry into the river "fire arms, uniform cloathing, other than that of the United States, medals, armbands or other jewelry, bearing devises or Emblems of any Prince, Potentate or foreign Power whatsoever"; that invoices of the merchandise intended for that trade were to be exhibited to territorial secretary Joseph Browne; and that all individuals engaged in the trade were to take an oath of fidelity to the United States and to abjure allegiance to any other power. When the proclamation was issued on 26 Aug. 1805, the prohibition on firearms was omitted. On 8 Sept. 1805 Wilkinson explained to Henry Dearborn that he had done this at the request of local merchants who had petitioned against it on 24 Aug. (ibid., 200, 201–3).

6. Wilkinson also enclosed copies (4 pp.; in French and English; in a clerk's hand, signed by Wilkinson; docketed by Wagner) of his 4 July 1805 proclamation (see Wilkinson to JM, 28 July 1805, and n. 1), and his 10 July 1805 proclamation, which prohibited all persons from ascending the Missouri into Indian territory and from going up the Mississippi "above the present Settlements" with the intention of entering any of its western branches or of trading with the Indians on the right bank except by permission from Wilkinson (ibid., 155–56, 160–61).

§ From James Brown. *24 August 1805*, *"German Coast."* "I had the honor to receive your favor covering my Commission as District Attorney of the United States for the District of Orleans,[1] and take the earliest opportunity of informing you that I have accepted the appointment."

RC (DNA: RG 59, TP, Orleans, vol. 7). 1 p.

1. For Brown's appointment, see Memorandum from Thomas Jefferson, 11 Mar. 1805, *PJM-SS*, 9:123, 125 n. 10.

§ From George W. Erving. *24 August 1805, London.* No. 64. "Immediately after Mr Monroes return to this place on the 23d. July I was preparing to depart for Madrid when Mr Bowdoin arrived from St Andero. You are already fully acquainted with the motives which induced him to quit Spain; I doubt not but that the measure will produce a good effect upon the disposition of the Spanish government, & it has not disappointed Mr. Bowdoins Expectations in regard to his health which happily has been most essentially benefitted by the medical assistance which he has received here.

"It has been determined within these few days that I shoud proceed without further delay thro Paris to Madrid to relieve Mr Pinkney; Mr Bowdoin himself will pass over to Paris in about a fortnight; in that situation he will probably await the orders of government & it will Enable him to preserve a quick & free communication with myself in all which concerns the publick interests, or is connected with the objects of the mission.

"Taking a few days to complete my final accounts & other documents connected with my late agency here, I propose on the first of the Ensuing month to leave London."

RC (DNA: RG 59, CD, London, vol. 9); RC (DNA: RG 59, DD, Spain, vol. 10). First RC 2 pp.; marked "Triplicate." Second RC marked "Duplicate."

§ From Joseph Nourse. *24 August 1805, "Treasury Department Register's Office."* "Upon application to Mr Wagner for information relative to the death of Judge Ker of the Missisippi Territory, I am informed that a letter mentioning that event has been forwarded to you in Philadelphia; permit me therefore to request a Certificate of the time of his decease in order to obtain a Settlement of his Account for salary to that period."[1]

RC (DNA: RG 59, ML). 1 p.; in a clerk's hand, signed by Nourse. Docketed by Wagner.

1. For letters announcing the death of David Ker, see Cato West to JM, 22 Jan. 1805, and Thomas Rodney to JM, 24 Jan. 1805, *PJM-SS*, 8:501.

To John Armstrong

SIR,   DEPARTMENT OF STATE August 25th. 1805

It is represented by the parties interested in the ship New Jersey and cargo, for which indemnity is claimed under the late Convention with France, that a disallowance of the claim is likely to proceed from an idea that Insurers do not in such cases take the place of the Insured.[1]

As the Convention has provided for its own exposition and execution, it has been thought best that these should be left, as much as possible to their own course; and an interposition of any kind in the present instance would be the rather declined, as it cannot be guided by communications from yourself relative to the nature of the difficulties which have arisen. Yet as the interest which the parties have at Stake renders them particularly anxious and urgent on the occasion; and as it cannot be injurious, and may be agreeable to yourself, to know the sentiments of the President on the question whether the title of the Insurers accrues to the insured, if that naked question be indeed the source of the difficulties, I am authorized to suggest for your information, that he considers the general principle, on which the questions turns, as supporting the claims of the American underwriters to the benefit of the Convention, where they have paid the loss of the original owners, citizens of the United States. I have the honor to be &c

JAMES MADISON

Letterbook copy (DNA: RG 59, IM, vol. 6).

1. See Philip Nicklin and Robert Eaglesfield Griffith to JM, 25 July 1805.

From Thomas Jefferson

DEAR SIR   MONTICELLO Aug. 25. 05
I confess that the inclosed letter from General Turreau excites in me both jealousy & offence, in undertaking, & without apology, to say in what manner we are to recieve & treat Moreau within our own country.[1] Had Turreau been here longer he would have known that the National authority pays honors to no foreigner, that the state authorities, municipalities & individuals, are free to render whatever they please, voluntarily, & free from restraint by us; & he ought to know that no part of the criminal sentence of another country can have any effect here. The style of that government in the Spanish business, was calculated to excite indignation: but it was a case in which that might have done injury. But the present is a case which would justify some notice in order to let them understand we are not of those powers who will recieve & execute mandates. I think the answer should shew independance as well as friendship. I am anxious to recieve the opinions of our brethren after their view & consideration of the Spanish papers. I am strongly impressed with a belief of hostile & treacherous intentions against us on the part of France, and that we should lose no time in securing something more than a neutral friendship from England.

Not having heard from you for some posts, I have had a hope you were on the road, & consequently that mrs Madison was reestablished. We are now in want of rain, having had none within the last ten days. In your quarter I am afraid they have been much longer without it. We hear great complaints from F. Walker's, Lindsay's Maury's etc of drought. Accept affectionate salutations & assurances of constant friendship.

P.S. I suppose Kuhn at Genoa should have new credentials.

Th:Jefferson

RC (DLC); FC (DLC: Jefferson Papers); Tr (MHi).

1. See Louis-Marie Turreau to JM, 14 Aug. 1805.

§ From George Tod. *25 August 1805, Youngstown, Ohio.* "Herewith is sent a letter from the judges of the supreme Court in this state. Should the President see fit to confer on me the appointment of judge in the Michigan Territory it will be thankfully recieved. Living as I do, remote from the active and informed parts of the Union, it is impossible for me to obtain other letters of recommendation, unless from people whose Characters are unknown to the President."

FC (OClWHi: George Tod Papers, MS. 3203). 1 p. For enclosure, see Samuel Huntington, William Sprigg, and Daniel Symmes to JM, 22 Aug. 1805.

§ From Carlos Martínez de Yrujo. *25 August 1805, "Neighborhood of Philadelphia."* "Having been absent from the City for some days, I did not receive until to day your letter of the 18th. current[1] in which you inform me of the capture of the American Brigantine Neptune by a French or Spanish privateer on her passage from the Island of St. Croix to Philada. and in which you enclose me various documents relative to the property[2] of her cargo. As Minister of a just King, desirous of respecting the rights of neutrals & more particularly of the neutrals, with whom he has connections so immediate and friendly as are those with the U.States I do not lose an instant in sending you enclosed a letter [not found] for the Governor of Porto Rico, who I doubt not will do the requisite Justice to the owners of the Brigantine, if as is supposed, she has been sent to any port of that Island: At the same time I permit myself to suggest, that it will be proper that in order to assure the good effects of my intervention, that the owners should transmit to the Governor of the said Island the documents necessary to prove the legality of their property.

"It is very painful to me, that the United States should still have causes of complaint respecting the injuries which you say the navigation of their citizens experience in some ports of the Island of Cuba. A long while ago I wrote upon the subject to the Captain General of that Island. I also am apprised that the King my master has given direct orders to the Captain Genl. of it in order that the navigation of the Americans employed in a legal and just commerce might be respected:

243

and it has also come to my knowledge, that the said Captain General has circulated those orders to the Governors and subaltern Commandants under him wherefore I am inclined to hope that in future, there cannot exist just cause of complaint. You will therefore be pleased to specify to me in the most detailed manner the cases and circumstances, which have excited the sensibility of the U.States and you may rely that I will send without lost [*sic*] of time the information you may give me on this particular to the said Captain General reminding him of the orders of H. M. upon this point and of the respect paid to the rights of a friendly nation."

Adds in a postscript: "The name of the capturing vessel and of its Captain leave me no room to doubt that it is a French Privateer; nevertheless by my letter to the Governor of Porto Rico you will see that I particularly recommend to him the cause of Justice. I return to you the documents transmitted."

RC (DNA: RG 59, NFL, Spain, vol. 2). 4 pp.; in Spanish; in a clerk's hand, except for Yrujo's complimentary close and signature; docketed by Wagner. Copytext is Wagner's interlinear translation.

1. See JM to George Armroyd, 18 Aug. 1805.
2. The word Yrujo used, *propiedad*, is better translated as "ownership."

From John Mason

DEAR SIR   GEO TOWN 26 Augt 1805
On the 15th. Inst your note for $500 endorsed by me became due in the Bank of Columbia. As I was not provided with a note of yours to offer for renewal I obtained leave to discount my own note in lieu thereof for 20 Days, to give time to receive yours.

I now take the liberty to enclose one in due form, which be pleased sign and return me so as to be here by the 4th of Septr: the day, on which, it must go into Bank.

Permit me Sir to offer my respects to Mrs Madison & my best wishes for her speedy restoration to perfect health. With great Respect & Esteem I have the honour to be Sir your very obt Sert

                                                          J. MASON

RC (DLC).

§ From William C. C. Claiborne. *26 August 1805*, *"120 Miles from New Orleans."* "The report of the retrocession to Spain of the Country west of the Mississippi had also prevailed in New Orleans: The Evening previous to my departure, being on a visit to the Marquis of Casa Calvo, I asked him if he Knew upon what Authority that report was circulated; he answered in the negative, and added that he had understood the negociation was suspended and that Mr. Monroe had left Madrid; he further said that 'the Minister of State (Cervalles) had informed him the (Marquis) that the desire of the Court of Spain was, to make the Mississippi river the Boundary, and in time it was expected that, that object would be attained.' The Marquis delivered himself in the French Language, From my imperfect knowledge of French, it is probable, I may have misunderstood some of his expressions; but I am sure I have given you the substance of what he said.

"The *prospect* of a *retrocession* of the West Bank of the Mississippi, *is* now, and has always been the Theeme of the Spanish Officers who remain in this Territory; and many Citizens seem to view *it* as an event likely to happen: An impression which I greatly regret, since it tends to lessen their confidence in the American Government, and to Cherish a Spanish party among us. Next therefore to a final adjustment of Limits with the Spanish Government, I most desire to see every Spanish Officer removed from the ceded Territory. There certainly must be a power some where vested, to Cause to be executed the Clause in the Treaty which directs 'the Spanish Forces to be withdrawn (within three months) from the Ceded Territory,' and I should indeed be pleased to have it hinted to me, that in my Character as Commissioner or Governor I could on this Occasion take (if necessary) compulsery Measures."

Adds in a postscript: "My last letter to you was dated the 23rd. Instant."

RC (DNA: RG 59, TP, Orleans, vol. 7); letterbook copy (Ms-Ar: Claiborne Executive Journal, vol. 15); Tr (DNA: RG 233, President's Messages, 9A–D1); Tr (DNA: RG 46, President's Messages, 9B–B1). RC 3 pp.; in a clerk's hand, signed by Claiborne; docketed by Wagner as received 1 Oct., with JM's added note: "2. copied for Congress." The second Tr is a letterpress copy of the first Tr, and the postscript is omitted from both.

§ From Anthony Merry. *26 August 1805, Philadelphia.* "I have received the Honor of your Letter of the 20th. Instant[1] inclosing a Copy of one from the Deputy Collector of Passamaquoddy respecting the Seizure of the American Schooner John in the Waters of that Bay, and the Impressment of Two Citizens of the United States from the American Revenue Boat, by His Majesty's Sloop Busy.

"I shall not fail, Sir, to transmit without Delay a Copy of your Representation on the above Subjects to the Commander in Chief of His Majesty's Ships on the Halifax Station in Order that proper Attention may be paid to it."

RC (DNA: RG 59, NFL, Great Britain, vol. 3). 2 pp.; in a clerk's hand, signed by Merry; docketed by Wagner, with his note: "Outrages of the Busy in Passamaquoddy."

1. The letter has not been found, but see Jacob Wagner to JM, 19 Aug. 1805.

§ From Peder Pedersen. *26 August 1805, Philadelphia.* "I herewith beg leave to inform you that His Majesty the King has been pleased to appoint G. Hammeken Esqr. hitherto His Vice Consul in New York, to be His Consul for the states of New Hampshire Massachussets Rhode Island Connecticut & New York, to reside in New York; and J. F. Eikard Esqr. hitherto His Vice Consul in Philadelphia, to be His Consul for the states of New Jersey–Delaware, Pennsylvania & Maryland, to reside in Philadelphia; and as His Majesty also on the same occasion most graciously has been pleased to honor myself with a new Commission as

Consul General for all the United States, I shall beg leave to request you will be pleased to lay before the President of the United States, the Three Commissions I herewith have the honor to transmit to you,[1] and according to their contents, to obtain the necessary *Exequatur's.*"

RC (DNA: RG 59, NFL, Denmark, vol. 1). 1 p.

1. Copies of the three commissions (3 pp.; in Latin) are filed in the National Archives, Record Group 360, Papers of the Continental Congress, item 129.

§ From Louis-Marie Turreau. *26 August 1805, Baltimore.* Has received JM's letter of 21 Aug. [not found] and the enclosures stating that the brig *Neptune* and cargo, which a French or Spanish privateer called *La Resource*, Captain Janet, had taken, belongs to U.S. citizens.[1]

Transmits them all to General Ferrand, commandant at Santo Domingo, asking that justice be done to the interested parties.

The general's decree, a copy of which he sends JM,[2] gives him reason to believe that complaints against the cruisers will be less frequent in future and that the parties who make claims against the violation of treaties or of the law of nations, if they themselves have not violated them, will obtain immediate justice, since no prize can any longer be judged in any place other than Santo Domingo and the privateer will be obliged to complete the formalities and give the bonds required by the laws.

General Ferrand has sent him a declaration of three sailors from which it appears that an American vessel, armed and cleared in May from Baltimore, while under a French flag had fired at sea on two American and one Danish ship. Did not communicate it to JM because in the declaration the names of the ship, the captain, and the owner are so frenchified that it cannot serve to identify either of the men or even to reveal what ship it may be except by a forced construction of the names. However this may be, the fact appears certain. It would be desirable if neutrals, who have so much to suffer from privateers, could stop those of their subjects whom a criminal greed leads to cover, under the flag of a belligerent power, the depredations which they commit on the vessels and trade of their own country.

Encloses his letter to General Ferrand about the *Neptune* [not found] because, not having a reliable occasion, fears that it may suffer the same fate as one of those which he wrote to the captains general of the colonies for the ship *Two Friends* of Charleston.[3] It was found attached to a piece of wood on the eastern shore of Chesapeake Bay, where it was thrown by the winds or the tide, its weight not having been heavy enough to make it sink to the bottom.

RC (DNA: RG 59, NFL, France, vol. 2–3). 2 pp.; in French.

1. For the case of the *Neptune*, see George Armroyd & Co. to JM, 17, 18, and 19 Aug. 1805.
2. The enclosure has not been found, but on 4 Sept. 1805 the *National Intelligencer* stated: "Gen. Ferrand has issued an order forbidding the officers under him from issuing commissions to cruisers elsewhere than at St. Domingo, where the sureties are to reside and the captures to be adjudged. He also revokes all authority, in prize matters and for issuing commissions, vested in the delegates from St. Dominga [*sic*] to other colonies."
3. For the case of the *Two Friends*, see *PJM-SS*, 9:459 n. 1, and Turreau to JM, 24 June 1805, ibid., 493–94.

¶ To Jacob Wagner. Letter not found. *26 August 1805*. Mentioned in Wagner to JM, 5 Sept. 1805, as suggesting that JM would leave Philadelphia in early September.

From Thomas Jefferson

DEAR SIR   MONTICELLO Aug. 27. 05.

Your's of the 20th. has been recieved, & in that a letter from Casenove and another from Mrs. Ciracchi:[1] but those from Turreau & to Yrujo were not inclosed. Probably the former was what came to me by the preceding post respecting Moreau: if so, you have my opinion on it in my last. Considering the character of Bonaparte, I think it material at once to let him see that we are not one of the powers who will recieve his orders.[2]

I think you have misconcieved the nature of the treaty I thought we should propose to England. I have no idea of committing ourselves immediately, or independantly of our further will to the war. The treaty should be provisional only, to come into force *on the event of our being engaged in war with either France or Spain*, during the present war in Europe. In that event we should make common cause, & England should stipulate not to make peace without our obtaining the objects for which we go to war, to wit, the ack[n]olegement by Spain of the rightful boundaries of Louisiana, (which we should reduce to our minimum by a secret article) and 2. indemnification for spoliations for which purpose we should be allowed to make reprisal on the Floridas & *retain them* as an indemnification. Our co operation in the war (if we should actually enter into it) would be a sufficient consideration for Great Britain to engage for it's object: and it being generally known to France & Spain that we had entered into treaty with England would probably ensure us a peaceable & immediate settlement of both points. But another motive much more powerful would indubitably induce England to go much further. Whatever ill humor may at times have been expressed against us by individuals of that country the first wish of every Englishman's heart is to see us once more fighting by their sides against France; nor could the king or his ministers do an act so popular, as to enter into alliance with us. The nation would not weigh the consideration by grains & scruples. They would consider it as the price & pledge of an indissoluble course of friendship. I think it possible that for such a provisional treaty they would give us their general guarantee of Louisiana & the Floridas. At any rate we might try them. A failure would not make our situation worse. If such a one could be obtained we might await our own convenience for calling up the casus federis.[3] I think important that England should recieve an overture as early as possible as it might prevent her listening to terms of peace. If I recollect rightly we had instructed Monroe, when he went to Paris to settle the deposit, if he failed in that object to propose a treaty to England immediately. We could not be more engaged to secure the deposit then, than we are the country now after paying 15. millions for it. I do expect therefore that considering the present state of things as analogous to that, & virtually within his instructions, he will very likely make the proposition to England. I write my thoughts freely, wishing the same from the other gentlemen that seeing & considering the grounds of each others opinions we may come as soon as possible to a result. I propose to be in Washington on the 2d. of October. By that time I hope we shall be ripe for some conclusion.

I have desired Mr. Barnes to pay my quota of expences respecting the Marseilles cargo, whatever you will be so good as to notify him that it is.[4] I wish I could have heard that Mrs. Madison's course of recovery were more speedy. I now fear we shall not see you but in Washington. Accept for her & yourself my affectionate salutations & assurances of constant esteem & respect

TH: JEFFERSON

RC (DLC: Rives Collection, Madison Papers); FC (DLC: Jefferson Papers).

1. The letter from Théophile Cazenove has not been found but may have been Cazenove to JM, 2 Jan. 1805, *PJM-SS*, 8:443. Jefferson received a 10 Mar. 1805 letter from Thèrése Ceracchi from Vienna on 22 Aug. He received JM's 20 Aug. letter on 26 Aug. (DLC: Jefferson Papers, Epistolary Record).

2. Jefferson is referring to Turreau's 14 Aug. 1805 letter to JM concerning government recognition of Gen. Jean Victor Moreau.

3. *Casus foederis:* "A situation or occurrence covered by the provisions of a treaty or compact, and so requiring the action of the parties thereto" (*OED Online*).

4. For this situation, see David Gelston to JM, 8 Aug. 1805, and JM to Jefferson, 9 Aug. 1805.

From Jacob Wagner

DEAR SIR   WASHINGTON 27 Augt. 1805.

Be pleased to sign and return to me the enclosed letters for the Secretary of the Treasury.[1] I enclose a letter, which as it appears to be addressed in the handwriting of your overseer, I have not opened.[2] Mr. Duffield has resigned the commission of Judge of Orleans Territory on account of the effect of the climate upon his health.[3] I have enclosed the resignation to the President.

A short time before your departure, Dr. Triplitt was induced by what he had heard from OBrien to apply to me for information, whether the government would probably send the Doctor requested by the Dey of

Algiers, proposing in that case to offer his services.[4] I promised to mention the subject to you but did not find the opportunity until the Dr. had left town; he has now returned and renewed his application. I have been acquainted with him but a short time, and therefore can say nothing more in his favor than that I hear him very favourably spoken of for his manners, temper and professional ability. He is a native of Virginia, has served in the Navy, is personally acquainted with Mr. Lear, and undertakes to offer the best testimonials of his personal and professional character. He thinks it reasonable, in case he is approved, that a moderate pecuniary aid should be allowed him by the government until his introduction to practise at Algiers should render it unnecessary. He observes that the Secretary of the Navy will be able to speak of the reputation he enjoyed in the Navy. I have the honor to remain with perfect respect & attachment Your most obed. servt.

JACOB WAGNER

RC (DNA: RG 59, LAR, 1801–9, filed under "Triplett"). Docketed by Jefferson "Triplett Dr. to go to Algiers."

1. The letters have not been found, but they may have included JM to Albert Gallatin, 17 Aug. 1805.
2. This was probably Gideon Gooch to JM, 28 July 1805.
3. This was George Duffield to JM, 23 July 1805.
4. For Mustafa Dey's request that an American doctor be sent to him, see *PJM-SS*, 8:446. Thomas Triplett was a naval surgeon from 14 Oct. 1799 to 4 July 1804. He was reinstated on 6 May 1806 and arrived in the Mediterranean in December 1806, expecting to become personal physician to Mustafa Dey; but in December 1807 Tobias Lear reported: "Dr. Triplett finds his expectations of doing well in his profession here, entirely defeated," so Lear employed him as his secretary (Knox, *Register of Officer Personnel*, 56; Knox, *Naval Documents, Barbary Wars*, 6:490; Lear to JM, 31 Dec. 1807, DNA: RG 59, CD, Algiers, vol. 7, pt. 2).

§From William C. C. Claiborne. *27 August 1805, "Territory of Orleans 150 Miles from New Orleans."* "I passed over to Batton Rouge on Yesterday, and partook of the hospitality of Governor Grandpré: I was introduced into a *Fort, where* the Governor has resided for several Months, from an apprehension that Kemper and his Associates, still meditate an Attack against his Government.

"The Fort of Batton Rouge, has lately been repaired; but the Works are ill constructed, and could not be defended (even from Assault) by a less number than One Thousand Men: the *Scite* also has been injudiciously selected, for *it* is commanded by ground not more than a Quarter of a Mile distant.

"I will endeavour to reach Fort Adams on tomorrow; from whence I shall pass by the Way of Natchez to Concordia, where I propose remaining for two Weeks, unless my earlier return to New Orleans, should be found expedient."

Adds in a postscript: "The Fort at Batton Rouge I am informd is Garrissoned by One Hundred and Twenty Men."

RC (DNA: RG 59, TP, Orleans, vol. 7); letterbook copy (Ms-Ar: Claiborne Executive Journal, vol. 15). RC 2 pp.; docketed by Wagner as received 1 Oct. Minor differences between the copies have not been noted.

§ From William Duane. *27 August 1805.* "Francis Brueil, a French merchant connected with the Spanish Ambassador in many transactions, has recently applied to a tinman in this city to make a lantern such as is used in the service of artillery by night; one was made, and it is understood that a large number more are to be made. The Tinman suspecting that they might be intended for some purpose hostile to the U.S. has hesitated whether he ought to execute them—and would not if there were to be any reason to confirm his suspicions; he advised with me, and I have told him he ought to go on, so that their direction may be the more easily detected or traced. As it is impossible for me to determine what opinion ought to be informed on this subject, I thought it best to apprize you of it, and should any steps be necessary to be made on the subject, I am sure the man would aid. I have not however intimated to any one that I have taken this step—as after all it may be of no moment."

RC (DLC). 1 p.

To William C. C. Claiborne

Sir.   DEPARTMENT OF STATE August. 28th. 1805.
In compliance with the request contained in your letter of the 26 ult.[1] I have to state it as my opinion (the office of Attorney General being vacant)[2] that the powers of the Legislative Council of the Territory of Orleans do not cease until the first Monday in November next; but, as under a contrary impression you intended to prorogue them on the third of July last, the true exposition of the Act of the last session of Congress[3] as far as relates to the subject is unimportant, unless some exigency, not to be calculated upon, should render it indispensible to convene the Council. I am &c.

JAMES MADISON

Letterbook copy (DNA: RG 59, DL, vol. 15).

1. See Claiborne to JM, 26 June 1805, *PJM-SS*, 9:495.
2. For the vacancy in the post of attorney general, see ibid., 107, 108 n. 11.
3. For section 8 of the 2 Mar. 1805 "Act further providing for the government of the territory of Orleans," stating that certain provisions of the prior act that divided the Louisiana Purchase into two territories should expire on the first Monday of November 1805, see *U.S. Statutes at Large*, 2:323.

To William Duane

PHILADA. Aug. 28 [1805]

J. M. prests. his respects to Mr. D. & in answer to his note of yesterday evening, observes that he is not acquainted with any circumstances denoting that the A⟨r⟩tillery Lanterns on which the Tinman is employed, may have a hostile reference to the U. States, or justifying an interposition in any form agst. the prosecution of the Job. Should the suspicions entertained by the Tinman have any real foundation the course which occurred to Mr. D. seems favorable to the requisite discoveries.

FC (DLC). Year not indicated; conjectural year assigned based on internal evidence and Duane to JM, 27 Aug. 1805.

To Frances Smith Prevost

SIR.   DEPARTMENT OF STATE August 28th. 1805.

I have received your letter of the 8th. July, expressing the wish of Judge Prevost to obtain the President's permission to leave the Territory for the benefit of his health. Though such a request on the part of an Officer, placed under the controul of the President, would be readily acceeded to, as far [as] the public service might permit, so on the other hand as Judge Prevost holds an office in a separate branch of the Government, he must be at liberty to act according to the urgency of circumstances. With my best wishes for his recovery, I am &c.

JAMES MADISON

Letterbook copy (DNA: RG 59, DL, vol. 15). Addressed to "T. W. Prevost." For the assignment of addressee as Frances Smith Prevost, see Prevost to JM, 8 July 1805, n.

From Jacob Wagner

DEAR SIR   DEP. STATE 28 Augt. 1805

I have the honor to enclose drafts of letters to Mr. Prevost & to Governor Claiborne.[1] It is so improbable that it will be found of importance to convene the Legislative Council of Orleans before November, and that thus the erroneous opinion of Govr. Claiborne will stand in need of correction, that I doubt the necessity of answering his letter: if you should suppress the draft, be pleased to inform me of it, that the copy I have preserved may share the same fate. In the mean time I think the opinion given in the draft a very obvious one as to correctness. The 8th. sect. of the Act of 2 March last repeals the repugnant parts of the former Act of 26 March 1804 "from & after the 1st. monday in Novr. next," which is the day, when, by the 3rd. sect. of the first mentioned act, the Representatives are to meet for the purpose of nominating a new Council. Although, therefore, according to the 2d. sect. of the Act of March last, so much of the ordinance of Congress as relates to the organization and powers of a general assembly was to be in force from the 4th. of July last, yet there could not be any actual practical repugnance between that part of the ordinance and the part of the Act of March 1804 which created the Legislative Council, before the day limited by the 8th. sect. of the other act for the repeal of the repugnant parts of the Act which it superseded: under such circumstances I cannot conceive a reason to refuse to that section its literal meaning. With great respect & attacht. I remain, Dear Sir, Your most obed. Servt.

JACOB WAGNER

RC (DLC).

    1. See JM to William C. C. Claiborne, and JM to Frances Smith Prevost, both dated 28 Aug. 1805.

§ From John Martin Baker. *28 August 1805, Palma, Majorca.* "With the expectation that the port of Mahon, will be considered, and prove useful at some period, to the Navy of the United States, within the Mediterranean—I have taken the liberty, and do herewith solicit your acceptance of a perspective view thereof, which I have had taken purposely; with the pleasing hope that it may meet your favorable acceptan⟨ce⟩."

    Adds in a postscript: "Permit me, sir, to observe, that the case contains two views—one of which, with the inclosed letter, I beg leave to solicit the favor of your having delivered to the President of the United-States of America."[1]

    RC, two copies (DNA: RG 59, CD, Port Mahon, vol. 1). First RC 3 pp.; docketed by Wagner. Second RC marked "Triplicate," with an additional paragraph to the postscript: "I beg leave to remark sir that the mentioned Case, containing the two Views, I sent per the Amer⟨ican⟩ Galliot Fortune, Captn. Thomas Sav⟨ille⟩ bound to Boston; to the particula⟨r⟩ care of General Benjamin Lincoln, Collector for said port &c." The *Fortune* arrived at Gibraltar on 9 Nov. 1805 and left there for Boston on 20 Nov. The ship arrived at Charleston, South Carolina, on 1 Feb. 1806, bound for Boston (Boston *Independent Chronicle*, 16 Jan. 1806; *New-York Gazette & General Advertiser*, 5 and 11 Feb. 1806). For enclosure, see n. 1.

    1. The enclosure was presumably Baker to Jefferson, 28 Aug. 1806, presenting him with a view of Port Mahon (DLC: Jefferson Papers; docketed by Jefferson as received 11 Feb. 1806).

§ From Henry Hill Jr. *28 August 1805, Havana.* "An Express boat arrived a short time since at Barracoa from Spain with dispatches for this Govt., which were received yesterday. Nothing has transpired of their contents, but orders were immediately given for equipping a frigate of 44 guns & a brig of 18, and to day 600 troops are ordered to be in readiness to embark. Conjecture destines this armament for Vera Cruz to take from hence the Marquis of Someruelos whom it is said is appointed to the Vice Royalty of Mexico, and that he is to be succeeded in the Govt. of this Island by a person daily expected[1]—of this there is no doubt; and that he is appointed to Mexico is very probable, the merchants of VeraCruz having remonstrated again(s)t the present Vice Roy, soliciting his removal; as he had taken various measures oppressive, and obnoxious to them.

"But I see not why so considerable a naval force should be required, nor so many troops to accompany the Marquis to VeraCruz. I am therefore induced to believe this force is destined to Pensacola. An Embargo is immediately expected, I write this in haste, and shall probably not have an opportunity of communicati(n)g farther before the sailing of this armament, which appearances indicat(e) will be immediately; when I shall have an opportunity of forming a more correct & certain opinion, and shall communicate the result of my inquiries and observations for your information.

"I embrace this oppy. of informing you that I have resumed my official functions, but without having been able to obtain from this Govt the object desired— that is, as(surance) of protection in my official character.

"I shall forward you without delay sir, copies of the correspondence that passed on this occasion, with other documents relating to the subject."

RC (DNA: RG 59, CD, Havana, vol. 1). 3 pp.; docketed by Wagner.

1. The report was erroneous. The marqués de Someruelos remained governor general of Cuba until 1812 (*Report on the Census of Cuba, 1899* [Washington, 1900], 697).

§ From William Jarvis. *28 August 1805, Lisbon.* "The last letter I had the honor to address you by the Brig Minerva, Captn. Colesworthy, for Boston, dated the 6th. Inst.[1] communicated an account of the capture of two Spanish Men of War, part of the Combined Squadron, by Sir Robert Calder, and of the arrival of the Combind Squadron at Vigo. They sailed from this Port the 31st. July & arrived at Corrunna & Ferrol the 2nd Inst., from whence they sailed the 11th being joined by Men of War in those ports, making in all 27 Line of Battle Ships 6 Frigates & 2 Corvettes. The 18th. they were seen of[f] Cape St. Vincents by the British Brig of War Halcyon. It is beleived they are bound to Cadiz & the report said to be brought by a Neutral, Yesterday, was, that they had got out the remaining part of the Cadiz Squadron & proceeded to Carthagena for the Squadron there, but whether they captured any part of the English Fleet off Cadiz is not said. Their having proceeded to Carthagena I imagine is at least primature but letters from Faro mention their arrival at Cadiz. An English Fleet under Sir Robert Calder passed here the 24th in persuit. It is said to consist of 23 Sail of the line. This is the only news we have here relative to the operations of Belligerent powers. The departure of Mr. Novozilltzoff from Berlin[2] is generally supposed must inevitably be followed by a Continental War. Whether, as some effect to think, this is only a fever fit of that Court, which will be succeeded by the paralysing Cold of the friged Zone, such as they pretend has been exhibited in one or two Instances already, or the conceived perpetual aggressions of the Emperor Napoleon, has drained to the very dregs the cup of forbearance, a few Months only can determine. From Spain I hear nothing regarding our affairs. But in politicks as in War I beleive it has been a principle ever held by sound statesmen, that the plan of the campaign is to be altered, or entirely changed if necessary, to meet any sudden or unexpected movement on the part of the enemy. Possibly this observations may in some sort apply to us as it regards the late iniquitous, impolitick & unexpected orders, which I understand by private Letters & which the public papers seem to corroborate, a certain power has lately given to enforce in part or in whole the obsolete principle, attempted to be established in 1793 not to allow any trade to Neutrals in time of War, that was not permitted in time of Peace. But I cannot be persuaded that I am correctly informed, for altho I have known so many instances of the monstrous doctrine, that the end sanctifies the means, being practised upon, that I am seldom surprised to hear of the most unjustifiable acts committed by Nations when prompted by interes⟨t⟩ or ambition, yet I confess it is a thing of some novelty for a Government, without any such object, to become a fele-do-se.[3] For my own part as I see no benifit, but many disadvantages that are certain to result to that Nation from it, I cannot with any plausibility of reasoning account for so extraordinary a proceeding. Be the cause what it may, if a fact, were we to let our difference with Spain prevent our pursuing strong measures to obtain redress, if Moderate will not answer, would it not Sir be, like neglecting a Cancer which was destroying the Vital principle of existence, to apply a remedy to a pimple? Besides Territory must always remain stationary: and that Court I imagine would be very well content with a declaration of our having from motives of mutual convenience—suspended our Territorial & Commercial claims till the disembarrassments of War had afforded on opportunity of discussing these points dispasionately & conformably to th⟨e⟩ true interests of both Nations. I find that my indignation has carried me beyond all boun⟨ds⟩ of reason & have to beg your excuse Sir, for the Warmth of expression that may have escaped me on this occasion; but to an administration who has the Welfare of the Country so much at heart, opinions offered with warmth, however inapplicable or absurd, from a want of knowledg⟨e⟩ of all the circumstances of the case, I am confident will be received with more satisfaction than an apathy to our National Welfare would upon such a supposed interesting accasion; & although my indignation has drawn from me such a freedom of observation, when I recall to mind the pre-eminent abilities, so superior to the most trying accasions, which at present direct the Machine of State, I feel perfectly Satisfied that such measures will be persued as will prove most for the honor, prosperity & Happiness of our Country.

"Inclosed is a letter from Messrs. Montgomery & Yznardi."[4]

RC (DNA: RG 59, CD, Lisbon, vol. 2). 6 pp.; marked "(Duplicate)."

1. The *Minerva*, Captain Colesworthy, arrived in Boston on 12 Sept. Jarvis's letter has not been found (Boston *Repertory*, 13 Sept. 1805).
2. For this incident, see John M. Forbes to JM, 16 July 1805, and n. 2.
3. *Felo-de-se:* suicide.
4. The enclosures have not been found, but they may have been Robert Montgomery to JM, 5 Aug. 1805, and Anthony Terry to JM, 20 Aug. 1805.

§ From Elias Vander Horst. *28 August 1805, Bristol.* "Above is a Copy of my last of the 10h Instn. ℀ the New York Packet, Capt. Dannett, Via New-York, by whom I also sent you under cover a London Paper & Price Currt. of the 9h. [not found]—since when I have not had the pleasure of hearing from you—nor has any thing particularly interesting occurred in the interval except what the enclosed papers will communicate to which (therefore) I beg leave to refer you.

"The Weather for the Harvest is now favorable—the appearance of the Crops in consequence are *much improved*, and should it continue fine for a few weeks longer the produce of our fields will in all probability be *much larger* than was a short time since expected, and of course render our want of Grain more limitted."

Adds in a 30 Aug. postscript: "I know of no cause that has been assigned for the detention of several of our Vessels of late by British Cruizers for Adjudication, than what the Public Papers have communicated.

"The Price of Grain continues rapidly to decline, owing to the general opinion that now prevails, that the Crops will be plentiful, though I am not myself *quite* so sanguine."

RC, two copies (DNA: RG 59, CD, Bristol, vol. 2). First RC 2 pp.; written at the foot of Vander Horst to JM, 10 Aug. 1805; verso of postscript docketed by Wagner "10. 28. 30 Augt. 1805." Second RC marked "(Copy.)." Word in angle brackets in the first RC has been supplied from the second RC. Minor differences between the copies have not been noted.

§ From Sylvanus Bourne. *30 August 1805, Amsterdam.* "I had the honor to write you a few days since via Baltimore mentioning the renewed depredations made on our navigation bound here by the British Cruisers in virtue of late orders from that Govt.[1]—and it appears now that it is a system become general on the Seas—our outward as well as inward bound Vessells in all the European Waters are brought up in British Ports & many of them have been already tried & condemned & it is asserted that orders have gone to the West Indies for their Cruisers to take all American Vessells laden with the produce of their enemies Colonies—not having yet recd any advice from our Consul in London on this important subject—I am not correctly informed of the motives & principles which have induced these proceedings nor can I say to what extent they are intended to be pursued. It seems pretty clear however that in the application of any general principle herein many of our vessells & cargoes will be *unjustifiably* condemned & our Citizens tho innocent be exposed to grave & severe losses.

"Every account from the various parts of Europe seem to justify the belief of a renewed War on the Continent. I must repeat as my opinion that the prospect in this regard Constitutes a prominent motive with the British Cabinett to treat neutrals in so rough a manner—as her political situation is found to influence most essentially her maritime adjudication but to what point we are bound to submit to the Rules G B may see fit to prescribe for our commerce is a que(s)tion which must of course be settled between the two Governments & I doubt not that ours will assume a firm & decided attitude under these untoward circumstances.

"By this opportunity I send for publication in Newyork a triplicate copy of the Statement referred to in my late letters in reply to those of Mess D & O[2]—and I flatter myself my respected Sir that you will [be] perfectly convinced from ⟨what⟩ I have said on this subject (that however awkward the first appe⟨rance⟩ of the matter was) I have been guided by pure & correct ma[*illegible*] through the whole transaction & that Govt will not fail to continue to me that confidence which I so highly value & which is *so necessary* to the welfare of my family—permit [me] to Say that I stand on high ground with both the french & Batavian Authorities here, & that I shall in future carefully avoid even the semblance of impropriety in all my conduct & with integrity & zeal pursue the duties of my Office & I hope with advantage to my fellow Citizens & with becoming personal honor & dignity."

Adds in a postscript: "The British appear to pursue a System of Blockade of their enemies Ports of insidious nature & which exposes Neutrals to great embarrassments as the Commanders of their fleets are found to have a discretionary power in this regard & often for a considerable length of time permit Vessells to enter blockaded Ports & all of a sudden withold this indulgence which tends to lead many into a security of which they are ultimately the victims—the practice upon this system has been of late evinced relative to the Port of Cadiz & a number of our Vessells have been taken & carried to Gibraltar for adjudication on the principle of having violated the blockade of that Port—Whereas they had only pursued the track which but a few days before was open & free to many of our Countrymen. The interests of our Commerce seems indeed to require that more precise rules should be agreed on relative to Blockaded Ports."

RC (DNA: RG 59, CD, Amsterdam, vol. 1). 3 pp.; docketed by Wagner.

1. See Bourne to JM, 18 Aug. 1805.
2. For the statement, see Bourne to JM, 10 Aug. 1805, and n. 1.

§ From Levett Harris. *30 August 1805, St. Petersburg.* "The letter you did me the honor to write to me of the 13. May came to hand the 10. inst. which mine to you of the 25. of same month has in some measure anticipated.[1]

"The importance of the subject you have treated Sir, rendered a special communication of it on my part to the Minister of foreign Affairs adviseable, altho.' my frequent conferences with the Minister of Commerce have established a perfect understanding between us on this point, I hastened to acquit myself of the charge submitted to me by a letter, copy as inclosed, which I addressed to the Prince de Czartoryski.[2]

"The Government of Denmark, I learn early last year, made known to Russia, Prussia, & Sweeden the measures which a just regard to its safety in preventing an introduction of the yellow fever into its ports would impell it to adopt; but, in guarding against this malady, a proper attention would be had that those measures, in their application to the Baltick trade, should be obedient to the engagements ixisting between the former government & these several powers relative to the passages of the Sound &c. and otherwise should be made to affect as little as possible the respective interests of their ports on this Sea.

"These Assurances, it is to be lamented for us, have not been as Strictly adhered to as an attachment to our own interests would have prompted us to have hoped for; detentions, amounting in Some instances to vexations, have been imposed upon many of our Ships at Christiansand; the place fixed on by Denmark for the quarantine of Vessels destined to the Baltick, and very loud complaints have been made to me by the masters of some of them thus detained who have since arrived at this place.

"Those Vessels left the United States at a season when we know that no disease, of the discription mentioned, could exist, and although provided with regular certificates of health have notwithstanding been arrested in the prosecution of their voyages.

"I entered into a correspondence early the present season, with our Consul at Copenhagen, and recommended his particular attention to this very important subject. The large private Concerns of this gentleman may perhaps have prevented his being as particular in his Correspondences with me as I could have wished, yet, I have reason to beleive, he was influencial in procuring a mitigation of the very onerous burthens with which our commerce was threatened at the commencement of the year, and I am alike inclined to think that some representations I made at the same time to Baron de Blome, the danish Minister resident here with whom I am on terms of familiar Acquaintance, & which representations he communicated to his Court may also have been of service.

"I am well convinced, in addition to all those very embarrassing restrictions, that others perhaps not less so would have been instituted by this Government, but my timely knowledge of them, by the friendly and polite communication on the part of the Russian Ministry of the measures thus Contemplated, enabled me most successfully to combat them: and I rejoice to add that even the naval force, which it had resolved to station at the entrance of the Gulph of Finland in order strictly to examine our Vessels in their way hither, has been deemed superfluous, and of sixty nine American Ships that have arrived to this period, not one of them has met with a moments detention.

"In a letter I had the honor to address you Sir, the 12/24. June last year,[3] I mentioned there had happened instances in the Winter that American Seamen were found here destitute, whose Situations were frequently such as prevented the Consular Authority, reaching them and Suggested the propriety of an adoption of special measures on the Subject; altho.' no recurrence of this evil took place last year yet, it is not difficult I conceive to foresee that, the increasing perplexities with which our navigation is threatened will occasion many wants to our Seamen, which in this Country would be in the extreme urgent. I now therefore take the liberty of recommending the establishment of an agency in this quarter, and of deligating to it the power to make suitable appointments at Christiansand & Elsineur, where proper officers are so highly necessary, also at some places within the Baltick, and instructing the person they authorized, to visit those places and regulate the duties of the several posts in such manner as may be deemed most eligible, by which the accumulating injuries resulting to our important trade to this quarter, by means of the indiscriminating prohibitions complained of, would doubtless be materially alleviated.

"If Government should deem it expedient to create such an Agency, I would solicit its union with my present post, as the establishment, that might be annexed to it, would enable me to meet the extraordinary expences my publick Character subjects me to in relation to which Sir, I was bold on a former Occasion to entertain you, whilst it could not in the Smallest degree interfere with a due discharge of my present duties.

"As respects the execution of my publick functions here, I have thus far had the most complete satisfaction, & not a Single instance has Occurred wherein I have been led to an application of the Ministry that has not been attended with the most happy result.

"I conceive it my duty to inform you Sir, that on my arrival at this place I found our commerce in a great measure under the controul of the English merchants; restrictions were imposed on us, fees claimed, and charges levied at the insistence of the English factory, and generally engrossed by the agents appointed to regulate its trade. Since my arrival I have by degrees succeeded in having most of them suppressed, and in placing our commerce on a footing totally independent. I have established seperate Agencies where they were deemed adviseable from which facilities have resulted benificial to our trade, and in all those undertakings I have had the immediate protection of the Minister of Commerce, to whom I have also suggested some improvements in the mode of entering & clearing of Vessels, and other custom house arrangements on which he has consulted me, calculated to promote dispatch to our Ships, so necessary an object in this Sea, and which are about to be adopted. I have peculiar pleasure in adding that I have accomplished these appendants of my duty without incurring the jealousy, oppositi⟨o⟩n or disrespect of the English Gentlemen resident here, who have had some influence with the Ministry in the commercial arrangements of the port. A disposition to conciliate, which I have encouraged, has been instrumental in Procuring me all the information I needed and has been a happy mean in the success of my undertakings, so that to my Successors in this honorable post, which I am highly proud in being the first to fill, little I hope will be left for them to do.

"If my humble efforts toward the faithful discharge of my duty shall be found in any degree deserving the approbation of my Government, it will be my greatest consolation."

RC and enclosure (DNA: RG 59, CD, St. Petersburg, vol. 1). RC 4 pp.; dated "18/30 August" in the Julian and Gregorian calendars; docketed by Wagner. For enclosure, see n. 2.

1. See *PJM-SS*, 9:345 n., 396–97.
2. The enclosure (3 pp.; in French; docketed by Wagner) is a copy of Harris to Prince Adam Jerzy Czartoryski, 15 Aug. 1805, stating that the rigorous quarantine rules that Denmark had instituted caused extreme hardship for U.S. ships trading with Russia. Harris assured the prince that yellow fever appeared to be on the wane in the northern American ports and that U.S. regulations demanded rigorous examination of all departing ships whenever there was the slightest trace of a contagious disease in the country, after which clean vessels were issued health certificates. For the imposition of the stricter Danish quarantine rules, see ibid., 246–47 and n. 3.
3. Ibid., 7:360–63.

§ From Henry Hill Jr. *30 August 1805, Havana.* "You are probably informed ere this by my letter of the 13th Inst. that I had suspended my official functions, in consequence of an order recd from the Govr. to embark from the Island. I have now the honor to address you, and inclose copies of the correspondence which has passed between His Excellency and myself since my letters of the 12th & 14 June, which were accompanied with what had passed previous to that time.[1] Also, to inclose You copies of Sundry documents relating to the Capture of several Vessels of the UStates, which gave rise to my correspondence with his Excellency,[2] and will serve to illustrate the abuses and depradations upon our commerce in and about this Island; to shew what justice our Citizens may expect in such cases from this Govt, and what in future we may expect from the aggressors, whose piracies wil⟨l⟩ increase in proportion to the impunity afforded them.

"From this correspondence you will also be able sir, to form a just estimate of my Situation; how far it will be in my power to aid my fellow Citizens in their just claims, to defend their rights, support my own, & the interests and honor of my Country.

"I conceive the circumstances which lead to this letter, of a serious and important nature to my Government, and they deeply affect my individual interests, character, and Situation; I shall therefore enter into a detail which will serve to explain the principles by which I have been actuated & governed.

"I was so unfortunate as to arrive at a time when my predecessor was just liberated from prison—when the office was placed in the most degraded and contemptible situation it had ever been, when he was granting documents under his private seal in a private manner, fearful to have the least appearance of exercising his functions openly, when the insult he had recd. was fresh in the mind of every one, and the light in which this Govt. considered a public agent was illustrated & exemplified in his disgraceful humble Situation.

"Although I held a commission of a higher rank, and direct from the president of the United States, yet as I succeeded to the same office, I also succeeded to the contempt & impotence attatched to it. It was my wish to make my commission respected, and to make it sufficiently evident by my conduct, that however little respectability this Govt might find it convenient to attatch to it, that I should consider it as my protection in the execution of my duty; but, I find it is not the Sentiments nor commission a man may hold which can make him respected in office, but the power he has of putting the duties of his commission into effect; impotence in a public officer ever attracts contempt and derision, & where a commission is held without the power and priviledges it ought to convey it naturally follows, that the holder & commission, are both treated with disregard & indifference.

"I experienced this particular⟨l⟩y on my arrival, and in many instances Since; and as every material circumstance relating to my public character is connected with, and will serve to elucidate the subject of this letter, permit me sir, to relate the insulting meanness of an act of the Govr on my first arrival, which was calculated to acquaint those who should treat me with any attention and respect, that they would become the objects of the jealousy and hatred of the Government.

"A Mr Herrera, a son of the Marquis of Villalta one of the most opulent and respectable families in the Island, to whom I came recommended from the Spanish Consul in New York, treated me with much distinction on my arrival, and without my knowledge invited a large party to dine with him in honor of myself, nameing me in his cards of invitation as being 'appointed Consul of the United States to this Island.'

"The Govr. came to the knowledge of this circumstance, called Mr Herrera before him, asked him by what authority he gave me the title of 'Consul,' and reprimanded him in terms of severity. This was three or four days after my arrival. A publication in the Aurora the Govt. paper—succeeded this insult, importing that I had arrived with a Commission as Consul from the United States, but that I could not be received and admitted as Such by this Govt, it being contrary to the laws of these dominions &c. Great pains were taken to impress upon the public mind that the Govt could not receive me as a public Character, nor afford me any protection and aid as Such. I take the origin of the conduct which has been pursued towards me, from the arrest and imprisonment of Mr Gray, and the seizure of his public papers. In which one department of this Government was directly implicated, and wished to draw in the Govr as having acknowledged public agents; at least tacitly so, by having permitted their residence in the Island. About this time, an order was sent to the Governor of St Yago de Cuba to embark Mr. Blakely from the Island. Hence I am inclined to think that the views of the Governor subsequent to the transaction respecting Mr Gray, and from the general tenor of his conduct with me since, have extended to the total exclusion of the residence of a public agent from the United States in the Island, to prevent facts from being substantiated relating to captured American property brought into the ports within his jurisdiction, the improprieties and abuse of which he finds it convenient to take no effectual Measures to repress; or at least to confine the functions of such agent to the mere act of granting certificates, without suffering him any representation, intimidating him by the fate awarded Gray, and by threats, or discouraging him by neglect and contempt, thereby rendering him insignificant and contemptible in the public opinion, and oblige him to abandon a situation disagreeable, perilous, and in fact dishonorable; as indeed it now is from the insecurity of the office, and disrespect this Govt attatches to it—which not only exposes the holder of it to insult and injury from those in power, but to abuse, from every one who may chuse to insult him.

"Notwithstanding all the disadvantages and disgrace which was attatched to the office when I arrived, the manner I was received and subsequently treated, I thought it my duty to take upon me the exercise of my functions, from a persuasion that I might be of some service to my fellow citizens, and that for the offic⟨e⟩ to be abandoned at a time when the duties of an agent were most required would materially affect the interests of those engaged in commerce with this Island, greatly to their prejudice. Concluding that from the extent and importance of our trade to this port, the abuse upon our commerce within this Govt by privateers, the procedure against Gray, and the persecution that would follow to myself, would either terminate in the total exclusion of an agent in the Island from the United States, or that measures would be taken to have his powers acknowledged & respected.

"The crisis has now arrived, when I conceive the Govt of the United states must either take such measures, or aband⟨on⟩ the idea of having an officer in a Country where his commission is treated with derision and insult, where he has no representation, no power; and consequently where he can be of no essential service to his fellow citizens or country.

"There can be no place where the interests of the United states would be benifited more by the residence of a Consul than at this place; but it is necessary he should have the powers of a consul in their full extent to make him respectable and of service to his country, and there never can be a more favorable moment to urge the acknowledgement of one than at this time. The Island is entirely dependent on our commerce, & the Government must accede to any demand persisted in by the United States.

"On receiving His Excellencys order to embark from the Island, it was my wish to avoid it, untill I could receive instructions from my government how to act, and to continue in office untill I should receive such orders—at the same time, I had some expectation that by taking the measures I did, it might persuade to a partial acknowledgement, which would lead to a general one. Finding tha⟨t⟩ I could gain no advantage, nor draw any direct assurances of protection in my official capacity, I did not think proper to reply to His Excellencys last letter, but consulted with those whom I knew were in his confidence, whether I could resume my functions without making any representations to the govt. and continue in granting the necessary documents to american citizens and for the protection of their property, without hazarding my personal liberty. Being assured by his secratary and another person on terms of intimacy with the Govr. whom I knew he consulted on this occasion, that I could grant such documents with safety, I again opened my office on the 27th. Inst. I have done this untill I can receive instructions how to act, in preference to vacating the consulate, and demanding my commission, which would preclude any further measures which it might be thought proper for me to adopt.

"In explanation of an inco[n]sistency in my conduct, having promised in my first letter to hold no communication with this Govt but by personal representations, It is my duty to inform you, that on some business with His Excellency on the part of Capt. Evans subsequent to the delivery of his memorials, I was peremptorily ordered not to appear to interfere in the behalf of any American citizen, and informed if they had any thing to desire of him it must be done through the public interpreter.

"It is impossible for you sir to have a proper idea, or for me to explain the impositions and abuses that are put upon us in this Island. The American character is treated with ridicule & contempt, they suppose us capable of bearing any insult, of pocketing any affront that may be offered, consider us a people dependent on commerce, and that we will descend to the most degrading meanness for the sake of gain. They have formed this opinion of our citizens and government, from the appearance and conduct of those who visit them which I confess is not surprising, since their conduct here entitles them to the treatment they receive. Each is governed by his individual interest without any regard to his national character, & are guilty of the greatest improprieties. I am ashamed of my countrymen, but cannot bear to see them imposed upon by Spaniards; people who in this Island are fed and cloathed by our commerce, and whose only revenue at present is derived from it. The officers of a Government who are paid by this revenue, whose authority is sustained by the means our commerce affords them, notwithstanding heap enormous impositions upon it, and suffer the greatest abuses upon our citizens.

Their Vessels are taken, brought into the ports of this Island and plundered of their cargoes, the crews maltreated, and no measures are taken to punish the aggressors, or to render justice to the aggrieved. Their complaints are disregarded. A public agent is denied any interference in their behalf, and if they resort to courts of justice, Their suits are purposily protracted to draw from them sums of money; justice is bought and sold as merchandize, and if they have less money than their competitors they are sure to be defeated. An enormous duty is imposed upon our trade, various impositions and abuses in the collection of that duty, american masters and sailors dragged to prison without any cause at the instance of any petty officer of the Govt. and enormous fees are demanded in every department.

"Being in a situation sir, where all complaints from these abuses are lodged, where I am looked up to by my fellow citizens to redress their grievances, and aid and assist them in their distress, I find myself totally without power to execute my duty—exposed to censure, to insult, injury, and the arbitrary and capricious will of this Govt. To be placed in this situation with a commission from the president of the United states, I feel it extremely disagreeable and humiliating to myself, and insulting & degrading to my Country, I therefore wait with impatience & anxeity for such instructions as it shall please the president to give, by which I shall be governed.

"I have not taken upon myself the appointment of agents in the different ports of the Island where they are necessary, because of the situation I found myself placed in, and of the consequences that might ensue from such a measure. I have a correspondence with the principal ports in the Island, which gives me information of any material circumstances relating to the interests of the United States, by every mail. The privateersmen make their grand rendavouz Barracoa. There are now ten or twelve american Vessels prizes there, principally Vessels from St. Domingo. There are no judicial proceedings had respecting them before their Cargoes are taken out and sold, as likewise the Vessels if purchasers offer. This is done openly and with the approbation of the officers of that port, who, there is no doubt share in the plunder, but which it is impossible to prove.

"No account reaches this Govt. of the transactions there, in an official manner. There are always purchesers principally our own citizens for those plundered Cargoe(s), no account is taken by the officers of either vessels or Cargoes that enter there and no entrance or clearance is made that appears on record—at St Yago there has been but few prizes taken in of late, but what are carried in there are plundered in the same manner as at Barracoa. At Trinidad there are no american prizes, but five large Jamaica Ships with Valuable Cargoes of sugars and coffee have been recently captured and sent in there. There is one American prize at Batavano, and three or four at the west end of the Island, where at present is the principle scene for plunder in this quarter of the Island.

"There are about 80 sail of American Vessels now in this port, all making very loosing Voyages. It is astonishing to me that our merchants will continue a trade where they are so much imposed upon, in which they must have sunk at least a Million of Dollars since the opening of the port.

"It may be calculated that the loss sustained by our merchants in this trade, is gained by the revenue here; about that sum arrising from duties having been paid into the treasury.

"I hope to be able shortly to forward you an official account of the last years exports of this Island, with a particular acct of its trade and resources from which you will be able to form a correct opinion of the importance of the commerce of the United States to this colony.

"Repeating my request tha⟨t⟩ you will be pleased to forward me such instructions as shall be deemed necessary in my present perplexd. & unpleasant Situation."

Adds in a postscript: "List of papers inclosed, on next page."[3]

RC and enclosures (DNA: RG 59, CD, Havana, vol. 1); Tr of enclosures (DNA: RG 233, President's Messages, 9A–D1); Tr of enclosures (DNA: RG 46, President's Messages, 9B–B1). RC 18 pp. For enclosures, see nn.

1. The enclosures (28 pp.; in English and Spanish) are copies of seventeen letters and memorials together with copies of JM's circular letters to consuls of 1 Aug. 1801 and 9 Apr. 1803, *PJM-SS*, 2:1–4, 4:491–93, that Hill submitted to Someruelos in his letter of 16 Aug. 1805. The documents date from late June 1805, when Hill certified the accuracy of documents about the case of John Evans, whose ship *Eliza* and crew were being held at Batabanó, Cuba, by privateers. Hill also enclosed a copy of a 25 June statement by a Havana notary that Hill was to stop intervening directly or indirectly in cases like that of Evans's, as Hill had been told twice before, and that if he did not do so, he would be required to leave Cuba. On 5 July, Hill wrote the marqués de Someruelos requesting a conference on matters of interest to U.S. citizens to which Someruelos replied the following day that Hill had been told repeatedly, both orally and in writing, that he could not be recognized in any public character whatsoever. The correspondence between the two continued in this vein, as the copies show, until the end of August, with Hill protesting that his government had given him a commission to look after the interests of U.S. citizens in Cuba and enclosing documents to prove this, and Someruelos stating repeatedly that he could not recognize Hill as a public character, and threatening to expel Hill from the island.

2. The enclosed protests and declarations (62 pp.; printed in *ASP, Foreign Relations*, 2:672–77) are those of several captains, mates, crewmembers, and passengers of the *Ann, Sea Horse*, and *Caroline* of Charleston, South Carolina, the *Success* of New York, the *Jason* of Philadelphia, the *Mary* of Camden, North Carolina, and the *Eliza* of Norfolk, stating that their ships had been seized near Cape San Antonio in western Cuba and brought to Batabanó, Cuba, to be plundered. Hill included his certification (1 p.) that the documents were accurate.

3. Hill enclosed a list (1 p.) describing 22 enclosures, among them "from A to G inclusive Sundry protests & declarations relating to the capture of Vessels of the United States" (see n. 2 above). Also filed with the RC are examples (3 pp.) of three forms used by Hill to certify the owners of a ship, the owners of the cargo, and the rôle d'equipage, as well as a report (4 pp.; in Spanish) of gold and silver specie minted at the Royal Mint in Mexico City from 1733 to 1793, totaling 854,361,070 pesos, and from 1793 to 1805, totaling another 616,000,000, for a final total of 1,470,000,000 [*sic*] pesos.

§ From James Simpson. *30 August 1805, Tangier.* No. 101. "By No 100 dated 11th. Inst [not found] and forwarded by the Ship Centurion for New York I had the honour of advising arrival here of a Tripoline Pinque[1] of eight Guns from that Port, Commanded by their Admiral (Lisle) bringing a Letter for Muley Soliman and in quest of the Meshouda. So soon as His Majesty received my Letter advising Peace was concluded between the United States and Tripoly he gave directions to Sid Muhammed Selawy to have that Ship got ready for Sea. Lisle has gone on a Cruize to the Westward.

"My Agent at Tetuan writes me under the 28h Inst as follows 'A Tunisien Xebeque of six Guns and seventy five Men is arrived here from thence, the news he gives is that he left twenty five sail of American Vessels of War at Anchor in that Bay, and that the Tunisiens talked of War with America.'

"I would gladly hope Commodore Rodgers presence may be a means of preventing any thing of that Kind happening.

"It is probable this Tunis Cruizer may also be bound to the Westward, for since those two Regencys have agreed with Portugal, that the terms of their Peace shall not be confined to the Mediterranean, the passage to the Atlantic is open to them. In No 99[2] I mentioned a deputation from Tremcen having arrived at Mequinez to acquaint Muley Soloman the people of that Country had proclaimed him their Sovereign and that His Majestys Brother Muley Mussa was gone to ascertain the truth of the matter. This Prince has returned to Fez without having proceeded farther than Tezza. It is said he has however sent on his Troops and a second detachment, to reinforce the Frontier Towns.

"We are assured the people of the Algerine dominions in Arms against Oran have now chosen a person in intelligence with Mohamet Derhany as their Chief. These outlines is all I can say by this conveyance by way of Faro and Lisbon. Lieut Gardner of the President told me I would very shortly see the Nautilus Schooner bound home. By such a conveyance I could be more detailed.

"The Batavian Republic has presented Muley Soliman with a Sloop of War laying at Malaga, where she has been a long time. His Majestys Ship Maimona returned to Larach and brought a Dogger of Lubeck with a Cargo chiefly of Naval Stores bound for Lisbon. The Emperour had engaged thro' the mediation of the Portuguese Consul that the Vessels of Hamburgh, Bremen & Lubeck should pass freely, but this Vessel is now brought in under the pretext of Lubeck being under the immediate protection of Prussia.

"The Cargo has been lodged in Store and triplicate Inventories taken of it by the Notaries, one for the Emperour another for the Governor of Larach and a third delivered the Master of the Dogger.

"The Ship has gone out again to Cruize but hitherto none of the other Vessels of War of this Country have been sent out this Season, which is not easily to be accounted for.

"The Keel of a Frigate was lately laid down at Rhabat & another ordered to be constructed at Sallé."

RC (DNA: RG 59, CD, Tangier, vol. 2). 3 pp.; marked "Duplicate."

1. Pink.
2. See Simpson to JM, 3 Aug. 1805.

From Albert Gallatin

Dear Sir   New York 31st. Augt. 1805

Mr Merry claims the exemption from duty for what may be imported by Mr Foster (for his own use) as Secretary of legation. If, and I believe it to be the case, no similar application has heretofore been made, I will want your directions: be, therefore, good enough to tell me whether the rule shall extend to every diplomatic character, excluding only consuls, but including Secretaries? Give our affectionate compliments to Mrs. Madison, and let us know how she is. Your's

Albert Gallatin

RC (DLC: Gallatin Papers). Docketed by Wagner, with his note: "Imports by Mr. Foster."

§ From John Brice Jr. *31 August 1805, Baltimore.* "By the Ship Robert, Michael Alcorn Master from Lisbon, there are consigned to you by Wm. Jarvis Esqr, Two pipes Lisbon Wine, which I have directed to be sent to the public Store 'till your instructions shall be received."[1]

RC (DLC). 1 p.

1. For the shipment of wine, see William Jarvis to JM, 5 and 12 July 1805.

§ From George Davis. *31 August 1805, "On Board the U: States Frigate Congress. Tunis Bay."* "By the U. States Frigate Congress, Capt. Decatur, who left this Bay on the 22d. Ulto., I had this honor, detailing my several recent conversations with the Bey of Tunis, relative to the Vessels captured off Tripoli, &c, &c⟨—⟩on the 31st. of the same, anchored in the Road of the Goletta, about 1 ⟨P.⟩M⟨,⟩ the Americain Squadron, consisting of 17 Sail, and the following morning Augt. 1st, went on board the Constitution Comodore Rodgers, where I had the satisfaction of meeting the Consul Gen⟨l.⟩ Tobias Lear Esqr.

"The measures which have been pursued Since the arrival of the Fleet, and which have forced me to leave, the Regency of Tunis, will be pointed out, with that Candour, which I owe *The Government, its authorised officers,* and myself. A copy of my dispatch of the 18th. July was handed the Consul Gen⟨l:⟩, and Comodore for perusal, as my letters, by the Congress, were not yet ⟨R⟩eceived—few remarks were made on its contents, few on the position of the Country, or probable intentions of the Bey; and no kind of conference took place between us⟨,⟩ on the proper measures to be pursued⟨,⟩ for⟨,⟩ an adjustment of our affairs altho frequently sollicited, on my part.

"The Comodore only observed⟨,⟩ that he would blockade the ports, untill every thing was Settled, 'one way, or the other,' and that he would not remain longer, than eight days. I told him, that such, a measure would not be recommended by me, and if he did blockade them, I would remain in the Regency, untill the Flag

Staff was cut, by order of the Bey, or a declaration of war, on our part—that any rash measure, would only force the Bey, to recede from his present position; or produce immediate hostilities—the former was most likely, and in doing which, our Affairs, would remain nearly on the same footing, they were at present—that however, I had only to sollicit, written instructions, from either, or both, as on such an important occasion, it was improper for me to act, under any verbal orders. I was inform'd that, both, would communicate with me fully the next day; and with this assurance left the Frigate, and went immediately to Tunis.

"I here beg leave to notice, particularly one or two questions of Col: Lear's, as unfair, and indelicate use have been made of my answers—the great object it was said, was to have a Security For the preservation of the peace, and I was desired to state, what were the most efficacious, means of obtaining it—he was answered in these words—'no Security can ever be had, for the peace, with any of these states, which are influenced, by two motives only, Interest and Fear—we must either keep a force in these Seas; or make pecuniary sacrifices.' Do you mean in this Bay? 'No—it is sufficient that it is kept, within the vicinity of these dominions'— but we shall always have a force in these Seas—'Then no Barbary State will ever declare war against us.'

"It was directly asserted that I had recommended a tribute, as the only means of Securing the Peace. The following day Augt. 2d. received the communications No. 1 & 2;[1] an express was sent on board the Comodore with the letter No. 3,[2] and at an early hour the next morning, waited on the Sapatapa, to whom, I communicated the contents of the Comodore's letter—he said that his master's way of thinking was changed; and consequently, would not put his threats into execution; that altho he conceived himself injured, and insulted, and, view'd the measure which the Comodore adopted, as an act, intended to force him into hostilities, still his Master would restrain his passions, and have recourse to the proper authority for Justice; and that he should hold the Comodore responsible for all the consequences—that Peace was his wish, because it was his interest—but that the actual situation of his country, seem'd to stimulate us, to outrage.

" 'These Sidi Jussuph are evils which His Excellency the Bey has drawn on himself; for nearly four years he has been in the constant habits of making unjust demands, accompanied with menaces; and our forbearance, has not been considered as arising from a desire to ma[i]ntain the peace, but from a want of energy, to resent the indignities So frequently offered us. The Interest and Policy of the U: States, is peace and harmony with all the world; and to secure it with this Regency we have frequently submitted to acts, which would have justified *strong measures.* I beg you to reflect on the repeated insults which have been offered particularly to my Govt., in the persons of its diffirent representatives; and to the nation entire by persisting in your unjust pretensions; and also consider the decided and unequivocal declarations of war made me by the Bey, unless we should comply with his demands; and then say, whether you have not forced us to this Crisis. It still rests with His Excellency to Secure our Sincere friendship, by assuring us that his threats, will never be put in execution, or again renewed; by a proper investigation of all the difficulties in question, and happy accomodation of the same. The Bey of Tunis will ever be treated as a Soverign, for whom the Govt. of the U: States, has the highest respect and most friendly consideration; as long as he will view us, as a free and independent Nation—but unless he assumes this position, and views us in that light, war must be, the inevitable consequence; a war however which you have Sought for, and brought on, by Injustice.'

"He left me, and in about half an hour was Sent for by the Bey; to whom I presented the letters, and at his request, read them in Italian. His Excellency said, that his decisions, had not only been revoked; but that he had already taken the proper measures for a redress of his grievances; and from which he would never deviate, as he had the fullest conviction that ample satisfaction, would be given him by the President of the U: States; and untill it was denied him, he should religiously observe the peace. If however his last attempt, was unsuccessful, the world should know, that the War, in which we would then be engaged, was not sought for by him, nor entered into, untill he had tried every means of accomodation—that he would write an answer to the Comodore's letter, but time was not allowed him; that he would give it, '*by word of mouth*,' and I might repeat it.

"Immediately, on my return from Bardo the letters No. 4 and 5 were addressed to the Comodore and Col: Lear,[3] and late in the evening received No. 6.[4]

"On the morning of the 4th. handed the Comodore the letter No. 7[5]—after reading it to Col: Lear, he observed, 'it is not admissible; and in one half hour from this, I will be at the Goletta If I can get five to coincide with me.' The Signal was instantly made for all Commanders to repair on board the flag; and a council of war was held, consisting of Capt: H: G: Campbell, Capt Stephen Decatur Master Commandant's Stewart, Shaw, Smith, Dent, Robertson [Robinson] & Lt Comdt. Evans—the Comodore Said that the object of his calling the Command⟨rs.⟩ together, was merely to know, whether, 'it would not be to the interest of the U: States, to declare war against the Regency of Tunis; and whether he would not be justifiable in commencing hostilities immediately'—adding, that he would be responsible for all consequences, and only wished five to coincide with him—my opinion was frequently offered constantly referring to the positive orders which the Honle. The Secretary of State had given to The Consul General, by letter bearing date, Washington June 6th. 1804—(an extract from which I had laid before the Members)[6] and I was as often answered by Col: Lear's declaring, 'that he had nothing to do in the Affairs here, that he would have no interference, and now washed his hands of it'—one or two of the Members expressed an opinion, contrary to the Comodores when Capt: Stewart's was asked; and as it was given more fully, than any of the others, I have taken it, as worded, by himself, in the paper No. 8. It was then proposed, that the Bey should revoke his declarations; and in order that all possible formality, might be given it, that two Consuls should be present to witness it. The measure I conceived necessary; but could not approve of the mode; as I was satisfied that great objections, would be raised, by the Bey; or that he would never acquiesce—but as Col Lear urged this point to be indispensably necessary; no farther objections were offered by me.

"After the Council was dismissed, the Comodore handed me, the letter No. 9[7]—left the Ship the same evening; arrived at Tunis about 8 oClock, on the morning of the 5th. and went instantly to the palace. Informed his Excellency that the Comodore, was neither satisfied with a verbal answer; nor with the manner in which it had been given—that he demanded a guarantee for the peace, which should be signed in the presence of the English, and French Consuls; and that a

Commander of one of the Frigates would come to the palace in the morning to see it executed—that if this was not acceded, his ports would instantly be block-aded, against all his Cruizers—a lengthy discussion took place. The Bey spoke much, and in vehement terms of the Comodore; constantly saying, he never could be authorised, either to make such a demand, or take any hostile measures against him—that the Guarantee would never be given, and if war was to be the consequence, of his refusal, he never would accord a peace to the U: States again; unless he should point out the punishment, which ought to be inflicted on the Comodore—if this was granted him by the president, *he Solemnly Swore*, that he would Sign, any treaty, and religiously adhere to it, which should be offered, even if he had to become tributary to the U: States; and for the faithful fulfillment of these promises he would obtain a Guarantee—that I might return in the morning, with the Commander, and he would again, talk over the business. Capt: Decatur arrived about 12 oClock: from whom I received the letter No. 10—he was also charged with *one*, from Col. Lear to the Bey,[8] which he was directed to deliver himself.

"Related to Capt: Decatur the conversation which had taken place at the pal-ace, he said, that he could not wait on the Bey, unless, he received assurances, that the Guarantee would be given, and begged that I would communicate his determination—on the 6th. was again at the palace; the conversation was, re-newed with considerable warmth, I repeated to His Excelly. the consequences, which must infallibly arise from his refusal; and as the commander had no com-munications to make, or business to transact, other than seeing the paper alluded to, signed; he would decline making his personal respects to His Excellecy., unless he was previously assured, that the business on which he came, would be done.

"Bey} he will never be assured of it, nor will it ever be given by me. I am already fatigued with these irregular messages, and I shall now finish them. I will write a letter to the Comodore, and Consul of Algiers, (whom I learn is the only person that has any authority to treat with me) if the letters are satisfactory, we are friends; if not, let your Comodore do; what he pleases. My conduct, shall be, in a great degree regulated by his.

"A:} Your Excellency is not yet aware of the consequences, of your refusal—nor ought you to complain of a measure, which you yourself have adopted—on more than two or three occasions, the Dutch Consul has been called to hear, your men-aces against my Gov't; and it is but a few days past, that you sent for the Dutch and Spanish Consuls, to witness a protest, against the Americain Comodore, and your solemn declarations of war, unless your demands, were aceded to. I have frequently remonstrated, against the presence, or interference, of any Christian Consul, in public transactions, which only interested my Govt. and yourself—and to these remonstrances, you have ever answered; you were a Prince, and I had no right, to object to the mode you wished, business to be transacted at your Court—but particularly to acts, which you were resolved, should have all possible publicity. If your Excellency's intentions are friendly, why should you not revoke your declarations, with at least the same formality they were made. I confess, it is, with much reluctance, that I again return on board, without obtaining that point, which however, *unimportant in itself,* will probably be made the cause of immedi-ate hostilities—the Comodore will never relinquish it; and I had rather obtain it, by 'reason, and argument,' than by force of arms.

"Bey} I again repeat, that you will never obtain it, by either; and I have nothing more to say, on the business—the letters shall be sent you, by twelve oclock; deliver them in person, and repeat my words. If they are not sufficient, you may remain on board—your flag, however, shall not be hawled down, untill you inform me, either by letter, or an attack on the Castle, that you do not return again to the Regency.

About 2 P:M: received the letters;[9] and in the evening Capt: Decatur, sent by the Drogerman, *the one*, he was charged with, from Col: Lear—on the morning of the 7th, previous to our, leaving the Goletta, Sidi Mahamet Coggia (Caid of Porto Farino, & Genrl. of Marines) spoke to me much, on the propriety of relinquishing the point, I had been contending for; and begged to know if war would really be the result; or if some means could not be devised, of avoiding it. I assured him, in the most solemn manner, my firm belief, was, that we could not remain three days longer in peace, unless his master was more accomodating—he informed me, an Ambassador was going to the U: States, and that he had every reason to suppose, the Bey would Select him; and asked Capt: Decatur, whether he would give him a passage, on board his Frigate; whether he would be well received by the President &c &c &c—arrived on board the Comodore, about 3 oClock, when the letters were delivered, and translated; and all the Bey's remarks repeated. Col: Lear said, he thought it would be well for the Bey to Send an Ambassador to the U: States; the Comodore added, if he had, or would, accord him what he had asked, he would then grant a passage on board one of the Frigates; but that he would bring the affairs to a conclusion, in less than forty eight hours. I asked Col: Lear to go on shore with me the next day, as I was confident the Bey would not deny his own words; and his presence, would doubtless have the happiest effects in any future attempts, to accomodate our difficulties; at any rate, it would be particularly gratifying to me—he informed me, '*that he washed his hands of the business altogether*'; that he would not interfere at such a moment; and never would set his foot on shore, untill the Guarantee was given, and in the form specified by the Comodore—on the morning of the 8th: Col: Lear wrote the Bashaw;[10] and Comodore Rodgers, directed me to return to Tunis, demand again the guarantee, and unless it was given by 6 oClock, the following morning to leave the Regency; '*as he was resolved to commence offensive and defensive operations.*'

"I stated the impossibility of receiving it, in so short a time; even if the Bey aceeded, *of which* I had many doubts; as also of the Justice of his according me, some little time, for the arangement of my private affairs—he said that his operations, could not be interrupted, for any private concerns; that however he would give the Bey untill 12 oclock, and myself till 4 P: M:, at which hour he would commence hostilities—he also directed me to declare to the Bey, that this was the last time, he should ever hear from him, on the subject of a Reconciliation; '*and that he would receive no more communications of any Kind, untill his demands were satisfied.*'

"I requested that it might be given me in writing, which was objected to; saying it was sufficient, that his declarations were made in the presence of Col: Lear. I told the Comodore that I had already refused to leave the Regency; and that the same just motives still existed—that I had no right to abandon a post assigned me by the Govt., unless I was satisfied that I could no longer, remain with honor to myself—that a declaration of war, or commencement of hostilities, on either side would be the only circumstance which could authorise me, to leave the Regency; and that his written order to that effect was indispensably necessary for my Justi-fication he then gave me the letter No. 11,[11] and added (Capt: Campbell & Col Lear being present) 'I swear, the moment I see you returning in the boat, I shall consider, that you have not obtained, the guarantee, and will instantly attack the Goletta; and that I will not wait one instant after 4 oClock.' No: 12 is a letter from Capt: Campbell.

"On my arrival at Tunis, I sent an express for Mr. Holck, His Danish Majesty's Consul, who was in the Country, as he had promised, in case of my death; or the U: States, being at war with this Regency, to take charge of our Affairs; and previ-ous to my going to the palace, made every arangement with him, which could be done in so short a time—on the morning of the 9th. delivered to His Excellency, the letter from Col: Lear—he observed that my return; together with the answer which he presumed, I brought him, augured a happy termination of our difficul-ties. I expressed my wishes of its being confirmed, but it now depended wholly on himself—that I had made use of every exertion, compatible with the dignity of my Country, to reduce things to a good understanding—that I now presented myself for the last time, to demand the Guarantee, and assured him, that no advance would ever be made again for a reconcilement.

"Bey} you have already been informed, and in the most decided manner, that I will never be reduced to that State of humiliation—you must consider it as such, or you would not have given So much consequence to it. I shall write an answer to the let-ter which you now bring me from the Ambassador, and it shall be ready by twelve oClock; but I again repeat to you, that I will never accede to your demand.

"A.} Then I must leave your Regency immediately; and hostilities will unques-tionably commence, before forty eight hours.

"Bey} you are at liberty to do so, but request that you will take the letters with you.

"A:} I will wait untill 12 oClock for any communications, which you may wish to make, but cannot stay longer—in taking my leave of your Excellency, I have only to repeat my regrets, at the manner in which I am compell'd to do it; and hopes that you are not dissatisfied with any part of my conduct Since I have been in your Regency.

"Bey} I have always endeavoured to convince you, that your manners, and con-duct, were agreable to me; and as a last proof of my friendship, my own guards shall accompany you to the Goletta, or take you on board, if you wish it.

"He then ordered the Sapatapa to prepare himself for going to the Goletta; again repeated his assurances of friendship, and left me—about 11 oClock received the letter No. 13, from the Chief Christian Secretary; sent immediately the an-swer No. 14; left the Regency at ½ past 12; and arrived on board the Flag, about ¼ before 4 P: M:. It was now said that I had left the Regency too soon; and that by remaining, untill the letters were written, I might have saved my country from a war; atho the Bey had refused in the most unequivocal manner, to give the *Guar-antee*, and I had been directed in the most positive terms, not, to wait '*one minute*,' after the specified time⟨,⟩ '*on any pretext whatever*'—I merely referred the Como-dore to his letter of the 8th: and his declarations, at the time it was ⟨given⟩.

"On the morning of the 10th. Col: Lear wrote the Bey,[12] expressing his regrets at not having received *an answer* to his last communication, *which might still enable him to settle all difficulties,* that hostilities had not commenced, and that the most respectful considerations should be paid to any Messages which His Excellency, might think proper to send him, it was sent by the Drogerman early in the morning, with the letter No. 15 to Mr. Holck—(took up my quarters on board the Frigate Constellation—) in the Afternoon received the note No. 16 from the Prime Minister—on the 11th. waited on the Comodore with Mr. Creuse, (Capts Clerk of the Constellation) who had translated the Bey's letter of yesterday as well, as all the others—as it was delivered in my presence, some parts of it were read to me, but the full contents were never made known—the Comodore, informed me, that he should again write the Bey,[13] as well as Col Lear, but did not mention the subject, or purport of their communications, which were forwarded in the Afternoon.

"12th. Col: Lear, and Mr. Creuse, left the Constitution about 8 A: M: for Tunis.[14]

"13th. The Comodore received letters from Tunis.[15]

"14th. The Comodore received letters from Tunis; in the Afternoon several shot, were fired at a Cruiser, standing into the harbour, from the Essex, John Adams, & Vixen; she entered without receiving any damage.

"15th, Col Lear arrived on board the Constitution (from tunis) about 1 P: M:, and I beleive Satisfied the Commander in Chief of the friendly intentions of the Bey.

"16th. Was sent for, by the Comodore, and Consul General—the former, stated, that, *as every thing was nerely settled,* and in the most friendly manner; he wished to know, whether I *had any particular desire to return to Tunis.*

"I told him, *under existing circumstances,* I certainly had not—but that I could not refrain from expressing my regrets; and speaking of, the injury done to my feelings, at not being replaced in a proper manner, previous to Col: Lear's going on shore, nor permitted to accompany him, when he did go—that I could not imagine it was ever the intention of the Govt, that I should be recalled at the pleasure or Caprice of the Comodore and Consul General—or that a Negociation, should have been carried on without my knowing any of the proceedings—that a Foreigner, as ignorant of the U: States, as he was of Barbary, had enjoyed their full confidence, while the representative of the Govt: had been kept at a distance—that to return, after being thus degraded, was to place me wholly in the power of the Bey—on the contrary, If I was reinstated, by the Govt. His Excellency, would then be convinced, that he must be as cautious his *words,* as he had been in his writings—and as I learnt there was an Ambassador going to the U: States, I conceived it of moment for me, to accompany him. The Comodore Said he beleived every thing, as related by me, and had no doubts, but the Honle. The Secretary of State, would also.

"Col. Lear, then informed me, that he had been received in the most friendly manner by the Bey, that he had talked with him much for two days past, and that *he really did not appear to be the Character represented that my dispatch of the 18th. Ulto.*[16] which he had taken with him, *was referred to, as being the cause, of the Comodore's proceedings*—and to which the Bey answered—'that I had never informed him, of the powers of the Consul Genrl: & that his refusal to receive him, arose from that circumstance—that he had never menaced us, with war; nor was it, his intention—that *his words*, the effect of disappointment or passion, *ought never to be beleived*, but his letters; and to these he referred him, for the truth of his friendly assurances—that the Dutch Consul only was present at the protest, (the Spanish remained in the Anti chambers) and that neither was called, for the express purpose of witnessing his declarations—that I had declared, he would be forced, to make changes in our Treaty, and that it was not to be an Act of mutual consent—in short, that his conduct to the Govt. of the U: States, had ever been the most friendly, and honorable.'

"I told Col: Lear, that I anticipated these remarks, from the Bey—but did not imagine, that an attentive ear, would ever have been given them, much less any credence by the Consul General—that it was calling me to the Bey's Tribunal, there to be accused and adjuged, without a hearing—that it was offering me a Sacrifice, to the falsehood, of a Prince, whose Perfidy, had become proverbial— that there were Serious consequences attached to such proceedings, which had escaped his penetration, or the importance of which he would not conceive—he offered no reply; and the Comodore merely observed, that he should write me, on the subject of returning to Tunis.

"17th. received the letter No. 17, the following day, wrote the Answer No. 18.[17]

"Many conversations have taken place since the formal establishment of Dr. Dodge but which I will not, at present, obtrude on the Honle. the Secretary of State.

"Since the arrival of the Consul Genrl. I have been in the habit of *suppressing every private feeling*, to what I conceived the good of my country; *and should have done it*, in this instance, had I not reason to suppose that unfair attacks would be made on my Character; and if any doubts existed of the propriety of my conduct, it was correct that these, should be done away, before I again entered on the duties of my office.

"My words have been misquoted, unfairly represented, and various *attempts*, made, to affix on the minds of the Commanders unfavourable impressions of my public deportment. It is true, I have opposed by every means in my power, a commencement of hostilities on our part; my sentiments have been declared with frankness, and with the purest intentions—but does this Justify the subsequent measures in relation to myself; excluding me from that right of opinion, which my actual situation entitled me to; and which not only countenanced but appear'd to support the Beys Falsehood, *the only resource that was left him.*

"Why was *His Excellency* so desirous that I should not be present at the conferences with Col: Lear? why accede to the demand that some person, other than myself might accompany him? Did not the request carry with it, a consciousness of guilt? and the acquiescence, a desire to Shield the Bey, if I could be made the Victim?

"The subject of correspondence, has been merely to ascertain one fact— whether the Menaces of his Excellency, for four years past, are truths; *or the fables of timid representitives.* The Bey's first letters on this head, consist of equivocation on the force of terms; but *in his last;* and conversations with Col: Lear, it appears, that an open denial is made of all the circumstances as related by me. Why?

"By Comodore Roger's letters of the 4th. & 5th Inst: I was directed to say, *'unless the Guarantee was given, and in the form specified, his ports Should instantly be blockaded*[']—and were they? By his letter of the 8th. I was ordered to declare, that no advance, should ever again be made by us, for a reconcilement, if I left his Regency; and with the solemn assurance, that hostilities would immediately commence—and on the morning of the 10th. was not a *more friendly letter,* written, than any, which had yet been forwarded? were not these proceedings declaring to the Bey, my representations false and unauthorised? and inviting him to take the same position? Why did Col: Lear *at the Council,* urge the Guarantee, as indispensably necessary, even to a declaration of war? and why relinquish it, at his first interview, with the Bey? why, *after being properly recognised by the Tunisian Govt* Did he refuse to act on his orders, or, accompany me on shore? and immediately after my recall prepare the way, for a negociation, and enter into it, without my knowledge? Is it not the first instance of official communications, being detailed to the Enemy? 'Examples' are supposed to Justify the most dangerous measures, and where they do not suit exactly, the defect is supplied by Analogy; one precedent thus, creates another. They soon 'accumulate, and constitute law.'

"The Bey's conduct to me througout the discussion, and particularly when taking my leave; his Secretary's letter of the Same morning; and Ministers of the 10th., Shew his disposition towards me, untill that period—why does he become so dissatisfied with me, after the arrival of Col: Lear? and why was the Consul General so anxious to establish this fact as to request His Excellency, to express his dissatisfaction in writing? and what was the Beys reply?

"It is worthy observing by what gentle degrees, the furious Zeal of Patriotism, had softened into moderation—untill the 9th. all was war—no respect for treaties, and no regard for our public faith; the *Imaginary Interest (War)* of our country was paramount, to every other consideration. On the 10th. and 11th. we confine ourselves to *defensive measures,* and *those* only which would secure the peace on honorable terms, and remove any improper impressions on account of the measures already pursued—and on the 14th. without any change having taken place in our affairs, (excepting my recall, and the Consul Genrls. being admitted to a private audience) we relinquish all pretensions for the (*Nominal*) *Guarantee; the importance of which, ought to be appreciated, by those, who proposed, and so strongly contended for it.* We certainly had arrived at that Crisis, when a conciliatory policy could scarcely be pursued, without its bearing the marks of weakness; and it was indispensably necessary, to come to, a final conclusion—but in doing which no points should have been advanced by us, from which we were ever to recede; nor no measures taken which could place protraction within his grasp. *The Spirit of our Government should have been evinced by a temperate and firm deportment;* for where *private pique,* or passion, could be distinguished, as interfering with the public interest, the acts would not certainly be traced to the *Supreme Authority,* but to the Man; and in which case much of the good effects we anticipated from the arrival of our Squadron must have been lost—*of our Enterprise and naval faculties, the Bey has already been well convinced;* and a serious impression, must necessarily have been made on his mind, by such a respectable force being placed before him; altho I must ever think, we should have obtained, *greater and more lasting advantages,* by less violent and more consistent procedures. It rests however with His Excellency the President to secure *them,* and place the flag of the United States, *in these Regencies,* on as solid, and independent basis, as *that,* of any power's on earth."[18]

Letterbook copy (NHi: George Davis Letterbooks). 29 pp. For enclosures, see nn. 1–5, 7–15, and 17. The RC has not been found, but it was delivered to JM by Davis after his arrival in the United States (see Davis to JM, 19 Dec. 1805).

1. The enclosures were probably copies of John Rodgers to Hammuda Bey, 2 Aug. 1805, and Tobias Lear to Hammuda Bey, 2 Aug. 1805, Knox, *Naval Documents, Barbary Wars*, 6:201–2.

2. This may have been Davis's first letter of 3 Aug. 1805 to Rodgers, ibid., 203–4.

3. Davis's second letter of 3 Aug. 1805 to Rodgers contained Hammuda Bey's verbal reply to Rodgers's 2 Aug. 1805 letter mentioned in n. 1 above, ibid., 204. The letter to Lear has not been found.

4. This was Rodgers to Davis, 3 Aug. 1805, ibid.

5. This was probably Davis to Rodgers, 4 Aug. 1805, ibid., 205.

6. For JM to Lear, 6 June 1804, see *PJM-SS*, 7:287–90.

7. This was Rodgers to Davis, 4 Aug. 1805, Knox, *Naval Documents, Barbary Wars*, 6:206.

8. For Lear to Hammuda Bey, 5 Aug. 1805, see ibid., 207.

9. For Hammuda Bey to Lear, 5 Aug. 1805, see ibid., 207–8. For his 5 Aug. 1805 letter to Rodgers, see ibid., 208–9.

10. For Lear to Hammuda Bey, 8 Aug. 1805, see ibid., 211–12.

11. This was probably Rodgers to Davis, 8 Aug. 1805, ibid., 212.

12. See Lear to Hammuda Bey, 10 Aug. 1805, ibid., 221–22.

13. For Rodgers to Hammuda Bey, 11 Aug. 1805, see ibid., 223.

14. One of these letters was probably Lear to Rodgers, 12 Aug. 1805, ibid., 224.

15. These were probably Hammuda Bey to Rodgers and Lear to Rodgers, both dated 14 Aug. 1805, ibid., 227–28.

16. Lear referred to Davis's 18 July 1805 letter to JM.

17. For Rodgers to Davis, 17 Aug. 1805, announcing the appointment of Dr. James Dodge to succeed Davis, and Davis's 18 Aug. 1805 reply, see Knox, *Naval Documents, Barbary Wars*, 6:234, 236.

18. For other documents dealing with the negotiations at Tunis, including a "Conversation between the Bey of Tunis and George Davis . . . ," Rodgers to Davis, 2 and 5 Aug. 1805, Hammuda Bey to Lear, 7 and 9 Aug. 1805, Lear to Rodgers, 10 Aug. 1805, Lear to Hammuda Bey, 11 Aug. 1805, Rodgers to Lear, 14 and 15 Aug. 1805, and Rodgers to Hammuda Bey, 16 Aug. 1805, see ibid., 200, 202, 208, 210–11, 221, 222–23, 228, 229–30, 233.

§ From Jussuf Hoggia. *31 August 1805, Bardo, Tunis.* Cannot allow Sidi Soliman Melimeni,[1] ambassador of his illustrious master to the president of the United States of America, to leave without remitting to him his letter for the gentleman, with which he has the pleasure of assuring JM directly of his distinguished esteem and of his pledge to maintain in the heart of his master friendly and peaceful feelings for JM's nation, as now he himself expresses it through the means of the ambassador, the bearer of this writing, sufficient to confirm such sentiments and such dispositions.

For all the delicate and agreeable attentions, that JM uses to the person he recommends, he shall be most grateful. Shall be even more so when he hears that by JM's valuable means he shall have succeeded in consolidating the friendship between the two nations upon a stable and reciprocally advantageous footing.

To Melimeni himself [he] has consigned a few souvenirs that he begs JM to accept as a small token of the ambition he cherishes to be useful to JM and to convince JM on all occasions that he will always sincerely be JM's most devoted servant and friend.

RC (DNA: RG 59, CD, Tunis, vol. 3). 2 pp.; in Italian; in a clerk's hand, with Hoggia's seal.

1. Throughout the documents there are many variations in the spelling of the ambassador's name. After consultation with Mohamed Sawaie, Arabic Faculty, Department of Middle Eastern and South Asian Languages and Cultures, at the University of Virginia; and noting how the ambassador, himself, spelled his name; how his "minder," former consul James Leander Cathcart, referred to him; and consideration of the difficulties of transliteration from the Arabic to the English alphabet, the editors have decided to use the form "Soliman Melimeni" for the name of the Tunisian ambassador.

§ From John Leonard. *31 August 1805, Barcelona.* "The preceeding is Copy of my last respects. I now have the Honor to transmit to you a list of the arrivals from Jany. to June 1805 [not found]. I Enclose you a Copy of an Office I Received from the French Consul.[1]

"I have not as yet the pleasure to receive the Commiss of Consul which I regret much, as it has been a considerable injury to my private arrangements as well as a drawback upon the respect due to my representations, in the Eyes of the Government. I have long been in anxious expectation of receiving it, & hope to Have the Honor of hearing from you on the Subject."

RC and enclosure (DNA: RG 59, CD, Barcelona, vol. 1). RC 2 pp.; written at the foot of a copy of Leonard to JM, 20 Feb. 1805. For surviving enclosure, see n. 1.

1. The enclosure (3 pp.; in French; docketed by Wagner as received in Leonard's 31 Aug. dispatch) is a copy of a 10 Aug. 1805 note to Leonard from French consul Viot, enclosing a copy of Napoleon's 18 Prairial an 13 (7 June 1805) decree issued at Milan. For the decree, see William Kirkpatrick to JM, 19 Aug. 1805, n. 1.

To Thomas Jefferson

DEAR SIR   PHILADA. Sepr. 1. 1805

I recd. yesterday yours of the 25th. The letter from Turreau appeared to me as to you, in the light of a reprehensible intrusion in a case where this Govt. ought to be guided by its own sense of propriety alone. Whether it be the effect of an habitual air of superiority in his Govt. or be meant as a particular disrespect to us is questionable. The former cause will explain it, and the latter does not seem to be a probable cause. Be it as it may, an answer breathing independence as well as friendship seems to be proper. And I inclose one to which that character was meant to be given. Just as I had finished it I was called on by Genl. Smith and considering him both in a public & personal view entitled to such a confidence, I communicated the letter & answer, in order to have the benefit of the impressions made on his mind by both. He was not insensible to the improper tone of the former, but regarded it as a misjudged precaution agst. proceedings which might be offensive to France & injurious to the harmony of the two Countries, rather than any thing positively disrespectful to the U.S. With respect to Turreau's part in the communication, he is entirely of that opinion. He says that Turreau speaks with the greatest respect and even affection towards the Administration; and such are the dispositions which it is certain he has uniformly manifested to me. With this impression as to the letter, he thought the answer tho' due to its manner, was rather harder than was required by its intention. I suggest for consideration whether it ought to be softened; and if so whether it will be sufficiently & properly done by substituting, (in line 8th.) for "the proper," "a sufficient" before "motive" and by inserting before "left" (in line 12) the words "of course" or by some other equivalant changes. If these alterations be approved, and the Answer be otherwise so, you can have them made & the letter forwarded thro' Washington to Baltimore. For this purpose the date is left blank, that you may fill it suitably. If the letter should not appear proper without material alterations which cannot be made within the copy sent, you will please to send it back with the requisite instructions for a new one. You will observe that I have not expressed or particularly implied the non responsibility of the Nation for the proceedings of the State or other local authorities. Whilst it can not be on one hand necessary to admit it, I think it would not be expedient, and might not even be correct, to deny it. Altho' the Govt. of the U.S. may have no authority to restrain in such cases, the Foreign Govt. will not be satisfied with a reference to that feature in our Constitution, ⟨in⟩ case a real insult be offered to it; and such an insult seems possible. A State Legislature or City Corporation, might resolve & publish that Moreau had been barbarously treated, or that Bonaparte was a Usurper & Tyrant. &c &c.

The more I reflect on the papers from Madrid, the more I feel the value of some mutual security for the active friendship of G. B. but the more I see at the same time the difficulty of obtaining it without a like security to her for ours. If she is to be *bound*, we must be *so too*, either to the same thing, that is, to join her in the war, or to do what she will accept as equivalent to such an obligation. What can we offer ⟨her⟩ negotiation? A mutual guaranty, unless so shaped as to involve us pretty certainly in her war would not be satisfactory. To offer commercial regulations, or concessions on points in the Law of nations, as a certain payment for aids which might never be recd. or required, would be a bargain liable to obvious objections of the most serious kind. Unless therefore some arrangement which has not occurred to me, can be devised, I see no other course than such an one as is suggested in my last letters. I have heard nothing from either of my Colleagues on the subject. Mr. Gallatin in returning the Spanish papers merely remarked that the business had not ended quite so badly as he had previously supposed, concurring in a remark I had made to him, that the instructions to Bowdoin would involved [*sic*] much delicacy.

Moreau was visited by a Crowd here; and it is said declined a public dinner with a promise to accept one on his return which wd. be about October. He did not call on me, & I did not see him. The fever is Still limited but very deadly in its attacks. The present rainy weather ⟨is⟩ giving it more activity. Mrs. M. is still on her bed, the apparatus of cure fixing her there. We hoped a few days ago that she would quickly be well; towards which ⟨gre⟩at progress is made; but a small operation which could not be avoided, will detain us yet a little longer. Yrs. always,

J. Madison

RC (DLC: Jefferson Papers). Docketed by Jefferson as received 6 Sept.

§ From William Riggin. *1 September 1805.* "I have the honor to inclose you a copy of my respects of the 1st. July.

"The public opinion is now general that a war between this Country and France is inevitable; the army is now on the war establishment, and if credit can be given to common report hostilities may be daily expected to commence."

RC (DNA: RG 59, CD, Trieste, vol. 1). 1 p.; in a clerk's hand, signed by Riggin.

§ From John Graham. *2 September 1805, New Orleans.* "A White Man by the Name of Le Grand, who is from St Domingo has lately been taken up in this City and is now confined in Jail here, for having endeavoured to bring about an Insurrection of the Negroes in this and the adjoining Territories.

"The details of his Plan, and of the Measures persue'd by the Mayor of the City to arrest him, & to obtain proof of his Guilt, shall be forwarded to you by the next Post. I was in hopes of being able to get them ready in time for this Post but I find it impossible. I therefore write this Letter in haste merely to let you know that nothing is now to be apprehended from this Plot, which was indeed only in Embryo, when it was discovered by a Slave who communicated to the Mayor the propositions which had been made to him by Le Grand. You will have heared before this reaches you that the Governor is on a Tour thro. the Upper parts of the Territory."

RC (DNA: RG 59, TP, Orleans, vol. 7). 2 pp.; docketed by Wagner as received 15 Oct.

§ From George Hay. *2 September 1805, Richmond.* "Mr Wagners letter of the 10th ult. requesting information concerning the estate of the late Major Ludeman was received on the 13th.[1]

"As to the real estate of which Major Ludeman died seised, I can learn nothing, except this, that at the time of his death, his lands in Kentucky were under the care of Colo. Richard C. Anderson, with whom the Executors Mr Heth and Mr Richardson, have had no communication. You know, Sir, that by our laws, the Executors do not represent the testator as to his lands.

"The history of the Military certificates ($1600) which Major Ludeman left, or rather was supposed to have left, is somewhat singular. They constitute at this moment the Subject of a controversy between the Agent of Mr Lekampe, acting for Ludeman's sisters in Europe, and Mr Heth. The accounts of Mr Heth as Executor, have been lately referred by an order of Court to a Commissioner. Having attended the Commissioner as Mr Heth's counsel, I became acquainted with the following circumstances.

"The certificates in question, it appears, were at the time of Ludemans death, in the hands of one Graves, a notorious speculator. Heth understood from his friend that they had been pledged as security for a small sum borrowed, and soon after his death offered to redeem them. Graves alledged that he had purchased them, and of course refused to surrender. A warm dispute arose, which was terminated by an agreement to leave the question to reference. Mr Pennock, now of Norfolk, and Mr Joseph Higbee now of Philada were the referrees. They decided in favor of Graves. Mr Heth at that time, a young man of warm feelings, indignant at the success of Grave's Villany, and influenced by sentiments of respect for his deceased friend, immediately purchased certificates of the same description and amount, saying that he made the purchase for the benefit of Ludeman's sisters. The money however, with which the purchase was made, was taken out of the funds of Heth and Munford. The latter was then in France. On his return, he and Mr Heth parted, and Munford took possession, without ceremony of the certificates thus purchased, as the Books proved that they were purchased with the Company's money. Heth afterwards commissioned Loff & Higbee to get $1600 in certificates for him, which he intended to apply in discharge of the legacy left by Ludeman to his sisters. Loff & Higbee executed their Commission, but Mr Heth being in arrears to them, the certificates were afterwards sold on his account. Thus the matter rested, until Mr Heth was called to account by the Agent of Lekampe.

"The foregoing facts I believe to be true: Mr   [2] consulted me as his friend as well as his Counsel and solemnly protested, I am sure with sincerity, that if I thought he was bound by law or by any principle of justice or honor to pay the value of the certificates, he would instantly make the sacrifice. My opinion was, and yet is, that he was under no obligation in law or conscience, to pay the legacy, without having received the certificates. That he never did and never could obtain the certificates is admitted: but it was conceived by some that he had made himself responsible by his subsequent acts. This idea however seems to be now abandoned.

"The other personal property of Mr Ludeman was very inconsiderable: and for that Mr Heth has been always ready to account.

"Mr George Tucker, attorney at law, was the Counsel opposed to Mr Heth. He will very readily, I have no doubt, if requested, communicate his ideas on the subject. Having acted as Mr Heth's Counsel, and having great confidence in his

Integrity, I may perhaps be favorable to him in my statement. I beg leave therefore to refer you to Mr Tucker."

RC, two copies (DNA: RG 59, ML). First RC 4 pp. Both RCs marked "Copy."

1. For the 12 May 1805 letter from Baron Jacobi-Kloest, Prussian minister at London, to George W. Erving, inquiring about Wilhelm Lüdemann, that was enclosed in Wagner's 10 Aug. 1805 letter to Hay, see *PJM-SS*, 9:424 n. 1. A copy of Wagner's letter is filed in the National Archives, Record Group 59, Diplomatic Letters, volume 15.

2. Left blank in both RCs. Hay presumably referred to Heth.

§ From Peter Kuhn Jr. *2 September 1805, Genoa.* "Nothing new in the Commercial Sphere has taken place since my last worthy of your notice.[1] On the 29th. Ulto. arrived here Mr. Jerome Bonopathe with a Squadron consisting of three Frigates and two Brigs, from Algiers bringing 201 Genoese Prisoners, released upon the demand of France for the consideration of 400,000 franks, and this day arrived a Brig appertaining to the same Squadron from Tunis with 29 Prisoners released.

"The Motions of the Austrian Armies have at length created the Suspicions of the Emperour Nepoleon who has caused new troops to be raised throughout the Italian Kingdom, and two regiments here are ordered to be in readiness for an immediate march to the Adige. The Old Genoese Regiments were removed to Savoy Some time past. All the fortified towns in Lombardy have been greatly Strengthened, the New Works at Alexandria and Mantua are of the greatest Magnitude, to the latter has been added a Strong fortress on the South of the Morass, completely Commanding the Causway & Bridge &c. Other considerable Out Works were forming during my Sojourn there in June last, which must by this time be Nearly if not entirely finished.

"A Carriage road has been made over Mont Cenis which is completed and practicable, & of obvious advantage(;) the Emperor has Also ordered Sometime back that Several Carriage roads be made to afford an easier Communication between Lombardy & this for the benifit of Commerce They have however Not yet Commenced upon them & as their want had proved in former times the guarantee of the independence of Genoa it is not likely that they will be undertaken in the present prospect of affairs.

"It is reported that the Emperors presence is expected at Milan shortly. What truth is to be attatched to it is not yet to be ascertained."

RC and enclosure (DNA: RG 59, CD, Genoa, vol. 1). RC 3 pp.; docketed by Wagner. The enclosure (1 p.) is a description of the tonnage, cargo, and papers of the *Matilda*, which arrived at Genoa from Philadelphia on 29 Sept. 1804.

1. See Peter Kuhn Jr. to JM, 10 Aug. 1805.

§ From Tobias Lear. *2 September 1805, "On board the U S ship Constitution Tunis Bay."* No. 11. "On the 7th. of July I had the honor to receive your respected letter of the 20th. of April,[1] by the U S Frigate John Adams, by which I find that the instructions given to me dated June 6th. 1804, were to be still followed, as nothing in the state or prospect of things subsequent thereto, made a change necessary. I have accordingly pursued the same, agreeably to the circumstances under which they were brought into operation; and I hope my Conduct will meet the approbation of the President.

"I claim for myself no superior merit for the highly favourable, and indeed unexpected manner in which our affairs have been settled with this regency. The moment was peculiarly happy for us, and the judicious and decided measures taken by Commodore Rodgers made so powerful an impression on the mind of the Bashaw, that the negociation afterwards became easy and unembarassed.

"I had the honor of addressing you on the 5th. of July, by the U.S. Ship President, and now forward duplicates of that dispatch, with its enclosures.

"On the 13th. of July we left Syracuse, and proceeded to Malta, with all the Vessels of war and Gun Boats, where we arrived on the 15th. After taking in the necessary supplies for the Squadron, the Commodore sailed, on the 22d., for Tunis, as I mentioned in my last was his intention: We had a tedious passage of 9 days to this place, owing to calms and head winds, in which the Gun Boats (altho' the most excellent Vessels of their kind, in the world) could make but little progress. On the first of August Mr Davis came off on board the Constitution, and shewed to the Commodore and myself, the Copy of a letter which he had Written to the Honorable the Secretary of State, detailing the interviews he had had with the Bey on the 12th. 13th. 14th. & 16th. of July, in which the Bey had repeatedly threatend our Country with immediate War as you will see by Mr. Davis's letter, or the Copy enclosed.[2] He also informed us of his determination to have gone to Malta or Syracuse, to have had a conference with the Commodore & myself. After some conversation with Mr D. on the Subject of our affairs here, I asked him what he considered would be the best means of securing the Peace of this Regency on solid grounds; he answered that he conceiv'd it would be best to give them an Annuity of 8 or 10,000. dollars and keep them two or three years in Arrears, the fear of losing which would prevent their making War upon us. Upon my expressing some surprize at such a proposal and saying that if we intended doing this it would have been sufficient to have sent a single Vessel for the purpose; he added that in his opinion we should either do this; or keep always a force in this Sea sufficient to prevent any evil from a sudden attack: I assured him I was certain our Government would never leave this Sea without a proper force to guard our Commerce; while we should have any   [3] it; and that we should never again agree to pay a tribute for peace with any Nation.

"In consequence of these declarations and hostile disposition of the Bey, as communicated by Mr. Davis, the Commodore assured him, that he should feel it his duty to take measures to prevent has [sic] carrying them into effect by preventing his Cruizers now in port, from going to sea, and those which were out, from committing any depredations on our Commerce; and even blockade his port, if necessary to reduce him to reason.

"Mr. Davis declared, that if the Commodore made such communication of his determination to the Bey he would pledge himself the Bey would cut down the Flag staff and declare War in twelve hours. The Commodore assured him he should write to that effect, as he conceived that the present state of things made it necessary for him to come to a decision without delay. Accordingly he wrote to the Bey, recapitulating the threats he had made, and the hostile disposition he had discovered towards the U.S. as stated by Mr Davis; and while he expressed an ernest desire to preserve peace, and restore a good understanding between the two Nations; yet, if he did not receive from the Bey within 36 hours assurances of his pacific and friendly disposition, he should feel it his duty to Commence defensive & offensive measures against his regency.[4]

"At the same time I wrote a Letter to the Bey No.   [5] and enclosed a Copy of the Presidents letter to him in my hands.

"On the 3rd. of August Mr. Davis wrote to the Commodore,[6] stating that it would not be practicable to obtain an Answer from the Bey within the 36 hours, and probably not untill the 5th or 6th. inst. A Council of War was called on board the Constitution when it was determined to extend the time for receiving an Answer to noon of the 6th. & Mr. Davis was accordingly informed thereof.

"At 10 a m on the 4th. Mr Davis came off and delivered to the Commodore two letters which he (Mr. D) had written to him[7] (he had not received the Commodores last letter) stating that he had an interview yesterday with the Bey, and delivered the Commodores letter of the 2nd. to him. The Bey said that as the time did not admit of his *writing* an answer to the Commodore, Mr. Davis might tell him, by word of mouth, that it was his determination to adhere to the letter and Spirit of our treaty with him, and that he would not make war upon the U. States, untill he should have heard from the President on the Subject of his Vessels captured and detained; and added, in a threatning and insulting manner, that if the Commodore should stop one Vessel of his; or fire a single shot; or do any other act which could be considered hostile, he would immediately declare war against the U. States.

"A Council of war was again called, and it was the opinion of the Commanders, as well as of myself, who was present at this & the proceeding [*sic*] consultation, that the Commodore should demand, in *writing* from the Bey, a declaration that he would not make war, nor commit any act of hostility against the U. States, so long as we should adhere to the Treaty now existing, nor until he should be denied reparation or indemnification for injuries or losses he may have sustained from us, after he should have made his reclamation agreeably to the Treaty existing between us; and, as the Bey had according to Mr. Davis's statement, called before him two Consuls to hear his protest agst. the United States and the Commodore, that this declaration should be made, in like manner, in presence of two Consuls. Should the Bey refuse to give such a declaration in writing, it would be concluded that he did not intend to adhere to his *verbal* declaration, and that the Commodore would be justified in taking measures to prevent his Cruizers from going to Sea, and secure our commerce effectually against any depredation.

"Mr. Davis had always positively declared that the Bey would never receive me as a person authorized to do business with him, and his letters both before and after my arrival in this Bay were pointed to that effect. I had, however (as I had the honor to inform you in my last) very little doubts of his receiving me in a proper manner, when he should be *justly* informed of the Character in which the President had ordered me to present myself to him.

"On the 5th. of August the Commodore sent Captain Decatur up to Tunis, with the form of a declaration to be signed by the Bey; or the substances thereof in other words:

"I also wrote to the Bey by Capt Decateur,[8] stating that as I could not be permitted to meet him on business, agreeably to the Presidents letter, I should impute all evils which might arise from this circumstance to their proper cause.

"On the 7th. Capt Decateur returned from Tunis, in company with Mr. Davis. Capt. D. had not seen the Bey, as he was informed by Mr. Davis, that they [sic] Bey refused to have any communication with him, on the Subject for which he was sent. Just before they came on board, a boat reached the Ship from the Goletta, bringing two letters from the Bey to me, which will be found in the Packet marked,   [9] saying that he had not before understood the nature of my Mission, that he was willing to see me on the Subject of our affairs and inviting me strongly to come to Bardo. Mr. Davis brought a Copy of one of these letters, and also a letter from the Bey to the Commodore.[10] Mr. Davis said that he yesterday presented to the Bey Commodore Rodger's demand of a guarantee to be given for the preservation of the peace, which irritated the Bey exceedingly and he told Mr. D *that he would take out his eyes if he persisted in offering it &ca. &ca. &ca. &ca.* The Bey says nothing on that Subject in his letters either to the Commodore or myself. Mr. Davis reports that great disorder and consternation prevails at Tunis—No business done—the Bey appearing like a Madman &ca.

"On the 8th. of August Mr. Davis returned to Tunis with a letter from me to the Bey (copy in packet)[11] and one from the Commodore to himself,[12] directing him to present to the Bey, without delay, the form of the assurance which was required from him for preserving the peace &ca. and saying that no longer time than tomorrow noon would be allowed for the Bey to decide on it; and if not then that he (Mr. D) would come off to the Constitution by 4 P.M prepared to leave the regency; as he was determined, if the Bey should persist in refusing to give the assurance required, to carry into execution his promise of preventing the departure of his Cruizers, and of examining every vessel going in or out of his ports to guard against any Clandestine attempts to annoy our Commerce; and Mr. Davis having declared in the most solemn manner that these measures would produce an immediate declaration of war on the part of the Bey; the Commodore did not think it would be prudent for him to remain in the power of the Bey, notwithstanding Mr. Davis had told the Commodore & myself that let the issue of the present differences be what it might, war or peace, he would continue in Tunis.

"In the afternoon of the 9th. Mr Davis came on board the Constitution, with his Baggage, Secretary & the Drogerman. He reported that the Bey would not give the Guarantee required by the Commodore before two Consuls; but that he would give the same thing under his Seal, and in the most formal manner, without the witnesses, if Mr. Davis would wait till to morrow morning, which from the Commodores orders he did not think himself warranted in so doing. Soon after Mr. Davis came on board, a Merchant Vessel got under way at the Goletta to go out, when she came within Gun Shot, the Commodore ordered a Shot to be fired at her to bring her too for Examination; the first shot not being regarded, a second was fired, upon which she immediately put about and went up to the Goletta again to anchor.

"On the 10th. I received a very lengthy letter from the Bey (in Packet marked   )[13] disavowing his threats—giving the most solemn assurance of his determination to keep the peace, and promising to send an Ambassador to the U States, to arrange and settle all differences, and give evidences of his friendly disposition; at the same time engaging me, in the most earnest manner, to come on shore, and settle all points of immediate difference.

"In consequence of this letter, which was deemed by the Commodore & myself sufficiently expressive of his earnest wish and sincere desire to maintain the peace, I wrote to the Bey that I would go on shore the day after to morrow to confer with him.[14]

"On the 11th. Mr. Davis came on Board the Constitution from the Constellation, where he had taken up his quarters, when I shewed him the letter I had received from the Bey, informed him that I was to go on shore to morrow, and invited him to accompany me. He expressed some surprize & resentment against the Bey, on reading the Letter, and said he should not go on Shore again, and never wished to put his foot in the Regency from this time.

"On the 12th. I went on Shore accompanied by Mr.   [15] Chaplin of the Constellation, who understood & spoke the Italian language perfectly, and whom I afterwards found very useful in the Course of our Negociations. At the Goletta met the Sapatapa, whom I requested to send a Messenger to inform the Bey of my being On Shore, and ready to confer with him at any time he might appoint. Proceeded to Tunis, from whence I sent the Drogerman to Bardo with the like message. On his return he informed me that the Bey had appointed to morrow morning at 7. O'clock to give me an Audience.

"In the evening I received a Visit from all the Consuls residing in Tunis.

"At 7 oclk. AM, of the 13th. I went to Bardo where I was immediately introduced to the Bey in his private Audience room my reception was cordial & flattering I delivered him the Presidents letter, which he received with great respect, and said that the Copy which I sent to him had been translated, and he knew its contents. After taking Coffee, he ordered all persons to retire excepting his first Secretary— Hadge Unis Ben Unis, one old man, and his Christian Secretary. He wished to know on what points I wished first to enter. I recapitulated to him his threats of making war upon us at different times as communicated by Mr. Davis, And that in consequence thereof, the Commodore had come here and taken the measures which he knew of, to avert or guard against that evil. Having a Copy of Mr. Davis's letter to the Secretary of State of the 18th. of July,[16] detailing his several interviews with the Bey in which he had threatened War, I recapitulated them in order.

First, that he had said he would make war upon Us, in consequence of his Cruizer and her two prizes having been taken, without asking a question about restitution, had not the situation of his Country forbid it. To this he replied by asking me If I thought him a wise man, or a fool? I told him the world gave him the Character of a Wise prince. Well, says he, if I am not a fool, do you think I would have made such a decleration of the distressed situation of my Country, to the representative of a Nation with whom I may expect to be at War? I told him he knew best what he had said; and asked him if the words mentioned by Mr. Davis as his were true, in effect or not. He replied, *that it was not true—he had never expressed himself in that manner, or to that effect.*

"Secondly That he (the Bey) had declared to Mr. Davis, that if the Commodore came into this Bay, with his Squadron, he would declare War against the U. States. He Answered, that he had told our Charge d'affaires, that if the Commodore came here with his Squadron he should consider it as a declaration of War on our part; as he could not conceive why we should come here with such a force, if our intentions were pacific; but that he had never said that *he* would declare War in that event.

"Thirdly: That he had called the Spanish and Dutch Consuls to hear him protest, that if the Government of the U. States did not pay him for his Cruizers and her two prizes, and make indemnification for taking and detaining the same, and give him satisfaction for the insults offered him by the Commodore, he would declare war agst. the U. States. The Bey answered—On that occasion there was only the Dutch Consul present. He was at Bardo and was called into the Hall, to hear him say that if he *was forced* into a War with the U. States he would never make peace with them as long as he lived. He desired me, (as this was a point on which there might be Witnesses) to ask the Dutch Consul, if this was not the case, and the Spanish Consul if he was there.

"On the Subject of blockaded ports, we had much conversation. The Bey saying that Altho' England was at war with France, yet his Vessels were permitted to enter the ports of those nations, and also, by them, permitted to enter the English Ports. I explained to him the nature of a Blockade, such as ours of Tripoli. He either did not, or pretended not to understand it. However, after some conversation with Hadge Unis, in Turkish, he appeared to have it explained.

"He acknowledged that after the Commodore had received the information from Mr. Davis, as before stated, he was perfectly right to take the measures he had done; but that the information was groundless.

"On the subject of sending an Ambassador to the U. States, he said he should rather wish to have all matters settled now, which would render that measure unnecessary. But I told him that the Commodore could not undertake to restore his Vessels, even were he inclined so to do, without becoming personally responsible for them.

"We had some conversation respecting the changing certain Articles in our Treaty, which bore hard upon us. He observed that he conceived our Treaty placed us upon the same ground as other Christian Nations stood with him; and that the alteration of a Treaty must be by the mutual consent of the parties. This I granted; but assured him we did not stand upon the same footing as other Nations. He said he would consider the Subject; but gave no assurance that he would make any change.

"With respect to demands upon the U. States for presents, or payments in any Shape, he declared he had none. He acknowledged that he had asked for a Frigate; but he had only made the request, as from one friend to another, which, if not convenient or agreeable to grant, should never produce any difference, and as we did not think proper to give him one, he had never made war or been disgusted in consequence thereof. We had made him an offer of 8 or 10,000 dollars annually in Cash; but he had not thought proper to accept it, which ought not to be a Subject of difference between our Nations.

"After a conversation of more than five hours, which was supported on his part with much good sense & shrewdness, and great, pleasantness, I took my leave, promising to wait upon him again to morrow morng at 7 O'clock to finish our business.

"On the 14th. I went to Bardo at 7 Oclock, agreeably to appointment. After taking Coffee, the Bey observed that we had yesterday conversed fully on all points between us, and had time to reflect on the Subject, which was the mode he liked to do business. After some general conversation, he asked what I had determined upon; or what I expected him to do. I told him I expected he would write a letter to the Commodore, giving him the fullest assurances of his determination to preserve the peace according to the Treaty between our Nations; and informing him of his intention to send an Ambassador to the U. States to lay before the President his requisition for a restoration of his Cruizer and her two prizes; and to make all arrangemts. which might prove mutually beneficial to the parties.

"This he promised to do this evening or to morrow morning. I assured him his Ambassador would be accomodated in the Frigate according to his rank; and would be received in the U. States with all the respect and attention due to his Character. He said the Ambassador would be ready to embark in 15 or 20 days.

"We then entered into the Subject of the Treaty. I told him that as it now stood we could have no commercial intercourse with his regency, as the duties we should have to pay (being the same as were paid in the U: States) were 3 or 4 times more than were paid here by the English or French, and unless we were put upon the same footing with those nations, we could never come in competition with them. I pointed out the advantages which would accrue to him from a commercial intercourse with us; besides it fixing our friendship on a more secure basis. He listened with great attention, and conversed on the Subject with his Minister & Hadge Unis who both appeared to advocate my proposition. The bey then observed, that he had thought we were, by our Treaty, placed upon same footing, as it respects commerce, as the French and English. I assured him he was mistaken. He sent for his Treaty with G. B and the U. S. and upon examination found I was right, as the English only pay 3 per cent duty. He then observed that it was his intention that we should be placed upon the footing of the most favored nation in this point. I told him I would put in writing the alterations or addittions which we wished in our treaty, and submit it to him; that it must be a matter of mutual consent, and both parties must find their interest in it.

"The Bey asked me if a Chargé d'affaires would not be placed here. I told him undoubtedly, and observed if Mr. Davis wished to return again, he would certainly be sent. The Bey replied that he had rather have some other person; for altho' he would not accuse Mr. Davis of wilful or intentional misrepresentation; he might have mistaken his expressions; or he might have forgotten some part of the Conversation between the time of its taking place & committing it to writing; Yet after what had happened, he could not suppose there would be that Cordiality existing between them which was so desirable for both parties, and he should prefer some other person.

"After leaving the Bey, the Prime Minister sent for me, with whom I found Hadge Unis. We had a long conversation on the several points which had been discussed by the Bey and myself this and the preceding day, and they appeared cordially disposed to promote the object of altering the Treaty: On their Assurances however, I place but little dependence.

"On the 15th. I return'd on board the Constitution, & on the 16th I communicated to Mr. Davis, who had come onboard the same Ship, all that had pass'd in my two interviews with the Bey. The Commodore asked Mr Davis if it was his wish to return again to Tunis as Chargé d'affairs; because, if it was, he would send him back again, in a proper manner, notwithstanding what the Bey had said; unless the Bey Shou'd give some very strong and substantial reasons for not receiving him. Mr. Davis Answer'd, that it was not his Wish to go back to Tunis; but to return to the U. States, as he conceived that the respect due to himself, after what had pass'd, made it proper for him to return home and lay his case before the Government, when he expected to be sent back again with marks of approbation. He urged very strongly the propriety & necessity there was of *Acting immediately* upon the information he had given of the Bey's threats; notwithstanding the Bey had denied them, and given the most pointed and unequivocal assurances of the reverse. I assured him that I did not doubt but the Bey had told him either the Very Words which he had written, or to the amount of them, and I was also confident that the Government wou'd not disbelieve him; yet when it came to the point of Acting, the written & Solemn Assurances of the Bey, & his revoking, or disavowing such language, must have its weight.

"As Mr Davis had declined returning to Tunis under any circumstances, the Commodore appointed Dr. James Dodge, Surgeon of this Ship, to take Charge of our Affairs here, untill the pleasure of the President shou'd be made known thereon.

"On the 18th I went to Tunis with Dr. Dodge to present him to the Bey as Chargé d'Affairs. On the 21st. went to Bardo & introduced Dr. Dodge, who was received, in form, as the Representative of our Nation, The Bey inform'd me that he had instructed his Prime Minister to confer with me on the Subject of making alterations in our Treaty. After our Audience, we waited upon the Sapatapa, and immediately enter'd upon the discussion of the Several points which we wish'd to have alter'd. He at once recapitulated them, and said they had long known that they were unfavorable to us, & expected that we shou'd have long before endeavour'd to get them Changed. I told him *I Knew* application had been made for that purpose but not effected. After a full conversation on the business, I promised to write him this day or tomorrow, state our wishes, and leave it for him to answer me in the same way.

"On the 22nd I return'd onboard the Constitution, where I remain'd 'till the 24th. when I went again to Tunis with Dr. Dodge, and a number of the Officers of the Squadron; to partake of an Entertainment provided for us at the Gardens of the Bey, a little beyond Bardo. We met with every mark of respect & attention, and found our entertainment prepared in an Elegant stile. After Dinner we met the Bey on a plane near Bardo, Where I introduced the Officers to him &ca.

"On the 30th. of August had my audience of leave of the Bey, when I presented him with an Elegant Watch Set with Brilliants. I gave also a Watch simalar, but inferior, to the Sapatapa; and to the First Turkish, & first Christian Secretaries each, an enammeld Snuff box ornamented with Brilliants. The Custom of the Country makes it unavoidable to give presents on Such an Occasion; And I reserved them to the last day of my being here, that they might not be considered as given with a View of Making favorable impressions for our obtaining any points with them which we wished to carry.

"I this day received a letter from the Prime Minister on the Subject of certain Articles in Our Treaty, Which you will find in the Packet Marked A.[17] The two most important points are granted, and the Other two left to be discussed & Settled by the Ambassador sent to the U. States.

"On the 1st. of September I came onboard this Ship with Sidi Soliman Mellamella, the Ambassador, Accompanied by Several of the first Officers of the Regency. The Wind blowing very fresh, obliged the Ambassador and the persons Accompa[n]ying him, to remain onboard all night. The Next Morning the Ambassador went onboard the U.S. Ship Congress, Cap Decateur, prepared to carry him to the U.States, & the rest returnd to Tunis.

"Thus, Sir; I have given you a faithful detail of *events* & *facts* as they have Occurred Since Our Arrival in this Bay, not from memory; but from Notes taken at the time When Such circumstances occurred; The Documents Which Accompany this letter,[18] will give a more minute account on some points than are Stated here. I shall make no comment, on what I have written, as I feel an honest pride in placing only plain fact, before those whom I know will receive them with candor, and draw from them the proper inferences. I will just observe, that the impression made here by the judicious display of our force, and the prompt and decided conduct of our Commodore, is such as had never before been felt, and has utterly Astonished the foreign representations at this Court. My path, as I before observed, was plain & easy. I had rather to guard against asking too much, least it should be imputed to an improper advantage after the moment, and I avoided pressing, with impetuosity, those points which were demanded, that they might See we were just as well as powerful.

"The recent situation of Algiers has been such, as to divert the attention of the Dey from foreign Nations. A formidable & threatning insurrection in the heart of his dominions,[19] a lawless and ungovernable Soldiery, who have lately committed the most horrid Massacre's in the City,[20] and Kept him in awe, have obliged him to attend to his personal Safety only. His Cruizers are disarmed & dismantled, from a fear that their Crews might Seize his Treasures, and carry it off, so that we can have nothing to apprehend from that quarter. As our bienial present becomes due this Month, I shall proceed to Leghorn, in this Ship to make arrangements for it, before I return to Algiers; And indeed the pressure of business which has been upon me during our Negociation at Tripoli, & Since, at this place, has very much injured my health, that I feel it necessary to have a few weeks relaxation, before I enter again into the Scenes of anxious business which always occurs in these Regencies.

"You will pardon my remarking that the salary of two thousand Dollars, will not allow a Public Character to live in Tunis, in a situation by any Means equal to his Standing—5 or 6 years ago it wou'd answer—now eve[r]y Article has increas'd

More than threefold. It is not possible for me to prepare my accounts for this op-portunity. The Month past has been occupied very Closely—And at this Moment the Congress is detain'd solely for My dispatches. I shall not fail to have them prepared & forwarded before I return to Algiers.

"To the President I pray you will be pleased to present my grateful respects, and Say, that in all my conduct both here, and at Tripoli, I have been Actuated with a confident belief, that I was conforming to his wishes and determination to support the honor & dignity of the U.States, while we convinced Nations of our Justice and Generosity."

RC (DNA: RG 59, CD, Tunis, vol. 2, pt. 2); enclosures and list of enclosures (DNA: RG 59, CD, Algiers, vol. 7, pt. 2); letterbook copy, letterbook copy of list of enclosures, and FC (owned by Stephen Decatur, Garden City, N.Y., 1961). RC 18 pp.; in clerks' hands; signed by Lear. For surviving enclosures and list of enclosures, see nn. 2, 5, 8–9, 11, 13–14, and 17–18.

1. *PJM-SS*, 9:261–63.

2. See George Davis to JM, 18 July 1805.

3. The clerk apparently omitted a word here.

4. See John Rodgers to Hammuda Bey, 2 Aug. 1805, Knox, *Naval Documents, Barbary Wars*, 6:202.

5. Left blank in RC. Lear referred to his letter of 2 Aug. 1805 to Hammuda Bey, ibid., 201. For Jefferson's 14 Apr. 1803 letter to the bey, copies of which were given to James Leander Cathcart and Lear, see *PJM-SS*, 4:495, 496 n. 4, 5:277, 278 n. 2.

6. See Davis to Rodgers, 3 Aug. 1805, Knox, *Naval Documents, Barbary Wars*, 6:203–4.

7. See Davis's second letter of 3 Aug. 1805 to Rodgers, and Davis to Rodgers, 4 Aug. 1805, ibid., 204, 205.

8. For Lear to Hammuda Bey, 5 Aug. 1805, see ibid., 207.

9. Left blank in RC. According to the list of enclosures, the bey's 5 and 7 Aug. 1805 let-ters to Lear were in packet *A* (see n. 18 below). For the letters, see ibid., 207–8, 210–11.

10. This was probably Hammuda Bey to John Rodgers, 5 Aug. 1805, ibid., 208–9.

11. For Lear to Hammuda Bey, 8 Aug. 1805, see ibid., 211–12.

12. For Rodgers to Davis, 8 Aug. 1805, see ibid., 212.

13. Left blank in RC. According to the list of enclosures, the bey's 9 Aug. 1805 letter to Lear was in packet *A*. For a truncated version of the letter, see ibid., 221.

14. For Lear to Hammuda Bey, 11 Aug. 1805, see ibid., 222–23.

15. Left blank in RC. Lear referred to Lawrence Cruise, acting chaplain of the *Constellation* (Knox, *Register of Officer Personnel*, 13).

16. See n. 2 above.

17. For Jussuf Hoggia to Lear, 31 Aug. 1805, see Knox, *Naval Documents, Barbary Wars*, 6:257–58.

18. Lear included a list of the contents of packets *A* through *E*. According to the list, packet *A* contained copies of the letters described in nn. 2, 5, 8–9, 11, 13–14, and 17 above, as well as Lear to Hammuda Bey, 10 Aug. 1805; Hammuda Bey to Lear, 11 Aug. 1805; Lear to Jussuf Hoggia, 22 Aug. 1805; and Lear's 1 Sept. 1805 instructions to James Dodge (for Lear's letters to Hammuda Bey and Jussuf Hoggia, see Knox, *Naval Documents, Barbary Wars*, 6:221–22, 244–45). Packet *B* contained copies of Lear's 5 July 1805 dispatch to JM and the treaty between the United States and Tripoli. There is no list for a packet *C*. Packet *D* con-tained copies of William Bainbridge to Lear, 11 Nov. 1804, 19 Dec. 1804 (two letters), 27 Jan. 1805, 11 Apr. 1805 (two letters), and 12 Apr. 1805; Samuel Barron to Lear, 13 Nov. 1804; Gerardo José de Souza Betancourt to Lear, 18 Dec. 1804 and 16 Apr. 1805; Nicolai C. Nis-

sen to Barron, 18 Mar. 1805; Bonaventure Beaussier to Lear, 10 Apr. 1805; John Rodgers to
Lear, 18 Apr. 1805; and John Ridgely to Lear, 6 June 1805 (surviving enclosures filed in
DNA: RG 59, CD, Algiers, vol. 7, pt. 2, and printed in Knox, *Naval Documents, Barbary
Wars*, 5:135–37, 139–40, 201–202, 311–12, 421–23, 500–502). Packet *E* contained correspon-
dence between Lear and Davis "from July 18th. 1804 to August 5th. 1805" (DNA: RG 59,
CD, Algiers, vol. 7, pt. 1). At the foot of the list, Lear added a 6 Sept. 1805 note: "N.B. Pack-
ets D and E are not enclosed, as there has not been time to make duplicates of them since the
dispatches sent by the Congress Sepr. 4h."

    19. For the revolt in Algiers, see *PJM-SS*, 9:176 and n. 5, 465.

    20. For the slaughter of the Jews in Algiers, see Peter Kuhn Jr. to JM, 16 July 1805, and
n. 2, and Robert Montgomery to JM, 5 Aug. 1805, and n. 1.

§ From James Seagrove.[1] *2 September 1805, "Town of St Mary's in Georgia."* "Although
I have not the pleasure of being personaly known to you, still I think it not improbable that you know something of my character: but if not, if you will please
enquire of the Senators or Representatives from Georgia in Congress, they will
inform you. For some time past, I have observed that the newspapers of our country have said much respecting a misunderstanding between the United States and
Spain; and of late it would seem as if a rupture between them, was at no great
distance. This, Sir, has led me to the freedom of addressing a line to you at this
time; and to communicate to you my candid opinion on the present state of the
Province of East Florida. Allow me in the first place to inform you, that I have
resided chiefly at this place ever since the year 1785. during which period I have
been several times commissioned by this State, and once by the United States,
on business of importance with the Spanish Government. This, together with a
personal, and intimate acquaintance with every Spanish Governor, and public Officer of that province since the year 1784, as well as a general and neighbourly intercourse with all the inhabitants, I have been enabled from year to year, to form a
prety correct statement of the population, Military force, as well of regular
troops as milita. The strength of their garrisons, the disposition of the Inhabitants toward the Spanish government; and what would be their conduct in case
the United States, should find it convenient to take possession of that country. At
the request of President Washington, a confidential correspondance took place
between him, and myself, on this subject which doubtless may be seen among his
papers. My early, and uniform attachment to our truly happy Republican government, will not allow me to pass over any opportunity wherein I think I can be
servicable to its interest. To be brief, Sir, should our Country, unavoidably be involved in a War with Spain, in my humble opinion the conquest of East Florida
would be an easy matter. And I should conceive it a wise measure to take immediate possession of both the Floridas. My motive for so doing at the commencement
of a War, or even befor a declaration, would be, to prevent these provinces being
strongly garrisoned by Spanish or French troops: or perhaps from political reasons, taken possession of by the latter: which in my opinion would be a most unfortunate event for our country. They would be restless bad neighbours, and rivals
in our Agricultural, and commercial pursuits. If any nation but the United States,
are to hold the Floridas: In Gods name, let it be the supine indolent one that now
has them. From it, we run no risque on any score: But should either France, or

Britain, possess them, they will have it in their power to injure the United States beyond calculation. They could from them, furnish lumber of almost every kind for the West India & European market—Also Ship timber such as live Oak & red cedar in abundance. Naviel Stores to a great extent. The culture of Cotton, Coffee, Sugar, Rice, Indigo, Corn, Hemp & Tobacco would in a few years be immense. The climat being good would invite numerous settlers; and these provinces would soon become heavy and troubleson [*sic*] on the most vulnerable flank of the union. I am unacquainted with the present situation or strength of West Florida: but as to that of East Florida, I can speak decidedly, and you may rely on the following as being correct. The only fortress in that province is St Marks Castle, or Fort, at St Augustine. This is a regular bull work, of stone in the modren stile of fortification tho now very old and much out of repair. It mounts about Twenty five pieces of cannon from 12 to 24 pounders, has a ditch and glacis—it stands at the North entrance to the town, and commands the approach by water from the bar. The grounds in front of the fort are on a level with it—there are old lines of earth in front of the Fort, which was thrown up by the British, during the American War; but are now nearly in ruins. Governor White is an old Soldier, and I believe as far as rests with him will do his duty to his country: But he has not the means of defence—not having more then Two hundred & fifty Spanish Soldiers, and these the meanest possible: And it's possible he might be able to get from 150 to 200 Men of all discriptions in Town and country to join him. There is no navil force whatever—so situated his defence could not be long. Nine tenths of the inhabitants in the Country are Americans born, the cheif part of whom have settled there on Account of giting lands on easy terms. These Men, as well as others, dispise the Spanish government; and with proper attention and management would take arms in favour of the United States. The force that I should conceive fully adequate to the reduction of, and keeping possession of East Florid would be as follow's—

2000 Infantry, Regulars & Militia
300 Militia Horse Men, from Georgia
50 Artillery Men
4 to 6 Gunboats such as these sent to the Mediteranean.

The Army to march by land from St Mary's, there being a good road all the way and but one river (the St Johns') to cross. In Florida would be found abundance of fresh beef and forage—Salt provisions & Flour must be brought from the Northward. The town & garrison of St Augustine never has beforehand, Six months provisions, and seldom three. A few Bomshells thrown into the Castle would cause a speedy surrender—whilst, & preceeding the attack, the Horse would cut of all supplies from the Town, & secure the Country and property therein. An expedition of this kind would I am convinced be very popular in Georgia, and that a large body of volunteers might immediately be had in this State.

If a War should take place, and an attempt on Florida be contemplated, I shall be happy in rendering every service in my power. And should the President of the United States, require further or more minute information I will with pleasure afford it, whenever he is pleased to call for it. Please excuse the freedom I have taken; and let this communication be confidential with the President & yourself."

Adds in a postscript: "There is now in this place, a Frenchman of the name of Verminet, who has been employed in the Comissareit line by the French in St Domingo: but now resides in Augustine. This man, is just returned from the City of Washington, where he has been to the French Minister to lay plans before him for takeing possession of Florida. I think well to mention this report tho' its, probable it may have come to your knowledge already."

RC (DLC). 4 pp.

1. Irish native James Seagrove (ca. 1747–1812) emigrated to America before the Revolution, became active in business in New York, Philadelphia, and Havana, and occasionally procured supplies for the American army. He moved to St. Marys, Georgia, in 1785, where he established relationships with both Spaniards and Indians along the Georgia border. He also had connections to the British firm of Panton, Leslie & Co. at Pensacola. In 1789 he was named collector at St. Marys, from which post he resigned in 1798. In 1791 he was named agent to the Creeks, and in 1792 he was named inspector for St. Marys (Richard K. Murdoch, ed., "Documents Pertaining to the Georgia-Florida Frontier, 1791–1793," *Florida Historical Quarterly* 38 [1960]: 323; Abbot et al., *Papers of George Washington: Presidential Series*, 3:307; *Senate Exec. Proceedings*, 1:15, 105, 262; Robbie Ethridge, *Creek Country: The Creek Indians and Their World* [Chapel Hill, N.C., 2003], 130).

§ From Fulwar Skipwith. *2 September 1805, Paris.* "I have the honor to inform you of my being about to depart from this for the United States and that I have authorized my Colleague Mr. Barnet to fill my place during my absence.

"The several marks of confidence and favour with which the President and yourself, Sir, have been pleased to honor this gentleman, leave me no doubt but my choice of him will meet your approbation—and under the belief that the Voyage I am going to undertake will be justified by the motives which have determined me to it and which I shall have the honor of making known to the President on my arrival at Washington—I shall say no more at present than to enclose Copies of the Letters I have addressed on this Subject—to the Ministers of the United States and of Exterior relations,[1] to which I respectfully beg your reference."

RC and enclosures (DNA: RG 59, CD, Paris, vol. 1); Tr and Tr of first enclosure (ibid.). RC 2 pp.; in a clerk's hand, signed by Skipwith. Minor differences between the copies have not been noted. For enclosures, see n. 1.

1. Skipwith enclosed copies of (1) his 29 June 1805 letter to John Armstrong (2 pp.), informing the latter of his impending visit to the United States and his designation of Isaac Cox Barnet as acting consul, and asking Armstrong to inform the French government of the change and to obtain an exequatur for Barnet allowing him to act as U.S. consul at Paris; and (2) his 2 Sept. 1805 letter to Talleyrand (2 pp.; in French), requesting a passport for his departure, offering to carry any dispatches Talleyrand might have for French agents in the United States, and announcing his selection of Barnet to serve as interim acting consul.

¶ To Jacob Wagner. Letter not found. *2 September 1805*. Mentioned in Wagner to Jefferson, 5 Sept. 1805, DLC: Jefferson Papers, as saying that JM had hoped Dolley was "considerably advanced to a cure, but that it was found unavoidable, in order to complete it, to resort to an expedient two days before, which retards the event a little."

From James Bowdoin

no. 78.

Conduit St. Hanr. square
London sep. 3d. 1805.

Sir,

In my last from this city dated on the 31st. of July last, I informed you of my safe arrival here, & that the voyage from St. Ander with the journey from the sea coast, had proved favourable to my health, which I have the satisfaction to add, has become so much improved, that I have reason to hope for a perfect re-establishment—insomuch that I contemplate quitting this city for Paris in the course of two or three weeks, or sooner if possible, where I shall wait to receive your further instructions. In the mean time, it is proposed, that mr. Erving shall proceed from hence to madrid as soon as possible, in order to relieve mr. Pinkney, & to attend to our political concerns, or to receive any overtures, which the Govt. of Spain may see fit to offer.

Immediately upon my arrival here, Mr. Monroe stated to me, that he was glad to see me in this country from political motives, admitting that the state of my health had not required my coming. I told him, that I had been much perplexed, whilst at St. ander, to know what course to pursue; that I had heard of the failure of his negociations, & readily foresaw, that the arrival of a new minister from the U.S. uninstructed upon the events of the negociation, would be placed in an awkward situation, & would serve to encourage the spanish governmt. in the belief of having pursued a judicious policy towards the U.S. So fully apprized were mr. monroe & Colo. armstrong of this circumstance, that mr. monroe informed me, that they had written a joint letter to mr. Pinkney, stating it as their opinion, that in the present posture of our affairs, it would be quite improper "to treat on the concerns, wch. formed the object of the late negociation, untill["] I should receive your further instructions, or at least untill the sense of our Govt. upon the failure of the negociation shd. be fully ascertained: and he added, that he should take the earliest opportunity of acquainting you with this circumstance. I should have gone to Paris to have sought the advice which I have happily found here, but my health was too feeble to admit of my traveling so great a distance by land, which added to the prospect of meeting both mr. monroe & mr. Erving in the event of coming here, determined me upon this place, rather than Paris.

Since my arrival here, I have become acquainted with the several points in our controversy with Spain, wch. I observe have been fully stated to you by mr. monroe in his details of the negociation. Although I think they point clearly to the cause of its failure, I shall yet forbear an expression of that opinion, untill I shall have investigated at Paris, the causes of its failure. I conceive it notwithstanding my duty to say, that mr. monroe appears to have done every thing, wch. could have been done under existing circumstances, & that I consider his communications with the spanish governmt. were both able & spirited.

The Negociations with Spain being broken up, one of two alternatives seems only to remain, either to relinquish our claims, or to vindicate them by spirited & decisive measures: In the latter case, it is probable that the Spanish govt. rather than take the consequences of an open rupture, would recede from the high ground, it has taken: Oppressed as Spain is on every side, her commerce ruined & the people from a thousand causes, dissatisfied, if the govt. was left to itself, & to the wisdom of its own councils, it is hardly to be supposed, it would risk a contest with the united States, at the present critical conjuncture of its affairs: but allied & connected as it is with france, spanish prudence must be taken in connection with the interest & views of her ally: not as they stood at the time the late negociation was broken up, but with all their present Bearings & Relations: whatever might have been the views of the french Cabinet respecting our Claims & Demands upon the Spanish Govermt., the friendship of the U.S. will become too important to be put to hazard at the present crisis: the continental Coalition, which has been formed against both france & Spain has an impending aspect, must stifle lesser considerations & will probably give opening, *for a time at least,* to an amicable adjustment of our affairs with Spain. It appears to me therefore, to be very important, that our Governmt. shd. be decisive, take its ground, & as soon as possible pursue such measures as its present policy shall dictate & require. But if unnecessary delay shd. take place & the continental Coalition shd. prove unsuccessful, wch. is not improbable from the number & Skill of the french armies, france may find herself in a situation to have no motive, to aid our measures or to settle our disputes with spain, especially shd. she find herself able to turn her attention to the reconquest of St. Domingo, whcre she must see, that the blacks will derive support & receive supplies from the U.S.

Whilst the great powers of europe are convulsed & contending, the moment will prove favorable for the adjustment of our differences; and it appears to me, that the U. S. shd. be prepared for the occasion, to assert their Rights & to vindicate their claims, not only against Spain, but with france or England, if their Relations require it: But it cannot be done by temporizing measures: Europe must be made to feel, that we know our Rights & we mean to vindicate them; and in that vindication we must take the Risk of decisive measures. It ought to be well understood in the U. S. that no european nation has prejudices to our advantage; that they all envy our prosperity, & that we have more to apprehend from the hatred, than to hope from the friendship of any power. It is [. . .]tation [. . .] of the moment wch. govern, [. . .] Interest [. . .]des or policy directs, concessions may be hoped for & obtained. Please to excuse the freedom of these opinions, they are given with the best motives; and spring from the best Facts, I am able to procure. Please to present my most Regards to the President, & to believe [. . .] with high consideration & esteem—Sir, Your faithful & obt Servt

JAMES BOWDOIN

FC (MeB). Extensively damaged at left margin of last page.

§ From Henry Cooper. *3 September 1805, St. Croix.* "I beg leave to hand you, under cover, copy of a letter from his Excellency Genl. Muhlenfels (Commander in Chief of this Island) communicating to me in my Official capacity, a late Ordinance from his Danish Majesty—expressly declaring that no Vessels from the United States of America shall be admitted into any Port within the Danish Dominions without producing a Health Certificate from his Majestys Consuls & Vice Consuls resident at the different Ports within the said States.[1]

"You will be pleas'd, Sir, to lay this, [(]together with the Original Ordinance, also inclos'd) before his Excellency the President of the United States for his consideration."

RC and enclosure (DNA: RG 59, CD, St. Croix, vol. 1). 1 p.; docketed by Wagner as received 30 Sept. For enclosure, see n. 1.

1. The enclosure (1 p.; docketed by Wagner) is a copy of governor general Balthazar Frederik Mühlenfels's 30 Aug. 1805 notice of the Danish requirement that no ships coming from the United States would be admitted to Danish ports without a health certificate from the Danish consul or vice-consul at the port of origin. For an earlier report of Danish quarantine regulations, see *PJM-SS*, 9:246–47 and n. 3.

§ From Armand Duplantier. *3 September 1805, Baton Rouge.* Has received the letter that JM wrote to him asking him to locate the lands that Congress has granted to Lafayette.[1] Accepts the charge with pleasure. Will do all he can to locate them advantageously, wishing to be useful to Lafayette and to show a small proof of his own gratitude. Has not forgotten the kindness Lafayette showed him. Did not answer JM sooner because the fever he caught at New Orleans, which lasted the greater part of the summer and kept him in the country, prevented him from taking care of business, collecting information, and seeing things for himself.

Says there is very little good land to grant in Orleans Territory. The greatest part, especially the best part, has been granted by earlier governments. According to the information he has received, there is, on the Amite River and the lake[2] some beautiful land, but it is claimed by the owners of the Houma lands on the river, who claim that their property line extends to there and that they acquired their lands from the government as well as from the Indians.[3] Since their line not only extends for a great distance, but also opens out considerably, they take in at least twenty-five to thirty thousand arpents in area. According to what he has been able to learn, their claims are not well-founded; consequently, he has written to Governor Claiborne. If these claimants do not really have legal rights to those quantities of land, they will not keep it, in which case he would find a way to place the greatest part of Lafayette's grants there. Those lands would perfectly fulfill the object that JM proposed. They are in reach of the city, likely to grow promptly in value, and of good quality. One might also find on the Carondelet Canal a small portion of land, which, although low, would not fail to become of great value shortly, the canal being developed, and with the perspective of the incalculable growth which the city of New Orleans offers. Does not know of any other good land in Orleans region. If that which he is mentioning cannot be granted, it will be necessary to provide some from the other bank of the river, and he knows that area only imperfectly.

Mr. de Nemours,[4] who is on the Ouachita, where it is said that there are beautiful lands, and who wants to serve Lafayette as much as Duplantier does, could locate some of the grants in that area. The Opelousas and Atacapas country is also very beautiful country with beautiful lands. Will go to get information to learn if any of them are to be granted. Will also get information about the lands near Avoyelles[5] and the Red River. Being nearer than the Ouachita, they would better suit. Will conduct himself according to the information he gets from Claiborne. Begs JM to believe that he will neglect nothing for the greater advantage of Lafayette's interest, as he is flattered by the confidence Lafayette shows in him. If JM would care to address him, he will try to answer. Being a fellow countryman and companion-in-arms with Lafayette, will do everything for him. Moreover, Lafayette has had misfortunes which give him the greatest right to Duplantier's friendship. If he can be of any use to JM in that country, begs of JM to dispose of him, and he will do his best.

RC (DLC). 4 pp.; in French; docketed by JM.

1. See JM to Duplantier, 2 June 1805, *PJM-SS*, 9:424–26.

2. Lake Pontchartrain.

3. In 1803 Daniel Clark described the Houma Indians to JM as a small group living on "the Eastern Bank of the Mississippi about 25 leagues above Orleans" (Carter, *Territorial Papers, Orleans*, 9:62).

4. This was probably Charles-François-Adrien Le Paulmier d'Annemours (1742–1821), former French consul at Baltimore (Anne Mézin, *Les consuls de France au siècle des Lumières [1715–1792]* [Paris, 1998], 398–99). For an earlier reference to him, see JM to Duplantier, 2 June 1805, *PJM-SS*, 9:425.

5. Avoyelles Parish is located on the Red River (Carter, *Territorial Papers, Orleans*, 9:729).

¶ From Michael Walton. Letter not found. *3 September 1805*. Described in Jacob Wagner to Walton, 6 Sept. 1805, as enclosing papers regarding a claim for transporting seamen. Wagner told Walton that his account, together with supporting vouchers, should be sent to the Treasury (DNA: RG 59, DL, vol. 15).

From Charles Pinckney

DEAR SIR,   MADRID September 4 1805.

In my last[1] I informed you that the non arrival of Mr. Erving & the departure of Mr. Bowdoin for England, with the alarming captures made by the Spaniards on our Vessels since Mr. Monroe's departure, had detained me here very much against my inclination to that time—that I had however suffered my sense of public duty to prevail over my private interest & wishes, & while I conceived there was a necessity had in conformity with Mr. Monroe's opinion remained to keep open the intercourse & prevent this Court taking hostile measures, which would have been the case had I retired before, there being no one with whom I could with the least propriety have left our affairs—during the two last & present Month, a great number of our Vessels have been brought into Spain—this has occasioned a variety of representations & replies—a few of them have, in consequence, been released, & many condemned—in the affair of the United States Gun Boat, captured, I demanded explicitly the punishment of the Captain of the Privateer who took her,[2] & he is now in jail to be tried for it. I have had occasion to make such a number of remonstrances on the almost daily captures & condemnations that it has occasion'd the inclosed Letter, to which I immediately sent the answer also inclosed, & am hopeful it will produce a good effect.[3]

Hearing of nothing of Mr. Bowdoin or Mr. Erving, I am now preparing to set out for Lisbon in a short time on my return, & shall leave Moses Young Esqr. our Consul & Agent (whose arrival I announced to you) charged with our affairs here until Mr. Erving arrives, which I trust the President will approve of, as it is impossible for me to remain longer from home. I have done so for the five last Months much against my inclination, & merely from the motive I mentioned, there not being before any proper person with whom I could leave our affairs. The List of Vessels taken & condemn'd since my last will be forwarded in my next, & I hope to leave this in   [4] days for Lisbon.

Please make my affectionate Respects to the President, and believe me Dear Sir, always, Yours truly.

I wrote you from Aranjuez that I hoped I had induced this Court to adopt measures that would put a stop to the injurious attempts many foreigners who had resided a short time in the United States & had become Citizens & then quitted them were making, to buy prize & other Vessels & fit them out under the American Flag, thereby committing the honor of the Flag & the interests of our true Citizens. The orders I induced this Court then to issue, & the short one I sent to our Consuls in the several ports, have, I trust, altogether checked it, & it may be proper for you to say something on this subject to my Successor, enforcing the directions— these foreigners who have become Citizens of the United States & left them after being made such, with intentions most of them never to return, may & will do us great injury, if strict provisions are not made to guard against it. On this subject I have much to say to you when I see you, & which can be better explained verbally than by Letter.

RC and enclosures (DNA: RG 59, DD, Spain, vol. 6A). RC unsigned; in a clerk's hand; marked "(Triplicate)" by Pinckney; docketed by Wagner. Day of month not indicated; day assigned based on Wagner's docket on the enclosures: "Rec'd. in Ch. Pinckney's 4 Septr. 1805." For enclosures, see n. 3.

    1. Pinckney to JM, 9 Aug. 1805.
    2. For the Spanish seizure of an American naval gunboat, see *PJM-SS*, 9:489.
    3. Pinckney enclosed copies of (1) a 3 Sept. 1805 letter from Pedro Cevallos to the director general of the fleet (1 p.; in Spanish; docketed by Wagner; translation printed in *ASP, Foreign Relations*, 2:669) stating that if the only reason for the detention of U.S. vessels at Algeciras was that they were carrying English goods, they should be released, since article 15 of the 1795 Treaty of San Lorenzo recognized the principle that free ships make free goods; (2) an undated letter from Lewis M. O'Brien, vice-consul at Santander, to Pinckney which covered the first enclosure; (3) Cevallos to Pinckney, 3 Sept. 1805 (1 p.; in Spanish; docketed by Wagner), stating that Cevallos had received a note from the minister of marine saying that the reason some of the American ships had been brought in was that they were navigating without the passport required by article 17 of the Treaty of San Lorenzo, and adding that since this explained the detentions of which Pinckney had complained in various letters, it had seemed necessary to inform Pinckney of this so he could direct American captains not to omit carrying the passport, thus avoiding a repetition of similar detentions; and (4) Pinckney to Cevallos (2 pp.), 4 Sept. 1805, stating that he would forward Cevallos's letter to the United States; that he was sure no American ship ever sailed without a proper passport or sea letter but that the privateers who encountered American ships seized their papers and then claimed the ships never had them; and that the only remedy was for the king to issue an order to all Spanish tribunals that, in cases of American ships brought in without papers, they defer judgment until the captains had time to send to the United States to prove that they had carried them. Pinckney further suggested that copies of the treaty be sent to all maritime tribunals with orders that its injunctions be observed, adding that there were some judges who not only refused to obey it but claimed they did not know there was such a treaty. For articles 15 and 17 of the 1795 Treaty of San Lorenzo, see Miller, *Treaties*, 2:328–30, 332–33.
    4. Left blank in RC.

§ From Levett Harris. *4 September 1805, St. Petersburg.* "Since my letter to you of the 18/30 Augst. transmitted by the Vessels hereunder named, I have been invited to an interview of the Minister of foreign affairs. The Prince de Czartoryski in acknowledgeing receipt of my note, informed me that Russia had judged it prudent to conform to those measures which Denmark had deemed adviseable to adopt in relation to the quarantine of Vessels at Christiansand; but was Sorry to learn that any of our Ships should have had reason to complain of improper detention: he would write to Copenhagen, and by representing the grievance contribute to prevent its recurrence.

"I was attentive on this occasion to repeat to the Minister the terms of your letter, and to hand him a Copy of that part of your Circular, referred to, relating to the Subject in question—he observed at the same time that when the certificates of health granted to our Vessels sailing from the Ports of the United States were Countersigned by the Danish Consuls resident there, little or no difficulty or delay would be made to a direct admission of such Vessels at the sound, and recommended this certificate, or attestation of the danish Consuls, as an essential addition to the documents furnished by us on these occasions.

"On the 28 July last, at a publick masquerade and Entertainment given at the Palace of Petershoff at which I attended, the Emperor did me the honor to address me in a particular manner & inquired if I knew whether the President had received his letter, I answered I hoped it had come to hand, but that I had yet received no advice of it; that it was conveyed by way of Amsterdam, but as the winter had been very inclement on the American Coasts, & many Ships were wrecked, it was not improbable that some Accident had befell the Vessel by which his Majestys letter had been forwarded.

"The Emperor rejoined by saying, 'je vous donnerai une autre et Je'vous prierai en même temps de communiquer au President que C'est un duplicat.'[1] Accordingly the Prince de Czartoryski at this meeting handed me the inclosed letters, copies of those I had the honor to transmit you Sir, with my letter of the 1st. of January last."[2]

RC, three copies, and enclosure (DNA: RG 59, CD, St. Petersburg, vol. 1). First RC 3 pp.; dated "23 Augt./4. September 1805" in the Julian and Gregorian calendars; marked at foot of page: "Letter of 17/30 Aug. p Severn Capt. Sinclair Via Baltimore / p Hero Appleton Portsmouth, N.H."; docketed by Wagner. Second RC marked "*Duplicate*," with Harris's note: "(Original pr. Ship Severn, via Baltimore)"; docketed by Wagner. Third RC marked "*Triplicate.*" The *Severn*, Sinclair, arrived from St. Petersburg on 4 Dec. 1805 (*Baltimore Weekly Price Current*, 5 Dec. 1805). The *Hero*, Appleton, arrived in Boston Harbor on 9 Dec. 1805 en route to Portsmouth, New Hampshire (Boston *Independent Chronicle*, 12 Dec. 1805). For enclosure, see n. 2.

1. "*Je vous donnerai une autre et Je'vous prierai en même temps de communiquer au President que C'est un duplicat*": "I will give you another and I will ask you at the same time to communicate to the President that it is a duplicate."

2. The enclosure (1 p.; in French; certified as correct by Pierre d'Oubril; docketed by Wagner, with his note that it was received in Harris's 4 Sept. 1805 dispatch) is a copy of foreign minister Alexander Vorontsov to JM, 1 Jan. 1805, *PJM-SS*, 8:441 n. 2. The original was enclosed in Harris to JM, 1 Jan. 1805, ibid., 440–41. Harris presumably also enclosed in that letter a copy of Alexander I to Jefferson, 19 Nov. 1804, ibid., 441 n. 1.

§ From Tobias Lear. *4 September 1805, "On board the U.S. Ship Constitution Tunis Bay."* "The bearer of this, Sidi Soliman Mellamella, goes to the U. States, to present himself before the President, as Ambassador from His Excellency the Bey of Tunis;

as his Credentials &ca. will fully shew. He has been Ambassador from this Court to Naples and Genoa, appears to be a Man of Correct observation, and much liberality of sentiment.

"My public dispatches, which accompany this, will fully detail all Matters here. I give this to the Ambassador, by his particular desire, as a personal recommendation.[1]

"If any proper person can be found in Washington, who is acquainted with the Manners & Customs of these people, it would be desireable that such an one shou'd see that they are accommodated, as much in the Style of their Country, as the difference of Climate & circumstances will permit; as I know they will be very backward in expressing their Wants or Wishes, least they might not accord with our ideas of the propriety of things.

"Mrs Lear unites with me in every good & friendly wish for Your good Lady and Yourself."

RC and enclosure (DNA: RG 59, CD, Algiers, vol. 7, pt. 1); letterbook copy (owned by Stephen Decatur, Garden City, N.Y., 1961). RC 1 p.; docketed by Wagner, with his note: "Introductory of the Tunisian Ambassadr." For enclosure, see n. 1.

1. The enclosure (1 p.; in Italian; undated; translation printed in Knox, *Naval Documents, Barbary Wars*, 6:226, where it is dated 14 Aug. 1805) is a copy of Hammuda Bey to Lear stating that in order to convince Lear of his peaceful intentions and friendship for the president, in case Lear and Rodgers did not intend to treat with him without new orders from the president, he proposed to send a distinguished person to the U.S. government to explain everything and remove all difficulties between the two countries. He added that if Rodgers would receive his representative on board his or any other ship of the squadron, the ambassador would be sent immediately; otherwise the bey would send him in a ship specially chartered for the purpose.

§ From Thomas Newton. *4 September 1805, Norfolk.* "I have made inquiry after Mr Jas McHenry in this place & Portsmouth & can hear nothing of him. Mr Ashley a respectable Merch(ant) of this place informd me that Mr McHenry would not Act as Agent at Jamaica & that he ha(d) forwarded his commission to you:[1] from the accounts I have heard there are a vast number of our Citizen(s) impressed at that Island, our vessels are taken & al(l) the Crew forced into the Brittish service from report. A vessel belonging to this place was taken & Condem'd with her Cargo as Spanish property when she had never been in a Spanish port, but wholly own'd here. You will have this case laid before you, when you'l see the injustice done to us. I can see no other way of getting our men which [*illegible*] are impressed but by sending an American Agent, in a vessel to demand & bring them away, as they can not get passages home & if they should it is probable they will be again pressed by some other Man (o)f War & as to a Brittish subject acting as an Agent it will have little effect & make him live, very uncomfortably, with the officers of the Governmen(t) Ships of War."[2]

RC (DNA: RG 59, ML). 2 pp.

1. JM had been informed of James M. Henry's disinclination to go to Jamaica but had written to him on 20 July 1805 in an attempt to persuade Henry to accept the post.

2. On 13 Sept., Newton wrote again, saying, "the first letter you sent to Mr McHenry was delivered him & I understood from Capt Ashly that he would not take the office of Agent. Two packets are here for him, from yr department. I have made every inquiry, without obtaining any knowledge where he is. We never shall obtain our impressed men until a vessel is sent for the purpose of bringing them home, as soon as they get Clear of one ⟨s⟩hip they are taken by another. The Centaur & some other Ships, who have many of our men, are now at Halifax I have heard dismasted in a gale" (DNA: RG 59, ML; 1 p.).

From Jacob Wagner

Dear Sir   Department of State 5 Septr. 1805.

I have been honored with your favor of the 2d. Having concluded from that of the 26th. ult. that you would commence your journey homeward early this week I have ceased to forward the letters to you: the arrears are however now enclosed; with the exception of letters from Genl. Hull and Genl. Wilkinson,[1] detailing their installation, and some other papers of a secondary nature, which I forwarded to the President, under the expectation that they would be returned at the time of your arrival.

I have advised Dr. Rogers to obtain a certificate from Governor Claiborne of his services to the English invalids at New Orleans, and what they were worth:[2] they will thereafter fall within Mr. Merry's engagement to pay the expenses occasioned by those unfortunate men's arrival.

Mr. Gray, who handed me the communications from the Norfolk insurance company, will wait here or at Baltimore for the passports.[3] He acceded to my advice, that the cargo contemplated to be put on board the Express should be omitted. The passports are alike except the last clause in that to Genl. Turreau. I have a blank which will enable me to furnish one from the Department of State.

No dispatches have yet arrived from Salem respecting Mediterranean affairs, from which I conclude that at least the part of the rumour, which promised them, is unfounded.[4] You will find in one of the Charleston papers herewith the arrival of the Eliza from Gibraltar & Malaga, which left the former place on the 25 July & the latter on the 20th. She was informed on the 21st. by a Portuguese 74, that the peace was made. Though I believe the fact of peace, yet it is surprizing that in nearly two months (Rogers' letter to Degen is quoted as dated 1st. June) it should not have been known at either of the abovementioned places officially and with details. It ought even to have been known at Madrid by the 12 July, the date of Yznardi's letters. I am inclined to think that fame has done more than justice to Mr. Eaton, and that truth will attribute the event, if at all a reality, to the apprehensions entertained of the attack from our maritime force.

As the enclosed application from Mr. Merry has travelled so much, I regret that it must experience some further delay;[5] but this must be excused by the importance of the precedent it involves. No similar exemption from duty is known at the treasury; and as any exemption is a courtesy not every where reciprocated, it does not seem adviseable to extend it. It was refused to Pedersen, until he obtained a formal credential. Yet if Mr. Merry would claim it as for articles imported for the use of his suite or household, as the precedent would be avoided, it might well pass. Without such a general claim, it might be inferred that Mr. Foster had the privilege of free importation.

The drought has been felt here and as far Westwardly as Fort Cumberland, but was relieved by copious rains succeeding in a few days those experienced at Philadelphia. We experience an intense heat but without any diminution of the general health. From the knowledge I have of the progress of yellow fever, I despair of Philada. escaping a general visitation this season, in the districts most exposed to its attack from local attractions. I have been informed that you are situated in eighth street between Chesnut and Walnut St. which has generally escaped and which I hope may exclude apprehension during your stay. With my best wishes and respects to Mrs. Madison, I remain, Dr. Sir, With affectionate respect, Your obed. servt.

JACOB WAGNER

PS. Barney has presented bills to the amount of 300,000 francs & makes no doubt of the receipt of upwards of 200,000, more under the Convention.[6]

RC (DLC). Docketed by JM.

1. Wagner probably referred to James Wilkinson to JM, 28 July 1805, and William Hull to JM, 3 Aug. 1805, both of which were received on 31 Aug.

2. For the British invalids from the *Hero* who were treated at New Orleans in 1804, see *PJM-SS*, 8:304 nn. 2–3, 415 and nn. 1–2. JM wrote to Anthony Merry on 16 Jan. 1806, requesting reimbursement for the charges (letterbook copy [UkLPR: Foreign Office, ser. 115, 15:7–7v]).

3. No communication from the Norfolk Marine Insurance Company to the State Department has been found. On 14 Sept. 1805 the department issued the following passport, signed by JM: "To all to whom these presents shall come Greeting: the bearer hereof Mr. George Lewis Gray, is a Citizen of the U. States of America, and being charged by the Marine Insurance company of Norfolk in Va. to reclaim and recover some property insured by them, which has been recently captured and carried into the West Indies. These are therefore to request all whom it may concern to permit him to procced in the American Cutter Express— (which is to be unarmed and without any Cargo)—to the Island of Puerto Rico, the City of Santo Domingo, and elsewhere as may be requisite for the object above mentioned, giving to him no molestation, but affording him every aid, protection and facil-[it]y he may need. In faith whereof I have caused the seal of the Department of State for the sd. United States to be hereunto affixed. Done at the City of Washington, this fourteenth September AD 1805, and of the Independence of these States the thirtieth" (DNA: RG 59,

DL, vol. 15; 2 pp.). On 5 Sept. 1805, notes were sent from the State Department to Anthony Merry, Louis-Marie Turreau, and Carlos Yrujo requesting passports for Gray and the *Express* (calendared in the index to the State Department notes to foreign legations, DNA: RG 59, Notes to Foreign Ministers and Consuls, vol. 1).

4. The 4 Sept. 1805 *National Intelligencer* carried several reports from Salem and Boston, Massachusetts, dated 28 and 29 Aug., stating variously that William Eaton had achieved a great victory over Yusuf Qaramanli's army, slaughtering a large part of it; that in a battle at Derne all the Americans had been killed except Eaton, who was wounded; and that Tripoli city had been captured by the forces of Ahmad Qaramanli and Eaton. All the reports agreed that a peace had been made between Tripoli and the United States, with credit for the peace being given both to Eaton and to Tobias Lear; most of the articles reported the release of the American prisoners, and one added that "Several parcels of dispatches, directed to the President, and to the Heads of Department . . . were lodged in the Post-Office last evening. They were noted to be of high importance and ordered to be forwarded to the seat of government, without delay." The *National Intelligencer* also printed a 22 June 1805 letter from Frederick Degen at Naples stating that Samuel Barron had resigned command of the squadron to John Rodgers and adding that the latter had written Degen on 1 June 1805 that peace with Tripoli had been concluded on terms "most advantageous and honorable to the United States." Degen also gave credit for the peace to Eaton's military activities.

5. The enclosure has not been found, but for Merry's request for an exemption, see Albert Gallatin to JM, 31 Aug. 1805.

6. For Joshua Barney's claim against France, see *PJM-SS*, 7:170 and n. 3, 240–41, 565, 8:276, 9:117.

§ From Sylvanus Bourne. *5 September 1805, Amsterdam.* "I have just recd. a letter from our Consul in London in reply to one I wrote him on the subject of the late proceedings of the British Govt towards our flag[1]—in which he mentions that their Commanders of the Cruizers had far exceeded their orders in many cases as their conduct had been disavowed by Govt which shewed a disposition of making due reparation & that he had reason to hope our navigation would here after be free from similar embarrassments—this is pleasing news particularly as every appearance supports the belief that the War will in a few days break out again on the Continent—in which case the u[n]molested neutrality of our flag will be precious indeed to our Country."

RC (DNA: RG 59, CD, Amsterdam, vol. 1). 1 p.; docketed by Wagner.

1. See Bourne to JM, 30 Aug. 1805.

§ From Benjamin Lincoln. *5 September 1805, Boston.* "Your request of the 10th. of July last has been attended to. The fine Muslins nor the Diaper could not be procured here & a Billit of the Sweet meats & Coffee is inclosed."[1]

RC and enclosures (DNA: RG 217, First Auditor's Accounts, no. 18,370). RC 1 p.; cover sheet addressed to JM at Washington and redirected to Philadelphia; docketed by Wagner, with his note: "remittance to be made." For enclosure, see n. 1.

1. The enclosures (2 pp.) are Lincoln's account with the United States for $213.40 for "the Cost of 7 Boxes of Confectionary and 1 bagg of Coffee . . . for the use of the Dey of

Algiers," and Elisha Tichnor & Co.'s 3 Aug. 1805 bill to Lincoln for the same amount for limes, oranges, pineapple, ginger, and pears, with Boston navy agent Samuel Brown's 3 Sept. acknowledgment of receipt of the goods at the bottom, and Wagner's 10 July 1806 note on the cover: "The within articles were procured by order of the Secretary of State and were shipped to Algiers on the public account. They ought to be charged to the Barbary appropriations"; countersigned by JM. The Treasury apparently neglected to pay Lincoln because he wrote again on 6 June 1806, resubmitting his account (DNA: RG 217, First Auditor's Accounts, no. 18,370; 1 p.). Filed before Lincoln's account is Account no. 18,369 (1 p.), Samuel Brown's 21 Dec. 1805 account with the War Department for $222.27 for receiving and shipping ordinance and merchandise to Kennebec, Maine, to be forwarded to Algiers in accordance with a 9 Aug. 1805 request from Wagner. On the verso is Wagner's 10 July 1806 note: "The within account is justly stated and may be paid out of the Barbary Appropriations"; countersigned by JM.

§ To John Patrick. *6 September 1805, Department of State.* "General Armstrong, our Minister at Paris, having instructions to patronise the claims of Citizens of the United States, circumstanced like that which is the subject of your letter of the 29th. ult. [not found] I must request you to address it to him for his support."

Letterbook copy (DNA: RG 59, DL, vol. 15). 1 p.; addressed to John Patrick at New York.

§ To Elisha Tracy. *6 September 1805, Department of State.* "In answer to your letter of the 27th. ult. [not found] I have to observe, that until something further is ascertained respecting the subjects of negotiation with Spain, it would be difficult to judge what effect in accelerating the issue of your claims might be produced by your presence at Madrid: for the present therefore it may be sufficient to have forwarded your documents to our Minister."

Letterbook copy (DNA: RG 59, DL, vol. 15). 1 p.

To James Monroe

SIR,   DEPARTMENT OF STATE 7th. September 1805

Mr. Erving having been applied to by the Prussian Minister in London to procure information respecting the estate of a Major Ludeman, who died in Virginia in the year 1786, I inclose a copy of a letter from Mr. Hay, the District Attorney, in which its situation is fully explained.[1]

It has been found that the Records delivered as those of West Florida, whilst a British Province, are but a partial mass;[2] and as it is of importance to possess the whole if attainable, I request you to have the remainder sought for. Any moderate expence incurred in the search will be justified by the nature of the object.

The inclosed order of His Britannic Majesty to his vessels of War, tho' dated so far back as the 23d. June 1803 has made its public appearance only this summer by the way of Tortola.[3] In the mean time there is reason to believe that its penal effect has been extended to our navigation. Be pleased to inform me whether it is genuine, and how it has happened, that like every just modification of existing rules, by which others are to be guided, it has not been notified or published. Should it be found to have originated in the regular source, its concealment will not form the only topic of complaint against it, as the principle on which it is founded is far from being conceded.

Some time since I received for the use of this Department the first volume of the Reports of Judge Marriott.[4] If any additions have been made to the publication I should be glad to possess them, as well as a continuation of the statutes at large from the 3 G. 3 C.72 in a quarto form.

It appears that Frederick Balcke the subject of a former enquiry from Baron Jacobi,[5] is living at the town of Clermont in the Manor of Livingston in the state of New York, where he has continued to reside ever since he came to this Country. I have the honor to be &c

JAMES MADISON

Letterbook copy (DNA: RG 59, IM, vol. 6).

1. For Baron Jacobi-Kloest's request, see George W. Erving to JM, 1 June 1805, *PJM-SS*, 9:423–24 and n. 1. For the enclosure, see George Hay to JM, 2 Sept. 1805.

2. For the British land grant papers sent to the State Department in 1804, see George W. Erving to JM, 6 Feb. 1804, ibid., 6:442–43 and nn.

3. The 24 June 1803 order in council to the commanders of Royal Navy warships and to privateers ordered them "not to seize any neutral vessel which shall be carrying on trade directly between the colonies of enemies, and the neutral country, to which the vessel belongs, and laden with the property of inhabitants of such neutral country: provided, that such neutral vessels shall not be supplying, nor shall have, on the outward voyage, supplied the enemy with any articles contraband of war, and shall not be trading with any blockaded port" (*ASP, Foreign Relations*, 3:265). For the article to which JM probably referred, see the Philadelphia *United States' Gazette*, 8 June 1805.

4. JM referred to *Decisions in the High Court of Admiralty: During the Time of Sir George Hay, and of Sir James Marriott, Late Judges of That Court*, vol. 1, 1776–1779 (London, 1801).

5. For Baron Jacobi-Kloest's request for information on Frederic Baléke, see Monroe to JM, 7 Apr. 1804, *PJM-SS*, 7:73, 74 n. 1.

From James Wilkinson

SIR   ST LOUIS Septr 7th. 1805.

In my last of the 24th. Ultmo. of which you have a duplicate under cover, I fear I intruded on you some details touching the Indian affairs, which in propriety appertained to the department of War; I shall therefore by the pending mail address the Sequel of that Business to General Dearborn.

You have under cover, copies of the Instructions of Governor Harrison, to the Surveyor General of this Territory, and of a Proclamation issued by Major S Hunt, Commandant of the District of St. Genevieve[1]—By misinterpretation of the first, a right was pretended to Survey all unlocated Concessions or Warrants, And the Tenor of the last having excited doubts, as to the propriety of Surveying any, excepting compleat Titles, I have deemed it expedient in conformity to the injunctions of the Act of the 2d. of March, for ["]Ascertaining and adjusting Titles &c" to give the Orders to the Surveyor, which you will find in the copy of my letter to him of the 28th. Ultmo. under cover.

I have recently been advised that all the Lead mineral raised in the vicinity of Minè a Burton the Property of Mr. M Austin,[2] is taken from the Public Lands, and on making enquiry from the Commandant, why this was permitted, he informed me, that it was an indulgence, which had been granted by the Spaniards, and that being at a loss how to Act in the case, he had written to the Secretary of War for advise, but had received no Answer—under our Law I must consider it a Trespass On the public Land, and shall order off the Workmen, untill the pleasure of Government may be made known.

Sordid Speculations, particularly in Land, have I am fearful frequently produced mischiefs in our Country; I am therefore solicitous to discourage the prevalence of that Spirit in this Territory, and some discussions have of consequence ensued, in which my opinions have proved unpalatable. I contend that it is manifestly improper, for a Public Officer of the Territory, to enter into the purchase of Such Spanish Concessions as may be fraudulent in their Nature or deemed illegal by our Government—because the example is derogatory and tends not only to generate a false confidence, to the injury of innocent and ignorant Persons, but to league the Servants of the Public against the Public itself. The Commandant of St Genevieve who had entered into this Speculation, after being gravely admonished for the impropriety, justifies his conduct by saying that the paper is a matter of fair purchase to Public Characters or private persons, and that he had conversed with no public Officer, who had not agreed with him in opinion. If I am wrong Sir And you should deem it worth your attention, I will thank you to correct me, Otherwise your approbation of my Opinion may produce salutary Effects.

We are exceeding embarrassed for the want of a Printing Press and our population will not Support a public paper; We have two good compositors in the Territory, who have offered their Services to print the Laws &c; And as we are destitute of Funds, we must implore the aid of Government; for at present no Law can be generally promulgated, before it has been sent to Kentucky, there printed and returned. Should it be consistent for the Government to send forward a small Font of Types, with Paper Ink and

Apparatus, it would releive our difficulties and if required, the Territory will doubtless reimburse the expense. With Great Respect I am Sir Your Most Obdt. Servant

JA. WILKINSON

RC and enclosures (DNA: RG 59, TP, Louisiana, vol. 1); draft (ICHi). RC 3 pp.; in a clerk's hand, signed by Wilkinson; docketed by Wagner as received 12 Oct., with his note: "Public officers speculate in fraudulent titles. Printing press wanting." Minor differences between the copies have not been noted. For enclosures, see n. 1.

    1. Wilkinson enclosed copies of (1) William Henry Harrison's 8 Nov. 1804 instructions to Antoine Soulard (2 pp.; certified as correct by Soulard on 7 July 1805; docketed by Wagner; printed in Carter, *Territorial Papers, Louisiana-Missouri*, 13:71–72); (2) Seth Hunt's 24 Mar. 1805 proclamation forbidding land surveys (1 p.; certified by Wilkinson; docketed by Wagner; printed ibid., 110); and (3) Wilkinson to Soulard, 28 July 1805 (1 p.; in a clerk's hand, except for Wilkinson's complimentary close, signature, and interior address; printed ibid., 175).

    2. For details on the lead mine, see ibid., 210–11, 274–75.

    3. Merchant Moses Austin (1761–1821) became involved in lead mining in Virginia in the 1790s and in 1796–97 explored the lead fields of southeastern Missouri. He obtained a Spanish land grant; established the town of Potosi; expanded the mine with an improved furnace, shot tower, and sheet-lead plant; and built saw and flour mills. He carried on these several businesses for the next twenty years but lost everything when the Bank of St. Louis failed in 1816. Following the panic of 1819 he moved to Texas and applied for a permit from the governor to settle three hundred families there. He died before completing this enterprize. Stephen F. Austin, colonizer of Anglo-American Texas, was his son.

§ From James Anderson.[1] *7 September 1805, Montpellier.* "I have had the honor to address You under date of the 28 June last,[2] in original, duplicate & triplicate, and then took the liberty to enclose a list of the American Vessels which have arrived in the Port of Cette, since the 31 december 1801. I also endeavoured to draw Your Excellency's attention to my particular & unpleasant situation, and from a firm persuation of the imposibility of paying my expences by residing at Cette, I have taken the resolution of going to Marseille, where I hope to be more fortunate.

"My good friend Mr. Walsh of this City, has promised me every possible assistanc⟨e⟩ in his power, and I flatter myself that our mutual efforts will redound to the commercial advantage of Our fellow-Citizens, as we are both determined to make use of promptitude & integrity, in their behalf.

"As the interest of The United Stat⟨es⟩ require, that during my absence from Cette, some One should fill the Office of Commercial Agent, I have therefore though⟨t⟩ fit to name Mr. Walsh, which appointment I sincerely wish may meet Your Excellency's approbation. Mr. Walsh will do himself the honor to write to You, Sir, upon the subject, and on my part, I beseech You to have me nominate⟨d⟩ Vice Consul for Marseille, provided it can be done without wounding the feelings of Mr. Cathalan.

"I cannot suppose, Sir, that Our truly worthy & respectable President, will ⟨be⟩ displeased at the step which I have taken, when I declare solemnly, that I have had many anxious moments, to know how to find the means to pay my expences, and I would rather cease to be an Agent of The United States, than to fill the Office in a manner unworthy of its dignity."

306

RC, two copies (DNA: RG 59, CD, Cette, vol. 1); RC (DNA: RG 59, LAR, 1801-9, filed under "Anderson"). First RC 3 pp.; marked "Duplicate"; docketed by Wagner. Second RC marked "Triplicate." Minor differences between the copies have not been noted.

    1. James Anderson (d. 1824) was a native of Charleston, South Carolina, who was in business in the West Indies in the 1700s and served as consular agent at Nantes after 1793. In 1803 he was appointed commercial agent at Sète (Cette); in 1807 he was named agent for seamen and commerce at Havana; and on 18 Jan. 1811 he was named consul at Gothenburg, Sweden. He died in Baltimore (Providence *Rhode Island American*, 19 Mar. 1824; Boyd, *Papers of Thomas Jefferson*, 24:423-24 and nn.; William Patterson to JM, 9 Nov. 1806, DNA: RG 59, LAR, 1801-9, filed under "Anderson"; JM to Anderson, 22 Jan. 1807, DNA: RG 59, IC, vol. 1; *Senate Exec. Proceedings*, 2:162).

    2. *PJM-SS*, 9:499-500.

§ From the Marqués de Someruelos. *7 September 1805*. By the schooner *Rose*, Capt. [*illegible*] Bolton, received on 8 July JM's letter of 11 June with a copy of another written to the marqués de Casa Yrujo,[1] both relating to JM's complaint about the seizure of the frigate *Huntress*, which is said to have been by a Spanish privateer, while the *Huntress* was carrying munitions to the Mediterranean squadron. Sent a circular order to the commanders with jurisdiction in the various ports of Cuba so that, if it should have arrived in one of their districts, they could proceed immediately to determine the case according to law and if the merits of the case result in the declaration of a good prize, the final steps should be taken accordingly and the original proceedings sent to Havana, so that the Departmental Tribunal may consider the merits of the case and decide on what is just.

    Has not yet received a reply about the result of this order; but the governor of Cuba, and the lieutenant governor of Puerto Principe have informed him that the *Huntress* has not been brought into those ports by any type of privateer: and, in order not to delay the answer to JM any longer, shares on this occasion the results of the decisions that the referenced individuals resolved on, waiting to give the other advices still pending, if by them the introduction of the vessel into any of the ports of this island should appear; adding to the knowledge of his government.

    As in case it should be certain that the indicated seizure was by a Spanish vessel, and the prize should arrive in a port of this island, the cognizance of the proceedings of the privateer in this matter belongs not to the jurisdiction of this government, but to that of the navy; has instructed the commander of the navy about the expressed complaint, so that in his wisdom he may take the precautions which he may consider suitable: has also immediately given the necessary warnings to the governor of the defenses of Cuba and the lieutenant general of the interior departments of the island, so that they may supply the assistance that might be needed and might be requested, for the fitting out of the frigate in question, if a suitable person should claim their assistance in order for it to continue its voyage.

    The navy commander answered on 12 July that no record existed in the fleet under his authority of the taking of the frigate *Huntress* and that, notwithstanding the uncertainty about the place where she may have been taken [. . .][2] that by the governments of the two Floridas, no notice has been given him that such a prize had been taken to those stations.

FC (AGI: Outgoing Papers from Cuba, vol. 1660). 6 pp.; in Spanish.

1. For JM's 11 June 1805 letters to Yrujo and Someruelos, see *PJM-SS*, 9:452–53, 454.
2. It appears that one or more pages are missing at this point.

§ From Peter Walsh. *7 September 1805, Montpellier.* "The inclosed Letter from Mr James Anderson[1] advises your Excellency of his determination to go immediately to Marseilles to Seek a livelihood, which he has not been able to make here, and of his leaving me encharged with the affairs of his Agency till your intentions respecting it are made known to us. And I beg leave to assure your Exy. that in the mean time every attention shall be paid by me to the duties of that Office.

"As a Citizen of the U S., holding a Commercial House here and at Cétte I would presume to offer myself to the President as a Candidate for that appointment, which I would endeavour to fill with advantage to them. I am known to Mr. Skipwith and to most of the Merchants in America."[2]

RC, two copies (DNA: RG 59, LAR, 1801-9, filed under "Walsh"). First RC 2 pp. Second RC marked "Triplicate." Both RCs docketed by Jefferson.

1. See James Anderson to JM, 7 Sept. 1805.
2. On 23 Dec. 1805 Jefferson named Walsh as commercial agent at Sète (Cette) (*Senate Exec. Proceedings*, 2:10–11).

§ From John Graham. *8 September 1805, New Orleans.* "I have now the Honor to inclose a Copy of all the Acts passed at the first Session of the Legislative Council of this Territory & shall very soon forward on a copy of those passed at their last Session."

RC (DNA: RG 59, TP, Orleans, vol. 7). 1 p. Enclosure not found, but see n. 1.

1. Graham doubtless enclosed a copy of *Acts Passed at the First Session of the Legislative Council of the Territory of Orleans* (Shaw and Shoemaker 9072).

§ From William Lee. *8 September 1805, Bordeaux.* "Should Mr Hammond of New York, or Capt. marner, commanding his ship Susan & Sarah make any complaint to you, of my official conduct I beg you will do me the favor to peruse the pieces accompanying this, relating to their improper discharge of Geo: Bender, the mate of the said Ship.[1]

"It is one of the many cases, I have every week to decide on, and I should not have troubled you with it, had not the above mentioned Gentlemen shewn particular acrimony, in this affair, and frequently expressed their determination of attacking me on it, in the United States. This appears to be the mode of revenge of every unprincipled person, to whose views I have been hostile.

"Permit me to observe that Mr Hammond & marner have protested against me for having detained as they state their Ship when the fact is she has been expedited from my office for these four days past and I find they have not yet left this City.

They have also offered to take their mate on board the Ship after he had been shipped ten days on board of another Vessel and after they had forced him by depriving him of lodging & sustenance to quit the Susan & Sarah on the 18th. August and to remain on shore nineteen days."

RC and enclosures (DNA: RG 59, CD, Bordeaux, vol. 2). RC 2 pp. For enclosures, see n. 1.

1. Lee enclosed copies of (1) his 24 and 27 Aug. 1805 summary judgment (9 pp.) in the disagreement between Capt. Richard Marner and mate George Bender of the *Susan and Sarah*, stating that Bender had complained to Lee on 18 Aug. that Marner had locked Bender out of the cabin and stateroom, locked up all Bender's clothes and other possessions, told the crew to ignore Bender's orders, fired him as mate, and refused to pay him the wages due him. On 24 Aug., Marner accused Bender of neglect of duty, sleeping on watch, getting drunk, refusing to paint the ship's trim, being absent from the ship without leave several times, and finally deserting the ship. He acknowledged doing what Bender accused him of but said it was because of Bender's own actions. Four members of the crew testified that although Bender had refused to paint the ship, it not being his duty, he had said he would have it done; that he sometimes lay down for an hour or so after dinner, and spent several nights on shore but always returned early enough to distribute work to the crew; that he would sometimes arise early, give the crew their tasks, and return to bed until breakfast; that they had never seen him drunk; and that they could not state that they had actually seen him sleeping on watch. In his 24 and 27 Aug. judgment Lee said that since the testimony did not uphold Marner's charges, and since Henry Hammond and Marner refused to have Bender back, Marner should pay the funds due into the consulate, after which he would be free to appeal the case in the courts of the United States; (2) Marner to Lee, 3 Sept. 1805 (1 p.), repeating his charges against Bender; (3) Lee to Marner, 4 Sept. 1805 (1 p.), enclosing an account of the funds due from Marner to Bender, stating that until the amount was paid, he would not release the papers for the *Susan and Sarah*, and asking Marner to point out any errors that existed; (4) an undated detailed account (1 p.) of the funds due Bender, those already paid, and the remainder; (5) a 30 July 1805 letter from Marner to Bender (1 p.) enclosing Lee's passport for Bender to be on shore and mentioning that it was only good for twenty days; (6) Lee to Bender, 27 Aug. 1805 (1 p.), stating that he had rendered judgment on the differences between Bender and Marner, that Bender could request a copy or read it in the consular records, and that Bender was free to sign on any vessel he could find, and if it was bound to the United States, Bender would receive, over and above his wages due from Marner, two months' pay; (7) Hammond's 5 Sept. 1805 protest before a local notary (3 pp.; in French) that he and Marner had done all that was required in offering to take Bender, the mate who had deserted, back on board, that Lee was acting contrary to U.S. maritime law in absolving Bender of everything and ordering Marner to pay the wages due to Bender plus three months' more, that because neither Hammond nor Marner would agree to this, Lee had refused to return the ship's papers, which were necessary for a safe voyage, that if Lee continued to refuse them, the ship would sail without them, and Lee would be responsible for anything that might happen to the ship because of the absence of the papers; the notary added that a copy of the protest had been left with a servant at Lee's home; and (8) Richard Marner's 6 Sept. 1805 declaration before another French notary (4 pp.; in French) claiming that Bender had been absent without leave from the *Susan and Sarah*, that he had neglected his duties, that he drank so much as to deprive himself of reason, to which the entire crew could attest, that once Bender left the ship, Marner had no desire to pursue him, that Marner was surprised, when he called on Lee to recover his papers, to learn that Lee demanded money for Bender, that he told Lee

U.S. law exempted him from paying anything to a deserter, that to put an end to the disagreements he had claimed Bender's return to the ship, that Lee refused this and continued to retain the ship's papers until the money for Bender was paid, and that Marner was now holding Lee responsible for any losses because of the delay in the ship's departure and the payment Marner was forced to make for Bender. For sections 3 and 4 of the 28 Feb. 1803 "Act supplementary to the 'act concerning Consuls and Vice-Consuls, and for the further protection of American Seamen,'" requiring ship captains to pay three months' wages to the consul for each seaman discharged in a foreign country, two months of which was for the seaman and one month of which the consul was to deposit into a fund for the transporation and care of such seamen, see *U.S. Statutes at Large*, 2:203–4.

§ From Anthony Merry. *8 September 1805, Philadelphia.* "I received to-day the Honor of your Letter of the 5th. Instant,[1] and have that to send you inclosed the Passport you have requested for Mr Gray, and for the Vessel in which he is about to embark."

RC (DNA: RG 59, NFL, Great Britain, vol. 3). 1 p.; in a clerk's hand, signed by Merry.

1. The letter has not been found, but for the probable contents, see Jacob Wagner to JM, 5 Sept. 1805.

To Albert Gallatin

Dear Sir   Philada. Sepr. 9. 1805

On the rect. of your favor on the subject to which the letter of Mr. Merry to you now inclosed relates,[1] I wrote to the office of State to know whether in any former instance the indulgence claimed by Mr. Foster had been allowed to a Secy. of Legation. It appears that there has not, during the presence of the Minister Plenipoy. I do not find however that it has been refused. The probability is that no application in such cases has been made in the name of the Secy., and that the privilege has been enjoyed under that of the Minister. If You think it not amiss to consider Mr. Merry's letter as a claim from him in right of the legation, you may consider this as giving my sanction to this request. If you doubt on the point, it may wait for the determination of the President.

Mrs. Madison is still in the hands of Docr. Physic. For several days appearances have been so favorable, that if there be no hidden flaw, which is certainly possible, We promise ourselves that we may get away in 7 or 8 days.

The fever has taken strong hold of Southwark, and cases begin to be sprinkled thro' a great part of the City. The best informed however indulge hopes that the precautions used will keep it under. I see with concern that N. York is threatened with a similar visitation.

310

Mr[s]. M's affectionate wishes accompany mine to Mrs. Gallatin your-self & the young ladies. Yrs. truly

JAMES MADISON

Gavino informs me that the late captives at Tripoli had arrived in Sicily. His letter is of July 12. He did not know the terms of the Treaty; but in-closed a copy of a letter to him from Rogers, speaking of them as favorable & honorable. He says the Bacris & Busnachs with all the other principal Jews at Algiers had been massacred by the rabble who wish to get an Arab Administration in place of a Turkish. The Pre[s]ident is to be in Washing-ton Ocr. 2. He is anxious to receive the opinions asked by him on the span-ish subject, and the measures it requires.

RC (NHi: Gallatin Papers).

1. The enclosure has not been found, but see Jacob Wagner to JM, 5 Sept. 1805, and n. 5.

From John Graham

SIR   NEW ORLEANS 9th. Sepr. 1805

I had the Honor to write you by the last Post[1] to let you know that a White Man had been taken up here for endeavouring to bring about an Insurrection among the Negroes, and I have now the Honor to inclose a Copy of a Letter from the Mayor of this City,[2] giving the best account that can be had of this Man, of his Plans, and of the Progress he had made towards their execution.

The Circumstance of an Insurrection having been planned, and the un-certainty how far the plan may have been acted upon, gives to the People here a very considerable degree of inquietude & alarm. I have the satisfac-tion however to say, that every possible precaution is taken by the Police Officers & I beleive that nothing is at present to be apprehended, more than at any other time; but I consider this country as in a state of constant danger & therefore as requiring the presence of a considerable Military Force—and if I might be permitted to give an opinion I would recommend an increase of the Regular Troops here, as a measure equally expedient, whether we have in view the Submission of the Black, or the Respect of the White Inhabitants of the Country. With Sentiments of the Highest Respect—I have the Honor to be, Sir, Your Mo Obt Sert,

JOHN GRAHAM

RC and enclosure (DNA: RG 59, TP, Orleans, vol. 7). Docketed by Wagner as received 15 Oct. For enclosure, see n. 2.

1. See Graham to JM, 2 Sept. 1805.

2. The enclosure (10 pp.; docketed by Wagner; printed in Carter, *Territorial Papers, Orleans,* 9:500–504) is a copy of John Watkins to John Graham, 6 Sept. 1805, reporting that a slave named Celestin had given him information that a white man called Le Grand had proposed that Celestin join in a conspiracy to incite a slave insurrection in New Orleans. Watkins arranged to have several "free people of colour" who would pretend to enter into the conspiracy introduced to Le Grand. After these men reported their conversations with Le Grand, Watkins, Col. Joseph Bellechasse, and Maj. Eugene Dorsière surrounded at night the cabin in which the conspirators, real and pretended, were meeting. Le Grand was arrested and confessed that his real name was Grandjean, that he was a French native who had lived for two years in Saint-Domingue, that he had fled the colony when the whites were being massacred, and that he had come to New Orleans by way of Baltimore and Kentucky. Watkins doubted Le Grand had revealed his proposed conspiracy to anyone other than Celestin and the free people of color sent by Watkins but expressed concern that the situation of the city, in which there were 4,000 whites and nearly 12,000 nonwhites, both free and enslaved, demanded the utmost vigilance on the part of the government. He added that more slaves were being introduced into the territory daily in spite of laws forbidding it. He suggested that the number of troops in the region be increased, that "native Americans" be encouraged to move to the territory, and that "we should root out from among [us] the agents and influence of foreign Governments."

§ From Jacob Ridgway. *9 September 1805, Antwerp.* "I have the honor to acknowledge receipt of your Letter of the 20th. May last relative to the ship Mac of Charleston[1] and of a Packet [not found] containing my Commission to this Agency adressed to the Emperor of the French, which Commission I have Sent to our Minister at Paris to be presented to this Government in order to obtain the necessary Exequatur.

"Enclosed you have Duplicates of my last Respects of the 31st July and of the Report List of the American Vessels entered and Cleared at this Port from the 1st Jany: to the 30th June 1805."

Adds in a postscript: "I have offered the ship Mac to Mr. Menet, a Merchant of this City who represents the owner on Condition of reimbursing the Expences already incurred, but have not yet received an answer.

"Should this Vessel not be accepted on these terms Please let me know if I may give her up, the United states sustaining the loss of the Expences incurred to this day. In this last event I shall wait your ulterior authorisation in as much as it may be practicable with my Obeying that part of your Letter which orders me, *in no event to incur expence in Keeping the attachment any longer in force.*"

RC (DNA: RG 59, CD, Antwerp, vol. 1). 2 pp.; in a clerk's hand, signed by Ridgway. Enclosures not found.

1. *PJM-SS,* 9:373.

§ From Louis-Marie Turreau. *9 September 1805, Philadelphia.* Encloses the passports requested in JM's 5 Sept. letter[1] for the cutter *Express* of Norfolk, sent by the insurance company of that city, and for George Lewis Gray, agent for the company in the different colonies.

RC (DNA: RG 59, NFL, France, vol. 2–3). 1 p.; in French; in a clerk's hand, signed by Turreau; docketed by Wagner.

1. The letter has not been found, but for the contents, see Jacob Wagner to JM, 5 Sept. 1805.

From John Armstrong

Sir   Paris 10th. Sept. 1805.

The note of which the annexed paper (Number 1)[1] is a copy was put into[2] by direction of Mr. Talleyrand who was then on the point of setting out for the camp at Bologne. The person charged with the delivery of it having no official relation to the minister and *but little personal acquaintance with me tho' sufficiently known as a political agent of the Govt. supposed that some introductory credential might be necessary* and *accordingly submitted the official manuscript. It was the handwriting of Mr. T—d. Informed[3] of communication he said had been prefered on account of greater security; it was a proof of the minister's habitual circumspection* and *of nothing else. The communication itself wanted no explanation. It obviously grew out of the interest taken by France in the adjustment of differences which ought not to become wider.* This interview ended with an assurance on my part that I was equally persuaded of the correctness of the motives which in this Step had influenced both the *minister and the government and that I should transmit the note to the president as early as possible. A second conversation took place between this person and myself on the 4 which you will find detailed in Number 2 annexed.[4] The note as illustrated presents a full development of French policy on this subject.* The moment of their putting it into motion may have been somewhat hastened by the expected war. *All possible means of raising money are tried and this may be regarded as one of the expedients.*

Mr. Skipwith will give you the current news of the day. A fact not publicly known & somewhat interesting is the plan of the projected Campaign. The grand army of 160,000 men in seven divisions, each commanded by a Marshal, & the whole by the Emperor, crosses the Rhine on the 30th. and takes the road to Vienna. Their movements will be, like those of their Leader, rapid & vigorous. Messina in upper and Jordan in lower Italy, will persue a defensive system. With the greatest possible respect, I am, Sir, Your most obed. hum. Servt

                                              John Armstrong

RC and enclosures (DNA: RG 59, DD, France, vol. 10). RC in code; decoded interlinearly by Wagner. For enclosures, see nn. 1 and 4.

1. The enclosure (1 p.; docketed by Wagner) is a copy of a note suggesting that the United States indicate to Spain that if that government would not negotiate the question of limits, the United States would be forced to take "such measures as shall appear to them the most efficacious." The note added that should Spain not agree to this, a copy of the communication from the United States to Spain should be sent to the French government mentioning "the evil consequences" that would follow and asking Napoleon to mediate, in which event Spain would no doubt agree to the U.S. proposal. The note listed the following conditions as acceptable to France: (1) Spain and France to have the same trading privileges in the Floridas as they had in Louisiana; (2) the boundary between U.S. and Spanish territory to be the Colorado River beginning "in the Bay of St. Bernard & a line northwardly including the head waters of all those rivers which fall into the Misisippi"; (3) thirty leagues on either side of the Mississippi to remain perpetually unoccupied; (4) debts due from Spain to U.S. citizens, except those for French spoliations, to be paid by bills on Spanish colonies; and (5) the United States to give ten million dollars to Spain.

2. "My hands" was probably omitted here.

3. Encoded "informed"; decoded "This form."

4. The enclosure (4 pp.; docketed by Wagner) is a copy of a transcription of the conversation between Armstrong and Talleyrand's emissary, "M," in which M stated that the submitted propositions had been tendered in confidence, that they could be sent to Jefferson but it was expected that the latter would not make them public; M then asked if Armstrong had had time to consider them, to which Armstrong replied that no consideration was necessary as a glance sufficed to show that they were totally lacking a reciprocity that could be the basis for a permanent and honorable agreement with Spain. Armstrong listed his objections, stating that the United States would yield three of the four points in controversy and settle the fourth in a way only advantageous to Spain. M responded that by the terms of the proposal, the United States would round out its territory to the south and the west, obtain clear unmistakable boundary limits, obtain command of the mouths of the rivers watering its interior territories, gain one of the finest harbors in that part of the world, add nearly twenty million acres in territory, and settle all this amicably and honorably and without disturbing the tranquility of its citizens. M warned that although the United States might have the power to start a war, the ability to end it might not be so certain. Armstrong replied that the United States could solve matters by taking possession of the territory between the Mississippi and the Rio Grande and seizing the Floridas as indemnity for Spanish debts, to which France could not object, having just acknowledged the legitimacy of U.S. claims. M then stated that it appeared the true sticking point was the sum of ten million dollars and suggested that seven million would do, to which Armstrong replied that he could "say nothing on the subject of money," and the discussion apparently ended.

From Jacob Wagner

DEAR SIR   DEPARTMENT OF STATE 10 Septr. 1805.

With this you will receive among other communications an interesting letter from Genl. Armstrong.[1] I have sent a duplicate of the List of claims liquidated finally and an extract of the letter respecting them, for the use of the Secretary of the Treasury. The 20,000 florins referred to in the correspondence respecting the Wilmington Packet stands in the name of the Secretary of State, to the use of the true owners, in the Bank of the U.States. There being other classes of claimants beside those who have applied to Genl. Armstrong, it is necessary that the clashing pretentions should be judicially decided upon by interpleading. I shall be obliged by your signing the exequaturs and the letter for Pedersen[2] & sending the package to him or to the Post office.

Dispatches have been received at the Navy office and forwarded to Mr. Smith at Baltimore, announcing the details of the cessation of hostilities with Tripoli and the liberation of the Prisoners. We have nothing by the conveyance. I do not know the particulars with a precision, which would authorize me to repeat them. I fear however that a considerable sum of money has been given, and that the intentions of the Govt. with respect to the Exile Achmet have not been so amply fulfilled as they would have desired.[3]

I this day forward to Genl. Turreau your answer to his letter respecting Genl. Moreau.[4]

The Secretary of War departed yesterday for Monticello. I remain, Dear Sir, faithfully & affecty. Your most obed. servt.

JACOB WAGNER

RC (DLC). Docketed by JM.

1. The enclosure has not been found, but it was probably John Armstrong's letter of 3 July, discussing the settlement of U.S. citizens' claims against France.

2. See Peder Pedersen to JM, 26 Aug. 1805.

3. For the article of the treaty with Tripoli dealing with the return of his family to Ahmad Qaramanli, see Tobias Lear to JM, 5 July 1805, n. 8.

4. The letter has not been found, but was doubtless the one of 30 Aug. 1805 described in the index to Notes to Foreign Ministers as "relative to Genl. Moreau" (DNA: RG 59, Notes to Foreign Ministers and Consuls, vol. 1). For Turreau's request that Moreau's stay in the United States not be marked by demonstrations, see Turreau to JM, 14 Aug. 1805.

§ From Carlos Martínez de Yrujo. *10 September 1805, "Near Philadelphia."* Last night received JM's much appreciated letter of 5 Sept.[1] and this morning takes up his pen in order to confirm the receipt and to enclose the passport JM requested for George Lewis Gray, agent of the Marine Insurance Company of Norfolk, to proceed to various ports in the West Indies for the purposes mentioned.

RC (DNA: RG 59, NFL, Spain, vol. 2). 1 p.; in Spanish; in a clerk's hand, with Yrujo's complimentary close and signature; docketed by Wagner.

1. The letter has not been found, but see Jacob Wagner to JM, 5 Sept. 1805, and n. 3.

To Charles Pitt Howard

Dear Sir   Philad. Sepr. 11. 1805.

I was presented a few days ago with a sample of Wheat from Buenos Ayres, and of Barley from Old Spain. Being deprived of the opportunity of putting them into the ground myself, I know not that I can dispose of them better than into your hands.[1] I have no particular reason to suppose that either has any peculiar merit; but it may be the case; or they may improve by a change of climate. Such experiments are at least curious, and multiply the chances of discovery.

You see that peace has at length been made with Tripoli, & our Captive Citizens delivered from the House of bondage. The particular terms are not yet officially known, but are every moment expected.

The yellow fever makes considerable havoc in Southw⟨ark,⟩ and creeps about in different parts of the City. A good many families have withdrawn from the Scene. I called on your father lately & found him very well.[2] I believe he is of that number. From a wish to keep my wife within a convenient reach of Dr. Physic, we have stood our ground thus long; but propose to remove this afternoon to Grays, where I have engaged quarters, a greater distance from the City would have been preferred; but the attendance of the Docr. even there is as much as can be reasonably expected.

I cannot yet say when I shall have the pleasure of seeing my friends in Orange. I anxiously wish it, and shall not lose a moment after the recovery of my wife will permit. She is considerably advanced towards it; but I fear it will be 8 or 10 days at least before she will be discharged by the Doctor. I wish it may not be longer. She offers her affectionate respects to Mrs. Howard, to which be so good as to add mine; & to accept for yourself assurances of the sincere esteem & regard with which I am Dr Sr Yrs.

JAMES MADISON

RC (ViHi).

1. Philadelphia-born Charles Pitt Howard (1765–1856) moved to Orange County, Virginia, around 1792 and served as sheriff, justice, and magistrate at different periods. He was married to JM's relative Jane Taylor Howard, and owned over five-hundred acres in the county. In 1811 he purchased land located just east of Montpelier known as "Howard Place." The antebellum plantation manor house "Mayhurst" now stands on the property (Ralph Dornfeld Owen, "Howard, An Early Philadelphia Family," in *Genealogies of Pennsylvania Families: From the Pennsylvania Genealogical Magazine* [3 vols.; Baltimore, 1982], 2:63–65; *Richmond Enquirer*, 6 Jan. 1829; Ann L. Miller, *Historic Structure Report: Montpelier, Orange County, Virginia; Phase II; Documentary Evidence Regarding the Montpelier House, 1723–1983* [Orange, Va., 1990], 73; DI: National Park Service, HABS No. VA-1082 [Rebecca Trumbull, "Historic American Buildings Survey: Howard Place (Mayhurst)," (unpublished manuscript, 1981), 1]).

2. John Howard (1727–1809) ran a joinery and furniture business in Philadelphia and owned many buildings and lots in the city. Several members of the Howard family were Quakers, and John apparently had lived in Orange County with Charles Pitt Howard for some years (Owen, "Howard, An Early Philadelphia Family," *Genealogies of Pennsylvania Families: From the Pennsylvania Genealogical Magazine*, 2:55–60).

From William Hull

Sir.   DETROIT 11th. Septr. 1805.

I have received your letter of the 1st. of August inclosing Mr. Grangers communication to the President of the United States.[1] Inclosed is a Copy of the proclamation, I have issued in consequence of it.[2] It has excited much uneasiness, and the best people here, are of the Opinion it will produce much distress, to those who have suffered by the calamity of the fire. Boards have allready risen four or five dollars pr. thousand, and none can now be obtained excepting from the British side of Lake and the River St. Clair. It is expected they will still take greater advantages of the situation in which the people are placed by this measure. Constant applications are making to me for releif, but the order from the government being possitive, I consider no discretion is left to me on the subject.

I do not learn that British Subjects have lately committed trespasses on this property. The people on this side, had long been in the habit of procuring timber from this pinery. Our own Citizens have been in the practice of it this summer. The Indian title having never been extinguished, no persons can have a legal title to the land, and consiquently it must be a trespass and a violation of the laws of the United States. It is however a fact, that improvements have been made for near thirty years on a part of these lands, and for a long time mills have been erected by private Individuals. They consider themselves entitled to the consideration of the government, in consiquence of their Indian title, and their long possession & improvement. A great part of the property in this territory is held by the same title, with this difference, that the property is of a different kind, (viz) cultivated farms, and more limited as to quantity. I put out of the question entirely Claims of large tracts under Indian titles, where there has been, neither possession or improvement.

The measure which has been adopted by the goverment seems to have made this impression, that it is their intention, in settling the titles, to observe rigid law, and that no consideration will be made for improvement and long possession.

The subject of Titles not being within my province, I should not have mentioned it, had it not been to explain one of the causes of the great sensibility which has been excited. Previous to this, every thing was tranquil, and satisfactory, the new Town was progressing in regular form & with great rapidity. I would therefore suggest for the consideration of the goverment, whether it would not be expedient, to authorize the government of this Territory, to grant permission to the suffering Inhabitants to cut and carry away as much of the timber as will be necessary to releive their immediate necessities. This however not to be general, but under a particular licence in each particular case. This will enable them to enclose their houses, so as to be comfortable, and prevent the unreasonable advantages which will otherwise be taken from the other Shore. It is painfull to me to make any suggestions against a measure, the goverment have thought proper to adopt. I have done it under a conviction, that had all the circumstances of the case been known, a different arrangement would have been directed. I am with very great respect, your most obedt. Servt.

WILLIAM HULL

RC and enclosure (DNA: RG 59, TP, Michigan, vol. 1). Docketed by Wagner as received 3 Oct. For enclosure, see n. 2.

1. For Gideon Granger's letter to Jefferson, see Jefferson to JM, 23 July 1805, and n. 1.

2. The enclosure (printed in *Michigan Pioneer and Historical Collections* 31 [1902]: 536) is a copy of Hull's 4 Sept. 1805 proclamation, stating that by the president's orders Hull was forbidding everyone from trespassing on the government lands and cutting government timber and that all government officers, particularly the marshal of the territory, and citizens were to apprehend offenders and bring them to justice. In 1902 the enclosure was in volume 1 of the Territorial Papers for Michigan in the National Archives; in 2013 it could not be found.

§ From William C. C. Claiborne. *11 September 1805, "Territory of Orleans Concordia."* "Since my letter of the 27th Ultimo, I have experienced a severe Indisposition. For sevn days my Fevers were incessant, and my Death was esteemed by myself and Physicians a probable event. But it has pleased Almighty God still to prolong my life and I feel now as if my Health would soon be restored. I had had in contemplation, to visit the Posts of Ouachita and Nachitoches; but my strength is so enfeebled from my late Attack, that I must thro' necessity decline the Journey.

"It is my intention to return to New Orleans, about the last of this Month; in the mean time, I am persuaded the public Interest will sustain no Injury by my absence: The care of the City is commited to the Mayor, Doctor John Watkins; a very vigilant and prudent Officer, and there is no doubt, but he will discharge with fidelity the Trust confided to him.

"I presume Governor Williams's communications will inform you, the particulars of the Arrest of the Kempers. The manner of the Arrest, was certainly

highly exceptionable, and it is not probable, that the Spanish Authorities will attempt to justify the measure.

"At the date of my last letters, every thing was quiet at New Orleans; there had
been some little Alarm, in consequence of an attempt made by a Frenchman to
excite the Negro's to Insurrection; but the Frenchman was arrested, and the uneasiness had subsided."[1]

RC (DNA: RG 59, TP, Orleans, vol. 7); letterbook copy (Ms-Ar: Claiborne Executive
Journal, vol. 15). RC 2 pp.; in a clerk's hand, signed by Claiborne; docketed by Wagner as
received 15 Oct. Minor differences between the copies have not been noted.

   1. For this incident, see John Graham to JM, 2 and 9 Sept. 1805.

§ From William C. C. Claiborne. *11 September 1805, Concordia.* "I now have the
Honor, to enclose you a Copy of the assurance given me in writing by Mr. Moralis, that he would not during his residence in this Territory, make any disposition
of Lands lying west of the Perdedo."[1]

RC and enclosures (DNA: RG 59, TP, Orleans, vol. 7); letterbook copy (Ms-Ar: Claiborne Executive Journal, vol. 15). RC 1 p.; in a clerk's hand, signed by Claiborne; docketed
by Wagner, with his note: "Parole of Morales."

   1. The enclosures (7 pp.; in English and Spanish; docketed by Wagner as enclosed in
Claiborne's 11 Sept. 1805 letter; printed in Carter, *Territorial Papers, Orleans,* 9:490–93) are
a copy of Juan Ventura Morales to Claiborne, 19 Aug. 1805, and an English translation. In
the letter Morales stated that the king's authority had been insulted in his person, that
Spanish interests might be damaged as a result of the inaction Claiborne demanded regarding the sale of lands in the unquestionably Spanish territory of West Florida, and that the
assurance that Claiborne had forced him to give, that he would not sell land, would not
prejudice in any way the titles to lands already sold and to those still vacant. Morales then
promised, while still maintaining his preceding objections, that he would not take any actions regarding the lands west of the Perdido River.

§ From Peter Kuhn Jr. *11 September 1805, Genoa.* "I have the Honour to transmit
you herewith Copy of my last under date 2d Inst original Via Bordeaux.

"I take the earliest occasion Sir to inform you that General Massena who takes
the Chief Command of all the Armies of Italy, passed through Milan on the 8th
Inst. and arrived the same day at Brescia where he stoped. The two regiments
under Orders since the 1st. departed from hence on the 7th. Inst."

RC (DNA: RG 59, CD, Genoa, vol. 1). 1 p.; docketed by Wagner.

§ From Joseph Seaward. *12 September 1805, "St. Juans (Porto Rico)."* "When depredations on neutral property by powers at war, become the order of the day, when
no respect is paid to existing Treaties, I conceive it a duty incumbent on every
individual to note every such infringement and to give advice of it to the Executive of that Government to which he belongs.

"As I am unaccustomed to a forensic style I shall simply relate my own case, and whatever has come under my immediate observation during my short stay in this Island. I left Norfolk on the 1st. June last in the Brig Catharine bound for the Island of Antigua, laden with a cargo of provisions & lumber, where I arrived, & sold said Cargo. I left the Island of Antigua on the 29th. July, with a return cargo, bound back to Norforlk [*sic*]—on the 4th. August in Lat. 23°, 10″ N. & Longte. 65°, 00″ west, was captured by the French Brig called General Blanshot, John Baptise de Brux, commander and sent into one of the ports at the west end of this Island.[1] The Privateer plundered me of my stores & ships provisions & part of the cargo. The Vessel was immediately striped of her sails & rigging & sent on shore, my people taken out put on board of another Vessel & sent out of the Island. Under these circumstances I came to the City & applied to the Governor requesting his interferance, stating to him that my papers were perfectly regular and that my capture was of course illegal—and I likewise requested him to order security to be given for the amount of my Brig & Cargo as the Agent of sd. Privateer was a resdt. Mercht. of this City. But all my representation has been to no effect. He has absolutely refused to take cognizance of my business. My papers remain in the hands of Mr. Duabon the Agent of the Captors. I may be detained here many months to come & the Vessel & Cargo exposed to a total loss. My trial, if any I am to have, must be by the determination of this Government either at Martinique or Guadeloupe—thus under the present circumstances this Island may become the Asylum of Pirates & Robbers. No pretence has been given for my capture, as I came from English Island I *might* have English property on board—at the time of my capture, my Cabin Boy was carried on board the Privateer, and put in Irons, threatened with severe chastisment unless he would declare that Specie was deposited in some part of the Vessel. This attempt proving fruitless, I now (in all probability) must be the victim of measures dictated by men without principles of honesty or honor. Thus far as relates to myself, I shall now take the liberty of relating to you some other particulars that have com(e) under my observations. At my arrival at the Port of my Entry on the West end of the Island & found at Anchor the Brig Susanna of Portland (Me.) the Captains name I do not recollect. Said Brig arrived the day before & prize to the same Privateer. She was from Portland bound to Jamaica & was taken on her outward bound passage with a Cargo of Fish & Lumber, said Brig was immediatly unloaded, & ballasted with sand, and without more ceremony the Capt. & Crew of sd. Vessel, together with the Mate & Crew of my own Vessel were shipped off with a very scanty supply of provisions & left to search for the first port they could make. On the 4th. inst. arrived the Brig Polley of Triverton [*sic*] (R.I) Capt. Trip; and the 5th. inst. the Schooner Mary Ann of Boston Capt. Anthony & bound to the Island of Barbadoes, loaded with Cattle & Horses and provision under Deck. They are prizes to a Spanish Vebeck [*sic*] from Cadiz bound to Vere Cruz. The Captains live still on board with their Crews, and may remain so for many days to come—*While* the Captor & his Agent are prosecuting every measure to effect the condemnation of sd. Vessels as lawful prizes."

Tr (DNA: RG 233, President's Messages, 9A–D1); Tr (DNA: RG 46, President's Messages, 9B–B1). Beneath Seaward's signature is written: "native of New Hampshire and resident of Virginia." First Tr 4 pp.; marked "No. 3." Second Tr is a letterpress copy of first Tr.

1. In a 10 Oct. 1805 statement at Antigua, Seaward said the privateer, which was called the "General Blarishot," was the brig *Leon* that had sailed from Charleston, South Carolina, to Africa and returned to Martinique with slaves. He said the ship was jointly owned by John B. de Brux, who served as supercargo, and Charleston merchant Stephen LaCoste. At Martinique, LaCoste sold the slaves, took on sugar, and carried it to St. Thomas, where he sold the sugar and converted the brig to a privateer. The *Catharine* was carried into Aguadilla, Puerto Rico, and stripped. Seaward said the agent at Puerto Rico was a Mr. Dubon. The privateer was also referred to as the "General Blanchet" (*New-York Commercial Advertiser*, 15 Nov. 1805; Hagy, *People and Professions of Charleston, South Carolina*, 55; *New-York Gazette & General Advertiser*, 9 Nov. 1805).

From Jacob Wagner

DEAR SIR   DEPARTMENT OF STATE 13 Septr. 1805
    The original of the enclosed letter from Mr. Monroe having become much disfiguered and rendered confused by the process of decyphering, I have had it copied, and the rather as it enabled me to send a copy to the President.[1] You will have seen the arrival of Mr. Monroe in London stated in the newspapers; and thus ends the negotiation with spain under any existing powers in Europe. Be pleased to sign the enclosed duplicate & Triplicate of the last letter to Mr. Monroe.[2]
    I received to day through the post office a small box containing two vials with a liquid resembling wine: being sealed I could not ascertain what it is.[3] The box was addressed to you, but is unaccompanied by any explanation, except that it came by the Ship Robert, Capt. Alcorn. With respect & attacht. Your obed servt.

                                                        J. WAGNER

RC (DLC).

    1. This was probably Monroe to JM, 30 June 1805 (*PJM-SS*, 9:504–7).
    2. See JM to Monroe, 7 Sept. 1805.
    3. For the wine, see William Jarvis to JM, 5 July 1805, and John Brice Jr. to JM, 31 Aug. 1805.

§ From Elias Vander Horst. *13 September 1805, Bristol.* "On the other side is Duplicate of My last of the 28h. with PS of the 30h. Ulto. ⅌ the Maine, Cap. Rossiter, for New-York, since which I have not been honored with any of your favors.
    "Enclosed I beg leave to hand you a few of our latest News-Papers, to which please be referred for what is now passing in this quarter of a Public nature. Politicks are so wrapped up in Intrigue & mystery here, that it is extremely difficult

to m⟨a⟩ke any calculation on them that can be depended on. My opinion on them however, is not materially alter'd 'though there is at present certainly a much greater *appearance* of a war on the Continent taking place than there was a short time since, but all this may possibly have a more speedy termination than People in general expect. The weather for the Harvest still continues favorable, from which I conclude our Crops of grain will be tolerably good as the greate⟨r⟩ part is now Housed; many suppose them abundant but I am not one of that number—the Crops of Roots are fine & that of Potatoes in particular will be very ample."

Adds in a postscript: "Enclosed is also a London Price Currt. of this date [not found]."

RC (DNA: RG 59, CD, Bristol, vol. 2). 2 pp.

¶ To Jacob Wagner. Letter not found. *13 September 1805*. Acknowledged in Wagner to JM, 16 Sept. 1805, as dated at Gray's Ferry, Pennsylvania.

To Thomas Jefferson

DEAR SIR   GRAY'S NEAR PHILADA. Sepr. 14. 1805

I inclose herewith sundry communications which I recd. yesterday. One of them is from Monroe at Paris, who appears by a letter from Erving to have arrived at London the latter end of July.[1] A letter from Armstrong went for you by the last mail.[2] He seems to have moderated the scope of his former advice as to Spain. In that now given, there is in my judgment, great solidity. If force should be necessary on our part, it can in no way be so justly or usefully employed as in maintaining the status quo. The efficacy of an imbargo [*sic*] also cannot be doubted. Indeed, if a commercial weapon can be properly shaped for the Executive hand, it is more & more apparent to me that it can force all the nations having colonies in this quarter of the Globe, to respect our rights. You will find in Erving's letters new marks of his talents.

I enclose also a sample of wheat from Buennos Ayres, another from Chili, and a sample of Barley from Galicia in Spain. The Wheat from B. A. I observe is weavel-eaten, and the paper when opened contained a number of the insects. If these are not known at Buennos Ayres, and the wheat, as I presume, was in this sample immediately from that province, it is a proof that the egg, if laid in the green state of the wheat, is also laid after it has been gathered. This fact however has been otherwise established, I believe. The whole was sent me by the Marquis d'yrujo to be forwarded to you. I have sent what he marked for myself to a careful gentleman in Orange;[3] so that there will be two chances for the experiment. The Marquis recd.

despatches by the vessel which brought Moreau. I did not doubt that they communicated his recall and the demand of it; till I was told by Merry a few days ago, that the Marquis signified to him that he should pass the next winter in Washington. Perhaps this may be a finesse, tho' I see no object for it. Mr. & Mrs Merry left Bush hill a few days ago, and are now at the Buck tavern about 11 miles on the Lancaster road, where she is sick with an intermittent, with which she was seized at Bush hill. Her maid was so ill that it was suspected hers was a case of yellow fever. It turns out to have been a violent bilious fever only, and she is on the recovery. Merry himself is at length discharged by Dr. Physic as *fundamentally* cured.[4]

The fever began to shew itself in so many parts of the City, & so far westwardly, that we thought it prudent to retire from the scene; the more so as it was probable that a removal would be forced, before my wife would be ready to depart altogether, and it was becoming very difficult to find in the neighborned [sic] quarters unoccupied by fugitives from the City. We were so lucky as to get rooms at this place, a day later and we should have been anticipated by others. How long we shall be detained here is uncertain. Mrs. M's complaint has varied its aspect so often, that altho' it seems now to be superficial & slight, it is not subject to any exact computation of time. If there be no retrograde perverseness hereafter, we are promised by appearances that she will be entirely well in a few days.

The fever rages severely in Southwark, and is very deadly. The cases in the city are as yet not perhaps very numerous. But no reliance is to be put in the accuracy of the statements published. There were certainly cases in 8th. Street two weeks ago which were never published. In the mean time the Medical corps continues split into opposite & obstinate opinions on the question whether it be or be not contagious. Each side puzzles itself with its own theory, and the other side with facts which the theory of the other does not explain. There is little probability therefore that the discord is near its term. The facts, indeed, which alone can decide the theory, are often so equivocal as to be construed into proofs on both sides.

I brought with me from Washington, the subject I had undertaken before you left it; I mean the new principle that a trade not open in peace, can not be opened by a nation at war to neutral nations; a principle that threatens more loss & vexation to neutrals than all the other belligerent claims put together.[5] I had hoped that I should find leisure in Philada. to pursue the subject & with the greater success, as some books not at Washington would be within my reach. In the latter particular I have not been entirely disappointed. But such were the interruptions Of visits of civility & of business, that with the heat of the weather, & the necessary correspondence from day to day with the office, I could make but little progress, particularly during the first three or four weeks after my arrival. I find my situation here more favorable, and am endeavoring to take advantage of it.

I shall in fact before I leave it, have a very considerable mass of matter, but it will be truly a rudis indigestaque moles.[6] From the authorities of the best Jurists, from a pretty thorough examination of Treaties, especially British Treaties, from the principles and practice of all other maritime nations, from the example of G. B. herself, in her laws & colonial regulations, and from a view of the arbitrary & contradictory decisions of her Admy. Courts, whether tested by the law of N. the principle assumed by her, or the miscalled relaxations from time to time issued by the Cabinet, the illegality of this mischevous innovation, seems to admit the fullest demonstration. Be assured of the respectful attachment with which I remain yrs.

JAMES MADISON

RC (DLC: Jefferson Papers). Docketed by Jefferson as received 2⟨1⟩ Sept., with his note: "Spain—neutral rights."

1. See Monroe to JM, 30 June 1805, *PJM-SS*, 9:504–7, and George W. Erving to JM, 25 July 1805.

2. The letter has not been found, but it may have been John Armstrong's of 3 July 1805, referred to in Jacob Wagner to JM, 10 Sept. 1805, and n. 1.

3. See JM to Charles Pitt Howard, 11 Sept. 1805.

4. For Anthony Merry's hemorrhoid surgery in the fall of 1804, see *PJM-SS*, 8:322 n. 1.

5. JM referred to his pamphlet, *An Examination of the British Doctrine, Which Subjects to Capture a Neutral Trade Not Open in Time of Peace* (Shaw and Shoemaker 10776), which was published anonymously and laid on the desks of the members of Congress in January 1806 (Brown, *William Plumer's Memorandum of Proceedings in the U.S. Senate*, 388).

6. *Rudis indigestuque moles:* a rude and undigested mass (D. E. Macdonnel, trans., *A Dictionary of Select and Popular Quotations, Which Are in Daily Use: Taken from the Latin, French, Greek, Spanish and Italian Languages. . . .*, 4th. Amer. ed. [Philadelphia, 1824], 261).

From George Jefferson

DEAR SIR   RICHMOND 14th. Septr. 1805

I have duly received your favor of the 9th.,[1] and am sorry to inform you, that the price of Tobacco still continues low; indeed I apprehend that even the price which Mr. G.[2] informed you he had been offered for yours, could not be now obtained.

There has been a very great drouth with us, of which probably you have heard—and which has injured the growing crop I am told immensely: this certainly ought to operate much in favor of the holders of the old crop, and I suppose will; unless a change still more unfavorable, takes place in the European markets. At present however, the fever which is making its appearance in the Northern Towns, operates much against us—when that subsides, I think we may look for a demand, which will almost insure a better price.

I think therefore it will be advisable still longer to hold your Tobacco. As to the Coal, I suppose it may be bought on some little credit; but if it cannot to the same advantage, the amount will be but trifling, and we'll advance it.

It will not be the smallest trouble for us to procure it, as I suppose the President will require his usual supply, & it can be shipped together.

Should your expensive trip, (which I take for granted must be so) or any other circumstance, cause you to stand in need of money, if you will send G.&J.[3] your note, *negotiable at the Bank of Virginia*, it can be discounted without any difficulty, or inconvenien[ce] to them and you can draw for its amount at a few days sight, should you meet with an opportunity of disposing of a draft; or if not, it can be remitted to you as you may direct.

This arrangement will give time to dispose of the Tobacco to the best advantage.

I most sincerely hope that Mrs. M. is fast recovering, and am Very respectfully Dear Sir Yr. Mt. Obt. servt.

GEO. JEFFERSON

RC (DLC). Docketed by JM.

1. Letter not found.
2. Gideon Gooch, JM's overseer.
3. For the firm of Gibson & Jefferson, see *PJM-SS*, 9:350 n. 2.

"Extracts from Longs Hist. Jamaica"

[ca. 14 September 1805]

"At the breaking out of the war with Spain in 1739, admiral Vernon was ordered 'to distress and annoy the Spaniards in the most effectual manner, by taking their ships, and possessing himself of such of their places & settlements as he should think it practicable to attempt, *and in convoying & protecting the British subjects in carrying on an open and advantageous Trade with the Spaniards in America.*' This instruction shewed much wisdom, and a perfect knowledge of what will always be our best interest upon these occasions"[1]

Vol. 1. p. 338–9.

"The first complaint of a scarcity, as well as I remember, was about the year 1760, when the island was drained extremely low by the sudden current its silver took to Hispaniola, on opening their ports there, & the Harbour of Monte Xti, to our illicit traders chiefly North American vessels, most of which went in Ballast under Jamaica Clearances; and carried off such great sums in gold & silver, *to lay up French produce*, that our Island was extremely distressed; the trade of it languished, & the assembly caused about 100,000 dollrs. to be stamped, & issued at two percent cash advance, on their former rate, in order to keep up a fund for the internal circulation"[2]

vol. 1. p. 535.

"In 1669 Spain, for want of ships & sailors of her own, began openly to hire Dutch shipping to sail to the Indies, tho' formerly so careful to exclude all foreigners from thence, And so great was the supply of Dutch manufactures to Spain &c that all the Merchandize brought from the Spanish W. Indies was not sufficient to make returns for them, so that the Dutch carried home the balance in money."

Note. page 598.[3]

Ms (DLC). Undated; conjectural date assigned based on the assumption that these notes, and the two documents following (which are filed together), are part of the material JM had accumulated for his writings about the British doctrine forbidding neutral trade with belligerents, mentioned in JM to Jefferson, 14 Sept. 1805. For Edward Long's *History of Jamaica*, from which JM quotes, see Peter S. Du Ponceau to JM, 8 July 1805, n. 14.

1. In the margin of this paragraph, JM has written: "proof of the avidity of England to share in the Spanish Colonial Trade in time of war."

2. In the margin of this paragraph, JM has written: "This might Stimulate the project of intercepting the neutral trade in French produce at Monte Xti: but was rather meant to prevent the N. Amns. from carrying money from Jama. & preferg. French produce to that of Jamaica, than as a measure agst. neutral commerce."

3. In the margin of this paragraph, JM has written: "proof of Trade with Spanish Cols. by Dutch &c. & that there was room for the Distinction &c. if it had then existed, as now alledged by G. B. ☞ subjoin this to the note from Apx. 4 Rob. as to colonl. trade of France in 1705." In his pamphlet *An Examination of the British Doctrine, Which Subjects to Capture a Neutral Trade*, JM quoted this paragraph on p. 40. In his marginal note JM referred to footnote (*a*) in Robinson, *Admiralty Reports* (London ed., 1799–1808), 4:appendix 3, 22.

Notes on Neutral Trade

[ca. 14 September 1805]

(31)

The immediate effect of this *new* rule[1] is to entrap all neutrals which British cruisers may have previously seized in defiance of the rules actually binding on them; and all others which can be seized before a knowledge of the new rule reaches the neutral vessels sailing under the faith of the only rule known to them: besides the vexation delays expence & frustration of mercantile expeditions resulting from the eagerness of cruizers to take the chance of prizes, where such a pretext is furnished for the arrest of neutral commerce & where they are further encouraged by the almost invariable [*illegible*] of the Courts, of throwing the costs on the claimants, even where compleat restitution is decreed.

May it not be fairly asked whether a proceeding like this can be reconciled with that common justice which every virtuous nation treats others; or with that respect which every enlightened nation pays to the favorable opinion of the world? May it not be asked whether any of the other Courts in G. B. of whose uniformity & impartiality the nation so loudly boasts, would be permitted, or would permit themselves, to tread a crooked path like that which the Admy. Courts pursue; and whether all pretensions of the Admiralty Courts to the same independent justice & to the same general confidence; which are allowed to the other Tribunals, must not necessarily be blasted by such a contrast in its proceedings?

May it not finally be asked, whether the British nation in the pride of its' strength, and the consciousness of its rights, would as a neutral nation receive, with acqueiseicse [*sic*], from any belligerent nation on earth, the same treatment which she does not scruple as a belligerent nation to inflict thro' its admiralty proceedings, on neutral nations? Let British honor answer this question; and let British Statesmen, in their wisdom reflect, that there is one other nation at least, which is equally conscious of its rights, and if less proud of its strength, is not ignorant of the sufficiency of its means for the vindication of its rights.

But what will be ultimate effect of this new principle of admiralty jurisprudence? Clearly & compleatly the subsidiary effect of driving the colonial trade now carried on circuitously thro' neutral ports, more especially *those* of the U. S. into *the British warehouses;* from which, after leaving all the *intermediate advantages* in her hands, it may find its way under her *own commercial regulations*, to its destined markets. By reducing the importation of each neutral nation *trading directly with colonies* to the amt. of its own consumption, all the supplies for other neutrals not trading directly with them, together with such as may ultimately find their way to the belligerent mother Countries, must become a monopoly in her own hands.

It is true that the late rule in the form made public seems to be limited to cases, where the voyage with colonial produce is from a neutral port to the Mother Country of the Colony. But both the reasoning of the Judge, and the sweep of the principle take in every indirect trade which the British regulations do not now or may hereafter allow to be directly carried on. If landing the goods, and paying the[2]

Ms (DLC). Undated; date assigned based on the assumption that these notes were part of the material JM had accumulated for his writings about the British doctrine forbidding neutral trade with belligerents mentioned in JM to Jefferson, 14 Sept. 1805.

1. For the tightening of British policy toward neutrals trading with the colonies of belligerents, see George Joy to JM, 26 July 1805, and n. 3.

2. Ms page ends here.

Notes on Treaties Relating to Neutral Trade

Treaties, to which Engd. not a party

Treaty of Munster one important source of Conventional & [illegible] Pub Law

Between Spain & U. P. see partr. art. Jenk. Vol. 1. p. 42[1]

Spain & France	1659.	Art. X–XVI	Id. V. 1. p. 110[2]
France & Holland	July 21. 1667.	art. 26–30.	Chalm. v. 1. 154[3]
Emper. Ch VI & Phil V	May 1. 1725.	art. VII.	Azuni v. 2. p. 129[4]
France & Hans towns	Sepr. 28. 1716.	Art. VIII.	Id. - - 129[4]
France. & Sweeden	1672		Dumont Tom. 7. p. 1. p. 166 Azuni v. 2. p. 130[5]
Denmark. & U. Provs	1701		Id. 166 Id. 130[6]
Naples & Holland	1752.		Azuni v. 2. p. 131[7]
✓ E. & Spain	May 13. 1667.	art. XXI–XXVI[8]	Chalm. vol. 1. p. 177.[9]
✓ Engd. & Holland	Decr. 1. 1674.	art. I–V.	Id. Vol. 1. p. 189[10]
do. do.	— 1. 1674.	explanatory of 1667/8. & 1674.	Chalm. vol. 2. 109[11]
G B. & Spain	Novr. 28./Decr. 9. 1713.	inserting May 13. 1667.	Jenk. vol. 2. p. 340[12]
✓ G. B. & S.	Jany. 14. 1739.	renewing 1713 & 1667.	Azuni v. 2. p. 129.[13]
x G. B. & Russia.	Decr. 2. 1734.	art. II.	

Do. to which Engd. a party

Cromwell & Lew XVI.	1655.	ar. XV. [Vs. all commerce for 4. years.]	Jenk. v. 1. p. 83[14]
✓ Cromwell & Sweeden	1654	Art XI	Jenk. Vol. 1. p. 70. Chal v. 1 p. 25[15]
✓ Id. wh Id.	1656.	art. III	Id. v. 1. p. 98[16]
All[i]ance x✓ Engd. with Sweeden	Ocr 21.1661.	Art. XI	See Collection &. p. 17. Chalm. v. 1. p. 25 Art. IV v. 1. p. 32[17]
✓ with Denmark also Ally.	1670.	art XVI[18]	do p:— Id. v. 1. p. 85.[19]
Engd. & Holland:	✓1668.	art. I. II.	Jenk. V. 1. p. 190 & Chal. v. 1. p 163[20]
Engd. & Holland.	July 21 ✓1667.	art III[21]	Chalmers v. 1. p. 153.[22]
Engd. & France	1677	art. I. II–IV	Id. V. 1. p. 209.[23]
✓ Engd. & UP.	1689.	pr. all commerce with F.	J. v. 1. p. 292[24]

✓ Engd. Sweeden & U. Hollan.	1700.	art. XII. to consult on for prohibg. comerce with enemies of one of allies	Jenk. v. 1. p. 315[25]
✓ Engd. Denmark & U. P.	1701.	art. VI. referg. to Convention betwn. Eng. & Hol. with Denm. in 1690	Id. v. 1. p. 333[26]
✓ G. B. & France	1713	art. XVII–XXI. explicit.	Jenk. v. 2. p. 50. Chal. v. 1. p. 390[27]
G. B with Holland	1674.	art. I–V.	Chalmers vol. 1. p. 177[28]
G. B & Spain	1713.	art. XXI–XXVI. renewing that of 1667.	Jenk. v. 2. p. 101–2[29]
✓ Idem & Idem.	Decr. 3. 1715.	art VII confirming the Above at Utrecht.	Chal. v. 2. p. 174[30]
✓ G. B & Sweeden	Jany 21. 1720.	art. XVIII: renewing that of. 1713.	Jenk. v. 2. p. 263.[31]
✓ G. B. & Spain	June 13. 1721.	Art 1. renewing all treaties	Id. v. 2. p. 265.[32]
✓ G. B. F. & Spain	Novr. 9. 1729.	renewg. all Treats	Id. v. 2. p. 307. Chal. v. 2. 200[33]
✓ G. B. Empr. & Holland	Mar. 16. 173⟨1⟩	Art III renewing that of Westphal & Utrech[t] & others.	Id. v. 2. p. 319 Id. v. 1. p. 312[34]
G. B. F. & U. P.	(Aixlachapell) 1748.		Jenk. 2. p. 37. Chalm. v. · p. 428[35]
acceded to by Austria. Spain. Sardinia, Modena & Genoa			
G. B. & Spain	1750.	Art. IX renewing those of 1713 & 1748.	Id. v. 2. p. 412[36]
G B. F & Spain (Portl. acceding)	*1763[37]	Art. 1. renewing Treaties of 1648. 1713. 1748.	Jenk. vol. 3. p. 180.
G. B. & Russia (during war	1766.	Art. X. pointed) to continue 20 years	Id. v. 3; p. 228[38]
G. B. & F.	†1788[39]	art. II renewing 1648. 1713 1748. 1763 et al.	Id. v. 3. p. 337
G. B. & Sp.	1783	art. II do. do. &c.	Id. V. 3. p. 377.[40]
G. B. & F.	1786.	art XX–XXIV. inserting those of Utrecht &c.	Chalm. v. 1. p. 531–2.[41]

☞ In the Treaty of Amiens—omitted—but proposed by on [sic] the part of G. B. in the negociations at Lisle (&ca) and opposed for sundry reasons alien to the point, same as to Treaty of Amiens

☞ Lord Malmesbury, in urging a renewal of article as to Treaties of 1713. 48. 63. & 83; observes that those Treaties were become the law of nations, and that if they were not renewed, confusion would ensue. They were certainly become the law of Nations as much on the subject of neutral (commerce?) as any other. See negociation of Ld. M. published by the Brit: Govt.[42]

✓ Treaty with Dantzic	Ocr. 11/23. 1706.	Art. XIV	Chal. v. 1. p. 108[43]
✓ Russia	*1734		Azuni v. 2. p. 129–30[44]
Russia	July 20. 1766.	Art. X.	Chalm. v. 1. p. 7.[45]
Holland	July 21. 1667.	Art III. adopting that with France.	Chalm. v. 1. 153.[46]
do. Breda	Feby. 9/19. 1673/4.	art VII. renewing the above of 1667.	Id. V. 1. 175.[47]
G. B. & Denmark	July 4. 1780.	Explany. of 1670.	Collect: p. 97.[48]
☞ G. B. & Do:	1669.	Art. 16*[49]	Dumont. tom. 7. part 1 p. 126. Azuni v 2. pa. 130

Curious to see the progress of G. B. from the first encroacht. founded on the idea of a naturalized ship, limited to a *Colony*, and a *direct* trade therewith; not being extended even to Coastg. trade or to case of Colonl. goods intermediatly landed at another Colony—thence extended to trade with Colonies on the general principle of its being an internal trade—then, after sleeping thro' the war of 1778, awaking with renewed strength, see orders of 1793—then again awed by at [sic] its own temerity & the shock given to neutral nations retreating under the orders of 94. & 98[50]—then again advancing under the constructions given in practice to those orders. Sr. W. S.[51] certainly displays great talents & much erudition; but the Englishman, if not the courtier is too often visible thro' the robes of the Judge:

G. B. denies to belligerents the right of a neutral trade to their Colonies whilst she exercise of the right of opening her own Colonies to neutral trade. She denies to neutral[s] the right to trade with beligant colonies on the pretext of distressing whilst the authorizing a trade supplies their wants herself by her own subjects & from her own ports

Reasons vs expoundg. the phrase "as before the war &c" are required by the British Doctrine
1. Such doctrine not previously know[n] not therefore referred to
2. consistent with other passages in same authors & treaties.
3. as they treat distinctly of contrabd. blockades—enemy/ property incon(ceiva)ble that they should pass over this so lightly & equivocally
4. the other exposition more obvious

Ms (DLC). Undated; date assigned based on the assumption that these notes were part of the material JM had accumulated for his writings about the British doctrine forbidding neutral trade with belligerents mentioned in JM to Jefferson, 14 Sept. 1805.

1. For the "particular Article concerning Navigation and Commerce" of the 1648 Treaty of Munster between Spain and the United Provinces of the Netherlands which allowed Dutch citizens to trade with Spain's enemies, barring contraband, see Jenkinson, *Collection of All the Treaties between Great Britain and Other Powers* (1968 reprint), 1:42–44.

2. Articles 10–16 of the 1659 Treaty of the Pyrenees between France and Spain stipulated that France was free to trade with any enemy of Spain, Portugal excepted, and described articles that would be considered contraband (ibid., 111, 113).

3. The Articles of Navigation and Commerce appended to the 31 July 1667 Treaty of Breda between Charles II of England and the United Provinces of the Netherlands incorporated articles 26–42 from a treaty between France and the Dutch Republic which stipulated that France was free to trade with the enemies of the Dutch Republic with the exception of those articles described as contraband (Chalmers, *Collection of Treaties between Great Britain and Other Powers*, 1:151–59).

4. JM referred to Domenico Azuni's *Sistema universale dei principi del diritto marittimo dell'Europa* (2 vols.; Florence, 1795–96). The 28 Sept. 1716 treaty of Paris between France and the Hanse towns, and the 1 May 1725 treaty of Vienna between Charles VI and Philip V prohibited only the transportation of contraband to the enemy (Domenico Azuni, *The Maritime Law of Europe*, trans. William Johnson [2 vols.; New York, 1806]; [Shaw and Shoemaker 9877], 2:131). For Azuni, see *PJM-RS*, 1:135 n. 1.

5. JM cited Jean Dumont's *Corps universel diplomatique du droit des gens.* For Dumont, see Peter S. Du Ponceau to JM, 8 July 1805, n. 12. JM's references note that the Franco-Swedish treaty of 1672 (which the New York edition of Azuni [see n. 4 above] mistakenly reported as a 1662 treaty) allowed neutrals all trade with enemies except for contraband (Azuni, *Maritime Law*, 2:132). For the error, see where Azuni cites Dumont, *Corps universel diplomatique du droit de gens*, vol. 8, pt. 1, p. 32, and not vol. 7, pt. 1, p. 166, which JM cites.

6. Article 12 of the 15 June 1701 Copenhagen treaty between Denmark and the United Provinces of the Netherlands allowed inhabitants of the Netherlands to trade with the enemies of Denmark, with the exclusion of contraband. Article 13 listed the items that constituted contraband (Clive Parry, ed., *The Consolidated Treaty Series* [231 vols.; Dobbs Ferry, N.Y., 1969–81], 23:377, 383, 391).

7. The Treaty of Commerce and Navigation between Naples and the United Provinces of the Netherlands, like those mentioned in nn. 4–5, above, allowed neutrals all trade with belligerents except contraband (Azuni, *Maritime Law*, 2:132). Azuni cited as a source the journal *Mercure historique et politique*, where the date of the treaty is given as 27 Aug. 1753 (*Mercure historique et politique* [September 1753]: 277).

8. Articles 21 through 26 of the 23 May 1667 Treaty of Madrid between Great Britain and Spain allowed citizens of each to trade with the enemies of the other, including foodstuffs, excepting contraband, which was described, and also allowed the merchandise of citizens of either country carried in belligerent vessels to be confiscated along with the rest of the ship and cargo (Chalmers, *Collection of Treaties between Great Britain and Other Powers*, 2:5, 17–19).

9. Articles 1 through 5 of the 1 Dec. 1674 Marine Treaty between Great Britain and the United Provinces of the Netherlands allowed citizens of each country to trade with the enemies of the other, listed contraband and acceptable trade items, and described the papers each was required to show to officials of the other as well as the technique to be used to examine them (ibid., 1:177–80).

10. The 30 Dec. 1675 Explanatory Declaration of the February 1668 and December 1674 treaties between Great Britain and the United Provinces of the Netherlands stated that citizens of the two countries could trade not only between neutral ports and those of an enemy but between one enemy port and another (ibid., 189–91).

11. The 9 Dec. 1713 Treaty of Navigation and Commerce between Great Britain and Spain included the words of the 1667 Treaty of Madrid (see n. 8 above) (ibid., 2:108–9). In his notes JM linked the treaties described in nn. 8–10, and here, with a brace.

12. The 14 Jan. 1739 Pardo Convention between Great Britain and Spain agreed to the appointment of ministers of the two countries who were to meet within six weeks to regulate the differences between them relating to trade and navigation and territorial limits, such regulation to be done "according to the treaties of the years 1667, 1670, 1713, 1715, 1721, 1728, and 1729" (Jenkinson, *Collection of All the Treaties between Great Britain and Other Powers* [1968 reprint], 2:339–43).

13. Article 2 of the 2 Dec. 1734 Treaty of Navigation and Commerce between Great Britain and Russia stated: "The subjects of either party may trade with all the states which may be at enmity with one of the parties, provided they carry no warlike stores to the enemy" (Azuni, *Maritime Law*, 2:131 and n. 108).

14. Article 15 of the 3 Nov. 1655 Treaty of Peace between Great Britain under Oliver Cromwell and France under Louis XIV stated that for "four years to come . . . ships of either nation may carry commodities of any kind to the enemies of the other" and excepted besieged places and military stores (Jenkinson, *Collection of All the Treaties between Great Britain and Other Powers* [1968 reprint], 1:81, 83).

15. Article 11 of the 11 Apr. 1654 Treaty of Peace between Great Britain and Sweden signed at Upsala stated: "By the previous articles is not to be understood that either nation may not trade with the enemies of the other, so the goods they carry be not deemed contraband" which would be defined within the ensuing four months (ibid., 69–70). Chalmers's version of the article is more detailed (Chalmers, *Collection of Treaties between Great Britain and Other Powers*, 1:20, 25–26).

16. Article 3 of the 15 July 1656 Treaty of Alliance between Great Britain and Sweden stated that either party might trade with the enemies of the other except to besieged places or when carrying the contraband listed in article 2 (Jenkinson, *Collection of All the Treaties between Great Britain and Other Powers* [1968 reprint], 1:98).

17. Article 11 of the 21 Oct. 1661 treaty between Great Britain and Sweden stated that each would be allowed to trade with enemies of the other, but that commerce in contraband, which the article listed, was forbidden. Also forbidden was trade with besieged places and giving any assistance to enemy endeavors. Article 4 allowed the citizens of each signatory full and free permission to travel and trade within the territories of the other, again barring contraband (Chalmers, *Collection of Treaties between Great Britain and Other Powers*, 1:44, 52–53, 48).

18. For article 16 of the 11 July 1670 Copenhagen Treaty of Alliance and Commerce between England and Denmark which allowed each participant to trade with the enemies of the other, excepting contraband and trade with blockaded ports, see ibid., 78, 85.

19. In the left margin here JM has inserted: "☞ Eng. ✓ & France 1697 art. V—same phrase in respect to neutral subjects—as of enemies-free trade restored as before the war—Jenk. V. 1. p. 300. See also Discourse, p. XI quoting Chartr. of Ed. III *prohibg* trade with Enemy So also Queen Eliz." Article 5 of the 20 Sept. 1697 Treaty of Ryswick between Great Britain and France allowed the "free use of navigation and commerce between the subjects of both the said kings, as was formerly in the time of peace" and allowed open trade between the two countries (Jenkinson, *Collection of All the Treaties between Great Britain and Other Powers* [1968 reprint], 1:299–300). For the prohibition by Edward III of trade with the enemy and its continuation by Elizabeth I, see Charles Jenkinson, *A Collection of Treaties of*

Peace, Commerce, and Alliance, between Great-Britain and Other Powers, from the Year 1619 to 1734: To Which is Added, A Discourse on the Conduct of the Government of Great-Britain, in Respect to Neutral Nations (London, 1781), 111–12.

20. For articles 1 and 2 of the 17 Feb. 1668 Treaty of Commerce between England and the United Provinces of the Netherlands which allowed British subjects to trade to any country at peace with England, even if that country should be at war with the United Provinces, and which extended that freedom to all non-contraband goods, see Jenkinson, *Collection of All the Treaties between Great Britain and Other Powers* (1968 reprint), 1:190.

21. Article 3 of the 31 July 1667 Articles of Navigation and Commerce between England and the United Provinces of the Netherlands acknowledged that the negotiators had been unable to reach agreement regarding the trade issue and incorporated into the contract articles 26–42 of the 21 July 1667 Treaty of Breda (see n. 3 above) (Chalmers, *Collection of Treaties between Great Britain and Other Powers*, 1:151, 153–59).

22. In the right margin here, JM wrote: "Hold. 1673/4; art VII. Chal v. 1. p. 175." Article 7 of the 19 Feb. 1674 Treaty of Westminster between England and the United Provinces of the Netherlands stated that the 1667 Treaty of Breda (see n. 3 above) and all treaties confirmed by it were to "be renewed, and remain in their full force and vigour" wherever they did not contradict the Westminster treaty (ibid., 172, 175).

23. Articles 1, 2, and 4 of the 31 July 1677 Treaty of Breda between England and France agreed on peace between the two countries, the cessation of all hostilities between them, and allowed that navigation and commerce should be as free as "before the late war" (Jenkinson, *Collection of All the Treaties between Great Britain and Other Powers* [1968 reprint], 1:186).

24. For the 22 Aug. 1689 convention between England and the United Provinces of the Netherlands in which, both countries being at war with France, they agreed to prevent all commerce, belligerent and neutral, with France, see ibid., 292–95.

25. Article 12 of the 23 Jan. 1700 Treaty of Alliance between Great Britain, Sweden, and the Estates General of the Netherlands bound the participants to "consult together, for prohibiting commerce with the enemies of such confederate or confederates," see ibid., 313, 315.

26. Article 6 of the 20 Jan. 1701 Odensee Treaty of Alliance between Great Britain, Denmark, and the United Provinces of the Netherlands stated that although the king of Denmark insisted on liberty of commerce for his subjects, in order to avoid fraudulent use by foreigners of Danish passports, the section of the convention made between the three signatories in 1690 regulating trade with France would come into effect and remain so until it could be examined and changed for the better prevention of fraud (ibid., 331, 333).

27. Articles 17–21 of the 11 Apr. 1713 Treaty of Utrecht between Great Britain and France stated that free ships make free goods, always excepting contraband which was described, and that subjects of either country were free to trade with and between ports of the enemies of the other. Article 20 listed as well all the merchandise that was not to be considered contraband, and article 21 listed the papers the ships had to carry to allow such free trade (ibid., 2:40, 50–52).

28. Articles 1–5 of the 1 Dec. 1674 Treaty of London between England and the United Provinces of the Netherlands allowed the subjects of each country to trade with the enemies of the other, listed contraband that was excepted, permitted non-contraband goods, also listed, and described the papers each vessel should carry and the methods to be used to inspect the ships (Chalmers, *Collection of Treaties between Great Britain and Other Powers*, 1:177–80).

29. For the 9 Dec. 1713 Utrecht Treaty of Navigation and Commerce between Great Britain and Spain that included the wording of the 1667 Treaty of Madrid, see Jenkinson, *Collection of All the Treaties between Great Britain and Other Powers* (1968 reprint), 2:88–107.

For articles 21–26, which allowed free trade between the subjects of either country and the enemies of the other, except for contraband and non-contraband items, see ibid., 101–2.

30. Article 7 of the 3 Dec. 1715 Madrid Treaty of Commerce between Great Britain and Spain stated that the 9 Dec. 1713 Utrecht Treaty of Commerce between the two countries would remain in effect except for articles contrary to the 1715 treaty which would be of no force (Chalmers, *Collection of Treaties between Great Britain and Other Powers*, 2:172–75). For the 9 Dec. 1713 treaty, see n. 29 above.

31. Article 18 of the 21 Jan. 1720 Treaty of Alliance and Assistance between Great Britain and Sweden stated that even after one of the signatories had fulfilled its obligation to send auxiliary troops to the other, if that country had not otherwise entered the war, its subjects were free to trade with the enemy of the other, excluding contraband (Jenkinson, *Collection of All the Treaties between Great Britain and Other Powers* [1968 reprint], 2:251, 263).

32. The 13 June 1721 Treaty of Madrid between Great Britain and Spain renewed the conditions of the 13 July and 9 Dec. 1713 treaties of Utrecht with certain exceptions (ibid., 264–68).

33. Article 1 of the 9 Nov. 1729 Treaty of Peace, Union, Friendship, and Mutual Defense between France, Great Britain, and Spain, signed at Seville, renewed and confirmed all former treaties of friendship and peace among them (ibid., 306–7).

34. Article 1 of the 16 Mar. 1731 Vienna Treaty of Peace and Alliance between Great Britain, the Holy Roman Empire, and the United Provinces of the Netherlands stated that all the former treaties between the three countries should have their full force and effect (Chalmers, *Collection of Treaties between Great Britain and Other Powers*, 1:310–11, 312–13).

35. Article 3 of the 18 Oct. 1748 Treaty of Aix-la-Chapelle between Great Britain, France, and the United Provinces of the Netherlands renewed the Treaty of Westphalia and ten other treaties (Jenkinson, *Collection of All the Treaties between Great Britain and Other Powers* [1968 reprint], 2:370, 374).

36. Article 9 of the 5 Oct. 1750 Madrid Treaty between Great Britain and Spain confirmed the Treaty of Aix-la-Chapelle (see n. 35 above) as well as all the other treaties mentioned in the Madrid Treaty (ibid., 410, 412).

37. JM placed an asterisk before the date and wrote in the left margin: "*This subsequent to captures of 1756." Article 2 of the 10 Feb. 1763 Paris Treaty of Peace and Friendship between Great Britain, France, and Spain renewed the treaty of Westphalia of 1648, the quadruple alliance of 1718, and the Aix-la-Chapelle treaty of 1748 (see nn. 35–36 above). Article 1 pledged "universal and perpetual peace" between the contracting parties (ibid., 3:177, 179–80).

38. Article 10 of the 20 June 1766 St. Petersburg treaty between Great Britain and Russia, which was to be in effect for twenty years, allowed the subjects of both countries to trade with the non-blockaded ports of the enemies of the other, excepting military stores, and required "men of war and privateers" to "behave as favourably as the reason of the war" would permit (ibid., 224, 228–29, 234).

39. JM placed a dagger before the date and wrote in the left margin: "†see p. 364. British declaration & p. 366 Fr. do. holding out idea of alterations witht. [*illegible*] the point in question. See p. 400 & 402. for British & Spanish *like* declarations." The 3 Sept. 1783 Versailles declarations by the British, French, and Spanish kings dealt with fishing rights and trade with India and permitted the commercial parts of the treaty to be changed as circumstances altered without changing the other parts of the treaty (ibid., 363–66, 375, 377–78, 400–402).

40. See n. 39 above.

41. For articles 20–24 of the 26 Sept. 1786 Treaty of Navigation and Commerce between Great Britain and France which basically repeated the descriptions in the 1713 Treaty of Utrecht, see Chalmers, *Collection of Treaties between Great Britain and Other Powers*, 1:517, 530–33, and n. 27 above.

42. In the failed negotiations between Great Britain and representatives of the French Directory in Lisle, France, in 1797, James Harris, Lord Malmesbury, offered a projet that would renew and confirm eleven treaties signed between 1678 and 1783; he also noted in his arguments that the treaties had become the law of nations, and "infinite confusion would result from their not being renewed" (*Papers Relative to the Late Negociation at Lisle, Laid before Both Houses of Parliament, by His Majesty's Command* [London, 1797], 15, 16, 25, 61–62).

43. Article 14 of the 23 Oct. 1706 Treaty of Commerce between Danzig and Great Britain stated that ships of Danzig carrying proper papers showing that they were carrying neither contraband nor enemy cargo should not be stopped by British vessels. JM wrote in the right margin here: "For reason's [*sic*] of G. B. see Jenkinson's Disc. Brown v. 2. P: [left blank]. Ward. Robinsons Rep." (Chalmers, *Collection of Treaties between Great Britain and Other Powers*, 1:100, 108).

44. JM placed an asterisk before 1734 and added a note in the left margin: "*The trade *between* the parties limited to Europe, & ports permitted & so as to exclude Colonies— bellig not trade—with Enemies also, if meant to be excluded." For the 2 Dec. 1734 Treaty of Navigation and Commerce between Great Britain and Russia, see n. 13 above.

45. Article 10 of the 1766 Treaty of Commerce and Navigation between Great Britain and Russia allowed subjects of both countries to trade with the enemies of the other, except to blockaded ports or with military stores, and ordered military vessels and privateers to act as favorably as the conditions of war would permit when searching trading vessels (Chalmers, *Collection of Treaties between Great Britain and Other Powers*, 1:2, 7).

46. For article 3 of the 31 July 1667 Articles of Navigation and Commerce between England and the United Provinces of the Netherlands, which incorporated articles 26–42 of the treaty between France and the United Provinces, see nn. 3 and 21 above.

47. For the 19 Feb. 1674 Treaty of Westminster that renewed the Treaty of Breda, see n. 22 above.

48. The 4 July 1780 explanatory article of the treaty of 1670 between Denmark and Great Britain specifically listed the military supplies that were to be considered contraband and were not to be provided to the enemies of either signatory (Lewis Hertslet et al., comps., *A Complete Collection of the Treaties and Conventions, and Reciprocal Regulations, at Present Subsisting between Great Britain and Foreign Powers, and of the Laws, Decrees, and Orders in Council, Concerning the Same; . . .* [31 vols.; London, 1827–1925], 1:203).

49. JM placed an asterisk here and added in the right margin: "*Trade to Enemy in all things not contraband, to all places not besieged." For article 16 of the 29 Nov. 1669 treaty between Great Britain and Denmark, which allowed the subjects of each party to trade with the enemies of the other in all goods but contraband, see *A Complete Collection of All the Marine Treaties Subsisting between Great-Britain and France, Spain, Portugal, Austria, Russia, Denmark, Sweden, Savoy, Holland, Morocco, Algiers, Tripoli, Tunis, &c. . . .* (London, 1779), 156, 158.

50. For the orders in council of 8 June and 6 Nov. 1793, see *ASP, Foreign Relations*, 1:240, 430. For those of 8 Jan. 1794 and 25 Jan. 1798, see ibid., 3:264–65. For the 18 Aug. 1794 instruction rescinding part of the order of 8 June 1793, see [James H. Causten], *A Sketch of the Claims of Sundry American Citizens on the Government of the United States, for Indemnity, . . .* (Washington, 1836), 30.

51. Sir William Scott, Lord Stowell.

§ From John Armstrong. *14 September 1805, Paris.* "In making up my dispatch by Mr. Skipwith, I omitted to enclose the copy of a second letter from the Minister of Exterior relations on the subject of the forced trade carried on between the United States & St. Domingo. It is sent herewith."[1]

RC and enclosures (DNA: RG 59, DD, France, vol. 10). RC 1 p.; in a clerk's hand, signed by Armstrong. For enclosures, see n. 1.

1. The enclosures (12 pp.; in French; docketed by Wagner) are copies of (1) Talleyrand to Armstrong, 16 Aug. 1805 (translation printed in *ASP, Foreign Relations*, 2:727), complaining that U.S. trade with the black rebels at Haiti (Saint-Domingue) continued and that U.S. merchants were supplying the blacks with military supplies; enclosing a copy of the condemnation of the *Happy Couple*, which had carried three cargoes of gunpowder to Haiti, had been captured on its return trip by the British, and carried into Halifax and there condemned; noting that even the British courts considered the island a French colony; and asking how, then, the Americans could continue aid, stating that Napoleon was convinced the U.S. government would end the trade; and (2) a summary of the condemnation of the armed vessel *Happy Couple* at Halifax, which noted that the crux of the case was the question of whether or not Saint-Domingue was still to be considered a French colony, and that the judge decided it was. For the case of the *Happy Couple*, see *PJM-SS*, 9:272 n. 6.

§ From William Lee. *14 September 1805, Bordeaux.* "I have the honor to enclose you a bill of Loading & Invoice of six Cases of Wine, one Tierce of Vinegar and two Cases of Cordials which I have shipped for you on board the Brig Lyon to the address of Mr Purveyance of Baltimore.[1] I hope they will arrive safe and be to your liking."

RC and enclosures (DLC). RC 1 p. For enclosures, see n. 1.

1. For JM's original order, see JM to Lee, 14 June 1805, *PJM-SS*, 9:469. The enclosures (2 pp.) are a copy of a 9 Sept. 1805 bill of lading for two cases containing thirty-six bottles of wine each, four cases containing thirty bottles of wine each, two cases containing fifty bottles of liqueurs each, and one tierce of vinegar, at four pounds sterling per ton freight "going for one ton and one sixth" sent aboard the *Lyon*, Peter Coursell, master; and a copy of an invoice dated 10 Sept. 1805 for seventy-two bottles of 1798 Pichon Longueville red wine, sixty bottles of red St. Julien wine, sixty bottles of unspecified red wine, two cases containing a total of twenty bottles of "huile de Jupiter," twenty bottles of "huile de Venus," twenty bottles of "huile de Rose," twenty bottles of orange liqueur, and twenty bottles of "huile de Noyeaux," and a barrel containing thirty-eight gallons of vinegar, plus various charges for packing, shipping, and attendant costs, for a total of 1,205 francs. The *Lyon* arrived at Baltimore on 10 Nov. 1805 (*Baltimore Weekly Price Current*, 14 Nov. 1805).

§ From Robert Williams. *14 September 1805, Washington, Mississippi Territory.* "The enclosed affidavits marked No, 1 to 11 inclusive will inform you of some outrages committed within this Territory by two Spanish parties.[1] The letters marked No. 1. to 5 and an Order to Colo Ellis will inform you of the steps which I have thought it advisable to take.[2] The Messenger with my letter to Governor Grand Pré has not returned altho he was requested and undertook to be back by this Morning. I have not rec'd any answer to my dispatch to you on this subject of the 14th of June [not found].

"If Sir I am to risque any thing on this occasion it shall be in the defence of the liberties and the property of the Citizens and in the support of the Honor and Independence of my Government. And I hope the Measures taken and advised by me will not be found adverse to the views of the Executive or to the Interest of the United States."

Letterbook copy and letterbook copy of enclosures 1, 4, and 5 (Ms-Ar: Executive Journal, 1805–1810); Tr and Tr of enclosures (DNA: RG 233, President's Messages, 9A–D1); Tr and Tr of enclosures (DNA: RG 46, President's Messages, 9B–B1). Second Tr and Tr of enclosures are letterpress copies of first Tr and Tr of enclosures. Tr and enclosures printed in *ASP, Foreign Relations*, 2:683–87.

1. The affidavits (14 pp.; printed in *ASP, Foreign Relations*, 2:683–86) describe the kidnapping of Nathan, Reuben, and Samuel Kemper from their homes in Pinckneyville, Mississippi Territory, on the night of 3 Sept. 1805 by a large group of men, residents of that territory and of Spanish West Florida; the Kempers being carried into West Florida and delivered to militia captain Solomon Alston, who placed them on a boat to be taken to Baton Rouge; their rescue by an American army unit when they called for help while passing Point Coupée; and an earlier invasion of American territory on 21 Aug. 1805 by a contingent of Spanish light horse in search of William Flanagan Sr., who had purportedly killed a man in West Florida and fled across the border into Mississippi Territory.

2. The letters (6 pp.; printed ibid., 686–87) are copies of (1) Williams to Carlos Grand Pré, 6 Sept. 1805, describing the kidnapping attempt on the Kempers and asking Grand Pré to explain the incident and to "provide against similar outrages"; (2) Lt. William Wilson, commandant at Point Coupée, to Williams, 5 Sept. 1805, describing his rescue of the Kempers and asking that Williams consult with William C. C. Claiborne, who Wilson assumed was visiting the town of Washington, and tell Wilson what to do; (3) Richard Sparks, commandant at Fort Adams, to Williams, 7 Sept. 1805, transmitting Wilson's letter and stating that he could send twenty-five men and a subaltern to Wilson's aid should Williams wish; (4) Williams to Wilson, 9 Sept. 1805, approving his conduct and asking him to send the Kempers and their assailants to Fort Adams under the guard of the men Captain Sparks would send to Point Coupée; (5) Williams to Sparks, 9 Sept. 1805, transmitting his letter to Wilson and asking Sparks to keep the men Wilson was to send under military guard until they could be delivered to civilian authority; and (6) Williams to Col. John Ellis, of the Fifth Regiment of the Mississippi militia, 9 Sept. 1805, ordering him to send one hundred and six troops in two companies to patrol the boundary with West Florida and to intercept any suspicious parties attempting to cross from there.

From Thomas Truxtun

Sir   Philadelphia September 15th. 1805.

Mr Robert Smith Secy of the Navy and myself have lately had a private correspondence explanatory of a misunderstanding or misconception between us, in consequence of my not having a Captain, or as I first proposed to him knowing that the Law for the peace establishment limitted the Number to Nine—a Lieutenant Commandant to Command under the Commodores broad pendnant [*sic*] his Ship, as *Morris* and *Morris's* Successors, have Since had, and as I have General Dearbourns letter of the 13th of June 1801 stating that the Government deemed such Officer necessary.[1] The result however of this Correspondence is, that we have mutually Agreed to throw A Mantle of oblivion over the whole, and thus the Affair is at rest.

The enclosed Copies are meerly forwarded to You that You Should Judge, or be enabled to Judge of the manner and terms I declined the Mediterranean

337

Service,[2] from my own relation of facts and to request that You will be good enough to cause the question to be ended whether, I am Considered in or out of the Navy which I made so many Sacrifices to Enter.

I Should be extreemly Sorry to wound the feelings of Mr Smith in the least and especially After what has passed, by this communication to You—Yet as it concerns myself alone and Something very mysterious to me and my friends Seem connected with the Affair in question—I cannot Conceive any impropriety in addressing a member of the Government So high as the Secy of State, by a private letter, Simply Asking his influence to end a question, I have applied in vain to Mr Smith to close; while he intimated it was an affair too delicate for him, and recommended an application to the Navy department. I have written him in consequence *officially*, and on this point am unanswered.

I cannot repeat too often my regret in not having been enabled to proceed to the Mediterranean in 1802 instead of *Morris* and of the desire I had, Not to let Slip, So glorious an Oppertunity of immortalizing the american Name, by a proper punishment of the Bashaw of Tripoli, and ending the Contest with him, as it ought to have been ended with the force we had there in June last—indeed I had my plan of attack and plan of procureing Gallies, Gunboats and Bomb ketches with fire Ships all fixt in 1801—provided the Government would have given me Latitude and I would have Sacrificed my private fortune Sooner, than been disappointed in distroying the City of Tripoli in 1802 or 1803, had I gone out to the Mediterranean, and this Should have been done without the Visionary projects of an exiled Prince or his Abetors being blended with the affair—I wished our Nation to have had all the Credit of the enterprize without any foreign or other aid.

It is No doubt in Your power to Make a Statement of My Affair to the President which will determine my Suspence So injurious to me, inasmuch, as it has prevented my attention to pursuits of a pecuniary kind for a great length of time & consequently has Still farther impared my impared fortune.

It would be painful to me and tedious for You to read details such as I have entered on in my late letters exchanged with Mr smith. Suffice it to Say I wish my Situation determined and should be extreemly Sorry at this time of day when I am verging towards half a century to find myself Considered by the *President* & Mr *Madison*, in a less honourable and useful point of view—than I seem to stand in the Opinion of mr Smith who uses the terms in his letters to me "No less honourable in private life than Illustrious in publick life."

On my own subject I shall not dwell—but beg leave to offer you also for Your perusal Copy of a private letter written to mr Smith on the subject of our Mediterranean Concerns, since the news of peace with Tripoli came to hand and the letters of Barron & Rodgers have been published by him at Baltimore. This you will be pleased to consider as a Confidential

Communication also, which being made by a naval military man may Not be unacceptable to You in taking a view of past Transactions Abroad, which I am Sorry to Say Appear to me Open to the animadversion of Government. I pray You Sir to Accept of my attachment and that Esteem with which I have the honor to be Your very Obt humble servant[3]

THOMAS TRUXTUN[4]

RC and enclosures (DLC). For enclosures, see n. 2.

1. On 3 Mar. 1802 Truxtun, who had been named to command the Mediterranean squadron, learned that, contrary to what he had been told by Robert Smith, he would have to serve as both captain of his flagship and commander of the squadron. Believing that the two responsibilities could not be efficiently handled by one man, Truxtun wrote to Smith and asked "leave to quit the service" unless he could have a flag captain. On 13 Mar. 1802 Smith replied that Truxtun's condition was "impossible" because of the reduction in officers under the 3 Mar. 1801 act "Providing for a Naval peace establishment." Although Truxtun wrote Aaron Burr on 22 Mar. 1802 that "it was with pain & reluctance I quit the Navy" and also told Charles Biddle that he had "quit the Navy," he very soon came to regret his action and as time passed he convinced himself that he had intended to resign only from the Mediterranean squadron and not from the navy. His efforts to be reappointed were unsuccessful, and in February 1806 Smith informed Truxtun definitively that he could not be reinstated (Knox, *Naval Documents, Barbary Wars*, 2:76, 83, 94; *U.S. Statutes at Large*, 2:110–11; Ferguson, *Truxtun of the Constellation*, 221–25, 227, 229–31, 238–40).

2. The enclosures (8 pp.) are copies of (1) Truxtun to Robert Smith, 7 Sept. 1805, enclosing letters from Charles Biddle and Richard Dale, and stating that although the serious illness under which he labored in March 1802 may have caused him to write a letter more ambiguous than he intended, he merely meant to resign from the Mediterranean squadron and not in any way to resign from the navy; (2) Truxtun to Charles Biddle, 7 Sept. 1805, stating that since it was being "said every where" that Truxtun had resigned from the navy, he was asking Biddle what his understanding had been, and was, of Truxtun's intentions then and now and also asking Biddle to ask Dale, who was Truxtun's immediate predecessor on the squadron and who had returned to Hampton Roads while Truxtun was there, what he understood Truxtun to have done; (3) Biddle to Truxtun, 7 Sept. 1805, stating that, based on what Truxtun had said in a letter to Biddle at the time, and on what he had since said, it was Biddle's belief that Truxtun had no intention of resigning his navy commission; (4) Biddle to Richard Dale, 7 Sept. 1805, asking if, on his arrival at Norfolk, he had understood from Truxtun that on giving up command of the squadron he had also resigned his commission and also asking if Dale had since then ever heard Truxtun say he had resigned from the navy; (5) Dale to Biddle, 7 Sept. 1805, stating that it was not then his understanding that Truxtun intended to resign his commission and from then to the present he had understood from Truxtun that it was not his intention; and (6) Truxtun to Smith, 14 Sept. 1805, offering his opinions on how the war with Tripoli should have been fought, and would have been fought had he been able to go to the Mediterranean, and criticizing Lear's peace as being premature, since Truxtun believed Yusuf Qaramanli could have been totally defeated and required to pay the United States rather than the latter pay him.

3. On the verso of the letter, Truxtun has written a list of ships and armature:

Force in Md. June 1805.

Frigate	President	44	Barron.
"	Constitution	44	Rodgers.
"	Constellation	36	Campbell.

"	Congress	36	Decature.
"	Essex	32	J. Barron.
"	J. Adams	32	Shaw.
Brig	Argus	18	Hull.
"	Siren	18	Stewart.
Schooner	Vixen	14	Smith.
"	Nautilus	14	Dent.
"	Enterprize	14	Robinson.
	4 Bomb Vessels		
	12 Gun boats		
	five Ships uncertain		

Officers, Seamen, Marines &c 3,200.

Force proposed to Mr Secy Smith by TT. in winter of 1804.

Frigate	President	44.	Guns
"	Constitution	44.	"
"	Congress	36.	"
"	Essex	32.	"

4 brigs of Guns 16 each.
4 Schooners   14 ditto.
4 Bomb Vessels.
12 Gallies (or an equivalent in Gun boats)
10 fire Ships.

4. Thomas Truxtun (1755–1822) was born on Long Island, New York, orphaned in 1765, and went to sea in 1767. In mid-adolescence, he was impressed into the Royal Navy but soon returned to merchant shipping and was commander of his own vessel by age twenty. He was a privateer during the American Revolution and became wealthy through his captures. After the war, he was again a merchant captain and sailed the first Philadelphia-owned ship to China. In 1794 he became a captain in the U.S. Navy and later won two battles against French frigates during the Quasi-War, for which he received Congressional thanks and a gold medal. He retired briefly after a peace was achieved but then received the assignment that led to his separation from naval service (see n. 1 above). During this last retirement he lived for several years in New Jersey and then moved to Philadelphia, where he was active in politics and in opposition to the Embargo in 1809. From 1816 to 1819 he was sheriff of Philadelphia. He wrote several instructional works on sailing.

§ From William D. Patterson. *15 September 1805, Nantes.* "I had this honor on the 18th. May last inclosing my official returns. I have now Sir to inform you that all Seamen on board American vessels, who may have been born either in France, Holland Italy or Genoa, are immediately taken out of their vessels and put on board Ships of War without any respect being paid to their Protections or the length of time they may have lived in America, I have always claimed them, and made many representations to the Marine office of this place, of the article in our Treaty, which protects American Seamen,[1] but have been answered, that there is a peremptory order of the Emperor's which they will always obey, the pressing of men of all kinds who may be useful on board of Ship, is here extremely severe.

I am informed that the Government of the United States, have resolved to grant no more Papers to ships purchased abroad, this resolution is necessary as it is impossible under the present regulations to prevent fraudulent Sales. I have used every precaution in my power and have exacted that the means of purchase and mode of payment should be exhibited to me supported by the testimony of the houses who had paid the money, yet have frequently entertained strong suspicions, that the Property still continued foreign, although unable to produce any positive fact to prove it, and American citizens think they have a right to take vessels under their name and when thier demands are refused they make loud complaints, which cause many embarassments, I therefore hope that Govt. will be pleased to adopt some regulations on this subject.

"I have had several visits from a Genl. Humbert the officer who commanded formerly the expedition to Ireland[2] he has much importuned me to offer his services to the United States, to which I have made him no answer he has repeatedly requested me to inclose an application to you, which I have equally declined but have sent a letter from him to Genl. Armstrong, he is one of those, who are out of favor, and proffers the services of many others who are in the same case.

"I took the liberty in my last to request a renewal of my commission to the Emperor, a want of which, prevents my obtaining an exequatur, although I meet no interruption in performing all my official functions, permit me to repeat this request."

RC (DNA: RG 59, CD, Nantes, vol. 1). RC 3 pp. Damaged by removal of seal.

1. Patterson referred to article 14 of the Convention of 1800, which agreed that free ships make free goods and extended the condition "to persons, who are on board a free ship" and who were "not to be taken out of that free ship, unless they are soldiers and in actual service of the enemy" (Miller, *Treaties*, 2:468).

2. Jean Joseph Amable Humbert (1767–1823) enlisted in the National Guard at the outbreak of the French Revolution in 1789. By 1792 he was a lieutenant colonel and participated in the pacification of the Vendée. He was made brigadier general in 1794 and the following year accompanied general Louis Lazare Hoche in fighting Royalists in Brittany. In 1798 he led an invasion of Ireland that ended in defeat. He accompanied Charles-Victor-Emmanuel Leclerc on the disastrous French invasion of Saint-Domingue in 1801. He was stripped of his rank and exiled to Brittany on his return to France in 1802. In 1812 he received permission to depart for the United States, and by August 1813 he had left Philadelphia for New Orleans, where he fought under Andrew Jackson in the Battle of New Orleans. In 1816 he participated in filibustering expeditions against Mexico in company with José Álvarez de Toledo y Dubois. He disbanded his troop of volunteers in 1817 after the collapse of Toledo's revolt and returned to New Orleans, where he taught at a French college (John A. Garraty and Mark C. Carnes, eds., *American National Biography* [24 vols.; New York, 1999], 11:458–59).

§ From Elias Vander Horst. *15 September 1805, Bristol.* "I had the Honor of addressing you on the 13h. Insta. ⅌ this conveyance—the object of the present is merely to advise that conformable to what I had the pleasure of writing you on the 12th of Feby. 1802[1] I forwarded your obliging Letter to Mr. Livingston on the subject of Messrs. Smiths Desaussure & Darrels claim for the value of 4 Casks of Indigo which were plundered from on board the American Ship Commerce by the Captn. & Crew of the French Privateer Tigre, of St. Malo, in May 1793. Mr. Livingston wrote me that he had referred it to Mr. Skipwith as a matter coming more immediately within his department. This claim in its earliest Stage (in 1793) was put into the hands of Mr. Morris, our then Minister at Paris, with every document to proscute & support it, from him it went to Mr, Monroe and was lastly, by that Gentleman, put into the hands of Mr. Skipwith, to whom I have written many Letters on the subject, as I had before done to his predecessors in Office, but I am sorry too say without the effect I had expected. On the 5 of Feby. 1802 Mr Skipwith wrote Mr. Livingston as follows (a Copy of which Mr. Livingston transmitted to me) 'the Papers which are in my hands are sufficient proofs of the Indigo's being the property of Messrs. Smiths Desaussure & Darrel, but by no means of their having been taken out of the Commerce by the *Tigre*, except the Protest of Capt. Preble, & this last Document never will be admitted by the French Courts as sufficient Title to the claimed restitution'—since then I have recd. another Letter from Mr. Skipwith dated the 22d of June 1804, an extract from which follows. 'I have but little to add to the information which you have acknowledged the receipt of through Mr. Livingston concerning the 4 Casks of Indigo—this Claim could not be brought before the Council of Prizes as you must have observed by the Minister of Marine's Letter to me, a Copy of which was forwarded to you by our Minister; It not being before the Council of Prizes it cannot be brought before the American board of Commissioners for reasons that must appear obvious to you on reading the 5th. Article of the Convention of 1803.[2] To pursue this business before the ordinary Tribunal at St. Malo, as indicated by the Letter of the Minister of Marine, you must be under the necessity of employing an Agent there. I am very respectfully &c. &c.' 'Fulwar Skipwith' Now Sir, if you will have the goodness to compare the contents of these two Letters you will, I am persuaded, find it no easy matter to reconcile them to the object of the busines(s) in question—first the proof of the property is *good*, but then the Captns. Protest cannot be admitted as evidence, and next the Claim could not be brought before the Commissioners because it could not be brought before the Council of Prizes, and lastly the business should be carried before the Ordinary tribunal at St. Malo &c.!! In reply to this Letter I wrote as follows on the 25th of July 1804: 'Sir I am favored with your Letter of the 22d of last Month, in which you say the claim for the 4 Casks of Indigo not having been brought before the Council of Prizes cannot be brought before the American board of Commissioners—in a former Letter you said that this Claim being supported only by Captn. Preble's *Protest* could not be admitted into any French Court—in my Letters to you of the 5t of Decr. & 1st. of June last I endeavored to remove that obstacle by mentioning to you where Capt Preble might be found or heard of at Havré, If however your obliging endeavors for that purpose should fail surely this business would then become a proper matter of investigation before our board of Commissioners at Paris, as it would be truly hard that Messrs. Smith, De Saussure & Co should be deprived of their property merely because the Council of Prizes refuse to admit that kind of evidence which I believe, is always allowed in every other Court of Law in the world, and which indeed is the only one that can be obtained in general in cases of this sort, You will therefore, I intreat Sir, be pleased to make a *full representation* of this matter to the Commissioners stating all the circumstances of the case, and as you possess every document that can be necessary to support it, I cannot for a moment doubt its success, as I am persuaded that, that board, will not permit a mere matter of form to deprive Citizens of the United States of their undoubted rights.

"[']You mention that an Agent to prosecute the matter at St. Malo will be nec-essary, but of what use will this be when you say the evidence of the *protest* will not be admitted? However, pray do in this business whatever you deem right as you have all the papers to establish & support the claim, the amount of which should certainly be paid some where, as otherwise the case of Messrs. Smith & Co will be hard indeed—you are Agent for them, and from the obliging disposi-tion which Mr. Livingston has shown in this business I am persuaded you will find him ready on all occasions to aid you therein as far as it may come within his province. In the hope of soon hearing satisfactorily from you on this vexatious subject, I remain &c &c. ELIAS VANDERHORST.'

"I have before observed that all the documents respecting this business with a proper Power of Attorney from Messrs. Smith, &C. are in the hands of Mr. Skipwith. If therefore an agent at St. Malo was necessary he certainly should have appointed one, especially, as I had before written him that his Drafts on me for any expence that might attend the business should be duly honored, but to my surprize & disappointment I have not since heard from him! I am extremely con-cerned to be under the painful necessity of making this very unpleasant represen-tation to you, but I flatter myself your goodness will not only pardon me, but lend me your powerful aid to obtain the object in view, the amount of which, with the Interest Justly due theron, will fall very little short of Five hundred pounds Stg. You will be pleased further to observe that Mr. Skipwith does not say that he ever attempted to enforce the claim or even make it, merely, it seems, from a presump-tion that the Protest would not be admitted, nor has he said what sort of evidence would be admitted—nor indeed, that the Indigo was ever Condemned! For my own part however, I have no Idea that it ever was, from the forcible manner in which it was taken from on board the Vessel.

"Thus Sir stands this very tedious & vexatious matter, but to which I promise myself, I shall by your kind assistance shortly witness a satisfactory termination."[3]

Adds in a postscript: "No part of this property was Insured."

RC (DNA: RG 59, CD, Bristol, vol. 2). 3 pp.; docketed by Wagner, with his note: "Indigo plundered by the Tigre."

1. *PJM-SS*, 2:464.
2. See Miller, *Treaties*, 2:518–19.
3. The ship *Commerce*, Enoch Preble master, of Baltimore, owned by Pierre Changeur and John Deyme Jr., was seized by *Le Tigre* on 1 June 1793. A claim of 56,869.11 livres was made and 28,993.13.09 livres was eventually awarded (Williams, *French Assault on American Shipping*, 107).

From Thomas Jefferson

DEAR SIR   MONTICELLO. Sep. 16. 05.

The inclosed letter from Genl. Armstrong furnishes matter for con-sideration.[1] You know the French considered themselves entitled to the Rio Bravo, & that Laussat declared his orders to be to recieve possession to that limit, but not to the Perdido:[2] & that France has to us been always silent as to the Western boundary, while she spoke decisively as to the Eastern. You know Turreau agreed with us that neither party should strengthen themselves in the disputed country during negotiation;[3] and Armstrong who says Monroe concurs with him, is of opinion from the character of the emperor that were we to restrict ourselves to taking the posts on the West side of the Misipi., & threaten a cessation of intercourse with Spain, Bonaparte would interpose efficiently to prevent the quarrel going further.[4] Add to these things the fact that Spain has sent 500. colonists to St. Antonio, & 100 troops to Nacogdoches, & probably has fixed or proposed a post at the bay of St. Bernard at Mattagordo. Supposing then a previous alliance with England to guard us in the worst event, I should propose that Congress should pass acts 1. authorising the Exve. to suspend intercourse with Spain at discretion; 2. to dislodge the new establishments of Spain between the Misipi & Bravo: and 3. to appoint Commrs. to examine & ascertain all claims for spoliation that they might be preserved for future indemnification. I commit these ideas merely for consideration & that the subject may be matured by the time of our meeting at Washington, where I shall be myself on the 2d. of October. I have for some time feared I should not have the pleasure of seeing you either in Albemarle or Orange, from a general observation of the slowness of Surgical cases. However should mrs. Madison be well enough for you to come to Orange I will call on you on my way to Washington if I learn you are at home. Genl. Dearborne is here. His motions depend on the Stage. Accept for mrs. M. & yourself affectionate salutations

TH: JEFFERSON

P.S. I am afraid Bowdoin's journey to England will furnish a ground for Pinckney's remaining at Madrid. I think he should be instructed to leave it immediately, & Bowdoin might as well perhaps delay going there till circumstances render it more necessary.

RC (DLC: Rives Collection, Madison Papers); FC (DLC: Jefferson Papers); Tr (MHi).

1. This was probably John Armstrong to JM, 3 July 1805, which arrived in early September.

2. For Pierre Clément de Laussat's opinion on Louisiana's boundaries, see William C. C. Claiborne and James Wilkinson to JM, 27 Dec. 1803, *PJM-SS*, 6:233.

3. For Turreau's opinion on the disputed territory, see JM to James Monroe, 23 May 1805, ibid., 9:381.

4. See Armstrong to JM, 3 July 1805.

From Jacob Wagner

DEAR SIR DEPARTMENT OF STATE 16 Septr. 1805

I have been honored with your's of the 13th. from Gray's, where I am happy you have secured a safe and agreeable retreat. I had kept a copy of your letter to Genl. Turreau. I think it adviseable to publish the list of bills drawn by Genl. Armstrong, because it will convey useful information to the claimants, will free us from the trouble of answering numerous enquiries, and it is not too voluminous for Mr. Smith's paper.[1] The other intimations and directions of your letter shall be attended to.

I enclose a passport for a Mr. Dugarcein, and as I doubt extremely his title to it, I have left the cover open to enable you to decide from an inspection of his papers. By the inhabitants of Louisiana, who were by the Convention to be considered as citizens of the U.States, were not meant transient persons, who had not the rights of citizens of the country whilst it was Spanish; and in the present instance it only appears that the person had resided at New Orleans for 18 months previously to the cession to the U.States. I also enclose some papers for franks, having nearly exhausted those left me by Genl. Dearborn.

Instructions from Com. Barron to Eaton, cautioning him against any permanent engagements with Hamet, has been published at Baltimore, with the date of 22 March. On my observing to Mr. Gouldsborough that this letter could have barely reached its destination previously to the attack upon Derna and consequently after every arrangement had been made for the common warfare, he assured me that it ought to have been dated 22 Decr. & not March.[2]

Another copy of the order of June 1803 lately mentioned in the letter to Mr. Monroe as having made it [*sic*] first appearance at Tortola, has been imported from the East Indies (Ceylon) and is published in our papers with criminating remarks that our government had not made it publick &c.[3] Among other proofs of the relaxation of the British navigation act to suit the various exigencies of war as it affects British commerce & manufactures, is the signal instance of the order lately enclosed by Mr. Erving, which admits British subjects, *with out a licence* specially obtained, to import and export certain articles in neutral vessels, from and to France Spain and Holland.[4]

Is any answer intended to be given to the memorial enclosed in Mr. Petit's letter respecting the New Jersey's case?[5] Sincerely & with attacht. Yrs.

J. WAGNER

RC (DLC). Docketed by JM.

1. See John Armstrong to JM, 3 July 1805, and n. 2.

2. For the published letter from Samuel Barron to William Eaton, dated 22 Mar. 1805, see *National Intelligencer*, 16 Sept. 1805.

3. For the article to which Wagner may have referred, see the Boston *Repertory*, 10 Sept. 1803. For an earlier mention of the order, see JM to James Monroe, 7 Sept. 1805, and n. 3.

4. See George W. Erving to JM, 16 July 1805 (second letter), and n. 3.

5. This letter has not been found, but it may have enclosed Philip Nicklin and Robert Eaglesfield Griffith's 25 July 1805 memorial to JM.

§ From John Graham. *16 September 1805, New Orleans.* "I had the Honor to forward to you by the last Post a Copy of a Letter from the Mayor of this City from which you would learn all that has transpired as to the Insurrection contemplated by Le Grand, or as he calls himself Grand Jean.[1] Present appearances justify a belief that this Man had formed no party among the Negroes.

"You will probably have learned before this reaches you, that a new General of Marine has lately been sent out to the Havanna to give vigour to that department there, and that he brought with him orders for the immediate embarcation of Six Hundred Men for Pensacola—Where I am told preparations have been made for their reception.[2] We have here a report that the Spanish Troops on the Frontiers of Mexico are also to be increased, of this, however, I presume, more certain information will be communicated to the President thro: the Department of War. Thro: the Same channel he will learn that some supplies sent from this place a few Weeks since, for the garrison of Fort Stoddart have been detained at Mobile, because the person who had charge of them refused to pay the Duties demanded by the Spanish Officer at that Post. In addition to this I hear that an American Vessel and her Cargo were lately seized at the same place, because she had a short time before passed by without paying Duties on a Cargo of Cotton,[3] which she was bringing from the Mississippi Territory to this City. These are circumstances well calculated to shew how important it is to us to have a free entrance into the Mobile River. I have great satisfaction in informing you that the City still continues healthy, at least there is no appearance of the yellow Fever."

Adds in a postscript: "The Election of Representatives for this County came on to day and the Votes for the lower District have been given in. They are generally in favor of Men who profess an Attachment to our Government. From what I hear I am greatly in hopes that Doctor Watkins and Mr. James Brown will be Elected."

RC (DNA: RG 59, TP, Orleans, vol. 7). 3 pp.; docketed by Wagner as received 22 Oct.

1. See Graham to JM, 9 Sept. 1805, n. 2.

2. For an earlier report on the Spanish troop movements, see Henry Hill Jr. to JM, 28 Aug. 1805.

3. See Harry Toulmin to JM, 8 Aug. 1805.

§ From William Jarvis. *16 September 1805, Lisbon.* "The original of the foregoing of the 28 Ulto. was forwarded by the Brig Three Brothers, Captain Lothrop for Boston with the inclosures described[1] I have now the Honor to acquaint you that advice has been received here that the French & Spanish Squadron was at Cadiz the 8th Instant, consisting of 34 Sail, & was blockaded by a British Squadron consisting of 25 Sail of the Line under Sir Robt. Calder. Advices have several times been received that the Rochfort Squadron consisting of 6 Line of Battle

346

Ships & 3 or 4 smaller Vessels were cruising off Cape Ortegal. Accounts by the last Packet say that a small Squadron has been detached from the Brest Fleet in pursuit of them, and a report was 2 days since in circulation that a Battle had taken place, but this wants confirmation. The latest accounts from the North favour much of a continental War, & I should think it inevitable was it not for a conversation I had with the Russian Minister[2] a few days since. When I mentioned the apparent certainty of English papers, of hostilities between Russia & France, he observed that he had no advice that would Justify him in giving Credit to such a report, & after some little conversation he seemed to enter pretty sincerely into arguments tending to show the impolicy of the measure, such as, the immense distance of the Two Countries, the lenght [sic] of time and dificulty thence arising to send a force adequate to make any sensible impression on France or Italy against the immence Force that France has now on foot, the danger of Germany being overrun before any succours could reach them: that the ability, policy, energy & Character of Bonaparte rendered success in a War still more improbable, that in the course of Natural events such an efficient Government was likely to be succeeded by one as week, thus circumstanced good policy dictated that such steps only be taken as to Check farther encroachments & to wait till time or accident afforded an opportunity for securing the equilibrium of Europe. As Ministers[3] commonly speak the language of their Courts[4] when they have no motives to deceive, as this Gentleman is generally esteemed a sincere person, as his Brother[5] holds an office of some consequence at home, it is likely he knows the sentiments of His Govmt.[6] & as I am not aware of any reason he could have to deceive me, & his manner left me to suppose he was giving his opinion, I have concluded, as he must have received advices from St. Petersburg[7] since the recall of Mr Novoziltszoff[8] that if that Court can possibly avoid coming to extremeties it will; and without assistance from that quarter Germany[9] cannot certainly engage. A short time since being in a company where was the Spanish Ambassador, His Excellency introduced a conversation relative to the difference between the two Countries. I observed to him that it was a pity that two Nations who had so long supported a good understanding & for whose convenience & interest it was to be on good terms, especially Spain's during the present contest, should have this harmony destroyed to accommodate the resentment of an individual, for I had too high an opinion of the good faith of the Court of Spain to believe that it would have conducted with so much injustice towards us as it had done, had it not been for the advice of the Marquis de Yrujo. His Exely replied, he was sorry for any misunderstanding that might exist & hoped it might be amicably settled. Some person coming up at the Moment stopped any farther conversation.

"An order has been given within these very few days for compleating the Regements which are only about half full; & to effect it a very hot press has been set on foot. No reason is assigned for it, but it is supposed by some to be a measure of precaution arising out of the expectation of a Continental War. A few days since arrived here a ship from Cadiz under American Colours. The Captain appearing to be a Scotchman I was induced to question him closely. He pretended that he was Born in Salem, but left there at 7 Years Old, that he had been educated in Scotland, & had served his tim(e) to the sea in that Country & since he was 21 had been Mate of a British Vessel, that he had been at Salem a short time when about 17 Years

347

Old, the only time he had been in the United States since he left there, when he got a protection, and that the Ship belonged to Mr. Crosselet of Philadelphia. After much trouble & a refusal to enter the Vessel unless the papers were brought me, I got them under a promise of returning them which I gave to avoid any unecessary or unadvised step. Finding that the Bill of sale & Consular Certificate were given in the Captains name, I was much in doubt what to do, whether it would be most adviseable to suppress the papers & not know the Vessel, or to make an application to the Government for her seizure. The first would have been attended with the advantage of making no noise, by consequence of not exciting suspicions against other Vessels similarly circumstanced & exposing our Certificate Vessels to unnecessary embarrassments from Privateers; in addition it would avoid the probability of placing this Government in any unpleasant situation from the possibility that some of the foreign Ministers might interfere, or at least in a situation of not wishing to act, least offence might be taken. The Consignee soon extricated me in part from this dilemma, by positively refusing to let me retain the papers unless I would enter the Vessel & thus acknowledge her an American's, which left me no alternative but to apply to this Government. Inclosed is a Copy of my Letters & of the papers, which I registered.[10] As I received no answer I waited on His Excellency last Thursday, when entering into a full explanation of the affair, He observed that he conceived that my request ought to be complied with, but it belonged to the Marine Departments, to which it should be sent in for an information. I also spoke about the freight of Schr. Trio which he assured me he would give an order to pay.[11]

"The Spanish Consul Yesterday informed me that the Ship would probably be claimed by the Spanish Ambassador as the Captain had not yet paid for her. Should he interfere & it renders the success of my application doubtful, I shall try to manage the matter so as to make it appear that I am, in behalf of Government, confering a favour on this Court, as well as His Excellency, in not pursuing the business farther. This step I feel more inclined to take as in the New York Gazette & General Advertizer of the 22nd July, handed me by a Captain Yesterday there is a paragraph stating, that Circular Letters from you dated the 12th. July last (one of which I have not yet had the pleasure to receive) desired the Consuls to desist from granting any Certificates whatever to Vessels purchased by Citizens of the United States in foreign Countries, which as it will effectually put a stop to the evil, in some measure obviates the necessity of rigidly pursuing this affair by entering into any unpleasant discussion, if the point is not to be obtained without; as an example will be no longer necessary to deter others from similar frauds. Beside which it is desirable, if it could have been consistently avoided, not to have taken any steps against her as it will be viewed as a thing of much severity in a Country were the Laws are so closely & badly executed & where things of this kind are considered as mere matters of course. I am much inclined to believe that Mr. Terry was deceived in this affair, either by a protection which Captain Roech had somewhere picked up or by Letters from Houses of respectability in London or Spain.

"A Report is in circulation that some disturbance has taken place in Madrid among the Citizens, that a Regiment of Spanish Horse, which was ordered to suppress the Riot, refused to act, that they & the rest of the Spanish Soldiery were sent into the Country & in their stead was ordered into the City the Swiss &

German Regiments. Inclosed is a Letter from Mr. Pinckney & another from Mr. Simpson."[12]

Adds in a 17 Sept. postscript: "An American Vessel which arrived here yesterday from Bordeaux brings advice that the Rochfort Squadron was seen by an American bound to Bordeaux, the 3rd. Instant off Bell-Isle,[13] that they then had a British Brig of War between them & the land, which was supposed must fall into their possession. It is supposed they are bound into Rochfort. They consisted of 5 sail of the line, 3 frigates & 2 smaller Vessels."

RC, two copies, and enclosures (DNA: RG 59, CD, Lisbon, vol. 2). First RC 7 pp.; in a clerk's hand, except for Jarvis's complimentary close, signature, and postscript; docketed by Wagner "16 Sept." Second RC is written at the head of Jarvis to JM, 26 Sept. 1805, and omits the postscript. For enclosures, see nn. 10–11.

1. The *Three Brothers*, Captain Lathrop, arrived at Boston the week of 3 Oct. 1805 (*Baltimore Weekly Price Current*, 17 Oct. 1805).

2. Left blank by clerk; "Russian Minister" inserted by Jarvis.

3. Left blank by clerk; "Ministers" inserted by Jarvis.

4. Left blank by clerk; "Courts" inserted by Jarvis.

5. Left blank by clerk; "Brother" inserted by Jarvis.

6. Left blank by clerk; "His Govmt." inserted by Jarvis.

7. Left blank by clerk; "St. Petersburg" inserted by Jarvis.

8. Left blank by clerk; "Mr Novoziltszoff" inserted by Jarvis.

9. Left blank by clerk; "Germany" inserted by Jarvis.

10. The enclosures (8 pp.; in Spanish and English; partly in Jarvis's hand) are copies of a 15 Mar. 1805 power of attorney from Antonio de Tastet & Co. to Miguel López & Co. to sell the ship; the 17 Apr. 1805 statement of Miguel López & Co. that for $6,000 in Spanish dollars they sold to John Reoch, an American citizen, the ship formerly called *Tastet* and now called *Venus of Salem* at Cádiz; the statement of consul Josef Yznardy that John Reoch said he had purchased the ship in question and "no foreigner or any other Person whatsoever" had any part of the said ship; a 24 Apr. consular certificate signed by vice-consul Anthony Terry and chancellor James McCann, describing the ship and giving Reoch permission to sail under the U.S. flag provided that he proceed directly from Cádiz to the United States "excepting the accidents of arriving to any other Port in case of distress"; and the 27 Sept. 1805 statement of Jarvis's clerk, Charles Gilman, that all the documents pertaining to the ship and deposited at the consulate had been returned to José Ventura Montano, the consignee, in accord with a promise he had extracted from Jarvis. Jarvis also enclosed two copies of his 6 Sept. 1805 letter to António de Araújo de Azevedo (4 pp.) explaining that Reoch had confessed that he had been hired by the London firm of Firmin de Tastet to go to Spain to purchase a ship supposedly for "Mr. Crosselet of Philadelphia"; that Reoch had purchased the ship in his own name and received a consular certificate giving him permission as an American citizen and owner of the ship to proceed directly to the United States; pointing out that Reoch had no power of attorney authorizing him to act for Crosselet and that the ship's papers should have been issued in Crosselet's name; that this was an infringement on the flag of a neutral nation; that such acts lessened the faith in all public documents of neutrals; that if the ship was truly the property of Reoch or de Tastet & Co., they had broken British law by trading with the enemy; that a British subject entering Spanish territory was breaking Spanish law; and that he was asking the prince regent to order the ship seized and to empower Jarvis to send the vessel to the United States, where it was ostensibly bound, and where the ship would be restored should it be proven that no U.S. laws were broken. He added that if he had exceeded the bounds of his

authority, he would be liable to the owners for damages and to the censure or punishment of the U.S. government.

11. Jarvis enclosed a copy of his 7 Aug. 1805 letter to Araújo (3 pp.) congratulating the prince regent on the recent birth of another child and transmitting the request of consignee John Turner that the freight charges for the American schooner *Trio*, Captain Storey, which had been carried into Lisbon by a privateer, be paid from the sale of the ship's cargo of wheat.

12. These were probably Charles Pinckney to JM, 4 Sept. 1805, and James Simpson to JM, 30 Aug. 1805.

13. Belle-Île-en-Mer is an island off Brittany, southwest of the Quiberon peninsula.

From Jacob Wagner

Sir   Department of State 17 Septr. 1805

The enclosed treaty[1] and dispatches from Mr. Lear were received by the Frigate President, Capt Barron, now in the river with about one hundred of the late captives on board. The Ex-Bashaw and his retainers were taken from the territory of Tripoli and are supported out of the Navy funds. Mr. Eaton is on his return, as I am informed, in a private vessel. I have sent to the President copies of almost the whole of Mr. Lear's dispatches and extracts of the leading articles of the treaty.

It is wished and confided at the Navy office, that the cargo of the Huntress may proceed to the Mediterranean, whence all the ships will not immediately return.[2] I have thrown out the hint respecting it, which you suggested and shall prepare a letter to Mr. Monroe on the subject of salvage and the devious route the re-captors carried her upon.

Captain Bainbridge, who is expected here this evening, has had a court upon his case, consisting of Captains James Barron, Decatur and Campbell, by whom he has been honourably exonerated from blame.[3] Capt. Barron has returned in a condition which is said to indicate his fate to be at hand. The disorder is an affection of the liver with dropsical symptoms.

Some of the young officers from Tripoli have passed through the City. They speak favourably of their mode of treatment, except as to the closeness of confinement. I have the honor to remain, Dr Sir, With the greatest respect & attacht. Your most obed. servt.

Jacob Wagner

RC (DLC). Docketed by JM.

1. For the enclosures, see Tobias Lear to JM, 5 July 1805, and nn. 2, 5, 7–8, and 11.

2. For the capture of the storeship *Huntress* by a Spanish privateer, see *PJM-SS*, 9:453 n. 1.

3. For the court of inquiry into the loss of the frigate *Philadelphia* under William Bainbridge in Tripoli harbor, see Knox, *Naval Documents, Barbary Wars*, 3:189–94.

§ From Vincent Gray. *17 September 1805, Havana.* "This goes from an out port, in Consiquence of there being an embargo at this place for the purpose of dispatching a Frigate to Pan⟨s⟩ecola with Troops.

"I have not ascertained the exact number of Troops on board, but I know that they have taken all the Spare Troops (Regulars) out of the city, and they say, that the militia is now to do duty. 600 is supposed to be the number, and it is said that Colo. Count O.Reily goes to Command them. This information fr[o]m present appearances may be useful to the president of the U States."

RC (DNA: RG 59, CD, Havana, vol. 1). 1 p. Unsigned; conjectural correspondent assigned based on Wagner's note: "Anonymous, supposed to be from V. Gray"; postmarked 5 Oct. at Baltimore.

§ From Robert Montgomery. *17 September 1805, Alicante.* "I had this day the honor of receiving your two Circular letters of the 1st. and 5 July last¹ and shall pay ⟨d⟩ue attention to the contents of each, We have not yet had ⟨a⟩ny return of the Epidemic nor do I learn that it has ⟨a⟩ppeared in any part of Spain this season Which now being far advanced, we generally beleive the Contagion to be ⟨e⟩ntirely extinguished and that without a fresh importation ⟨w⟩e Shall not have it again.

"The Frigate Congress Capn Decatur touched ⟨in here⟩ on the 12 Currt from Tunis and demanded ⟨water?⟩ ⟨and?⟩ provisions but as she was put under Quara⟨ntine⟩ ⟨a⟩nd the Wind freshning from the East she sailed withou⟨t⟩ ⟨th⟩em and I hope will arrive with you long before this.

"Inclosed please find Copy of a letter I recei[v]ed. ⟨fr⟩om Mr Mountford at Algiers [not found] which as it is highly ⟨in⟩teresting I shall hand you duplicates by Other ⟨co⟩nveyances."

RC (DNA: RG 59, CD, Alicante, vol. 1). 1 p.; docketed by Wagner, with his note: "Affairs at Algiers." Damaged by removal of seal.

1. No circular letter of 5 July 1805 from JM has been found. Montgomery may have referred to JM's 12 July 1805 circular.

¶ From Stanley Griswold. Letter not found. *17 September 1805.* Presumed to have covered the undated enclosure (DNA: RG 59, TP, Michigan, vol. 1; 2 pp.) docketed by Wagner: "Recd. in Mr S. Griswold's 17 Septr. 1805." For the law referred to, see *U.S. Statutes at Large,* 1:285–86.

[Enclosure]

Questions submitted by the Secretary of the Territory of Michigan, to the Secretary of State.

1. Is it the duty of the Secretary of the territory, to attend the Governor and Judges in their legislative capacity, to engross, or prepare the manuscript of their laws, previous to signature—or must they prepare them themselves, or by a clerk, and deliver them over to the secretary in a state of completion?

2. Is it the duty of the secretary to attend on the Governor in his executive capacity, to prepare his acts previous to signature, and minute his proceedings—or must the Governor prepare and minute them himself, or by a private secretary, and deliver them over in a state of completion?

3. Must the executive acts, and the laws of the governor and judges, and their proceedings respectively, be transcribed by the secretary of the Territory into *books*, or *volumes*, in order to "keep and preserve them safely"—or is it sufficient, that the *originals* be kept on file, or in rolls, in the secretary's office?

4. Is the secretary of the territory at liberty to procure at this place, the stationary &c. necessary for his office, at the public expence—or may he expect to be supplied by government from the city of Washington?

5. To what amount may it be expected that government will authorise expence for *office-rent*, in the present situation of this town, where rent is excessively high and difficult to be procured, in consequence of the fire? And will an allowance be made for office-rent, in case the papers of the office are kept (safely) in a desk, or case, in a house hired for family use?

6. If it should fall to my lot to be called to execute the duties of *Governor* of this Territory for a considerable length of time, may an extra allowance of salary be expected for such extra service? Or is it adviseable for me to incur the expences necessary to support the usual stile of Chief Magistrate during that time, depending on something more to reimburse those expences, than the small and very insufficient salary of Secretary?

7. Do the provisions contained in the act of congress, passed the 8th. day of May, 1792, entituled, "An Act respecting the government of the territories of the United States, Northwest and South of the river Ohio," apply to the Territory of Michigan?

8. Is the secretary of the Territory, who, in case of the death or absence of the Commander in Chief of its militia, must supply his place, liable to be called on to do military duty in any station subordinate to that *nearest* to the Commander in Chief? To state it in the extreme, would it be proper for a private soldier to step forward from the ranks, to command General officers, in any case?

From Thomas Jefferson

Dear Sir   Monticello Sep. 18. 05.

I return you Munroe's letter[1] most of the views of which appear to me very sound, & especially that which shews a measure which would engage France to compromise our difference rather than to take part in it and correct the dangerous error that we are a people whom no injuries can provoke to war. No further intelligence being now expected on this subject, & some measures growing out of it requiring as early consideration as possible, I have asked of our collegues a cabinet meeting at Washington on the 4th. of Oct. at 12. oclock, where I hope mrs. Madison's situation will permit you to be altho I despair of it's admitting your visit to Orange. It is most *unfortunate that Monroe should be coming home so precipitately.* I cannot but hope that Bonaparte's return to Paris about the 13th. of July would find & detain him there till it would be too late to get to England & wind up there in time to arrive here before winter. Accept for Mrs. Madison & yourself affectionate salutations.

Th: Jefferson

RC (DLC: Rives Collection, Madison Papers); FC (DLC: Jefferson Papers).

1. Jefferson referred to Monroe's letter of 30 June 1805, a copy of which had been sent to him by Jacob Wagner, in addition to the copy sent him by JM on 14 Sept. (see Wagner to JM, 13 Sept. 1805).

§ From Henry Hill Jr. *18 September 1805, Havana.* "I had the honor to address you on the 28th. Augt. respecting the Equipment of a frigate and a Brig which were to convey troops on a secret expedition.

"The brig sailed a few days after with some gunboats to convoy some drogers[1] from the coast, laden with sugars. Therefore I conclude is not destined on the expedition alluded to.

"But the frigate which is called the Pomona of forty four guns with four hundred troops on board and cannon, powder and other warlike stores and ammunition sailed yesterday.

"I am confirmed in my opinion from the circumstance of her having soldiers and military stores that she is bound to Pensacola.

"For at Vera Cruz they are in no want of military stores and it is from thence this island is supplied with powder from the manufacture of Mexico. The most profound secresy has been observed respecting her destination therefore it is mere matter of conjecture with me; but her force is not so great as to excite much alarm.

"As in the present situation of our affairs with Spain it may be useful to our government to be informed the force of this place, I have taken pains to acquaint myself with it.

"The Military consists of four regiments of Veterans which are very incomplete and could not muster more than two thousand five hundred effective men including the four hundred embarked in the pomona which were drawn from these regiments four companies of artillerists and about four thousand militia. These are well disciplined and a part of them are now ordered to do duty in garrison.

"This place would require at least fifteen thousand men to defend all its fortifications and the city in the event of an attack. So that its present situation is very weak and defenceless particularly as the marine force is very inconsiderable consisting only of one ship of seventy four guns one corvette and six gunboats.

"Don Juan Villavicencio arrived here the last of August in quality of commander in chief of the marine forces in America.

"A new governor is daily expected. An embargo took place the 13th. and continued till this day. A British frigate having been off."

Adds in a postscript: "The frigate has one hundred and twenty convicts on board criminals who have been condemned to the Kings works. She has also fifty thousands dollars in specie and was accompanied by a small armed Brig and Schooner."

RC (DNA: RG 59, CD, Havana, vol. 1). 4 pp.; in code; key not found; decoded interlinearly by Wagner. Docketed by Wagner as received 15 Oct., with his note: "Secret expedition from Havana."

    1. Droger: a West Indian coasting vessel (*OED Online*).

§ From William Lee. *18 September 1805, Bordeaux.* "I have shipped your wines &c on the Brig Lyon Capt Coursell to sail in a few days for Baltimore. Would it not be adviseable for you to cause insurance thereon as I understand our Vessels are much harrassed by the English.

"Mr Holmes the bearer of this will hand you a file of the moniteur and a work on the Commerce of the Black Sea[1] which contains some useful information."

RC (DLC). 1 p.

    1. This volume has not been identified but may have been Antoine-Ignace Anthoine de Saint-Joseph's *Essai historique sur le commerce et la navigation de la Mer-Noire: ou Voyage et entreprises pour établir des rapports commerciaux et maritimes entre les ports de la Mer-Noire et ceux de la Méditerranée: . . .* , which was published at Paris in 1805.

¶ From John F. Dumas. Letter not found. *18 September 1805.* Described in Jacob Wagner to Dumas, 24 Sept. 1805, as enclosing a certificate which Wagner said had been transmitted to Richard Harrison, auditor of the Treasury, "to whom the subject belongs." Wagner stated that any further communication on the matter should be addressed to Harrison (DNA: RG 59, DL, vol. 15).

¶ From John Gavino. Letter not found. *18 September 1805.* Acknowledged by Wagner on the verso of the enclosure, dated 13 Sept. 1805: "Recd. In John Gavino's 18 Septr. 1805." The enclosure (3 pp.; DNA: RG 76, Preliminary Inventory 177, entry 322, Spain, Treaty of 1819 [Art. XI] [Spoliation], Misc. Records, ca. 1801–24, box 5, envelope 6, folder 22; printed in Knox, *Naval Documents, Barbary Wars,* 6:247) is the deposition of Commander John Allen and master's mate John Thomson of the sloop *Ranger*, certified by Gavino. Transcriptions of the deposition were sent to the House of Representatives and the Senate (DNA: RG 233, President's Messages, 9A–D1; transcription (DNA: RG 46, President's Messages, 9B–B1). The second is a letterpress copy of the first transcription. The *Ranger* left Boston about 21 July 1805 and was stopped on 23 Aug. by a schooner manned by what appeared to be Spaniards, who robbed the captain, the doctor, the mate, and the men of many articles of clothing in addition to brandy and various foodstuffs from the ship's stores. The *Ranger* had been bought in New York by the U.S. government at the request of Gov. Alexander John Ball of Malta and was on its way to Malta when it was stopped (Knox, *Naval Documents, Barbary Wars,* 6:123, 149, 313).

¶ From Alexander Wolcott. Letter not found. *18 September 1805.* Acknowledged in Daniel Brent to Wolcott, 3 Oct. 1805, as dealing with impressed seaman Anthony Powers, whose father, Gregory Powers of Stow, Ohio, had also written to the State Department in a letter received "about the first of Sepr" (DNA: RG 59, Preliminary Inventory 15, entry 929, Misc. Correspondence with Collectors of Customs regarding Impressed Seamen, 1796–1814, box 12).

To James Monroe

Sir,   Department of State September 20th. 1805
    The Ship Huntress Capt Stinson,[1] loaded with Naval and Military stores and provisions for the supply of the squadron in the Mediterranean was taken about the beginning of June last, shortly after she left the Capes of the Chesapeake by a French or Spanish Privateer. Whilst the Captors had possession of her she is [s]tated to have been recaptured by two British Letters of Marque near the Bermudas Islands and to have been carried to and to have arrived at some port of England. As, besides the usual marine papers, she was provided with a special passport under the signature of the President and seal of the United States and the passports of the British and French Ministers, she could not at the time of the recapture have been in circumstances from which a danger of condemnation could be presumed, nor on that or any other account liable to pay salvage, she ought to have been liberated without being carried so far from her destination. This forced deviation is the more inexcusable as the operations of our squadron depended in a great measure upon the safe and timely arrival of the supplies in the Mediterranean. Inclosed are the usual documents[2] to support a claim which you will be pleased to cause to be made in the name of the United States to the cargo, if an application to the Ministry does not produce a summary restitution. Should no person be present to represent the owners of the vessel it may be well to include her also in the judicial claim. So censurable has been the conduct of the recaptors in carrying

355

the property to England and so clear are the principles which forbid their claim to salvage that should a decree of the Court of Admiralty have ordered it before this letter comes to hand, I request you to cause an appeal to be prosecuted from the adjudication. I have the honor to be Sir, with my great respect your most Obt Sevt

JAMES MADISON

RC, enclosures, and letterpress copy of RC (DNA: RG 76, Preliminary Inventory 177, entry 180, Great Britain, Treaty of 1794 [Art. VII], British Spoliations, ca. 1794–1824, box 3, folder H); letterbook copy (DNA: RG 59, IM, vol. 6). RC in a clerk's hand, signed by JM.

1. For an earlier mention of the seizure of the *Huntress*, see JM to Yrujo, 11 June 1805.
2. The enclosures are JM's 2 Oct. 1805 certification "that the writing hereto annexed contains a true copy of a passport issued under the signature of the President of the United States and the seal thereof for the ship Huntress therein mentioned, and also of the sailing orders, charter party bill of lading and invoice of the same vessel given at the time and applicable to the voyage also therein mentioned"; copies of Jefferson's 18 May 1805 passport for the *Huntress* (printed in Knox, *Naval Documents, Barbary Wars*, 6:21); the 18 May 1805 charter party between Alexandria merchant William Hodgson, agent for Robert Elwell of Wiscasset, and the Navy Department for the *Huntress* to go from Washington to the Mediterranean (printed ibid., 73–74); the 18 May 1805 invoice of goods shipped on the *Huntress*; a second copy of JM's certification of the enclosed documents; a second copy of the charter party; a second copy of the invoice; Robert Smith to Capt. John Stinson of the *Huntress*, 15 May 1805, ordering him to proceed to Malta with the ship and goods; Samuel Sterett's 11 Oct. 1805 certification of the copy of the insurance policy on the *Huntress*; and a copy of the 21 May 1805 policy with the Maryland Insurance Company. Also filed with the other documents is a copy (1 p.; printed ibid., 278–79) of the 12 Sept. 1805 decision of the Admiralty Court for "Restitution of the Ship and Cargo decreed upon payment of the Recaptors Costs."

From Jacob Wagner

DEAR SIR   WASHINGTON 20 Septr. 1805
   The case of the passport requested by Lafonta,[1] to whom the enclosed packet is addressed, resembles one I sent you a few days ago, and will therefore follow its fate. The Navy Department is to furnish me with the documents to be enclosed in the letter to Mr. Monroe respecting the Huntress: they are to be the bill of lading, invoice, sailing orders, insurance &c.[2] The London advices make it probable that some severe sanction has been added to the restraint of the colony trade by G. Britain, and that besides the direct modification of it by Executive orders, the Court of Appeals have decided new precedents of rigor upon the old doctrine. Capt. Bainbridge and some of his officers arrived her[e] last evening and are to be entertained at a public dinner to morrow. Mr. Henry, to whom the office of Agent at Jamaica has been tendered,[3] is traced to NewYork,

whence I expect that we shall soon have his decisive answer. With great respect & attacht. yr. ob. servt.

J.WAGNER

RC (DLC).

1. Request not found.
2. See JM to James Monroe, 20 Sept. 1805.
3. For James M. Henry's appointment, see Jefferson to JM, 11 Mar. 1805, and JM to Henry, 25 Mar. 1805, *PJM-SS*, 9:123, 171–72, and JM to Henry, 20 July 1805.

§ To Norman Butler. *20 September 1805.* "I have received your letter of the 9th. stating that you have revoked a power of Attorney formerly given to Messrs. Capper & Perkins of Bermingham to receive the compensation awarded to you by the Commors. under the 7 Art: of the British Treaty, and requesting that the third instalment of the award may be paid only to your future order.

"It appearing from documents filed in this Office by Mr. Thomas Marston of New York, that you assigned the interest of the award to him for a valuable and other considerations on the 10 Jany. 1804, and that the revoked power was no more than an instrument to receive it, the less essential as his own power would suffice for the purpose, and Mr. Marston having executed an indemnity with the security approved by the Branch Bank of the U. States at New York, I shall as at present advised cause the third instalment to be paid to Mr. Marston after the 1st. Novr. next, if in the mean while it shall not appear to have been paid in London."[1]

Letterbook copy (DNA: RG 59, DL, vol. 15). 1 p.; addressed to Butler at Hartford.

1. For the award to Butler and its assignment to Marston, see *PJM-SS*, 9:199 and n. 2, 472 and n. 1.

§ From George Mathews Jr. *20 September 1805, Oglethorpe County, Georgia.* "I received a few days since, from the President of the United States, a Commission, bearing date on the first of July, by which it appears I am appointed a Judge of the Mississippi Territory;[1] and this being the earliest opportunity, I take the liberty through you, of informing the President, that I accept said appointment & am making preparations for my journy to that Country, where I hope to arrive early in November & will enter on the duties of my Office."

RC (DNA: RG 59, LAR, 1801-9, filed under "Mathews"). 1 p.; docketed by Wagner and Jefferson.

1. Because his was a recess appointment, Mathews's name was not submitted to the Senate until 20 Dec. 1805. George Mathews Jr. (1774–1836) was born in Virginia and moved with his family to Georgia in 1785, returning to Virginia in 1792, where he studied at Liberty Hall (now Washington and Lee University) in Lexington from 1794 to 1795. He returned to Georgia, studied law, and was admitted to the bar in 1799. In 1806 Jefferson appointed him to the bench in Orleans Territory, and on Louisiana's achieving statehood in 1812, he was elevated to the state supreme court. Shortly thereafter he became presiding judge, a position he held until his death (*Senate Exec. Proceedings*, 2:8–9; Charles Watts,

"Discourse on the Life and Character of the Hon. George Mathews," *La. Historical Quarterly* 4 [1921]: 190–91; *PJM-SS*, 6:71 n. 5).

§ From Mr. Plumard Jr. *20 September 1805, Nantes.* "An Intimate relation of mine Mr. Plumard Derieux of Virginia,[1] has indicated to me your address, in the confidence you would be so good as to forward him the Letters I might send you. I crave your obliging in this Circumstance and send you one inclosed.

"Being accountable to him for ₶504.11 tournois I Applied here to mr Patterson the commercial agent of the united states, in nantes, whose brother you are acquainted with, and who will p⟨rocur⟩e that sum for the account, of mr Plumard Derieux. Be so good, Sir, as to receive it and please to inform the said, of it.

"For the receipte of mr Patterson, that I have sent to mr Plumard Derieux, the Dollar is to be settled at 5 ₶livre.8!⸗!—this for your regulation."

RC (DNA: RG 59, ML). 1 p. Postmarked 2[1] Nov. at New York. Cover sheet bears note: "Forwarded by Sir Your most obt. hbe. Ser. Thos: Shields Newyork 21st. Novembr. 18⟨05⟩."

1. For Justin Pierre Plumard Derieux, see Derieux to JM, 19 May 1805, *PJM-SS*, 9:371 and n. 1.

§ From William Riggin. *20 September 1805.* "I had this honor on the 1st. Inst, and have now that of inclosing to you an important state paper [not found], a few Copies of which have been distributed by this Government: it will explain to you fully how the affairs of Europe remain with regard to a renewal of hostilities. At the same time I must further remark to you that every thing in this neighborhood is on the War Establishment."

RC (DNA: RG 59, CD, Trieste, vol. 1). 1 p. In a clerk's hand, signed by Riggin.

From James Wilkinson

SIR   ST: LOUIS. September 21st: 1805

Being desirous to submit my every act to the Executive scrutiny, I take the liberty of trespassing upon You, a copy of my instructions to Colonel Hammond,[1] whose authority *has* been extended to the adjacent district of St: Genevieve, in consequence of the abdication and arrest of Major Seth Hunt.[2]

I have thought proper also to offer information to the poor and ignorant Setlers of the Territory, to save them from the rapacity of a band of Speculators, combined first to frighten and then to defraud them of their rights.[3]

Under the peculiar circumstances of the population of this Territory, I find the establishment of District Commandants highly useful, and should derive great assistance from their cooperation, was the number authorized by the Act of the 26th: March 1804,[4] completed, with Suitable Characters; At new madrid and the sequestered position of the Arkansan village, Such Officers are peculiarly necessary to instruct our unlettered Magistrates, and to secure the honest and impartial execution of the Laws.

We have here some Scintillations of faction, emitted from the collisions of a few Ardent discontents, who having failed to inlist me in oposition to an ideal French part⟨y⟩ would turn their Batteries directly against me, if they could do s⟨o⟩ with effect, and as is not uncommon in such cases, will probab⟨ly⟩ ⟨e⟩ndeavour to carry by sap,[5] what they cannot accomplish by open assault—I infer from a variety of strong indications, that a Mr: Moses Austin, has been the prime mover of these d⟨is⟩cords—this gentleman whom I have not the pleasure of Knowing, became a voluntary subject of Spain about nine ye⟨ars⟩ since, and having under the patronage of that Governmen⟨t,⟩ from small beginings secured a large fortune; now alledg⟨es⟩ that he has been cruelly persecuted for his americanism, an⟨d⟩ on this ground lays claim to extraordinary patronage from the united States: it is to be regretted that this Gentleman should have been able to seduce, Several of the junior Territorial Officers, to make common cause with him, in the excitements, which have agitated the District of St: Genevieve— Ye⟨t⟩ I am pursuaded Sir, these agitations cannot affect the concord and tranquillity of the Territory, and I venture to intrude this detail on you, to prevent any uneasiness whic⟨h⟩ might be produced by misrepresentation.

We are much at a loss for the Law affecting the Land claims of the Territory.[6] I have received two copies only—we have no press—and I am this day informed, by letters of a recent date from New Madrid and the Arkansan, that this Law had not reached those places.

Being informed some of our erratics are entering illicitly upon the public Lands, on the river St: Francois, and near its mouth—I shall make an immediate Detachment to remove them, and destroy their Huts: But I may find some difficulty (I fear) in dislodging eight families, which have taken refuge with a strong tribe of Cherokee Indians high up on the same river, yet the attempt will be made under Such precaution, as may Save disagreable consequences. With perfect Respect I am Sir Your obdt: Servant

JAMES WILKINSON

RC and enclosure (DNA: RG 59, TP, Louisiana, vol. 1); FC (ICHi). RC in a clerk's hand, emended and signed by Wilkinson. FC in a clerk's hand, except for Wilkinson's emendations and docket. Words and parts of words in angle brackets in the RC have been supplied from the FC. Minor differences between the copies have not been noted. For enclosure, see n. 1.

1. The enclosure (2 pp.; marked "Copy"; in a clerk's hand, signed by Wilkinson; printed in Carter, *Territorial Papers, Louisiana-Missouri*, 13:220–21) is a copy of Wilkinson's 19 Sept. 1805 letter to Col. Samuel Hammond, commandant of the district of St. Louis (printed

ibid., 24), stating that the district of St. Genevieve was to be annexed to his command; that he should remove and punish the "intruders" who were reported to be mining and smelting lead on public lands; that Colonel Hunt had said that such actions were allowed by Spanish license and were not prohibited by U.S. law, which Wilkinson denied, advising Hammond to proceed with "every degree of kindness" in ejecting the miners; and that "one Russel" was surveying land along the Meramec River and should be prosecuted if he had broken the law.

2. Col. Seth Hunt had objected to Wilkinson's appointment as governor as being unconstitutional, had disagreed with Wilkinson about ejecting one John Smith from public lands, had bought and later sold a doubtful land title, and had written letters to Wilkinson that were "not only imprudent, but highly improper," all of which resulted in his 11 Sept. 1805 arrest by Wilkinson and ultimately in his dismissal by Henry Dearborn (ibid., 204–7, 225–26, 241–42).

3. Wilkinson referred to his 18 Sept. 1805 notification to the "uninformed Inhabitants" who were "appalled by false alarms, and imaginary difficulties" not to sell their claims at a price less than their true value, adding that he stood ready "to instruct and assist them gratuitously in the prosecution of their just rights" (DNA: RG 46, President's Messages, 9B–A3).

4. *U.S. Statutes at Large*, 2:287.

5. Sap: "Applied to stealthy or insidious methods of attacking or destroying something" (*OED Online*).

6. For the 2 Mar. 1805 "act for ascertaining and adjusting the titles and claims to land, within the territory of Orleans, and the district of Louisiana," decreeing how French and Spanish land grants issued before 1 Oct. 1800 were to be confirmed, see *U.S. Statutes at Large*, 2:324–29.

From Charles Pinckney

DEAR SIR   September 22: 1805 IN MADRID

My last informed you that I was still under the necessity of remaining here until the 2d: October[1] on account of all the Mules being embargoed for the Kings Service until that day so that I could not before go to the Sitio to take leave—that I had still been without the pleasure of seeing Mr Erving or Mr. Bowdoin & that not being able to wait for them any longer I should when I went away leave Mr: Young charged with our affairs until they or one of them came—that during this time & constantly I had been busily employed with this Court in endeavouring to arrest the numerous depredations of their Privateers on our commerce & their condemnations of our Vessels & that to do this my Exertions have not only been unceasing but more than twenty letters have passed between Mr Cevallos & myself on the subject. I have now the pleasure to send you the result by enclosing the copy of a Letter which I have just recieved from Cadiz[2] & which I have recieved in such an unquestionable shape as to leave no doubt of its authenticity—by this it appears my exertions have been effectual & will probably prevent future captures on that ground. I attribute this change in the Spaniards to the expected consequences of the formidable Coalition formed against France & I think the same reason will make both of them much more complaisant to us & much more ready to yield to our claims than before—the fact is Spain wishes success to the Coalition: & this I know from the highest authority & things have taken such a favourable change for us in Europe that if You have held out on our claims as I am sure you have all will end well yet, but the universal opinion in Europe is that You will now make the Spaniards send a special Mission to You & not send another to them.

I am hopeful to be with You in December & request You to present me always respectfully & affectionately to the President being dear sir with regard Yours Truly

Charles Pinckney

RC and enclosure (DNA: RG 59, DD, Spain, vol. 6A); extract (DNA: RG 233, President's Messages, 9A–D1; extract and translation of enclosure (DNA: RG 46, President's Messages, 9B–B1). Second extract is a letterpress copy of first extract. Extract and translation of enclosure printed in the *National Intelligencer*, 13 Dec. 1805. Filed with the RC, and probably meant as a postscript, is a 20 Oct. 1805 note in Pinckney's hand (1 p.): "Mr Erving ⟨nor⟩ Mr. Bowdoin have yet arrived. I expect to leave this to morrow or the next day for Lisbon to embark." For enclosure, see n. 2.

 1. Pinckney's last known letter, of 4 Sept. 1805, does not specifically mention 2 Oct. as his departure date nor does it discuss the embargo on mules.
 2. The enclosure (1 p.; in Spanish; docketed by Wagner as received in Pinckney's 22 Sept. dispatch) is a copy of the 3 Sept. 1805 letter from Pedro Cevallos to the director general of the fleet that Pinckney had also enclosed in his 4 Sept. 1805 letter.

§ To John Brice Jr. 22 *September 1805, "Gray's near Philada."* "Having mislaid your letter of Aug. 31, with an expectation constantly of finding it, it has remained thus long unacknowledged. I now thank you for your attention to the wine shipped to me from Lisbon, and request the favor of you to procure a conveyance of it to Washington. If it be not too inconvenient, I should be glad to have it secured by cases agst. improper liberties with it on the way. I must request the favor of you also to let me know the amount of duties &c &c which I am to remit."[1]

RC (owned by Joseph M. Maddalena, Profiles in History, Catalog 22 [1994], item 23). 1 p. Cover sheet addressed by JM to "John Brice Esqr. Depy. Colr." at Baltimore.

 1. Noted on the cover sheet are the following charges:

260 Galls @ 30 Ct.	78.00
Dray & Porterage	1.12½
Dray to Wharf	.50
Storage	1.00
P & Blks	.20
	80.82½
Freight	14.70
2 Cases & casing	7 —
	102.52½

361

§ From Thomas Auldjo. *22 September 1805, Cowes.* "I had the honor to write you 27th July last—since which time affairs have materially changed for the Worse in regard to the navigation in these parts of the Ships of the United States which are now detained & brought into port in considerable numbers. On the 23d. of July the Judge of the Admiralty passed Sentence on the Enoch—Capt Doen of which inclosed is copy[1] & since that time no less than 7 Ships have been brought into the ports of my district of which I have sent regular accounts to the Minister in London thro' the Consul at his desire. Of these ships 2 were immediately released on examination of the papers, 1 vizt the Eagle Capt Terry[2] from Boston to Cherburgh[3] with West India produce, has had Sentence passed on her this last week as on the other side & the other 4 remain under prosecution. Our harvest is nearly over & the Crops are estimated to be good—no new wheat at market—prices cannot be ascertained at present."[4]

Adds in a postscript:

Eagle—Terry—New York to Cherburgh
        133 hogsheads Sugar & 20 Bales Cotton Condemned with some trifling things besides
Ship & remainder of the Cargo—restored.

RC, two copies, and enclosure (DNA: RG 59, CD, Southampton, vol. 1). First RC 2 pp.; in a clerk's hand, signed by Auldjo. Second RC in a clerk's hand, signed by Auldjo; marked "Copy"; enclosed in Auldjo to JM, 11 Oct. 1805. Minor differences between the copies have not been noted. For enclosure, see n. 1.

    1. For the *Enoch,* see George Joy to JM, 26 July 1805, and n. 3. The enclosure (2 pp.; docketed as enclosed in Auldjo's 22 Sept. 1805 dispatch; printed in the *New-York Evening Post,* 16 Sept. 1805) is a copy of the 23 July Admiralty Court decision of Sir William Scott that unloading the cargo and paying duty did not signify the end of a voyage, and it must be proved that the original intent was for a ship to go to its own, neutral, country. If it appeared that a ship had merely touched at the neutral country and then pursued its voyage, the trip must be treated as a continuous voyage from the enemy colony to the enemy mother country. Scott added that there was proof that the *Enoch* intended to go from Martinique to Antwerp as was planned in a charter party before the ship left Boston. However, he ordered that the part of the cargo originally loaded at Boston be restored.
    2. The section from "1" to "Terry" is in Auldjo's hand.
    3. Here and in the postscript of the first RC, the clerk wrote "Amsterdam," then wrote "Cherburgh" over it.
    4. This sentence is omitted from the second RC.

§ From Samuel Snow. *22 September 1805, Providence.* "Herewith I have the honour to transmit to you two semi-annual returns of Vessels entered and cleared at the Port of Canton between the first day of January and the last day of December 1804 [not found], also copies of sundry letters received by a late arrival from my Agent at Canton relative to the impressment of some American Seamen on board the Carolina, and Grampus two of his Britanic Majestys Ships, and the demand made by him for their releasement.[1]

"From the tenor of the reply of Captain B.W. Page, which seems intended merely to evade giving a possitive refusal, and the scheme of Captain Caulfield, it appears clerely to be the determination of those gentlemen (and I fear also of many other Commanders of Foreign Ships) to take every advantage of our defenceless Seamen wherever they may fall in with them, and however contrary to treaty and the most solomn engagements they appear determined to impress indiscriminately all those whom they may concieve would be in the least servicable to them, or that caprice might dictate.

"The Chinese are a Nation who invariably refuse to interfere, or meddle with the laws, or Government, of any other Country, and leave the controle of all Foreigners who may be among them, or within their ports (so long as they do not break, or infringe, upon their own laws and regulations) entirely to the direction of those who may have been empowered by their own Government to watch over them, or to the Commanders of Ships who are under no such restrictions, to act in the disposal of their Crews as in their opinions may seem best.

"A Consul or Agent therefore, thus situated, finds it impossible to enforce his demands by any legal process, or aid, in China, and is too frequently obliged to submit to the painful necessity of barely receiving an evasive refusal to his request without any means whatever in his power to exact a compliance. To guard our Seamen from oppression, insult, and cruelty abroad, appears to be a subject of great magnitude. I cannot therefore Sir, but submit it to your consideration, whether it would not be expedient, and important, for Government to provide more effectually if possible, against so growing an evil, an evil so destructive to our commerce, so painfull to our Citizens, and so humiliating to every freind to his Country."

RC and enclosures (DNA: RG 59, CD, Canton, vol. 1). RC 3 pp.; docketed by Wagner. For surviving enclosures, see n. 1.

1. The enclosures (8 pp.) are copies of (1) Edward Carrington to Snow, 31 Dec. 1804, transmitting copies (not found) of three protections from American seamen held on the British warship *Caroline*, one protection from a seaman on the *Grampus*, the letters from the seamen to Carrington, and Carrington's correspondence with the captains of the ships; (2) Carrington to Benjamin William Page of the *Caroline*, 6 Dec. 1804, asking for the release of Samuel Endicott, George Christie, and Charles Moody, who had protections stating that they were U.S. citizens; (3) Carrington to Thomas Gordon Caulfield of the *Grampus*, 6 Dec. 1804, asking for the release of John Barton, who also had a protection; (4) Page to Carrington, 7 Dec. 1804, stating that Carrington would have to address his request to the Admiralty Lords at London or to the Admiral, Commander in Chief in India, since Page could not discharge any man without orders from them; (5) Carrington to Page, 11 Dec. 1804, stating that the men appeared to have been impressed under Page's command and he was therefore "the proper person to grant them their liberation," adding that he had had no opportunity to apply to the Admiralty Lords or to the Admiral, Commander in Chief, and if the men were not released, he would report the incident to the U.S. government; and (6) Page to Carrington, 11 Dec. 1804, stating that he had no orders to attend to demands like Carrington's. In his 31 Dec. 1804 letter to Snow (see enclosure 1 above), Carrington said that Caulfield had not replied to his 6 Dec. letter.

§ From James Simpson. *23 September 1805, Tangier.* No. 102. "In the last Letter I had the honour of addressing you[1] I touched on the affairs of the Algerine dominions on their Western Frontier, since that time an intimation was sent in the name of the Emperour to the Governours of Salle—Larach—Tangier and Tetuan, stateing that the presence of the Troops His Majesty had sent into that Country, had given such confidence to the Inhabitants as had induced them to declare in favour of Muley Soliman, and that the Fortress of Oran had also open'd its Gates and submitted to him. At same time rejoicings on the occasion were commanded & actualy observed for three days at all but Tangier, where one sufficed.

"Notwithstanding this, I have it from good authority that the person I mentioned to you as holding intelligence with Mohamet Derhawy retains the Command of all the Country outside of Oran and that the Turkish Garrison defend that place against every thing he can do. As this Sidy Mohamet Derhawy has by his exertions to expell the Turks from Algiers brought his name to be known and as its possible he may yet become a still more conspicuous Character, I have stated for your information some circumstances of his private history, may not have reached you before.

"The declaration he made to the Regency of Algiers that the people with him were determined to be Independent of all others, was tantamount to saying their intention was to get quit of the Turks. The promised Warfare against the Christians was what he well knew would be the strongest inducement with the ignorant and bigoted people he led, to attach themselves the more to him. The cause he had espoused was theirs, but it is generaly believed Derhawy had views far beyond that of overturning the present Government in Algiers. Should he succeed there, we may expect to hear of him in this Quarter.

"Whether from resentment, or by inspiration I will not say, but he seldom fails of threatening Muley Soliman with distruction whenever he has an opportunity of speaking with people of this Country, passing thro' that where he at present is—he treats them courteously and grants them escorts.

"Mohamet Derhawy is well acquainted with every circumstance relating to the internal concerns of this Empire. He knows the serious discontents prevail in the very populous Provinces of Schedma Duquella and Abda in consequence of their having for several years back been prevented from selling their Grain for exportation. In the latter years of Sidy Mohamet and during the contest for the Succession the extensive Corn Country I have mentioned, was immensely enriched by the Export of Wheat and Barley then allowed: for some time they have not only been denied that but all the three have been repeatedly subjected to heavy fines, from one hundred to three hundred thousand dollars at a time, on very frivolous pretexts.

"These discontents bear no sort of appearance of giving rise to immediate disturbances in the Country, but should any attempt from abroad threaten Muley Soliman, he must either abandon the system he has undoubtedly adopted, of reducing his people to poverty that they may be the more easily governed, or he will run a very serrious risque of provoking a revolt in the three Midland Provinces. Spain has great influence with those people and would readily foment troubles did they shew any disposition for such, in hopes thereby to obtain an extraction of Grain from this Country.

"I have taken the liberty of noting at top of this Letter the nature of its contents, that it may be seen at opening. I persuade myself you will direct its being kept as such."

RC (DNA: RG 59, CD, Tangier, vol. 2). 3 pp.; marked "Confidential"; docketed by Wagner.

1. See Simpson to JM, 30 Aug. 1805.

¶ From John M. Peck. Letter not found. *23 September 1805*. Described in Wagner's 30 Sept. 1805 reply, addressed to Peck at Providence, Rhode Island, as enclosing a bill for one thousand dollars drawn on JM on 8 July by James Simpson (see Simpson to JM, *8 July 1805*) in favor of Richard Worsam Meade and endorsed by "Mr. Clark." Wagner told Peck that subsequent to the acceptance of that bill, another had been received endorsed by Robert Murray of New York, who stated he had a power from Clark. Wagner advised Peck that if the second presentation was not explained, it might present obstacles to payment on the bill Peck had presented (DNA: RG 59, DL, vol. 15).

To James Monroe

private

DEAR SIR   PHILADA. Sepr. 24. 1805

The decision in the Admiralty Courts of G. B. disallowing the sufficiency of landing, and paying duties on, Colonial produce of belligerent Colonies, re-exported from ports of the U. S., to protect the produce agst. the British Cruisers & Courts,[1] has spread great alarm among merchants & has had a grievous effect on the rate of insurance. From the great amt. of property afloat subject to this new & shameful depredation, a dreadful scene of distress may ensue to our Commerce. The subject was brought to attention by the case of the Aurora, which gave rise to the observations & instructions contained in my letter of 12 April last.[2] I omitted in that letter to refer you to a case in Blackstone's reports, where Ld. Mansfield says, that it was a rule settled by the Lords of appeal, that a transhipment off a neutral port, was equivalent to the landing, of goods from an enemy's colony, and that in the case of a landing there could be *no color* for seizure.[3] As Mr. King's correspondence may not be in London I think it not amiss to remind you of what passed with the British Govt. in 180(1), in consequence of such seizures as are now sanctioned. A copy of the doctrine transmitted by the Govt. to the vice admy. Courts as the law for their guidance is inclosed.[4] If such a condemnation out of their own mouths has no effect, all reasonings will be lost; and absolute submission, or some other resort in vindication of our neutral rights, will be the only alternative left.[5]

I hope you will have recd. the instructions above referr(e)d to, and that your interposition will have had a good effect. I am engaged in a pretty thorough investigation of the original principle, to which so many shapes are given, namely, that "a trade not open in peace is not lawful in war," and shall furnish you with the result as soon ⟨as⟩ my resea⟨r⟩ches are digested. If I am not greatly deceived, it will appear that, the principle is not only agst. the law of nations, but one which G. B. is precluded from assuming by the most conclusive facts & arguments derived from herself. It is wonderful that so much silence has prevailed among the neutral authors on this subject. I find scarcely one that has touched on it; even since the predatory effects have been known to the world. If you can collect any publications which can aid in detecting & exposing the imposture, be so good as to send them.

I have been here eight weeks with Mrs. Madison, who was brought hither in order to have the assistance of Dr. Physic in curing a complaint near her knee; which from a very slight tumor had ulcerated into a very obstinate sore. I believe the cure is at length effected, and that I shall be able to set out in a few days for Washington. The Presidt. is to be there on the 2d. of Ocr. I postpone all reflections of a public nature, untill I can communicate the result of his Cabinet consultations. Mrs. M. presents her affece. respects to Mrs. Monroe. Yours sincerly [*sic*]

JAMES MADISON

RC (DLC); letterbook copy (DNA: RG 59, IM, vol. 5). RC cover sheet bears a note in an unidentified hand: "[. . .] Monticello ⟨C⟩apt Wilson to care of J. Maury Esq Consul USA Liverpool"; docketed by Monroe. Words and parts of words in angle brackets in the RC have been supplied from the letterbook copy. Minor differences between the copies have not been noted. Cover sheet extensively damaged; docketed by Monroe; docketed at a later date by JM.

1. For the decision, see George Joy to JM, 26 July 1805, and n. 3, and Thomas Auldjo to JM, 22 Sept. 1805, and n. 1.

2. *PJM-SS*, 9:234–39 and n. 1.

3. JM referred to the decision of William Murray, Lord Mansfield, in the 1761 case of *Berens v. Rucker.* A Dutch ship had taken on a cargo of French produce at the Dutch island of Saint Eustatius, partly from on shore and partly from ships afloat. Mansfield decreed that because the cargo had not been taken in at a French port it was not good prize (Lester H. Woolsey, "Early Cases on the Doctrine of Continuous Voyages," *American Journal of International Law* 4 [1910]: 838).

4. For the enclosure, see Rufus King to JM, 1 June 1801, *PJM-SS*, 1:251–52 and n. 1.

5. A letterbook copy of Wagner's 28 Sept. 1805 transmittal letter (DNA: RG 59, IM, vol. 5; 1 p.) covering this letter reads: "The preceding is a copy of a private letter addressed to you by Mr Madison, which he entrusted to me in order that I might multiply the copies and furnish the envelopes. At the time of writing it he had not a copy of Mr Kings letter before him, or he might have noticed the consent of Lord Hawkesbury to the publication of the enclosures, as binding them in an official manner not to change the rule they contain without giving sufficient notice to prevent those who might act upon it from being entrapped, if indeed they were competent to make the alteration they have."

From Robert Slade

The Memorial of Robert Slade of Doctors Commons London Proctor Sheweth

That your Memorialist was applied to in the Beginning of the year 1795 as a Proctor of the High Court of Admiralty of England and of the High Court of Appeals in Prize Causes by Samuel Bayard the Agent appointed by the Government of the United States of America to prosecute Claims and Appeals in Prize Causes on Behalf of Citizens of said States, to undertake in his said Capacity of Proctor the Management of certain Causes to be prosecuted by him as Claims and Appeals in the said Courts.[1]

That your Memorialist consenting to undertake the said Causes, the said Samuel Bayard as the Public Agent of the United States agreed to pay your Memorialist his regular and accustomed Bills in the same way as was done by his other Clients according to the constant Usage of his Profession and as there were a great many Causes the Expences of which would be very heavy it was also expressly stipulated by the said Samuel Bayard on Behalf of the Government of the said United States that your Memorialist was to be paid Twenty Pounds in each Cause on entering the Appeal, Eighty Pounds more on setting down the Cause for Hearing and the Remainder as soon as each Cause was actually heard and the Bill made out, though the said Samuel Bayard could not in his Capacity of Public Agent make himself personally responsible, yet he pledged the Faith of the American Government thereto, sanctioned by the Authority of Mr. Jay the American Minister then in London.

That your Memorialist in consequence of such Agreement undertook the Management of the Causes entrusted to his Care by the said Public Agent and prosecuted the same with great Zeal and unremitted Diligence so as to receive the repeated Approbation of the said Samuel Bayard himself and also of his Successors in office.

That notwithstanding the Pledge and Assurances given by the said Samuel Bayard to your Memorialist that he should be paid in the manner already stated as the said Causes were proceeded in, the Payments were suffered to run in Arrear, for want of his receiving Remittances from the Treasury of the United States in so much that on your Memorialist furnishing the said Samuel Bayard with a General Account on his leaving England, to return to America there was due to your Memorialist the accumulated Balance of:

£10174.12.0

That the Balance due to your Memorialist on the
26th July 1799 was   £14184.13.8
on the 31st Decr. 1799   11332.11.9
on the 31st Decr. 1801   13362.14.9

which last Balance was reduced by Degrees till the 11th October 1803 when it was Two Thousand Seven Hundred and Thirty two Pounds five Shillings and two Pence and which Sum is still justly due and owing to your Memorialist.

That your Memorialist frequently applied to the said Samuel Bayard and also to Rufus King Esqre. the American Minister in London for Payments of Money on Account of said Causes in manner originally stipulated but without Effect notwithstanding your Memorialist was put to great Pecuniary Embarrassment to raise the Money necessary to carry on the said Causes.

That after the Causes were finally heard in the Courts of Admiralty and Appeals they were referred by the Parties concerned to the Board of Commissioners appointed under the Treaty of Amity and Commerce concluded between the Governments of Great Britain and America to ascertain the Amount to be paid in each Cause by the British Government and the said Board of Commissioners having resolved that the British Government should only be subject to pay the Costs as taxed of the American Claimant Your Memorialist's Bills were accordingly taxed to comply with the Regulation made by the said Board of Commissioners, but which could not in Law or Equity preclude your Memorialist or the other Proctors concerned for American Citizens from receiving the full Amount of a fair and regular Bill.

That such Taxation being seldom adopted except for the sake of ascertaining the Costs necessarily incurred between Party and Party Cases where the Judge has seen fit to condemn one of them to pay the Costs of the other your Memorialist submits it cannot by any fair or liberal Construction be resorted to in the present Instances more especially as part of said Extra Costs have been occasioned by Payments actually disbursed in employing a third Counsel or otherwise with a View to benefit the Client.

That your Memorialist confiding in the Liberality as well as Justice of the United States, the Honour of their Public Agents and the Fairness of his Bills did on the Delivery of his Accounts from Time to Time carry out their full Amount to the Debit of the United States noticing therein at the same Time the Sums deducted by the Registrars Taxation and no Objection having been made till the Period of final Settlement he considered the Acquiescence of the Agents successively appointed as an Admission that he would be paid his full Costs according to the general Practice of British Merchants in which Expectation he was confirmed by the Agents of the United States themselves accepting Payment of full Costs in many Instances from the Parties and by receiving the same himself by such of the Parties as occasionally of their own Accord came to a Settlement with your Memorialist.

That George William Erving Esqre. the late Agent of the United States for Claims and Appeals having directed the Account between your Memorialist and the said States to be furnished to him in order to its being settled and the Balances discharged has refused to pay your Memorialist's Bills as made out and charged by him to the Account of the United States, saying that he does not consider himself authorized to pay your Memorialist any Thing beyond the Costs as taxed under aforesaid Regulation of the Board of Commissioners.

That prior to Mr. Bayards Return to the United States your Memorialist and the other Proctors to whom the Interests of the Citizens of said States in the Management of their Causes had been confided requested a personal Interview with the aforesaid Rufus King Esqre. with respect to the more regular Payment of their Costs in Future and the Taxation of them by the Registrar of the Court at which Interview Mr. King gave such Assurances of the Honor and Liberality of the government of the United States as induced them to rest satisfied that if the Bills were fairly made out and the Business properly conducted their said Extra Costs would be paid by the United States And your Memorialist craves leave for the Information of your Excellency to annex a Copy of the Minutes made on occasion of said Interview immediately after the same had taken Place the Original of which was signed by your Memorialist and the other Proctors present and now remains in their Custody.[2]

That Independent of the foregoing Considerations your Memorialist submits that the Loss of Interest alone on the Balances due to him on the Accounts delivered by him at different Times and to which he submits he is justly entitled would more than equal the Extra Costs in Question.

That your Memorialist has moreover suffered a Loss of Two Thousand Pounds by the Failure and Bankruptcy of Messrs. Bird Savage and Bird the Bankers of the United States in consequence of his having consented to postpone for a few Days the Payment of an Order on them to that Amount received from the said Mr. Erving the Public Agent in part Payment of his Account and which Postponement he would not have agreed to if the Respectability of their Situation as Bankers to the United States had not induced him thereto.

Under all these Circumstances your Memorialist trusts that the Government of the United States will order his Bills and Accounts to be settled and paid on the same Footing with other Clients, the Taxation of his Bills not being applicable to them and having been made solely in complia⟨nce⟩ with the Regulation of the Board of Commiss⟨ioners⟩ appointed by the Treaty of Amity and Commer⟨ce⟩ between the United States and Great Britai⟨n.⟩

ROBERT SLADE

RC and enclosure (DNA: RG 59, Communications from Special Agents). RC in a clerk's hand, dated and signed by Slade; enclosed in Samuel Bayard to JM, 20 Jan. 1806 (ibid.), in which Bayard stated Slade's claim was just. For enclosure, see n. 2.

1. In the British Admiralty Court, proctors prepared the papers and initiated proceedings. They functioned much like solicitors in the criminal court (Moore, *International Adjudications*, 4:34). For earlier discussions of the proctors' claims, see *PJM-SS*, 7:263–64, 271, 9:364–65.

2. The enclosure is a copy of a memorandum (4 pp.; signed by James Townley, Robert Slade, and James Bush) of a 27 Feb. 1798 meeting between the three proctors and Rufus King. They stated that Samuel Bayard introduced them to King, who told them that Samuel Williams, who was expected daily, was replacing Bayard, and read them the part of Williams's appointment that authorized him to act as agent. They suggested that, since the Admiralty claims were in Bayard's name, Bayard should name Williams as his attorney, but King replied that an extract or copy of the appointment should suffice. King added that although he did not personally assume responsibility for the expenses they and others incurred while acting for Bayard or Williams, he could assure them that "the United States would honorably satisfy their just Demands" for business done at the agents' orders, adding: "Gentlemen you run no Risk in this Business." They replied that as their bill had already been taxed by the registrar, which was unusual between a proctor and his client, and as cases might arise where extra charges might occur, it would be hard for them not to be reimbursed for these. King apologized for appearing to pay "strict Attention to Fees" but said that since he was responsible for obtaining approbation by proper persons of the bills, he hoped he would be excused, adding that considerable sums had been advanced on account by the United States but that "the Reimbursements had not followed as had been expected," which prevented Bayard from satisfying the proctors' bills, and that he had no doubt that a statement justifying the extra charges would be paid by the United States. King recommended that Bayard be supplied with statements of each proctor's account so that he could leave a copy with Williams and could exhibit them on arrival in the United States as an explanation of the state in which he had left affairs.

From Jacob Wagner

DEAR SIR   DEP. STATE 24 Septr. 1805

I had put aside the letters of recall of Mr. Olsen and Mr. Freire, in order that the answers might be made on the return of yourself and the President. As he however has given me notice that nothing will reach him before his setting out on his journey, I shall have answers to both made out for your approbation; expecting their return before his arrival. I do not suppose the order of the British Government, to capture all merchandise found on board our vessels, except such as is the production of our country, to be genuine:[1] it is more probable that the report has originated in the rigourous decision of the Lords of Appeal respecting carrying of colonial produce where the intent to continue to the voyage indirectly from the colony is presumed. The minor letter you wrote upon this subject will have fortified

Mr. Monroe both with the views of the government and many strong arguments to support them.[2] I have looked at the Logan Act and have satisfied myself that it could not be made to bear upon the purchasers at N. Orleans of the W. Florida lands.[3] I have this day received from Dr. Sibley the book you were promised as calculated to throw light upon the boundaries of Louisiana. It is a manuscript of many quires, purporting to be an historical journal concerning the establishment of the French therein, compiled from the works of Iberville, Bienville and Benard de la Harpe, Commandant of the Bay of St. Benard. It was found among the papers of M. Messier, late Govr. of Texas, whose family, after his death at St. Antonio, returned to their former residence at Natchitoches, where the son, who furnished the manuscript from which the present is copied, is County Treasurer. The history is deduced to the year 1724. Notwithstanding the evident and conspicuous superiority of the means and manner of discussing our claim over the Spanish Minister's efforts at Madrid, has already given us a great advantage in the appearance of the argument, I am in hopes that we can derive further succour, before the meeting of Congress, from this manuscript. It cost Dr. Sibley, as he states, 85 dollars for the copying: I suppose we ought to devise a means of repaying him, if indeed he does not mean to draw, of which he is silent. I shall await your instruction, whether I shall retain it for the President, who may be expected in about a week, or forward it to you. I have enclosed the salary account for your signature. Unless you direct otherwise, Mr. Thom will place your salary in the bank to your credit.

I have heretofore sent you an appointment, by the commander of the Nautilus, of a Navy Agent at Algesiras, with a sweeping clause which might be construed to make him an Agent for every purpose.[4] Other Naval officers have undertook to make provisional *Consuls*. Perhaps you will think they ought to be checked. I am informed at the Navy Office that they do not consider even a Commodore as competent to appoint a *Navy Agent;* and Mr. Smith would therefore readily take the steps necessary to prevent the practice in future.

Except the 2 & 3 articles, Mr. Lear's treaty is copied from Cathcart's projet with but few alterations and additions.[5] I have compared them together. The circumstance is remarkable as Mr. Cathcart cannot be supposed to have stopped short of the utmost scope of concession, as to terms, expected from the Bashaw. It was drawn up before the loss of the Philada. and therefore is silent about money. With my best wishes and respects to Mrs. Madison, I have the honor to remain, with the greatest respect & attachment Your obed. Servt.

JACOB WAGNER

RC (DLC).

1. American newspapers reprinted a 7 Aug. 1805 article from a London paper that stated: "an order, we understand, was sent to all the out ports some days ago, instructing our cruizers to detain all American vessels which have on board property not the produce of the United States. This order has been already acted upon, and several ships have been stopped. The American Consul, it is reported, applied to government yesterday for an explanation: but, we are not acquainted with the answer he received" (Boston *Independent Chronicle*, 16 Sept. 1805).

2. Wagner may have referred to JM's 12 Apr. 1805 letter to Monroe, *PJM-SS*, 9:234–39.

3. The 30 Jan. 1799 "Logan Act" forbade U.S. citizens to negotiate with foreign governments "with an intent to influence the measures or conduct" of such governments without express permission from the U.S. government (*U.S. Statutes at Large*, 1: 613).

4. For Capt. Charles Stewart's appointment of Pedro Porral as U.S. Navy agent at Algeciras on 14 May 1805, at the suggestion of John Gavino, see Josef Yznardy to JM, 12 July 1805, and n. 1. Stewart was commander of the *Syren*.

5. Articles 2 and 3 of Tobias Lear's treaty with Yusuf Qaramanli deal with the return of the officers and crew of the *Philadelphia*, which ran aground in Tripoli harbor in October 1803; and the removal of all American forces from Tripoli, a reference to William Eaton's expedition against Derna, which took place in the spring of 1805. Neither article could have been mentioned in the treaty draft that Cathcart included in his 5 May 1803 letter to JM; the wording of the other articles is the same (Miller, *Treaties*, 2:529–30, 550; *PJM-SS*, 6:58–59 and n. 2, 172–74 and n. 1, 8:67 n. 2, 9:101, 4:575–76 and n. 4).

§ From William Bushby.[1] *24 September 1805, "Washington Navy Yard."* "Last summer I waited on you with a line from Mr. George Hite[2] wishing your favour with Mr. Latrobe to obtain for me employment as a Painter on the Publick buildings in the City. As Mr. Latrobe was then absent, and you observed might return when you was not present—you advised me on his coming to show him my recommendations—(as at your request)—which wou'd answer my purpose. I did so, and had the satisfaction of being promised a share of the work as soon as the Capitol shou'd be ready—adding, that for want of appropriation nothing cou'd be done to the renewing the Work to the Publick buildings already finished. Shortly after this I understood there was one of my business wanting in the Navy Yard, which induced me to wait on the Secretary, and was engaged by him with my Apprentice. I have now been 13 Months constantly in the service on monthly wages, and have been induced thereby to build me a house for the reception of my family contiguous to the Yard—not being able to obtain one on Rent. I flatter myself that I have given satisfaction to Capt. Cassin[3] who superintends the business of the Navy Yard—and am very well satisfied with the Service. But lately I have been informed that there is a person trying to procure some Interest to be made to the Secretary to get the preference to the employ—(presuming on my having no permanent engagement)—which induces me to trouble you with this. For tho' I am conscious that I need not fear being superseeded for want of faithfulness, or abillity in my business—yet I know not what affect a Gentlemans immediate application may have—as only my general Character was made known to him—without the aid of any personal interest whatever. And as you have so kindly shewn your desire to serve me—it will greatly add to my former obligation—Your signifying to Secretary Smith—that if I have answered the character given me—your wish, that I may be continued in the employment."

RC (DLC). 2 pp. Docketed by JM.

1. Painter William Bushby (ca. 1746–1810) owned considerable property in and around Alexandria, Virginia, where he lived before moving to the vicinity of the navy yard in 1804. He also sold paints in Georgetown (*National Intelligencer*, 13 July 1810; *Centinel of Liberty, or George-Town and Washington Advertiser*, 10 June 1800; *Alexandria Advertiser and Commercial Intelligencer*, 31 Aug. and 10 Sept. 1803).

2. George Hite was the brother of Bushby's wife, Mary Hite Manning Bushby. They were both cousins of Isaac Hite who had married Nelly Conway Madison Hite, JM's sister, who died in 1802 (*Historical Sketches: A Collection of Papers Prepared for the Historical Society of Montgomery County, Pennsylvania* [7 vols.; Norristown, Pa., 1895–1925], 4:128–30; *PJM-SS*, 4:180 n. 6).

3. John Cassin (d. 1822) was named to supervise the Washington navy yard in April 1803 and served in that post until 1812, when he was transferred to the Norfolk navy yard (Knox, *Naval Documents, Barbary Wars*, 2:388; Henry B. Hibben, *Navy-Yard, Washington: History from Organization, 1799, to Present Date* [Washington, 1890], 47; Charleston *City Gazette and Commercial Daily Advertiser*, 30 Mar. 1822).

§ From John Teasdale. *24 September 1805, Charleston.* "Being persuaded the following statement of facts may come under your attention that in September 1803 I loaded my Schooner the Hiram John Fiott master with Provissions to the Bay of Honduras that on her passage the Capt⟨n.⟩ touched at Cape Mole St Nicholas & was boarded by the Port officer who told him that the government must have his Provissions & Cargo for wch. they woud give him an order on the Commanding Officer at Cape franceway to pay him in money or Coff⟨ee.⟩ His Letter to me says that they was in a distressd state, haveing had nothing for the people to subsist on for some days that they would only allow him the price they pleased. On arrival at Cape france way he applyd agreeable to the order on the government for pay & was informd there was no produce or money there but woud give him Bills on france for the amount, which finally Cap⟨n.⟩ fiott was oblidged reluctantly to receive, dureing this time the place was invested by the brigands & in about a week after Cape Francois was lost, compelling the Schooner to bring as many of the inhabitants as he could from there, on comeing out of that port, he was boarded by an Officer of an English man of war, who sent her down to Jamaica as french Property on the day he landed he was took sick & in four days he died in Kingston, the Bills was forwarded the day on his arrival there in a letter to me & agreeable to their tenor I sent them to Mr Skipwith at Paris for payment, from the account I have recd they yet remain unpaid nor is there any probability of their being soon settled, from the Information of a gentleman who has had some lately paid, that if a representation of facts attending my Bills was represented by the minister resideing there they would have great Influence with the heads of that government. I shoud think myself greatly oblidged could I prevail on you to forward a Statement Of this to the minister at Paris for him to make application & to urge payment of said Bills now in the hands of Mr Skipwith.

"My situation with that of many other⟨s,⟩ here are much distressd intirely oweing to the transactions of this nature with also the spoliations committed on my property on which account am now oblidged to apply for your aid in obtaining for me that Justice they are so unwilling to grant & which the present case requires with much Esteem I am &c[1]

373

Copy of the Bills[2]

No 279   Cape 12 brumair year 12 90 days sight pay to the order of John F(i)att
          master of the Schooner Hiram 6222—franks—14—for provissions &
          Tobacco deliverd at Cape
          Mole St Nickolas on the french government at Paris
          Indorsed John Fiott & John Teasdale & Signd by B(i)souard & others
No. 280. same date same sight to John Fiott at 90 dys sight for 39333 franks 12—for
          provissions deliverd to the french Government at Cape Mole s Nickolas
          on the french marine at Paris. Indorsed John fiott & John Teasdale.[3]

Tr and enclosures (DNA: RG 76, Preliminary Inventory 177, entry 123, France, Con-
vention of 1803 [Spoliation], Misc. Claims, ca. 1798–1804, envelope 3, folder 3). Tr 3 pp.
Unsigned; conjectural correspondent assigned based on contents of letter and enclosures.
For enclosures, see n. 1.

1. The enclosures (3 pp.) are copies of (1) Teasdale to Fulwar Skipwith, 20 Apr. 1804,
which enclosed the two bills of exchange, asking Skipwith to have them paid and converted
to cash to be sent to the firm of Andrews & Cook at Bordeaux, who had Teasdale's order to
spend the money on "articles suitable for the consumption of this City," and to acknowledge receipt of the letter and bills; (2) Teasdale to Skipwith, 31 Oct. 1804, reminding him
of the 20 Apr. letter, stating that several of his friends had had such bills negotiated at Paris
and Bordeaux at eight percent and the money sent to England, noting that he was not disposed to let a sum as large as that owed to him "lay dormant," asking Skipwith again to
convert the bills into cash, stating that merchant houses in Charleston were distressed because of the seizures in the West Indies by French ships and the withholding of funds by
the French governments there, lamenting his own involvement, and suggesting that if the
government would not pay, then Skipwith should attempt to have the claim included in
those to be paid out of the Louisiana Purchase Claims Convention funds; (3) Teasdale to
Andrews & Cook, 31 Oct. 1804, acknowledging receipt of their 18 July 1804 letter, stating
that Skipwith's silence left him ignorant of the fate of the bills he had sent and that he had
written Skipwith again asking him to convert the bills into cash to be sent to Bordeaux,
asking them to have half the funds laid out on "Course Linen, Brittanies a few cambricks &
boxes of fruit in Brandy" and the other half spent on "Clarret Wine in Hhds a few pipes of
Brandy & 50 Cases of Oil to be shipped by a good American vessell," adding that there was
an abundance in Charleston of everything but woolen goods and that the hurricane there
in early September had done "great Injury" to the cotton crop; and (4) Teasdale to Skipwith, 26 Apr. 1805, acknowledging receipt of the latter's letter of 4 Jan. explaining his silence, stating that Andrews & Cook had not informed him of Skipwith's request for
information, observing that he saw that commissioners had been named to look into the
Saint-Domingue bills and that the wording of the ones he had sent made it clear they were
in exchange for provisions for the garrison at Môle Saint-Nicholas, adding that had Captain Fiott been able to sell the provisions to the residents of Cap Français, he could have
obtained four times as much money and asking Skipwith to explain this to the commissioners, stating that the current state of the local market discouraged him from having the
funds laid out on goods and asking Skipwith to keep them and inform Teasdale that he had
them at which point he would be advised to send the money on.

2. In 1827 Secretary of State Henry Clay's report to Congress on ships seized by France
between 1793 and 1800 included a list of unpaid claims among which was John Teasdale's
claim for $8,427.67 for two unpaid bills of exchange (Williams, *French Assault on American
Shipping*, 37, 370).

3. English-born merchant John Teasdale (ca. 1752–1818) had been a resident of Charleston, South Carolina, for forty years when he died. He left the city with the British army when they evacuated it in 1782 but returned to marry, build a home, and open up the cotton trade (Charleston *City Gazette & Daily Advertiser*, 23 Nov. 1818; *PJM*, 6:30 n. 5; C. Irvine Walker, *The Romance of Lower Carolina: Historic, Romantic and Traditional Incidents of the Colonial and Revolutionary Eras* ... [Charleston, 1915], 116).

From James Monroe

No. 34.
Duplicate.
Sir   London Septem 25. 1805.

    I have already forwarded you copies of two letters to Ld Mulgrave respecting the late seizure of American vessels,[1] and you will receive with this a Copy of a third one.[2] His Lordship has endeavourd to manage this business without writing, from a desire which has been very apparent to get rid of it, without any compromitment. With that view he gave me in an early interview, a report of the King's Advocate-General and Proctor on my first letter, which had been referred to them, which gave Some explanation on the Subject, which he might Suppose would be Satisfactory. I Soon however assured him that it was not, and pressed an answer to my letters which was promised, but which has not yet been given. A few days before Mr. Erving left this for the Continent I requested him to ask Mr. Hammond when I should be favored with one. I Send you a note of the conversation between them.[3] Having waited Some time longer I thought it my duty to press the point again, and in So doing to expose as fully as I could, the fallacy and injustice of the principle on which G. Britain asserts the right, to interdict our commerce with the colonies of her enemies, and elsewhere in the productions of those colonies. I do not Know that I Shall be able to obtain an answer to this or the other letters. The presumption is against it, because She does not wish to tie up her hands from doing what her interest may dictate, in case the new combination with Russia and Austria Should be Successful against France.[4] In the mean time She Seeks to tranquillize us by dismissing our vessels in every case that she possibly can. It is evident to those who attend the trials that the tone of the Judge has become more moderate: that he acquits whenever he can acquit our vessels, and Keeping within the precedent of the Essex,[5] Seizes every fact that the papers or other evidence furnish, in the cases which occur, to bring them within that limit. If any thing can be done in our affairs, it may be in a week or ten days; and if not done in that time it most probably will not be during the present winter. I Shall do every thing in my power to bring them to a Satisfactory conclusion. I am, Sir, with great respect and esteem, Your very obedient Servant

JAS. MONROE.

P. S. I enclose you a copy of my letter to Genl. Armstrong by Mr. Erving.[6]

RC (DNA: RG 46, President's Messages, 10B–B1); RC (DNA: RG 233, President's Messages, 10A–D1, vol. 1); letterbook copy (DLC: Monroe Papers); enclosures (DNA: RG 59, DD, Great Britain, vol. 12); Tr of enclosures (DNA: RG 46, President's Messages, 9A–E3; Tr of enclosures (DNA: RG 233, President's Messages, 9A–D1). First RC in a clerk's hand, signed by Monroe; docketed by Wagner. Second RC in a clerk's hand, except for Monroe's complimentary close and signature; docketed by Wagner. Minor differences between the copies have not been noted. For enclosures, see nn. 2–3, and 6.

1. See Monroe to JM, 6 Aug. 1805, and n. 9, and Monroe to JM, 16 Aug. 1805, and n. 2.
2. The enclosure is a copy of Monroe to Mulgrave, 23 Sept. 1805 (16 pp.; printed in *ASP, Foreign Relations*, 2:734–37), protesting the British doctrine that forbade neutral trade with the colonies of Britain's enemies during a war, if that trade had been forbidden by the belligerents in peacetime. Monroe argued that the doctrine was a violation of the law of nations, that the multiple orders that the British government had issued over the years showed that it had changed its own views from time to time, that Rufus King and Lord Hawkesbury had had similar correspondence on the subject, and that the principle was in opposition to decisions made under the seventh article of the Jay Treaty. He also touched on the subjects of boundaries between the two countries in North America and especially of impressment, which was important for both nations, adding that he would be glad to discuss those points with Mulgrave at any time.
3. The enclosure (3 pp.; docketed by Wagner) is a copy of George W. Erving's report on his 30 Aug. 1805 farewell meeting with British undersecretary of state George Hammond. Erving told Hammond that he would be traveling through France, and that Monroe had asked him to inquire as to when he could expect a reply from Mulgrave, to which Hammond replied that he did not know but would ask Mulgrave. Erving stressed that Monroe strongly wished to be able to report to the U.S. government what the British had to say about the issues he had raised and he was thinking of writing to Mulgrave again, which Hammond seemed to discourage. They discussed the recent increase in seizures of U.S. ships by the British, which both men attributed to recent Admiralty Court decisions. Erving reported: "It is impossible to State his words distinctly. His manner was ⟨more⟩ important."
4. For the alliances among Great Britain, Russia, and Austria, see Sylvanus Bourne to JM, 17 May 1805, *PJM-SS*, 9:362 and n. 1.
5. For the case of the *Essex*, see George Joy to JM, 26 July 1805, and n. 3.
6. The enclosure was a copy of Monroe to Armstrong, 2 Sept. 1805 (3 pp.; docketed by Wagner; printed in Hamilton, *Writings of James Monroe*, 4:311–15), referring Armstrong to George W. Erving for any questions he might have about U.S. relations with either Great Britain or Spain; discussing Bowdoin's arrival in England, the state of his health, and his plans to join Armstrong in Paris; offering suggestions for how Erving should be introduced to the Spanish government; speculating that an intensification of the European war might alter the French government's opinion on U.S. relations with Spain; and discussing his attempts to resolve the problem of increased British seizures of U.S. ships.

§ From William C. C. Claiborne. *25 September 1805, Concordia.* "I am still in a state of Convalescence; but continue very fible; so soon as I feel enabled to undertake the Journey, I shall return to New Orleans. In the mean time I do not suppose that my absence from *that City,* will prove injurious to the public Interest. The enclosed letter from Mr. Graham will present You with the latest intelligence.[1]

"The conduct of the Spaniards in this Quarter evidence a settled hostility to the United States, and I am inclined to think that such conduct is encouraged by the Court of Spain. I am anxious to know the result of the late Negociation. I have not been honored with an official letter from you, for two Months past, and I very much fear you[r] Communications have miscaried."

RC and enclosure (DNA: RG 59, TP, Orleans, vol. 7); letterbook copy (Ms-Ar: Claiborne Executive Journal, vol. 15). RC 1 p.; in a clerk's hand, except for Claiborne's complimentary close and signature; docketed by Wagner as received 22 Oct. On the right and left sides of the cover sheet of the enclosure, Graham added an updated current report of the election returns. For enclosure, see n. 1.

1. The enclosure (3 pp.; printed in Carter, *Territorial Papers, Orleans,* 9:504–6) is John Graham's 16 Sept. 1805 letter to Claiborne, commenting on the candidates for the election beginning that day; reporting that the alarm over the plotted slave insurrection had died down; describing recent U.S. troop movements and stating the general belief that the federal government should increase the number of regular army troops in the region; repeating reports that 600 Spanish troops were ordered for Pensacola, and 5,000 for the U.S.-Mexican frontier; stating that Casa Calvo had been quite ill and was rumored to have received letters from Madrid saying the government would request diplomatic status for him; and touching on the arrest of the Spaniards who had taken the Kempers, the seizure of an American ship at Mobile for failure to pay duties, and the confiscation there of goods bound for Fort Stoddart for the same reason.

From James Leander Cathcart

SIR   WASHINGTON Septr: 26th: 1805.

A few days ago I made application to General Dearborn as a candidate for an Agency that is vacant at the post of Natchitoches; finding I had a rival in the person of Mr. Rodgers, I waited upon the general this morning who inform'd me that a number of respectable persons having applied for the said appointment he had determined to lay their pretensions before the President who would select the person most eligible to fill the vacancy; in my application I took the liberty to refer him to the President & yourself for any information he might conceive necessary to acquire relative to me, & now take the liberty to request you to mention me favorably to the President & to General Dearborn in order that I may not be disappointed, being fully persuaded that a few lines from you to either before the appointment takes place will insure the desired success.

The place in it self is no great acquisition, but as it is situated in a new acquired territory where the knowledge of the French & Spanish languages which I possess will be of infinite service to myself as well as render me more useful to the service I conceive it opens a road to preferment which makes it desireable.[1]

Mrs. Cathcart & myself frequently hears of the state of Mrs. Madisons health & are happy to find it meliorates. She desires me to request you to make her respects acceptable & to assure your lady that she is very anxious to have the pleasure of congratulating her on her perfect recovery & happy arrival at Washington. I have the honor to continue with the most respectful esteem Sir. Your Obnt. Servt.

JAMES LEANDER CATHCART

RC (DLC). Docketed by JM.

1. Cathcart did not receive the Indian agency appointment; it went instead to Philip Reibelt, who lingered so long at New Orleans that Dearborn at length gave up on him and appointed Thomas Linnard in his place (Carter, *Territorial Papers, Orleans*, 9:563 and n. 56).

From Jacob Wagner

DEAR SIR   DEPARTMENT OF STATE 26 Septr. 1805
I have examined the point you refer to relative to the British order of 8 Jany. 1794,[1] in the appendix to the 4th. vol. of Robinson. This government was very far from recognising the right of a belligerent to confine neutrals within the limits of their commerce in time of peace. The order of Novr. 1793[2] was known at the Admiralty only a few days before the 26th. Decr. It was superseded therefore in about a fortnight after it was published: of course it could not have admitted of any actual opposition from Philada. and it appears that on the 9th. Jany. Mr. Pinckney, in an interview with Lord Grenville, in remonstrating against the order of the 8 Jany. observed "that we did not admit the right of belligerent powers to interfere further in the commerce between neutral nations and their adversaries, than to prevent their carrying to them articles, which, by *common usage*, were established as contraband, and any articles to a place *fairly blockaded;* that consequently the two first articles, though founded upon principles of not suffering in war a traffic, which was not admitted by the same nations in time of peace, and of taking their enemies property when found on board of neutral vessels, were nevertheless contrary to what we contended to be just principles of the modern law of nations."[3] At the time Mr. Pinckney received the order of Novr. Ld. Grenville was absent, and after his return

an interview was avoided by him until it was agreed in the Cabinet to re-scind the order. Mr. Robinson is therefore mistaken in his assertion that we made representations analogous to the British doctrine.[4]

In one of the Moniteurs you sent me is a detail of the massacre of the Jews at Algiers, coming in all probability from the French legation. It seems that Basnach was the first sacrifice. It ended by a stipulation of the Dey, that no jews, except Artisans, should be permitted to reside at Algiers, and that their number should be limited as agreed upon in a treaty be-tween Barbarossa and their nation. It is probable that at least the pecuniary corruption, necessary to the management of affairs, will be diminished by the fall of the Jews.

I am preparing details of Spanish depredations for the Spanish Minis-ter, but I am fearful as they are in most instances authenticated by our Consuls in Cuba, the Spaniards may act vindictively towards them.

There is an Indian Agency at Natchitoches vacant, which Cathcart is desirous of obtaining. He has applied to the Secretary of war for it, and as he has no intimate acquaintance with him, he is about to apply for your assistance. I observed to the Secretary of war, that there was a disposition to provide reasonably for Cathcart in what he might be competent to perform; and the appointment is to remain open until the return of the President. As C. understands French & Spanish and knows enough of the quality of goods and keeping accounts to qualify him, he seems not[5] be very unfit. The Secretary of war, wishing a person who would stand behind the counter and attend with patience to the minute wants of the Indians, is fearful that in practice Mr. C's dignity may be found an inconvenience. The emolument I am told is a salary of 1000 dollars, with a Clerk at 500, which he wishes to unite if he obtains the appointment. I have the honor to remain, Dear Sir, With great attachmt. & respect, Your most obed. servt.

JACOB WAGNER

RC (DLC).

1. For the British instructions of 8 Jan. 1794 that eased the restrictions in the Novem-ber 1793 order, see *ASP, Foreign Relations,* 3:264.

2. The British instructions of 6 Nov. 1793 said naval commanders and privateers "shall stop and detain all ships laden with goods the produce of any colony belonging to France, or carrying provisions or other supplies for the use of any such colony, and shall bring the same, with their cargoes, to legal adjudication in our Courts of Admiralty" (ibid.).

3. Wagner quoted from a 9 Jan. 1794 letter that Thomas Pinckney sent Secretary of State Edmund Randolph, enclosing a copy of the instructions of 8 Jan. 1794. On 28 Jan. 1794 Pinckney told Randolph that he had nothing to do with the revocation of the instruc-tions of 6 Nov. 1793, since the foreign secretary had avoided meeting with him until 9 Jan., by which time the British cabinet had already decided on the revocation (DNA: RG 59, DD, Great Britain, vol. 3). The italics were added by Wagner.

4. Robinson's statement, to which Wagner objected, was: "*American* vessels, had been admitted to trade in some articles, and on certain conditions, with the colonies both of this Country and of *France*. Such a permission had become a part of the general commercial arrangements, as the ordinary state of their trade in time of peace. The commerce of *America* was therefore abridged by the foregoing [November] *instructions*, and debarred of the right generally ascribed to neutral trade in time of war, that it may be continued, with particular exceptions, on the basis of its ordinary establishment. In consequence of representations made by the *American* government to this effect, new instructions to our cruizers were issued, 8th *Jan.* 1794, apparently designed to exempt *American* ships, trading between their own country, and the colonies of *France*" (Robinson, *Admiralty Reports* [London ed., 1799–1808], 4:appendix A, 2).

5. Wagner apparently omitted the word "to" here.

§ From William Jarvis. *26 September 1805, Lisbon.* "The first of the foregoing went by the ship Harriot, Captn Winslow Harlow, for Baltimore with the inclosures.[1]

"The press set on foot here has already subsided here to a certain extent without many Men being impressed.[2]

"A Report has been whispered about that the Emperor Napoleon has made a farther demand on this Government of Six Million of Crusados ie 3,000,000 dollars, whether in the shape of a loan or contribution it is not said, nor is it said what is the determination of this Government. In fact I have some doubts whether such a demand has been made, it not coming from a quarter deserving of much Credit.

"It appears certain that the Camp of Boulogne is broken up & the troops are marching toward the Rhine & Italy, also several of the Regiments nea(r) Paris. It was currently circulated here yesterday, that the Emperor Napoleon being satisfied of the hostile disposition of the Emperors of Russia & Germany was determined to anticipate a junction of their forces by an attack on the latter, in hopes of striking an effectual stroke before any assistance could be afforded by the Russians.[3] This report I have every reason to suppose came from the French Ambassado(r) Genl. Junot, & that it was circulated by his orders or consent.

"I have heard nothing about my application relative to the ship Venus except that my letter was translated & sent to the Minister of Marine.[4] The advice I mentioned in my last of the Rochfort Squadron being seen off Bell-Isle the 3rd. Instant, I presume is correct, as it is certain they have disappeared from off Cape Ortegal."

RC (DNA: RG 59, CD, Lisbon, vol. 2). 2 pp.; written at the foot of Jarvis to JM, 16 Sept. 1805; docketed by Wagner.

1. The *Harriot*, Harlow, arrived at Baltimore on 29 Nov. 1805 (*Baltimore Weekly Price Current*, 5 Dec. 1805).

2. See Jarvis to JM, 16 Sept. 1805.

3. In the summer of 1805, Austria and Russia had agreed that Austria would join Russia in the coalition against France, and both began moving troops closer to territory held by Napoleon. In response, he began in late September to move his troops from Boulogne towards the east and south (Acton, *Cambridge Modern History* [1969 reprint], 9:249–53).

4. See Jarvis to JM, 16 Sept. 1805, and n. 10.

§ From Louis-Marie Turreau. *26 September 1803*. Encloses a decree of Napoleon I naming Pierre Lemarois undersecretary of commercial relations for the state of Georgia, residing at Savannah. Asks JM to present it to the president and obtain the usual exequatur.

RC (DNA: RG 59, NFL, France, vol. 2–3). 1 p.; in French; in a clerk's hand, signed by Turreau; docketed by Wagner.

§ From Carlos Martínez de Yrujo. *26 September 1805, near Philadelphia*. Guided by the sentiments of justice which characterize the king, Yrujo took the liberty to call the royal attention to certain expressions in JM's letter in response to the letter Yrujo wrote giving JM the news that the king had declared war on Great Britain,[1] which referred to the hope that the United States would see the rights of neutrals respected. Now encloses JM a copy of a 14 July 1805 letter just received from Pedro Cevallos[2] so JM may see with satisfaction that the most efficacious means have been taken by the Spanish government, through the medium of a royal circular dated the ninth of the same month, making known to the privateers the circumspection with which they must conduct themselves towards neutral vessels, making them responsible for complaints that result in justice against their conduct.

RC and enclosure (DNA: RG 59, NFL, Spain, vol. 2). RC 2 pp.; in Spanish; in a clerk's hand, except for Yrujo's complimentary close and signature. For enclosure, see n. 2.

1. See JM to Yrujo, 4 Apr. 1805, *PJM-SS*, 9:216.
2. The enclosure (2 pp.; in Spanish; docketed by Wagner) is a copy of Pedro Cevallos to Yrujo, 14 July 1805, stating that in view of what Yrujo had reported in a letter about JM's reply to the communication Yrujo had made of the Spanish declaration of war against England, Cevallos had sent a dispatch to the navy secretary, warning that the king might want to take measures respecting the neutrality of the United States to carefully avoid molestation of American commerce by Spanish privateers. Cevallos added that in reply the navy secretary told him that a royal circular, dated 9 July [1805], had been issued, warning the privateers again about the circumspection with which they must conduct themselves toward neutral vessels, and holding them responsible for any complaints that might result against their conduct. Cevallos added that it seemed opportune to reveal this to Yrujo, so he might put it to an appropriate use.

§ To Charles Pettit and James S. Cox. *27 September 1805, Department of State*. "I have received your memorial respecting the proceedings at Paris in the case of the ship New Jersey and cargo, in which the Companies you represent are interested as insurers, and I have the honor to inform you, that on the previous application of other parties (Messrs. Nichlin & Griffith) the step has been taken which the circumstances seemed to render proper."[1]

RC (TU: Papers of the Insurance Company of North America); letterbook copy (DNA: RG 59, DL, vol. 15). RC 1 p.; in a clerk's hand, signed by JM; addressed by Wagner. Postmarked 30 Sept. at Philadelphia.

1. Pettit and Cox's memorial has not been found. For the other correspondence to which JM refers, see Philip Nicklin and Robert Eaglesfield Griffith to JM, 25 July 1805, and JM to John Armstrong, 25 Aug. 1805.

§ From William C. C. Claiborne. *27 September 1805, Concordia.* "In consequence of a letter, I received on last Evening from Mr. Graham, of which the enclosed is a Copy,[1] I shall set out on this Morning for New Orleans.

"I cannot conjecture the unpleasant *Rumors* alluded to by Mr. Graham; but I persuade myself they will not prove of serious importance. I am indeed illy fitted for a Journey; my Health is far from being restored and I fear the fatigue to which I shall be exposed, may occasion a Relapse. But I shall nevertheless proceed, and will be in New Orleans as soon as possable."

RC and enclosure (DNA: RG 59, TP, Orleans, vol. 7); letterbook copy (Ms-Ar: Claiborne Executive Journal, vol. 15). RC 1 p.; docketed by Wagner as received 30 Oct. For enclosure, see n. 1.

1. The enclosure (1 p.; docketed by Wagner; printed in Carter, *Territorial Papers, Orleans,* 9:513) is John Graham's 19 Sept. 1805 letter, stating "rumours of an unpleasant nature have got abroad; how far they are to be relyed on, I do not know; but I feel it my duty to recommend to you *immediately* to return Here," and adding that since he did not know if this opportunity of conveying his letter was a safe one, he would say no more.

¶ From William Lewis. Letter not found. *27 September 1805.* Described in Jacob Wagner to Lewis, 4 Oct. 1805, as dealing with Lewis's claim against France (DNA: RG 59, DL, vol. 15). For Lewis's claim, see JM to John Armstrong, 26 Mar. 1805, *PJM-SS,* 9:178, and Armstrong to JM, 3 July 1805, and n. 3.

To Robert R. Livingston

SIR,　　　　　　　　　　　DEPARTMENT OF STATE 28th Septr 1805

The case of Mr William Lewis, whose vessel was carried into Tobago by a French Cruizer, as stated and referred to in the letter I had the honor to write to you on the 27th Octr 1803, has been since renewed to Genl Armstrong, who returns for answer, that he has neither seen nor heard any thing of it, that none of your papers have been left with him, and that Mr. Skipwith's memory does not supply the defect.[1] I therefore beg the favor of you to forward to me these and any other official papers respecting unfinished demands which may remain with you and which you may judge necessary to their furtherance at Paris. As Mr Lewis's case has taken a peculiar course here, I will thank you for his papers in particular, as soon as you can make it convenient to forward them. I have the honor to be, Sir Very respectfully your most obt Sert.

JAMES MADISON

RC (NjP); letterbook copy (DNA: RG 59, DL, vol. 15). RC in a clerk's hand, signed and franked by JM; addressed by Wagner. Docketed by Livingston.

1. See John Armstrong to JM, 3 July 1805, and n. 3.

From Samuel Smith

The inclosed extract of a Letter (also from Mackenzie & Glennie)[1] differs from that to Mr Taylor by the Words "Scored" which were interlined in the letter to Mesrs. Gilmor & Sons & not in that to Mr. Taylor—those words give a quite different turn to the whole Case. But there is in this extract a New Principle not before known—to wit—all Vessels & their Cargoes bound from an Enemies Port direct to the East or West Indies are good Prize—this Doctrine is New—from the Mother Country to a Colony in either we knew, was not Considered legal. Indeed It does appear that when we Conform to One declared System, as in the Correspondence between Mr. King & Lord. Hy. they the British institute a New System, that Involves the Neutrals in unforeseen Ruin.[2] The Trade of the U.S. Subject to Condemnation under this Novel doctrine, Cannot be less than Five Millions of Dollars. I should Suppose It would be Eight Millions. I am Dr. sir with Mrs Smith's Love to Mrs. M. your friend & servt

S. SMITH

RC and enclosure (DLC). For enclosure, see n. 1.

1. The enclosure (1 p.; filed at 25 July 1809) is an extract from Scottish merchants Mackenzie & Glennie to Baltimore merchants Robert Gilmor & Sons, 25 July [1805], which stated: "In consequence of some new instructions issued by our Government, the British cruizers are bringing into port for adjudication, all American vessels bound direct to ports in Holland or France that have plantation property on board; and two cargoes have been condemned that had been brought from St. Domingo (or) Guadaloupe to America, there landed, and the duties bonded, and reshipped in the same vessel, and consigned to Antwerp. Upon this last voyage they were stopped, and it seems to be the judges determination to condemn all French or Dutch Colonial property if it is found going to ports in the mother Country *in the same vessel it was brought from the Colony in*, unless it is clearly proved that it has been bona fide sold in America; and all vessels and their cargoes bound from ports of France or Holland, direct to the East or West Indies will be condemned. This last mentioned trade our confidential counsel admits is illegal, being contrary to the acknowledged laws of nations."

2. For JM's earlier discussion of the new British marine regulation, see JM to Monroe, 24 Sept. 1805.

From Jacob Wagner

Mr. Erving has acknowledged the receipt of your letter respecting the colony-trade as involved in the case of the Aurora.[1] Your private letter to Mr. Monroe has been copied[2] and partly transmitted with the enclosures from the Gazettes, to which I have added Mr. King's letter in which they were received, whence it will appear that Lord Hawkesbury knew of

Mr. King's intention to procure their publication, as a guide to the public, before they were drawn up. This circumstance seems to me to strengthen the complaint of the doctrine being departed from suddenly, in such manner as to entrap those who had regulated themselves by it.

We have nothing new, but the death of Mr. Wayman.[3] Affectionly. Your obed. servt.

JACOB WAGNER

RC (DLC).

1. For Erving's acknowledgement of the receipt of JM to James Monroe, 12 Apr. 1805, see Erving to JM, 10 July 1805, and n. 5.
2. See JM to Monroe, 24 Sept. 1805.
3. Charles Wayman of Georgetown, D.C., died on 26 Sept. 1805 (*Alexandria Daily Advertiser,* 1 Oct. 1805).

¶ From Stephen Kingston. Letter not found. *28 September 1805.* Described in Wagner's 3 Oct. 1805 reply as dealing with the capture of the *Ann & Susan.* Wagner informed Kingston that copies of his documents had been sent to John Armstrong together with general instructions on vessels captured at Curaçao (DNA: RG 59, DL, vol. 15). For the case of the *Ann & Susan,* and the captures at Curaçao, see *PJM-SS,* 9:34–35 and n. 2, 174, 200–201.

§ From John Elmslie. *29 September 1805, Cape of Good Hope.* "I am sorry to observe, that from a general neglect in Masters of Vessels for these six months past of not reporting their vessels and in departing from the ports of the Cape without exhibiting their marine Papers, have not only prevented me from inspecting Registers &c. but also forwarding the usual semi annual List of vessels which have entered this district. As soon as the Customhouse Book of reports comes from Simons Bay where entries are made from April to September I shall endeavour to procure a correct list in order to show to Government who have been so remiss in their duty. The delinquents may make a plea of a late Customhouse regulation at the Cape, detaining Ships papers till clearing—though this regulation prevents Masters of vessels from fulfilling that part of the Act which requires them to deposite their Registers &c. with the Consuls—They can have no excuse after having received their clearances and papers in not exhibiting them for inspection before their departure—I now beg leave to mention a practice which I have remarked some Masters of Vessels to be guilty of, by procuring their vessels to be condemned as unseaworthy when they were notoriously otherwise. The Brig Molly of Nantuckett David Joy Master is a recent instance of this kind & which diserves particular animadversion.

"The Molly arrived here in March last, having received some triffling damage in a gale of wind off the Cap*—Capt. Joy in consequence had a survey held

---

*sec 4 "Regulations proposed." Many Caps. are not overnice in making such representation.[1]

& by the report made the Molly was declared not seaworth[y], accordingly the Capt. had her condemned and sold at public Auction. John Clements a Citizen of the United States & Agent for Wm. H Bordman & Thos. Clements junr residing in Boston Massachusetts, purchas(ed) said Vessel for their account and in order to show to his Principals, th(e) situation of the Molly before any repairs were done to her; order(ed) a very full survey to be held, copy of the report made being deposited in my Office I herewith enclose the same for your information.[2] The Molly after undergoing some small repairs, was loaded here by Mr. Clements & sent on a voyage to the Eastward. Respecting the Mollys marine papers whic(h) were left in my Office by Capt. Joy to be forwarded to the U.S. in order to cancel his bond passed at the Customhouse for the faithful use of the same—I was at a considerable loss how to Act, Capt. Clements having demanded them when the Molly was ready to proceed to Sea in consequence of the vessel being owned by American Citizens & navigated according to Law, and even threatened in case of my not delivering then to protest agains(t) me for all loss which should happen to the Vessel & cargo for want of her marine papers. This being the first Case of the kind that had come before me, and the clause in the Registry Act respecting the faithful use of Certificates of Registry &c. being to my apprehension not sufficently clear, I deliver(ed) over the Mollys papers to the Master first taking the usual Oaths administered in cases of granting Registers with the enclos(e)d Bond which I hope will justify me to Government if I hav(e) erred in delivering up the Mollys papers to Capt. Clements.[3] Respecting the delivery up of Registers, Sea Letters &c. I have known some masters of Vessels even doubt the propriety of delivering over vessels papers to lawful Owners when transfers were made in foreign ports. This however I take to be a mistake. A similar miscomprehension of a like clause in the British Registry Act by some British masters, no doubt occasioned the succeeding Act of Parliament 28th. Geo: III. Chap 34 Sec: 13. inflicting a penalty on masters of Vessels withholding Registers from the lawful Owners.

"I shall now beg leave to suggest for the consideration of Government the following regulations in order to check unprincipled Masters from committing similar malpractices as before noticed.

1st.   That no Surveys shall be held on Vessels belonging to Citizens of the U.States coming in distress into ports where Consuls reside or upon Goods damaged belonging to Citizens without first making a report in writing to the Consul.

2nd.   That the Consuls of the U.S. be empowered to nominate one or more of the surveyors & the Capt. or Supercargo the others & that before any survey on vessels or Goods shall be taken, the surveyors shall take an Oath before the Consul, that they will examine the same with such strictness & integrity as their judgement is capable of and report accordingly which report to be authenticated by the Consul.

3rd.   That all accounts respecting disbursements for repairing of Vessels in foreign ports shall be certified by two reputable Merchants of the place that the charges are at the market prices, said certificate to be authenticated by the Consul if any there be at such port.[4]

4th.   That all protests against sea damages, made in ports where Consuls reside, shall be confirmed by the affidavits of the Master & two other officers belonging to the vessel & authenticated as aforesaid. And that none other coming from ports where Consuls reside shall be held valid in Law.

I have only now to beg your excuse for troubling you wi⟨th⟩ so long a letter."[5]

RC, two copies, and enclosures (DNA: RG 59, CD, Cape Town, vol. 1). First RC 4 pp. Second RC marked "*Duplicate*," with note: "Or⟨ig.⟩ ℔ the Betsy via N York." Both RCs docketed by Wagner. Minor differences between the copies have not been noted. For enclosures, see nn. 1, 3, and 5.

1. This note is omitted from the second RC.

2. The second RC has an asterisk here, with a note at the bottom of the page: "*Notarial copy of Survey forwarded in the Origl." Elmslie enclosed a copy (2 pp.; docketed by Wagner) of the "Certificate of Survey of Brig Molly of Nantucket," signed by John Osmond and H. Phillips on 18 May 1805, stating that they had examined the *Molly* and found it to be "a Strong and well Built vessel," that all parts of the ship were "perfectly good the Vessel tight and Sea worthy and fit to proceed on a voyage to any part of the world." Written at the bottom of this is a second certification, signed on 20 May by James Callander and Thomas Nevill⟨e⟩, also testifying to the seaworthiness of the *Molly*.

3. Filed with this dispatch are two copies (2 pp. each; both certified by Elmslie: the first on 29 Sept. 1805; the second copy, marked "Duplicate," on 20 Nov. 1805) of the 20 May 1805 bond of Capt. Robert Inott and John Clements, agent, pledging to pay the U.S. Treasury 1,200 "Spanish milled Dollars" if they failed to return the brig's papers to the collector of the port of the United States at which Inott or any other person with command of the ship should arrive in the United States. The second copy contains a stipulation that the papers would also be delivered to the said collector should any foreigner obtain an interest in the vessel.

4. "If any there be at such port" is omitted from the second RC.

5. On the verso of the brig *Molly*'s certificate (see n. 1 above) is a note in Albert Gallatin's hand, initialed and addressed by him: "For the Secretary of State. The Consul is certainly mistaken in supposing that he has a right to detain Registers, particularly where the vessel is transferred to citizens; but it is to the former owners or captain that they should be returned by the Consul. It is the business of the purchasers to obtain them from those who sell." Elmslie wrote to Gallatin on 7 Oct. 1805 (DNA: RG 59, CD, Cape Town, vol. 1), enclosing his accounts of funds collected and dispersed, and explaining the problems he was having collecting from ships' captains the funds required by law. On the verso of the last page is a note in an unidentified hand: "Referred to the Secretary of State, that he may reply to the same in case he should think proper" (ibid.).

To Thomas Jefferson

Dear Sir   Gray's Sepr. 30. 1805

I duly recd. your favor of   [1] from which I learn your purpose of
meeting the Heads of Depts. in consultation on the 4th of Ocr. It is no
little mortification that it will not be in my power to obey the summons.
Mrs. M's afflicted knee which has already detained me so long, tho' I trust
perfectly healed, is in so tender a state, and the whole limb so extremely
feeble, that she could not be put on the journey for some days to come
without a manifest risk, the more to be avoided on the road, as she would
be out of reach of the necessary aid. If it were possible to place her in such
a situation here as would justify my leaving her, I shd. not hesitate to set
out without her, and either return or send for her. But no such situation
can be found out of the City, and there the attempt is forbidden by the
existing fever, which is understood too, to be growing considerably worse.
There is another obstacle in my way which will oblige me to wait a few days
longer. On the whole, I shall not be able to set out before thursday or friday.
I shall make it the first of these days if possible & shall be as expeditious on
the journey as circumstances will permit.

Since I recd. your letter I have turned in my thoughts the several subjects which at the present moment press on the attention of the Executive.

With respect to G. B. I think we ought to go as far into an understanding on the subject of an eventual coalition in the war, as will not preclude
us from an intermediate adjustment if attainable, with Spain. I see not however much chance that she will positively bind herself not to make peace
whilst we refuse to bind ourselves positively to make war; unless indeed
some positive advantages were yielded on our part in lieu of an engagement
to enter into the war. No such advantage as yet occurs, as would be admissible to us and satisfactory to her.

At Paris, I think Armstrong ought to receive instructions to extinguish
in the French Govt. every hope of turning our controversy with Spain
into a French job public or private; to leave them under apprehensions of
an eventual connexion between the U.S. & G.B. and to take advantage of
any change in the French Cabinet favorable to our objects with Spain.

As to Spain herself one question is whether Bowdoin ought to proceed
or not to Madrid. My opinion is that his trip to G.B. was fortunate, and
that the effect of it will be aided by his keeping aloof untill occurrences
shall invite him to Spain. I think it will be expedient not even to order
Erving thither for the present. The nicest question however is whether
any or what step should be taken for a communication with the Spanish
Govt. on the points not embraced by the late negociation. On this question my reflections disapprove of any step whatever, other than such as
may fall within the path to be ⟨wo⟩rked out for Armstrong; or as may lie

387

⟨within⟩ the sphere of Claiborne's intercourse with the Marquis de C. Calvo.

Perhaps the last may be the best opportunity of all for conveying to Spain the impressions we wish, without committing the Govt. in any respect more than may be adviseable. In general it seems to me proper that Claiborne should hold a pretty strong language on all cases, and particularly that he should go every length the law will warrant agst. Morales & his project of selling lands. If Congs. should be not indisposed, proceedings may be authorized that will be perfectly effectual, on that as well as other points. But before their meeting there will[2] time to consider more fully what ought to be suggested for their consideration.

The Merchts are much alarmed at the late decisions in G.B. agst. their trade. It is conjectured that several millions of property are afloat, subject to capture under the doctrine now enforced. Accept assurances of my constan⟨t⟩ & most respectful attacht.

JAMES MADISON

RC (DLC: Jefferson Papers). Docketed by Jefferson as received 3 Oct.

1. Left blank by JM. See Jefferson to JM, 18 Sept. 1805.
2. JM may have omitted the word "be" here.

§ From David Airth. *30 September 1805, Gothenberg.* "I had the honour to address you last on the 1st. of January[1] giving an Account of the Shipping and trade of the United States at this Port for the Year 1804. Since that time Nothing particular has occurred worthy of your Notice. The Trade this Season is more enlarged than the foregoing year, of which I will have the honour to transmit you a particular Account at the Close of the Season. This Country will to all appearance⟨s⟩ soon be actively engaged with its allies in War against France. This will make not the Smallest interruption in the Friendly Intercourse with the United States as both this Government and the Country at large wish by every means in their Power to enlarge their Commercial Connections with America.

"Should at any time henceforward anything occur which I think can in the Smallest degree merit your attention, I will immediately have the Honour to advise you thereof."

RC (DNA: RG 59, CD, Gothenburg, vol. 1). 2 pp.; in a clerk's hand, signed by Airth; docketed by Wagner.

1. See *PJM-SS*, 8:441.

§ From DeWitt Clinton. *30 September 1805, New York.* "Capt. Alexr. Coffin[1] of the Ship *Penman* of this Port has some business with your department of great importance to himself & connexions. I beg leave to recommend him to your patronage as highly worthy of it."

RC (DNA: RG 76, Preliminary Inventory 177, entry 180, Great Britain, Treaty of 1794 [Art. VII], British Spoliations, ca. 1794–1824, Unsorted Papers, box 5, folder P & Q).

1. Nantucket native Alexander Coffin Jr. (1764–1836) was the son of one of the founders of Hudson, New York. He was educated in England and served as a midshipman during the American Revolution until he was captured and confined to prison ships in New York harbor. In 1804 and 1805 he commanded the *Penman* on a voyage to the Persian Gulf, but the ship and cargo were seized by the British and condemned. During the War of 1812 he was captured while sailing to France and confined to Dartmoor prison. In 1814 he published two volumes of poetry dealing with the American attack on Quebec and the Battle of Bunker Hill. For a time he was a merchant in New York City and from 1815 to 1824 agent of the state prison. In 1829 he was named an inspector of customs, a position he held until his death (Robert Barry Coffin, "The Coffin Family: The Hudson Branch," *American Historical Record* 2 [1873]: 65–67).

From Christopher Johnston, Mark Pringle, and John Sherlock

SIR,   BALTIMORE October 1st. 1805

We conceive it a Duty we owe ourselves and the Public to lay before you a Statement of the Case of the Schooner Hannah Maria, Peter Sorensen, Master.

This Vessel, owned by us, was loaded in this Port in the Month of March last and destined for Porto Bello on the Spanish Main, but conceiving it might facilitate her Admission into a Spanish Port, if she was cleared out for Curraçoa, we cleared her for that Port accordingly, and having given the Master Orders to Porto Bello, he proceeded there direct and to no other Po⟨rt⟩ whatever. On his homeward Passage from ⟨thence⟩ he was captured by His Britannic Majesty's Ship Diana, John Thomas Maling Master, Who proc⟨eeded⟩ to take the said Schooner's Cargo, consisting chiefly of Specie, on board the Frigate, an⟨d⟩ fitted out the Schooner with Guns, and h⟨as⟩ since kept her cruizing as a Tender, detai⟨ning⟩ at same Time the Captain, Supercargo a⟨nd⟩ Crew on board as Prisoners for upwards ⟨of⟩ Two Months, as appears by the enclosed Letters from Henry Bingham, late Super-⟨cargo⟩ of said Schooner Hannah Maria, which I⟨s⟩ further corroborated by the Affidavit of A. S. [*sic*] Thomas, a respectable Citizen of this Place ⟨to⟩ which we beg Leave to refer you.[1] Viewing ⟨the⟩ Conduct of Captain Maling to be contrary ⟨to⟩ the Law of Nations, as well as a direct Viol⟨ation⟩ of the Treaty between the United States an⟨d⟩ Great Britain, we rely with Confidence on the ready Interposition of the President to obtain Restitution of the Schooner Hannah Maria and Cargo, by Representation to the Minister of His

Britannic Majesty, or otherwise as to him may seem meet.[2] With Sentiments of high Respect &c. &c.

(signed) CHR: JOHNSTON
MARK PRINGLE
JOHN SHERLOCK.[3]

Tr and Tr of enclosures (UkLPR: Foreign Office, ser. 5, 45:297–299v); letterbook copy and letterbook copy of enclosures (UkLPR: Foreign Office, ser. 115, 14:143–145v). Tr and Tr of enclosures, marked ⟨"(C)opy),"⟩ enclosed in Merry to Mulgrave, 2 Nov. 1805 (ibid., ser. 5, 45:293–294v). Words and parts of words in angle brackets in the Tr have been supplied from the letterbook copy. For enclosures, see n. 1.

1. The enclosures (4 pp.) are copies of (1) Henry Bingham to Christopher Johnston, 3 Aug. 1805, "on board the British Frigate Diana off the Havana," stating that he had written Johnston by every opportunity since his detention on the *Diana;* that the *Hannah Maria* had arrived safely at Portobelo after 28 days' passage; that he had sold all the cargo for $19,101, except for "about 15 or 16 Hundred Dollars of Goods" and "three Trunks of Merchandize" belonging to Johnston's son that remained unsold; that they had left Portobelo on 17 Apr. 1805 but were detained on 2 June on grounds that they had cleared out of Curaçao, which was blockaded; that the money was on board the *Diana;* that the *Hannah Maria* had been armed and sent on a cruise; that he and Captain Sorensen were held on the frigate, which had been down the Gulf of Mexico and was then off Havana; that the *Diana* was short of provisions and would soon get into a port which he believed would be New Providence; that he would write as soon as they arrived; and that he "never suffered as much in [his] Life"; and (2) the 28 Sept. 1805 deposition of Baltimore merchant A. J. Thomas before Baltimore notary public Samuel Sterett that on 24 June 1805, while he was sailing from Campeche to New Orleans in the *Flying Fish,* his ship was captured by the *Diana,* "then lying in the Mouth of the River Mississippi"; that he saw Sorensen, Bingham, and the crew of the *Hannah Maria* on board the frigate; that Sorensen and Bingham had told him about their capture and detention, and that they were to be held until the *Diana*'s cruise ended in about two months; that he saw the *Hannah Maria* acting as tender to the *Diana;* and that while he was on board the frigate, the *Hannah Maria* was fitted out and sent on a cruise.

2. On 17 Oct. 1805 Jacob Wagner informed Johnston, Pringle, and Sherlock (DNA: RG 59, DL, vol. 15) that JM would call Anthony Merry's attention to the case but advised them in the meantime to pursue the case in the British courts.

3. Merchant Christopher Johnston (1750–1819) was a director of the Bank of the United States and the National Bank of Baltimore, an elder of the First Presbyterian Church, and one of the founders of the Maryland Insurance Company. Baltimore merchant Mark Pringle (d. 1819) was also a director of the Bank of the United States. His estate at Havre-de-Grace, Maryland, was set afire by the British during the War of 1812 but was saved through the efforts of William Pinkney and two marines. Merchant John Sherlock (d. 1813), who was in business with Pringle in 1800, was one of the founders of the Maryland Insurance Company and the Baltimore Insurance Company. All three men were directors of the Marine Insurance Office (George Norbury Mackenzie, ed., *Colonial Families of the United States of America* . . . [7 vols.; New York, 1907–20], 4:270; *Baltimore Patriot & Mercantile Advertiser,* 8 Mar. 1819; J. Thomas Scharf, *History of Baltimore City and County from the Earliest Period to the Present Day: Including Biographical Sketches of Their Representative Men* [Philadelphia, 1881], 452, 454, 455, 546; William Kilty, comp., *The Laws of Maryland* . . . [2 vols.; Annapolis, 1800], 2: Nov. 1795, ch. 60; Edgar Erskine Hume, "Letters Written During the

War of 1812 by the British Naval Commander in American Waters (Admiral Sir David Milne)," *WMQ*, 2d ser., 10 [1930]: 290 n. 24; *New-York Evening Post*, 13 Jan. 1819; *New-York Gazette & General Advertiser*, 28 Dec. 1813; Philadelphia *Claypoole's American Daily Advertiser*, 26 Jan. 1796; *Federal Gazette & Baltimore Daily Advertiser*, 4 Sept. 1800, 8 Apr. 1801).

§ From Jacob Wagner. *1 October 1805, Department of State.* "According to you[r] directions [not found] are enclosed three drafts in your favor for one hundred dollars each on the Bank of the U.States and ten bank notes of the office of Disct. & Deposit in this city for ten dollars each, notes of the Bank at Philadelphia not being to be had."

Adds in a postscript: "Mr. Thom will pay the balance into the bank to your credit."

RC (DLC). 1 p.; docketed by JM.

§ From Robert Williams. *1 October 1805, Washington, Mississippi Territory.* "By my communication of the 14th. Ulto. you were informed of some outrages committed within this Territory near the Spanish line, and of the steps I had taken in relation thereto.

"I have now the honor to enclose for your further information, Governor Grandpré's letter in answer to mine of the 6th. ulto. and my reply to him marked and numbered 1. and 2.—also the documents marked 1. 2. 3. which will inform you of the further steps taken in this affair.[1]

"The military Patrol which I ordered out on the line were organized, and disbanded on holding themselves in readiness, places appointed to rendezvous under a standing order of the officers commanding, to check any disorders that might appear.

"I have the satisfaction to inform you that things in that quarter have become very quiet and settled, which I believe would not have been the case, but for the measures which were authorized.

"Some of our citizens were concerned in this business, and are bound over to Court for prosecution.

"I am afraid affairs are not going on well in and about Orleans. Governor Claiborne was called from here a few days ago by a letter from the Secretary Mr. Graham, urging him to return immediately, without assigning particular reasons; and I have not such information as will authorize me to even give an opinion.[2]

"I am really concerned for the personal safety of the Governor. He was in so low a state of health as might have justified his not going down; but his remark to me on the subject was, 'I will go if I were sure to die the week after I get down.'"

Letterbook copy and letterbook copy of enclosures 2 and 3 (Ms-Ar); draft (CSmH); extract and Tr of enclosures (DNA: RG 233, President's Messages, 9A–D1); extract and Tr of enclosures (DNA: RG 46, President's Messages, 9B–B1). The second extract and Tr of enclosures is a letterpress copy of the first extract and Tr of enclosures. Draft docketed "Letter to Madison Secretary of State" and "Recorded." Extract and enclosures enclosed in

Jefferson's 6 Dec. 1805 message to Congress; extract printed in *ASP, Foreign Relations*, 2:687. For enclosures, see n. 1.

1. The enclosures (12 pp.; printed in *ASP, Foreign Relations*, 2:687–89) are copies of (1) Carlos Grand Pré to Williams, 9 Sept. 1805, acknowledging receipt of Williams's 6 Sept. letter about the kidnapping of the Kempers, and stating that he had been told by a Spanish officer that the officer had intercepted "a party of men disguised and armed who were conducting three others, who they immediately abandoned"; that the officer was conducting the three Kempers to Bayou Tunica, whence they were to be delivered to Grand Pré; that the American officer at Point Coupée had stopped and detained the party; that Grand Pré had sent an express for more information, listing the various disorders that had been taking place in West Florida, trusting that Williams would be happy with the measures he was going to take, and asking for the return of the inhabitants who had been escorting the Kempers, since they were not participants in the whole business; (2) Williams's 30 Sept. 1805 reply, stating that Grand Pré's equivocal letter had caused him to delay his answer until he had more information; reporting that he had learned that the raid on the Kempers was committed by U.S. citizens and Spanish subjects and that he had sent the Kempers and their Spanish guard to Fort Adams; naming the six Spanish subjects who had been conducting the Kempers, adding that he had released them under escort to Spanish territory and had the Kempers "bound to their good behavior" and to keep the peace toward Spain; describing the seizure and detention of William Flanagan Jr. and his wife by twelve men commanded by Lieutenant Glascock "of Capt Jones's Company of Spanish Light Horse," who also stole Flanagan's horse, and asking Grand Pré to look into this; and refusing Grand Pré's demand for the return of the Kempers; (3) Williams to Judge Thomas Rodney, 23 Sept. 1805, covering Williams's 23 Sept. letter to Capt. Richard Sparks at Fort Adams, asking Sparks to deliver the prisoners from Point Coupée to Rodney, to have the Spanish subjects, should the civil authorities release them, escorted to the boundary with West Florida and released; and expressing his hope that the Kempers would be dealt with as the law authorized; and (4) Thomas Rodney to Williams, 30 Sept. 1805, stating that his examination revealed that a party composed of twelve white and seven black men had broken into the Kempers' houses, taken them prisoner, and carried them below the boundary, where the Kempers had been handed over to Captain Alston and a party of twelve; that the original group then had left; that Alston had ordered the Kempers and six of his men onto a boat for Baton Rouge; that as this party was passing the American fort at Point Coupée the Kempers had been rescued by the Americans who had also seized the Spanish guards, who were released when the Kempers testified that those men had done nothing within U.S. territory. He added that the Kempers had been ordered to post bail that they would keep the peace and "to do no injury to any one below the line."

2. See William C. C. Claiborne to JM, 27 Sept. 1805.

From Andrew Ellicott

DEAR SIR   LANCASTER October 2d. 1805.

With this you will receive a packet directed to our Minister Mr. Armstrong: it contains a number of astronomical observations for Mr. Delambre, one of the perpetual secretaries to the national institute of france.[1] I wish your interest with Mr. Armstrong, to have my letters delivered, and the answers, when put in his hands, either forwarded with his dispatches to you, or sent to our consul Mr. Lee at Bordeaux: to this subject Mr. Livingston paid particular attention.

I should have written to you long ago on the political situation of this State, but the ferment was daily assuming such a variety of forms, that it was impossible to draw any rational conclusions respecting the final result. One point may now be considered as fixed; because we may with certainty calculate upon the re-election of Mr. Mc. Kean. But in this event, there will be involved a number of delicate, and interesting considerations, as Mr. Mc.Kean will certainly be indebted to the federalists for his re-election, because the constitutional republicans are by no means so strong as the Snyderites.[2] On this great, and leading point, a union is therefore necessarily, and unavoidably produced between a large portion of the federal, with a part of the old republican interest, and this union will probably become stronger, as it is certainly the effect of self preservation: a defence against the unbridled licence of Duane's press, and the ambitious views of Lieb, Clay, and a few other similar characters, whose consequence, and weight, arises from two sources: *first* their influence with the populace which composes a large portion of the inhabitants of all countries, and *secondly*, with a superior class, who are led to believe by artful insinuations, that Duane, Clay, and Leib are in the full confidence of the President of the United States, and that their plans are in concert with the views, and wishes of the administration of the general government. By this finesse, the popularity of the president is brought forward by a few unprincipled adventurers, to aid them in their attacks upon our governor, and constitution. And however, absurd as it may appear to us, that those men should be in the confidence of the President, I assure you as an old friend, that it is not only believed by the followers of Duane, but by the great body of the federalists in this State, and may be considered as one of the principal causes, which has induced them to cooperate so chearfully on the present occasion with the constitutionalists.

I should extend this to a much greater length, but have this moment recollected, that my opinions may be considered as intruders into a select company, on the score of good manners I shall therefore wait the reception of this, before I send forward any more of my political speculations. I am sir, with great respect, and esteem, your sincere friend

ANDW. ELLICOTT

RC (DLC); FC (DLC: Ellicott Papers). The FC is a letterpress copy of the RC.

1. For similar previous requests, see *PJM-SS*, 2:480 and n. 1, 3:33, 4:251, 5:20, 6:333.

2. By the fall of 1805 the Republicans in Pennsylvania had split completely. One wing, under William Duane and Michael Leib, held a caucus and nominated Simon Snyder to oppose incumbent Republican governor Thomas McKean. McKean won the election only by dint of garnering support from the Federalists. For a discussion of politics in Pennsylvania

in 1805, see Higginbotham, *Keystone in the Democratic Arch*, 77–101. For warnings that JM had received previously about the political turmoil in the state, see JM to Unidentified Correspondent, 29 May 1805, Hugh Henry Brackenridge to JM, 31 May 1805, *PJM-SS*, 9:416 and n. 1, 421 and n. 5.

From John Armstrong

SIR   PARIS, October 3d. 1805.

Since the date of my letter by Mr Skipwith[1] I have become acquainted with some circumstances which have a near relation to the subject of that letter, and which may tend to illustrate the course to be taken in our business with *Spain*. They are as follows: *soon after Mister Monro left Madrid a detailed account of his late negotiation with the Spanish government* was transmitted by *Mister Cevallos to Richlan where the Emperor then was*. A digest was immediately made of it and presented *to the Emperor who after having read it attentively remarked that he had nothing to do with it* and that *Spain must settle her own business*. This determination on the part of *the Emperor* was not altogether acceptable to *his Minister* and on *their retur[n] to Paris the lat[t]er told a person of the utmost respectab[il]ity* that means must be employed to alter it. *A chief of a bureau accordingly prepared a paper with the view of producing this effect, the heads and substance of which have been thus presented.*

1st. The right of the U. S. to *redress herself.*

2d. Her means of doing it.

3d The consequences to *Spain* of this policy.

4th. The means of *Spain* to obviate these consequences

& 5th. What, under these circumstances, ought to be the Policy of *France?*

In examining these points—the right and the means of the U. S. to *redress herself* were both admitted, but with these qualifications, that the right did not go beyond a reasonable compensation for the nonpayment of debts acknowledged by *Spain* to be due to Citizens of the U. S. and that the means were merely incidental to the present state of things in Europe.

Under the 3d head were stated the certain loss of the *Floridas* and the probable dangers awaiting *other of the Spanish colonies* provided (as was natural and almost necessary) that the principle of reprisal should run into that of open hostility, and make *the U.S. a party to the present war.*

Under the 4th head, it was conceded that *Spain* was in no condition to multiply the number of her enemies, or to pursue any policy which should make new demands upon her present resources either proper, or necessary.

The fi[f]th point was examined with great care and under different views, and the result was that *France ought to interpose her good offices promptly* and *efficiently* and that some middle and reasonable terms between what *we demanded and what Spain was willing to admit* might be suggested: that *if Spain refused to accede to these, France would be exonerated from al[l] obligation to take part in her quar[r]el;* and that if the *refusal came from the U.S. and they should proceed to make reprisals upon Spain,* that it then would become a question whether *this government* should, or should not resort to the means within her power of counteracting this system. These means were then indicated, according to my information, in nearly the following words— "they are of two kinds; one of which is to be found in ourselves; the other, in our Adversary. Of the first I shall say nothing, because it would be useless to number our Legions, or to expatiate on their skill or their courage. Our fleets too are sur[e] to be in a condition to transport and co-operate with them, wherever their service may be required. Of the last I will but suggest—that the maxims of a Government which abhors war, and regards fleets and armies as nuisances or scourges; that the habits of a people who have known nothing at home but peace and prosperity for twenty years; that a public revenue, increasing rapidly and beyond all calculation, but entirely dependent on the present state of things: that towns and harbours, large and affluent but wholly defenceless; that a neutral flag rendering tributary to them one half of all the Nations of Europe; that a Commerce, filling all the parts of the Globe, and spread over every sea, but no where in a state to defend itself against the attacks which may be made upon it; that a mediterranean war, recently terminated but easily rekindled, and with a tenfold effect, form altogether a mass of circumstances, which, if we are to be viewed in the light of enemies, sufficiently indicates the course and the issue of the Contest."

Whether this memoir was carried to the Emperor or whether it was placed in the portfolio of the minister to be employed or not as contingencies might direct I can not learn, as well from the temper in which it seems to have been written, as from the striking resemblance it bears to the *informal propositions communicated in my letter of the 10th* ² *which appears to have been the first step in the execution of the plan it offers.*

The public papers will have informed you of the sudden irruption of the Austrian Army into Bavaria and a part of Suabia. Their first movements indicated a design of forming a line from Londau to Ingolstadt of which Ulm would have been the central and salient point, but this plan (if it ever was their plan) is abandoned, and we now find them presenting a front to the Rhine, and occupying a chain of posts from the famous passes of the Black forest to the foot of Mount St Gothard, and thence through the Tyrol and along the Adige quite to Venice. These dispositions, together with the appointment of the Archduke to the command of the left of this long but powerful line, look as though Austria intended that Italy, as it has been in a great degree the cause, should also be made the principal theatre of this war.

On the other hand, the Emperor seems determined to defend Italy in the plains of Germany, and the greater part of his force is accordingly drawn to the right bank of the Rhine, where, by its present positions, it forms the segment of a circle, of which Homberg, in Suabia, and Nuryberg in Franconia are the extremes. It is said, and his movements warrant the belief, that leaving Bernadotte, with the armies of Hanover and Batavia and the Bavarian Regiments which have joined his standard, to menace, or assail as the case may require, the rear of the Austrian Army, he will himself turn the sources of the Danube and attack General Mack, at Hockach.[3]

I annex, to this, a letter from Mr. Talleyrand accompanying a collection of Official papers on the subject of the rupture between this Government and that of Austria;[4] and am, with the greatest respect, your most Obedient, and very humble Servant,

JOHN ARMSTRONG

RC and enclosures (DNA: RG 59, DD, France, vol. 10); RC and enclosure (DNA: RG 59, Preliminary Inventory 15, entry 98, Misc. Duplicate Consular and Diplomatic Dispatches, 1791–1906). First RC marked "Duplicate"; in a clerk's hand, signed by Armstrong. Italicized words are those encoded by Armstrong in a State Department code also used by John Quincy Adams at St. Petersburg and by Jacob Lewis at Saint-Domingue; code key not found but substantially reconstructed by the editors; first RC decoded by the editors with omissions supplied from JM's interlinear decoding. Second RC encoded but not decoded. For surviving enclosures, see n. 4.

　　1. Armstrong to JM, 14 Sept. 1805.
　　2. Left blank in RC. Armstrong referred to his 10 Sept. 1805 dispatch.
　　3. For the movements of the Austrian and French armies at this time, see David G. Chandler, *The Campaigns of Napoleon* [New York, 1966], 382–402.
　　4. The enclosures (2 pp.) are (1) copies of Talleyrand to Armstrong, 4 Vendémiaire an 14 (26 Sept. 1805), stating that he was communicating, as Napoleon had ordered, an account of the reciprocal conduct of France and Austria since the signing of the treaty of Lunéville, and adding that he was about to join the emperor at Strasbourg, but this would not interrupt the usual course of business, since Armstrong's correspondence would be forwarded there and passports would continue to be issued by the foreign office; and (2) Armstrong to Talleyrand, 26 Sept. 1805, acknowledging receipt of his letter, and stating that he would take the first opportunity to transmit the papers enclosed there to the U.S. government.

From Alexander Coffin Jr.

Sir   NewYork 3d. Octr. 1805

Altho' a painful task to me to be Oblij'd to address you on a subject so
very distressing to my feelings yet beleiving it a duty which I owe to myself, my owners, & my Country, I could not forego the unpleasant task.
I am sensible, Sir, that I am addressing one of the first officers of the
freest, & one of the greatest nations on Earth, & I Know also that I do
not possess the power to express myself In a manner that may do Justice
to the Subject, having been a Seaman from my earliest Youth. Should any
language escape me that is not perfectly correct, I hope you will be Kind
enough to excuse it, & attribute it to my inexperience & want of education
to express myself in a more correct manner. I shall, Sir, with as much brev-
ity as the subject will admit of, & with the simplicity of an American Seaman, State to you, that being Part Owner, Commander, and Supercargo of
the Ship Penman of New York, of the Burthen of 447 Tons, I arriv'd in her
from Canton in March 1803, with a Cargo of Teas, the Duties on which
were secur'd according to Law. In NewYork, part of sd. Cargo with other
lawful goods to amount of 73,000 Dollars, were loaded on board Sd. Ship
for Antwerp for which port I sail'd from Newyork the 14th May 1803.

My Owners & myself made an agreement with the agent & partner of
a House in Antwerp who resided in NYk. to consign the Cargo to Sd.
House, he agreeing in their name that they should furnish Dollars, to the
probable amount the Cargo would sell for, without delay, that is, so soon as
they had receiv'd the Cargo into their hands, to enable me to prosecute my
Voyage to Canton where I intended to proceed from Antwerp, but, on my
arrival there in June the House was either unable, or unwilling To make
the advances, & after a detention of four months all I was able to obtain
on so Valuable a Cargo was $4000 in Specie, 9800 Guilders in Copper
money; & an Invoice of goods of about 33,000 Guilders, Consisting of
Cloths, beer wine, Glass ware &c. This property I shipped on board Said
Ship on the sole account & risk of the Owners all Citizens of, & residents
in the United States of America. I forwarded Invoices & bills of Lading to
them, to enable them to Insure the same, which Insurance was so made in
Newyork (& warranted bona fide American property) from Flushing to
Madeira. I sail'd from Flushing the 31st Octr. 1803, for Madeira, but meeting with very severe Weather after leaving the British Channel, & after
beating in Vain for a considerable time I found it would be impossible to
gain that place perhaps for the winter—it being then the month of Novr.
& worse weather to be expected. I therefore with the advice of my Officers, bore away for St. Jago's one of the Cape DeVerd Islands for Water &
Stock when we arriv'd at St. Jago's our water was nearly out, from thence
we Saild the   [1] Decr. & after a long tedious passage arriv'd at the Cape

of Good Hope the 29th. Jany. 1804. where I was Oblig'd to touch for water & Stock, & to receive some Dollrs for bills of exchange which I had on
the Cape. I there landed the goods & dispos'd of them, and Sail'd from
thence, the 17th. April, & arriv'd at Batavia the 8th. June. At the Cape I
drew on my Owners in favo'r of Capt Joseph King of Newyork for 21.000
Dollars, which money consisted of Copper doits which Capt. K like myself had been oblij'd to receive in Holland, & as he obtain'd a Cargo at the
Cape for bills on his owners Messrs. Franklin & Robinson, that money
was useless to him as it would not pass at the Cape. My intention when I
left the Cape was, to have touch'd at Batavia, & turn the Copper money
into Dollars, & proceed on to Canton to fulfill an agreement I had made
on my last Voyage with Mr. James Oliver an American Gentleman residing there, but, On my Arrival at Batavia I found that the exportation of
Dollars was totally prohibited. It therefore became necessary to purchase
my Cargo there, as the money I had would not answer in any other part of
India. There being no produce at Market at the time of my Arrival I
petition'd the Governo'r & Director General to grant me permission to
proceed up the Coast of Java in search of a Cargo. This I did for dispatch
& the preservation of the health of my Crew it being very sickly at Batavia. I was up the Coast about 2 Months, & in that time could procure but
one half of a Cargo. I therefore return'd to Batavia, & fill'd the Ship up, as
the new Sugar was Just coming in, and Sail'd the 13th. Sept. for Muscat,
the 15th. pass'd Java Head; & on the 16th. I was taken Sick with a violent
nervous fever; on the 27th. being tho't past recovery without speedy releif,
5 of my Crew at the same time sick, being therefore weakly mann'd, & the
Ship proving very leaky, It was the opinion of my officers that we could
not, with any degree of safety, or, prudence continue the Voyage without
more men. I therefore orderd the Ship's Course alter'd for the Isle of
france, it being the nearest, & in fact only port where we could touch at,
to procure assistance and relief. We made the Island on the 3rd. of Octr.
In the Afternoon; on the morning of the 4th. Saw two Ships of War to
windward of us; and one between us & the Harbour, which we soon
discover'd to be British, we hoisted American, & they, British Colours; we
Kept on our Course as I was conscious we were pursuing a perfect legal
Voyage, had I have tho't otherwise We could have escaped very easily, as
we could out Sail them. At 8 AM being within hail of a 74 Gun Ship we
bro't too, & he sent an officer on board to examine the papers, which
done, he order'd me to go on board of the Ship of War but being unable to
leave my Cabbin my Cheif Officer was order'd to go with the papers in my
stead. In about 3 or 4 Hours he was sent back on board of the Penman
with an officer and fourteen men with orders to carry the Ship into Colombo in the Island of Ceylon, when Mr. Gardner my officer, inform'd me
of this I was amaz'd. I Knew that my papers were perfectly in order, & I

398

was well convinc'd in my own mind, that I was pursuing a perfectly legal Voyage, agreeably to treaty & the Laws of Nations. On what acct. the Ship was thus seiz'd I could not learn; for Altho' Mr Gardner requested Capt. Osborn to inform him for the Satisfaction of his Commander, on what grounds the Ship was Seiz'd, he told him, that it was none of his, nor His Commanders business, but, that she was Seiz'd because he chose to Seize her. We arrivd at Colombo the 24th. of Novr. last & on the [2] Decr. the Ship, Cargo, & my private adventure were Condemn'd. My adventure was condemn'd, because I was part Owner of Ship & Cargo.

So soon as the Ship was condemn'd my officers & Crew were turn'd on Shore in a Strange Country, without a Shilling, and without a friend!! I was sick on Shore at the time, but was plunder'd of pretty much every thing but my wearing apparel, by the Prize agent, John Robbin, Purser of the Pheaton Frigate, notwithstanding being thus strip't of every thing I was charg'd, & oblij'd to pay, to the Hospital 107 Rix Dollars for 3 of my Crew who had been sent there sick, the money to pay that bill as well as every other absolute necessary expence I was oblij'd to borrow of my Cheif officer, whose private adventure after having been condemn'd, was restor'd him by the particular request of Mr. Johnson the Advocate fiscal, & not, Sir, rest assur'd, on acct. of a Spark of humanity in the breast of Walter Bathurst, Commander of the Terpsichor Frigate, who was there, or in that of John Robbin whose very name is a satire on Humanity. I will now Sir Annex an extract from the Condemnation.

"He the said Alexander Coffin being a Citizen of the United States of America & master of the said Ship & part Owner thereof having during the Voyage in which the sd. Ship was Captur'd as aforesaid, Carried on and Being at the time of the Capture thereof Carrying on an illicit trade between the Batavian Republic & her Colonies in the East Indies & the Colonies of her Allies, & that the Sd. Ship Cargo & private adventure were therefore or otherwise subject & liable to confiscation & condemn'd the Same &c &c &c." Now Sir It is an Absolute falsehood that I was carrying on trade between the Colonies of the Batavian Republic & the Colonies of her Allies, for I had been at no Colony in India but Batavia— from thence I was bound to Muscat which my papers & the Solemn declaration of myself & officers will fully prove, & my letters to my Owners from Batavia to enable them to Insure for Muscat, when taken I was bound to the Isle of france, to be sure, & my protest States the Cause fully for my being bound there, which was, absolute necessity for assistance & releif.

As to my having carried on trade between the Batavian Republic & her Colonies in the E. Indies I have before stated in what manner, I carried on that trade. I took on board a few goods in Holland because I could get nothing else for a very Valuable Cargo which I had left in the hands of the above mention'd House in Antwerp, & among those goods there was not a single contraband Article. I was bound to Madeira but could not get there on acct. of the bad weather as before Stated, this was an Act of God, which I could neither foresee, nor prevent. From the Cape of Good Hope to Batavia I had nothing on board but Cash, & with that Cash, I purchas'd my Cargo, at Batavia, 21.000 Dollrs. of which I rec'd at the Cape for bills on my Owners, about 5000 Ds. I rec'd for a bill of Exchange on the Cape & the remainder I bro't with me from Europe. Judge Carrington however told me, that my being bound from Batavia to Muscat, ["]if true," as he expressd himself, was of itself sufficient grounds for him to condemn Ship & Cargo, for that agreeably to Lord Pelham's Instructions lately sent out, the Voyage was illegal. Ship masters & Super cargoes, direct from America & Mr. Buchannan our Consul where astonish'd, when at the Isle of france after my Arrival there a passenger in a Danish Brig from Colombo I shew them a Copy of those Instructions many of those Gentlemen were pursuing exactly Similar Voyages to the one I was pursuing when Captur'd, & suppos'd, as I did, that they were pursuig a perfectly legal voyage, but certain it is, should they fall in with a British Ship of War they will share my fate. I take it for granted Sir that the American Government is either not acquainted with those instructions, or being acquainted with them view them in a very different light to what they are viewed in India, in fact, on the trial those Instructions seem'd to be the only plausible pretext urged, to condemn the Ship & Cargo.

The unjust capture & condemnation of my Ship & Cargo is not only a loss to myself & the rest of the Owners, but is also a loss to Governmt. for my Cargo would have Sold at Muskat for about 100,000 Ds. there I could have procur'd a full load of Coffee at 12 Cents PrH the Duties on which in America, would have been between 40 & 50 thousd. Dollrs. Thus Sir, it is not only a loss to a few individuals, but a loss to the community at large, moreover, if the British are to be suffer'd to harrass us in this way it will finally tend to damp that, universally acknowledg'd, enterprising spirit of American Seamen and Merchants, who have so largely contributed to the astonishing prosperity of our Common Country, & who in return expect that protection in their lawful pursuits which they are so Justly entitled to.

I have now Sir I beleive given you a faithful statement of facts, & have been induc'd to mention the Conduct the British have, & seem inclin'd to pursue in the India Seas. I consider it a duty, which every Citizen owes to his Country to give to government every information he possibly can, relative to the Conduct of the Beligerent Powers, in matters which so immediately interests the Country generally to Know, & Sir I consider the Seizure And Condemnation of my Ship & Cargo as an Arbitrary Stretch of Arbitrary power, & unwarranted, either, in Law, or

Justice, & I appeal to the magnanimity and Justice of my own Government, for Support in my legal demands on the British Government, for the unwarranted & Arbitrary proceedings of its officers towards me & my Owners. In behalf of myself & Owners of the Ship Penman of Newyork I am Sir, with the highest Consideration and Respect Your very Obedt. Hm'ble Servt.[3]

ALEX. COFFIN JR

P.S. The Names of Ships & Commanders by which I was Captur'd, British King's Ships Tremendous of 74 Guns, John Osborn Commander, Lancaster of 64 Do. Willm. Fotheringale, Do—Pheaton Frigate George Cockburn Do.—Terpsichore Frigate—walter Bathurst Do.

A.C. JR:

RC (DNA: RG 76, Preliminary Inventory 177, entry 180, Great Britain, Treaty of 1794 [Art. VII], British Spoliations, ca. 1794–1824, Unsorted Papers, box 5, folder P & Q).

1. Left blank in original.
2. Left blank in original.
3. On 23 Oct. 1805 Jacob Wagner wrote Coffin: "The Secretary of State has directed me to intimate to you, in answer to your statement of the case of the Ship Penman, that it is expedient for you to prosecute an appeal from the sentence of the Court of Vice Admiralty at Ceylon. He has already apprised you of the advantage of proving, that the sources of trade, on account of the use of which the condemnation was passed, were open in time of peace. Independently however of this matter of fact, it is to be hoped, that, from the discussions upon which our Minister in London has been instructed to enter and which he has commenced, some advantageous impression may be made upon the British Government of a nature to repel or avoid the effect of the doctrine itself, upon which the sentence is founded" (DNA: RG 59, DL, vol. 15). The condemnation at Ceylon was upheld by the appeals court in London (*ASP, Foreign Relations*, 2:765; New York *Columbian*, 26 Dec. 1811).

From William Thornton

DEAR SIR   CITY OF WASHINGTON October 3rd: 1805.

We have been lately much flattered with the hope of soon seeing you again; and I assure you there is a general pleasure expressed in hearing that your amiable Partner is compleatly recovered. I was certain that it would only require attention and great patience; but it is a severe tax upon a Lady to be obliged to stay at home in Philada: where she would have given and received so much pleasure.

We often talk here of the Insults and Injuries we receive from the Spanish and English. Being educated a Quaker I would willingly curb any Disposition to fight; but if we do not receive prompt Satisfaction from both I think we could take the Floridas and Cuba by Volunteers, and we could do the English more injury by our armed Vessels than France & Spain combined. The Executive will be supported I know by all Classes of the People, for though we are a pacific Nation we cannot be imposed on. I am pleased when I hear on all Sides a general Concurrence in Support of our Honor and Dignity. The present opportunity is a glorious one— The nations themselves at war, and our late preparations for humbling Tripoli now disengaged. I think the extension of our Empire fraught with wisdom and humanity. By it we should prevent those Contentions that so embroil Europe; and being ourselves the only compleatly free people on Earth, Benevolence more than Interest implants a desire to extend this System of happiness to a larger portion of mankind. Excuse me for what I have expressed—This liberty may border on presumption; for those who are better acquainted with the relations of the different Powers may be better enabled to see both sides of the Shield.

I have just heard that Mr: Grainger is dead.[1] If so he is to be lamented, being an useful Character. I would not willingly be indelicate or antici- pate the Consequences of the Event; but if the report be true a post of honor will be vacant. No change of this kind can take place without many applications to fill the vacancy, and I doubt not the President has great choice of Individuals. Since he became President there have been many Gifts of Office in his power. I waited with patience, because I knew there were many Persons whose Services entitled them to a preference, but I had the presumption to imagine I should not totally be forgotten, when it was considered that under the former Administrations I had been hon- ored by the possession of a respectable office at the very time I was using every possible exertion to forward the Election of the present President, and openly took hundreds to the Hustings. My first appointment induced me to reside here, where I have in every Sense of the word lost many years of my Life. You have been my Friend and your kind attentions will ever live in my Memory. You had it not in your power to serve me more than you have done. The President perhaps had it not in his power to gratify my wishes, consistently with those Arrangements wch. his Executive Du- ties imposed. He made me a Magistrate & Commissioner of Bankruptcy I presume, in some degree, to shew me that he thought me not unworthy of his Confidence. They cannot be considered as Offices; for, by the first I have had never-ceasing Trouble and no Emolument—by the last—I re- ceived about $ 150 in abt. 18 months—when the Office ceased.[2] If I am worthy of his Confidence he has now an opportunity of shewing me his Friendship, supposing the Event to have taken place which I have so re- peatedly heard is the Case. The P. M. G. must reside in this City, and perhaps a resident might be permitted to urge this as some Claim. I know you are my Friend and I wish I may prove worthy of a continuance of your Friendship—If you think an Application to the President can benefit me I will presume to solicit your favour in my behalf. I am, dear Sir, very sincerely & respectfully Yrs. &c.

WILLIAM THORNTON

P. S. I have just heard the President is arrived.

W.T.

RC (DLC). Docketed by JM.

1. The report of Granger's death was premature. Connecticut native, Yale graduate, and lawyer Gideon Granger (1767–1822) spent nine years in the Connecticut state legislature. A staunch Republican in a Federalist state, he strongly supported Jefferson in the election of 1800 and was named postmaster general in 1801, in which post he served until JM forced him to resign in 1814. He then moved to upstate New York, where he practiced law and served in the state senate, 1820–21, before his health failed.

2. Thornton was at this time serving as a clerk in the State Department, having been appointed to supervise the patent office in 1802, a position he held until his death in 1828. He also raised horses and engaged in multiple business endeavors, none of which were particularly successful.

§ To Anthony Merry. *3 October 1805, Department of State.* "I beg leave to trouble you with Duplicate Copies of two Documents concerning Nathaniel Bartlett, who appears to have been impressed into the British Schooner Whiting, on the Halifax station; and to ask the Interposition of your good Offices, to effect the Release of this man, whose Citizenship is fully proved by the Documents alluded to. The Copy of a letter from Ephraim Spooner is likewise enclosed, & I take the liberty of also referring you to that."

FC (DNA: RG 59, Notes to Foreign Ministers and Consuls, vol. 1). 1 p.; in Daniel Brent's hand; initialed "J M." at bottom; marked "Office Copy." Enclosures not found.

§ From Cyrus Griffin.[1] *3 October 1805, Williamsburg.* "Will you have the Goodness to pardon this Intrusion.

"My Son John Griffin is anxious to change his position from Indiana to Michican, principally on account of health.[2] Having been Judge for Some years, a young man of good Genius, and speaking the French language with fluency, perhaps he might be an acquisition to the new Teritory, if there shall be a vacancy in the Judiciary department.

"Not having fatigued our most excellent president, or you, my dear Friend, with any applications for myself or my dear Children, may I hope that this Solicitation will not be rejected, if convenient to grant it. With my very best Respects to the president."

RC (DNA: RG 59, LAR, 1801–9, filed under "Griffin"). 1 p.; docketed by Jefferson.

1. Cyrus Griffin (1748–1810) was born in Virginia and educated in London and Edinburgh. He was a member of the Virginia legislature, 1777–78 and 1786–87; of the

403

Continental Congress, 1778–80 and 1788–89; and judge of the Court of Appeals in Cases of Capture, 1780–87. The last president of the Continental Congress, he was appointed a federal district judge for Virginia in 1790 by George Washington, a post in which he served until his death (*Senate Exec. Proceedings*, 1:40).

2. John Griffin (ca. 1771–1849) received this appointment to Michigan but was unhappy and in poor health there and soon began applying for an appointment to the bench in Indiana, where he had previously served for six years, or in Illinois. He resigned from his Michigan post in 1823 and moved to Philadelphia where he died (New York *Weekly Herald*, 8 Aug. 1849; Carter, *Territorial Papers, Michigan*, 10:99, 276, 304, 337, 383, 384, 417–18; Robert B. Ross and George B. Catlin, *Landmarks of Detroit: A History of the City* [Detroit, 1898], 276).

§ From James Monroe. *3 October 1805, London*. "The object of this is to present to your acquaintance Major Forman with whom I became acquainted soon after my arrival in this country in 1803. I have had much communication with him on the subject of Louisiana, of which he now is an Inhabitant, having movd lately from the Natchez to the neighborhood of N. Orleans, & derived from it much satisfaction. He is in my opinion a very sensible & worthy character, & is animated with the best views & intentions towards our common country. As he is desirous of being known to you I have taken the liberty of giving him this introduction."

Adds in a postscript: "This is forwarded to Liverpool in the expectation it may find Major Forman there, but will be sent on if he is not."

RC (DLC: Rives Collection, Madison Papers). 1 p.

¶ From Robert and John McKim. Letter not found. *3 October 1805*. In a 17 Oct. letter to Robert and John McKim, Jacob Wagner acknowledged receipt of their letter and stated that: "the Minister of the United States in London, will on the application of your Agent, furnish him whatever official aid and countenance may be proper and necessary, according to the stage in which your memorial may be" (DNA: RG 59, DL, vol. 15). Robert and John McKim were Baltimore merchants. Robert was later president of the Union Manufacturing Company of Maryland, which made cotton yarn and cloth ("Cotton Factories in Maryland, January, 1859," *Hunt's Merchants' Magazine and Commercial Review* 40 [1859]: 374; Baltimore *North American, and Mercantile Daily Advertiser*, 18 July 1808).

From George W. Erving

Private

DEAR SIR　　　　　　　　　　　　　　　　BOURDEAUX Oct: 4. 1805

Pursuant to the determination which I mentioned in my last official letter to you from London,[1] to have been taken in concert with Mr Monroe & Mr Bowdoin, I left that place on the 5th of Septr. for Paris, where I arrived on the 14th. We supposed that some sensations might have mani-

fested themselves on the part of the French government since the departure of Mr Monroe from Paris, favorable to the hope of a satisfactory
adjustment of our affairs with Spain; that the manner in which the late
negotiations had terminated, & the return of Mr Monroe to London,
must have produced apprehensions of a total rupture, necessarily leading
that government to seek for an opportunity of making some Explanations
as to the share which it had taken in those negotiations, ⟨& thus?⟩ evincing
the interest which it felt in the preservation of harmony: It was also presumed that the late blow aimed by great Britain at ⟨a⟩ very important branch
of our commerce, & the dignified & firm tone with which it had been met
by our minister in London, (in as much as those measures proved that we
had not a previous understanding with England hostile to France or its
ally, ⟨we?⟩ were not disposed to make any undue concessions to their disadvantage, & how reluctantly we parted with the Expectation that France
herself woud ultimately manifest a candor & good faith suitable to our
just claims, & due to the honor & consistency of her own character) woud
Excite ⟨a⟩ strong sentiment of friendly acknowledgement, & induce an
anxiety to quiet the troubles which seemed consequent upon the rupture
of the negotiations; that she woud therefore shew a disposition to place
the relations between the United States & Spain upon that safe & satisfactory footing which she certainly has it in her power to give them:
These probabilities were much strengthened by the very unexpected
change in the aspect of continental affairs which took place about the
time of my arrival in Holland. It was for the purpose of consulting with
General Armstrong & of obtaining information upon these important
subjects that it was determined I shoud take Paris in my way to Madrid:
we had doubts also whether in the course of Enquiry motives might not
occur for me to attend the arrival of Mr Bowdoin at that place, & to wait
with him for the orders of the President; whether the public considerations which woud prevent Mr Bowdoins going immediately to Madrid,
(& which have been Explained to you by him & Mr Monroe) did not apply
in some degree to myself. Upon all these points I conversed fully with
General Armstrong: whatever has passed between him & the French
Minister he has of course presented to you, such part as he communicated
to me does not bear the favorable aspect which we hoped for: he thinks
also that Mr Monroes departure produced no sensation, and that they
have no apprehension of any serious rupture between the United States &
Spain. I infer his opinion to be that if any future discussions take place
they must be had with the government at Paris: in such case it seems that
M. Tallyrand promises to produce documentary proofs against the claim
for indemnity to our citizens for certain spoliations; what the proof referred to may be I cannot distinctly understand, & it is a little Extraordinary that if any such exists it shoud not have been brought forward to

support the Extreme imbecillity of Mr Cervallos's argument upon that
point in his discussions with Mr Monroe, since there is every reason to
presume that his share in those discussions, to say the least, passed under
the view of the French government. General Armstrong did not seem to
think that we derived any advantage from the transactions in England, he
beleives that the French government are fully persuaded of our intention
to smooth over all difficulties in that quarter, that they annex no importance to the tone which we have assumed, & in fine that nothing but an
open rupture with Great Britain, will produce such dispositions as had
been calculated upon.

In all this business the important points of consideration seem to be;
how France may be brought to act in our favor; at what course she woud
take if we were to pursue the measures against Spain which the conduct &
pretensions of that power will justify. If Spain were left Entirely to herself
either by negotiation or means less mild we shoud doubtless soon bring
the subsisting differences to a very satisfactory termination: France aught
to be convinced that she can derive no mony from the present state of this
controversy; yet whatever pains may have been taken to inform her correctly upon this subject, I am persuaded that such a hope is amongst the
strongest of her motives for still resting upon the ground which she took
in the negotiations, & that she never will abandon that hope till she is
undeceived in the most formal & unequivocal manner: It is Extremely to
be regretted that the measures of our government both with respect to
England & France are continually weakened by the intrigues & misrepresentations of certain interested individuals, & those of our citizens actuated by mere political malevolence who are found in both countries; It
is thus that France is supported in the Expectation referred to, & in the
same way its opinion has been formed on the state of our affairs in England,
& in the same way also England herself has from time to time been led
into Measures of unfriendly policy: But I learn from a source generally
good, the accuracy of whose information however is not entirely to be
depended upon, that the Sum Expected is Extremely moderate even as
low as 5,000,000 livres: by giving no Opinion as to the Western boundary
she certainly has left the means open of forming an amicable arrangement
upon some temptation of this sort, and however inconsiderable the Sum
may appear, yet when the mode in which it woud probably be employed
and certain wants are considered, its importance is very much enhanced.
But there is another view of this subject which I have received from one
who has the very best means of information, how far he has been faithful
in his representation I cannot pretend to say, but it is altogether different
from that which appearances induce to. He says that there was nothing
like dictation or any undue interference on the part of the French government in the late negotiations, that they kept aloof from the subject, except

when they were applied to on such points as it was incumbent on them to attend to; that they Exercised no secret influence whatever, and that upon the same principles which regulated their conduct on that occasion they are now determined not to move till they are applied to by the U. S: or by Spain, or till our hostilities & their treaties make it necessary for them to act: He does not pretend to say that they have no hope of money, but that it is expected to be paid only for the territory not contested, & that a moderate sum (without stating the amount) woud be sufficient; the points in contest to be adjusted by arrangements as to the western limits.

It seems that much more importance is annexed by the French government to an acquisition of E. Florida by the Un States than we give to that object; the idea is held out that this favorable moment is the only one in which it can be procured; that in time of peace & without the aid of France it woud be impossible to obtain a foot of territory [*sic*] in that quarter, from the obstinacy with which the Spanish government adhere to their possessions; it being a very essential principle of their monarchy that none of the dominions of the Crown shall be alienated, which the most imperious circumstances only have ever induced them to deviate from.

With respect to the other important point, how France woud act in a certain Event; from all I can learn it does seem that if we do not conclude to use money to the Extent & for the object suggested, that the most decided & vigorous course woud be the safest policy; that too much reliance is now placed in our pacific disposition, & that a respect woud be created by strong measures very favorable to an ultimate adjustment upon terms the most satisfactory to us: I know that Mr Monroe has Expressed this opinion to you, & all that I have since heard or observed recommends to such a course: whether the affairs of Europe still further recommend to it cannot perhaps be well judged of at present; it may prove otherwise, even the hopes of negotiation between the parties now so hostilely arrayed are not yet abandoned, but long before congress rises these questions will have been settled.

It is whispered that the French either have attempted to negotiate or are now negotiating with Spain for E. Florida, thus to take the contest with us partly into their own hands; this as I suppose Genl Armstrong has informed you is denied by M. Tallyrand, it bears indeed very little probability of truth.

I left Paris on the 27th of Septr. & arrived here on the first instant: I have staid here only long Enough to allow time for Mr Lees agent at Bayonne to prepare the means necessary for carrying me on to Madrid, for which place I shall depart to morrow & shall proceed with all possible dispatch: I learn from a Spanish courier that Mr Pinkney was yet at Madrid four days ago. Mr Bowdoin has applied thro Genl Armstrong for a passport to Enable him to land at Calais, which will doubtless be obtained, & he will probably be there in about three weeks. I am Dear Sir always with sincere respect your very obliged & obt St

GEORGE W ERVING

PS. As I took the liberty of mentioning to you in a former letter some reports which I had heard respecting Mr Alexander,[2] I ought now in justice to that gentleman to mention that I saw him on my passage thro Rotterdam in perfect health; & I have reason to think that the Accounts which we heard in England were very exaggerated representations founded upon an illness which he had some time since, & which as he confesses did for a time affect his mind; but since then he says he has not been ill, & he certainly has not the least appearance of derangement; he is moreover a very amiable man & appears to be very desirous & very capable of doing his duty satisfactorily; & having waited with him upon the French general I had an opportunity of observing that he stood well with him, & as I heard he has a similar good intelligence with the other authorities there.

GWE

RC (MHi: Winthrop Family Papers). Damaged by removal of seals.

1. See Erving to JM, 24 Aug. 1805.
2. See Erving to JM, 25 Oct. 1804, *PJM-SS*, 8:215.

§ From William Kirkpatrick. *4 October 1805, Málaga.* "I had last the honor of addressing you on the 19h. August. Your respected Letters of the 1st: & 12. July have since come to hand, with a Copy of the Laws past at last Session of Congress, which will serve for my Government, but you have omitted to forward me, or at least I have not receiv'd, those of the second Session of the seventh Congress, or first of the Eighth, which would be of Service, and I will be oblig'd by your ordering to be transmitted by first conveyance to a Port in Spain.

"I take proper note of the construction which the late Attorney General has put on the 3 Section of the Act of the 28. February. 1803,[1] of what you mention regarding Registers of Vessels lost, or condemned as not Sea worthy, and that no judicial Authority appertains to the Office of Consul, except what is expressly given by a Law of the United States, and may be tolerated by the Government, in which they reside, as also that I am to grant no Certificates whatever to Vessels purchased here, it having been considered proper to annul the Instructions transmitted of 1st. August 1801, to all which, I shall pay due attention, in such cases as may occur.

"I have in conformity to your Instructions, sent on a Bond sign'd by me, to Joseph Head Esq. of Boston, in order that he may procure the Signature of two Merchants of respectability as security for me, and transmit it to you in due form; As the Sureties must be Citizens of the United States, have Property, or a Commercial Establishment therein, I can meet with none here at present that would

Answer, and consequently have been under the necessity of recurring to my Friends on the Continent.

"Should any Publications be made in the district of this Consulate on the subject of Epidimical disorders, or quarantine Regulations which may be considered worthy the attention of Government, I shall have a particular pleasure in transmitting them as you desire, although I am apprehensive little Knowledge can be collected from this quarter, where the study of Medicine is in such a backward State, Our Physicians during the Sickness of last, and preceding Year, pursued no fix'd Plan in it's Cure, Some applied to one remidy, others to another, generally with equally bad success.

"Towards the end of August, the Brig Louisa, Captain Peter Billings arrived here from Bristol in England, under American Colours, when called upon to present his Papers, I found the Vessel was purchased in England and that he sailed her with a Bill of Sale, the two Certificates, and List of the Crew, of which I hand you a Copy;[2] as no doubt existed of his being a Citizen of the United States, and your Letter of the 12. July had not reached me, I returned them to him, but gave no document under my hand, or Seal of the Brig being American, and he proceeded on his Voyage; Should however any other of that description arrive here, I shall now consider myself as authorized to retire any Consular Certificates he may have, and not to acknowledge the Vessel as belonging to the United States.

"On the 28. Septr. the Brig Friendship of Boston, Richard Keating, Master, was brought into this Port, by a French Privateer, she had proceeded from Boston in July last in ballast, to the Coast of Labrador, where the Captain purchased a Cargo consisting in 1533 quintals of Cod Fish, for a Market in the Miditerranean. Thro' a strange neglect he had neither an Invoice or Bill of Lading for the Cargo on board, only a memorandum of the quantity of Fish purchas'd, and from whom, without a date, or Signature. After the Papers were brought on Shore, I assisted at the French Commercial Agents Office, at the opening of the Packet which contain'd them, those of the Vessel were in perfect Order, and thereon I founded the Captain's defence with the Convention between the two Nations in my hand; after two lengthy conferences on the subject, in which I would not admit that the French Marine Ordinances were in any respect binding on Americans, as the Commercial Agent wish'd to establish, but that the case was to be determined according to the tenor of the Convention mutually agreed on, I am happy to inform you the Papers of the Brig Friendship were deliver'd to me the day following, and Captain Keating proceeded on his Voyage to Alicante, after having furnish'd himself with the two essential documents which were wanting.

"Altho' it is probable you may already be inform'd by our Minister in Madrid of the two Orders that have been dispatch'd to the Marine Tribunals in the Ports of Spain, to give up all Property which had been condemned as English on board of American Vessels, and henceforward to respect our Flag, I enclose a copy of them; which I have procured thro' the Interest of a Friend.[3]

"This City continues to enjoy the most perfect Health, no Symptoms whatever of the Yellow Fever have appear'd, or at any of the other Cities in Spain, where it raged last Season, I consequently flatter myself there is now no danger to be apprehended.

"I have always made it a point to live on friendly terms with the Governor, and other Authorities of this Place, and treat them with the [d]eference they merit, you may depend I shall, if possible, never deviate from this Sistem, as by pursuing it, when difficulties occur, I generally get over them in a satisfactory manner, of which I have several proofs in my hand."

RC and enclosures (DNA: RG 59, CD, Málaga, vol. 1). RC 4 pp. For enclosures, see nn. 2–3.

    1. See JM's 1 July 1805 Circular to American Consuls and Commercial Agents, and n. 2.

    2. Kirkpatrick enclosed copies of (1) a 29 Apr. 1805 certificate (1 p.) of Josef Yznardy at Cádiz that Peter Billings of Boston had appeared and sworn he was the master of the brig *Louisa* of Baltimore, Richard Billings of Baltimore sole owner, and that the ship was "foreign built" and was seventy-one feet, six inches long, fifteen feet wide, of sixty-two tons and forty-two parts burden, with a square stern and a single deck; (2) a 27 July 1805 certification (1 p.; written on the verso of Yznardy's certificate), signed by chancellor Richard Vigor at Bristol in the absence of Elias Vander Horst, that Billings had appeared and sworn that the dimensions given in Yznardy's certification were erroneous, that the brig was measured at Bristol and was fifty-four feet, nine inches long, sixteen feet, seven and one-half inches wide, nine feet in depth, the burden the same as above, and that he swore it was the same ship; (3) a 27 July 1805 certification (1 p.) over Vander Horst's name that the annexed crew list contained the names and places of birth and residence of the crew of the *Louisa* bound for Málaga from Bristol; and (4) a list (1 p.) dated 27 July 1805 at Bristol and signed by Billings, mate Josiah Jackson, and Vigor, showing that besides the captain, mate, and second mate, the crew was composed of six seamen, two Americans, a Portuguese, a Prussian, a Swede, and a native resident of "Port o Port."

    3. The enclosures (3 pp.; in Spanish) are copies of offical notices from late August 1805, warning Spanish privateers to avoid irregularities, such as Charles Pinckney had complained of, when detaining American vessels, and to see that all legal matters were handled justly and expeditiously. For a 3 Sept. 1805 notice from Pedro Cevallos reiterating the same warning, see Pinckney to JM, 22 Sept. 1805, and n. 2.

§ From Robert Purviance. *4 October 1805, Baltimore.* "According to your request, I had put on board Capt Mann's Packet yesterday your two Pipes of Wine, completely cased, which I hope will arrive safe.

"I have inclosed you an Account of the Expenses thereon."[1]

RC and enclosures (DLC). RC 1 p.; in a clerk's hand, signed by Purviance. For enclosures, see n. 1.

    1. The enclosures (2 pp.) are a 3 Oct. 1805 receipt for the wine, signed by Capt. Zachariah Mann, and an invoice for $102.52 to which JM has added $44.95. For the wine, see William Jarvis to JM, 5 and 12 July and 1 Aug. 1805, Jacob Wagner to JM, 13 Sept. 1805, John Brice Jr. to JM, 31 Aug. 1805, and JM to Brice, 22 Sept. 1805.

To Thomas Jefferson

At the date of my last I entertained hopes of being at this time half way to Washington. Instead of that I am unable to say when I shall be able to commence the journey. The ride which we took in order to train Mrs. M. for it has been succeeded by sensations & appearances which threaten a renewal of her complaint in some degree & in some form or other. I flatter myself that as the appearances are rather in the vicinity than in the spot before affected, the cause may not be of a nature to re-open the part healed. Perhaps it may be very superficial and be quickly removed. My situation is nevertheless rendered peculiarly painful & perplexing. She will be infinitely distressed at my leaving her, with a gloomy prospect as to her relapse, and in a place which solitude would not be the only circumstance to render disagreeable. On the other hand, I feel the Obligations which call me to my post at this particular moment. In this dilemma, I shall wait a few days, to see whether my hopes of a favorable turn are justified: and if I should be disappointed shall wait a few more, in order to be decided by a letter from you. If the business of the consultation should have been carried into execution,[1] or can be so conveniently, without my share of service, or if what belongs to my duty can be executed under your instructions sent hither, I shall avail myself of your indulgence by remaining with my wife. If this indulgence be found improper, I shall do the best I can for her accomodation & comfort during my absence, and set out for Washington. Should my continuance here be the result, I shall make it subservient to the task of examining & disproving & exposing the British principle which threatens to spread wide the havoc on our neutral commerce, and which has already by its effects thrown our merchants into general consternation.[2] I have found it impossible to do what seemed to me, any thing like justice to a question so new, so important, and involving so many points, witht. going thro' a wide field, and drawing together a large volume of matter. The result, however, fairly viewed, will I think fully establish the heresy of the British doctrine, and present her selfishness & inconsistences [*sic*] in a light, which it would be prudent in her to retreat from. I have been for several days engaged in reviewing the judgments of Sir. W. Scott in cases involving that doctrine. I find them more vulnerable than I had supposed. The decisions are often at variance with each other, and the arguments some times shamefully sophistical, at others grossly absurd. It were to be wished that some legal critic of leisure and talents would undertake to overturn this Colossal champion of Belligerent usurpations. He could not fail to succeed, and the task is becoming absolutely necessary in order to save our admiralty jurisprudence from the misguidance which threatens it. The decisions and even dicta of Sir. W. Scott are in a manner laws already in our Courts; and his authority if not checked will be as despotic here as it is in England.

Cathcart I find is a candidate for a factorship among the Indians. He has written to me on the subject.[3] You know him so well that I can give no information that could aid your estimate of his pretensions. I believe him honest & capable, and cannot but think his knowledge of French & Spanish may balance in some measure the defect of his temper. It has been doubted I understand, whether his habits wd. descend to the functions to which he would be subjected. I am not so intimately acquainted with him as to be a judge on that point. Perhaps an idea of dignity would have less effect in the Wilderness, than in scenes of fashion. I hazard these remarks without knowing the competitions which probably exist, and chiefly under the influence of a sensibility to his need and expectation of some appt. which will testify the favorable opinion of the Govt. and give subsistance to his family. With respectful & constant attacht. I re⟨main⟩ Yrs.

JAMES MADISON

RC (DLC: Jefferson Papers). Docketed by Jefferson as received 8 Oct.

1. For the proposed cabinet meeting, see Jefferson to JM, 18 Sept. 1805.
2. For an earlier mention of this project, see JM to Jefferson, 14 Sept. 1805, and n. 5.
3. See James Leander Cathcart to JM, 26 Sept. 1805.

§ From William C. C. Claiborne. *5 October 1805, New Orleans.* "I arrived here on last Evening, and altho' my Health is much improved since my departure from Natchez, I am nevertheless far from being well.

"The unpleasant Reports alluded to by Mr. Graham in his Letter of the 22d. Ultimo, (a Copy of which I forwarded you from Natchez)[1] related to the Menaces of our Spanish Neighbours; the Warlike preparations at Havannah, and the apparent willingness of a portion of the Inhabitants of this place, to support Spanish Measures. I am happy however, to inform you that I have found every thing tranquil, nor do I apprehend any event (in which the people of the Territory would take an agency) which would subject the Government to serious embarrassment.

"A Rupture betwe[e]n the United States and Spain is esteemed here highly probable, and has excited much anxiety; I have however ventured an opinion that War was not likely to ensue, and I delivered this opinion with the more confidence, since no communications from the department of State have been received by me, which give the slightest intimation of a prospect of Hostilities."

RC (DNA: RG 59, TP, Orleans, vol. 7); letterbook copy (Ms-Ar: Claiborne Executive Journal, vol. 15). RC 2 pp.; in a clerk's hand, signed by Claiborne; docketed by Wagner. Minor differences between the copies have not been noted.

1. See Claiborne to JM, 27 Sept. 1805, and n. 1.

§ From William Davy.[1] *5 October 1805, Germantown.* "The Bearer Mr John Joseph Fraissinet is a Gentleman of such high Character, & Estimation, in the Opinion of a number of the most respectable Merchants of Philadelphia, that I may plead it as an Excuse for the liberty I take, of obliging him with this Line of Introduction to You. It is thought that he may render essential Services to the Commerce of the United States if favoured with the Appointment of Consul at Martinique which he applies for, & is strongly recommended to, by a Document he will present to You.

"I hope your Journey, has not incommoded Your good Lady. My whole Family unite, in best Wishes for her perfect Recovery, & in respectfull Remembrance."

RC (DNA: RG 59, LAR, 1801-9, filed under "Fraissinet"). 2 pp.; docketed by Jefferson.

1. Philadelphia merchant William Davy (d. 1827) was named consul at Kingston upon Hull, England, in 1816 (*Journal of the U.S. House of Representatives,* 10th Cong., 1st sess., 48; *Senate Exec. Proceedings,* 3:61, 68, 580).

§ From Sylvanus Bourne. *6 October 1805, Amsterdam.* "It seems that the British Cruizers Still continue to capture our Vessells bound to Europe with W India produce & although many are released after examination & trial which Subjects the owners to heavy charges—others are condemned upon principles new & extraordinary & such as must operate very injuriously to our trade—among them is to be cited the case of the Briga. Adair of Newbury Port lately taken into England while on her voyage to this port—part of whose cargo has been condemned because the Captain in his declaration asserted that while loading in the UStates he waited for some arrivals from the West Indies to make up his cargo—that portion therefore of the Cargo brought by said Vessells was confiscated on the grounds that it proved that the property was imported with intent to reship to Europe—which they will not permit Saying that we can import what we want for our home consumption & if it shoud happen that a surplus remains they will graciously permit as [*sic*] to send said Surplus to Europe for Sale—but not allow an importation made with *view* to exportation. This indeed is the essence of their reasoning & is truly humiliating towards an independent nation you will perceive by the last account from Europe that a wide extended War is about to be renewed upo⟨n⟩ the Continent—involving most of the nations thereof & which must in effect render the neutrality of our flag precious indeed to our Country & it may be that the British Govt is from this led to conclude that we shall consent to suffer much rather than expose ourselves to the consequences of a War to protect our Rights—& to the loss of what share of neutrality we now enjoy—how far this may be the case must depend on the force of public sentiment in our Co⟨un⟩try & its sense of what we owe to ourselves & the rising interest of our Commerce.

"Confiding that I shall soon have the pleasure of a favorable reply to my late interest⟨ing⟩ Communications."

RC (DNA: RG 59, CD, Amsterdam, vol. 1). 2 pp.

§ From William Buchanan. *6 October 1805, Île de France.* "I have the pleasure of forwarding you by this occasion two returns, one a copy of the return commencing the first July 1804 and one commencing the first of January 1805. which I hope will arrive Safe.[1] Since I had the pleasure of addressing you last no change has Taken place in the Commercial regulations at this Island, nor do I expect any."

RC and enclosures (DNA: RG 59, CD, Port Louis, vol. 1). RC 1 p.; in a clerk's hand, signed by Buchanan. For enclosures, see n. 1.

1. The enclosures (2 pp.) list thirty-seven American ships that arrived at Île de France between 1 July 1804 and 31 Dec. 1804, and fifty-three that arrived between 1 Jan. 1805 and 30 June 1805.

§ From Anthony Terry. *8 October 1805, Cádiz.* "Begging reference to what I had the honor of addressing you ⅌ Duplicate on the 5th. & 31st. January 25 march 3d. & 10. April,[1] 15th. May, 11th. June, 4th. 11th. 19th. 23d. & 30 July, 16th. & 20th. August & 3d. & 14th. September ultimo.[2]

"I am now honored with your verry esteem'd Circulars of the 1st. & 12th. July last, accompanied with the Book of Acts passed at the 2d. Session of the 8th. Congress, and have with due attention read the Contents, and to which I pledge you my word of honour I shall not deviate in the least in complying therewith, as I have done heretofore and which I will continue doing as long as the Office is under my charge.

"I shall have particular care to forward now & then every interesting Paper that may make its appearance on the Subject of Epidemic disorder and Quarenteen regulations.

"They continue to put this City in a proper State of defence, in case of any attack; all the Boats to be found are arming, a numbe⟨r⟩ of Artilliry & Troops arrived here last week. The Fleet off this Port is daily augmenting it is actually composed of Forty Sail of the Line, a number of Frigates, Corvettes Brigs & Sloops. A Convoy of about Seventy Sail arrived at Gibraltar with Troops on the 30th. ultimo.

"Monsr. Lauriston General of the French troops on board the Fleet, with his Etat Major has set out for France ⅌ Post on the 2d. instant.

"By all accounts there can be no doubt, but a Continental war will take place." Adds in a postscript: "Governmt. Notes 56½ a 57."

RC (DNA: RG 59, CD, Cádiz, vol. 1). 3 pp.; in a clerk's hand, signed by Terry.

1. *PJM-SS*, 8:459, 9:209, 231. The 31 Jan. and 25 Mar. 1805 letters are from Josef Yznardy, ibid., 8:520–21, 9:177.

2. No letters of 15 May, 11 June, 16 Aug., and 3 and 14 Sept. 1805 have been found. The only July 1805 letter found from Cádiz is one of 12 July from Yznardy, which Terry may have meant by his reference to an 11 July letter.

From Peder Pedersen

S<small>IR</small>,   P<small>HILADELPHIA</small> 9th. October 1805.

In addition to the communications I have had the honor to make to
you, under date of the 18th. and 28th. of May last,[1] concerning such
Quarantine Regulations as lately have been adopted by the Danish Government, I have now the honor to inform you, that by a Royal Ordinance
dated 15th. of May, every Danish subject, commanding a Vessel bound
from any port in North America to any port in Europe, is obliged to
demand from the Consul or Vice-Consul residing at the place whence
he commences his Voyage, a particular Certificate, for which a certain
form is prescribed, and whereby the state of health of the place at the
time when the Vessel was laying there in lading, may be known with
certainty.

From the result of the later years Experience, it seems to appear, that
the United States scarcely at any time can be considered as being absolutely free from contagious diseases, and that the yellow fever, almost
every year, prevails in some of the principal ports, whence Vessels may be
expected to arrive in Danish or other ports on the Baltic; hence the Quarantine Department must lay this down as a general rule, that Vessels coming from the United States, at all times are suspicious of carrying with
them contagion, either by their Crews, or by their Cargoes; yet as it would
occasion too great a loss and expence to Commerce, if, on account of this
Suspicion, all Vessels coming from the United States should be subjected
to a regular quarantine, my Government has, by the regulation prescribed
in the above Ordinance, deemed same to be the most advantagious way
of uniting the interest of Commerce with the preservation and security
of the public health.

But as the same danger with which Vessels proceeding from the United
States for Danish ports, are liable to treaten the public state of health, no
less exists with those bound to other ports on the Baltic: the Danish Government has deemed it proper to invite the Neighbouring powers, border-
ing on the Baltic, to adopt similar measures with respect to Vessels from
the United States, bound to their respective ports; that they thereby may
avoid being treated as suspicious on their arrival at the Sound, and consequently subjected to the quarantine Ordinance; The Swedish the Russian
and the Prussian Governments, to whom such proposal, on the part of His
Majesty's Government, was made, have signified their approbation of it,
and it has consequently been agreed upon, that Consular Certificates shall
henceforth be furnished, either by Danish Consuls or Vice Consuls, where
those powers themselves have no Commercial agents, or by theirs, vice
versa, where no Danish Consul or Vice Consul reside.

Having thus had the honour, Sir, of explaining to you the measures of precaution lately adopted, as well as the causes whence they originated, you will no doubt, acknowledge that what applied to Danish or other foreign Vessels bound from any port in the United States, to any Danish or other ports on the Baltic, does as fully apply to American Vessels bound from one of their own ports to any Danish European port, or any port on the Baltic, for the same reasons, is it desirable that American Vessels having the above destination, should at the place, whence they commence their voyage, provide themselves with such a Consular Certificate as before is mentioned; as the want of this, will absolutely subject every American Vessel, deficient in this point, to be treated, on its arrival at the Sound, or at its destination, as suspicious of Contagion, and consequently to undergo all what in such case is prescribed by the Quarantine Law—a Copy of which in the french language, as well as one of the herethofore mentioned Royal Ordinance, I here beg leave to enclose.[2]

I have therefore been directed to inform you of this, and at the same time have herewith the honour, Sir, to acquaint you with the wish entertained by His Majesty's Government, that the Government of the United States would enjoin its Citizens commanding Vessels bound to any of the above mentioned ports, to provide themselves with such Certificates, as before stated; my Government does so much the less doubt that the Government of the United States will do Justice to the motives, to which the adopted Regulations owe their existence, as it by them has had in view, not only the security of His Majesty's dominions as well as that of the neighbouring powers, but also in particular, the wish, to secure the Commerce with the United States, and their Navigation, so far as possible, from all unecessary constraints and from every obstacle, which can be avoided. I have the honour to be with the most distinguished Consideration and very respectfully Sir, Your most obedient humble servant

PR. PEDERSEN

RC and enclosures (DNA: RG 59, NFL, Denmark, vol. 1). RC docketed by Wagner, with his note: "Quarantine." For enclosures, see n. 2.

1. *PJM-SS*, 9:369–70, 412–13.

2. The enclosures are (1) a copy (2 pp.; printed in the 2 Oct. 1805 New York *Republican Watch-Tower*) of the 15 May 1805 ordinance requiring the consular certificates, and (2) a printed copy (51 pp.; in French) of the 8 Feb. 1805 quarantine regulations with tables of merchandise susceptible and non-susceptible to contagion.

From Jacob Wagner

DEAR SIR   DEPARTMENT OF STATE 9 Octr. 1805

I have received your favor of the 5th.[1] and now enclose the papers accumulated since I suspended communicating them.

The two enclosures with Mr. Monroe's letter of 6 Augt. were not received with the copy you have read. I have sent to Genl. Smith the extract from Blakeley's letter marked by crotchets, that the fraud may be repelled.[2] The answer to Messrs. McKims' complaint may perhaps be a reference of their correspondent to Mr. Monroe for his aid, which he will afford as of course. Johnson's case requires the judicial remedy to be attempted, though it may not be amiss to send a copy of the deposition to Mr. Merry, that he may find a balance against the prize taken by Com. Preble and used as a cruiser before condemnation:[3] the long detention of the supercargo and crew on board the ship of war is another grievance. I suppose Mr. Coffin may be advised to prosecute his appeal in the case of the Penman and informed that the principle assumed by the judge will be opposed in London by our Minister. You may recollect that Sir Wm. Scott makes a distinction between the oriental and western colonies of belligerents as to neutral trade. With respect to the latter, he says, the illegality is decided upon the general presumption that it was not permitted in time of peace; but with respect to the other no presumption is regarded but the fact must be proved.

I have spent some of my vacant time in tracing the three points you desired: 1st. the rule of coasting & colony trade as deducible from the practise of Sir James Marriott: 2d. examples of Acts of parliament relaxing the commercial and navigation laws of G. Britain in time of war: & 3rd. treaties stipulating expressly or impliedly such an universal free trade as would be incomptable with the existence of the British restrictive rule. Of the 1st. I have collected all the cases in the vol. we have[4] and abstracted the material facts; of the 2d. I have added a few to a series, given in Reeves with the history and effects of the relaxations,[5] as calculated to answer the temporary exigencies of war and literally limited to its duration; and I have also collected a number of references to treaties, though not to such an host of them as would be possible. I have the honor to remain, Dr sir, With respectful attachment Your most obed. servt.

JACOB WAGNER

RC (DLC).

1. The letter has not been found, but like JM's 5 Oct. 1805 letter to Jefferson, it probably informed Wagner that JM would not be returning to Washington as soon as he had expected.

2. See Josiah Blakeley to JM, 1 July 1805.

3. Wagner probably referred to the case of the *Hannah Maria* (see Christopher John-ston, Mark Pringle, and John Sherlock to JM, 1 Oct. 1805). For the case of the *Transfer*, see Anthony Merry to JM, 9 July 1805 (first letter), and n. 1.

4. For the work on the decisions of James Marriott, see JM to Monroe, 7 Sept. 1805, and n. 4.

5. Wagner may have referred to John Reeves's *History of the Law of Shipping and Naviga-tion* published in London and Dublin in 1792.

§ From John Dawson. *9 October 1805*. "I have pleasure in presenting to you Mr. Fuller—a gentleman, and a member of the legislature of S. Carolina, who, with an amiable lady, has been on a visit to the Eastern states, and is now on his return.[1] I pray your civilities to them and a belief in the regard of Your friend & Sert."

RC (DLC). 1 p.

1. This was Christopher Fuller (1777–1818), a physician and planter who owned a plan-tation on the Ashley River and a house in Charleston. He served in the South Carolina legislature from 1800 to 1808. He was married to Jennet Innes McDonald (Edgar et al., *Biographical Directory of the South Carolina House of Representatives*, 4:215).

§ From William Jarvis. *9 October 1805, Lisbon*. "I have only time to inform you that a Courier arrived here the last night from Paris in 10 days, to Genl. Junot, & proceeded to the Caldres where the General now is. It is confidently reported that he said that the 26th. Ultimo war was declared on the part of France against Austria, but this will not be Known to a certainty for two or three days, altho: such an event appears very probable."

Adds in a postscript: "Inclosed is a letter from Mr Pinckney one from Mr Terry & one from Mr Montgomery."[1]

Adds in a second postscript on verso, dated 10 Oct.: "This Vessel being stopped by contrary winds affords me the opportunity of informing you that General Junot met the Courier on the road to Town & has informed several persons of War being declared, also that he is to return to France in a few days."

RC (DNA: RG 59, CD, Lisbon, vol. 2). 1 p.

1. The enclosures may have included Charles Pinckney to JM, 22 Sept. 1805, and Robert Montgomery to JM, 17 Sept. 1805. No September 1805 letter from Anthony Terry has been found.

§ From Anthony Merry. *9 October 1805, "Near Philadelphia."* "I have received the Honor of your Letter of the 3rd. Instant, with the Documents inclosed respect-ing the Impressment of Nathaniel Bartlett, a Citizen of the United States, by the British Schooner Whiting, said to be on the Halifax Station.

"I have lost no Time, Sir, in transmitting Copies of those Documents to the Commander in Chief of His Majesty's Ships on that Station, in order that, should the Schooner Whiting be under his Command, immediate Attention may be paid to your Application for the Release of the Seaman in question."

RC (DNA: RG 59, NFL, Great Britain, vol. 3). 1 p.

From Robert R. Livingston

Dear Sir   ClerMont 10th. Octr. 1805

I received on the fifth Inst your favor of the ⟨2⟩8th. Septr. I began immediately to unpack my papers and have been since employed in examining them, this took ⟨s⟩ome time, as they were all unsorted & put into a trunk for the convenience of transportation. I can find none of the papers you refer to. It was my practice in all ship cases t⟨o⟩ put the papers into the hands of Mr. Skipwith for ex⟨a⟩mination who reported to me his opinion thereon, so that I have few or no papers relative to that subject except ⟨s⟩uch as arrived after Mr. Skipwith had declined transac⟨t⟩i⟨n⟩g that business, & I employed Mr. Hawkins as sec⟨r⟩etary for that department. The papers therefore ⟨if⟩ they ever came to hand must be with Mr Skipwith, ⟨bu⟩t I much doubt whether they have ever been recd, because I have but one copy of your letter of 27 Octr. 1803[1] ⟨n⟩or can I find that I have in any of my letters to you acknowledged the rect of those papers. Nor do my books present me with any note or memorandum upo⟨n⟩ the subject so that I much fear they have been lost on their passage. It may seem singular to you that Mr Armstrong should have no papers from me. The follo⟨wg.⟩ statement will however shew that it is not owing to me that ⟨he⟩ has them not. So soon as his office was established, (in November last) I sent him six boxes of papers containin⟨g⟩ all I had of every sort except your Letters, & mine to you. These I presumed you had yourself communicated as far as you thought adviseable. I requested him to take copie⟨s⟩ of any of my notes that he conceived might be useful to him & to keep all the other papers that he might want. Five months after this just as I was about to e⟨m⟩bark he returned them to me observing that they w⟨ould⟩ be of no use to him I requested him to keep at leas⟨t⟩ the papers that related to individuals & ship busi⟨ness.⟩ This he declined & I was compelled to burden myself w⟨ith⟩ them. I do not find upon examination any or at leas⟨t⟩ very few papers that relate to unfinished business. Those which respected prize c⟨au⟩sses having been all in Mr Skipwiths hands or been with drawn for the use of the courts or the board of commissioners. Few or no new cases have occurred during the present war which has [*illegible*] both cheafly to applications for oppressions in the ports of france Seamens claims & claims of Citizens who f⟨e⟩ll under the censure of the police or were mistaken for British subjects all or most of these I was happy enough to finish. I will however put up these papers & have them sent by water to the post office at New York to your address. I propose within six or eight days to set out for Washington where I hope to have the honor of paying my respects to the president ⟨&⟩ to you & to afford you every information in my power relative to such objects as have demanded my attention during my mission. I have the honor to be with the sincerest essteem & attatchment Dear Sir Yr Most Ob Hum. Servt

R R LIVINGSTON

RC (DNA: RG 59, DD, France, vol. 9); FC (NHi: Livingston Papers). FC dated 11 Oct. RC and FC differ considerably in wording but convey the same information.

1. *PJM-SS*, 5:579–80.

From Alexander Coffin Jr.

SIR,   HUDSON. 11th. Octr. 1805.

I have only been able to obtain one Of the nuts of the Vegetable soap, which I inclose, & which I hope will prove acceptable.[1] The manner the Javanese use it is, to cut the nut in two, then wet the Cloth, & rub it on 'till the Soapy Quality of the nut be totally extracted, which it will by this friction. By a Chemical Analises the Quantity, & Quality of each component part might doubtless be ascertain'd. & it may not be a wild opinion, that, the Vegetable Kingdom in our own Country may contain similar qualities which by experiments might lead to some useful discoveries. Useful I say, because the easier & the cheaper the necessaries of life; & soap certainly, is a very desirable one, comes to us the less dependant it will make us on foreign Nations.

I dont Know, Sir, wether you have ever Seen any of the Birds nests of which the delicious Soup, so much admir'd in India is made, & which has, as we are told by the Indians, the wonderful quality of Stimulating, a certain favorite passion of theirs, to a great degree; without the least injury to the Physical, whatever it may be to the moral *System*.[2] I inclose you a Small piece, it's all I have. These Nests are form'd on the high Rocky Shores of Islands in those Seas, & consist of a Glutinous substance which the birds collect on the beach. They are form'd with great art, & generally against the highest projecting Rocks; for Nature, it Seems, has taught them that they have enemies, & instructed them to Keep as much out of their reach as possible. Great Quantities of the(ir) nests are yearly Collected by the natives, & sold to the different traders who visit their Islands. Great quantities find their way to China, for most certainly the Chinese are the greatest Epicures on Earth, & the most Voluptuous, & a rich Chinaman will grudge no expence to gratify his Sensual inclinations. With the highest respect I am Sir your most Obedt. & oblig'd. Hmble Servt.

ALEX COFFIN JUNR.

RC (DLC).

1. Coffin referred to one of several species of the *Sapindus* genus (M. K. Seth, "Trees and Their Economic Importance," *Botanical Review* 69 [2003]: 348).

2. Coffin presumably enclosed a piece of a nest of the edible-nest swiftlet (*Collacalia unicolor*), which breeds on the Malabar coast of India in the early spring (H. E. Barnes, "Nesting in Western India," *Journal of the Bombay Natural History Society* 4 [1889]: 5–6).

From Thomas Jefferson

DEAR SIR   WASHINGTON Oct. 11.05

The only questions which press on the Executive for decision are Whether we shall enter into a provisional alliance with England to come into force only in the event that *during the present war* we become engaged in war *with France?* leaving the declaration of the casus federis ultimately to us. Whether we shall send away Yrujo, Casacalvo, Morales? Whether we shall instruct Bowdoin not to go to Madrid till further orders? but we are all of opinion that the first of these questions is too important & too difficult to be decided but on the fullest consideration in which your aid & counsel should be waited for. I sincerely regret the cause of your absence from this place and hope it will soon be removed; but it is one of those contingencies from the effects of which even the march of public affairs cannot be exempt. Perhaps it would not be amiss to instruct Bowdoin to await at London further orders; because if we conclude afterwards that he should proceed, this may follow the other instruction without delay.

I am glad we did not intermeddle with Armstrong's decision against the Insurance companies.[1] I am told these companies have a great mixture of English subscribers. If so, the question becomes affected by the partnership. What is become of our hermitage?[2] As you are in the neighborhood of Butler I presume the claim upon us could be easily settled & apportioned. Present my respects to mrs. Madison & my prayers for her speedy & perfect reestablishment, and accept your self affectionate salutations

TH: JEFFERSON

RC (DLC: Rives Collection, Madison Papers); FC (DLC: Jefferson Papers).

1. For the issue of John Armstrong and the *New Jersey*, see Philip Nicklin and Robert Eaglesfield Griffith to JM, 25 July 1805, and n. 7. For additional correspondence on the case, see JM to Jefferson, 9 Aug. 1805, Jefferson to JM, 17 Aug. 1805, and JM to John Armstrong, 25 Aug. 1805.

2. For the hermitage wine that JM, Jefferson, and Pierce Butler bought from Stephen Cathalan Jr., which was intercepted by the British, see *PJM-SS*, 8:78 and n. 2, 359–60, 9:503 and n. 1, and David Gelston to JM, 8 Aug. 1805, JM to Jefferson, 9 Aug. 1805, Anthony Merry to JM, 19 Aug. 1805, and n. 1, and Jefferson to JM, 27 Aug. 1805.

§ From Thomas Auldjo. *11 October 1805, Cowes.* "I had the honor to address myself to you 22nd. ultimo of which inclosed is Copy. Since then the Ship Merchant of & from New York with East & West India Goods for Amsterdam, has been released & proceeded on her voyage, but has not had any Compensation for the delay or the Charges incurred. The Ship Palinurus of New Bedford from New York with Sugar &c for Amsterdam detained at Portsmouth, has been released by decree of the Admiralty, but 169 hogsheads Sugar of the Cargo are unloaden & retained for further proof.[1] No Expences are allowed this Ship. I have also to advise that Since my last the Ship Little Cornelia Ichabod Clarke master with West India produce from New York for Amsterdam has been brought into Portsmouth by a man of War & is under prosecution in the Admiralty."[2]

RC, two copies (DNA: RG 59, CD, Southampton, vol. 1). First RC 2 pp. Second RC, marked "Copy," enclosed in Auldjo to JM, 1 Nov. 1805. Minor differences between the copies have not been noted.

1. On 15 Sept. 1805 Capt. Stephen Merrihew of the *Palinurus* wrote his owners from Portsmouth that he had been taken, sent into Plymouth, and released. He had departed on 9 Sept., was taken again on 10 Sept., and on 12 Sept. sent to Portsmouth, where he was held prisoner and incommunicado for two days. "General opinion" there was that so much of the cargo as came from French colonies would be condemned or held for further proof. Since the deputy U.S. consul at Portsmouth was acting as agent for the captor, Merrihew was having nothing to do with him. He added that the *Eagle* was also there, and the *Merchant* had just arrived (*New-York Commercial Advertiser*, 14 Nov. 1805; Williams, *French Assault on American Shipping*, 272).
2. The *Little Cornelia* carried sugar from Martinique to New York, where it arrived on 23 July 1805. About 12 Aug. the ship and cargo cleared for Amsterdam. On 6 Nov. 1805 Sir William Scott of the Admiralty Court condemned the ship and that part of the cargo that had been brought from Martinique on the grounds that the testimony given indicated that James Arden, owner of both the ship and the sugar, was aware of the British position on the doctrine of continuous voyages and had attempted to hide the fact that the sugar was intended for Holland all along (New York *Morning Chronicle*, 12 Aug. 1805 and 17 Jan. 1806).

§ From William Hull. *11 October 1805, Detroit.* "From letters, I have received from my agent in Boston, I find, my private affairs render my return indispensably necessary. Had these letters arrived in time, I should have stated the fact, and asked this indulgence from the President. I believe however no ill consiquences will result from my absence, as every arrangement has been made, which at present will be necessary. Mr. Griswold the Secretary will perform the duties of Governor in my absence. I have the pleasure to inform you the Territory is perfectly tranquil, and the people satisfied.

"It is my intention to be at Washington the beginning of the winter, to propose some measures, which seem indispensably necessary, for the prosperity of the Territory."

RC (DNA: RG 59, TP, Michigan, vol. 1). 1 p.; docketed by Wagner as received 19 Nov.

§ From William Jarvis. *11 October 1805, Lisbon.* "Inclosed is a copy of my letter of the 26 Ulto, which went by the Bark Pompey, Captn Orne for Salem, mine of the

9th Inst that went by the ship Baltimore, Captn Long for Baltimore with the letters from Messrs Pinckney, Montgomery & Terry inclosed, a copy of which went
by the ship Nanking, Captn Dorr for New York.[1]

"As I at first supposed in case any interference took place, the inclosed copy of
a letter from His Excy Mr de Araujo will inform you of the decision of this Government to let the affair be decided in the Courts of this Kingdom.[2] The trials in
the Tribunals are commonly so slow that little prospect remained of this affair
being brought to an issue under four or five years if the claimants of the Vessel
thought proper to keep it off so long. It would also be attended with a considerable expense & I think would ultimately be likely to eat out the Vessel. Beside
which there is no certainty of a decision according to the true merits of the case
being finally had, for the reasons I offered in my letter of the 8th: Inst to His
Excy. (a copy of which goes inclosed)[3] and for others which will readily suggest
themselves to your mind. Under all these circumstances I thought it better to
leave the affair with this Government to decide as it might deem mos⟨t⟩ consonant
to strict justice. Several advantages it appear'd to m⟨e,⟩ would attend this mode of
proceeding. In the first place it not only would prevent any altercation with this
government, but might be construed into a handsome compliment. To the Spanish Ambassador it indicated a disposition on the part of Government, as far as it
could be supposed that I knew its sentiments, to adjust amicably any difference
between the two Countries: and after the spirit of justice his Court discovered in
the orders of the 3d. Sept⟨r⟩. for restoring all American Vessels captured by Spanish privateers, that its Officers would not strain a point of Law to the injury of a
Spanish subject. To add to the favour I conceived it would be well enough to state
the ground upon which I founded my request to send her to the U.S. for Trial.
Copies of a letter & Note from the Spanish Consul General go inclosed.[4] I have
been very doubtful how to act in this affair, and if Gover⟨n⟩ment thinks I have
taken the worse course, it will add to the numberless proofs that the best intentions in the world will not always free us from error. But a⟨s⟩ there were only two
ways of proceeding, after this Government determined that the affair must be
decided in its Tribunals; either to pursue it through this channel at considerable
expense, much time & great trouble, when I was persuaded that a decision according to the true merits of the case was at least uncertain, which therefore I deemed
would have been contrary to the Consular Instructions of the 9th. April 1803;[5] or
to leave it with this Government to decide, recommending the situation of the late
Spanish owner to favour; which method I imagined would be more consonant to the
liberal views of Government & hope my Conduct will not meet its disapprobation.
In my letter to Mr. de Araujo I am afraid that you will think I have made use of an
improper expression ('altho it might be contrary to the strict letter of the Law') to
convey the idea that Govmt. would not under the circumstances of the late owner,
wish to strain or rigidly inforce a point of Law to his injury.

"A formal declaration of War was not made on the 26th. Ultimo, but only virtually in a speech made by the Emperor Napoleon to the Senate, in consequence
of the Austrian forces having passed the River Inn;[6] the French Minister at Vienna
some weeks ago having Officially declared that the Emperor would consider the
invasion of Bavaria by Austria as a declaration of War. Genl. Junot is appointed to
a command in the Army.

"Amidst those shocks of War this Country seems to be secure of its Neutrality. The impressment of soldiery has entirely ceased. Nothing is doing in the Navy beside coppering one frigate.

"All conversation has subsided relative to a farther demand for money, nor do I believe that any has lately been made.

"This Court has lately gon⟨e⟩ into mourning for the Countess of Artois & the Duke of Gloucester. A Copy of the Notice goes herewith.[7] About 3 months since the same formality was gone thro⟨ugh⟩ for the queen Dowager of Prussia.

"Inclosed is a Copy of a letter from me to Mr Lyman at London regarding an impressed seaman, to which I must beg leave to refer for particulars.[8]

"I have been honored with your circulars of the 1st. & 12th. July past & was much pleased with the instructions relative to Judicial proceedings. It will save the Consuls from much censure; at the same time that it no longer leaves his discretion as the measure of his conduct. The Laws of 1804–5 I also received.

"I am extremely solicitous to know the measures pursued by Government relative to Spain. Events have proved as favourable as We could desire either to urge a compliance with our territorial claims, or of receding without the appearance of weakness. In fact not to enforce them at such a moment must be considered as the highth of generosity. I presume from the extremely embarrassed state of the Spanish finances, no compensation for or settlement of our monied claims need be expected during the War, without some territorial arrangement should take place & it should be included in that."[9]

RC, two copies, and enclosures, two copies (DNA: RG 59, CD, Lisbon, vol. 2). First RC 5 pp. Second RC in a clerk's hand, unsigned; marked "(Dup)"; written at the head of Jarvis to JM, 24 Oct. 1805. Words and parts of words in angle brackets in the first RC have been supplied from the second RC. Minor differences between the copies have not been noted. For enclosures, see nn. 2, 4, 7, and 9.

1. The *Pompey*, Capt. William Orne, arrived at Salem, Massachusetts, about 7 Nov. 1805; the *Baltimore*, Captain Long, arrived at Baltimore about 16 Dec.; the *Nanking*, Captain Dorr, arrived at Norfolk about 17 Dec. (*New-York Evening Post*, 14 Nov. 1805; *New-York Gazette & General Advertiser*, 20 Dec. 1805; Philadelphia *United States' Gazette*, 23 Dec. 1805).

2. The enclosure (3 pp.; in Portuguese and English) is a copy of António de Araújo to Jarvis, 27 Sept. 1805, in reply to Jarvis's letter of 6 Sept. about the *Venus*. Araújo said the prince regent had decreed that the government could not proceed against the ship and the captain on the basis of a mere allegation, especially in so delicate a matter as commerce, therefore the case should be decided in the proper court and after that such steps as were found necessary would be taken.

3. In his 8 Oct. 1805 reply (4 pp.; in a clerk's hand, signed by Jarvis) to Araújo's 27 Sept. letter (see n. 2 above) Jarvis repeated the personal information about John Reoch and the sale of the *Venus* that he had sent to JM on 16 Sept. 1805; enclosed the documents he had about the *Venus;* stated that had it become known that Reoch was not American, as he had claimed in order to get American papers for the ship, the vessel would have been liable to seizure by any of the belligerents. He asked how far any nation had a right to claim jurisdiction over a foreign flag for a breach of the laws of the country to which the ship belonged when the breach occurred out of the territory of the nation claiming jurisdiction. Jarvis acknowledged that although some writers on international law upheld the principle, in practice it was so difficult to enforce that most governments waived that right when an

official request for custody had been made by the nation where the crime was committed. He cited two recent examples from England, one of an American captain accused of killing a seaman who was released from jail at Rufus King's request and sent to the United States for trial, and the other of Portuguese citizens who had forged Portuguese financial paper and who were "indirectly given up" to the Portuguese minister and sent to Lisbon. He also cited the difficulties of translating United States laws affecting the *Venus* case, of deciding cases by the laws of a foreign country whose language the judges didn't understand exacerbated by the different legal customs of Portugal and the United States, all of which might make it difficult to achieve a decision based on the merits of the case, leading to unpleasant discussions. He added that the American government had too high an opinion of the wisdom of the prince regent not to be satisfied with whatever steps he decided to take and that the U. S. Constitution forbade public officials from spending sums not expressly appropriated by law, which would prevent him from pursuing the case in the Portuguese courts without express orders from his government. His correspondence with Spanish consul general Lugo (see n. 4 below) had suggested a solution. Because those who sold the ship to Reoch had taken bills from him, and because he was not "a man of property," if the ship was condemned, they would be the losers. Should Portugal approve the restoration of the *Venus* to Tastet & Co., he was convinced that the U.S. government would be satisfied with that step "although it might be contrary to the strict letter of the Law."

4. The enclosures (5 pp.; in French and English) are copies of (1) Spanish consul general José de Lugo to Jarvis, 4 Oct. 1805, stating that Tastet & Co., merchants at St. Sebastián, informed him that the *Venus*, which had entered Lisbon from Cádiz under the American flag, was sold by them to John Reoch, but the sale was being canceled for lack of payment, and they wished Lugo to reclaim the ship; that Lugo had just learned that Jarvis had placed an embargo on the ship because the papers shown him were not according to regulation; that the owners wanted the ship sold at Lisbon; and asking Jarvis to lift the embargo so the proposed sale might take place; (2) Jarvis to Lugo, 6 Oct. 1805, noting that Lugo had not mentioned the ship's papers, and adding that whatever steps Jarvis might take were contingent on an unqualified promise from Lugo that they would be returned; (3) Lugo to Jarvis, 6 Oct. 1805, apologizing for neglecting to mention the papers, and assuring Jarvis that the American papers of the *Venus* would be delivered to him so that this unpleasant business would be quickly drawn to a close; (4) and Jarvis to Lugo, 9 Oct. 1805, saying that the affair of the *Venus* was in the hands of the Portuguese government for a decision; that in his 8 Oct. letter to Araújo (see n. 3 above) he had mentioned the case of the Spanish owners favorably; and that the decision of Charles IV ordering the release of American ships captured by Spanish privateers in violation of the Treaty of San Lorenzo would dispose the U.S. government to "grant every consistent favour" to Spanish subjects.

5. For JM's 9 Apr. 1803 Circular Letter to American Consuls and Commercial Agents, see *PJM-SS*, 4:491–93.

6. In his 23 Sept. 1805 speech to the senate, Napoleon announced that he was just leaving Paris to lead the French army, that Austria had crossed the Inn, that Munich had been invaded, that war had broken out in Germany, and that Russia and Austria had allied themselves with Great Britain (*Annual Register for 1805*, 659).

7. The enclosure (1 p.) is a copy of Araújo's 3 Oct. 1805 letter announcing that the court had decreed two months' mourning for the Countess of Artois and noting that within that period would also be included fifteen days' mourning for the Duke of Gloucester. Marie Thérèse of Savoy, Countess of Artois, died on 2 June 1805, and William Henry, Duke of Gloucester, died on 25 Aug. (Francis Lieber, ed., *Encyclopaedia Americana: A Popular Dictionary of Arts, Sciences, Literature, History, Politics and Biography, Brought down to the Present Time . . .* [13 vols.; Philadelphia, 1829–33], 3:82; *Times* [London], 27 Aug. 1805).

8. In his 30 Sept. 1805 letter to William Lyman (2 pp.; in a clerk's hand, signed by Jarvis), Jarvis stated that American seaman John Robinson of Wiscasset had been impressed at Lisbon into the British sloop-of-war *Constance*, Captain Griffiths, who denied to Jarvis's secretary that Robinson had a protection. Robinson had written Jarvis that, although he had declared that he had one, no one at any time had asked to see it. Jarvis presumed that in view of this the Admiralty would issue orders for Robinson's discharge. Jarvis himself had seen the protection, which described Robinson, who was a destitute seaman discharged from the French fleet, but Jarvis could not send Lyman the description because he took only the date, the number, and the district where issued from protections when he aided American seamen. He added that he presumed Captain Griffiths was unaware of this, since he could not believe "a person holding so reputable a station" would lie.

9. Also filed with this letter is the 10 Oct. 1805 deposition of consulate clerks Charles T. Gilman and Thomas Carter (4 pp.; in a clerk's hand, signed by Gilman and Carter, certified by Jarvis). The deposition stated that they were present in the office when John Reoch appeared to request entry at the customhouse on or about 2 Sept. 1805. Their testimony repeated much of what Jarvis had written about the case in his 16 Sept. 1805 letter to JM, adding only that the twenty-seven-year-old Reoch said he had been sent to Cádiz by Firmin de Tastet & Co. of London to purchase the ship for Mr. Crousillat of Philadelphia, that he had been shown no power of attorney from Crousillat, and that he could not present the protection he had received at Salem, Massachusetts, when he was seventeen because he had lost it.

§ From Harry Toulmin. *11 October 1805*. "Duties are still rigorously insisted upon at Mobille, Cargoes unladed and inventories taken of them, in order to ascertain the duties to be paid.[1] The Schooner Cato which wen⟨t⟩ down the river without calling, is still detained and will probably be confiscated, if not her Cargo. I could not even get a few articles belonging to the United States from on board of her, which I had requested to apply for when there, in behalf of Mr. Dinsmoor and Mr. Chambers. If they continue their exactions, this Country must inevitably be ruined: I mean that the settlements will be abandoned. Many are now preparing to go: some probably for other reasons, but the greater part, I believe, on this account, and most who go will become Subjects of the Spanish Government."

Extract (DNA: RG 233, President's Messages, 9A–D1); extract (DNA: RG 46, President's Messages, 9B–B1). The second extract is a letterpress copy of the first extract. Printed in *ASP, Foreign Relations*, 2:683.

1. See Toulmin to JM, 6 July 1805 (second letter).

¶ From Samuel Emery. Letter not found. *11 October 1805*. Described in Wagner to Emery, 23 Oct. 1805, as inquiring about Thomas Appleton's account (DNA: RG 59, DL, vol. 15). In his letter, addressed to Emery at Philadelphia, Wagner enclosed a statement from the Treasury Department showing $219.73 due to Appleton.

From Jacob Wagner

Dear Sir   Department of State 14th. Octr 1805

With the concurrence of Genl. Dearborn, I have given the following Sketch for publication: "We understand that on the 15th. Augt. Mr. Monroe our Minister in London had an interview with Ld. Mulgrave, the Br. Secretary of State for foreign affairs, on the Subject of the recent captures, when it appeared that no new order had been issued, but that they proceeded from the decisions recently made in the High Court of Appeals, Subjecting the trade between European hostile countries and their colonies, through a neutral State, to a much narrower rule than had been before contemplated. At this interview the Subject was not discussed in detail, between Mr. M. and the Minister, but the latter assured him that there was nothing in the disposition of his government, which would admit of an unfriendly measure against the U.S. Another conference having been requested by Mr. M. for the purpose of entering more fully into the affair it remains to be seen what will be the issue of this important business."[1] Your former hint on this Subject, the importance and anxiety attached to it, and the unfounded and contradictory rumours in the gazettes, prompted this as a step I thought proper and useful. In the enclosed N.Y. paper you will see an article, so particular as to details and circumstances as to challenge Some attention.[2] To reconcile it with the Silence of Mr. Monroe in his letter, dated a day later, it may be supposed perhaps, that it relates to the direct trade by British Subjects in neutral vessels between hostile colonies and G-Britain, under the Act of Parliament, as further explained in the enclosed Baltimore paper. I have the honor to remain, Dear Sir, affectly. Your obed. servt.

Jacob Wagner

RC (DLC). Docketed by JM.

1. For the source of this information, see Monroe to JM, 16 Aug. 1805. Wagner's sketch was printed in the 16 Oct. 1805 *National Intelligencer*.

2. Wagner may have referred to an item published in the New York papers the previous week stating that a 13 Aug. letter received from London, said that "in consequence of a remonstrance to the British government by Mr. Munroe, the American minister, that government had suspended, for three months, the late order for the detention of American vessels, for the purpose of making such arrangements as the necessity of the case may require" (*New-York Gazette & General Advertiser*, 8 Oct. 1805).

§ To Anthony Merry. *14 October 1805, Department of State.* "I beg leave to trouble you with Duplicate Coopies [*sic*] of a letter to this Office from the Collector of the Customs at Nyork, enclosing one that he had received from Doctor Rose, a Gentleman of Suffolk County, in the State of Nyork, (of which Duplicate Copies are also herewith enclosed) soliciting his aid to procure the release of Daniel

Talmage from the Cleopatra, frigate, into which, it seems, he has been impressed, from the American Sloop, Experiment. As Talmage is unquestionably an American Citizen, and the Cleopatra is still probably on the American Coast, I must take the liberty of asking the Interposition of your good Offices in this Case."

FC (DNA: RG 59, Notes to Foreign Ministers and Consuls, vol. 1). In a clerk's hand, marked "(Office Copy)."

§ From William C. C. Claiborne. *14 October 1805, New Orleans.* "The Marquis of Casa Calvo has communicated to me his intention of passing by way of the Bayou Laforche and the River Tache to the Sea, and from thence to the Mouth of the *Sabine,* which *River* he proposes to ascend as far as the Old Post of Adais. In making this excursion, the Marquis states that he has two *objects* in view; the *one,* to enjoy the amusement of Hunting; the *other,* to acquire some geographical Knowledge of the Country, and in particular to ascertain the Latitude of the Post of Adais, and to make an examination for some *Stone Posts* which are said to have been deposited some where *in its vicinity,* and immediatly on the *line* which was formerly established betwe[e]n the French and Spanish possessions west of the Mississippi. I expressed to the Marquis a wish, that on his Arrival at the Post of Adais, he should be joined by an American Officer from the Garrison of Nachitoches, who should witness his *proceedings,* and make report to *me thereof;* To which proposition, the Marquis having assented Captain Turner (who speaks the French Language) has been selected to accompany him. A Copy of my Instructions to Captain Turner is herewith enclosed for your perusal."[1]

Adds in a postscript: "I shall take measurs to ascertain the General deportment of the Marquis on his excursion."

RC and enclosure (DNA: RG 59, TP, Orleans, vol. 7); letterbook copy and letterbook copy of enclosure (Ms-Ar: Claiborne Executive Journal, vol. 15). RC 2 pp.; in a clerk's hand, signed and addressed by Claiborne; docketed by Wagner, with his note: "To be answd." For enclosure, see n. 1.

1. The enclosure (2 pp.; docketed by Wagner; printed in Rowland, *Claiborne Letter Books,* 3:196–98) is a copy of Claiborne to Capt. Edward D. Turner, 14 Oct. 1805, ordering Turner to join Casa Calvo when the latter arrived at Adaïs and (1) to note the latitude and longitude of Adaïs, ascertain when the garrison was established and when evacuated, and if the French had at any time objected to Spanish retention of the post; (2) to ascertain, if the stone posts were found, by whom and when they were deposited and "with *what object!*"; (3) to ask, should Turner learn that the line of demarcation had been partly determined, how far it had been extended, why it was not completed, the name or names of the commissioners employed on it, and under whose instructions they acted; (4) to inquire about any settlements made on the Red River or elsewhere before the settlements now possessed by the United States, and to obtain on oath and in writing the statements of anyone who might have any personal knowledge of them; and (5) to communicate any other information that he might acquire that could be useful to the United States. Claiborne added that the mission would probably last only eight or ten days, that Turner's expenses would be reimbursed, that Col. Constant Freeman would send orders to the commanding officer at Natchitoches, and if ill health or other good cause prevented Turner from fulfilling the mission, the order would be given to such other person the commanding officer might select.

§ From Carlos Martínez de Yrujo. *14 October 1805, Philadelphia*. Has the honor to send JM the attached copy of a letter just received from the governor of Puerto Rico,[1] to the effect that the American brigantine *Neptune*, which was supposed to have been captured by a French or Spanish cruiser called *Resource*, Captain Janet, has not come to his port nor any of the others in his district. Asks JM to observe with satisfaction the just and friendly disposition of the governor toward American citizens and vessels, as a necessary consequence of those which characterize the king in this regard.

RC and enclosure (DNA: RG 59, NFL, Spain, vol. 2). RC 2 pp.; in Spanish. For enclosure, see n. 1.

1. The enclosure is a copy of Toribio de Montes to Yrujo (2 pp.; in Spanish; undated), acknowledging receipt of Yrujo's 25 Aug. 1805 dispatch and the papers pertaining to the *Neptune*, captured by a French or Spanish privateer and said to have been sent to one of the western ports of Puerto Rico. After making the most effective and diligent inquiries, he said that the ship had not arrived anywhere on the island, that the capture and entry could not have happened without his knowledge, and he asked Yrujo to make that known to the owners and JM. He further added that in his jurisdiction the rights of neutrals were respected, particularly those of American citizens, with whom the king had intimate connections, demanding conduct that did not give the lie to the sentiments of justice that characterize him, as all American ships and crews that have come to Puerto Rico have experienced. He said that if he could find out the fate of the *Neptune*, he would inform Yrujo and proceed appropriately (editor's translation).

From Rufus King

Secret

SIR   JAMAICA LONG ISLAND Oct. 15. 1805.

You will probably recollect that soon after my return from England I communicated to you the Extract of a Letter that I had received and which related to an object respecting which we cannot be in different.[1] For some time past I have heard nothing further on the Subject: A few days since however I received a Letter from the same Person, dated London Aug. 8. the following Extract of which I have thought it Expedient confidentially to communicate to you.

Extract viz

"Après des inconsequences, et des retards inconcevables & insupportables, nous voila sur le point de partir. Je compte m'embarquer dans le courant de ce mois." P.S. "C'est pour le 15. de ce mois (Aout) que notre depart est fixé."[2]

Whether any adequate succour has been furnished by England or favourable Expectations are derived from a supposed State of things between the U.S. & Spain, is what at present I have no satisfactory means of deciding. I may however shortly receive more exact information.

With Sentiments of Respect & Esteem I have the Honour to be Sir yr. ob. Servt.

RUFUS KING

Draft (NHi: Rufus King Papers). Docketed by King: "Extr. of Gen. M. Letter of Aug. 8h."

1. For Rufus King to JM, 11 Oct. 1803, which contained an extract from Francisco de Miranda's 23 Aug. 1803 letter to King, see *PJM-SS*, 5:507–9 and n. 4.

2. "After inconsistencies, and delays inconceivable & unbearable, here we are about to leave. I intend to embark later this month. P.S. It is for the 15th of this month (August) that our departure is fixed (editor's translation)."

§ From Sylvanus Bourne. *15 October 1805, Amsterdam.* "I have the honor to advise the due rect of your Circulars of July 1t & 12h last & shall give a strict & scrupulous attention to the instructions they contain in every respect.

"The war on the continent is to all appearances about commencing under circumstances which presage a wide extended scene of horror & carnage to afflicted Europe. It will probably involve most of the powers of the continent & leave our flag the only truly neutral on the Seas—which will render it very precious to our Country I therefore hope that some arrangments may be concluded on between GB & the UStates of a nature to relieve us from the injurious vexations to which our navigation has been subject—while it shall preserve harmony & peace between the two Countries.

"I have the pleasure to inform you that since M⟨r⟩ Alexander has officiated as my agent at Rotterdam agreeably to the arrangment suggested to you in a form⟨er⟩ letter.[1] I have heard no complaints whatever & have reason to believe that the course of public service I⟨n⟩ that department goes on with propriety & correctness. His mind however will be prepared to meet such other disposition of the place as Govt may see proper to make as I gave him fully to understand that he could count on the present one only *as temporary.*

"As two of the Vessels having my Statemen⟨t⟩ on board in reply to Mess D&O have been carried into England it may be uncertain when they arrive if at all. I have therefor thought best to send another Copy to my Kinsman Mr Taylor at Balte for publication there Should neither of the others have arrived—it is left open for your perusal—when you will please Cause it to be sealed & forward⟨ed⟩ to its direction[2]—in this as well as *one* of the Copies before sent I have noticed the buisn⟨ess⟩ of Mr Hogelan⟨t⟩s agency during my absence in su⟨ch⟩ a manner as to assert the fact—without exposing to the need to bringing forward that kind of proof which Mr D has cunningly put it out of my power to do—that he did act there as agent during my absence is well known & that it was with Mr D.'s suggestion & connivance—is evident as he is the particular friend of D & concerned with him in all buisness relative to the Amn. trade. I shall never more touch on this subject at large but rely on your candid & just interpretation of the whole matter & on the continuanc⟨e⟩ of your confidence & you may be persuaded that I will never again expose myself to the shadow even of blame or Cause of reprehension."

RC (DNA: RG 59, CD, Amsterdam, vol. 1). 3 pp.; docketed by Wagner.

1. See Bourne to JM, 22 July (first letter) and 23 July 1805.
2. The enclosure has not been found, but for Bourne's apologia, see Bourne to JM, 10 Aug. 1805, and n. 1.

§ From William C. C. Claiborne. *15 October 1805, New Orleans.* "During my late Illness at Natchez I receivd your private Letter of the 20th July [not found], and I immediatly transmitted by a safe conveyance to Mr: Duplantier, the Packet which you committed to my care.

"I am inclined to think, that the Land near this City, which has been mentioned to Genl. Lafayette, is not in a situation to be located; There is indeed, some dispute as to the Title, but it is supposed that the present Claimant, Mr: Marigney, will maintain his claim to the grater portion of the Tract; and indeed were it otherwise, a location for the General, could not be made under the Act of Congress, since there is not 1000 Acres in the Tract.

"I am in the expectation of seeing Mr. Duplantier in a few days, and will *again* consult with him the means, of best promoting 'the Interest of A Man who enjoys by so good a Title, the affections of this Country.'"

RC (DLC); letterbook copy (Ms-Ar: Claiborne Executive Journal, vol. 15). RC 1 p.; in a clerk's hand, signed and marked "(Private)" by Claiborne; docketed by JM.

To Thomas Jefferson

DEAR SIR   GRAY'S OCT. 16. 1805.

I recd. duly your favor of the 11th. at this place, where I am still very painfully detained by the situation of Mrs. M. The appearance of her knee is still equivocal; I am afraid discouraging as to a very prompt and compleat cure. I am the less able however to pronounce on this point, as the Dr. has been prevented by indisposition from seeing his patient for several days, and I cannot be guided by his judgment. We expect he will visit her tomorrow. I am not the less distressed by this uncertainty, in consequence of the indulgent manner in which you regard my absence; but it would have been a great alleviation to me, if my absence had not suspended important questions, on which my aid would have been so inconsiderable. The suspension however I hope will not be continued if circumstances should press for early decisions. The latest accounts from Europe may perhaps suggest a little delay with respect to any provisional arrangements with England. Considering the probability of an extension of the war agst. France, and the influence that may have on her temper towards the U.S: the uncertainty of effecting with England such a shape for an arrangement as alone would be admissible, and the possible effects elsewhere of abortive overtures to her, I think it very questionable whether a little delay may not be expedient, especially as in the mean time the English pulse will be somewhat felt by the discussions now on foot by Mr. Monroe. With respect to Morales, my idea is that he should be instantly ordered off, if Claiborne has the legal power necessary; to which ought to be added perhaps some public admonition agst. the purchase of lands from him. Casa Calvo has more of personal claim to indulgence. I lean to the opinion nevertheless that he should receive notice also to depart; unless Claiborne should be very decided in thinking his stay useful. The stronger his personal claim to indulgence may be, the stronger would be the manifestation of the public sentiment producing his dismission. Yrujo's case involves some delicate considerations. The harshness of his recall, as made by our Ministers,[1] and then the footing of a voluntary return on which his leaving the U. S. was put, seem to suggest a degree of forbearance. On the other hand the necessity of some marked displeasure at the Spanish Conduct, a necessity produced as is believed by his own mischeivous agency, and the indelicacy of his obtruding his functions here, if that should be the case, plead strongly for peremptory measures towards him. As it is not yet formally known, that he has heard from his Govt. in consequence of the letter of recall, altho' rendered pretty certain by a recurrence to dates, it may be well perhaps to see whether he manifests a purpose of remaining here. If he should the question will arise whether he shall receive notice that his departure was expected, or that he can no longer be received as the organ of communication with his Govt. Thro' private channels I collect that he proposes to be at Washington the ensuing winter. The idea is also given out by his family that they are to go to Spain. It cannot be long before some occasion will arise for knowing his real intentions, and therefore for expressing those of the Executive. As to Bowdoin I think it clear he ought to remain in England for the present, and if Erving should have not proceeded to Madrid, I think he also should remain there. Pinkney if, as is to be wished & his last letter promised, he should have left Spain, will have named Young or some one else, to be the shadow of a representative and if shd. have named no one, perhaps so much the better.

If you think it proper that Mr. Wagner should write to Bowdoin or Claiborne or both, he will on an intimation of what you wish to be said, write letters of which he is very capable, either in his own name referring to my absence, or to be sent hither for my signature.

I find it necessary to mention, what I thought I had done before, that on receiving your sanction, I intimated, to Armstrong the opinion here that Insurers stood in the shoes of the insured, under the Convention.[2] I was particularly careful however to use terms that would not commit the Govt. on the question of a mixture of British subjects in the transaction.

The question had occurred to me on reading the papers concerning the N Jersey and I suggested it Mr. Dallas, who confirmed the fact of such a mixture. It appeared to me however, that it was best not to bring the matter into view by countenancing a different decision in a particular case, from what had taken place in similar cases. Probably ⁴/₅ of the payments under the Convention involve the question.

I wrote long ago to Gelston to send me the precise amount of what is due on the Hermitage, with a promise to remit the money. I have not yet recd. an answer, which I ascribe to the confusion produced in N.Y. by the fever. In the same manner I explain his not having forwarded the wine to Washington.

I inclose a letter &c from Truxton which explains itself.[3] Also one from Fraissinet, with a recommendation of him for Consul at Martinique.[4] I explained the obstacle to the appt: of a Consul. He was not altogether unaware of it, but seemed to think that an informal Agency at least would not be offensive, but otherwise, and would be very useful. I believe he wd. suit very well for such a purpose, probably better than any other to be had; and, it is possible that Turreau might give some sort of sanction. Prudent guardians of our affairs in the W. Indies would probably prevent much loss to individuals, and much perplexity to the Govt. If you think the proposition in this case admissible, and that it ought to depend on Turreau, Wagner could communicate with Petry on the subject unless any other mode of ascertaining the disposition in that quarter be thought better.

I put under the same cover with this the last letters from Monroe, which you will please to send to the office when You think proper.[5] I am sorry he did not transmit copies of the law opinions given him by Lord Mulgrave. With constant & respectful attacht I remain Yrs.

JAMES MADISON

RC (DLC: Jefferson Papers). Docketed by Jefferson as received 19 Oct.

1. For the request for the recall of the Spanish minister, see James Monroe to JM, 16 Apr. 1805, and Monroe to JM, 3 May 1805, *PJM-SS*, 9:250, 251 nn. 8 and 12, 313, 314 n. 6.
2. See JM to Armstrong, 25 Aug. 1805.
3. See Thomas Truxtun to JM, 15 Sept. 1805.
4. No letter from John Joseph Fraissinet to JM has been found. For the letter recommending Fraissinet as consul, see William Davy to JM, 5 Oct. 1805.
5. JM probably enclosed Monroe to JM, 16 and 20 Aug. 1805.

From Lafayette

La Grange 24h trad. 16h Octobre 1805

Your Letter of the 6h. June, My dear friend, or Rather a Copy of it from the press Has Come to Hand. I think it is the duplicate of one Which Has Been Lost, and By the Bye I Caution You Against the Ink of Your Copying press, as the Whiteness of it Has Rendered it Very difficult for General Armstrong and for me to Read the Respective dispatches You Have on that day Adressed to Us.[1]

Yet I Have properly found out How kind, How Constantly and Affectionately Good You are to me—I Wish I Could properly Express the Sense I Have of Your friendship—Let me Here offer to You, to our Respected president, to Mr. Gallatin, the Warm Gratitude and Unbounded Confidence with which My Heart feels the Obligations I Am Happy and proud to Have to You and to them.

I Have Hitherto Received No Answers, to My Long Confidential Letters—the first of Which I Conclude, from a Hint in Yours of the 6h June, Have Not Miscaried. As to those Entrusted to Mr. Livingston and Colonel Touzard, I Know they are Safely Arrived[2]—and Considering they Must Have Been in the president's Hands and Yours Before the 10th. of July, I am Every day Expecting the Wished for Answers.

Gnl. Armstrong Will Let You Know in What Manner the New Coalition Has Been formed, What part prussia Has Been Acting, How the Austrian Emperor Has, in His Wisdom, found Means to Be the Agressor, Yet to Let His Ennemy Be Every Where Before Hand With Him, and How, While the Russians are on the March, the Austrians Have Advanced to Meet the first Blow Which Has So Gloriously for the french Arms Oppened the Campaign, and Has, I think, decided its fate—My Son Serves in the Grand Army as an Aid de Camp to General Grouchy—My Son in Law Louïs Lasteyrie Serves there also as an officer of dragoons—two Young Wives, a Sister, and Mother Are With Me at La Grange—and While I Consider their Anxiety and My Own for the Sake of our Young Soldiers, I am inclined to feel Less Regret, and I know You Will find More Cause to Approve me for Having Yelded to the Opinion of the Ambassadors and Mine Respecting the present obstacles to An immediate Voyage—Yet I Anxiously Waït for An Answer to My Letters and particularly those Entrusted to Mm. Livingston and Touzard.

I See With Great pleasure, My dear Sir, that You Have Adopted My ideas for the disposal of the Bountiful Gift of Congress, the Value of Which, owing to the friendship of the president, To Your, and Mr. Gallatin's Kindness Will fulfill, Nay Exceed all My Wants and Wishes.

You Have felt With me the first object Ought to Be to Relieve me from present Embarassments and Wholly to Clear My fortune—Your Letter of

434

the 6th June Reproached me with Having Neglected to Express a Quantum—You Will Have found it in My dispatches to Mm. Livingston and Touzard—there I Numbered the Sum Which is Necessary to fulfill the Above Mentionned object[3]—and as I know those papers are in Your Hands I Would Not Have troubled You With a Repetition, But for this Reason—that altho' One Half of that Sum, owing to Mr. Baring's Loan, to Mr. Waddel's kind Advance of two thousand dollars,[4] to An other of the Same kind I Expect from Mr. parker[5] &c. May be prorogued to the 1st. January 1807, it Becomes of the Highest importance for me that Your kind Exertions With the proprietors of the Banks, or Any other Lenders, May Authorise me By the Next first January to Receive Monney or draw Bills to the Amount of One Half of the Capital I found Myself obliged to Mention as Necessary to answer the purpose.

I know, My dear Madison those Wants Will Even to My intimate friends, Appear Enormous, and Would By Malevolent, and perhaps By indifferent People Be Called Very Blameable—Yet I Have Hinted to You in former Letters the political and private Circumstances Which did Render My Case Quite particular, and My Pecuniary Situation More Eazy to Be Understood—and While I Refer You, as an Apology for it, to A Rememberance of My Stormy Life, While I Must Here Repeat that, Exclusive of pleasurable plans, it Becomes a Necessity for me to Conform to My Statement, and an Urging one to Have one Half of it immediately at My disposal, You Will More and More feel the Obligations I am Under to My American friends.

The two other articles of an actual Revenue, and the Best disposition to Be Made for the Remainder of the Grant, as Well as the object Relative to my Brother in law, I Will Refrain from Mentionning Again Untill I Have Received Your Answer to My former letters.

Permit me However to Give You a piece of information Which I Wholly Submit to Your Better Judgment—A french Louisiana Merchant Now in paris, Who in Every Respect deserves Confidence, Tells me that Besides the tract of Land Near New orleans about Which I wrote to You, He is Sure that there are *Near pointe Coupée, on the Bayoue Saarah* Some thousands Acres of Lands, of Very Great Value, two or three thousand He Believes, Still in the Hands of the United States— that is the Best Cotton Land of the Country—the Situation pleasant and Healthy—and Upon the Whole So desirable, Says He, that planters Should Be Very True friends Who instead of Aiming at it for themselves Would point it Out to the American Government as Grounds Still in ⟨their⟩ power, and to Me as a Location to Be Asked for—the intelligence I Give to You as I Have Received it—Cotton Land, Near pointe Coupée, on the Bayoue Saarah—You are Better Able than Myself to Ascertain the Truth of it.

435

I Have Received a Letter from Colol Touzard Notifying His Safe Arrival With My dispatches—Give me leave to inclose My Answer as I don't know Where it May find Him—this Letter Will Be Carried By Mr. Waddel, an American Citizen, to Whom I Am particularly Obliged for His friendly, and in the Most Amiable Manner offered advance of two thousand dollars to Be Added To Mr. Baring Advance—I am Going to Have a Similar Obligation to My friend daniel parker to Whom You know I am Already Indebted for Every Act of Affectionate kindness. Adieu, My dear Sir, I am With all My Heart Your old affectionate Grateful friend

LAFAYETTE

RC (PHi: Dreer Collection, Lafayette Letters). Docketed by JM.

1. No letter of 6 June 1805 to Lafayette has been found. For JM to John Armstrong, 6 June, see *PJM-SS*, 9:432–36.

2. Anne-Louis de Tousard carried Lafayette's 22 Apr. 1805 letter, ibid., 276–79. Lafayette may have sent a copy with Robert R. Livingston who left France on 26 May, ibid., 501–2.

3. See Lafayette to JM, 22 Apr. 1805, ibid., 276–79.

4. Lafayette may have referred to Henry L. Waddell who left Paris on 25 Oct. 1805, carrying letters from John Armstrong (Waddell to JM, 22 Jan. 1806, NN).

5. For an earlier loan from Daniel Parker to Lafayette, see Lafayette to JM, 10 Oct. 1804, *PJM-SS*, 8:146.

§ From Peter Audrain.[1] *16 October 1805, Detroit.* "In compliance with the instructions which I have received from William Hull, Governor of the territory of Michigan, I have the honor to transmit to Your Excellency Copies of four acts of the legislature of the Said territory—to wit—An act Concerning the Supreme Court—An act concerning the district Court—An act Concerning the Militia, and An act for the encouragement of litterature, and the improvement of the City of Detroit.

"The Governor and the Chief Justice Woodward left this place, on the 11th. inst. for fort Erie on their way to the Fœderal City,[2] I hope you will pardon the liberty I take to inclose few lines for each of them.

"As the Secretary, now acting as Governor, will no doubt write to you, I leave to him to acquaint you with the occurences of this place, Since the departure of the Governor; Please to accept the tender of my humble Services to the General Government."

RC (DNA: RG 59, TP, Michigan, vol. 1). 1 p.; docketed by Wagner, with his note: "Laws of the Territory." Printed in *Michigan Pioneer and Historical Collections* 31 (1902): 541.

1. Peter Audrain (ca. 1725–1820) was born in France and swore allegiance to America in 1781. After living in Pittsburgh, he went to Michigan with Anthony Wayne in 1796, where at various times he held the offices of prothonotary, probate judge, register of probate, register of deeds, justice of the peace, clerk and interpreter to the board of land commis-

sioners and land commissioner, and superintendent of the sale of public lands. He was clerk of the territorial Supreme Court for fourteen years (Clarence M. Burton, *History of Detroit, 1780–1850: Financial and Commercial* [Detroit, 1917], 19–20; Carter, *Territorial Papers, Michigan*, 10:293 n., 306–7, 780).

2. See William Hull to JM, 11 Oct. 1805.

To Andrew Ellicott

DEAR SIR   GRAY'S NEAR PHILADA. Ocr. 17. 1805

I recd. some days ago your favor of the 2d. inclosing a letter to Genl. Armstrong, which will be forwarded with a few lines from myself, of the purport you suggest.

I perceive by the printed reports of the election that your estimate of the event is not likely to be disappointed. The schism among those heretofore united in the scale of republicanism, could not but be regretted, whatever the cause might be, by those in the same general scale elsewhere. That the President should regret such an occurrence in so important a State as Pennsylva. is naturally to be supposed; that the tendency of the precedent to endanger that general Union which was the basis of his administration, and its bulwark agst. the warfare so unceasingly made on it, could not fail to excite his particular regret, is equally to be supposed. As far as this state of things might exact his attention I have no doubt that it was regulated by principles and intentions which no considerate friend of his administration, could fail to approve; and I infer with confidence that if any representations have been made not consistent with a proper line of conduct, they have been founded in the grossest misapprehension, or a wilful perversion of his sentiments.

I have been detained in Philada. & its neighborhood since the last of July by a complaint of Mrs. Madison requiring the medical skill of Dr Physic. A cure was compleated about ten days ago; but an anxiety to be at Washington led to a premature trial of its stability, which has caused a further detention. I hope it will not continue many days longer. If it should threaten to do, I shall proceed without her. I am Dr. Sir very respectfully Your friend & servt.

JAMES MADISON

RC (MHi); Tr (DLC: Ellicott Papers). RC addressed and franked by JM. Minor differences between the copies have not been noted.

437

To Anthony Merry

S<small>IR</small>,   D<small>EPARTMENT OF</small> S<small>TATE</small> October 17th. 1805

I have the Honor to enclose Copies of a Letter from Messrs. Johnston, Pringle and Sherlock of Baltimore, Owners of the Schooner Hannah Maria and her Cargo,[1] and of the Deposition of Mr. A. S. Thomas of Baltimore referred to therein, exhibiting the Circumstances of the Detention of that Vessel by the British Ship of War Diana. It must be evident that whatsoever might be the Cause or the Pretext, which induced the Capture, the Detention, on board of the Ship of War, of the Supercargo, Master and Crew of the Schooner for so long a Peri(od) as is stated in the Letter from the Supercargo, of which a Copy is enclos(ed) and the Conversion of her into a Crui(zer) before any legal Adjudication took p(lace) whereby the Proprietors are debarre(d) from the usual Means of vindicating their Rights, are Irregularities with(out) Excuse and perhaps without Preced(ent) and I am led by the Persuasion th(at) you will look upon them to be such, to request for the Parties concerned the Benefit of your Go(od) Offices in promoting the Justice which is due to them.[2] I have the Honor to be &a.

(Signed) J<small>AMES</small> M<small>ADISON</small>

Tr (UkLPR: Foreign Office, ser. 5, 45:296–296v); letterbook copy (UkLPR: Foreign Office, ser. 115, 14:142–143). Tr enclosed in Merry to Mulgrave, 2 Nov. 1805 (ibid., ser. 5, 45:293–294v).

1. See Christopher Johnston, Mark Pringle, and John Sheldon to JM, 1 Oct. 1805, and nn.

2. On 25 Oct. 1805 Merry replied: "I have received the Honor of your Letter of the 17th. Instant, with its Inclosures, stating the Circumstances of the Detention of the American Schooner Hannah Maria, and her Cargo, by His Majesty's Ship Diana.

"I shall not fail, Sir, to avail myself of the earliest Opportunity to transmit Copies of the Papers with which you have been pleased to furnish me respecting this Occurrence to the Commander in Chief of His Majesty's Ships on the Jamaica Station, to which it is probable that the Diana belongs, as well as to His Majesty's Government, in Case that Ship should be returned to Europe, in order that Inquiry may be made into the Case, and Justice rendered upon it, in the most expeditious Manner" (DNA: RG 59, NFL, Great Britain, vol. 3; 2 pp.; docketed by Wagner as received 27 Oct.). A 2 Oct. 1805 Baltimore newspaper reported that the *Hannah Maria* had been retaken by the Spanish armed brig *Volador* and carried into Campeche, Mexico (*New-York Gazette & General Advertiser*, 5 Oct. 1805).

From Jacob Wagner

Dear Sir   Department of State 17 Octr. 1805

Enclosed are the abstracts from Sir J. Marriott's reports, the references to treaties, and an extract from Reeves, respecting the modifications of the navigation laws to suit the course of war. To the latter I have not found time to add the references I have collected to additional acts, including the late order issued by Ld. Hawkesbury: they will follow to morrow.[1] The communication from Mr. Yznardi's deputy exhibits such an importance in the captures by the British under pretence of the blockade of Cadiz and St. Lucar, as almost to compare with the captures of vessels bound to Holland.[2] A communication similar to this from Mr. Hill was received some time ago and is now in the hands of the President: it was in a feigned hand, supposed to be that of Mr. Gray, but without signature.[3] I had calculated to send you to day the answers to the letters of recredence of Messrs. Freire & Olsen, with the necessary letters to accompany them,[4] but the former have been accidentally so much disfigured as to make other copies necessary: they will be ready to morrow, as also a letter to Mr. Merry respecting the Hannah Maria's case.[5] I have written to Johnston and to Mc.Kim. I believe I have not before mentioned, that the effect of the pardons I have from time to time sent you has been anticipated by my writing to the Marshall to consider them as actually completed, when no more than the fiat of the President had been given. The curiosities from Mr. Coffin, occupying but a small space, I have thought it not improper to send them to you.[6]

Dr. Thornton received a letter, yesterday, from Peacock,[7] who dates at Bath, England. He observes that as *his expedition was fortunate*, he considers it the harbinger of future prosperity. I remain with affecte. respect Your ob. Servt.

Jacob Wagner

RC (DLC). Docketed by JM. Enclosures not found.

1. Wagner's 18 Oct. 1805 letter to JM has not been found. The enclosure (4 pp.; in a clerk's hand with additions by Wagner) is a copy of the 29 June 1805 order in council issued by Lord Hawkesbury listing the articles neutral vessels were allowed to carry between British ports and unblockaded European ports of Britain's enemies. It was published in the United States on 6 Sept. 1805 under a 10 July dateline and in Great Britain in *Cobbett's Weekly Register.* Wagner added references to 6 Ann c. 3 7 s. 19 and s. 20, 13 Geo. 2. c. 3, and 39 Geo. 3. c. 98. The first and second authorized the reduction of the component of British seamen of crews of privateers and trading ships to only one fourth and provided that foreign seamen serving on such ships would be considered naturalized after two years of service; the last allowed the importation of Spanish wool in any type of neutral vessels and from any country (*National Intelligencer*, 6 Sept. 1805; *Cobbett's Weekly Political Register* 8 [1805]: 92–93; John Raithby, *The Statutes Relating to the Admiralty, Navy, Shipping, and*

Navigation of the United Kingdom, from 9 Hen. III. to 3 Geo. IV. Inclusive [London, 1823], 108, 112, 182, 626).

2. See Anthony Terry to JM, 20 Aug. 1805, and n. 1.

3. See Henry Hill Jr. to JM, 28 Aug. 1805, and Vincent Gray to JM, 17 Sept. 1805.

4. See Wagner to JM, 24 Sept. 1805.

5. See JM to Anthony Merry, 17 Oct. 1805.

6. See Alexander Coffin Jr. to JM, 11 Oct. 1805.

7. This was probably Washington attorney, boardinghouse keeper, and real-estate investor Robert Ware Peacock, who was acquitted in January 1805 of forging a bill of exchange endorsed by himself and William Thornton. He was convicted at the same court term of forging another bill and was imprisoned and disbarred. On 22 Mar. 1805 he escaped from jail and evidently fled to England (Allen C. Clark, "The Mayoralty of Robert Brent," *Records of the Columbia Historical Society* 33–34 [1932]: 275–78; *United States v. Peacock*, 1 Cranch, C.C. 215–18; *Ex parte Levi S. Burr*, 2 Cranch, C.C. 387–88).

§ Circular to the Governors. *17 October 1805, Department of State.* "Agreeably to an act of Congress, entitled 'an act for the more general promulgation of the Laws of the United States, passed 3d. March 1795,['] and the acts in addition thereto passed on the 2d.: March 1799, and on the 27th. March 1804,[1] I have transmitted to the Collector of the Customs   copies of the Laws of the United States, 2d. Session 8th. Congress, being the proportion for the state of *   2 with a request that he would forward them to your Excellency."

Letterbook copy (DNA: RG 59, DL, vol. 15). 2 pp.

1. *U.S. Statutes at Large*, 1:443, 724–25, 2:302–3.

2. Blanks left in copytext. In the first column of the table below the circular, the clerk placed an asterisk:

*Name of States &c.	No. Boxes & no copies in each. (57 copies for each Member)		No. Memrs. of Congress	no copies for each State & Territory
New Hampshire	1 Box	contg. 285 copies	5	285
Massachusetts	3 Do.	Do. 323 Do each	17	969
Vermont	1 Do.	Do. 228	4	228
Rhode Island	1 Do.	Do. 114	2	114
Connecticut	1 Do.	Do. 399	7	399
New york	3 Do.	Do. 323 do. each	17	969
New Jersey	1 Do.	Do. 342	6	342
Pennsylvania	3 Do.	Do. 342 do. ea:	18	1026
Delaware	1 Do.	Do. 57	1	57
Maryland	1 Do.	Do. 256 & 1 Do. 257	9	513
Virginia	3 Do.	342 & 1 Do. 228 ea.	22	1254
North Carolina	2 Do.	342 each	12	684
South Carolina	2 Do.	228 do.	8	456
Georgia	1 Do.	228 do.	4	228
Kentucky	1 Do.	342 Do.	6	342
Tennessee	1 Do.	171	3	171
Ohio	1 Do.	57	1	57
Indiana Ty.	1 Do.	57	1	57
Mississippi, Do.	1 Do.	57	1	57

Orleans Ty.	1 box	75 cops. of 1 & 2		
		Session 8th Congress	1	75
Louisiana. Do.	1 Do.	25 do. Do. Do.		25
Michigan, Do.	1 Do.	57 copies		57
			145	8365

From James Monroe

Triplicate,
No. 35.

SIR   LONDON October 18. 1805.

I Sent you lately by Col. Mercer my note to Lord Mulgrave of the 23d. ulto. relative to the late seizure of our vessels,[1] in which I thought proper to advert, at the conclusion, to the other topics that were depending when I left this country for Spain. I endeavoured to touch those topics, especially the insults in our ports and the impressment of our seamen, in a manner to Shew a due sensibility to Such outrages, and if possible to conciliate this government to concur in a Suitable arrangement to prevent the like in future. It Seemed to be improper and it was certainly useless to touch them without expressing the Sense which the President entertained of the injury and indignity to which the United-States had thereby been exposed. The acts were of a nature to require it, and the conduct of this government Since had increased the obligation to do it. It appeared also by your letters which were received by Mr Purviance in my absence,[2] that the President expected that this government would make such an example of the officers who had most Signalized themselves, by their misconduct, as would Serve as a warning to the commanders of other vessels, who may hereafter Seek Shelter, or hospitality in our ports. This had not been done. On the contrary, I was informed, by the best authority, that Captn. Bradley of the Cambrian, whose conduct had been most offensive, had been promoted immediately on his return to the command of a ship of the line. By that measure which prejudged the case this government seemed to have adopted those acts of its officers as its own, and even to announce to all others that the commission of like aggressions within our jurisdiction would pave the way to their preferment. It is said it is true that the translation of an officer from a frigate to a ship of the line, is not considered in all cases a promotion; or more correctly speaking is not such an one as ⟨is⟩ Sollicited by the officers of the Navy. The command of a frigate on a separate station especially one which affords an opportunity to make prizes is often preferred by them to that of a Ship of the line in a fleet, and may perhaps be deemed a more important trust by the government. Ostensibly

441

however and in effect it is a promotion; the least therefore that could be Said of the dispositi(on) which this government had shewn respecting the misconduct of that officer was(,) that if it had not been the cause, it certainly formed no obstacle to his. Under Such circumstances it Seemed to be impossible to Separate the officer from the government in those Outrages, and quite useless to demand the censure of him. I thought it therefore most adviseable in the present Stage at least, to treat the affair in a general way, rather than in reference to a particular occurrenc(e,) and in looking to the offensive object, and paying any regard to what was du(e) to the U.States, the manner was as conciliating as I could make it.

Having waited near three weeks after my letter of the 23 ulto to Lord Mulgrave without hearing from him, I wrote him again on the 10. inst. and stated, that by the permission of the President I proposed to Sail to the U. States thi(s) autumn, and as the favorable Season was far advancd wished to depart with the least possible delay: that I Should be happy to See the interesti(n)g Concerns depending between our governments satisfactorily arranged befor(e) I Sailed; that I had been and Should Continue to be prepared to enter on them while I remained in England, and that the time of my departure would be ma(de) Subservient to that very important object. To this note I received some days after a Short Answer, which promised as early a reply to my communications as the additional matter contained in that of the 23rd. ulto. would permit.[3] Having taken the liberty to inform you from Madrid that I Should sail for the U.States soon after my arrival here,[4] it was my intention after making a fair experiment to arrange the concerns with this government, to have departed forthwith be the Success of it what it might. I Considered myself as having the permission of the President to return home, after Such an experiment, And it was very much my wish and that of my family to avail ourselves of it. But unfortunately at that period the Seizures which had just before commenced began to assume a Serious form. It became my duty in my first letter to Lord Mulgrave to notice them, and they soon claimed the principal attention. On the 10th. however I thought myself perfectly at liberty to give notice of my intention to depart, in a guarded manner. I had already Said every thing in my several communications, on the subjects that were depending that I intended to Say, unless it should be made necessary to add more by a reply to them: I had also waited a Sufficient time for a reply: I could not depart without giving timely notice of it, especially after the late correspondence; and the Season was so far advanc'd that if I withheld it longer, I Should be exposed to a winter's passage or compelled to remain 'till the Spring. It was on these considerations that I wrote the abovementioned note to Lord Mulgrave, in the hope of promoting without longer delay a Satisfactory arrangement of the points alluded to. But so vague is his answer that it is quite out of my power to determine at this time whether it will be proper for me to Sail or not in the course of the present Season. Indeed there is but one Vessel now in the port destined to the U. States in which I Should wish to embark with my family, at so late a period. She will be commanded by Capt. Tomkins, for Norfolk, who I understand proposes to Set out in the beginning of next month. By that time I Shall probably see more fully into the ultimate intentions and policy of this government towards the U. States, and I think I may venture to Say that if I Sail during the present Autumn it will be in that vessel.

I have no doubt that the Seizure of our vessels was a deliberate Act of this government. I do not Know that the measure was regularly Submitted to and decided in the Cabinet, but I am Satisfied that that departmen⟨t⟩ of it having cognizance of and controul over the business dictated the measur⟨e.⟩ The circumstances attending the transaction justify this opinion. Before the coalition with Russia and Sweden the commerce was free. The blow was given when that coalition was formed. Great-Britain has Shewn much political arrangement in the whole of this affair. By the amendatory article of her treaty with Russia in 1801. the latter abandons the right to the direct trade with the Colonies of an enemy and the parent country,⁵ and agrees to rest on the ground which the United-States might hold in that respect. It is to be presumed that She declined the Seizure before the coalition was formed with the Northern powers lest it might alarm them and endanger the coalition and that She made the Seizure afterwards on the idea that as they were embarked in the war with her, they would become indifferent to the object, and leave her free to push her pretentions against us. The manner in which the pressure is made, being thro' the Admiralty Court, on a pretext that the trade is direct, altho' the articles were landed in our ports and the duties paid On them, is equally a proof of management on her part. It was obviously intended to urge, indeed Lord Mulgrave in our first interview, began by urging, that there had been no⁶ measure, that the government had not acted in the business, while the Court by Considering every species of that Commerce, direct, and every accommodation on the part of our citizens with previous regulations fraudulent and evasive, Should push the pretention of the government to Such an extent as to Anihilate it altogether. Lord Mulgrave insisted in express terms, in the Second interview, that we ought not to carry it on at all with the parent country; that the importation into our country ought to be Confined to the Supplies necessary for the home consumption. I am equally confident that if G. Britain Should Succeed in establishing her pretentions against us, She would avail herself of the e⟨x⟩ample hereafter with the Northern Powers. It is therefore a question of great importance to them also.

443

With respect to our other concerns with G. Britain I am sorry to say that I do not See any prospect of arranging them on just and reasonable terms at the present time. No disposition has been shewn to prescribe by treaty any restraint on the impressment of our seamen, whenever the government may be so disposed, or even when any of its officers in the West-Indies or elsewhere may think fit. On the Subject of boundary nothing has been lately Said, nor does there appear to be any inclination to enter on it. I have also reason to think that this government is equally disposed to postpone an arrangement of our commerce in general, by treaty, for any number of years. On this point however I cannot Speak with So much confidence as on the others, having never made any proposition, which was calculated to obtain an explicit declaration of its Sentiments. The conversations which I had with Lords Hawkesbury and Harrowby before I went to Spain, on the other Subjects, naturally brought this into view, but being incidentally it was only slightly touched. The proposition which was made by the latter to Consider the treaty of 1794. in force,[7] was as a temporary expedient, not a permanent regulation. From that circumstance and the manner in which they both Spoke of that treaty, I Concluded that their government would be willing to revive it, for an equal term. It might however have been made only to obtain delay. You will observe that in my note of the 23d: ulto. I have taken the liberty to mention the Subject, in a manner to Shew that it is not one to which the U. States are indifferent, or which the President wishes to postpone. Altho' I have no power to form a treaty, of so comprehensive a nature, yet I thought I might with propriety open the Subject, So far at least as to ascertain the views of this government on it, for your information.

On a review of the conduct of this government towards the United-States, from the commencement of the war, I am inclined to think that the delay which has been so Studiously Sought in all these concerns is the part of a System, and that it is intended, as circumstances favor, to Subject our commerce at present and hereaft(er) to every restraint in their power. It is certain that the greatest jealousy is entertained of our present and encreasing prosperity, and I am Satisfied that nothing which is likely to Succeed, will be left untried to impair it. That this sentiment has taken a deep hold of the publick councils here, was sufficiently proved by t(he) late Seizures, being at a time when the state of our Affairs with Spain menaced a rupture, from which G. Britain could not fail to derive the most Solid advantages. It was natural to expect, especially if we advert to the then critical Situation of this country, that the government would have Seized the opportunity to promote that tendency by a more just and enlightened policy. The part however which it acted was calculated, So far as depended on it, to prevent one. It proved Satisfactorily that no event is deemed more unfavorable to G.Britain than the growing importance of the U.States and that it is a primary object of her government to check if not to crush it. It is possible that this government may b(e) influenced in its conduct by a belief that the U. States will not revive the treaty of 1794., unless they be driven to it by such means. It may also be attributab(le) to a policy Still more unfriendly. There is cause to believe that many prejudices are Still fostered here, in certain circles at least, which the experience of multiplied and Striking facts ought long Since to have Swept away. Among these it is proper to mention an opinion which many do not hesitate to avow, that the U. States are by (the) nature of their government, being popular, incapable of any great, vigorous, or persevering exertion: that they cannot for example resist a System of commercial hostility from this country, but must yield to the pressure. It is useless to mention other prejudices Still more idle, which had influence on past measur(es) and certainly Still exist with many of great Consideration. With Such a view of their interest, of the means of promoting it, and the confidence which is entertained of Success, it cannot be doubted that it is intended to push their fortune in every practicable line at our expence. The late Seizure is probably an experim(ent,) on this principle, of what the U. States will bear, and the delay which is observe(d) in answering my letters only an expedient to give the government time to see its effect. If it Succeeds they will I presume pursue the advantage gained to the greatest extent in all the relations Subsisting between the two countries, more especially in the impressment of our Seamen, the prostration and pillage of our commerce thro' the war, and in the more elevated tone of the government in a future Negotiation. If it fails I am equally confident that their whole system of conduct towards the U. States will change, and that it will then be easy to adjust our affairs with this country, and place them on an equal and a reciprocally advantageous footing. Perhaps no time was ever more favorable for resisting these unjust encroachments than the present one. The conduct of our government is universally Known to have been just, friendly and conciliating towards G. Britain, while the attack by her government on the U. States, is as universally Known to be unjust, wanton and unprovoked. The measure has wounded deeply the interests of many of her own people, & is not a popular one. The U. States furnish them at all times one of the best markets for their manufactures, and at present almost the only one. Her colonies are dependant on us. Harassed as they already are with the war, and the menaces of a powerful adversary, a State of hostility with us, would probably go far to throw this country into Confusion. It is an event which the Ministry would find it difficult to resist, and therefore cannot I presume be willing to encounter.

But is it Safe for the U. States to attempt a vindication of their rights and interests in a decisive manner with Spain and Britain at the same time? Will it not unite them against us and otherwise do us the most essential

445

injury? This is certainly a very important consideration and will of course be maturely weighed by our government. In my view of the Subject the cases do not interfere. We probably never shall be able to Settle our concerns with either power, without pushing our just claims on each with the greatest decision. At present, tho' at war with each other they harmonize in a System of aggression against us, as far as it is possible in Such a State. Is it not presumeable then that at peace their harmony will be greater and its effect more injurious? It seems to be a question Simply whether we will resist their unjust pressure at this time or defer it to Some other opportunity, and Surely none can be more favorable for us or less so for them. They are now respectively muc⟨h⟩ in our power. We can wound both essentially, Should it be necessary to push things to that extremity, without receiving much comparative injury in return. I am Strong in the opinion that a pressure on each at the Same time would produc⟨e⟩ a good effect with the other. Success with either could not well fail to produce it with the other. I am far from thinking that the incident with Britai⟨n⟩ Should change our conduct towards Spain, or that the necessity we may be under to push our pretentions with Spain should relax our exertions against Britain. Some considerations indeed occur which make it probable that the latter incident was a fortunate one. By pressing both at the Same time France may find herself relieved from a dilemma, in which a pressure on Spain alone, might place her, in consideration of her conduct in the late negotiation; and being desirous to encourage our misunderstanding with England She ma⟨y⟩ be prompted to promote an adjustment of our differences with Spain, to lea⟨ve⟩ us free to push the object with England. As these Subjects have been practically much under my view in the trusts with which I have been honored by the President, and have entirely engrossed my attention, I have thought that it would be agreeable to you to receive the result of my reflections on them. I am, Sir, with great respect & esteem, Your very obedient servant,[8]

JAS. MONROE

P.S. Oct 25.

I have just had an interview with Mr Hammond in which I asked him when I Should obtain an answer from Lord Mulgrave. He assured me that the Subject was under the consideration of the Cabinet, and that it was intended to give me as early an answer as its own importance, and the other very important Concerns of the government would permit: that I Knew they were contending for their existence &c. I told him that I was detained here by that business alone and Should have Sailed long Since for the U. States, had his government placed our affairs on Such a footing as to have enabled me: that we wanted nothing but what was just and reasonable. Nothing else material passed in the interview. Mr Bowdoin

Sailed for the Continent about 10 days Since; I have not heard of his arrival in Holland, and fear as the winds have been unfavorable, that he has had a bad passage. Capt. Tomkins will not sail 'till February, So that there is no prospect of an immediate passage in his vessel.

RC and enclosures (DNA: RG 59, DD, Great Britain, vol. 12); RC (DNA: RG 46, President's Messages, 10B–B1); extract (DNA: RG 233, President's Messages, 9B–B4); letterbook copy (DLC: Monroe Papers). First RC in a clerk's hand, signed by Monroe; docketed by Wagner. Second RC is a letterpress copy of the first RC. Words and parts of words in angle brackets in the first RC have been supplied from the letterbook copy. Minor differences between the copies have not been noted. For enclosures, see nn. 3 and 8.

    1. See Monroe to JM, 25 Sept. 1805, and n. 2.

    2. For JM's letter about the British ships *Boston*, *Cambrian*, and *Driver*, and John Henry Purviance's 19 Oct. 1804 acknowledgment, see *PJM-SS*, 7:484–86, 8:188.

    3. Monroe enclosed copies (2 pp.; docketed by Wagner) of his 10 Oct. 1805 note to Lord Mulgrave, and Mulgrave's 12 Oct. reply stating that he had not been aware of Monroe's proposed departure, and he would reply with as little delay as possible, adding that "the additional matter" in Monroe's latest paper "necessarily calls for some further deliberation."

    4. For Monroe's desire to return to the United States, see Monroe to JM, 26 May and 30 June 1804, *PJM-SS*, 9:406, 505–6.

    5. The "Declaration explanatory of the second Section of the third Article" of the 1801 convention between Russia and Great Britain stated that "the freedom of commerce and navigation granted by the said article to the subjects of a neutral power, does not authorize them to carry, in time of war, the produce or merchandize of the colonies of the belligerent power direct to the continental possessions, nor *vice versa*, from the mother-country to the enemy's colonies" (*Annual Register for 1801*, 217–18).

    6. Monroe inserted a caret here and probably meant to insert the word "new," which is in the letterbook copy.

    7. For Lord Harrowby's suggestion that the temporary Jay Treaty provisions be considered as still in force, see Monroe to JM, 7 Aug. 1804, *PJM-SS*, 7:569–70.

    8. Monroe also enclosed copies (4 pp.; docketed by Wagner) of the condemnation of the *Essex*, Orne, by Judge John Kelsau of the Nassau, New Providence, vice-admiralty court for carrying a cargo from Spain to Havana with a stop for unloading and paying duties at Salem, Massachusetts, and the 22 June 1805 confirmation of the sentence by the Lords Commissioners of Appeals.

§ To Joseph Sansom.[1] *18 October 1805, Department of State.* "Mr. Madison presents his compliments to Mr. Sansom, and encloses a letter to the Director of the Mint, containing permission to use the Machinery of the Mint as desired."[2]

Letterbook copy and letterbook copy of enclosure (DNA: RG 59, DL, vol. 15). Letterbook copy 1 p. For enclosure, see n. 2.

    1. In 1805 and 1806 Philadelphia Quaker and silhouettist Joseph Sansom (1767–1826) issued a series of commemorative medals designed by him and engraved by John Matthias Reich depicting American historical events. His medal of George Washington, available in gold at fifty dollars, or in silver at five dollars, was advertised for sale in the winter of 1805–6. John Matthias Reich (1768–1833), an engraver and diesinker at the Mint, was a German who had worked in Paris before settling in Philadelphia in 1800. His medals were exhibited at the Pennsylvania Academy of the Fine Arts from 1811 to 1814 (Philadelphia *United States'*

Gazette, 28 Dec. 1805; *Washington Federalist,* 12 Mar. 1806; Joseph Sansom and Charles
Coleman Sellers, "Joseph Sansom, Philadelphia Silhouettist," *PMHB* 88 [1964]: 395, 397,
401; Charles Coleman Sellers, *Benjamin Franklin in Portraiture* [New Haven, 1962], 362).
    2. The enclosure (1 p.; DNA: RG 59, DL, vol. 15) was JM to Robert Patterson, 18 Oct.
1805, stating: "Mr. Joseph Sansom of Philadelphia being desirous of using the machinery
of the Mint for striking a medal of Genl. Washington, you will be pleased to indulge him
with the permission, at such time and to such a degree, as may not materially interfere with
the public work."

§ From William Lee. *18 October 1805, Bordeaux.* "I profit of a good opportunity
which has this moment offered, to forward to yourself the moniteur, and to the
President the argus.[1] These papers will now become more interesting from the
operations on the Continent, which have at last commenced with some vigour. A
part of the Division of the French Army under the command of Prince murat have
defeated a column of Austrians, and taken eight thousand prisoners before Ulm,[2]
and from thence have proceeded on to munich while Marshal Davout's division,
have entered Bohemia by Neuburg. It seems the Austrians had taken a strong position in the *Foret Noir* through which, the French had made a feint to pass, but by a
manouvre of the Emperor they suddenly left this forest, on their right and pene-
trated into the Country without opposition, leaving the austrians in their rear who,
appear now to be retiring in every direction with a view most military men, think
to concentrate their forces, and draw the French into the heart of Germany, from
whence if they should meet with a check, it will be very difficult for them to retreat.
Thinking men consider the game both Sovereigns are playing as a very hazardous
one and that everything depends on the conduct of the King of Prussia.[3] Should he
remain neuter the house of austria will be ruined and the Elector of Bavaria elevated but, should he join the Confederacy (as there is great reason at present to
believe is his intention) the French will in all probability be driven back to the
netherlands and out of Italy. Such a reverse of fortune, under the present *temper* and
distress of this nation, would lead to incalculab(le) evils.
    "We were led to believe a few days since, that Mr Monroe had put a stop to the
attack on our Commerce, by the British cruisers but it appears by accounts recd.
yesterday; that some very late captures have been made, and if these measures
should be persisted in, they will be productive of much mischief. They are already
so sensibly felt by the merchants of this City that they talk loud of representing to
the Emperor the necessity of their being permitted, to arrest American Ships with
English property on board. Should the chamber of Commerce build on these rumours and take any steps, that may prove injurious to the interests of the united
States, I shall loose no time in communicating the same to yourself and Genl.
Armstrong. I am sorry to have it in my power to say that several Americans, who
are settled here, forgetting the duty they owe their Government unite, with the
enemies of the present administration and not understanding their true interests,
instead of endeavouring to appease, the inquietude of the French merchant, lead
him to believe that our government wink at the conduct of the English.
    "With the constituted authorities I find no difficulty in creating a right con-
struction of the business but, as I stand ill with the merchants of Bordeaux, and
ever shall (unless I consent to give up every principle of justice & duty) I have it

not so much in my power to counteract the misrepresentations to say the least of misguided individuals.

"The Schooner Mercury of Salem and the Schr. Sophia of Provincetown have lately arrived here from England, where they had been conducted by private armed Vessels, and after an examinat(ion) released. The modifications of the Law of the first of Messidor An 12. admit such Vessels, but great detention is necessary before the minister of the Interiors decision can be had on such cases, which detention, when added to that they have already recd. in England, proves destructive to their Voyages.

"The Prefect of this department has arrested Capt. James Drummond, of the Brig Fox of Boston accused of having run from Martinico without settling with the Custom house for about eleven thousand francs duties which he owed them.[4] If the facts are proved against him he will be severely handled."

RC (DNA: RG 59, CD, Bordeaux, vol. 2). 5 pp.

1. The *Argus* was an English-language newspaper at Paris founded by Lewis Goldsmith in 1802 (*Times* [London], 27 Dec. 1805).

2. For the actions of the French and Austrian armies in October 1805, see Chandler, *Campaigns of Napoleon*, 390–402.

3. After vacillating for months between allying Prussia with France, or with the members of the Third Coalition, Frederick William III opted to join the latter in late 1805, shortly before it was broken up by the French defeat of Austria at Austerlitz in December 1805 (Georges Lefebvre, *Napoleon: From 18 Brumaire to Tilsit, 1799–1807* [New York, 1969], 204–6, 240–42).

4. For the charge against Drummond, see Louis-Marie Turreau to JM, 4 Aug. 1805. For Jefferson's comments on the case, see Jefferson to JM, 17 Aug. 1805.

§ From Philip Reed.[1] *18 October 1805, Kent County, Maryland.* "Not having the honor of being personally known to you, it might perhaps appear presuming in me to trouble you with this letter, if the occasion did not seem to Justify it, I must therefore rely on this circumstance for my apology.

"The death of Judge Winchester, having vacated his Seat, as district Judge, of the district of Maryland,[2] I have taken the liberty to mention Major Robert Wright,[3] as a proper person to fill that place. I have no doubt it would be agreeable to the major, should he meet the approbation of the President of the U. States.

"This gentleman being a senator of the U. States, must be known to the government. The sense of the State of Maryland, of his worth, has been tested by his appointment at an important crisis of our political affairs, and his political reputation in tha(t) appointment has gratified public expectation. But there are some particulars attaching to the charactor and pretintions of Major Wright, which may not be so well known; It remains therefore for me to speak of those facts. He was one of the most early, active and zealous supporters of the revolution. In 1776, he Served a campaign as a private Voluntier, in a minute company, In the fall of that year he was electe(d) in the Legislature of this State, in which he served (with the exception of one year) during the war. He joined the campaig(n) of 1777 in the same Regiment with me, and was justly considered one of the most active and meritorious officers in the Corps. As a Lawyer he has practised for upwards of thirty years, in the General,

449

and Several of the County Courts of this State, with great reputation. Having had the honor of a Seat on the bench of Kents County Court, for nearly eleven years, I have had an opportunity of being a witness of Mr. Wrights conduct as a practitioner at that Bar, during which time, he has discharged his duty as a Lawyer with attention, candour, integrity and distinguished ability. His Standing at the general Court Bar, is well known to Judge Duval, near the U. States, to whom permit me to refer. As a republican Mr. Wrights conduct has been firm and uniform and his exertions have contributed not a little to the present happy state of things. I must beg leave, further, to observe, that with the exception of M(r) Paca (deceased) who formerly held the office of Judge for the district of Maryland,[4] the Eastern Shore has had no appointment of any importance under the Federal government. Our Situation with regard to the Chesepeak, is so insulated that we Seem to be cut off from public notice, altho of eighteen Counties in the State, the E. Shore compose eight.

"Pardon the freedom I have taken and ascribe it to a desire of lending my feeble efforts to serve a person who I think merit(s) a portion of the attention of the govt."

RC (DNA: RG 59, LAR, 1801–9, filed under "Wright"). 4 pp.; docketed by Jefferson. Extensively damaged at margins.

1. Revolutionary War veteran Philip Reed (1760–1829) was one of the original members of the Society of the Cincinnati and also served in the Maryland militia in the War of 1812. He served in the U.S. Senate from 1807 to 1813, and in the U.S. House of Representatives from 1817 to 1819 and again from 1822 to 1823. He was an associate justice in Kent County from 1794 to at least 1816 (Papenfuse et al., *Biographical Dictionary of the Maryland Legislature*, 2:674–75).

2. Reed was mistaken: Judge James Winchester did not die until 5 Apr. 1806 (Maryland *Republican Star or Eastern Shore General Advertiser*, 15 Apr. 1806).

3. Revolutionary War veteran Robert Wright (1752–1826) was admitted to the Maryland bar in 1773. He served in the military from 1776 to the conclusion of peace, after which he was elected to the Maryland House of Delegates. In 1801 he was chosen to represent the state in the U.S. Senate, where he was a staunch Jeffersonian. He resigned in 1806 to become governor, a post he held until 1809. In 1810 he was elected to the U.S. House of Representatives, where he served until 1817 and again from 1821 to 1823. In 1822 he was named district judge for Maryland's lower Eastern Shore, a position he held until his death.

4. William Paca (1740–1799) was educated to the law in Annapolis and London. He was a member of the Continental Congress and a signer of the Declaration of Independence. He was governor of Maryland from November 1782 to November 1785 and was a delegate to the 1788 state convention that ratified the Constitution. In 1789 Washington named him judge of the U.S. court for Maryland, where he served from 1789 until his death.

To Thomas Jefferson

DEAR SIR   PHILADA. OCT. 19. 1805
Doctor Park of this City is setting out with his daughter,[1] on a trip Southwards and proposes to be in Washington before he returns. He is an old acquaintance in the family of Mrs. Madison, and is truly an amiable & respectable man. That he may present his respects with the greater facil-

ity I have asked him to accept a few lines making him known to you. With sentiments of respectful attachment I am Your mo. Obedt hble servt.

JAMES MADISON

RC (NjP: Jasper E. Crane Collection of James and Dolley Madison).

1. Quaker Thomas Parke (1749–1835) was a Philadelphia physician, who was variously the director of the Library Company, a member of the American Philosophical Society, and president of the College of Physicians of Philadelphia. At his death he left his daughter Hannah a house and lot and the ground rents from several of the many properties he owned (Mattern and Shulman, *Selected Letters of Dolley Payne Madison,* 409; Frederick Watts and Henry J. Sergeant, *Reports of Cases Adjudged in the Supreme Court of Pennsylvania* [9 vols.; Philadelphia, 1853–55], 7:19–22).

§ To John Teasdale. *19 October 1805, Department of State.* "I have received your letter of the 30th. Ult. respecting your claim upon the French government.[1] The Minister of the United States at Paris being possessed of instructions on the subject of such demands, it would be superfluous to repeat them with a view to any general purpose. There cannot therefore be a doubt that Mr. Skipwith will receive from him every assistance in supporting your case, which may be proper & necessary."

Letterbook copy (DNA: RG 59, DL, vol. 15). 1 p.

1. Teasdale's 30 Sept. 1805 letter has not been found. For his claim against France, see Teasdale to JM, 24 Sept. 1805.

§ From Isaac Cox Barnet. *19 October 1805, Paris.* "I have the honour to transmit to you herewith, a list of the Vessels of the United States which have entered the port of Cherbourg Since the 1st. of January last [not found] and a note furnished me by my Agent there of the State & prospect of the American Trade to that port—to this I have to add the following from his last letter dated on the 15th. Inst [not found]—viz: that a few days before 'The amn. Brig Three Thomas' Captn. Foster arrived at Cherbourg with Colonial produce, after having been taken into England and there released' and that 'another Amn. Brig had arrived in the Roads of Chrg. (the Eagle) after having been carried into England where a part of her Cargo Was Confiscated.'

"In the Same letter Mr Chantereyne informs me that Several Amn. seamen had arrived from Caen at Cherbg. to Seek a passage home—but that the Mayor of that Town had refused to suffer them there until their passage was Secured and that in consequence he had ordered them to *Valognes,* a Town 15 miles interior. These men had been engaged at Antwerp for a foreign built Vessel fitting there by an American Citizen but which it appears he has changed the destination of—this case and several others not unlike it, added to the fact of the french Navigation act not permitting the alienation of french built or prize vessels which, when cleared as Neutral are Still expressed to be french property in the permission granted to that effect—enduces me to Solicit your attention to the Subject as one connected with the interests and policy of our flag in time of war.

451

"Mr. Charles St. Jore being recommanded to me as a fit person to attend to the interests of americans who frequent *Caen* and believing from his Knowledge of the English language and what I have Seen of him personally that I could not make a better Selection I have appointed him deputy Commercial Agent for the Department of *Calvados*—and shall be happy Sir, if my choice of him and Mr. Chantereyne for the department *de la Manche* should obtain your approbation.

"The enclosed copies of two letters from Captn: Hawthorn of the Brig Hannah of Philada. and Mr. Ridgway,[1] will perhaps be considered as further evidence of some omissions in the regulations concerning the duties of Consuls. The Minister of the United States, General Armstrong, to whom I have Submitted them for his advice in what applies to the conduct of Capt. Hawthorn tells me he does not See that any thing can be done with him—(except the refusing the papers he wants) and that his vessel—Sold under the circumstances mentioned, will of course be out of the Controul of either Consul or owners. This Vessel, when I was at Cherbourg in June last, was ready for Sea—having been completely repaired and waiting: as Captn. Hawthorn told me, for payment of his freight from Lisbon due by a House of Rouen: without venturing upon conjecture as to the present cause of her Sale which is about to take place—I see that the object is to obtain papers for the Same Vessel, doubtless in connection with the famous Captn. Alexr. Black who is Settled at Cherbourg and to whom Cap: H. consigned himself. In this therefore they will not be indulged and I hope a legislative remedy will ere long put it into the power of consuls to arrest the progress of proceedings which appear in this instance to be so flagrantly prejudicial to Ship owners.

"During the last absence of the Minister of the U. States from Paris—I address'd to the Minister of Exterr. Relations of this Empire—the late Commission issued to Mr. Ridgway—with a request for an *exequatur*—but none has yet been granted—tho' I presume its delay is owing to no other cause than the momentous objects which occupy his Majesty's attention—in mentioning this, allow me sir, to add that neither Mr. Skipwith nor myself have yet been favoured with Similar new Commissions and that when it may please the President to grant them to the Emperor & King—it would be very desirable to have the Departments specified over which the agency is to extend. I experienced some difficulty for the want of that Specification from my Exequatur's being limited to the Department of *Lower-Seine* (Copy of which I have had the honour of transmitting to you) and after some remarks made at the Office of foreign affairs, I was told that 'if the *new* Commission which I should doubtless soon receive did not mention the departments—there was no other way to make up for the omission than for the Minister of the United States to state those it was intended to embrace, and request an Exequatur to that effect'—but that, under my Commission addressed to the *first Consul* it was impossible to change the Exequatur.

"I was obliged therefore, to take the minister's passport (gen: Armstrong's) for 'the Departments of Seine-inferieure, Calvados, la Manch. L'Eure and l'orne,' over which he determined my agency, (upon a inspection of the Map,) to extend—and I obtained, upon due explanation, and as a matter of courtesy, my recognition in the Port of Cherbourg thereon."

RC, two copies, and enclosures, two copies (DNA: RG 59, CD, Paris, vol. 1). First RC 4 pp.; docketed by Wagner. Second RC headed "Commercial Agency of the United States for the District of Havre de Grace." For surviving enclosures, see n. 1.

1. The enclosures (2 pp.) are copies of Thomas P. Hawthorn to Barnet, 11 Oct. 1805, stating that an American ship was wrecked at Cherbourg, the captain was unable to pay for the repairs, the ship was seized, and would be sold for the debt, and asking, if it should be bought by an American, could it obtain a certificate to navigate to any port in Europe or America, and would it be possible to obtain the vessel's Mediterranean pass. He asked Barnet to reply to him in care of merchant Alexander Black at Cherbourg. Barnet also enclosed Jacob Ridgway to Barnet, 17 Oct. 1805, saying he believed Hawthorn was trying to defraud the ship's owners. Hawthorn had arrived at Antwerp fifteen months earlier from Charleston with a cargo consigned to Ridgway's merchant house and with orders to go thence to Lisbon and take on a cargo of salt for Philadelphia. Ridgway's firm gave him a bill on Lisbon and also a line of credit to use if the bill was refused. Hawthorn used both and bought no salt but accepted a freight for Cherbourg where his ship ran aground. He asked Ridgway for more funds for repairs but was refused by him and every merchant house at Antwerp, after which he told Ridgway the ship was to be sold for the repairs. Since then Ridgway had heard nothing. Ridgway added that if Barnet could prevent Hawthorn from defrauding his owners, he would "be doing a piece of justice."

§ From Carlos Martínez de Yrujo. *19 October 1805, Neighborhood of Philadelphia.* Encloses a true copy of documents lately sent him by secretary of state Pedro Cevallos at the king's order[1] by the contents of which JM will see the offensive threat made by two U.S. citizens called John and James Callier, brothers, one a justice of the peace and the other principal magistrate in the Tensas[2] district of the Mississippi Territory, to burn all Spanish ships that should come into their district and to throw the sailors into the water. Leaves it to JM to judge with what fitness there could be left as judges and defenders of the peace two persons so disposed to violate and to break it, as the aforementioned two brothers, if declarations given by several U.S. citizens, who testified to these and other threats of the same tendency many times, can be credited. Persuaded as he is of the good will of the U.S. government in preserving peace and harmony on that border, hopes that in view of these acts, so contrary to preserving them, and supported by irrefutable testimony from American citizens, JM will take appropriate measures so that discord and resentment might not be spread by the same people who by their situation have the double obligations of preventing similar disorders; and so that with time and anticipation, any attempt against the good understanding that ought to rule between individuals of two friendly nations might be prevented.

RC and enclosures (DNA: RG 59, NFL, Spain, vol. 2). RC 3 pp.; in Spanish; in a clerk's hand, except for Yrujo's complimentary close and signature; docketed by Wagner, with his note: "Threats of Messrs. Calliers against W. Florida." For enclosures, see n. 1.

1. The enclosures (9 pp.; in Spanish; docketed by Wagner) are copies of Vicente Folch's 18 Sept. 1804 letter to the marqués de Someruelos, with its enclosures Nos. 1 and 2. Enclosure No. 1 is a copy of Carlos Howard to Vicente Folch, 18 Sept. 1804, stating that he was sending his dispatch open to the marqués de Casa Calvo so that he could be aware of the documents he, Howard, was enclosing and might come to an understanding with Governor Claiborne should anything new occur. Howard said that he agreed with [Joaquín] Osorno,

[commanding officer at Mobile], that the Calliers' remarks were empty boasts, but since several of the justices of the peace and magistrates on the American frontier were ignorant or half-civilized, one could not always trust their decisions. Howard enclosed several documents including the 10 Sept. 1804 statement of Joaquín Osorno that he had called several Americans who had just returned from the Calliers' district to depose, that army lieutenants Francisco Hemeterío de Hevia and Francisco Cañedo had witnessed the depositions with Francisco Fontanilla as the translator. Osorno attached the statements of Robert Chess, John Muirell, and Henry Harvey, who testified variously and with minor differences to the information about the Calliers given by Yrujo. Also enclosed is a copy of Osorno to Folch, 12 Sept. 1804, stating that the inhabitants of Mobile were afraid to go up to American territory because of the Calliers' threats. Enclosure No. 2 is a copy of Folch to Howard, 8 Oct. 1804, stating that the Calliers' threats should be considered as the work of foolish individuals, that the government was responsible should their actions fall short of what the law of nations and the treaties between the two countries demanded, advising shipmasters going to the American settlements to conduct themselves moderately, and to inform Spanish officials should they be molested in spite of that. Folch added that the threats were not sufficient to suspend the traffic between West Florida and the settlements, first, because what West Florida got from them was necessary, and second, because if Spanish ships were not to be allowed up the river, the Americans must be prevented from coming down, which would cut off all communication between the two countries, which would be equivalent to a threat of war. Folch further added that so serious a decision was beyond his power and that things should remain as they were until higher authorities could make a decision.

2. Tensaw.

¶ From William Spencer. Letter not found. *19 October 1805.* Described in Jacob Wagner to Spencer, 26 Oct. 1805 (DNA: RG 59, DL, vol. 15; addressed to Spencer at "George Town crossroads") as referring to a claim against France. Wagner told Spencer that the latest information received from Paris about bills drawn for claims under the Louisiana Purchase Claims Convention had been published in the papers, which Spencer must have seen. Wagner added that the claim to which Spencer referred was not on the list, dated 3 July, so it was probable that "further progress must have been made in the business" of which the State Department had not been informed. For earlier correspondence on this claim, see *PJM-SS*, 9:99–100, 394, 395 n. 2.

To Thomas Jefferson

DEAR SIR   PHILADA. Oct. 20. 1805.

The decrease of the fever in the City has induced me to return with Mrs. M. to it, with a view to place her in a situation that would justify me in leaving her for a while. She is likely to be detained several weeks longer, before the Docr. will approve of her entering on a journey; but I hope she is now or will be in a day or two advanced towards her recovery beyond the occasion of particular anxiety. I propose therefore to set out with little delay for Washington. Perhaps I may reach Washington by the last of the Week. I have nothing to add but the respectful attachment with which I remain yrs.

JAMES MADISON

I took the liberty of givg. yesterday a line of introduction to Dr. Parke of this City who is on a visit with a daughter to Washington. He is in his political connections of the Old School I presume. But he is at least candid in his judgmt: of executive measures, and sincere in his personal esteem & respect. I am not sure that he will make use of the letter; but I think it probable. If he should not it will happen from circumstances incident to his movemts. His daughter is of the demure Quaker manners, but sensible & accomplished.

RC (DLC: Jefferson Papers). Docketed by Jefferson as received 22 Oct.

§ From William Clark. *20 October 1805, Emden*. "I had the pleasure to address you under date of Septr. 18Th. 1804.[1] and have since remained without any of your favors or Commands.

"Herewith, I have now the honor to transmit an official report of the American Vessels, which have entered the River Embs during my ⟨r⟩esidence here. By this Document it will be perceived, that contrary to general expectation at the commencement of the present War, (& of the Blockade of the Elbe & Weser,) the Port of Embden, has not been found so convenient for the Trade carried on between the United states & Hamburg & Bremen, as Tonningen & the Ports on the Jahde. In the course of the present year, but few of our Vessels have unloaded at this place. These were all destined for Holland, & came here only, in consequence of the Regulations of the Dutch East India Company, which prohibit the Importation of Teas into the Ports of Holland, in foreign Vessels, unless they are from china direct; & without having broken bulk.

"Thus, from the little prospect of any important lasting commercial Intercourse between the United States & the Port of Embden, I am discourage⟨d⟩ from forming a permanent Establishment here; This place, presenting scarcely any opening to me, either for the American Trade, or of being officially usefull to my country."

RC (DNA: RG 59, CD, Elberfeld, Rostock, and Lübeck, vol. 1). 2 pp.; docketed by Wagner. Enclosure not found.

1. *PJM-SS*, 8:65–66.

To an Unidentified Correspondent

PHILADELPHIA, 21 October 1805.

I have this moment received yours of the 18th. I regret most sensibly that Dr. Winston should be under the inconveniency he describes, and that you could not fall on some expedient for his relief more expeditious than a remittance from this place. I enclose a check for 200 dollars and by that it may be presented at the Bank, if any conveyance can serve to forward the money. I have inclosed a check to Mr. Voss for a half years rent. Please ask him for a receipt. These drafts with expenses here will oblige me to renew the note to Mr. Cox—and one to General Mason. I shall set out tomorrow or next day for Washington. Yours affectionately,

JAMES MADISON

RC (offered for sale by Gary Combs Autographs, Inc., New York, N.Y., 2005, ref. 2307).

From William Prichard

SIR,   RICHMOND, October. 21st. 1805.

In obedience to your directions of August last,[1] I have shipped for *New York* two cases of books containing 366 Vols of Researches into the History of the United States, and directed them to Mr. Mazzei, at Leghorn Italy,[2] to the particular care of Mr. Archd. Campbell Merchant, New York; who, jointly with a friend of mine of the name of John Byrne at that place, promised to see the said Cases reshiped in a safe Vessel, for Leghorn. The bill of Lading from this place to NewYork, I take the liberty to enclose.[3] During the long period of time they remained in my hands, none of these books were sold by me, and they are now all returned save eleven setts that would not go in the boxes. Consequently I take them, in some measure to renumerate me for expences incurred thereon, and in order, finally to close that account on my books. Should you deem it necessary to write at the same time to Mr. M, if you address to the care of either Archibald Campbell, or John Byrne, both Merchants, NewYork, it will be forwarded. That you and Lady may long live to enjoy health & happiness are the sincere wishes of, Honble. Sir, Your Obt. hble Servt.

WM. PRICHARD[4]

RC and enclosure (DLC). RC docketed by JM. For enclosure, see n. 3.

1. This letter has not been found.
2. For Philip Mazzei's books, see Jefferson to JM, 2 Mar. 1798, Mazzei to JM, 30 Aug. and 15 Dec. 1804, *PJM*, 17:87, 88 n. 5, *PJM-SS*, 6:243 n. 1, 7:660, 8:385.

3. The enclosure (1 p.) is a copy of the 17 Oct. 1805 bill of lading for "Two Boxes Merchandize" to be shipped in the schooner *Weymouth*, Capt. W. W. Weymouth, from Richmond to Campbell at New York. The freight charge was two dollars. "Mr. Mazzei Leghorn Italy No. 1—2." is written in the margin.

4. William Prichard (d. 1815) sold books and musical instruments and operated a lending library in Philadelphia for many years before moving to Richmond in the early 1790s. "Probably the principal music merchant in Richmond during the last decade of the eighteenth century," he continued to sell books and musical instruments for at least another decade (Philadelphia *Freeman's Journal: or, The North-American Intelligencer*, 12 Sept. 1781; Philadelphia *Pennsylvania Packet, and Daily Advertiser*, 24 Jan. 1788; Philadelphia *Dunlap's American Daily Advertiser*, 1 May 1792, 28 July 1794; Albert Stoutamire, *Music of the Old South: Colony to Confederacy* [Rutherford, N.J., 1972], 97).

§ From Sylvanus Bourne. *22 October 1805, Amsterdam*. "Inclosed are the two last Leyden Papers by which you will find that the war on the Continent has again recommenced with vigor & as yet with success on the part of the French—whose great object is to force the Austrians to battle before the arrival of the Russians. The situation of Prussia at this moment is delicate & full of difficulty. Its Govt. notwithstanding the declaration of a Strict neutrality has permitted the Russians to enter Prussian Silesia because the french faced their passage through his territory of Anspach & caused the magazines of the King to be opened for feeding their troops.[1] It is by some even thought that the K Prussia will declare in favr of the Allies. I however much doubt if its policy or interest will dictate such a measure. He will at least be disposed to wait the probable issue of Affairs & then agreeably to the System of that Court join with the Stronger party.

"It is now near a month we had scarcely any ariva⟨ls⟩ here from the U States The late conduct of the British appears to have struck a deadly blow to our trade in this quarter. What will be the issue of this matter I am unable to say, unless our Govt. takes firm & vigorous measures in this important Crisis which I am led to believe will produce a relaxation on the other Side & resto⟨re⟩ our Commerce to its wonted freedom so far as may be consistent with its really *neutral* Character.

"Your late Circulars of July last have been duly received & Shall be Strictly observed."

RC (DNA: RG 59, CD, Amsterdam, vol. 1). 2 pp.

1. During the previous European war, Prussia had exempted Anspach from the neutrality agreement that encompassed northern Germany because the province lay between the belligerent countries of France and Austria. The only restrictions were that any troops should pass through quickly, refrain from actual hostilities in Prussian territory, and pay for anything they might take. Alexander I had been pressuring Frederick William III to join the Third Coalition, but the latter had been resisting, hoping to maintain his neutral position. Napoleon's transit through Anspach gave Frederick the opportunity to grant the Russian troops passage without giving up neutrality (Thiers, *History of the Consulate and the Empire of France under Napoleon*, 2:61–62).

§ From Levett Harris. *22 October 1805, St. Petersburg*. "Since I had the honor to address you under date of 23 Aug. 4. September ℔ Ship Severn via Baltimore

Copy via Amsterdam: I have received a letter, of which the inclosed A is Copy, from Commodore Rogers,[1] advising that a peace had been concluded with the Tripolitans, and that the Russian Vessel St. Michael, which had been captured by a part of the Squadron in September last year in an attempt to enter Tripoli in defiance of its blockade, together with the amount of the Sales of her Cargo in Malta, he had taken upon himself to restore to the original owners.

"On my receipt of this intelligence I immediately communicated it to the Russian Ministry by a Letter of which the inclosed Bb is Copy.[2]

"The pacifick Sistem in which the Emperor has persevered, Since the recommencement of the War between France & England, is, to all appearance, to be abandoned. The Correspondence which has taken place at Paris Vienna & Berlin between the ministers of the respective Continental powers, & to which you will be fully known Sir, before this can reach you, will apprise you of the actual State of the Political Affairs of Europe.

"It is yet to be hoped from the line of policy pursued by Prussia, & by which its Monarch maintains a most important position, that the calamities inseperable from the impending State of things will be materially mitigated.

"An Armament however which the Emperor, in conjunction with the King of Sweden, has deemed it proper to establish in Pomerania, has produced a Strong remonstrance from the Prussian Minister Count de Goltz resident at this Court. This minister has made great efforts to divert the ostensible object of a force very onerous to the views of the Prussian King; but he has not Succeeded. About fifteen thousand men have been embarked here and at Riga within the last five weeks destined for the above object, & News have just come to hand that between thirty & forty transports employed on these Occasions have been wrecked, and that one intire regiment of Cosacks have perished.

"The Emperor left this on the 11th. ulto., to proceed to the review of his respective Armies, now on their march to Germany and Italy: he was accompanied on this journey by two Privy Counsellors, M. de Novosiltzoff & Count Tolstoy, & his Minister of foreign Affairs Prince de Czartoryski. In the absence of the Latter the Portefeuille is held by the Privy Counsellor de Weydemeyer, of which I have been notified by a letter copy as inclosed C.[3]

"If any thing particularly interesting Should occur here during the winter, I shall be attentive to its due Communication. The period is approaching when a suspension will take place for six months in our direct intercourse with America; I Shall thus be impelled to have recourse to the Conveyances by Holland or England, whither, in the Winter, the Communications from hence are tardy & uncertain, and which, in the present State of things, are likely to meet with additional difficulties.

"I Shall necessarily avail myself of them in the event of circumstances rendering it adviseable.

"By my next I Shall transmit you Sir, a report of our trade here the present year. In the mean time, I beg leave to Accompany the present with the inclosed list of Exports by the Vessels which have sailed [not found]."

Adds in a 25 Oct. postscript: "News Arrived here last night by express, that Prussia had determined to take an Active part in the war against France, in consequence of this power having forced a passage though a part of the Prussian Territory with an Army destined to the succor of Bavaria."[4]

RC, two copies, and enclosures, two copies (DNA: RG 59, CD, St. Petersburg, vol. 1). First RC 3 pp.; dated "10/22 October, 1805" in the Julian and Gregorian calendars. Second RC marked "duplicate." Both RCs docketed by Wagner. Minor differences between the copies have not been noted. For enclosures, see nn. 1–3.

1. Enclosure "A" (3 pp.; filed with Harris's 18/30 Aug. 1805 dispatch; printed in Knox, *Naval Documents, Barbary Wars*, 6:190) is a copy of John Rodgers to Harris, 18 July 1805, regarding the Russian ship *St. Miguel* (*St. Michael*), seized while trying to violate the U.S. blockade of Tripoli. Rodgers stated that since the establishment of peace between the United States and Tripoli he had released the ship and its cargo as a gesture of friendship towards Russia. For earlier notice of the seizure of the *St. Michael*, see *PJM-SS*, 9:396, 397 n. 3.

2. Enclosure "B" (2 pp.; in French) is a copy of Harris's 14 Sept. 1805 note to privy councillor Ivan Andreevich Weydemeyer (Veidemeier) notifying him of the *St. Michael*'s return.

3. Enclosure "C" (2 pp.; in French; one copy docketed by Wagner as enclosed in Harris's 23 Aug./2 Sept. 1805 letter and filed there; the other copy docketed as enclosed with this dispatch) is a copy of Prince Jerzy Czartoryski's 9 Sept. 1805 letter informing Harris that in his absence foreign affairs would be entrusted to Weydemeyer. On the same sheet Harris included "b," which is a copy of Weydemeyer's 16 Sept. 1805 note acknowledging Harris's 14 Sept. 1805 note (see n. 2 above).

4. For this incident, see Sylvanus Bourne to JM, 22 Oct. 1805, and n. 1.

§ From Louis-Marie Turreau. *22 October 1805*. Has told JM in conversation of his just discontent with the commercial relations which the citizens of different states maintain with the rebels of every color who have momentarily withdrawn Saint-Domingue from the legal authority.

The principles injured by such a commerce, or rather by such a system of brigandage, are so evident, generally acknowledged, and adopted, not only by all nations that have a colonial system to defend, by those who have none, and even by wise people of every political view, that a statesman, if he has not lost every idea of justice, humanity, and public law, can no more contest their wisdom than their existence. And certainly he, finding himself called by duty as well as inclination, in the bosom of a friendly people, and near the respectable chief of government, could not have expected that his first political relations would have for their object a complaint so serious, an infraction so manifest, of a most sacred law, well observed by every civilized nation.

It was not enough for some U.S. citizens to convey munitions of every kind to the rebels of Saint-Domingue, to that race of African slaves the reproach and the refuse of nature; it was necessary to insure the success of this ignoble and criminal traffic by the use of force. The vessels destined to protect it are constructed, loaded, and armed in every port of the union, under the eyes of the American people, of the authorities, and of the federal government itself, and that government, which has taken for the basis of its political career the most severe equity and the most impartial neutrality, does not forbid it.

Without doubt, notwithstanding the profound consideration for the American government with which he is filled, he might enlarge still further upon the

459

reflections suggested by such an important and unexpected state of things. It would be equally as afflicting for him to dwell upon it and to state the results as it would be for the government to hear them.

JM, who knows perfectly the justice of the principles and the legitimacy of the rights referred to, will be of opinion, that neither are susceptible of discussion because a principle universally assented to, a right generally established, is never discussed, or at least is discussed in vain. The only way open for the redress of these complaints is to put an end to the tolerance which produces them and which daily aggravates their consequences.

Moreover, this note, founded upon facts no less evident than the principles which they infract, does not permit him to doubt that the U.S. government will take the most prompt and effectual prohibitory measures in order to put an end to its cause.

RC (DNA: RG 59, NFL, France, vol. 2–3); RC (DNA: RG 76, Preliminary Inventory 177, entry 125, France, Convention of 1803 [Spoliation], Misc. Records, ca. 1798–1804, box 2, envelope 1, folder 7); Tr (AAE: Political Correspondence, U.S., 59:11–12). First RC 2 pp.; in French (editors' translation); marked "Note officielle"; in a clerk's hand, signed by Turreau. Second RC dated 14 Oct. 1805; in French; marked "Pour copie conforme" and countersigned by Turreau; docketed by Wagner as received in Turreau's 3 Jan. 1806 letter. Tr enclosed in Turreau to Talleyrand, 15 Jan. 1806 (AAE: Political Correspondence, U.S., 59:10). Translation printed in *ASP, Foreign Relations*, 2:725–26.

From Peter S. Du Ponceau

Wednesday, [23 October 1805]

Mr Du Ponceau presents his respects to Mr. Madison, & is very happy that any of the Books that he is possessed of can be useful to him, & by his means to our Country, whose interests he has to Support. Mr. Madison is welcome to make such use of them & as long as he pleases. Mr D. thinks it may be acceptable to add to the other Books Ompteda's Litterature of the Law of Nations or Catalogue of Writers on that Subject.[1] As Mr Wagner understands German he may point out some useful Books to Mr. Madison.

Mr. D. takes the liberty to enclose an attempt at a more correct Translation of the passage in the 9th. Chapter of Bynkershoek in which he has tried to reconcile the idiom & the sense.[2]

He wishes to Mr. Madison a Safe & pleasant Journey, & begs leave to present to Mrs Madison his respects & wishes for her Speedy recovery.

RC (DLC). Undated; conjectural date assigned based on JM's departure from Philadelphia for Washington on Wednesday, 23 Oct. 1805.

1. Du Ponceau referred to Dietrich Heinrich Ludwig von Ompteda's *Literatur des gesamten sowohl natürlichen als positiven Völkerrechts* (2 vols.; Regensburg, 1785). Ompteda

(1746–1803) was born in the Hoya region of Hanover and became a bureaucrat after completing his education in 1767. In 1783 he was minister plenipotentiary to the Bavarian court and representative to the diet at Regensburg for George III, posts he held until his death (Stolberg-Wernigerode et al., *Neue Deutsche Biographie*), 19:535.

2. Du Ponceau enclosed the following note:

Text

Non licit *igitur* advohere ea &c. & quorum praecipuus in bello usus, milites; *quin &* milites variis gentium pactis excepti sunt &c.

Translation

It is not *therefore* (referring to his preceeding Argument) to carry those things &c. nor soldiers which are particularly useful in War; *nay*, Soldiers have been (*expressly*) excepted by various Treaties &c.

Du Ponceau omitted a word in his transcription and his translation. The phrase might better be translated: "It is not *therefore* allowed to carry those things &c. nor those which are particularly useful in War, soldiers; *nay &* soldiers have been expressly excepted by various Treaties &c." JM quoted this in full in his pamphlet *An Examination of the British Doctrine, Which Subjects to Capture a Neutral Trade, Not Open in Time of Peace* (Madison, *Letters* [Cong. ed.], 2:244 n.).

From Thomas Jefferson

Dear Sir   Washington Oct. 23. 05.

Yours of the 20th. came to hand last night. I sincerely regret that mrs. Madison is not likely to be able to come on so soon as had been hoped. The probability of an extensive war on the continent of Europe strengthening every day for some time past, is now almost certain. This gives us our great desideratum, time. In truth it places us quite at our ease. We are certain of one year of campaigning at least, and one other year of negociation for their peace arrangements. Should we be now forced into war, it is become much more questionable than it was, whether we should not pursue it unembarrassed by any alliance & free to retire from it whenever we can obtain our separate terms. It gives us time too to make another effort for peaceable settlement. Where shall this be done? Not at Madrid certainly. At Paris: through Armstrong, or Armstrong & Monroe as negociators, France as the Mediator, the price of the Floridas as the means. We need not care who gets that: and an enlargement of the sum we had thought of may be the bait to France, while the Guadaloupe as the Western boundary may be the soother of Spain providing for our spoliated citizens in some effectual way. We may announce to France that determined not to ask justice of Spain again, yet desirous of making one other effort to preserve peace, we are willing to see whether her interposition can obtain it on terms which we think just; that no delay however can be admitted, & that in the mean time should Spain attempt to change the status quo, we shall repel force by force, without undertaking other active hostilities till we see what may be the issue of her interference. I hazard my own ideas merely for your consideration. The present state of things does not so far press as to render it necessary for you to do violence to your feelings by prematurely leaving Mrs. Madison. Accept for her & yourself my affectionate salutations.

TH: JEFFERSON

P.S. Let Mr. Smith know as you pass thro' Baltimore & he will come on.

RC (DLC: Rives Collection, Madison Papers); FC (DLC: Jefferson Papers).

From Dolley Madison

23d. October 1805

A few hours only have passed since you left me my beloved, and I find nothing can releave the oppression of my mind but speaking to you in this *only* way. The Doctor called before you had gone far and with an air of sympathy wished you could see how much better the knee appeared. I could only speak to assure him it felt better. Betsey Pemberton[1] and Amy are sitting beside me and seem to respect the grief they know I feel, at even a short seperation from one who is all to me. I shall be better when Peter returns, not that any length of time could lessen my just regret, but an assurance that you are well and easy will contribute to make me So. I have sent the books and note to Mrs. Dallas. B. Pemberton puts on your hat to divert me, but I cannot look at her.

24th. of October. What a sad day! The watchman announced a cloudy morning at one clock, and from that moment I found myself unable to sleep from anxiety for thee my dearest husband—detention cold and accident Seemed to menace thee! B. Pemberton who lay beside me administered three or four drops of Laudinum, it had some effect before the Dr. came, who pronounced a favorable opinion on the knee.

Yesterday the Miss Gibbons called upon me, in the evening Mrs. Dallas and daughter[2] with Mrs. Stuart and Nancy Pemberton. Every one is kind and attentive.

25th. This clear cold morning will favor your journey and enliven the feelings of my darling! I have nothing new to tell you. Betsey and myself sleep quietly together and the knee is mending. I eat very little and sit precisely as you left me. The doctor during his very short visits, talks of you, he says he regards you more than any man he ever knew and nothing could please him so much as passing his life near you—sentiments so congenial with one's own, and in *such cases*, like dew drops on flowers, exhilarate as they fall! The Governor, I hear, has arrived and is elated with his good fortune.³ General Moreau is expected in town in a few days, to partake of a grand dinner the citizens are about to give him.

Adieu, my beloved, our hearts understand each other. In fond affection thine

DOLLEY P. MADISON

Tr (owned by Mrs. George B. Cutts, Wellesley, Mass., 1982).

1. Elizabeth (Betsy) Pemberton Waddell (1780–1859) married Henry L. Waddell in 1806, and in 1812 the family moved to a farm in Bucks County, Pennsylvania (Thomas Allen Glenn, ed., *Genealogical Notes Relating to the Families of Lloyd, Pemberton, Hutchinson, Hudson and Parke and to Others, Connected Directly or Remotely with Them* [Philadelphia, 1898], 58; Mattern and Shulman, *Selected Letters of Dolley Payne Madison*, 415).

2. This was probably Sophia Burrell Dallas Bache (d. 1860), the daughter of Arabella Maria Smith Dallas and Alexander James Dallas. She married Benjamin Franklin's grandson Richard Bache Jr., who later abandoned her and their numerous children and moved to Texas, where he was a member of the legislature (Glossary, *DMDE*; Bernard S. Katz and C. Daniel Vencill, eds., *Biographical Dictionary of the United States Secretaries of the Treasury, 1789–1995* [Westport, Conn., 1996], 101; Washington *Constitution*, 10 July 1860; Hugh Richard Slotten, *Patronage, Practice, and the Culture of American Science: Alexander Dallas Bache and the U.S. Coast Survey* [Cambridge, 1994], 6–8; Victoria, Tex., *Texian Advocate*, 30 Mar. 1848).

3. For Gov. Thomas McKean's reelection, see Andrew Ellicott to JM, 2 Oct. 1805, n. 2.

§ From John Graham. *23 October 1805, New Orleans.* "I have the Honor to forward to you by this mail a copy of the Official Journal of the Governor of this Territory, from the 22d. of January (the time when mr Brown left this Office) to the 1st. July [not found].

"Circumstances over which I had no controul, prevented me from transmitting this Copy sooner; but in future I will take care to comply more strictly with the Injunctions of the Law.

"The appointments made by the Governor are not as yet placed upon the Records in this Office, but he tells me they will be so soon as he can ascertain who have, and who have not accepted the Commissions sent to them."

RC (DNA: RG 59, TP, Orleans, vol. 7). 1 p.; docketed by Wagner as received 26 Nov.

From William C. C. Claiborne

I am sorry to inform you of the embarrassments to which the Citizens of the United States are subjected who navigate the Mobile River. All american Vessels passing by the Town of Mobile, are brought to and a duty of ¹ per cent exacted both on imports and Exports. These duties are even required on Articles passing to and from the Garrisons and Factories of the United States. I have addressed on this occasion, a Letter to Mr. Morales, by whom it is said this proceeding was Authorized, but in his answer, which was this morning received,² he professes to be unacquainted with the particulars, and declines any interference until he should advise upon the subject with the Governor of West Florida.

I have certain information of the arrival at Pensacola of four hundred troops from Havana and that a much larger number is daily expected. *I also learn from a* source entitled to credit *that three hundred men are ordered from Pensacola to Baton Rouge and that eight hundred Spanish troops have lately been posted on the frontier of the Province of Taxus.* It is a fact known to me that a *Spanish Agent has contracted with a Merchant of this City for the delivery at the Town of Mobille of four thousand barrels of flour* and that this same *Agent not being able* to effect *a contract for the delivery of four thousand pair of shoes at Mobille*, has purchased a quantity *of leather.* The Marquis of Casa Calvo being absent from this City it is my intention to enquire of Governor Folch an explanation of the object of *these military movements.* I flatter myself that Hostilities between the United States and Spain may be avoided and that an honorable adjustment of our differences may ensue. But I am inclined to think that the Spanish Agents calculate on a Speedy rupture and are making all the preparations which their means permit to commence the War in this quarter to advantage. *New orleans would* unquestionably *be the first object of attack* and with a view to *its security* I should be pleased to see *Fort St. John repaired and put in a state of defence; that fort commands the mouth of the Bayou St. John and if strengthened* would present a great impediment to *the passage of troops from Pensacola and Mobille by the way of the lakes to this City* at present *the works are in ruins* but might readily *be repaired and made defensible* without any considerable expenditure. I have communicated to Colonel Freeman the officer Commanding here my Ideas of the *importance of Fort St. John* but he does not agree with me in opinion and Says further that, *he has not the means of strengthening any fort.* If our differences with Spain should Still be unsettled, I beg leave to suggest for consideration the propriety of taking some immediate measures for the *security of this territory and particularly the City of New Orleans.* I can only calculate with certainty *on the valour and patriotism of a part of the militia of this territory* and I know that from the *Mississippi Territory speedy support* would in the event of *danger be given.* But I nevertheless think that the strengthening *of Fort St. John and Fort St. Philip*³ *the mounting of cannon* as well those suited *for Forts as for use in the field the collecting of* ample Supplies of ammunition and the stationing *on the River Missippi and the Lakes a few gun boats would be measures*⁴ *of precaution.* I have the Honor to be Sir very respectfully your Hble Sert

WILLIAM C. C. CLAIBORNE

RC (DNA: RG 59, TP, Orleans, vol. 7); letterbook copy (Ms-Ar: Claiborne Executive Journal, vol. 15); extract (DNA: RG 233, President's Messages, 9A–D1); extract (DNA: RG 46, President's Messages, 9B–B1). RC in a clerk's hand, signed by Claiborne; docketed by Wagner. Italicized words are those encoded by Claiborne in a State Department code; key not found; copytext is Wagner's interlinear decoding. Second extract is a letterpress copy of first extract. Extract printed in the *National Intelligencer,* 9 Dec. 1805.

    1. Left blank in original. In his 9 Dec. 1805 letter to JM, Claiborne said the duty was twelve percent.
    2. On 22 Oct. 1805 Claiborne asked Juan Ventura Morales if the collection of duties at Mobile was connected with Morales's ban on the American deposit at New Orleans in 1802, or with some later edict of Governor Folch. Claiborne suggested, should Morales be responsible for such collections, that he suspend the duties until he received orders from Madrid, noting that doing so would not weaken any right the king might then have and would show Morales's disposition to prevent an increase of difficulties already felt in the negotiations between their two countries (Rowland, *Claiborne Letter Books,* 3:205–6; *PJM-SS,* 4:30 n. 1). Morales's reply has not been found.
    3. Fort St. Philip was located at Plaquemine, downriver from New Orleans (Carter, *Territorial Papers, Orleans,* 9:782).
    4. Letterbook copy has "wise measures."

§ From William Jarvis. *24 October 1805, Lisbon.* "The foregoing of the 11th. I had the honor to forward by the Brig Neptune Captn. Delano, for New York, with the inclosed papers.¹ Duplicates of those from me go inclosed.

"A few days since three sailors belonging to the Laura of Boston Captn. Higginson, were imprisoned for striking the Mate. One who was not protected as an American, having wrote to Mr. Gambier the British Consul General claiming his protection as a British Subject, he sent the letter to me by his secretary & demanded him. I replied as a matter of right I certainly could not give him up, but as the Seaman wished to go on board a Man of War & Captn. Higginson did not want him, I might consent to his release from prison as a favor. This Mr. Gambier declined accepting contending that he, (Michl. Chase) ought to be given up as a thing of right. For which purpose, Mr Gambier's Secretary & the Merinho General, informed me that, Mr. Gambier had written to the Secretary of State. Upon which I wrote the inclosed to His Excellency.² I am sorry to be under the necessity of troubling you Sir about such trifles; but when they are attempted to be made matters of consequence it is unavoidable. This Government has done nothing about the seaman.

"Inclosed is also a Copy of my letter to His Excellency to try to obtain some alteration in the arrangement relative to the franquia of Bread Stuffs,³ but I doubt any thing coming of it, as the present method was introduced by the Minister of

465

Finance, who is administrator of the Corn Market, & therefore it is probable will not consent to an alteration.

"It appears that a Bill of Lading of the Cargo of the Schooner Trio of Boston Captn. Storey was unthinkingly shown to one of the House of Messrs. John Bulkley & Son, Agents of the Privateer Admiral Saumarez that captured her, by Mr. Turner the Consignee, by which it appeared that the Cargo was French property; upon which Messrs. Bulkely & Sons wrote to Mr. Gambier retracting their permission for the payment of the freight, and Mr. Gambier inclosed Copy of their Letter to His Excellency Mr. de Araujo & which occasioned the original of the inclosed of the 15th: Instant.[4]

"Nothing as yet has been done about the Venus,[5] altho the Spanish Minister applied ten days ago for her to be delivered up.

"General Junot left this Court for France the 26th. Instant; leaving the Secretary of Embassy Chargé d'Affaires. Madam is now drinking the Waters at the Caldres. So soon as she is restored to health she will follow him.

"The Rochfort Squadron made its appearance off this Coast about a fortnight ago consisting of 5 Ships of the line 2 frigates and a Brig of War. It has captured several Merchantmen & among the rest two or three of a Convoy from England for Porto. A Man of War had come within shot of the Frigate in which Lord Robt. Fitzgerald the British Minister was returning; which had nearly a Million sterling on board for Malta; but the port Convoy heaving in sight, a signal was made to the Man of War to give over the Chase. His Lordship was landed at Faro & reached here four days since.

"Twenty nine Transports & two Frigates, part of the British expedition, has put in here from stress of Weather. There is on board two s(c)ots regiments. It is supposed they are for Italy. Much field & heavy artilery & equipage is said to be on board. A transport loaded principally with Cannon Balls foundered a short distance off the Bar and the Crew perished.

"Mr. Pinckney writes me that he shall be on here in a few days, to embark for the United States. He says not a word about Spanish Affairs. Inclosed is a Packet from him.

"Common fame says that hostilities have commenced between France & Austria and a Battle been fought; the friends of each side alternately claiming the Victory; but as this Lady has not the best reputation in the World for truth, those who pretend to think, give no Credit to these reports. It is asserted however upon better grounds, that the King of Prussia has refused a passage to the Russains [sic] troops through His Dominions; and it is added, declared he would repel force with force if attempted.

"This Country is in the most perfect state of Tranquility; altho the paragraphists in the English & French papers occasionally involve it in a War."

RC, two copies, and enclosures, two copies (DNA: RG 59, CD, Lisbon, vol. 2). First RC 4 pp.; in a clerk's hand, except for Jarvis's complimentary close, signature, and address. Second RC marked "(Dup)." Minor differences between the copies have not been noted. For enclosures, see nn. 2–4.

1. The *Neptune*, Captain Delano, arrived at New York about 28 Dec. 1805 in seventy-two days from Lisbon (*New-York Commercial Advertiser*, 28 Dec. 1805).

2. The enclosure (5 pp.; in a clerk's hand, signed by Jarvis) is a copy of Jarvis to António de Araújo, 20 Oct. 1805, stating that Michael Chase had shipped on the *Laura* from Boston to Lisbon and thence to India and back to the United States; that he had been arrested in Lisbon for striking the first mate, an act that would have brought him a court-martial and the death penalty in the British navy; that there was "not the Shadow of Proof" that Chase was British; and that a letter written for Chase by a third party, in which Chase asked the protection of British consul James Gambier as a British subject and offered to serve in the British navy, was not proof. Jarvis said that for one nation to claim a subject who was guilty of a crime against another state would allow criminals to evade the laws and subject the persons and property of any community to crimes by foreigners. He noted that whenever an American citizen entered the British service, he was treated as a subject of Great Britain, and he argued that Chase had signed a contract to serve on the *Laura*, which Britain had no right to abrogate. He contrasted Gambier's demand for Chase's release with "the almost weekly impressments" of Americans in Lisbon and asked Araújo to arrange the release of five impressed American seamen then being held on British ships at Lisbon including two who had disappeared from their American ships leaving their clothing and possessions behind.

3. The enclosure (3 pp.; in a clerk's hand, signed by Jarvis) is a copy of Jarvis to Araújo, 18 Oct. 1805, stating that because of "an abundant harvest" the United States would have much flour and grain to spare, but that there were delays in obtaining franquia (admission) to Lisbon because of the papers ships were required by Portuguese law to have. He noted that since American captains were often also the owners of the cargoes, they carried no charter party or letters of orders. He said that if Americans decided to take their cargoes elsewhere, Portugal would be denied the opportunity to buy flour at a cheaper rate than in Europe as well as to sell return cargoes of wine, salt, and fruit, and he asked that the government approve a return to the previous regulations.

4. The enclosures (4 pp.; in Portuguese and English) are a copy and translation of Araújo to Jarvis, 15 Oct. 1805, stating that after the Bukeleys had written the letter identifying themselves as agents for the owner of the *Admiral Saumarez*, and agreed to pay the freight out of the proceeds of the cargo, "some circumstances occurred which hindered their agreeing to the said payment." As a result the matter was to be decided in the courts. Araújo added that the Portuguese government would not hesitate in facilitating the payment in that manner.

5. For the *Venus*, see Jarvis to JM, 16 Sept. 1805, and n. 10, 26 Sept. 1805, and 11 Oct. 1805, and nn. 2–4, and 9.

§ From Anthony Merry. *24 October 1805, Washington.* " I have received the Honor of your Letter of the 14th. Instant, with its Inclosure, respecting the Impressment of Daniel Talmage, a Citizen of the United States, by His Majesty's Ship Cleopatra; and I have the Honor, Sir, to acquaint you that I have lost no Time in transmitting a Copy of the Document with which you have furnished me on this Subject to the Commander in Chief of His Majesty's Ships on the Halifax Station, in order that immediate Attention may be paid to your Application for the Release of the Seaman in question."

RC (DNA: RG 59, NFL, Great Britain, vol. 3). 1 p.; docketed by Wagner as received 27 Oct.

From John Armstrong

⟨DE⟩AR SIR,   25 October 1805. PARIS.

You will see by an article in the enclosed paper that the Emperor (Napoleon) has begun the war by throwing Sixes. In twenty four days from that on which he crossed the Rhine he has traversed Suabia, assembled the Several column[s] of his army at Newburg, forced the passage of the Danube, and either killed or captured the whole of the Austrian Army under Prince Ferdinand & Gen. Mack.[1] He has now no force to combat or destroy in his march to Vienna, excepting what may be presented by the first Russian Column of 50,000 men which has recently gained the Eastern banks of the Inn, they Cannot occupy him either long or seriously. Where this Career is to end, or what will be its consequences to Europe, are problems highly interesting. Should Prussia see in this new & extravagant Success only new motives to her old System of neutrality, or sufficient ones for taking part with the Conqueror, the fate of Austria is inevitably fixed. My last letter from you is dated the 6th. of June.[2] Mr. Bowdoin is still in England. With much respect & esteem, I am Sir, Your most obedient & very hum. Servant

JOHN ARMSTRONG

RC (DNA: RG 59, DD, France, vol. 10). In a clerk's hand, signed by Armstrong.

1. See Chandler, *Campaigns of Napoleon*, 382–402.
2. *PJM-SS*, 9:432–36.

§ From George W. Erving. *25 October 1805*, *"Escurial."* "I have the honor to inform you that I arrived at Madrid on the 23d Instt: finding that Mr. Pinckney had left it on the 22d with an intention of returning to the United States by way of Lisbon & that he woud stop at the Escurial to take an audience of leave, I proceeded immediately to this place: Mr Pinckney had expected to meet me here on my way to the capital, but I went by another rout, & it seemed important that I shoud see him before his departure. I found that he had appointed yesterday to wait upon the secretary of state, & it was concluded that this occasion shoud be taken of introducing me to the government. I preferred this mode, to that of waiting Mr Pinckneys departure, & then introducing myself in the ordinary way; since this latter course woud more probably have Encouraged a beleif that I had preceded Mr Bowdoin in consequence of late orders from you, an inference might thence arise of some alteration in the views of our government, & any effect which may have been produced by the rupture of the late negotiations might be thus in some degree impaired: At the same time it seemed proper that the presentation shoud be grounded upon the appointment of the President, & there Existed no motive sufficiently important to authorize a deviation from the arrangement which you had made; but on the contrary it seemed better calculated to Encourage & meet any conciliatory dispositions which may arise in this government: I therefore presented your letter to Don Pedro Cevallos, taking care at the same time that he shoud observe the date of the appointment, & Mr Pinckney gave him Explicitly to understand that I had not arrived in consequence of any late orders, but merely to releive him from his station, & to enable him to return home pursuant to the permission which he has long since received. The secretary made many polite & amicable professions public & personal suited to the occasion, & the interview of Mr Pinckney with their Majesties, & my introduction were fixed for, & took place accordingly to day.

"I avail myself of the occasion to send this by Mr Pinckney who departs Early to morrow, & who will give you particular information of the Situation in which he leaves our affairs here, & of the important circumstances belonging to the present critical state of European politics."

RC (DNA: RG 59, DD, Spain, vol. 10). 3 pp.; docketed by Wagner.

From Dolley Madison

MY DEAREST HUSBAND,   26th. of October 1805.

Peter returned safe, with your letter,[1] and cheared me with a favorable account of your prospect of getting home in the stage. I was sorry you could not ride further in our carriage, as you would have felt less fatigue. In my dreams of last night, I saw you in your chamber, unable to move, from riding so far and so fast. I pray that an early letter from you may chase away the painful impression of this vision. I am still improving and shall observe strictly, what you say on the subject of the Doctor's precepts, he has given me no new instructions. Betsey sends you love and kisses in *return*, with "a word to Cousin Isaac."

28th. I have the letters this moment which you enclosed at Washington, I rejoice to find you there and I see that you can write—shall now expect the next post with impatience, by that you will speak of yourself. The Marquis and Marchoness came to see me yesterday, with several other ladies. I am getting well as fast as I can, for I have the reward in view of seeing my beloved, when I do. Please enclose Mamma's letter with those of the other friends you will send me tomorrow. Anna's was dated on the 14th. before she received my last, I have every reason to expect her the end of this week. Tell me if Mrs. Randolph is expected and all the other news, you shall have time and patience to give me. I have written you every day since we parted, but am so shut up that I can say nothing to amuse, when I begin to ride, shall become a more interesting correspondant. Doctor Physic has had a letter from Mrs. Merry at Baltimore, written in great gaity. Did you see the Bishop or engage a place for Payne?

Farewell, until tomorrow, my best friend! think of thy wife! who thinks and dreams of thee!

D.

Tr (owned by Mrs. George B. Cutts, Wellesley, Mass., 1982).

1. This letter has not been found.

From James Monroe

DEAR SIR   LONDON Octr 26. 1805.

You will receive within a copy of a note recd. yesterday evening from Mr. OReilly of Phila., of certain reports in circulation yesterday at the exchange.[1] That with respect to the Prussian minister has been confirm'd in the gazettes of this morning, tho' no notice is taken in them of that wh. more particularly regards us. I send so much of the Chronicle as respects publick concerns.[2] No allusion of the kind was made me yesterday by Mr. Hammond, tho' as our conversation was lengthy an opportunity was furnished for it. If the report is true the prospect with respect to Prussia has confirmed them in the policy, if indeed it has not long since been decided on. I shall be able to inform you more correctly in a few days by the Bristol Packet an American ship wh. sails for N. York.[3] Mr. Hammond mentioned to me an interesting circumstance wh. he said had an irritating tendency. Admiral Collingwood had taken a dispatch of Yrujo to his govt. from an american vessel, stating a proposition from commodore Truxton accompanied with a plan for taking the Island of Jamaica, in which he informed him that he had certain plans of the fortifications &ca of the Island, wh. had been given him by admiral Parker, wh. wod. be or were at the ministers service. He shewed me the dispatch in spanish, wh. as I read that lang[u]age imperfectly, & the room was dark, I do not state on that evidence but give it only on Mr. Hammonds report to me. I will send you by the Bristol packet a copy of a late pamphlet called "war in disguise" alluding to neutral trade, wh. advises direct war on us in pretty plain terms.[4] It is said to be a ministerial work, or rather under its auspices. How truly will soon be seen. Yr. friend & servt.

JAS. MONROE.

RC (DLC: Rives Collection, Madison Papers); enclosure (DNA: RG 59, DD, Great Britain, vol. 12). Cover sheet marked "private" by Monroe. For enclosure, see n. 1.

1. Monroe enclosed a 25 Oct. 1805 letter from Thomas O'Reilly at St. Paul's Coffee House (1 p.; docketed by Wagner as received in Monroe's dispatch No. 35 of 18 Oct. 1805), stating that "official notification" from the Prussian minister had been sent to Lloyd's Coffee

House "importing that no Prussian Vessel would be safe in the Ports of France or Holland" and adding that there was a rumor on the Exchange that orders had been issued that day from the Admiralty that British cruisers were to detain all neutral vessels bound to enemy ports. O'Reilly added that a 15 Sept. 1805 letter received the previous day from Moses Young said that Charles Pinckney was still at Madrid but said nothing about George W. Erving's arrival.

2. The London *Morning Chronicle*, 26 Oct. 1805, said that Baron Jacobi-Kloest had told Mr. Freydag, the Prussian consul at London, to instruct all Prussian ships there "not to clear out for any French or Dutch ports." The paper speculated that this meant Prussia would soon be joining the coalition against France, which could strengthen it to such a degree as to bring about the defeat of Napoleon. The rest of the article contained news of the movements of various nobles, kings, and generals throughout Europe. Monroe may also have included other articles from Berlin, reporting Frederick William III's actions, and from Portugal, describing ship movements there and at Madeira.

3. The *Bristol Packet* of Boston arrived at New York on 10 Jan. 1806 (*New-York Commercial Advertiser*, 11 Jan. 1806).

4. James Stephen wrote *War in Disguise; or, The Frauds of the Neutral Flags* (London, 1805) at the behest of the ministry. It urged the British government to end the neutral trade with Europe (William M. Sloane, "The Continental System of Napoleon," *Political Science Quarterly* 13 [1898]: 219).

§ From Peter Kuhn Jr. *27 October 1805, Genoa*. "The present serves to convey you the Bulletins Nos 10 & 11 of the Grand Army of France,[1] which has been addressed to his Serene Highness the Arch Treasurer of the Empire of France by expresses of last night & this afternoon from the French Emperor.

"Genl. Massina has crossed the Adige and arrived at Vicenza without penetrating further.

"The Circuitious rout of Bordeaux, which is preferable, (to that of Leghorn) by which I forward my letters makes me diffident in Communicating the political events which occur in this quarter upon the supposition that you receive Sir the same information much earlier from the Consuls at more approximate ports to the United States, to whom certain oppertunities offer.

"The Mail being upon the eve of Closing, I beg leave to refer you Sir to my Next for a translation of the decree of the Arch-Treasurer relative to the Conduction of the Porto Franco of Genoa."

RC (DNA: RG 59, CD, Genoa, vol. 1). 2 pp. In a clerk's hand, except for Kuhn's complimentary close and signature.

1. The Tenth Bulletin, issued at Augsburg on 22 Oct. 1805, listed the military supplies captured and number of prisoners taken when Gen. Joachim Murat defeated the armies of Gen. Franz von Werneck and Archduke Ferdinand Karl Joseph of Austria-Este. Werneck surrendered, but the archduke escaped. The Eleventh Bulletin, printed in the 1 Nov. 1805 *Moniteur universel*, announced the arrival of Napoleon at Munich on 24 Oct. and his praise of the French troops who left untouched 200,000 guilders they had found in order to pursue the Austrians; mentioned that escaped Austrian soldiers in Franconia had "occasioned great disorder"; that all the Austrian baggage was seized; and added that the Grande Armée was "in full march for the Inn" (*Cobbett's Weekly Political Register* 8 [1805]: 726–28, 791).

To Dolley Madison

My dearest,   Washington Octr. 28. 1805
I reached the end of my journey on Saturday evening; without accident and in good health. I found your friends here all well. Payne arrived about an hour after I did. I inclose a letter from him, with several others. During my halt at Baltimore, I made two efforts to see Bishop Carroll, but without success. Genl. Smith had not returned to Town from his Country Seat. I could do nothing therefore towards getting a birth for Payne in the seminary of Mr. Dubourg.[1] I have lost no time however in making an attempt for the purpose, by a request which is gone in a letter to Bishop Carroll, and if his answer authorizes me, I shall take immediate steps for preventing any further loss of time. Docr. Willis has signified to Gooch that he wishes if we should not load the waggon ourselves on its return from Washington, to provide a conveyance for some of his furniture, and will with that view contribute a pair of Horses to the Team. May I not assent to this arrangement, without inconvenience to our own plans? Let me know as soon as possible. The Yellow Woman of Docr W. has applied to me for a passage in the Waggon, and I have given her to understand that there would probably be no objection to it.[2] Docr. & Miss Park had before my arrival gone to Alexa. They are to return hither tomorrow. I hope you did not fail to execute my commission as to Miss P. I had the pleasure of dining yesterday with Cousin Isaac at the Presidents, and can venture to say that——.[3]

Present my best respects to Dr. Physic, and let me know that I shall soon have you with me, which is most anxiously desired by your ever affectionate

J. Madison

This is the first mail that has been closed since my arrival.

RC offered for sale by Early American History Auctions, Inc., 10 June 2000, item A024317; Tr (owned by Mrs. George B. Cutts, Wellesley, Mass., 1982). Cover sheet addressed to "Mrs. Madison at Mrs. Woods Market near 8th Street Philada."

1. Louis Guillaume Valentin Dubourg (1766–1833) was born at Saint-Domingue but was sent to his grandparents at Bordeaux when he was two. He was educated in France and ordained in 1790. Forced to leave after the French Revolution, he arrived in Baltimore in 1794, where he joined the Sulpicians of St. Mary's Seminary. In 1796 he was named president of Georgetown College, a post he held for two years. He founded St. Mary's College in 1805 and served as its head until 1812, when Archbishop John Carroll named him Administrator Apostolic of New Orleans, where he was opposed by Father Antoine de Sedella. In 1815 he went to Rome to enlist more clergy and religious for the diocese, and while there he was ordained bishop. He returned to the United States in 1817 and went to live at St. Louis because of the opposition of Sedella and his followers. Dubourg returned to New Orleans in 1820, but five years later he again encountered disaffection among the clergy

and resigned. The following year he returned to France, where he was named bishop of Montauban and later Besançon (Conrad, *Dictionary of Louisiana Biography*, 1:257–58).

2. The preceding sentence is omitted from the Tr.

3. Left blank in RC.

From John G. Jackson

DR. SIR.   CLARKSBURG 28th. Octr. 1805

I have paid considerable attention to the land memo. of Mr. Lovell[1] & had supposed I should be enabled ere this to state explicitly my opinion which however I have deferred until a survey of the land is made by a person now doing that business—at first I supposed that from the investigation I made the land was Sold for taxes, & not redeemed in time; that fact is somewhat doubtful & can only be confirmed either way by recurrence to the direct tax books now at Richmond—Independant of this difficulty I have been informed tho' not in a way which makes it decisive that the land was not worth any thing; it is certainly in the neighborhood of extreme bad land, & to ascertain its value is what the survey was directed for—the desire of making this enquiry a preliminary step to perfecting the title to Mr. L—relatives, was guided by a regard to economy & the interests of those persons—when we meet, I shall be able to decide what I would recommend to be done. I had oft times intended writing to you during the past Summer; but as I could only have given an account of domestic & agricultural concerns, & I know your important public engagements do not even give you time to peruse the communications of your private correspondents, I denied myself the pleasure. Mrs. J joins me in assurances of the highest regard for yourself and our dear Sister. Your mo. obt Servt.

J G JACKSON

PS Mrs. M has informed us that the Lisbon wine has arrived at W. I shall be prepared when we meet to pay the price & charges on it—& to crack a Bottle of it with you.

JGJ

RC (DLC). Docketed by JM.

1. For James Lovell's land issues, see *PJM-SS*, 9:297, 298 n. 3, 318.

§ From George W. Erving. *28 October 1805, Madrid.* "*Private No 1.*" "I wrote to you officially from the Escurial on the 25th Inst by Mr Pinckney, who left that place on his way home on the 26th., merely to inform you of my arrival & introduction;

Mr Pinckney had Expected me, but a ship being at Lisbon on the point of departure, he feared that if he delayed his journey thither he might lose his passage in
that Vessel, & had therefore concluded to introduce Mr Young as chargé d'affaires
for the interim. The Conversation which passed with Don Pedro Cevallos did not
appear sufficiently important to be detailed in the public letter; yet as he evidently
intended that we shoud understand his reception of us to be marked with peculiar
attention, & as it has been since intimated to me that the Prince of peace has some
conciliatory dispositions towards us, it may be proper that you shoud be more particularly informed of it.

"After Mr Pinckney had introduced me & expressed his intention of going, I
presented your letter; Don Pedro said that he was happy to receive & shoud at all
times be ready to Enter into communication with me, that I shoud always find in
him the most friendly dispositions, & a sincere desire to preserve the best intelligence: this was the substance. His Expressions were a little more amplified: I
acknowledged his politeness, & added that if it conformed to the Etiquette I shoud
be happy in having the honor of being presented to his Majesty in such form as
might be suitable, & whenever he might judge proper. He observed that the form of
presentation for persons in my situation differed from that of Ministers Plenipotentiary, that I coud not be introduced at the "circle" but might be at the Dinner; that
he woud speak to the king & arrange it, & woud further procure permission that I
shoud be *presented to the Queen*,[1] which he gave us to understand is uncustomary;
how far it is so, & what degree of consideration this act of politeness merits I have
not yet been able to ascertain: To Mr Pinckney he said at parting, that he shoud be
always happy either in his public or individual character to render him Every service possible. All this perhaps was the mere unmeaning language of a courtier, yet
considering it in connection with the present situation of European Affairs, &
more particularly with certain dispositions which are said to have existed here for
some time past, & which the little I have as yet been able to learn tends to convince
me do in fact Exist, it affords some hope that they look to a means of accommodation. The disposition to which I allude, more particularly those *of the Prince of Peace
are to throw off[f] the French yoke on the first favorable occasion*. This was first intimated
to Mr Monroe & myself by the Swedish Minister in London, & the communication
was made to him *his colleague here who has been lately*[2] *raised to the rank of a Minister*[3]
Plenipoy. This Opinion derives force from the *appointment*[4] *made* by *Russia of an
Embassador*[5] *whom* I *left* in *London where he Staid* a considerable time and *who* has
now *arrived at Lisbon* in *his way hither*. The measures which our government will
probably take, must I am persuaded by rousing them into a true sense of their
danger, & by correcting the false impressions which have been given by their minister Yruco, tend very much to promote this disposition: It cannot be beleived that
if left to themselves they shoud be so blind to their own interests & the peril of
their situation as to persevere in the absurd pretensions which they have set up:
Their means of coping with us at any time are not very great, & they have now
absolutely none: However splendid the first Efforts of their Ally may be, & however decisive his ultimate success; the utmost may be Expected from his vast powers & from the Energy & Enterprize of his character, yet there can be no doubt
but that the present contest will demand all his attention & occupy all his resources for a long time to come.

"There is a report here that the President has summoned Congress to an extraordinary session, & Mr Pinckney was of opinion that it had produced considerable Effect. The King & Queen received us with much affability⟨;⟩ Mr Pinckney addressed to Each of them a neat speech conformable to the sentiments which as I understood him he was instructed to deliver; He said that in taking leave he was directed by the President to Express to them the high regard which he Entertained for them, & for their illustrious family, & his best wishes for the prosperity of the Spanish Empire. Their Majesties were not prepared with any answer, but appeared to be pleased with the address.

"On my return to Madrid I received from Mr Young your letters of March 18.[6] & that to Mr Monroe of May 4th[7] the former partly in cypher. The papers of the legation have been from time to time delivered to Mr Young & mixed with the consular & agency papers, so that he has not hitherto been able to seperate & deliver over such as may be necessary or useful to me, nor has he yet been able to lay his hand on the Cypher; That which I have used in this letter is Mr Monroes."

Adds in a 29 Oct. postscript: "I called yesterday on all the foreign Ministers. Genl Bournonville speaking of Mr. Monroe professed the highest respect for him. This indeed the others did, but he is the only one who mentioned particularly the late Negotiations: he said, that he had Endeavoured *to assist*[8] him as much as possible & to promote the object of his mission: but that the parties were so "Eloigné"![9] The US demanded *so much*[10] & the Spanish govt woud give so *little*,[11] that he found it impossible to bring them together. You are already informed of the facts; yesterday the news arrived of the Entire defeat of the combined fleets by the English.[12]

"Mr Young informs me that he has searched Every where for the Cypher without success. What is Equally unfortunate the Correspondence of the late special Mission cannot be found. In hopes that a letter may overtake Mr Pinckney at Lisbon I write to him upon these subjects, & shall also write to Mr Bowdoin who will probably be at Paris soon to procure from Genl Armstrong a copy of the Correspondence."

RC (PHi: Miscellaneous Collection). 6 pp.; docketed by Wagner as received 27 Jan. 1806. Italicized words are in code, except as noted; decoded interlinearly by Wagner, and decoded here, with punctuation added, by the editors (for the code, see *PJM-SS*, 4:352 n. 1).

1. Underlined by Erving.
2. Underlined by Erving.
3. Encoded "opportunity"; decoded "Minister."
4. Encoded "aprilointment"; decoded "appointment."
5. Coded word underlined by Erving.
6. *PJM-SS*, 9:143–46.
7. Ibid., 319.
8. Underlined by Erving.
9. *Eloigné:* far apart.
10. Underlined by Erving.
11. Underlined by Erving.
12. On 21 Oct. 1805 the combined French and Spanish fleets were destroyed off Cape Trafalgar by the British fleet under Lord Horatio Nelson, who was killed in the battle (David G. Chandler, *Dictionary of the Napoleonic Wars* [New York, 1979], 448–50).

§ From Frederick Jacob Wichelhausen. *28 October 1805, Bremen.* "I had the honor to write to you on the 9th July. and have now the pleasure to acknowledge receipt of your high esteemed favor of the 13th May[1] the contents of it, I find partly answered by my letters of the 20th. March[2] and 9th. of July. In compliance with my duty I have immediately on the receipt of your instructions given me in the above mentioned letter, wrote again to the Governments of Oldenburg and Bremen, and communicated to them the contents of yours which solely concerns the quarantaine measures adopted in this Country against vessels coming from the United States; I at the same time inclosed them a copy and translation of the circular letter directed in July 1801, to the respective Collectors of the Custom,[3] in the United States, adding such remarks which I considered most expedient to procure my applications a more certain access. I received immediately a provisional answer from both Governments wherein they acknowledge the receipt of mine, and that they would not fail to communicate to me in a short time, the result of their deliberations on the subject.

"The Senate of Bremen, who from the beginning has evinced a most extraordinary fear about importing the yellow fever in this Country, begins now to feel the inconvenience of its own councils given that time to the Government of Oldenburg, however it being entirely out of its power to make any alteration in the quarantaine laws published by said Government it has likewise wrote to Oldenburg on the subject to solicit a moderation. Mr. Mentz, who is at the head of the quarantaine commission at Oldenburg and with whom I entertain a regular correspondence is rather of a fearful dispositi(on) and having applied since a year the greatest part of his time to inform himself about the nature and qualities of this dreadful malady called the yellow fever, his fear has constantly increased, and he at present perceives danger, where really no danger exists. As in my abovementioned letter to him, I insisted on it, to have its contents communicated to his serene Highness the Duke, & I have now, by his order, received a long and circumstancial report, wherein they vindicate their conduct in regard to vessels coming from the United States. As this letter is in my opinion written with much knowledge and penetration, and may, in future, when some new regulations are thought necessary to be adopted in the different Seaports of the United States, it may perhaps be serviceable, I thought it advisable to transmit you a faithful translation thereof, which I have the honor to enclose herewith.[4]

"I likewise inclose you herein copy of a protest made before me, by an American Sailor,[5] who escaped from on board an english frigate and saved himself on board the Ship Mary of Charleston, Capt. Fuller, bound from Charleston to the Jahde and ordered to Christiansand for quarantaine; I have furnished this boy with the necessary clothing and returned him to America on board the abovementioned Ship Mary bound for Charleston.

"As the french troops have redrawn from the Shores of the Elbe and Weser, the blockade of these Rivers, which has lasted upwards of two years, has been raised again; this agreeable news has been officially notified to the Senate of this City by its commercial Agent in London, and by the british Minister in Hamburg Edwd. Thornton Esqre.

"It will be known to you some time, that the War on the Continent has at last broke out again, and that hostilities have actually taken place in the Circles of

Bavaria and Swabia between the french and austrian troops; the reports of those engagements are so various and contradictory, that it is very difficult to form a true judgment about them; however agreeable to some official accounts received here by the french Commissary, it appears, the french have been victorious in several engagements.

"The last accounts received here by an express, mention of Ulm being surrendered to the french, whereby they made 34,000 Prisoners of War, amongst whom 36 Generals and the Commander in Chief General Mack himself, this great news however wants still a further confirmation.

"At Straubingen the first russian army consisting of 45,000 men have joined an austrian column of 25,000 men under General Kienmayer, and the report says that also an engagement had taken place there between this combined army and those commanded by Generals Marmont and Bernadotte, wherein the Austrians have been victorious. General Marmont should have been killed and General Bernadotte with 4000 men taken prisoners. The russian troops disembarked in Pomerania are marching in conjunction with the Swedes through Mecklenburg and the advance guard is arrived already on the 25th Inst. at the frontier of Hannover.

"General Barbon, who is commander in chief of the remaining french troops in Hannover, left that City on the 25th. Instant with all his troops and went to Hameln, which place is strongly fortified and provisioned for one year. A news of the greatest importance and which is authentic, is, the arrival of the Emperor Alexander at Berlin on the 23rd Inst. and that very little doubt is entertained of Prussia's taking an active part in this War, as it has delivered a very severe and energetic note to the french ministers in Berlin Laforest, and General Duroc, respecting the march of the french and bavarian troops through its dominions in the circle of Franconia. Should any thing further occur, concerning the continental war, in this neighbourhood, which may be interesting to you, I shall avail myself of every opportunity that offers to communicate you the same."

RC and enclosures (DNA: RG 59, CD, Bremen, vol. 1). RC 4 pp.; docketed by Wagner. For enclosures, see nn. 4–5.

1. See JM to John Armstrong, James Bowdoin, and James Monroe, *PJM-SS*, 9:344–45 and n.

2. Ibid., 160–63.

3. For the 15 July 1801 Treasury Department circular to the collectors of customs, see Albert Gallatin to JM, ca. 1 July and 22 July 1801, ibid., 1:366–67, 453–54 and n. 1.

4. The enclosure (5 pp.) is a translation of an 11 Oct. 1805 letter from Holstein and Oldenburg chamberlain C. F. Mentz replying to Wichelhausen's 20 Aug. 1805 letter requesting an alteration in the strict quarantine regulations. Mentz stated that although the earlier regulations had been based on what was known of the yellow fever in 1801, namely, that contagion of the fever was based on personal contact, now that it was scientifically believed that the "venom" of the disease could also live in "infectible" commodities for up to a year, newer, stricter regulations were required. He pointed out that cargoes often came from North American ports without any official attestation as to whether they were the produce of healthy areas surrounding the ports or of suspicious West Indian islands. He noted that if infectible goods from the West Indies, especially such dangerous goods as cotton and rawhides, were quarantined in the United States, it would lessen northern European suspicions of them, but they had never seen certification of any such quarantine.

He denied the accusation that whenever a few areas of the extensive territory of the United States were infected, the whole seacoast was considered infected; his country's laws carefully differentiated between such areas. He also noted that on the long voyage from North America to Europe, and with the large number of cruisers and merchantmen abroad on the ocean, it was almost impossible to avoid contact with infected or suspicious ships, adding that for the past year all English ships coming from the Jamaica station "certainly or most probably" had yellow fever on board. Mentz stated that the six- to eight-day quarantine and careful inquiry about persons aboard ship were now standard in northern Europe, but the inquiries could be lengthened by the thoughtless answers of some crews to their questions. In view of all this, the duke had not seen fit to make any alteration in the 12 Mar. 1805 quarantine regulations. He had, however, in view of the accounts of the state of health at New Orleans, Savannah, and Charleston, declared that ships coming from those places with non-infectible cargoes should be admitted after examination and a modified quarantine and need no longer go to Christiansand for quarantine after showing papers stating that until the end of August no further traces of yellow fever had been seen in those ports.

5. The enclosure (2 pp.) is the 10 Oct. 1805 deposition of seaman William Cochlin that he was born in Great Choptank, Maryland, about 1785; that he had sailed from Alexandria, Virginia, to Boston in 1803, where he had received a protection from the collector at Salem. In June 1805 he had joined the schooner *Lucy*, Capt. Jonathan Smith, bound for Copenhagen. In late July, north of Fair Isle, Scotland, he and Samuel Warey of Alexandria were impressed into the *Adolphus*, Captain Downs. About six weeks after Warey drowned himself on 1 Aug., sooner than be flogged, Cochlin jumped overboard in a Norwegian harbor and swam to an island where he was picked up by a fishing boat that brought him to Christiansand. There Capt. Gilbert Fuller of the ship *Mary* of Charleston took him on board and brought him to the Jahde. The deposition was sworn to by Fuller and Capt. Eliakin Gardner of the *Lovely Nan* of Baltimore, and sealed and certified by Wichelhausen. The *Mary* arrived in Charleston harbor on 17 Jan. 1806 (*New-York Commercial Advertiser*, 1 Feb. 1806).

From John Carroll

HONORABLE AND DEAR SIR,   BALTIMORE October 29th. 1805

I was very much concerned at my absence from home, when you did me the honor of a visit. Though it was late when I returned, I went to Bryden's[1] in hopes of finding you there, but understood at the bar that you had not put up there, and feared, as it was nine o'clock, intruding on the repose of a wearied traveller, if I had sought you elsewhere. I had spent the afternoon with Mr. Carroll of Carrollton, who was then here and would have been happy to see you, if he had known of your being in Baltimore. I am sollicitous to know, that Mrs. Madison has returned to the city in perfect health, and have often anxiously enquired of her during your residence in and near Philadelphia. Mr. Dubourg will assuredly have a place ready to receive Mrs. Madison's son in a month from this date, and perhaps sooner. On the first mention of your request, he said it was impossible, there being above twenty on the list for admission, whom he could not accomodate. I urged, in behalf of your son in law,[2] a claim, which has been mentioned

478

heretofore in my presence, tho' perhaps an unfounded one, but of which I made use; that Mrs. Madison had bespoken a place a year ago, and perhaps more. Mr. Dubourg then said, that such being the case, he would certainly make a proper provision within the time above mentioned. He could not furnish me with a copy of his regulations; they are out of print; but he promised to have them reprinted immediately, when I will have the honor of transmitting one to you. In the meantime, you may obtain every necessary information, and perhaps a printed prospectus from Mr. Brent, the mayor of Washington.[3] On this and every other occasion, I shall be happy to execute your commissions, without considering them as any interruption to other business; and therefore hope you will often enable me to prove my attachment and esteem. I beg Mrs. Madison to accept the tender of my respectful wishes for her health and happiness. With the same sentiments I have the honor to be dear Sir, your most obedient servant

J. CARROLL.[4]

Tr (owned by Mrs. George B. Cutts, Wellesley, Mass., 1982).

1. Scottish native James Bryden (ca. 1762–1820) operated the Fountain Inn in Baltimore from 1795 until he leased it to John H. Barney in 1808 in order to move to New York, where he leased and operated the Tontine Coffee House. In 1812 he leased and operated the Greenwich Hotel two miles north of New York City. He later returned to Baltimore, where he died on 11 Apr. 1820 (*Federal Intelligencer, and Baltimore Daily Gazette*, 16 Sept. 1795; Baltimore *North American and Mercantile Daily Advertiser*, 1 Mar. 1808; New York *American Citizen*, 30 Apr. 1808; New York *Columbian*, 2 May 1812; *Baltimore Patriot & Mercantile Advertiser*, 12 Apr. 1820).

2. JM's stepson, John Payne Todd.

3. Robert Brent (1764–1819), the first mayor of Washington City, was John Carroll's nephew. Brent was appointed mayor by Jefferson in 1802 and was reappointed to the non-salaried post by both Jefferson and JM through 1812. He also served as justice of the peace for the District of Columbia from 1801 to at least 1817, was judge of the district's Orphan's Court from 1806 to 1814, and paymaster of the army from 1808 to shortly before his death in September 1819. He was also the first president of the Patriotic Bank (*PJM-PS*, 1:193 n. 1; James Dudley Morgan, "Robert Brent, First Mayor of Washington City," *Records of the Columbia Historical Society* 2 [1899]: 236, 243–44, 247).

4. John Carroll (1735–1815) was born in Maryland and educated at an English college in France. In 1753 he entered the Jesuit novitiate at Watten, France, and was ordained into the Society of Jesus at Liège in either 1767 or 1769. After the suppression of the Society in 1773, he lived in England before returning to America in 1774, where he lived quietly except for a brief trip to Canada with the American commissioners in 1776. In 1783 he joined in agitation for a reform of the American Catholic Church, was named prefect-apostolic shortly thereafter, and was consecrated bishop in 1790. He was raised to archbishop in 1808. Carroll was particularly interested in education and encouraged the establishment of several secondary schools and colleges. He supported JM's administration during the War of 1812.

From George Jefferson

Dear Sir   Richmond 29th. Octr. 1805

The season being so far advanced that we may shortly expect the new crop of Tobacco to be coming in, which may have an unfavorable effect upon our market—and supposing too from the length of time your last crop has been kept on hand, that you were probably getting impatient to have it sold—I to day concluded to make sale of it to Pickett Pollard & Johnston[1] at 6. ¼ $ for their draft on New York at 60 days.

I should have preferred a note payable here, which could be discounted at the Bank, but could not effect a sale in that way.

I have at times had hopes of being able to do better with your Tobacco, and am sorry that I could not. I am Very respectfully Dear Sir Yr. Mt. Obt. servt.[2]

Geo. Jefferson

RC and enclosure (DLC). For enclosure, see n. 2.

1. Pickett, Pollard & Johnston was a Richmond merchant firm belonging to partners George Pickett, Robert Pollard (d. 1842), who was a member of the Richmond Committee of Vigilance during the War of 1812, and Charles Johnston, who was later the president of the Farmers' Bank in Lynchburg. The firm also dealt in Western lands (Samuel Mordecai, *Virginia, Especially Richmond, in By-Gone Days; With a Glance at the Present,* 2d ed. [Richmond, Va., 1860], 94, 97; "The Vigilance Committee: Richmond during the War of 1812," *VMHB* 7 [1900]: 225, 229–30, 241).

2. Jefferson enclosed an account (1 p.) for the sale of twelve hogsheads of tobacco totaling 16,201 pounds at $6.25 per pound for a total of $1,012.56, from which he deducted his two- and-one-half-percent commission and $13.33 in tobacco inspection charges paid on 15 May; $182.00 paid for half a ton of coal on Sept. 30; and $3.42 in interest charges, leaving $788.50 due to JM.

§ To George Hay. *29 October 1805, Department of State.* "In answer to your letter of the 23d: inst. [not found] I have to state that passports or sea letters were at no time in the year 1796 withheld from our Vessels by the Government. How far the inability alleges [*sic*] of procuring one from the Custom House at Norfolk may have been produced by a casual defect of those documents in the hands of the Collector may be judged from the enclosed letter of Mr. Jones, the Chief Clerk in the Office of the Secretary of the Treasury, whence the Sea letters are distributed among the Collectors."

Letterbook copy (DNA: RG 59, DL, vol. 15). 1 p.

§ From William Jarvis. *29 October 1805, Lisbon.* "A British frigate sent to England with despatches, in passing this port last evening, communicated the following information to the British Minister; that the french & Spanish fleet to the number of 33 sail of the line, put to sea from Cadiz for the purpose of engaging the

British Blockading Squadron consisting of 27 sail of the line. The Battle took place the 21st. Inst 7 leagues S.S.E. of Cadiz, which was very severe and terminated in favour of the British, who captured 18 French & Spanish Men of War, sunk one & another was blown up. The other 13 got into Cadiz. In the course of two days two of the captured Ships sunk. Among the captured was the French Admirals ship with Admiral Villeneuve on board.[1] Three of the English fleet were dismasted & most of them much shattered. Lord Nelson was Killed in the Engagement."

RC (DNA: RG 59, CD, Lisbon, vol. 2). 1 p.; docketed by Wagner. Cover marked "⊕ Schr. Antelope Captn. Pittman Via New York." The *Antelope* arrived at New York on 30 Dec. 1805 after a voyage of fifty-nine days (*New-York Price-Current*, 4 Jan. 1806).

1. Vice Adm. Pierre-Charles-Jean-Baptiste-Silvestre de Villeneuve (d. 1806) was carried to England, where he lived for about six months with Henry Addington, Viscount Sidmouth. He was exchanged for four British captains in April 1806 and returned to France where, a few days later, it was reported that he had committed suicide by stabbing himself several times (Roy Adkins, *Nelson's Trafalgar: The Battle That Changed the World* [New York, 2005], 322–23).

§ From William Lee. *29 October 1805, Bordeaux.* "I had the pleasure of addressing you on the 18th giving you a short sketch of the movements of the French Army in Germany. Since then the accounts have been so contradictory, that it has been impossible to come at facts. For several days past we have been led to believe that the French had received a great check, were retreating in confusion, that the Emperor had been wounded and Prince Murat killed. The silence of the moniteur confirmed in a measure these reports, and the public mind has been in consequence greatly agitated and confidence destroyed to a degree that can only be credited by those who are accustomed to these vibrations of public sentiment.

"The people have this morning been relieved from this distressing suspense by the arrival of a Courier who brings intelligence of a very decisive victory, having been gained by the French over the Austrians before Ulm. The particulars of this battle have not yet been published, and I can only learn that the austrians having concentrated nearly all their forces at Ulm, the Emperor surrounded them with the main body of his Army, and after a more obstinate and bloody battle, than ever has been fought during the Revolution, completely defeated them, taking twenty thousand prisoners and Seventeen General Officers among whom is General Mack. It is said that the Emperor refused to receive the sword of Genl Mack, telling him he was at liberty to return home to his master whom he expected to meet in Vienna, in the course of a few months. This battle is said to have taken place on the 14 inst. at the same moment that Marshal Soult gained a decisive victory over a body of the austrian(s) at Memminghen taking six thousand prisoners and while Prince Murat attaked the rear Guard of a body of twenty thousand men who had escaped from Ulm under the command of Prince Ferdinand and made three thousand, prisoners. These several victories have cost the French sixteen thousand men, and notwithstanding they appear so decissive still they have not had that effect in restoring public confidence that one would imagine. The distress of all classes of people is daily increasing and Commercial credit is totally destroyed. We have various reports concerning the armies of Italy but nothing

Official. It is thought that the austrians will have to abandon the Tirol, and that the Emperors plan is to leave for a moment Vienna on his left in order to form a junction with the army of Italy, when he will proceed on toward that Capital. We hear nothing of the Russians and are kept much in the dark respecting the intention of the King of Prussia."

Adds in a postscript: "By the arrival of an american Gentleman from Paris I have just learnt that Genl. Armstrong is very dangerously ill."[1]

RC (DNA: RG 59, CD, Bordeaux, vol. 2). 3 pp.

1. John Armstrong's health was poor for much of the time he was in France. He suffered from rheumatism, malarial fever, and several other ailments (Skeen, *John Armstrong*, 58).

§ From Carlos Martínez de Yrujo. *29 October 1805, "Near Philadelphia."* Because some Spanish privateers have detained several ships that seemed to be American and taken them to Spanish ports, the United States minister in Madrid has made several complaints on the subject; the ministry of state having informed the ministry of marine about them, some of the said vessels have been set at liberty and others are pursuing their cases in the admiralty courts according to the privateer ordinance, the treaty existing between the two nations, and the laws on the subject.

To this end, it has been observed that some American ships were sailing without a passport, contrary to the arrangement in article 17 of the treaty between the two countries, and since this circumstance could have provided scope for the detention of some of the American ships about which minister Pinckney has complained, the king has commanded that information be given about it, which has been done by the first secretary of state, so that this government might be notified of it with the goal of warning American captains not to omit carrying the said passport with them in order to avoid the repetition of such detentions.

He has the honor to communicate this decision to JM, so that JM might see with satisfaction the right intentions and disposition of the king to avoid further reasons for complaints on the part of the United States, like those which minister Pinckney has lately made on this point.

RC (DNA: RG 59, NFL, Spain, vol. 2). 3 pp.; in Spanish; in a clerk's hand, except for Yrujo's complimentary close and signature.

From Dolley Madison

30th. October 1805 PHILA.

I have this moment perused with delight thy letter,[1] my darling, with its enclosures—to find you love me, have my child safe and that my mother is well, seems to comprise all my happiness. You consult me on the subject of Dr. Willis's request, which I should assuredly comply with. I do not know as yet what we have to send home, but I shall be ever desirous to oblige Nelly and every other of our connexions. The knee is acquiring strength every day but my nerves are often weak—the Doctor ordered me some drops yesterday which I took—he also directed me to eat meat and drink porter, I take but a morsel of either, having no appetite. I walk about the room and expect a few days more will enable me to ride, no inflamation and the little incission nearly fast, so that you may expect me to fly to you as soon—ah! I wish I could say how soon! I had a visit from Mr. Lewis yesterday, who repeated most pressingly his wife's invitation. I gave him the reason I had in store for resisting the many temptations held out for my removal to their house.

Madam Pichon writes me an affectionate letter and begs me to accept a pair of earrings for her sake, I suppose you may have them if they are not with the letter. I am punctual in delivering to Betsey your commands she insists on adding a postcript to this which I am not to see, but she must go home to dinner and I must not miss the post. You will continue to write me and say whether you get all mine—adieu, my beloved

your DOLLEY.

Tr (owned by Mrs. George B. Cutts, Wellesley, Mass., 1982).

1. JM to Dolley Madison, 28 Oct. 1805.

§ From William C. C. Claiborne. *30 October 1805, New Orleans.* "I enclose for your perusal and information copies of several Depositions which have been forwarded to me, by Doctor Sibley; These documents prove the establishment of a Garrison on the Trinity River, & state the particulars of several outrages committed on the Citizens of the United States by Persons in the Employ of the Spanish Government. I shall not fail to make suitable Representations on this Subject, to the Marquis of Casa Calvo, and to the Governor General of the Province of Taxus; but it is not probable that adequate redress will be offer'ed for the Injury done."[1]

RC (DNA: RG 59, TP, Orleans, vol. 7); letterbook copy (Ms-Ar: Claiborne Executive Journal, vol. 15). RC 1 p.; in a clerk's hand, signed by Claiborne; docketed by Wagner as received 3 Dec. 1805, with his note: "Same day gave the enclosures to the Secy. of War."

1. The enclosures have not been found, but on the same day Claiborne wrote Henry Dearborn that two hundred men, most of whom were cavalry, were stationed at a fort that had been built on the Trinity River (Rowland, *Claiborne Letter Books*, 3:216–17).

§ From James Maury. *30 October 1805, Liverpool.* "I had this honor on the 22d. August. The sickness of the Clerk, who assists me in my Consular office, has occasioned a considerable delay in the table of imports & exports for the first six months of this year. I now have the honor to lay it before you, as also a price current for the produce and exports of the United States."

RC (DNA: RG 59, CD, Liverpool, vol. 2). 1 p.; in a clerk's hand; signed by Maury. Enclosures not found.

To Dolley Madison

WASHINGTON Oct. 31. [1805]

Your second letter my dearest, of the 26. continued on the 28. is this moment recd; and flatters my anxious wishes & hopes for your perfect recovery, and your *safe* return to Washington. I am glad to find you so determined in your adherence to the Drs. prescriptions. Be assured that he will give none that are not indispensable, & that you will not rejoice in having strictly observed.

I had not the pleasure of seeing Dr. P. & his daugh⟨ter⟩ till this morning. They intended to set out for Philada. this afternoon. I had therefore no opportuny of shewing them some attentions which I wished. They will tell their own story of Washington, the Races &c. Mrs. Randolph is expected by the Presidt. but he does not consider her coming as absolutely certain.[1] My last informed you that I had written to Bishop Carrol with respect to Payne. He was so good as to lose not a moment in attending to the contents of it. I inclose his answer.[2] I am sorry for the delay; but a birth seems at last to be secured for our son, & I hope it will prove a fortunate one. Tell me whether there be any steps in the mean time that you wish to be taken. We are all well. Inclosed are a letter from Mrs. Washington & another sent in by Mrs. Thornton. I believe I have already referred to Bishop Carroll's to me also inclosed. I can give you no acct of the races nor of the Theatre, having not been at either. The arrears of business formed an objection, which was not combated by the slightest inclination. I repeat my kisses to Miss P. I wish I could give her more substantial ones than can be put on paper. She shall know the difference between them the moment she presents her sweet lips in Washington—after I have set the example on those of another person whose name I flatter myself you will not find it difficult to guess. I shall comply with all the ⟨com⟩mands in your letter. With unalterable love I remain Yrs.

JAMES MADISON

Our worthy old friend Judge Jones death is published frm Fredg.[3]

RC (NjP).

1. Martha Jefferson Randolph arrived in Washington in early December and remained until the following May. While staying with Jefferson she gave birth to her son, James Madison Randolph, who was the first child born in the presidential mansion (Betts and Bear, *Family Letters of Thomas Jefferson*, 283–84 and n. 1, 295 n. 4).
2. See John Carroll to JM, 29 Oct. 1805.
3. James Monroe's uncle, Joseph Jones, died on 26 Oct. 1805.

§ To Stephen Kingston. *31 October 1805, Department of State.* "Your letter of the 20th. instant, respecting the Ship Robert [not found] has been duly received.

Altho' the accommodation you entered into with the captors should not be considered as barring the responsibility of Great Britain, yet as no redress was applied for under the Treaty within the time limited the recourse to the British Government appears to be cut off, if it ever existed. You are therefore left to pursue the captors in the manner you may deem advisable, and the documents you transmitted are herewith returned."

Letterbook copy (DNA: RG 59, DL, vol. 15). 2 pp.

§ From William C. C. Claiborne. *31 October 1805, New Orleans.* "In consequence of the embarrassments to which the *Commerce* of the United States *is* exposed by the exaction of heavy duties at the Town of Mobile; the various reports which have reached me of the Hostile disposition of the Spaniards, and of the War-like preparations at Pensacola and at other places in the vicinity of this Territory, I have been induced to address a Letter to Governor Folch, of which the enclosure is a copy.[1]

"I have avoided introducing in my communication any sentiment or expression that could give offence, and I trust I have said nothing that will be deemed exceptionable by the President of the United States. My Friend Mr. Graham (who on this occasion is good enough to be the Bearer of my Dispatch[)] will take his passage in the first Vessel passing from hence to Mobile or Pensacola; and on his return, I shall be enabled to write you more particularly."

RC and enclosure (DNA: RG 59, TP, Orleans, vol. 7); letterbook copy and letterbook copy of enclosure (Ms-Ar: Claiborne Executive Journal, vol. 15). RC 1 p.; in a clerk's hand, signed by Claiborne; docketed by Wagner as received 3 Dec. For enclosure, see n. 1.

1. The enclosure (3 pp.; printed in Rowland, *Claiborne Letter Books,* 3:221–22) is a copy of Claiborne to Juan Vicente Folch, 31 Oct. 1805, asking that the collection of the twelve percent duty on U.S. ships passing Mobile to and from U.S. territory be suspended, stating that doing so would not invalidate any rights the king might have, asking if the rumors that the garrisons at Mobile and Baton Rouge were to be augmented were true, adding that he had hoped no augmentation of military force in the disputed territories would take place and that "such Measures on the part of Spain" would probably cause the United States to increase its forces, and introducing John Graham.

§ From Alexander Coffin Jr. *31 October 1805, Hudson.* "I Yesterday received a letter written by Mr. Jacob Wagner by your direction[1] expressing your Opinion of the expediency of my prosecuting an appeal from the sentence of the Vice admiralty Court of Colombo in the case of the Penman, but Sir I apprehend that you must have forgotten to return the papers I left with you, as without them we can do nothing towards instituting the appeal. I will therefore thank you to forward them as soon as you can conveniently. As to myself, I see but little prospect of being able to bear the expense that will necessarily arise in prosecuting an appeal. I had with me in the Penman the greater part of the property I possess'd. Having been robb'd of that, precludes the possibility of bearing an additional expense, as I have a large family dependant solely upon me for Support. Now Sir, being render'd, in a pecuniary point of view, unable to Seek redress, what am I to do? must I in consequence of my Inability to prosecute an appeal give all up for lost?

This I intended to have mention'd to you personally but I found the Subject rather too delicate for my feelings. I am no Stoic Sir. I do not possess the Philosophy of Socrates, & if I did our situations are extremely different, he died by an unjust decree of his Country but left all Athens a Husband to his Wife, & a father to his Children, but, should I suddenly make my exit I should leave my wife a Widow and my children fatherless indeed: & pennyless too. No Sir, I can't bear the expense of an appeal, the rest of the Owners can. I therefore appeal to my Country & urgently request that Government would assist me, in some way or other, to obtain Justice. Sixty thousd. Dollars which certainly is the least I could Calculate as my proportion of Ship & Cargo, & private adventure, is too much for me to be robb'd of, & particularly after a perseverance and Industry second to no American of Sixteen years as Commander of a Ship in the East India trade. I was one of the first Sir, who led the way in the Lucrative pepper trade, on the Coast of Sumatra, from thence to Madrass & Calcutta 'till Mr. Jay's treaty put an end to it, & I presume I have render'd as much service to my Country as most Americans in my line of business. Add to which I served my Country faithfully, 'tho very young, during our revolutionary War. I was a Midshipman on board of the South Carolina Frigate commanded by Commodore Gillon. I left Holland with him, in that Ship when new, & Sir, I do not mean to arrogate any digree of merit when I say that I was particularly notic'd and patronised by that Commander. I mention these things merely, to Show that I have not been an Idle Citizen during my life, & on that ground I certainly think myself intitled to protection in property as well as in person. This is an unpleasant Subject for me to dwell upon, but I should have consider'd myself reprehensible not to have stated my situation to Government. In this I have done *my* Duty & now rely wholly on them to point out to me some mode of releif, & redress."

RC (DNA: RG 76, Preliminary Inventory 177, entry 180, Great Britain, Treaty of 1794 [Art. VII], British Spoliations, ca. 1794–1824, Unsorted Papers, box 5, folder P & Q). 3 pp.

    1. See Coffin to JM, 3 Oct. 1805, and n. 3.

§ From John Graham. *31 October 1805, New Orleans.* "I had the Honor to forward to you by the last mail a copy of the official Journal of the Governor of this Territory from the 22d Jany to the 1st of July last, as it stands on Record in this office. Both the Governor & myself wish to know whether you consider this the proper kind of Journal to be kept in the Secretarys Office, under the Ordinance of 1787. That Ordinance speaking of the Secretary says that 'it shall be his Duty to keep and preserve the Acts & Laws passed by the Legislature, and the Public Records of the District, and the proceedings of the Governor in his Executive Department; and transmit authentic Copies of such Acts & proceedings every Six months to the Secretary of Congress.'[1] I have no difficulty in understanding that I am to transmit copies of the acts of the Legislature and of the proceedings of the Governor in his Executive Department; but I am somewhat at a loss to know, what are to be considered as his proceedings in his Executive Department and therefore beg leave to ask for Instructions on that Subject. I do this not only with the approbation, but by the advice of Governor Claiborne, who is not less anxious than myself, that the Journal of his proceedings should be kept in the manner, the President deems most proper.

"From the Ordinance it would seem that the Records of the Territory were considered as something different from either the Acts of the Legislature, or the proceeding of the Governor in his Executive Department: am I to take charge of the Land Papers? or would they more properly remain with the Register who now has them In making these enquiries I am actuated solely by a wish faithfully to discharge the Trust reposed in me & I flatter myself that my Motive will induce you to pardon me for the trouble I now give you."

RC (DNA: RG 59, TP, Orleans, vol. 7). 2 pp.; docketed by Wagner, with his note: "To be answd?."

1. *U.S. Statutes at Large*, 1:51 n. (*a*).

§ From Anthony Terry. *31 October 1805, Cádiz*. "Referring to what I had the honor of writing you on the 8. inst. Copy herewith—The object of the present is to inclose you a List of the Combined Fleet that left this Port on the 19th. & 20th.[1] it is reported that the motives that Admiral Villeneuve had for Sailing, was, that as a new Admiral was expected daily from France to take the Command of the Fleet, he thought it verry hard to deliver up the Command; that having received intelligence that Nelson's fleet was only composed of 22. Ships & some Frigates determin'd him to go out & give him battle, let it be what it will, the whole Fleet has been Sacrificed, as a most dreadfull action at the distance of 8. or 10 leagues began on the 21st. at 11. oClock in the morning, which lasted without intermission untill 7. oClock in the Evening—the results down to this date are agreable to the enclosed Sheet, shall continue giving you every information I may be able to obtain on the Subject.

"The French General Mr. Rosigny that was expected arrived here on the 24th.—say Admiral.

"The American Ship Huntress John Cunnyngham Master bound from Belfast to Gibraltar wth. Provisions has been sent in here by the French Ship Heroe on the 19th. the Cargo will be condemned & freight paid.[2]

"By the enclosed Paper you will see the glorious beginning of the French on the Continent."

Adds in a postscript: "Governmt. Notes 55 ¾ a 56."

RC and enclosures (DNA: RG 59, CD, Cádiz, vol. 1). RC 2 pp.; in a clerk's hand, signed by Terry. For enclosures, see n. 1.

1. The enclosures (19 pp.) are several lists of the thirty-three ships of the line, five frigates, and two brigs of the combined French and Spanish fleets in the 21 Oct. 1805 Battle of Trafalgar. The lists describe the state of the ships after the battle, how many survived and their condition, and how many were lost. Also enclosed is a transcript of an article from a 13 Oct. 1805 Bayonne newspaper, describing French victories in Germany, a sheet listing the total number of ships in the British squadron, and a note that Lord Nelson had survived for six hours after the battle.

2. The *Huntress*, John Cunningham, carrying a cargo of soap, candles, butter, potatoes, cider, rum, and cloth was taken by the *Héros* and carried into Cádiz, where French commissary Le Roy reported to Denis Decrès that, according to the U.S.-French Convention of

1800, carrying enemy property did not make the ship liable to condemnation. Le Roy authorized the captain to make a provisory sale of the cargo. The French council of prizes did not decide on the case until 1814, when it declared that the ship had all proper documentation, and depriving the enemy of the cargo could have been accomplished by driving the *Huntress* away from the port instead of seizing it. The ship and cargo were ordered released (Bonnel, *La France, les États-Unis et la guerre de course*, 209–10).

§ From Benedict Van Pradelles.[1] *31 October 1805, New Orleans.* "Permit me to do myself the honor of informing You, that I accept, With gratitude, the appointment, which it has pleased the President of the United States, to bestow on me, of commissioner under the act of March 2d. 1805, 'for ascertaining & adjusting the titles & claims to land in the Territory of Orleans & District of Louisiana' for the Eastern district of the Territory of Orleans.

"The length of the time, elapsed between the date of my Commission & that of this letter will, I hope, Justify my accounting & Serve as my apology for it: I have been detained by the low State of the Water, on the Ohio & Mississipi rivers from the 26th of July till yesterday that of my arrival here, Where my commission came to hand."

RC (DNA: RG 59, TP, Orleans, vol. 7); RC (DNA: RG 59, LAR, 1801–9, filed under "Van Pradelles"); FC (PPGi: Girard Papers). First RC 1 p.; docketed by Wagner. Second RC docketed by Jefferson. Wording varies between the copies, but the content is the same.

1. Benedict Van Pradelles (d. 1808) was a Flemish-born ex-soldier who came to America about 1780 and explored the lands in upstate New York. From 1798 to 1801 he was in Lexington, Kentucky. He was named notary public at New Orleans in 1806 and register of the land office for the eastern territory of Orleans in April 1808 (R. W. G. Vail, "The Lure of the Land Promoter: A Bibliographical Study of Certain New York Real Estate Rarities," *University of Rochester Library Bulletin* 24 [1969]: 42–44; Lexington *Stewart's Kentucky Herald*, 6 Mar. 1798, 24 Feb. 1801; Carter, *Territorial Papers, Orleans*, 9:701, 782, 810).

To George W. Erving

Private

DEAR SIR   WASHINGTON Novr. 1. 1805

By Mr. Smith to whom this is committed[1] you will receive the public letter in which the course approved by the P. is marked out for your conduct at Madrid. The grounds for it are strengthened by the posture of things in Europe, and by the approach of the Session of Congs. The impression made on this Country by the proud & perverse conclusion given by Spain to the endeavors of Mr. M. & Mr. P. to adjust our differences, ought if faithfully reported to her, to teach her a lesson salutary at all times & particularly so at the present moment. She may be sure that she will never better her stipulations with this Country by delay. If she calculates on the friend at her elbow or be jogged by him into follies not altogether

her own, she is so far to be pitied or despised, as she avails herself of such explanations. But here again she receives a lesson from the scene which appears to be opening in Europe agst. the Imperial career of France. England seems as ready to play the fool with respect to this Country as her enemies. She is renewing her depredations on our Commerce in the most ruinous shapes, and has kindled a more general indignation among our merchts. than was ever before expressed. How little do those great nations in Europe appear, in alternately smiling and frowning on the U.S: not according to any fixt sentiments or interests, but according to the winds & clouds of the moment. It will be the more honorable to the U.S. if they continue to present a contrast of steady and dignified conduct, doing justice under all circumstances to others, and taking no other advantage of events than to seek it for themselves.

For our domestic news I refer to the newspapers which go by Mr. S. Congs. do not meet till December. Their session will involve important questions & measures relative to the nations of Europe having unsettled relations to this Country, or committing wrongs agst. it.

The attention which you have been so good as to pay to the sending us publications useful for this Dept. of State induces me to request that you will during your stay at Madrid procure whatever Books on diplomatic & commercial subjects deserve a place on the office shelves; also such as may relate to America generally, and particularly the ordinances &c relating to the Indies and Islands belonging to Spain. This general intimation will readily be applied by your own judgment to the pertinent objects. With my sincere esteem & regard I remain Dr. Sir Your friend & sert

JAMES MADISON

Letterpress copy (DLC). Docketed by JM at a later date "Nov. 6. 1805."

1. Sen. Samuel Smith's son, Louis B. Smith, planned to sail from Baltimore to Lisbon and "to Spend the Winter at Madrid" (Samuel Smith to Jefferson, 30 Oct. 1805, DLC: Jefferson Papers).

To George W. Erving

SIR,   DEPARTMENT OF STATE November 1st. 1805

In a letter from Mr. Monroe of 20 Augt. and from yourself of the 24th. of same it is signified that according to an arrangement formed under the existing state of things, you were to proceed to Madrid; Mr. Bowdoin remaining away, until he should be furnished with new instructions. On the supposition that this arrangement will have been adhered to, and that you will be found at Madrid, I avail myself of the present conveyance by

Mr. Smith, to communicate the line of conduct which the President has charged me to mark out for you.

Considering the manner in which the late negotiation with the Spanish Government terminated, and the present posture of the relations between the two countries, it is thought proper that you should take no step whatever for reviving any part of the negotiation, and that you should not conceal from the Spanish Government the cause of this reserve. Your duty therefore at Madrid will be confined to a mere observance of the ordinary civilities incident to a state of peace, to a watchfulness over the rights and remedies of our citizens within your purview, particularly of those suffering from irregularities of Spanish Cruizers, and to the transmission of any communications of which the Spanish Government may choose to make you the organ; to which will of course be added every information from yourself, which may be thought to claim or deserve the attention of the President.

Mr Pinckney it is presumed will have left Madrid, immediately on your arrival, if not before it.

Mr Smith will take charge of a packet of late newspapers, to which I refer for the current information. I have the honor to be Sir, Very respectfully, your most Obt Sert

JAMES MADISON

RC (DLC: Curry Autograph Collection); letterbook copy (DNA: RG 59, IM, vol. 6). RC in a clerk's hand; amended and signed by JM; docketed by Erving as received 14 Jan. 1806, with his note: "it shoud have arrived on the 10 Jay. with the Presidents speech but Mr Jarvis forgot to forward it." Marked in an unidentified hand: "duplicate in Madrid."

To William Jarvis

private

DEAR SIR   WASHINGTON Novr. 1. 1805

Having just recd notice of the proposed trip of Mr. Smith to Madrid thro' Lisbon I avail myself of the opportunity to thank you for your attention to the Wine, and for the extras on their way for Mrs. Madison.[1] The two pipes are arrived. Having just returned to this place, after a long detention at Philada. by the situation of Mrs. M.'s health at length happily restored, I have not yet broached them, or even tasted the samples in the little box. The bills are not yet presented. They will be duly honored.

Congs. do not meet this year till Decr. Their Sessi(on) will involve important topics growing out of the conduc(t) of different nations of Europe towards this Country.

For the current information at home, I refer to a few newspapers inclosed. Our Seasons throughout the presen(t) year have been somewhat irregular; but have given Crops of Wheat liberal in quantity, and almost without example in excellence of quality. The crops of Maiz are diversified, on the whole rather deficient: In Penna. Maryland & New. Jersey very short indeed. With my best wishes I remain very respectfully Yr. friend & sert.

JAMES MADISON

RC (offered for sale by Christie's, New York, N.Y., 9 June 1993, sale 7700, lot 248). Cover sheet marked in an unidentified hand: "By Capt. Migee Ship Resource"; docketed by Jarvis. Captain Magee and the *Resource* left Baltimore for Lisbon on 18 Nov. (*New-York Gazette & General Advertiser*, 21 Nov. 1805).

    1. For JM's wine and the dainties for Dolley Madison, see Jarvis to JM, 1 Aug. 1805.

From Dolley Madison

PHILADELPHIA Novr. 1st. [1805]

I have great pleasure, my beloved in repeating to you what the Doctor has just now said, that the knee would be well in one day more and in two or three I might begin to ride—so that I may reasonably hope that a fortnight more will be the extent of my stay in Philadelphia, I am so impatient to be restored to you.

I wish you would indulge me with some information respecting the war with Spain and disagreement with England, as it is so generally expected here that I am at a loss what to surmise. You know I am not much of a politician but I am extremely anxious to hear (as far as you may think proper) what is going forward in the Cabinet—on this subject, I beleive you would not desire your wife the active partizan, such as her neighbor Mrs. L,[1] nor will there be the slightest danger whilst she is conscious of her want of talents, and her diffidence in expressing her opinions always imperfectly understood by her sex. In my last I told you every thing the state of my finances &c &c. I have sent Peter to the office for letters and I hope to hear from you and to receive some account of Anna. I expect to see her every day.

Kiss my child for me and remember me to my friends. Could you speak a word to General Dearborn in favor of poor Mrs. Jackson—the Doctor's widow[2] who used to supply so well the soldiers—adieu, my dear husband, Peter brings me no letters which really unfits me for writing more to any one, your ever affectionate

D.

Tr (owned by Mrs. George B. Cutts, Wellesley, Mass., 1982). Year not indicated; conjectural year assigned based on internal evidence.

1. Dolley Madison's neighbor has not been identified.
2. Dolley Madison referred to Susanna Kemper Jackson, the widow of Dr. David Jackson, who died in 1801 (Joseph W. England, ed., *The First Century of the Philadelphia College of Pharmacy: 1821–1921* [Philadelphia, 1922], 396; *Philadelphia Repository, and Weekly Register,* 19 Sept. 1801).

§ To William Eustis. *1 November 1805.* "Will you permit me to inclose for your consideration, a commission whch may be recommended by the advantage of local conveniency? It will not be put on record untill your decision shall warrant, which it will be agreeable to receive as soon as it may be reasonably expected."

RC (offered for sale by James D. Julia, Inc., Fairfield, Maine, 4–5 Feb. 2010, lot 2043). 1 p.

§ To Albert Gallatin. *1 November 1805, Department of State.* "I have the honor to request that in virtue of the power of Attorney of Tobias Lear Esqr., enclosed in my letter to you of the 5th. Septr. 1803 [not found], there may be remitted to George Long,[1] of Portsmouth N.H. five hundred dollars, from the appropriations for Barbary Intercourse. Mr. Lear to be charged with the same and held accountable."

Letterbook copy (DNA: RG 59, DL, vol. 15). 1 p.

1. George Long was the half brother of Lear's first wife, Mary (Polly) Long, who died in the Philadelphia yellow fever epidemic of 1793. When Lear left for Algiers, he left George Long in charge of financial arrangements for the support of his son, Benjamin Lincoln Lear, and his mother, Mary Stillson Lear (Brighton, *The Checkered Career of Tobias Lear,* 91, 114–15, 285, 367, 368).

§ From Thomas Auldjo. *1 November 1805, Cowes.* "I had the honour to write you 11th. ultimo by a Ship direct to Baltimore & of which inclosed is Copy.

"I have now to give you as below an account of four more Valuable American Ships sent into the port of Portsmouth by British Cruizers[1] & that they will all be prosecuted in the Admiralty Court, as soon as the terms begin which will be in a few days. The Blockades of the Elbe & Weser are raised & of which I presume you will have received from the Minister official accounts. Our Crops of grain are considered abundant & prices of Wheat are now 9/ ℔ bushel with a probability of reduction to 7/6 soon."

RC (DNA: RG 59, CD, Southampton, vol. 1). 2 pp.

1. Below his signature Auldjo wrote "please turn over." On the verso of the letter, is the following list:

> Ship Cicero—Jona: Parker Masr from New York with
> West India. produce for Amsterdam
> Ship Misisippi—Hubbard Skidmore—from New York with
> Wt India produce for Nantes

Ship Young Elias—Linzey Riddell Masr from
              Philada for Amsterdam—Wt India Produce
Brig Vigilant—Geo Dodd—Boston to Bourdeaux
              W India produce."

To Dolley Madison

[ca. 2 November 1805]

The last mail brought me, my dearest yours of the 30 Ocr. I am happy to find you able to walk about. I hope that will help to restore your appetite & strength, and that it will not belong before you will be able to undertake a journey hither; tho' anxiously as I sigh for it, I can not wish it to be precipitated agst. the fullest approbation of Dr. P. I inclose a letter from the President and another from Mrs. Jackson.[1] I have one from the latter but it says nothing except as to Lovells land.[2] I find that the letter from Mrs. Pichon was brought by the black maid who went with her, and that a little box remains in her hands, containing probably the trinket referred to. If you wish it to be procured & forwarded, say so. Payne is well, and I am endeavoring to keep him in some sort of attention to his books.

All my affection embraces you. A Carté blanche to Miss P.

J. M.

Inclosed. $300.

RC (ViU: Madison Papers, Special Collections). Undated; conjectural date assigned based on internal evidence and surviving enclosure (see n. 1 below).

1. Mary Payne Jackson's letter has not been found. Jefferson's 1 Nov. 1805 letter asked Dolley to buy "a fashionable wig of the colour of the hair inclosed. a set of combs for dressing the hair. a bonnet a shawl & white lace veil for paying morning visits 2. lace half-handkerchiefs" for Martha Jefferson Randolph (MHi: Thomas Jefferson Collection).

2. See John G. Jackson to JM, 28 Oct. 1805.

From Dolley Madison

Saturday 4 oClock [2 November 1805]

Your charming letter[1] my beloved, has revived my Spirit, & made me feel like another being—so much does my health peace, & every thing else, depend on your Affection & goodness. I am very greatful for the prospect you have opened for our child—& shall now look forward to his Manhood, when he will bless—and do honour to his guardians. I wrote you yesterday, & have but a moment now—as the 2 hours since I reccd: yours, has been devoted to the inclosed—pray take as much relaxsation, & pleasure as you can—alltogether, business will not agree with you, & unless you amuse yourself as usial I may travel too soon.

Betsy P. is almost frantic with the prospect of seeing W. & says she feels already your sweet kisses—what must some body else do—farewell til tomorrow—your own

D

Please to put a wafer in Lucys Letter & send it without delay.[2]

RC (CLO: Elizabeth and Stuart Chevalier Autograph Collection). Undated; conjectural date assigned based on internal evidence.

1. JM to Dolley Madison, 31 Oct. 1805.
2. This letter has not been found but was probably Dolley's reply to the letter from her sister Lucy Payne Washington (later Lucy Payne Todd), which was enclosed in JM's 31 Oct. letter (see n. 1 above).

§ From Thomas Auldjo. *2 November 1805, Cowes.* "I had the honor to write to you yesterday & have now to convey Copy of letter from Ld. Mulgrave Secretary of State for Foreign Affairs as transmitted me by Mr. Monroe relative to the blockades of Cadiz & St. Lucar."[1]

RC and enclosure (DNA: RG 59, CD, Southampton, vol. 1). RC 1 p.; docketed by Wagner, with his note: "Relaxation of the blockade of Cadiz & St. Lucar." For enclosure, see n. 1.

1. The enclosure (1 p.; docketed by Wagner as received in Auldjo's 1 Nov. 1805 dispatch) is a copy of Lord Mulgrave's 27 Oct. 1805 letter to James Monroe (printed in the 17 Dec. 1805 *New-York Commercial Advertiser*) stating that the blockades of Cádiz and Sanlúcar de Barrameda had been eased, and neutral vessels could now enter and leave those ports provided they were not carrying any warlike articles or naval stores beyond what the ship itself needed.

§ From John Page. *2 November 1805, Richmond.* "I have to acknowledge the receipt of your favor of the 30th. Ultimo,[1] notifying me of your having forwarded by Captain Caleb Creighton, as the proportion due under certain acts of Congress to this Commonwealth, 1254 Copies of the acts of the 2d. session of the 8th. Congress, which have not been received. So soon as they come to hand a receipt will be given to them to the Captain who delivers them."

Letterbook copy (Vi: Executive Letterbook). 1 p.

1. The letter has not been found, but for the transmission of the laws by the State Department, see JM's 17 Oct. 1805 Circular to the Governors.

From Dolley Madison

Monday night PHILADELPHIA [4 November 1805]

I received, my dear Husband's, two last letters this morning, one enclosing Anna's and the other a commission from the President to procure several articles for Mrs. Randolph,[1] which I shall now be able to do by riding to the shop doors, he did not send money but I can get them notwithstanding, as General Morland has paid me $100[2]—and I have the sum you sent.

How I grieved at the loss of your estimable friend Judge Jones. I hope it was not his son who fought the duel.[3] Anna will not be here until the 18th. or 20th. of the month, owing to the illness of her nourse. I have had many ladies to see me today, Mrs. Lenox and Miss Keen came to invite me to a party[4] and were very pressing, but I could not think of it—and this evening General Tourrea[u] and two or three frenchmen with him, I declined seeing them as you were absent and I upstairs, the General sent word up that he was anxious to see and speak to me, but I resolved not to admit a gentleman, into my room, unless entitled by age and long acquaintance. It is now past 9 o'clock and I cease to write but to dream of thee. Miss P. is beside me as usual and sends you abundance of love and fills up the blank with Cousin Isaac. Tuesday morning. I was so entirely exhausted with my short ride of yesterday that the Doctor thinks I had better be still today, and I shall be helped down stairs to see my acquaintance. Doctor and Mrs. Rush called after I had bid you adieu last night, and left word they must see me this morning. I have been interrupted with company—Mr. Baldwin, Dr. Physic, Dr. Logan and General Tourreau. The General seems to have forgotten his English. I could not understand when he intends going to Washington, or what he was about here. He said he had been afflicted with every thing this summer but yellow fever. Mr. Baldwin is waiting the arrival of his sister Mrs. Barlow and her husband. Mr. Patton[5] has just called to say I must sell my horses and take a pair he is acquainted with they are very fine and handsome. I told him I would consult you directly. I must again leave you as I am down in the parlor and surrounded with visitors. Tell Mrs. Thornton that I am having a model of a bonnet made for her, the new ones are just coming in. Write to thy ever affectionate

DOLLEY.

Tr (owned by Mrs. George B. Cutts, Wellesley, Mass., 1982). Undated; conjectural date assigned based on the fact that the Monday following JM's 2 Nov. letter (see n. 1 below) was 4 Nov. 1805.

1. For Jefferson's commission, see JM to Dolley, ca. 2 Nov. 1805, and n. 1. The letter from JM transmitting one from Dolley's sister Anna Payne Cutts was probably his 31 Oct. letter, which conveyed the news of Joseph Jones's death.

2. Irish-born merchant Stephen Moylan (1737–1811) was educated in Paris and had a shipping business in Lisbon before coming in 1768 to Philadelphia, where he was the first president of the Friendly Sons of St. Patrick from 1771 to 1773. During the Revolution he served as George Washington's secretary, as quartermaster general, and as commander of a cavalry regiment. In 1783 he was made brevet brigadier general. Washington appointed him commissioner of loans at Philadelphia in 1793, a position he held until his death. In 1796 he was elected as the last president of the Friendly Sons of St. Patrick. He rented Dolley Madison's Philadelphia house from 1796 to 1807 (Campbell, *History of the Friendly Sons of St. Patrick*, 124–25; Mattern and Shulman, *Selected Letters of Dolley Payne Madison*, 408).

3. Dolley probably referred to the duel in Virginia between Skelton Jones and William Upshaw, which was reported in both the Philadelphia *Aurora General Advertiser* and the Philadelphia *United States' Gazette* of 31 Oct. 1805.

4. Sarah Lukens Keene (d. 1866) was the niece of Tacy Lukens Lenox (d. 1834), the wife of Revolutionary War veteran David Lenox (*New York Times*, 17 June 1866; Campbell, *History of the Friendly Sons of St. Patrick*, 274).

5. Irish-born Robert Patton (1755–1814) fought in the American Revolution. He was a member of the Society of the Cincinnati and was elected treasurer in 1804. Patton was postmaster at Philadelphia from 1789 until his death on 2 Jan. 1814 (Glossary, *DMDE*; Campbell, *History of the Friendly Sons of St. Patrick*, 501; Philadelphia *Poulson's American Daily Advertiser*, 4 Jan. 1814).

§ From Tobias Lear. *4 November 1805, Leghorn*. "I have this day drawn on you, three setts of exchange, as follows

$16776.31[1]

4934.22 at thirty days sight, to the order of mrs.

3947.36[2]   Degen Purviance & Co.

$25657.89 say for twenty five thousand six

hundred and fifty Seven Dollars, and eighty nine Cents being for value, received on account, of the Department of State of the U.S. for the Service of the Barbary affairs, which please to honour accordingly."

RC (DNA: RG 59, CD, Algiers, vol. 7, pt. 1); letterbook copy (owned by Stephen Decatur, Garden City, N.Y., 1961). RC 1 p.; marked "*fifth letter of advice*"; in a clerk's hand, signed by Lear; docketed by Wagner. Letterbook copy marked "Copy of Letter of advice from No. 1. to No 7."

1. A letterbook copy (owned by Stephen Decatur, Garden City, N.Y., 1961; 1 p.) of the first bill of exchange reads: "Thirty days after sight please to pay this my Seventh of Exchange (first, second, third, fourth, Fifth & Sixth not paid) to the Order of Messrs Degen, Purviance & Co. Sixteen thousand seven hundred and seventy Six dollars, thirty one Cents, Value received on account of the United States of America, for the Barbary service, and place the same, with or without advice." Two added notes read: "One Sett of the same tenor and date for four thousand nine hundred and thirty four dollars, twenty four Cents," and "One Sett of the same tenor and date for three thousand nine hundred and forty seven dollars & thirty six Cents."

2. The RC of the third bill of exchange (NHi: 1 p.; marked "Fifth"; in a clerk's hand, signed by Lear; endorsed on the verso on 4 Nov. 1805 by Degen, Purviance & Company to Philip and Anthony Filicchy & Co., and on 8 Nov. 1805 by the latter firm to Frederick and Philip Rhinlander) reads: "Thirty days after sight please to pay this my Fifth of Exchange

(First, Second, Third Fourth Sixth & Seventh not paid) to the Order of Messrs Degen Purviance & Co. Three Thousand nine Hundred Forty Seven Dollars & Thirty six Cents, Value received on Account of the United States of America for the Barbary Service & place the same with or without advice."

§ From John Mitchell. *4 November 1805, Paris.* "I am honord with your Circular letters of the 1st. & 4h. july last,[1] with a Volume of the Laws; and a New Commission as Vice Commercial Agent for Havre. I have handed the Commission to His Excellency Gl. Armstrong for to Obtain My Exequatur. Agreably to your instructns, I have Advertized, that, in future no Certificate will be granted for Vessells purchased in france, & shall carefully attend to your instructions.

"The ports in the Channel are still continued under Blockade by the British, but, with an inferior force since the sailing of the flotilla. Yet No Vessel attempts to enter. Havre is without the appearance of Commerce, and more than half the houses are deserted.

"Since it is known here that no Certif[i]cates will be granted for Vessells purchased in a forreign Country, I have received from Mr. Omealy (of Baltimore in Maryland doing Business in france)[2] Info⟨r⟩mation that, The Brig Maryland, James Petrie Masr. purchased at Havre by John Newel⟨l⟩ of Norfolk for Fras & Alexr. Tubeuf of Norfolk—Virgin⟨ia.⟩

"deposition dated 6 July—1803.—

Brig Franklin Shadk: Hill Masr. purchased at

Dieppe by F. X. Mazza for Account of said John Newell. Deposn. 31 July 1804 at Havre Brig Virginia, William Bass purchased by same fo⟨r⟩ same "deposition 28 decr. 1804—at Hav⟨re⟩ & transmitted to Marsailles—to obtain Certificat⟨e⟩ are all the property of Mr. F. X. Mazza or the House of Dolla Mazza & Co of Havre together with the ship Martha Cap. Petrie (late of the Marylan⟨d⟩.⟩

"for the Brig Maryland, Mr. Newell Appeard in person & subscribed the deposition sent with the Vessell. This Vessell has since been Condemnd & Sold & the Sea Letter & mediteranean pass⟨port⟩ transmitted you by Me.

"for the Franklin and Virginia, Mr Mazza Appeard Made Oath & Subscribed the same which went with the Vessells papers. Where the Ship Martha Appears to be purchased by or for Account ⟨o⟩f Mr. Newell, I can't inform you. But the three sail constantly out of Norfolk where Mr Newell resides.

"Here I beg leave to observe that, Mr John Newell 'tho a young Man Appeard at Havre to posess property, but Wether his own or Consignments I cant say. & was of good Character. Mr. Mazza is a Mercht long established at Havre & Officiates as Commercial Agent for Portugal. He and Mr. Omealy are long Aquainted, and as Mr. Omealy frequently called about the papers for the Brig Maryland—it is very probable he knew all of that transaction, And I presume is aquainted with the others from his giveing the information. To Obtain a proof here from Mr Mazza I believe is impossible, and no doubt but evry after declaration would Conform to the former. From Mr. Newell perhaps more may be known.

"As the Information of Mr. Omealy was so positive I have considered it my Duty thus early to Communicate it and especially as the imposition if it exists, is upon Me. and of which I had no suspision, 'till the Communication of

Mr. Omealy, for before I granted the Certificate I convened with Mr Mazza, Who, produced Me the orders in Writeing of Mr Newell to make the purchases, a note of whic⟨h⟩ was made & sent with the Vessells papers, that I consider myself free from blame, and shall gladly learn from you that you do not attatch any to Me."

RC (DNA: RG 59, CD, Havre, vol. 1). Marked "duplicate"; docketed by Wagner.

1. No circular letter of 4 July 1805 has been found. Mitchell probably referred to JM's second circular of 12 July 1805.

2. Baltimore merchant Michael O'Mealy had lived in France since 1793 and was still there in 1810 (Yvon Bizardel, *The First Expatriates: Americans in Paris during the French Revolution* [New York, 1972], 225; *New-York Gazette & General Advertiser*, 23 Aug. 1810).

§ From Robert Williams. *4 November 1805, Washington, Mississippi Territory.* "For several weeks past I have expected the land business would have been in such forwardness as to admit my starting to North Carolina the next, but it turns out to be such a perplexing business as to baffle all reasonable calculation; however, my final determination was to have started about this time; but the last mail from New-Orleans brought me a letter from Governor Claiborne (a copy of which I enclose)[1] confirming some reports in circulation here relative to our Spanish neighbours which has determined me not to leave the Territory 'till Congress meets, and until I can hear from our Government, and know what is likely to be our political standing with Spain, which I hope to know by the first of January, by which time I expect to have nearly completed the land business, so far at least as it can be, previously to the surveying; after which I shall immediately start for North Carolina, should not the situation of affairs demand my remaining.

"On receiving this Government I found the militia in such a state of disorder as to render it impracticable to have them yet organized tho' I am making every exertion to that effect, and which I hope to have completed in a very short time.

"We have several volunteer companies of horse, composed of the most wealthy and active men amongst us, who hold themselves in readiness, and I am persuaded would render services equal to any, if called upon.

"I have the satisfaction to inform you that there is at present more unanimity and concord amongst the people of this Territory, than at any other period since the American Government, and perhaps as much if not more harmony towards the General Government than in any other quarter.

"I have not had the honor of an answer to any of my letters or communications addressed to you since my appointment as Governor."

Adds in a postscript: "will you be so good as to give Mr. Gallatin the perusal of this letter as I have not time to write him now?"

Letterbook copy (Ms-Ar: Executive Journal, 1805–1810); FC (Ms-Ar). Letterbook copy 3 pp. FC in a clerk's hand, signed by Williams. Minor differences between the copies have not been noted.

1. The enclosure has not been found, but it was probably a copy of Claiborne to Williams, 24 Oct. 1805, reporting the same information about Spanish troop movements in West Florida and Texas, and the actions of a Spanish purchasing agent, as that in Claiborne's letter to JM of the same date (Rowland, *Claiborne Letter Books*, 3:213–14).

§ To John Joseph Fraissinet. *5 November 1805, Department of State.* "Enclosed you will receive the passport requested for yourself & family. As it is not at present thought advisable to institute a commercial or consular agency to Martinique,[1] I can only observe in answer to the other parts of your letter, that the circumstances which may be thought to recommend you to fill it, will be estimated with those which may be presented by other candidates, whenso[e]ver it may be expedient to make the appointment."

Letterbook copy (DNA: RG 59, DL, vol. 15). 1 p.

1. For Fraissinet's desire to be consul at Martinique, see William Davy to JM, 5 Oct. 1805, and JM to Jefferson, 16 Oct. 1805, and n. 4.

§ From William C. C. Claiborne. *5 November 1805, New Orleans.* "The members of the House of Representatives of this Territory, to the amount of nineteen assembled on yesterday, at the Hotel de Ville in conformity to my Proclamation of the 26. of July last.[1] I attended them in person, and after administering to each member an oath to support the Constitution of the United States, and an oath of Office, I delivered a short address, of which the inclosed, marked (A) is a copy.[2]

"It is reported here, and generally believed, that the Marquis of Casa Calvo, who has gone to the Post of Adais, took with him Thirty two thousand dollars. Various are the conjectures as to the real objects of the Marquis's journey; some have said, that he is to meet, on the Frontiers of the province of Taxus, Three thousand troops, of which he is to take the command; others, that he is engaged in sowing discontents among the people of this Territory; and there are some again who suppose that the conciliating the Indian Tribes to the Spanish interest, in the event of a rupture with the United States, is deemed important, and that to this object the Marquis proposed appropriating the money he carried with him. New Orleans however is fruitful in reports, and it is difficult to say how far those now in circulation may be correct; But if any reliance can be placed in the assurances given me by the Marquis himself, he had no object in view hostile to the United States, that on the contrary, he only proposed a short excursion on a hunting party, and if the weather permitted, to ascend the Sabine as far as Adais—the Latitude and Longitude of which place he proposed taking; but on this subject, my letter to you of the 14th. ultimo, was explicit, and to which I beg leave to refer you.

"It is certain that great exertions are making to fortify *strongly* Pensacola and Mobile, at the former place new Barracks are erecting for the reception, as is said, of four thousand Troops whose arrival is daily expected; there is also no doubt but that two hundred troops have been ordered to Baton Rouge, and it is supposed they are now on their march.

"Doctor Sibley writes me on the 14. ultimo that 'some troops had arrived at Nacesdoches, 'tis said 220—and 'tis likewise said they are going to fortify, in a short time, within five or six Leagues of Nachitoches. Considering the attachment to them of their militia, and the contrary towards us of our militia, they are stronger than we are, counting numbers.'

"I have little doubt of the correctness of Doctor Sibley's information; nor do I hesitate to give it as my opinion, that the Spanish authorities in the vicinity of this Territory, contemplate a speedy rupture with the United States and are making every preparation to commence the War on their part, to advantage. Under these impressions, I deem it a duty to advise some immediate measures for the protection of Louisiana, and particularly of the City of New Orleans; the regular troops here are few in number, nor can I rely with certainty on the Body of the militia. I believe many of the Creoles of the Country would be faithful to the American government; but perhaps a majority of them would remain neutral, and I am inclined to think that most of the Frenchmen, and all the Spaniards, who reside here, in the event of war, would favor the Spanish interest.

"These are my impressions, and I deem it a duty freely to impart them to you.

"It remains now for me to advise—that the force now here be used to the best advantage, and that it be augmented as soon as possible. I advise that Fort St John and Plaquimine be repaired and placed in a state of defence, that the Troops at Fort Adams (leaving a small guard for the public property) be removed to Point Coupée, that the troops in this City (leaving only a necessary guard for the public Stores and Barracks) should be posted at Fort St. John, and above and below New Orleans, at suitable positions; not more than six miles distant from this City. Thus situated, a degree of discipline might be introduced, which the best Commander cannot enforce among troops stationed in a City; protection also might be given to Plaquimine, if threatned with attack, the passage of a hostile army by the way of the Lakes or from Baton Rouge, might be opposed, various rallying points would be presented for the patriotic portion of the Militia, and if any unforeseen circumstances should render the presence of the army in New Orleans necessary, it might easily be reacquired.

"I further advise, that the command of the Troops in this quarter be committed to a Colonel of tried military talents. Of Lieutenant Colonel Freeman's patriotism or integrity, I have no reason to doubt; but I am inclined to the opinion, that neither his mental or personal Energies are equal to the Command which at this time devolves upon him."

RC, two copies, and enclosure (DNA: RG 59, TP, Orleans, vol. 7); letterbook copy and letterbook copy of enclosure (Ms-Ar: Claiborne Executive Journal, vol. 15); letterbook copy (Ms-Ar). Both RCs in a clerk's hand, docketed by Wagner. First RC 4 pp.; signed by Claiborne. Second RC emended, signed, marked "Duplicate," and addressed by Claiborne. The first paragraph in first RC is omitted from second RC and second letterbook copy. Minor differences between the copies have not been noted. For enclosure, see n. 2.

1. First letterbook copy has "20th. of July." For the proclamation, see Claiborne to JM, 27 July 1805, and n. 2.

2. The enclosure (2 pp.; marked "(A)"; docketed by Wagner; printed, with minor differences, in Rowland, *Claiborne Letter Books*, 3:223–24) is a copy of Claiborne's 4 Nov. 1805 address to the territorial house of representatives congratulating them on their election; requesting that they choose ten persons "residents in the Territory, possessing each, a freehold estate of five hundred acres of land"; and asking them to send their names to the president, who would choose five from the list to serve as legislative councilors. Claiborne suggested that their choices come from among the several districts of the territory in order to assure better representation to local interests.

§ From George Davis. *5 November 1805, "Hampton Roads on Board U. S. Frigate Congress."* "I have the honor to inform you that I arrived at this place yesterday, on board the U.S. Frigate Congress, forty days from Tangiers, in company with Sidi Solyman Meli Meli (late Bashaw Ambi of the Turks) Ambassador from the Court of Tunis to the Govt. of the U.States. I presume we shall Sail the first fair wind for Washington, where I will wait the orders of the Honb. The Secretary of State."

Letterbook copy (NHi: George Davis Letterbooks). 1 p.

§ From Joseph Rademaker. *5 November 1805, Philadelphia.* "The 2d. Instant I had the honor to receive your Letter dated 27th. ultimo [not found] with an enclosed Package addressed to the Chevr. Freire. I have transmited the said Package by this day's mail to London to the care of the Portuguese Minister there, requesting him to remit it to the Chevr. Freire."[1]

RC (DNA: RG 59, NFL, Portugal, vol. 1). 1 p.; docketed by Wagner.

1. For Cipriano Riberio Freire's recall from the United States and the gift promised him, which was presumably in the packet Rademaker mentioned, see Freire to JM, 20 Apr. 1805, and James Monroe to JM, 26 May 1805, *PJM-SS*, 9:266–67, 404.

¶ From John H. Greene. Letter not found. *5 November 1805.* Acknowledged in Daniel Brent to John H. Greene, 16 Dec. 1805, as regarding the impressment of his brother, Thomas Rice Greene, into the British sloop of war *Raisonable* (DNA: RG 59, Preliminary Inventory 15, entry 929, Correspondence with Collectors of Customs regarding Impressed Seamen, 1796–1814, box 5).

To Nathaniel Lawrence and John Patrick

GENTLEMEN.   DEPARTMENT OF STATE Novr. 6th. 1805.

I have received your letter of the 1st. inst.[1] respecting the capture of the Ship Eugenia, off the Harbour of New york by the Cambrian British Frigate.[2] That you may be correctly acquainted with what passed on the complaint made by the British Minister of the rescue of the former Vessel in the last year, from the British captor, who had her in possession, I enclose a copy of my answer dated 5th. Septr. 1804.[3] In relation to the present seizure, it will be incumbent on you to prosecute a legal claim in the Court at Halifax in which she may be proceeded against; and should the decision be unfavorable, it may be proper for you after appealing to communicate to this Department the documents in which it is contained, and such as may explain it. Respecting the rigorous & injurious usage of the

Master of the Eugenia, after the capture, it may not be amiss for you to send me the details authenticated in due form, as soon as you obtain them. I am &c.

JAMES MADISON.

Letterbook copy (DNA: RG 59, DL, vol. 15).

1. Letter not found.
2. The *Eugenia*, Capt. John Mansfield, bound from Bordeaux to New York, was taken by the *Cambrian* near Sandy Hook, New Jersey, and sent to Halifax for adjudication. The ship was held for further proof on the questions of the need for certificates of origin for the cargo, the certificates under which the cargo was admitted to France, whether foreign or reduced duties were paid, what the French laws on the subject were, and what the limitations on return cargoes were (New York *Morning Chronicle*, 10 Aug. 1804; Philadelphia *United States' Gazette*, 10 Sept. 1805; *New-York Commercial Advertiser*, 25 Nov. 1805).
3. For JM's 5 Sept. 1804 letter to Anthony Merry, see *PJM-SS*, 8:19–20. For the capture of the *Eugenia* by the British on 4 Aug. 1804, and its recapture in Long Island Sound on 7 Aug., see Jacob Wagner to JM, 16 Aug. 1804, and Merry to JM, 24 Aug. 1804, *PJM-SS*, 7:613, 631–34 and n. 1. For Albert Gallatin's 26 Sept. 1804 letter to JM about the *Eugenia*, see ibid., 8:94 and n. 1. For more details on the 1804 capture, see George Lockhart Rives, ed., *Selections from the Correspondence of Thomas Barclay, Formerly British Consul-General at New York* (New York, 1894), 183–87.

To Dolley Madison

[ca. 6 November 1805]

Yours of the 1st. instant, my dearest gives me much happiness, but it can not be compleat till I have you again secure with me. Let me know the moment you can of the time you will set out that I may make arrangements for paying th(e) Dr. &c. My Tobo. has been sold in Richd, but unfortunately th(e) bills are not yet come on, and are on N. York at 60 days,[1] so that some negociation will be necessary. I did not expect you wd. receive much from your Tenants. Don't forget to do something as to insuring the Buildings. Your question as to our situation in regard to Spain & England is puzzling. As one gets into ill humor it is possible the other may change her countenance. If a general war takes place in Europe Spain will probably be less disposed to insult us; and England less sparing of her insults. Whether a war will be forced by either is more than can be foreseen. It certainly will not if they consult their interest. The power however of deciding questions of war—and providding [*sic*] measures that will make or meet it, lies with Congress, and that is always our answer to newsmongers. Madam Turreau is here. The Genl. not. Your friends are al(l) well: except Capt. Tingey who has been in extreme danger but is mending. Mrs. Tingey also has been unwell. I inclose a letter from Payne, and one from Mrs. K.[2] Miss P's postscript makes my mouth water. Cousin Isaac's would too, if he had ever had the taste which I have had. Your ever affece.

J.M.

I have written to Gooch to hurry on with the Waggon, & to bring the Carpet if it can be secured agst. injury from the greasy & dirty companions it will have.

RC (Greensboro Historical Museum, Greensboro, N.C.). Undated; conjectural date assigned based on internal evidence and the assumption that it would have taken several days for Dolley Madison's letter to arrive at Washington.

1. See George Jefferson to JM, 29 Oct. 1805.
2. This was possibly Dolley's longtime Philadelphia friend Mary Phille Knapp whose husband, Irish-born John Knapp (d. 1820), was a clerk in the comptroller's office for many years before his death (Mattern and Shulman, *Selected Letters of Dolley Payne Madison*, 404; Washington *Daily National Intelligencer*, 31 July 1820; *ASP, Miscellaneous*, 2:308).

From James Monroe

DEAR SIR   LONDON Novr. 6th. 1805.

I have yet recd. no letter from Lord Mulgrave or other communication on the subjects depending. A note relative to the blockade of Cadiz & St. Lucar, wh. opens the ports to let in British manufactures, in consequence I presume of the decision of the Sph. govt. to respect our treaty in that point, has been published by Genl. Lyman with mine to him.[1] I did not expect it wod. have been published, as none of mine of the kind ever were before: tho' it is not material, as it happens that in treating the measure in a manner respectful to this govt., I spake of its effect in reference to us hipothetically. I advert to it here to shew you how attentive they are to every incident in which their commerce is interested. To day an important question is before the court, wh. turns, I am told on the principle established in the case of the Essex.[2] It has been postpon'd once or twice, I presume for the deliberations of the Cabinet. I may probably get the result before I conclude this letter, as I shall keep it open to the latest moment for the opportunity of the vessel wh. takes it "the Bristol packet" early to morrow morning.[3]

As soon as Mr. Bowdoin recovered his health he was impatient to get on the Continent, not being willing to take the responsibility of remaining here longer, & feeling also some desire to be in the way to render some service in his mission. There appeared to me to be reasons both for his going & staying; as however he was resolved to go, I did every thing in my power in conversation with him, & by letter to Genl. Armstrong, to promote a perfect harmony between them. I gave it as my opinion to Mr. Bowdoin that he had nothing to do with the French govt., and ought to leave every thing with it concerning Spain to Genl. Armstrong: that he ought even to decline informal conversations with those who might be sent to sound him in the business on its part, & refer such agents to the Genl.: that such attempts wod. not be made but in the hope of dividing our ministers to profit of it: that he wod. go to Paris under circumstances materially different from those wh. existed when I went there; then a negotiation was actually to be held with Spain, in which France was called on to fulfill a promise made to our govt. to me in person, while a minister there; that I went by the order of my govt. &ce: that at present the negotiation with Spain till new instructions from you were recd., was at an end; that he had never been accreditted with France, had no instructions &ce. To this doctrine he fully acceded.[4] Still it is probable, if a treaty is formed, indeed I do not see how it can be otherwise, that it must be with Spain, in which he wod. of course be the party. My effort was to push France into an acquiescence, with the terms we were willing to give Spain, & pressing the latter, keep the former out of the business. But that could not be done for reasons you have seen. At present the thing comes back to France, of whom in case it is done in a manner quite amicably, without an essential change of the attitude at home, wh. certainly has its dangers, she will be the sole party; spain will have to thank her for taking the whole into her hands. Under such circumstances might it not be well to unite them in a power to make a treaty, such as may be necessary with Spain? If it be made at Paris with the Sph. ambassidor it will be easy. If at Madrid, they may correspond & sign by agreement. I merely hint these things to draw yr. attention to them. They are both good men, with sound principles, & where they may be respectively gratified not only without injury, but even with advantage to the publick, it may be well to do it. These remarks bring to my recollection what occurr'd in the case of Mr. Pinckney, wh. I may not have sufficiently explained in my other letters. Having begun the negotiation with him, before I recd. a seperate commission, it seemed to be left in a great measure with me, either to consider him as removd or continued after I recd. one. Your letter to him was an acceptance only of his resignation, without expressing any dissatisfaction with his conduct; nor was any expressed in yrs. to me. The question was, whether his continuance was likely to do any injury? I was clear in the opinion that it was not. Indeed I thought his discontinuance likely to do injury, & had frankly told him so, when he offered to withdraw, as far as he could, soon after my arrival, before I recd. the seperate commission. He wished to continue because (in addition to publick motives wh. he appeard to me to feel strongly) he thought his removal wod. degrade him in the UStates. Under those circumstances I told him, that I knew it would be perfectly satisfactory to the President and yourself that he shod. continue to act with me, & in requesting him to do it, that I shod. comply with his & yr. wishes.[5] In this light we proceeded in the business together, & he has since continued to act. He appeared to be highly sensible of the delicacy shewn him by the President, & will withdraw with sentiments of the highest regard for him & yr.self. What I stated in my other letters of him is correct. With certain defects of a personal nature, wh. are also unsuited to his publick station, he has as a publick character, some very excellent qualities; such as integrity, independance of foreign influence, a contempt for what is called being a favorite at court, when the favoritism is to be obtained at the expence of the interest of his country, of his political principles &ce. These are comparatively inferior topicks, but yet an explanation of them may be useful.

I have just recd. an account of a complete victory obtd. by Ld. Nelson over the French & Spanish squadrons off Cadiz, in wh. 19. ships are taken & destroyed.[6] The details will be communicated by the gazettes wh. accompany this. The event is very important in respect to this country, & not otherwise in a more general view, as it may tend to preserve a balance between the parties at war. The overthrow of Genl. Mack had produc'd some degree of consternation, which this event has in a great measure dissipated. Our attitude with respect to both is I think better, if any thing, than before they took place.

I have also just heard that Judge Scott has condemned the vessel alluded to in the commencment of this. There were I am told some circumstances wh. distinguishd the case from that of the Essex, such as that it did not appear that the duty had been paid; tho' as the cargo was landed that was of course. It is stated that the judge enter'd fully in to the subject; adverted to rumors &ce of new orders and a new doctrine being introduc'd by the govt. which he disavowd insisted that the doctrine in the case of the Polly Lasky still govd. & was that which he applied to the case before him. He then stated that the landing of the goods & paying the duties, was never considered as conclusive proof, that the voyage was not continuous; that they were only circumstances, which might be controuled by others. I understand that the sum of his doctrine amounted, in clear terms, to this, that a trade in the productions of the Islands between the UStates, & their parent country might be lawful; that it would be so if the productions were landed, the duty on them paid, & they incorporated into the stock of the country, which might be done by their not having been imported for exportation, which wod. be judged to be the case if they were purchased in the country, by the Exporter. I do not know that he determined that in no case the Importer might not export the goods; I rather think he did not go into that question, or whether they might not be put in the same ship; but in laying down the general principle as above, cautiously evaded adverting to such facts, as would tie him up hereafter, in the application of it. I suspect that this is the ground which will be taken by Ld. Mulgrave in his answer to my letters, if he makes one. Our merchants here say that the rule of this court may be easily complied with, & will do no harm except in the cases that have or may occur before it is known in America: that cargoes may be sold &ce., & that that fact is known & anticipated here by those who make the rule. Was this step then taken to make an experiment of what we would bear, with intention to go further if it was found it might be done with safety? Or has the govt. repented of it, and only seeks some to cover its retreat from the ground it had in part taken? It is hardly presumeable that it contemplated going no further at first than it has done: indeed I understood Ld. Mulgrave, as insisting that the trade between the UStates & the parent country could not be tolerated, tho' it is true he said that our conversation was to be considered as informal. The impression here too among the merchants & others, taken from the decisions of the court, & what was said by the judge in the argument, was that it was intended to go further, & even cut up the trade except between the UStates & the Colonies. That such was the intention in the begining is also presumeable from the consideration that little is done if nothing farther is done. Be the motive for halting what it may, there is then much cause to apprehend that the object will be resumed when the occasion favors. It seems probable that the opposition which the measure is likely to produce in the UStates, is one among the principal causes which have produc'd the hesitation. If that be true it proves that it is not intended to hazard a war with us for the object, and of course that the way to obtain a change of policy is to take the affair up seriously in some mode or other. Such a proceeding on our part wod. be likely to produce a good effect in reference to the object with the northern powers. It seems to me to be impossible that they shod. be indifferent to the object, if they were made to understand the question. At present they might not be able or willing to aid us in it, but it wod. draw their attention to the march this govt. was stealing on them, and dispose them to interpose their good offices, when their danger from another quarter was less eminent. I am persuaded that to tranquilize them was one of the objects in the publication of the late pamphlet.[7] I have conferr'd with *the Minister of Sweden* on the subject who is far from wishing any concession to be made on our part in it. He thinks the interest of the northern powers with us in the question. If the subject is acted on, the merits shod. be opend to the publick, so that they may be understood every where. I think such an issue as shewed us a party, & made a question in the case, leaving the door open not to accomodation only, but which preserved the existing relations, wod. also produce a good effect in France. To do nothing is to acknowledge the doctrine. For us to make a question & illustrate it, is what this govt. does not appear to wish; It is possible Ld. Mulgrave may give such an answer to my letters as may aid in designating the course to be taken; but the presumption is that none will be given.

Many circumstances which have just come to hand seem to indicate that Prussia is abt. to take or has taken the part of the allies in the war.[8] It is said that her troops have taken possession of Hanover in the name of G. Britain; that some of her troops have taken the field & are approaching the Inn, so as to favor their cause. The fact will be known in a few days if so. If these powers were to succeed agnst France I do not think that their union afterwards wod. last long. This very attempt of G. B. to wound them thro us, while they were aiding her in another tho' common cause wod. tend to weaken it. What effect this measure will have among our merchants & others I know not: much will doubtless depend on it. I have communicated freely with those here, to draw facts & information from all who possessed them, without regard to shades of political opinion. Indeed I have thought it my duty to give them information of the state of the business for their own use & that of their friends.

Two circumstances I will mention while I think of them, for I shall keep the letter open a day longer, as the opportunity admits it. On my return thro' Holland I saw Mr. Alexander, & found him in much better health than when I saw him before, & the reports I have since heard make the same favorable representation.[9] He bears a good character, & has other claims to consideration. A Mr. Hargrave formerly British consul at Algiers, now here in distress, claims some recompense for services rendered us in our Barbary business under the auspices of Mr. King.[10] I soon informed him, that I had no documents illustrative of his claim, & altho' his were strong, yet I cod. only submit his case to you, wh. I wod. do. That you wod. communicate with Mr. King, ascertain how much if any thing was due, & direct the pament of it. He was not satisfied, but continued to harrass me with letters wh. I wod. not answer. I recd. from him 7. of wh. I send you such as will illustrate his pretentions.

On the subject of my expences on the Continent I shall probably write you by this opportunity. I shall postpone the final settlement of them till my return home,

8th. I send you the morning paper wh. I believe adds nothing to the statement of yesterday. Shod. the vessel be detained longer in port I shall certainly write you again by it. Shod. I be detained here to receive an answer to this, it will give Mrs. Monroe & myself much pleasure to be able to render Mrs. Madison & yrself any service, in bringing any articles you may want. I am dear Sir yr. friend & servt

JAS. MONROE

I have sent you a box of pamphlets &ce. wh. are charged to the govt. This is given to Mr. Parish a respectable young man.

RC (DLC: Rives Collection, Madison Papers); letterpress copy (NN: Monroe Papers). Underlined phrase in RC in code; decoded interlinearly by JM, and decoded here by the editors. For the code, see *PJM-SS*, 4:352 n. 1.

1. The 1 Nov. 1805 London *Times* printed a copy of Monroe's 28 Oct. 1805 note to William Lyman and a copy of Mulgrave's 27 Oct. 1805 letter to Monroe reporting the modification of the blockades of Cádiz and Sanlúcar de Barrameda. For the modification, see Thomas Auldjo to JM, 2 Nov. 1805, and n. 1.

2. Sir William Scott's 6 Nov. 1805 condemnation of the ship *Little Cornelia*, which belonged to James Arden of New York, and part of the cargo, was printed in the 17 Jan. 1806 New York *Morning Chronicle*. The ship had carried a cargo of sugar from Martinique to New York and shortly thereafter carried sugar to the Netherlands. Scott based his decision on actions taken in unloading and reloading the cargo at New York that indicated they were done in an attempt to hide the fact that the sugar imported was the same sugar that was reloaded less than a week later and sent to Europe.

3. The *Bristol Packet* sailed from Gravesend, England, on 15 Nov. 1805 and arrived at New York on 11 Jan. 1806. In addition to passengers and cargo, the ship carried over four thousand letters (*New-York Gazette & General Advertiser*, 6 and 11 Jan. 1806).

4. Either Monroe misunderstood Bowdoin or the latter changed his mind upon arriving in Paris on 1 Nov. 1805, since he was soon complaining that John Armstrong did not keep him informed of events. Bowdoin also responded eagerly when approached by "the agent of the agent" of Manuel Godoy to reestablish negotiations with Spain, and he passed on to George W. Erving, with instructions to show them to Godoy, the propositions made earlier to Armstrong by an agent of Talleyrand for the U.S. acquisition of the Floridas that Armstrong had shown Bowdoin only after swearing him to secrecy. Bowdoin's imprudent actions caused a serious rift between him and Armstrong (Skeen, *John Armstrong*, 77–80; "The Bowdoin and Temple Papers," *Collections of the Massachusetts Historical Society*, 7th ser., 6 [1907]: 262, 269, 279–85).

5. On the contrary, on 8 Jan. 1804 Jefferson told Monroe to use whatever methods were necessary to induce Pinckney to return, saying that if Monroe did so, he would "render us in this the most acceptable service possible"; and in a 9 Nov. 1804 coded letter JM told Monroe that Pinckney was "*well* off in *escaping reproof* for his agency has been very *faulty* as *well as feeble*" (*PJM-SS*, 8:271 n. 9, 270).

6. The Battle of Trafalgar.

7. Monroe referred to James Stephen's *War in Disguise*.

8. For Prussia's position at this time, see William Lee to JM, 18 Oct. 1805, and n. 3.

9. For Lawson Alexander's mental health, see Sylvanus Bourne to JM, 29 Dec. 1803, and Monroe to JM, 14 Sept. 1804, *PJM-SS*, 6:244 and n. 1, 8:48.

10. Lewis Hargreaves was apparently never British consul at Algiers. He lived in Tunis and in 1802 he carried a box of jewels intended for the bey of Tunis, purchased by Rufus King and sent to William Eaton (*PJM-SS*, 2:316, 317 n. 3, 387 and n. 1, 433; 3:293, 457).

From James Wilkinson

S<small>IR</small>,   S<small>T</small> L<small>OUIS</small> November 6th. 1805

When I arrived in this Territory I found Rufus Easton Esqr occupying the Office of Attorney general, under the appointment of Governor Harrison, which was vacated by his acceptance of the Office of Territorial Judge.

Particular reasons prevented my filling the vacancy, but on the 29th. Ulto. the day when the General Court commenced its first term, I appointed a District Attorney to attend the same, believing no exception would be taken to the appointment, since the Territory is divided into Districts; This Officer was however rejected by the Judges, on the grounds set forth in the report (of Mr. Donaldson) No. 1, herewith enclosed,[1] and I the next day appointed him Attorney general, but have to regret that this measure of accommodation, did not meet the approbation of the Court, as will appear by the report No. 2. from the same Gentleman.[2]

Whilst I lament this incident, because of its unfavorable aspect, towards that Spirit of conciliation and harmony which I had flattered myself would mark the intercourses of the Territorial Officers, I must hope that my conduct may be justified by usage immemorial, by Precedents innumerable, by the arrangements of my Predecessor, and by the first, fifth and ninth sections of the Act "further providing for the Government of the District of Louisiana."[3]

It had been proposed to commence the first session of the Legislature on the 4th. Instant but the intervention of the Court prevented, and I shall now endeavor to postpone all legislative proceedings, until the heats and animosities which have occurred, between the Judges and the grand Jury have Subsided; indeed the high powers claimed by the Judges, and the extravagant doctrines held forth by them, would probably widen the breach they have made, and which I am desirous to close, was the legislature to be immediately convened; I shall however watch over the Public Interests, and will promote those of the community, with my best skill and Judgement.

In my letter of the 29th. Ulto., I transmitted you the depositions of David Fine and his wife and Lt. Hughes, respecting the conduct of Judge Easton;[4] having previously furnished the Judge Copies of those Documents, and warned him in the presence of Governor Harrison of my intention—I since understand the Judge has attempted to extenuate his conduct in the case of Fine, buy endeavoring to prove the validity, of the concession purchased from Masterson, which renders it necessary for me to apprize you, that this concession was forfeited by the 14th. Article of the Spanish Regulations respecting the granting of lands, uttered on the 9th. of September 1797, by the then Governor General of the Province of

Louisiana, Don Manuel Gayoso de Lemos, which sets forth that "the new Inhabitant to whom a concession of land shall have been granted, shall forfeit the same, if within one year he does not begin to settle it, and the same with him who by the third year shall not have cultivated six acres on every hundred" and by the 15th. Article of the same regulations it is also declared that "the Settler will not be permited to sell his lands unless he has raised three crops, the produce of the tenth part of his cultivated land." It is also equally clear that this concession of Mastersons, was excluded by the settlement of Fine, under the Act of Congress of the 2nd. of March last,[5] and I beg leave for illustration of this transaction, to refer you to the Deposition of Masterson, which will be found under cover.[6]

I trespass on your attention the Copy of a Notification which has caused me great trouble, and drawn on me much obloquy, and I have no doubt, the Proclamation I have this day issued of which you have also a Copy enclosed,[7] will draw on me a load of unmerited opprobrium, yet I feel myself justified in both cases, by a sense of duty to the Public and to Individuals—But I do sincerely regret that the conduct and declared opinion of the Judges, should have rendered the last Act necessary, for I have been taught by experience, that if license was given to all persons without qualification or responsibility, to return Plats of Survey to the Recorders Office, a door would be opened to excessive frauds, and endless confusion would ensue.

This letter will be handed to you by Mr Parke the Representative to Congress from the Indiana Territory,[8] who is well acquainted with this Territory, its Population and trading Characters. With perfect respect I am Sir your Obedt Servt[9]

JA: WILKINSON

RC, two copies, and enclosures (DNA: RG 59, TP, Louisiana, vol. 1); Tr of enclosures (DNA: RG 46, President's Messages, 9B–A3). First RC in a clerk's hand, signed by Wilkinson; docketed by Wagner. Second RC marked "Duplicate"; in a clerk's hand, signed by Wilkinson; docketed by Wagner. Minor differences between the copies have not been noted. For surviving enclosures, see nn. 1–2, 6–7, and 9.

1. The enclosure (5 pp.; in a clerk's hand, except for Donaldson's complimentary close and signature; addressee inserted by Wilkinson; printed in Carter, *Territorial Papers, Louisiana-Missouri,* 13:256–59) is a copy of James L. Donaldson to Wilkinson, 29 Oct. 1805, stating that when he appeared before court that day and presented his commission as district attorney for St. Louis to judges Rufus Easton and John B. C. Lucas, they rejected it on the grounds that the governor could only appoint an attorney general and that a district attorney could not argue in a superior territorial court. They then required Donaldson to spend much time presenting arguments in defense of his commission and again rejected it, after which observing that they had no personal objections to Donaldson, they offered him the post as prosecuting attorney under an appointment from the court. Donaldson declined the post because acceptance "would be a formal renunciation of the right of the Governor," whereupon the judges named William Carr prosecuting attorney instead.

2. The enclosure (4 pp.; in a clerk's hand, except for Donaldson's complimentary close and signature; addressee inserted by Wilkinson; docketed by Wagner; printed ibid., 261–63) is a copy of Donaldson to Wilkinson, 3 Nov. 1805, reporting that the court had nullified the appointment as territorial attorney general that Wilkinson had conferred on him on 30 Oct. He listed the reasons the court had given for rejecting his appointment and argued against them.

3. Section 1 of the 3 Mar. 1805 "Act further providing for the government of the district of Louisiana" vested the executive power of the territory in the governor; section 5 stated: "for the more convenient distribution of justice, the prevention of crimes and injuries, and execution of process criminal and civil, the governor shall proceed from time to time as circumstances may require, to lay out those parts of the territory in which the Indian title shall have been extinguished, into districts, subject to such alteration as may be found necessary; and he shall appoint thereto such magistrates and other civil officers as he may deem necessary"; section 9 stated: "the laws and regulations, in force in the said district, at the commencement of this act, and not inconsistent with the provisions thereof, shall continue in force, until altered, modified, or repealed by the legislature" (*U.S. Statutes at Large*, 2:331–32).

4. Neither Wilkinson's 29 Oct. 1805 letter nor the depositions of the Fines have been found. Lt. Daniel Hughes's 16 Oct. 1805 deposition (2 pp.; certified by Auguste Chouteau) stated that about 25 Sept. 1805 one Henry Cassidy told Hughes that he had engaged Rufus Easton as agent to obtain the American land commissioners' sanction to the title to one-and-a-half-million acres of land granted by the Spanish governor general to several proprietors and that Cassidy had agreed to grant Easton ten thousand acres of that land as compensation to be delivered as soon as title was established. At the bottom of the deposition is an undated note by Wilkinson stating that he had read the deposition to Easton in Gov. William Henry Harrison's presence and that Easton had acknowledged the fact, stating that since the governor was advising the poor gratuitously, Easton thought he had an equal right "to advise the rich for what they would freely give Him." Easton blamed Wilkinson's exposure of his conduct on Wilkinson's federalism and said he and his friends would "demolish" Wilkinson and Harrison. For Easton's dealings with David Fine, see Carter, *Territorial Papers, Louisiana-Missouri*, 13:249, 321–22.

5. The 2 Mar. 1805 "act for ascertaining and adjusting the titles and claims to land, within the territory of Orleans, and the district of Louisiana" stated, among other things, that anyone who claimed under a Spanish grant had to have actually been settled on the land prior to 20 Dec. 1803 (*U.S. Statutes at Large*, 2:324–26).

6. Wilkinson enclosed the 4 Nov. 1805 deposition of Michael Masterson (1 p.; docketed by Wagner; printed in Carter, *Territorial Papers, Louisiana-Missouri*, 13:263–64) that in 1797 he had received a grant of four hundred acres of land near the Meramec River from the Spanish commandant, that he had planted turnips on it and cut down some trees, but hearing that someone else claimed the land, and having married a woman who preferred to stay in Indiana Territory, he had done nothing further. In 1804 he visited the plat where David Fine was apparently squatting, told Fine he had a title to the land, and offered to transfer it to Fine if the latter would pay Masterson for the improvements he had made, which Fine refused. In the spring of 1805 Rufus Easton stopped by Masterson's house and offered to buy the land. Masterson accepted the offer and received "ten Cows and Calves." Easton then contracted with Fine for whatever title the latter had to the land. Although evidence was given that Fine was able to read and write, he signed a 27 Dec. 1805 memorial to Jefferson with an *X*. On 30 Dec. 1805 the St. Louis bar issued an opinion that Easton's conduct in the transaction had "not been in the most distant degree, fraudulent or *mala fide*" (ibid., 249, 321–22, 329, 343, 366–68).

7. Wilkinson enclosed copies of (1) his 18 Sept. 1805 public notice regarding land sales (1 p.; in a clerk's hand, signed by Wilkinson; docketed by Wagner as received in this letter;

for the notice, see Wilkinson to JM, 21 Sept. 1805, n. 3) and (2) his 4 Nov. 1805 proclamation (1 p. each; in English and French; printed ibid., 264–65) stating that because "certain unauthorized Persons" had "presumed to enter upon the survey of the lands of this Territory" in opposition to the act providing for the government of Louisiana (see n. 3 above), causing confusion, "a perplexity of titles," and "endless litigation," he was prohibiting all persons except those authorized by the surveyor general from "prosecuting Such pernicious and unlawful proceedings."

8. New Jersey native Benjamin Parke (1777–1835) later moved to Lexington, Kentucky, where he studied law. On admission to the bar, he moved to Vincennes, Indiana Territory, where he was a strong supporter of Gov. William Henry Harrison. He served as attorney general from 1804 to 1808; he also served two terms in Congress. He resigned from both in 1808 to become a judge in the territory. He was a delegate to the state constitutional convention in 1816, and in 1817 was named federal district judge. He was for many years active in the state militia and fought at the Battle of Tippecanoe. He promoted public education and public libraries and was the first president of the Indiana Historical Society.

9. Wilkinson also enclosed copies (2 pp. each; certified on 3 Nov. 1805 by William Prince, clerk of the general court; docketed by Wagner) of the judges' 29 and 30 Oct. 1805 opinions on Donaldson's commissions as district attorney and attorney general (printed in Carter, *Territorial Papers, Louisiana-Missouri*, 13:259–61). They stated that Donaldson could not as district attorney be an officer of the court that embraced the entire territory, that no such officer had any power defined by law, that the position of attorney general existed when the territorial government was created and no subsequent law had changed that, and because, so far as the law recognized public prosecutors, it referred only to an attorney general and his deputies. They rejected his commission as attorney general on the grounds that the act creating the territory authorized the governor to appoint district officers, which did not include the attorney general; that under that law there was no provision for an attorney general and, if there were, there would still be no authorization for the governor to make the appointment.

§ From William Jarvis. *6 November 1805, Lisbon.* "My last letter of the 24th. Ultimo went by the schooner Antelope Captn. Pittman for New York;[1] Since which I have received the inclosed account [not found] of the Naval engagement off Cadiz, which I have no doubt is correct. Inclosed is also a Copy of the progress of the French Armies [not found] and the subsequent operations it appears by the advices recd. by the post of yesterday, have been still more favourable. It is confidently said that ten thousand Men have been killed & made prisoners by the French with a very small loss on their own part; but Genl. Massena had lost a leg & Genl. Launes severely wounded in both thighs.[2] Among the taken were several Officers of distinction. It is also said that between forty & fifty thousand Austrians were so situated that they would unquestionably be made Prisoners. These reports were confidently given out by the French Chargé & Consul as from actual, but not detailed advices.

"Not having time to send by this conveyance duplicates of my last, I must postpone it to the next opportunity.

"I have the pleasure to inclose a packet from Mr Pinckney. He will be here after to-morrow. Mr. Erving had reached Madrid, the 29th. Ultimo."

Adds in a postscript: "N.B. Genl. Massena is killed."[3]

RC, two copies (DNA: RG 59, CD, Lisbon, vol. 2). First RC 3 pp. Postscript omitted on second RC, but a marginal note in Jarvis's hand reads: "Sir The post of to day does not confirm the Battle in Italy: but it is now reported from the same quarter 15000 Austrians are made Prisoners in Bavaria." Minor differences between the copies have not been noted.

    1. Jarvis's last letter was dated 29 Oct. 1805, five days after his 24 Oct. letter.
    2. No report exists of Gen. Jean Lannes being injured during Napoleon's 1805 Austrian campaign.
    3. André Massena died on 4 Apr. 1817 (Chandler, *Campaigns of Napoleon*, 1123).

§ From Richard Worsam Meade. *6 November 1805, Cádiz.* "I have the honor to inclose you copy of a letter written to General Armstrong, Our Minister at Paris on the Subject of the detention of the American Ship Huntress, & to refer you to it, for the particulars of the Case.[1] I feel confident in assuring you, that if the General is enabled to procure an order from the Minister of Marine, for the cancelling of the security given, that It will put a Stop to a vast deal of the Piracies that are committed in this neighbourhood: But sir, one measure must be adopted, before our Citizens can expect to obtain any attention or protection from this Government; I mean the appointment of a Citizen of Respectability, as Consul here. Our present Consul does not reside at Cádiz, nor has he been for the last 8 months within 450 miles of his Station, His Deputy has neither Capacity or Respectability. At Algeciras a port under the jurisdiccion of this Consulate, we have no Agent, nor can it be expected any man of Respectability would reside in such a Place, unless put on the footing of a Salary. I sincerely hope this session will not pass over without a change taking place.

    "Conceiving it interesting to you, to have some details respecting the late Naval Combat in our neighbourhood, I hand inclosed a particular account [not found] made out by myself & on which you may place full reliance of the Ships returned to this port, & those whose loss we know of. I also hand you a manuscript account in Spanish [not found] kept by the Spanish officer of the Tour with a journal of the occurrences as seen from there. This account tho: the same nearly as mine any Spaniard on yr. side as coming from one of his own nation, he probably would place more confidence in. Whenever my services can be the least utility to my Country or yourself I pray you to Command me."

RC (DLC: Jefferson Papers); enclosure (DNA: RG 59, CD, Cádiz, vol. 1). RC 3 pp.; docketed by Jefferson "Meade R. W. to remove Yznardi." For surviving enclosure, see n. 1.

    1. The enclosure (5 pp.; marked "Copy") is Meade to John Armstrong, 3 Nov. 1805, describing the case of the *Huntress*, for which he was acting as agent; stating that the French and Spanish commanders seemed inclined to return the ship, but a commission of officers and the French consul had ordered the case to be sent to French minister of marine Denis Decrès; noting that most of the privateers sailing from Cádiz were owned or manned by the French; asking Armstrong to attempt to procure an order from Decrès that the fourteenth article of the convention between France and the United States would be strictly observed; and expressing surprise that the U.S. government had not done more to protect its citizens by appointing as consul at Cádiz a "Citizen of Respectability." For the case of the *Huntress*, see Anthony Terry to JM, 31 Oct. 1805, and n. 2. For article 14 of the Convention of 1800, see Miller, *Treaties*, 2:468.

¶ From Caleb Gardner, Constant Taber, and Pardon Gray. Letter not found. *6 November 1805*. Described in Jacob Wagner to Gardner, Taber, and Gray, 18 Nov. 1805 (DNA: RG 59, DL, vol. 15) as asking that the third installment of the award due them be paid by the collector at Newport, Rhode Island. Wagner stated that it would be inconvenient to depart from the prescribed form for payment, which required them to execute a power of attorney authorizing someone to receive the money for them, and that one of those who would execute the business for them was James Davidson Jr., cashier of the Bank of the United States at Washington.

From David Gelston

Private

DEAR SIR   NEW YORK NOVR. 7th. 1805

Enclosed is Capt. Bells bill of lading for two cases, I also enclose an account of the duties and expenses I have paid.[1]

The articles have received so much damage in the several changes they have undergone & the marks being so imperfect, perhaps some of the articles shipped to the President may belong to you. I have made a statement (enclosed) of the different proportions of Messrs. Robinson & Hartshornes bill of tonnage, but you will see it must be guesswork. You will have the goodness to arrange the whole.

I shall not trouble the President with another long statement, only beg leave to refer him to you.

Mr. Butler has paid his proportion of all expenses but tonnage money $168. If the statement is correct his proportion is $30.44.

The articles are all shipped to the care of the Collector at Alexandria I dare not wait longer—but unfortunately, the next day after I had engaged Capt Bell—Capt Lee, bound direct to Washington made his appearance from Connecticut. Sincerely yours

DAVID GELSTON

RC and enclosures (DLC). For enclosures, see n. 1.

1. The enclosures (4 pp.; each dated 7 Nov. 1805) are (1) a list of expenses for tonnage and light money on the *Adventure* ($168), duties on the imported goods ($45.50), and cartage and storage ($8.44), from which was deducted $9.64 received from Pierce Butler, for a total of $211.85. JM further deducted the $30.44 due from Butler for tonnage; (2) a bill of lading for two cases shipped on board the *President* from New York to the collector at Alexandria, signed by Boaz Bell Jr.; (3) a detailed statement of the $45.50 in duties; and (4) a breakdown (docketed by JM) of the $168 tonnage showing $102.34 due from Jefferson for seven boxes and two jars, $9.54 from JM for one box, $30.44 from Butler for two boxes, $15.41 for one box marked MM, and $10.27 for an unmarked box, from which JM again deducted the $30.44 due from Butler. For JM's wine that was captured by the British and brought to Halifax, see Gelston to JM, 8 Aug. 1805.

§ From Sylvanus Bourne. *7 November 1805, Amsterdam.* "I send you herewith Sundry Leyden Gazettes by which you will perceive the astonishing progress the french are making in the heart of Germany as well as in Italy & indeed unless the Prussian Cabinet decides on uniting with the allies I regard their cause as lost. What the latter powers will determine is yet problematical though by some a declaration of war on their part against France is daily expected. While the french continue to triumph on Land we find the English hold fast to their Superiority at Sea. Their victory in the late important naval engagement off Cadiz has been decisive & will operate to sustain the Superiority on that element against all the powers of the world yet for years to come & to prolong the present war in Europe for should France succeed to destroy this third coalition against her I doubt if England would consent to a peace on terms acceptable to France. The continuanc(e) of the war will cause enormous expences to GB & force her in a manner (to [*illegible*] them) to a war on the trade of neutrals seeing that her avowed enemies have not at Sea those riches which they had in former times. Such indeed is the language lately held by a Govermental writer in England as preparatory step to a predatory system they are about to pursue against the trade of the neutral nations. It does not appear by the last advices I have from London that any Satisfactory reply has been given to the remonstrances made on the subject of our trade & I fear that their late sucesses at Sea will not favr our views in this regard but America is no longer in leading Strings & has much in her power towards the support & protection of her just rights."

RC (DNA: RG 59, CD, Amsterdam, vol. 1). 2 pp.

§ From Peder Pedersen. *7 November 1805, Philadelphia.* "I have the honor to acknowledge the receipt of your Letter of the 17th. Ult.[1] enclosing the answer to M: Olsen's Letter of recredence and which accordingly has been forwarded to its destination."

RC (DNA: RG 59, NFL, Denmark, vol. 1). 1 p.; docketed by Wagner.

1. The letter has not been found, but see Jacob Wagner to JM, 17 Oct. 1805.

§ To Albert Gallatin. *8 November 1805, Department of State.* "I request you to be pleased to issue a warrant for three thousand three hundred & Seventeen dollars & eight cents, on the appropriations for the relief of Seamen, in favor of James Davidson Jnr. the holder of the enclosed bill of exchange drawn upon me on the 26th. Septr. last, for the same sum, by Josiah Blakely, Consul of the States, for St. Jago of Cuba, who is to be charged with the same."

Letterbook copy (DNA: RG 59, DL, vol. 15). 1 p.

§ From David Airth. *8 November 1805, Gothenburg.* "I had the Honour of addressing your Excellency last on the 30th. Septr. by Capt. Dillingham of an American Ship to NewYork,[1] a Copy of which is here inclosed, along with a Copy of my Letter and Memorandum of the 6th. Currt. to Count Ehrenheim the Swedish Secretary of State for Foreign Affairs.[2] The Complaints they carry to him are not of very great Importance, but still I judged it necessary not to pass them over in Silence and I hope from the Counts known estimation by all who have the pleasure of his acquaintance, that it will be the Means of preventing such things in future; I have endeavoured to put the Letter in Such language, that it cannot easily be construed as meant to give unnecessary Offence, but at same time to convey the Truth. Agreeable to your General Instructions—I will have the honour at the Close of the Year to wait upon you with a particular Acct. of the Trade of the past Season which has much exceeded both my own and the general Expectation."

RC and enclosures (DNA: RG 59, CD, Gothenburg, vol. 1). RC 2 pp. For enclosures, see n. 2.

1. The *Pomona*, Capt. John Dillingham, arrived in New York from Gothenburg about 4 Nov. 1805 (New York *Mercantile Advertiser*, 13 Apr. 1805; *New-York Commercial Advertiser*, 5 Nov. 1805).

2. The enclosures (6 pp.) consist of a copy of Airth to Frederick von Ehrenheim, 6 Nov. 1805, stating that thirteen American ships had visited Gothenburg over the summer, carrying away almost twenty thousand ship pounds of iron together with other Swedish produce; that two of the captains had "innocently" been brought into lawsuits, the particulars of which Ehrenheim would see in an enclosed memorandum. Airth pointed out that should this sort of thing continue, Americans might avoid coming to Sweden to trade. In the enclosed 6 Nov. memorandum, Airth reported that although it had been proven in court in June 1805 that the shipbroker for Capt. David Crafts had "by a mistake" not entered fifteen barrels of raw sugar with the rest of the cargo and that there was no intent to smuggle, the sugar was nevertheless confiscated by the customhouse. In the second case, Airth stated that two West Indian or Spanish seamen on board Capt. Moses M. Derkheim's ship had repeatedly disobeyed orders, neglected duties, and finally deserted. Airth had summoned all three parties to the consulate and judged that, under U.S. law and the rôle d'équipage they had signed, the men had forfeited their wages and Derkheim was not required to receive them back on board. The city magistrates "at the Intercession of some inferior and deseigning Lawyers" sentenced Derkheim to pay the men damages for being expelled from the ship, although they had deserted and had "since attempted on Shore to murder the Captain Mate and several of the Crew." The case was referred to a higher court, but Airth had been held answerable for the funds so that the ship would not be detained until that court's final decision. Airth added that he had been told by several people familiar with Swedish law that the magistrates' decision was "in direct opposition" to Swedish maritime and common law.

§ From William C. C. Claiborne. *8 November 1805, New Orleans.* "I enclose you a copy of the *answer* which the House of Representatives have returned to my address,[1] You will perceive that *it* is respectful and friendly. I am happy to find that nothing of party spirit has yet been manifested, and I indulge a hope that the Members generally will pursue a conduct which will be approved.

"Believing that a *declaration* of the devotion of the House of Representatives of this Territory to the interest of the United States, would, at this particular crises, produce a happy political effect, I shall endeavor to bring *it* about; but at present I cannot say how far my wishes may be gratified. I am however impressed with an opinion that the Creoles of the Country are, for the most part, well disposed—and several influential natives of France, who are here, seem fully to appreciate the merits of the American Government."

RC and enclosure (DNA: RG 59, TP, Orleans, vol. 7); letterbook copy (Ms-Ar: Claiborne Executive Journal, vol. 15). RC 1 p.; in a clerk's hand, signed by Claiborne; docketed by Wagner. Minor differences between the copies have not been noted. For enclosure, see n. 1.

1. The enclosure (1 p.; with Claiborne's appended note: "*unanimously adopted*"; docketed by Wagner; printed in Carter, *Territorial Papers, Orleans*, 9:520) is a copy of the 8 Nov. 1805 reply of the territorial house, signed by speaker Jean Noël Destréhan, to Claiborne's 4 Nov. 1805 address, promising their best efforts to promote the good of the country and trusting that the persons recommended as councilors to the president would "prove worthy of his approbation."

From James Monroe

DEAR SIR   LONDON novr. 9. 1805.
It is probable I may sail in the remittance Captn. Law in Jany. to be with you the last of Feby or first of March. Nothing will prevent it but the season, especially shod. it be unfavorable. However I will write you by the John Bulkeley for Phila. which sails next week. I shall be able then to bring you full information of the state of our affairs in this Country, & on the continent, & it is possible that it may be better for me to come then than even at this time. My family are all in delicate health, & having an infant of only three years old, are circumstances wh. make it an arduous undertaking. I am Dear Sir your friend & servt

JAS. MONROE

Shod. you intimate yr. wish for me to remain a while, or come directly it will be conclusive either way.

RC (DLC: Rives Collection, Madison Papers).

§ To Alexander Coffin Jr. *9 November 1805, Department of State.* "Herewith are returned, as you request, the papers respecting the Ship Penman, which accompanied your letter of the 3d. ult. It would be a precedent contrary to the established usage of the Executive, to afford pecuniary aid in prosecuting the appeal in a case like the present. But as the other owners do not lie under the same inability as yourself, with respect to the means, and as their interest will doubtless engage them to take the necessary steps for a reversal of the condemnation, it would seem that your portion of the vessel & cargo would necessarily participate in the benefit of their measures."

Letterbook copy (DNA: RG 59, DL, vol. 15). 1 p.

§ To Anthony Merry. *9 November 1805, Department of State.* "I beg leave to trouble you with Duplicate Copies of two Documents concerning John Harl⟨a⟩n, who appears to have been impressed into the British Ship of war, Petterell, which is supposed to be at this time on the American Coast, off the Harbor of Charleston, in South Carolina;[1] and to ask the Interposition of your good Offices, to procure the Release of this man, whose Citizenship is fully proved by the Documents alluded to."

FC (DNA: RG 59, Notes to Foreign Ministers and Consuls, vol. 1). 1 p.

1. The British sloop of war *Peterell* was reported as having engaged in a brief battle with the French privateer *Superb*, Captain Dominique, off North Edisto Island in the middle of October (*New-York Commercial Advertiser,* 29 Oct. 1805).

§ From George Jefferson. *9 November 1805, Richmond.* "I was by last post favor'd with yours of the 4th. [not found], and (not being able to exchange a draft agreeably to your wish) now inclose you Pickett Pollard & Johnston's dft. on Leroy Bayard & Mc.Evers of New York at 50 d/s for $:788.^{50}/$_{100}$; that being the amount of the balance due on rect. of your Tobo."

RC (DLC). 1 p.

§ From William Willis. *9 November 1805, New Bedford.* "I have to request the favor of you to enclose me one of the authenticated coppies of the affadavit of Benjamin B Mumford and Willm. B Bouen before Mr. Cathalan at Marseilles, the 5th of Feby. 1802. respecting the sailing of the Ship Pomona in my absence to France &c.[1]

"I suppose there are two of those Coppies in the office of State, authenticated, under Mr. Cathalans Seal of Office, as I sent one of them to Mr. Pinckney at Madrid to be forwarded to you, after he should read it, and the other I enclos'd you direct. One of those coppies is now become essentially necessary to me, in a weighty law suit, the tryal of which may come on in a few days. I therefore Sir request you to forward one of them, to me, at Boston as soon as you conveniently can."[2]

RC (DNA: RC 59, CD, Barcelona, vol. 1). 1 p.

1. Copies of the affidavit were enclosed in Willis to JM, 15 Dec. 1802, and 6 July 1803, *PJM-SS,* 4:192, 5:146.
2. On 20 Nov. 1805 JM sent Willis a copy of "the depositions of Benj. B. Mumford and Wm. B. Bowen taken before Mr. Cathalan on the 5th. February 1802" (DNA: RG 59, DL, vol. 15; 1 p.).

§ From Henry Hill Jr. *10 November 1805, Havana.* "I have the honor to acknowledge the recpt. of your circulars of 1st. & 12th. of July, and am happy that the instructions contained in that of the 12th., are such as in future will prevent an abuse which has been largely acted upon in this Island, to the prejudice of our legitimate commerce.

"I have also the honor, to enclose you a statement of the abuses upon our commerce in this Island, with some observations thereon, which I wrote with the intention of publishing in the United states for the information of our merchants;[1] but on reflecting that it might militate against the views of the Govt., which it is my duty and wish to promote, and conceiving them, the best judges of the propriety of publishing, & of the expediency of correcting the abuses enumerated, I transmit it to your department to be made use of as may be deemed convenient.

"My returns in January will furnish matter & proofs to authenticate facts, which I hope to have the hono⟨r⟩ of delivering myself, as I propose visiti⟨n⟩g the United States at that time, and leaveing here a substitute till my return, unless instructions from you should direct me otherwise.

"I hope that this exposition of abuses with other proofs you are already in possession of, will call the attention of our government to the adoption of measures which may speedily alleviate from oppressive impositions a considerabl⟨e⟩ branch of our commerce.

"I am aware of the delicacy of placing any restrictions upon the enterprize of our merchants, but conceive that in this instance it might be made a popular measure, & would be ultimately greatly to their advantage & the country generally. It could not but have the desired effect. I know the sentiments of the people of this Island are such, of the planters particularly who are the prevailing interest, that they would oblige this Govt. to admit our trade on any terms we should please to dictate.

"I view the abuses upon us of an enormous & flagrant nature, and the object of restraining them by legislative aid, not alone as a matter of interest to our merchants, but in a national light, and conceive the honor, character, & interest of the nation concernd, to prevent them. This statement of abuses is accompanied with the orders of the 28th. of may & June therein refered to.

"I also inclose you copy of a sentence passed against Josiah Blakely Esqr. which will serve to shew you the punishment annexed to the act of officiating as Consul of the United states in this Island.[2] I appealed for Mr Blakeley from this sentence to the Council of the Indies in Madrid, to prevent its being carried into effect; but this sentence so much alarmed him that he left StYago immediately on receiving intimation of it, and has gone to NewOrleans. He is a persecuted and unfortunate man, I know him well, and has not deserved the malice of his enemies, nor the persecution he has suffered. He left a Mr. Andrew Hadfeg in charge of his office, whom I have confirmed in it, conceiving an agent necessary in that place. Captures by french privateers have not been so frequent of late as hither to. This Government have taken more effectual measures to suppress their piracies—many of them have assumed the Spanish flag. But at Barracoa a scene of iniquitous plunder is still continued by them, which is the only port in the Island where they now carry any prizes. At the West End of the Island there is a number of privateers cruizing, which plunder almost every Vessel they meet with, and send their prizes to campeachy.

"In this quarter there has been three recent captures by Spanish privateers. The schooner Lititia of Phila. Capt Franklin bound from Phila. to New Orleans, sailing under a coasting licence, with a valuable Cargo of dry goods—Brig Argo of Dresden Capt Lilly bound from Jamaica to New York with a Cargo Rum & Brig

Mary of newbern N.Carolina, Capt. Barnet, bound from Jamaica to newbern with a cargo of Rum and $12.000 in specie.[3]

"The former of these Vessels was given up without being libelled with $250 damag(es.) The second was cleared in the marine Court of admiralty and damages awarded, the latter is now under adjudication. The present Genl. of Marines seems favorably disposed towards our commerce and if he persecutes the privateersmen as he promises to do, I hope our commerce may be subjected to less interruption than hitherto. It is only Captures by spanish privateers or Ships of War he has cognizance of. Those made by french privateers come under the jurisdiction of the Govr. and Auditor of War; from neither of whom justice can be expected. The former is timid, and fearful of exposing himself to some responsability, therefore will do nothing without the consent of the latter which exhonerates him from any responsability, and the auditor is a venal character who will do nothing without money, and sells his authority and decrees, to the party that will pay the most for them.

"Sea Letters and certificates of property are esteemed indispensable documents here, and every Vessel navigating these seas ought to be furnishd with them."

Adds in an 11 Nov. postscript: "An Embargo is this day laid on, in consequence of a Schooner sailing with some troops & 50.000 Dollars said to be destined to St. Augustine, which is probable as the troops of that place have not been paid for some time."

RC, enclosures, and duplicates of enclosures (DNA: RG 59, CD, Havana, vol. 1). RC 8 pp.

1. The enclosure (29 pp.; marked "*duplicate*") is a copy of Hill's 1 Nov. 1805 statement of "Abuses on the commerce of the United States in the Island of Cuba." Hill listed thirteen examples of Spanish regulations and practices that hindered U.S. trade with Cuba, including a duty of 32½ percent on goods imported in American ships and on the sale of American ships there to non-Spanish buyers, the requirement of a vast number of documents describing the cargoes, the corruption, and the insistence that American merchants and captains hire Spanish translators and brokers. He argued that because the war impeded Spanish trade with the colony, it was dependent on Americans for goods and provisions; he noted that when no ships had arrived for several days, the alarmed authorities lowered the duty by 7 percent, and in January and March of 1805, they had opened ten ports to neutral trade and allowed neutrals to import products that had previously been allowed to enter only in Spanish vessels. He reported that Cuban exports amounted to $12,000,000 annually and since the port of Havana was opened to trade six hundred American ships had arrived; he added that without them to carry away Spanish produce, the plantations and merchants would fail, and he suggested that an interdiction on trade from the United States would demonstrate that. He cited figures to support his argument that American merchants failed to make a profit on goods they sold in the island, except for the slave trade, but the merchants were unable to see that. The local authorities argued that the Americans must be gainers by the trade, since they flocked to the island while knowing well what awaited them. He compared trade conditions at Cuba with those at other West Indian islands, Spanish, British, and French, to Cuba's detriment. In an added note he further broke down the duties paid in Spain and in Cuba and differentiated between overall cost of duties on goods imported from the United States via Spain and those directly imported. In a postscript dated ca. 11 Nov., he said he had been told the intendant had resolved "to prohibit all British manufactured goods." In a second undated note following the postscript, he analyzed more minutely the method of calculating the duties using soap as an example and proved

that the duty was not the stated 32½ percent but was actually 37 percent. He said "[i]t was a long time before" he could ascertain how the duties were calculated, adding that "not three merchants in this city" could understand it.

2. The enclosure (3 pp.; in Spanish) is a copy of the decree affirming a 15 Sept. 1803 decree banishing Josiah Blakeley from Cuba with the added condition that should he return, he would be imprisoned for five years. He was sentenced for having, with the connivance of others, issued fraudulent papers to cover a shipment of goods in 1799.

3. The schooner *Letitia*, Captain Franklin, bound from Philadelphia to New Orleans, was captured off Matanzas, Cuba, on 16 Oct. 1805 by the Spanish privateer *Vengeance*, Capt. Antonio Rouett; the brig *Argo*, Captain Lilly, was bound from Jamaica to New York with a cargo of rum, when it was captured by the Spanish privateer *Flor de Mays*, Captain Lissard, and carried into the west end of Cuba (*New-York Commercial Advertiser*, 6 Nov. 1805; New York *Mercantile Advertiser*, 15 Nov. 1805).

To Dolley Madison

WASHINGTON Monday [ca. 11–18] Novr. [1805]

I have recd. my dearest your letter by the last mail. As the Horses have been bought, the bargain must not only be maintained but Mr. Patton must understand that I am particularly indebted to him for his kindness on that as well as on other occasions.[1] I inclose a note from Mr. Ker relating to the Cook. It implies that she was hired for a year and must be paid for accordingly. Let me know what answer is to be given; and what deductions are to me [*sic*] made for Cloaths &c. I inclose also the little bundle from Miss Wheeler. Cousin Isaac was duly reminded of the reward in store for his share in the trust. Mrs. Forrest has also just sent in a letter to be inclosed, to which Payne adds another. I wish it were possible for you to get nearly at the Dr's Bill. Why might you not request it in order to be forwarded to me? I forgot to mention that the 2 other Vols. of Dallas might follow the 1st. in the same channel. Mr. Livingston arrived here last night.[2] We are to have as a guest an Ambassador from Tunis who is on board one of the Frigates arrived from the Mediterranean.[3]

I am rejoiced to hear that your knee remains perfectly healed. Take care of it I beseech you, till it can defy ordinary exercise, and that you may the sooner undertake your journey home. Being obliged to write in a hurry, I can only add my best love to you, with a little smack for your fair friend, who has a sweet lip, tho' I fear a sour face for me.

J. M.

RC (NjP). Day of month and year not indicated; conjectural date assigned based on the fact that 4, 11, 18, and 23 were the Mondays in November 1805, and internal evidence.

1. This letter has not been found: the earliest surviving letter from Dolley mentioning that the horses had already been bought was her first letter of 12 Nov. 1805.

2. According to a newspaper report with a dateline of Thursday, 14 Nov. 1805, Robert R. Livingston arrived in Washington "on Monday last," or 11 Nov. 1805 (Philadelphia *Aurora General Advertiser*, 18 Nov. 1805).

3. Tunisian ambassador Soliman Melimeni, arrived at Norfolk in the *Congress* on 7 Nov. 1805 (*New-York Commercial Advertiser*, 18 Nov. 1805).

From Tench Coxe

SIR   PHILADELPHIA November 11t. 1805

I have the honor to transmit to you official copies of two Patents of the King of Great Britain for Land in West Florida, this day received from William Lyman Esquire, Consul of the U.S. in London. One of them is to George Tead for 2000 acres on Mobile River, recorded May 4. 1770 in Book E fo. 14 Recorders office West Florida, as certified by Fras. P(on)ssett D. Recorder. The other is to Mrs. Rebecca Blackwell for 1000 as. in West Florida on Thompson's Creek recorded July 28. 1772 in Book A N.1. p. 374 as certified by Ph. Livingston Jr D. Secy. At the request of Mr. Lyman I beg leave to present this letter as a claim to the lands in the two patents [*illegible*] & described in behalf of the concerned. The original patents were proposed by Mr Lyman to be sent to the U.S. by the next ship. They were lodged in his office on the 10th. of September 1805. If it should happen, that the Department of State is not the right place of destination for these papers, I beg the favor of your directing them to be transmitted with this letter or with a copy of it to the Commissioners office or other proper place. It may serve Mr. Lyman, if you would be so good as to have me informed what other steps of any kind it may be proper or necessary to take. I have the honor to be, Sir yr. respectful h. Servant

                                                              TENCH COXE

Draft (PHi: Tench Coxe Papers).

From James Monroe

No. 36.

SIR   LONDON November 11. 1805.

Of the destruction of the austrian army, consisting of 100,000 men, and near Ulm on the Danube, under Gen. Mack, by the French commanded by the Emperor, you will have heard before this reaches you, as you likewise will of the naval victory which was obtained by Lord Nelson, who perished in the action, over the combined squadrons of France and Spain near Cadiz. I decline therefore giving the details of those very important events.[1] These naval *disasters ought* to *prompt* the *French government to hasten* an *adjustment* of our *affairs with Spain*, since it must *sell*[2] that *we stand* almost *alone* of the *asserters* of the *rights of the neutral flag. I trust* that *Genl. Armstrong* will be *able* to *impress this with effect* on the *ministry* of *that government.*[3] I gave to *Mr. Bowdoin* a *copy of my correspondence* with *Lord Mulgrave* on the subject of the *late seizures here, which I requested* him to *impart to general A.*[4] *Thi*[5] *motive was, that by seeing distinctly the ground on which* the *question stood,* he might *urge with more confidence* and *effect* the *necessity* of such a *policy* on the part of *the French government. I shall inform these gentlemen* by a respectable *American who leaves this in a few days for Paris,* that I shall most probably *not sail 'till* the middle of *January, when I shall be happy to carry home* such a *result* of *our affairs with Spain, as will leave our governmemorial*[6] at *liberty* to look to the other *object. They will* of course *shew* no *official document,* or make any *compromitment whatever of thi*[7] *President.* The *pamphlet*[8] called "*War in Disguise*" will furnish *evidence* sufficiently *strong* of the extent *to which this governmemorial*[9] is *disposed* to *push its pretentions,* if not *checked* by the *apprehension* of a *vigorous resistance from us.* It is proper to add that in a late decision of the court of admiralty here, it was declared by the Judge that it was not intended to introduce any new doctrine relative to the trade in question, or to interdict it to neutrals, in such productions of the Colonies of their enemies, from the neutral to the parent Country of the colony as had been incorporated into the stock of the neutral country. It is possible that this *governmemorial*[10] may *rest* the *affair on this ground,* and that Lord Mulgrave *may soon officially announce it* to me. It is my present intention and expectation to sail some time in January for New York in the Remittance, Captn. Law, when I hope to be able to bring you *such a view of our affairs,* as may be *satisfactory in respect to all these powers,* or at least *mark in more distinct colours* the course *which may ultimately be taken with each.* I am Sir with great respect & esteem yr. very obt. servant

JAS. MONROE

RC (DNA: RG 59, DD, Great Britain, vol. 12); letterbook copy (DLC: Monroe Papers). RC in a clerk's hand, except for Monroe's complimentary close and signature; docketed by Wagner. Italicized words are those encoded by Monroe's secretary and decoded here by the editors (for the code, see *PJM-SS*, 4:352 n. 1).

1. Here the letterbook copy has: "Another success is just announced of the British over the French by which four more of their ships are taken." The 11 Nov. 1805 London *Times* reported a 4 Nov. battle off Ferrol in which four French ships were defeated by a British squadron under Adm. Richard Strachan. For the defeat of the Austrians at Ulm, see William Lee to JM, 18 Oct. 1805, and n. 2. For the Battle of Trafalgar, see George W. Erving to JM, 28 Oct. 1805, and n. 12.

2. Encoded "sell"; letterbook copy has "see."

3. Encoded "country"; letterbook copy has "government."

4. For Monroe's correspondence with Lord Mulgrave about British seizures of U.S. ships, see Monroe to JM, 6 Aug. 1805, and n. 9, 16 Aug. 1805, and n. 2, and 25 Sept. 1805, and n. 2.

5. Encoded "Thi"; letterbook copy has "the."

6. Encoded "memorial"; letterbook copy has "ment."

7. Encoded "Thi"; letterbook copy has "the."

8. Encoded "painphlet"; letterbook copy has "pamphlet." For the pamphlet, see Monroe to JM, 26 Oct. 1805, and n. 4.

9. Encoded "memorial"; letterbook copy has "ment."

10. Encoded "memorial"; letterbook copy has "ment."

Wagner's Notes on Neutral Trade with Belligerents

[ca. 11 November 1805]

10 April 1805.

By 45 Geo. 3. C. 34. The King & Council are authorized to grant licences to *British Subjects* to import in *neutral vessels* for their *own* or *neutral* account, the productions of American colonies belonging to any European power, which productions are allowed to be used or consumed in G. Britain. No greater duties are to be paid than would be payable if they were imported in a British Ship. Foreign sugar and coffee thus imported cannot be consumed in G. Britain. The *license* is to be granted to such persons only as may have exported, or who give security to export, to the Possessions in America of the Same European power goods & commodities bearing such a proportion of value to the imports as the King and Council may direct.

The Act is limited to the war & six months after a peace.[1]

An Act was passed 27 June 1805 to consolidate and extend the provisions respecting the free ports in the W Indies.

Wool, cotton, indigo, cochineal, drugs, cocoa dyewoods, hides, furs tallow tortoise shell mahogany & other woods of the hard kind, horses and cattle, the production of the British plantations or of countries on *the continent* of America belonging to European Powers and coin, bullion & precious stones, may be imported into certain ports in Jamaica, Grenada, Dominica, Antigua, Trinidad, Tobago, Tortola, New Providence Crooked Island, St. Vincents & Bermuda—in small vessels belonging to & navigated by inhabitants of the plantations or such countries in America.

2. Tobacco, of any Island or country in America, belonging to an European Power, may be imported into those free ports in such vessels, and

reexported to Great Britain on the same terms as Tobacco, the growth of British colonies or of the US.

3. Sugar & Coffee may be carried to the Bahamas in similar foreign vessels & reexported without paying any duty; but if carried to G. Britain they are to pay foreign duties.

4. Rum, negroes and goods legally imported into the free ports except certain naval stores may be exported in British vessels to the British colonies and plantations and to the colonies on the Continent of America in their respective vessels.

5. Provision is made for the exportation in British vessels from the free ports to the other British American colonies of the goods imported from the foreign colonies in America.[2]

Instructions to the Admiralty & to British Cruisers
29 June 1805.

In consideration of the *present state of commerce*, British subjects may trade *without licence*, directly or circuitously in neutral vessels between the ports of G. Britain and those of her enemies, in Europe, not being blockaded—by *exporting* all kinds of British manufactures (except naval & military stores) as well as an enumerated variety of other goods; and by *importing* from the enemy goods contained in another list.[3]

3 Augt. 1805

The Privy Council determined not to allow the trade with hostile American colonies, except through the free ports in the West Indies according to the act of June 27. 1805; and except as to the trade to and from the River Plate and the Western part of S. America.

As a misapprehension had taken place, vessels cleared from such colonies before the 1st. Novr. Were not to be molested.[4]

Ms (DLC). Undated; date assigned based on the fact that the 3 Aug. 1805 Privy Council decision was printed in American newspapers on 11 Nov. 1805 (see n. 4 below). In Wagner's hand.

1. The 10 Apr. 1805 "Act to permit the Importation of Goods and Commodities . . ." was printed in the Philadelphia *Aurora General Advertiser,* 13 June 1805, where it was dated 27 Apr. 1805.
2. The 27 June 1805 act, 45 Geo. III c. 57, was printed in the Philadelphia *United States' Gazette* of 7, 9, and 11 Nov. 1805.
3. For the 29 June order in council, see Wagner to JM, 17 Oct. 1805, and n. 1.
4. The 3 Aug. 1805 decision was printed in the Philadelphia *Poulson's American Daily Advertiser,* 11 Nov. 1805.

§ To Anthony Merry. *11 November 1805, Department of State.* "I beg leave to trouble with Duplicate Copies of a Document concerning James Gunnill, who appears to have been lately impressed into the British Ship of War Cambrian, which is supposed to be at this time on the American Coast, or at Halifax, to which is added the Copy of a letter from the said Gunnell to General Mason of George Town; and to ask the Interposition of your good offices, to procure the Release of this man, whose Citizenship is fully proved by the Document alluded to."

Letterpress copy (DNA: RG 59, Notes to Foreign Ministers and Consuls, vol. 1). 1 p.; in Daniel Brent's hand, signed by JM.

§ From Albert Gallatin. *11 November 1805, Treasury Department.* "I have the honor to enclose a letter from Andrew Allen junr., the British Consul at Boston, together with a copy of my answer."[1]

RC and enclosures (DLC: Gallatin Papers). RC 1 p.; docketed by Wagner. For enclosures, see n. 1.

1. The enclosures (3 pp.) are Andrew Allen Jr. to Gallatin, 28 Oct. 1805, stating that Capt. Randall McDonald of the British schooner *Union*, who had carried from Halifax to Boston the crew of the American brig *Sally*, which was condemned at Halifax, had applied to the customs collector at Boston for fifty dollars payment for passage and food for the seamen, whose names Allen included in an annexed list (not found), and had been refused on the ground that the collector lacked instructions "to make disbursments under such circumstances," enclosing vouchers, and requesting in "considerations of equity" that McDonald be remunerated; and Gallatin to Allen, 11 Nov. 1805, stating that since there was no fund at the Treasury out of which such a claim could be paid, he was transmitting Allen's letter to JM, who superintended "expenditures, for the relief of American Seamen abroad."

§ From Robert Purviance. *11 November 1805, Baltimore.* "I have the honor to inclose you a Letter from Mr. Lee of Bordeaux, accompanied with Invoice and Bill of Loading, for Sundries for your Account by the Brig Lyon, which arrived this morning.[1]

"I have taken a Copy of the Invoice for my goverment in making the Entry & retained the Bill of Loading.

"You will please to give the necessary directions about the transportation of the goods to you."

RC (DLC). 1 p.; in a clerk's hand, signed by Purviance.

1. For the shipment, see William Lee to JM, 14 and 18 Sept. 1805.

From John B. C. Lucas

SIR   ST LOUIS 9ber. 12. 1805

From the statement here in Contained[1] and the vouchers in support thereof[2] and also from my solemn obligation to support by every other means its Correctness and accuracy, if controverted it appears that a plot had been Laid to prostrate the authority of the general-court of the territory of Louisianna or bring about som[e] Commotion or open resistance to its authority.

I was quite unprepared for the event, I had not the Least expectation that the grand jury would wantonly wander from their duties and insult the Court. I was on terms of friendship with several persons of the Jury specially those Called french; and I knew not of one foe among the whole; True it is several of them were unknown to me. That their zeal for vendicating what they term the right and power of the governor should excite so much acrimony and rancour, and Lead them so far astray as to commit themselves very much indeed is unaccountable to me; One would think that it should be of Little importance to the jury which of the courts or of the governor, had better right to appoint a prosecutor of the pleas of the united states. It is certain that the publick service hath not suffered nor could suffer from that Circumstance, Nor can it be supposed that the Court exercised that power for the purpose of conniving and preventing the means of making a fair and thorough inquiry.

Mr. Donaldson the recorder and Commissioner of the Land Claims having been the person whom the governor had Commissioned attorney of the District of st Louis, and on the day following attorney general, the Court after having refused to acknowledge him as being Duely Commissioned by the governor requested him to act as prosecutor of the pleas of the united states, *pro tempore;* On his refusal the Court appointed mr. Carr the agent of the u.s. for the Land Claims—I am persuaded that mr. Carr hath properly discharged his Duties on that occasion; This being the Case we must recurr to some other Cause for the strange conduct of the jury— from the affidavit here inclosed of mr. Caulks a justice of the peace, and one of the Jurors, it appears that the governor had directed the sheriff to summon for grand jurors, a certain description of Persons—Independent of that testimony it appears that this grand jury was composed of allmost all persons of the town of st Louis; the remaining part were from the district of st Louis. The best part of them are holding office, under the governor. One is his relation, and to my certain knowledge at Least, two are expectants for offices from him. Several of them Claim Large concessions of Land, are high toned monarchists, are fond of the pageantry of the governor, and hold civile authority in perfect contempt; whilst on another hand they, have a pretty good guess that I am not disposed to Countenance antidated Concessions, or fraud in any shape; that my manners and political Character, is a perfect contrast to theirs; in addition to these, judge Easton is supposed by them, to have denounced their fraud to some of the heads of Department; his politicks also give them a great umbrage; and he hath the misfortune to have incurred the displeasure of the governor. All these Circumstances Combined together, perhaps will account for the insults which a majority of the grand Jury have offered to the Court.

I Beg Leave to observe to you, sir, that as early as august Last, the governor, Judge Easton, and My self, had several conferences together; and

had agreed on the out Lines and principles of several subjects of Legislation. In pursuance of these, several bills have been drawn by mr Easton;
others, were to be drawn by the governor. I intimated at different times
since to the governor that in my opinion, it would be proper to Convene
the Legislature, for the purpose of examining the Bills drawn on the principles agreed at our first Conferences; and pass some of the most necessary
Laws. He answered me that he did not wish to Legislate much, Seeing that
the term of the session of the superior Court was first [*sic*] approaching,
mr. Easton and my self thought proper to write twice to the governor, to
request him to Convene the Legislature. We were twice answered that
other business did prevent him from giving his attendance to Legislation.
This appears from the copy of his Letters here inclosed.[3] Thus in this
Loose state of things the superior Court did sit.

There was then a bill drawn for Creating the office of attorney general
&c; but the governor, who had not been able to find time to Legislate,
Could spare time to issue two Commissions on the two first days of the
session of the court. The one of district attorney, the other of attorney
general; and all that, without any Law previously Creating such offices and
defining and regulating the powers and duties of the same. I have discovered that the governor entertains exagerated ideas of his authority, that he
is as fond of issuing proclamations and Commissions, as he is averse to
Legislation, I am disposed to believe that the military pomp which sur-
rounds him; That the former minions of the spanish government, at st
Louis, and all the tribe of monarchists that are Crowding in his house,
make him Some time Loose sight of the Line which necessarily exists between Civile[4] and military authority.

I am not one of those that believe that the opinion of two or three families is the standard of the general opinion of the inhabitants of this territory. These families were once the Cankers of the Country, when it was a
spanish colony. The industrous and independent part of the population,
both french & american, knows perfectly that their Country never Could
rise to Consequence, as long as those monopolizers should have the management of it. I neither Covet nor dispute the merit that som[e] may Claim,
in having them enrolled under their Banners. They may set their french or
spanish Machinery into action I dont dread the effects of it I have endeavoured to be an american. I hope I have succeeded. Should genuine american manners & principles be never so unfashionable among a certain
description of men at St Louis, I shall not however Change them for the
sake of humouring either great or small.

I have thought it my duty to give you sir, an accurate and a minute
account of the proceedings of the Court; of the conduct of the jury and
other circumstances; together with two Letters of the governor and the
affidavit of justice caulks and Lawyer hempstead, that government may

make such a use of the whole information as in its wisdom it may seems meet. I have the honnour to be Sir with great respect your most humble & obdt. svt.

JOHN B. C. LUCAS.

RC and enclosures (DNA: RG 46, President's Messages, 9B–A3). The enclosures may have been sent to Albert Gallatin with a request to transmit them to JM (see Lucas to Gallatin, 12 Nov. 1805, Carter, *Territorial Papers, Louisiana-Missouri*, 13:269). For enclosures, see nn. 1–3.

1. Lucas enclosed the presentment of the grand jury of the territory to the court (5 pp.; dated "October Term"; printed in Carter, *Territorial Papers, Louisiana-Missouri*, 13:248–51), denouncing Rufus Easton for obtaining "from a poor man by the name of David fine, Who resides near the River Merrimack and who has a wife and Seven Children, a Deed for about Six hundred Acres of land, Without giving him any consideration for the same"; stating that they had been hearing witnesses on the matter when they were called before the territorial supreme court and treated to conduct that was "highly indecorous, extremely insulting to the feelings of the Grand Jury, and most derogatory to the honor and dignity" of the court; complaining that the court, in violation of the general method of summoning jurors randomly at the door of the courthouse, had added six jurors to the original panel called by the sheriff; also complaining that under a court ruling they were restrained from exercising their right of inquiry without receiving permission from the prosecuting attorney to call witnesses; complaining further that the court had not allowed them to choose their own meeting room but had confined them "Twenty one in number, in a Room . . . scarce Sufficient to contain their bodies, being no more than Eleven feet by Eight an[d] ahalf feet"; stating that by annulling Wilkinson's appointment of James L. Donaldson as attorney general, "in open contempt and defiance" of the governor's authority, the court presented an example of resistance that would "encourage all the disaffected and Turbulent Spirits of the country, to oppose the laws" and lead to "utter disorganization and confusion"; and adding that the court had acted as both interested party and judge in the case and should have appealed to Congress as the proper tribunal "to define and if necessary to restrain the authority of the Governor." The document was signed by jury foreman Charles Gratiot and fourteen others.

2. Lucas enclosed (1) Edward Hempstead's 11 Nov. 1805 statement sworn before Rufus Easton (2 pp.), stating that when then sheriff Josiah McLanahan took from the court clerk's office the venire "requiring him to summon a Grand Jury," he asked for a piece of paper on which to write the names of some grand jurors; that he named five men, and when Hempstead asked why, McLanahan said he had been ordered to summon every magistrate in the St. Louis district for the grand jury and (2) Richard Caulk's 4 Nov. 1805 statement before Lucas (1 p.) that when McLanahan came to summon him to serve on the grand jury, the sheriff commented that he had been ordered to summon every judge and justice of the peace for the jury, and when Caulk asked who had so ordered him, McLanahan replied that the governor had.

3. Lucas enclosed Wilkinson's 12 and 28 Oct. (2 pp.; in a clerk's hand, signed by Wilkinson) and 2 Nov. 1805 (1 p.; in Wilkinson's hand) letters to him and Easton. The first acknowledged receipt of their 12 Oct. letter to him and stated that he would have convened the legislature before that time had not his "particular attention been called by the executive authority, to an object of National Interest now pending, at a very considerable daily expense to the General Government"; Wilkinson added that he expected the business to be concluded within a week, after which he would be ready to cooperate with them. The second acknowledged receipt of their letter of 24 Oct. 1805, which he found when he returned to

town on 26 Oct., after having been called away by "an Interesting Indian Occurrence" and "a slight indisposition, and an unexpected engagement, with the Sacque Nation," which kept him from meeting with them on 28 Oct.; he added that since their "Judicial engagements" would begin on 29 Oct., he preferred to meet them on 5 Nov. in whatever location shall have been "found most convenient for holding the Sessions, and Securing the records of the Legislature." The third letter stated that since the general court had been adjourned until 4 Nov. and that it was "probable your Judicial avocations, may occupy your attention several Days longer," Wilkinson thought it proper to postpone the proposed convening of the legislature to a future date.

4. "Civil" is interlined here in a different hand.

From Dolley Madison

PHILA. Novr. 12th. 1805

I received yours containing Payne's letter yesterday,[1] my best beloved, which gave me great pleasure, and immediately after was surprised and pleased by a visit from our brother John, he says his anxiety to see me was so great that he could not control it and I only regret that he should have indulged it without informing you. He travelled in the mail and had not slept for 3 nights—and now my darling I must tell you that our poor horse is considered incurable and that Mr. Patton has so interested himself as to procure one of the finest pairs of Sorrel, he knows them perfectly and gives ours in exchange with three hundred and fifty dollars difference I told him I was extremely averse to the purchase, until I could hear from you, but he insists on paying for them, himself taking an order on Mr. Lewis, as he knows the opportunity will be lost.

I wish I could now appoint a day for returning, tho' my knee is perfectly healed and gains strength I am unable to ride two days together a few days without sinking under fatigue—but as I am well I shall expect to be quite ready for Mr. Cutts and Anna about the 20th. No tongue can express my anxiety to be with *you*, at home. The Doctor is much concerned at the idea of my journey, as I have freely told him I would risk every thing to join you, he says he hopes it will be sufficiently firm by that time to travel with great care. Adieu for the present my dear husband your

D.

Tr (owned by Mrs. George B. Cutts, Wellesley, Mass., 1982).

1. JM to Dolley Madison, ca. 6 Nov. 1805.

From Dolley Madison

MY DARLING,   PHILADELPHIA 12th. November 1805

I have just parted with Col. Patton who is well satisfied with the term of payment for the horses and congratulated me on possessing them, our own poor grey being on a meadow, but not any change in him for the better. I have been this morning to make several visits and on my return found Anthony Morris, who had come with a petition from his wife that I would let him wait upon me to her house; I was not strong enough to go directly, but wish greatly to visit this old and dear friend, if the Doctor should think well of my going for two days. I expect Anna next Sunday, and as soon as your arrangements are made from New York, I will set out with or without her.

I see that Jackson's paper has announced the Declaration of War from Spain against us, and that the Marquis d'Yruho has requested his passport. He was here the other evening with other company, Mrs. Steward enquired of him if this was true, he was terribly angry and declared it was "a lie." Teaureau is ill, but goes abroad—the impression of him in Philadelphia is a sad one—he is recollected as the cruel commander at La Vendé, and the fighting husband[1]—and tho Morris's company went to salute him with their drums and fife, he says, that the Americans hate him.

13th. The doctor says I must not go to Molly Morris's so that I must think no more of it.

I am about to put up the articles for the President[2] and will enclose a note for him, to you farewell, my beloved.

Tr (owned by Mrs. George B. Cutts, Wellesley, Mass., 1982).

1. The relationship of the Turreaus was notoriously volatile. In June 1805 Dolley wrote her sister Anna that rumor had it that Turreau "whips his wife, and abuses her dreadfully," and Anthony Merry reported to Lord Mulgrave that Turreau's treatment of his family "was carried latterly to so barbarous an excess as to oblige them to fly from his house." The following month Dolley reported to Anna that the Turreaus had gone to Baltimore, where they went on "fighting and exposing themselves" (Brant, *Madison*, 4:268–69, 505 nn. 4–5).

2. For Jefferson's request that Dolley Madison buy some items for his daughter, Martha, see JM to Dolley Madison, ca. 2 Nov. 1805.

From James Wilkinson

SIR(,)   TERRITORY OF ORLEANS ST. LOUIS. Novr. 12(th.) 05.

When I reached this territory, I found a surveyor general in office, authorized by the regulations of Spain to appoint his deputies, and I continued him in commission, as I have done every other appointment of my Predecessor, Governor Harrison.

As we have no territorial law, which recognises a surveyor general, or defines the duties of such station, the propriety of the appointment, has been questioned by some, & the functions of the officer denied by others, which together with the variety of interpretations, applied to the Act of the 2d. of March, "for adjusting land claims,"[1] has involved some doubts and perplexities.

Perceiving that the opinion of the Judges (Lucas & Euston) favoured the right of individuals to survey & return plats to the Recorders office, at their discretion, & understanding that one Person, without qualification or responsibility, had actually proceeded to Survey under the sanction of Judge Euston's countenance, my active interference, became necessary, to prevent the confusion frauds & pillage which were about to ensue.

On scrutinizing the Land Law applicable to the Territory, I observed that the 4th section of it required, "a plat of the tract or tracts claimed["] to substantiate any incomple[te] title, or to effect its admission to record, & I also discovered, in the 5th. Section of the same act, the recognition of an "officer exercising in the District, the authority of Surveyor General." These facts & the circumstances which I have stated, determined me to pursue my own Judgement, and to avail myself of the reservations of the 9th. Section of the Act, providing for the Government of the Territory, to avert the impending mischief.[2]

I accordingly Sir, in conformity with the authority, heretofore exercised by the Spanish Governors, digested regulations for the government of the Surveyor general & his deputies, passed a letter of Office to him on the subject of which you have copies under cover, & issued the proclamation forwarded you by Mr Parke the 6th. inst. of which the enclosed is a duplicate.[3]

The Spanish fees for surveying were four sous per acre, or thirty three reals ℞ day exclusive of travelling expences: these had been reduced one half by Governor Harrison, & I have deemed it just to reduce them still lower, as you will perceive from the regulations.

I flatter myself these steps may suffice to protect the interests of Government, & secure the rights of Individuals, against the sinister speculations of a band of Swindlers of which you may have a glimpse, by glancing at the original Documents marked Russell[4]—I feel humiliated Sir, by the imposition of such frivolous details on your time, but under existing circumstances, I believe it may be necessary if, for no other reason, to meet the misrepresentations which disappointed avarice may send forth.

In my letter of the 21st. September I communicated the measures I had adopted, respecting the intrusion of sundry persons on the public domain at the Mine of Bretau, and I now transmit you the result of our enquiries. The report of Col: Hammond was not handed me, untile [sic] the 20th. ultimo, and I have since held it in reserve, that it might be accompanied by the representation of the People of St Genevieve, which I have recently recieved, & now forward them together.[5]

It remains with government to determine which shall ultimately be done in this case, in order to furnish, a correct view of the local, I shall direct an exact survey to be made of the mine lands, & the approximate settlements, to be transmitted to you; But in the mean time I have yielded to a spirit of conciliation, & the rights of prescription set up by the inhabitants who have been permitted to prosecute their labours as usual, untill the pleasure of Government shall be expressed.

The "act for ascertaining & adjusting titles & claims to lands," appears to be too close in some respects & too loose in others; In the latter view I am at a loss to devise, how we are, to protect our Mines & salines, against the Head rights recognised by the 2d section of the Act, or even against ancient Legitimate French or Spanish concessions, unless by forfeiture for non improvement under the Spanish regulations, of which I have the honor to transmit you an authentic copy [not found]. With perfect respect I am Sir your obt. Servt.

(signed) JA: WILKINSON

Tr and enclosures (DNA: RG 46, Territorial Papers of the U.S. Senate, 8th–14th Congress, Louisiana Territory). Enclosed in Gallatin to Thomas Worthington, 8 Feb. 1806 (ibid.; printed in Carter, *Territorial Papers, Louisiana-Missouri*, 13:432–35). For surviving enclosures, see nn. 3–4.

1. For the act, see *U.S. Statutes at Large*, 2:324–29.

2. For section 9 of the act providing for the government of Louisiana, see Wilkinson to JM, 6 Nov. 1805, n. 3. The act allowed laws and regulations then in force to remain until changed by the territorial legislature and since the legislature had not yet met, Wilkinson was operating under the assumption that Spanish regulations still applied.

3. The enclosures are a copy (3 pp.) of Wilkinson's 2 Nov. 1805 "Regulations for the Government of the Surveyor General and his Deputies," and a copy of Wilkinson to Antoine Soulard, 5 Nov. 1805, in which the regulations were enclosed (1 p.; printed in Carter, *Territorial Papers, Louisiana-Missouri*, 13:437–38). For the proclamation, see Wilkinson to JM, 6 Nov. 1805, and n. 7.

4. Wilkinson enclosed a 1 Nov. 1805 agreement between William Russell and Michael Masterson (1 p.; endorsed by Wilkinson; printed ibid., 439), stating that Masterson claimed title to a tract of land on Sandy Creek by virtue of an improvement claim Masterson had bought from a Michael Null; that William Russell would "pay for surveying, recording and all other lawful charges, & expences" that might arise from having the title recorded; and he bound himself "to use all lawful endeavors . . . to bring forward said claim in a lawful manner," in exchange for which Masterson had deeded to Russell one third of however much land would be covered by the rights Masterson had bought from Null. Wilkinson added his own note: "This paper was handed to me, by a poor & ignorant Man in its present condition (accidentally in the presence of Mr Jno Smith of the Senate) who beged my advice for his conduct." Wilkinson added that Masterson claimed "920 acres, of which an unlicensed Surveyor was to have 300 for walking round the tract & paying about $10.—& the land estimated at $3 per acre." Wilkinson also enclosed William Russell's 6 Nov. 1805 statement (2 pp.; printed ibid., 439–40) that on 3 Sept. 1804 he had stopped in St. Louis on his

way to the Meramec River region and was told that there was no one authorized to survey land in the district; that in conversation with Rufus Easton, Russell had asked the judge if he wanted any surveys done, to which Easton replied that he had an interest in two small tracts near the Meramec; and that he and Easton had traveled to David Fine's property, where Russell, Easton, Fine, and his son had surveyed the property for which there apparently was a contract between Easton and Fine, with Fine to retain four hundred acres. Russell added, "the parties appeared to be well pleased with the survey & with each other."

5. Samuel Hammond's report and the representation from the people of St. Genevieve district have not been found but they no doubt dealt with the lead ore on public land near St. Genevieve, which the residents had been accustomed to mine. On 19 Sept. 1805 Wilkinson wrote Hammond that the St. Genevieve district had been annexed to Hammond's command and repeated reports he had heard about the mining of the ore, which it was claimed the Spanish had allowed (printed ibid., 220–21).

§ From William C. C. Claiborne. *12 November 1805, New Orleans.* "Since my letter of the 5. instant, I have received further intelligence of the progress of the Marquis of Casa Calvo. He is said to have arrived at the Sea-shore, and proposed prosecuting his voyage to the mouth of the Sabine, and from thence to the old Post of Adais.

"The Marquis is stated to have taken with him an assortment *of Goods* calculated for Indian Presents—but whether *they* were designated (only) to ensure the safety of his person in the excursion, or for the *advancement of some important national object*, is a question on which my present information is not such as to enable me to give a conclusive opinion: I am however inclined to think the *latter* is the most probable. The journey of the Marquis has excited much attention in this quarter, and gives rise to a variety of reports; the prospect of war between the United States and Spain, is the constant theme of conversation; the Spanish officers in our vicinity speak of it as an inevitable event. I have received but *one letter* from the Department of State for three months past,[1] and in *that* nothing was said as to our relations with Spain.

"I reviewed, on the 10. instant the Batalion of Orleans Volunteers. It is composed, principally, of Americans, and Creoles of Louisiana, who possess a great share of military ardor. The inclosed is a copy of a general Order which I have issued on the occasion."[2]

RC and enclosure (DNA: RG 59, TP, Orleans, vol. 7); letterbook copy (Ms-Ar: Claiborne Executive Journal, vol. 15). RC 2 pp.; in a clerk's hand, signed by Claiborne; docketed by Wagner. Filed with this letter is an 11 Nov. 1805 letter from Jean Noël Destréhan to Jefferson (3 pp.; in a clerk's hand, signed by Destréhan; docketed by Wagner; docketed by Jefferson as received 16 Dec.; printed in Carter, *Territorial Papers, Orleans*, 9:523–25), enclosing a list of ten persons nominated by the house of representatives, from which the president was to choose five to serve as members of the legislative council, together with the 11 Nov. 1805 resolution of the house that Destréhan send the list to the president. For enclosure, see n. 2.

1. See JM to Claiborne, 28 Aug. 1805.
2. The enclosure (1 p.; docketed by Wagner) is a copy of Claiborne's 11 Nov. 1805 general order praising the militia battalion for its performance during the review and urging the officers to attend to the discipline of the corps.

§ From Peter A. Guestier. *12 November 1805, Baltimore.* "I have the honor of inclosing you a draft for $241. drawn by Mr. Wm. Lee consul for the U.S at Bordeaux at thirty days Sight order of cap. Peter Coursell of my brig Lyon I Beg you to accept it and please to Send it back to me."[1]

RC (DLC). 1 p.

1. For the original shipment on the *Lyon*, see William Lee to JM, 14 Sept. 1805.

§ From Peter Kuhn Jr. *12 November 1805, "Cornigliano 5 Miles from Genoa."* "I have the honour to inform you that on the 28 Ulo. in the evening came to anchor in this harbour the United States armed Brig Syren Captn. John Smith from Leghorn, and was admitted to immediate pratique.

"Upon the enterence of the Brig into port she was visited according to Custom by an Officer from the Frigate Commanding in the harbour, who I am sorry to say, put very uncommon questions to Captn. Smith; some of which he did not think proper to satisfy; such as, 'what brings you here, how long do you intend to stay,' &c &c. It is but seldom, I believe that our Ships of War are seen in French ports in the Mediterranean, and the Syren the only one that has ever appeared in Genoa; which induced the Commandant Afloat (as I have Since been informed) to suspect her to have been an English Vessel under the disguise of American Colours.

"I presented Capn. Smith the next day to His Serene Highness the Arch Treasurer of the Empire, as also to the Prefect & Mayor who were there present; they received him with every mark of respect. In the course of Conversation Capn. Smith mentioned the questions which were put to him on his arrival. H. S. H. express'd his displeasure at the Officers conduct, and promised an explanation from the Commandant.

"At an early hour the following morning I received a note from the Arch Treasurer requesting me to send Capn. Smith to him as soon as possible. Capn. Smith waited immediately upon him.

"'I am informed by the Commandant, said the Arch Treasurer to Capn. Smith, that you did not conform to regulations established in the Ports of France with respect to Armed Vessels on your enterence here.' Capn Smith replied that he observed the same rules in Coming into the port of Genoa as he had been accustomed to in entering other Ports. It was his care to respect them equally with Government and Officers in every place he came to. That if there were different regulations established in the ports of France from what were general elsewhere, he requested to be informed what they were and he should conform to them as far as was practicable; he had however to complain to his Highness of an order he had that morning recieved from the Commandant to take down his Colours and not to hoist them untill those of the Frigate were hoisted; he did not think proper to attend to the order, nor Could he accord to any regulation of that Nature.

"His Serene Highness demanded if he Saluted the Port on entering. Capn. Smith said it was not a general custom, more especially for small Vessels—he had not: H. S. H. replied it was always the custom in the Ports of France, & his want of observing it was the cause of what had happened.

535

"A fair wind Offering on the 1st. the Syren was about to leave Genoa but an unlucky accident threw her upon a French Corvette and Carried away her jib: boom. The Syren had some of her sails torn, her fore yard Carried away, and much rigging Cut by the french crew. She was consequently obliged to remain in Port to repair the damage received. This accident produced another note from the Arch Treasurer demanding my presence. I went immediately to him. 'The object of his calling me, he Said, was to mention that Capn. Smith had been insulting anew the Imperial Navy that he had run his vessel against one of their Corvetts and broken her PS—all done with premeditated intention—that it was a matter of high importance and Could Only be settled by the Governments.['] Knowing well the disposition of his Serene Highness, I regulated my Answers so as to obtain from him, the different charges which the Commandant had made against Captn Smith. I then told him he was much misinformed and the charges not just—that I accompanied Capn Smith on board of the Syren at his expected departure, was an eye witness to the accident and should relate to him the occurences precisely as they occured. The Harbour of Genoa as H. S. H was acquainted, is of Circular form and surrounded by Mountains where the wind blew from the Land (except-ing gales) it was never settle'd but subject to instantanious shifts from one point of the port to the other, which was the unfortunate Case that morning at the moment the Syren was geting under way; her Anchors from the ground, a sudden flow from the eastward filled her head Sails and turned her upon the Corvette, doing her some little damage which Capn. Smith immediately offered to repair accidents of the like were not uncommon in the port of Genoa altho' they might not come under the notice of his S. H.

"I could not forbear expressing that I thought H. S. H's informent a very jelous or a very Malicious Man, as I could not for a moment suppose from the post he held in the Imperial Navy that he was wanting in a Knowledge of Sea affairs, by which he would be acquainted that the occurence was altogether accide[n]tle.

"His Serene Highness appeared well satisfied with my explanation In the in-terim however Capn. Smith reced. a Message that he could not leave the port without permission from the Prince; greatly astonished he Came to the Consulate where I found him on my return from the Palace. The Arch Treasurer had not communicated a word to me of this order. I immediately requested an interview in company with Capn. Smith which was soon granted. He assured that the Syren was not detained, but could depart when ever Capn Smith should think proper—that it had been a missunderstanding.

"The next morning at day break Capn Smith called upon me to inform that he had received a new order not to leave the Port I address'd H. S. H. a note upon the subject, to which an answer was returned (Copy inclosed)[1] repeating that the Syren was not detained in the port of Genoa, and the sole cause of what had arrived, was the want of adhearence to the general established rules.

"Capn. Smith left this the following day for Naples.

"I have thought it my duty Sir to communicate these particulars to you, & to express my opinion in favor of the Conduct of Capn. Smith which did not deviate from proper Consistency during these proceedings whose origin were entirely owing to the Missrepresentations made by the Commandant to his Serene High-ness the Arch Treasure⟨r⟩."

RC and enclosure (DNA: RG 59, CD, Genoa, vol. 1). RC 3 pp.; docketed by Wagner. For enclosure, see n. 1.

1. The enclosure (1 p.; two copies; in French; first copy docketed by Wagner) is the 2 Nov. 1805 note from Charles-François Lebrun, repeating that Smith was not detained and was free to leave the port. Lebrun added that a failure of protocol and a neglect of forms known in European, especially French, ports was the sole cause of what had happened and, in addition, that all the ships belonging to the United States would always find in the ports of the Empire, when the vessels conformed to the established usage, the consideration and treatment that treaties and French hospitality guaranteed to them.

§ From Anthony Merry. *12 November 1805, Washington.* "I have received the Honor of your Letters of the 9th. and 11th. Instant, the former on the Subject of the Impressment of John Harlan [*sic*], an American Citizen, by His Majesty's Sloop Peterell, the latter respecting that of James Gunnell [*sic*], also a Citizen of the United States, by His Majesty's Ship Cambrian; and I have the Honor, Sir, to acquaint you that I shall forward, by the earliest Opportunity, to the Commanders in Chief on the Station to which those Ships respectively belong, the Documents which you have been pleased to transmit to me proving the Citizenship of the Seamen in Question, in order that immediate Attention may be paid to your Application for their Discharge."

RC (DNA: RG 59, NFL, Great Britain, vol. 3). 2 pp.; in a clerk's hand, signed by Merry.

§ From James Taylor. *12 November 1805, Jefferson County, Kentucky.* "This by Doctr. Nicholas a Respective Young Gentn. out of My Neighbourhood, Who Can Inform you of our Connections in this Neighbourhood of their Healths &c We have had the greatest drouth this Summer I ever Saw, but Still there Will be good Crops of Corn Where the land was Tolerable Well Tended I think I Shall Make about 400 Barrells from about 50 Acres of Land. Pork at 15/ ℔. Ct. Wheat @ 4/ pr. Bushl. Money is Scarce With us & Foreign Articles Very high. Doctr. Nicholas Accompynies Some Indians going in to the Federal City.[1] My Compliments to Mrs. Madison."

RC (DLC). 1 p.

1. In the fall of 1805 Benjamin Hawkins, agent to the Creek Nation, traveled to Washington with six of the Creek chiefs, where they signed a treaty amending a treaty originally agreed to on 3 Nov. 1804, by which the tribe sold land to the United States. The Senate had refused to ratify the 1804 treaty until modifications to the amount and method of payment for the land were made (Merritt B. Pound, *Benjamin Hawkins: Indian Agent* [Athens, Ga., 1951], 184–87).

§ From Anthony Terry. *12 November 1805, Cádiz.* "The order respecting the devolution of the Cargo on board of American Vessels detained by Spanish Privateers & condemn'd, Copy of which had the pleasure to forward you on the 14th. Sepr.

last [not found]—Am sorry to inform you that the Government has not as yet made any notification to the Tribunals where it corresponds; as applications have been made here by Sundry Merchants empower'd by the owners of the Cargo, and have obtained no redress, as the Judges say they know nothing of said order; for fear of miscarriage I inclose a third Copy [not found].

"By the Paragraph on the other side of a Letter received from Mr. Gavino of Gibraltar,[1] you will be informed how the English act with Americans that have W. I. produce on board."

RC (DNA: RG 59, CD, Cádiz, vol. 1). 1 p.; in a clerk's hand, signed by Terry.

1. The paragraph on the verso, dated at Gibraltar, 29 Oct. 1805, reads: "An American Cargo of Havana Sugar has been tryed in this Vice Admiralty Court and released, yet One before it was Condemned, which is verry odd, and Government can only get this matter put in a proper train."

§From Robert Williams. *12 November 1805, Washington, Mississippi Territory.* "Since my dispatch of last week to you,[1] I have been informed from a source which may be relied on, that four thousand Spanish troops are destined for the Floridas, and that five hundred will be immediately sent to Baton Rouge. Also, that considerable military preparations have commenced between Natchitoches and the province of Taxas; and that the foundations of two very considerable fortifications have been formed—one within about two days journey of Natchitoches, and the other at the Sabine River, besides a number of intermediate military stations."

Letterbook copy (Ms-Ar: Executive Journal, 1805–1810). 1 p.

1. See Williams to JM, 4 Nov. 1805.

§From William C. C. Claiborne. *13 November 1805, New Orleans.* "I have the pleasure to inclose you a copy of a Resolution, which was this day unanimously adopted by the House of Representatives of this Territory."[1]

RC and enclosure (DNA: RG 59, TP, Orleans, vol. 7); letterbook copy (Ms-Ar: Claiborne Executive Journal, vol. 15). RC 1 p.; in a clerk's hand, signed by Claiborne; docketed by Wagner. For enclosure, see n. 1.

1. The enclosure (1 p.; docketed by Wagner) is the 13 Nov. 1805 resolution of the Orleans territorial house of representatives that a committee be appointed to draft an address to the president "expressive of the sentiments of respect, confidence and esteem" entertained by the members of the house.

§From Levett Harris. *13 November 1805, St. Petersburg.* "A copy of what I had the honor to address you the 10/22 Ulto. p. the Hermoine via New York I now inclose You, & transmit you at same time a report of our trade here this season;[1] by which there will be perceived an increase of some consequence over that of last year.

"I Am very happy to be able to contradict the Account stated in my last, of the loss of russian troops by shipwreck. This news came in so unquestionable a form that it was deemed fully intitled to credence. I therefore did not hesitate to communicate it; it since appears that the ships therein mentioned to be lost, though correct as to number, did not, with the exception of one Vessel, contain any troops, & on this, very few were embarked.

"The Emperor has not yet returned, & the disasterous turn which the cause of his Majesty has espoused Appears to have taken in Germanny, will perhaps protract his absence. He is now at Berlin."

Adds in a postscript: "The difference that appears between the printed list herewith sent, and my general Statement, arises from the custom house reports, from which the former is taken, & the entries made by the merchants, which are Submitted to my inspection & which govern me in my report of these particulars."

RC, two copies, and enclosure (DNA: RG 59, CD, St. Petersburg, vol. 1). First RC 2 pp.; dated "1/13. November" in the Julian and Gregorian calendars; docketed by Wagner. Second RC marked "Duplicate" and, following the postscript, "Original via London"; docketed by Wagner. Parts of words in angle brackets in the first RC have been supplied from the second RC. Minor differences between the copies have not been noted. For enclosure, see n. 1.

1. The enclosure (1 p.; docketed by Wagner) is a printed form showing that sixty-nine American ships visited Russia in 1805, four more than in 1804. The form breaks down the ships by home ports, with the nineteen from Boston being the greatest number from any port, followed by twelve from New York, eleven from Salem, and six from Providence. No other U.S. port sent more than three ships to Russia in 1805, and many sent only one. The form also lists all the Russian products exported, chief among them iron, tallow, and textiles, and further breaks down the exports by showing the amount of each that went to each of the eighteen American ports listed.

To Dolley Madison

WASHINGTON Novr. 15. 1805

I was not disappointed my dearest, in my expectation of a letter by the last mail,[1] which continues to give me favorable reports of your returning health & strength. I hope by this time Mrs. Cutts will have joined you and that the event will accelerate that of your setting out. Proceed nevertheless with all the caution the Dr. may recommend. The inclosed letter came by yesterdays mail. I have no news for you; unless you wish to know that Col. Hawkins with his Indians is about leaving us,[2] that Mr. Skipwith is just arrived from France, and that the Tunisian Ambassador is expected soon from Norfolk.[3] I have but just seen Mr. S. and had no time to enquire of your friend Mrs. Pichon &c. Mr. Livingston went off yesterday. I can give you no city news. The wedding at Mr Simmon's[4] has produced a round of parties; but I have not attended one of them. I send a letter by the mail which came inclosed to me for Mr⟨s?⟩ Barlow. It is addressed to Philada.

which you may mention to Mr Baldwin if you have an oppy. Give Miss P⟨:⟩ a kiss for me & accept a thousand for yourself. Yr. affte. husband

JAMES MADISON

Why don't you send on the other vols. of Dallas.

RC (owned by Charles M. Storey, Boston, Mass., 1961). Cover addressed and franked by JM to Dolley Madison "[. . .] at Mrs. Woods." Torn.

1. JM probably referred to Dolley's letter to him of 12 Nov. 1805 (first letter).
2. For the visit of Benjamin Hawkins and the Creek chiefs to Washington, see James Taylor to JM, 12 Nov. 1805, n. 1.
3. Tunisian ambassador Soliman Melimeni arrived at Washington in the *Congress* on 29 Nov. 1805, left the ship on 30 Nov., and went with his "two Turkish secretaries and two black domestics to the house provided for him on the Capitol Hill," after which he proceeded to the State Department for an audience with JM (*National Intelligencer*, 2 Dec. 1805).
4. William Simmons was an accountant in the War Department. On 7 Nov. 1805 Catherine C. Simmons, who may have been Simmons's sister, married George G. Macdaniel (Mattern and Shulman, *Selected Letters of Dolley Payne Madison*, 412; *National Intelligencer*, 11 Nov. 1805; Ford, "Diary of Mrs. William Thornton," *Records of the Columbia Historical Society* 10 [1907]: 191).

From Dolley Madison

PHILA. 15th. November 1805

I was so unwell yesterday, my dearest husband, that I omitted writing. Dr. Physic has been ill for two days and so surrounded by young students, who attend his lectures that I have not ventured to send for his bill. I will do it however. I was persuaded to take a social dinner yesterday with Mrs. Dallas and on my return found your short letter of the 13th.[1]

17th. I am much better this morning, my dear husband, and should take a short ride but for unfavorable weather, tomorrow I propose to call on as many as I can, as one preperation for my journey to you—that is the object to which my wishes all tend. I have yet seen little of the city—the Museum &c I hope to peep into Monday morning.

Mr. Cutts and Anna arrived last evening, my beloved, and so pleased and agitated was I that I could not sleep. We leave Monday, if I am quite strong enough—but I must wait a little for your commands.

I have received visits and invitations from the Lewis's, and am to dine with them on Thursday and at the Governor's on Wednesday—tomorrow at Dr. Bache's, all my engagements are made conditionally and with the approbation of the Doctor. Mrs. Wingate will have called to tell you about us.

Your own D.

Tr (owned by Mrs. George B. Cutts, Wellesley, Mass., 1982).

1. Letter not found.

§ To Andrew Allen Jr. *15 November 1805, Department of State.* "I have this day written to the Collector of the Customs at Boston to pay what he may deem reasonable for the passage of the American Seamen from Halifax to Boston as mentioned in your letter of the 28th. ultimo to the Secretary of the Treasury."[1]

Letterbook copy (DNA: RG 59, DL, vol. 15). 1 p.

1. For Allen's letter to Albert Gallatin, see Gallatin to JM, 11 Nov. 1805, and n. 1. In his 15 Nov. 1805 letter to Benjamin Lincoln, JM stated: "I request you to be pleased to pay what you may deem reasonable for the passage of the American seamen from Halifax to Boston as mentioned in the enclosed document, taking a receipt from the British Captain or his Attorney for the same, and on transmitting it to this Department, you will be reimbursed the expence" (DNA: RG 59, DL, vol. 15; 1 p.).

§ From Francis J. Le Breton Dorgenoy. *15 November 1805, New Orleans.* "I have received with Gratitude and regard the honour of your circular to the marshals.[1] Enclosed in the same packet, you have favoured me with an act of Congress passed 'at the last cession for the more preservation of peace in the ports and harbours of the United states and in the waters under their Juridiction.[']"[2]

"Be pleased, sir to accept my further thanks for the Second session of the eight congress you have forwarded me together with a new commission dated June 12th. instant from the president of the united States whom I am very much indebted to & in return for this favour, Give me leave to Express here my great veneration for his virtues which gain him the affection and love of the good people of america.

"I wish, Sir, you would be Conscious that I am as much devoted to the General government and constitution of the union as disposed faithfully To discharge the duties of my office."

RC (DNA: RG 59, TP, Orleans, vol. 7). 1 p.; docketed by Wagner.

1. For JM's 29 May 1805 Circular Letter to the Marshals, see *PJM-SS*, 9:414–15.
2. For the act, see Circular Letter to the Governors, 29 May 1805, ibid., 414 n. 1.

§ From Peter Freneau. *15 November 1805, Charleston.* "Having published in the two Gazettes of which I am now the proprietor, the Laws passed at the different Sessions of the 7th. and 8th. Congress and all the Notifications that have issued from the Department of State, for four years past, I beg leave to call upon you to say, what is the compensation to be allowed for those services; you will find on enquiry that I have received none hitherto. Whatever the sum may be you will confer a particular favor on ma [*sic*] if you will direct the payment of it to be made. I mention above that the publications were made both in the City and Country paper, nevertheless I do not urge a claim for double payment; whatever you have paid to other printers I presume will be allotted to me."

RC (DNA: RG 217, First Auditor's Accounts, no. 17,515). RC 1 p. Filed with this letter is Freneau's account with the State Department (1 p.) for $346.50, certified as correct by Wagner on 8 Jan. 1806.

§ From Joseph Warner Rose. *15 November 1805, Worcester.* "I have taken the earliest opportunity on my arrival in this place from the Island of Antigua of acknowledging the receipt of your Letter dated in April last Original and Duplicate of which has never been received.[1]

"I quitted the above Island on the 15th of last Month and on the 17th a Vessel was dispatched after me to Montserrat where I received your Triplicate by which I find that The President had honored me with the Appointment of Commercial Agent for the Island of Antigua.

"I shall do myself the honor of waiting on the President and yourself as soon as my Health will permit when I shall have an opportunity of thanking you personally."

RC (DNA: RG 59, CD, Antigua, vol. 1). 1 p.; docketed by Wagner.

1. No April 1805 letter from JM to Rose has been found. For JM's 19 Apr. 1805 letter to Richard Cutts inquiring about Rose, see *PJM-SS*, 9:254. For JM's 13 May 1805 letter to Rose informing him of his appointment, see ibid., 347–48.

From Robert R. Livingston

Dear Sir   Baltimore 16h. Novr 1805

Mr ⟨F⟩ Skipwith may probably have brought letters for me. If so I shall deem it a favor to have them sent to me at Philadelphia where I shall remain till the 23d. of this month. I saw here the new order of council relative to colonial commerce.[1] It led me to reflect upon what you observed with respect to Russia but not only Russia but Sweden Austria & Germany are deeply interested in a change of this system since while it lasts England will engross the whole west India trade & sell at her own price & as the articles we purchase from those powers are paid in colonial produce they must be doubly injured by our being driven from this markets—prusia must be sensibly affected as she disposes of an immense quantity of linnen by this means & her merchants are our factors to a considerable extent.

It appears to me therefore that this would be the moment to engage all Europe in compelling England to change her system, & that ministers should not only be sent to Russia but to Austria and Germany. And the object of the embassies should be avowed to france that she may take no umbrage at our fixing on this time for sending them & that her aid may be procured at the diet & wth. prusia. I pray you to be assured of the sincerity

of the attachment with which I am Dear Sir respectfully Your most Obt
hume Servt

R R LIVINGSTON

RC (DLC).

1. The minutes of the 3 Aug. 1805 meeting of the king's council stated that the council
had resolved to continue to allow neutral trade with the American and West Indian colonies of
Britain's enemies to be carried on only through British free ports in the West Indies, but
because some neutral ships may have sailed under an impression that the regulations would
be enforced less strictly, the council ordered that naval commanders, privateers, and admiralty courts be instructed that ships that had sailed from Havana and other enemy ports prior
to 1 Nov. 1805 should not be molested or condemned (Philadelphia *Aurora General Advertiser*,
15 Nov. 1805). Lord Hawkesbury's 17 Aug. 1805 letter conveying these instructions to admiralty courts, commanders of warships, and privateers is printed in *ASP, Foreign Relations*,
3:266. On 11 Nov. 1805 Phineas Bond, the British consul at Philadelphia, sent a copy to the
State Department, and both Bond and Thomas Barclay, the British consul general at New
York, submitted copies to the newspapers (DNA: RG 59, NFC, vol. 1; Philadelphia *Poulson's
American Daily Advertiser*, 11 Nov. 1805; *New-York Gazette & General Advertiser*, 12 Nov. 1805).

From James Monroe

DEAR SIR   LONDON novr. 16. 1805.

I have this moment recd. yr favor of sepr. 24. the only one for a great
length of time. You will find by mine forwarded by Col: Mercer[1] & subsequent letters how the business stands, on which you touch, with this govt.
Lord Mulgrave has given no answer to my letters, nor have I heard anything of late from him, or indeed since the short one to that notifying my
intention to sail to the UStates by permission of the President. It is impossible for him to justify the conduct of his govt., and therefore he may
possibly conclude that more is gained by silence, than by a weak defence.
The pamphlet sent you was I think written by a person who saw my note.[2]
It undoubtedly shews what the govt. wod. do if it did not dread the consequences with us & the northern powers. It will give me great pleasure to
recieve yr. veiw of the subject. The decision of Ld. Mansfield was intirely
unknown to me.[3] The correspondence of Ld. Hawkesbury with Mr. King
was communicated to me by Mr. S. Williams, and is relied on in my note,
as you have seen. That correspondence is interesting in many views. You
will observe that it bears date abt. 3. months before the Russian treaty,[4]
and is in precise sentiment with that treaty as amended, especially; there
can be no doubt that it was entered into on the part of this govt., with a
view to subserve its interest with the northern powers. However having
written fully on this point to the President it is not necessary to add any

thing here.[5] I had sent you by anticipation what I could collect wh. might be supposed to have any reference to the question depending with this govt. In making the question, that is denying the right, it may perhaps be best to take at the present time the most moderate ground. By so doing this govt. wod. be deprived of any pretext for other measure(s,) & the attention of France, (an object important in respect to Spain) & what is still more likely to be felt here that of the northern powers wod. be drawn to the object. That seems to me to be all that is necessary in the present stage. How far it may be proper to submit to the Congress, so as that it may become publick, my letters or any of them, to Lord Mulgrave, in case I am to have any future agency in the business, you will decide. Mrs. monroe & my daughter desire their best regards to Mrs. Madison, whose indisposition we very much regret; tho' hope she was recovered so as to accompany you to washington. My daughter has been much indisposed lately, & her mothers health in a delicate state, on which acct. by advice of the phisician we intend going soon to Cheltenham, a days ride from London. I shall be here when necessary of wh. Mr. Purviance will give me due notice. I am Dear Sir sincerely your friend & servt

JAS. MONROE

RC (DLC: Rives Collection, Madison Papers).

1. See Monroe to JM, 18 Oct. 1805, and Monroe to JM, 25 Sept. 1805, and n. 2.

2. See Monroe to JM, 26 Oct. 1805, and n. 4.

3. For this decision, see JM to Monroe, 24 Sept. 1805, and n. 3.

4. Monroe referred to letters exchanged between Rufus King and Lord Hawkesbury in March and April of 1801 dealing with the case of an American ship condemned for carrying Málaga wine to a Spanish colony. The cargo was condemned by the Nassau vice-admiralty court in spite of its having been landed in the United States and later reshipped. As a result of King's complaint, the Advocate General decreed broken voyages licit. For the correspondence and the decision, see *ASP, Foreign Relations*, 2:490–91. The Anglo-Russian treaty was signed in June 1801 (*Annual Register for 1801*, 212–18).

5. For Monroe to Jefferson, 26 Sept. 1805, in which he discusses the British use of King's letter as a talking point in their negotiations with Russia, see Hamilton, *Writings of James Monroe*, 4:334–38. For a 6 Oct. 1805 letter to Jefferson in which Monroe stated King's letter was also used in British negotiations with Prussia, see ibid., 338–51.

§ To Messrs. Ketland & Field.[1] *16 November 1805, Department of State.* "The enclosed documents are all that this Department afford of those requested by you in relation to the seizure by the French of American property at Leghorn in the year 1796."

Letterbook copy (DNA: RG 59, DL, vol. 15). 1 p.

1. John and Thomas Ketland and John Field all had property that was shipped from Philadelphia to Leghorn in 1795 and stored in the warehouse of the English firm Earl, Hodgson & Drake. When Napoleon entered Tuscany in June 1796, he seized all the goods

on the grounds that they were British property (Williams, *French Assault on American Shipping*, 370). See also John Field to JM, 14 Aug. 1804, *PJM-SS*, 7:599–600 and nn. 2–3.

§ From William Findley.[1] *17 November 1805.* "I herewith enclose a Statement of Otho Shraders character and wishes.[2] Since I had the pleasure of Conversing with you I was informed by Mr. Gallatin that he apprehended that a Judges place in Louisiana was or soon would be vacant and enquired if Mr. Shrader could attend without delay if he was appointed to that office.[3] He arrived here on Saturday and informed me that he would thankfully accept of that office and attend on very Short notice. He is under the Necessity of making his stay here very Short, you would oblige me by informing yourself on the Subject as soon as you can conveniently. I introduced him and Another Gentleman to the view of the president but without any oppertunity of mentioning the Subject."

RC and enclosure (DNA: RG 59, LAR, 1801–9, filed under "Shrader"). RC 1 p. For enclosure, see n. 2.

1. William Findley (ca. 1742–1821) came from Ireland to Philadelphia in 1763. He fought in the American Revolution, and after the war moved to Westmoreland County, Pennsylvania. He held several state elective offices before being elected to Congress for four terms, 1791–1799. In 1794 he initially opposed the federal government during the Whiskey Rebellion. He served in the state senate from 1799 to 1802, and again in Congress from 1803 to 1817.

2. The enclosure (1 p.; printed in Carter, *Territorial Papers, Louisiana-Missouri*, 13:285–86) is Findley's undated statement that Shrader was a thirty-one-year-old German immigrant who had been in the United States for about ten years. Educated in Europe, Shrader wrote excellent French and correct English. He studied law in Pennsylvania, was admitted to the bar, and served as county prothonotary and register.

3. Somerset County, Pennsylvania, resident Otho Shrader (ca. 1774–1811) was named one of the judges in Louisiana Territory in April 1806 and served in that post until his death. He was also the captain of militia cavalry regiments in the St. Charles and St. Genevieve districts (ibid., 452, 14:211, 263, 375, 481–82).

§ From William Jarvis. *17 November 1805, Lisbon.* "My last letter of the 6th. Inst. is sent by the ship Columbia Captn. Lewis Via NYork and the duplicate by the Bg. Commerce, Captn. Price, the former inclosing a letter from Mr Pinckney.[1] This Gentleman reached here nine days since & sails to-morrow for Charleston in the danish Ship Henry the fourth, Captn. Rees.[2]

"Inclosed I have the honor to hand you a copy of my letter to His Excy Mr. de Araujo relative to the quarantine, in which I took the liberty to insert a part of your letter of the 12th. May.[3] This was applying it to the thing which of all others I know you have nearest you⟨r⟩ heart, the benefit of our Country⟨,⟩ and I hope will be an excuse for my plagiarism. Not to let the matter cool I waited (the 14th., the Minister's Diplomatique Audience day) on His Excy. who assured me that the most liberal arrangements should be adopted consistent with the health of His Royal Highness⟨'s⟩ subjects. I also waited on the Marquis of Pombal, the President of the Junta of Health who after a conversation of about half an hour, very politely said to me that he had no doubt I should be satisfied with the arrangements. I took the liberty to suggest that where Vessels had clean Bills of Health & with Crews in health. I apprehended five days de prove would be sufficient, without Bills of health but with Crews in health 15 days, but if the Crews were sickly or any had died possibly a few more days, and in the two latter cases the advantage of airing the apparel & fumigating the Vessel with brimstone a day or two before admission to Prattic. I was desirous of discovering the utmost liberality & fairness in my respresentations [*sic*], being persuaded that a confidence being placed in my candor would be likely to have a very beneficial tendency; in which I hope I shall not be mistaken. With His Excellency Mr. de Araujo I likewise entered pretty largely upon the Subject of Franquia for grain. He observed that he was entire⟨l⟩y of opinion that every possible degree of freedom should be given to Commerce, that he had my letter[4] translate⟨d⟩ & sent to the Minister of Finan⟨ce⟩ who is administrador of the Corn market & would also speak to His Excellency *on* the Subject. I do not however expect that any alteration will take place but I am of opinion that no future difficulty will be made about the want of the papers pointed out by the franquia Law. The Ship Venus likewise became a subject of conversation.[5] I observed that I was fully persuaded it would give my Government satisfaction if upon investigation it should be deemed just & equitable to restore the Vessel to the original owner but even under this view of the case it must be received as a favour done the Spanish Court, for the original owner after having divested himself of the property by a Bill of Sale & acknowledged a valuable consideration deprived him of all claim in Law on the Vessel; whether the bills received which at the time must have been viewed as money, were paid or not; but I must again repeat that in a question between the two Nations, I was fully satisfied that my Government was not desirous of straining a point of Law to the disadvantage of a Spanish subject, who had the shadow of justice on his side. His Excellency replied that the Ministry could not do anything in the affair, other than to recommend an immediate decision to the tribunals, to which effect he should write to the Spanish Ambassador at the same time advise an immediate application to the proper judge, (the Judge Conservador) for the purpose. As I shall not take an active part against her, for the reasons I formerly offered, it is probable she will be restored to the Spanish owners, on a trial of equity somewhat like a suit in Chancery. Impressment was a subject I also spoke about. His Excellency observed that every step had been taken to prevent these Kinds of aggressions against Foreigners in this port, but if I would give Certificates of Citizenship to all our seamen as the Vessels came into port, I might depend on their being respected. I informed His Excellency that all I could extend my Official protection to had documents of this nature, granted by the proper authorities in the U.S. or by the Consuls under proper evidence. He observed, if I would send him a copy, it should be sent to the Officers of police with strict injunctions to afford such seamen as held them the utmost protection.

"The only news We have here is the capitulation of Ulm, with twenty seven thousand Men made prisoners of war & the Arms, Ammunition, & a train of artillery fallen into the possession of the French, subsequently between twenty & thirty thousand prisoners in several engagements, whi⟨ch⟩ with the ten thousand befor⟨e⟩ make sixty seven thousand prisoners in all, according to the Continental papers; add t⟨o⟩ which the killed wounded⟨,⟩ & deserted, makes near⟨l⟩y 100,000 Men—as is stated. Inclosed are the Gibra[l]tar acco'ts. of the Naval engagement off Cadiz [not found], which I presume you will have recd., befor⟨e⟩ this will reach you."

RC, two copies, and enclosures (DNA: RG 59, CD, Lisbon, vol. 2). First RC 8 pp.; docketed by Wagner. Second RC marked "Dup," dated 18 Nov. 1805. Minor differences between
the copies have not been noted. Filed with the enclosures is a copy of Jarvis to Araújo, 25
Nov. 1805 (2 pp.), in which Jarvis had enclosed copies (not found) of the protections granted
to seamen by American collectors and consuls, who were the only persons legally authorized
to grant them. For surviving enclosures, see n. 3.

1. The *Columbia*, Lewis, bound from Lisbon for New York, went on shore at Little Egg
Harbor, New Jersey, ca. 5 Jan. 1806, and was a total loss. The *Commerce*, Price, arrived at
Norfolk ca. 11 Jan. 1806 (*Boston Gazette*, 16 Jan. 1806; Robert F. Marx, *Shipwrecks of the
Western Hemisphere: 1492–1825* [New York, 1971], 160; New York *Mercantile Advertiser*, 22
Jan. 1806).

2. Charles Pinckney arrived at Charleston, South Carolina, on 11 Jan. 1806 (*New-York
Evening Post*, 25 Jan. 1806).

3. Jarvis referred to JM's 13 May 1805 letter to John Armstrong, James Bowdoin, and
James Monroe, which was also sent to Jarvis (*PJM-SS*, 9:344–45 and n.). The enclosures
are (1) a copy of Jarvis's 6 Nov. 1805 letter to António de Araújo (5 pp.), reporting the existence of yellow fever in Philadelphia and New York; explaining that the epidemics occurred only between midsummer and the first frost; that moving as little as one league
away from the site of an outbreak removed people from danger of infection, thus showing
that there was no reason to ban ships from American cities where there was no disease; and
asking for relaxation of the rigid Portuguese quarantine of all American ships for the above
reasons; and (2) Araújo's 11 Nov. 1805 acknowledgement (1 p.; in Portuguese, with English
translation [1 p.]) of Jarvis's letter stating that the prince regent had ordered the contents of
it "to be communicated to the Board of Inspection upon the Providences for the Plague,
that the necessary cautions may be taken which circumstances exact."

4. For Jarvis's 18 Oct. 1805 letter to Araújo about admission of American ships to Lisbon, see Jarvis to JM, 24 Oct. 1805, and n. 3.

5. For the case of the *Venus*, see Jarvis to JM, 11 Oct. 1805, and nn. 2–4 and 9.

To William C. C. Claiborne

Sir.   Department of State, November 18th: 1805.
   You will find enclosed a list of your letters which remain unacknowledged.
   From the public papers you will have learnt the unfavorable result of
the negotiations for the settlement of the controversy with Spain. In truth
Mr. Monroe left Madrid without being able to accomplish any object of
his mission; the councils of Spain obstinately rejecting our demands &
declining not only to accept our proposals of compromise, but to offer
any of their own. Under such appearances of an obstinate and unfriendly
temper on her part, heightened by the reinforcements lately landed at Pensacola, the similar movements reported to have taken place on the western
frontier accompanied by the violent and predatory acts committed by the
Spanish troops in that quarter, as communicated to the Secretary of War
by Dr. Sibley,[1] the President has come to the resolution, that the Marquis

Casa Calvo and all other persons holding commissions or retained in the service of His Catholic Majesty should be ordered to quit the Territory of Orleans as soon as possible. As the pretext for the Marquis remaining as a Commissioner for delivering possession has ceased, or seems to be exchanged for another arising from his character of Commissioner for settling limits, it may be proper to remark that he has never been accredited in any such character and that no arrangement has ever been proposed to us for setting such a Commission on foot, that the Marquis and nearly all his attendants are military characters, some of them of considerable rank, and that as long as such a difference of opinion continues respecting the lines to be run, there can be no necessity for the commission. You will therefore lose no time in notifying the Presidents order upon this subject to the Marquis and through him to the persons whom it comprehends, in such terms as may leave no room for a further discussion, and as whilst they are attempered to the present state of things may not wear the aspect of hostility. In what manner the relations between the United States & Spain may be affected by the views of Congress on the subject will be known at the approaching Session. With them also it will lie to extend the intermediate provisions for the safety of the Country, in case the new posture of things in Europe should draw Spain into manifestations of a readiness to terminate the difference with us on reasonable & amicable grounds. I am &c.

JAMES MADISON.

Letterbook copy (DNA: RG 59, DL, vol. 15). 2 pp.

1. For extracts from John Sibley to Henry Dearborn, 1 and 31 May, 2 July, and 8 Aug. 1805, reporting the movements of Spanish troops, see *ASP, Foreign Relations*, 2:690–91.

From Christopher Gore

SIR.   BOSTON November 18. 1805.

The ship Indus, David Myrick master, was taken by his Britannic Majesty's Ship the Cambrian, Captain John P. Beresford, in Latitude 31.30 North & Longitude 61.56 West, & sent to Halifax, where she & all the property on board, belonging to the Owners, Master & Supercargo, were condemn'd on the ground, as is said, of the illegality of the trade, which she was prosecuting at the time of the capture. An appeal has been claimed, & will be duly prosecuted before the Lords Commissioners of Appeal, in Great Britain, by the Insurers to whom the said Ship & Cargo have been abandoned. These insurers consist of four companies in the town of Boston, incorporated under the names of the Massachusetts Fire and Marine

Insurance—The Suffolk Insurance—The Boston Marine Insurance—&
the New England Insurance, who are not only interested in the above
decision as it relates to the particular case, in which it was rendered; but
are deeply concerned on account of insurances made by them on Vessels
& Cargoes that may be embraced, as they fear, by rules & principles, said
to have been adopted in the case of the Indus. These fears derive but too
much weight from decisions, that have taken place in London, condemning property, for being in a commerce, always by them understood to be
lawful, not only from their own sense of the Law of Nations, but also
from the assent of Great Britain, discover'd by her former practice, & by
principles advanced by her Judges, in support of such decrees.

The amount of property witheld, & ultimately depending on the decisions, of the High Court of Appeals, in the case of the Indus, is sufficient,
of itself, to demand their serious attention; but when combined with the
effect of principles, supposed to have been applied in this instance, they
are apprehensive of further & still greater injuries to their own property &
that of their fellow citizens in this quarter of the Country—and these
losses, should they be realized, would be encountered in the prosecution
of a trade, in which they felt themselves as unoffending against the rights
of others—as secure from the interruption of the power that now molests
them, as in coasting voyages between different parts of the United States.

They hope therefore not to be thought intrusive, in asking of the Government its interference, through their Minister at the Court of London,
or otherwise, as the President in his wisdom may judge proper, to protect
their commercial rights, & to obtain redress of the particular injury of
which they complain. They have even felt it a duty, due from them to the
Government of their Country, to apprize those, entrusted with the administration of its concerns, of events, so injurious in themselves, & preg-
nant with consequences so momentous to their individual properties & the
general prosperity of the Country. Such reflections have influenced these
several Companies to request me, to present you a statement of the case of
the Indus, for the inspection of the Government, & the purposes above
alluded to; & also to subjoin some of the reasons which have occasioned
the security with which they have hazarded their property on voyages
now pretended to be unlawful.

In the summer of 1804 Messrs. David Sears & Jonathan Chapman,[1] native citizens of the United States & residents in Boston, owned a Ship
called the Indus, which they fitted out for a voyage to India. They put on
board her 63,640 Dollars & three sets of Exchange, drawn by themselves
on Messrs. John Hodshon & son of Amsterdam at ninety days sight for
twenty five thousand three hundred Gueldres, which amount of specie &
bills they confided to Abishai Barnard, a native citizen of the United

States, & Supercargo. This Ship & property, altogether owned by themselves they dispatched, with orders to go to the Isles of France & Bourbon,
& if able, to purchase a cargo there, so to invest the specie & bills: if not,
to proceed to Batavia, for the same purpose: if not practicable there, to go
on to Calcutta, and obtain a cargo; with which cargo, wherever procured,
the said Ship was directed to return to Boston; unless, before the vessel
should quit the Isle of France or Batavia, a peace should take place in Europe; in which event, she was ordered to proceed to Falmouth in England,
& conform herself to the orders of her owners' correspondents in London.
All the papers on board showed these facts; & such, and such only was the
property & destination of the Vessel & her lading. In a memorandum
relating to the purchase of the cargo, given to the Supercargo, he was reminded, not to forget to insert in the manifest, after the arrival of the
vessel in the tide waters of Boston the words "*and Embden*," viz from the
Isle of France or Batavia, to Boston "and Embden," as this would not deprive the owners of the priviledge of unloading wholly in Boston. The
object of this request was, in case of peace, to avoid an expence & inconvenience, which, Mr. Sears, the principal owner of this Ship & Cargo,
suffered at the last peace, viz the unloading of the entire cargo of a vessel
called the Arab, from India in the port of Boston, which under the then
existing circumstances, viz. a state of peace, he inclined to send immediately to Europe, but which he would not have contemplated, had not peace
have taken place, and which he did not anticipate when the vessel sailed
from Boston, as he did not foresee a termination of the War. Such being
the construction, put by the Collector of the port of Boston & Charlestown, on the laws in force, when the Vessel referred to arrived, & when the
Indus sailed in 1804. The expence of unloading & reloading this vessel,
would have amounted to several thousand dollars; and in case of the law
being at her arrival as when she sailed, & of a peace in Europe, & the owners sending her there (in which event alone did they ever entertain the
least intention of not closing the voyage in America) this expence might
have been saved.

   With this property, & under these instructions, the Indus proceeded on
her voyage to the Isle of France. Not being able to procure a cargo there,
she went to Batavia, where she loaded with the proceeds of her specie &
one set of her bills. In the prosecution of her voyage from Batavia to Boston, the ship was so damaged by storms, that she was obliged to put into
the Isle of France, where the vessel was condemn'd as no longer sea worthy,
the cargo was taken out, a new vessel purchased by the Supercargo, which
he named the Indus, & such of the articles as were on board the former
Indus, & not damaged, were reshipped in the new Indus; these articles
together with some Tea, taken on freight for certain Citizens of Boston,
there to be landed, composed her entire cargo. With this property, she

was within a few days' sail of her destined port of Boston, in the Latitude & Longitude aforesaid, when she was captured by the Cambrian, sent to Halifax & condemned as beforementioned.

The assumed ground of condemnation was, as the Underwriters are informed, that the direction to insert the words "and Embden" after the arrival of the vessel in the port of Boston, disclosed an intention in the owners to continue the voyage to Europe, whereas the only object was to reserve to themselves the right to obviate any objection, from the Custom House here, to her proceeding thither, in the event of a peace between the present Belligerents.

This is manifest from the testimony of the owners, & is confirmed by their instructions to the conductors of this voyage, as to its destination, in case of a peace before they quitted India. On this contingency only were they to proceed otherwise than to Boston. The reason why Mr. Sears directed the words "and Embden" to be inserted, is obvious from what he suffered in the case of the Arab, as related by himself & the Collector of the Customs: and that it was only in the event of peace, that he contemplated sending to Europe the Vessel & Cargo to which his memorandum referred, is confirmed by his former practice & course of trade—viz During the last ten years, he has been engaged in voyages to India, & likewise, in shipping the produce of the East & West-Indies to Europe; & in no case, during the existence of war, has he sent to Europe, articles imported by himself, in the same vessel in which they were brought from India. (Further, in the case of the Ship Lydia which arrived from India at Boston, in the Summer of 1804, & on board which vessel there was the like instruction as in the Indus, which instruction was complied with by the master, yet as the War continued, on her arrival at Boston, he sold the whole cargo to a merchant of this town; & also that of the Indus, in the voyage preceeding the one in which she was lost, wherein the like precaution was also taken, & for the like purpose, but as it was war when she arrived the voyage terminated here[)]—Thus, Sir, in this case there exists the most plenary evidence, that the voyage which the Indus was performing, when captured, was direct from Batavia to Boston there to terminate. A trade perfectly legal, not only in the understanding of the Owners, but so acknowledged, admitted & declared by Great Britain in her practice, for ten years past, in her instructions to her cruizers, in the decrees of her Courts, & in the rules & principles advanced by her Judges in promulgating their decrees.

The principle understood to be assumed by Great Britain, is, that in time of war, a trade carried on between two independent Nations, one neutral, and the other belligerent, is unlawful in the Neutral, if the same trade was not allowed & practised in time of peace. This principle though assumed by Great Britain, is now, & always has been resisted as unsound, by every other nation. She always assumes as a fact, that the trade with a

Colony has always been confined exclusively to ships of the Parent Country. In virtue therefore of this assumption of principle and fact, she deems unlawful & derogatory to her rights, the trade of a Neutral with the colonies of her enemies. How ever, in the last war, she so far modified her principle as to assent to the lawfulness of the voyage of a Neutral,[2] if direct between the ports of the Neutral & the colony of the Enemy; & also a trade in such colonial articles from the country of the Neutral to any other Country, even to the parent Country of such colony;[3] provided, such articles were imported, bona fide, for the use of the Neutral, and there purchased or afterwards shipped by himself; and also in articles the produce of the parent kingdom from the neutral state to the colony of that metropolitan kingdom, provided the exporting & importing were bona fide, as in the other case. But this modification she always affected to consider as relaxation of her strict rights, & from this consideration assumed greater authorities to interfere with the permitted trade, as she would say, of Neutrals.

The underwriters have therefore thought it important to examine how far the doctrine is sanctioned by the law of nations, & the grounds on which it is supposed to rest, are conformed to, or contravened by the practice of Belligerents themselves.

This principle was first brought forward in the war of 1756, & was then attempted to be supported on the doctrines advanced by Bynkershoek. You, Sir, to whom the writings of this eminent Civilian are doubtless familiar, must be aware, that the rule laid down by him is brought forward to a very different purpose, & from the manner in which he treats on the rights of Neutrals, & the historical fact quoted from Livy, to illustrate & sanction the principle asserted, shows, that it can by no means warrant the proceedings which it has been attempted to justify; & that there is no analogy between the case cited, & that of the mere peacable trade of a Neutral with a Belligerent, in articles not contraband of war, nor to places under blockade.

His general position is, that whatever Nations had the power & faculty to do in time of peace, they have the right to do in time of war; except that they have not a right to carry to either of two enemies, articles contraband of war, or, to trade to blockaded places, because this would be to intermeddle in the war.

The author before cited is the principal, if not the only one, whose opinions are adduced, as capable of affording support, or in any way bearing upon this doctrine. An authority however, to interrupt the trade of a Neutral in war, which he was not free to carry on in peace, is assumed as a legitimate consequence of his acknowledged rights. The law of Nations not only prescribes rules for the conduct & supports the rights of nations at war; but also contains regulations & principles by which the rights of such as remain at peace, are protected & defined.

The intercourse between independent Nations, must exclusively rest on the Laws which such Nations may choose to establish. This is a natural consequence of the equality & independence of nations. Each may make such commercial & other internal regulations, as it thinks proper. It may open its whole trade to all foreign Nations, or admit them only to a part: it may indulge one nation in such a commerce & not others; it may admit them at one time & refuse them at another; it may restrict it's trade to certain parts of it's dominions & refuse the entrance of strangers into others. In this respect, it has a right to consult only it's own convenience, & whatever it shall choose to admit to others, may be enjoyed by them, without consulting a third power. Great Britain acts upon this principle—at one time she executes her navigation law with strictness; at other times she relaxes most of its regulations, according to the estimate she forms of advantage or disadvantage to be derived from its execution or relaxation: neither does she allow the competence of any foreign power to call in question her right so to do. In time of peace she compels a strict adherence to the principles & letter of her navigation act: in time of war she suspends most of its provisions, and to this she is doubtless induced by the paramount interest of manning her navy; whereby she is enabled to employ a much greater number of Seamen in her own defence, & to destroy the commerce of her Foes.

In consequence of a superiority derived, in some degree, from this relaxation, England is rendered an entrepot for receiving & supplying all the products of the world; and after reaping a considerable revenue from the merchandize thus introduced, she furnishes not only the continent of Europe generally; but her own Enemy with such articles as are wanted, many of which she prevents his receiving in the ordinary course.

The other nations of Europe, possessing foreign Colonies, & influenced by motives of convenience, certainly not by considerations of an higher nature than actuate Great Britain, find their advantage in a similar change of their commercial systems.

The mere circumstance that the innocent property of a Neutral is engaged in a trade permitted now, though prohibited at a former period, is in itself perfectly innocent, & does not seem capable of interfering with the rights, or justifying the complaints of a third power.

The ordinary policy of a nation may be to encourage the manufacture or growth of a certain article, within its own dominions, & for this end may prohibit or restrict the importation of the like articles from other countries. Does the repeal or suspension of such restriction confer any right to impede the transportation, by a third, of the article, the prohibition whereof is suspended? Because the Corn laws of a Nation operate three years in five, as a prohibition to the importation of all corn, can it be inferred that a friendly power should abstain from carrying its surplus corn to market? Has any belligerent a right to stop the corn owned by neutral merchants, on the way to its enemy, whose crops have failed, & prohibitory laws have been repealed? The simple state of the case, that the trade, though illegal in peace, is legal in war, decides the question.

Recourse is therefore had to another principle, in order to render that unlawful, which on every ground of the equality & independence of Nations is lawful.

The belligerent has a right to distress the person & property of his enemy, & thereby compel a submission to his demand, & for this purpose, he may use all the means in his power.

By interrupting the trade of Neutrals, which is opened to them in war, & was prohibited in peace, the belligerent distresses his enemy, lessens his revenue, prevents the exercise of his commercial capital and the employment of his merchants; & deprives him of the enjoyment of those articles which administer to his comfort & convenience, therefore such interruption is lawful.

An obvious answer to this reasoning is, that it proves too much, is founded on a principle, so comprehensive, as to embrace all trade between Neutrals & a Nation at war. If it distress a nation to interrupt that commerce which has become lawful since the war, it would distress him much more to cut off all trade, that which was allowed in time of peace, as well as that which was not: and the same reason which is used to authorize an interruption of the one, would as well justify the other. Indeed we have several times seen the like doctrine extended this length, in the heat of contest; but no instance has occurred of an attempt to vindicate it, in time of peace: for the legality of a trade in innocent articles, to a place not blockaded, & the right of the Neutral to carry it on, depends entirely on the laws of the two Countries, between which, & by whose inhabitants it is prosecuted, & in no degree on the consent of the belligerent. If this argument of distress, combined with that of an unaccustomed trade, should be admitted in all its latitude, no trade with belligerents would be legal to Neutrals. The enemies of Great Britain would be disposed to attribute much weight to a consideration of the peculiar advantages which a power constituted as hers, may be supposed to derive, & such evils as she may be presumed to prevent, by the relaxation of her commercial system. A continental power may derive some accomodation, & some convenience from relaxing her commercial restrictions; but nothing essential to her safety, nothing, as was demonstrated in the last war, materially affecting the great objects of the contest. She might obtain the articles of east & west India produce a little cheaper by these means, than if compelled to procure them by her own ships, or through the medium of her enemy: for it is a circumstance which very much impairs the argument of distressing the foe, that in modern wars, it is the practice of commercial nations, notwithstanding they respectively capture each others' property, to open their ports, for the exchange of their merchandize, by the assistance of Neutrals; & in this way afford the succour they mutually need. It will, however, be said, that [it] is not the trade between neutral countries & the metropolitan dominions of Europe, which is deemed illegal, but the trade of Neutrals with their colonies. It is not easy to perceive the grounds on which this distinction rests, but without complaining of an exceptionable rule, because the practice under it is not as extensive as its principle might be supposed to warrant, it may be examined in the case to which it is applied.

The argument of distressing the enemy is adduced, to vindicate the interruption of the trade of Neutrals with enemies' colonies. This distress can be inflicted in two ways; by depriving the Colony of the necessary supplies, or the parent country of the colony'[s] productions. To supply the enemies' colonies is now considered legal, provided it be done from the neutral Country; & also to furnish the parent country with the produce of the Colony, provided it be done from the neutral country. The argument therefore of distress, is narrowed down to a mere trifle; to the addition of a fraction in the price of the article supplied to the parent country: for so far as respects the supply of the colony & the finding a market for its produce, & the arguments flowing from thence, these, surely the most plausible, on the score of inflicting distress, are utterly abandoned. But further, the same commercial spirit which has been before noticed, leads the great Nations of Europe themselves, to contribute to those very supplies, the depriving the enemy whereof, is alledged as a justification for interrupting the trade of Neutrals. Not only a trade in Europe, but a regular & authorized trade, to the extent of every necessary & almost every other supply, was carried on during the last war, between the British & Spanish Colonies; & instances have again & again occured, & before the close of the late war, ceased to be considered as extraordinary, where the cargoes of neutral vessels bound to the spanish Colonies, were seized by the British & condemned in the vice admiralty Courts, on pretence that the trade was illegal; & the articles thus stopped & made prize of, under the plea of distressing the enemy, were shipped on board a Spanish or British Vessel, supplied with a British licence, & sent to the original port of their destination. Surely, such a mode of distressing the enemy, may be more properly denominated distressing the Neutral, for the purpose of supplying the enemy, at the exclusive profit of the belligerent.

Such, Sir! are some of the observations, which these Gentlemen make, on the difference between the practice & avowed principles of Belligerents, & the unavoidable consequences of such principles; & which satisfy their minds, that according to the practice of Belligerents themselves, there is no foundation for the arguments raised on pretence of distressing the enemy—and that interrupting a trade in war, because not exercised in peace, is inconsistent with the equality & independence of nations, & an infring[e]ment of their perfect rights. It is also evident, that the wants & interests of all nations at war, even of those who possess the most powerful commercial & military Navy, require them to contradict, in their own practice, those principles, which are avowed in justification of the injuries they inflict on Neutrals.

To support this doctrine it is also necessary to assume as true, that all trade & intercourse between the colonies of the different European powers, & other countries, have been constantly & uniformly interdicted in time of peace, & that such colonies depended exclusively on the Metropolitan kingdom for supplies of every kind—that nothing could be received by or from them, but through the mother country; except when the overpowering force of the public Enemy had prevented all such communication. This supposed exclusive trade, so confidently assumed, will, on examination, be found subject to many exceptions. It is well known that some of the British west India Colonies, during the commotions, which existed in England, in consequence of the disagreement between Charles the first & his Parliament, exported their produce to Europe by Dutch ships, manned with Dutch seamen, & that the navigation act originated in the double view of punishing some of these colonies, who had discovered an attachment to the cause of defeated Royalty, and of curtailing the means enjoyed by the Dutch of encreasing their wealth, influence & power. An intercourse has always been admitted, at some times, very restrained at others, more extended; as suited the caprice of the Governours, or as the necessity of the Colonies required.

Until a period subsequent to the Treaty of Utrecht, France seems to have paid no attention to her West India Colonies—previous to that time, they do not appear to have enjoyed any constant correspondence, or direct intercourse with the Mother Country; and at all times, as well as before, as since the independence of the continental Colonies of Great Britain, a direct trade has existed, between the colonies of France, & those of Great Britain in the West Indies, & also with the settlements on the continent of North America, more or less limited, as real or pretended convenience demanded.

Great Britain, prior to the independence of the United States, had less occasion to admit the entry of vessels & merchandize from, or the export of the produce of her colonies to any other, than her own dominions: yet instances are not wanting of the relaxation of her Navigation Act, for both purposes, & in the year 1739 a bill passed the Parliament, allowing the Sugar Colonies, for a limited time, to export their produce to foreign Ports.[4] In fact, Colonies depending on other countries for their supplies, and at a distance from their Parent Country, must, at times admit the intercourse of foreigners, or suffer the greatest impoverishment & distress. It will not be denied, that the British provinces in the West Indies, depend in a great measure, if not altogether on the United States for their Corn. True it is, that the shipment is generally made in British Vessels, but should the United States deem it for their interest, to insist on its being transported thither, in American Ships, it is not certain, that the convenience not to say the necessities of the Colonies, would not render an acquiescence advisable. The fact is, in regard to the Colonies in the West Indies, whether belonging to France or Great Britain, that the monopoly has not been, & in the nature of things never can be very strict, constant and exclusive. The United States always have enjoyed, & without hazarding much, one may pronounce with confidence, that they always must enjoy a direct intercourse with their colonies, however adverse to the dispositions or supposed interest of the Parent Countries in Europe. Thus stands the fact of an accustomed trade, in time of peace as relates to the West Indies. In regard to the East Indies, it is certain that the vessels of the United States have always gone freely to the British settlements, there, & it is believed, that the vessels of our Country were the first to export Sugars from Bengal, & that their exportations have augmented immensely the culture of that article in that Country. To many of the Dutch settlements, our vessels have gone, with but little interruption; and to some of these, & to the French possessions; more especially to the Isles of France & Bourbon, the trade of the United States has been constant, uninterrupted & increasing ever since the year 1784. It is difficult then, Sir! for these Gentlemen to conceive how the doctrine or the fact assumed by Great Britain can be supported by the Law of Nations, or reconciled to the truth.

Moreover Great Britain professes that the decisions of her Admiralty Courts are always regulated by the Law of Nations, that they do not bend to particular circumstances, nor are guided by the orders, or instructions of the Goverment. The principles of this law are immutable; being founded on truth & justice, they are ever the same. Now it appears from the practice of Great Britain herself, that in the war of 1744, & in that which was concluded in 1788, whether the trade was an accustomed one in time of peace, made no part of the discussion, nor was it pretended, that the trade not having been prosecuted in peace, subjected the vessel or cargo to forfeiture, in war. It seems more like the offspring of her pre-eminent power on the ocean, in the two wars of 1756 & that which lately ended, than the legitimate doctrine of right & justice. In the war of 1756 Dutch vessels, by special license from France, were permitted to export the produce of the French Colonies. These were captured & condemned, on the ground that, by adoption they had become French vessels. Afterwards the property was carried to Monte Christi, and exported thence in Dutch Vessels. Particular trades & special priviledges were also allowed by France, to vessels belonging to Citizens of Amsterdam, as a gratification for their peculiar exertions to induce the Stadtholder to take part with France against Great

557

Britain—Vessels & their cargoes so circumstanced, were captured & condemned by the British and this principle was then brought forward to justify their conduct, as covering, in their Courts, all the cases, by a rule as extensive as was the power and cupidity of their cruizers on the sea.

In the war for the independence of America, this principle, set up for the first time in that which preceded it, & contrary to former practice, was abandoned. This is exemplified in the following case, vizt. a vessel bound from Marseilles to Martinico, & back again, was taken on the outward voyage; the vice admiralty Court at Antigua gave half freight—on appeal the Lords of Appeal gave the whole. It is said in answer to this, that France opened her Colonies, & though it was during the existence of war, yet it was the profession of keeping them always so, but was afterwards found delusive. The Lords of Appeal however, in the case of the Danish vessel, could not have acted upon such grounds: for their decision was in 1786, three years after the peace, & after it was manifest, if any doubt had before existed, that the general opening of the trade, between the Colonies & the Mother Country, to foreigners, was a temporary expedient, & dependent on the duration of the war. The claim before them was merely equitable, being for freight of that part of the voyage, which had not been performed & to obtain which, the party claiming is bound to show, that he has offended no law & interfered with no rights of the belligerent.

What renders the conduct of Great Britain, peculiarly injurious to the merchants of our Country at this time, is the extension of this offensive doctrine, contrary to her own express & public declaration of the law, during the last war; for it was then declared, that the importation from an Enemy's colony, to the Country to which the Ship belonged, & the subsequent exportation was lawful; & so of property the produce of the parent country, going from the United States to the Colony—vide Cases of Immanuel & Polly in Robinson's Admiralty Reports before cited, Whereas property going from the United States, the produce of an Enemy's country, to her colony, although bona fide, imported & landed in the United States, and exported on the sole account & risk of the American merchant, is now taken & condemned, on the ground that the same person & vessel imported & exported the same articles; & thus by an arbitrary interpretation of the intention of the merchant the second voyage is adjudged to be a continuance of the first. If this new & extraordinary doctrine of continuity is maintained on the part of Great Britain, & acquiesced in by the United States; a very large property, now afloat, may be subject to condemnation, and it must follow, that an extensive trade, which has been carried on with great advantage by the United States, for these twelve years, & admitted to be lawful, will be totally annihilated.

The Indus & cargo have been condemned on the mere possibility, that the same might go to Europe from Boston, in case of a peace; in which event Great Britain could pretend no authority to question the voyage she should make.

Now, to adopt a principle of dubious right, in its own nature, & then to extend such principle to a further restriction of the trade of the neutral, without notice, is spreading a snare to entrap the property, & defeat the acknowledged rights to which he is entitled.

Such are its effects, both on the individual owners of this property, as well as on the Underwriters. For Mr. Sears & Mr. Chapman, in planning this voyage, & indeed in every one they ever prosecuted, have endeavoured to ascertain what the law authorized them to do, as that law was understood & practised by the Belligerents & for this purpose they examined the orders to the British Cruizers, the adjudications in the British Courts during the last war, & conceived themselves clearly within even the narrowest limits to which Great Britain professed to circumscribe the trade of Neutrals. The Underwriters also, have been uniformly guided, in insuring property, by the rules, declared & promulgated by the belligerents themselves. In the present case, they considered that according to the clearest evidence of those rules, they incurred no risk from British Cruizers.

Should then Great Britain undertake to presume that the law would authorize the interruption of such a trade, these Gentlemen cannot bring themselves to believe, that under even such impressions of her rights, she would so far forget what is due to her former understanding of the law, & to the encouragement given to such a commerce; as without notice of her altered sentiments to seize & confiscate the property of those, who had so conformed their voyages to rules pronounced by herself. I have the Honour to be, Sir, with great Respect, Your very obed. Servant

C. GORE

RC (DNA: RG 46, President's Messages, 9A–E3); Tr (DNA: RG 233, President's Messages, 9A–D1). RC in a clerk's hand, except for Gore's date, complimentary close, and signature; docketed by Wagner. Enclosed in Gore to JM, 26 Nov. 1805.

1. David Sears (1752–1816) was a wealthy Boston merchant who was successful in trade to China and India, and a director of the Bank of the United States. After his sudden, unexpected death in 1816, he left his namesake and only child $800,000. Jonathan Chapman (1756–1832) was born in Charlestown, Massachusetts, and first went to sea in 1775. He made two commercial voyages to Saint-Domingue before being drafted into the Royal Navy in January 1777. After being captured by the Americans, he was released in Virginia and in the summer of 1779 returned to Boston, from where he shipped in privateers until he was captured by the British in 1782 and sent to Halifax. He escaped, again made his way to Boston, and returned to privateering. After the Revolution he sailed in merchant ships to Europe and the West Indies. In 1789 he made his first voyage to India, in which trade he continued for several more years, becoming quite wealthy. During the Quasi-War with France he briefly held a captain's commission in the American navy but soon gave it up to return to merchant shipping. He retired in 1804 but continued to invest in trading voyages while building a wharf and a distillery in Charlestown. From 1803 to 1806 he was a selectman

in Boston, and from 1813 to 1815 he was a member of the Massachusetts legislature (Dorus Clarke, "Necrology," *New-England Historical & Genealogical Register* 26 [1872]: 207; Edmund H. Sears, *Pictures of the Olden Time, as Shown in the Fortunes of a Family of the Pilgrims* [Boston, 1857], 93–94; "Autobiography of Captain Jonathan Chapman," *Publications of the Colonial Society of Massachusetts* 11 [1910]: 208–39; *Newburyport Herald*, 14 Dec. 1832).

2. The clerk wrote in the margin here: "Polly. Lasky Robinsons Admy Repts page 361." For the *Polly* case, see *PJM-PS*, 5:38 n. 7.

3. The clerk wrote in the margin here: "Immanuel. Robinson page 186 particularly. "203." Page 203 discusses the disadvantage to trade of unloading and storing belligerent goods in a neutral country and notes that during wartime, belligerents frequently changed their commercial rules to allow the admission of neutrals. The *Immanuel* was a Hamburg ship that stopped at Bordeaux in 1799 to load French products as part of a cargo to be carried to Saint-Domingue. The French goods were condemned under the "rule of '56," which stated that a trade not allowed in peacetime was also not allowed in wartime (Robinson, *Admiralty Reports* [London ed., 1799–1808], 2:186–87, 190–91, 197–98, 205–6).

4. The 1739 act allowing the export of sugar from British colonies directly to foreign ports required the sugar to be carried in British ships that were to stop at British ports before proceeding on to European ports (*The Statutes at Large, Containing All the Publick Acts of Parliament from the Seventh Year of the Reign of His Present Majesty King George the Second, to the Fourteenth Year of His Present Majesty's Reign Inclusive* [7 vols.; London, 1734–42], 7:307–12).

§ To Ambrose Vasse. *18 November 1805, Department of State.* "In answer to your letter of the 16th. [not found] respecting the Cargo of the Ship Olive Branch,[1] I have to observe that none of the considerations stated by you or which have presented themselves to reflection are deemed sufficient to entitle you to receive the compensation recovered in your name by the Agent of the United States in London for the condemnation of the Cargo shipped in your name on board that Vessel. It will therefore be restored to the British Government if you shall not in the course of the present year take such measures or Afford such elucidations to support a title to the same, as may vary the determination."

Letterbook copy (DNA: RG 59, DL, vol. 15). 1 p.

1. For Vasse's *Olive Branch* claim, see *PJM-SS*, 9:230 n. 1.

§ From Thomas Lewis & Son. *18 November 1805, Boston.* "In the month of May last our Thomas Lewis Jr. made representation to you (at Washington)[1] concerning a claim we have upon the Government of France under the Treaty of 1800. Then you was good enough to write to General Armstrong on the subject;[2] those Letters with our papers on the affair reached Paris early in July last—since when we have not heard any thing relative to the business.

"Our losses by the French have been peculiarly hard, for beside (the Ship Hope & Cargo) the claim above alluded to, we have lost two other Vessells & cargoes without any hopes of indemnification.

"We would now represent to you a recent depredation on a vessell and Cargo owned by us, by a spanish privateer. On the 18th July last the Schooner Mary Ann, Captn. John Anthony, sailed from Boston for Guadeloupe (to touch at Barbadoes) on her outward passage was captured by a Spanish Vessell from Cadiz upon pretence—'War was declared by Spain against the United States'—and carried into St. Johns Porto Rico on the 3d. Septr. last, and our Captain confined. As late as the 20th October last the Governour of that Island detained her. Considerable part of her cargo was perishable goods—some of it the Governour had caused to be sold, and the proceeds he had taken charge of—the remainder was exposed to destruction—and the Vessell to be eaten up by worms.

"We have received three Letters from the Captain, but neither gives us any hopes of our Vessell or Cargo's being released or in any way restituted. We think it our duty to make this representation to our Government, hopeing it will meet such attention as the affair deserves."

Adds in a postscript: "If you have received any communication from General Armstrong concerning our claim forwarded to him, we should be very happy for a line of information from you."

RC (DLC: Causten-Pickett Papers, box 58, folder "Mary Ann," Brig. New York, N.Y. [. . .] 1797.". 3 pp.; docketed by Wagner, with his note: "Spanish 1804 Sch's Mary Ann (Anthony)."

1. See Thomas Lewis & Son to JM, 8 May 1805, *PJM-SS*, 9:336–37.
2. See JM to John Armstrong, 23 May 1805, ibid., 378–79.

To Dolley Madison

Wednesday Tuesday [*sic*] [19–20] Novr. 1805

I have recd. my dearest yours begun on the 15. & continued on the 16th. The low spirits which pervade it affect mine. I sho⟨uld⟩ be still more affected, if you did not tell me that your knee grew better and stronger. I am much consoled by that information, and think you ought to be also, as your knee has been the source of both our disquietudes. I hope your next will manifest better spirits, and be a cordial to mine. I hope also that the company of Your sister will prove a good medicine to you, and accelerate all the requisites to our reunion, my anxiety for which you can better feel I trust than I can express. I have been exerting myself to provide a remittance for you, but shall not be able to get it ready before the mail of thursday. In the mean time I hope to learn something particular as to the Drs. Charge, and thence to estimate the better, the sum necessary. Should there be time however after you receive this to let me know how much would be desireable to you for your Philada. purposes, let me know without reserve, and I will do all I can in that as in all cases, to evince the happiness I feel in giving proofs of my unlimited affection & confidence. Gooch tells me he has hopes of making up nearly our quota of Bacon, & in general gives a favorable acct. of things. Your friends here are all well. Tingey is recovering from a tedious & dangerous attack. I send inclosed a letter from Mrs. Washington. Col. Burr & Genl. Dayton are here from the Western Country.

They were at Clarksburg, and speak highly of Mrs. Jackson's blooming resurrection from the puerperal bed.[1] She was to set out the day after they left her, accompanied by Capt Washington whose health was also much improved. I inclose also $60 from the President to replace your advances. The things arrived safe. I hope you have not been unmindful of the civilities recd. from your friends, and among them the particular attentions of Mrs. Leiper. I inclose a specimen of Capt. W's tobo. Present it to Mr. L. and tell him with my complts. I wish to have his judgmt. of it.[2] Payne is well. I endeavor to keep him a little in the path of the Student; but the close employment of my time, at this juncture leaves much to his own disposition. I have not yet heard from Mr Dubourg. As I hope soon to see Miss P. and settle all ballces. with her, I will pay her no more at 2d. hand, reserving to myself the payment & receipt of all kisses on both sides of the acct. Accept my dearest love the warmest affections of your

                                                                    J. M.

RC (NjP). Day not indicated; conjectural days assigned based on Jefferson's having repaid JM for "sundries bot for Mrs. Randolph" on 19 Nov. 1805 (Bear and Stanton, *Jefferson's Memorandum Books*, 2:1168). Addressed and franked by JM to "Mrs. Madison at Mrs. Wood's."

1. Dolley's sister, Mary Payne Jackson, gave birth to Mary Elizabeth Payne Jackson in 1805 (Glossary, *DMDE*).

2. Scots-born Thomas Leiper (1745–1825) came to America in 1763 and settled in Maryland, moving to Philadelphia two years later to work with his cousin who was a tobacco exporter. He later formed his own business and became one of the most important tobacco merchants in Philadelphia. He also owned mills and stone quarries and constructed a horse-drawn railway in 1809 and a tramway in 1810. He was a strong supporter of the American Revolution and belonged to a troop of Philadelphia cavalry. One of Pennsylvania's most influential Republicans, he was a presidential elector in 1808 and 1825, member and later president of the Philadelphia common council, a member of the St. Andrew's Society, and a founder and officer of the Franklin Institute.

From James Sullivan

SIR   BOSTON 19th. Novr. 1805
    The idea of preserving the post offices, and mails inviolable is almost too sacred to allow a petition for mitigating the punishment of any one who may have been convicted of robbing them. We are very unfortunate here. A young man, labouring under an accidental, but nearly inpenetrable, deafness of respectable connexions; and one whose character stood well before; has been duly and fairly, as I suppose, convicted of stealing money from a letter in the post office.[1] He had long been employed in the office

without any suspicions. By the Law, the Judges were *obliged* to sentence him to be whiped. A late law of this state, fostered by some of our Judges and principal men, has done away this infamous kind of punishment. The ideas on which that act was supported, through the forms of Legislation, was, that such punishment was incongenial to the nature of our constitutions; that it had no tendency to reclaim the offender, but cast him out of civil society; fixing a deep and indelible stain on his character, and doing an incurable injury to that of his friends. That it was founded in principles of a government of Terror, and unsuitable to be applied to a citizen. The manner of punishment has become odious in the public opinion here, and the execution of it, in this instance, as I firmly beleive, will be of no advantage to the national government. I do not know whether the president holds a power of a conditional pardon, and therefore say nothing on that point. I feel a diffidence to interfere in a concern, where I have no privity authority, or interest, but a confidence that the attempt will tend to save a respectable, and numerous connexion from most excruciating torture, as well as to serve the interest of the government, urges me to give you this trouble and gives me an opportunity to assure you with how much respect I am your most humble Servant.

JA SULLIVAN

RC (DLC: Jefferson Papers).

1. In May 1804 Richard Quince Hoskins (1770–1825), chief clerk at the Boston post office, was accused of stealing from the mail four hundred dollars sent by Edmund M. Blunt to Joseph White Jr. at Salem. Hoskins paid Blunt four hundred and forty dollars with the proviso that the money would be refunded if the letter was returned with proof that Hoskins had nothing to do with its disappearance; if such proof did not accompany the letter, only four hundred dollars would be returned. In the July 1805 federal court term, Hoskins was convicted and sentenced to receive twenty lashes, to spend three years at hard labor, and to pay court costs. In addition to Sullivan's appeal through JM, fifty-two distinguished Massachusetts citizens, among them Christopher Gore, Harrison Gray Otis, and merchants Peter Chardon Brooks and Perez Morton, submitted a petition requesting a pardon for Hoskins. Because Hoskins refused to admit any guilt, Jefferson did not sign a pardon until 12 Aug. 1808, after Hoskins had spent fifty months in jail (Lucius B. Marsh and Harriet F. Parker, *Bronsdon and Box Families* [Lynn, Mass., 1902], 224; Fredericktown, Md., *Bartgis's Republican Gazette*, 22 June 1804; Edmund M. Blunt to Richard Q. Hoskins, 10 May 1804, Harrison Gray Otis et al. to Jefferson, ca. 27 Dec. 1805, and Hoskins to Jefferson, 14 and 28 Aug. 1808, DLC: Jefferson Papers; Pardon No. 147, DNA: RG 59, PPR, 1:156).

To Alexander J. Dallas

Dear Sir   Washington Nov. 20. 1805

It is inferred from some indications that the Marquis d'Yrujo, has it in view to visit this place and even to pass the Winter with the Govt. The footing on which he stands, renders it improper to continue the diplomatic intercourse with him, and will make it necessary that he should not remain indefinitely in this Country in his public Character. It can hardly be supposed that he is left unapprized by his own Govt. of this state of the case. It is however possible that he may be under some illusion. At any rate it is not expedient for himself, nor wished by the President that any step should be taken by him, which might give him needless pain, or needless publicity to his personal situation. May I presume so far on your goodness, and your friendly relations to the family, as to request you to find some means, the more delicate the better, of conveying impressions that will put a stop to the intensions of the Marquis, if they be such as they have been understood to be. A line from you intimating the result of this request, for the liberty of which I put myself on your goodness, will further oblige Dear Sir, Yr. Obedt. hble servt.

James Madison

Draft (DLC: American Academy of History, Letters Collection, 1961).

From John Carroll

Dear and hond. Sir   Baltre. Nov. 20. 1805.

Your much esteemed favour of the 1st. inst. would have received a much earlier answer, if Mr. Dubourg had determined sooner the time, when he would be ready to receive your Son. I have the pleasure to inform you now, that the College will be ready for his reception on the first of next month, Decr.[1]

I was sorry indeed to hear that you were under the necessity of leaving Mrs. Madison at Philada., & that this was occasioned by the tediousness of her recovery. Not having been since informed of her having passed thro this place, I fear that she has not been yet able to travel, and feel that concern for it, which no one, who has the happiness of knowing her, can avoid feeling.

I am much obliged to you for your goodness in furnishing the inclosed prints respecting New Orleans; they had been forwarded to me before, &

I had read them attentively. With my assurances of the sincerest regard, respect & esteem, I am, Dr. Sir, Your most obedt. hble St.

†J. CARROLL

RC (DLC).

1. John Payne Todd attended St. Mary's College in Baltimore from December 1805 to at least June 1812 (MdBS: Student Index, St. Mary's College Collection, Archives of the Associated Sulpicians of the U.S., Associated Archives; Account with St. Mary's College, 1 June 1812, *PJM-PS*, 4:444).

§ From William C. C. Claiborne. *20 November 1805, New Orleans.* "The inclosed paper will furnish you with a Copy of an address from the House of Representatives of this Territory to the President of the United States:[1] it was unanimously adopted, and evinces a degree of Patriotism which I hope may have a good effect.

"I contemplate convening the Legislature, some time about the last of February, and am therefore solicitous for an early appointment of the Councillors; a list of the Citizens recommended by the House of Representatives, has been transmitted to the President.[2]

"I received, yesterday, a letter from Mr. Graham, dated the 14. Instant, on the Lake; he had experienced opposite winds, and apprehended a long passage to Pensacola."

RC and enclosure (DNA: RG 59, TP, Orleans, vol. 7); letterbook copy (Ms-Ar: Claiborne Executive Journal, vol. 15). RC 1 p.; in a clerk's hand, signed by Claiborne; docketed by Wagner. For enclosure, see n. 1.

1. Claiborne enclosed a section (2 pp.) from the 19 Nov. 1805 *Louisiana Gazette* containing a copy of the 14 Nov. 1805 letter from the territorial house of representatives to Jefferson, expressing their esteem for and confidence in him and praising his "conduct in the aquisition [*sic*] of Louisiana."

2. For the list of nominees to the council, see Claiborne to JM, 12 Nov. 1805, n.

§ From George W. Erving. *20 November 1805, Madrid.* No. 2. "I had the honor to write you on the 25th. Ulto. from the Escurial, by Mr. Pinckney who proceeded to Lisbon on the 26th.

"Mr. Pinckney will have informed you particularly of the state in which he left our affairs here, of the means which he took, (but without success,) towards the close of his Mission, to obtain a Ratification of the Convention, & of the actual dispositions of this Government. Since his departure nothing of very material importance has occurred: their proceedings in the capture & trial of our vessels do not seem to be regulated by any uniformity of system, or to be founded on any determined principles. Whether owing to a policy in the Government perpetually varying, to a want of due organization in its Tribunals, to the insubordination of the inferior to the superior departments of the Government, or to the interference of personal interests & influence, it is difficult to say; probably at times to each of these. However this may be, the effect is very prejudicial to us, rendering it almost impossible (the great points of question apart) to preserve that perfect cordiality & uninterrupted harmony of intercourse which it is so desirable to have with this Country; for under such a state of things the Commerce of our Citizens must always be subjected to insufferable vexations, even if it can be secured from actual depredation.

"In consequence of the repeated & strong representations of Mr. Pinckney, an order was passed last year, intended, as it would seem, to secure a due respect to the 15th. Article of the Treaty[1] on the part of the inferior executive departments, the tribunals & the Commanders of armed vessels, public & private; more particularly to repress the excesses of the privateers-men which had been so much complained of, & to establish a sort of code to regulate their conduct which appears to have been before that time perfectly lawless. I am informed from Cadiz that to this day no notification of the order has been given to the Tribunals there, & we have unfortunately abundant proof of its total inefficacy in other places; so that whether any vessel engaged in carrying enemies goods may or may not be brought in, & if brought in whether she will or will not at this moment be condemned, remain loose & uncertain questions.

"Having received from Nathaniel F. Adams, lately Commander of the Ship 'Recovery' from Norfolk, a copy of a decree made by the Court at Algesiras in July last, by which it appears that the Cargo of that vessel was condemned upon the ground of its being English property,[2] I have thought this a fit occasion & the present a suitable time to make such a representation to this Government as is calculated to ascertain whether or not it will explicitly abandon the pretention of capturing enemies property on board our vessels, & properly inforce the order which it formerly issued upon the subject.

"I have thought it my duty to make a representation at the same time upon the case of the 'Hudson,' Bailey—a vessel which was robbed by a privateers-man of her papers, & then condemned for the want of them, with a view not only of obtaining an immediate restitution of the ship & cargo, but the infliction of such punishment on the privateers-man as the enormity of his offence seems to require, & which may operate beneficially as an example to others. I have the honor to inclose a copy of these notes,[3] together with a copy of a decree lately given in a Court constituted by the french Admiral at Cadiz to try an American vessel (the 'Huntress,' Cunningham)[4] which was taken by the combined fleets on the day of their sailing. By this last document it appears that whilst the Spaniards are harrassing our Commerce in such a variety of modes, the french authorities here are disposed to respect the neutrality of our flag to the full extent of our treaty stipulations—thus, though the Cargo of the 'Huntress' was proven to be enemies property, it has been delivered over to an Agent for the Owners, appointed by the Captain, the question only as to the blockade of Gibraltar being reserved for the decision of a superior Tribunal.

"The claim of Messrs. Dulton & Tombarel, which you have been pleased to recommend to the care of Mr. Pinckney,[5] he has not been able, with every exertion, to bring to a favorable issue, & I am now informed by Mr. Tombarel that he has learnt, tho' not from a source immediately official, that he cannot hope to be paid the compensation which he has been so long seeking for; since the Government having received accounts from the United States, giving them reason to apprehend hostilities in that quarter, have concluded not to attend to individual reclamations.

"What calculation they make here as to the future, it is difficult to conjecture; wholly deprived of the means even of defensive operations, they must needs rely upon the interference or intermediation of their powerful ally: Whether on assurances from that quarter, or whether from an ignorance of, or an insensibility to, their true situation with respect to the United States, they seem, as far as I can observe, to repose in a state of perfect security.

"I did not write to you immediately upon the important meeting of the combined fleets & that of the British, because I concluded that you would receive intelligence from various other quarters much earlier than I could transmit it from hence in any correct form, for even to this day the whole extent of the loss on either side, is not generally known here. I inclose herewith the best reports which I have been able to obtain. I hear further that only two of the Spanish Ships are considered to be worth the expence of repairs. The King has rewarded the bravery of his Officers, by promoting each a grade, & by additional honors given to those of the highest class."[6]

Adds in a postscript: "21st. The following is extract of a letter which I have this day received from Mr. Montgomery of Alicante, dated 16th. November.

" 'Last night I received a letter from Mr. Mounbird, Agent of the United States at Algiars. He advises that the new Dey has entirely quietted the insurrection within the City, & dispersed the rebellious Army without, so that tranquility has taken place of terror and disorder, & American affairs in the Regency were on the best footing. Colonel Lear had not yet returned from his mission in Tripoli.[']"

RC and enclosures (DNA: RG 59, DD, Spain, vol. 10). RC 3 pp.; in a clerk's hand, signed by Erving; docketed by Wagner. For enclosures, see nn. 2–3.

1. For article 15 of the 1795 Treaty of San Lorenzo, which allowed either country to trade with the enemies of the other, see Miller, *Treaties*, 2:328–30.
2. For the *Recovery*, see Charles Pinckney to JM, 24 July 1805, and n. 2. Erving enclosed a copy of Erving to Pedro Cevallos, 14 Nov. 1805 (3 pp.; marked "(Triplicate.)"), transmitting a copy of the 26 July 1805 decree of the Algeciras court and noting that the cargo was condemned (1) for want of certain certificates specifying cargo particulars as required by article 17 of the Treaty of San Lorenzo; (2) because this defect could not be supplied by customhouse clearances; and (3) because the bills of lading did not specify that the freighters were American citizens, which led to a suspicion that the goods were not American. Erving stated that because the lack of the certificates could be made up by customhouse clearance papers showing the ship as American in spite of the requirements of article 17, because the fifteenth article of the treaty allowed that free ships make free goods, and because the cargo, when examined in a Spanish port, was clearly shown not to be contraband, the decree was unjust. Erving stated that Cevallos must see that the rights of the United States, founded on the Treaty of San Lorenzo, had been violated by the Algeciras court; that he did not doubt that Cevallos would annul the decree; and that the king would issue an immediate order for restitution of the cargo. He added in a postscript that to save Cevallos trouble, he was enclosing a copy in French but stated that he could not be answerable for the accuracy of the translation. For article 17 of the 1795 Treaty of San Lorenzo, see Miller, *Treaties*, 2:332–33.
3. The enclosure (3 pp.) is a copy of Erving to Cevallos, 16 Nov. 1805, repeating the details of the case of the *Hudson*, Bailey, which was stopped by a Spanish privateer while en route to Naples in May 1805. All the ship's papers were in order, the cargo was owned by neutrals, and it was bound to a neutral port. The captain of the privateer took away the ship's papers, and Captain Bailey, unable to continue his voyage without them, followed the privateer

into Cádiz, where the privateer's captain, instead of returning them, hid them. Bailey's agent later found two of the documents in the health office, but because an essential one was missing, the ship was condemned. The king ordered the proceedings delayed until evidence could be obtained from the United States. Erving announced that this had just arrived, was enclosed, and would prove that the ship had every necessary document when it left the United States. He added that since the guilt of the privateer's captain had been established, he trusted Cevallos would take the measures "which a love of justice will naturally declare."

4. For the case of the *Huntress*, see Anthony Terry to JM, 31 Oct. 1805, and n. 2.

5. For Thomas Dulton and John Francis Tombarel's case, see Jacob Wagner to JM, 17 Aug. 1801, *PJM-SS*, 2:49, 52 n. 3.

6. In addition to promoting the officers who were at Trafalgar, the Spanish awarded every soldier and sailor who had been there treble pay for the day, since they were considered to have acted courageously and endured an honorable defeat. The French, on the other hand, considered Trafalgar "a disgraceful disaster," and those who had participated were rewarded with "oblivion" (Adkins, *Nelson's Trafalgar*, 346–47).

§ From Robert Purviance. *20 November 1805, Baltimore.* "I had the honor to receive your Letter of the 13th. Inst. [not found] and have conformable to your request shipped the articles imported in the Brig Lyon, on board the Schooner Betsy & Charlotte Alexander Lammond master for George Town.

"I have inclosed you Capn. Lammonds receipt, the Bill of Loading [not found], and Mr. Guestier's receipt for the freight,[1] and given you as below a statement of the expenses."

Purviance added the following account below his signature:

Amount of Duties	20.63
Drayage to the Ware House	62
Freight ℔ rect	23.20
Drayage to the Packet	50
	Drs. 44.95

RC and enclosures (DLC). RC 1 p.; in a clerk's hand, signed by Purviance. For surviving enclosures, see n. 1.

1. The enclosures (2 pp.) are (1) a 20 Nov. 1805 account from Peter A. Guestier for $23.20, or £5.4.6, for freight and primage on the brig *Lyon* for eight cases and one tierce marked JM, marked payment received from Purviance; and (2) a 20 Nov. 1805 receipt from Alexander Lammond of the *Betsy & Charlotte* for eight cases and one tierce to be delivered to JM's order at Georgetown, D.C. For the contents, see William Lee to JM, 14 Sept. 1805, and n. 1.

To Dolley Madison

Novr. 21. [1805]

I mentioned in my last my dearest that I should put into the mail today the remittance promised you. Having failed to sell the bill on N. York I was obliged to enter into an arrangement with the Bank here bottomed on the Credit of that Bill. It has enabled me to forward you the enclosed post note which I hope will arrive safe, and remove all (pecuni)ary obstacles to your setting out. Should it be insufficient, You will be able doubtless to get credit till I can make a further remittance which can be done on your return to Washington. The Horses I understand are to be paid for some time hence. I think your brother to blame to precipitate a sale of lands. He can not be so pressed as to require it, I shd. imagine, and the Moment is certainly not favorable to such a transaction. Mrs. Randolph is not arrived nor does the President know the precise time that she will. I have nothing to add to my last but repeated expressions of my anxiety to have you safe with me, and with best regards & respects to Dr. Physic & love to our Sister & Miss P. assurances of the truest affection of Yrs.

J. M.

RC (PWbW: Gilbert S. McClintock Collection).

§ From George W. Erving. *21 November 1805, Madrid. "Private* No. 2." "Having heard thro a variety of channels, (not officially) that the British still continue their depredations, & as it is to be apprehended that their late successes will neither add to the wisdom of their policy, or to their love of justice, presuming therefore that Mr. Monroe will find it necessary to continue amongst them, I have sent to him Copies of two of the papers herewith inclosed; not however very confidently expecting that either the Endeavours which we make to secure the neutrality of our flag under the protection of which they derive such great advantages, & which is indeed so essential to them at this time, or the good faith manifested by France on this point, can produce much effect upon a government always calculating its measures for existing circumstances, & always building upon temporary Expedients.

"I cannot add to the information which you have received from France respecting the rapid progress & unparalled [*sic*] success of the French Armies in Austria; that of Napoleon in Italy as you will also hear has not been inactive; it seems as tho' the Archduke now placed in Carniola between three French armies cannot escape by any possibility. It is reported here on the authority of letters from Genoa of the 5th. Instant that Massena has been obliged to recross the 'Adige' with the loss of 30,000 men. This however is not to be beleived in any degree, because by authentic accounts, he had beaten the Archduke twice, before, he was joined by 25,000 men under St. Cyr; & the Austrians have not been Reinforced.[1]

"The attention of all Europe is at this moment turned towards the King of Prussia: in Every body's opinion Except that of Buonaparte, his force thrown into Either scale woud decide the contest; the probability however is that he will preserve his Consequence by Remaining Neuter; his interest is also clearly in favor of that course; or if he must take a part Buonaparte has greater boons to offer him than any body Else. A little Expression of ill humour & some threatening movements of his troops intended however only to assert his importance bristling himself up, as it were, to defend his neutrality, have Encouraged the hopes of great Britain always very Easily raised, & in the good honest conviction that he may be induced to join the coalition they have sent an Extraordinary mission; to which Mr Hammond, who is considered as particularly adroit in foreign affairs is joined: There can be very little Expectation that G. B. will succeed in this courtship further than to induce his Prussian Majesty to occupy Hanover, which in the Event will render their Ever seeing it again more improbable than it was before. It is said here that the king of Prussia has actually Entered Hanover; if so doubtless with the consent of the allies under the idea of his hostility to France, & with the consent of France also under the better arrangement of securing it from the allies for the use of indemnities & equivalents after the war, or what is still more probable for his own use as the price of his neutrality. The successes of Buonaparte must necessarily open to him vast views; is it improbable that he will undertake to reerect the kingdom of Poland; totally to destroy the house of Austria with the assistance of the Turks whom he can reward with a great part of Hungary, & to Elevate & Establish his ally the Elector of Bavaria in the intermediate territory.

"You will expect from me some interesting information respecting the Sentiments & views of this government but from a variety of causes, extremely little of these can be known from any ordinary sources; or can any probable conjectures be founded on what may be called public Opinion; since if that can be heard by the government it cannot be supposed to influence its conduct. One is astonished to observe how little sensation is excited by Events of the greatest importance of either character, & at the perfect Equanimity which is preserved in situations of the greatest trial. The general state of the Country bad enough certainly before, is of course rendered infinitely worse by the late disaster; it is now absolutely destitute of a naval force, & as is beleived of the means of creating one. Its government a *compost* of *imbecility and corruption* has driven from its *support all the patriotism* and *character* which Existed in the *Grandees* a *class* now broken down & as to *political influence annihilated*. It is said that such a state of things is not to last long, yet I cannot learn what is to terminate it; as far as one can judge from any visible cause it must not only last but during the continuance of the war grow worse. If they were before *dependent on France* they are still more so now If they have been impoverished *by that alliance*, this is an evil not likely to be remedied by the new wants for money which are created. What can be more melancholy than this fact, that money was never so scarce & the necessaries of life never dearer here than at this moment, a coincidence that speaks their distress more distinctly than the most laboured description can do: To this Evil is added a paper currency amounting to 6 or 7 millions of dollars the circulation of which is confined to Madrid, which is made a legal tender *Except for payments of duties*[2] &c. & which is now at a depreciation of nearly 25 per Ct.!!*

"Mr Bowdoin has arrived at Paris but as all Opinions have concurred in the propriety of his not proceeding to this place till he shall receive your instructions, he has therefore concluded to continue in the mean time where he is. I am very much concerned to be obliged to tell you that after the most strict search I have not been able to find Mr. Pinckneys Cypher. He has not replied to the letter which I wrote to him at Lisbon upon the subject, & Mr. Youngs letter to him remains upon that point unanswered. I am therefore very apprehensive that the Cypher has been *lost*. That which I have used herein is Mr. Monroes, of which he gave me a copy before I left London.

"I learnt from Mr. Pinckney that our Ministers here have Employed a french translator & interpreter at the Expence of the government. Upon this recommendation I have therefore continued Mr. Barrett (the gentleman who for a long time past has held that Office & who is also well spoken of by Mr. Monroe) in Employ at his former salary of 40 Ds. per Month, till you shall direct otherwise. I understand also that the Expences of travelling occasionally to & from the Royal residences have been included in the Account of Contingent Expences."

Added below Erving's signature: "*It is probable that this government has sent out orders to South America calculated to meet hostilities in that Quarter, for it is not supposable that they are insensible to the Value or to the Vulnerability of their Colonies; but as they cannot send troops, so they must ultimately depend on France to protect them from Whatever dangers may arise. France at this time can give no aid but by intermediation, or is it probable that she even contemplated any other; she wishes to see a state of things which will render her Umpirage necessary, & doubtless calculates to derive advantages from Either side for holding the ballance."

RC (DNA: RG 59, DD, Spain, vol. 10). 7 pp.; in a clerk's hand, signed by Erving. Damaged by removal of seal. Italicized words are those encoded by Erving and decoded here by the editors (for the code, see *PJM-SS*, 4:352 n. 1).

1. After two days of fierce fighting with the French forces under Gen. André Massena on 30–31 Oct. 1805, Archduke Charles of Austria ordered his troops to retreat from Caldiero, Italy, on 1 Nov. 1805 (George Armand Furse, *Campaigns of 1805: Ulm, Trafalgar & Austerlitz* [1905; reprint, Felling, Eng., 1995], 283–86).

2. Underlined by Erving's clerk.

From Thomas Jefferson

Nov. 22. 05.

Will you be so good as to give this a severe correction both as to stile & matter, & as early a one as you can, because there remains little enough time to submit it to our brethren successively, to have copies made &c.[1] Think also what documents it requires, & especially as to Spanish affairs. Before we promise a subsequent communication on that subject, it would be well to agree on it's substance, form, and accompaniments, that we may not be embarrassed by promising too much.

RC (DLC: Rives Collection, Madison Papers). Unsigned. In Jefferson's hand.

1. The enclosure presumably was a draft of Jefferson's fifth annual message to Congress, 3 Dec. 1805 (Ford, *Writings of Thomas Jefferson*, 8:384–96). For his 6 Dec. 1805 message and its enclosures dealing with Spanish depredations on American commerce and the failed negotiations at Madrid, see *ASP, Foreign Relations*, 2:613–95.

From Thomas Jefferson

Nov. 22. 05.

The inclosed barbarous Italian would require more consideration to be perfectly understood than I have time to bestow on it.[1] I believe Mr. Wagner reads Italian. If he does, a good translation should be made; and it sets up such serious pretensions as that I think we should give it to Eaton & desire him to make a statement of what passed between him & the Ex bashaw & such a one as we may communicate to the latter with our determinati(on) on it.

RC (DNA: RG 59, ML). Unsigned. In Jefferson's hand.

1. The enclosure was probably Ahmad Qaramanli to Jefferson, 5 Aug. 1805 (printed in *ASP, Foreign Relations*, 2:720), stating that William Eaton had promised him a pension should their joint attempt to overthrow his brother Yusuf fail, that Isaac Hull had then sent him a ship loaded with supplies, that he and Eaton had conquered Derna but had been refused further assistance from the U.S. Navy after word arrived of the treaty Tobias Lear had signed with Yusuf, and that Yusuf was refusing to return Ahmad's family as promised. Ahmad said that he and his retinue were living in Syracuse, Sicily, on two hundred dollars a month and that he felt abandoned "by a great nation"; he asked Jefferson for mercy and justice. In a 1 Sept. 1805 letter to the American people, Ahmad noted that after paying the expenses of his thirty dependents, he was left with $1.50 for himself (Knox, *Naval Documents, Barbary Wars*, 6:263–64). For the secret agreement between Lear and Yusuf Qaramanli allowing the latter to hold Ahmad's family for four years further, see Lear to JM, 5 July 1805, n. 8.

From James Monroe

Dear Sir   London Novr. 22. 1805.

I wrote you on the 16th. in haste by the "John Bulkley"[1] a letter in which I observed that in making the question of right with this govt. it might perhaps be best to take *at*[2] *this time the most moderate*[3] *ground. As those terms are indefinite and* may be misunderstood, some explanation may be necessary to convey an idea of what I shod. consider in that light. The seizure is a positive violation of right, subjects to great loss & even ruin many of our people, and is in effect an act of hostility to our country. Under such circumstances what ought to be considered *as moderate ground*? Reprisals are unquestionably justifiable: *but I would not resort to that measure*[4] *or to any other which broke* the relations subsisting between the two countries. You will have seen my letter to a friend of ours of the 1st. instant which touches this point.[5] The sentiment expressed in it, was that which I meant to convey in mine to you to which I refer. I really think that the measures suggested in that letter *would be moderate* & such as are eminently called for, by the injuries complained of. Every days experience confirms me more fully in this opinion, as in those which are communicated in my publick letter to you of the 16th. ulto. I have no reason to presume that in the points in question any accomodation can be obtained *voluntarily;* am strong in the opinion that if they are successful in the war & no measure of counteraction taken on our part at this time, that they will push their aggressions still further in comparison with the injury *and think the prospect fair that a suitable[6] pressure* on our part *which would be deemed moderate* in comparison with the injury *but also firm and decisive would produce* the desired effect. *Perhaps an embargo would be better,* but I am aware that the course to be pursued by our government in this business is a question which depends on so many circumstances, many of which are entirely domestick, and of course out of my sight, that it is impossible for me to give an opinion on it worthy much attention. In what estimation is the commerce held by the American people? How is their sensibility affected by the seizure of their vessels? What injury have they sustained in the various branches to which its influence extends? What sacrifices are they willing to hasard & even make to put our concerns in this & other respects on a just footing with this government? To form a safe opinion of the measures which the present juncture may require, correct information shod. be had on these & other points, in which I am defective. I can only venture to judge of the *attitude it may be proper* for our government to take to *support[7] negociation here* the facts relative to which are before me.

The progress of the war on the continent, the ultimate fortune of which must essentially dictate the terms of peace, has so far greatly disappointed the expectation of this country. The hope of a favorable termination of it, seems now to rest principally on the part which Prussia takes in it, & her conduct is quite œnigmatical. It is believed that a bargain had been struck between France & her before the violation of her neutrality to divide Holland between them, by the antient courses of the Rhine, as the price of her neutrality, or on some other terms. That bargain seems to have been set aside since, & the King of Prussia to have taken a new attitude, wh. under the character of an armed mediation, presents the exterior of an half quarrel with France. About the time that Ld. Harrowby left this for Berlin, Count or Baron Haugwitz left Berlin for the French camp,[8] which I believe continues to move on towards Vienna. The object of Prussia is I presume to get as much territory as possible, at the lowest price. She wants Holland & Hanover. France is willing to give the latter & part of the former. The allies the whole of the former only. It is said that the ministry here was willing to give both, but was overruled by those above it. It is probable that the mission of Mr. Haugwitz to the French camp, was to secure his govt. by a negotiation with both parties at the same time, the means of making the best bargain with either. In this state of things the result is quite uncertain, as it depends altogether on the abilities & energy of the Prussian Cabinet. In the mean time delay is most probably favorable to France, in wh. case she will become in the degree, more independant daily of the allies, and if successful of Prussia herself.

I expect to leave this in the Roba & Betsey, Captn. Tomkins for Norfolk, sometime abt. the middle of Feby. unless I receive some instructions from you, to prevent it. The delicate state of health both of Mrs. Monroe & my daughter compels me to leave London for the country, Cheltenham, where we shall probably stay till we sail, except that I shall be here occasionally especially if business requires it.

Two packets from you taken in an american vessel coming to Europe, to Mr. Bowdoin at Madrid, were sent me lately by Sir William Scott, in a polite note, & were forwarded to day to Mr. Alexander at Rotterdam, by Mr. Caldwell of Phila. I wrote Mr. Alexander & requested him not to put them in the mail, but if a private safe opportunity could not be had in a week or ten days, to forward them, by a special messenger with my letters accompanying them, to Mr. Bowdoin, & one which I also wrote to general Armstrong. I apprized those gentlemen that I proposed sailing in Feby. for the U States, & expressd a wish that they wod. previously put in my possession what they might wish me to communicate to you, on my arrival. I am dear sir your friend & servant

JAS. MONROE

25th. I send you the paper of this & some preceeding days. Your packets to Mr. Bowdoin, were large, one was directed "not to be put in the post office," & might be the laws: the other, was I think marked no. 7—it was large.

RC (DLC: Rives Collection, Madison Papers); partial FC and partial letterpress copy of RC (NN: Monroe Papers). Unless otherwise noted, italicized words in the RC were written in code; decoded interlinearly by JM; decoded here by the editors (for the code, see *PJM-SS*, 4:352 n. 1).

1. The *John Bulkley* arrived at Wilmington, Delaware, on 23 Jan. 1806 (Philadelphia *Aurora General Advertiser*, 24 Jan. 1806).

2. Encoded "ask"; decoded "at."

3. "Moderate" was omitted in the encoding and supplied at the State Department.

4. Encoded "massure"; decoded "measure."

5. In his 1 Nov. 1805 letter to Jefferson, DLC: Jefferson Papers, Monroe included several copies of James Stephen's *War in Disguise* and suggested, as one possible response to the renewed seizure of American ships, that "it would be proper for the congress to act on it, and declare its sense of the law of nations, taking perhaps the ground of the Russian treaty & pledging the representative body that is both branches, to support the Executive in the maintenance of those rights. As an indemnity to those who may have suffered by a violation of them, it may be advisable to impose a discriminatory duty on British manufactures of 15. or 25. pr. Cent."

6. Encoded "suitble"; decoded "suitable."

7. Encoded "ntport"; decoded "support."

8. In October 1805 the British government sent Dudley Ryder, Baron Harrowby, to Berlin to offer Frederick William III a £2,500,000 subsidy for his troops and the acquisition of more territory if he would join the coalition against France. The revelation that Prussia had signed a treaty with Russia guaranteeing acquisition of Hanover to the former, and the news of the defeat of Russia and Austria by the French at Austerlitz, ended the negotiations. On 15 Dec. 1805 Prussia signed a treaty with Napoleon that ceded Hanover to Prussia (J. Holland Rose, *William Pitt and the Great War* [London, 1911], 536–45, 553; Hague, *William Pitt the Younger*, 562, 564).

§ To John Beckley. *22 November 1805, Department of State.* "I have the honor to enclose a certificate of the election of a new member of the House of Representatives for the State of Delaware[1] with the letter of Mr. Robinson in which it was transmitted to me."

Letterbook copy (DNA: RG 59, DL, vol. 15). 1 p.

1. The new member of the House of Representatives from Delaware was James Madison Broom (Connecticut *Windham Herald*, 3 Oct. 1805).

§ To Albert Gallatin. *22 November 1805, Department of State.* "I have the honor to request that you will be pleased to issue a warrant on the appropriations for Barbary Intercourse, for Seven hundred & Sixty dollars & Sixty nine cents in favor of James Davidson Jnr. the holder of the enclosed bill of exchange, drawn on me on the 4th. Novr. 1803, by James Simpson Esqr. Consul of the U. States at Tangier,[1] in favor of Edward Humphry. Said Simpson to be charged with the same."

Letterbook copy (DNA: RG 59, DL, vol. 15). 1 p.

1. See Simpson to JM, 4 Nov. 1803, *PJM-SS*, 6:18.

§ From William C. C. Claiborne. *22 November 1805, New Orleans.* "An American Schooner which was lately captured and carried into the Havanna, has been released, and the Owners of the Privateer that made the capture, have been ordered to pay a considerable sum of money for the injury done. This circumstance has afforded much pleasure to the Merchants here, and will doubtless greatly benefit the commerce of the Port.

"You will read with pleasure the Address of Mr. Detréhan to the House of Representatives;[1] he seems at this time to be a good American, and I think I have observed of late, a very favorable change in the public sentiment. No man entertains a greater regard for the ancient Inhabitants of Louisiana than myself or more appreciates their many private virtues; and I entertain Strong hopes that, in a few years, they will become very zealous members of the American Republic."

RC and enclosure (DNA: RG 59, TP, Orleans, vol. 7); letterbook copy (Ms-Ar: Claiborne Executive Journal, vol. 15). RC 1 p.; in a clerk's hand, signed by Claiborne; docketed by Wagner. For enclosure, see n. 1.

1. The enclosure (2 pp.) is from the 19 Nov. 1805 *Louisiana Gazette* and contains Jean Noël Destréhan's 14 Nov. 1805 address to the members of the territorial house of

representatives thanking them for naming him speaker, congratulating them on how well they had fulfilled their task as legislators, and urging them to study during the recess all the materials that would "accelerate the accomplishment" of their legislative duties (Carter, *Territorial Papers, Orleans*, 9:523).

To Dolley Madison

[23 November 1805]

This is the last mail My dearest that will be likely to find you in Philada. and I am not without some hope that this will be too late. I take the chance however for enclosing a few letters which as they will be returned in case of your previous departure, you will receive them as soon as if they were kept here. I am desirous that you shd. get Mr Carrol, before you arrive in Baltimore. You will see that Payne is admissible the 1st. of next month. I hope to learn this evening from your wish as to the arrangemt. & time for his being in Baltimore. I write this in haste, being sent for to dine with the P. at the moment of my t⟨akin⟩g up the pen, and it will be too late to write after I get home from dinner. Consoling myself now with the expectation of soon having you with me, I conclude with best regards to Mr. & Mrs. C. and Miss P. who I hope will not fail to be a travelling companion, and with the ardent affection which I know I feel. Yours &c

Say every thing to Dr. Physic that can express my gratitude esteem & regard.

RC (MHi: Charles Edward French Autograph Collection). In JM's hand. Undated; conjectural date assigned based on the fact that this letter was written after JM had received the 20 Nov. 1805 letter from John Carroll, and the fact that JM was Jefferson's dinner guest on 23 Nov. 1805 (Charles Cullen, "Jefferson's White House Dinner Guests," *White House History* 17 [2006]: 31).

From Dolley Madison

Saturday 23d. Novr. [1805]

The letters of my beloved Husband are allways a cordial to my heart—particularly the one reced. yesterday which breaths that affection so precious that I wept over it in joy.[1] I thought to have written in reply by the last night's post but dined at Mr. Lewises where I saw a very large party of the first inhabitants in point of rank, among them the Bishop. I sent the Tobaco with a note to Mrs. Leaper for whose civilitys I have been careful to make every return she expected—& I have call'd at the doors generally of those who visited me—they all seem satisfied with my [. . .] at acknowledgments. M Morris has been [. . .]e. Yours containing the Check [. . .] arrived this moment[2] which will be quite ⟨suff⟩icient for the Docr. & every other purpose & I will make my preperations to sett of on monday the weather for 3 days has been bad for the roads but hope to get along as far as Chester the first night & small stages, or as long as I can bear until I am safely lodged in your arms.

I go to Gilpins to dinner & must make an abreviation in the Vol I could write you for the Horses we pay 3 months hence. I could have ha⟨d⟩ of Anna what mony I wanted, & regret that you should have the slightest uneasiness about it—pray take care of your health & keep up your spiri⟨ts⟩ & when we are again together I hope never more to lose sight of you. I will say more tomorr⟨ow⟩ til then farewell my best love. Anna Mr C. & Betsy with old Amey offer their kindest affection to ⟨you⟩.

RC (DLC: Papers of Dolley Madison). Damaged by removal of seal.

1. Probably JM to Dolley Madison, 19–20 Nov. 1805.
2. Probably JM to Dolley Madison, 21 Nov. 1805.

§ To George William Murray. *23 November 1805, Department of State.* "I have red. your letter of the 19th. inst.[1] Should the delay you have experienced in the transmission of the papers, necessary to prosecute the appeal, from the Court of Vice-Admiralty at Antigua be further continued, it is probable that some judicial measure may be taken to question the pace of those, by whose inattention you are suffering. Mr. Rose was appointed Agent at that Island in April last, but as he is now in Ms. his instruction to execute the business cannot be expected till his return."

Letterbook copy (DNA: RG 59, DL, vol. 15). 1 p.

1. The letter has not been found, but for Murray's claim against Great Britain, see *PJM-SS,* 9:209 and n. 1, 210 n. 2.

§ From Anthony Terry. *23 November 1805, Cádiz.* "Referring to what I had the honor of addressing you on the 12th. ultimo Copy enclosed;[1] I now have the pleasure of transmitting you Copy of a Letter passed to me by the French Commissary residing here, respectg. Neutral Subjects found on board English Vessels;[2] also to advise you that notwithstanding what I expressed in my Letter of the 31st. Octr. that the Cargo of the American Ship Huntress detained by a French Man of War would be condemned, nothing has been determined as yet, as all the Papers are forwarded to Paris to the *Ministre de Marine* who is to decide the business; mean time the Cargo is to be Sold and the amount deposited being all perishable Articles."

Adds in a postscript: "Governmt. Notes. 46½ a 48%."

RC and enclosure (DNA: RG 59, CD, Cádiz, vol. 1). RC 2 pp.; in a clerk's hand, signed by Terry; docketed by Wagner "Joseph Yznardi 23rd Novr. 1805." For enclosure, see n. 2.

1. For the letter, see Terry to JM, 12 Nov. 1805.
2. The enclosure (2 pp.; in French) is a copy of Denis Decrès's 8 Vendémiaire An 14 (30 Sept. 1805) letter to Colonel Le Roy, the French consul at Cádiz, stating that Admiral Villeneuve had sent him a letter concerning consuls of various countries claiming the return of their seamen who had been found on captured British vessels, and that he was writing Villeneuve that Napoleon had ordered that all neutrals found on board British ships, whatever their countries or the nature of their voyages, be considered prisoners of war.

To Thomas Jefferson

[24 November 1805]

(a) after 'others'—the insertion of "with commissions"—seems necessary, as others refers to the armed vessels, not to commissns.[1]

(b) Instead of "under the controul," it may be well to insert some such phrase as "unreached by any controul"[2] in order not to sanction a plea agst. indemnification, drawn from an acknowledgment on our part that the enormities were uncontroulable

(c) "as unprofitable as immoral"[3] seems to be applicable to both parties. Some such substitute as the followg is suggested—"as painful on one side as immoral on the other"

(d) It is suggested whether naming the ages, particularly that of 18 years may not be too specific, and perhaps incur p[*illegible*]ace objections.[4] It might be generalized in some such manner as this "From the last Census it may be deduced that upwards of 300,000 able-bodied men will be found within the ages answering that character.["] These will give time for raising regular forces after the necessity of them shall become certain, and the reducing to the early period of life all its active service, can not but be desirable to our younger Citizens of all times, inasmuch as it engages to them in more advanced stages an undisturbed repose in the bosom of their families.

RC (DLC: Jefferson Papers). In JM's hand. Undated; unaddressed; conjectural date and recipient assigned based on Jefferson's docket: "Departmt State. Recd. Nov. 24. 05. Message."

1. JM referred to Jefferson's discussion, in the third paragraph of his 3 Dec. 1805 fifth annual message, of privateers that "infested" American coasts (Ford, *Writings of Thomas Jefferson*, 8:389).
2. Jefferson made the change JM suggested in the third paragraph of the message (ibid.).
3. Jefferson removed this phrase entirely from the sixth paragraph of the message (ibid., 391).
4. Jefferson retained the reference to specific ages in the sixth paragraph of the message (ibid., 392).

From Thomas Jefferson

Nov. 24. 05.

How will it do to amend the passage respecting England to read as follows?

'New principles too have been interpolated into the Law of Nations, founded neither in justice, nor the usage or acknolegement of nations. According to these a belligerent takes to itself a commerce with it's own enemy, which it denies to a Neutral on the ground of it's aiding that enemy. But reason revolts at such an inconsistency: and the Neutral having equal right with the belligerent to decide the question, the interests of our constituents, & the duty of maintaining the authority of reason, the only Umpire between just nations, impose on us the obligation of providing an effectual and determined opposition to a doctrine' so injurious to peaceable nations.[1]

Will you give me your opinion on the above immediately, as I wish to send the paper to Mr. Gallatin? Should we not lay before Congress the act of parl. proving the British take the trade to themselves, & the order of council proving they deny it to Neutrals?

RC (DLC: Jefferson Papers). At the foot of the page is JM's penciled note: "Altho' it is strictly true as here applied that reason is the sole umpire, yet as G.B. abuses the idea, in order to get rid of the instituted L. of Nations, and as it may not be amiss to invite the attention of other neutrals—suppose there be added after an doctrine 'as alarming to all peaceable nations as it is illegal/against all law in itself'—or some similar expression. This however is merely for consideration. The passage as it stands has a good countenance and is made of good stuff."

1. See the fourth paragraph of Jefferson's fifth annual message to Congress (Ford, *Writings of Thomas Jefferson*, 8:390).

§ To Robert Purviance. *24 November 1805, Washington.* "I inclose a note on the office of D. & D. at Baltimore for 147 $^{47}/_{100}$ dollrs. to replace the advances which you have been so obliging as to make for me on two late importations,[1] one from Lisbon the other from Bourdeaux; to which I beg leave to add my thanks."[2]

RC (CCamarSJ). 1 p.

1. For the shipments, see John Brice Jr. to JM, 31 Aug. 1805, and Purviance to JM, 4 Oct. and 20 Nov. 1805.
2. On 26 Nov. 1805 Purviance acknowledged receipt of $147.47 as payment in full for "Wines &c Imported by him ℗ the Brig Robert from Lisbon & the Brig Lyon from Bordeaux" (DLC: Rives Collection, Madison Papers; 1 p.).

§ From John Gavino. *24 November 1805, Gibraltar.* No. 21. "Not having been honourd with any of your Commands since my last respects under 5: & 6th: Instant No. 19 and 20. [not found] from that time the Tryal of the Brig Indefatigable with wheat & Conceald Copper in sheets &c. from Bordeaux for Villa real not having proper Ships Papers came on, when Ship, freight, and Cargo was Condemnd, the Capns: adventure given up. The Schooner Jane Capn. Barry[1] from Belisle with Fish, and the Brig Mary Parsons with Staves from Edenton N.C. both bound to Cadiz were also tryd and liberated by the Judge as he supposed there was a probability when they left the U.S. that they did not know of the Blocade of Cadiz, but as there was cause for the detention Condemnd the Captains in Charges, and to have no Damages. The Cause of the Ship Aurora Capn: Hall from Leghorn for Trancabar[2] with $45,000 in Cash, & Ballast. The Super Cargo Mr: Linzie, with the Captain and Mate had adventures to the amount of $6000 in Oil, Soap, anchovies, Olives &ca. was finally decided by the Judge of the Vice ady. Court the 22d: Inst: when after a long speetch Recapitulating, orders, Cases. &ca., that took place since 1757 to the present time, he Decreed the Ship &ca: was Nutral property, adding that by the Charterparty and other minutes found on board there was grounds to lead to beleive she was going to the Isle of France, the Captain being subjected to the Super Cargos orders, yet he liberated the ship without freights Damages or detention and Condemnd the rest, that is the Cash &ca., as going from a Port of a Country which neither the ship or Owners of the Property belongd, to a Colony of the Enemy; after some Arguments on the subject I stated that hitherto in General all adventures were given up, except in this Instance; the Agents for the Captors aledged they were large & of Consideration, yet the Judge decided that they should be given up, as he did not look upon them to be of so great a Consideration as was going to India, so that ultimately only the 45,000$ were Condemnd, from which sentence the Super Cargo Mr. Linzie will Appeal to the Superior Court in London they belong to Messrs. Ths. C. Amory & Co. with other Respectable Gentlemen of Boston.

"I inclosed you in mine No: 20, two Cutts out of four of the Sea Letter and Turkish Pass granted the Brig Sally of Boston Capn: Stepn. D. Turner, the Vessel having been Sold here by the owner Mr. Stepn. Rawson, & inclosd you have other two.[3]

"Most of the Criple Ships of the action of the 21st. Ulto. have gone for England & only 5 now here: adl: Collingwood proceeded to the Eastward, & admiral Duckworth is off Cadiz.

"A Convoy arrived from England with the first Batallion of the 42d. Regt. & the 2d. of the 78h: both Highlanders. The 2d: 13h. & 54h: Regs. have Embarkd & supposed gone for England."

Adds in a 26 Nov. postscript: "This day the Brig Ann of & from Charleston S.C. for Malaga with a Cargo of upwards of 500 Boxes Havana Sugar some Coffe & Staves, Commanded by W. Cory, shipd by Mr. Chrr. Fitzimons[4] & Mr. Ryan both Citizens of the U.S. residing as said Port of Charleston and for their account & Risk, which they are going to libel for tryal being Colonial produce bound to the Mother Country."

RC (DNA: RG 59, CD, Gibraltar, vol. 3). 4 pp.; docketed by Wagner.

1. The *Jane* was from Norwich, Connecticut (Norwich *Courier*, 15 Jan. 1806).
2. Tranquebar, a Danish colony on the east coast of India (Donald Ferguson, "The Settlement of the Danes at Tranquebar and Serampore," *Journal of the Royal Asiatic Society of Great Britain and Ireland* [1898]: 625–29).

3. Boston merchant Stephen Rawson went bankrupt in August 1805 and fled from his creditors to Gibraltar, where he was arrested in 1806 (*Union Bank v. U.S. Bank*, 3 Tyng, 74–75; Boston *Columbian Centinel*, 24 May 1806).

4. Charleston merchant and shipowner Christopher Fitzsimons (1752–1825) was born in Ireland and came to the United States in 1783. He also owned a large cotton plantation near Augusta, Georgia (Charles Coleman Sellers, "Portraits and Miniatures by Charles Willson Peale," *Transactions of the American Philosophical Society*, n.s., 42, no. 1 [1952]: 77; Harold D. Woodman, *King Cotton and His Retainers: Financing and Marketing the Cotton Crop of the South, 1800–1925* [Columbia, S.C., 1990], 48).

§ From Richard Willson. *24 November 1805, Washington.* "Having very considerably impaired my Paternal Estate in the service of my Country when an Officer in the Revolutionary War and having a large Family to support on very scanty means, I am irresistibly impelled to solicit the President of the United States, through you Sir, for some appointment under the Government.

"And as I have not the honor of your acquaintance, I must refer to Letters to the President from Robert Wright and Joseph H Nicholson Esquires in my favor for the appointment of Librarian to Congress and which Letters are in your possession.[1]

"Should further Testimonials of my capacity be necessary, the Treasurer of the United States can give correct information of my promptitude, correctness and indefatigable attention to business.

"The establishing of a Navy yard down the Bay is an event that appears to me must very soon take place, and I beg leave to solicit the appointment of Navy Agent, should the Establishment take place."

RC (DNA: RG 59, LAR, 1801–9, filed under "Willson"). 1 p.; docketed by Jefferson.

1. For Willson's earlier applications to JM for appointment, see *PJM-SS*, 6:505 and n. 1, 8:562.

To William C. C. Claiborne

SIR.   DEPARTMENT OF STATE Novr. 25th. 1805.
     Since my letter of the 18th. instant, I have received yours of the 14th. October relating to the excursion of the Marquis of Casa Calvo to the Saline River.[1] In the present situation of our affairs with Spain, it would have been preferred that the liberty he has used to travel and explore the Country should not have been indulged, and particularly that it should not have been countenanced by the attendance of an American Officer at Adais. As however my letter of the 18th: (of which one copy has been sent by the Mail, and another by Sea) will have occasioned such a different impression with respect to the Marquis and the other persons in the service

of Spain, it is not to be apprehended that any future question will arise with respect to a similar courtesy. I am &c.

JAMES MADISON.

Letterbook copy (DNA: RG 59, DL, vol. 15). 1 p.

1. Sabine River.

To John R. Livingston

SIR.   DEPT. OF STATE Novr. 25th. 1805.

An intimation from this Department to Mr. Erving, that from the report of the assessors, it would appear, that you had been overpaid for the 1st. and 2d. installments of the award in the case of the Somerset, Miller, and Mr. Erving's concurrence in the belief that such an error was committed, were the causes of the partial protest of your bill.[1] The same suggestion having been made to you before it was conveyed to him, it was to be expected that you would not have included the amount of the alledged overpayments in the bill, but as you nevertheless have done so, the inconvenience of their being deducted ought not to excite complaint. In order to bring your claim to the disputed sum to a conclusion you could perhaps, if you are not possessed of documents to establish it, procure a release from Capt. Miller or his representatives, in whose name this portion of the award stands; or if you rely on your documents to establish your title, and transmit them hither, they shall on the arrival of the Attorney General, be laid before him for his opinion. I am &c.

JAMES MADISON.

Letterbook copy (DNA: RG 59, DL, vol. 15).

1. For John R. Livingston's claim against Great Britain, see *PJM-SS*, 6:135, 136 n. 1, 9:365, 366 n. 6, 424.

From Thomas Jefferson

[ca. 25 November 1805]

Additions proposed on some subjects suggested by mr. Gallatin submitted to mr. Madison by

TH: J.

The object of the 1st. addition is to give a practical or ostensible object to the observations on Yellow fever: The true one however being to present facts to the governments of Europe, which in the ordinary course of things, would not otherwise reach them in half a century.

RC (DLC). Undated; conjectural date assigned based on Gallatin to Jefferson, 25 Nov. 1805 (see n. 1 below).

1. In his 25 Nov. 1805 "Remarks on the Message," Albert Gallatin suggested to Jefferson: "the second paragraph on the yellow fever ends rather abruptly, nothing is proposed or suggested for Congress to do, which can remedy the inconvenience complained of" (DLC: Jefferson Papers).

From Rufus King

private
Sir   NEW YORK Novr. 25. 1805
    I had the honour to write to you on the 15. of last month, since when I have received by General Miranda who has arrived here, a letter from Mr. N. Vansittart(,) a member of the British parliament, and who was likewise a member of the late Administration of Mr. Addington. Mr. Vansittart being a man of distinguished Probity, and in a situation to understand fully the subject on which he writes, I send you his letter for the President's perusal,[1] requesting that it may afterwards be returned to me. With great Respect I have the Honour to be Sir Your obt: & faithful Servt.
                                      RUFUS KING

RC (DNA: RG 59, ML); FC and enclosure (NHi: Rufus King Papers). RC docketed by Wagner. For enclosure, see n. 1.

1. The enclosure (11 pp.; docketed by King as received from Francisco de Miranda on 10 Nov. 1805 and returned from JM on 5 Dec.) is a copy of Nicholas Vansittart to King, 14 Aug. 1805, stating that Miranda had embarked on the execution of his long-planned invasion of South America, and reminding King of his familiarity with the offers of support tendered Miranda by the British government "as well as on some occasions by certain continental powers." Vansittart said that soon after the war with France was renewed he had received permission to collect arms, clothing, and stores for Miranda's project to be used should a rupture take place between Britain and Spain, but the British government, hoping that Spanish neutrality might be preserved, had diverted the supplies to other service. He added that Miranda had hoped for some time after war broke out between Great Britain and Spain "for active & cordial assistance," but since the British government continued to expend its efforts elsewhere, Miranda had determined "to try what can be effected by such resources as America can furnish," be it government or private funding. Vansittart told King, "your influence will be of the utmost importance to him." He said the British merchant community was "anxious for an extension of trade" and "a removal of the restraints which . . .

exclude them from the rich market of South America" and that "a great body of our most reasonable & judicious men consider a well combined system of independence" the best way to prevent Spain's colonies "from falling, like the mother country under the dominion of France and furnishing resources" that would enable Napoleon "to complete the subjugation of Europe." Other men, "of great weight & authority," had such an abhorrence of anything resembling revolution that they believed all such ideas should be dismissed or directly resisted. Vansittart stated that it was futile to try to convince the latter that the separation of rapidly growing colonies "from a feeble, decrepit & degraded government" was inevitable, and that Britain should try to influence the direction of such a change in order "to secure the gratitude & attachment of the new" governments because they would argue that the outcome would be so uncertain that Britain should not "incur the guilt & risque the consequences of cooperating to produce it." Vansittart said he believed the present administration was inclined to the first position, and had formed "a serious intention" of supplying Miranda, but had given up the plan from an unwillingness to divert supplies from objects which they felt were more important. He added that he was less acquainted with the opinion of the opposition party but believed that Charles James Fox and his friends were favorable to the emancipation of South America. He stated that the great national advantage that would accrue to Great Britain in the event of Miranda's achieving a successful commencement assured that, barring the conclusion of peace, "the general disposition of the Country" would "compel almost any government" to support Miranda. Vansittart added that the British "blockading squadrons in Europe & . . . fleets in the West Indies will be nearly as vigilant & useful in intercepting any succour which the Spaniards or French may attempt to send to the Colonies as if they were stationed for that express purpose." He said that he had addressed King so openly from a conviction that "the views & interests of this Country & the United States must be indissolubly united" on this matter.

§ To John Hollins. *25 November 1805, Department of State.* "In consequence of your letter of the 22 inst. [not found] I have to inform you, that, according to a letter received from Mr. Blakely, dated 20 Septr. [not found] the Government of St. Jago of Cuba has taken possession of the Industry and her Cargo, and ordered them to be sold. Two days before the date of that letter, Capt. Johns had been committed to prison."

Letterbook copy (DNA: RG 59, DL, vol. 15). 1 p.

§ From Edward Carrington. *25 November 1805, Canton.* "I have the honor to inclose you, a Duplicate of the Deposition of John Gardnier,[1] first Officer of the Ship New Jersey of Philadelphia, stating the outrage committed onboard that Ship, by the Officers of His Britanic Majesty's Brig, Harier, commanded by Captain Ratsey, and Duplicates of two Letters, address'd to Captain Ratsey on the subject of that violence.[2]

"Some days having pass'd, without receiving any answer to the Letters address'd to Captain Ratsey, I conceived it necessary, to make a representation to the Chinese Government, of the indignity offered to the Flag of the United States, in the Port of Canton, by the Officers of His Britanic Majesty's Brig Harier, and claim that protection due to a friendly nation.

"Accordingly I prepared a representation, (a Copy of which I now inclose you)[3] Stating the circumstances of this outrageous violence, but I lament, that I have not been able to present it to the Government.

"All communications from Foreigners to the Chinese Goverment, are made by the Hong or Security Merchants, to whom I have made repeated application, but without success; they always answering, that their Goverment do not, nor will not, take cognizance of disputes between Foreigners, altho' they arise within their Territory; however I am not disposed to receive this answer as a Conclusive one of the Goverment, and it is my intention, to make a further exertion to present the representation.

"As the Chinese Goverment do not recognize Foreign Ministers or Consuls, I considered it advisable, to join the American Merchants residing at Canton, and the Super Cargoes and Commanders of the American Ships, with me in the representation, hoping it would have the desired influence with their several Security Merchants, to encourage them to present the same to their Goverment, and give to our Complaints their full force; but as the Hong Merchants are So extremely cautious of meddling with anything that regards their Goverment, I fear it will not be possible thro' them, ever to obtain any satisfaction.

"The Brig Harier left this Port about the 25th. October, (carrying with her the Said Richard Weldon) and has taken her Station in the River of Canton a small distance without the Bocca Tygris, where She has been joined by His Britanic Majesty's Ships the Phaeton and Cornwallis, and where they bring too all Amercian [sic] vessels bound to or from this Port, for the purpose of examining their Papers and Seaman."

RC and enclosures (DNA: RG 59, CD, Canton, vol. 1). RC 3 pp.; docketed by Wagner. For enclosures, see nn.

1. The enclosure (3 pp.) is a copy of John Gardnier's deposition, dated both 17 Oct. and 17 Nov. 1805, and certified by Carrington on 25 Nov. 1805, that on 13 Oct. 1805, while Capt. James Cooper was away from the *New Jersey*, two officers and a boat crew from the *Harrier* came alongside asking for seaman Richard Weldon. Weldon appeared and said he was a British subject who wished to go on board the *Harrier*, after which the British officers ordered him to take his personal effects and go into the boat. When Gardnier forbade this and attempted to restrain Weldon, one of the British officers drew his dagger and ordered the boat crew to board the *New Jersey*, which they did with drawn cutlasses, and forcibly removed Weldon. The officers threatened to return for Weldon's wages and to take every *New Jersey* crewmember who wished to enter the *Harrier*, even if this should deplete the crew. Gardnier added that Weldon had shipped on the *New Jersey* at Philadelphia, where he represented himself as an American, had sailed with the ship to Antwerp and Canton, and had a protection held by Captain Cooper.

2. The enclosures (4 pp.) are copies of Carrington to Edward Ratsey, 14 Oct. 1805, reporting the event of 13 Oct., expressing his hope that this direct violation of the law of nations and the neutrality of China was done without Ratsey's authority, and requesting the return of Weldon; and Carrington to Ratsey, undated but probably of 16 Oct. 1805 (see n. 3 below), noting that he had received no reply to his previous letter demanding Weldon's return, and stating that if Ratsey did not comply, Carrington would complain to the Chinese and American governments about "this unprecedented and Outrageous violence against the rights of Nations."

3. The enclosure (4 pp.) is a copy of the 23 Oct. 1805 representation to "John Tuck Governor of the Province of Canton," signed by Carrington and twenty-seven others and certified as accurate by Carrington, describing the events of 13 Oct. 1805, stating that Carrington had written to Captain Ratsey on 14 and 16 Oct. 1805 and had received no reply, that Ratsey

had informed an American that he intended to visit the American ships at Whampoa, that the American captains feared "that they would be robbed of their Seamen" and were determined to repel by force any attack made on their ships, reminding the governor of the extensive trade of America with China, and asking the governor to effect the return of Weldon and to prevent any further such aggressions.

§ From Christopher Ellery. *25 November 1805, Newport, Rhode Island.* "The present editor of the 'Rhode Island Republican,' in which the Laws of the United States have been, for four years past, printed in this State, supposes that the benefit of publishing them in his paper will be continued as heretofore; but there being a possibility of application for this favour from some one or more of the printers in R. Island, he wishes, in such case, that the Secretary of State may be assured of the propriety of continuing their publication in the 'Rhode Island Republican,' and requests me to write a few lines to this purport—and in compliance with his desires, I have the honor to declare to the Secretary, that, in my opinion, not only all the reasons which might have contributed, formerly, to a preference of the 'Rhode Island Republican' must still be in full force, but that new and stronger reasons exist to render the preference, at this time, highly proper."

Adds in a postscript: "Noah Bisbee junr. esqr. is now the editor of the 'R.I. Republican,' formerly published by Oliver Farnsworth."

RC (DNA: RG 59, Preliminary Inventory 15, entry 151, Letters Concerning the Printing of the Laws, 1790–1809).

§ From William Lee. *25 November 1805, Bordeaux.* "Since my respects of the 18th. and 19th [not found] of October and 12th inst. [not found], I have been favored with your instructions of the 1st and 12th of July.

"In the numerous transfers of American Ships Papers that have taken place in my office, I do not recollect one, that falls under that section of the act passed the 27th of March 1804. which you have quoted, and I shall take good care that the description of persons therein mentioned, shall not own within my district in whole, or in part, any Vessel sailing under the flag of the United States.

"The frequent discussions I have had with masters of Vessels respecting the discharge of their seamen, have often led me to wish to have the attorney Generals construction of the third section of the Act, supplementary to the Consular Act, and I am happy to find that my decisions have been in conformity with his interpretation. This is one of the best regulations that could have been adopted for the protection of our seamen and I am persuaded it saves many thousand of Dollars annually to the United States.

"When registered or other Vessels have been last condemned, or sold to foreigners, I have when the papers came into my possession canceled them. In two or three instances I returned them to the Custom houses they were issued from, but of late had determined to send them to the Minister at Paris who, has already received several sets from me. In future they shall be disposed of as you have directed.

There is no one point upon which I have received so much abuse and been subject to such gross impositions as in the transfer of American Vessels at this port. Those only who have witnessed the conduct of Americans abroad, and who are acquainted with the characters of the merchants of this City, would credit the representations I could make.

"The duties of the Consuls of the United States are so little understood, and we are so frequently at a loss how to act that, I could have wished you had dwelt longer on this head. In all disputes that have arisen between the Captains and Crews of Vessels on account of wages, I have found it necessary to interpose but all differences, that have taken place between american merchants settled here, I have ever refused to meddle with, and have referred them either to the Tribunals here, or to the Courts of their own Country.

"I have sent by this conveyance to my friend Mr Barlow my official Bond, requesting him to see it properly executed, and lodged with You, and I shall as you have directed, with pleasure forward every publication, that may tend to the cure of epidemical disorders, or to the progress of useful improvements. The salutary Quarantine Laws of Marseilles, would prove beneficial in the United States and no doubt mr Cathalan who is very *particular* will send you a copy of them.

"My advertisement occasioned by your instruction under date of the 12th of July has not proved very pleasing to the merchants of this City, and some of my Countrymen (the very men who have before abused me for granting so many of these Consular Certificates) have taken care, to make them believe that my representations, have caused the American Government to issue this unfavorable order. Such is the inconsistency of mankind. Those Vessels which are mentioned in the enclosed letter to General Armstrong[1] I shall permit to proceed to the United States the bills of sales conveying them to American Citizens having been registered in my office before your Instruction came to hand and these will be the last expeditions of this nature.

"I have always studied to gain the esteem of the Constituted Authorities near whom I have the honer to reside, by treating them with great deference and I have so far succeeded as to find myself on all public, as well as private occasions, noticed by marked attentions. In my Contestations the last year, with the Custom house and my correspondence with the Chamber of Commerce, I was fully supported by Monsr. Charles delaCroix, the former minister of foreign affairs and the then prefect of this Departmen⟨t⟩ whose kindness toward myself and family I shall never forget. During the embarrassments of my house of Perrot & Lee[2] this officer, was directed by the minister at Paris, not to permit my person or furniture to be molested for any debts, I might owe on that concern.

"In little cases of disputes between artisans, tavern keepers, and american Captains, before the Justices of the peace, or Court of Commerce, cite the Latter to appear they usually address the French Citizens to me, begging my intervention in obtaining them justice, and in all breaches of the police by american Citizens not of a criminal nature, I am generally requested before the police go to extremities, to remedy the abuses as you will observe by the enclosed correspondence with the mayor of this City.[3] This harmony arising from mutual good offices, renders my situation as far as respects my relations with the Government extremely pleasant, and compensates in a great degree for that calumny, and jealousy, which is continually set on float against me among my Countrymen by unprincipled [*sic*] office seekers and political enemies.

"The file of papers I have the honor to send you by this conveyance, will make you acquainted with the state of affairs in Germany. The opinions on the question of peace or War are various, and the best informed men do not calculate on the long continuation of a pacific system, until France shall set bounds to her ambition."

RC and enclosures (DNA: RG 59, CD, Bordeaux, vol. 2). RC 6 pp.; docketed by Wagner. For enclosures, see nn. 1 and 3.

1. The enclosures (4 pp.) are copies of (1) Lee to John Armstrong, 12 Nov. 1805, enclosing an advertisement which stated that Lee would issue no certificates after 25 Oct. 1805; that he had been approached by several captains wanting to take advantage of the exception; that he had refused certificates to those whose sales were not registered with him before the announcement of the change; and listing five ships to which he had given certificates, the brigs *Peggy* and *General Armstrong*, and the ships *General Armstrong*, *Highland Mary*, and *Peggy*, the last "owned by Genl Stevens of Newyork who covers more property than any other Merchant in the United States"; and (2) Armstrong to Lee, 31 Oct. 1805, stating that his health had left him unable to pursue the case Lee had submitted to him but that JM's 12 July 1805 circular had, in any event, forbidden consuls to issue certificates of ownership to vessels sold within their districts, except those that had been sold before the owners had knowledge of the new regulations, and warning Lee that this exception could lead to much fraud.

2. For the bankruptcy of Perrot & Lee, see *PJM-SS*, 7:92, 8:412, 9:343.

3. The enclosures are (1) an English translation (1 p.) of Mayor Laurent Lafaurie de Montbadon to Lee, 5 Nov. 1805, complaining that several American captains had behaved "in a very indecent manner" at the theater the previous evening and that the captain of the *Ulysses*, in particular, "was very boisterous"; asking Lee to impose on American captains "the necessity of their behaving with more decorum at the Theatres," since Montbadon would regret having to use the police against citizens of a nation so friendly to France; and adding that he trusted that with Lee's instructions the Americans would remember "when they frequent public places [to] comport themselves with that deference & decency which polite people owe each other"; and (2) Lee to Montbadon, 6 Nov. 1805 (1 p.), acknowledging his letter, stating that he would use his best endeavors to prevent the behavior of "these unruly beings," and adding that, having been himself a witness to "their disorderly behaviour at public places," he wished Montbadon had "made an example of them," and that his not having done so was proof of the friendly disposition towards Americans that Lee had always observed on the part of the Bordeaux police.

§ From Anthony Terry. *25 November 1805, Cádiz.* "It is with great Satisfaction & pleasure I have the honor to enclose you Copy of a Letter received this day from the Danish Consul residing at this City; requesting you will be so obliging as to make it public for the benefit of our trade."[1]

RC (DNA: RG 59, CD, Cádiz, vol. 1). 1 p.; in a clerk's hand. Written above Terry to JM, 6 Dec. 1805.

1. The enclosure has not been found, but it probably reported the relaxation of the terms of the blockades of Sanlúcar de Barrameda and Cádiz. See Thomas Auldjo to JM, 2 Nov. 1805, and n. 1.

To Tench Coxe

SIR   DEPARTMENT OF STATE 26 Novr. 1805.

In pursuance of the 5th. sect. of the Act of March 2d. respecting the lands claimed in the Mississippi Territory, I have sent your letter of the 11th. inst. and the copies of the patents it enclosed, in the names of George Tead and Rebecca Blackwell, to the Register of the Land Office West of Pearl River. The tract described in one of the patents appears to lie in that territory, but it is not certain, whether the other tract is not within the country held by Spain as West Florida. I have intimated to the Register, that you would provide for paying to him his fees.[1] I have the honor to be Sir, Very respectfully, Your most obd. servt.

JAMES MADISON

RC (PHi: Tench Coxe Papers); letterbook copy (DNA: RG 59, DL, vol. 15). RC in Wagner's hand, signed by JM. Minor differences between the copies have not been noted.

1. On the same day JM wrote Thomas Hill Williams saying: "Agreeably to the request of Mr. Coxe, I enclose copies of the grants of the British Government to George Tead & Rebecca Blackwell respectively, together with Mr. Coxe's letter explanatory of his object in sending them to me. You will of course dispose of these documents according to the directions of the law. On acquainting Mr. Coxe with the course which is given to his business, I shall intimate to him of providing for paying any fees which may be due to you on this occasio⟨n⟩" (DNA: RG 59, DL, vol. 15; 1 p.). On 13 Feb. 1806 JM wrote Coxe: "Having forwarded the originals and duplicates of the patents, in the names of Fead [*sic*] and Blackwell, to the Register of the land office west of Pearl River, he has returned them with the remarks contained in the enclosed letter [not found]. The patents and duplicates are therefore herewith returned" (RC [PHi: Tench Coxe Papers; 1 p.; in Wagner's hand, signed by JM; docketed by Coxe]; letterbook copy [DNA: RG 59, DL, vol. 15]).

From John Armstrong

SIR,   PARIS 26 November 1805.

I had the honor, within the last week, of receiving your letter of the 25th. of August—expressing the Sollicitude of the parties interested in the Ship New Jersey and Cargo,[1] least "their claim should be rejected on the idea, that the rights of the insured, did not pass to the insurers;" and communicating also the opinion of the President, that "American underwriters, who had paid the loss to the original owners, citizens of the United States, were entitled to the benefits of the treaty of 1803."

In my next dispatch I shall furnish you with documents, from which you will see, that the difficulties in this case, have in no Stage of it, arisen from the causes to which they have been ascribed; that it's admission by the American board was long suspended under Colo. Mercer's objection, that, "no evidence had been produced of the insolvency of the captors"; that its rejection, by the Council General of liquidation, proceeded from the belief, that "the Ship and Cargo were partially, or altogether, British property; and from certain other causes"—and that when this belief concerning the national character of the property was done away by the production of certain policies of insurance, which had been effected in different parts of the United States, (but which till then had been carefully kept out of sight) the claim, so far from being opposed on the principle that "the rights of the insured did not vest in the insurers" as indeed on any other principle, was, on my suggestion, sent back to the council, relieved from the first and apparently the principal objecti[o]n, and left subject only to the "other causes" mentioned in the rejecting Arrete of the 28 of Frimaire. These "other causes" are fully exhibited in the report of the Director of the 4th. Division, dated on the 15 Germinal, and may be digested into the following heads—

1st. that the judgment of the 17 Prairial year (6). pronouncing the confiscation of the N. Jersey & cargo is still subsisting—inasmuch as it has not been annulled by the decree of the Council of Prizes, which directs only, the restitution of the sum deposited by the owners with Gen. Hedouville.

2d. that the claimants having neglected to prosecute their appeal within six years after the capture, were precluded, by the laws of France, from a right of appealing.

3d. that the New Jersey, not having a role d'Equipage, as provided by the treaty of 1778, was excluded from the provisions of the 4th. Article of the treaty of 1800.

4th. that the Capt and Agent of the Privateer, not having been heard in their defense, nor even summoned to appear before the Tribunal, the decree of the Council of Prizes was illegal.

5th. that no evidence having been produced of the abandonment of the Ship and Cargo to the Underwriters, and the Agents having even denied the right of either Government to question them with regard to an abandonment of the property, and having besides acknowledged, that the original owners, or a part of them, had acquired the N. Jersey by a new title; by yielding to the Underwriters "Un droit convenable de reprise dans le depot"[2]—it may be fairly inferred, that the loss never was paid by the insurers, & that the receits (which by the way do not correspond in number with the policies), are merely fictitious.

& 6th. that were it in proof that the owners had abandoned, and that the under-writers had paid, still the Claim of the latter could not be admitted—inasmuch as it could not now be liquidated under the rules prescribed by the Treaty—the American Commission having no longer an existence.

You will readily perceive that in all this, there is not a single syllable pointed at the rights of insurers "who have paid the loss of the original owner." It only remains for me therefore to shew, that in no after act either of the Council or of Mr Marbois & myself, was the broad principle which has given So much alarm to our under-writing Citizens, or even the qualified one to be found in the President's opinion, adopted or applied to the case of the N.J. The report, of which I have already given you the Substance, not having been agreed to by all the members of the Council, and the Liquidator Genl. not choosing to decide the difference, transmitted the case a second time to the Treasury with a wish, that Mr. Marbois & myself might determine it. We complied with this wish—we did determine it, and admitted it for its' full proportion of the Marginal fund. It is true, that Mr. Marbois & I differed somewhat concerning this proportion. He, would have given 333,000 francs, whereas I, thought that 300,000 were quite as many as fell to its share; and that you will think as I did, I have no doubt, when I inform you, that there are claims amounting to more than Three Millions, as sound in point of principle, less objectionable in point of form & better recommended by the pecuniary circumstan[c] es of the Claimants, for which I have not yet got a Single sous. In my last letter I gave you the commencement of the war, and in this, you will find its conclusion. The two events are worthy of each other. They certainly have never had a parralel. Bavaria restored to its Sovereign—a French functionary residing in Vienna and exercising dominion over Austria— the house of Lorraine flying to the most remote of its provinces—Hungary withdrawing itself from the fortunes of Austria—Germany preparing to receive a foreign Master—the Coalition at an end—the Russian Columns offering to capitulate and seeking no better or other condition than that of being permitted to go home—the German army driven into Ci-devant Poland, and Poland itself about to rise from the dead! These are the miracles of a Campaign of 64 days.

Prussia has begun her agency where it ought to have ended, and without yielding any assistance to the Allies, has unmasked herself with regard to France. The basis she took for negociation, was little different from that of which the Russian Minister, Novolitzoff, was the bearer. But she is now of no consequence, and her propositions will probably be accomodated to her humiliation.

These events cannot fail to have their effect on the British Councils. If they are not mad, they will abandon the absurd & wicked system they have adopted towards us. With the highest consideration, I am, Sir, Your most Obed. hum. Servt.

JOHN ARMSTRONG.

RC (DNA: RG 59, DD, France, vol. 10); RC (DNA: RG 59, Preliminary Inventory 15, entry 98, Misc. Duplicate Consular and Diplomatic Dispatches, 1791–1906); extract (DNA: RG 46, President's Messages, 9B–B3). First RC in a clerk's hand, signed by Armstrong. Extract printed in the *National Intelligencer*, 3 Mar. 1806.

1. For the case of the *New Jersey*, see Philip Nicklin and Robert Eaglesfield Griffith to JM, 25 July 1805, and n. 7.

2. *"Un droit convenable de reprise dans le depot"*: an appropriate right of recovery in the deposit.

From James Monroe

No. 37.

SIR   LONDON NOVr. 26. 1805.

I hasten to transmit to you a copy of a letter which I received yesterday from Lord Mulgrave in reply to mine of augt. 12. and Sepr. 23d.[1] From the length of time which had elapsed, and other circumstances, I had almost concluded that his government had resolved not to enter on the subject, but to leave me to get its determination as I could⟨,⟩ from the decisions of the admiralty. I find however with much satisfaction that it is intended to take it up, whence there is some cause to presume that the business may yet be placed on a satisfactory footing. I shall not fail to cherish a disposition to such an adjustment, by all the means in my power, or to inform you with out delay of whatever may occur in it. I am Sir with great respect & esteem yr. very obt. servant

                                                    JAS. MONROE

RC, Tr, and enclosure (DNA: RG 46, President's Messages, 10B–B1); RC (DNA: RG 233, President's Messages, 10A–D1, vol. 1); letterbook copy and letterbook copy of enclosure (DLC: Monroe Papers). First RC in a clerk's hand, except for Monroe's complimentary close and signature. The second RC is a letterpress copy of the first RC. Minor differences between the copies have not been noted. For enclosure, see n. 1.

1. The enclosure (2 pp.; marked "Copy"; printed in *ASP, Foreign Relations*, 3:108) is Lord Mulgrave to Monroe, 25 Nov. 1805, stating that after "due deliberation" on the question Monroe had opened in his two notes, he had "deemed it indispensably necessary" to refer the subject "to those who are best acquainted with all the circumstances respecting the decisions which have taken place, and the rules which have been established" in the courts of admiralty and appeal and adding that he had not yet received a report but hoped to be able "at no distant period" to give Monroe a "full and . . . conclusive answer."

From James Wilkinson

SIR   ST. LOUIS Novr. 26th 05

To promote the presidential Views relatively to the transfer, of our wide spread Setlers in the lower Districts of this Territory, to some other Quarter of our Domain,[1] I have availed myself of the agency of a few Persons of observation & influence, and have the enclosed communications of a Mr. Bond,[2] (whose Letters have before been transmited to you). The Object appears to be attainable, provided the necessary measures are adopted by Government, & a sound cooperation of the territorial officers should be faithfully observed.

But sir in regard to this very desirable cooperation, I must acknowledge my expectations are faint; and it mortifies me to be obliged to expose to you, the chief cause of my apprehensions, in the Memoranda under cover,[3] which portray the public Conduct of Judge Lucas, who before a lisp of controversy between us, pursues me from the great Landed Interests of the Country, where he had rendered my Interference necessary, to Scenes of private amusement, in which I have neither Agency nor participation.

You have under cover the Proclamation which has excited so much resentment, & an official Letter to the Recorder on the same subject,[4] the motives of my Conduct on this occasion are set forth in these Documents, and I rest their Policy & expediency on the nature of the case, the Judgment of my predecessor (Governor Harrison) and the 9th. Section of the Law, "further providing for the Government of the District of Louisiana."[5] If I have Erred the intention will I hope extenuate my Error, but the conflicting opinions of the first officers of this Government, on a point of such Magnitude, appear to render the interposition of the competent Authority necessary, to the preservation of the rights & Interests of Individuals & of the public.

I have been warned by the public denounciations of a Cabal of public officers, who have opposed themselves to me, that Effectual measures would be taken to remove me from office, but I had no Idea until a recent detection, that attempts could be made to suborn testimony for the purpose; This foul Measure is exposed in the Documents marked No. 1[6] & I hold in my possession the Deposition of which you have a Copy, in the Hand writing of Major Seth Hunt,[7] I make this exposition with pain, but I have deemed it necessary, to guard against the Effects of similar attempts, which may be more successfully made.

You sir will I hope excuse me for trespassing such details upon you, and I hope the president will pardon my Solicitude to defend my Conduct against sinister Intrigues, since I am bound by an awful responsibility to justify his confidence, by a fair, Honourable & (as far as my capacities extend) able administration of the trust, which he has been pleased to re-pose in me. With perfect respect I am sir Your Obe Svt

JA WILKINSON

RC and enclosures (DNA: RG 46, President's Messages, 9B–A3). For surviving enclo-sures, see nn. 2–3 and 7.

1. See Wilkinson to JM, 24 Aug. 1805, and n. 1.

2. The enclosure (3 pp.; certified by Wilkinson) is a copy of Edward F. Bond to Wilkin-son, 15 Nov. 1805, stating that sentiment in the Cape Girardeau region for exchanging the settlers' land there for lands east of the Mississippi was gaining ground, partly because "many of the Inhabitants of this District [are] of such a turbulent restless Character, and have such predilection for wandering, [they] would move any where for the sake of change novelty and a new and unpeopled Country where they could indulge themselves in their favorite amuse-ments and occupations, of hunting and raising Stock in what they term Range"; that others, who had formerly boasted of their attachment to the United States, were thinking of "going to the Spaniards, their Old Masters"; that it was rumored that the Spanish were very gener-ous with land grants to new settlers; that some of these men were going because they had heard that Louis and William Lorimier, who were unpopular, had been nominated as mili-tia officers, but Bond believed the complainers would join the militia in the end; that no new settlers had arrived at Cape Girardeau; and that Col. John B. Scott had suggested raising a light horse company, which could become very popular with the younger men.

3. The enclosure is a copy (1 p.; certified by Wilkinson) of Robert Wescott's 25 Nov. 1805 statement that in a conversation with him, Judge John B. C. Lucas had remarked that "the Judiciary were not in any degree subordinate to, but coequal with, the Executive in this Territory," that the judges had a right to make laws independently of the governor because Congress had given the power of legislation "to a Majority of those to whom it was dele-gated," that the governor's opinion was not *essential* in framing Laws," and that he consid-ered Rufus Easton "full as respectable as Genl. Wilkinson."

4. The enclosures have not been found, but they were probably copies of Wilkinson's 4 Nov. 1805 proclamation regarding land surveys, and his 5 Nov. letter to Antoine Soulard. For the proclamation, see Wilkinson to JM, 6 Nov. 1805, n. 7; for the letter to Soulard, see Wilkinson to JM, 12 Nov. 1805, n. 3.

5. For the act "providing for the Government of the District of Louisiana," see Wilkin-son to JM, 6 Nov. 1805, n. 3.

6. These enclosures have not been identified but may have been the documents de-scribed in n. 7 below.

7. The enclosure (1 p.; printed in Carter, *Territorial Papers, Louisiana-Missouri*, 13:292) is a copy of Sheriff Israel Dodge at St. Genevieve to Wilkinson, 20 Nov. 1805, stating that he had received the enclosed writing on 19 Nov. from William C. Carr, who stated that it had been sent to him from St. Louis; that Dodge was to swear to it and return it; that "the nature of this writing, and the evident use intended to be made of it, are so repugnant" to his senti-ments that he considered it his duty to transmit it to Wilkinson; that the document was in the hand of Maj. Seth Hunt; that he knew nothing of Rufus Easton's purported influence; that he knew nothing of the views of "the Junto" named in the document; and that he be-lieved that any attempt to "weaken the attachment" of the people of the territory to Wilkinson was "as futile as malicious." Dodge enclosed a model (3 pp.; printed ibid., 292–93) of an affidavit to be made by him, which stated that he had known Rufus Easton since Easton arrived at St. Genevieve about 1 May 1804; that Easton was respectable, upright, and as an attorney, "superior to that of any other counsellor in this Territory"; that his

appointment was approved by the populace except for "a few individuals, (*Monarchists* and *antidated land Claimants*) at St. Louis"; that the idea of a combination against Wilkinson existing between Moses Austin, Seth Hunt, William C. Carr, Easton, and Dodge was "ridiculous and absolutely void of any foundation"; that Easton had been Wilkinson's best friend and ardent supporter "until he found himself denounced to Mr. Austin by Gover Wilkinson as concerned in a Combination with the persons above named, to render him obnoxious to the people and prevent his confirmation as Governor." Appended to the affidavit is a 24 Nov. 1805 paragraph, signed by Joseph Browne and Thomas H. Cushing, stating that they had compared the handwriting on the document with that of Maj. Seth Hunt, and they had "no hesitation" in declaring that it was from Hunt's pen. A similar copy of the affidavit sent by Wilkinson to Henry Dearborn is marked: "Deposition prepared for Isreal [*sic*] Dodge by Majr. S. Hunt" (printed ibid., 293).

§ From Christopher Gore. *26 November 1805, Boston.* "Since making the Statement herewith enclosed,[1] the Underwriters find themselves called upon to represent a new Cause of Complaint, founded on a still further Extension of the Principle, before remarked on, and which is now made the Ground of condemning Property, going to Europe, merely because it was imported into the United States, & exported by the same Person, although it had been landed & subjected to the Payment of Duties here, and was transporting in another Vessel & belonging to different owners.

"It is the Case of Property, belonging to the same Mr. Sears, who shipped sundry Goods (some of them imported by Himself in various Vessels, & others purchased here) on board the George Washington, Capt. Porter, a general freighting Ship, bound for Amsterdam from Boston.

"That Vessel has been captured & the Property imported and then exported, has been condemned in London. This is also abandonned to the Underwriters.

"This Proceeding of the British has been so unforeseen, & unexpected by even the most prudent & circumspect, that very serious & general consequences are to be apprehended in this Part of the Community.

"Should the Facts related in the Statement of the Case of the Indus, or of the Geo.: Washington, now mention'd, require any further Verification, than what accompanies these Papers, and you will please to notify me thereof, I will endeavour to supply the same."

RC (DNA: RG 46, President's Messages, 9A–E3); Tr (RG 233, President's Messages, 9A–D1). RC 2 pp.

1. See Gore to JM, 18 Nov. 1805.

§ From Samuel S. Hamilton.[1] *26 November 1805.* "Mr. Madison borrowed of the Library of Congress
"The Annual Register for the Years 1758, 1759, 1778, 1779–1784 and 1797.
"Grotius Puffendorf and Sir William Temple's Works.[2]
"Which he is respectfully requested to return before the meeting of Congress."

RC (DLC). 1 p.; signed by Hamilton "for John Beckley Librarian."

1. Samuel S. Hamilton (ca. 1783–1832) was a clerk in the War Department by 1816. In 1830 he was named superintendent for the Bureau of Indian Affairs (Mark Grossman, *The ABC-CLIO Companion to the Native American Rights Movement* [Santa Barbara, Calif., 1996], 148; *ASP, Miscellaneous*, 2:309; *Rhode Island American, Statesman and Providence Gazette*, 10 Sept. 1830).

2. Filed in JM's papers in the Rives Collection at the Library of Congress is a four-page extract in an unidentified hand, except for JM's date and names of writer and recipient, of a letter from Sir William Temple to Sir Joseph Williamson, dated 6 Nov. 1674, describing his treaty negotiations with Holland, in which he argued the British position that free ships make free goods. JM later cited the correspondence in the pamphlet he was writing in late 1805 (*The Works of Sir William Temple, Bart.* [4 vols.; London, 1770], 4:55–57; [Madison], *Examination of the British Doctrine* [Shaw and Shoemaker 10776], 57–59 and n. [1]).

§ From Joseph Rademaker. *26 November 1805, Philadelphia.* "I beg leave to transmit to You the enclosed Letter of participation from H. R. H. The Prince Regent of Portugal to the United States on the happy event of His newly-born Doughter."[1]

RC (DNA: RG 59, NFL, Portugal, vol. 1). 1 p.

1. Maria de Assunção, fifth daughter of Prince Regent João and Princess Carlota Joaquina, was born on 25 July 1805 (*Burke's Royal Families*, 1:445–46).

§ From Robert Williams. *26 November 1805, Washington, Mississippi Territory.* "The Citizens in that part of this Territory composing Washington County, are becoming very restless in consequence of the treatment they have lately received from the Spanish authorities.

"I have used my influence to keep them quiet, which thus far has been sucessful; but I am really doubtful it will not be the case long if those authorities continue to conduct themselves as heretofore.

"They say one of two things must be done—either to abandon the country, or protect and defend their property in its' way to New-Orleans which the Spaniards inhibit and very much embarrass by imposing duties &c.

"In some instances I am informed, after receiving the duties, they have under certain pretences, taken the whole cargo. For your further information on this subject, I herewith enclose a representation [not found] made to me from some of the most respectable and influential characters residing in that quarter."

Letterbook copy (Ms-Ar: Executive Journal, 1805–1810); draft (Ms-Ar). Letterbook copy 2 pp.

To Thomas Jefferson

[27 November 1805]

will become able to regulate with effect their respective functions in these departments. The burthen of Quarentines is felt at home as well as abroad. Their efficacy merits examination. although the health laws of the states should not at this moment be found to require a particular revisal by Congress yet Commerce claims that their attention be ever awake to them.[1]

(a) "will become more able to regulate with effect their respective functions in these Departmts." instead of what is between the first [   ]
(b) omit what is between the 2d. [   ]

(a) the first alteration is suggested on the ground that an Executive definition of the constitutional power of an Indept. Branch of Govt. may be liable to criticism.

(b) the 2d. on the ground that it takes, apparently, side with the sect of Infectionists. If "really infected" be struck out after vessels, and "in a state dangerous to health" were substituted, or some other neutral phrase, the objection would be taken away.

The pencilled words have reference to the idea & anxiety of some that the State laws should be revised.

RC (DLC: Jefferson Papers). Unsigned; undated; unaddressed; conjectural date assigned based on Jefferson's docket "recd. Nov. 27. 05. Messag(e)."

1. This paragraph, in Jefferson's hand, was also written by him, with minor differences, in the margin of his draft of his fifth annual message to Congress (DLC: Jefferson Papers). For a transcript of the draft, see Ford, *Writings of Thomas Jefferson*, 8:384–96. From this point on, document in JM's hand.

§ From William C. C. Claiborne. *27 November 1805, New Orleans.* "Mr. Cobourn has not Yet arrived in this City, and it is apprehended, that he either has or will decline accepting the Commission which has been offered him.[1]

"The Economy observed in the Salaries of the Judicial officers of this Territory, will I fear effect the respectability of our Judiciary; The Compensation of a Supreme Judge is really Sir inadequate to a comfortable support. Judge Hall altho' by no means extravagant in his mode of Living, cannot I am sure, make his Salary meet his expences, and as for Judge Prevost, who has a large Family to maintain, he cannot possibly avoid making inroads on his private Fortune.

"From a principle of duty to the Government, and Justice to the Judges, I have been induced to address You this Letter. Permit me to add, that the same reasons, which suggest the pr[o]priety of encreasing the Salary of the Judges, wil[l] apply to the Secretary for the Territory."

RC (DNA: RG 59, TP, Orleans, vol. 7). 2 pp.; in a clerk's hand, signed by Claiborne; docketed by Wagner.

1. For John Coburn's refusal of his appointment as judge in Orleans Territory, see *PJM-SS*, 9:62 n. 2.

§ From William Eaton. *27 November 1805, Washington City.* "Permit me to request that my unsettled acounts, long since submitted for decision, may be reviewed; compared with facts; and admitted or rejected. In case I should again be obliged to apply to Congress,[1] I believe it would now be no difficult matter to convince that body that, if my arrangements, out of which some of the most considerable items have arisen and which were inconsiderately and hastily rejected by Captain Murray, had been properly respected, we should have saved the United States four or five millions of dollars. I believe it will be no difficult task to show them that I have consumed eight years of my life and embarked all the property I possessed or have acquired in establishing the point that *Our relations with Barbary may be maintained without the humiliation of tribute;* and that, in doing this, I have made no cession of their honor nor their interests which my efforts could resist. I hope the Government are already convinced of the truth of these facts.

"The Committee of Claims have, nearly two years ago, plainly expressed their opinion by a report to the house that a competence exists in the ordinary authorities to adjust and settle my claims. It would be peculiarly gratifying to me if they may be there adjusted & settled—and with as little delay as possible. It would be injurious to me to be obliged to pass the winter at the capital—My finances are low—And I am extremely desirous of returning to domestic life.

"I have received a formal letter from the Chevalier, Don Antonio Porcile, stating that he had been released from my claim against him by an act of the Government. It is certain that the only surety I held for his fidelity and such as the usage of the country where the debt was contracted admitted, has been set at liberty in conformity to instructions from the Department of state.[2]

"I expressed my wish to the acting Commodore Rodgers when in Tunis Bay, that the brig Franklin or one of the other homeward bound vessels might be permitted to touch at Cagliari with me to renew this claim but he could not reconcile the indulgence to his sense of duty: consequently my tour to the Mediterranean has afforded me no opportunity to prosecute my claim at the Court of Sardinia. I therefore desire to transfer this claim to Government, together with the document I hold in support of it."[3]

RC (DNA: RG 59, CD, Tunis, vol. 2, pt. 2). 3 pp.; docketed by Wagner.

1. For Eaton's earlier application to Congress for reimbursement for his expenses at Tunis, see *ASP, Claims,* 299–307. For previous correspondence about his accounts, see *PJM-SS*, 5:126, 131, 6:328, 369, 465–66, 9:42 and n. 1.
2. For Eaton's rescue of Maria Anna Porcile and her father's refusal to repay Eaton the ransom, see *PJM-SS*, 7:214, 8:66, 67 nn. 1 and 3. For JM's instructions to George Davis not to suggest that the United States had any right to hold her in captivity, see ibid., 8:574.

3. In his March 1807 statement of account, Eaton listed the total due him for the ransom of Maria Anna Porcile as $4,837.25 (DNA: RG 217, First Auditor's Accounts, no. 19,140).

To Thomas Jefferson

[ca. 28 November 1805]

Resol. 1. (Substitute within any part of the former Louisiana comprehended in the delivery of possession thereof to the U.S.)

2. (omit)—(substitute as may consist with the honor of the U. States) this change will look less towards advances by the U.S. ["] *to effect*" the adjustment.

4. (omit, as embarrassing and inefficacious)

5. (quer. if not unnecessary and provided for by the succedg. Resol.)

6. (omit, on the idea that witht. this specification—amicable expense of adjustmt. will be in fact authorized, with an apparent reference to the use of force previously authorized)

The difficulty lies in covering an application of money to *a new purchase* of territory. As a means of adjustment it will be covered; but by a construction probably not entering into the views of Congs.[1]

RC (DLC: Jefferson Papers). In JM's hand. Undated; unaddressed. Conjectural date and recipient assigned based on Jefferson's docket: "recd. Nov. 28.05. Resolns Spain."

1. JM's notes referred to the wording of a list of suggested resolutions on Spain that Jefferson drew up for discussion by the cabinet before it was submitted to Congress. For the initial list and a revised list that Jefferson sent to Gallatin on 4 Dec. 1805, see Ford, *Writings of Thomas Jefferson*, 8:398–400 n.

§ From Tench Coxe. *29 November 1805, Philadelphia*. "I am honored with your letter relative to the copies of the two patents to Mrs. Rebecca Blackwell and Mr. Geo. Fende or Fead.[1] I have just recd. the originals and I take the liberty to transmit them for the purpose of being forwarded to the proper officer or officers, whether register or commissioners. I will take the necessary measures for the discharge of the Registers fees, if I shall be favored with information of his name and place of residence."[2]

FC (PHi: Tench Coxe Papers). In an unidentified hand.

1. See JM to Coxe, 26 Nov. 1805, and n. 1.

2. On 3 Dec. 1805 Jacob Wagner wrote Coxe: "The Secretary of State has caused the two original patents, enclosed with [your] letter, to be forwarded to the Register of the Land Office West of Pearl River, viz Thomas H. Williams Esqr. at Washington in the Mississippi Territory (PHi: Tench Coxe Papers).

§ From George W. Erving. *29 November 1805, Madrid. "Private No. 3."* "In my last unofficial letter dated Novr. 20 which was sent by way of Bourdeaux with the original of my official letter No. 2[1] I intimated an apprehension that the Cypher of this legation had been lost; but having today received a letter from Mr. Jarvis by ⟨w⟩hich I find that Mr. Pinckney has carried it to Lisbon, & has now delivered it to him for the purpose of being forwarded to me by some private opportunity, I hasten to communicate this circumstance to you."

RC (DNA: RG 59, DD, Spain, vol. 10). 1 p.

1. No private letter dated 20 Nov. from Erving to JM has been found; he probably referred to his 21 Nov. private letter. For his official letter No. 2, see Erving to JM, 20 Nov. 1805.

§ From George W. Erving. *29 November 1805, Madrid, "At Night."* "Private No. 4." "I have a moment before the post goes out to communicate to you the very important telegraphick news which has just been received here in private letters from Paris."

[Below Erving's signature is a note:] "Blle Generale. au 16 & 17 devant Vienne les françois [*sic*] victorieux le 18 & 19 les franç⟨a⟩is entrerent victorieux dans Vienne—100 Millions de florins d'imposition—12 places fortes en otages le Tirol & Venise reunis au Roya[u]me d'Italie Messrs. Raugwitz [Haugwitz] & Taleyrand appelés a un traité de paix-continental." [*Trans.* General Bulln. On the 16 and 17 the French victorious against Vienna. The 18 and 19 the French enter Vienna victorious—100 thousand florins levy—12 strongholds surrendered as security. The Tirol and Venice united with the Kingdom of Italy. Messrs. Raugwitz and Talleyrand called to make a continental peace treaty.]

"N.B. The dates are according to the French Calendar. P.T.O."

RC (DNA: RG 59, DD, Spain, vol. 10). 1 p.; marked "via Lisbon." On verso: "Raugwitz is (as I think) a Prussian Minister GWE." Docketed by Wagner.

From John Graham

SIR   PENSACOLA 30th. Novr. 1805

After a very tedious passage I arrived here, via Mobile, on the 23d. Inst and the next morning delivered to Governor Folch the Letter with which I had been charged by Governor Claiborne & of which I beleive a Copy has been sent to you.[1] I am sorry to say that neither this Letter, nor any representations I have been able to make to Governor Folch have induced him to suspend the execution of the Order for the exaction of Duties on American Property passing the Town of Mobile—he tells me that before he took possesion of this Government the Order had been issued by Mr Morales the Intendant—that it had since been approved of by the King and that he could not agree to its suspension unless he received an equivalent on the Mississippi. He takes it as a position that the Spanish Inhabitants of Baton Rouge have as much Right to pass Orleans without paying Duty as the American Inhabitants of Washington County have to pass Mobile & he says that so soon as Governor Claiborne shall give him assurances that Spanish Vessels are permitted to pass to & from Baton Rouge without paying Duties at Orleans, he will suspend the Order now in force at Mobile: & if it shall be found that Spanish Vessels have not hitherto been prevented from freely going to Baton Rouge, that he will refund the Money which has been paid *this Year* at Mobile on the passage of American Property. He limits the refunding to this Year because the Accounts of former Years have been settled & are not now under his controul.

As I did not know that any vessel would be permitted to pass Orleans without paying Duty unless she was bound for Natchez, I endeavoured to convince Governor Folch that the cases which he thought parallel were not so. Finding however that I could not succeed in this, I took him upon his own Ground of Reciprocity & proposed, as the Inhabitants were permitted to send off from Baton Rouge all their Produce free of Duty, that no Restriction should be placed on the Export Trade of the Mobile or rather that he should *immediately* withdraw those already placed & leave the question of Imports as it now stands until he could hear from Governor Claiborne. He pointedly objected to this, saying that to us the Export Trade was the most important & to them the Import Trade.

On the Subject of Military preparations Governor Folch assures me that none are made here with a view to Hostilities against the United States. He says that the propriety of sending Reinforcements to the Garrisons of Mobile & Baton Rouge was suggested by recent occurrences in the neighbourhood of those places & that as to the Garrisons of this Town & the Fort; below, they fall short of their full number by 600 Men. With Sentiments of the Highest Respect I have the Honor to be, Sir Your Mo Obt Sert

JOHN GRAHAM

1st Decr. I have received the Official Answer to Governor Claiborne's Letter & expect to sail this Morning for Orleans.

RC (DNA: RG 59, TP, Orleans, vol. 7). Postmarked 5 Dec. 1805 at Fort Stoddert, Mississippi Territory; docketed by Wagner.

1. See Claiborne to JM, 31 Oct. 1805, and n. 1.

§ From Christopher Gore. *30 November 1805, Boston.* "In making up the packet containing the Statement of the Ship Indus's case, which I had the honour to transmit to you by post 27th: instant;[1] the enclosed documents were omitted—viz Copy of the sentence of the Vice Admiralty Court at Halifax—copy of the Master's protest—copy of a letter from James Stewart Esqr: proctor."[2]

RC and enclosures (DNA: RG 76, Preliminary Inventory 177, entry 174, Great Britain, Treaty of 1794 [Art. VII], Papers Relative to the Commissioners, 1796–1804, vol. 4). RC 1 p.; in a clerk's hand, signed by Gore. For enclosures, see n. 2.

1. See Gore to JM, 18 and 26 Nov. 1805.
2. The enclosures (11 pp.; certified as accurate by Boston notary public William Stevenson) are copies of (1) Jonathan Chapman's 26 Nov. 1805 deposition that he owned one-eighth share of the *Indus*, its specie and bills, when it sailed from Boston in June 1804 as well as one-eighth share of the replacement vessel bought at Île de France when the first *Indus* was declared unseaworthy; that he and David Sears were the sole owners; that he had owned one-eighth share on five previous voyages to India and had always sold his share of the cargo in Boston; that he had no intention of sending the ship or cargo to Europe; that Sears had never mentioned sending the ship to Europe; and that the words "of Emden" that were to be added to the manifest at Boston were only intended to come into effect in case of a peace and that the ship would not have gone to Europe had the war continued; (2) the 4 Sept. 1805 protest at Halifax before notary James Stewart of *Indus* master David Myrick, mate Jacob S. Rayner, and carpenter Benjamin Brentnall that the *Indus* left Batavia for Boston on 26 Dec. 1804, encountered a violent storm on 15 Jan. 1805 that required it to put in at Île de France on 21 Feb. 1805, where the cargo, most of which was damaged, was unloaded and the ship condemned; that another ship was bought and laden with the undamaged cargo and a freight of tea, and had sailed for Boston on 20 May 1805; that it was stopped by John Poo Beresford of the *Cambrian* on 10 Aug. 1805; that a prize crew was placed aboard and the ship sent to Halifax on 24 Aug., arriving on 31 Aug.; (3) the 9 Oct. 1805 condemnation by Judge Alexander Croke of the Halifax vice-admiralty court of the ship and the part of the cargo belonging to Sears and Chapman; and (4) the 10 Oct. 1805 letter of James Stewart, who acted as advocate for Sears and Chapman, to David Sears stating that although the advocates for the captors had advanced several reasons for the ship to be declared good prize, the only ground Croke accepted was that of Sears's instruction to supercargo Abishai Barnard to insert "and Embden" in the manifest upon arrival at Boston lighthouse, which Croke interpreted as trading from an enemy colony to the mother country in contravention of the British "rule of '56." Stewart added that he confidently expected the condemnation to be overturned on appeal.

§ From Edward Meeks. *30 November 1805, New York.* "Having been Informed previous to my departure from the State of Ohio of which I am a resident, that the Office of Ma[r]shal would be vacated at the Opening of the present Session of Congress, I was solicited by Mr. Baldwin & others of that State to make the Application. Since in this City on a Visit to my friends (which by the bye is the place of my Nativity) I have accordingly addressed the Members from Ohio particularly Mr. John Smith who has a perfect Knowlege of me and my General Character having been in the Western Country Some years.

"I could wish worthy sir a reference might be made to his Honor George Clinton Vice President who has a General Knowlege of my family and with whom I have served as an Officer and I flatter myself will Give every Satisfaction touching my Reputation that is So essentially Necessary before a choice can be made.

"Should you conceive me pocess'd of Sufficient Merit to intitle me to your patronage it will make a lasting Impression of Gratitude on my mind—& rest Assured the Greatest punctuality Should be Observed in the discharge of the functions of Sd. Office."

RC (DNA: RG 59, LAR, 1801–9, filed under "Meeks"). 1 p.

§ From James Simpson. *30 November 1805, Tangier.* No. 103. "The approaching close of Rhamadan requiring a supply of piece Goods, as well as of Sugar, Tea and Coffee being provided for the usual Presents made on the occasion of that Festival, I have the honor (agreeably to your Instructions of the 8th. October last year)[1] of subjoining a Schedule of the sundry Articles I have this day requested of Mr. John Gavino of Gibraltar to procure and send me by first safe conveyance, for the Public Service in the Consulate under my charge.[2]

"For payment of those Articles, and to provide for the farther Current Contingent Expences, I have this day drawn a Bill on you to Mr. Gavinos order, payable thirty days after presentation for one thousand two hundred dollars, which request you will be pleased to direct being paid accordingly.

"The Accounts of receipt and expenditure of Articles for Service and of disbursements for the Current Year will be ready to be transmitted by the first probable safe conveyance may offer, after its expiration."

RC and enclosure (DNA: RG 59, CD, Tangier, vol. 2). RC 2 pp.; marked "Triplicate"; docketed by Wagner. For enclosure, see n. 2.

1. *PJM-SS*, 8:135.
2. The enclosure (1 p.) is a list of the required goods, including cambric and flowered muslin, plain muslin "for Turbans," Irish linen, broadcloth, two dozen silk handkerchiefs, dimity, coffee, sugar, and pearl and hyson teas.

From Jonathan Williams

SIR,   WEST-POINT, December 1 1805.

WITH *a view to collect and preserve the Military Science, which must still exist among the Veterans of our Revolutionary Contest, and those of our Fellow-Citizens, who may have gathered Scientific Fruits in the course of their Travels, the* Corps of Engineers *have, under the Auspices of the* President of the United States, *commenced an Institution for the purpose of establishing and perpetuating a Repository so evidently beneficial to our Country.*

As soon as the Constitution *of the* United States Military Philosophical Society *was formed,*[1] *the Plan was submitted to the Chief Magistrate of the Union, who not only honored it with his approbation, but authorized the Society to consider the* President of the United States *as their perpetual Patron.*

The Corps of Engineers *feel assured,* Sir, *that, however feeble this attempt may appear, in the infant state of their own Institution, you will, notwithstanding, take pleasure in granting the aid of your instructive Communications.*

The Military Academy of the United States *is the permanent place of meeting of the Society, and on the* fourth *of* November *you were elected one of its Members. I am, with respect, Sir, Your obedient servant,*[2]

Jon Williams[3]
President, U. S. M. P. S.

RC and enclosure (DLC: Madison Collection, Rare Book and Special Collections Division). RC is a printed sheet with dates and address inserted in a clerk's hand, signed by Williams. For enclosure, see n. 2.

    1. The United States Military Philosophical Society was founded by Jonathan Williams at West Point on 12 Nov. 1802 to promote military science and supplement the activities of the Army Corps of Engineers and of the United States Military Academy. Officers and cadets of the Corps of Engineers were the initial members, but civilians were also eligible for membership. Members presented technical papers at meetings and assembled a library. During the War of 1812 the members were scattered to various military posts, and the society was dissolved after a last meeting on 1 Nov. 1813 (Sidney Forman, "The United States Military Philosophical Society, 1802–1813: Scientia in Bello Pax," *WMQ*, 3d ser., 2 [1945]: 273–85).
    2. The enclosure (2 pp.) is a printed copy of the 12 Nov. 1802 letter announcing the establishment of the society together with the society's constitution.
    3. Jonathan Williams (1750–1815) was Benjamin Franklin's great-nephew and joined Franklin in London in 1770 to further his business education. He later accompanied Franklin to France, where he worked as purchasing agent for Congress, returning to Philadelphia with Franklin in 1785. A member of the American Philosophical Society, Williams published scientific papers in the society's *Transactions* and was named the first superintendent of the United States Military Academy at West Point at its founding in 1802. Faced with inadequate funding and staffing, Williams struggled to improve and expand the academy. Frustrated in his efforts and unhappy about not having been placed in charge of military fortifications at New York, he resigned from the army in 1812 and joined the New York militia. He was elected to Congress in 1814 but died before he could take his seat.

§ From François de Navoni. *1 December 1805, Cagliari.* Although he has not received any answer to several of his letters, at the beginning of the new year he can do no less than fulfill very humbly his duty, wishing JM a good beginning and a better end, with every kind of prosperity and good fortunes and that the good Lord may cover JM with all his desires together with his illustrious family.
    Asks JM to present his respects to the president and his wishes for all that the president can desire of happiness and prosperity for the good of the state. Recommends himself to the president's authority and protection so that he may be honored with the patents of an agent as Commodore Morris honored him which he has already represented in preceding letters.[1] Has not yet learned of the decision that will put him at ease and make him happy. Asks JM to procure this favor for him.
    Continues his efforts to establish a trade with Cagliari for salt as he has already informed JM. Has learned that the commodore may at any moment come in there

with the squadron to be nearer Tunis. Will do all he can to render him service and to procure his esteem and protection.

Continues his correspondence with the United States consuls in the ports of the Mediterranean with the aim of causing merchant ships to load salt for America. JM may assure American merchants that he will engage to serve and favor them.

Begs an answer from JM, should JM think it suitable, to put him more at ease and asks JM to honor him with any commands.

RC (DNA: RG 59, CD, Cagliari, vol. 1). 2 pp.; in French.

1. For Navoni's earlier letters, see *PJM-SS*, 3:605, 5:62, 7:214.

§ From David Ramsay. *1 December 1805, Charleston, South Carolina.* "The bearer Dr. Alexander Garden[1] being about to visit Washington on private business I take the liberty of mentioning to you that he is a Gentleman of high respectability both in his professional & private character. He is one of the committee of our Botanick society & an active zealous promoter of that institution. Should it be in your power to favor him with anything new curious or useful in the Botanic or Agricultural way you would oblige a numerous & respectable association of more than 200 of our inhabitants who are engaged in enriching our Botanick Garden with valuable productions from all parts of the world. The President has been liberal to our Agricultural society & I doubt not of his readiness to oblige our Botanic association. Would you have the goodness to introduce Dr. Garden to him & to such of your friends as may be at Washington. You will find him worthy of any attention you may bestow on him."

RC (DLC). 1 p.; complimentary close and signature clipped. In David Ramsay's hand.

1. Revolutionary War veteran and Charleston, South Carolina, native Alexander Garden (1757–1829) was educated in England and Scotland and admitted to Lincoln's Inn in 1779. His Loyalist father forbade him to return to enlist in the American cause, but in 1780 he returned and fought under Nathanael Greene until the evacuation of Charleston in December 1782, after which he retired to the 1,689-acre property outside Charleston his father had left in trust for him. He traveled extensively and was a member of the South Carolina Society of the Cincinnati. He served one term in the South Carolina legislature and wrote two books of anecdotes about the Revolution.

§ From Joseph Willcox. *1 December 1805, Killingworth, Connecticut.* "With permission, I wish to observe, that the commission with which the President of the United States has been pleased to honor me, as Marshal of the District of Connecticut, will expire on the 20th. Instant—the office has produced but very little business the last four years, none of which is unsettled, yet I shoud be glad to be reappointed to the Office, & will thank you for your influence in Obtaining it."[1]

RC (DNA: RG 59, LAR, 1801–9, filed under "Willcox"). 1 p.; docketed by Jefferson: "Willcox Joseph to be reappointed Marshl. of Connecticut."

1. Jefferson submitted Willcox's name for renewal as marshal to the Senate on 16 Dec. 1805, and the appointment was approved the following day (*Senate Exec. Proceedings*, 2:5).

From Thomas Jefferson

[ca. 2 December 1805]

As we omit in the 2d. message to enumerate the aggressions of Spain & refer for them to the documents, we must furnish the documents for every act, particularly

    1. The capture of the Huntress

    2. The carrying our gunboats into Algesiras

5   3. The late depredations on our commerce in Europe. Extracts from Pinckney's letters

⟨3⟩   4. Oppressions on our commerce at Mobille

⟨2⟩   5. Delays in the evacuation of N.Orleans

5   6. Dissemination of rumors of the probable restoration of Louisiana to Spain.

    7. The new post taken on the bay of St. Bernard.

    8. The reinforcement of Nacogdoches

    9. The robbery near Apelousa

    10. that at Bayou Pierre

    11. The Patroles established on this side Sabine

5   12. The aggression on the Missisipi territory in the case of the Kempers.

⟨5⟩.   13 The subsequent one in the case of Flan⟨a⟩gen and his wife

⟨5⟩.   14. The negociation at Madrid.

    No. 1.2. from the Navy department

    7:8.9.10.11. from the War office

    4.5.6. from the offices both of War and state

    3.12.13.14. from the office of state.[1]

RC (DNA: RG 59, ML); FC (DLC: Jefferson Papers). RC in Jefferson's hand. Undated; conjectural date assigned based on the docket "file Dec. 2. 1805" in an unidentified hand and on Wagner's docket: "President's list of documents for 1st. session of Congress of 1805." Unaddressed; conjectural addressee assigned based on Jefferson's direction at the head of FC: "ThoJ. to mr. Madison." Parts of words in angle brackets in the RC have been supplied from the FC. Minor differences between the copies have not been noted.

1. For the documents concerning U.S. relations with Spain assembled and sent to Congress on 10 Dec. 1805, see *ASP, Foreign Relations*, 2:669–95.

§ From Jacob Barker. *2 December 1805, New York.* "I here enclose Capt Smith's protest and a notarial copy of Captn. Grants protest, who commanded two Vessels belonging to my friends of Kennebunk and were at Cuba for Cargoes of Wood to my Address, when the British Privateer Alexandrine captur'd and[1] them to Nassau, on the passage they run the schr. on the rocks and injur'd her so much that she was not worth repairing, & they robb'd the Brig of her sails and rigging and took the men on board the privateer, so that the masters in a strange country without money, had no alternative but to abandon both vessels, which they did, and left them in possession of the privateersmen at Newprovidence, I have written there, ordering claims to be made for the property and the master and Owners prosecuted for damages."

RC (DNA: RG 76, Preliminary Inventory 177, entry 180, Great Britain, Treaty of 1794 [Art. VII], British Spoliations, ca. 1794–1824, box 6, folder "Unnamed Ships"). Dated "12 month 2d. 1805." Enclosures not found.

1. Barker evidently omitted a word here.

¶ From James Eaton. Letter not found. *2 December 1805.* Acknowledged in Daniel Brent to Eaton, 1[0?] Dec. 1805, as an inquiry about Eaton's two impressed sons, in which Brent stated: "The Secy of State has duly received your letter of the 2d inst in relation to John & Wm Eaton, your two Impressed Sons, and enclosing sundry Documents concerning them, of the sufficiency of which you wish to be informed. I am directed to signify to you, in reply, that authenticated Copies of the papers in these two Cases, which were sent hither in June last by Mr Hodge, a Notary Public at Newburyport, containing the substance of those now sent by you, were forwarded in the same month from this Department to Mr *James M Henry* our Agent at Kingston, Jamaica, with a request that he would do all in his power to procure the discharge of the persons to whom they related. But Mr Henry being unluckily at that time on a visit to this Country, a Circumstance unknown to this Departmt., these papers failed in producing the desired effect, and they were returned to this Department. As it is to be presumed, however, that he is now at Kingston, other Copies of them will be sent to him, and Copies will likewise be sent to Genl Wm Lyman, our Agent in London" (DNA: RG 59, DL, vol. 15; 1 p.; addressed to Eaton at "Salisbury, near Newburyport").

From Stanley Griswold

SIR,   TERRITORY OF MICHIGAN, DETROIT, 3. December 1805.

It is reduced to a certainty, that this government cannot proceed, without some additional pecuniary aid from Congress. Its seat is established at a place, which combines all the *disadvantages* of an old and of a new settlement, without one of the *advantages* of either. Luxury, the relic of British fortunes formerly squandered here, and of a once flourishing commerce, continues its empire, tho' I am happy to think it is on the decline. Fashion, ceremony and expence are great, far beyond the present abilities of the inhabitants. We are in the neighborhood of a proud, rich and shewy government, which has frequent intercourse with us through characters of wealth and distinction. Our compensations are scanty for the most retired, internal situations, where house-rent and provisions are cheap, and expensive company is not known—as was the case at the seat of the government of the North Western Territory, in the year 1787, by the Ordinance of which date, our salaries are regulated.[1]

Of all the salaries, that annexed to the office which I sustain, is most scanty and inadequate, especially considering the circumstances in which I may be called to act, and am now in fact acting, viz. as *Governor* of the Territory. In short, Sir, I have no hesitation to affirm, that I am *ruined*, absolutely *ruined*, by the acceptance of this place, unless relief can be afforded. Imagine to yourself a man expending the little savings he had been able to make amidst incessant persecutions for ten years, in fitting out and removing his family a thousand miles—and finding himself at the end of his journey compelled to pay for rent and the necessaries of life, *more* than he would be obliged to pay in the most expensive city of the United States, or of the world—with the extraordinary duties and expence of *Chief Magistrate*, devolved on him for eight months out of twelve; of *Commander in chief* of a militia, which is relied on for effective defence; and of *Superintendent of Indian affairs* to numerous and powerful nations, whose Chiefs are frequently at his house; and imagine this man receiving but $750 per annum! What would $750 do to support a *private* gentleman and his family, a year, at Washington, Philadelphia, or New York? Much more a *public* man, who must meet every occurance and receive every company, in a manner becoming the dignity of the government of the United States? With my very narrow and restricted provision, I feel a mortification which I shall not attempt to describe. I cannot refuse to go *beyond* what I know to be warranted by my compensation, relying on the justice and magnanimity of the government under which I serve. If that government should think proper to allow me an adequate provision, I should be thankful. Otherwise, I must retire with my family, in despair, to some sequestered situation, to retrieve, if possible, my affairs, and think no more of public employment.

Governor Hull will be with you the ensuing winter, and will amply confirm the statement given above. I enclose a letter and some papers which I wish you to commit to him; or if any cause should prevent his being at Washington, you will be good enough to make such use of the papers as the nature of their contents requires.

One is a *Petition* to Congress in my own behalf.[2] Perhaps it will not be necessary to present it, in case the Governor should be there in person. Of this, however, you and he will be judges.

Another of the enclosed papers is a *Bill* of expences I have been obliged to incur in my office, for the public service.[3] I waited many weeks to receive stationary from, or by the order of Government. None arriving, I was compelled to take up a small quantity for my office, and become responsible. The office-rent is the lowest that a decent or comfortable place can be obtained for in this town, near the centre. The Indian annuities could not be opened in the only surviving public store, which is not large, and extremely crouded. Of course, I was obliged to bring them to my chambers, where they were opened and delivered. This, together with the charge for victualing the Chiefs at my table, while waiting the distribution of the goods, and transacting all the business concerning them, would not have been mentioned, if my salary had been equal to an expence of this weight. But in my present circumstances, it appears to be just that these items be allowed. Still, I submit the propriety of retaining them in the bill, to your and Governor Hull's judgment. I have the honor to subscribe, with great respect, Sir, Your most obedient Servant,

STANLEY GRISWOLD.

RC and enclosure (DNA: RG 59, TP, Michigan, vol. 1). RC docketed by Wagner. For enclosure, see n. 3.

1. For the Northwest Ordinance, see *U.S. Statutes at Large*, 1:51 n. (*a*).
2. Griswold's petition was presented to the House of Representatives on 8 Jan. 1806 (*Journal of the U.S. House of Representatives*, 9th Cong., 1st sess., 229).
3. The enclosure (1 p.; printed in *Michigan Pioneer and Historical Collections* 31 [1902]: 544–45) is a list of expenses amounting to $122.79 that included stationery and a record book totaling $14.46; a year's office rent of $50; wood and candles estimated at $20; $5 for the delivery of $4,500 worth of goods, "annuities for five Indian Nations, from the public wharf" to Griswold's house; and $33.33 for one hundred meals fed to the Indian chiefs at Griswold's house.

From John R. Livingston

duplicate

SIR   NEW YORK December 3. 1805

I have the honor to enclose you sundry documents to prove that the £54 Stg. exclusive of Int. did not belong to Captain Miller or was ever considered by the Commissioners as his. If an attention is paid to the Freight of one box of Cambricks and Two bales of Britania[1] you will find that Clarkson & Cross have their names mentioned and the Sum of £3. charged on their Goods and Creditted to the Ship. Besides this Captain Millers adventure is distinctly marked as is also Mr. Hendersons. In Mr. Ervings Letter dated 13th. Augt. 1803 a Reference is made to the Names of C. & C. advising my purchasing them out or settling the business among ourselves so as to be enabled to draw. In Mr. Ervings second Letter Jany. 11. 1804 he acknowledges the Receipt of the assignment from C. & C. & others. In Mr. Ervings third Letter January 20. 1804 He more particularly mentions C. & C and advises my procuring their signatures—If a Sale of the Award Should take place. These several Letters will Show that Mr Erving had no doubt but that the property was awarded to C. & Cross. It is unnecessary to make any farther Comments on this business but that Captain Miller or his Heirs have never claimed the Sum in question—And that it was claimed by their Assignee (C & C) from whom I purchased. If a release from the Heirs of Captain Miller will answer to procure the amount Awarded to him I will endeavor to obtain it for his Sister in Law Mrs. Daubigny who avers that it of right belongs to her she having sent an adventure by him for which she had no bills Lading or Receipt of any kind. But to procure a Release that I may be enabled to draw for money not claimed or ever having belonged to Cap Miller wd. be an acknowledgement that the sum in question is theirs. I must therefore decline doing it on that account. I beg leave to inclose you a Statement of my account I flatter myself I shall receive the ballance which I consider justly due to me. I am Sir With every respect Yours—*&c* &c[2]

JRL

RC (DNA: RG 76, Preliminary Inventory 177, entry 180, Great Britain, Treaty of 1794 [Art. VII], British Spoliations, ca. 1794–1824, box 10, folder 1d). Written above Livingston to JM, 29 Dec. 1805. Enclosures not found.

1. Britannia: "standard lengths of medium-quality linen or linen-cotton plain-weave fabric used for clothing, sheeting, etc., originally made in Brittany in northern France and often exported through Great Britain to North and South America in the 18th and 19th centuries" (*OED Online*).

2. See JM to John R. Livingston, 25 Nov. 1805.

From William Pennock

Sir   Norfolk, Decr: 3. 1805

I have been selected by the Merchants of this place to forward to you memorials upon the cases of spoliation committed by the Belligerent Powers on their commerce: In consequence of which I have the honour to address you and to forward memorials with copies of documents accompanying, in the following cases

1. Conway and Fore Whittle, Ship Eliza, John Evans Master[1]
2. John Granbery, Sloop George Reynolds master[2]
3. Donaldson Thorburn & Co, Ship Charles Carter Tompkins Master[3]
4. James Dykes & Co. Schooner Iris Saml. Pearson Master[4]
5. Edward Chamberlain Brig Nancy, John Christy Master[5]
6. Alexander Leckie Brig Catherine, Jno. Seward Master[6]
7. Moses Myers[7] Ship Argus E. Chamberlain. Master[8]
8. Moses Myers Schooner Adeline, Nathl. Strong Master[9]
9. Richard Drummond. Schooner Favorite Fletcher Master[10]
10. John Burke, Schooner Two Brothers, Canby Master[11]

I am directed to state that the originals in each case are lodged with me or will be subject to my order provided they are considered by you as requisite and if they should be so considered they will be forwarded whenever you direct them. There are I am informed sundry other cases but the Owners either have not received Protests from the Masters, or have neglected to send them to me as I receive them I shall do my self the honour to transmit them to your department. I have the honour to be with consideration and respect Sir Your Obed Servant

WM. PENNOCK

RC (DNA: RG 46, President's Messages, 9A–E3); Tr (DNA: RG 233, President's Messages, 9A–D1). RC in a clerk's hand, signed by Pennock.

1. For the *Eliza*, owned by Conway and Fortescue Whittle, see Henry Hill Jr. to JM, 12 and 27 June 1805, *PJM-SS*, 9:462, 464 n. 4, 496.

2. The sloop *George*, Captain Reynolds, was taken at Turks Island by the French privateer *Resource* under Captain Jeanett. An award of $7,663.51 was granted in recompense under the 1831 treaty with France (*New-York Gazette & General Advertiser*, 20 Aug. 1805; Williams, *French Assault on American Shipping*, 160).

3. The *Charles Carter*, Capt. John Tomkins, was captured by the Puerto Rican privateer *Maria*, Capt. Anthony Lobo, recaptured off Bermuda by British merchant ships bearing letters of marque, and brought to England (*Alexandria Daily Advertiser*, 6 July 1805; New York *Daily Advertiser*, 29 Aug. 1805; Boston *Independent Chronicle*, 9 Sept. 1805).

4. For the *Iris*, see Robert Patton to JM, 25 May 1805, Louis-Marie Turreau to JM, 2 June 1805, and JM to Patton, 13 June 1805, *PJM-SS*, 9:402 and n., 403 n. 1, 426, 466.

5. For the *Nancy*, Christy, see Samuel Sterett to JM, 21 Apr. 1805, ibid., 271, 272 n. 7.

6. For the *Catherine*, see Joseph Seaward to JM, 12 Sept. 1805, and n. 1.

7. Moses Myers (1753–1835) arrived in Norfolk from New York in 1787. He flourished in Virginia and became one of Norfolk's richest merchants. He was a board member of the Bank of Richmond, a militia officer, served as French and Spanish consul in Norfolk, and as president of the town council. His firm failed in the Panic of 1819. From 1828 to 1830 he was collector of customs (George Holbert Tucker, *Norfolk Highlights, 1584–1881* [Norfolk, Va., 1972], 101; Jacob Rader Marcus, *United States Jewry, 1776–1985* [4 vols.; Detroit, 1989–93], 1:143–44, 596; *Senate Exec. Proceedings*, 3:594, 4:63).

8. The *Argus*, Captain Chamberlain, was seized along with several other ships coming out from Cádiz, which was blockaded. They were sent to the vice-admiralty court at Gibraltar, where it was expected all would be condemned (Boston *Columbian Centinel*, 18 Sept. 1805).

9. When the *Adeline*, Captain Strong, was about to be brought to trial on 24 Sept. 1805 in the vice-admiralty court in Nassau, it was predicted that the cargo of two hundred and thirty boxes of white sugar would be condemned (New York *Mercantile Advertiser*, 14 Oct. 1805).

10. The *Favorite*, Captain Fletcher, was captured by a British frigate while entering Curaçao and condemned by the vice-admiralty court at Jamaica (ibid., 9 Aug. 1805).

11. The cargo of the *Two Brothers*, Captain Canby, was condemned by the vice-admiralty court at Jamaica, but the captain's personal cargo was released (Philadelphia *United States' Gazette*, 26 Aug. 1805).

§ To Albert Gallatin. *3 December 1805, Department of State.* "I have to request that you will please to issue your warrant on the appropriations for Barbary purposes for one thousand dollars in favor of Daniel Brent, for defraying the expences of the Tunisian Embassy now in this City; the said Daniel Brent to be charged and held accountable for the same."[1]

RC (DNA: RG 59, DL, vol. 15). 1 p.

1. JM made similar requests for warrants of a thousand dollars each to defray the expenses of the Tunisians in Washington on 24 Dec. 1805, and 4 and 25 Jan., 3 and 31 Mar., and 7 May 1806, DNA: RG 59, DL, vol. 15; 1 p. each.

§ From Sylvanus Bourne. *3 December 1805, Amsterdam.* "The inclosed Gazette of to day will be found peculiarly interesting as it contains a detailed relation of the great & extraordinary events which have lately taken place in Germany, Viz the Capture of Vienna by the Armies of France[1]—the desire manifested by the Austrians to retreat from the Coalition & that of the Russians to return home the neutrality of Hungary, & in fine a combination of Events which presage a Speedy close of the war on the Continent & should Prussia keep aloof which will probably be her policy & interest to do under existing Circumstances—Great Britain will soon be left alone again to combat with the Power of France & will be less haughty in her conduct towards neutrals as she will have enough to combat with the Power France without provoking the enmity of other nations.

"The moment is indeed important to all Europe & we may expect in the ten first years of the new age to see the developements of Still more interesting scenes than what the ten last years of the last Century presented."

RC (DNA: RG 59, CD, Amsterdam, vol. 1). 1 p.; docketed by Wagner.

1. As the main coalition armies retreated east across the Danube before Napoleon's advancing forces, the Austrians declared Vienna an open city, thus sparing it the effects of a seige. After entering the capital, the French seized five hundred cannon, one hundred thousand muskets, and a large quantity of ammunition (Chandler, *Campaigns of Napoleon*, 402–7).

§ From William Jarvis. *3 December 1805, Lisbon.* "The foregoing Mr Pinckney did me the favour to take charge of. He sailed the 19th.[1] & left the inclosed letters addressed to you, to himself to your care & to his daughter(s) to be forwarded.

"In my haste I omitted to inclose a Copy of my letter to Mr de Araujo of the 6th. Ulto. relative to the quarantine, I now send it with a Copy of his answer.[2]

"Two days after I waited on him & the Marquis Pombal, a Vessel from Alexandria was cleared. She had 30 days passage & only lay 8 days. One from Baltimore & one from Plymouth, which arrived two days after, being detained longer, I sent to learn of the Secy. of the Junta the cause; he returned for answer that advices had been given by the Portugee Ambassador at Madrid, that a Vessel which had arrived at St. Ander from Philada. had brought Accounts that the yellow fever was raging in that place & in New York with much violence & that the Spanish Government had given orders for a rigid quarantine from the U.S., and that he supposed the quarantine would be more strictly enforced here. I thereupon wrote the inclosed of the 28th. Ulto. to the Marquis Pombal,[3] having two days before made a second Petition for them; petitions in these cases being customary they were released the 28th after laying 15 days, I rather believe before the letter was delivered.

I have heard nothing farther about it but I am much inclined to believe that our Vessels will not lay longer than 5 to ten days with clear Bills of health.

"From the Army of Germany our advices are only to the 15th. Bulletin & the 4th. from Italy, which I presume you will have rec(ie)ved before this reaches you."

RC and enclosure (DNA: RG 59, CD, Lisbon, vol. 2). RC 3 pp.; written at the foot of the 18 Nov. 1805 duplicate of Jarvis to JM, 17 Nov. 1805. For surviving enclosure, see n. 3.

1. For Charles Pinckney's arrival at Charleston, South Carolina, see Jarvis to JM, 17 Nov. 1805, and n. 3.

2. For Jarvis to António de Araújo, 6 Nov. 1805, and Araújo's reply, see Jarvis to JM, 17 Nov. 1805, and n. 3.

3. The enclosure (8 pp.) is a copy of Jarvis to the marquis de Pombal, 28 Nov. 1805, flattering Pombal's wisdom and knowledge, stating that the lengthy detention of the *Governor Carver* and *Truxton*, must have been owing to Jarvis's poor French when he spoke personally to Pombal. He described yellow fever as a disease of hot climates and noted that it began to the north of the equator in August or September and sometimes continued into November when cool weather began but generally disappeared in the West Indies at the beginning of the heavy fall rains. He attributed the cause to "a foul, poisonous atmosphere" occasioned by the air emanating from putrid substances and from low situations where air did not circulate freely. He noted that in hot weather with prevailing southern winds, the miasma was most virulent, fading with clear weather, northerly winds, and frequent rainstorms. He added that in the past year the cold rainy summer in the United States and hot weather in Spain had accounted for the lack of yellow fever in the former and its prevalence in the latter country. Jarvis continued that "many of the ablest physicians" who had studied the disease had decided it was not contagious but was caused by "a miasma." He argued that in a country like Portugal, blessed with pure air, excellent drinking water, and a diet composed chiefly of vegetables, it was impossible for the disease to be communicated without an extreme change in the weather. Jarvis added that his government would never hazard the health of other countries and had given orders in July 1801, that were strictly enforced, to collectors of customs. He extolled the virtues of the collectors, adding that their large salaries and the fear of being deposed from office, which was held at the will of the president, placed them above temptation. He stated that even beyond this, the immediate detection of any false news in the papers required everyone to adhere to the truth. Jarvis apologized for discussing a disease Pombal and Araújo knew better than himself but asked "whether Bills of Health granted under such circumstances ought not to have the utmost Credit given them"? He assumed Pombal would agree and asked that the prince regent give orders that ships from the United States with clean bills of health and healthy crews be admitted to pratique immediately or at least detained for no longer than five days, excepting always those vessels that had no, or limited, bills of health.

§ From Benjamin Rush. *3 December 1805, Philadelphia.* "To a person acquainted with the great events which characterised the first years of the French Revolution, it might be sufficient barely to say—the bearer of this letter is General Miranda. But much more may be said of him. He is still the friend the [*sic*] liberty, and a beleiver in the practicability of governments that shall have for their objects the happiness of nations, instead of the Greatness of individuals. He knows your Character, and longs to do homage to your principles. He will repay you for your Civilities to him, by streams of knowledge, and information upon all Subjects."

RC (DLC). 1 p.

To John Carroll

Dear Sir   Washington Decemr. 4. 1805
I received in due time your favor of the 20th. Ulto. and had hoped that less time would have been lost in availing my son in law[1] of the opening for him with Mr. Dubourg. For some days however previous to the arrival of his mother, he had a complaint in his bowels, which rendered several doses of medicine necessary. The little delay required by her affection, after her arrival, was prolonged by the disagreeable idea of sending him with crouds of drunken sailors who now fill every Stage,[2] and without any particular acquaintance to take charge of him. All difficulties are at length removed by the patronage of him on the journey by our neighbor Mr Forrest[3] who sits out with him tomorrow morning & will be so good as to present and introduce him into the care of his preceptor. The kind attention which you have shewn on the occasion, and the friendly sentiments expressed in your last letter, have not lost the effect they ought to have on our gratitude, and I beseech you to be assured that I shall always be happy in evincing that sentiment as well as every other with which I ought to remain My dear & right Revd. Sir Your Most Obedt. hble. sert.

James Madison.

RC (Archives of the Archdiocese of Baltimore). Docketed by Carroll.

1. JM's stepson, John Payne Todd.
2. JM presumably referred to sailors from the frigate *Congress*, which had arrived at Greenleaf Point on 29 Nov. 1805 (Knox, *Naval Documents, Barbary Wars*, 6:312).
3. "High toned federalist" Richard Forrest (ca. 1767–1828) was secretary to the commissioners of bankruptcy for the District of Columbia in 1803 and was a clerk at the State Department from 1806 until his death. JM nominated him in 1809 to be consul at Tunis, and in 1811 to be consul at Tripoli, both of which nominations were rejected by the Senate (New York *American Citizen*, 4 Mar. 1808; Washington *Daily National Journal*, 10 Oct. 1828; *Washington Federalist*, 25 Nov. 1803; DNA: RG 217, First Auditor's Accounts, no. 17,985½; *PJM-PS*, 3:195 n. 1).

To Rufus King

private

Sir   Washington Decr. 4. 1805
I have recd. your favor of the 25th. Ulto. inclosing one to you from Mr. Vansittart; which I now return as you requested, after having submitted it to the Perusal of the President. As it is of importance to understand the way of thinking in Great Britain with respect to Spanish America, and what the Government there does not at this particular time mean to undertake,

as well as what under other circumstances it may probably undertake towards the object pursued by General Miranda, the communication of Mr. Vansittart's information thereto, claims acknowledgments which I pray you to accept. With assurances of the high respect with which I have the honor to be Your Mo: Obedt. servt.

JAMES MADISON

RC (NHi: Rufus King Papers); letterbook copy (DNA: RG 59, DL, vol. 15).

§ To John Armstrong, George W. Erving, and James Monroe. *4 December 1805, Department of State.* "Inclosed is a copy of the message of the President yesterday delivered to the two houses of Congress.[1] The importance of its contents makes it desireable that you should receive it with as little delay as possible."

Letterbook copy (DNA: RG 59, IM, vol. 6); RC (DLC: Curry Autograph Collection); RC (DLC: Rives Collection, Madison Papers). Letterbook copy 1 p. Addressed to: "The Ministers of the United States in London, Paris and Madrid (Circular)." First RC 1 p.; in a clerk's hand, signed by JM; docketed by Erving. Second RC in Wagner's hand, signed by JM; docketed by Monroe, with his note: "recd: Wednesday M:g 19 Mar." The cover sheet of the second RC is marked "Collectors office Norfolk" and "⅌ Eliza, Capt Doggett from Norfolk, left there 31 Jany."

1. For Jefferson's fifth annual message to Congress, 3 Dec. 1805, see Richardson, *Compilation of the Messages and Papers of the Presidents*, 1:370–76.

§ From William C. C. Claiborne. *4 December 1805, New Orleans.* "I have had no late intelligence from Mr. Graham; it is probable he has met with some detention at Pensacola, for it is (I presume) well known to you, that dispatch in business is not a trait in the spanish character.

"I am sorry to inform you that much confusion exists in the County of Atachapas; the Citizens in that quarter are divided into parties, and their personal resentments so great, that it has been difficult to preserve the public peace.

"During the provisional Government in Louisiana, Lieutenant Hopkins, late of the army, acted (under my orders) as Civil Commandant of Atachapas, and discharged his duties in a manner very satisfactory to me; he preserved the most perfect good order, and acquired for himself, the esteem and confidence of the People.

"The gentlemen whom, under a Law (passed by the legislative Council) providing for the establishment of inferior Courts I appointed to Offices within Atachapas, have not profited by Mr. Hopkins's good example; on the contrary they have neither commanded, for themselves, or for the Law, the public respect; and such is (at this time) the state of things, that my presence in the County has become advisable. I contemplate setting out in a few days, and will be accompanied by Colonel Bellechasse, a very worthy and influential Citizen; our personal expenses, *which will be inconsiderable,* I purpose defraying out of the Fund allowed for the contingent expenses of this government.

"The divisions in Atachapas owe their origin to the affair of St. Julien, of which you have, long since, been made acquainted;[1] no very *serious acts* of disorder have yet been committed, but to prevent *such*, and if possible to restore harmony; but in any event to remove from Office, the Officer or officers who may have acted improperly, are the objects of my visit.

"I shall not be absent from this City more than Eighteen days, and if, in the mean time, any important dispatches from the Seat of Government should arrive at New Orleans, they will be forwarded to me by Express."

RC (DNA: RG 59, TP, Orleans, vol. 7). 2 pp.; in a clerk's hand, signed by Claiborne; docketed incorrectly by Wagner "4 Decr. 1806."

1. For the St. Julien case, see Daniel Clark to JM, 3 Dec. 1803, Claiborne to JM, 24 Jan. and 24 May 1804 (first letter), JM to Claiborne, 19 June 1804, Jefferson to JM, 5 July 1804, JM to Claiborne, 10 July 1804, and Claiborne to JM, 30 July and 10 Aug. 1804, *PJM-SS*, 6:138, 139 n. 4, 377–78, 379 n. 3, 7:250 and n. 2, 251 nn. 3–4, 331, 420, 435–36, 542, 586.

From William Bartlet and Others

[ca. 5 December 1805]

To the Honorable James Maddison, Secretary of State of the United States.

The Memorial of the Merchants, of Newburyport and its vicinity respectfully represents.

That while pursuing a just and legal commerce we have suffered great and aggravated losses from unwarrantable depredations on our property by several of the Belligerent powers of Europe.

In conducting our commerce we have endeavoured strictly to conform ourselves to the Laws of Nations & existing Treaties, to the regulations of our own government and to those of the Belligerent powers. Yet nevertheless, our property has, in various instances, been taken from us on the high seas, in a piratical manner, in some others, it has been seized by the cruizers of one Nation, carried into the ports of another, and there embezzled with scarcely the semblance of a trial and in many cases our Vessels and cargoes have been captured, tried and condemned in Courts of Law, under unusual and alarming pretences, which, if permitted to continue, threaten the ruin of our commercial interests.

So far from obtaining redress our grievances by the ordinary modes and processes of Law, we have in most cases been subjected to heavy costs, and suffered embarassing and distressing detention of property even where no pretence could be found to authorize the seizure of it.

In this alarming situation of our commercial affairs, both our duty and interest strongly urge us to embrace the earliest opportunity to communicate to the constituted guardians of our rights such facts and documents, as may enable them effectually to demand indemnification for past losses and security from future aggressions.

You will therefore have the goodness as soon as may be to lay before the President of the United States the enclosed List of Losses sustained by the Merchants of Newburyport and vicinity, together with this Memorial.[1]

Having sustained these Losses and injuries, in the prosecution of our lawful commerce, & in the exercise of our Just rights, we rely with confidence on the wisdom, firmness, and Justice of our Government to obtain for us that compensation and to grant to us that protection which a regard to the honor of our country, no less than to the rights of our citizens must dictate and require. We have the honor to be very respectfully Sir Your Obedient Servants

> WM: BARTLET
> MOSES (BR)OWN
> WILLIAM FARIS
> JOHN PEARSON   } *Committee.*
> EBENEZER STOCKER
> STEPHEN HOWARD
> EDWARD TOPPAN[2]

RC and first enclosure (DNA: RG 46, President's Messages, 9A–E3); Tr and Tr of enclosures (DNA: RG 233, President's Messages, 9A–D1). RC in a clerk's hand. Undated; date assigned based on the date on the certification of the first enclosure. RC and enclosures printed in *ASP, Foreign Relations*, 2:746–49. For enclosures, see n. 1.

1. The first enclosure (3 pp.; certified as a correct copy on 5 Dec. 1805 by notary Michael Hodge) is the 2 Dec. 1805 deposition of William Morris and William Kloot, captain and mate respectively, of the brig *Lucretia*, that they had sailed from Newburyport for Martinique on 24 Aug. 1805; that on 20 Sept. 1805 they had been stopped by the British privateer *Andromeda* under Captain Carrol; that the crew of the *Andromeda* had robbed the *Lucretia* of naval supplies, food, medicine, and dry goods, and robbed the captain, the mate, and the cooper of their trade articles, and the crew of their clothing; and that they had beaten the captain and several crew members. The second enclosure (3 pp.) is a list of sixteen vessels captured by the British or the French, together with the names of the captains and the owners, the details of the captures, and the value of the properties. The total valuation of the captured ships and cargoes was $283,377.22. Most of the vessels captured by French privateers were carried into Cuba and plundered without trial, while those captured by the British were usually tried in vice-admiralty courts.

2. Federalist William Bartlet (1747–1841) began to accumulate property during the Revolution, eventually owning wharves, warehouses, and a fleet of ships. By 1807 he was worth over $500,000. In addition to investing in a woolen mill, a bank, an insurance company, and a turnpike, he donated time and funds to various local charities. Bartlet also served in the Massachusetts state legislature in 1801 and 1802. Federalist Moses Brown (1742–1827) began as a carriage maker who invested in the sugar and molasses trade before the Revolution.

After the war he became a full-time merchant and accumulated a fortune second only to Bartlet's, much of which he lost after the War of 1812. Like Bartlet, he invested in a woolen mill, a bank, an insurance company, and a turnpike. Irish-born Federalist William Faris (or Farris) (d. 1837) came to Newburyport about 1765. He became a ship's captain, commanded several letters of marque, and invaded Canada with Benedict Arnold. After the war he joined Ebenezer Stocker in a banking and importing partnership which failed owing to losses during the Quasi-War with France. By the time of his death he was dependent for income on his Revolutionary War pension. Merchant and shipowner John Pearson was also an insurance underwriter who owned a wharf and a mill in Newburyport. He served for several years as director of the Newburyport Bank. In 1815 he retired from his retail mercantile pursuits. Stephen Howard (ca. 1764–1825) represented Newburyport in the state legislature from 1806 to 1820 and was joined from 1806 to 1809 by John Pearson. Howard was a shipowner and a director of the Essex Merrimack Bridge corporation. Revolutionary War veteran Edward Toppan became a merchant and shipowner who was also an insurance underwriter. Pearson was a partner in the Merrimack Marine and Fire Insurance Company, as was Howard, and Bartlet, Brown, and Stocker were directors. Bartlet and Pearson were managers of the Merrimack Bible Society. For Ebenezer Stocker, see *PJM-SS*, 2:286 n. 2. All of the men were active in the town administration and among themselves held many positions over the years. On 30 Nov. 1805 the seven men were chosen at a meeting of Newburyport merchants to serve as a committee "to collect and report a list of vessels and property belonging to this town" that had been captured or detained by the belligerent European nations (Labaree, *Patriots and Partisans*, 207–8, 212; Currier, *History of Newburyport, Mass., 1764–1905*, 540, 678, 680–81; *Newburyport Herald*, 14 Feb. 1800, 6 Apr. 1802, 25 Mar. 1803, 23 Mar. 1804, 27 Aug. 1805, 9 June 1807, 29 Mar. and 15 Apr. 1808, 6 Feb. 1810, 14 Aug. 1812, 22 Oct. 1813, 15 Mar. 1814, 27 Jan. 1815, 9 Jan. 1816, 27 Mar. 1818, 11 Jan. 1820, 31 May 1825; Boston *Republican Gazetteer*, 12 Mar. 1803; Williams, *French Assault on American Shipping*, 120, 201, 243, 421, 433, 467; Philadelphia *United States' Gazette*, 10 Dec. 1805).

§ From William C. C. Claiborne. *5 December 1805, New Orleans.* "Mr. Graham has this moment returned from Pensacola, and brought me Governor Folch's reply to my communication of the 31. of October last.[1]

"The answer is not as explicit as I could have wished; but it is probable that the difficulties to which our commerce is at present subjected at Mobile may soon be removed. I will inclose you a copy of Governor Folch's letter, and write you more particularly upon this subject by the next mail."

RC (DNA: RG 59, TP, Orleans, vol. 7). 1 p.; in a clerk's hand, signed by Claiborne; docketed by Wagner.

1. For Claiborne's 31 Oct. 1805 letter to Vicente Folch, see Claiborne to JM, 31 Oct. 1805, and n. 1.

§ From William Jarvis. *6 December 1805, Lisbon.* "Inclosed are 3 letters from G W Erving Esquire And by the mail two minutes since 5."

Adds in a postscript: "The capture of vienna, Tyrol & Venice given up—a Million sterling Contribution. 12 strong places given as a security for an Armistice whilst negotiating a peace. This on the authority of news from Report."

RC (DNA: RG 59, CD, Lisbon, vol. 2). 1 p.; docketed by Wagner.

§ From John Patrick and Nathaniel Lawrence. *6 December 1805, New York.* "We had the honor to receive Your letter under date of 6th. Ulto, & pay due respect to the Contents thereof.

"We have a few days ago recd. Copies of the Proceedings at Halifax in the Case of the Ship Eugenia, (which formd the Subject of our former application to You) and as these proceedings involve in themselves principles highly interresting to the United States, and we conceive highly injurious to our rights as American Citizens, we think proper to transmit to You such Vouchers, as may serve to inform You on the Subject, & to Communicate such other information as may further explain the same.

"You will therefore please receive herewith

"No. 1 The Masters Protest[1]

    2 Copy of interlocutory Decree,[2]

    3 Copy of letter from our attorney James Stewart Esqr. to our Agent, Michael Wallace Esq[3]

"The Protest as you will see, states the Capture to have taken place within 4 or 5 miles of the Land, and as we understand the Jurisdiction of every independent Power, agreeably to the acknowledged Laws of nations, extends to three marine Leagues from its Shores, we therefore view this Capture as having taken place within the Jurisdictional limits of the United States, & consequently illegal. The Decree requires certain proofs to be produc'd within three months, from the date thereof, say 4th. Novr. The letter of Mr Stewart, No. 3, will explain to You the Nature of these proofs. The object of the first article of these proofs, is no doubt to ascertain whether or not the articles composing the outward Cargo, were French—Colonial Produce, & if such, & imported from the Colonies, by the same person exporting them to France, to Condemn them or their Value, on the principles on which some late decisions in Great Britain, have been founded. As American Citizens we solemnly protest against the admission of the right on the part of Great Britain to exact such Conditions, because we conceive that by the Laws of Nations Neutrals have a right to import into any Foreign Country, such articles as the Laws of that Country permit, (Contraband of War excepted), and because we view it as contrary to the principles of Justice, & the Spirit of the British Laws themselves, to compell individuals who are Claimants of property wrested from them, to produce such testimony, as may have the effect of Criminating themselves, & Occasioning the Condemnation of their property, and because we consider that by the same principles, the Onus probandi, ought to rest with the Complaimants [*sic*]. To the Second article we make the same objections, only adding that as respects the right of Capture & Condemnation, we consider it irrelevant to the point in Question under what revenue Law of France the goods were imported, or what per Centum of Duty was paid, So that the right of property was in the neutral Individual. Against the third Condition required, we also most pointedly protest, for the same reasons as before-mentioned, & because we do not consider it to compose any part of a duty incumbent on neutral individuals, to become the Expounders of Foreign Laws. We therefore claim the Support & protection of our Government, against the hardships & injuries arising from this decision, & hope that such measures may be adopted, as may produce for us the proper redress, & guard us against the repetition of such hardships.

"Should the proofs that are there required, not be produced within the limited time, it is understood the property will be condemn'd, & in the principles of this decision many of our fellow Citizens are involved, for independent of the Eugenia, there are now three other ships in Halifax, to which it extended. Should that fail, however, another plea, as You will also see by Mr Stewarts letter, is set up against the Eugenia, under which he appears to think She will be condemn'd, unless certain proofs are brought forward.

"That Plea is for having been *forcebly rescued* from a British Prize Master off NewLondon—and the Proofs required, are that this rescue was made by a revenue officer, authorised by the Collector of the Port of NewLondon, in Consequence of the Noncompliance, by the Prize Master on board the Eugenia, with the revenue Laws, and not by the Master of the Ship.[4] We should therefore be glad to receive Your advice on the Subject, & to be furnish'd with such documents, & in such form as will be received as proofs at Halifax.

"As innocent & unoffending individuals, we certainly cannot expect to be Sufferers by an act in which we had no agency, having in every thing *that we have done*, been Sanctiond by the Laws of the United States.

"As the term allow'd us is very short, we should be glad if this would receive Your early attention, as we shall take no measures whatever witht. Your Sanction & approbation, & shall be govern'd by the advice & recommendations You may be pleased to give us. We beg leave to add that we are in possession of the affidavit of the Prize Master, & Masters mate, on which the Allegation against the ship at Halifax is founded, & that from the whole tenor of it, it appears that the whole proceedings before NewLondon were under the direction of a Revenue officer.

"We are also in possession of a Copy of the charge exhibited by the King's advocate against the Ship on that account, Copies of both which can be sent to You if required.

"In hopes of being honor'd with Your reply, at as early a date as possible."

Add in a postscript: "As You will see by the Protest, Capt Fleming has waved any discussion relative to the improper treatment he was said to have recd. from the Commander of the Cambrian."

RC and enclosures (DNA: RG 76, Preliminary Inventory 177, entry 180, Great Britain, Treaty of 1794 [Art. VII], British Spoliations, ca. 1794–1824, Unsorted Papers, box 2, folder E). For surviving enclosures, see nn. 1–3.

1. The 29 Sept. 1805 protest of Capt. Mathias Fleming before Halifax notary public James Stewart (2 pp.; signed by Fleming, mate Peter Hass, and seaman Peter Coffee) stated that he left Bordeaux in the *Eugenia* on 25 July 1805 with a cargo of "Brandy, Wine, Oil and Dry Goods bound for New York" and that on 7 Sept. 1805 "being in Sight of Sandy Hook Light House and about four or five miles distant from the Land," he was stopped by the *Cambrian* under John Poo Beresford who, after examining the ship's papers, took possession of the *Eugenia* and the cargo and placed a prize master and crew on board with orders to take the ship to Halifax for adjudication.

2. The 4 Nov. 1805 decree of vice-admiralty court Judge Alexander Croke (2 pp.) stated that after having heard the arguments and proofs of the prosecutor and the defending proctor, he "directed further proof to be produced on the part of the Claimant" within three months.

3. The enclosure has not been found, but a copy of James Stewart to Michael Wallace, 8 Nov. 1805, explaining Judge Alexander Croke's reasoning and listing the further proofs he

required, was included with the list of losses paid and claims against the United Insurance Company of New York submitted to Congress (DNA: RG 46, President's Messages, 9A–E3); printed in *ASP, Foreign Relations*, 2:766–67).

4. For the capture and recapture of the *Eugenia* in 1804, see Jacob Wagner to JM, 16 Aug., Anthony Merry to JM, 24 Aug., and JM to Merry, 5 Sept. 1804, *PJM-SS*, 7:613, 614 n. 3, 631–34 and n. 1, 8:19–20 and n. 2.

§ From Anthony Terry. *6 December 1805, Cádiz.* "After having forwarded to Algeziras the Original of the above; I have obtained a Copy of the order issued by the British Government, and received by the Danish Consul, respecting the free entry to this Port & St. Lucar of neutral Vessels, by which you will be informed that it is not in the least favourable for our Citizens to face said Ports with the Produce of the United States.[1]

"I expect however that as Soon as the British Government is informed that there is no fleet in this Port, it will mitigate Said order.

"This Place with respect to business is quite at a Stand, nothing whatever doing, on⟨ly⟩ a few negociations in Government Paper; a grea⟨t⟩ quantity of Wheat & flour remains in Stores witho⟨ut⟩ a purchaser offering."

Adds in a postscript: "Governmt. notes 46 a 46½ ⅌."

RC and enclosures (DNA: RG 59, CD, Cádiz, vol. 1). RC 2 pp.; in a clerk's hand, signed by Terry; marked "[*illegible*] ⅌ [*illegible*] of Capt. [*illegible*] Nicholl." Written at the foot of Terry to JM, 25 Nov. 1805. For enclosures, see n. 1.

1. The first enclosure (1 p.) is a copy of a 29 Oct. 1805 letter from Jens Wolff, Danish consul general at London, to John Kroger, Danish consul at Plymouth, announcing the free entrance of neutral ships to Cádiz and Sanlúcar de Barrameda, providing they did not carry, when entering or leaving, naval or military supplies. Terry also enclosed a printed copy (1 p.) of a Spanish translation of Adm. Cuthbert Collingwood's 19 Nov. 1805 letter to the marqués de Solano announcing the relaxation of the blockade for neutral vessels. Collingwood's letter was printed in the 22 Feb. 1806 *New-York Herald*.

§ From Carlos Martínez de Yrujo. *6 December 1805, Philadelphia.* The extreme effort with which I have endeavored to maintain the harmony and good understanding between Spain and the United States have made me read with a peculiar sensation the article of the message of the president sent to Congress the third of this month on political relations between the United States and the king my master. As in the exposition to which I allude, there exist, it seems to me, various equivocations of a delicate and important propensity, although I do the president of the United States the justice due upon the motives that could have caused this apparent lack of exactitude, my character imposes on me the obligation to enter into the examination of some of his assertions to show that, whether through lack of exact information, or through faulty translations, they appear in some cases not to be correct.

In the article of the said message relative to Spain, the president, after mentioning that the negotiations for ending existing differences had not had a felicitous issue, continues: "Compensation for the spoliations produced during the previous War, and for which Spain had formally acknowledged herself responsible, she now denies us except under conditions that affect other claims that *have no connection with her.* Nevertheless, she has renewed the same practice in the present War, and these new spoliations are already to a great amount."[1] It is well known that in a state of war [there] exists, and probably will always exist, some abuse of the power entrusted to subordinate hands. Even the United States has been unable to be an exception to this general rule, and in the short period of hostilities towards France in the year 1798, in spite of not having armed privateers, and reducing its defensive force to a small number of frigates, neutrals experienced from [the United States] many annoyances, well demonstrated by the numerous claims of the injured powers on this Government, principally on the part of Denmark and Sweden. In the past War there perhaps could have been some abuses of this nature, although very rare, on the part of the royal navy of Spain; but the king my master, animated by the spirit of justice that characterizes him, authorized his chief secretary of state to sign a convention with the American minister near his person by which was stipulated reciprocal compensation for the damages that the subjects and citizens of both might have experienced on the part of officers or individuals of either [country] contrary to human rights or to the Law of Nations. This stipulation resembled that of the same kind in the treaty of friendship and limits made in 1795,[2] and fulfilled religiously by my sovereign, would have now had the same effect, through the ratification of the convention, if there had not been inserted in it an article whose tendency was to impose on Spain an obligation for a responsibility as grave and important in its consequences as [it was] little supported by reason and justice under the circumstances.[3] My court, by direct means as well as through me, has repeatedly shown the American government that it was disposed to carry out the said stipulations provided that the article in the same convention relative to the said responsibility be suppressed, or altered in a way that it believed conformed to justice; and it has been so far from refusing to fulfill the said compensation for claims that *have no connection with it*, that in reality this *connection* has been precisely the reason that the said convention has not been carried into effect as the king my master has always wished. It is certain that the two points in their nature do not have *a connection* with each other; but it is also true that this *connection is very great* when it is considered it attempts to make these two things, diverse in themselves, *parts of the same whole;* hence results the disagreeable dilemma for the king my master, whether to refuse to ratify a stipulation that he believes fair, and that he consequently wishes to carry out, or to impose upon himself a responsibility more or less direct in favor of the United States that they, as is well proven, have no right to claim.

    As for the new spoliations, I can assure you, there are very few Spanish vessels that strictly merit this denomination, many of the seizures frequently listed in the American gazettes originating either in acts of contraband trade, or from the lack of papers that they ought to carry on board according to our treaty of 1795,[4] or from other circumstances that the captains or owners of the said seized ships have been very careful to hide; leaving this aside, the citizens of the United States would find the same justice that they experienced on this point under the treaty of 95. I can do no less than observe, having had the honor of informing you some two months ago, that the most strict orders had been given by the king my master that the navigation of Americans employed in licit commerce should not be interrupted;[5] the president has not made any mention of this circumstance as important in its effects for American navigations, as for demonstrating [the king's] just and peaceful intentions.

Without it being my intention to use recrimination, I am obliged to notice that when violations of the rights of neutrality occur infinitely more frequent and extensive on the part of England, whose *Royal Navy* vessels have almost constantly blockaded the ports of the United States; and what is more, when this power daily decrees new principles upon the rights of neutrals, that really undermine them and reduce them to nothing, the name of Great Britain is not found in any column of the president's message. These circumstances in themselves would not give me the right to accent them if it were not for one, extremely essential, that immediately affects the interests of the king my master; I allude to the *huge numbers of American sailors carried off by force from the shelter of the flag under which they ought to find themselves protected*, and who find themselves forced to fight in British ships against the subjects of the king my master. This conduct cannot but excite in me the obligation to remind the Government of the United States of it in order that in its wisdom it may take suitable means to correct an abuse that at the same time that it actually violates its neutrality continues so greatly damaging to Spain.

The president goes on to say: "Our commerce through the River Mobile continues to be obstructed by arbitrary duties, and troublesome searches." Although this assertion is not accompanied by any remark that could make it look like a national offense, I cannot but observe in passing that according to what I am informed the import and export duties on the Mobile are very moderate, of only six percent;[6] that each power can arrange these matters within the limits of its jurisdiction as it thinks; and that this practice of Sovereignty is executed by the American government at Fort Stoddert, being within its boundary, without Spain pretending to interfere in its regulations. Ultimately, this might be an inconvenience, but in no way can it be presented as a national offense.

After, he says: "Propositions *for adjusting amicably*[7] the limits of Louisiana have not been acceded to." This proposal is not strictly correct, since it is, and has been, the wish and the intention of Spain to *adjust amicably*[8] the limits of Louisiana: but although her dispositions toward this end may have been, and are, friendly, she cannot sacrifice to them either the dignity or the rights of her crown; so that this matter not having been concluded has not been because of the lack of will *for adjusting amicably*[9] as the president supposes, but because of the nature of the propositions, which were inadmissible.

The same paragraph continues: "While the *title* continues *undecided* we have abstained from changing the state of things, from taking new positions, or fortifications in the *disputed* territories with the hope that the other power will not compel us, by a contrary conduct, to follow its example, and generate conflicts of authority whose consequences would not be easy to contain; but we now have reasons to lessen our confidence in this hope." Truly I cannot comprehend what it is that the president could call *unsettled title*, much less if he wishes to apply it to that part of West Florida between the Mississippi and Iberville, the Lakes, and the Perdido River. The title to this territory cannot be considered as *undecided* or *unsettled*, since putting aside that given by possession, and the treaty of retrocession of Louisiana to France, there is another conclusive circumstance, well known to the American government, that ought to and must dissipate all doubts, if they should exist on this point. The most distinguished publicists[10] agree that the true interpreters of a treaty doubtful in any of its clauses or expressions are the contracting parties themselves when this can be achieved. Spain and France are these in the treaty of *retrocession* upon which the sale of 30 April[11] is based, from which emanate the pretensions of the American Government; they have declared, as is evident to you, that Spain had no intention to give France more than she had received from her, as the title and the word *retrocession* used in it indicate; and France had neither claimed nor expected an inch of land to the east of the Mississippi, Iberville, and Lakes. The *true intention of the contracting parties* being stated and shown in this manner, I will content myself with copying to you here a short paragraph from Vattel among the many other publicists who one could present in support of the rights of the king my master upon this point. In paragraph 274 of the interpretation of treaties,[12] Vattel says: "When we manifestly see what is the sense *that agrees with the intention of the contracting Powers*, it is not permitted to turn their words to a contrary meaning. The intention *sufficiently known furnishes the true matter of the convention* of what is promised & accepted, demanded & granted. *To violate the Treaty is to go contrary to the intentions sufficiently manifested, rather than against the terms in which it is conceived; for the terms are nothing without the intention that ought to dictate them.*"[13] In view of this, the position that the president has taken in the cited paragraph that the right (no doubt alluding to a territorial right) could be doubtful, or *unsettled*, cannot be admitted, and all persuasions and conclusions emanating from this supposition fall of themselves; leaving that aside, as I have had the honor to inform you previously, whatever alteration may have existed in the territories of His Catholic Majesty, either could have been the effect of a new plan for the frontier that the alienation of Louisiana made necessary, or must have proceeded from the circumstances of the war in which Spain is now engaged with England, and in no way has the goal of disturbing the peace, and good harmony between Spain and the United States.

The president goes on to say: "Lately forays or incursions have been made into the territories of Orleans, and Mississippi. Our Citizens have been seized, and their property stolen in those same places that Spain has transferred to us and this by *regular officers* and soldiers of this Government."

Although on this point I have no more news than that received from the American gazettes, whose reports one cannot expect to be very impartial, nevertheless, supposing them correct in all their extent, it does not follow from those that I have read, nor does it seem to me credible, that *the officers* and soldiers of the king my master, might have crossed the American line in order to commit within the jurisdiction of these states the insults that are surmised. *The first example of these incursions was given by a lot of American citizens* in the month of August 1803,[14] penetrating the territory of Baton Rouge, aided by the Kemper brothers and other malcontents from the Spanish side with them, who made an attempt to seize the fort of Baton Rouge, and imprisoned some mayors and other persons of note. About this matter I had the honor to speak and write to you, but I have not until now had the least response. If seizing the person of American citizens (*our citizens have been seized*)[15] has some reference to the apprehension of the Kemper brothers inside the American line,[16] I must declare first that, according to what I am informed, the said Kempers are not *American citizens;* having been established in Spanish territory, they have become subjects of the king my master, and consequently have lost their rights as American citizens; and second, because in the arrest of these subjects according to the extract of a letter from Natchez of 8 Oct. last, published in the Gazette of the United States at Philadelphia,[17] their arrest was accomplished by *negroes, mulattoes,* and *American citizens,* who no doubt expected some recompense for delivering them inside the Spanish line, *from where* it seems some Spanish soldiers were charged with conducting them to Baton Rouge. It is true, it is said also, that part of a cavalry company commanded by a certain Captain Jones had crossed another part of the border and had conducted themselves in a hostile and violent manner toward two families;[18] but if a story of this nature should be certain, I can assure you that the government of the United States shall not fail to receive the appropriate satisfaction from Spain, whose government has too well established its reputation for one to attribute to it knowledge or approbation of acts as improper in their character as useless in their effects. Incidents of this nature often occur on the borders of all countries and only deserve attention when they receive the sanction of the government of the aggressors, or the satisfaction due in such cases is denied.

I have examined step by step the article of the president's message relative to Spain, and I have tried to present with candor and truth, although lightly, whatever can elucidate correct ideas about its nature and tendency. Having discharged this obligation belonging to my station, I place myself at your service.[19]

RC (DNA: RG 59, NFL, Spain, vol. 2); Tr (AAE: Political Correspondence, U.S., 59:4–9); Tr (Danish National Archives); letterbook copy of second Tr (UkLPR: Foreign Office, ser. 115, 15:33v–41). RC 10 pp.; in Spanish; in a clerk's hand, except for Yrujo's complimentary close and signature. First Tr is a translation of the RC, in French, enclosed in Turreau to Talleyrand, 15 Jan. 1806 (AAE: Political Correspondence, U.S., 58:292). Second Tr is an English translation. Italics are Yrujo's underlings. Quoted passages from the message are in Spanish in the RC, and quotation marks are as placed by Yrujo, except as noted in n. 13 below.

1. Jefferson's fifth annual message was printed in the Philadelphia *United States' Gazette* on 5 Dec. 1805. For the paragraph dealing with U.S. relations with Spain, see Ford, *Writings of Thomas Jefferson,* 8:390–91.

2. For articles 20 and 21 of the 1795 Treaty of San Lorenzo dealing with claims, see Miller, *Treaties,* 2:334–37.

3. Yrujo referred to article 6 of the Convention of 1802, under which Spain would have accepted responsibility for condemnations of U.S. property by French consuls in Spanish ports. For earlier correspondence on these claims, see *PJM-SS,* 4:442–43, 596–97, 5:358, 7:55, 8:166, 171–72, 198–99, 9:410.

4. For article 17 of the 1795 Treaty of San Lorenzo detailing the nature of the papers merchant ships were required to carry, see Miller, *Treaties,* 2:332–33.

5. See Yrujo to JM, 26 Sept. 1805.

6. In the second Tr, and in copies printed in contemporary newspapers, and in *Annals of Congress,* Ninth Congress, Second session, pages 688–93, there is an asterisk here with the following note: "It is necessary to remark that the navigation of the Mobille, which appears to furnish to the President a motive of complaint, is enjoyed by the Americans in consequence of a gracious indulgence on the part of Spain; as no right does yet exist, to navigate the waters of that River within the boundaries of Spain, who holds exclusively that right

grounded on Sovereignty possession, on the opinions of the most celebrated Civilians an[d] supported by the very principles established by the American Government, thro' the medium of their Attorney-General Bradford, in the case of the Prize Grange, taken on the waters of the Delaware. After this it is necessary to confess, that the animadversions of the President upon this head are as unjust as they are impolitic" (*Washington Federalist*, 5 Feb. 1806). Yrujo referred here to the case of the British merchant ship *Grange* that was captured in Delaware Bay within U.S. territory on 25 Apr. 1793 by the French privateer *L'Embuscade* and carried into Philadelphia. The *Grange* was released after the U.S. government insisted that the capture of the ship in neutral waters was a violation of U.S. sovereignty (Boyd, *Papers of Thomas Jefferson*, 25:637–40, 26:43–44, 75).

7. Yrujo repeated the phrase "for adjusting amicably" in English here.

8. Yrujo repeated the phrase "for adjusting amicably" in English here.

9. Yrujo repeated the phrase "for adjusting amicably" in English here.

10. Publicist: "An expert or writer on the law of nations or international law" (*OED Online*).

11. For the 30 Apr. 1803 Treaty for the Cession of Louisiana, see Miller, *Treaties*, 2:498–505.

12. Vattel, *Law of Nations* (1793 ed.), 230–31.

13. The quoted paragraph is in English.

14. Yrujo was mistaken. It was in August 1804 that the Kemper brothers attempted to capture the fort at Baton Rouge, and JM did reply to Yrujo's complaint about the raid. See *PJM-SS*, 7:638 n. 2, 657 and n. 1, 8:203–4, 237, 263, 281.

15. Yrujo repeated these words in English.

16. For the seizure and subsequent rescue of the Kemper brothers, see Robert Williams to JM, 14 Sept. 1805, and nn. 1–2, and 1 Oct. 1805, and n. 1.

17. The 14 Nov. 1805 *United States' Gazette* carried an 8 Oct. 1805 report from Natchez of the results of an inquiry before Thomas Rodney at Fort Adams. On 3 Sept. 1805 nineteen individuals, twelve whites and seven slaves, broke into the houses of Nathan and Samuel Kemper, seized them and their brother Reuben, carried them below the border, and turned them over to Spanish soldiers. The Kempers were rescued by U.S. troops when the party passed Pointe Coupée. The raiders included citizens of Mississippi Territory and Spanish citizens, and most of them escaped. Two whites and the blacks were held in custody for trial; the Spanish troops were released because they had only been acting under orders. Several of the raiders were enemies of the Kempers, and the Spanish government had also offered a reward of $1,500 for each of the Kempers (Philadelphia *United States' Gazette*, 14 Nov. 1805; Robert V. Haynes, *The Mississippi Territory and the Southwest Frontier, 1795–1817* [Lexington, Ky., 2010], 113).

18. For this incident, see Robert Williams to JM, 1 Oct. 1805, and n. 1.

19. On 21 Jan. 1806 Yrujo sent a copy of this note in French to the other foreign ministers, stating that since he had received no reply nor had the U.S. government printed his note, he was transmitting copies to show the truth of the king's actions toward the United States. Translations of his letter to the ministers and his note to JM were printed in the 27 Jan. 1806 Philadelphia *United States' Gazette*.

From James Bowdoin

Duplicate.

Sir,   Paris Dec. 2nd [7th] 1805.

My last letter to you was dated at London Sep 3., which place I did not leave untill the 14. of Octo, owing to some disappointment in receiving a passport from hence. My passage from Gravesend to Rotterdam was no less, than eight Days, and part of the time very dangerous. By industriously pursuing our journey after landing, we arrived here on the eveng. the 1st of Nov. I have been since engaged in making myself known to our minister and to some of the public functionaries in this City. Mr Tallerand, the minister for foreign affairs, I found to be with the Emperor, who had put himself at the head of his armies in Germany. Upon the 12. nov. Gen Armstrong communicated and delivered to me your letter of the 23 of May last to Mr Monroe,[1] accompanied with yours of the 16th of June,[2] stating to me at the same time, that he apprehended a few days would give other instructions upon the subject of our controversy with Spain: and that he had transmitted to you certain informal propositions from this Govt., accompanied with suggestions of his own upon the same subject:[3] to which, it could not be long before, he should receive your reply. I then stated to him, that from a conference, held in London with Mr Monroe and Mr Erving, it had been thought adviseable under existing circumstances, and that it had been agreed, that Mr E. should proceed to Madrid to relieve Mr Pinckney, be there introduced as Secretary of Legation, or as charge d'affaires under Mr Pinckney's appointment, as he should deem best, taking care, that the Spanish Govt. should be duly impressed with the idea, that he was uninstructed and uninformed as to the ground our Govt. meant finally to take in consequence of the failure of Mr Monroe's negotiations.[4] That I was to proceed to this City, here to confer with him, General Armstrong, as to the views and designs of this Govt., and to wait for the arrival of your further instructions before I proceeded to Madrid. This plan I have litterally pursued, as being the best, that could be devised in the present posture of our affairs; and to this plan I shall continue to adhere, unless diverted from it by circumstances, which shall promise a favorable issue. Perhaps you may enquire why I did not immediately upon the receipt of your letter to Mr Monroe of the 23 of May proceed for Madrid, and act under that Instruction. To which I reply, that I daily expected to receive direct dispatches from you: that it appeared by the Letter itself as well, as by that of the 16th. of June to Genl. Armstrong, that you were not in possession of all the facts and documents, relating to the failure of the negotiations; that it would have been contrary to the opinions of Mr Monroe and General Armstrong as well, as to the concerted arrangement, aforementioned. That Mr Erving was already at Madrid, and had not been heard from, but had doubtless given the impression, which had been preconcerted and which in the nature of things would have weakened the ground of any propositions, not predicated upon direct and positive instructions. In confirmation of these facts permit me to transcribe a few extracts from letters, which I have lately received from Mr Erving at Madrid. "In this view" says Mr E in his Letter of the 29. of October "I thought it necessary, that it should be distinctly understood, that my appointment was of an old date; that I had preceded you merely for the purpose of relieving Mr Pinckney, and to hold the ground, till the orders of the Presidt. should authorize your taking it. The same reasons, which operated to prevent your coming, applied, in a less degree to myself. Mr Pinckney fully agreed with me upon this point" &c. In another part of the same letter he observes, "that you will be much gratified in knowing, that nothing has occurred here, since your first landing in St. Ander, to occasion regret on account of the measures which you took. Since the departure of Mr Monroe every thing has remained in statu quo. Mr Pinckney has not received a word for many months. There is therefore no discussion upon the tapis, and not the least probability, that they will ratify the convention." In his last letter of the 19th. Nov. received only three days since, he says, "you will best determine as to the time of leaving Paris, but my opinion extremely concurs with Mr Monroe's, and in the presumption, that this line of conduct was fixed, I have given it to be understood, that you will not move till directed expressly to do so: You see therefore, that a great effect, and probably a prejudicial one, would be produced by your coming hither at this time, but you will determine how far &c."

From these extracts it is pretty clear, that no advantage can be expected from departing from the plan concerted with Mr Monroe in London, and I conceive my self in the best possible position, Mr Erving being at Madrid, to receive your further instructions, and to act to effect under every contingent. My powers, to be sure, are at present very limitted, resting chiefly upon my commission upon conditional rather, than positive instructions. I have happily recovered my health, am tolerably acquainted with the posture of our affairs, and am anxiously disposed to execute to effect the commission with which I am charged: my situation is however somewhat delicate as well, as difficult, and I hope, I shall continue to receive the President's and your confidence as far at least, as I may be thought worthy of it, to relieve me as much, as possible, from local or particular embarrassment, whether it may arise from etiquette, or any other cause in reference to our controversy with Spain.

The events of Mr Monroe's negotiations with other circumstances have given rise to opinions unfriendly to the independence of Spain: and it is now made a clear case, that without the officious interference of this Govt. our negotiations at Madrid would have had a more favorable issue:

permit me then to suggest to you, whether your instructions in future should not provide for this contingent? That those who negotiate should execute the treaty: or if it should prove a mixed transaction and be made under the influence of both Govts., whether coincident powers may not be required? The peculiar situation of the Spanish to this Govt., and the political connection of both, induce me to the enquiry. Delicacy to Gen. Armstrong's situation, as connected with my own responsibility, leads me to hope, that with whatever powers the president may see fit to charge me, they should be explicit in their terms, efficient to the purpose, and clear and definitive in their expression. What renders this circumstance the more important is, that whilst Gen. Armstrong supposes, that the controversy is to be adjusted here, Mr E. in his last letter observes to me, "I never was of the opinion, that the business was to be done at Paris, and I am much less so now": "on the contrary I am well persuaded" &c "that it should be settled here" &c. I hope Sir, I shall neither incur suspicion or blame, or be thought too particular in making these suggestions; They are grounded upon no hostility to Genl. Armstrong, but are suggested with the best views to the continuance of our friendship and harmony, and that the President's and your expectations may be finally realized.

With respect to the course which our disputes with Spain will probably take, it is very uncertain. It is however an ascertained fact both by Mr Pinckney & Mr Erving, that the convention of 1802 will not be ratified: Gen. Armstrong is also of the same opinion: whether this arises from the secret intervention of this Govt. to engraft its own views upon our disputes with Spain, I know not: It is however pretty clear, that if this Government should actually interfere, and a treaty should be attempted under its influence, four principal points will be insisted on. 1. That the eastern boundary of Louisiana does not include West Florida, but is limitted to the Rivers Mississippi and Ibberville, and to the Lakes Maurepas and Portchartrain 2. That a tract of country should remain unoccupied by either party on the western limits forever. 3. That she *will* not permit Spain to stipulate to indemnify our citizens for spoliations by french cruizers fitted out of Spanish ports; and lastly: that she will endeavor to obtain as large a sum, as possible, from the UStates for east and West Florida.

In confirmation of the first of these points, you will permit me to refer you to Mr Tallerand's letter of the 25th. Dec. last in reply to Mr Monroe's note of the 8th of Nov. preceeding;[5] in which you will find the arguments and detailed view of the opinions of this Govt. respecting the eastern boundaries of Louisiana. With respect to the Second point; altho' the western boundary is well known to the Spanish and French Govts. to be the Rio del norte or Rio Bravo, yet it will insist upon a tract of land to lay uncultivated and unoccupied for a term of years at least, if not forever, with a view of rendering the frontier the more secure, as well, as to palliate the disadvantages of having ceded Louisiana to the US., more especially, as she may suppose, that the U States may hold that part of the territory in no high estimation, and as one of Mr Monroe's propositions went to the same object. With respect to the third point: french spoliations authorized in Spanish ports, it is true, that Mr Tallerand's letter of the 25th. is silent as to this part of Mr Monroe's note, probably owing to Rules which govern his official proceedings, and which may be explained by his letter to Mr Livingston, dated the 14. of ventose 14. year[6] wherein he says, "il est tout-a-fait contre les maxims du gouvernement de la republique de mettre ensemble rapports importants et delicats de la politique avec des ca[l]culs de solde et des interêts d'argent."[7] But I understand that both the spanish and french Govts. conceive those demands to be satisfied by the ratification of our treaty with France in the year 180   :[8] and from the energy with which this claim was repelled by the Spanish,[9] and probably at the instance of this Government, and renders it quite unlikely it will ever be admitted. With respect to the fourth and last point (the sum to be paid) it will doubtless be required to be to as great an amount, as the U States can in any way be induced to allow: not less with a view of obtaining the approbation of the Spanish Government, than with the design of drawing into its treasury through a loan from Spain as great a supply of Cash, as possible, to meet present exigencies, and for the want of which this Govt. is known to be greatly embarrassed: and with the view of enlarging this sum, it will be expected, that the indemnities for Spanish spoliations shall be discharged by bills upon the Spanish Colonies: There is more reason I apprehend to distrust the success of our negotiations from these money projects, than from any other cause.

With respect to the late capture of our vessels by British cruizers, implicating the peace of the U States & aimed as a direct blow at the commerce of France and Spain, it appears, as yet to have produced no effect upon this Govt. The Emperor and minister for foreign affairs being both absent and engaged in affairs which, require their whole attention, it is not probable, that their sentiments upon this subject can be ascertained, untill their return to Paris, which is shortly expected, and certainly, as it is said, before the 1st. of January. No satisfactory opinions can be drawn from other sources upon this subject, as there is a certain reserve in the ministers of all the departments, arising from an extreme jealousy of each other. But as our commerce and the principles on which it is maintained must be of great importance, both to France and Spain not only in reference to their colonies, revenues, manufactures and produce, but in the supply of both with the goods and productions of the east and west Indies, our present difficulties with England, and the terms upon which we may sustain our neutrality, are of great consequence and offer strong motives on the part of both governments for an equitable adjustment of our disputes with Spain.

Having thus stated to you my present situation, and the best facts I am able to procure upon the subject of our differencies, it does not belong to me to recommend to the President the measures to be pursued, to give force and effect to the pending negotiations: But it is my opinion, that unless some favorable circumstance shall grow out of our complaints for the capture of our vessels by British cruisers, or some decisive step be taken by taking possession of some part of the contested territory, or the payment of a large sum be authorized, our negotiations will be languid and inefficient, and probably trained out to an interminable length.

In whatever point of view this subject may be regarded, whether in reference to France or Spain, I think it my duty to suggest, that one principle should be kept steadily in view: That the U States should pursue that line of conduct, which best comports with their present interest, regardless of the views or feelings of this or the Spanish Govt., I take it, that they are neither in a situation to bring their force to bear, nor in a condition to go to war with the U States, and that our commerce is absolutely necessary to both; from which I infer, that if they should be pressed to the alternative of an open rupture, or to yield the points in controversy, they will be obliged to give way. The politicians of Europe in the present day are governed more by the interests of the moment, than by speculations upon future contingencies. That as gratitude or past favor among nations produces no influence against a present object of national interest or aggrandizement, so upon the other hand, if they find themselves obliged to yield to the effects of a like interest in other nations, altho' it may induce a present irritation, it will prove only transient and momentary. If this is a just principle, the U States can have nothing to fear from these Govts, especially the Spanish by a decisive line of conduct. Please to present my most respectful regards to the President, and believe me always with the greatest esteem and respect Sir, Your faithful and most obedient Servant

JAMES BOWDOIN

RC, two copies (DNA: RG 59, DD, Spain, vol. 9); Tr (NN: Monroe Papers). First RC marked "Duplicate"; in a clerk's hand, signed by Bowdoin; docketed by Wagner. Second RC in Bowdoin's hand. Second RC dated 7 Dec. 1805, which is the correct date based on Bowdoin to JM, 18 Dec. 1805. Minor differences between the copies have not been noted.

1. *PJM-SS*, 9:380–83.
2. No letter from JM to John Armstrong dated 16 June 1805 has been found. Bowdoin meant JM's 6 June 1805 letter (ibid., 432–36).
3. Armstrong probably referred to his 10 Sept. 1805 letter to JM.
4. See James Monroe to JM, 20 Aug. 1805.
5. For Talleyrand's 21 Dec. 1804 reply to Armstrong concerning Monroe's 8 Nov. 1804 note to him, see *PJM-SS*, 8:431 n. 2.

6. Second RC has "14th of ventose 11th. year." No letter of 5 Mar. 1803 from Talleyrand to Robert R. Livingston has been found.

7. *"Il est tout-a-fait contre les maxims du gouvernement de la republique de mettre ensemble rapports importants et delicats de la politique avec des ca[l]culs de solde et des interêts d'argent"*: It is completely against the principles of the government of the republic to place together important and delicate political relations with calculations of payment and money interests.

8. Left blank in both RCs. Bowdoin referred to the Convention of 1800 with France.

9. In the second RC there is an asterisk here, and at the foot of the page: "see mr. Cevallos's notes of the 16 & 28th. of feb last." For Pedro Cevallos's letters of 16 and 28 Feb. 1805 to Pinckney and Monroe, see *PJM-SS*, 9:81 n. 1, 82 n. 3.

From George W. Erving

No. 3.

Sir,   Madrid December 7th. 1805.

I had the honor to write to you (No. 2.) on the 20th. Ulto. by way of Bordeaux, and to inclose copies of my notes to Dn. Pedro Cevallos on the case of the "Recovery, Adams," the cargo of which vessel was condemned at Algesiras as being English property, and on that of the "Hudson, Bailey," condemned at Cadiz for want of papers, which as it appears, were taken from her by the Commander of a Privateer.

The inclosed are translations of the answers which I received to those,[1] and copy of another note on the case of the "Recovery" which I thought it my duty to make in reply to that of Dn. Pedro;[2] this last was transmitted yesterday after an interview which I had with the Prince of Peace. My object in waiting upon the Prince, who, considering his situation, is frank & communicative, was to learn something more of the dispositions of his Government than I could expect to collect from any official correspondencies with the Secretary of State.

He received me with his usual attention; but though he was not wanting in friendly professions to the United States, yet, I was concerned to find that he would not give me reason to believe that any favorable change had taken place in the policy of his government towards us, and I came away in the full conviction that at this moment it stands upon precisely the same ground where the negotiations were broken off—somewhat confirmed by the late successes of France.

I herewith transmit minits of all which occurred in the conversation, of importance;[3] and have the honor to be, Sir, With perfect Respect & Consideration, Your very obedient Servant

George W. Erving

RC and enclosure (DNA: RG 59, DD, Spain, vol. 10). RC in a clerk's hand, signed by Erving. For surviving enclosure, see n. 2.

1. Enclosures not found.

2. The enclosure (5 pp.; marked "(Triplicate)") is a copy of Erving to Pedro Cevallos, 6 Dec. 1805, in response to Cevallos's 21 Nov. 1805 reply (not found) to Erving's 14 Nov. note about the *Recovery* (see Erving to JM, 20 Nov. 1805, and n. 2). Cevallos had apparently informed Erving on 21 Nov. that orders had been given to the tribunals at Algeciras and elsewhere to adhere strictly to treaty provisions when judging seizure cases, to which Erving replied on 6 Dec. that if the orders had been obeyed, there would be no grounds to complain or to request the annulment of the decree on the *Recovery*. Cevallos apparently also stated that the owners of the ship had the right of appeal to the Council of War and that the king wished justice for all who were entitled to it, to which Erving replied that it was his knowledge of the latter that had caused him to appeal to Cevallos in the hope that Cevallos shared those sentiments and would immediately repair the injury done and that Cevallos's referral to the Council of War implied that there was a possibility that the condemnation might be upheld. He added that a decision that was unjust and in violation of a treaty could not be sanctioned by any tribunal and, should the council uphold the decree, he would have to appeal to Cevallos again, thus accumulating the grievances and expenses of delay. He continued that Spanish professions of friendship could not fail to impress the U.S. government, particularly if they resulted in the reversal of unjust decisions such as the present one. He concluded that he could not advise the captain to appeal to the council but instead to the American government because the case involved the neutrality of the American flag and fidelity to treaty terms.

3. Not found.

§ From Sylvanus Bourne. *7 December 1805, Amsterdam.* "I had the honor to address you a few days past[1] since which no thing specially new or important has occurred in the scene of the war. Prussia's conduct still remains Enigmatical, & undiceded [*sic*]—very much will depend on the resolution of that Cabinete touching the affairs of the Continent, which causes us to Expect its definitive resolution with interest & anxiety. I am happy to find that the *major* part of the Vessells carried into England are released after examination which encourages me to hope that we may preserve peace with that Country & continue to enjoy the benefits of a neutrality which is daily becoming more precious to us."

RC (DNA: RG 59, CD, Amsterdam, vol. 1). 1 p.; docketed by Wagner.

1. See Bourne to JM, 3 Dec. 1805.

§ From John Dawson. *7 December 1805, Washington.* "I inclose a letter [not found] from Mr. Poinsett of South Carolina with whom I am well acquainted and believe him to be a young gentleman of much merit[1]—if you think proper to comply with his request you will be pleasd to forward your letter to me."

RC (DLC). 1 p.

1. Joel Roberts Poinsett (1779–1851) was born in Charleston, South Carolina, and educated in England and Scotland. Except for a visit to the United States in 1804–6, he spent the years from 1801 to 1809 traveling in Europe. In 1810 JM named him special agent to Chile and Río de la Plata where he encouraged movements for independence from Spain. In 1815 he returned to South Carolina and entered politics, serving in the state legislature in 1816–17 and 1818–19. He was a member of Congress from 1821 to 1827, after which he

was appointed minister to Mexico. He returned to South Carolina in 1830 and defended the union cause during the nullification controversy. In 1837 he was named secretary of war under Martin Van Buren. He returned to private life in South Carolina in 1841 (Bailey et al., *Biographical Directory of the South Carolina Senate*, 2:1287–88).

§ From William Lee. *7 December 1805, Bordeaux.* "We are led to suppose by the enclosed handbill [not found] and the general satisfaction that has prevailed in this City to day, that Austria has made overtures of peace.[1] Whether Russia is to be included or not, in the negotiations we have yet to learn. It is whispered that Russia Prussia & Sweden are to sustain the contest against France. This however wants confirmation, and the prevailing opinion appears to be, that the Continent will be at Peace this winter and England left to struggle alone. Koziusko and some other influential Poles who reside at Paris having been called near the Emperor has given rise to a conjecture that Poland is to be restored to its ancient state in order to form a barrier to the future inroads of Russia. The Moniteur you will receive with this will give you the position of the contending Armies up to the 23d. of November at which date the French had their head quarters at Brinn the Capital of Moravia.

"My last respects were of the 25th Ulto."

RC (DNA: RG 59, CD, Bordeaux, vol. 2). 2 pp.

1. After Napoleon's decisive defeat of Russia and Austria at Austerlitz on 2 Dec. 1805, Francis II began peace negotiations which led to the Treaty of Pressburg on 26 Dec. 1805. Under the terms of the treaty, Austria recognized Napoleon and his successor as kings of Italy, ceded all its Venetian, Tyrolean, and south German territory, agreed to recognize Bavaria and Würtemberg as independent kingdoms, and agreed to pay France forty million francs (Chandler, *Dictionary of the Napoleonic Wars*, 31–36, 348; de Clercq, *Recueil des traités de la France*, 2:145–51).

§ From Samuel Vernon Jr. *7 December 1805, Newport, Rhode Island.* "Subjoined you have a list of American Vessels insured by the Rhode Island Insurance Company established at this place, which have been captured by Some of the powers at war and in consequence thereof abandoned to Said Company.

No 1. Schooner Polly of Newport.	Owners, John Bigley & Charles Cozzens both of Sd. Newport. Master. Sd. Bigley of New Port Burthen of Vessel, about one hundred Tons.
Circumstances of the Capture.	On the 18th of June 1803 She Sailed from Newyork, bound On a Voyage to Jamaica & thence back to Newyork—With a Cargo of lumber and provisions Vessel & Cargo of the Value of about five thousand dollars; on the 13th day of July following on her outward passage lat. 20°.20 North. She was captured by a french Privateer, called the Two friends commanded by [1] Beson if his name be rightly recollected The master with his papers was taken and detained on board the privateer; the

mate & Crew put onboard a boat & compelled to leave the Schooner and provide for their Safety as they might. Fortunately they arrived Safe to land. Capt Bigley was put on Shore at Miaguiagua.[2] SW. part of Port Rico, being first Stripped of his papers and the property about him. The prize master and men put onboard the Schooner conducted her to Samana in the Island of Hispaniola, Vessel & Cargo, according to information were Sold there by order of the government and the proceeds deposited in the public Treasury to be paid over to the concern. The amount of these proceeds is not known, but report makes it a trifle compared to the Value of the property, What or whether any process was instituted against her by the Captors is not known or whether they had any commission. It is Supposed they had none. Owing to the difficulty & unfrequency of the communication it has not yet been in the Power of the concern to Obtain the proceeds.[3]

Brige! Orange of Newport	Owner. Thomas Dennis of Newport—Master Stephen A Wanton of ditto, Burthen of the Vessel about [4] Tons.
Circumstances of Capture &c.	On the 15h. day of June 1804 She Sailed from Newport bound on a Voyage to Jamaica & from thence back to Newport with a Cargo of dry & pickled fish &c. Valued at about Eight thousand dollars. On the [5] day of August 1804 She was captured by a french privateer called the [6] commanded by [7] and carried into Barricoa, and there disposed by the Captors but in what manner is not known.[8]
Schooner Sea Flower Newport	Owner John Clarke of Newport Master the Same John Clarke Burthen of the Vessel of about ninety three Tons.
Circumstances of the Capture &c.	On the 26th. day of December 1804 within one mile of the Shore of the Island of Cuba, & in Sight of the Moro Castle & bound to havanna, She was captured by a french privateer called the Napoleon, and commanded by [9] Master. Capt. Clarke petitioned the government at the havanna to have the property liberated, as being captured within that jurisdiction. Pending this petition to avoid delay & expence, Capt. Clarke made a compromise with the Captors, by which he agreed to pay them nine hundred dollars and they agreed to release the property. He paid the $900. & they executed the Release, and the prize master & french men quitted the Vessel, Clarke then informed the government of what had been done, produced the release & requested the Spanish guard onboard the Sea Flower might be withdrawn, The Spanish government demurred from day to

day on one pretence and another till at length one of
the Officers of the Privateer, presented a new petition
claiming the Prize anew. Thereupon the government
immediately decreed, that the property Should be delivered to the Captors, upon their giving bonds to abide
the decree of the french government at St. Domingo.
The agent of Clarke Offered, to take the property on
deposite in Court Twenty four thousand dollars to abide
the Decree at St. Domingo, this was refused and Bond
of the Captors was accepted for only Eighteen thousand
dollars and the only Security required to this Bond, was
A Mortgage of Some land in a distant part of the Island
of Cuba Whether any decree at St. Domingo has Since
been passed, we are not assertained, but from the best
information we presume a decree has been passed, The
information is contradictory One report States that the
Vessel was acquitted and the Cargo condemned, Another that both were condemned.

Schooner Ann & Harriot of Newport } Owners, Robert Stevens & Robert Rogers of Newport Master William Shearman of Newport Burthen of the Vessel about Ninety three Tons.

Circumstances of the capture &c } On the 17th. day of June 1805, She was captured by a french privateer called the Lucerne on her passage to Jamaica. Afterward on the ¹⁰ day of ¹¹ 1805 She was recaptured by an English Frigate of War called the Diana, and commanded by ¹² Molony and was Sent into, Jamaica, where Vessel & Cargo, were libelled & Sold for Salvage, Value of Vessel & Cargo about Ten Thousand dollars.[13]

Brigt. Mary of Newport } Owner, Thomas Dennis of Newport Master, John Dennis of Ditto Burthen of the Vessel about 100 Tons.

Circumstances of the capture &c } On the 8th day of April 1805 She Sailed from Newport for Jamaica, loaded with Cod fish provisions &c That the 26h. Same month She was captured by a french armed boat, whether, commission'd or not unknown. The Crew of the Brig, were forced into a boat, with Some provisions, and driven Off to Seek their Safety as they could. They got to one of the Bahama Islands. The master was afterwards put on shore at one of the Bahama Islands, The Brig & Cargo were carried to Barricoa, in the Island of Cuba, no process whatever was instituded [sic] against the property by the Captors, they there embezzled the Cargo & Sold the Vessel. The loss is about Ten Thousand dollars.[14]

"The Office has an interest in the Brig Rowena, Robinson Potter Master condemned in England in the course of the Summer past but the circumstances of that case are not here detailed, as other Offices who have a greater interest in the Same Vessel have already or will represent them.[15] The Vouchers in proof of the foregoing Statements will be forwarded if necessary With perfect confidence that these lawless depredations on our commerce will be properly felt & noticed by our government."

RC (DNA: RG 46, President's Messages, 9A–E3; Tr (DNA: RG 233, President's Messages, 9A–D1). RC 4 pp.; docketed by Wagner. Minor differences between the copies have not been noted.

1. Left blank in RC and Tr.
2. Mayagüez, Puerto Rico.
3. The Rhode Island Insurance Company paid John Troup, owner of the cargo, $4,214 (Williams, *French Assault on American Shipping*, 286).
4. Left blank in RC and Tr.
5. Left blank in RC and Tr.
6. Left blank in RC and Tr.
7. Left blank in RC and Tr.
8. The privateer was *La Voltiguese*, Captain Moisson. Captain Wanton and his crew "were robbed of everything, 'even to the clothes on their backs'" and the *Orange*, valued at $2,000, was said to be burned at Baracoa. The Rhode Island Insurance Company incurred a loss of $10,000 (ibid., 270).
9. Left blank in RC and Tr.
10. Left blank in RC and Tr.
11. Left blank in RC and Tr.
12. Left blank in RC and Tr.
13. Another report says the *Ann and Harriot* was captured on 8 May 1805. While attempting to escape the *Diana*, the prize crew ran the vessel on shore. Captain Maling of the *Diana* had most of the cargo thrown overboard and the ship refloated. Under the 1831 treaty between the United States and France, $2,965.50 in damages was awarded (ibid., 59–60).
14. Under the 1819 treaty between the United States and Spain, the Rhode Island Insurance Company was awarded $9,400 (ibid., 236).
15. For the *Rowena*, see Samuel Elam to JM, 11 Dec. 1805.

§ From Frederick Jacob Wichelhausen. *7 December 1805, Bremen.* "It is with much pleasure I embrace this opportunity, of testifying you my most hearty and obliging thanks, for the agreable present of 2 boxes peach brandy, you have been kind enough to transmit me, through my brother; I received the same with the Ship United States, Capt. Bounds from Baltimore[1] in the best condition, and found the quality most delicate. I am likewise under the highest obligation to you, for the kind and hospitable reception, you have been pleased to shew my brother, during his stay at your city. My brother in passing through Washington, considered it his duty to wait upon you, and to pay you his most dutiful respects. He by no means had the least idea to intrude upon your so valuable time, which he mentions you have been kind enough to sacrifice him frequently. Indeed those speaking testimonies of your kind and friendly sentiments towards me, contribute greatly to make me happy, and it will be my constant study to preserve for ever the present good opinion you so kindly entertain of me. Should opportunity offer, when it might be in my power, to be useful to you, I beg you to dispose of my services at all times, and I assure you it will give me much pleasure to be soon honoured with your commands."

RC (DLC). 2 pp.; marked "not official Duplicate" by Wichelhausen. Docketed by JM.

1. The *United States*, Captain Bounds, left Baltimore for Varel, Germany, on 31 July 1805 (*Baltimore Weekly Price Current*, 1 Aug. 1805).

§ From Frederick Jacob Wichelhausen. *7 December 1805, Bremen.* "I had the honor to write to you on the 28th Octr. and am since deprived of your further kind commands. The large bodies of troops of different powers which are now assembling in our neighbourhood occasion frequent applications to the Senate of Bremen, respecting the marching through or quartering in this city, which has always been refused by this Government from the principle, that the strict neutrality of this city, could not allow admittance or a free passage to troops which were engaged in war. However the foreign powers do not always look upon this in the same light; on the 23rd Ult: a prussian regiment of Infantry marched into this city and was billeted with the citizens, although the most solemn protestations were made on the part of the assembled Senate and Citizens, to the Duke of Brunswick, who rejected the same, saying, that the troops of a neutral power could on no account, injure the neutrality of Bremen. The other day a brigade of english riflemen passed through the city, against which strong remonstrances were made likewise, and the bar at the gates shut in consequence, which however was forced by the carpenters. On the 29th Ult: the prussians quite unexpectedly left the city again leaving about 100 men to watch the considerable corn magazines expected in the Weser for prussian account. The other day a brigade of british guards arrived near the city and wanted to be quartered in it; however the representations made to the Commander in chief, General Don, that the admittance of british troops in the city, would be highly injurious to our commerce and navigation, induced the General to withdraw his demand, insisting nevertheless earnestly to have his men quartered in its Suburbs, which, although it was also positively refused, was accordingly done, and the bar at the entrance likewise cut open. All these different troops keep a severe discipline and behave orderly and in a modest manner, and business continues with the same briskness and safety as before."

RC (DNA: RG 59, CD, Bremen, vol. 1). 2 pp.; marked "Duplicate"; in a clerk's hand, signed by Wichelhausen.

§ From Adam Goodlett.[1] *8 December 1805, Cane Run, Scott County, Kentucky.* "After ten years absence from Virginia, where your obliging attention often supported and encouraged me, I take the liberty to sollicit one last favour. My eldest son, who has practised medecine for some time in this state with considerable success, has been invited to the Indiana Territory: Mr. Mansfield Surveyor General informs, that immediately after the present session of Congress, a land office will be opened for that Territory: May I presume on your influence to procure the

Registry of that Office for me? Integrity and assiduity are all I have to recommend me. Declining years and attachment to my son as well as anxiety for my still large family induce me to sollicit you. Excuse the freedom I have taken."

RC (DLC). 1 p.

1. Adam Goodlett had taught in Virginia before moving to Kentucky. Goodlett's son, John Goodlett, appears not to have moved to Indiana, since he was practicing medicine at Bardstown, Kentucky, as late as 1817 (Garraty and Carnes, *American National Biography*, 10:591; *Acts passed at the First Session of the Twenty-fifth General Assembly, for the Commonwealth of Kentucky* . . . [Frankfort, Ky., 1817; Shaw and Shoemaker 41189], 62).

From Soliman Melimeni

SIR   WASHINGTON CITY December. the 9 1805

I take the liberty of Writing you these few lines for the trouble I have given, We have been here these ten days, and We have been very Well treated, and in ten days more our fas⟨t⟩ will be over, and my people will want Wine And I dont wish them to have aney, for fear they Should fight amongh one Another, For that Reason I wish if it is agreeable to you to Send me the money that you Spend every day for us. And I will purchase what ever we want, and as the Winter is coming on, And I dont wish too much Expence for the Sake of our Country. That is only What I think, But You may do as please.

N.B. I have not writing this letter without the Consent of Mr Davis.

SOLIMAN MALMAL⟨1⟩
Ambassador of the
Queen [*sic*] of Tun⟨is⟩

RC (DNA: RG 59, CD, Tunis, vol. 3). Signed in English and Arabic.

§ From William C. C. Claiborne. *9 December 1805, New Orleans.* "The enclosures Nos. 1. 2 & 3[1] will present you with copies of the Several Letters, which have passed between Govr. Folch and Myself, relative to the exaction of Duties at the Town of Mobile on American Vessels, and the late Military Movements in West Florida. The Enclosure No. 4 is a copy of a Letter from me to Mr. Brown the Collector of this Port, and that No. 5 of his answer.[2] Governor Folch proposes to put the American Trade on the Mobile, on the Same footing in which the Spanish trade is placed on the Mississippi; But inasmuch as Foreign Vessels with Negroes on Board, cannot be permitted to pass New Orleans, I fear the Governor will Seize upon this circumstance as a pretext for continuing at Mobile the present regulations. In this event, I solicit your instructions how to act. A continuance of the duty of 12 ₱ ct, amounts very nearly to a prohibition to our Citizens, of the Navigation of the Mobile Waters; and cannot but prove ruinous to our Settlements on the Tombicbee.

"Mr. Graham Supposes that at Pensacola and its Dependencies, there are about 800 Troops and at Mobile 150. He represents the Fort below *Pensacola*, called the Barances, which defends the entrance to the Bay as already Strong, and undergoing considerable improvements, but that the Fortifications near *the Town* are in a State of Ruin. The Fort at Mobile has lately been repaired, and in the opinion of Mr. Graham is a regular work, and capable of making a good defence; It is Supported by about 32 Pieces of Heavy Can'on. Mr. Graham States that on Dauphin Island near the mouth of Mobile, the Spaniards are about to erect a Block House, and from thence to Pensacola at convenient distances, they propose rearing Signal Posts to convey intelligence. Mr. Graham understood that more Troops were expected at Pensacola; report Said 2000, and that new Barracks were to be erected, but the truth of this, he much doubts.

"At Baton Rouge I presume there are about 200 Men. I shall Set out on Tomorrow for the County of Atakapas, on the Business which I communicated to you in my last Letter.³ It is not probable that I shall be absent from the City more than 15 or 16 days."

RC and enclosures (DNA: RG 59, TP, Orleans, vol. 7). 3 pp.; in a clerk's hand, signed by Claiborne; docketed by Wagner, with his note: "Proposal to Govr. Folch about opening the Mobille." For surviving enclosures, see nn. 1–2.

1. Enclosure No. 1 has not been found but presumably was a copy of Claiborne to Vicente Folch, 31 Oct. 1805, enclosed in Claiborne to JM, 31 Oct. 1805. Enclosure No. 2 (4 pp.; marked "Copy / translation" by Claiborne; docketed by Wagner) is Folch to Claiborne, 28 Nov. 1805, replying to the two points in the latter's 31 Oct. 1805 letter. Folch stated that he would be willing to suspend the duties paid by American ships passing Mobile, ad interim, pending royal approval, provided that Spanish ships passing to Baton Rouge should not be detained or charged duties; that the Treaty of San Lorenzo stated that Spain should receive most-favored-nation status, therefore vessels sailing from New Orleans to West Florida should receive the same drawbacks granted merchandise sailing to other foreign ports; that if the United States had a right to use of the waters of Mobile river and bay, Spain should have the same right to the Mississippi; that the treaty nowhere exempted U.S. ships from paying duties in Spanish ports; and that Claiborne's argument that international law gave the United States such a right was refuted by the fact that all ships passing through the Oresund paid duties to Denmark, and those passing through the Dardanelles paid duties to the Ottoman Empire. In reply to Claiborne's objection to Spanish troop movements, Folch stated that they had occurred in response to the disruptions of good order caused by the Kempers at Baton Rouge and by another disruption at Mobile caused by U.S. citizens from the Tombigbee River region; he reminded Claiborne that in 1804 a detachment of U.S. troops had arrived at New Orleans from Philadelphia, that another had come down the Mississippi bringing artillery, that another had "traversed the whole Indian Nation of Creeks to come to Fort Stoddart," and that in none of these instances had Folch objected to Claiborne, since they all occurred within U.S. sovereignty, and that Claiborne might follow his example and not inquire into movements occurring in territory under Spanish sovereignty. Enclosure No. 3 (4 pp.; in a clerk's hand, signed by Claiborne) is a copy of Claiborne to Folch, 9 Dec. 1805, stating that while he regretted that he and Folch interpreted international law differently, he was pleased to find that the situation might be resolved to their mutual satisfaction and that Folch was willing to put U.S. trade on the Mobile on the same footing as Spanish trade on the Mississippi; that Spanish vessels were never detained at New Orleans provided it was manifest that the cargo was destined for a Spanish port and not for New

Orleans; that this being the case, he presumed Folch would suspend the orders in effect at Mobile, adding that Folch would understand "that no foreign Vessel with negroes on board, will be permitted to pass the First Military Post on the Mississippi," but that this would not injure Spanish trade, since if the inhabitants of Baton Rouge wanted blacks, the Mississippi was not the route by which they would introduce them. Claiborne added that no distinction was made with regard to drawbacks between Spanish and any other foreign ports; that Congress had legislated that "no Drawback shall be allowed on Goods exported to the Territories of any foreign power adjoining those of the United States"; that since this was a general regulation, he believed it could not be used by Folch as justification for keeping the orders at Mobile in force; that he had assumed Folch had not objected to U.S. military movements because there were too few troops to excite alarm and because any explanation that might be desired "was long since given . . . unsolicited" to Casa Calvo; that he appreciated Folch's courtesy in explaining the movements; and that he trusted his desire for an amicable adjustment of any misunderstandings would be a prelude for "a long and honorable Peace" between their two countries.

2. Enclosure No. 4 (1 p.; docketed by Wagner) is a copy of Claiborne's 7 Dec. 1805 letter to William Brown, collector at New Orleans, asking first, if any Spanish vessel passing to or from Baton Rouge had been detained or required to pay duties at New Orleans, and second, if any drawbacks were granted on merchandise exported from the United States to the territory of any foreign power adjacent to U.S. territory. Enclosure No. 5 (1 p.; docketed by Wagner) is a copy of Brown to Claiborne, 7 Dec. 1805, stating that no such detention had occurred, but that ships with slaves on board would not be allowed past the first military post on the Mississippi even if bound for a Spanish port, and that no drawbacks of the type described could be granted.

3. See Claiborne to JM, 4 Dec. 1805.

From Thomas FitzSimons and Others

SIR   PHILADELPHIA 10th December 1805

Among the numerous Captures of American Vessels, lately made by British Cruizers the Circumstances attending four Vessels taken on their passage from Bourdeaux (three for New York the other for this place)[1] has particularly attracted the Attention of the Merchants & Insurance Companies of this place where the property has been principally Insured. Those Vessels carried Cargoes from the U. S. to Bourdeaux & were returning with Articles, the Manufacture or Growth of France, partly the proceeds of the Goods they Carried out & partly purchased with other funds. The Vessels & their Cargoes were libelled in the Vice Admiralty Court at Halifax & are held over for further proof.

By a letter received from the Proctor of the Claimants (Copy of which accompanies this)[2] it appears that the Kings Advocate advanced on the Trial principles new and Extraordinary, which was favorably received by the Judge who has called for proofs that has never been required on any former occasion.

Such proofs as has been usual, have actually been sent forward, but strong doubts exist whether the others called for if obtainable ought to be adduced. Wishing to act with due Circumspection in an Affair which may involve important Consequences It has been deemed advisable to submit the Case with such Observations as have occurred to us to the Department of State that We may benefit of any advice or opinion You may favour us with.

The proofs required by the Judge which to us appear exceptionable are

1st. Of what Colony or Country the Outward Cargo was the growth product or Manufacture.

2d. Under what Certificates were the same admitted to entry in the Ports of France and whether liable to foreign or reduced Duties.

3d. What are the french Laws on this subject, and what limitations are imposed on return Cargoes.

We Consider the 1st. as exceptionable in as much as it has not been heretofore required. It has been held under former decisions of the British Courts—that return Cargoes are not questionable on Account of the Outward One except the latter consisted of Articles Contraband of War. In the last order of the British King the exception is confined to the product of Articles Contraband of War. The embarrassment which the establishing this as a principle would Occasion is too obvious to require Explanation.

2nd. Under what Certificate were the same admitted to entry in the ports of France and whether liable to foreign or reduced duties.

To this besides the objection already stated, it seems utterly irreconcilable to the principles of Justice; that the Claimants should be called upon either to prove a negative or furnish a Cause of Condemnation of their property.

It was suggested by the Judge in his reasoning that the permission of importing into France the produce of her Colonys by neutrals, while those of the British Dominions were excluded was of itself—a breach of Neutrality—and if on reduced duties—that would be an additional reason.

The fact (as respects those ships) is that they Carried from the United States Cargoes taken on freight from various people and Consisting of Articles the produce of the U. S. and of the French and Spanish Colonies. The Cargoes with which they were returning are not precisely the proceeds of the outward ones nor all belonging to the same persons it is therefore imposing upon the Owners of the present one a most unreasonable task & has this still further disadvantage—that if those proofs are furnished in Cases in which they are attainable—In every instance in which that could not be done it may be made a ground for Condemnation—besides that it would be used for a precedent on all future occasions.

To the third, there is no other Objection, but that it puts upon the Claimant a proof which if material ought to be adduced by the Captors; if as they contend the Laws of France which provides for neutral Commerce is a ground of Condemnation, the proof of the existence of such Law in reason rests with the Captors.

As the French Laws are explained to us, they provide against the introduction into that Kingdom of any Goods or Merchandize the Manufacture or Growth of any of the Dominions of Britain. And it is therefore required that all Goods carried there should be accompanied with Certificates shewing of what Country they are the Manufacture or Growth—and such Certificates are to be verified by the Commercial Agent of France at the Port of their shipment or his Deputy. These are called Certificates of Origin and are indispensable.

With respect to the reduced duties We understand that there has existed in France (many Years previous to the Revolution) a regulation, which provided that the Exporters of Goods from her Colonies, by paying certain duties at the place of Export would be allowed an Abatement on the duties, to which they would otherwise be liable on their introduction into France. When that Law was decreed—French subjects *only* could export the products of her Colonies to the Mother Country Since the Revolution the like provision has been extended to all persons exporting those products but We are informed, that it is embarrassed with so many provisions & difficulties, that the Abatement in France is seldom Claimed & much seldomer obtained. Some imperfect notices extracted from Letters found on board those Ships has probably suggested this inquiry and not any certain Knowledge of the Law or its effect on the Goods in question.

To the latter part of the 3d. proof required—it can be established that no Condition is exacted from the Exporters of Goods from France to any neutral Country.

In the present state of our Commerce the principles to which We have referred cannot be viewed by the Merchants & Underwriters of this City without extreme Anxiety. Relying on the decisions which formerly took place in the British Courts the Merchants of this Country have risked property to an immense Amount much of which is now at hazard & depending on the establishment of the principles which are the subject of this Communication.

The time limited for exhibiting our proofs at Halifax expires on the 8th. february. If you shall deem it necessary to favour us with any Communication on the subject it may be in time & will be used in such way as you may advise. We are with Respect sir Yr Mo hble servts

THOS. FITZSIMONS
Presidt Delaware I Co of Philada
JAMES S COX, Prest.
Ins Co. *Pennsa*
JOSEPH BALL, President
Union Insure. Co. of Philada.
CHAS. PETTIT, Prest. of the Inse.
Co. of N America

RC (DNA: RG 46, President's Messages, 9A–E3; Tr (DNA: RG 233, President's Messages, 9A–D1). RC in a clerk's hand, except for FitzSimon's complimentary close and signature; signed also by Cox, Ball, and Pettit; docketed by Wagner, with his note: "British." Minor differences between the copies have not been noted.

    1. FitzSimons probably referred to the *Eugenia*, the *Enterprise*, Thompson, and the *Jefferson*, Crocker, all bound from Bordeaux to New York, and to the *Zulima*, bound from Bordeaux to Philadelphia. The *Hamilton*, Masterton, bound from Bordeaux to New York, was also captured and sent into Halifax (Boston *Democrat*, 26 Oct. 1805; *ASP, Foreign Relations*, 2:765–66). See also James Stewart to John Black, 8 Nov. 1805, ibid., 770. For the *Eugenia*, see JM to Nathaniel Lawrence and John Patrick, 6 Nov. 1805, and nn. 2–3.

    2. Enclosure not found.

Estimate for the Service of the Year 1806

DEPARTMENT OF STATE December 10th. 1805

Foreign Intercourse.

Salaries of three Ministers viz: to London, Paris and Madrid @ $9000 is	$27.000	
Ditto for their three Secretaries @ 1350 ea.	4.050	
Their Contingent expences other than personal	2.000	
Extra expense of the Mission to Madrid.	6.000	
Contingencies	26.950	$66.000
Deficiency of former appropriation to carry into effect the Convention with France of April		6.000

Barbary Intercourse.

Salary allowed to the Consul at Algiers	$4.000	
Do. to those at Morocco, Tunis & Tripoli @ 2000 ea	6.000	
Their expences other than personal	3.500	
For difference between the cost of the articles in which the annuity to algiers is payable and the price at which they are received, making a difference between the permanent appropriations & the annual charges of	36.000	
Contingent expense of Intercourse with Barbary not to be foreseen	50.000	$99.500

Seamen.

For the relief & protection of distressed Seamen		5.000

Captures.

Salary of an Agent at Paris to prosecute claims in relation to captures	$2,000	
Do. one at Madrid $2000. Do. one at London $2000	$4.000	$6.000

Carried forward   Dols. 182.500
Estimate continued, amot. brot. forward $182,500.

Salaries of the Dept. of State.

Of the Secretary of State	$5,000	
Of his Clerks	5,900	
Of additional Clerk hire in the year 1806, and for a deficiency in the year 1805	1.200	
Of his Messenger	410	$12,560 [sic]

Contingent expences of the Dept. of State

For printing and distributing 10,000 copies of the laws of the first Session, ninth Congress	$4.250
For printing the laws in Newspapers	4.000
Fire and Candles	200
Newspapers for the Office, & public Agents abroad	150
Mediterranean passports, Printing and Parchment	1,350
Blank patents, personal papers Circulars, &ca	1.000
Purchasing Books	400
Stationary	600
Miscellaneous	500
For Special messengers charged with dispatches	2,000

$14,450

$209.510

JAMES MADISON.

Letterbook copy (DNA: RG 59, DL, vol. 15).

§ To Jacob Ridgway. *10 December 1805, Department of State.* "I have received your letter of the 9th. September. It was the meaning of my letter to which it refers, not in any event to incur a further expence in detaining the Ship Mac, and that if the owner, or his representative would not reimburse the expence before incurred, to suffer him to take her without such reimbursement."

Letterbook copy (DNA: RG 59, IC, vol. 1). 1 p.

§ From William Hull. *10 December 1805, Washington.* "Governor Hull wishes to enquire of the Secretary ⟨of⟩ State, whether he received his letter inclosing a Copy of the proclamation,¹ he was directed to issue, and whether for the reasons stated in his Letter the President, thought it expedient, to authorize the Governor, or any other Officer, to grant permissions to cut such quantities of pine timber as was absolutely necessary, under the peculiar circumstances of the People of Detroit."²

RC (DNA: RG 59, TP, Michigan, vol. 1). 1 p.; docketed by Wagner. A note by Jefferson interlined above the address and dateline reads: "It was our joint opinion that altho' it would not do to lay open the public timber to all persons indiscriminately, yet that the calamity which happened at Detroit rendered it proper that the public should permit the poorer sufferers to get timber from their lands, and that it should be left to the discretion of Govr. Hull to grant the special licences. Th: J."

    1. For the proclamation, see Hull to JM, 11 Sept. 1805, and n. 2.
    2. On 13 Dec. 1805 JM replied: "In answer to your note of the 10th. inst. I have the honor to observe, that altho' it is not expedient to lay open the public timber to the Inhabitants of Detroit indiscriminately, nevertheless the President leaves it to your discretion to grant special licenses to the poorer sufferers by the conflagration" (DNA: RG 59, DL, vol. 15; 1 p.).

§ From Tobias Lear. *10 December 1805, Algiers.* "I have this day drawn on you a sett of Exchange for twelve thousand Dollars, at thirty days sight, to the Order of Messrs. Degen, Purviance and Co. being for Value received, on Account of the Department of State, for the Service of the United States of America in their Barbary Affairs, which please to honor Accordingly."

RC (DNA: RG 59, CD, Algiers, vol. 7, pt. 2); letterbook copy and letterbook copy of the 10 Dec. 1805 bill of exchange (owned by Stephen Decatur, Garden City, N.Y., 1961). RC 1 p.; in a clerk's hand, signed by Lear; docketed by Wagner, with his note: "Accepted 16 April 1806 Payable at the Department of State."

§ From Francisco de Miranda. *"Stelle's Hotel Tuesday December the 10th."* "Genl. Miranda presents his respectful Compliments to Mr. Madison—is very sorry that the Note he sent to him dated yesterday, monday the 9th., did not come to him until this day after 2 oC:; which circumstance has prevented him from waiting upon Mr. Madison at the hour he had the goodness to appoint for this day: but he will do himself the honour to wait on him tomorrow at 2 o'C:, in hopes of finding him at his Office, and Amending the Retard produced by this mistake."

RC (DLC). 1 p. Year not indicated; assigned to 1805 based on Rufus King to JM, 25 Nov. 1805, and Benjamin Rush to JM, 3 Dec. 1805.

From Samuel Elam

Sir.   Newport, R.I. December 11th. 1805.

The Newport Insurance Company, deem it their duty to exhibit to the Government, a statement of the losses they have sustained, during the present War, by the depredations of the belligerent powers. Compared with its limited capital & enterprize, it is presumed there are few offices in the United States that have suffered more.

From the instances mentioned in the sequel, it may be collected that since the 23d. day July 1804, the aggregate of loss to the Merchants and the Country by lawless captures exceeds Fifty seven thousand dollars, and that the part thereof that falls to the share of this Company exceeds Thirty thousand Dollars. The Company conceive themselves to be justified in stating that these losses arose from contingencies which no commercial intelligence could foresee, & upon which no commercial prudence was bound to calculate.

The losses they have to enumerate were sustained in the course of a legal *accustomed* & *honestly neutral* Commerce, carried on by *native* American Citizens, with American Capitals, in *american* bottoms.

These losses may be arranged under two Heads.

1st. Captures in the West Indies by piratical Privateers with real or pretended French Commissions. The property plundered by these Privateers has been uniformly taken into the ports of the Island of Cuba; and there with the connivance or under the protection of the Spanish Government, without any form of trial or pretence for legal condemnation has been sold and distributed.

2d: Captures in the British Channel by British armed Vessels in consequence of the new principle lately announced by the Courts of Admiralty: viz: that in case a Vessel has brought goods from the Colony of a Belligerent altho' she brings them to the U. States, and the owners there unlade them, pay the importation duties, finish the concerns of the old Voyage, & select & undertake another, with the same Vessel & goods; it shall not be deemed evidence of a new Voyage, but on the contrary conclusive evidence of a continued & uninterrupted Voyage from the Colony of the Belligerent.

Under the first head have occurred the following cases.

No. 1. Brig Orange,[1] S. A. Wanton Master, Thomas Dennis of Newport Rhode Island, Merchant Owner, laden with Fish & Provisions, bound from Newport to Jamaica. Vessel & Cargo valued at $10,000 Dollars. Insured by the Newport Insurance Company $4,000 Dols. on Cargo.

Circumstances ⎱
of Capture &c. ⎰ The Orange was taken on the 21st. July 1804, by the French Privateer Valtegeuse Capt. Moisson, about Six leagues from the

Island of St. Domingo. The Officers & men were stript of everything even to the Cloaths on their backs, and left entirely destitute. The property was taken to *Barracoa*, in the Island of Cuba. No form of Trial or Condemnation was had. The Cargo was distributed by the Captors in their own way and the vessel it is *believed burnt.*

No. 2—Brig Sally[2]—Stephen Chase Master, Seth Hoard owner, bound from Jamaica to the U. States, vessel & Cargo estimated at 4000 Dollars. Insured by the Newport Insurance Company 2700 Dollars.

Circumstances of Capture &C. } The Captain in his Protest declares that after being detained by an Embargo at Falmouth in Jamaica, he sailed from thence for Montego Bay on the 28th. of April 1805. That he had been out about four hours when he was captured by a *Feluca*, within a mile of the Shore. The Captain of the Feluca informed Capt. Chace he was a good prize, and that he had orders to *capture all American Vessels* on the coast of Jamaica. The Sally was taken to cape *Coure* in the Island of Cuba—no condemnation or form of trial was had and Capt. Chace, and three out of Six of his Men, after being stript of their Cloaths were ordered to take to their *boat.* They did so, and fortunately arrived at Montego Bay, on the 29th. of the same Month.

No. 3 Schooner American Lady, Enoch Tobey Master, owned by Bowen & Ennis of Newport Merchants & others, Cargo Rum &C bound from Jamaica to the U. States, value of Vessel & Cargo $4000 Dols. Insured by the Newport Insurance Company $2950 Dollars.

Circumstances of Capture &c. } This Vessel sailed on the 16th: Feby. 1805 from Morant Bay, South side of Jamaica bound for Camden State of North Carolina. On the 20th. of the same Month, being about five leagues distant from the Isle of Pines, she was brought to by a small Privateer under French Colours, mounting one Swivel Gun and manned with about fifteen men principally *Spaniards.* The Vessel was taken possession of carried to the Isle of Pines, the captain and men plundered, and abused and left on shore at this desert Island, without any means of subsistence except a dozen of Biscuit and a Bottle of Rum. They would have perished there had it not been for the compassion of a Spaniard the only Inhabitant of the Island. The Captain & Crew remained at this place until another French Privateer arrived there: when they were taken at the request of Capt. Toby near Savannah La Mar on the South side of Cuba. From whence they travelled to the *Havana.* The Captain noted his protest with the American Consul, who attended him to the Governor. Captain Tobey explained to the Governor the ill treatment he had encountered, demanded a restoration of his Vessel which was *now within the Governors jurisdiction*, and the release of Moses Henly a free black one of his Crew, who had left a wife & family in the United States, and who was in the greatest distress as the Captors were

648

determined to sell him a Slave for life. The Governor made little or no reply to Capt. Tobey's remonstrances or petitions. After waiting some time, finding himself unable to obtain redress he was compelled to abandon the property, and returned to the United States.

No. 4. Schooner Ann & Harriet, Wm. Shearman Master. Vessel & Cargo valued at $10,400 Dols. Vessel owned by Robert Rogers & Robert Stevens, and the Cargo by John Mein all of Newport Merchants—bound from the U. States to Jamaica. 5000 Dollars was insured by the Newport Insurance Compy.

Circumstances of Capture &c. } This Vessel was captured on the 8th. of May last by a French Privateer off Cape Marie in the Island of Cuba and was ordered for St. Jago de Cuba, but upon being chased by the English Ship of War Diana, she was run on shore by the *Prize Master.* After considerable exertions & throwing overboard a great part of her Cargo she was got off by the *English Recaptors,* and taken by them to Kingston Jamaica, where the Vessel and the remainder of her Cargo were sold under the process of the Court of Vice-Admiralty there. The Salvage of one eighth which was awarded the Recaptors, the destruction of part of the Cargo and the disadvantages under which the resedue was sold render this little less than a total loss.[3]

These are the principal losses sustained by this Company arising from the piratical depredations of Privateers in the *West Indies.* In all these cases abandonments have been made to, and the sums insured paid by this Company.

Under the second head of loss, the two following important cases have occurred.

No. 1. The Brig Rowena. Robinson Potter Master.

Voyage from Newport to Antwerp. Vessel & Cargo valued at $26,735 Dollars owned by Christopher Grant Champlin, Esqr. for himself in his own right and as administrator of Christopher Champlin Esq decd. Sum insured by the Newport Inse. Cy. $15,000.

Circumstances of Capture—Grounds of Condemnation &c. } The owners of the Rowena had imported in her from Martinique a Cargo of *Sugar & Coffee.* This Cargo was legally landed & the duties payable to the United States secured. The Owners finding no advantageous domestic market for their Coffee & Sugar, made general enquiries into the State of the European Market. They began to contemplate generally an exportation but whether that exportation would be to Copenhagen, Amsterdam or Antwerp or whether it was to be totally abandoned was a matter in deliberation & to be determined by the result of their enquiries. After a delay of some weeks it was ultimately decided to send the Sugar & Coffee to *Antwerp.* For this purpose a new Voyage was

concerted; a new crew hired, a quantity of Staves the growth of our Country (and so expressly & minutely certified by the Brigs papers) was added
to the original Cargo. On the 6th. of May last the Rowena sailed from
Newport, and on the 16th. of June was captured Off Ostend by His Britannic Majestys hired armed Cutter the Griffin commanded by Lieut. Forbes.
The alleged pretence of capture was a suspicion that the Rowena intended
to violate the Blockade of Ostend. This pretence however, totally unsupported by facts or by appearances was speedily abandoned; and the sole
question at the trial in the Court of Admiralty was, whether the Voyage
was to be treated upon the footing of one continued Voyage from Martinique to Antwerp i.e. from the Colony of the *Enemy* to the Mother Country. The Judge Sir Wm. Scott without entering into any discussion of the
above question or detailing at all the particular facts of this case referred to
his decision in a case immediately pending viz: The Enoch, Doane Master,[4]
and declared as he did not see sufficient reasons to distinguish this from
the case of the Enoch, it must meet the same fate. The case of the Enoch is
without doubt in the possession of Government, and altho', therefore
comment is unnecessary and may be even deemed improper, yet we cannot
forbear to remark that the case of the Enoch is distinguishable from that of
the Rowena in a very important particular. The Enoch as Sir Wm. Scott
states was under a Charter party before she quitted Boston to perform the
Voyage she did perform. Addmitting a moment for the purposes of argument (what can never be admitted in fact without the prostration of Neutral rights and the destruction of the Commerce of the Country) that the
newly announced principle of Great Britain *is* one deducible from the law
of Nations and that its *application* was correct in the case of the Enoch, it by
no means follows that its application was likewise correct in the case of the
Rowena. There was no Charter party in the latter case. There was nothing
indicating a primary & preconceived intention viz: at the outset to go to
Europe with the Cargo procured in the West Indies. There existed nothing of which the case was first to be cleared for the claimants to be entitled
to the benefit of the rules of evidence as laid down by the British Courts.
There was nothing to speak in the language of those Courts to *shift the
burden of proof.* But waving any observations on a difference so obvious, it
does seem somewhat extraordinary that the sentence in the case of the
Rowena should have been in reality one of *more* severity, than the sentence
in the *preceding* case. In that the property put on board at Boston was favorably considered & restored. In the case of the Rowena, staves of the growth
of the U: States, and put on board at Newport were not restored, but included in the undistinguishing clause of condemnation, which in its style
of absurd formality, pronounces the Ship & Cargo to have belonged at the
time of the Capture & seizure thereof to the Enemies of the Crown of
Great Britain, and as such or otherwise liable to confiscation.

Besides the total loss the company have paid 556 Dols. their proportion of 876 Dollars being the law Costs attending the Claim.

No. 2. Ship Hope—Robert Robinson Master, Owners George Champlin Esqr.—Christopher Grant Champlin Esqr. as administrator of Christopher Champlin Esqr. *and the Master.* Voyage from Newport to Amsterdam. Value of Ship & Cargo 108,631 Dollars insured by the Newport Insurance Company $15,000 Dols.

Circumstances
of the Case, Capture &c } The Voyage in which this Ship was engaged previous to the one in which she was captured was from Newport to Batavia. She sailed from Newport in Feby. 1804, and arrived at *Batavia* in the following May—Owing to the scarcity of produce and the number of Ships endeavoring to procure it: After selling a small quantity of Iron which made a part of his Cargo the Capt. proceeded with his Ship & Specie to Manilla. He there purchased a Cargo of Sugar & Indigo & sailed about the 20th. of Novr. 1804, for Newport where he arrived on the 12th. of May 1805. The Cargo was landed & delivered and the importation duties secured to be paid. After a lapse of about Six weeks the Owners not finding a sufficiently favorable Market at home, concluded on a *new* Voyage to Amsterdam for the purpose of re-exporting their Sugar & Indigo. The Ship was consequently partially repaired, a *new* crew hired, and the Sugar & Indigo taken from *Warehouses* & re-shipt. This Ship sailed for Amsterdam on the 30th. of June, and was captured by his Britannic Majesty's hired armed Cutter Swan Lieut. Cameron & brought into Yarmouth, where in consequence of the recess of the Admiralty Court she was detained until the 12th. of Septr. 1805, when upon trial the Ship & Cargo was *restored* but without Costs or Damages. The condemnation was pressed on the part of the Captors, on the ground of its being a Cargo taken in at an Enemy's Colony, and after touching at America having been brought on to the Enemy's Country in Europe, without breaking the *continuity* of the Voyage by any *Act done.* And in respect to this question, the Judge declared there was *no evidence* that the *continuity* of the Voyage was interrupted. The Cargo of the Hope was purchased in Manila in time of profound peace between England & Spain. The Ship sailed from Manila three weeks before the Declaration of War by Spain against G. Britain which took place the 14th. Decr. 1804, and about Seven weeks before Reprizals on the part of Great Britain. Yet still it was urged by the Captors that the Cargo was purchased in *contemplation* of war, and the Judge agreed that if that had been proved it would have operated exactly the same effect as if actual Hostilities had taken place. But he said as no proof appeared, and the fact being that War did not commence till after the Vessel sailed, he thought it unlikely that Americans would speculate upon the Subject. But supposing says he that it was an *importation* from *Manila* to Amsterdam, *at this*

period it would have been an importation *perfectly legal:* and all transactions in America may be laid out of the question. Yet for being engaged in a Voyage perfectly legal, after having had that Voyage ruined by an illegal capture, the owners of the Hope were denied indemnity for damages sustained, and compelled to pay Costs, Expences & law Charges to the amount of £260 Sterling about £40, of which were exactions for light money & Ramsgate and Dover Harbour Dues.

Such is the Statement which this Company at the present juncture has to make to the Government of the United States. The various protests, decrees and other documentary evidence conformatory of this Statement, shall be forwarded when deemed necessary by Government.

The Newport Insurance Company have a hope and confidence, that the general government, whose right it is to regulate, would feel it their duty to protect commerce—that means will be found in the wisdom & energy of government to procure *speedy compensation* to the sufferers and redress to the Nation for its *violated* rights and dignity. With sentiments of high respect I remain, on behalf of said Company, your obedt. Servt.

(Signed) SAMUEL ELAM
President.

Tr (DNA: RG 233, President's Messages, 9A–D1).

1. For the *Orange*, see Samuel Vernon Jr. to JM, 7 Dec. 1805, and n. 8.

2. In the report of captured vessels enclosed in his 1 July 1805 letter to JM, Josiah Blakeley said that the captain of the *Sally* was John Chase, that the cargo was rum, and that the brig was captured by the privateer *Jalousie*, Captain Camile, on 25 Apr. 1805.

3. For the *Ann and Harriot*, see Samuel Vernon Jr. to JM, 7 Dec. 1805, and n. 13.

4. For the *Enoch* decision, see George Joy to JM, 26 July 1805, and n. 3.

From James Monroe

No. *38*.
Copy.
SIR   CHELTENHAM Dec. 11. 1805.

The delicate state of health which my family has enjoyed of late, attributable as is supposed in a great measure to the atmosphere of London induced me to come here last week. A letter from Lord Mulgrave, which I received just before I left town, having revived the expectation that I should hear from him on the subject of my former ones; I thought it proper to apprize him of my proposed absence, as that it would be short; that Mr. Purviance would remain behind to receive and forward me his letters, and that I would repair to London to wait on him whenever it might be necessary.

I informed him also that I had postponed my departure for the U. States 'till Feby. to give full time for the arrangement of the affairs depending between our governments without interfering with his other engagements.[1] It is my intention to visit London occasionally and to call on his Lordship when I do, to see if it is possible to accomplish that interesting object before I leave the country. Having done every thing in my power to place our concerns with this government on a satisfactory and secure footing, since the trust was reposed in me, I shall Continue to make the same exertions while I am charged with it.

By late acccounts from the continent it appears that the French have entered Vienna almost without opposition, the Austrian and Russian armies having left it open to them. It was a while reported and believed that the Emperor of Austria had made a separate peace the conditions of which had been dictated to him by his adversary in the spirit of conquest; but this is now contradicted and disbelieved. The Emperor it seems plays a bolder game and is willing to hazard all, rather than make the sacrifices which it is supposed were insisted on. Thus the campaign seems to be hastening t⟨o⟩ its crisis, which will unfold the policy of some movements in the field and Cabinet which may not have been heretofore well understood. It will soon be seen whether the Emperor of France has been drawn on without system⟨,⟩ by the brilliancy of his success against Gen. Mack, to hazard more than an able and prudent Commander ought to have done; or having in view the accomplishment of a vast object, his movements have been combined with those of Gen. Massena in Italy, were judicious and conformable to a plan wisely laid down in the commencement. It will soon be seen whether Prussia who cannot be an indifferent spectator and has much in her power, intend⟨s⟩ to act a part in the adventure, and performs it well, or governed by circumstanc⟨es⟩ makes and breaks her resolutions as they change, and finally becomes a vict⟨im⟩ to unsteady and feeble councils. Whatever may have been the motive of the Emperor of France to take his present position it is certainly a daring and hazardous one. It gives in plain terms the defiance to Europe, and if Prussia takes part against him he may be considered as fairly pitted against Europe, for the powers that are on his side are not volunteers in the cause. If he experiences a serious reverse of fortune they will I think quickly fall off. He must either succeed, that is make at least a good and safe retreat in case of necessity, or he is utterly undone. It remains to be seen, whether in case he succeeds, by completely vanquishing the armies opposed to him, he will be able to make a prudent use of his victories for the purpose of consolidating and securing his own power, and of course whether his victories are to prove of any solid and permanent advantage to him. It may perhaps require greater talents in the present State of the world, in respect to that object, to turn such victories to the best account, than at the head of the veteran armies of France to gain them.

The situation of the U. States in respect to all these powers is in every view a very favorable one. So circumstanced are they respectively that while we have the means of doing each irreparable injury, all are interested in preserving the relations of peace and frien[d]ship with us, and none have it in their power to do us comparatively equal harm. As things now stand each of the parties forms a complete counterpoise to the other, in a way best adapted to its own Safety, and to our interest. Victorious by land France has scarcely a ship at sea and is therefore interested in the prosperity of our commerce. Victorious at sea G. Britain finds herself compelled to Concentrate her force so much in this quarter, with a view to her own security, that she would not only be unable to annoy us essentially in case of war, but even to protect her commerce and possessions elsewhere which would be exposed to our attacks. As to Spain, she ought not perhaps to be considered as a party to this controversy. If she were asked in which scale her interest lay, which party she wished to prevail, her friends or her enemies, she would most probably be at a loss to decide. I think it must be her interest that neither should succeed but that the scales should stand suspended as they now are. If her enemies succeeded completely she would be undone; and the same thing would happen if her friends did. Thus it appears that from none of these powers, have we any serious danger or injury to apprehend in the present state of affairs; nor from what I can see is it likely that we soon shall have. While the powers of Europe are contending against each other, none of them can venture to break with us, in consideration of such motives, as the just pretentions and claims of our government may furnish; and by many causes they seemed to be destined to remain in that state some years longer, or at least in one of great jealousy and rivalry of interests, which may produce the same effect.

I have just received your letter of Sep. 20. respecting the Ship Huntress, which has been given up to Gen: Lyman, as I understand, by the order of the Admiralty. The cargo, consisting in provisions having been much injured by the detention, was at his suggestion, and by my direction to have been lately disposed of. I shall communicate with him on the subject and transmit you shortly a correct account of the business. I am, Sir, with great respect and esteem, Your very obedient Servant.

JAS. MONROE

RC and enclosure (DNA: RG 59, DD, Great Britain, vol. 12); letterbook copy (DLC: Monroe Papers); Tr (DNA: RG 46, President's Messages, 10B–B1). RC in a clerk's hand, signed by Monroe; docketed by Wagner. Words and parts of words in angle brackets in the RC have been supplied from the letterbook copy. Minor differences between the copies have not been noted. For enclosure, see n. 1.

1. The enclosure (1 p.; docketed by Wagner) is a copy of Monroe to Lord Mulgrave, 29 Nov. 1805, conveying the information in this paragraph and adding John Henry Purviance's address in London.

From Peder Pedersen

   The Legislature of the United States having again assembled, and the first Session of the Ninth Congress being now opened, I consider it my duty to avail myself of the earliest opportunity for again representing to your attention the case of the Danish Brig Henrick,[1] and to request your interference for obtaining a speedy and favorable decision of same; the Documents, submitted to your consideration, and deposited with you— have sufficiently proved the injury done on that occasion to the Kings subjects by commissioned officers of the United States, and consequently also the equity of the demand for a satisfactory compensation which by order of my Government has been presented to you; yet, as it appears, that in a debate which in the last Session of Congress took place,[2] on the merits of this case, a doubt was expressed of Mr. Humphreys's being a Danish Subject and Citizen at the time when the purchase of the Brig Henrick by his order was effected, and as such a circumstance materially would have affected the merit of the case, the concerned lost no time in procuring a Certificate of Mr. Humphreys's Citizenship, which Certificate, issued and signed by the first Magistrate of the City of Altona, I beg leave here to enclose with an annexed translation.[3] For the authenticity of said Certificate I do not hesitate to pledge myself; From its contents it will appear, that Mr. Humphreys became a Danish Citizen in the year 1796. From the other Documents it has appeared that the purchase of the Brig Henrick for his account did not take place before some time in the year 1799, consequently about 3 years after he had obtained the rigths of citizenship; having thus furnished ample Testimony on the only head where, during nearly 6 years in which this case has been under the consideration of Government, proofs had appeared to be wanting, I shall now recommend the decision of this affair to the justice of the Government of the United States. I shall hope that tho' the injury done to the Kings Subjects be great, and tho' the relief due to them has long been withold, it at last will be granted in such a manner as shall be satisfactory to them, and worthy of a Nation justly jealous of her own neutral rigths, and consequently it is expected, will be no less scrupulous in redressing wrongs committed under her authority, towards other Neutrals; I shall hope, Sir, that the Issue of this affair, far from interrupting the friendly intercourse which hidhertho' so happily has existed between the two Nations, rather will serve to increase Same, and justify the friendly disposition which in many instances His Majesty has manifested towards the United States. I have the Honor to be with great Respect Sir, Your most obedient humble Servant

                                        PR: PEDERSEN

RC (DNA: RG 59, NFL, Denmark, vol. 1); Tr (Danish National Archives). Minor differences between the copies have not been noted.

1. For previous correspondence on the *Hendrick*, see *PJM-SS*, 4:312 and n. 1, 318, 327 n. 1, 337–38 and nn., 339–40, 383, 384 n. 1, 5:145, 6:245 and n. 1, 7:226 and n. 1, 8:277 and n., 464 and nn. 2–3, 475.

2. On 5 Feb. 1805 Jefferson submitted to Congress several documents concerning the case of the *Hendrick*, which were referred to the committee on claims. On 20 Feb. 1805 the committee returned its report and referred the case to the Committee of the Whole House for discussion (*ASP, Foreign Relations*, 2:609–12; *Annals of Congress*, 8th Cong., 2d sess., 1202–3.

3. The enclosure has not been found, but at the bottom of this letter's first page, a note by Wagner, countersigned by Richard Söderström, reads: "April 1806 Recd the certificate above mentioned." For earlier references to John Humphreys's Danish citizenship, see *ASP, Foreign Relations*, 2:609–10.

From Willink and Van Staphorsts

Sir!   Amsterdam 12. December 1805.

We have the honor to acknowledge your esteemed favor of 22. April last[1] forwarded to us by His Excellency James Bowdoin Esqe: which directs us to hold at His Excellency's disposal the Sum of $9000. as his outfit, an equal Sum as His Salary as Minister plenipotentiary of the U.S. at Madrid, together with the contingencies of the legation, the reimbursements to Consuls and at the termination of His mission a quarter's Salary. We shall of course duly attend to these directions, honoring Mr Bowdoin's drafts and carrying our payments to the department of State.

We further observe that G. W. Erving Esqr Secretary to the Legation and provisionally and eventually Chargé des Affaires is authorised to value on us for his Salary in the former capacity at the rate of $1350. one quarter's Salary as outfit and the Same on returning; that he is authorised to draw in the latter Capacity whilst he holds the Same at the rate of $4.500 ⅌ annum; to all which we shall equally attend placing the Sums to the debit of the Department of State. We have the honor to be Sir Yr. mo Obed Serts

WILHEM VAN WILLINK
N. & J. & R. VAN STAPHORST

RC (DNA: RG 59, Letters Received from Bankers). Docketed by Wagner.

1. *PJM-SS*, 9:280.

§ From Daniel Elliot. *12 December 1805, Machias.* "You will be pleased to lay the Inclosed before His Excellency the President."[1]

RC and enclosure (DNA: RG 59, LAR, 1801–9, filed under "Elliott"). RC 1 p. For enclosure, see n. 1.

1. The enclosure (1 p.; docketed by Jefferson as received 4 Jan. [1806]) is Elliot to Jefferson, 12 Dec. 1805, covering letters of recommendation for him (not found), and asking to be appointed collector at Machias, Massachusetts.

§ From Albert Gallatin. *12 December 1805, Treasury Department.* "I have the honor to enclose an extract of a letter from James Brown Esqr. the Agent of the United States at New Orleans in relation to Land Claims.[1] As the Intendant and other Spanish Officers may, in consequence of the late orders, be expected to leave the Territory in a very short time, permit me to suggest the propriety of giving to Govr. Claiborne positive instructions, at all events, to obtain possession of the title papers and other documents which of right pertain to Louisiana."[2]

RC and enclosure (DLC: Gallatin Papers). RC 1 p.; in a clerk's hand, signed by Gallatin; docketed by Wagner, with his note: "Land titles in the possession of the Spanish Surveyor General." For enclosure, see n. 1.

1. The enclosure (2 pp.) is an extract from James Brown to Gallatin, 30 Oct. 1805 (printed in Carter, *Territorial Papers, Orleans,* 9:517–18), stating that he and land register John W. Gurley had hired Ferdinand Ibañez to make abstracts of the grants for land in the districts of Louisiana and western Orleans at a price of a third of a dollar each up to a total of one thousand dollars. When Ibañez applied to Spanish surveyor general Charles Laveau Trudeau for the papers, Trudeau told him that intendant Juan Ventura Morales had ordered Trudeau to be ready "to depart for Pensacola, and to carry with him all the Surveys, Grants, Concessions and other papers which were in his possession relative to lands in the ceded Country." Trudeau added that many title papers were still held by the marqués de Casa Calvo's secretary, Andrés López Armesto, who was on a hunting trip with Casa Calvo. Brown said he had immediately passed this information to Claiborne.

2. On 14 Dec. 1805 JM wrote Claiborne: "You will have been apprized of the intention of the Spanish Officers to withdraw from New Orleans the Land Archives of the late Province of Louisiana, and in particular the surveys, grants, concessions and other papers in the possession of the late Surveyor General. Many of the title pape(rs) of the people of that Country are stated to remain [in] the hands of Don André, the late Secy. of the Govt. and are probably intended to be disposed of in like manner. The President therefore directs in order that the 2d. Art: of the Treaty of cession may not longer remain unfulfilled, that you take all legal & proper measures for gaining possession of these 'archives, papers & documents, relative to the domain & Sovereignty of Louisiana'—but he expects from you, that they will in no event be permitted to be carried out of the Territory" (DNA: RG 59, DL, vol. 15; 1 p.). For more details on the history of Spanish land grant records in Louisiana, see Edward F. Hass, "Odyssey of a Manuscript Collection: Records of the Surveyor General of Antebellum Louisiana," *Louisiana History* 27 [1986]: 5–26.

From Soliman Melimeni

Sir.   Washington City December 13th. 180⟨5.⟩
I am very much Oblige to the Presiden⟨t⟩ for the Arrival of my horses.[1]
I have received 2 horses, the best one them is dead, Sir if the President,
wants I send him one of them Sadd[l]ed, if not I send it without the Sadle.
I am Yours

Solimon,
Ambassador

RC, two copies (DNA: RG 59, CD, Tunis, vol. 3). Signed in English and Arabic.

1. Melimeni brought four Arabian horses with him as gifts for Jefferson (Brown, *William Plumer's Memorandum of Proceedings in the U.S. Senate*, 334, 344, 351).

From William A. Burwell

Dr Sir,   Richmond December 14th 1805
I take the liberty of naming the Lynchburg Star as a fit paper for the
publication of the Laws of the UStates.[1] Its character is decidedly Republican, Situation central, & circulation extensive in the western parts of the
State; If these circumstances were not Sufficient to recommend the Star, I
would add, that the Editor, is a man of Talents, & means to devote himself
to the diffusion of information among the people; Be assur'd if this application is improper, it is not So meant by me.

Shortly after we Separated last summer I experienced, a most severe
indisposition, & though engaged, in my duty on the L.—. my health is far
from being perfectly reestablis'hd. There are still intervals of debility, &
indisposition, which indicate the necessity of attention to my constitution.
Present my respects to your family, & yourself accept my gratitude, for
your uniform civility.

Wm. A Burwell[2]

RC (DLC).

1. The *Lynchburg Star* was founded by James Graham on 31 Oct. 1805 (Brigham, *American Newspapers*, 2:1121).

2. Virginia native William Armistead Burwell (1780–1821) spent a year at the College of William and Mary, after which he used his inheritance from his father, who died shortly after Burwell was born, to invest in extensive landholdings. From 1804 to 1806 he repre-sented Franklin County in the Virginia House of Delegates while also serving sporadically as private secretary to Jefferson. In 1806 he was elected to the U.S. House of Representa-tives, where he served until his death (John T. Kneebone et al., eds., *Dictionary of Virginia Biography* [3 vols. to date; Richmond, Va., 1998—], 2:439–40).

§ From George W. Erving. *14 December 1805, Madrid.* "Private *No 6.*" "I wrote to you in great haste unofficially on the 27th. Ulto.[1] to announce some telegraphic news which had just been Received from Paris. It did not however prove to be well founded. The annexed may be depended upon as I had it from the Prussian Minister who Received it from his Court yesterday, & by the French mail to day it is confirmed. One letter which I have received from a private individual to day mentions that the guns in Paris had been fired on this occasion; if so, it is not improbable that the Preliminaries are signed.

"You will certainly receive more correct & probably quicker intelligence from Paris than ⟨I⟩ can possibly transmit to you from hence; yet ⟨b⟩eing informed that a vessel is on the point ⟨of⟩ departure from Cadiz, at such a critical moment, ⟨I⟩ ⟨c⟩an not omit the chance of conveying this to you."

Adds in a postscript: "Messrs Talyrand, Studion, & de Guilai sont reunis a Brunn pour y traiter de la paix avec l'autriche. Messrs Haugwitz devoit aussi s'y' rendre, & on croit que sous peu des jours le paix pourrait etre faite."[2]

RC (DNA: RG 59, DD, Spain, vol. 10). 2 pp.

1. Erving referred to his letter of 29 Nov. 1805 (second letter).
2. "Messrs. Talleyrand, Studion, & de Guilai have met at Brunn to treat there for the peace with Austria. Messr. Haugwitz is also supposed to go there, & it is believed that within a few days, the peace could be made" (editors' translation). For the results of the peace negotiations, see William Lee to JM, 7 Dec. 1805, n. 1.

From Thomas Leiper

DEAR SIR   PHILADA. Decr. 15th. 1805

Your Twist of Tobacco I duly received from Mrs. Madison[1] it has certainly been very good but has been kept too long for it has got what we Tobacconist call the rotten sweet which is the very next stage to its being rotten. I should be glad to be informed more of the Process of this manufacture. I think you told me it was stoved or sweated to a very high degree.[2] Does your information extend so far as to be informed whether it is put into kegs before the tobacco has got the Hh'd sweat or after on this subject I am differently informed some say before others say it is after it has had the Hhds sweat. I have long been of the opinion that we could make new Tobacco old by putting it into a sweating Room and raising the Heat to such a degree as to give it the Hhds sweat so as to render it fit for our manufacture. But if we can take it in the Green State and sweat it in Kegs it will make the process shorter still. You know the common method is to let the Tobacco sweat in Hhds from our summer heat by this means Tobacco of this years growth is not fit to manufacture before the first of next Octr. whereas the people in Europe always have it old for the Hold of the Vessel gives it a compleat sweat and their was never any such thing seen there as new Tobacco. David Ross[3] informed me in the Year our non ex-portation took place[4] he ship't a large quantity of New Tobacco which you know most have been cleared out before the 11th. of September and that this new Tobacco sold higher at the market of London than the Old so from this very circumstance the Tobacco most have had a compleat sweat in some Five or Six weeks for had it remained in the same state it would have remained here they would not have given any thing for it indeed it is good for no purpose on earth but dung till it has had the Hhd sweate. I built a Vault some years ago with a view of sweating Tobacco but the Chimney and funnels were never compleated. I now intend to go about it immideately and I wish to try the experiment with Tobacco of known quality and if your present Crop is not sold and your Agent can vouch for the quality being good which it most be if it is properly handled I will im-medeately take it at Richmond at the present market price. Or if you like it better I will take it now and give you the market price of any month you may fix on next year. The Presidents Message is will received by every friend of this country Altho' Three Fourths of us believe he is not correct in his statement of the Yellow fever I am with much respect and esteem Your Obedient Hum: Sert.

THOMAS LEIPER

RC (DLC).

1. See JM to Dolley Madison, 19–20 Nov. 1805.

2. After harvesting, tobacco is hung to dry, with or without the use of artificial heat sources (James F. Chaplin et al., *Tobacco Production* [Washington, 1976], 15–18, 19–21).

3. Scots-born David Ross (ca. 1739–1817), of Richmond and Petersburg, Virginia, was a merchant who owned ships and iron mines, and at one time possessed over 100,000 acres of Virginia land as well as 254 horses, more than any other farmer in the state, and 400 slaves. He was commercial agent for the state from 1780 to 1782 and a delegate to the 1786 An-napolis Convention (Charles B. Dew, "David Ross and the Oxford Iron Works: A Study of Industrial Slavery in the Early Nineteenth-Century South," *WMQ*, 3d ser., 31 [1974]: 189–90; Jackson T. Main, "The One Hundred," ibid., 11 [1954]: 354, 362–63; *PJM*, 3:60 n. 8).

4. Leiper referred to the short-lived embargo of 1794 (*PJM*, 15:287–88, 294–95 and n. 1, 328 and nn. 2–3).

§ From William C. C. Claiborne. *15 December 1805,* "*120 Miles from New-Orleans.*" "Previous to my departure from the City, I informed you of the dissentions in Attackapas, and of my intension to visit that County.[1] These *dissensions* have not assumed a serious aspect, nor would *they* alone, have induced my absence from New-Orleans. But as several objects of Importance awaited my presence in Op-palousas and Attackapas, I have hastened my Journey, and propose to avail myself of the occasion, to make suitable efforts to adjust the differences & to produce harm(o)ny. The general objects of my visit, to which I allude, are—first: To (a)cquire a more accurate knowledge of the Country, and of the Interest of the Inhabitants, than I at present possess. Secondly—To assist in the more perfect organization of the Militia. Thirdly—To give such explanations of the late Act of Congress, concerning the Lands in this Territory, as will tend to remove certain discontents which are said to exist.[2] And lastly to conciliate (by such Means as may be in my power) the Affections of the People, as well towards the General, as the local Government.

"Next to the Island of New-Orleans, Oppalousas and Attackapas are the most important Districts of the Territory; the Land is fertile, and well adapted to Cultivation; the Improvements are considerable, and the Settlers numerous and respectable; But on my return, I shall be enabled to give you more accurate information, and will write you in detail.

"My Journey has been so much delayed by bad weather, that I shall necessarily be longer absent, than I at first contemplated; But unless some unforeseen event, should prevent, I shall return to New-Orleans on or before the fourth day of January next."

RC (DNA: RG 59, TP, Orleans, vol. 7). 3 pp.; docketed by Wagner.

1. See Claiborne to JM, 4 Dec. 1805.
2. For the 2 Mar. 1805 "act for ascertaining and adjusting the titles and claims to land, within the territory of Orleans, and the district of Louisiana," see *U.S. Statutes at Large*, 2:324–30.

§ From Justin Pierre Plumard Derieux. *15 December 1805, Greenbriar Courthouse.* "My cousin Plumard of Nantz inform'd me that he had remitted to the Commercial Agent of that Town, a Small sum to Forward to me through your hands.[1] I hope you will be so good as to excuse that liberty, and oblige me in sending it to me in Small notes on the Bank of the United States as I should found extremely difficult in this part of the Country to negociate any large one. I have the honour of inclosing you two receits of Mr. Patterson. I am with respectfull thanks for Your many Favours."

Adds in a postscript: "Will you be so obliging, Sir, as to inform me if Mr. Wam. Lee late agent at Bordeaux is return'd to the U. S. and where he now resides, as I have a little Business to transact with him."

RC (DLC). 1 p.

1. See Mr. Plumard Jr. to JM, 20 Sept. 1805.

§ From Richard Worsam Meade. *15 December 1805, Cádiz.* "I have the honor to hand you inclosed, a letter forwarded me by Mr. Erving from Madrid, with (inst)ructions to Send on, by Some carefull person.[1] C(o)nsidering the departure of Capt. Lindsay as a favorable occasion, I inclose it with our last Madrid Gazette, containing the particulars of (th)e Successes of the french armies on the Continent.

"I also take the liberty of inclosing a copy [not found] (o)f an official letter from Adml. now Lord Collingwood t(o) The marquez de Solana our Governor here, res(p)ecting the blockade of this port.[2] It differs most (e)ssentially from the official communication made by Lord Mulgrave to Mr. Munroe, in as much (a)s the ingress of provisions, was prohibited, whereas Lord Collingwoods letter, the original of which The Governor was polite enough to shew me, expressly says, 'All Cargoes whatsoever except Contraband of War shall freely pass in & out.[']"

RC and enclosure (DNA: RG 59, CD, Cádiz, vol. 1). 2 pp.; docketed by Wagner. For surviving enclosure, see n. 1.

1. The enclosure (1 p.; in Spanish; marked "No. 11," with an appended note by Meade: "The above is copy of the decision of the Governor of Cadiz forwarded to Geo W Erving Esqe.") is an 11 Dec. 1805 communication from Solano dealing with a complaint about a royal decree.

2. The *Two Mothers*, Captain Lindsay (also Lindsey), bearing Collingwood's letter to the governor, arrived at Marblehead, Massachusetts, from Cádiz, about 12 Feb. 1806 (*New-York Gazette & General Advertiser*, 21 Feb. 1806).

¶ From John Chew Jr. Letter not found. *15 December 1805.* Described in Daniel Brent to Chew, 23 Dec. 1805, as enclosing documents relating to James G. Garland, alias James Green, an impressed seaman. Brent said he had been directed to inform Chew that authenticated copies would be sent to William Lyman in London with instructions to use them to obtain Garland's discharge. Brent added that the documents might not apply in the case since "the Report upon which the notice in the Gazettes" to which Chew alluded stated only that "a person of that name, who was possessed of a Custom House protection, was, on the 29th Novr 1803, on Board the British Ship of War Hero" but did not give the state to which the man belonged. Brent referred to a 25 Oct. 1805 State Department notice and list of 271 "persons, representing themselves to be American seamen, impressed and detained in the British service for want of documents to prove their citizenship. As the former places of residence of these men are unknown at the department of state, their friends are in this manner, requested to procure proof of their citizenship, with descriptions of their persons, and forward the same to the secretary of state" that was published in a number of newspapers (DNA: RG 59, Preliminary Inventory 15, entry 929, Misc. Correspondence with Collectors of Customs regarding Impressed Seamen, 1796–1814, box 12; Philadelphia *Aurora General Advertiser*, 29 Oct. 1805).

To John Patrick and Nathaniel Lawrence

GENTLEMEN.   DEPARTMENT OF STATE. Decr. 16th. 1805.

I have received your letter of the 6th. instant and its enclosures, respecting the capture of the Eugenia. Though the further proof respecting the trade in which the Vessel was concerned is believed to be unwarranted by the law of Nations, both in its object and the channel required for obtaining it, it is most proper for the injured individuals to judge, whether the inconvenience or injury involved by the proof may be counterbalanced or not by any prospect of benefit from the impression it may have with the

Court of Vice Admiralty. The Executive have not omitted to cause suitable representations to be made at London, against the principles assumed in the British prize Courts, on which the measures taken at Halifax have been grafted; nor will the occasion be passed by of exemplifying their unjust tendency by yours and the similar cases.

The passages in your letters relating to the allegation, founded on the seizure of the Vessel when in the hands of former British Captors, has been transmitted to the Secretary of the Treasury in order that he may be pleased to furnish you with the report of the Officers of the Customs at New London concerning their proceedings on the subject. From this compliance with your wishes it is not however to be inferred, that the matter of the allegation is believed to be legally susceptible of an effect to your disadvantage, were it verified in its fullest extent. It is hardly necessary to suggest the advantage of causing an appeal to be entered in case a condemnation ensues. I am &c.

JAMES MADISON.

Letterbook copy (DNA: RG 59, DL, vol. 15).

From David Gelston

DEAR SIR NEW YORK Decer, 16. 1805

I received in due course your letter of the 24th. ultimo with $137.56 and supposed after you had arranged the small amount paid for duties &ca. you would remit the remaining sum.

But by a letter received this day from the President, I am persuaded my accounts transmitted the 7th. ultimo were not sufficiently explicit, as he says—"for the wines from Marseilles via Halifax Mr. Madison remitted for him & my self."

The $137.56 received from you with the $30.44 to receive from Majr. Butler make only $168—which I repaid Messrs. R. & Hartshorne for tonnage &ce. You will observe by my Account enclosed to you the 7th. Ulto. I paid duties on those wines &ca

from Halifax	45 –5
I received from Mr Butler	9.64
	35.41
paid sundry cartage Storage &ce.	8.44
which sum of	dollars 43.85

yet remains due to me. If, upon re:examination you find the statement correct, you will whenever convenient, be pleased to remit the amount.

I am sorry to have occasioned you this trouble by My statement not being sufficiently clear in the first instance Very sincerely yours

DAVID GELSTON

RC (DLC). Docketed by JM.

1. Letter not found.
2. Jefferson's letter to Gelston is dated 13 Dec. 1805, DLC: Jefferson Papers, Epistolary Record.

§ From Anthony Merry. *16 December 1805, Washington.* "Having transmitted to the Commander in Chief of His Majestys Ships on the Halifax Station Copies of the Documents which accompanied your Letter to me of the 14th. October respecting the Impressment of Daniel Talmage, an American Citizen, who was supposed to have been impressed by His Majesty's Ship Cleopatra, I have the Honor, Sir, to acquaint you that I have received an Answer from the Commander in Chief, in which he states that no such Man has ever appeared on board the Cleopatra, but that should he be on board any other Ship under his Command that was then at Sea, he would order him to be discharged."

RC (DNA: RG 59, NFL, Great Britain, vol. 3). 2 pp.; in a clerk's hand, signed by Merry.

1. On 17 Dec. 1805 JM replied: "I have the Honor to acknowledge the receipt of your letter of the 16th Inst in relation to Daniel Talmage, the Impressed American seaman, concerning whom I wrote to you on the 14th October last; and to inform you that I have just received Intelligence of this man's being detained on board of His Britannic Majesty's Ship of War, the Hawk, on the Halifax station. I have, therefore, to request that you will be pleased to communicate this Circumstance to the Commander in Chief of the Ships on that station" (DNA: RG 59, Notes to Foreign Ministers and Consuls, vol. 1; 1 p.; marked "(Office Copy)").

To Thomas FitzSimons and Others

GENTLEMEN.   DEPARTMENT OF STATE Decr. 17th. 1805.

I have received your letter of the 10th. inst. and its enclosures respecting the capture of the Enterprize, Eugenia and other Vessels lately sent to Halifax.

Though the further proof respecting the trade in which these Vessels were concerned is believed to be unwarranted by the law of Nations, both in its object & the Channell required for obtaining it, it is most proper for the aggreaved persons to judge, whether the inconvenience or injury involved by the proof may be counterbalanced or not by any prospect of benefit from the impression it may have with the Court of Vice Admiralty.

The Executive have not omitted to cause suitable representations to be made at London against the principles assumed in the British Prize-Courts, on which the measures taken at Halifax have been grafted, nor will the occasion be passed by of exemplifying their unjust tendency by the present and similar recent cases.

It is hardly necessary to suggest the advantage of causing appeals to be entered in case a condemnation ensues. I am &c.

JAMES MADISON

Letterbook copy (DNA: RG 59, DL, vol. 15). Addressed to "Messr. Fitzsimons, Cox, Ball & Pettit."

§ To Christopher Gore. *17 December 1805, Department of State.* "I have received your communications of the 18. 26 & 30th. November respecting the cases of the Ship Indus & George Washington, with the just and forcible observations you have made upon them. In pursuance of instructions early transmitted to our Minister in London, he has not failed to make proper representations to the British Government against the principle which has been assumed as the ground of these condemnations, and its injustice will be further exemplified to that Government by the present & similar recent cases."

Letterbook copy (DNA: RG 59, DL, vol. 15). 1 p.

§ To John and William Wood. *17 December 1805, Department of State.* "I have recd. your letter of the 2d. inst. [not found]. It may be necessary for you to forward to Genl. Armstrong our Minister in France the papers which substantiate the nature of the voyage, the ownership, capture & disposal of the Schooner Vigilant & Cargo: for if the case is such as you represent, the seizure was illegal.

"An abandonment of the Ship Enterprize to the British Captors would be by no means advisable; as such a step would diminish the force of a representation to the British Government, which may become necessary, if redress should fail to be received in the prize-Courts."[1]

Letterbook copy (DNA: RG 59, DL, vol. 15). 1 p.

1. The *Enterprize* was returning from Bordeaux when it was captured by the British and sent to Halifax for adjudication. John and William Wood were New York merchants whose partnership was dissolved in 1807 (*Baltimore Weekly Price Current*, 8 Nov. 1805; Boston *Democrat*, 5 Sept. 1804; New York *American Citizen*, 14 Apr. 1807).

§ From Frederick Degen. *17 December 1805, Naples.* "Through the medium of my friend Comodore Preble and mr. James Purviance of Baltimore, I some time Since received Intelligence that the President of the United States had thought proper to honor me with the appointment of Consul for Naples.[1] I have further Subsequently received by the Ship Charles from newyork, Your Circulars dated from the Department of State the 1st. & 12th. July.

"As however the original Instructions and Commission for the office have never yet reached me, I am led to Suppose that these Documents must have miscarried, and I conceive it my Duty to make the Circumstance Known to you.

"While I consider myself highly flattered by this mark of the confidence of the President of the United States, I would Sollicit the favor of you Sir, to assure His Excellency of my Zealous exertions to do justice to the charge which he has been pleased to confer on me."

RC, two copies (DNA: RG 59, CD, Naples, vol. 1). First RC 2 pp.; docketed by Wagner. Second RC marked "(Duplicate)"; docketed by Wagner. Minor differences between the copies have not been noted.

1. On 20 Dec. 1805 Jefferson submitted Degen's name to the Senate for confirmation of his interim appointment as consul at Naples (*Senate Exec. Proceedings*, 2:7).

§ From James Bowdoin. *18 December 1805, Paris.* "I had the honour to write to you very fully on the 7th. inst. by Capt. Jarvis of the brig dispatch a fast sailing vessell bound from Rochélle for Savannah in Georgia: I understand it is probable, that this Letter may reach Rochélle before Capt. Jarvis may have sailed, wch. gives me the oppty. to transmit to you this Govt.'s acco. of a late decisive victory obtained by the french over the Russian & Austrian-Armies.[1] This being the hour for the departure of the Post."

RC (DNA: RG 59, DD, Spain, vol. 9). 1 p.; docketed by Wagner.

1. For the French defeat of the Russian and Austrian armies, see William Lee to JM, 7 Dec. 1805, and n. 1.

§ From Stanley Griswold. *18 December 1805, Detroit.* "An unfortunate affair took place in the heart of this city, and of the next settlement below, on the 8th. instant, between some military men from the British Shore, and our citizens. I am taking measures to obtain an impartial and authentic statement of the whole transaction, to transmit to your department, as there is reason to apprehend the honor of our country, as well as the peace of our citizens, to be implicated. In this opinion I am supported by the Judge and all the civil magistrates here. It is uncertain whether I can complete the statement, to be forwarded by this mail, which is expected every hour. But I thought it my duty to give you this information, that the ill effects of any partial, or unauthenticated accounts, might be anticipated."

RC (DNA: RG 59, TP, Michigan, vol. 1). 1 p.; signed by Griswold: "Acting as Governor of the Territory of Michigan."

§ From Joseph Rademaker. *18 December 1805, Philadelphia.* "The 16th. Instant, I had the honor to receive Your Letter dated 9 instant [not found], with the President's answer to the communication of the Prince Regent of Portugal of the birth of a Princess.[1] I have this day forwarded the said answer to Lisbon by the American Ship Romulus Captn. Prior, and have reserved the Copy which You were pleased to send me."

RC (DNA: RG 59, NFL, Portugal, vol. 1). 1 p.

1. See Rademaker to JM, 26 Nov. 1805.

§ From George Davis. *19 December 1805, New York.* "I had the honor to lay before you a dispatch under date of the 31st. of August, detailing the transactions of our Squadron off Tunis; and the reasons which forced me to return to the U. States. It affords me some Satisfaction to find that no charges exist against me, nor, that any part of my conduct, has been disapproved of; in as much, as I am disposed to infer, that the *Distrust, evinced towards me, by the Agents of Govt.* is not sanctioned, by the Honle. The Secretary of State.

"I have there fore the honor to report myself ready, to return to the duties of the office lately assigned me."[1]

RC (DNA: RG 59, CD, Tunis, vol. 2, pt. 2); letterbook copy (NHi: George Davis Letterbooks); Tr (DLC: Preble Papers). RC 1 p.; docketed by Wagner. Tr in Davis's hand. Minor differences between the copies have not been noted.

1. Davis did not return to Tunis. On 28 Feb. 1806, Jefferson named him consul at Tripoli (*Senate Exec. Proceedings*, 2:25).

§ From Robert Power. *19 December 1805, Tenerife.* "On the third Ulto. anchor'd in the Bay of Santa Cruz a French Squadron commanded by le Chef d'Escadre Allemand, which had sailed from Rochfort 112 days before, and consisted of the following Ships

Le Majestueux	120 Guns
Jemappe	80
Magnanime	74
Suffrein	74
Lion	74
Calcutta	⟨5⟩4 English captur'd Ship
Armide	44
Gloire	44
Thetis	44
Sylphe Brig	18
Paleneire [Palinure] do	18

Having learnt that Said Squadron had destroyed every Neutral Vessel they had met at Sea, and among them Some American vessels, I immediately applic'd in my Official capacity to the Commodore, as you will see viz the enclosed note,[1] which was deliver'd to him in person by Capt. Henry Hughes of the Brig Peggy of New York, accompanied by Capt. James Riley of the Brig Eliza and Mary of Same place, for the delivery of all the American Citizens who were detained by him on board of her Squadron, but he never thought proper to answer, altho Capt. Riley returned on board two days after and dema⟨nd⟩ed an answer in my name, the Commodore's reply being always, that he wou'd send it.

"The American Vessels burnt at Sea by his order, without examination of papers and cargos, and whose crews were detained on board of his Squadron are the following The Brig Two Friends of New York, Solomon Pennick Master, bound from Said port for Nante in Latt: 47. 30. Long: 14. burnt on the 22d. of July. The Schooner Alpha of Marblehead, Francis Sargent Mast(er) bound from Said port for Bilboa in Latt: 43. 30 Long: 9. 30. burnt on the 31 of July. The Schooner Hart of Boston, John Tuck Master, bound from said port for Bilboa in Latt: 43. 48. Long: 10. 30. burnt on the 31st. of July. The Brig Minerva of New York Perkins Salter Master,[2] bound from Said port for Bordeaux in Latt: 45. 40. Long: 16. 50. burnt on the 20th. Sepr. There were also on board, the crews of 25 other Neutral Vessels burnt at Sea, and of a number of English taken during the cruize amounting in the whole to near 1100 prisoners, none of whom were released. The Squadron sailed on the 17th. of Novr. it's destination unknown."

RC and enclosure (DNA: RG 59, CD, Tenerife, vol. 1). RC 3 pp. For enclosure, see n. 1.

1. The enclosure (1 p.) is a 7 Nov. 1805 letter from Power to Adm. Zacharie Allemand, which stated: "Having this day learnt that there are on board of your Squadron several masters and crews belonging to sundry American Vessels destroyed at sea, and who are detained by you contrary to the laws of Amity and Friendship subsisting between The United States of America, and The Emperor of The French, as Agent for, and in the name of the said United States of America, I hereby demand the release of such Citizens of the said States as may be found on board of your Squadron." The Rochefort squadron, under Allemand, had sailed out when the British blockade of that port was lifted in July 1805 and spent the next five months cruising the Atlantic during which time Allemand captured a British frigate, seized over forty merchant vessels, and took about 1,200 prisoners (James, *Naval History of Great Britain* [1902 ed.], 4:47–50).

2. On 11 Feb. 1806 Perkins Salter wrote from Rochefort to a friend in Marblehead, Massachusetts, that he had been held on the French squadron for four months "in a most deplorable situation"; he added "if they had burned me with the brig, it would not have been much worse." He also said that Francis Sargent had died in the marine hospital at Rochefort on 9 Feb. 1806. Under the terms of the 1831 treaty between the United States and France, $17,049 was awarded in compensation for the *Alpha*, $11,650 for the *Hart*, $35,759 for the *Minerva*, and $24,750 for the *Two Friends* (Windsor, Vt., *Post-Boy*, 13 May 1806; *New-York Gazette & General Advertiser*, 9 July 1805; Williams, *French Assault on American Shipping*, 52, 174, 249, 348).

§ From Joseph N. Thomas. *19 December 1805*, *"Oxen Ferry," Maryland*. "I had the Houner of recievg a Letter from the Departmt, of State informing me that the President had been pleased to appoint me a Justice of the Peace in and for the County of Washington in the District of Columbia. I beg Leave Sir, to Inform the Departmt, of State that I am not a resident of the District of Columbia, my Dwelling-House being outside the Line in the County of Prince Geo, State of Maryland, Consiquently am not Eligible to the Office."[1]

RC (DLC: Jefferson Papers). 1 p.; docketed by Jefferson.

1. Joseph N. Thomas (ca. 1755–1815), who had formerly lived in Alexandria, Virginia, lived near Oxon Hill, Maryland, where he operated a ferry to and from Alexandria. Jefferson named him justice of the peace for Washington County on 20 Dec. 1805 (*Alexandria*

Gazette Commercial and Political, 17 Jan. 1805; T. Michael Miller, ed., *Pen Portraits of Alexandria, Virginia, 1739–1800* [Bowie, Md., 1987], 5; *Senate Exec. Proceedings*, 2:8; *Centinel of Liberty and George-town Advertiser*, 7 Apr. 1797; *Alexandria Daily Advertiser*, 15 Feb. 1806, 10 Nov. 1807).

¶ From William Dubourg. Letter not found. *19 December 1805*. Acknowledged in JM to Dubourg, 21 Dec. 1805, where it is described as referring to John Payne Todd's acceptable deportment and lackluster scholarship, suggesting a personal French tutor for him, and enclosing a list of advances made on his account.

From Joseph Hamilton Daveiss

SIR   CORNLAND NEAR YELLOW BANKS 20. Decr 1805

From the answer to my letter respecting the panther creek lands with which you honoured me about three years ago,[1] I was obliged to pursue the caveat against the heirs of your respected Father, and by the Judgment of our District court theron, recovered the premises in controversy, together with $66.45.3 costs, as you will perceive by an extract from the clerks office enclosed.[2]

I have deemed it more proper to apply to you for payment of these costs, than to pursue by execution the recovery of them out of the lands owned by yourself & your coheirs in this country. Should you approve of this course, be pleased to pay that sum to the Hon. Albert Gallatin & enclose me his rect. or a copy therof. But if you think it inexpedient to do so, be so kind as to notify me of such decision. I am very respectfully yo mo ob. servant

J. H. DAVEISS

RC (ViU: Madison Papers, Special Collections).

1. Daveiss may have referred to JM's letter of 26 Nov. 1801, *PJM-SS*, 2:273.
2. Enclosure not found.

§ From William Lee. *20 December 1805, Bordeaux*. "Since my last respects of the 7th inst the flattering prospects of a peace, being about to take place on the continent, have been diminished. It appears that at the moment Austria, was making through her Envoys pacific proposals, she was also collecting her scattered forces, to join the newly recruited armies of Russia, in order to strike a decissive and she hoped fortunate stroke. The Emperor of the French, suspected their designs from the high tone the Russian, and Austrian Ambassadors, had taken and from the active movements of their different corps. It is stated they went so far as to demand his abdicating the throne of Italy, and giving up Belgium, 'when like you (said he) I shall be driven from my States, from my capital, and be fighting on my last frontier, with my remnant of soldiers, I would answer such propositions with my cannon; may cannon now punish such audacity, such impudence.' The french Army, then lay within three or four leagues of Olmutz, and consisted of fifty five thousand men; The Russian, and Austrian forces, amounted some accounts say to eighty thousand, men, others to ninety. The position of the French not being very good, the Emperor retreated to a more advantageous one, at Austerlitz, about two leagues from Brinn, where his right, was supported by a wood, and marsh, his left by heights, which could not well be surrounded, and his centre, covered by hillocks, which being garnished by Artillery, made a formidable fortification. The Russian General, was deceived by this manoeuvre and calculating from the great superiority of his numbers, on a complete victory, pushed on in pursuit of the French by the great road from Olmutz to Brinn. The french laying on their arms, and refreshed waited the arrival of the Russians, at their centre, when they fell on them with great impetuosity turning with immense carnage their right, upon the marsh where they found themselves so completely surrounded, that all who escaped the sword, were forced to surrender. While the right, and centre, of the French were thus victorious the left, composed of Marshal Lannes division, and Prince Murats horse, were equally successful, which by two oClock in the afternoon decided the contest with a loss to the Russians it is said, of forty five thousand men, one hundred and fifty pieces of cannon, ten general officers, and two Princes. The two Emperors who commanded the combined army, escaped narrowly into Olmutz, where they are now penned up and it is expected will be made prisoners of. The official account of this battle, has not yet reached Bordeaux. When it arrives I shall forward it by the first Vessel. If the king of Prussia should be deterred by this event, from joining the confederates a peace on the continent, will in all probability follow these unheard of successes, in which case the British forces under Genl Don, that have landed at Bremin and are about occupying Hanover, will all be cut off by the French as their retreat is already rendered impossible, by the severity of the weather, which has frozen up all their transports.

"Notwithstanding these brilliant successes the distresses of the people augment daily, and mercantile credit is at as low an ebb as it ever experienced during the revolution; within these six weeks there have been failures, in this City, and Paris, for upwards of fifty million of francs, and others daily expected. Coloni(al) produce of every species is at a peace price, & much cheaper than in the United States, so much so that I am confident our merchants are now sinking forty per Cent on their voyages to this Country."

RC (DNA: RG 59, CD, Bordeaux, vol. 2). 4 pp.; docketed by Wagner.

To William Dubourg

Sir   WASHINGTON Dcr. 21. 1805

I have duly recd. your favor of the 19th. instant. It affords me very great pleasure to learn that the dawn of my son in law's deportment is found to be so acceptable. I was fully aware of the little progress he had made in his studies, and was the more anxious on that account, that in future he might have the aids which I doubt not he will experience under your superintendance [*sic*]. The advances which you have been so obliging as to make for his establishment will be remitted by an early oppy.[1] I entirely approve the expedient of engaging a ⟨private?⟩ teacher of French, in order to bring him up, in that necessary part of his instruction, and will be thankful if you will have one provided. The expence will be attended in the remittance otherwise to be made.

Mrs. Madison is very sensible to the polite & friendly sentiments you express towards her, and joins ⟨in⟩ those of the high respect & esteem which I pray you to accept from Sir Your most Obedt. hble servt.

JAMES MADISON

RC (MdBS: St. Mary's College Collection, Associated Archives, Archives of the Associated Sulpicians of the U.S.).

1. The advances made were probably those listed in the account with St. Mary's Seminary (MdBS: Account Book, 1805–1807, St. Mary's College Collection, Associated Archives, Archives of the Associated Sulpicians of the U.S.; 1 p.) charged to "James Madisson, Esqr., for Mr: John Todd, of Washington," enclosed in Dubourg to JM, 19 Dec. 1805, itemizing the following expenses:

December 7	for 2 pair of sheets	$16.	
	" 1 Matrass	10.	
	" 1 Pillow	3.	
	" 3 Blankets	7.50	
	" 1 Cot	4.25	40.75
	" 3 yd blue Cloth	18.	
	" 3 " brown Linen	.75	
	" ¾ " black velvet	2.25	
	" ⅝ " Casimer	1.56	
	" Buttons Silk & Trimming	1.	
J/A	" making a uniform coat	3.	
⟨$⟩/ 33./	" making a uniform jacket	1.50	
	" making a Patloon & Furnishings	2.	
	" a leather Cap	1.50	31.56
	one Silver Spoon and Tumbler	12.	
	a black Silk Cravat	1.	
	45 yard White Linen	11.75	
	making six Shirts	5.	
	4 pair Woolen Stockings	2.75	

	4 pair Cotton Do.	4.	
	6 White percal Cravats	3.	
	6 Hankerchiefs [sic]	4.50	44.
December 7	Six Months Boarding and Tuition		
	in advance	100.	
	Entrance	20.	
			120.
			$236.31

From Alexander J. Dallas

DR. SIR.   PHILA. 21 Dec. 1805.

In an accidental conversation, with the Marchioness Yrujo, yesterday, I found that the Marquis was determined, without his family, to visit Washington after Christmas. I observed to her, that I wished he would not go, while the discussion on the Spanish papers continued. She answered, that it was her wish too; but that the Marquis declared, he thought it was his duty, at least, to appear at the seat of Government.

On this information, you will take any steps you think proper.[1] Or, if you wish me to speak to the Marquis more explicitly, I will do it. With sincere esteem, I am, Dr. Sir, Yr. mo. obed Sert

A. J. DALLAS

RC (PHi: Gratz Collection).

1. Yrujo arrived in Washington in January 1806, prompting JM to write on 15 Jan. 1806, informing him that his continued presence there was "dissatisfactory" to the president who, while not insisting on Yrujo's departure from the United States "during an inclement season," expected that it would "not be unnecessarily postponed, after this obstacle" had ceased. On 16 Jan. 1806 Yrujo replied that he intended to remain in the city and that he received orders only from his king (*Annals of Congress*, 9th Cong., 1st sess., 1221–24).

From Stanley Griswold

SIR,   TERRITORY OF MICHIGAN, DETROIT 21. Dec. 1805.

A more particular and authenticated statement of the aggression, committed by some British officers and soldiers in this vicinity and town, on the 8th. instant, I have now obtained, and am under the necessity of transmitting for the information of government.[1] I requested our Magistrates, who on the following day had legal cognizance of the transaction, to furnish me with the testimony, as it appeared on oath before them, which they were so obliging as to do, and certified an abstract of the same with their signatures. This is enclosed, and marked No. 1.[2]

On the ground of the facts stated in this testimony, together with certain information communicated to me, about the same time, by our public Interpreter and other citizens, I conceived it my duty to take notice of the affair in a *national* point of view, as the *rights* and the *honor* of our *government* and *country* appeared to be implicated. Of course, I wrote to the British commanding officer of the garrison at Malden, (Amherstburgh,) from whence the aggressors came; a copy of which letter is enclosed, marked No. 2.[3]

The information given me by our Interpreter, corroborated by that of other citizens, and some Indians, was, that a number of *Indians* are hired, or enlisted, and kept under pay by the British, to come over occasionally to the Indian villages between this town and the settlements at the southward, to apprehend deserters passing on the great road leading through those villages, and convey them to the British shore. I was informed, that some *Americans* had already met with trouble from those Indians; and some citizens, I am told, are now fearful to pass on that road, particularly strangers. I am also informed, that an *unusual intercourse* has recently been kept up with certain Indians in our territory, by an individual, or individuals, from the British shore, possessing great influence with them.

Our civil magistracy and courts of justice are doubtless sufficient to cause satisfaction to be rendered for the outrage committed on the *private rights* and *peace* of the citizens. If the general government should be of opinion, that the affair ought to end here, and that our *national rights, sovereignty* and *honor* have not been infringed, I shall be happy to be corrected of my mistake, and shall receive its orders with pleasure.

I think it my duty to state, that the *insult* upon the government is conceived to be aggravated by the circumstance, that one of the British officers, concerned in this outrage, viz. *Lieutenant Lundie*, waited on the legislative board last fall, at this place, to take the opinion of government on this very point, *Whether British deserters might be pursued & forcibly arrested in this Territory?* And after due consultation, *Governor Hull* delivered to him a decided opinion, *that it might not be done, to the disturbance of the peace of our citizens.* He has now come and done it, in a very high-handed manner.

To justify my viewing it as an *act of hostility*, I will summarily describe the facts as they appeared to me from the testimony I have seen. A boat full of armed British soldiers, commanded by officers of no small rank, cross in open day the boundary line of the United States, and entering one of our small rivers, proceed into the heart of a flourishing settlement—on the way hailing and searching the boat of a Deputy Marshal. Arriving in the settlement, they enter the house of a citizen, and place a centinel at the door, with Indians in their employ. A canoe on our river is announced in sight! immediately they man their boat and pursue, for the purpose of taking by violent means whom they pleased, some being left to guard the house, which was a tavern. A stranger arrives and calls for refreshment—he is forcibly seized—our Deputy Marshal interferes—the stranger is wrested from his protection and abused—the Deputy, by summoning more aid and procuring arms, rescues the stranger and brings him off to Detroit for safety. The two officers, hearing of this, fly to Detroit, where, after visiting the garrison, late in the evening, they enter the house of a citizen in the centre of the town, and seize the stranger, presenting pistols at the heads of the family and other citizens, threatening to blow their brains out, if they should offer to interfere! A bustle ensues—pistols are fired—the citizens prevail, and wrest the arms from the assailants: the Marshal appears and takes the aggressors into custody. For subsequent events, I refer to the enclosed abstract of our magistrates.

Placing all these things together, I have been unable to conceive of the transaction in a less aggravated light than an *open insult* upon the government, and an *act of hostility* on the part of the British concerned therein. Under this impression, I ordered the arms, which fell into the hands of our citizens, to be detained, until the pleasure of the General Government should be known. These arms consist of very elegant pistols and a sword, and were ordered by the Magistrates, previous to my interference, to be kept as evidence of assault *vi et armis*,[4] at the ensuing Supreme Court. They are now in possession of the Marshal of the Territory.

As to those officers of the United States army, or other citizens, named in the enclosed abstract of testimony, no one can feel greater regret than myself for the circumstances of their implication in a part of the transaction; but it is not for me to offer either apology or accusation, having myself interfered only as it respects the members of *another government*. I will only say, that when I observed *their* names to be contained in the abstract, I thought it my duty to transmit a copy of it to the commanding officer of our garrison, and shall detain this packet a suitable time, to receive any communications they may wish to forward along with these documents.

December 22.

I have received from the commanding officer at Malden, (Amherstburgh) a letter in answer to mine of the 16th. instant, and a copy is enclosed, marked No. 3.[5]

If further correspondence should take place, I have prepared a few articles, expressive of *my own* ideas on certain points, in respect to which satisfactory explanation appears to me to be necessary, subject however to the future orders of government. These are marked No. 4.[6]

The foregoing, with the enclosures, are respectfully submitted by, Sir, With great respect, Your most obedient Servant,

STANLEY GRISWOLD,
Acting as Governor of the Territory of
Michigan.

RC and enclosures (DNA: RG 59, TP, Michigan, vol. 1). RC docketed by Wagner, with his note: "Breach of the Peace by the British Officers from Malden." For enclosures, see nn. 2–3 and 5–6.

1. For the initial report of this incident, see Griswold to JM, 18 Dec. 1805.

2. The enclosure (5 pp.; docketed by Wagner; printed in *Michigan Pioneer and Historical Collections* 31 [1902]: 551–53) is a copy of the 14 Dec. 1805 report of James Abbott and William Scott stating that, according to depositions given before them, deputy marshal Thomas Nowlan was going by boat to the River Rouge when he was hailed by a boatload of British soldiers who searched his boat. When Nowlan stopped for breakfast, he found two British officers, Captain Muir and Lieutenant Lundee, several soldiers, and some Indians already at the house. The officers ordered some of the soldiers to pursue a passing canoe and others to follow on foot, lest the men in the canoe take to the land. While this was happening, one Morrison, for whom the party was searching, arrived and was arrested by the British. Nowlan called nearby citizens to come to his aid, and with their help, recaptured Morrison, and brought him to Detroit. That evening two American officers, Captain Brevort and Lieutenant Hanks, and a companion, asked local resident Richard Smyth if he had seen a British deserter and left his house after receiving a negative reply. When the British discovered Morrison was staying with Conrad Seck, Muir and Lundee, together with Brevort, all armed, burst into the house and dragged Morrison out. Muir threatened to shoot Morrison if he continued to resist, and in the ensuing struggle Muir was shot in the leg. The scuffle continued with Brevort supporting the British. American citizens gathered, and took away the deserter. The British were conveyed to Smyth's house where they were arrested by Nowlan. Lieutenant Hanks and the governor's son, Abraham Hull, ordered the crowd to disperse and threatened to bring troops from the fort to drive the citizens away and to level their homes with artillery. The judges said that after hearing all this, they required Muir, Lundee, Hanks, and Brevort to post bond that they would appear at the general court the following September.

3. Enclosure No. 2 (1 p.; docketed by Wagner; printed ibid., 553–54) is a copy of Griswold's 16 Dec. 1805 letter to Maj. Alexander Campbell stating that he considered the incidents on the River Rouge and in Detroit an insult to the American government and an act of hostility and would transmit a statement to Washington immediately. He added that the weapons that were seized from the British would be held until the administration's wishes were known, that he expected Campbell to take the proper measures in relation to the offenders, and that he would be happy to forward any correspondence from Campbell to Washington.

4. *Vi et armis:* by force and arms.

5. The enclosure (1 p.; docketed by Wagner; printed ibid., 554–55) is a copy of Campbell to Griswold, 19 Dec. 1805, stating that "whatever impropriety may have taken place" on American territory by any of his troops was "entirely unauthorized" by him and he was always ready to surrender a miscreant to punishment. He said that his information was that "a single ignorant *unarmed* soldier" had seized a British deserter at the River Rouge but had given him up to the Americans when they had demanded it. He added that so far as the incident at Detroit was concerned "the officers on that occasion also acted without the least

sanction or order" and "if they have violated the laws of the United States," he left them to American justice. He said that his extralegal opinion was that the arms should be returned once the parties were bound to appear in court. He added further that it was his "earnest desire to cultivate the most amicable & friendly intercourse with the inhabitants and government of the Territory of Michigan."

6. The enclosure (1 p.; docketed by Wagner; printed ibid., 555–56) is a copy of Griswold's memorandum of five suggestions for future interactions between representatives of the two countries in the region. These are: (1) the British officers "should declare *on what authority* they acted, and if on *none,*" should be dealt with by Campbell in a manner that would evince the "*perfect friendship* and *good understanding*" between the two countries; (2) Lieutenant Lundee should be required to explain to William Hull why he so pointedly ignored Hull's answer the previous fall to Lundee's query whether British deserters could be pursued and arrested in Michigan Territory; (3) the evil consequences arising from the pursuit and detention of deserters by the citizens of one government in the territory of the other required the total abandonment of the practice; (4) an explanation should be required for the report that Indians were hired by the British to visit Indian villages in U.S. territory and apprehend deserters on the roads; and (5) that "*no more than the usual intercourse*" should be held by the members of one government with Indians within the territory of the other.

From William Madison

DEAR BROTHER   RICHMD. 21th. Decr. 1805
Inclosed I send you the Weights of 4 Hhds Tobo. inspected in your name. $6. may be had for them. Yesterday the House of Deligates passed two Resolutions, one expressing their confidence in the President of the US & his Administration, Ays 16.1. noes 8 the second—their readiness, when Congress shall direct, to join in a contest with any Nation that has injured us, and, "try which party can do the other the most harm," unanimously.[1] Mr. Taylor will thank you to procure him a Parliamentary Manuel, by Mr. Jefferson, and send it to Richmond.[2] The current price of Tobo. from 30.33/.
I hope my Sister has entirely recove(r)d. Yr &c

                                                WM MADISON.

RC (NN: Arents Tobacco Collection).

1. After a preamble decrying the blockading of U.S. ports and the impressment of U.S. seamen by foreign nations as well as the trespasses of Spanish officers on U.S. territory, the House of Delegates resolution stated "that the Legislature of Virginia have the highest confidence in the wisdom, virtue and firmness of the President of the United States, and that they are ready, whenever Congress shall direct, to join in a contest with any nation that has injured us, and 'try which party can do the other the most harm'" ("Journal of the House of Delegates of the Commonwealth of Virginia . . . [1805]," 38–39, in *Records of the States of the United States of America* [DLC microfilm ed.], Va. A.1b, reel 5).

2. Jefferson's *Manual of Parliamentary Practice. For the Use of the Senate of the United States*, was published on 27 Feb. 1801, a day before he resigned as presiding officer of the Senate (Boyd, *Papers of Thomas Jefferson*, 31:401 n.).

§ From Thomas T. Davis. *21 December 1805, Jeffersonville, Indiana Territory.* "In the news Papers in this Quarter I see a number of Accusations published against Govenor Harrison; which are said to be laid before the President by you.[1] To One of those Charges I find myself named as a Witness: If such facts exist I declare my total Ignorance of them. Though I do not pretend to defend all the charges: Some may be True: But if they are, they are unknown to me;

"And if the charges alluded to are laid before the President, I wish this Letter to be laid before him also."

RC (DLC: Jefferson Papers). 1 p.; postmarked 24 Dec. at Jeffersonville; docketed by Jefferson.

1. The accusations against Harrison may have concerned land speculation. The governor, while acting as superintendent of sales of public lands, was a member of a company that purchased public lands and offered to pay individuals not to bid on certain parcels. Treasury Secretary Gallatin concluded in 1808 that Harrison was not involved in the offers, but he also stated that, although there was nothing improper in Harrison as an individual bidding on public lands, his being a member of a company for that purpose was improper because the main object of such companies was to prevent competition and lower the prices paid for the land, thus diminishing the funds the government acquired from the sales. Gallatin suggested that the administration express dissatisfaction "at such conduct" and prevent a recurrence by sending "a circular to . . . Superintendents in other districts" (Carter, *Territorial Papers, Indiana*, 7:328, 548, 562–63). For Gallatin's 30 Apr. 1808 circular to that effect, see ibid., 563–64.

From John Armstrong

SIR,   December 22d 1805. PARIS

Since the date of my last dispatch[1] I have been so much indisposed as to be quite ⟨un⟩able to write, and it is now with extreme difficulty that I can keep my chair ⟨lo⟩ng eno' to make up even a short letter.

The negociation I mentioned between France & Austria, was of short continuance ⟨a⟩nd to no effect. Francis in his proclamation of the causes of the new rupture, declared ⟨the⟩ terms offered by his brother Napoleon to be such, as could not be accepted with any ⟨reg⟩ard either to his honor or his Safety—& closed, by putting his trust in God and his ⟨il⟩lustrious allies, the Kings of England & Prussia & the Emperor of Russia. Of these Alexander is the most forward, if not the most faithful. He fought the battle of Austerlitz, lost one ⟨h⟩alf of his army, and withdrew with the other, under conditions which approach the ⟨tr⟩ansaction very nearly to a Surrender. This ill-judged exertion of courage & friendship ⟨h⟩as been followed by another Armistice, devoted to another negotiation in which Napoleon may be more generous, or Francis more humble. In either event a peace ⟨be⟩tween these powers will be the consequence & will probably bring after it a general ⟨pa⟩cification. I may here notice, that it was at the moment, the most unfortunate ⟨f⟩or the Allies, that the King of the two Sicilies, with his appropriate wisdom, thought proper to declare for them. He has

677

thus brought down upon himself a vengeance that will be satisfied only with his expulsion. An army of 60,000 men are destined to ⟨t⟩his service, and it is already whispered, that Joseph is to be his successor.[2] Nothing ⟨i⟩s yet known of the terms prescribed to Austria except by inference from the fact, that Wurtemberg & Bavaria are to be enlarged & erected into King-doms. This can only be done out of the clippings of Austria. The Voral-berg, the Tyrol & ci-devant Venice, will probabl⟨y⟩ form these.[3] Another negociation is opened at Berlin, & will no doubt produc⟨e⟩ some arange-ments, corresponding with these, in the North of Germany. Hanover must be severed from England, & Pomerania from Sweden. To make this dose palatable to Prussia, she is to have the Hanse towns, but not without giving up Nev[*illegible*] & Vallangin to France. It is expected that Turkey, European & Asiatic, will furnis⟨h⟩ reasons sufficiently solid for renewing a correspondence between France & Russia & the more so, as Constantine, instead of following his brother to Petersburg, has directed his course to Berlin. The effect anticipated from all this most interest⟨ing⟩ to us, is, a law of Nations, which shall adopt the principle of free bottoms ma⟨ke⟩ free goods, & which shall secure the means of enforcing itself.

The intended marriage between Beauharnois & the Princess Augusta, of Bavaria will detain the court at Munich 'till the 1st. of February.[4]

Mr. Bowdoin Arrived here some time since from London, and means to remai⟨n⟩ where he is, untill he shall hear from you. I furnished him with a copy of Your letter of the 23 May immediately on his arrival. It is some-what r⟨e⟩markable that neither Mr. Monro nor Mr. Pinckney had, as I un-derstand, received copies of this letter. Mr. Irving thinks, that the terms of accomodation indicated in it, would not be acceptable to the Span. Governm⟨ent⟩ but supposes that the whole ground of Mr. M's negociation might be advantageously opened with them. The reasons for either opin-ion, have not been given.

I have, with respect to the Dutch business, preferred a correspondence directly with Mr. Schimmelpennick, to one with Mr. Brantzan.[5] I cannot yet say, how the thing will turn. With very great respect, I have the honor to be, Sir, Your Most Obdt. & very hum. Servt.

JOHN ARMSTRONG

RC (DNA: RG 59, DD, France, vol. 10).

1. Armstrong to JM, 26 Nov. 1805.

2. On 31 Mar. 1806 Napoleon named his older brother Joseph king of Naples in place of Ferdinand IV (Chandler, *Dictionary of the Napoleonic Wars*, 62).

3. For the terms of the Treaty of Pressburg, see William Lee to JM, 7 Dec. 1805, n. 1.

4. Napoleon's stepson Eugène de Beauharnais married Princess Augusta of Bavaria on 15 Jan. 1806 (Lefebvre, *Napoleon: From 18 Brumaire to Tilsit*, [New York, 1969], 250).

5. For "the Dutch business," see JM to Armstrong, 2 Apr. 1805, *PJM-SS*, 9:200–201.

From Thomas Jefferson

Dec. 22. 05.

The Tunisian Ambassador put into my hands the packet now sent, & at his request I promised it should be safely returned to him before he went away, as it contains the originals of letters—it presents a chronological view of the Bey's correspondence with our officers, with explanatory statements of facts connecting them. I found the whole worth reading, tho' I had read the letters hastily before. He appears to feel deep indignation against Davis, whom he considers as having alimented the whole by an unfaithful mediation, & by misrepresentations from the one to the other.

RC (DLC).

From James Monroe

No. 39.

Sir   London Decr: 23. 1805.

I came to town on the 20th. in consequence of a letter from General Lyman of which a copy is enclosed.[1] Altho' the suggestion which it communicated as proceeding from Doctor Lawrence, a proctor in the admiralty, who has no connection with the Ministry, that the government would suspend on my application the seizure of our vessels 'till the principle could be adjusted, might be founded on mere conjecture yet I did not feel myself at liberty altogether to disregard it. After what had passed, it did not seem probable that the government would expect any new application from me before it had answered those I had already made, or that it would adopt such an expedient to obtain one. If it was disposed to accomodate, the invitation already given was surely sufficiently strong. Still it was not an impossible case. Doctor Lawrence's standing in the court is a very respectable one, and I knew that reference had been made to him in some of the cases that were depending altho' he was employed by our citizens, on the receit of my first letters, and that on his opinion the vessels were discharged. But what gave more countenance to the presumption was certain extraneous circumstances, which were likely to be felt by the government. A Strong Paper extracted from the National Intelligencer, which reprehended in decisive terms the conduct of this government towards our Commerce had appeared in the Morning Chronicle and produced some sensation in the City, in addition to which the character of events on the continent, under the most favorable aspect in which they might be viewed, still wore an equivocal face. My experience here, without going further back in our history has satisfied me⟨,⟩ that nothing inspires those in power with such friendly sentiments towards u⟨s,⟩ or brings to their recollection with such glowing feelings and expressions th⟨e⟩ circumstances of our common origin, language &C, as adversity. Before I went to Spain when this country stood alone pitted against its adversary, and I pressed a decision on the propositions I had presented, I heard some eloquent discourses on that topick, to which I was not insensible. But as soon as the prospect improves, the relationship is forgotten and Scouted; nothing is thought of then but their maritime rights, which by their pretentions, comprize a complete monopoly of the ocean, sovereignty over all Islands belonging to their enemies &C. This change has been very visible of late, and is to be traced to the period of the organization of the new coalition. What the disposition of this government is, at this moment on these Subjects I Shall endeavor to ascertain. It is my intention to Sound it thoroughly, in some suitable mode, and to profit of the opportunity, if one is offered, to arrange them on satisfactory terms.

The latest accounts from the Scene of action state, with some degree of credibility, that the Conflict was continued between the contending parties near Austerlitz, on the 3d. 4th. and even the 5th., and that fortune finally proved favorable to the Allies: in what degree however is variousl⟨y⟩ represented. Some accounts State that the French army was completel⟨y⟩ broken and put to rout, while others represent it only as a handsome check. In truth less confidence is now due to official statements than they used to obtain. Since they have begun under the pretext of "ruses de guerre" to mistate Simple facts, people at a distance do not well Know what to believ⟨e.⟩ From every thing I can collect it does not seem probable, that any event has taken place, to decide the fate of the campaign, much less of the war; nor is there any certainty that Prussia has taken a more decisive attitude towards France as yet, tho' it is often reported to be the case. On this point you will doubtless receive better information from the Continent than I can give you.

It is probable that negotiations for peace will be opened in the course of the winter, as it may be that most of the parties seriously wish it. The mission of Coint Haugwitz was supposed to present to the Emperor of France a species of ultimatum, which if adopted, would put an end to the war; or being rejected bring Prussia into it on the Side of the Allies. The following are Said to be its conditions, that he should Separate the crown of Italy from that of France, and withdraw his troops from Naples, Holland and Switzerland, and leave those countries to the enjoyment of their independence. It is reported that the conditions, be they what they may, were known to and approved by the Emperor Alexander, whence it is inferr'd that they are such as Austria and G. Britain also would accede to. It is likewise reported that a provisional treaty was formed between Russia and Prussia when Alexander was at Berlin which stipulated that Prussia Should join the Allies in case France rejected the propositions of the latter. But I should not be Surprized if it Should ultimately appear that this mission was adopted by the King of Prussia, to get rid at the time, in a handsome manner, of the pressure of the Emperor Alexander, or being adopted in good faith for the ostensible purpose, should nevertheless produce no immediate effect, either with respect to a general peace, or the union of Prussia with the Allies in the war against France. It is not probable that the King of Prussia sent to the Emperor of France a positive unqualified ultimatum, which Should admit of no modification. A measure so bold and hazardous is not consistent with the character of the Prussian cabinet which is more remarkable for its hesitation and deliberation than the promptitude of its action; for its desire to preserve what it has by peace, than to risk every thing in an attempt to gain more by war. And if the propositions which were to be made by the Prussian envoy were liable to modification, I cannot well discern how his mission is to be distinguished from ordinary ones, which commence in negotiation, have a regular course and termination. In this view it is not unlikely that the business may be referred to Conferences, or a Congress to be held elsewhere⟨,⟩ which by management may be prolonged for a Considerable time, and whose result may finally depend on the fortune of other battles between the existing parties; unless indeed by the Successes of France over her present opponents, and the high pretentions of her chief, Prussia should hereafter have no alternative, but be forc'd into the war in her own defence. Be the fact however as it may, with respect to Prussia, that is whether She abstains from the war or becomes a party to it, and at an earlier or later period, I do not think that there is much prospect of a general peace in the course of this winter. I rather think that the war will go o⟨n⟩ 'till it produces some great change in the ⟨Cond⟩ition of one of the parties. The Contest is in truth between France and her dependencies and the rest of Europe, and seems to be now so deeply laid, that I cannot well perceive how a Solid and permanent peace can be established between them⟨,⟩ 'till one or other gains so far the ascendancy as to be able to dictate the terms. The gigantick Struggle of the French revolution had so far extended the bounds and contributed to the aggrandizement of France, at the expence of other powers, that it seemed to be impossible for them to reconcile their safety with her existing state. The new dynasty too which grew out of the revolution, did not diminish if it did not encrease the difficulty. It seems to have made up its mind that it was impossible for it to incorporate itself with the antient ones, even by alliances if Such were to be formed, in Such a manner as to establish confidence, friendship and an opinion of Security[2] between them. The French Emperor has not been able to attach to him the antient nobility of France. He has taken many into his service, but even these are not the persons in whom he reposes his chief confidence. Thus while he possesses powers utterly incompatible with the principles of the revolution, he finds himself under the necessity to rely principally for his support on the revolutionary party in the publick councils, in the armies and among the people. It cannot be doubted that he draws to his aid every species of support, from every quarter, and by means which he deems best adapted to the end: still the revolutionary party are his chief counsellors, his generals and body-guard. Where that business will end is a problem to be solved, which time alone can Solve. Perhaps the result is connected with other causes in embrio, which may hereafter unfold themselves. From what I can See he appears to think that foreign war tends to Consolidate his power at home, and thus that consideration encreases much the interval between him and foreign powers and also gives an additional impulse to the revolutionary movement, tho' directed to a different end. Should the issue be fairly made between France and the other powers, it is by no means certain, provided the parties live, in whose favor the Scale will preponderate. On one side there is a vast Superiority of population; on the other an extraordinary concentration of talents with proportional activity and enterprize in the leaders of a great and powerful people. On both, the regular force is nearly equal, but the character of the troops as well as of the people is essentially different. On the side of France they feel the impulse of the revolutionary movement, while on that of Austria there seems to be a consciousness of imbecillity, an entire want of enterprize, and an evident indispositio(n) to the conflict, which cannot be attributed to the want of courage for there are no braver troops. Under Such circumstances the Superiority of population promises to be of little avail: we have already Seen by the incursion into Germany that no part of it, or but a very inconsiderable one, has been brought into action; that it is a lifeless mass Subject to the command of the victoriou(s) army in the field tho' perhaps inferior to the force to be found in the smallest provinces. It Seems probable if the Emperor of France beats the armies opposed to him, that he may demolish the dynasties; but then would arise a question whether in case those events happened, the nations were Subdued? The world has Seen with astonishment that Austria who has among her people Several millions of fighting men, has not been able to call into the field at this great crisis, above 200,000. Surely it cannot be said that the defeat of that force is the Subduction of Austria. Does it not on the contrary give good Cause to presume that her governmen(t) has lost its influence, that the people have withdrawn their confidence fro(m) it, that it is tottering and that every thing is ripe for a change which the Slightest external pressure may produce? If I may judge of Austria by what I saw of spain, and I am told that in many respects the lines are parallel, there is much ground for these Suggestions. I did not believ(e) that there existed in Europe, if there did on the earth, a government s(o) completely worn out and exhausted in all its institutions and function(s,) as I found that to be; or that it was possible for any government to produce such an impoverishing and destructive effect on the moral character of the people which is naturally a manly one, and on the face of the country, its cultivation and even on the Soil itself, as is evident there. These considerations afford Sufficient cause at least to doubt that altho' the armies be defeated and the dynasties overthrown the nations ought not to be considered as Subdued, or liable to be disposed of as a conquered people, by arrangements that are likely to be durable. This is however in Some measure a digression from the Subject. In stating that I did not think it probable that the existing strife between the powers at war would be Soon settled I have thought that it might not be improper to explain the reasons of that opinion.

I will conclude these with a few additional remarks. Under existing Circumstances I think our attitude with all these powers is a very imposing one; that altho' with their loose System of political morality, inordinate pride and extravagant pretentions, they will respectively commit all Kinds of injustice and outrage against us, if permitted, it is nevertheless in our power, and will be while the present state lasts to obtain of either by a Suitable pressure, any just and reasonable demand we may have against it; that nothing will be obtained without Some Kind of pressure, Such an one as excites an apprehension that it will be encreased in case of necessity; and that to produce that effect and protect ourselves against unexpected and unfavorable results, which are always to be Supposed & provided for, it will be proper to put our Country, by invigorating the militia System and encreasing the naval force, in a better State of defence. I am with great respect and esteem, Your very obedient servant

JAS. MONROE

P.S.[3] Since I came to town I have endeavored to ascertain whether any thing had lately occurred to invite from me a new application to the ministry respecting the proceedings against our commerce, and the result has been to satisfy me that there had not. Gen. Lyman has had a conference with Doctor Laurence,[4] with whom he is acquainted, on the Subject, in which the Docr. informed him that he had heard it intimated by persons in power, as their opinion, that there would be a Suspension of those proceedings if an application was made for it. But who those persons were he declined to mention. It did not appear, and it is not presumeable that either the Doctor or those to whom he referred Knew the present State of the intercourse, what applications had already been made or that any had. I called on my arrival at Downing Street to see Lord Mulgrave who, as I was informed was a(t) Bath with Mr Pitt, as he had been more than a fortnight. I asked the young man in the office who is charged, in the absence of Mr. Hammond, with the American business if Lord Mulgrave had prepared an answer for me, to which he replied in the negative. In conversation he gave me reason to infer that no decision had been made upon the subject. I requested him to inform his Lordship that I had come to town to see him on that business, and should remain some time in the hope of hearing from him, which I was desirous of doing at this time as the Congress was Sitting, and Several opportunities offered to bear my dispatches to our government. He promised to do So immediately and assured me that if he received his Lordship's instructions to make any communications to me that I Should hear from him without delay. Four days were more than Sufficient for the correspondence between them; whereas twice that term has now elapsed without my hearing any thing on the subject, so that I conclude that no change has take⟨n⟩ place in the disposition of the cabinet on it. The business is in th⟨e⟩ regular train between the government and myself. It appears t⟨o⟩ me that I have done every thing that it was proper to do, and must attend an answer which if much longer withheld cannot be considered otherwise than as a decision of the government to Support present measures, 'till Some Stronger motive presents itself.

It is unnecessary to add that in giving my sentiments on these important Subjects, I am far from being wedded to them: that being founded on a partial view only, that which is presented here, of those facts and circumstances which ought to be taken into consideration in making a decision, I have always given them with diffidence; and as I well Know that a Combined view of all the great interests and Concerns which merit attention will be taken by our government in making the decision, by whom alone it can be taken with advantage, that I Shall from that and many other Considerations have much greater Confidence in its judgment than my Own.[5]

RC and enclosures (DNA: RG 59, DD, Great Britain, vol. 12); letterbook copy (DLC: Monroe Papers); Tr (DNA: RG 46, President's Messages, 10B–B1). RC in a clerk's hand, signed by Monroe. Words and parts of words in angle brackets in the RC have been supplied from the letterbook copy. Minor differences between the copies have not been noted. For enclosures, see nn. 1 and 5.

1. The enclosure (2 pp.; docketed by Wagner as received in Monroe's dispatch of 23 Dec. 1805) is a copy of William Lyman to Monroe, 16 Dec. 1805, stating that the proctors had told him that the appeal in the case of the *Huntress* was lost, and promising Monroe a report on the case which would fully state the reason for the decree, saying that he had heard from third parties that Dr. French Laurence of the Admiralty Court and some other had hinted that if the U.S. should ask for a suspension of proceedings in cases of American vessels taken for trading from enemy colonies to the mother country, it would be granted until the government decided on final procedures to implement the regulation. For the case of the *Huntress*, see *PJM-SS*, 9:453 n. 1. Lyman also commented that an extract from the *National Intelligencer* that was printed in the 16 Dec. London *Morning Chronicle* had "excite[d] a little sensation." The article from the 8 Nov. 1805 *National Intelligencer* criticized the British for allowing their warships, "with lawless violence, to seize the property of the honest trader," questioned how England would react to "heavy duties on all her manufactured fabrics," and

suggested that the new Congress might inflict "a just and honorable retaliation" for British actions. The *Chronicle* noted that the *National Intelligencer* "is supposed to speak only the sentiments of the Executive."

2. Letterbook copy has "confidence and friendship" only.

3. The postscript, which is undated in the RC, is dated 28 Dec. in the letterbook copy.

4. French Laurence (1757–1809) was a civil lawyer and follower of Edmund Burke who entered Parliament in 1796. He was an advocate in the Admiralty Court and eventually rose to become a judge in that court (*European Magazine and London Review* 55 [1809]: 241).

5. Monroe also included a copy (3 pp.; docketed by Wagner as received in Monroe's dispatch of 23 Dec. 1805) of (1) Lyman to Monroe, 14 Nov. 1805, stating that the court had decreed that the *Huntress* and cargo should be returned to the U.S. government on payment of the expenses of the recaptor; that the ship was so badly damaged that the cargo would have to be unloaded and the ship undergo considerable repair; that the captain wished to leave the cargo warehoused in England and return to the United States, to which Lyman had agreed; and that Lyman had paid all expenses and charges, which could be reimbursed to the United States by the sale of part of the cargo; and (2) to which is appended, Monroe to Lyman, 16 Nov. 1805, agreeing that the perishable part of the cargo, which was probably damaged and might not be needed by the Mediterranean squadron should it continue on there, should be sold and the funds placed with Barings; that any permanent cargo, such as cannon or shot, could be returned as ballast to the United States in any ship that would take them; and recommending Lyman to James Maury for any aid he might need. For Robert Smith's protest to Jefferson against how the matter was handled, see Knox, *Naval Documents, Barbary Wars,* 6:409.

§ From William Jarvis. *23 December 1805, Lisbon.* "The foregoing is a Copy of the letter I had the honor to write you the 3rd. Inst. by the Brig Rebecca Captain Wilson for Philadelphia. Since which no arrangement has taken place relative to Quarantines, except two orders sent to the Health Office of Bellem the 18th. & 26 Ulto. the former very mild the latter very rigid. This may be imputed to advice received from Spain; how ever, I am inclined to think, that from some Quarter or other some unfavourable representations have been made. Among other things, I understood to day, that the Providor Mor should say two days since, that he heard several persons had died of the Yellow fever in Boston. This must have originated in a letter received by a mr. Gould of this place, he having received advice from his correspondent in Boston, that a Mr. Scobic [*sic*] of Marblehead died of the Yellow fever in Boston, three of [*sic*] four days after he reached there from New York; the infection supposed to be received at the latter place. If this observation was founded on this fact, which in itself is nothing but as it tends to excite alarm, it is an extraordinary thing to me. Another circumstanc⟨e⟩ has recently taken place which I augured no advantage from. The early part of the Summer the British Vice Consul had a dispute with the Health Officers of Bellem, in which the Chargé d'Affaires & the Consul General took a very warm and active part. Several representations were made to Mr. de Arauj⟨o⟩ against them; sometimes the board of Health immediately deciding in all case⟨s,⟩ at others sending the Petitions to Bellem to be informed. But the latter part of the last month the British Minister & Consul ordered the Vice Consul at Bellem to make no more compliments as they shou⟨ld⟩ not attend to any more of them; since when the business of the Health Office h⟨as⟩ gone on in the Ancient Track, with this indifference, that the Officers at

Bellem seem much more disposed to embarrass Trade than before. I hope the thus suddenly ceasing from all complaint, is not with a view to countenance the very absurd (to say the least of them) Quarantine regulations adop[t]ed the last Spring in England. To Morrow the Junta sits. I shall wait on the Marquis Pombal before Junta hours; if I should not effect any thing, I shall wait on His Excellency Mr. de Araujo the next day. An American Seaman by the name of Thomas F. Carling of the Age of twenty three Years, five feet 4 ½ Inches high, brown hair, darkish Complexion, born in New Bedford in the State of Massachusetts, as appears by a protection granted by David Gelston, Collector of the District of New York the 7th. June 1804, was impressed out of a British Merchantman in this port by the boats belonging to the English frigate Pomona, Captn. Lobb, Commander. The Frigate Sailing the next morning after I received the information, the Officers having refused to give him up, prevented my making a more efficient application. As the frigate is Stationed off this Coast, she will probably be in again in a few days, when I hope to obtain his release. Several other instances of impressments of our Seamen have lately occurred, but they were directly given up on producing their protectio⟨ns.⟩"

Adds in a postscript: "Inclosed I have the pleasure to hand you a letter from Mr. Erving. By a Vessel that Sails in a few days I shall forward the Semi-annual list, & other documents ending the 30th June to Mr. Gallatin."

RC (DNA: RG 59, CD, Lisbon, vol. 2). 4 pp.; marked "(Dup:)." Sent in the *Commerce*, Captain Adams, according to Jarvis's 24 Dec. 1805 letter. The *Commerce* arrived at Baltimore on 10 Feb. 1806 from Setúbal, Portugal (*Baltimore Weekly Price Current*, 13 Feb. 1806).

§ From William Lambert.[1] *23 December 1805, Washington*. "Being now out of the service of the House of Representatives, and desirous of being employed in such a manner as that I may be useful to the public, allow me, Sir, to enquire whether I may be considered as an applicant for a station in your department, that I may be deemed competent to fill with propriety, whenever a vacancy occurs, provided I do not unjustly interfere with the pretensions of any other person."

RC (DLC). 1 p.

1. William Lambert (d. 1834) was a clerk in the State Department from November 1790 through September 1792 under Jefferson. He was one of the clerks of the House of Representatives under Chief Clerk John Beckley from 1801 to 1805, often serving as acting chief clerk in Beckley's absence. In early December 1805 he offered himself as a candidate for chief clerk, but the House voted for Beckley and against Lambert, 85 votes to 18, and Beckley fired Lambert. JM was well enough acquainted with Lambert that, in contrast to his usual wont with applicants, he wrote Lambert on 6 Jan. 1806, explaining that there was no current opening in the department nor was there the prospect of one in the near future, and should one occur, a successful applicant would have "a knowledge of some of the modern languages" (Boyd, *Papers of Thomas Jefferson*, 26:234–35 n.; Richmond *Enquirer*, 6 Dec. 1805; *PJM-SS*, 2:419 n. 1, 459 n. 1, 4:285 n. 2, 317 n. 1, 350 n., 494 n. 7, 8:487 n. 1; DLC).

From John Breckinridge

Quest(o). for the Opinion of the Atto. General

"In the award rendered by the Commissioners, under the 7th. Article of the treaty with G. Britain, in the case of the Somerset, in favor of John R. Livingston Wm. Henderson, Messrs. Clarkson & Cross & Chr. Miller; Mr. Livingston claims £54, which in the report of the assessors appears to be considered as the property of C. Miller; it being alledged by Mr Livingston that C. Miller had no right to that sum, & that it was the property of Clarkson & Cross, of whom he is the assee. The question is, Does the award & papers in that case herewith inclosed, justify the payment of this sum of £54 to Mr. Livingston?["]]¹

Answer.

The award being rendered in favor of *several persons*, who do not appear to be in partnership, the right to its amount, is in *all collectively*, & not in any individually: of consequence, the right to transfer, must be in all. No transfer from Miller is produced. Evidence to shew (as has been attempted in this case) that Miller had never any interest in this sum, nor indeed in the award, & that it was so understood by the commrs., is, I conceive, wholly inadmissible. This would be going into a reexamination of the matter referred to, & decided on, by the Commrs., of which under the Treaty, they had the exclusive and final Jurisdiction.

It would be contesting the verity of the award, by setting up a claim contrary to its very letter. If the Parties cannot adjust their respective interests in the Award, or if either of them shall receive more than his proportion, they must resort to a court of Justice for redress. The Goverment has only to see, that the monies are paid to those in whose favor they were awardd, or to those, who are legally entitled under them.

The award not ascertaining the separate interests of the Parties, and the report of the assessors not being referred to, nor made part of the award, the Goverment has not, I conceive, either the means, or the power, of examining into such facts. The report of the assessors may furnish evidence for the parties in a contest among themselves, with regard to their respective interests in the Award: But as the Commrs. in making up their awards were not bound by the Reports of the Assessors, but might depart from them as they thought fit, the award alone, appears to me, to be the only portion of their proceedings, from which the Goverment can draw that information, of which it is bound to take notice. If those concerned have neglected to have inserted in the award the amount of their respective interests; or if they disagree as to their several proportions, the embarrassments are attributable to themselves; & the Goverment cannot without endangering the rights of the parties, as well as the interest of the public, interpose, (and that too ex parte) & undertake to decide among them.

Cases may probably occur where it might be very difficult, perhaps impossible, to procure complete evidence of the transfer of the claims of some of the persons in whose favor awards like the present have been rendered. Such cases must rest on their own circumstances, & may no doubt furnish such satisfactory proof of the equitable right of the claimant as to induce the Govrment to direct payment upon receiving from him an indemnity against all future demands on the same account.

JOHN BRECKINRIDGE

Atto. Genl

RC (DNA: RG 59, LOAG). Docketed by Wagner, with his note: "J. R. Livingston's case."

1. See JM to John R. Livingston, 25 Nov. 1805, and Livingston to JM, 3 Dec. 1805.

§ From Sylvanus Bourne. *24 December 1805, Amsterdam.* "The inclosed Gazettes will give you a relation of the very surprising & splendid events which have lately taken place on the Theatre of the War in Germany & which have led to an Armistice that will in all probability be followed by a peace on the continent, leaving Great Britain once more to combat alone with the colossal power of France which is much enhanced by the issue of the late short but brilliant campaign. I am inclined to beleive that the actual position of Great Britain will tend to inspire the Govt. with moderation & produce a relaxation of its high toned pretensions relative to the trade of neutrals & that of course our Commerce will be there by relievd in a considerable degree from those vexations which have of late been so perplexing & injurious to its interests.

"The consequences of the late campaign must be peculiarly important to the future fate of Europe & lead to events which the most sagacious & penetrating mind cannot at that moment in any degree appretiate with certainty. I am yet without the favr. of your reply to my interesting letters of July & August last, although I find by th⟨e⟩ papers that they duly arrived. Cogent reasons Cause me however to indulge the hope of a continuance of your confidence & protection & I have consequently wrote to my friend⟨s⟩ & relations George Salmon & Wm. Taylor Esquires[1] of Baltimor⟨e⟩ on the subject of a bond to be given in my behalf agreeably to your late circular & they will have the honor to communicate with you on this subject.

"The inclosed letter for the President of the U. States is relative to a Works [*sic*] published lately by Mr S Luciu⟨is⟩ Professor of Chemistry at Delft on the subject of a Bathometre or Sonde de mer,[2] which with a model thereof I have Sent by this vessell to the President by his des⟨ire⟩ & have addressed the same to care of the Collector at Ba⟨l⟩timore & hope they may all arrive in safety."

RC (DNA: RG 59, CD, Amsterdam, vol. 1). 2 pp. For enclosures, see n. 2.

1. Irish-born Baltimore merchant George Salmon (d. 1807), a partner in the firm of Woolsey and Salmon, was for several years a judge of the Court of Oyer and Terminer and a justice of the peace for Baltimore County, as well as founding director and first president of the Bank of Baltimore. In 1783 he was involved in a plan to transport British convicts to Maryland. Barnstable, Massachusetts, native William Taylor was a flour merchant and purveyor of general merchandise at Baltimore for over thirty years; he also had a deputy at New Orleans. During the Quasi-War with France, he sold one of his ships to the U.S. Navy for $28,000 (Thomas W. Griffith, *Annals of Baltimore* [Baltimore, 1833], 64–65, 104; J. Thomas Smith, "The National Bank of Baltimore," *Bankers' Magazine* 52 [1896]: 621; *Manual of the First Presbyterian Church . . . Baltimore* [Baltimore, 1877], 16; A. Roger Ekirch, "Great Britain's Secret Convict Trade to America, 1783–1784," *American Historical Review* 89 [1984]: 1285, 1287; Abbot et al., *Papers of George Washington: Presidential Series*, 7:341 n.; *Archives of Maryland*, 72:51, 70, 76, 89, 170, 245, 256, 317; Lewis E. Atherton, "John McDonogh—New Orleans Mercantile Capitalist," *Journal of Southern History* 7 [1941]: 457 n. 16; G. Terry Sharrer, "The Merchant-Millers: Baltimore's Flour Milling Industry, 1783–1860," *Agricultural History* 56 [1982]: 147; Knox, *Naval Documents, Quasi-War*, 1:123, 143).

2. The enclosures (3 pp.; in English and French; docketed by Jefferson as received 7 Apr. [DLC: Jefferson Papers]) are copies of Bourne to Jefferson, 23 Dec. 1805, covering a letter and publication from Abraham Gerardus van Stipriaan Luiscius, with a model of his bathometer, and reporting on an apparent armistice between Russia, France, and Austria; and Bourne to van Stipriaan Luiscius, 16 Dec. 1805, stating that he had sent the model to the president. Bourne's letter to Jefferson presumably enclosed van Stipriaan Luiscius to Jefferson, 1 Dec. 1805, enclosing his publication and a model of his device to which Jefferson replied on 3 May 1806, thanking van Stipriaan Luiscius and saying he had sent the treatise and model to the American Philosophical Society (ViW: Tucker-Coleman Collection, Jefferson Papers, Special Collections Research Center, Swem Library). The enclosed treatise was Abraham Gerardus van Stipriaan Luiscius's *Description d'une sonde de mer, ou Bathometre, qui pourra servir a sonder toutes les profondeurs des mers . . .* (The Hague, 1805).

§ From John Church. *24 December 1805, Cork.* "I have the Honor to acknowledge Receipt of your different Circular Letters, & also of the recent Acts of Congress both which shall have my Attention.

"I now profit with the Opportunity of the Ship Six Sisters via Baltimore[1] to hand you the inclosed Schedule for the Current Year of the Imports into this City of American Produce [not found] & I also accompany herewith a Statement of what Money I have received for Account of the United States [not found] the Balance whereof I have transferred being £31.1. or 127 Dols. 38.

"I have at this Time to request you will be so kind as to allow me to nominate my Son James B. Church, to be my Vice Consul for the American Consulate in this City. You may rest assured of his Attention & Abilities to represent me, as Occasion may require, having the Advantage of many Years Experience in Trade & long been one of the Firm of my Mercantile House, Church, Sons & Busteed.

"I am induced to this Application under the Supposition that I may find it necessary to absent myself from here for the Benefit of the English Watering-places & perhaps at some Time when the Interest of the United States might require Attention. Our Port being so conveniently situate & so open for Vessels passing between your Continent & these Countries seldom leaves this Harbor without Cases that require to be attended to.

"Not doubting of your Approbation on the Occasion & expecting you will forward the *Needful Authority* for this Arrangement."

Adds in a postscript: "For your Governmt. is subscribed the Signature of, JAMES B. CHURCH."

Adds in a second postscript: "Should this Mode of Application not be quite regular, may I request of you to forward it in the right Channel, as we are seperated by too gre⟨at⟩ a distance to admit of a Correspondence hereon."

RC, two copies (DNA: RG 59, CD, Cork, vol. 1). First RC 2 pp.; docketed by Wagner. Second RC marked "Duplicate"; cover sheet addressed "⅌ Packet" and docketed by Wagner.

1. The *Six Sisters*, Auld, arrived at Baltimore on 28 Apr. 1806 (*Baltimore Weekly Price Current*, 1 May 1806).

§ From William Jarvis. *24 December 1805, Lisbon.* "I had the honor to write to you yesterday by mr Adams of the Ship Commerce from St. Ubes for Baltimore inclosing a letter received from Mr Erving the preceding day & five duplicates or Triplicates to His Excy Mr de Araujo & the Marquis Pombal.

"At 1 p m I have returned from waiting on the latter Gentleman, who positively assured me that all the Vessels under Quarantine except those from New York & Philadelphia should be released immediately, but those from these two Ports must lay a few days longer."

Adds in a postscript: "Private letters by the Post from Paris, which has just arrived, state that the Preliminaries of Peace between France & Germany are positively signed. The terms are not mentioned. Inclosed is the Official Notice from Admiral Collingwood to the Governor of Cadiz announcing the alteration in the Blockade. You will se⟨e⟩ that Provisions, as in the Official Notice to Mr. Munroe, are not here excepted."[1]

RC and enclosure (DNA: RG 59, CD, Lisbon, vol. 2). RC 2 pp.; marked "(Copy)"; sent via the brig *Truxton*, Mooney, according to Jarvis's 17 Jan. 1806 letter. The *Truxton* arrived at Baltimore on 5 Feb. 1806 (New York *Daily Advertiser*, 10 Feb. 1806). For enclosure, see n. 1.

1. Appended to this dispatch is a copy of a 19 Nov. 1805 letter from Cuthbert Collingwood to Solano, announcing the relaxation of the terms of the blockade. For earlier notice of this, see Anthony Terry to JM, 6 Dec. 1805, and n. 1.

¶ To David Gelston. Letter not found. *24 December 1805.* Acknowledged in Gelston to JM, 27 Dec. 1805, as containing two bills of exchange.

§ From Jonathan Warner. *25 December 1805, Saybrook.* "Suffer me once more to trouble you With a Letter on the Subject of our Loss of the Brig Matilda of Saybrook taken by the french in the Harbour of St Bartholemews Carried to St Martins & Condemnd at Gaudeloop Contreray to the Laws of nations.[1]

"We have Made evry Possible exertion to forward to the Secretary of State the Necessary Docements and expect and trust that the Claim will be persued with energy and faithfullness. At the same time, we Wish to hear from you Sir what

Situation the buisness is in you will not think strange that we trouble you so often, when you Consider the Loss that we met with and the need we stand in for releaf."

RC (DNA: RG 59, NFC, vol. 1). 1 p.; postmarked 3 Jan. [1806] at New Haven; docketed by Wagner.

1. For earlier references to the case of the *Matilda*, see *PJM-SS*, 3:193 n., 8:465, 9:138 and n. 1, 179. The brig *Matilda*, Capt. Ira Canfield, was bound for St. Bartholomew in 1799, carrying beef, pork, flour, stock, corn, meal, lumber, lard, beans, and cheese when bad weather forced it into the British island of Anguilla for repair. It was captured near St. Bartholomew by two French privateers and brought to St. Martin where the ship and cargo were condemned because Canfield had sold horses and tack at Anguilla and taken on a load of sugar. From 1809 to 1826 Warner heard nothing about this claim. In 1836 he and co-owner Gideon Leet received $23,947.33 under the 1831 U.S. claims treaty with France (Williams, *French Assault on American Shipping*, 242; Hopkins et al., *Papers of Henry Clay*, 5:132).

To Levett Harris

SIR.   DEPARTMENT OF STATE Decr. 26th. 1805.

I have received yours of the 30th. August & 4th. Septr. last, with a copy of the letter of Count Worontzow, the original of which with that which it enclosed from His Majesty the Emperor to the President had previously got to hand. In acknowledging their receipt you will not omit to express the respect which has been attached to the magnanimous and truly amicable sentiments they contain.

From the prevalence of the Yellow fever at New York and Philadelphia, during the last Season, it is not improbable that you will have new rigours of the quarantine regulations to combat. In this duty you will receive support from the observations contained in the President's Message at the opening of the Session of Congress, copies of which have been forwarded through England, nor is it unreasonable to expect that these explanations, coming from such a source, and upon so solemn an occasion, will have the most advantageous effect in extinguishing the prejudices, which have so much embarrassed our trade.

The special agency in the Baltic in relation to Seamen, is not under present circumstances deemed expedient. I am &c.

JAMES MADISON.

Letterbook copy (DNA: RG 59, IC, vol. 1).

From Isaac Winston

DEAR SIR   AUBURN Decr 26th 1805

At no time since I have had the Happiness of being acquainted with you,[1] have you had it in your power to render me so essential, and important a service, as at the present moment. For some Time past, I have been Writing to Colo. John Nicholas about a Tract of Land he offers for sale near F.burg,[2] but have recd. no Answer. I have thought it best therefore, that Walter should in person negotiate the Business, and make the purchase—but both himself, and me, being Strangers to Colo Nicholas, I would take it extremely kind of you, to write to him, both of Walter, and myself.

Under existing Circumstances, I can only offer Walter as my Security in case of Purchase. As he possesses an Estate in Land, and Negroes, in his own Right, he could only by a Stranger be tho't objectionable, but possibly, Colo. Nicholas might think otherwise. Should this be the Case, a delay must unavoidably ensue, and there being several Gentlemen, who talk of purchasing the Land, I might, from this Circumstance be disappointed I anticipate a difficulty too, which may arise from another Source—Ample as my Funds are, Colo. nicholas, from the View I have given of them, may in some respects think them Objectionable—now my Dear Sir, as I wish to be guarded at all points, I will ask the Favor of you to say to Walter, whether you would have any Objection to joining us in Bonds given to Colo Nicholas, and afford me pecuniary aid, if in your power, in the Course of the next Year—these Favors, I ask in Confidence of your Friendship, and would avail myself of, in Case of absolute Necessity only. To me, they might be great, as your Name alone, thus mentioned, would have more weight, than every thing I could possibly Write on the Subject to Colo Nicholas.

You will observe in my Instructions to Walter, the mention of Chewing Tobo. This is an article above all others, I wish Colo. N. to receive in paymt. as I have had some dealings with you in this way, I would be much obliged to you to, give Walter a Memo. of the 4 Barrels, and three Boxes, which you obtained of me, Stating the Cost of it, which was 2/ ℔ pound, and the Price it brought you, which I have been informed, for the first 2 Bls. delivered, was 3/ M.Currency.

I had for a great length of Time, been under great uneasiness, and suffered the most painful anxiety on account of your precious, And my ever beloved Dolley, but rejoice now, in having the power of congratulaling [sic] you on her Recovery—an Afft Remembrance to her, and all Frends, if you please, and be assured of my Sincere, and unalterable Affection

ISAAC WINSTON

RC (offered for sale by Historical Collectible Auctions, Burlington, N.C., 24 June 2004, item 436). RC cover marked "W Winston"; docketed by JM.

1. Isaac Winston was married to Dolley Madison's maternal aunt, Lucy Coles Winston. Walter Winston was one of their sons (Glossary, *DMDE*).

2. Winston probably referred to John Nicholas of Geneva, New York, who had advertised for sale his property in Stafford, Virginia, before he moved out of the state in 1803 (Fredericksburg *Virginia Herald*, 18 June 1802; *PJM-SS*, 6:271 n. 2).

§ From James Simpson. *26 December 1805, Tangier*. No. 104. "I beg leave to acquaint you Mr Gwyn advises me the arrival at Mogadore on the 9th. Inst of a Portuguese Vessel from the Canaries with intelligence that a French Fleet of ten sail of the Line, two Frigates and two Brigs had been there and sailed again on a secret Expedition, after having taken on board a large supply of Water and fresh Provisions.[1]

"On the Voyage from France they detained and destroyed twenty five sail of Neutral Vessels, to prevent intelligence of the course they stand being carried to Europe; among those were the Brig Two Friends of Charlestown from New York for Nantes and the Minerva Captain Salter also from New York bound for Bourdeaux.[2] These Vessels were burnt. Three French Officers were Passengers in them landed at Mogadore and are on their way to Tangier. The Masters and Crews (as well as those of the other Neutrals) were left at the Canaries. Some English Vessels taken by the Fleet were all destroyed.

"On the ninth this Month the two Moors sent to England & Hamburgh by Muley Soliman[3] arrived here from London in a Swedish Ship, laden with Cloathing for the Troops and a variety of other Articles for the Emperour. They also bring a Ship mounting 24 Guns bought in London for His Majestys Service; this Vessel brings eighteen hundred Barrels Gunpowder, which has been all landed here, and the Ship is ordered round to Larach.

"The Tripoline Ship Meshouda sailed from thence for Tripoly in October last, and carried the Wheat Muley Soliman has so long been desirous of sending for the poor of that Town.

"All prospect of any part of the Algerine Dominions being annexed to this Empire has vanished—even difficulty is found to bring back the Chief of the Ludaya and some of that race were sent to Tremecen; whether they be detained by the people of that Country, or remain with them from inclination is not yet fully ascertained. A dismasted Ship was picked up at Sea in the end of October or beginning of last Month, by the Fishing Boats of Sta. Cruz and carried to that Port. It is asserted there was not a paper found on board, nor any other circumstance discovered to lead to the knowledge of what Nation she is. The Cargo being Sugar in Hogsheads and some Coffee I have instructed my Agent at Mogadore to be particular in his enquiry respecting the Vessel, as it appears not improbable but it may be an American; few others at this time navigate with those Articles in a course would expose them to drift to Sta. Cruz after being dismasted."

RC (DNA: RG 59, CD, Tangier, vol. 2). 3 pp.; marked "Duplicate"; docketed by Wagner.

1. For the French squadron at the Canary Islands, see Robert Power to JM, 19 Dec. 1805.
2. For the *Two Friends* and the *Minerva*, see ibid., and n. 2.

3. For the Moroccan agents sent to Europe to buy ships, see Simpson to JM, 24 Dec. 1804, William Jarvis to JM, 9 Feb. and 20 Feb. 1805, and Simpson to JM, 2 Apr. 1805, *PJM-SS*, 8:422, 9:25–26, 56–57, 206.

From David Gelston

Private

DEAR SIR   NEW YORK 27th Dec: 1805

I have received your letter of the 24th. instant with its enclosures, which have both been presented and paid. The ballance due you 49 $^{81}/_{100}$ dollars will be handed to you by my friend John Smith. Very sincerely your friend & servant

DAVID GELSTON

l. s.	
1 bill 404 11 in dolls. at ex: 5.8 is	74.91
1 " 100 f: " " " " 5.8 is	18.75
	93.66
from which deduct	43.85
due J.M.	49.81

RC (DLC). Docketed by JM.

§ From Timothy Bloodworth. *27 December 1805, Wilmington, North Carolina.* "Inclosed herewith I have the honor of transmitting a Copy of an Official Protest,[1] taken by John Tomkins master of the Ship Charles Carter of Norfolk Virginia for depradation committed on him on his outward bound passage to Europe and Certified here.

"This would have been sooner sent but for the absence of Capt. Tomkins in the Country."

RC (DNA: RG 59, Preliminary Inventory 15, entry 929, Correspondence with Collectors of Customs regarding Impressed Seamen, box 12). 1 p.; in a clerk's hand, signed by Bloodworth.

1. The enclosed protest has not been found but probably dealt with the seizure of the *Charles Carter.* For the incident, see William Pennock to JM, 3 Dec. 1805, n. 3.

§ From John James Armstrong. *28 December 1805, Tenerife.* "I beg leave to acknowledge, rect. of my Commission and appointment with which I have been honored, as Consul of the United States of America for this Island. It will allways be my particular Study to meritt the confidence, which the Government of the United States, hath thought propper to place in me, and shall on every occasion adher to the Instructions which have accompanied my Commission received the twenty fifth ulto."

RC (DNA: RG 59, CD, Tenerife, vol. 1). 1 p.; in a clerk's hand, signed by Armstrong; docketed by Wagner.

§ From John R. Livingston. *29 December 1805, New York.* "I have the honor to transmit to your Excellency the proceedings of the Court of Vice Admiralty at Bermuda [not found] which will elucidate the Award of the Commissioners respecting the Adventure of Clarkson & Cross on Board the Ship Somerset—As these papers do not appertaine to me I could wish their return as soon as the necessary Use have been made of them.

"Having received a few days since a Letter from Mr Skipwith a Copy of which is enclosed[1] respecting a Claim of mine upon the Goverment of france, for the Embargo of the Ship Somerset, the demurrage of the Same Vessel the Second Voyage—and that of the Brig. Hawk and Two Brothers to amount of $41000 the bussiness for which under a power of Substitution for my Brother R. R. Livingston he had in his hands. And being unable to procure any information respecting a liquidation of this account but through a Clue just obtained that it is probable the Bills have come out in the names of the Several Captains or of the Agents who transacted the bussiness (under the direction of the Owner). Under the reference Mr. Skipwith has directed I am induced to apply to your Excellency to know whether any liquidation of Such an account has taken place—and if so whether Bills have been issued for the amount either in the names of my Captains or agents and to beg they may not be paid untill the proprietor is determined."

Adds in a postscript: "I understand there has been a dispute between Mr Skipwith & Mr. Fenwick respecting the Agency for Claims of Embargo and demurrage—how settled I could not learn."

RC and enclosure (DNA: RG 76, Preliminary Inventory 177, entry 180, Great Britain, Treaty of 1794 [Art. VII], British Spoliations, ca. 1794–1824, box 10, folder 1d). RC 3 pp.; marked "*duplicate.*" Below the body of the letter is the following list:

> Christopher Miller, C. Ship
> Somerset 2 Voyages
> Moses G. West. Capt. Brig Hawk
>   I. Cox Barnet Super Cargo
> Robert Carman. Captain Brig. Two Brothers
>   Robert. J. Livingston Super Cargo.

For enclosure, see n. 1.

1. The enclosure (1 p.) is a copy of Fulwar Skipwith to Livingston, 5 Dec. 1805, acknowledging receipt of Livingston's 18 Nov. 1805 letter inquiring about the latter's claim for "the Somers[e]t Brig. Hawk & Brothers"; stating that since he had no private agency in the cases, he was referring Livingston to the State Department for information; saying he had requested his friend "Mr Hickly of your City to apply to you for paym⟨ent⟩ of 1 pCent Commission" still due him for the amount Livingston had received "for supplies of Leather"; adding that he had "ample documents" to support his demand that were in a trunk on the way to Washington from Norfolk; and saying he hoped that "a due sense of Justice" would

induce Livingston to honor his demand without his being compelled to put Livingston or himself "to trouble" in order to obtain what was due him.

§ From William Lee. *30 December 1805, Bordeaux.* "By the mail of to day it appears that the Russians are in full march home with their Emperor at their head: That the king of Prussian, has accommodated his differences with Napoleon, and accorded him permission to march a division of his troops, through his territory in order to attack the English. That the negotiations for the peace, on the continent are far advanced, and that the Emperor of the French, is expected at Paris between the first and tenth of January.

"The Rochfort Squadron called the invisible fleet, have returned into port after having destroyed a large number of British merchantmen, and several neutrals, among which I find the Brig Minerva of NewYork commanded by Capt. Salter and owned by Ebenr. Stevens of that City.[1]

"The Bank bills of Paris that had a few weeks Since experienced a depreciation of ten PCen⟨t⟩ are nearly at par, and letters from that City would lead us to believe, that there exists a faint glimmering of the restoration of Mercantile cred⟨it⟩ but the distressing failures that are daily taking place in this City, and its neigbourh⟨ood⟩ mark the contrary. I have been instrumental in saving the last week, upwards of three hundred thousand francs, belonging to Citizens of the U States.

"By this Vessel I have the honour to forward you a file of the Moniteur. My last respects were of the 20th & 25th."[2]

RC (DNA: RG 59, CD, Bordeaux, vol. 2). 2 pp.

1. For more on the *Minerva,* see James Simpson to JM, 26 Dec. 1805, and n. 2.
2. Lee's 25 Dec. 1805 letter has not been found.

§ From Perez Morton.[1] *30 December 1805, Boston.* "I have taken the Liberty to introduce to your acquaintance & Civility, my friend Jas. Temple Bowdoin Esqr:[2] the Nephew & adopted heir of our Ambassador to Spain. The high respectability of his Connections are well known to you, & you will find him on acquaintance not less deserving in his personal Qualifications; he sustains the highest Character as a Man of honor & Principle, is interesting in conversation, & completely the Gentleman in his manners & deportment. Mrs. Morton desires her best regards may be presented to Mrs. Madison."

RC (PHi: Dreer Collection, American Lawyers). 1 p.; cover marked "honored by Jas T Bowdoin Eqr."

1. Republican lawyer Perez Morton (1750–1837) was a member of the Boston Committee of Correspondence and held various other public positions during the Revolution. In the late 1700s he invested in real estate and was a founder of the Union Bank. From 1794 to 1796 and again from 1800 to 1811 he was a member of the general court, and in 1806, 1807, 1810, and 1811 he was elected speaker; he resigned when he was named state attorney general in 1811, a post he held until 1832. Sarah Apthorp Morton (1759–1846) was a renowned beauty who was painted three times by Gilbert Stuart, and a prolific poet known as "the American Sappho." Connected socially with many of the most prominent Bostonians, the

Mortons were the center of a notorious scandal in 1788, when Mrs. Morton's younger sister, Frances Apthorp, who was living with them, gave birth to a daughter supposedly fathered by Perez Morton. Morton denied this; James Apthorp, the father of the two sisters, demanded a family council so the truth could be ascertained, and Frances Apthorp, distraught, committed suicide at the age of twenty-two. A coroner's inquest produced a verdict of deliberate suicide and implicated Morton, but John Adams and James Bowdoin made a public declaration that they had investigated the matter and the accusations were not supported. The incident was discussed at length in contemporary newspapers and fiction (Emily Pendleton and Milton Ellis, *Philenia: The Life and Works of Sarah Wentworth Morton, 1759–1846*, University of Maine Studies, 2d ser., vol. 34, no. 20 [Orono, Maine, 1931], 19, 21, 22, 24–26, 29, 32–35, 41–50, 52, 53–59, 60, 77, 80, 82, 86, 92–95, 102).

2. James Temple Bowdoin (ca. 1776–1842) was the second son of James Bowdoin's sister Elizabeth and her husband Sir John Temple. Born James Bowdoin Temple, he was a British army officer when he legally changed his name in June 1805 in order to become his childless uncle's heir. He moved from England to the United States in 1808 but by 1810 had returned to England where he died (Conrad Edick Wright, *Revolutionary Generation: Harvard Men and the Consequences of Independence* [Amherst, Mass., 2005], 184–86; Looney et al., *Papers of Thomas Jefferson: Retirement Series*, 7:67 n.; *Gentleman's Magazine: and Historical Chronicle* 80, pt. 2 [1810]: 590; Rhode Island *Newport Mercury*, 26 Nov. 1842).

To the House of Representatives

DEPT. OF STATE 31 Decr. 1805

The Secretary of State, to whom, by a Resolution of the House of Representatives of the 16th. inst.,[1] the memorial of Peter Landais[2] was referred, has examined the same, and thereupon makes the following report.

That it appears from the documents hereunto annexed,[3] that the Alliance, a Frigate belonging to the United States, whilst she was cruising in concert with several other armed Vessels under the command of the Chevalier Jones, in the year 1779, captured three British Vessels & sent them to Bergen into Norway. That at the time of the said Capture, the Frigate Alliance was under the command of the memorialist: that the distribution of the prize money which might accrue from the success of the cruize was regulated by the commanders of the Squadron in the agreement of which a copy is subjoined. That on the arrival of the prizes at Bergen, where they were consigned to the French Consul, they were seized by order of His Majesty the King of Denmark, and restored to the original British proprietors, on the ground as appears, that as Denmark did not acknowledge the Independence of the United States, the captures were to be considered illegal.

That the sentiments of Congress have been expressed upon the subject in their resolutions of the 25th. Octr. 1787, of which a copy is annexed: but notwithstanding the application for compensation made in pursuance thereof and an antecedent demand by Doctor Franklin, then the Minister of the United States at Paris, nothing has been accorded by Denmark as a satisfaction for the injury sustained. Extracts of Doctor Franklin's corre-spondence upon the subject are annexed. It would be superfluous to add any remarks to evince the illegality of this interposition in the war between the United States and Great Britain, for were it admissible that it should be considered in the view of Denmark as merely a civil war, the restoration of the prizes to either party in the war would still be unau-thorized, and the right of the United States to compensation consequently remain valid. All which is respectfully submitted.[4]

JAMES MADISON.

Letterbook copy (DNA: RG 59, DL, vol. 15); Tr and Tr of enclosures (DNA: RG 233, Transcribed Reports and Communications from the Secretary of State, 5C–B1, 3:339). Minor differences between the copies have not been noted. For enclosures, see n. 3.

1. For the resolution (DNA: RG 59, ML; 1 p.; docketed by Wagner), see *Journal of the House of Representatives of the United States, Being the First Session of the Ninth Congress* (Washington, 1826), 5:198.

2. Pierre (Peter) Landais (ca. 1731–1820) was born in Brittany and served in the French navy. He entered American service in 1777 and sailed the *Flamand* from Marseilles to Ports-mouth, New Hampshire, with military supplies, for which Congress voted him an award of twelve thousand livres. In 1778 he was named commander of the *Alliance* and was natural-ized as an American citizen. After Landais averted a mutiny, the *Alliance* arrived in France, where Benjamin Franklin ordered Landais to join John Paul Jones's squadron. Landais and Jones were totally incompatible and made charges against each other to Franklin, who re-ferred their quarrel to Congress and gave Jones command of the *Alliance*. Landais was sup-ported by Arthur Lee who encouraged him to take unauthorized possession of the *Alliance* from Jones and return to America, on which voyage he again encountered a mutinous crew. Landais was found guilty at a court-martial that also recommended him to government in-dulgence because of all he had suffered. He spent the rest of his life in New York City except for the years 1792 to 1797, which he spent in the French navy during that country's revolu-tion. In 1785 Congress voted to give him $1,814.40, and in 1806 he was paid $4,000 on ac-count on his Danish claim. In 1848 Congress awarded £50,000 to Jones and his squadron members; the share for the by then deceased Landais, after the previous $4,000 had been deducted, was $3,457.40, but no next of kin could be found to receive the funds (Charles O. Paullin, "Admiral Pierre Landais," *Catholic Historical Review* 17 [1931]: 296–305, 307).

3. The enclosures (9 pp.; printed in *Public Documents printed by Order of the Senate of the United States, First Session of the Twenty-Fourth Congress* [6 vols.; Washington, 1836], doc. 198) are (1) extracts from Benjamin Franklin to Continental Congress member James Lovell, 17 Oct. 1779, reporting that "two of the most valuable prizes taken by the Alliance" had arrived at Bergen; (2) Franklin to Continental Congress president, Samuel Hunting-ton, 4 Mar. 1780, reporting that three prizes sent to Bergen had been seized and returned to the British and that he was sending a memorial to the Danish government reclaiming them; (3) Franklin to Danish foreign minister Count Andreas Peter Bernstorff, 22 Dec. 1779, describing the capture of the ships and their conveyance to Bergen and asking their return; (4) Franklin to Huntington, 31 May 1780, enclosing a reply from Bernstorff, stat-ing that the Danish minister at Paris had told him that the return of the ships to Britain had been in accordance with a treaty between the two countries, but he did not show Franklin a copy of such a treaty, and adding that the Americans left at Bergen had been "treated with the greatest kindness" by order of the Danish court; (5) Bernstorff to Franklin, 8 Mar. 1780, saying that had Franklin's letter come from anyone less distinguished he would have con-

sidered it calculated to embarrass the Danes, reminding Franklin that there were "perplexing situations in which it is impossible to avoid displeasing one party," and adding that the Danish minister at Paris would speak to Franklin in confidence on the subject; (6) an undated agreement between John Paul Jones, head of the American squadron and captain of the *Bonhomme Richard*, Pierre Landais of the *Alliance*, Dennis Cottineau of the *Pallas*, Joseph Varage of the *Stag*, and Philip Ricot of the *Vengeance*, that they would act under their United States brevet and fly the American flag, that the division of prizes would be agreeable to American laws and that they would answer to the French minister of marine and Franklin, and that all prizes would be remitted to Jacques-Donation Le Ray de Chaumont, who had paid for arming the squadron "for the purpose of injuring the common enemies of France and America"; (7) the 25 Oct. 1787 resolution of Congress to instruct Thomas Jefferson, then minister to France, to remind the Danish king that the United States expected compensation for all prizes returned to Great Britain by Denmark; (8) Timothy Pickering to Pierre Landais, 4 Jan. 1798, stating, in reply to Landais's question of whether Denmark had ever paid the claim, that they had not; and (9) Pickering to Landais, 17 Jan. 1798, stating that the United States had, at various times, renewed the claim, that Jefferson had appointed John Paul Jones as agent, who went to Copenhagen in March of 1788 and again pressed the claim, that Jones had been told the Danish minister at Paris would deal with Jefferson, after which Jones went into the service of Russia, "and here the business appears ever since to have rested."

4. On 3 June 1813 Landais wrote to JM about his claim, describing his supporting documents with his arguments. On 8 Oct. 1814 he wrote again and explained that he was having his former letter and the current one printed in New York lest his papers had been destroyed when the British burned Washington during the War of 1812 ("May it please your excellency, To receive my hearty and sincere congratulations on your reelection to the presidentship of the United States of America . . ." [New York, 1813 [*sic*]]; Shaw and Shoemaker 28905).

§ From David Airth. *31 December 1805, Gothenburg.* "I had the honour of addressing your Excellency last on the 8th. Ulto. by the Susanna of Baltimore Capt. John Arnold bound to NewYork[1] and as therein promised and agreeable to my Instructions, I now beg leave to wait on you with a Specified Acct. of the Trade of the United States at this Port during the past Year,[2] which as hinted before has been more considerable than the two preceeding Years and I hope it will still continue to increase.

"The East India Company's Charter here is expired and will not be renewed. They have therefore resolved to dispose of their Ships, a list of which I have the honour to send here inclosed, in case the United States should wish to purchase any of them to be employed as Ships of War."[3]

RC and enclosures (DNA: RG 59, CD, Gothenburg, vol. 1). RC 1 p. For enclosures, docketed by Wagner as received in Airth's 31 Dec. 1805 dispatch, see nn. 2–3.

1. The *Susanna*, Captain Arnold, arrived at New York on 15 Feb. 1806 in ninety-six days from Gothenburg (*New-York Price-Current*, 22 Feb. 1806).
2. Airth enclosed a list (1 p.; dated 31 Dec. 1806 [*sic*]) of twelve American ships that had traded at Gothenburg in 1805. Of the twelve, eight had arrived in ballast and eleven departed with cargoes of iron.
3. Airth enclosed a list (1 p.; dated 31 Dec. 1805) of six ships that were to be sold by the Swedish East India Company, describing them as built of oak, coppered, with complete inventories of sails, anchors, cables, etc., and carrying from fourteen to twenty guns each; he added that two were "old French Ships and I believe nearly wore out."

§ From George Joy. *31 December 1805, London.* "I wrote you on the 26 July to which I have yet recd no reply. The Subject of that Letter continuing important I have occasionally attended the Court of Admiralty, and hearing Sir Willm, Scott aver that the last Judgements were neither new in principle nor the Consequence of any fresh orders from the Government; Explicitly declaring that none such had issued, I immediately advised Mr. Monroe thereof. Excepting this and sending him printed Copy of the Law of the U.S. passed I think the 13th., and approved 22d., Feby, last,[1] I have not had any intercourse with Mr. Monroe on this Subject since I wrote you.

"I am not the less advised of the copious remonstrances he has made and the fair footing upon which he has offered to negotiate. The most intelligent Americans here are perfectly satisfied with his Efforts; and none of them dissatisfied as I firmly believe. But thinking I might possibly be of some use in a line that ought not to contemplate any special intercourse with him, I have purposely avoided it. The enclosed Correspondence,[2] (which I think it would be indelicate to make public, and therefore pray you not to communicate unnecessarily to any one,) having in the Opinion of a confidential Friend, who has since attended the Court, been the cause of some observations, and some little hesitation on the part of the Judge; I take the liberty to submit to your perusal. I cover also the Sentence in the Case of the Fame, being the first that occured after my Letter was recd. The Little Cornelia[3] follow'd shortly after, but on her Sir Willm., deferred his Judgement from time to time with remarks, on the necessity of giving it more consideration than the press of business would allow, utter'd in a way that led my friend, and others, to suppose he might be hoping for Orders from Government, relaxing the Principle, so far as to relieve him from the necessity of condemng, the Property—the Judgement in this case was not finally given till the 6th, Novr. It is too prolix to trouble you with occupying 13 folio pages and as I know Copy to have been sent to Messrs, Jas, & Thomas Perkins of Boston; and think it must also have been sent to Mr, Jas, Arden of New York, of whom it may be had in case of need; I shall here subjoin only a few short Extracts and Abridgements. The Property is admitted to be American—the Master circumspect and wary in his testimony—the Question for the Court—were not the Goods imported from Martinique to New-York with the *original intention* of sending them to Holland? The Master had reason to *imagine* the Judge to *conclude* that they were the identical Goods that were imported from Martinique and merely landed to save appearances; 'still' says the Judge [']that Conclusion (i,e, that they are the same Goods) will not dispose of this Question: tho' they might be the same Goods imported from Martinique to New-York; yet if it was done with *no original intention* of pursuing this destination to Europe—if imported bona fide into America they would not be subject to any unfavourable determination of the Court. This is the Material Question in this case, whether it was the intention of the Party *originally* to send the Goods to Europe,' and here I must observe, *en passant* that the Judge has always insisted on the Evidence of such intention being positive and palpable. At one time he said it must be obtruded upon him; at another that he must be *provoked* into it, before he would condemn *any* of those Vessells; but in the latter case he added that he must be blind—he must absolutely shut his Eyes against all Conviction to acquit her. To return to the Little Cornelia—the shortness of the time the Judge would not allow to be conclusive against her, if it were otherwise shewn that she went to New York for a Market but the presumption must be that the Goods were *originally intended* to be carried further. From the Evidence before the Court, however, it clearly appears that there was a management on the part of the Owners to withold from the View of the Court the true Case; to draw a Veil over the transaction—and that it was their original intention to carry this Cargo to Europe. 'The studious attemp[t]s which have been made in this Case and other Cases,' say's the Judge, 'to conceal the fact shews the parties were fully aware of the Law.' This was an unfortunate Conclusion for my Contendment, but it remains to be ascertained whether this Management was not a Consequence of the decision in the Case of the Essex Orme[4] which took place on the 23d. May and was probably known in America before the Little Cornelia arrived from Martinique at N, York. Refering to the Case of the Polly Laskey,[5] which you will observe I had brought under his notice as well as yours, he says—'the Rule meant to be pursued was that it should be a bone fide Importation into America and that the Landing and paying the Duties were Tests of it, and Tests that would lay; but it was open to the other parties to produce Evidence to shew that no such intention existed—that the intention was merely to touch at America and actually to carry on the Cargo to Europe.' In another Case he said such Evidence was satisfactory unless countervailed by other facts—for instance, if a Ship were to arrive from an Enemys Colony and Land her Cargo and pay the Duties; yet if a Charter Party were found on board whereby she contracted to take in the Cargo at such Colony, land, pay the duties, or secure them, and reship it to the Neutral port, and proceed with it to the Mother Country; it could never be contended that this was a bone fide Importation into the neutral Country or Exportation from it. He finishes the sentence of the Little Cornelia by saying—'I am sorry if a mistake has prevailed in America. Certainly it did not reach these Owners they have according to my view of their Conduct, studiously attempted to withdraw the fact from the Eye of the Court, knowing perfectly well what the discovery of that fact would expose them to; therefore I shall condemn that part of the Cargo and the Ship.' In the Inclosed Letter to Sir Wm. Scott you will perceive that I did not introduce the Correspondence between Mr. King and Lord Haukesbury; presuming that if he Attended at all to the business, this would occur to him and thinking it would be better to state the difficulty as arising cheifly from his own decisions. I know moreover that this had already been urged by Mr. Monroe, having been a Subject of Conversation between him and my friend Mr. Williams with whom I had previously conferred thereon. I think it always useful to leave something to suggest itself in the mind of the party I am addressing favorable to my objects, in addition to the Arguments adduced by myself: It is evident that this Correspondence did not escape Sir Wm, from the following which I omitted to quote from this Case of the Little Cornelia—'I am perfectly aware if the decisions of the Courts of this Country, and still more if the public Declarations of the Country have led that Country into mistakes, it should be amended; but no public Declarations of *Government* have been *notified:* and with respect to this Court and the Court above, a contrary Doctrince [sic] has been held upon this Subject.' I certainly have a most exalted opinion of Sir Wm, Scott, tho' I did not know, till since this Correspondence, that his Celebrity was so great abroad as well as at home.

"It is impossible to attend his Judgements without perceiving the labourious Efforts with which he brings the resources of a great and enlightened mind to bear upon the subject before him; and the conscientious integrity with which he endeavours to discharge the trust reposed in him. I have absolutely known Americans to express their admiration and respect for the Man, at the moment that he was condemning their property, which, before they heard his doctrines, they had thought innocent and safe.

"I am afraid this anxious solicitude for the equal Rights of Neutrals and belligerents does not exist in the Quarter where alone Mr, Monroe can with propriety apply. You know my opinion on the principles of Policy, which are alone to be looked to here—these I think are fortunately with us, and I am now endeavouring to inculcate this Opinion in a quarter where if I do no good, wch. is probable enough, it will at worst be only labour lost. There is the hour of insolence and the hour of humiliation; and it is matter of serious regret for the advocates of rational policy that the Affairs of Nations should be in the hands of those that consult the effect of adventitious Events on their feelings in preference to the eternal principles of Justice and mutual Benefit.[6] I am now turning my attention to an Establishment in Rotterdam in which I am advised that the Consulship of that port will be advantag[e]ous to me. I would not dispossess the present Agent whom I apprehend to be poor. I think him also honest and a Young Man of good Abilities while he retains his senses; but he is now subject to such frequent fits of entire derangement (of which indeed he is never without some symptoms, as I am credibly informed) that I understand it is the intention of the Government of the U,S, to appoint a Consul for that port. I have not time to write to my friends in America on this Subject by this Conveyance; but I beg you to consider me as a Candidate for the Situation and that I shall be ready to undertake it as soon as a Commission can arrive.[7] On this Subject I shall write you further."

RC and enclosures (DLC); Tr (ViFreJM). RC 8 pp.; in a clerk's hand, except for Joy's note "(Copy) 1st. ⅌ Packet," signature, and cover address with its note "⅌ Remitance via New York." Written at the head of Joy to JM, 15 Jan. 1806. The *Remittance*, Captain Law, arrived at New York about 22 Mar. 1806 (*New-York Commercial Advertiser*, 22 Mar. 1806). For enclosures, see n. 2.

1. Joy referred to the 22 Feb. 1805 "Act supplementary to the act intituled 'An act to regulate the collection of duties on imports and tonnage'" granting "the same terms of credit . . . for the payment of duties on articles the produce of the West Indies, . . . shall be allowed on goods, . . . imported by sea into the United States from all foreign ports and islands lying north of the Equator, and situated on the eastern shores of America, or in its adjacent seas, bays and gulfs," and stating "that it shall be lawful for any ship or vessel to proceed with any goods, wares or merchandise, brought in her, and which shall in the manifest delivered to the collector of the customs, be reported as destined or intended for any foreign port or place, from the district within which such ship or vessel shall first arrive, to such foreign port or place, without paying or securing the payment of any duties upon such goods . . . as shall be actually re-exported in the said . . . vessel: Provided, that such manifest so declaring to re-export such goods, wares, or merchandise, shall be delivered to such collector, within forty-eight hours after the arrival of such ship. . . . And, Provided also, that the master or commander of such ship . . . shall give bond as required . . ." (*U.S. Statutes at Large*, 2:315–16).

2. The enclosures (7 pp.) are copies of (1) Joy's prolix and fulsome letter to Sir William Scott of 24 Oct. 1805, praising Scott's wisdom, fairness, and renown as a jurist both in Great

Britain and the United States; expressing his agreement with the decision on the *Enoch*; quoting Scott's comment in the *Polly* case about what was evidence of bona fide intention of importation to a neutral port; noting that merchants who had trusted to that would be surprised to be stopped; urging relaxation of the *Essex* decision which, without intending to, operated as a snare and which Scott's decision on the *Enoch* seemed to show a reluctance to follow; saying he had heard that the Admiralty Lords had decreed that any ship seized under the *Essex* decision before 1 Nov. 1805 should be released and believed it was Scott's wisdom that had influenced their decree and that he was "mortified" to learn the decree applied only to neutral ships coming from enemy colonies to Great Britain; and asking Scott to add to his glory by urging the Lords to apply the first interpretation and give merchants "fair warning" of the change in interpretation of proof of what constituted bona fide importation; and (2) Scott's terse 27 Oct. 1805 reply acknowledging receipt of Joy's letter, expressing appreciation for the communication and its "obliging terms," and adding that Joy's "own good sense & Candour" would prove the impossibility of Scott's "entering into a private Correspondence" on such subjects. For the *Enoch* decision, see Joy to JM, 26 July 1805, and n. 3; for the *Essex* decision, see n. 4 below.

  3. For the case of the *Little Cornelia*, see Monroe to JM, 6 Nov. 1805, and n. 2.

  4. For the case of the *Essex*, Orne, see Monroe to JM, 18 Oct. 1805, and n. 8.

  5. For the case of the *Polly*, Lasky, see *PJM-PS*, 5:38 n. 7.

  6. The remaining part of the letter following this sentence is omitted from the Tr.

  7. For Lawson Alexander's mental state, see *PJM-SS*, 6:244 and n. 1, 8:47–48, Sylvanus Bourne to JM, 22 July (first letter), 23 July, and 10 Aug. 1805, George Erving to JM, 4 Oct. 1805, and Monroe to JM, 6 Nov. 1805. For Joy's appointment as consul at Rotterdam, see Joy to JM, 26 July 1805, n. 1.

§ From Aaron Vail. *31 December 1805, Lorient.* "I confirm my last respects of 20th. Ult. [not found] and now have the honour to enclose the returns of vessels, since the 30th. June last [not found], and having nothing interesting to communicate."

  RC (DNA: RG 59, CD, Calais, vol. 1). 1 p.; docketed by Wagner.

§ Account with St. Mary's Seminary for John P. Todd. *31 December 1805.*

96. James Madison for divers items		$236.31
for the amount of his account detailed in Account		
Book at Folio 15 furnished 7		
.74	for Underwear $116.31	
for divers items furnished & fashioned		116.31
.77	to Literary Instruction $20	
called Entry of Pupils		
for Entry to the Seminary		20.
.95	to Instruction $25.	
for six months board in advance		25
.94	to Board Expenses $75.	
for six months board as above		75.
		236.31[1]

  Letterbook copy (MdBS: Journal, 1805–1808, St. Mary's College Collection, Associated Archives, Archives of the Associated Sulpicians of the U.S.). 2 pp.; in French.

  1. A second page of the account book lists under account No. 96 an advance payment of $125 received from JM for John P. Todd.

Index

NOTE: Persons are identified on pages cited below in boldface type. Identifications in previous volumes of this series are noted within parentheses. Page numbers followed only by n (e.g., 272n) refer to the provenance portion of the annotation.

Bushby, Mary Hite Manning (Mrs. William), 373n2
Bushby, William, **373n1**; letter to JM, 372
Bush Hill (Philadelphia estate), 323
Busnach, Naphtali, 379; murdered, 80n2, 175n1
Busnach family: massacred, 311
Busy (British armed brig), 172, 245
Butler, Norman: letter from JM, 357
Butler, Pierce: buys wine, 190, 421, 421n1, 514, 514n1, 663–64; goods captured, 188, 228, 228n1
Bützow, University of, 42n6
Byrne, John (N.Y. merchant), 456

Cádiz, Spain, 26–27, 66, 139, 190, 206–7n1, 207n3, 320, 347, 360, 487n2, 512, 515, 560, 567–68n3; American merchants in, 47; blockaded, 233, 233n1, 256, 414, 439, 481, 494, 494n, 494n1, 503, 508n1, 580, 588n1, 611n8, 621, 621n1, 661–62, 690; combined fleet at, 233, 253, 346; commerce in, 621; Danish consul at (*see* Bekelman, Mr.); defenses of, 414; French admiral's court at, 566; French and Spanish fleets at, 480; French consul at (*see* Le Roy, M.); French consul at in *1797*, 207n3; governor general of (*see* Solano Ortiz de Rozas, Francisco, marqués del Socorro y de la Solana); Spanish warships at, 63; trade with France, 97; trade with U.S., 11. *See also* Terry, Anthony; Yznardy (Yznardi; also Iznardi), Josef
Caen, France, 451, 452
Cagliari, Sardinia, 598; U.S. agent at, 604
Calais, France, 407
Calcutta (French warship captured from British): at Tenerife, 667
Calcutta (now Kolkata), India, 486; U.S. trade with, 550
Caldas da Rainha, Portugal, 418, 466
Calder, Robert: of Royal Navy, 216, 253, 346
Caldiero, Italy, 569, 571n1
Caldres. *See* Caldas da Rainha, Portugal

Caldwell, Mr. (Philadelphian in Europe), 574
Callander, James, 386n1
Callier (also Caller), James: threats against Spanish citizens, 453–54n1
Callier (also Caller), John: threats against Spanish citizens, 453–54n1
Calvados, Department of, France, 452
Cambacérès, Jean-Jacques Régis de: arch-chancellor of France, 178
Cambrian (British frigate), 441, 447n2, 501–2, 502n2, 548, 551, 602n1, 620, 620n1; and impressed seamen, 525–26, 537; retakes prize ship, 133n1
Cambridge University, 138
Camden, N.C., 263n2, 648
Camden, William, 38, **42n8**
Cameron, John (of *Swan*), 651
Camile, Capt. (of *Jalousie*), 652n2
Campbell, Alexander: commander at Fort Malden: and British incursions into Mich. Territory, 673, 674, 675n3, 675nn5–6
Campbell, Archibald (N.Y. merchant), 456, 457n1
Campbell, Hugh G., 209, 211n4, 267, 270, 339n3; and Bainbridge trial, 350
Campeche, Mexico, 390n1, 438n2, 519
Canada, xxix, 162n1, 479n4; citizens in U.S. territory, 105n1; invaded, 617–18n2; trade in U.S. territory, 147, 238–39, 240nn4–6, 317–18
Canary Islands: French fleet at, 693
Canby, Capt. (of *Two Brothers*), 58n11, 610, 611n11
Cañedo, Francisco, 453–54n1
Canfield, Ira (of *Matilda*), 691n1
Canton, China, 134; seamen impressed at, 362–63, 585, 585nn 1–2; trade with U.S., 397, 398, 584–85, 585n4
Cape Antonio, Cuba, 263n2
Cape (Cabo) Codera, Venezuela, 88
Cape Coure, Cuba, 648
Cape François. *See* Cap Français
Cape Girardeau, La. Territory (now Mo.), 238, 240n3, 594n2
Cape Marie, Cuba, 649
Cape Nicholas Mole. *See* Môle Saint-Nicolas, Haiti

Graham, James: publisher of
Lynchburg Star, 658, 658n1
Graham, John (*see* 9:312n3): secretary
of Orleans Territory, 598; carries
letter to Pensacola, 485, 485n1, 600,
615; commission for, 101, 101n2;
corresponds with Claiborne, 377,
377n1, 382, 382n1, 391, 412, 565;
estimates Spanish troop strength,
640; recommends U.S. standing
troops, 311; returns from Pensacola,
618; letters to JM, 277, 308, 311,
346, 463, 486–87, 600–601
Grampus (British warship), 362, 363n1
Granbery, John: ship seized, 610
Grand Banks, Newfoundland, 173n14
Grand Decide (French privateer), 82n1
Grandjean. *See* Le Grand, Mr.
Grand Pré, Carlos: governor at Baton
Rouge, 200n1, 249, 336, 337n2; and
raids into Miss. Territory, 391, 392n1
Grange (British merchant ship),
625–26n6
Granger, Gideon: postmaster general,
403n1; and appointments, 172;
corresponds with Jefferson, 104,
105n1, 153, 317; death rumored, 402
Grant, Capt. (protests ship capture),
606
Grant, Forbes & Co. (N.Y.
merchants), 92
Grant, Harry: consul at Leith, 56
Granville, 2nd Earl, 7th Seigneur of
Sark (John Carteret), 72, 154, 154n2
Gratiot, Charles, 148n2; grand jury
foreman, 529n1
Graves, Mr. (speculator in military
certificates), 278
Gravesend, England, 508n3, 627
Gray, George Lewis, 300, 301n3, 310,
312, 315
Gray, Pardon: letter to JM, 514
Gray, Vincent (*see* 9:9n1): vice-consul
at Havana, 439; arrest of, 4, 5n3,
101–2; imprisoned, 259, 260; letter
to JM, 351
Gray, William: impressed seaman, 91
Gray's Ferry, Pa., 316, 322, 323, 361,
387, 411; JM at, 345; Madisons at, 431
Great Britain, xxvi, xxix, 8, 34;
abolition of slave trade in, 117,

126n28; acts of Parliament, 109–12,
417; Admiralty, 94n, 109, 139, 140,
142, 216, 225n1, 231–32, 324, 356,
356n2, 362, 365, 367, 370, 370n1,
375, 376n3, 378, 388, 401n3, 422,
422n1, 426n8, 427, 443, 447n8,
470–71n1, 492, 503, 523, 548, 557,
580, 619, 647, 650–51, 684n1, 685n4,
700; admiralty courts, 92, 112, 327,
379, 417, 447n8, 579–80; Admiralty
Lords, 363n1, 702–3n2; army, 375n3,
466, 580, 638, 666, 672–75, 675n2,
697n2; blockades, 233, 256, 346,
414, 439, 476, 481, 492, 494, 494n,
494n1, 497, 503, 580, 583–84n1,
661–62, 690; boundaries with U.S.,
xxvi, 172, 376n2, 444; and broken-
voyage rule, 365–66, 366n3, 366n5,
544n4, 647, 650, 700–701; coalition
with Sweden, 443; colonies, 74n3,
107–8, 556; commercial regulations,
5, 5n2, 11, 11n3, 38–39, 111, 524–25,
552–57, 560n3; consuls in North
Africa, 209, 211n3; crops in, 322;
customs duties, 158; and E.Fla., 290;
emigrants from, 133; and fishing
rights, 334n39; and free trade, 417,
596n2; government of, 43–44n17,
71, 72, 73, 77, 108, 110, 115–16, 117,
125n17, 139, 176, 178–79, 216, 235,
236n1, 446, 503, 524–25, 556, 560n4,
685n4; histories of, 42n8; and
Huntress, 350, 355–56, 654; and
impressment, xxvi, 173n14, 362,
363n1, 441, 444–45, 585, 585nn1–3;
instructions to privateers, 116;
invalids in New Orleans, 300,
301n2; Jefferson suggests alliance
with, 166–67, 247, 344; king's
advocate general (*see* Nicholl, John);
king's proctor (*see* Bishop, Charles);
land grants, 589, 589n1; letters of
marque, 611n3; marine regulations,
78, 110, 302, 324, 362, 383–84, 385;
and Maryland bank stock, 177n2;
and Miranda's attack on S. America,
583n1, 614; monopoly on West
Indian trade, 117–18, 542; murder
by ship captains, 170; and
Napoleon's *1805* campaigns, 591;
and naturalized U.S. citizens,

508n5; instructs Wilkinson, 238, 240n2; introductions to, 151, 298; and inventions, 688, 689n2; JM dines with, 472, 576n; and judicial branch, 46, 46n, 251; and La. boundaries, 219; and Lafayette, 163, 164n4, 434; on La. Purchase, 247; and La. Territory, 238, 240n2; W. Lee sends newspapers to, 448; letters for, 656; memorials and petitions to, 511n6, 617; mentioned, 21, 24, 67, 84, 86, 128, 130, 130n4, 152, 203, 267, 273, 274, 290–91, 294, 296, 302n4, 306, 338, 361, 419, 487, 523, 538n1, 545, 604, 614, 629, 631; messages to Congress, 140, 141n4, 201n1, 490n, 571, 571n1, 578, 578nn1–4, 579, 597, 606, 615, 621–25, 625n1, 625n6, 660, 691; as minister to France, 698–99n3; and Miranda, 583; at Monticello, 12, 185, 366; and navy, 142n6; and neutral rights, 579; orders Spanish officials to leave Orleans Territory, 547–48; and Orleans Territory, 218, 218n; and Pa. politics, 393, 437; and pardons, 131, 131n1, 439, 562, 562n1; and passports, 355, 356n2; and C. Pinckney, 505, 508n5; and Portuguese princess, 666; and protection of U.S. coast, 52; and public lands, 104–5, 153, 317, 646, 646n, 646n2, 657n2; and purchase of W.Fla., 599, 599n1; and M. J. Randolph, 484, 484n1, 569; receives specimens from M. Lewis, 205, 205n1; receives views of Port Mahon, 252, 252n1; reimburses D. Madison, 562; and resettlement of landowners, 238, 240nn2–3, 593; and resignations, 106, 158, 248; returns to Washington, 311, 344, 370, 371; secretaries, 658n2; as secretary of state, 686n1; and Spanish troops, 346, 351; and territorial governors, 223, 422; and treaty with Tripoli, 350; and Tunis, 281, 288; and U.S. claims against France, 242, 589; and U.S. claims against Great Britain, 389, 549; and U.S. claims against Spain, 139, 344; and U.S. Military

Philosophical Society, 603; and U.S. relations with France, 242–43; and U.S. relations with Great Britain, 166–67, 183, 219, 247–48, 276, 344, 421, 441; and U.S. relations with Spain, 156, 183, 219, 313, 314n4, 344, 461–62, 490; Wagner sends letters to, 145, 149, 300, 321, 439; and war in Europe, 461; and war with France, 421; writes *A Manual of Parliamentary Practice*, 676, 676n2; and Yrujo, 564, 672n1; letters from JM, 98, 127, 156–57, 190–91, 229–30, 275–77, 322–24, 387–88, 411–12, 431–33, 450–51, 454–55, 578, 597, 599; letters to JM, 104–5, 131, 166–67, 183–84, 219–20, 242–43, 247–48, 343–44, 353, 421, 461–62, 571, 572, 579, 582–83, 606, 679
Jefferson (U.S. brig), 151, 151n3
Jefferson (U.S. brigantine) (Richmond), 192
Jefferson (U.S. ship) (Crocker), 644n1
Jefferson County, Ky., 226
Jeffersonville, Indiana Territory, 677
Jemappe (French warship), 667
Jena, Germany, 41n5
Jenkins, Leoline (*see* 8:416n1), 113
Jenkins' Ear, War of (1739), 70, 74n7, 107, 325, 557
Jenkinson, Charles: *Collection of all the Treaties*, 328–29; *Collection of Treaties of Peace, Commerce and Alliance*, and *Discourse*, 332n19, 335n43
jewelry, 483
Jews: in Algiers, 79, 80n2, 175n1, 209, 211n2, 215, 287, 311, 379; in Tripoli, 211n3; in Va., 611n7
João (prince regent of Portugal), 349n10, 424–25n3, 547n3, 596, 596n1, 613n3; birth of daughter, 350n11, 666
John III (of Sweden), 38
John (U.S. schooner): captured by British, 234, 245
John (U.S. ship): captured by Spain, 53, 228n1
John Adams (U.S. frigate), 271, 279, 339–40n3
John Adams (U.S. schooner) (Ramsdale), 130n4

La Rochefoucauld, Alexandre-
François de: French minister to
Holy Roman Empire, 423
Laskey, Capt. (of *Polly*), 141–42n5, 701
Lasteyrie, Louis de, 434
Lasteyrie, Virginia Lafayette de
(Mrs. Louis), 434
Lathrop, Capt. (of *Three Brothers*):
carries dispatches, 346
La Tour-Maubourg, Anastasie
Lafayette de (Mrs. Juste-Charles),
434
Latrobe, Benjamin Henry: and U.S.
Capitol, 372
Latvia: Polish territory in, 42n6
Laura (U.S. ship) (Higginson), 465,
467n2
Laurence, French: British counsel in
Admiralty court, 232, 679, 683,
684n1, **685n4**
Laurie, Robert (of *Ville de Milan*),
173n14
Laussat, Pierre Clément de (*see*
4:130n2), 167, 168, 168n1; and La.
boundaries, 343–44
La Voltiguese (French privateer)
(Moisson), 637n8, 647
Law, Capt. (of *Sally*), 227n1
Law, Jacques Alexandre Bernard,
marquis de Lauriston, 414
Law, Richard, Jr. (of *Remittance*), 517,
523, 702n
law of nations. *See* international law
Law of Nations (Vattel), 624,
626nn12–13
Lawrence, Dr. *See* Laurence, French
Lawrence, Nathaniel: letters from
JM, 501–2, 662–63; letter to JM,
619–20
Leander (British frigate): and
impressed seamen, 83n1, 150, 171
Lear, Benjamin Lincoln, 492n1
Lear, Frances Henley (Mrs. Tobias),
299
Lear, Mary (Polly) Long (Mrs.
Tobias), 492n1
Lear, Mary Stillson (Mrs. Tobias, Sr.),
492n1
Lear, Tobias (*see* 1:13n5): consul
general at Algiers, 14–21, 225, 249,
249n4, 302n4, 492, 492n1; and

annuities for Algiers, 220;
corresponds with S. Barron, 15;
corresponds with Hammuda Bey,
299n1; draws funds, 172, 173n8, 177,
187, 204, 496, 496nn1–2, 646, 646n;
introduces Melimeni, 298–99; JM
instructs, 279–80; leaves Tripoli for
Tunis, 21; at Malta, 20; negotiations
with Tripoli, 567; negotiations with
Tunis, 83–86, 265–73, 280–88;
opposes W. Eaton's attack on
Derna, 20; peace with Tripoli, xxvii,
14–21, 22n8, 23, 98n1, 128, 175–76n1,
339n2, 350, 371, 372n5, 572n1; and
secret treaty article, xxvii, 22n8;
sends wheat to Algiers, 20; letter
from JM, 214–15; letters to JM,
14–21, 279–88, 298–99, 496,
646
Lebeau, Sylvain, 126n34
Lebrun, Charles-François: arch-
treasurer of France: at Genoa, 79,
471, 535–36, 537n1
Leckie, Alexander: ship seized, 610
Leclerc, Charles-Victor-Emmanuel,
195, 341n2
Leda (U.S. ship) (Williamson), 235
Lee, Capt. (of sloop *Mary Ann*), 514
Lee, Arthur, 698n2
Lee, Hancock: and Madison family
lands in Ky., 226
Lee, Silas: U.S. attorney for Maine,
81n1; letter from JM, 81
Lee, William (*see* 2:18n2): consul at
Bordeaux, 203–4, 393, 407, 661;
accounts, 97; corresponds with J.
Armstrong, 80, 80n1, 196, 198n7;
corresponds with Jefferson, 131,
132n2; draws on JM, 535; and local
officials, 587–88; recommends J.
Erving, 138; sends goods to JM, 336,
336n1, 526; sends newspapers, 448;
and ship *Easter*, 194–95; and ships'
papers, 94–97; letters to JM, 80,
94–97, 98, 138, 169, 308–9, 336, 354,
448–49, 481–82, 586–88, 634,
669–70, 696
Lee, William Raymond (*see* 3:401n3):
collector at Salem, Mass.: corresponds
with JM, 172, 173n14
Leet, Gideon, 691n1

Morning Chronicle (London): 470, 471n2; quotes *National Intelligencer,* 679, 684n1

Morning Chronicle (N.Y.), 508n2

Moro Castle, Havana, Cuba, 635

Morocco, 65, 264; and annexation of Algerian territory, 693; army of, 166; buys ships and military supplies, 693, 694n3; commerce, 364; disease in, 65; presents for, 27; revolt in, 363–64. *See also* Simpson, James; Sulaiman, Mawlay

Morris, Mr. (head of militia company), 531

Morris, Anthony: invites D. Madison to visit, 531

Morris, Gouverneur: as minister to France, 342

Morris, Mary Smith Pemberton (Mrs. Anthony), 531, 577

Morris, Richard Valentine, 38, 337; appoints navy agent, 604

Morris, Robert, Jr., **220n1**; letter from JM, 220

Morris, Robert (*see* 3:545n): Revolutionary financier, 220n1

Morris, Thomas, 220n1

Morris, William (of *Lucretia*), 617n1

Morrison, Mr. (British deserter), 675n2

Mortefontaine, Convention of. *See* Convention of *1800* (with France)

Morton, Perez (*see* 5:195n5): Boston merchant, **696n1**; petitions for clemency, 563n1; letter to JM, 696

Morton, Sarah Apthorp (Mrs. Perez), 696, **696n1**

Mountbird, Mr. *See* Mountford, Timothy

Mountford, Timothy: acting consul at Algiers, 204, 214, 351, 567; corresponds with JM, 187, 187n2; corresponds with R. Montgomery, 175, 175n1

Mountfort, Joseph (of *White Oak*), 88–90

Mount St. Gotthard, 395

Moylan, Stephen: pays rent, 495, **496n2**

Muhlenberg, John Peter Gabriel: collector at Philadelphia, 81n2; letters from JM, 87, 92

Mühlenfels, Balthazar Frederik: governor-general of St. Croix, 294, 294n1

Muir, Adam: British Army captain, 675n2

Muirell, John, 453–54n1

Muley Mussa (brother of Mawlay Sulaiman), 166, 264

Mumford, Benjamin B., 518, 518n2

Munich, Germany, 425n6, 448, 678; Napoleon at, 471n1

Munroe, Lovise (of *Sampson*): and ship's papers, 93

Munster, Treaty of (*1648*), 328, 331n1

Murad Rais (Peter Lisle), 263

Murat, Joachim: French marshal, prince, and husband of Caroline Buonaparte, 481, 670; defeats Austrians, 448, 471n1

Murray, Alexander, 172; rejects W. Eaton's plans, 598

Murray, George William: letter from JM, 577

Murray, John J.: consul at Glasgow, 5

Murray, Robert, 365

Murray, William. *See* Mansfield, 1st Earl (William Murray)

Murray, William Vans: minister to the Netherlands, 8–9n2

Muscat, Oman, 398–400

Mustafa Dey (of Algiers), 14, 84, 214–15, 302n1; captured, 80, 80n2; and Jews, 379; requests doctor, 248–49, 249n4; and revolt, 175–76n1

Myers, Moses, **611n7**; ships seized, 610

Myrick, David (of *Indus*), 548, 602, 602n1

Nacogdoches, Texas, 183; Spanish troops at, 344, 499, 606

Nancy (U.S. brig) (Christy), 610, 611n5

Nanking (U.S. ship) (Dorr), 423, 424n1

Nantes, France, 661, 668, 693; consuls in, 307n1; trade with U.S., 492n1

Nantucket, Mass., 384, 386n1, 389n1

Naples, Kingdom of the Two Sicilies, 116, 210, 302n4, 536, 678, 678n2; French minister at (*see* Alquier,